PART FOUR

## SUMMARY PROCEEDINGS TO RECOVER POSSESSION OF REAL PROPERTY

29. Summary Proceedings; Introductory Matters
30. Grounds for Summary Proceedings; Tenant Wrongfully Holding Over
31. Grounds for Summary Proceedings; Employee Wrongfully Holding Over
32. Grounds for Summary Proceedings; Non-payment of Rent
33. Grounds for Summary Proceedings; Non-payment of Taxes
34. Grounds for Summary Proceedings; Illegal Use and Bankruptcy
35. Grounds for Summary Proceedings; Additional Cases
36. Grounds for Summary Proceedings; Forcible or Unlawful Entry and Detainer
37. Grounds for Summary Proceedings; Mobile Home Dwellers
38. Summary Proceedings; Against Whom Maintainable
39. Summary Proceedings; By Whom Maintainable

## VOLUME 3

40. Summary Proceedings; Jurisdiction and Venue
41. Summary Proceedings; The Petition
42. Summary Proceedings; The Notice of Petition
43. Summary Proceedings; The Answer
44. Summary Proceedings; Pretrial Proceedings; The Trial
45. Summary Proceedings; The Judgment
46. Summary Proceedings; The Warrant
47. Summary Proceedings; Stays
48. Summary Proceedings; Redemption
49. Rent Strike Proceeding

## APPENDICES

Appendix A. Articles 7 and 7-A of the Real Property Action and Proceedings Law
Appendix B. Article 7 of the Real Property Law
Appendix C. Pertinent Provisions of General Obligations law
Appendix D. Article 7-C of the Multiple Dwelling Law

**TABLE OF CASES**

**TABLE OF STATUTES**

**INDEX**

(684) NY Landlord 3d

# NEW YORK PRACTICE LIBRARY

## New York Landlord and Tenant

including
## Summary Proceedings

Third Edition

by

**Joseph Rasch**
of the New York Bar

*Author of
New York Landlord and Tenant
Rent Control and Rent Stabilization
Second Edition
and
New York Law and Practice of Real Property*

**Volume 1
§§ 1:1-16:20**

1988

THE LAWYERS CO-OPERATIVE PUBLISHING CO.
Aqueduct Building
Rochester, New York 14694

Copyright © 1988
by
The Lawyers Co-operative Publishing Company

The paper used in this publication meets the minimum requirements of American National Standard for Information Sciences—Permanence of Paper for Printed Library Materials, ANSI Z39.48-1984.

*Library of Congress Catalog Card Number 88–81921*

## Preface to the Third Edition

During the 16 years which have elapsed since the second edition of this book, the changes in the statutory and decisional law of landlord and tenant have made a new edition necessary. The basic plan and scope of the previous editions have been retained in this edition.

I trust that this third edition will receive the same warm reception as the previous editions and will be found even more helpful to my fellow practitioners

JOSEPH RASCH

New York, July 1988

## PREFACE TO THE SECOND EDITION

During the twenty years which have elapsed since the first edition of this book, the changes in both the statutory and decisional law of landlord and tenant have been so extensive that a complete rewriting of the book is necessary. Every part of the original book has been reconsidered and weighed in the light of late authorities and modern developments. In addition, to render the book more valuable and useful to the practitioner, much additional material has been added.

The basic plan and scope of the first edition have demonstrated their soundness and efficiency over long years of service and therefore have been retained in the present edition. The objective of the author is to give the practitioner a practical working tool in the field of landlord-tenant law—one that not only gives him the fundamental principles of the substantive and procedural law of landlord and tenant, but also tells him how these principles can be co-ordinated and utilized to best serve his clients' needs. Many new forms and practical suggestions have been added.

I trust that this second edition will receive the same warm reception as the first, and will be found even more helpful to my fellow practitioners.

JOSEPH RASCH

New York, July 1, 1971

# PREFACE TO THE FIRST EDITION

The relationship of landlord and tenant is a prolific source of litigation. The reports abound in cases involving landlord-tenant disputes. But it is significant to observe that in case after case dealing with the construction of leases the courts repeat with monotonous frequency that they cannot be expected to guess at what the parties meant. Time and time again they say that courts cannot order that to be done which the parties were able to do for themselves, and probably would have done had they thought of it.

A textbook confined to fundamental principles of landlord and tenant law is, therefore, inadequate for the practitioner. What he needs is a textbook which will not only give him these fundamental principles, but will in addition tell him how they can be co-ordinated and utilized to express adequately and fully the intent of the parties. This book, developed out of the author's active experience in this field for many years, has been written to fill this need. It has been designed to give the practitioner a practical working tool.

To adapt a work of this size and scope for maximum use by the busy practitioner engaged in the general practice of the law, the sections have been made short. Each section pinpoints its subject. Each chapter commences with a syllabus of all the sections contained therein. In this manner the reader is enabled to focus attention quickly on the particular problem which concerns him, and at the same time to consider it in conjunction with related subject matter. Citations of cases have been limited to those which are squarely in point, so that the reader need not waste time looking up a great number of cases which are either cumulative or are not usable by him as " authorities".

The author has omitted a detailed discussion of any specific emergency rent law, since such laws are transitory. Rather, he has set forth and discussed the principles established by the courts to apply to all emergency rent situations regardless of the specific provisions of any particular set of acts.

Although basically this is not a form book, many forms have been inserted in the text to illustrate the principles discussed. Forms for the more complex provisions of a lease have been given. In the text dealing with summary proceedings the practitioner will find a complete set of forms for all phases of the proceeding.

JOSEPH RASCH

New York, September, 1950

# TABLE OF CONTENTS*

## VOLUME 1

## PART ONE

## THE COMMENCEMENT OF THE LANDLORD-TENANT RELATIONSHIP

### CHAPTER 1
### GENERAL PRINCIPLES

A. IN GENERAL
- § 1:1. Definitions of Fundamental Terms
- § 1:2. Nature of a Lease
- § 1:3. Lease as Personal or Real Property
- § 1:4. Interest of Tenant in Term to Commence in Future
- § 1:5. Possession of Tenant as Possession of Landlord
- § 1:6. Governing Law (Conflict of Laws)

B. NOTICE OF TENANT'S RIGHTS
- § 1:7. Notice of Tenant's Rights by Recording Lease
- § 1:8. Form of Memorandum of Lease for Recording
- § 1:9. Notice of Tenant's Rights by Recording Modification of Lease
- § 1:10. Notice of Tenant's Rights from Possession

C. FORMS OF COMPLETE LEASES
- § 1:11. Introduction
- § 1:12. Loft Lease
- § 1:13. Office Lease
- § 1:14. Store Lease

D. RESEARCH REFERENCES
- § 1:15. Generally

### CHAPTER 2
### REQUISITES AND VALIDITY OF LEASES

A. IN GENERAL
- § 2:1. Necessity for Contract, Express or Implied
- § 2:2. Necessity of Privities of Contract and of Estate
- § 2:3. Necessity of Attornment

---

* Chapters 1-16 are in Volume 1; Chapters 17-39 are in Volume 2; Chapters 40-49, Appendices, Table of Cases, Table of Statutes and Index are in Volume 3.

§ 2:4. Creation of Landlord-Tenant Relationship by Attornment to Title Paramount
§ 2:5. —By Attornment to Purchaser at Mortgage Foreclosure Sale
§ 2:6. —By Attornment to Stranger
§ 2:7. Necessity for a Valid Contract
§ 2:8. Lease Must Not be Unconscionable
§ 2:9. Delivery and Acceptance of Written Lease
§ 2:10. Necessity for Acknowledgment
§ 2:11. Fraud; Effect and Remedies
§ 2:12. Illegal Use; Effect
§ 2:13. Use in Violation of Subsequently Enacted Laws
§ 2:14. Subsequently Enacted Laws Prohibiting Principal Use
§ 2:15. Subsequently Enacted Laws Limiting Use
§ 2:16. Inability to Comply with Requirements of Law; Tenant at Fault
§ 2:17. —Landlord at Fault
§ 2:18. Violation of Departmental Orders
§ 2:19. Violation of Certificate of Occupancy
§ 2:20. Landlord's Failure to Obtain Certificate of Occupancy
§ 2:21. Zoning Violation
§ 2:22. Conditioning Lease to Protect Tenant in Event of Illegal Use
§ 2:23. Perpetual Leases
§ 2:24. Non-technical Language for Residential Lease (Plain English Law)

B. PARTIES TO A LEASE

§ 2:25. Generally
§ 2:26. The State of New York
§ 2:27. Aliens
§ 2:28. Tenants in Common or Joint Tenants
§ 2:29. Infants
§ 2:30. Insane Persons
§ 2:31. Life Tenant
§ 2:32. Trustees

C. DESCRIPTION OF PREMISES

§ 2:33. Generally
§ 2:34. Form of Description

D. STATUTE OF FRAUDS

§ 2:35. Generally
§ 2:36. Necessity for Pleading Statute
§ 2:37. Effect of Part Performance

E. RESEARCH REFERENCES

§ 2:38. Generally

TABLE OF CONTENTS

## CHAPTER 3
## AGREEMENT FOR A LEASE

A. IN GENERAL
- § 3:1. Nature and Effect
- § 3:2. Distinguished from Option for Lease
- § 3:3. Provision for Execution of Formal Lease
- § 3:4. Necessity for Valid Contract
- § 3:5. Immateriality of Acts Done in Anticipation of Lease
- § 3:6. Certainty of Terms Essential
- § 3:7. Provision for Attorney's Approval of Lease

B. STATUTE OF FRAUDS
- § 3:8. Generally
- § 3:9. Requirements for Note or Memorandum
- § 3:10. Effect of Part Performance

C. DEPOSIT
- § 3:11. Stipulated as Liquidated Damages
- § 3:12. No Purpose Specified for Deposit
- § 3:13. Effect on Deposit Where Lease Not Consummated

D. BREACH
- § 3:14. Action for Damages
- § 3:15. Rescission
- § 3:16. Specific Performance
- § 3:17. First Option to Lease; Damages for Breach

E. RESEARCH REFERENCES
- § 3:18. Generally

## CHAPTER 4
## LEASES AND OTHER INTERESTS IN REAL PROPERTY DISTINGUISHED

A. IN GENERAL
- § 4:1. Test of Distinction
- § 4:2. Board and Lodging Agreement
- § 4:3. Occupation by Purchaser of Premises
- § 4:4. Occupation by Grantor After Conveyance
- § 4:5. Occupation by Mortgagor or Mortgagee
- § 4:6. Contract to Cultivate Land or Farm on Shares
- § 4:7. Occupation of Premises by Employee
- § 4:8. Effect of Deduction from Wages of Employee for Occupancy of Employer's Premises
- § 4:9. Effect on Nature of Occupancy Where Tenant Becomes Employee
- § 4:10. Expense Sharing Arrangement

B. DISTINGUISHING BETWEEN LEASE AND LICENSE
- § 4:11. Test
- § 4:12. Effect of Owner's Right to Regulate Use of Property

§ 4:13. Effect of Cancellation Clause
§ 4:14. Use of Wall or Roof for Advertising Purposes
§ 4:15. Business Concession
§ 4:16. Washing Machine Concession
§ 4:17. Storage of Automobile in Public Garage
§ 4:18. Importance of Distinguishing Between Lease and License
§ 4:19. Non-assignability of License
§ 4:20. Effect of Grantor's Conveyance on License
§ 4:21. Revocability of License

C. PROPRIETARY LEASE (CO-OPERATIVE OWNERSHIP)
§ 4:22. Generally
§ 4:23. Form of Proprietary Lease

D. RESEARCH REFERENCES
§ 4:24. Generally

## CHAPTER 5

## TITLE AND REVERSION OF LANDLORD

A. IN GENERAL
§ 5:1. Reversion Defined
§ 5:2. Title of Landlord Implied
§ 5:3. Necessity of Title and Possession
§ 5:4. After-acquired Title
§ 5:5. Possession of Tenant as Possession of Landlord
§ 5:6. Acquisition of Appurtenances by Tenant as Property of Landlord
§ 5:7. Possession of Persons Holding Under Tenant as Possession of Landlord

B. ESTOPPEL TO DENY LANDLORD'S TITLE
§ 5:8. Generally
§ 5:9. Where Attornment Void
§ 5:10. Duration of Estoppel
§ 5:11. Effect of Expiration of Landlord's Title
§ 5:12. Effect of Fraud or Mistake
§ 5:13. Tenant's Acquisition of Title to Attack Landlord's Title
§ 5:14. Where Landlord a Grantee

C. TRANSFER OF REVERSION
§ 5:15. Generally
§ 5:16. Rights and Obligations of Grantor
§ 5:17. Rights and Obligations of Grantee
§ 5:18. Rights on Transfer of Reversion to Tent Due or to Become Due
§ 5:19. Waiver of Grantor Binding on Grantee
§ 5:20. Concurrent Lease as Transfer of Reversion
§ 5:21. Death of Landlord
§ 5:22. Injury to Reversion by Third Person
§ 5:23. —Particular Injuries

D. RESEARCH REFERENCES
§ 5:24. Generally

## CHAPTER 6
## CONSTRUCTION OF LEASES

A. IN GENERAL
- § 6:1. General Rule
- § 6:2. Ascertaining Intent
- § 6:3. Practical Construction by the Parties
- § 6:4. Statutes as Part of a Lease
- § 6:5. Meaning of Words
- § 6:6. Surrounding Circumstances
- § 6:7. Reconciling Inconsistencies
- § 6:8. Construction Against Draftsman of Lease
- § 6:9. Construction in Favor of Tenant
- § 6:10. Repugnancy Between Printed and Typewritten Matter
- § 6:11. Reasonable Construction
- § 6:12. Additional Liability to be Avoided
- § 6:13. Unconscionable Lease or Clause

B. PAROL EVIDENCE RULE
- § 6:14. Generally
- § 6:15. Exceptions to the Parol Evidence Rule
- § 6:16. Merger Clause and the Parol Evidence Rule
- § 6:17. Form of Provision Against Oral Misrepresentation or Promises
- § 6:18. Ambiguity or Uncertainty in Instrument
- § 6:19. Incomplete Instrument
- § 6:20. Independent Collateral Agreements
- § 6:21. Condition Precedent to Lease Rule

C. MODIFICATION OF LEASE
- § 6:22. Generally
- § 6:23. Necessity of Consideration
- § 6:24. Necessity of Recording
- § 6:25. Oral Modification
- § 6:26. —Provision Against Oral Modification
- § 6:27. Form of Provision Against Oral Modification

D. RESEARCH REFERENCES
- § 6:28. Generally

## PART TWO

## THE RESPECTIVE RIGHTS AND OBLIGATIONS OF LANDLORD AND TENANT

## CHAPTER 7
## PREMISES LEASED; EASEMENTS AND APPURTENANCES

A. IN GENERAL
- § 7:1. What is Included in a Lease?
- § 7:2. Lease of Entire Building as Including Land

§ 7:3. Lease of Dwelling as Including Land, Garden and Curtilage
§ 7:4. Lease of Building as Including Roofs and Walls
§ 7:5. Appurtenances Defined
§ 7:6. Appurtenances Necessary to Enjoyment of Premises as Included in Lease
§ 7:7. Illustrations of Appurtenances Included in a Lease
§ 7:8. Conveniences Not Included in a Lease
§ 7:9. Other Land Not Included in a Lease

B. WHAT IS INCLUDED IN LEASE OF PART OF BUILDING
§ 7:10. Generally
§ 7:11. Basement
§ 7:12. Means of Access and Exit
§ 7:13. Land Not Included
§ 7:14. Roofs and Walls for Common Use
§ 7:15. Roof for Tenant's Sole Use
§ 7:16. Services
§ 7:17. Lobby Attendant Services

C. RIGHT TO LIGHT, AIR, UTILITIES, ETC.
§ 7:18. Light and Air from Adjoining Premises
§ 7:19. —From Lot on Which Leased Premises are Situated
§ 7:20. Heat and Hot Water; Absent Covenant
§ 7:21. Extent of Obligation Under Covenant to Furnish Heat or Hot Water
§ 7:22. Elevator Service
§ 7:23. Water
§ 7:24. Air Space Rights

D. FARM LANDS LEASE
§ 7:25. Generally
§ 7:26. Right to Crops
§ 7:27. Rights with Respect to Hay, Straw, and Manure
§ 7:28. Right to Emblements
§ 7:29. —Special Agreements
§ 7:30. —Effect of Custom or Usage
§ 7:31. —Right of Subtenant

E. RESEARCH REFERENCES
§ 7:32. Generally

CHAPTER 8

**OBLIGATIONS TO DELIVER POSSESSION AND TO OCCUPY PREMISES**

§ 8:1. Landlord's Obligation to Deliver Possession
§ 8:2. Right of Rescission Against Landlord
§ 8:3. Right to Damages Against Landlord
§ 8:4. —Measure of Damages
§ 8:5. —Right to Special Damages
§ 8:6. —Right to Loss of Profits and Time
§ 8:7. Action to Recover Possession

# TABLE OF CONTENTS

§ 8:8. Equitable Relief Against Landlord
§ 8:9. Remedies for Inability to Get Full Possession
§ 8:10. Remedies Against Third Persons
§ 8:11. Form of Covenant to Deliver Possession
§ 8:12. Form of Provision to Protect Landlord Against Inability to Deliver Possession
§ 8:13. Tenant's Obligation to Occupy
§ 8:14. Research References

## CHAPTER 9

## ASSIGNMENT AND SUBLETTING

A. IN GENERAL
§ 9:1. Scope of Chapter
§ 9:2. Assignment and Sublease Defined
§ 9:3. Requisites of Assignment

B. DISTINGUISHING BETWEEN ASSIGNMENT AND SUBLEASE
§ 9:4. Fundamental Test
§ 9:5. Pro Tanto Assignment and Sublease
§ 9:6. —Illustrations of Pro Tanto Assignment
§ 9:7. —Determination of Rent Payable Under Pro Tanto Assignment
§ 9:8. Materiality of Name or Form of Instrument
§ 9:9. Effect of Right of Re-entry
§ 9:10. Effect of Different Rental or Terms
§ 9:11. Effect of Transfer for Period Exceeding Tenant's Term
§ 9:12. Effect of Covenant to Surrender at End of Term
§ 9:13. Explanation of Suggestion that Assignment be Treated as Sublease in Certain Situations
§ 9:14. Distinction Between Assignment and Sublease Summarized
§ 9:15. Importance of Distinguishing Between Assignment and Sublease

C. PRESUMPTION OF ASSIGNMENT
§ 9:16. From Possession by Stranger
§ 9:17. From Payment of Rent by Stranger
§ 9:18. Overcoming Presumption

D. ASSIGNOR'S LIABILITY
§ 9:19. Importance of Privity of Contract and Privity of Estate
§ 9:20. Assignor's Liability on Express Covenants
§ 9:21. Ineffective Termination of Assignor's Liability
§ 9:22. Effective Termination of Assignor's Liability
§ 9:23. Form of Clause Consenting to Assignment with Release of Tenant

E. NON-ASSUMING ASSIGNEE'S LIABILITY
§ 9:24. Nature of Problem

§ 9:25. Liability on Covenants Running with Land
§ 9:26. Liability on Covenant to Pay Rent
§ 9:27. Liability on Covenant to Pay Taxes
§ 9:28. Liability on Pro Tanto Assignment
§ 9:29. Liability Where Assignment in Violation of Lease Restriction
§ 9:30. Termination of Non-assuming Assignee's Liability
§ 9:31. —Effect of Termination
§ 9:32. —Requisites of Bona Fide Assignment
§ 9:33. —Necessity of Consideration; Motive for Assignment
§ 9:34. Liability as Between Non-assuming Assignee and Assignor

F. ASSUMING ASSIGNEE'S LIABILITY

§ 9:35. Definition of "Assumption"
§ 9:36. Scope and Extent of Liability
§ 9:37. —Illustrations
§ 9:38. Landlord's Right to Enforce Assumption Agreement
§ 9:39. Requirements of Assumption Agreement
§ 9:40. —Illustrations
§ 9:41. Form of Assignment with Assumption Agreement
§ 9:42. Liability as Between Assuming Assignee and Assignor

G. ASSIGNEE'S RIGHTS

§ 9:43. Generally

H. LIABILITY OF TENANT'S ASSIGNEE FOR BENEFIT OF CREDITORS

§ 9:44. Generally
§ 9:45. What Constitutes Acceptance of Lease by Assignee for Benefit of Creditors
§ 9:46. Scope of Liability
§ 9:47. Summary of Liability
§ 9:48. Terminating Liability
§ 9:49. —Illustration
§ 9:50. Liability on Lease Not Accepted
§ 9:51. Valuation of Use and Occupation by Assignee

I. SURVIVAL OF DECEASED TENANT'S LIABILITY

§ 9:52. Generally
§ 9:53. Nature of Liability of Personal Representative
§ 9:54. —Illustration

J. SECURITY DEPOSITS

§ 9:55. Effect of Assignment of Lease on Security Deposit
§ 9:56. Effect of Mortgage on Lease on Security Deposit

K. SUBTENANT'S LIABILITIES AND RIGHTS

§ 9:57. Form of Sublease
§ 9:58. Liability to Paramount Landlord
§ 9:59. Liability to Sublessor

§ 9:60. Rights Limited by Terms of Paramount Lease
§ 9:61. Right to Perform Paramount Lease
§ 9:62. —Illustration
§ 9:63. Right to Compel Sublessor's Performance of Paramount Lease
§ 9:64. Form of Agreement Permitting Subtenant to Remedy Sublessor's Default
§ 9:65. Right to Contest Summary Proceedings Brought Against Sublessor
§ 9:66. Rights on New Lease to Sublessor

L. SUBTENANT'S RIGHTS ON CANCELLATION OF PARAMOUNT LEASE
§ 9:67. Right to Vacate
§ 9:68. Effect of Subtenant's Failure to Vacate on Cancellation of Paramount Lease
§ 9:69. Right to Possession
§ 9:70. Effect of Assignment of Sublease After Cancellation of Paramount Lease
§ 9:71. Right to Vacate on Threat of Cancellation
§ 9:72. Summary of Rights

M. SUBTENANT'S RIGHTS ON VOLUNTARY SURRENDER OF PARAMOUNT LEASE
§ 9:73. Generally
§ 9:74. Illustrative Cases

N. RIGHT TO ASSIGN AND SUBLET
§ 9:75. Generally
§ 9:76. Effect of Personal Relationship
§ 9:77. Effect of Emergency Rent Laws
§ 9:78. Residential Tenant's Statutory Right to Assign
§ 9:79. Residential Tenant's Statutory Right to Sublet
§ 9:80. Mobile Home Tenant's Statutory Right to Assign and Sublet
§ 9:81. Form of Agreement to Assign Proprietary Lease (Co-operative Ownership)
§ 9:82. Form of Assignment of Proprietary (Co-operative Apartment) Lease

O. RESTRICTIONS ON RIGHT TO ASSIGN AND SUBLET
§ 9:83. Restrictions Not Favored by Courts
§ 9:84. Covenant Restricting Assignment and Subletting in Proprietary Leases (Co-operative Ownership)
§ 9:85. Effect of Consent or Waiver on Covenant Restricting Assignment
§ 9:86. Effect of Consent or Waiver on Covenant Restricting Subletting
§ 9:87. Effect of Emergency Rent Laws on Restrictions
§ 9:88. Statutory Modification of Restrictions Because of Race or Color
§ 9:89. Breach of Restriction; Voluntary Acts of Tenant
§ 9:90. —Operation of Law

§ 9:91. —Sale by Judicial Officer
§ 9:92. —Bankruptcy
§ 9:93. —Assignment for Benefit of Creditors
§ 9:94. —Acts of Personal Representatives of Deceased Tenant
§ 9:95. Form of Clauses Restricting Assignment and Subletting
§ 9:96. Right of Landlord to Withhold Consent
§ 9:97. Contractual Modification of Right to Withhold Consent
§ 9:98. Criteria for Determination of Reasonableness
§ 9:99. Statutory Modification of Right to Withhold Consent in Case of a Deceased Residential Tenant
§ 9:100. Tenant's Remedies for Landlord's Breach of Covenant to Consent
§ 9:101. Landlord's Remedies for Breach of Restriction Against Assignment or Subletting
§ 9:102. —Equitable Relief
§ 9:103. —Damages

P. RESEARCH REFERENCES
§ 9:104. Generally

## CHAPTER 10

## EFFECT OF HOLDING OVER

A. IN GENERAL
§ 10:1. Effect of Holding Over by Tenant
§ 10:2. Terms and Conditions of Holdover Tenancy
§ 10:3. Holding Over; Burden of Proof
§ 10:4. Leaving Property on Premises as Holding Over
§ 10:5. Breach of Covenant to Surrender in Good Condition as Holding Over
§ 10:6. Holding Over Where Term Ends on Saturday, Sunday, or Holiday
§ 10:7. Holding Over by Assignee or Subtenant
§ 10:8. Retention of Key as Holding Over
§ 10:9. Measure of Damages for Holding Over
§ 10:10. Double Rent Not Recoverable as Damages

B. STATUTORY TENANCY
§ 10:11. Holding Over by Virtue of Emergency Rent Laws
§ 10:12. Duration of Tenancy
§ 10:13. Expiration of Tenancy on Death of Tenant
§ 10:14. Terms and Conditions of Tenancy
§ 10:15. —Waiver of Jury Trial Clause
§ 10:16. —Security Clause
§ 10:17. —Provision for Attorney's Fees
§ 10:18. —Option to Purchase
§ 10:19. —Automatic Renewal Clause
§ 10:20. Damages on Termination of Tenancy

## C. RESEARCH REFERENCES
§ 10:21. Generally

## CHAPTER 11
## RENEWAL OF LEASES

### A. RIGHT TO RENEWAL ABSENT COVENANT
§ 11:1. Generally
§ 11:2. Protection of Tenant's Expectancy of Renewal
§ 11:3. —Effect of Landlord's Refusal to Renew
§ 11:4. —Against Persons in Positions of Trust and Confidence
§ 11:5. —As Between Cotenants
§ 11:6. —As Between Tenant and His/Her Assignee
§ 11:7. —As Between Tenant and His/Her Subtenant
§ 11:8. Mobile Home Park Tenancy

### B. COVENANT TO RENEW
§ 11:9. Phraseology of Covenant
§ 11:10. —Illustrations
§ 11:11. Necessity of Certainty
§ 11:12. Terms Implied in Renewal Covenant
§ 11:13. Form of Covenant to Renew at Lessee's Election
§ 11:14. Provision for Determination of Renewal Rental
§ 11:15. —Form of Provision
§ 11:16. Rights of Parties Pending Appraisal to Determine Renewal Terms
§ 11:17. Illustrations of Indefinite Renewal Covenants

### C. WHO CAN ENFORCE COVENANT TO RENEW
§ 11:18. Right of Renewal at Tenant's Sole Option
§ 11:19. —Landlord's Covenant to Pay for Improvements or Renew
§ 11:20. —Landlord's Covenant to Sell Property or Renew
§ 11:21. —Summary of Rule
§ 11:22. Renewal at Landlord's Sole Option
§ 11:23. "First Privilege of Renewal" Clauses
§ 11:24. Assignee or Sublessee
§ 11:25. —Where Assignor Reserves Right of Renewal
§ 11:26. —Where Assignment is in Violation of Lease Restriction
§ 11:27. Personal Representative of Deceased Tenant
§ 11:28. —Liability of Personal Representative upon Renewal
§ 11:29. Joint Tenants
§ 11:30. Surviving Partner
§ 11:31. Partner Remaining After Dissolution

### D. AGAINST WHOM COVENANT TO RENEW ENFORCEABLE
§ 11:32. Landlord's Grantee
§ 11:33. Trustee or Personal Representative

## E. EXERCISING RIGHT TO RENEW
§ 11:34. Necessity of Strict Performance of Conditions Precedent
§ 11:35. Necessity of Timely Notice to Renew
§ 11:36. When Performance of Other Provisions of Lease Necessary
§ 11:37. Rent Payment as Condition Precedent
§ 11:38. Provision for Renewal "at Expense of Tenant"
§ 11:39. Equitable Relief from Failure to Give Timely Notice of Election to Renew
§ 11:40. Waiver of Performance of Conditions to Renewal
§ 11:41. Effect of Non-waiver of Conditions to Renewal
§ 11:42. Exercising Right of Renewal Where No Notice Required

## F. RENEWAL LEASE
§ 11:43. Necessity for New Lease
§ 11:44. Terms of Renewal Lease Absent Provision Therefor
§ 11:45. Modification of Lease as Projected into Renewal Term
§ 11:46. Modification of Rent as Projected into Renewal Term
§ 11:47. Right to Perpetual Renewals
§ 11:48. Form of Provision for Perpetual Renewals
§ 11:49. Effect of Emergency Rent Laws
§ 11:50. Nature and Effect of Renewed Lease
§ 11:51. —Illustrative Cases
§ 11:52. Tenant-Assignor's Liability Under Renewal Lease

## G. AUTOMATIC RENEWALS
§ 11:53. Form of Automatic Renewal Clause
§ 11:54. Statutory Protection of Tenants Against Automatic Renewal Clauses
§ 11:55. —Effect of Non-compliance with Statute
§ 11:56. —Waiver of Statutory Protection

## H. REMEDIES FOR BREACH OF COVENANT TO RENEW
§ 11:57. Damages Recoverable
§ 11:58. —Measure of Damages
§ 11:59. Specific Performance
§ 11:60. Action for Declaratory Judgment

## I. RESEARCH REFERENCES
§ 11:61. Generally

## CHAPTER 12
### RENT

## A. IN GENERAL
§ 12:1. Nature and Definition
§ 12:2. Distinguished from Other Payments to be Made by Tenant

§ 12:3. When Other Payments to be Made by Tenant Constitute Rent
§ 12:4. Cost of Repairs as Rent
§ 12:5. Mortgage Interest and Taxes as Rent
§ 12:6. Attorney's Fees as Rent
§ 12:7. Attorney's Fees as Rent; Mobile Homes
§ 12:8. Forms of Clauses Making Other Payments Rent
§ 12:9. Importance of Ascertaining When Other Payments to be Made by Tenant Constitute Rent
§ 12:10. Express Covenant to Pay Rent
§ 12:11. Interest on Rent
§ 12:12. Implied Agreement to Pay Rent
§ 12:13. Percentage Rentals
§ 12:14. When Percentage Rent Payable
§ 12:15. Tenant's Obligation Under a Percentage Rental Provision
§ 12:16. Executory Modification of Rent
§ 12:17. Executed Modification of Rent

B. PAYMENT OF RENT
§ 12:18. To Whom Payable
§ 12:19. Duty of Landlord to Provide Written Receipt
§ 12:20. When and Where Payable
§ 12:21. —Sunday or Public Holiday
§ 12:22. Application of Rent Payments
§ 12:23. When Payable in Advance
§ 12:24. —Form
§ 12:25. Course of Conduct Establishing Mode of Payment
§ 12:26. Provision for Acceleration
§ 12:27. —Form
§ 12:28. Recovery by Tenant of Rent Paid
§ 12:29. Separate Actions for Installments
§ 12:30. Liability for Rent upon Death of Tenant

C. RESEARCH REFERENCES
§ 12:31. Generally

## CHAPTER 13

## DEPOSIT TO SECURE PERFORMANCE OF LEASE

A. IN GENERAL
§ 13:1. Provision for Security Deposit; Form
§ 13:2. Importance of Determining Nature of Deposit
§ 13:3. Difficulty of Ascertaining Nature of Deposit
§ 13:4. Nature of Deposit Determined as of Execution of Lease
§ 13:5. Immateriality of Names Used, in Determining Nature of Deposit
§ 13:6. Criteria for Determining Nature of Deposit
§ 13:7. Effect of Agreement to Apply Deposit to Rent
§ 13:8. Penalty Construction Favored

- § 13:9. Construction Where Performance of Several Covenant Secured
- § 13:10. Construction Where Deposit Limited to Breach of a Material Covenant
- § 13:11. Rent Security Deposit by Social Service Officials
- § 13:12. Exempt from Satisfaction of Judgment
- § 13:13. Determination of Nature of Deposit Binding on Both Parties

B. RIGHTS TO DEPOSIT
- § 13:14. On Renewal of Lease
- § 13:15. On Creation of Holdover Tenancy
- § 13:16. On Conveyance of Fee
- § 13:17. On Assignment of Lease by Tenant
- § 13:18. Assignability of Deposit
- § 13:19. Rights of Assignee of Lease
- § 13:20. Rights to Deposit Assigned in Violation of Lease

C. DUTY WITH RESPECT TO DEPOSIT ON CONVEYANCE OF LEASED PROPERTY
- § 13:21. Landlord's Statutory Duty on Conveyance
- § 13:22. Liability of Grantee or Assignee for Deposits Made by Tenant on Conveyance of Rent Stabilized Dwelling Units
- § 13:23. Liability of Grantee or Assignee for Deposits Made by Tenant on Conveyance of Non-Rent Stabilized Dwelling Units
- § 13:24. Form of Clause for Landlord-Grantor's Protection on Conveyance
- § 13:25. Liability for Interest
- § 13:26. Federal Income Tax on Security Deposit Interest

D. CONVERSION OF DEPOSIT
- § 13:27. Deposit as Trust Fund
- § 13:28. —Mobile Home Park Lease
- § 13:29. Conversion of Deposit
- § 13:30. —As Bar to Summary Proceeding

E. AGREEMENT TO APPLY DEPOSIT TO RENT
- § 13:31. How Applied
- § 13:32. Agreement Binding on Grantee

F. RESEARCH REFERENCES
- § 13:33. Generally

## CHAPTER 14

## TENANT'S OBLIGATION TO PAY TAXES AND WATER CHARGES

A. TENANT'S OBLIGATION ABSENT COVENANT
- § 14:1. Generally
- § 14:2. On Buildings Erected by Tenant
- § 14:3. On Buildings Owned by Tenant

# TABLE OF CONTENTS

§ 14:4. —Effect of Landlord's Agreement to Pay All Taxes "Assessed Against Premises"
§ 14:5. Water Taxes and Water Rents Distinguished
§ 14:6. Tenant's Obligation to Pay for Water Absent Covenant

## B. COVENANT TO PAY TAXES

§ 14:7. Problems Raised by Covenant
§ 14:8. Rule of Practical Construction Not Applicable
§ 14:9. Special Assessments
§ 14:10. —Effect of Covenant to Comply with Laws
§ 14:11. Landlord's Income Tax on Rentals
§ 14:12. —When Landlord Exempt
§ 14:13. Covenant to Pay Increase in Taxes
§ 14:14. Covenant to Pay Tax on Amount of Increase in Assessed Valuation
§ 14:15. Obligation to Protest Increase Where Tenant to Pay Increase
§ 14:16. Covenant to Pay Increase in Taxes Caused by Tenant's Improvements
§ 14:17. Covenant to Pay Increase in Taxes Caused by Landlord's Improvements
§ 14:18. Effect of Renewal of Lease on Covenant to Pay Increase in Taxes
§ 14:19. Form of Covenant to Pay Increase in Taxes
§ 14:20. Effect of Change in the Law
§ 14:21. Liability to Pay Taxes as of Due Date or Date of Imposition
§ 14:22. Covenant to Pay Taxes as of Date of Imposition of Tax
§ 14:23. Covenant to Pay Taxes "Levied or Imposed During Term"
§ 14:24. Covenant to Pay Taxes "Imposed in Any and Every Year During the Term"
§ 14:25. Covenant to Pay Taxes "Assessed During Term"
§ 14:26. Covenant to Pay Taxes as of Date of Imposition of Tax; Rule Summarized
§ 14:27. Form of Covenant to Pay Taxes as of Date of Imposition of Tax
§ 14:28. Covenant to Pay Taxes as of Due Date of Tax
§ 14:29. Covenant to "Keep Premises Free, Clear, Discharged and Unincumbered from All Taxes"
§ 14:30. Covenant to Pay Taxes "So That Landlord Shall Receive a Net Rental"
§ 14:31. Covenant to "Pay Carrying and Maintenance Charges"
§ 14:32. Covenant to Pay Taxes "Charged During Term"
§ 14:33. Covenant to Pay Taxes as of Due Date of Tax; Rule Summarized
§ 14:34. Liability of Assignee on Covenant to Pay Taxes
§ 14:35. Right of Grantee to Enforce Covenant to Pay Taxes

§ 14:36. Remedies of Landlord for Breach of Covenant
§ 14:37. Remedy of Tenant for Taxes Paid by him

C. COVENANT TO PAY FOR WATER AND SEWER RENTS
§ 14:38. Remedies of Landlord for Breach of Covenant
§ 14:39. Obligation to Install Water Meter
§ 14:40. Tenant's Obligation to Pay Sewer Rents
§ 14:41. Form of Covenant to Pay for Water and Sewer Rents

D. RESEARCH REFERENCES
§ 14:42. Generally

## CHAPTER 15

## TENANT'S RIGHTS IN THE USE OF THE LEASED PREMISES

A. IN GENERAL
§ 15:1. General Rule
§ 15:2. Where Lease is of Portion of Building
§ 15:3. Right of Tenant to Permit or Invite Persons upon Leased Premises
§ 15:4. Sharing of Apartment
§ 15:5. Landlord's Right to Waive Tenant's Unlawful Use of Lease Premises

B. WASTE
§ 15:6. Tenant's Obligation Not to Commit Waste; Definitions
§ 15:7. Structural Alterations as Waste
§ 15:8. Structural Alterations Made in Good Faith
§ 15:9. Ability to Restore Premises as Justification for Structural Alterations
§ 15:10. Structural Alterations Beneficial to Landlord

C. WHEN TENANT MAY MAKE ALTERATIONS
§ 15:11. Generally
§ 15:12. Necessity for Written Consent to Make Structural Alterations
§ 15:13. Consent Granted by Lease "To Make Inside Alterations Provided Premises Not Injured"
§ 15:14. Form of Provision Consenting to Tenant-Alterations
§ 15:15. Tenant May Not Go Beyond Consent Granted to Make Alterations
§ 15:16. Consent to Alterations Required by Lease; as Affecting Structural Alterations
§ 15:17. —As Affecting Non-structural Alterations Necessary to Carry on Business
§ 15:18. Form of Provision Requiring Landlord's Consent to Alterations and Improvements
§ 15:19. When Landlord May Withhold Lease-required Consent to Alterations

§ 15:20. Right of Tenant in Multiple Dwellings to Install Locks
§ 15:21. Statutory Authorization to Make Alterations
§ 15:22. Forms for Obtaining Statutory Authorization to Make Alterations

D. REMEDIES FOR UNAUTHORIZED ALTERATIONS
§ 15:23. Right of Injunction to Restrain Unauthorized Alterations
§ 15:24. Injunction to Compel Restoration of Premises Altered Without Authorization
§ 15:25. Right to Damages for Unauthorized Alterations

E. RIGHT TO DISPLAY SIGNS
§ 15:26. Where Entire Building Leased
§ 15:27. —Limitations
§ 15:28. Where Part of Building Leased
§ 15:29. —Limitations

F. MISCELLANEOUS RIGHTS
§ 15:30. Erect Television Aerials
§ 15:31. Cut Trees and Timber
§ 15:32. Tenant's Right to Form, Join, or Participate in Tenants' Groups
§ 15:33. Protection from Harassment of Landlord

G. EXPRESS RESTRICTIONS ON USE OF PREMISES BY TENANT
§ 15:34. General Rule
§ 15:35. Binding on Tenant's Assignee
§ 15:36. Binding on Subtenants
§ 15:37. Enforceable by Landlord's Grantee
§ 15:38. Rule of Construction
§ 15:39. Specification of Purpose as Description or Limitation of Use of Premises; Forms
§ 15:40. No Implied Covenant or Warranty that Premises Fit for Restricted Use
§ 15:41. Includability of Covenant of No Legal Impediments
§ 15:42. Display of Signs
§ 15:43. —Where Entire Building Leased
§ 15:44. Restriction by Rules and Regulations of Landlord
§ 15:45. —Form of Clause
§ 15:46. —Rules and Regulations Must be Reasonable
§ 15:47. Mobile Home Parks
§ 15:48. Form of Rules and Regulations
§ 15:49. Projections from Window of Lease Apartment
§ 15:50. Racial Discriminatory Restrictions Under Statute
§ 15:51. Statutory Restrictions Against Children in Dwellings

H. WAIVER OF EXPRESS RESTRICTION
§ 15:52. Generally
§ 15:53. Parol Waiver

§ 15:54. By Acceptance of Rent with Knowledge of Breach
§ 15:55. Waiver Binding on Grantee

I. INJUNCTION TO RESTRAIN IMPROPER USE OF PREMISES
§ 15:56. Against Tenant
§ 15:57. Against Tenant's Assignee
§ 15:58. Against Subtenant

J. RESTRICTION ON LESSOR'S USE OF OTHER PREMISES
§ 15:59. Generally
§ 15:60. Restriction of "Same or Similar Business"; Form
§ 15:61. Restriction of Sale of Specified Articles
§ 15:62. Remedies at Law Against Lessor for Breach
§ 15:63. Paying Rent as Waiver of Breach
§ 15:64. Measure of Damages for Breach
§ 15:65. Equitable Relief Against Lessor
§ 15:66. Remedies at Law Against Competing Tenant
§ 15:67. Equitable Relief Against Competing Tenant

K. RESEARCH REFERENCES
§ 15:68. Generally

## CHAPTER 16

## FIXTURES

A. IN GENERAL
§ 16:1. Fixture Defined
§ 16:2. Trade and Domestic Fixtures Defined

B. REMOVAL OF FIXTURES
§ 16:3. Tenant's Right to Remove Trade and Domestic Fixtures
§ 16:4. —Limitation on Tenant's Right
§ 16:5. —Duty on Removal
§ 16:6. —Illustrative Cases
§ 16:7. Agreement Restricting Tenant's Right to Remove Fixtures
§ 16:8. Effect of Provision that "Tenant's Fixtures Shall Belong to Landlord"
§ 16:9. Effect of Provision that "Alterations Except Movable Fixtures Shall Belong to Landlord"
§ 16:10. Effect of Provision that "Alterations, Additions, Etc. Except Movable Office Furniture Shall Belong to Landlord"
§ 16:11. Tenant's Right to Remove Fixtures as Against Grantee of Fee
§ 16:12. When Tenant May Remove Fixtures
§ 16:13. When Tenant Holding Over May Remove Fixtures
§ 16:14. Tenant's Right to Remove Fixtures Where He Takes New Lease
§ 16:15. Tenant's Right to Remove Fixtures upon Abandonment of Possession

§ 16:16. Tenant's Reservation of Right to Remove Fixtures
§ 16:17. Right of Removal of Substitutions or Replacements of Fixtures Made by Tenant
§ 16:18. Tenant's Right to Personal Property Left on Premises After His/Her Removal or Eviction
§ 16:19. Landlord's Obligation as to Tenant's Personal Property Left on Premises After His/Her Removal or Eviction
§ 16:20. Form of Provision for Removal of Fixtures

C. RESEARCH REFERENCES
§ 16:21. Generally

# VOLUME 2

## CHAPTER 17

## IMPROVEMENTS MADE BY TENANTS

A. IN GENERAL
§ 17:1. Improvements, Defined
§ 17:2. Permission to Make Improvements; Tenant's Duty
§ 17:3. Landlord's Obligation to Pay for Improvements Voluntarily Made by Tenant
§ 17:4. Tenant's Rights to Improvements Voluntarily Made by Tenant
§ 17:5. Tenant as Agent of Lessor Within Mechanic's Lien Statutes

B. TENANT'S COVENANT TO MAKE IMPROVEMENTS
§ 17:6. Duty to Get Building Department's Consent
§ 17:7. Accrual of Liability for Breach
§ 17:8. Measure of Damages for Breach
§ 17:9. Delay Caused by Authorities as Defense for Breach
§ 17:10. Dispossession as Defense for Breach

C. LANDLORD'S COVENANT TO PAY FOR IMPROVEMENTS
§ 17:11. Where Improvements Optional with Tenant
§ 17:12. Conditions Precedent to Payment
§ 17:13. Importance of Determining if Covenant Dependent on Performance of Lease
§ 17:14. When Covenant Independent of Tenant's Performance of Lease
§ 17:15. Dependency of Covenant on Tenant's Performance of Lease by Express Provision
§ 17:16. Dependency of Covenant on Tenant's Performance of Lease by Construction
§ 17:17. Submission to Appraisal as Waiver of Default in Performance of Lease
§ 17:18. Equitable Relief for Default in Performance of Lease
§ 17:19. Covenant to Pay "At Expiration of Term"

§ 17:20. Action at Law to Enforce Landlord's Covenant
§ 17:21. Lien on Land for Enforcement of Landlord's Covenant

D. LANDLORD'S COVENANT TO PAY FOR IMPROVEMENTS OR TO RENEW LEASE
§ 17:22. Generally
§ 17:23. Finality of Landlord's Election
§ 17:24. Delay of Appraisers as Extension of Landlord's Time to Elect
§ 17:25. Tenant's Right of Possession after Expiration of Term
§ 17:26. Tenant's Liability for Use and Occupation on Retaining Possession Until Performance by Landlord of Covenant
§ 17:27. Tenant's Right to Possession After Expiration of Term Where Landlord Covenants Only to Pay for Improvements
§ 17:28. Tenant's Obligation to Take a Renewal Offered Under Landlord's Covenant
§ 17:29. Effect of Tenant's Rejection of a Renewal Offered Under Landlord's Covenant

E. APPRAISAL TO DETERMINE VALUE OF IMPROVEMENTS
§ 17:30. Procedure
§ 17:31. When Courts Will Interfere with Appraised Value
§ 17:32. Who Pays Expenses of Appraisal
§ 17:33. Damages for Landlord's Refusal to Proceed with Appraisal
§ 17:34. Enforcement of Landlord's Agreement to Submit Value of Improvements to Appraisal

F. RESEARCH REFERENCES
§ 17:35. Generally

## CHAPTER 18

## LANDLORD'S DUTY TO PUT AND KEEP LEASED PREMISES IN REPAIR

A. DUTY TO PUT NON-RESIDENTIAL PREMISES IN REPAIR
§ 18:1. Landlord's Duty Absent Covenant
§ 18:2. Covenant of Quiet Enjoyment Imposes No Obligation
§ 18:3. Express Restriction on Tenant's Use Imposes No Obligation on Landlord
§ 18:4. Form of Clause Exculpating Landlord for Condition of Commercial Premises at Commencement of Term
§ 18:5. Landlord's Implied Obligation Where Premises Rented for Public Purpose.

# TABLE OF CONTENTS

### B. DUTY WITH RESPECT TO RESIDENTIAL PREMISES

§ 18:6. Statutory Warranty of Habitability of Residential Premises
§ 18:7. Illustrations of Breach of Warranty of Habitability
§ 18:8. Remedies for Breach of Warranty of Habitability
§ 18:9. Mobile Home Park Owner's Statutory Warranty of Habitability
§ 18:10. Protection Against Criminal Acts of Third Person

### C. DUTY TO KEEP NON-RESIDENTIAL PREMISES IN REPAIR ABSENT COVENANT OR STATUTE

§ 18:11. General Rule
§ 18:12. Effect of Voluntary Repairs
§ 18:13. Effect of Reservation of Right to Repair
§ 18:14. Duty with Respect to Parts of Building Under Landlord's Control
§ 18:15. Buildings Abutting on Public Streets
§ 18:16. Projections from Building
§ 18:17. Tenant's Projection from Building
§ 18:18. Premises Damaged or Destroyed by Fire
§ 18:19. Landlord's Obligation to Comply with Municipal Orders and Regulations

### D. AGREEMENT TO REPAIR

§ 18:20. Oral Agreement Made Prior to Execution of Lease
§ 18:21. Agreement Made After Execution of Lease

### E. COVENANT TO REPAIR NON-RESIDENTIAL PREMISES

§ 18:22. Must be Express
§ 18:23. Will Not be Enlarged by Construction
§ 18:24. Covenant "To Comply with Violations Existing at Time of Execution of Lease"
§ 18:25. Covenant "To Keep in Repair"
§ 18:26. Covenant "To Put and Keep in Repair"
§ 18:27. Binding on Grantee
§ 18:28. Enforceable by Tenant's Assignee

### F. REMEDIES FOR BREACH OF COVENANT TO REPAIR NON-RESIDENTIAL PREMISES

§ 18:29. Necessity for Notice of Disrepair
§ 18:30. Non-payment of Rent
§ 18:31. Damages Recoverable
§ 18:32. —Special Damages
§ 18:33. —Loss of Profits
§ 18:34. —Loss of Rent
§ 18:35. —Property Damage
§ 18:36. Continuing in Possession as Waiver of Damages
§ 18:37. Tenant's Right to Make Repairs at Landlord's Expense
§ 18:38. —When Landlord is Under Statutory Duty to Repair
§ 18:39. Specific Performance

## G. LIABILITY IN NEGLIGENCE FOR DEFECTIVE CONDITION OF NON-RESIDENTIAL PREMISES

§ 18:40. Basis of Liability
§ 18:41. Premises Rented for Public Use
§ 18:42. Premises Abutting on Public Street
§ 18:43. —Effect of Deed or Lease
§ 18:44. Voluntary Repairs Done Negligently
§ 18:45. —Removal of Snow
§ 18:46. Validity of Agreement Exempting Landlord from Liability
§ 18:47. Tenant's Right of Rescission

## H. STATUTORY RIGHT OF ENTRY ON ADJOINING PREMISES TO MAKE IMPROVEMENTS AND REPAIRS

§ 18:48. Generally

## I. RESEARCH REFERENCES

§ 18:49. Generally

# CHAPTER 19

# TENANT'S DUTY TO PUT AND KEEP NON-RESIDENTIAL PREMISES IN REPAIR

## A. DUTY ABSENT COVENANT

§ 19:1. Tenant's Implied Duty
§ 19:2. Basis for Rule
§ 19:3. Extent of Duty
§ 19:4. To Restore or Rebuild

## B. COVENANT TO REPAIR

§ 19:5. Effect on Implied Duty
§ 19:6. Covenant to Keep "in Good Order" or "In Good Repair"
§ 19:7. Covenant to "Put and Keep in Good Repair"
§ 19:8. Covenant to "Keep in Repair"; Form
§ 19:9. Effect of Cause of Disrepair
§ 19:10. Effect of Covenant to Surrender in Certain Condition
§ 19:11. Duty to Rebuild or Reconstruct
§ 19:12. Enforceable by Grantee
§ 19:13. Enforceable Against Assignee of Lease
§ 19:14. When Liability for Breach of Covenant Accrues
§ 19:15. Damages Recoverable
§ 19:16. Deduction for Value of New Over Old to be Allowed Tenant
§ 19:17. Right to Recover Interest on Cost of Repairs
§ 19:18. Right to Recover Cost of Repairs Where Landlord Replaces Instead of Making Repairs
§ 19:19. When Summary Proceedings May be Maintained for Breach
§ 19:20. Statutory Right of Entry on Adjoining Premises to Make Repairs to Leased Premises

## TABLE OF CONTENTS

### C. COVENANT TO COMPLY WITH STATUTES AND GOVERNMENTAL ORDERS
§ 19:21. Nature of Problem; Three Situations
§ 19:22. Structural Work or Changes Defined
§ 19:23. Intent and Not Character of Work Important
§ 19:24. Ascertaining Intention
§ 19:25. Forms of Covenant to Comply with Statutes and Governmental Orders, and with Certificate of Occupancy

### D. COVENANT TO COMPLY WITH STATUTES AND GOVERNMENTAL ORDERS; FIRST SITUATION
§ 19:26. General Rule
§ 19:27. Effect of Covenant Not to Make Alterations Without Consent
§ 19:28. Effect of Covenant "To Abate Nuisances"
§ 19:29. Effect of Covenant to "Conform"
§ 19:30. Tenant of Part of Premises

### E. COVENANT TO COMPLY WITH STATUTES AND GOVERNMENTAL ORDERS; SECOND SITUATION
§ 19:31. General Rule
§ 19:32. What Constitutes Changes in Governmental Policy

### F. COVENANT TO COMPLY WITH STATUTES AND GOVERNMENTAL ORDERS; THIRD SITUATION
§ 19:33. General Rule

### G. DUTY WITH RESPECT TO CONDITION OF PREMISES AT EXPIRATION OF TERM ABSENT COVENANT
§ 19:34. Generally
§ 19:35. "Reasonable Use and Wear" Defined
§ 19:36. Removal of Rubbish and Debris

### H. COVENANT AS TO CONDITION OF PREMISES AT EXPIRATION OF TERM
§ 19:37. Effect of Covenant to Repair
§ 19:38. Obligation to Paint
§ 19:39. Effect of Destruction of Premises
§ 19:40. Effect of Alterations Consented to by Landlord
§ 19:41. When Liability Accrues for Breach of Covenant
§ 19:42. Covenant Runs with the Land
§ 19:43. Effect of Renewal of Lease
§ 19:44. Burden of Proving Breach of Covenant
§ 19:45. Damages Recoverable for Breach
§ 19:46. Form of Covenant to Surrender Premises in Specified Condition

### I. RESEARCH REFERENCES
§ 19:47. Generally

## CHAPTER 20

## OPTIONS TO BUY CONTAINED IN LEASES

A. IN GENERAL

§ 20:1. Validity
§ 20:2. Option to Buy as Covenant Running with Land
§ 20:3. Requisites for Enforceability
§ 20:4. Effect of Lessee's Breach of Terms of Lease
§ 20:5. Effect of Inclusion of Lands Additional to Leased Premises in Option
§ 20:6. Validity in Lease by Trustee
§ 20:7. General Rule of Construction
§ 20:8. "Premises" Defined
§ 20:9. Form of Option to Buy

B. "FIRST OPTION TO BUY"

§ 20:10. Validity
§ 20:11. Not Absolute Option
§ 20:12. Landlord's Obligation
§ 20:13. Necessity for a Bona Fide Offer
§ 20:14. When "First" Option to Buy Must be Exercised; What Constitutes a "Sale"
§ 20:15. Offer for a Sale of an Entire Tract of Which the Leased Premises Form a Part

C. EXERCISING OPTION

§ 20:16. Time is of the Essence
§ 20:17. Effect of Holding Over
§ 20:18. Effect of a Renewal of Lease
§ 20:19. Effect of Emergency Rent Laws
§ 20:20. Effect of Earlier Termination of Lease
§ 20:21. Method of Exercising Option
§ 20:22. When Tender of Purchase Price Must be Made
§ 20:23. Exercise of Option on Landlord's Death
§ 20:24. Exercise of Option on Tenant's Death
§ 20:25. Exercising Option on Conveyance of Fee by Landlord
§ 20:26. Right of Assignee of Lease
§ 20:27. Tenant Entitled to Title Free from Encumbrances
§ 20:28. Status and Interest of Parties on Exercising Option
§ 20:29. Right of Assignment Upon Exercising Option

D. REMEDIES FOR BREACH

§ 20:30. Specific Performance
§ 20:31. Injunction
§ 20:32. Damages Recoverable

E. RESEARCH REFERENCES

§ 20:33. Generally

TABLE OF CONTENTS xxxi

## CHAPTER 21

## FIRE INSURANCE ON LEASED PREMISES

A. IN GENERAL
- § 21:1. Obligation to Insure Leased Premises Absent Covenant
- § 21:2. Necessity for Insurable Interest; Definition
- § 21:3. Landlord's Insurable Interest
- § 21:4. Tenant's Insurable Interest
- § 21:5. Tenant's Rights in Proceeds of Landlord's Insurance
- § 21:6. Recording Insurance Information for Multiple Dwellings

B. TENANT'S COVENANT TO INSURE
- § 21:7. Generally
- § 21:8. Tenant's Covenant to Insure Lease Premises Runs with Land
- § 21:9. Landlord May Insure and Charge Tenant Therefor on Breach of Covenant to Insure
- § 21:10. Measure of Damages Where Landlord Knew of Breach of Covenant to Insure
- § 21:11. Measure of Damages Where Landlord Does Not Know of Breach of Covenant to Insure

C. TENANT'S COVENANT TO PAY INCREASE IN COST OF INSURANCE
- § 21:12. Validity
- § 21:13. Interpretation of Covenant to Pay Increase in Cost of Insurance
- § 21:14. Covenant to Pay Increase in Cost of Insurance Collateral or One Running with the Land

D. RESEARCH REFERENCES
- § 21:15. Generally

## CHAPTER 22

## BANKRUPTCY

- § 22:1. Validity of Bankruptcy Termination Clauses
- § 22:2. Bankruptcy Trustee's Options
- § 22:3. Trustee's Assumption of Lease
- § 22:4. Assignment of Lease by Trustee
- § 22:5. Trustee's Rejection of Lease
- § 22:6. Effect of Trustee's Rejection of Lease
- § 22:7. Ouster of Trustee from Possession of Leased Premises
- § 22:8. Claim for Accrued Rent
- § 22:9. Claim for Future Rent
- § 22:10. Research References

## PART THREE

## TERMINATION OF THE RELATION OF LANDLORD AND TENANT

### CHAPTER 23

### TERMINATION AND FORFEITURE OF LEASES

A. INTRODUCTION
- § 23:1. Generally
- § 23:2. Enforceability of Termination Provisions by Governmental Agency

B. COVENANTS
- § 23:3. Defined
- § 23:4. Types of Covenants
- § 23:5. Dependent or Independent
- § 23:6. Real or Personal
- § 23:7. Remedies for Breach

C. CONDITIONS
- § 23:8. Defined
- § 23:9. Not Favored by Courts
- § 23:10. Creation
- § 23:11. Personal Liability for Breach
- § 23:12. Re-entry and Forfeiture for Breach
- § 23:13. Remedies for Breach when Coupled with Covenant
- § 23:14. Landlord's Election of Remedies for Breach
- § 23:15. Waiver of Forfeiture
- § 23:16. Acceptance of Rent with Knowledge of Breach as Waiver of Forfeiture
- § 23:17. Provision Against Waiver of Breach of Terms of Lease; Form
- § 23:18. Acceptance of Rent Without Knowledge of Breach as Waiver of Forfeiture
- § 23:19. Effect of Waiver of Forfeiture
- § 23:20. Equitable Relief from Forfeiture for Breach

D. CONDITIONAL LIMITATIONS
- § 23:21. Defined
- § 23:22. Fundamental Difference Between Condition Subsequent and Conditional Limitation
- § 23:23. Use of Word "Expire" Not Essential
- § 23:24. Relevance of Intention
- § 23:25. Importance of Distinguishing Between Condition and Conditional Limitation
- § 23:26. First Type; Objective Event
- § 23:27. Second Type: Event Set in Motion by Landlord
- § 23:28. —Illustrations
- § 23:29. Third Type; Event Set in Motion by Tenant's Breach of Lease
- § 23:30. —Illustrations
- § 23:31. Summary of Rules for Determination

# TABLE OF CONTENTS

§ 23:32. Effect of Clause Permitting Tenant to Remedy Default During Running of Notice
§ 23:33. Effect of Additional Clause permitting Landlord to Relet
§ 23:34. Forms
§ 23:35. Runs with Land
§ 23:36. —Dependency on Intent
§ 23:37. Effect of Use of "Legal Representatives"

### E. OPTION TO TERMINATE

§ 23:38. When Exercisable
§ 23:39. Necessity for Breach of Material Covenant
§ 23:40. On Sale of Premises
§ 23:41. —Purchaser's Right
§ 23:42. —Grantee's Right
§ 23:43. Necessity for Good Faith
§ 23:44. Necessity for Timely Notice of Termination
§ 23:45. Notice of Termination on Sunday
§ 23:46. Notice of Termination Between Rent Days
§ 23:47. Effect of Payment of Rent in Advance
§ 23:48. Who May Give Notice of Termination
§ 23:49. Effect of Assignment of Lease
§ 23:50. Consent to Continuation of Possession After Exercise of Termination Option

### F. WAIVER OF TERMINATION OPTION

§ 23:51. Abortive Attempt to Terminate
§ 23:52. Acceptance of Rent
§ 23:53. Equitable Relief from Termination ("Yellowstone" Injunction)

### G. TERMINATION BY SUMMARY PROCEEDING

§ 23:54. Generally
§ 23:55. Termination by Removal During Pendency of Summary Proceeding
§ 23:56. Discontinuance of Summary Proceeding After Removal of Tenant
§ 23:57. Reversal of Judgment After Removal of Tenant
§ 23:58. Removal of Tenant After Dismissal of Summary Proceeding

### H. TERMINATION OF LEASE BY PERSON ENTERING MILITARY SERVICE

§ 23:59. Generally

### I. TERMINATION OF OIL AND GAS LEASE

§ 23:60. "Thereafter" Clause

### J. SURVIVAL OF LIABILITY

§ 23:61. Necessity for Provision Therefor
§ 23:62. Interpretation of Survival of Liability Provision
§ 23:63. On Re-entry
§ 23:64. On Re-entry "By Force or Otherwise"

§ 23:65. —Effect of Tenant's Removal During Pendency of Summary Proceeding
§ 23:66. —Effect of Reversal of Judgment After Tenant's Removal
§ 23:67. On Re-entry by "Process of Law or Otherwise"
§ 23:68. Under Provision, "Resume Possession and Relet"
§ 23:69. Under Provision, "If Premises Become Vacant"
§ 23:70. Effect of Transfer of Reversion
§ 23:71. Nature of Liability
§ 23:72. —Effect of Word "Rent" in Survival Clause
§ 23:73. —Effect of Inability of Landlord to Re-rent
§ 23:74. When Action Maintainable for Survival Damages
§ 23:75. Provision for Periodic Actions to Recover Survival Damages
§ 23:76. Effect of Survival of Liability on Return of Penalty Deposit
§ 23:77. Right to Return of Penalty Deposit Where No Survival of Liability
§ 23:78. —Where no Further Claims Possible
§ 23:79. Condition Precedent to Action for Return of Penalty Deposit
§ 23:80. Form of Survival of Liability Clause

K. RESEARCH REFERENCES
§ 23:81. Generally

## CHAPTER 24

### TERMINATION OF LEASES BY POWER OF EMINENT DOMAIN

§ 24:1. Eminent Domain Defined
§ 24:2. Effect or Lease Where Whole of Leased Premises Taken
§ 24:3. Liability for Rent Where Whole of Leased Premises Taken
§ 24:4. Effect on Lease Where Part of Leased Premises Taken
§ 24:5. Liability for Rent Where Part of Leased Premises Taken
§ 24:6. Respective Interests of Landlord and Tenant in Condemnation Award
§ 24:7. Tenant's Right to Compensation
§ 24:8. Value of Leasehold
§ 24:9. Tenant's Right to Compensation for Options to Purchase and Renew
§ 24:10. Tenant's Right to Compensation Where Lease Provides for Cancellation on Condemnation
§ 24:11. Tenant's Right to Compensation "In Case of Destruction of Premises by Fire or Otherwise"
§ 24:12. Tenant's Right to Compensation for Fixtures
§ 24:13. Value of Fixtures

§ 24:14. What are Fixtures for Condemnation Purposes
§ 24:15. Forms of Condemnation Clause
§ 24:16. Research References

## CHAPTER 25

## TERMINATION OF LEASES BY DESTRUCTION OF PREMISES

### A. COMMON LAW RULE
§ 25:1. Lease of an Entire Building
§ 25:2. Lease of Part of Building

### B. MODIFICATION OF COMMON LAW RULE BY STATUTE
§ 25:3. Generally
§ 25:4. Options Granted to Tenant under Statute
§ 25:5. Landlord's Obligation to Repair or Rebuild
§ 25:6. Necessity of Notice of Termination
§ 25:7. Tenant's Obligation to Remove Debris
§ 25:8. When Surrender to be Made
§ 25:9. Payment of Rent on Election to Terminate
§ 25:10. Payment of Rent on Election to Continue in Possession

### C. APPLICABILITY OF STATUTE
§ 25:11. Dependent upon Cause of Destruction or Injury
§ 25:12. Where Destruction Caused by Defect When Lease Made
§ 25:13. When Destruction Results from Disrepair or Deterioration
§ 25:14. Where Destruction Caused by Vermin or Disease
§ 25:15. Extent of Injury

### D. MODIFICATION OF STATUTORY RULE BY LEASE
§ 25:16. Generally
§ 25:17. Necessity of Providing for the Statutory Contingency
§ 25:18. Ineffective Modification; Covenant to Pay Rent for Whole Term
§ 25:19. —Acceleration of Rent on Abandonment
§ 25:20. —Tenant's Covenant to Repair
§ 25:21. —Provision for Partial Untenantability
§ 25:22. Effective Modification of Statutory Provision

### E. DESTRUCTION CLAUSES; PREMISES PARTIALLY UNTENANTABLE
§ 25:23. Repairs to be Made "With all Proper Speed"
§ 25:24. Tenant's Rights on Landlord's Failure to Repair with all Proper Speed
§ 25:25. Landlord's Duty to Repair or Rebuild Under Provision for Cessation of Rent Until Premises Rebuilt or Repaired

§ 25:26. Landlord's Obligation to Remove Debris Under Provision Requiring Rebuilding or Repair
§ 25:27. Necessity for Surrender of Possession Under Provision Suspending Rent in Event of Untenantability

F. DESTRUCTION CLAUSES; PREMISES WHOLLY UNTENANTABLE
§ 25:28. "Untenantable" Defined; Effect of Possession
§ 25:29. Liability for Rent Under Provision Suspending Rent in Event of Untenantability
§ 25:30. Right of Surrender Under Provision Suspending Rent Pending Repairs
§ 25:31. Liability for Rent Under Provision Terminating Lease if Landlord Elects to Rebuild

G. DESTRUCTION CLAUSES; PREMISES WHOLLY DESTROYED
§ 25:32. Total Destruction Defined
§ 25:33. Substantial Destruction, Defined
§ 25:34. Form of Destruction Clause

H. RESEARCH REFERENCES
§ 25:35. Generally

## CHAPTER 26

## TERMINATION OF LEASES BY SURRENDER AND ACCEPTANCE

A. IN GENERAL
§ 26:1. Surrender Defined
§ 26:2. Express Surrender; Defined
§ 26:3. —When Writing Required
§ 26:4. Express Surrender of Lease to Commence in the Future
§ 26:5. Destruction of Instrument of Lease as Surrender

B. SURRENDER BY OPERATION OF LAW
§ 26:6. Defined
§ 26:7. Problems Created
§ 26:8. Requirements as to Writing
§ 26:9. Of Lease to Commence in the Future
§ 26:10. By New Lease to Same Tenant
§ 26:11. —Requisites of New Lease
§ 26:12. By Modification of Lease
§ 26:13. Importance to Liability of Tenant-Assignor of Lease—Modification Constituting Surrender

C. OFFER OF SURRENDER
§ 26:14. Relinquishing Possession
§ 26:15. Relinquishing Possession at Expiration of Term
§ 26:16. Return of Keys

# TABLE OF CONTENTS

## D. ACCEPTANCE OF SURRENDER
§ 26:17. Resumption of Possession
§ 26:18. —To Protect Property
§ 26:19. —To Repair
§ 26:20. Acceptance of Keys
§ 26:21. Reletting; General Rule
§ 26:22. —Landlord's Obligation to Relet
§ 26:23. —Reletting with Tenant's Consent
§ 26:24. —Reletting without Tenant's Consent
§ 26:25. —Reletting Beyond Tenant's Consent
§ 26:26. —Attempting to Relet
§ 26:27. —Delay in Authorized Reletting
§ 26:28. Who May Accept; Generally
§ 26:29. —Renting Agent
§ 26:30. —Superintendent of Building
§ 26:31. —Managing Agent
§ 26:32. Ratification of Unauthorized Acceptance
§ 26:33. Burden of Proving Surrender and Acceptance
§ 26:34. Waiver of Requirement for Written Acceptance
§ 26:35. Effect of Surrender and Acceptance on Continued Liability of Tenant
§ 26:36. Effect of Surrender and Acceptance on Accrued Liability of Tenant

## E. RESEARCH REFERENCES
§ 26:37. Generally

# CHAPTER 27

# QUIET ENJOYMENT OF LEASED PREMISES

## A. COVENANT FOR QUIET ENJOYMENT
§ 27:1. Scope of Covenant
§ 27:2. Covenant Implied from Landlord-Tenant Relationship
§ 27:3. Implication of Covenant Not Prohibited by Law
§ 27:4. Breach of Covenant for Quiet Enjoyment
§ 27:5. When Covenant for Quiet Enjoyment Dependent on Tenant's Performance
§ 27:6. Injunctive Relief for Disturbance of Tenant's Possession
§ 27:7. Recovery of Damages for Interference with Tenant's Right of Removal from Premises
§ 27:8. Interference with Tenant's Right of Removal from Premises as Conversion

## B. LIMITED COVENANT FOR QUIET ENJOYMENT
§ 27:9. Generally
§ 27:10. Breach without Eviction

## C. RESEARCH REFERENCES
§ 27:11. Generally

## CHAPTER 28
## ACTUAL AND CONSTRUCTIVE EVICTION

A. ACTUAL EVICTION
- § 28:1. Actual and Constructive Eviction Defined
- § 28:2. Total and Partial Actual Eviction Defined
- § 28:3. Landlord's Right of Entry on Leased Premises
- § 28:4. Landlord's Right of Entry When Leased Premises Unoccupied
- § 28:5. Trespass by Landlord
- § 28:6. Trespass by Landlord and Acts of Exclusion
- § 28:7. Landlord's Right to Repair, Alter and Improve Leased Premises, Generally
- § 28:8. Landlord's Right to Repair, Alter and Improve Leased Premises to Comply with Governmental Orders
- § 28:9. Repairs and Improvements of Leased Premises by Landlord
- § 28:10. Repairs by Landlord in Parts of Premises Under Landlord's Control
- § 28:11. Repairs by Landlord to Leased Premises with Tenant's Consent
- § 28:12. Repairs to Leased Premises by Landlord Outside Scope of Reserved Right
- § 28:13. Demolition of or Repairs to Leased Premises Required by Governmental Orders
- § 28:14. Deprivation of Appurtenances
- § 28:15. Interference with Right of Ingress and Egress
- § 28:16. Changing Means of Access to Leased Premises
- § 28:17. Exclusion from Use of Abutting Street
- § 28:18. Change of Grade of Street
- § 28:19. Eviction of Subtenant by Paramount Landlord
- § 28:20. Interference with Subtenancy by Paramount Landlord

B. CONSTRUCTIVE EVICTION
- § 28:21. Constructive Eviction Distinguished from Actual Eviction
- § 28:22. Material Deprivation of Enjoyment of Premises Essential
- § 28:23. Permanent Deprivation of Enjoyment of Premises Essential
- § 28:24. Materiality of Intent of Landlord
- § 28:25. Landlord's Acts Must be Wrongful
- § 28:26. Abandonment of Possession Essential
- § 28:27. —Effect of Unreasonable Delay in Abandoning Possession
- § 28:28. —Effect of Delay in Reliance on Landlord's Promises
- § 28:29. —Abandonment After Landlord Commences Repairs
- § 28:30. —Abandonment After Condition Rectified

§ 28:31. Constructive Eviction Question of Fact
§ 28:32. Failure to Maintain Common Appurtenances in Repair
§ 28:33. Leaks and Seepages from Common Appurtenances
§ 28:34. Failure to Repair
§ 28:35. Making Repairs or Improvements
§ 28:36. Misconduct of Landlord's Employees
§ 28:37. Operation of Machinery
§ 28:38. Infection of Premises with Contagious Disease
§ 28:39. Infestation of Vermin Where Entire Building Leased
§ 28:40. Infestation of Vermin Where Part of Building Leased
§ 28:41. Offensive Odors
§ 28:42. Deprivation of Light and Air from Adjoining Premises
§ 28:43. Deprivation of Light and Air from Lot on Which Leased Premises are Situated
§ 28:44. Failure to Furnish Heat and Hot Water
§ 28:45. Deprivation of Elevator Service
§ 28:46. Arbitrary Restriction of Elevator Use
§ 28:47. Conversion from Manually Operated to Automatic Elevator
§ 28:48. Deprivation of Water

C. EVICTION BY TITLE PARAMOUNT

§ 28:49. Breach of Covenant of Quiet Enjoyment
§ 28:50. Elements
§ 28:51. Apprehension or Threat of Eviction
§ 28:52. Wrongful Eviction of Subtenant
§ 28:53. Yielding Possession Pursuant to Judgment
§ 28:54. Yielding Possession Voluntarily
§ 28:55. Attornment
§ 28:56. Eviction of Subtenant by Forfeiture of Paramount Lease
§ 28:57. Landlord's Obligation to Prevent Mortgage Foreclosure
§ 28:58. —Where Lease Expressly subordinated to Mortgage
§ 28:59. —Survives Conveyance of Fee
§ 28:60. Form of Clause Protecting Landlord Against Mortgage Foreclosure
§ 28:61. Eviction by Mortgage Foreclosure; Tenant Not a Party
§ 28:62. Necessity for Sale and Conveyance in Foreclosure
§ 28:63. Danger of Vacating Prior to Sale in Foreclosure
§ 28:64. Appointment of Receiver in Mortgage Foreclosure Action
§ 28:65. Foreclosure Receiver's Rights to the Rent

D. EVICTION BY STRANGERS

§ 28:66. Generally

§ 28:67. Burden of Proving Eviction by Strangers Done with Landlord's Sanction
§ 28:68. Eviction of Subtenant by Paramount Landlord as Eviction by Sublessor
§ 28:69. Acts of Other Tenants in Their Own Apartments
§ 28:70. Acts of Tenants in Parts of Building Under Landlord's Control
§ 28:71. Acts of Other Tenants Where Landlord Reserves Right to Terminate Leases
§ 28:72. Acts of Public Authorities
§ 28:73. —Where Landlord at Fault

E. REMEDY FOR TOTAL EVICTION
§ 28:74. Discharge from Rent Accruing After Eviction
§ 28:75. Discharge from Rent Accruing Prior to Eviction
§ 28:76. Damages Recoverable for Total Eviction by Landlord
§ 28:77. Damages Recoverable for Total Eviction by Title Paramount; Necessity for Covenant for Quiet Enjoyment
§ 28:78. —Where Landlord Not at Fault
§ 28:79. —Where Landlord at Fault

F. REMEDY FOR PARTIAL EVICTION
§ 28:80. Discharge from Rent Accruing After Eviction; by Landlord
§ 28:81. Discharge from Rent Accruing After Eviction; by Title Paramount
§ 28:82. Damages Recoverable for Partial Eviction by Title Paramount; General Rule
§ 28:83. Damages Recoverable for Partial Eviction by Landlord; Tenant Remains in Possession and Admits Liability for Rent
§ 28:84. —Tenant Remains in Possession and Disputes Liability for Rent
§ 28:85. —Tenant Vacates from Possession of Entire Premises

G. FAILURE TO FURNISH HEAT AND UTILITIES
§ 28:86. As Defense to Rent
§ 28:87. Damages Recoverable for Breach of Implied Covenant to Furnish Heat
§ 28:88. Damages Recoverable for Breach of Express Covenant to Furnish Heat
§ 28:89. Alternative to General Damages for Breach of Express Covenant to Furnish Heat
§ 28:90. Statutory Right to Deduct from Rent Payments for Heat Failure in Multiple Dwelling
§ 28:91. Discontinuance of Utility Services to Building; Tenant's Right to Offset Payment and Damages

H. RESEARCH REFERENCES
§ 28:92. Generally

# PART FOUR

# SUMMARY PROCEEDINGS TO RECOVER POSSESSION OF REAL PROPERTY

## CHAPTER 29

### SUMMARY PROCEEDINGS: INTRODUCTORY MATTERS

§ 29:1. Landlord's Right to Regain Possession Without Process of Law
§ 29:2. Landlord's Right to Maintain Possession Regained Without Process of Law
§ 29:3. Landlord's Legal Possessory Remedies
§ 29:4. Landlord's Equitable Possessory Remedies
§ 29:5. History of Summary Proceedings
§ 29:6. Summary Proceedings a Special Proceeding
§ 29:7. Summary Proceeding Relates Only to Real Property
§ 29:8. Statutory Sources; Right to Maintain Summary Proceeding
§ 29:9. —Procedure in Summary Proceeding
§ 29:10. Summary Proceeding Not a Bar to Other Remedies at Law
§ 29:11. Summary Proceeding Not a Bar to Other Remedies Without Process of Law
§ 29:12. Consent of Parties Ineffective to Confer Jurisdiction in Summary Proceeding
§ 29:13. Necessity for Compliance with Statutory Requirements in Maintaining Summary Proceeding
§ 29:14. Outline of Procedure in Summary Proceeding
§ 29:15. —Effect of Rent Control or Rent Stabilization
§ 29:16. Research References

## CHAPTER 30

### GROUNDS FOR SUMMARY PROCEEDINGS; TENANT WRONGFULLY HOLDING OVER

A. IN GENERAL

§ 30:1. Elements
§ 30:2. Effect of Acceptance of Rent on Holdover Proceeding
§ 30:3. Expiration of Term Prior to Commencement of Proceeding
§ 30:4. Expiration of Term by Lapse of Time Essential
§ 30:5. Forfeiture of Term for Breach of Condition
§ 30:6. Occurrence of Conditional Limitation
§ 30:7. Right to Self-operative Renewal
§ 30:8. Right to Non-self-operative Renewal
§ 30:9. Definition and Duration of "Term"

§ 30:10. —Where no Expiration Date Specified
§ 30:11. —Where Expiration Date Specified
§ 30:12. Expiration of Fixed Term on Sunday
§ 30:13. Effect of Death of Lessee on Fixed Term
§ 30:14. Effect of Death of Lessor on Fixed Term
§ 30:15. Necessity for Notice to Quit for Fixed Term
§ 30:16. Waiver or Revocation by Landlord of Notice to Quit
§ 30:17. Effect of Dismissal of Proceeding on Notice to Quit

B. MONTHLY TENANCY IN NEW YORK CITY

§ 30:18. Monthly Tenancy Defined
§ 30:19. Necessity for Notice to Quit
§ 30:20. Contents of Notice to Quit
§ 30:21. Form of Notice to Quit
§ 30:22. Service of Notice to Quit
§ 30:23. —After Tenant's Death
§ 30:24. —When Must be Served
§ 30:25. Who Must Give Notice to Quit
§ 30:26. Waiver by Tenant of Notice to Quit

C. MONTHLY TENANCY OUTSIDE NEW YORK CITY

§ 30:27. Necessity for Notice to Quit
§ 30:28. Manner of Serving Notice to Quit

D. TENANCY AT WILL

§ 30:29. Creation
§ 30:30. Creation by Entry Under Void Lease
§ 30:31. Necessity for Notice to Quit
§ 30:32. Manner of Serving Notice to Quit
§ 30:33. Who Must Give Notice to Quit
§ 30:34. When Notice to Quit Must be Served
§ 30:35. Effect of Second Notice to Quit
§ 30:36. Form of Notice to Quit

E. TENANCY BY SUFFERANCE

§ 30:37. Creation
§ 30:38. Lessee of Deceased Life Tenant
§ 30:39. Necessity for Notice to Quit
§ 30:40. Manner of Serving Notice to Quit

F. PERIODIC TENANCIES

§ 30:41. Defined
§ 30:42. Creation
§ 30:43. Determining Period
§ 30:44. Creation by Entry Under Invalid Lease
§ 30:45. Notice to Quit be Given Year-to-Year Tenant

G. MONTH-TO-MONTH TENANCY IN NEW YORK CITY

§ 30:46. Necessity for Notice to Quit
§ 30:47. Contents of Notice to Quit
§ 30:48. Form of Notice to Quit for Month-to-Month Tenancy

# TABLE OF CONTENTS

§ 30:49. Manner of Serving Notice to Quit
§ 30:50. Service of Notice to Quit After Death of Month-to-Month Tenant
§ 30:51. When Notice to Quit to be Served
§ 30:52. Who Must Give Notice to Quit
§ 30:53. Waiver of Notice to Quit

### H. MONTH-TO-MONTH TENANCY OUTSIDE NEW YORK CITY
§ 30:54. Necessity for Notice to Quit
§ 30:55. Manner of Service of Notice to Quit

### I. INDEFINITE TENANCY
§ 30:56. Expiration in New York City
§ 30:57. Tenancy at Will
§ 30:58. Periodic Tenancy

### J. OBJECTIONABLE TENANCY
§ 30:59. Ground for Summary Proceeding
§ 30:60. Who is an Objectionable Tenant
§ 30:61. Harboring an Animal in Violation of Terms of Lease

### K. ILLEGAL USE
§ 30:62. Necessity for Notice of Termination

### L. RENT CONTROLLED AND RENT STABILIZED TENANCIES
§ 30:63. Rent Controlled Tenancy; Grounds for Eviction
§ 30:64. Rent Stabilized Tenancy; Grounds for Eviction
§ 30:65. Contents of Notice of Termination to Rent Stabilized Tenant

### M. RESEARCH REFERENCES
§ 30:66. Generally

## CHAPTER 31

## GROUNDS FOR SUMMARY PROCEEDINGS; EMPLOYEE WRONGFULLY HOLDING OVER

§ 31:1. Importance of Determining Whether Employee or Tenant Relationship
§ 31:2. Right to Continued Possession upon Termination of Employee Relationship
§ 31:3. Employer's Common Law Right of Removal
§ 31:4. Nature of "Termination" of Employment Required for Common Law Removal
§ 31:5. Employer's Right to Summary Proceeding
§ 31:6. Nature of "Termination" of Employment Required for Summary Proceeding
§ 31:7. Creation of Tenant Relationship After Termination of Employment
§ 31:8. Research References

## CHAPTER 32

## GROUNDS FOR SUMMARY PROCEEDINGS; NON-PAYMENT OF RENT

A. IN GENERAL
- § 32:1. Elements
- § 32:2. Effect of Pending Action for Rent
- § 32:3. Effect of Recovery of Judgment for Rent
- § 32:4. Effect of Right of Forfeiture for Non-payment of Rent
- § 32:5. Effect of Action to Recover Real Property
- § 32:6. Consent to Holding Over After Default in Payment of Rent
- § 32:7. —Form
- § 32:8. Default in Rent Prior to Commencement of Proceeding Essential
- § 32:9. What is Rent?
- § 32:10. Proceeding After Lapse of Three Days After Service of Notice
- § 32:11. Proceeding Brought by Landlord's Successor in Interest
- § 32:12. Proceeding Brought After Tenant's Death

B. DEMAND OR NOTICE
- § 32:13. Generally
- § 32:14. Landlord's Election Between Demand and Notice
- § 32:15. Burden of Proving Demand or Notice
- § 32:16. Sufficiency of Demand
- § 32:17. Service of Notice of Petition as Demand
- § 32:18. Demand by Mail
- § 32:19. Demand by Phone
- § 32:20. Demand Made by Agent
- § 32:21. When Demand Must be Made
- § 32:22. Sufficiency of Notice
- § 32:23. Form of Notice
- § 32:24. Method of Serving Notice
- § 32:25. —Alleging Method of Serving Notice

C. RESEARCH REFERENCES
- § 32:26. Generally

## CHAPTER 33

## GROUNDS FOR SUMMARY PROCEEDINGS; NON-PAYMENT OF TAXES

- § 33:1. Elements
- § 33:2. Effect of Acceptance of Rent
- § 33:3. City Property Only
- § 33:4. Effect of Right to Forfeit Term for Failure to Pay Taxes
- § 33:5. Necessity for Demand or Notice
- § 33:6. Form of Notice to Pay Taxes or Assessments
- § 33:7. Research References

## CHAPTER 34

## GROUNDS FOR SUMMARY PROCEEDINGS; ILLEGAL USE AND BANKRUPTCY

A. ILLEGAL USE

§ 34:1. Elements
§ 34:2. Necessity for Preliminary Notice
§ 34:3. What Constitutes Illegal Use?
§ 34:4. —Where Landlord Obligated to Comply with Statute
§ 34:5. Necessity for Continuity of Use
§ 34:6. Failure to Have Required License for Business or Profession
§ 34:7. Violation of Departmental Orders
§ 34:8. Burden of Proof
§ 34:9. Discontinuance of Illegal Use
§ 34:10. Landlord's Knowledge or Consent as Defense to Proceeding

B. TENANT-FACTORY LAW VIOLATION

§ 34:11. As Ground for Summary Proceeding
§ 34:12. Necessity for Notice of Termination
§ 34:13. Necessity for Covenant to Comply with Labor Law
§ 34:14. Necessity for Allegation of Factory Tenancy

C. BANKRUPTCY

§ 34:15. As Ground for Summary Proceeding

D. RESEARCH REFERENCES

§ 34:16. Generally

## CHAPTER 35

## GROUNDS FOR SUMMARY PROCEEDINGS; ADDITIONAL CASES

A. EXECUTION SALE SUMMARY PROCEEDING

§ 35:1. Elements
§ 35:2. Necessity for Valid Judgment
§ 35:3. Necessity for Valid Execution and Sale
§ 35:4. Necessity of Perfected Title
§ 35:5. Occupant's Rights Must be Subordinate to Judgment
§ 35:6. Necessity for Notice to Quit
§ 35:7. Form of Notice to Quit

B. MORTGAGE FORECLOSURE SUMMARY PROCEEDING

§ 35:8. Elements
§ 35:9. Form of Notice to Quit

C. SHARECROPPER SUMMARY PROCEEDING

§ 35:10. Elements
§ 35:11. Form of Notice to Quit

### D. SQUATTER PROCEEDING

§ 35:12. Elements
§ 35:13. Squatting and Intruding, Defined
§ 35:14. Original Entry Without Right Essential
§ 35:15. Effect of Entry with Permission of Tenant
§ 35:16. Effect of Revocation of Permission to Enter
§ 35:17. Effect of Entry by Collusion of Tenant
§ 35:18. Against Vendee in Possession
§ 35:19. Against Lessee of Life Tenant After Lessor's Death
§ 35:20. Against Widow of Tenant
§ 35:21. Against Immediate Family of Deceased Tenant
§ 35:22. By Spouse Against Spouse
§ 35:23. Against Tenant Changing Apartment Without Landlord's Permission
§ 35:24. By Tenant Against Guest
§ 35:25. To Remove Television Aerials
§ 35:26. Necessity for Notice to Quit
§ 35:27. Form of Notice to Quit

### E. TAX SALE SUMMARY PROCEEDING

§ 35:28. Generally
§ 35:29. Right of Assignee of Tax Sale Bid to Bring Proceeding
§ 35:30. Statutory Conditions Precedent
§ 35:31. Necessity for Notice to Quit
§ 35:32. Form of Notice to Quit

### F. SUMMARY PROCEEDING AGAINST LESSEE OF DECEASED LIFE TENANT

§ 35:33. Elements
§ 35:34. Form of Notice to Quit

### G. SUMMARY PROCEEDING AGAINST LICENSEE

§ 35:35. Elements
§ 35:36. Form of Notice to Quit for Licensee

### H. SUMMARY PROCEEDING AGAINST VENDEE OR MORTGAGEE IN POSSESSION

§ 35:37. Elements

### I. SUMMARY PROCEEDING AGAINST VENDOR IN POSSESSION

§ 35:38. Elements

### J. SUMMARY PROCEEDINGS BY SPOUSE AGAINST SPOUSE

§ 35:39. Elements

### K. SUMMARY PROCEEDING AGAINST OCCUPANT OF LAND APPROPRIATED BY CONSERVATION COMMISSIONER

§ 35:40. Elements

## L. ADULT HOME RESIDENTS
§ 35:41. Generally

## M. SMOKE DETECTOR TAMPERING
§ 35:42. Generally

## N. RESEARCH REFERENCES
§ 35:43. Generally

## CHAPTER 36

# GROUNDS FOR SUMMARY PROCEEDINGS; FORCIBLE OR UNLAWFUL ENTRY AND DETAINER

§ 36:1. Generally
§ 36:2. Other Remedies Available
§ 36:3. Elements of Forcible or Unlawful Entry and Detainer Summary Proceeding
§ 36:4. Necessity for Landlord and Tenant Relationship
§ 36:5. Ouster of Employee or Licensee
§ 36:6. Proceeding Available Between Tenants in Common
§ 36:7. Proceeding Available Between Co-lessees
§ 36:8. Necessity for Actual or Constructive Possession
§ 36:9. —Actual Possession Defined
§ 36:10. —Constructive Possession Defined
§ 36:11. Defenses
§ 36:12. —Better Title
§ 36:13. Research References

## CHAPTER 37

# GROUNDS FOR SUMMARY PROCEEDINGS; MOBILE HOME DWELLERS

§ 37:1. Generally
§ 37:2. Research References

## CHAPTER 38

# SUMMARY PROCEEDINGS; AGAINST WHOM MAINTAINABLE

## A. IN GENERAL
§ 38:1. Generally
§ 38:2. Corporations
§ 38:3. Incompetent Persons
§ 38:4. Diplomatic Officers of Foreign States
§ 38:5. Necessity for Conventional Relation of Landlord and Tenant
§ 38:6. —Creation of Conventional Relation
§ 38:7. —Necessity for Agreement to Pay Rent

## B. PARTICULAR PERSONS
§ 38:8. New Tenant Against Holdover Tenant
§ 38:9. Vendor Against Vendee

§ 38:10. Landlord Against Tenant-Vendee
§ 38:11. Grantee Against Grantor
§ 38:12. Assignee of Leasehold Against Assignor
§ 38:13. Assignor of Leasehold Against Assignee
§ 38:14. Lodgers and Boarders
§ 38:15. Mortgagee of Fee Against Mortgagor's Tenants
§ 38:16. Mortgagee of Fee Against Mortgagor
§ 38:17. Paramount Landlord Against Subtenant
§ 38:18. Landlord Against Assignee
§ 38:19. Landlord Against Assignee Where Assignment Prohibited
§ 38:20. Widow of Tenant as Assignee
§ 38:21. Estate of Deceased Tenant
§ 38:22. Tenants in Common

C. NECESSITY FOR POSSESSION
§ 38:23. Generally
§ 38:24. Possession Through Subtenants or Agents
§ 38:25. Possession through Assignee; Assignment with Landlord's Consent
§ 38:26. Possession through Assignee; Assignment Prohibited
§ 38:27. Effect of Removal Prior to Commencement of Proceeding
§ 38:28. Effect of Removal after Commencement of Proceeding

D. ADDITIONAL PARTIES
§ 38:29. Necessary and Proper Parties Defined
§ 38:30. General Rule
§ 38:31. Subtenant
§ 38:32. Children, Wife, Guests of Tenant
§ 38:33. Person Hiring Desk Space

E. RESEARCH REFERENCES
§ 38:34. Generally

## CHAPTER 39

### SUMMARY PROCEEDINGS; BY WHOM MAINTAINABLE

§ 39:1. General Rule
§ 39:2. Corporations
§ 39:3. Partner-Lessor of Partnership
§ 39:4. Landlord After Conveyance of Reversion
§ 39:5. Landlord After Contracting to Convey Reversion
§ 39:6. Landlord After Giving New Lease to Premises
§ 39:7. Landlord After Assigning Rents
§ 39:8. Lessee Entitled to Possession
§ 39:9. Tenant of Concurrent Lease as Assignee
§ 39:10. Assignee of Rents Only
§ 39:11. Assignee of Lease by Partner to His Partnership

TABLE OF CONTENTS  xlix

§ 39:12. Legal Representative, Attorney, or Agent
§ 39:13. Mortgagee in Possession Under Assignment of Rents as Agent
§ 39:14. Co-Owner
§ 39:15. Authorized Not-for-Profit Corporations and Tenant Associations
§ 39:16. Temporary Administrator
§ 39:17. Receiver
§ 39:18. Landlord's Rights After Receivership Vacated
§ 39:19. Assignee of Landlord for Benefit of Creditors
§ 39:20. Neighbor of Illegally Used Real Property
§ 39:21. Form of Notice to be Given by Neighbor of Illegally Used Real Property
§ 39:22. Research References

## VOLUME 3

### CHAPTER 40

### SUMMARY PROCEEDINGS; JURISDICTION AND VENUE

§ 40:1. Jurisdiction, Generally
§ 40:2. Jurisdiction over Subject Matter
§ 40:3. Jurisdiction of District Courts, City Courts, and Justice Courts
§ 40:4. Housing Part of New York City Civil Court
§ 40:5. —Who May Represent Parties in Housing Part
§ 40:6. —Trials and Relief
§ 40:7. Jurisdiction of Supreme and Surrogate's Courts
§ 40:8. Supreme Court Power of Consolidation and Removal
§ 40:9. Venue
§ 40:10. Procedure for Change of Venue
§ 40:11. Research References

### CHAPTER 41

### SUMMARY PROCEEDING; THE PETITION

A. IN GENERAL

§ 41:1. Generally
§ 41:2. Form of Papers
§ 41:3. Contents of Petition
§ 41:4. Pleading by or Against Corporation
§ 41:5. Appearance by Attorney for Corporate Petitioner

B. VERIFICATION

§ 41:6. Verification Jurisdictionally Required
§ 41:7. Requirements of Verification
§ 41:8. Notary's Omission to Sign Jurat
§ 41:9. Omission of Date of Verification
§ 41:10. Omissions on Copy Served

§ 41:11. Form of Verification; Individual
§ 41:12. —Corporate
§ 41:13. Waiver of Failure to Verify; Amendability of Defective Verification

C. DESCRIPTION OF PREMISES
§ 41:14. Description Jurisdictionally Required
§ 41:15. Waiver of Defective Description

D. INTEREST OF PARTIES
§ 41:16. Statement of Interest of Parties Jurisdictionally Required
§ 41:17. Waiver of Defective Statement
§ 41:18. Stating Petitioner's Interest
§ 41:19. —Illustrative Statements
§ 41:20. —In Squatter Proceeding
§ 41:21. —In a Forcible Entry Proceeding
§ 41:22. Statement of Respondent's Interest
§ 41:23. Unknown Parties

E. FACTS AUTHORIZING REMOVAL
§ 41:24. Generally
§ 41:25. Alleging Service of Required Notice
§ 41:26. —Manner of Service
§ 41:27. —Annexing Proof of Service
§ 41:28. —When Waived
§ 41:29. —Authority of Agent to Give Notice
§ 41:30. —Waiver of Defective Allegation
§ 41:31. Alleging Holding Over by Subtenant
§ 41:32. Allegations of Multiple Dwelling Registration
§ 41:33. Allegations Required in Rent-Controlled and Rent Stabilized Areas

F. PRAYER FOR RELIEF
§ 41:34. Generally
§ 41:35. Forms of Petition; Checklist for Contents

G. POWER OF AMENDMENT
§ 41:36. Generally

H. RESEARCH REFERENCES
§ 41:37. Generally

## CHAPTER 42

### SUMMARY PROCEEDINGS; THE NOTICE OF PETITION

A. IN GENERAL
§ 42:1. By Whom Issued
§ 42:2. Contents; Forms
§ 42:3. When and Where Returnable
§ 42:4. Short Notice in Holdover Proceeding

## B. SERVICE
§ 42:5. Personal Service
§ 42:6. Substituted Service
§ 42:7. Conspicuous Place Service
§ 42:8. Who May Serve Notice of Petition
§ 42:9. Time of Service
§ 42:10. Waiver of Irregularity in Service
§ 42:11. Filing Proof of Service
§ 42:12. Forms

## C. RESEARCH REFERENCES
§ 42:13. Generally

# CHAPTER 43
# SUMMARY PROCEEDINGS; THE ANSWER

## A. IN GENERAL
§ 43:1. When Interposed
§ 43:2. Contents and Form
§ 43:3. Amendment
§ 43:4. Motion to Dismiss in Lieu of Answer; Objection to Jurisdiction
§ 43:5. Right of Interpleader

## B. WHO MAY ANSWER
§ 43:6. Right of Intervention
§ 43:7. Assignee of Rents
§ 43:8. Subtenant
§ 43:9. Assignee of Lease
§ 43:10. Form of Intervenor's Answer

## C. DENIALS
§ 43:11. Requirements

## D. DENIAL OF LANDLORD'S TITLE
§ 43:12. Generally
§ 43:13. Necessity for Landlord-Tenant Relationship for Estoppel to Deny Landlord's Title
§ 43:14. Tenant's Attack on Lease
§ 43:15. Expiration of Landlord's Title
§ 43:16. Tenant's Acquisition of Title at a Judicial Sale
§ 43:17. Tenant's Acquisition of Title at Tax Sale
§ 43:18. Landlord a Grantee
§ 43:19. Void Attornment
§ 43:20. Effect on Jurisdiction

## E. DEFENSES
§ 43:21. Generally
§ 43:22. Payment
§ 43:23. Extension of Time of Payment
§ 43:24. Reduction of Rent
§ 43:25. Compromise of claim for Rent

§ 43:26. Accord and Satisfaction
§ 43:27. Failure to Obtain Certificate of Occupancy
§ 43:28. Violations
§ 43:29. Loft Occupied as Residence
§ 43:30. Agreement to Give New Lease
§ 43:31. Breach of Covenant
§ 43:32. Equitable Defenses
§ 43:33. Stale Claims (Laches)
§ 43:34. Retaliatory Eviction
§ 43:35. Retaliatory Eviction; Mobile Homes
§ 43:36. Waiver of Defense by Failure to Interpose It

F. COUNTERCLAIM
§ 43:37. Generally
§ 43:38. Equitable Counterclaim
§ 43:39. Cases Illustrative of Distinction Between Equitable Counterclaims and Equitable Defenses
§ 43:40. Waiver of Right to Interpose Counterclaim
§ 43:41. Relief Obtainable on Counterclaim
§ 43:42. Limitation on Amount of Recovery on Counterclaim
§ 43:43. Effect on Counterclaim of Dismissal of Proceeding
§ 43:44. Effect of Failure to Interpose Counterclaim

G. RESEARCH REFERENCES
§ 43:45. Generally

## CHAPTER 44

## SUMMARY PROCEEDINGS; PRETRIAL PROCEEDINGS; THE TRIAL

A. IN GENERAL
§ 44:1. Disclosure Proceedings
§ 44:2. Bill of Particulars
§ 44:3. Motion Practice
§ 44:4. Mode of Trial
§ 44:5. Adjournments
§ 44:6. Trial Practice

B. TRIAL BY JURY
§ 44:7. Generally
§ 44:8. New York City Civil Court
§ 44:9. City Courts Outside New York City
§ 44:10. District Courts
§ 44:11. Justice Court
§ 44:12. Waiver of Jury Trial by Lease Provision

C. RESEARCH REFERENCES
§ 44:13. Generally

## CHAPTER 45

## SUMMARY PROCEEDINGS; THE JUDGMENT

A. IN GENERAL
§ 45:1. What It Is

§ 45:2. On Default
§ 45:3. Effect of Removal After Service of Notice of Petition
§ 45:4. Effect of Demolition of Building After Service of Notice of Petition
§ 45:5. Effect of Landlord's Loss of Right to Possession
§ 45:6. Direction for Entry of Judgment
§ 45:7. Must be Determinative of Issues Raised
§ 45:8. Must Not Award Less Space than Rented to Tenant
§ 45:9. Must Correctly Specify Issues Determined
§ 45:10. Must be an Unconditional Determination
§ 45:11. Adjudication of Title
§ 45:12. Judgment for Rent and Value of Use and Occupancy
§ 45:13. —Jurisdictional Limitation on Amount of Judgment for Rent
§ 45:14. —Necessity of Personal Jurisdiction for Judgment for Rent
§ 45:15. —Judgment on Counterclaim
§ 45:16. —Forms of Decision and Judgment
§ 45:17. Docketing

B. COSTS

§ 45:18. Costs
§ 45:19. —Forcible Entry or Detainer Proceeding

C. CONCLUSIVENESS OF JUDGMENT; RES JUDICATA

§ 45:20. Applicability of Res Judicata to Summary Proceeding
§ 45:21. Conclusiveness of Judgment Dependent upon Jurisdiction
§ 45:22. Scope of Estoppel of Judgment, Generally
§ 45:23. —As to Immaterial Findings
§ 45:24. —Where Several Grounds for Prior Determination
§ 45:25. Applicability of Res Judicata to Default Judgment
§ 45:26. Conclusiveness of Judgment; as to Valid and Subsisting Tenancy
§ 45:27. —As to Tenant's Possession
§ 45:28. —As to Surrender and Acceptance
§ 45:29. —As to Constructive Eviction
§ 45:30. —As to Agreement for Application of Security to Rent
§ 45:31. —As to Liability of Non-Assuming Assignee
§ 45:32. —Rules Summarized
§ 45:33. Pleading Res Judicata as Defense
§ 45:34. Judgment as Bar to Affirmative Equitable Relief
§ 45:35. —As Bar to Damages for Fraud
§ 45:36. —As Bar to Action to Recover Real Property

D. RESEARCH REFERENCES

§ 45:37. Generally

## CHAPTER 46

### SUMMARY PROCEEDING; THE WARRANT

A. IN GENERAL
- § 46:1. What It Is
- § 46:2. When to be issued
- § 46:3. To Whom Issued
- § 46:4. Contents of Warrant
- § 46:5. Form of Warrant
- § 46:6. Execution of the Warrant
- § 46:7. Pendency of Proceeding Until Warrant Executed
- § 46:8. —Effect of Emergency Rent Laws
- § 46:9. When Warrant Can be Executed
- § 46:10. Persons Removable
- § 46:11. Property Affected by Warrant
- § 46:12. Tenant's Liability for Expense of Removal
- § 46:13. Tenant's Liability for Storage of His Property
- § 46:14. Liability for Damage to Tenant's Property
- § 46:15. Form of Officer's Return
- § 46:16. Re-execution upon Wrongful Re-entry by Evicted Tenant
- § 46:17. Re-execution After Returned as "Unused"
- § 46:18. Cancellation of Lease by Issuance of Warrant
- § 46:19. Cancellation of Lease by Voluntary Removal Before Issuance of Warrant
- § 46:20. Effect of Discontinuance of Summary Proceeding on Cancellation of Lease
- § 46:21. Effect of Reversal on Appeal on Cancellation of Lease
- § 46:22. Effect of Dismissal of Proceeding on Cancellation of Lease
- § 46:23. Effect of Acceptance of Rent After Issuance of Warrant

B. SURVIVAL OF LIABILITY
- § 46:24. Liability for Rent
- § 46:25. Liability for Use and Occupation
- § 46:26. —Value of Use and Occupation
- § 46:27. Liability for Breach of Covenant to Surrender
- § 46:28. Liability for Rent upon Cancellation of Lease by Removal of Tenant Before Issuance of Warrant
- § 46:29. Survival of Liability by Agreement

C. RESEARCH REFERENCES
- § 46:30. Generally

## CHAPTER 47

### SUMMARY PROCEEDINGS; STAYS

A. IN GENERAL
- § 47:1. General Power to Grant Stay

# TABLE OF CONTENTS

§ 47:2. Stay by Another Court; Pending Outcome of Another Action
§ 47:3. —After Judgment in Proceeding
§ 47:4. Stay Against Persons in Military Service
§ 47:5. Stay in Case of "Constructive Eviction" Violations or Lack of Repairs
§ 47:6. —Definition of "Constructive Eviction" Violations
§ 47:7. Stay on Discontinuance of Utilities
§ 47:8. Stay on Appeal

B. STAYING ISSUANCE OF WARRANT

§ 47:9. After Default in Rent or Taxes
§ 47:10. After Insolvency or Bankruptcy
§ 47:11. After Sale Under Execution
§ 47:12. In Dwelling Holdover Proceeding in New York City; Inability to Find Other Accommodations; Breach of Lease
§ 47:13. —Forms
§ 47:14. In Local Courts
§ 47:15. Form of Undertaking to Stay Issuance of Warrant

C. RESEARCH REFERENCES

§ 47:16. Generally

## CHAPTER 48

### SUMMARY PROCEEDINGS; REDEMPTION

A. IN GENERAL

§ 48:1. Nature of Redemption
§ 48:2. Who May Redeem
§ 48:3. Right of Partner to Redeem
§ 48:4. Right of Corporate Receiver to Redeem
§ 48:5. When Redemption Available
§ 48:6. —Non-payment of Taxes or Assessments
§ 48:7. Waiver of Right of Redemption
§ 48:8. —Form
§ 48:9. Tender or Payment Condition Precedent to Tenant's Redemption
§ 48:10. Costs and Charges Defined
§ 48:11. "Rent" Defined
§ 48:12. Keeping Tenant's Tender Good
§ 48:13. Procedure in Tenant's Redemption Proceeding
§ 48:14. Redemption Judgment Must Adjust Equities
§ 48:15. Allowance in Redemption Proceedings; For Substantial Alterations
§ 48:16. —For Use of Landlord's Property
§ 48:17. Rights of New Tenant on Redemption Proceeding
§ 48:18. Forms

B. CREDITOR'S REDEMPTION PROCEEDING

§ 48:19. When Proceeding Available
§ 48:20. Procedure

§ 48:21. —Where Two or More Creditors
§ 48:22. —Execution of Warrant Condition Precedent
§ 48:23. Effect of Proceeding
§ 48:24. Forms

C. RESEARCH REFERENCES

§ 48:25. Generally

## CHAPTER 49

### RENT STRIKE PROCEEDING

§ 49:1. Generally
§ 49:2. When Maintainable
§ 49:3. Where Maintainable
§ 49:4. Owner Defined
§ 49:5. Dwelling Defined
§ 49:6. Notice of Petition
§ 49:7. Manner of Service of Petition and Notice of Petition
§ 49:8. Notice to Non-petitioning Tenants
§ 49:9. Filing Proof of Service
§ 49:10. Contents of Petition
§ 49:11. Answer
§ 49:12. Defenses
§ 49:13. Trial
§ 49:14. Judgment
§ 49:15. Service of Judgment
§ 49:16. Application by Mortgagee or Lienor of Record
§ 49:17. Waiver of Rights Void
§ 49:18. Appointment of and Duties of Administrator
§ 49:19. Presentation or Settlement of Accounts of Administrator
§ 49:20. Research References

## APPENDICES

Appendix A. ARTICLES 7 AND 7-A OF THE REAL PROPERTY ACTION AND PROCEEDINGS LAW
Appendix B. ARTICLE 7 OF THE REAL PROPERTY LAW
Appendix C. PERTINENT PROVISIONS OF GENERAL OBLIGATIONS LAW
Appendix D. ARTICLE 7-C OF THE MULTIPLE DWELLING LAW

TABLE OF CASES

TABLE OF STATUTES

INDEX

# PART ONE
# THE COMMENCEMENT OF THE LANDLORD-TENANT RELATIONSHIP

## CHAPTER 1
## GENERAL PRINCIPLES

A. IN GENERAL
  § 1:1. Definitions of Fundamental Terms
  § 1:2. Nature of a Lease
  § 1:3. Lease as Personal or Real Property
  § 1:4. Interest of Tenant in Term to Commence in Future
  § 1:5. Possession of Tenant as Possession of Landlord
  § 1:6. Governing Law (Conflict of Laws)

B. NOTICE OF TENANT'S RIGHTS
  § 1:7. Notice of Tenant's Rights by Recording Lease
  § 1:8. Form of Memorandum of Lease for Recording
  § 1:9. Notice of Tenant's Rights by Recording Modification of Lease
  § 1:10. Notice of Tenant's Rights from Possession

C. FORMS OF COMPLETE LEASES
  § 1:11. Introduction
  § 1:12. Loft Lease
  § 1:13. Office Lease
  § 1:14. Store Lease

D. RESEARCH REFERENCES
  § 1:15. Generally

---

## A. IN GENERAL
### § 1:1. Definitions of Fundamental Terms

It has been observed that the law concerning landlord and tenant came into existence in the infancy of civilization, and, by gradual accretion of new rights, privileges, and principles during the centuries of its development, has come to be one of the most momentous, extensive, and far-reaching branches of the law.[1]

The relationship of landlord and tenant is always created by contract, express or implied,[2] by the terms of which one party, ordinarily designated as the "tenant" or "lessee," enters into possession of the land of another party, ordinarily designated as the "landlord" or "lessor."

---

1. 49 Am Jur 2d, Landlord and Tenant, § 1.

2. § 2:1, infra.

"Lease" designates the contract by which the relation of landlord and tenant is created.[3] A lease, in other words, is merely a particular type of agreement which is made by a landlord with a tenant[4] for the occupation of real property, and contains provisions, or clauses, for the protection of both parties, and expires upon a definite date agreed upon by the parties,[5] or fixed by the law.[6]

Although the terms "landlord" and "tenant" are frequently used interchangeably with "lessor" and "lessee," the use of the words "landlord" and "tenant" is preferable when it is intended to designate one who owns or possesses some estate in real property without reference to the existence of a written lease between them. "One who holds land by any kind of title, whether for years, for life, or in fee," it has been said,[7] "is tenant, and he of whom land is held subject to the rendering or payment of rent or service is landlord." But a "tenant" necessarily may not be a "lessee," since he may be an assignee of the lessee.

"Provision," means a distinct clause in the lease.[8] Such provision may be a covenant,[9] a condition,[10] or a conditional limitation.[11]

Although the word "lease" is used to designate the contract by which the relation of landlord and tenant is created, it must be observed that the instrument of lease is not the estate of the lessee, but merely the evidence of the conveyance thereof to him. This distinction is important in considering the effect of tearing up a lease-instrument.[12]

For the purposes of the administration of a decedent's estate, the Estates, Powers and Trusts Law declares,[13] that estates for years in real property, estates from year

3. Rochester Poster Advertising Co. v State (1961) 27 Misc 2d 99, 213 NYS2d 812, affd (4th Dept) 15 AD2d 632, 222 NYS2d 688, affd 11 NY2d 1036, 230 NYS2d 30, 183 NE2d 911.
4. Gaulang Realty Co. v Dyer (M Ct Bx 1954) 207 Misc 480, 138 NYS2d 817, affd 207 Misc 489, 138 NYS2d 826.
5. Nussbaum v Garstaff Realty Co. (S Ct Bx Co 1950) 197 Misc 527, 96 NYS2d 161.
6. See § 30:10, infra, where no definite expiration date is agreed upon.
7. Hosford v Ballard (1868) 39 NY 147, 151.
8. People ex rel. Home Mortg. Inv. Co. v State Board of Tax Com'rs (AD2 1918) 182 AD 699, 169 NYS 978.
9. §§ 23:4, et seq., infra.
10. §§ 23:8, et seq., infra.
11. §§ 23:21, et seq., infra.
12. See § 26:5, infra.
13. EPTL 13-1.1(a)(1) and (2).

to year, estates which were held by the decedent for the life of another person, and estates for years in real property given to an executor for the payment of debts, are personal property, and pass to the "personal representative," that is, the person who has received letters to administer the estate of a decedent.[14] Upon the death of the holder of a leasehold, his interest is not terminated, but passes for the purposes of the administration of his estate to his "personal representative," that is, the person who has received letters to administer his estate. And, until the distributees or legatees receive the leasehold through the process of administration, the legal title thereto is in such personal representative.[15]

Under some statutes leaseholds are treated as real property for certain specified purposes only. For example, for purposes of recording, leases, except leases for a term not exceeding three years, are treated as real property.[16]

§ 1:2. Nature of a Lease

A lease has a twofold aspect. It is an executory contract creating mutual obligations by the landlord and tenant. A lease also is the present conveyance of an estate in a designated portion of real property, whereby the lessor yields up to the lessee exclusive possession of such designated portion of real property for a specified term.[17] For the purposes of recording, however, only a lease for a term exceeding three years is deemed a conveyance.[18] But, a lease is not a "conveyance of real property" within the meaning of Real Property Law § 251, which provides that a "covenant is not implied in a conveyance of real property, whether the conveyance contains any special covenant or not." Therefore, it is a settled rule of property

14. EPTL 1-2.13, which further provides that this term "personal representative" does not include an assignee for the benefit of creditors, or a committee, conservator, curator, custodian, guardian, trustee or donee of a power during minority.

15. Mayor, etc., of New York v Mabie (1858) 13 NY 151.

16. Real Prop L § 290, subd 1.

17. Park West Management Corp. v Mitchell (1979) 47 NY2d 316, 418 NYS2d 310, 391 NE2d 1288, cert den 444 US 992, 62 L Ed 2d 421, 100 S Ct 523; Geraci v Jenrette (1977) 41 NY2d 660, 394 NYS2d 853, 363 NE2d 559; Feder v Caliguira (1960) 8 NY2d 400, 208 NYS2d 970, 171 NE2d 316.

An estate for years is an estate in property. EPTL 6-1.1.

18. Real Prop L § 290.

A lease for more than 3 years is a recordable instrument. Commission on Ecumenical Mission & Relations of United Presbyterian Church v Roger Gray, Ltd. (1971) 27 NY2d 457, 318 NYS2d 726, 267 NE2d 467.

§ 1:2    LANDLORD AND TENANT

law that the implication of a covenant for quiet enjoyment in a lease is not prohibited by law.[19]

Thus, a lease achieves two ends: The conveyance of an estate in real property from lessor to lessee, and the designation of the parties' rights and obligations pursuant thereto.[20]

However, to constitute a lease, the estate transferred must be less than the lessor has in the designated premises. Thus, in the case of the fee owner of real property, when he grants a lease to the property, he carves out of his fee a term of years. But, by so doing, he does not divest himself of his inheritance. He still has his inheritance in the land, technically, a reversion. His prior absolute and unqualified estate has been divided into two estates, one in the lessee, the nature and quality of which is determined by the terms of the lease, and the other in himself. Since a reversion is essential to the concept of a lease, the term granted by a lease must not exceed the lessor's own term.[1]

Leases may be either for a fixed term or in perpetuity.[2]

Although a tenancy is an estate, the word "seized" is not properly used to refer to a tenure or holding under a tenancy. "Seized" is applicable to possession by one claiming an estate in freehold, and the proper term to use for a tenancy is "possessed."[3] By virtue of the enactment of Real Property Law § 235-b,[4] which created the statutory warranty of habitability in every written or oral lease or rental agreement for residential premises, a *residential*

---

19. Fifth Ave. Bldg. Co. v Kernochan (1917) 221 NY 370, 117 NE 579, reh den 222 NY 525, 118 NE 1057.

20. 219 Broadway Corp. v Alexander's, Inc. (1979) 46 NY2d 506, 414 NYS2d 889, 387 NE2d 1205.

1. Kernochan v New York E. R. Co. (1891) 128 NY 559, 29 NE 65.

2. Genesee Conservation Foundation, Inc. v Oatka Fish & Game Club, Inc. (1978, 4th Dept) 63 AD2d 1115, 405 NYS2d 869.

Even though a lease may be perpetual, if the ownership of the grantor-lessor is kept alive by a power of re-entry on non-payment of the rent, a right of preemption in case of sale, or a certain control over the use of the land, it has been held that the legal status of the parties is that of landlord and tenant, and not that of grantor and grantee. Munro v Syracuse, L. & N. R. Co. (1910) 200 NY 224, 232-233, 93 NE 516; Bradt v Church (1888) 110 NY 537, 544, 18 NE 357, 359; First Religious Soc. v Socony Mobil Oil Co. (S Ct Oneida Co 1964) 44 Misc 2d 415, 253 NYS2d 839; Kavanaugh v Cohoes Power & Light Corp. (S Ct Albany Co 1921) 114 Misc 590, 187 NYS 216.

3. Brinn v Slawson & Hobbs (AD1 1947) 273 AD 1, 74 NYS2d 825; Fink v Liberman (S Ct Monroe Co 1920) 183 NYS 693.

4. See § 18:6, infra.

## GENERAL PRINCIPLES § 1:3

lease is now also effectively deemed a sale of shelter and services by the landlord who impliedly warrants: first, that the premises are fit for human habitation; second, that the condition of the premises is in accord with the uses reasonably intended by the parties; and third, that the tenants are not subjected to any conditions endangering or detrimental to their life, health, or safety.[5] Leases acquired the character of conveyances of real property when their primary function was to govern the relationship between landowners and farmers. Unlike the original medieval tenant, the modern apartment dweller rents not for profit but for shelter.[6]

### § 1:3. Lease as Personal or Real Property

Although a lease is an interest or estate in real property, it has none of the characteristics of real property.[7] Under decisional law it is well established that a lease for years is to be deemed personalty,[8] regardless of the num-

---

5. Park West Management Corp. v Mitchell (1979) 47 NY2d 316, 418 NYS2d 310, 391 NE2d 1288, cert den 444 US 992, 62 L Ed 2d 421, 100 S Ct 523.

6. See, McGovern, "The Historical Conception of A Lease for Effect," 23 UCLA Rev 501.

7. Re Althause's Estate (AD1 1901) 63 AD 252, 71 NYS 445, affd 168 NY 670, 61 NE 1127; Rodack v New Moon Theatre (AT2 1923) 121 Misc 63, 200 NYS 237.

Former Real Prop L § 33 declared that estates for years were chattels real, and that estates at will or by sufferance were chattel interests, but were not liable as such to sale on execution. This statute was repealed by EPTL 14-1.1, eff Sept 1, 1967, and accordingly the designation of an estate for years as a chattel real, as well as the distinction between estates for years and estates at will or by sufferance, have been eliminated. [Nevertheless, CPLR 105(s) still provides that as used in the CPLR "real property" includes chattels real; and Real Prop Act & Proc L § 111(2) still provides that "real property" as used in § 1921 thereof (discharge of mortgages) includes chattels real, except a lease for a term not exceeding three years.] It should be observed that although the repealed statute also provided that estates at will or by sufferance were not liable as such to sale on execution, nevertheless, the law still remains that such estates are not liable to sale on execution, because CPLR 5201(b) provides that a money judgment may be enforced against any property which can be assigned or transferred. Since estates at will and by sufferance are not assignable or transferrable (§ 9:75, infra), they therefore are not property interests against which a money judgment may be enforced.

8. Ft. Hamilton Manor, Inc. v Boyland (1958) 4 NY2d 192, 173 NYS2d 560, 149 NE2d 856 (a leasehold is not subject to tax upon real property); Grumman Aircraft Engineering Corp. v Board of Assessors (1957) 2 NY2d 500, 161 NYS2d 393, 141 NE2d 794 (a leasehold is not taxable under statute providing for taxation of real property), remittitur amd 2 NY2d 1012, 163 NYS2d 620, 143 NE2d 352, cert den 355 US 814, 2 L Ed 2d 31, 78 S Ct 14, reh den 355 US 885, 2 L Ed 2d 115, 78 S Ct 145; First Trust & Deposit Co. v Syrdelco, Inc. (AD4 1936) 249 AD 285, 292 NYS 206 (a mortgage upon a lease is a mortgage upon personalty), app dismd 275 NY 468, 11 NE2d 301; Ehrsam v Utica (AD4

ber of years involved in the term of the lease, even if it be for hundreds of years.[9]

### § 1:4. Interest of Tenant in Term to Commence in Future

A lease for a term to commence in the future is valid,[10] whether oral or written.[11] But, if the term is for more than one year, the requirements of the statute of frauds must be met.[12]

From the time of the making of a lease for a term to commence at a future date, a present interest vests in the tenant. This interest is called an "interesse termini." This is merely an interest resting in contract, but it is not an estate in the land. Moreover, the time between the making of the lease and its commencement is no part of the term granted. The term is that period which is granted for the lessee or tenant to occupy and have possession of the leased premises.[13] Thus, although one who holds a lease of premises to begin at a future time, does not have a present estate in the land, nevertheless he owns a present interest in the property with the right to future possession which will be protected by equity by injunctive relief to prevent the destruction or demolition of buildings on the premises either by the lessor or by a third person.[14]

It has been held that the interest of the tenant which vests in him at the time of the making of a lease to commence in the future is assignable before the term commences,[15] unless the lease contains an express restriction against assignment.[16]

---

1899) 37 AD 272, 55 NYS 942; Susskind v 1136 Tenants Corp. (NY Civ Ct NY Co 1964) 43 Misc 2d 588, 251 NYS2d 321 (leasehold of a co-operative apartment is personalty); Nemmer Furniture Co. v Select Furniture Co. (S Ct Erie Co 1960) 25 Misc 2d 895, 208 NYS2d 51; Re Miller's Estate (Surr Ct NY Co 1954) 205 Misc 770, 130 NYS2d 295 (leasehold of a co-operative apartment is personalty, and does not pass by devise of "all the real estate owned by me").

9. Averill v Taylor (1853) 8 NY 44, 52.

10. EPTL 6-3.3, which provides that an estate (and an estate for years is an estate, EPTL 6-1.1) may be created to commence at a future time.

11. Ward v Hasbrouck (1902) 169 NY 407, 62 NE 434; Jay-Washington Realty Corp. v Koondel (AD1 1944) 268 AD 116, 49 NYS2d 306.

12. § 2:35, et seq, infra.

13. Young v Dake (1851) 5 NY 463, 467; 39 Cortlandt Street Corp. v Lambert (AD1 1924) 209 AD 575, 205 NYS 161.

14. Evans v Prince's Bay Oyster Co. (S Ct Kings Co 1915) 154 NYS 279, affd 170 AD 909, 154 NYS 1120.

15. Becar v Flues (1876) 64 NY 518, 520.

## § 1:5. Possession of Tenant as Possession of Landlord

It is well settled by decisional law that once the relation of landlord and tenant has been established, the possession of the tenant and his assignees is the possession of the landlord, and not hostile or adverse, at least until there has been a repudiation of the holding under the landlord, which is brought home to the landlord.[17] A statute provides that where the relation of landlord and tenant has existed between any persons, the possession of the tenant is deemed the possession of the landlord until the expiration of ten years after the termination of the tenancy; or, where there has been no written lease, until the expiration of ten years after the last payment of rent; notwithstanding that the tenant has acquired another title or has claimed to hold adversely to his landlord. But, this statute further declares, this presumption shall cease after the prescribed periods (10 years), and "such tenant may then commence to hold adversely to his landlord."[18]

## § 1:6. Governing Law (Conflict of Laws)

The principle is well established by decisional law that all matters concerning the title and disposition of real property, and the incidents of ownership thereof, are determined by what is known as the lex loci rei sitae, that is, the law of the situs of the property, which can alone prescribe the mode by which a title to it can pass from one person to another,[19] or an interest therein of any sort can be gained or lost.[20] However, this principle does not apply indiscriminately to leases. A distinction has been drawn between what may be regarded as personal covenants of the lease giving rise to personal rights and obligations, and covenants creating rights and inter-

---

16. See § 9:75, infra.
17. Bedlow v New York Floating Dry-Dock Co. (1889) 112 NY 263, 19 NE 800; Whiting v Edmunds (1884) 94 NY 309, 314.
18. Real Prop Act & Proc L § 531.
19. Moscow Fire Ins. Co. v Bank of New York & Trust Co. (1939) 280 NY 286, 20 NE2d 758, reh den 280 NY 848, 21 NE2d 890 and remittitur amd 281 NY 818, 24 NE2d 487 and affd 309 US 624, 84 L Ed 986, 60 S Ct 725, reh den 309 US 697, 84 L Ed 1036, 60 S Ct 706; Mount v Tuttle (1906) 183 NY 358, 76 NE 873.

Possessory rights under sublease of property in New Jersey, executed by sublessor, a New York corporation, in New Jersey, and by sublessee, a Massachusetts corporation, in Massachusetts, is determined by New Jersey law. Regal Knitwear Co. v M. Hoffman & Co. (1978) 96 Misc 2d 605, 409 NYS2d 483.

20. Van Cleaf v Burns (1892) 133 NY 540, 30 NE 661.

ests in the land itself. As has been seen, a lease creates a tenancy, an interest in real property.[1] But, a lease also creates rights in personam, as distinguished from rights in rem; that is, a lease, in addition to creating rights in the property itself, also gives rise to personal rights and obligations. Insofar as the lease creates personal rights and obligations, rights in personam, such rights are to be governed by the lex loci contractus, the law of the situs of the transaction, and not by the law of the situs of the property. Thus, if the question involved relates solely to the rights and liabilities of the parties as a matter of contractual obligation, it is to be determined by the law governing the contract, even though the subject matter of the contract may be land in another state.[2] For example, rights of the parties arising from a deposit made by a lessee to secure the performance of the lease are rights in personam, are not concerned with the creation or transfer of any interest in real property, and are to be governed, therefore, by the law of the place where the lease or the deposit agreement was made, if it was made at a place other than the situs of the property.[3] However, a lease, insofar as it affects the creation of an interest in real property, is governed by the law of the situs of the property, and, therefore, questions relating to the rights in rem of the parties to the lease, that is, covenants affecting rights and interests in the land itself, will be governed by the law of the situs of the property.[4] An action in New York for rent due on a building located in another state is governed by the laws of such other state.[5] Similarly, it was held that the rights of a lessee and a sublessee under a lease and an accompanying agreement, as respects the question whether the failure of the lessee to make certain structural repairs in the building, as a result of which public safety authorities of the state in which the property was situated closed the building as

1. § 1:2, supra.
2. Mallory Associates, Inc. v Barving Realty Co. (1949) 300 NY 297, 90 NE2d 468, 15 ALR2d 1193, reh den 300 NY 680, 91 NE2d 331, 15 ALR2d 1193.
3. Mallory Associates, Inc. v Barving Realty Co. (1949) 300 NY 297, 90 NE2d 468, 15 ALR2d 1193, reh den 300 NY 680, 91 NE2d 331, 15 ALR2d 1193.
4. Mallory Associates, Inc. v Barving Realty Co. (1949) 300 NY 297, 90 NE2d 468, 15 ALR2d 1193, reh den 300 NY 680, 91 NE2d 331, 15 ALR2d 1193.
5. Bowen v Frank (S Ct Queens Co 1949) 92 NYS2d 527.

## GENERAL PRINCIPLES § 1:7

unsafe, constituted constructive eviction of the sublessee so as to relieve him from the payment of rent under his sublease, were governed by the laws of the state where the demised premises were located, and not by the laws of New York where the action was brought.[6]

### B. NOTICE OF TENANT'S RIGHTS

### § 1:7. Notice of Tenant's Rights by Recording Lease

A lease for a term exceeding three years, being a conveyance for the purposes of recording,[7] "may" be recorded.[8] But recording is not necessary for its validity. The failure to record it does not make it void as between the parties to the lease. Under the statute, every conveyance of real property which is not recorded is void as against subsequent purchasers in good faith, and for value, whose conveyances shall be first recorded.[9] "The recording acts,"[10] said Andrews, J.,[11] "however, do not declare what effect shall be given to the recording of conveyances, upon the point of notice. They declare that unless recorded, they shall be void as against subsequent purchasers in good faith, and for value, whose conveyances shall be first recorded. But the courts, by construction, make the record of a conveyance, notice to subsequent purchasers; but this doctrine is subject to the limitation, that it is notice only, to those claiming under the same grantor or through one who is the common source of title." Therefore, a purchaser of property is chargeable with notice of a recorded lease of such property, and of the terms therein contained.[12]

---

6. Galland v Shubert Theatrical Co. (AT1 1918) 105 Misc 185, 172 NYS 775, later app 124 Misc 371, 208 NYS 144, revd 220 AD 704, 221 NYS 437.

7. § 1:2, supra.

8. Real Prop L § 291.

9. See § 1:10, infra, as to necessity for a lessee out of possession to record his lease.

10. Real Prop L Art 9.

11. Tarbell v West (1881) 86 NY 280, 288.

12. Lent & Graff Co. v Satenstein (AD1 1924) 210 AD 251, 205 NYS 403; Carney v Pendleton (AD2 1910) 139 AD 152, 123 NYS 738; Stolts v Tuska (AD1 1902) 76 AD 137, 78 NYS 687; Fulway Corp. v Liggett Drug Co. (S Ct NY Co 1956) 1 Misc 2d 527, 148 NYS2d 222.

Bank of New York v Hirschfeld (1975) 37 NY2d 501, 374 NYS2d 100, 336 NE2d 710, holding that where memorandum of lease is duly recorded, purchaser of leased premises is charged with notice of the covenants and obligations under the lease. (Lease provided: In event of sale of said land and building, it shall be deemed construed without further agreement between the parties or their successors in interest that the purchaser has assumed and agreed to carry out any and all covenants and obligations of Landlord hereunder.)

The recording of a lease with its attendant public disclosure of all of its terms may not always be desirable. To overcome this, the statute[13] provides a method of recording whereby a short memorandum of lease referring to an unrecorded lease may be recorded with like effect as if the original lease is recorded. Such memorandum must be duly acknowledged, must set forth the names and addresses of the parties, a reference to the lease and its date, the description of the property, the dates of the commencement and termination of the lease, and a digest of the renewal privileges. When the memorandum is presented to the recording officer, the original lease must be submitted for inspection to determine whether any mortgage tax is due.

## § 1:8. Form of Memorandum of Lease for Recording

### Form No. 1

### Memorandum of Lease for Recording

The undersigned, Landlord Realty Co. Inc., a domestic corporation having its principal office at 1 Oak Street, Albany, New York, as LANDLORD, and Lessee Realty Co. Inc., a domestic corporation having its principal office at 2 Elm Street, Albany, New York, as TENANT, entered into a certain lease of real property on January 2, 1985.

The said lease covers the store on the street floor in premises known as and by No. 63 Sycamore Street, Albany, New York.

Under the terms of said lease, the said premises were leased by LANDLORD to TENANT for a term of 10 years, commencing on February 1, 1985, and terminating on the 31st day of January, 1995. Under the terms of said lease TENANT has an option to renew the lease for a further period of 10 years, provided TENANT exercises said option on or before June 1, 1994. The said lease does not grant the parties any other or further rights of extension or renewal.

The said lease provides that LANDLORD will not during the term thereof or any renewal thereof rent or permit any other portion of the premises of which the leased premises form a part to be used or occupied for the

---

13. Real Prop L § 291-c.

GENERAL PRINCIPLES § 1:9

sale of toys, sporting goods, bathing suits, and any other articles which come under the classification of sporting goods.

Dated: New York, July 1, 1985.
      Landlord Realty Co. Inc.
      by John Lessor, President
      Lessee Realty Co. Inc.
      by Richard Lessee, President

[ACKNOWLEDGMENTS]

### § 1:9. Notice of Tenant's Rights by Recording Modification of Lease

Where a lease or memorandum of such lease has been recorded, an unrecorded agreement modifying such lease or memorandum is void as against a subsequent purchaser in good faith and for a valuable consideration, and the possession of the tenant shall not be deemed notice of the modification, unless the agreement of modification or a memorandum thereof is recorded prior to the recording of the instrument by which the subsequent purchaser acquires his estate or interest.[14]

A memorandum of an agreement modifying a lease which is to be recorded must contain at least the following information with respect to the agreement: (a) the names of the parties and the addresses, if any, set forth in the agreement; (b) a reference to the agreement with its date of execution; (c) a brief description of the leased premises in form sufficient to identify the same; (d) any changes made by the agreement in the term of the lease; (e) the date of the termination of the lease as modified; and (f) any changes in the provisions of the lease as to the rights of extension or renewal.[15] The word "purchaser" as used in this statute includes a person who purchases or acquires by exchange, or contracts to purchase or acquire by exchange the leased premises or the real property of which the leased premises are part or any estate or interest therein, or acquires by assignment the rent to accrue from tenancies or subtenancies thereof in existence at the time of the assignment.[16]

14. Real Prop L § 291-cc(1).
15. Real Prop L § 291-cc(2).
16. Real Prop L § 291-cc(3).

### § 1:10. Notice of Tenant's Rights from Possession

The recording statute makes an unrecorded lease void only as against certain persons, specified in the statute, who acquire an interest in the property in good faith and for a valuable consideration.[17] However, it is well established by decisional law that actual possession of real property is notice to all the world of the existence of any right which the person in possession is able to establish.[18] As was said by the Court of Appeals,[19] "Actual notice of a prior unrecorded conveyance, or of any title, legal or equitable, to the premises, or knowledge and notice of any facts which should put a prudent man upon inquiry, impeaches the good faith of the subsequent purchaser." In other words, where a purchaser of land has knowledge of any facts sufficient to put him on inquiry as to the existence of some right or some title in conflict with that which he is about to acquire, he is presumed either to have made the inquiry and ascertained the extent of such prior right, or to have been guilty of a degree of negligence equally fatal to his claim to be considered as a bona fide purchaser.[20]

A new owner is under no duty to inquire whether or not a tenant in possession pays his rent on time; therefore, the new owner in the absence of actual knowledge cannot be charged with constructive knowledge of, and accordingly is not bound by, his predecessor's waiver of strict compliance with a provision of the lease requiring payment of rent on the first day of the month.[1]

The character of the possession which is sufficient to put a person on notice, and which will be equivalent to actual notice of rights or equities in persons other than those who have a title upon record, must be actual, open, and visible; it must not be equivocal, occasional, or for a special or temporary purpose; neither must it be consis-

---

17. § 1:7, supra.
18. Phelan v Brady (1890) 119 NY 587, 591, 23 NE 1109.
19. Brown v Volkening (1876) 64 NY 76, 82.
A purchaser is charged with knowledge of the exact rights claimed by all persons in possession, and therefore is charged with knowledge that the tenant occupying the premises entered into a contract to purchase the premises. Raines v Moran (S Ct Ontario Co 1945) 57 NYS2d 800, affd 270 AD 979, 62 NYS2d 817.
20. Sweet v Henry (1903) 175 NY 268, 276, 67 NE 574, remittur amd 177 NY 583, 69 NE 1132.

1. Tehan v Thos. C. Peters Printing Co. (1979, 4th Dept) 71 AD2d 101, 421 NYS2d 465 (citing text).

# GENERAL PRINCIPLES § 1:11

tent with the title of the apparent record owner.[2] Therefore, a purchaser of real estate which is occupied by a tenant whose lease is unrecorded, even though for a term exceeding three years, is put upon inquiry, and is bound by what such an inquiry would reveal. Such a purchaser is not a bona fide purchaser, and will take subject to the rights of the tenant in possession.[3] "It may be true," said the Court of Appeals,[4] "as has been argued by the plaintiff's counsel, that when a party takes a conveyance of property situated as this was, occupied by numerous tenants, it would be inconvenient and difficult for him to ascertain the rights or interests that are claimed by all or any of them. But this circumstance cannot change the rule."[5] However, where a lease for a term exceeding three years commences at a date subsequent to the date of its execution, prior to taking actual possession the lessee must record the lease to protect himself.[6] Otherwise the lessee runs the risk of subordinating his interest to a subsequent grantee, mortgagee, lessee, contract vendee, or a person holding an option to buy the property or take a lease thereto.

## C. FORMS OF COMPLETE LEASES

### § 1:11. Introduction

The following forms are those prepared by The Real Estate Board of New York, Inc.[7] It must be emphasized that forms—even the best—must not be followed blindly. It is the attorney's obligation to read each provision carefully, and determine whether the lease should be

---

**2.** Brown v Volkening (1876) 64 NY 76, 83.

**3.** Tarbell v West (1881) 86 NY 280, 288; Gilbert v Van Kleeck (AD3 1954) 284 AD 611, 132 NYS2d 580, motion to modify den 284 AD 857, 134 NYS2d 193 and app dismd 308 NY 882, 126 NE2d 383, motion den 308 NY 1045, 127 NE2d 873; Re Ehrlich's Estate (AD4 1949) 275 AD 742, 87 NYS2d 682; City Bank of Bayonne v Hocke (AD1 1915) 168 AD 83, 153 NYS 731.

**4.** Phelan v Brady (1890) 119 NY 587, 591, 23 NE 1109.

**5.** Also, see, Gilbert v Van Kleeck (AD3 1954) 284 AD 611, 132 NYS2d 580, motion to modify den 284 AD 857, 134 NYS2d 193 and app dismd 308 NY 882, 126 NE2d 383, motion den 308 NY 1045, 127 NE2d 873; Re Ehrlich's Estate (AD4 1949) 275 AD 742, 87 NYS2d 682.

**6.** Raisin v Shoemaker (AD1 1923) 206 AD 122, 200 NYS 615, affd 238 NY 630, 144 NE 921.

**7.** These forms are copyrighted by The Real Estate Board of New York Inc., and reprinted by its permission. Reproduction in whole or in part is prohibited, and all rights are reserved by The Real Estate Board of New York. I have eliminated from these forms the bankruptcy clauses, which are no longer enforceable.

15

used without change, or whether the needs of his client would be better served by amendment or omission or even substitution of a particular provision. The prime object of the attorney, especially one representing the lessee, is to obtain an agreement which will best fit the needs of his client, and carry out the client's objectives in seeking to occupy the leased premises rather than to fit the client into a Procrustean lease-form.

However, the value of these forms is in their use of carefully worked out, time-tested language, and in their inclusion of many provisions which otherwise might not be thought of.[8]

### § 1:12. Loft Lease

#### FORM NO. 1.1

#### LOFT LEASE*

**Agreement of Lease,** made as of this        day of       19 , between       party of the first part, hereinafter referred to as OWNER, and       party of the second part, hereinafter referred to as TENANT,

**Witnesseth:** Owner hereby leases to Tenant and Tenant hereby hires from Owner       in the building known as       in the Borough of       , City of New York, for the term of       (or until such term shall sooner cease and expire as hereinafter provided) to commence on the       day of       nineteen hundred and       , and to end on the       day of       nineteen hundred and       both dates inclusive, at an annual rental rate of       which Tenant agrees to pay in lawful money of the United States which shall be legal tender in payment of all debts and dues, public and private, at the time of payment, in equal monthly installments in advance on the first day of each month during said term, at the office of Owner or such other place as Owner may designate, without any set off or deduction whatsoever,

---

[8]. For example, see suggestions as to additions for the benefit of the lessee, Form No. 44, § 19:25, or suggestions as to alternative form, Form No. 53 § 24:15.

* This loft lease is adopted and copyrighted by The Real Estate Board of New York Inc., and reprinted by its permission. Reproduction in whole or in part is prohibited and all rights are reserved by The Real Estate Board of New York Inc.

# GENERAL PRINCIPLES § 1:12

except that Tenant shall pay the first    monthly installment(s) on the execution hereof (unless this lease be a renewal).

In the event that, at the commencement of the term of this lease, or thereafter, Tenant shall be in default in the payment of rent to Owner pursuant to the terms of another lease with Owner or with Owner's predecessor in interest, Owner may at Owner's option and without notice to Tenant add the amount of such arrears to any monthly installment of rent payable hereunder and the same shall be payable to Owner as additional rent.

The parties hereto, for themselves, their heirs, distributees, executors, administrators, legal representatives, successors and assigns, hereby convenant as follows:

**Occupancy:**

1. Tenant shall pay the rent as above and as hereinafter provided.

**Use:**

2. Tenant shall use and occupy demised premises for    provided such use is in accordance with the Certificate of Occupancy for the building, if any, and for no other purpose.

**Alterations:**

3. Tenant shall make no changes in or to the demised premises of any nature without Owner's prior written consent. Subject to the prior written consent of Owner, and to the provisions of this article, Tenant at Tenant's expense, may make alterations, installations, additions or improvements which are nonstructural and which do not affect utility services or plumbing and electrical lines, in or to the interior of the demised premises using contractors or mechanics first approved by Owner. Tenant shall, at its expense, before making any alterations, additions, installations or improvements obtain all permits, approval and certificates required by any governmental or quasi-governmental bodies and (upon completion) certificates of final approval thereof and shall deliver promptly duplicates of all such permits, approvals and certificates to Owner. Tenant agrees to carry and will cause Tenant's contractors and sub-contractors to carry such workman's

compensation, general liability, personal and property damage insurance as Owner may require. If any mechanic's lien is filed against the demised premises, or the building of which the same forms a part, for work claimed to have been done for, or materials furnished to, Tenant, whether or not done pursuant to this article, the same shall be discharged by Tenant within thirty days thereafter, at Tenant's expense, by filing the bond required by law or otherwise. All fixtures and all paneling, partitions, railings and like installations, installed in the premises at any time, either by Tenant or by Owner on Tenant's behalf, shall, upon installation, become the property of Owner and shall remain upon and be surrendered with the demised premises unless Owner, by notice to Tenant no later than twenty days prior to the date fixed as the termination of this lease, elects to relinquish Owner's right thereto and to have them removed by Tenant, in which event the same shall be removed from the demised premises by Tenant prior to the expiration of the lease, at Tenant's expense. Nothing in this Article shall be construed to give Owner title to or to prevent Tenant's removal of trade fixtures, moveable office furniture and equipment, but upon removal of any such from the premises or upon removal of other installations as may be required by Owner, Tenant shall immediately and at its expense, repair and restore the premises to the condition existing prior to installation and repair any damage to the demised premises or the building due to such removal. All property permitted or required to be removed, by Tenant at the end of the term remaining in the premises after Tenant's removal shall be deemed abandoned and may, at the election of Owner, either be retained as Owner's property or removed from the premises by Owner, at Tenant's expense.

**Repairs:**

**4.** Owner shall maintain and repair the exterior of and the public portions of the building. Tenant shall, throughout the term of this lease, take good care of the demised premises including the bathrooms and lavatory facilities (if the demised premises encompass the entire floor of the building) and the windows and window frames and, the fixtures and appurtenances therein and at Tenant's sole

## GENERAL PRINCIPLES § 1:12

cost and expense promptly make all repairs thereto and to the building, whether structural or non-structural in nature, caused by or resulting from the carelessness, omission, neglect or improper conduct of Tenant, Tenant's servants, employees, invitees, or licensees, and whether or not arising from such Tenant conduct or omission, when required by other provisions of this lease, including Article 6. Tenant shall also repair all damage to the building and the demised premises caused by the moving of Tenant's fixtures, furniture or equipment. All the aforesaid repairs shall be of quality or class equal to the original work or construction. If Tenant fails, after ten days notice, to proceed with due diligence to make repairs required to be made by Tenant, the same may be made by the Owner at the expense of Tenant, and the expenses thereof incurred by Owner shall be collectible, as additional rent, after rendition of a bill or statement therefor. If the demised premises be or become infested with vermin, Tenant shall, at its expense, cause the same to be exterminated. Tenant shall give Owner prompt notice of any defective condition in any plumbing, heating system or electrical lines located in the demised premises and following such notice, Owner shall remedy the condition with due diligence, but at the expense of Tenant, if repairs are necessitated by damage or injury attributable to Tenant, Tenant's servants, agents, employees, invitees or licensees as aforesaid. Except as specifically provided in Article 9 or elsewhere in this lease, there shall be no allowance to the Tenant for a diminution of rental value and no liability on the part of Owner by reason of inconvenience, annoyance or injury to business arising from Owner, Tenant or others making or failing to make any repairs, alterations, additions or improvements in or to any portion of the building or the demised premises or in and to the fixtures, appurtenances or equipment thereof. The provisions of this Article 4 with respect to the making of repairs shall not apply in the case of fire or other casualty with regard to which Article 9 hereof shall apply.

**Window Cleaning:**

5. Tenant will not clean nor require, permit, suffer or allow any window in the demised premises to be cleaned

from the outside in violation of Section 202 of the New York State Labor Law or any other applicable law or of the Rules of the Board of Standards and Appeals, or of any other Board or body having or asserting jurisdiction.

**Requirements of Law, Fire Insurance, Floor Loads:**

**6.** Prior to the commencement of the lease term, if Tenant is then in possession, and at all times thereafter, Tenant shall, at Tenant's sole cost and expense, promptly comply with all present and future laws, orders and regulations of all state, federal, municipal and local governments, departments, commissions and boards and any direction of any public officer pursuant to law, and all orders, rules and regulations of the New York Board of Fire Underwriters, or the Insurance Services Office, or any similar body which shall impose any violation, order or duty upon Owner or Tenant with respect to the demised premises, whether or not arising out of Tenant's use or manner of use thereof, or, with respect to the building, if arising out of Tenant's use or manner of use of the demised premises or the building (including the use permitted under the lease). Except as provided in Article 30 hereof, nothing herein shall require Tenant to make structural repairs or alterations unless Tenant has, by its manner of use of the demised premises or method of operation therein, violated any such laws, ordinances, orders, rules, regulations or requirements with respect thereto. Tenant shall not do or permit any act or thing to be done in or to the demised premises which is contrary to law, or which will invalidate or be in conflict with public liability, fire or other policies of insurance at any time carried by or for the benefit of Owner. Tenant shall not keep anything in the demised premises except as now or hereafter permitted by the Fire Department, Board of Fire Underwriters, Fire Insurance Rating Organization and other authority having jurisdiction, and then only in such manner and such quantity so as not to increase the rate for fire insurance applicable to the building, nor use the premises in a manner which will increase the insurance rate for the building or any property located therein over that in effect prior to the commencement of Tenant's occupancy. If by reason of failure to comply with the foregoing the fire insurance rate shall, at the beginning of this lease or at any time thereafter, be higher than it otherwise would be, then Tenant shall reimburse Owner, as additional rent hereunder, for that portion of all fire insurance premiums thereafter paid by Owner which shall have been charged because of such failure by Tenant. In any action or proceeding wherein Owner and Tenant are parties, a schedule or "make-up" or rate for the building or demised premises issued by a body making fire insurance rates applicable to said premises shall be conclusive evidence of the facts therein stated and of the several items and charges in the fire insurance rates then applicable to said premises. Tenant shall not place a load upon any floor of the demised premises exceeding the floor load per square foot area which it was designed to carry and which is allowed by law. Owner reserves the right to prescribe the weight and position of all safes, business machines and mechanical equipment. Such installations shall be placed and maintained by Tenant, at Tenant's expense, in settings sufficient, in Owner's judgment, to absorb and prevent vibration, noise and annoyance.

**Subordination:**

7. This lease is subject and subordinate to all ground or underlying leases and to all mortgages which may now or hereafter affect such leases or the real property of which demised premises are a part and to all renewals, modifications, consolidations, replacements and extensions of any such underlying leases and mortgages. This clause shall be self-operative and no further instrument of subordination shall be required by any ground or underlying lessor or by any mortgagee, affecting any lease or the real property of which the demised premises are a part. In confirmation of such subordination, Tenant shall execute promptly any certificate that Owner may request.

**Property—Loss, Damage, Reimbursement, Indemnity:**

8. Owner or its agents shall not be liable for any damage to property of Tenant or of others entrusted to employees of the building, nor for loss of or damage to any property of Tenant by theft or otherwise, nor for any injury or damage to persons or property resulting from

any cause of whatsoever nature, unless caused by or due to the negligence of Owner, its agents, servants or employees; Owner or its agents shall not be liable for any damage caused by other tenants or persons in, upon or about said building or caused by operations in connection of any private, public or quasi public work. If at any time any windows of the demised premises are temporarily closed, darkened or bricked up (or permanently closed, darkened or bricked up, if required by law) for any reason whatsoever including, but not limited to Owner's own acts, Owner shall not be liable for any damage Tenant may sustain thereby and Tenant shall not be entitled to any compensation therefor nor abatement or diminution of rent nor shall the same release Tenant from its obligations hereunder nor constitute an eviction. Tenant shall indemnify and save harmless Owner against and from all liabilities, obligations, damages, penalties, claims, costs and expenses for which Owner shall not be reimbursed by insurance, including reasonable attorney's fees, paid, suffered or incurred as a result of any breach by Tenant, Tenant's agents, contractors, employees, invitees, or licensees, of any covenant or condition of this lease, or the carelessness, negligence or improper conduct of the Tenant, Tenant's agents, contractors, employees, invitees or licensees. Tenant's liability under this lease extends to the acts and omissions of any sub-tenant, and any agent, contractor, employee, invitee or licensee of any sub-tenant. In case any action or proceeding is brought against Owner by reason of any such claim, Tenant, upon written notice from Owner, will, at Tenant's expense, resist or defend such action or proceeding by counsel approved by Owner in writing, such approval not to be unreasonably withheld.

**Destruction, Fire and Other Casualty:**

**9.** (a) If the demised premises or any part thereof shall be damaged by fire or other casualty, Tenant shall give immediate notice thereof to Owner and this lease shall continue in full force and effect except as hereinafter set forth. (b) If the demised premises are partially damaged or rendered partially unusable by fire or other casualty, the damages thereto shall be repaired by and at the expense of Owner and the rent, until such repair shall be

## GENERAL PRINCIPLES § 1:12

substantially completed, shall be apportioned from the day following the casualty according to the part of the premises which is usable. (c) If the demised premises are totally damaged or rendered wholly unusable by fire or other casualty, then the rent shall be proportionately paid up to the time of the casualty and thenceforth shall cease until the date when the premises shall have been repaired and restored by Owner, subject to Owner's right to elect not to restore the same as hereinafter provided. (d) If the demised premises are rendered wholly unusable or (whether or not the demised premises are damaged in whole or in part) if the building shall be so damaged that Owner shall decide to demolish it or to rebuild it, then, in any of such events, Owner may elect to terminate this lease by written notice to Tenant, given within 90 days after such fire or casualty, specifying a date for the expiration of the lease, which date shall not be more than 60 days after the giving of such notice, and upon the date specified in such notice the term of this lease shall expire as fully and completely as if such date were the date set forth above for the termination of this lease and Tenant shall forthwith quit, surrender and vacate the premises without prejudice however, to Owner's rights and remedies against Tenant under the lease provisions in effect prior to such termination, and any rent owing shall be paid up to such date and any payments of rent made by Tenant which were on account of any period subsequent to such date shall be returned to Tenant. Unless Owner shall serve a termination notice as provided for herein, Owner shall make the repairs and restorations under the conditions of (b) and (c) hereof, with all reasonable expedition, subject to delays due to adjustment of insurance claims, labor troubles and causes beyond Owner's control. After any such casualty, Tenant shall cooperate with Owner's restoration by removing from the premises as promptly as reasonably possible, all of Tenant's salvageable inventory and movable equipment, furniture, and other property. Tenant's liability for rent shall resume five (5) days after written notice from Owner that the premises are substantially ready for Tenant's occupancy. (e) Nothing contained hereinabove shall relieve Tenant from liability that may exist as a result of damage from fire or other casualty. Notwithstanding the foregoing, each party shall look first to any insurance in its favor before making any claim against the other party for recovery for loss or damage resulting from fire or other casualty, and to the extent that such insurance is in force and collectible and to the extent permitted by law, Owner and Tenant each hereby releases and waives all right of recovery against the other or any one claiming through or under each of them by way of subrogation or otherwise. The foregoing release and waiver shall be in force only if both releasors' insurance policies contain a clause providing that such a release or waiver shall not invalidate the insurance. If, and to the extent, that such waiver can be obtained only by the payment of additional premiums, then the party benefitting from the waiver shall pay such premium within ten days after written demand or shall be deemed to have agreed that the party obtaining insurance coverage shall be free of any further obligation under the provisions hereof with respect to waiver of subrogation. Tenant acknowledges that Owner will not carry insurance on Tenant's furniture and or furnishings or any fixtures or equipment, improvements, or appurtenances removable by Tenant and agrees that Owner will not be obligated to repair any damage thereto or replace the same. (f) Tenant hereby waives the provisions of Section 227 of the Real Property Law and agrees that the provisions of this article shall govern and control in lieu thereof.

**Eminent Domain:**

10. If the whole or any part of the demised premises shall be acquired or condemned by Eminent Domain for any public or quasi public use or purpose, then and in that event, the term of this lease shall cease and terminate from the date of title vesting in such proceeding and Tenant shall have no claim for the value of any unexpired term of said lease.

**Assignment, Mortgage, Etc.:**

11. Tenant, for itself, its heirs, distributees, executors, administrators, legal representatives, successors and assigns, expressly covenants that it shall not assign, mortgage or encumber this agreement, nor underlet, or suffer

or permit the demised premises or any part thereof to be used by others, without the prior written consent of Owner in each instance. Transfer of the majority of the stock of a corporate Tenant shall be deemed an assignment. If this lease be assigned, or if the demised premises or any part thereof be underlet or occupied by anybody other than Tenant, Owner may, after default by Tenant, collect rent from the assignee, under-tenant or occupant, and apply the net amount collected to the rent herein reserved, but no such assignment, underletting, occupancy or collection shall be deemed a waiver of this covenant, or the acceptance of the assignee, under-tenant or occupant as tenant, or a release of Tenant from the further performance by Tenant of covenants on the part of Tenant herein contained. The consent by Owner to an assignment or underletting shall not in any wise be construed to relieve Tenant from obtaining the express consent in writing of Owner to any further assignment or underletting.

**Electric Current:**

12. Rates and conditions in respect to submetering or rent inclusion, as the case may be, to be added in RIDER attached hereto. Tenant covenants and agrees that at all times its use of electric current shall not exceed the capacity of existing leeders to the building or the risers or wiring installation and Tenant may not use any electrical equipment which, in Owner's opinion, reasonably exercised, will overload such installations or interfere with the use thereof by other tenants of the building. The change at any time of the character of electric service shall in no wise make Owner liable or responsible to Tenant, for any loss, damages or expenses which Tenant may sustain.

**Access to Premises:**

13. Owner or Owner's agents shall have the right (but shall not be obligated) to enter the demised premises in any emergency at any time, and, at other reasonable times, to examine the same and to make such repairs, replacements and improvements as Owner may deem necessary and reasonably desirable to any portion of the building or which Owner may elect to perform in the

§ 1:12　　　　　　　　　LANDLORD AND TENANT

premises after Tenant's failure to make repairs or perform any work which Tenant is obligated to perform under this lease, or for the purpose of complying with laws, regulations and other directions of governmental authorities. Tenant shall permit Owner to use and maintain and replace pipes and conduits in and through the demised premises and to erect new pipes and conduits therein provided, wherever possible, they are within walls or otherwise concealed. Owner may, during the progress of any work in the demised premises, take all necessary materials and equipment into said premises without the same constituting an eviction nor shall the Tenant be entitled to any abatement of rent while such work is in progress nor to any damages by reason of loss or interruption of business or otherwise. Throughout the term hereof Owner shall have the right to enter the demised premises at reasonable hours for the purpose of showing the same to prospective purchasers or mortgagees of the building, and during the last six months of the term for the purpose of showing the same to prospective tenants and may, during said six months period, place upon the premises the usual notices "To Let" and "For Sale" which notices Tenant shall permit to remain thereon without molestation. If Tenant is not present to open and permit an entry into the premises, Owner or Owner's agents may enter the same whenever such entry may be necessary or permissible by master key or forcibly and provided reasonable care is exercised to safeguard Tenant's property, such entry shall not render Owner or its agents liable therefor, nor in any event shall the obligations of Tenant hereunder be affected. If during the last month of the term Tenant shall have removed all or substantially all of Tenant's property therefrom. Owner may immediately enter, alter, renovate or redecorate the demised premises without limitation or abatement of rent, or incurring liability to Tenant for any compensation and such act shall have no effect on this lease or Tenant's obligations hereunder.

**Vault, Vault Space, Area:**

14. No Vaults, vault space or area, whether or not enclosed or covered, not within the property line of the building is leased hereunder, anything contained in or

indicated on any sketch, blue print or plan, or anything contained elsewhere in this lease to the contrary notwithstanding. Owner makes no representation as to the location of the property line of the building. All vaults and vault space and all such areas not within the property line of the building, which Tenant may be permitted to use and/or occupy, is to be used and/or occupied under a revocable license, and if any such license be revoked, or if the amount of such space or area be diminished or required by any federal, state or municipal authority or public utility, Owner shall not be subject to any liability nor shall Tenant be entitled to any compensation or diminution or abatement of rent, nor shall such revocation, diminution or requisition be deemed constructive or actual eviction. Any tax, fee or charge of municipal authorities for such vault or area shall be paid by Tenant, if used by Tenant, whether or not specifically leased hereunder.

**Occupancy:**

**15.** Tenant will not at any time use or occupy the demised premises in violation of the certificate of occupancy issued for the building of which the demised premises are a part. Tenant has inspected the premises and accepts them as is, subject to the riders annexed hereto with respect to Owner's work, if any. In any event, Owner makes no representation as to the condition of the premises and Tenant agrees to accept the same subject to violations, whether or not of record. If any governmental license or permit shall be required for the proper and lawful conduct of Tenant's business, Tenant shall be responsible for and shall procure and maintain such license or permit.

*[Provision 16 of this lease is a bankruptcy termination clause, which no longer is enforceable, and therefore has been omitted. See Chapter 22, infra.]*

**Default:**

**17.** (1) If Tenant defaults in fulfilling any of the covenants of this lease other than the covenants for the payment of rent or additional rent; or if the demised premises becomes vacant or deserted "or if this lease be rejected under 11 USCS § 365 (bankruptcy code); or if any execution or attachment shall be issued against Tenant or any of Tenant's property whereupon the demised premises shall be taken or occupied by someone other than Tenant; or if Tenant shall make default with respect to any other lease between Owner and Tenant; or if Tenant shall have failed, after five (5) days written notice, to redeposit with Owner any portion of the security deposited hereunder which Owner has applied to the payment of any rent and additional rent due and payable hereunder or failed to move into or take possession of the premises within fifteen (15) days after the commencement of the term of this lease, of which fact Owner shall be the sole judge; then in any one or more of such events, upon Owner serving a written five (5) days notice upon Tenant specifying the nature of said default and upon the expiration of said five (5) days, if Tenant shall have failed to comply with or remedy such default, or if the said default or omission complained of shall be of a nature that the same cannot be completely cured or remedied within said five (5) day period, and if Tenant shall not have diligently commenced during such default within such five (5) day period, and shall not thereafter with reasonable diligence and in good faith, proceed to remedy or cure such default, then Owner may serve a written three (3) days' notice of cancellation of this lease upon Tenant, and upon the expiration of said three (3) days this lease and the term thereunder shall end and expire as fully and completely as if the expiration of such three (3) day period were the day herein definitely fixed for the end and expiration of this lease and the term thereof and Tenant shall then quit and surrender the demised premises to Owner but Tenant shall remain liable as hereinafter provided.

(2) If the notice provided for in (1) hereof shall have been given, and the term shall expire as aforesaid: or if Tenant shall make default in the payment of the rent reserved herein or any item of additional rent herein mentioned or any part of either or in making any other payment herein required: then and in any of such events Owner may without notice, re-enter the demised premises either by force or otherwise, and dispossess Tenant by summary proceedings or otherwise, and the legal representative of Tenant or other occupant of demised prem-

GENERAL PRINCIPLES § 1:12

ises and remove their effects and hold the premises as if this lease had not been made, and Tenant hereby waives the service of notice of intention to re-enter or to institute legal proceedings to that end. If Tenant shall make default hereunder prior to the date fixed as the commencement of any renewal or extension of this lease, Owner may cancel and terminate such renewal or extension agreement by written notice.

**Remedies of Owner and Waiver of Redemption:**

18. In case of any such default, re-entry, expiration and/or dispossess by summary proceedings or otherwise, (a) the rent, and additional rent, shall become due thereupon and be paid up to the time of such re-entry, dispossess and/or expiration, (b) Owner may re-let the premises or any part or parts thereof, either in the name of Owner or otherwise, for a term or terms, which may at Owner's option be less than or exceed the period which would otherwise have constituted the balance of the term of this lease and may grant concessions or free rent or charge a higher rental than that in this lease, (c) Tenant or the legal representatives of Tenant shall also pay Owner as liquidated damages for the failure of Tenant to observe and perform said Tenant's convenants herein contained, any deficiency between the rent hereby reserved and or covenanted to be paid and the net amount, if any, of the rents collected on account of the subsequent lease or leases of the demised premises for each month of the period which would otherwise have constituted the balance of the term of this lease. The failure of Owner to re-let the premises or any part or parts thereof shall not release or affect Tenant's liability for damages. In computing such liquidated damages there shall be added to the said deficiency such expenses as Owner may incur in connection with re-letting, such as legal expenses, attorneys' fees, brokerage, advertising and for keeping the demised premises in good order or for preparing the same for re-letting. Any such liquidated damages shall be paid in monthly installments by Tenant on the rent day specified in this lease and any suit brought to collect the amount of the deficiency for any month shall not prejudice in any way the rights of Owner to collect the deficiency for any subsequent month by a similar proceed-

ing. Owner, in putting the demised premises in good order or preparing the same for re-rental may, at Owner's option, make such alterations, repairs, replacements, and/or decorations in the demised premises as Owner, in Owner's sole judgment, considers advisable and necessary for the purpose of re-letting the demised premises, and the making of such alterations, repairs, replacements, and/or decorations shall not operate or be construed to release Tenant from liability hereunder as aforesaid. Owner shall in no event be liable in any way whatsoever for failure to re-let the demised premises, or in the event that the demised premises are re-let, for failure to collect the rent thereof under such re-letting, and in no event shall Tenant be entitled to receive any excess, if any, of such net rents collected over the sums payable by Tenant to Owner hereunder. In the event of a breach or threatened breach by Tenant of any of the covenants or provisions hereof, Owner shall have the right of injunction and the right to invoke any remedy allowed at law or in equity as if re-entry, summary proceedings and other remedies were not herein provided for. Mention in this lease of any particular remedy, shall not preclude Owner from any other remedy, in law or in equity. Tenant hereby expressly waives any and all rights of redemption granted by or under any present or future laws.

**Fees and Expenses:**

**19.** If Tenant shall default in the observance or performance of any term or covenant on Tenant's part to be observed or performed under or by virtue of any of the terms or provisions in any article of this lease, then, unless otherwise provided elsewhere in this lease, Owner may immediately or at any time thereafter and without notice perform the obligation of Tenant thereunder. If Owner, in connection with the foregoing or in connection with any default by Tenant in the covenant to pay rent hereunder, makes any expenditures or incurs any obligations for the payment of money, including but not limited to attorney's fees, in instituting, prosecuting or defending any action or proceedings, then Tenant will reimburse Owner for such sums so paid or obligations incurred with interest and costs. The foregoing expenses incurred by reason of Tenant's default shall be deemed to be additional rent hereunder and shall be paid by Tenant to Owner within five (5) days of rendition of any bill or statement to Tenant therefor. If Tenant's lease term shall have expired at the time of making of such expenditures or incurring of such obligations, such sums shall be recoverable by Owner as damages.

### Building Alterations and Management:

**20.** Owner shall have the right at any time without the same constituting an eviction and without incurring liability to Tenant therefor to change the arrangement and or location of public entrances, passageways, doors, doorways, corridors, elevators, stairs, toilets or other public parts of the building and to change the name, number or designation by which the building may be known. There shall be no allowance to Tenant for diminution of rental value and no liability on the part of Owner by reason of inconvenience, annoyance or injury to business arising from Owner or other Tenant making any repairs in the building or any such alterations, additions and improvements. Furthermore, Tenant shall not have any claim against Owner by reason of Owner's imposition of any controls of the manner of access to the building by Tenant's social or business visitors as the Owner may deem necessary for the security of the building and its occupants.

### No Representations by Owner:

**21.** Neither Owner nor Owner's agents have made any representations or promises with respect to the physical condition of the building, the land upon which it is erected or the demised premises, the rents, leases, expenses of operation or any other matter or thing affecting or related to the demised premises or the building except as herein expressly set forth and no rights, easements or licenses are acquired by Tenant by implication or otherwise except as expressly set forth in the provisions of this lease. Tenant has inspected the building and the demised premises and is thoroughly acquainted with their condition and agrees to take the same "as is" on the date possession is tendered and acknowledges that the taking of possession of the demised premises by Tenant shall be conclusive evidence that the said premises and the building of which the same form a part were in good and satisfactory condition at the time such possession was so taken, except as to latent defects. All understandings and agreements heretofore made between the parties hereto are merged in this contract, which alone fully and completely expresses the agreement between Owner and Tenant and any executory agreement hereafter made shall be ineffective to change, modify, discharge or effect an abandonment of it in whole or in part, unless such executory agreement is in writing and signed by the party against whom enforcement of the change, modification, discharge or abandonment is sought.

**End of Term:**

22. Upon the expiration or other termination of the term of this lease, Tenant shall quit and surrender to Owner the demised premises, broom clean, in good order and condition, ordinary wear and damages which Tenant is not required to repair as provided elsewhere in this lease excepted, and Tenant shall remove all its property from the demised premises. Tenant's obligation to observe or perform this covenant shall survive the expiration or other termination of this lease. If the last day of the term of this Lease or any renewal thereof, falls on Sunday, this lease shall expire at noon on the preceding Saturday unless it be a legal holiday in which case it shall expire at noon on the preceding business day.

**Quiet Enjoyment:**

23. Owner covenants and agrees with Tenant that upon Tenant paying the rent and additional rent and observing and performing all the terms, covenants and conditions, on Tenant's part to be observed and performed, Tenant may peaceably and quietly enjoy the premises hereby demised, subject, nevertheless, to the terms and conditions of this lease including, but not limited to, Article 34 hereof and to the ground leases, underlying leases and mortgages hereinbefore mentioned.

**Failure to Give Possession:**

24. If Owner is unable to give possession of the demised premises on the date of the commencement of the term hereof, because of the holding-over or retention of possession of any tenant, undertenant or occupants or if the

## GENERAL PRINCIPLES § 1:12

demised premises are located in a building being constructed, because such building has not been sufficiently completed to make the premises ready for occupancy or because of the fact that a certificate of occupancy has not been procured or if Owner has not completed any work required to be performed by Owner, or for any other reason, Owner shall not be subject to any liability for failure to give possession on said date and the validity of the lease shall not be impaired under such circumstances, nor shall the same be construed in any wise to extend the term of this lease, but the rent payable hereunder shall be abated (provided Tenant is not responsible for Owner's inability to obtain possession or complete any work required) until after Owner shall have given Tenant notice that the premises are substantially ready for Tenant's occupancy. If permission is given to Tenant to enter into the possession of the demised premises or to occupy premises other than the demised premises prior to the date specified as the commencement of the term of this lease. Tenant covenants and agrees that such occupancy shall be deemed to be under all the terms, covenants, conditions and provisions of this lease, except as to the covenant to pay rent. The provisions of this article are intended to constitute "an express provision to the contrary" within the meaning of Section 223-a of the New York Real Property Law.

### No Waiver:

25. The failure of Owner to seek redress for violation of, or to insist upon the strict performance of any covenant or condition of this lease or of any of the Rules or Regulations, set forth or hereafter adopted by Owner, shall not prevent a subsequent act which would have originally constituted a violation from having all the force and effect of an original violation. The receipt by Owner of rent with knowledge of the breach of any covenant of this lease shall not be deemed a waiver of such breach and no provision of this lease shall be deemed to have been waived by Owner unless such waiver be in writing signed by Owner. No payment by Tenant or receipt by Owner of a lesser amount than the monthly rent herein stipulated shall be deemed to be other than on account of the earliest stipulated rent, nor

shall any endorsement or statement of any check or any letter accompanying any check or payment as rent be deemed an accord and satisfaction, and Owner may accept such check or payment without prejudice to Owner's right to recover the balance of such rent or pursue any other remedy in this lease provided. All checks tendered to Owner as and for the rent of the demised premises shall be deemed payments for the account of Tenant. Acceptance by Owner of rent from anyone other than Tenant shall not be deemed to operate as an attornment to Owner by the payor of such rent or as a consent by Owner to an assignment or subletting by Tenant of the demised premises to such payor, or as a modification of the provisions of this lease. No act or thing done by Owner or Owner's agents during the term hereby demised shall be deemed an acceptance of a surrender of said premises and no agreement to accept such surrender shall be valid unless in writing signed by Owner. No employee of Owner or Owner's agent shall have any power to accept the keys of said premises prior to the termination of the lease and the delivery of keys to any such agent or employee shall not operate as a termination of the lease or a surrender of the premises.

**Waiver of Trial by Jury:**

**26.** It is mutually agreed by and between Owner and Tenant that the respective parties hereto shall and they hereby do waive trial by jury in any action, proceeding or counterclaim brought by either of the parties hereto against the other (except for personal injury or property damage) on any matters whatsoever arising out of or in any way connected with this lease, the relationship of Owner and Tenant, Tenant's use of or occupancy of said premises, and any emergency statutory or any other statutory remedy. It is further mutually agreed that in the event Owner commences any summary proceeding for possession of the premises, Tenant will not interpose any counterclaim of whatever nature or description in any such proceeding.

**Inability to Perform:**

**27.** This Lease and the obligation of Tenant to pay rent hereunder and perform all of the other covenants and agreements hereunder on part of Tenant to be performed shall in no wise be affected, impaired or excused because Owner is unable to fulfill any of its obligations under this lease or to supply or is delayed in supplying any service expressly or impliedly to be supplied or is unable to make, or is delayed in making any repair, additions, alterations or decorations or is unable to supply or is delayed in supplying any equipment or fixtures if Owner is prevented or delayed from so doing by reason of strike or labor troubles or any cause whatsoever beyond Owner's sole control including, but not limited to, government preemption in connection with a National Emergency or by reason of any rule, order or regulation of any department or subdivision thereof of any government agency or by reason of the conditions of supply and demand which have been or are affected by war or other emergency.

### Bills and Notices:

28. Except as otherwise in this lease provided, a bill, statement, notice or communication which Owner may desire or be required to give to Tenant, shall be deemed sufficiently given or rendered it, in writing, delivered to Tenant personally or sent by registered or certified mail addressed to Tenant at the building of which the demised premises form a part or at the last known residence address or business address of Tenant or left at any of the aforesaid premises addressed to Tenant, and the time of the rendition of such bill or statement and of the giving of such notice or communication shall be deemed to be the time when the same is delivered to Tenant, mailed, or left at the premises as herein provided. Any notice by Tenant to Owner must be served by registered or certified mail addressed to Owner at the address first hereinabove given or at such other address as Owner shall designate by written notice.

### Water Charges:

29. If Tenant requires, uses or consumes water for any purpose in addition to ordinary lavatory purposes (of which fact Tenant constitutes Owner to be the sole judge) Owner may install a water meter and thereby measure Tenant's water consumption for all purposes. Tenant shall pay Owner for the cost of the meter and the cost of

the installation, thereof and throughout the duration of Tenant's occupancy Tenant shall keep said meter and installation equipment in good working order and repair at Tenant's own cost and expense in default of which Owner may cause such meter and equipment to be replaced or repaired and collect the cost thereof from Tenant, as additional rent. Tenant agrees to pay for water consumed, as shown on said meter as and when bills are rendered, and on default in making such payment Owner may pay such charges and collect the same from Tenant, as additional rent. Tenant covenants and agrees to pay, as additional rent, the sewer rent, charge or any other tax, rent, levy or charge which now or hereafter is assessed, imposed or a lien upon the demised premises or the realty of which they are part pursuant to law, order or regulation made or issued in connection with the use, consumption, maintenance or supply of water, water system or sewage or sewage connection or system. If the building or the demised premises or any part thereof is supplied with water through a meter through which water is also supplied to other premises Tenant shall pay to Owner, as additional rent, on the first day of each month, _____% ($\_\_\_\_) of the total meter charges as Tenant's portion. Independently of and in addition to any of the remedies reserved to Owner hereinabove or elsewhere in this lease, Owner may sue for and collect any monies to be paid by Tenant or paid by Owner for any of the reasons or purposes hereinabove set forth.

**Sprinklers:**

**30.** Anything elsewhere in this lease to the contrary notwithstanding, if the New York Board of Fire Underwriters or the New York Fire Insurance Exchange or any bureau, department or official of the federal, state or city government recommend or require the installation of a sprinkler system or that any changes, modifications, alterations, or additional sprinkler heads or other equipment be made or supplied in an existing sprinkler system by reason of Tenant's business, or the location of partitions, trade fixtures, or other contents of the demised premises, or for any other reason, or if any such sprinkler system installations, modifications, alterations, additional sprinkler heads or other such equipment, become necessary to prevent the imposition of a penalty or charge against the full allowance for a sprinkler system in the fire insurance rate set by any said Exchange or by any fire insurance company, Tenant shall, at Tenant's expense, promptly make such sprinkler system installations, changes, modifications, alterations, and supply additional sprinkler heads or other equipment as required whether the work involved shall be structural or nonstructural in nature. Tenant shall pay to Owner as additional rent the sum of $_____, on the first day of each month during the term of this lease, as Tenant's portion of the contract price for sprinkler supervisory service.

**Elevators, Heat, Cleaning:**

**31.** As long as Tenant is not in default under any of the covenants of this lease Owner shall: (a) provide necessary passenger elevator facilities on business days from 8 a.m. to 6 p.m. and on Saturdays from 8 a.m. to 1 p.m.; (b) if freight elevator service is provided, same shall be provided only on regular business days Monday through Friday inclusive, and on those days only between the hours of 9 a.m. and 12 noon and between 1 p.m. and 5 p.m.; (c) furnish heat, water and other services supplied by Owner to the demised premises, when and as required by law, on business days from 8 a.m. to 6 p.m. and on Saturdays from 8 a.m. to 1 p.m.; (d) clean the public halls and public portions of the building which are used in common by all tenants. Tenant shall, at Tenant's expense, keep the demised premises, including the windows, clean and in order, to the satisfaction of Owner, and for that purpose shall employ the person or persons, or corporation approved by Owner. Tenant shall pay to Owner the cost of removal of any of Tenant's refuse and rubbish from the building. Bills for the same shall be rendered by Owner to Tenant at such time as Owner may elect and shall be due and payable hereunder, and the amount of such bills shall be deemed to be, and be paid as, additional rent. Tenant shall, however, have the option of independently contracting for the removal of such rubbish and refuse in the event that Tenant does not wish to have same done by employees of Owner. Under such circumstances, however, the removal of such refuse and rubbish by others shall be subject to such rules and

**§ 1:12**    LANDLORD AND TENANT

regulations as, in the judgment of Owner, are necessary for the proper operation of the building. Owner reserves the right to stop service of the heating, elevator, plumbing and electric systems, when necessary, by reason of accident, or emergency, or for repairs, alterations, replacements or improvements, in the judgment of Owner desirable or necessary to be made, until said repairs, alterations, replacements or improvements shall have been completed. If the building of which the demised premises are a part supplies manually operated elevator service, Owner may proceed with alterations necessary to substitute automatic control elevator service upon ten (10) day written notice to Tenant without in any way affecting the obligations of Tenant hereunder, provided that the same shall be done with the minimum amount of inconvenience to Tenant, and Owner pursues with due diligence the completion of the alterations.

**Security:**

32. Tenant has deposited with Owner the sum of $_____ as security for the faithful performance and observance by Tenant of the terms, provisions and conditions of this lease; it is agreed that in the event Tenant defaults in respect of any of the terms, provisions and conditions of this lease, including, but not limited to, the payment of rent and additional rent, Owner may use, apply or retain the whole or any part of the security so deposited to the extent required for the payment of any rent and additional rent or any other sum as to which tenant is in default or for any sum which Owner may expend or may be required to expend by reason of Tenant's default in respect of any of the terms, covenants and conditions of this lease, including but not limited to, any damages or deficiency in the reletting of the premises, whether such damages or deficiency accrued before or after summary proceedings or other re-entry by Owner. In the event that Tenant shall fully and faithfully comply with all of the terms, provisions, covenants and conditions of this lease, the security shall be returned to Tenant after the date fixed as the end of the Lease and after delivery of entire possession of the demised premises to Owner. In the event of a sale of the land and building or leasing of the building, of which the demised premises

# GENERAL PRINCIPLES § 1:12

form a part, Owner shall have the right to transfer the security to the vendee or lessee and Owner shall thereupon be released by Tenant from all liability for the return of such security; and Tenant agrees to look to the new Owner solely for the return of said security, and it is agreed that the provisions hereof shall apply to every transfer or assignment made of the security to a new Owner. Tenant further convenants that it will not assign or encumber or attempt to assign or encumber the monies deposited herein as security and that neither Owner nor its successors or assigns shall be bound by any such assignment, encumbrance, attempted assignment or attempted encumbrance.

## Captions:

33. The Captions are inserted only as a matter of convenience and for reference and in no way define, limit or describe the scope of this lease nor the intent of any provision thereof.

## Definitions:

34. The term "Owner" as used in this lease means only the owner of the fee or of the leasehold of the building, or the mortgagee in possession, for the time being of the land and building (or the owner of a lease of the building or of the land and building) of which the demised premises form a part, so that in the event of any sale or sales of said land and building or of said lease, or in the event of a lease of said building, or of the land and building, the said Owner shall be and hereby is entirely freed and relieved of all covenants and obligations of Owner hereunder, and it shall be deemed and construed without further agreement between the parties or their successors in interest, or between the parties and the purchaser, at any such sale, or the said lessee of the building, or of the land and building, that the purchaser or the lessee of the building has assumed and agreed to carry out any and all covenants and obligations of Owner hereunder. The words "re-enter" and "re-entry" as used in this lease are not restricted to their technical legal meaning. The term "rent" includes the annual rental rate whether so-expressed or expressed in monthly installments, and "additional rent." "Additional rent" means all sums which

shall be due to new Owner from Tenant under this lease, in addition to the annual rental rate. The term "business days" as used in this lease, shall exclude Saturdays (except such portion thereof as is covered by specific hours in Article 31 hereof), Sundays and all days observed by the State or Federal Government as legal holidays and those designated as holidays by the applicable building service union employees service contract or by the applicable Operating Engineers contract with respect to HVAC service.

**Adjacent Excavation and Sharing:**

**35.** If an excavation shall be made upon land adjacent to the demised premises, or shall be authorized to be made, Tenant shall afford to the person causing or authorized to cause such excavation, license to enter upon the demised premises for the purpose of doing such work as said person shall deem necessary to preserve the wall or the building of which demised premises form a part from injury or damage and to support the same by proper foundations without any claim for damages or indemnity against Owner, or diminution or abatement of rent.

**Rules and Regulations:**

**36.** Tenant and Tenant's servants, employees, agents, visitors, and licensees shall observe faithfully, and comply strictly with, the Rules and Regulations annexed hereto and such other and further reasonable Rules and Regulations as Owner or Owner's agents may from time to time adopt. Notice of any additional rules or regulations shall be given in such manner as Owner may elect. In case Tenant disputes the reasonableness of any additional Rule or Regulation hereafter made or adopted by Owner or Owner's agents, the parties hereto agree to submit the question of the reasonableness of such Rule or Regulation for decision to the New York office of the American Arbitration Association, whose determination shall be final and conclusive upon the parties hereto. The right to dispute the reasonableness of any additional Rule or Regulation upon Tenant's part shall be deemed waived unless the same shall be asserted by service of a notice, in writing upon Owner within ten (10) days after the giving of notice thereof. Nothing in this lease contained shall be construed to impose upon Owner any duty or obligation to enforce the Rules and Regulations or terms, covenants or conditions in any other lease, as against any other tenant and Owner shall not be liable to Tenant for violation of the same by any other tenant, its servants, employees, agents, visitors or licensees.

**Glass:**

**37.** Owner shall replace, at the expense of the Tenant, any and all plate and other glass damaged or broken from any cause whatsoever in and about the demised premises. Owner may insure, and keep insured, at Tenant's expense, all plate and other glass in the demised premises for and in the name of Owner. Bills for the premiums therefor shall be rendered by Owner to Tenant at such times as Owner may elect, and shall be due from, and payable by, Tenant when rendered, and the amount thereof shall be deemed to be, and be paid, as additional rent.

**Estoppel Certificate:**

**38.** Tenant, at any time, and from time to time, upon at least 10 days' prior notice by Owner, shall execute, acknowledge and deliver to Owner, and/or to any other person, firm or corporation specified by Owner, a statement certifying that this Lease is unmodified in full force and effect (or, if there have been modifications, that the same is in full force and effect as modified and stating the modifications), stating the dates to which the rent and additional rent have been paid, and stating whether or not there exists any default by Owner under this Lease, and, if so, specifying each such default.

**Directory Board Listing:**

**39.** If, at the request of and as accommodation to Tenant, Owner shall place upon the directory board in the lobby of the building, one or more names of persons other than Tenant, such directory board listing shall not be construed as the consent by Owner to an assignment or subletting by Tenant to such person or persons.

**Successors and Assigns:**

**40.** The covenants, conditions and agreements contained in this lease shall bind and inure to the benefit of

Owner and Tenant and their respective heirs, distributees, executors, administrators, successors, and except as otherwise provided in this lease, their assigns.

IN WITNESS WHEREOF, Owner and Tenant have respectively signed and sealed this lease as of the day and year first above written. Witness for Landlord:

..........................

.................................
[Corporate Seal]
.................................
[L. S.]

Witness for Tenant:

..........................

.................................
[L. S.]
[Corporate Seal]

## ACKNOWLEDGMENTS
### CORPORATE OWNER

**STATE OF NEW YORK,**   ss.:
**County of** ..........

On this ........ day of ........, 19..., before me personally came ........, to me known, who being by me duly sworn, did depose and say that he resides in ........; that he is the ........ of ........ the corporation described in and which executed the foregoing instrument, as OWNER; that he knows the seal of said corporation; that the seal affixed to said instrument is such corporate seal; that it was so affixed by order of the Board of Directors of said corporation, and that he signed his name thereto by like order.

.................................

### INDIVIDUAL OWNER

**STATE OF NEW YORK,**   ss.:
**County of** ..........

On this ........ day of ........, 19..., before me personally came ........, to me known and known to me to be the individual described in and who, as OWNER, executed the foregoing instrument and acknowledged to me that he executed the same.

.................................

## CORPORATE TENANT

**STATE OF NEW YORK,**
**County of** .......... ss.:

On this ........ day of ........, 19..., before me personally came ........, to me known, who being by me duly sworn, did depose and say that he resides in ........; that he is the ........ of ........ the corporation described in and which executed the foregoing instrument, as TENANT; that he knows the seal of said corporation; that the seal affixed to said instrument is such corporate seal; that it was so affixed by order of the Board of Directors of said corporation, and that he signed his name thereto by like order.

..............................

## INDIVIDUAL TENANT

**STATE OF NEW YORK,**
**County of** .......... ss.:

On this ........ day of ........, 19..., before me personally came ........, to me known and known to me to be the individual described in and who, as TENANT, executed the foregoing instrument and acknowledged to me that he executed the same.

## IMPORTANT—PLEASE READ RULES AND REGULATIONS ATTACHED TO AND MADE A PART OF THIS LEASE IN ACCORDANCE WITH ARTICLE 36.

1. The sidewalks, entrances, driveways, passages, courts, elevators, vestibules, stairways, corridors or halls shall not be obstructed or encumbered by any Tenant or used for any purpose other than for ingress or egress from the demised premises and for delivery of merchandise and equipment in a prompt and efficient manner using elevators and passageways designated for such delivery by Owner. There shall not be used in any space, or in the public hall of the building, either by any Tenant or by jobbers or others in the delivery or receipt of merchandise, any hand trucks, except those equipped with rubber tires and sideguards. If said premises are situated on the ground floor of the building, Tenant

thereof shall further, at Tenant's expense, keep the sidewalk and curb in front of said premises clean and free from ice, snow, dirt and rubbish.

2. The water and wash closets and plumbing fixtures shall not be used for any purposes other than those for which they were designed or constructed and no sweepings, rubbish, rags, acids or other substances shall be deposited therein, and the expense of any breakage, stoppage, or damage resulting from the violation of this rule shall be borne by the Tenant who, or whose clerks, agents, employees or visitors, shall have caused it.

3. No carpet, rug or other article shall be hung or shaken out of any window of the building; and no Tenant shall sweep or throw or permit to be swept or thrown from the demised premises any dirt or other substances into any of the corridors or halls, elevators, or out of the doors or windows or stairways of the building and Tenant shall not use, keep or permit to be used or kept any foul or noxious gas or substance in the demised premises, or permit or suffer the demised premises to be occupied or used in a manner offensive or objectionable to Owner or other occupants of the buildings by reason of noise, odors, and or vibrations, or interfere in any way, with other Tenants or those having business therein, nor shall any animals or birds be kept in or about the building. Smoking or carrying lighted cigars or cigarettes in the elevators of the building is prohibited.

4. No awnings or other projections shall be attached to the outside walls of the building without the prior written consent of Owner.

5. No sign, advertisement, notice or other lettering shall be exhibited, inscribed, painted or affixed by any Tenant on any part of the outside of the demised premises or the building or on the inside of the demised premises if the same is visible from the outside of the premises without the prior written consent of Owner, except that the name of Tenant may appear on the entrance door of the premises. In the event of the violation of the foregoing by any Tenant, Owner may remove same without any liability and may charge the expense incurred by such removal to Tenant or Tenants violating this rule. Interior signs on doors and directory tablet

shall be inscribed, painted or affixed for each Tenant by Owner at the expense of such Tenant, and shall be of a size, color and style acceptable to Owner.

**6.** No Tenant shall mark, paint, drill into, or in any way deface any part of the demised premises or the building of which they form a part. No boring, cutting or stringing of wires shall be permitted, except with the prior written consent of Owner, and as Owner may direct. No Tenant shall lay linoleum, or other similar floor covering, so that the same shall come in direct contact with the floor of the demised premises, and, if linoleum or other similar floor covering is desired to be used an interlining of builder's deadening felt shall be first affixed to the floor, by a paste or other material, soluble in water, the use of cement or other similar adhesive material being expressly prohibited.

**7.** No additional locks or bolts of any kind shall be placed upon any of the doors or windows by any Tenant, nor shall any changes be made in existing locks or mechanism thereof. Each Tenant must, upon the termination of his Tenancy, restore to Owner all keys of stores, offices and toilet rooms, either furnished to, or otherwise procured by, such Tenant, and in the event of the loss of any keys, so furnished, such Tenant shall pay to Owner the cost thereof.

**8.** Freight, furniture, business equipment, merchandise and bulky matter of any description shall be delivered to and removed from the premises only on the freight elevators and through the service entrances and corridors, and only during hours and in a manner approved by Owner. Owner reserves the right to inspect all freight to be brought into the building and to exclude from the building all freight which violates any of these Rules and Regulations of the lease of which these Rules and Regulations are a part.

**9.** No Tenant shall obtain for use upon the demised premises ice, drinking water, towel and other similar services, or accept barbering or bootblacking services in the demised premises, except from persons authorized by Owner, and at hours and under regulations fixed by Owner. Canvassing, soliciting and peddling in the building is prohibited and each Tenant shall cooperate to prevent the same.

10. Owner reserves the right to exclude from the building between the hours of 6 p.m. and 8 a.m. on business days, after 1 p.m. on Saturdays, and at all hours on Sundays and legal holidays all persons who do not present a pass to the building signed by Owner. Owner will furnish passes to persons for whom any Tenant requests same in writing. Each Tenant shall be responsible for all persons for whom he requests such pass and shall be liable to Owner for all acts of such persons. Notwithstanding the foregoing, Owner shall not be required to allow Tenant or any person to enter or remain in the building, except on business days from 8:00 a.m. to 6:00 p.m. and on Saturdays from 8:00 a.m. to 1:00 p.m.

11. Owner shall have the right to prohibit any advertising by any Tenant which in Owner's opinion, tends to impair the reputation of the building or its desirability as a loft building, and upon written notice from Owner, Tenant shall refrain from or discontinue such advertising.

12. Tenant shall not bring or permit to be brought or kept in or on the demised premises, any inflammable, combustible or explosive fluid, material, chemical or substance, or cause or permit any odors of cooking or other processes, or any unusual or other objectionable odors to permeate in or emanate from the demised premises.

13. Tenant shall not use the demised premises in a manner which disturbs or interferes with other Tenants in the beneficial use of their premises.

### § 1:13. Office Lease

#### FORM NO. 1.2

#### OFFICE LEASE WITH FORM* OF GUARANTY

**Agreement of Lease,** made as of this       day of       19 , between       party of the first part, hereinafter referred to as OWNER, and       party of the second part, hereinafter referred to as TENANT,

---

* This office lease is adopted and copyrighted by The Real Estate Board of New York Inc., and reprinted with its permission. Reproduction in whole or in part is prohibited, and all rights are reserved by The Real Estate Board of New York Inc.

## GENERAL PRINCIPLES § 1:13

**Witnesseth:** Owner hereby leases to Tenant and Tenant hereby hires from Owner       in the building known as       in the Borough of      , City of New York, for the term of       (or until such term shall sooner cease and expire as hereinafter provided) to commence on the       day of       nineteen hundred and       , and to end on the       day of       nineteen hundred and       both dates inclusive, at an annual rental rate of       which Tenant agrees to pay in lawful money of the United States which shall be legal tender in payment of all debts and dues, public and private, at the time of payment, in equal monthly installments in advance on the first day of each month during said term, at the office of Owner or such other place as Owner may designate, without any set off or deduction whatsoever, except that Tenant shall pay the first       monthly installment(s) on the execution hereof (unless this lease be a renewal).

In the event that, at the commencement of the term of this lease, or thereafter, Tenant shall be in default in the payment of rent to Owner pursuant to the terms of another lease with Owner or with Owner's predecessor in interest, Owner may at Owner's option and without notice to Tenant add the amount of such arrears to any monthly installment of rent payable hereunder and the same shall be payable to Owner as additional rent.

The parties hereto, for themselves, their heirs, distributees, executors, administrators, legal representatives, successors and assigns, hereby convenant as follows:

**Rent:**

1. Tenant shall pay the rent as above and as hereinafter provided.

**Occupancy:**

2. Tenant shall use and occupy demised premises for ........ and for no other purpose

**Tenant Alterations:**

3. Tenant shall make no changes in or to the demised premises of any nature without Owner's prior written consent. Subject to the prior written consent of Owner, and to the provisions of this article, Tenant at Tenant's

expense, may make alterations, installations, additions or improvements which are nonstructural and which do not affect utility services or plumbing and electrical lines, in or to the interior of the demised premises by using contractors or mechanics first approved by Owner. Tenant shall, before making any alterations, additions, installations or improvements, at its expense, obtain all permits, approvals and certificates required by any governmental or quasi-governmental bodies and (upon completion) certificates of final approval thereof and shall deliver promptly duplicates of all such permits, approvals and certificates to Owner and Tenant agrees to carry and will cause Tenant's contractors and sub-contractors to carry such workman's compensation, general liability, personal and property damage insurance as Owner may require. If any mechanic's lien is filed against the demised premises, or the building of which the same forms a part, for work claimed to have been done for, or materials furnished to, Tenant, whether or not done pursuant to this article, the same shall be discharged by Tenant within thirty days thereafter, at Tenant's expense, by filing the bond required by law. All fixtures and all paneling, partitions, railings and like installations, installed in the premises at any time, either by Tenant or by Owner in Tenant's behalf, shall, upon installation, become the property of Owner and shall remain upon and be surrendered with the demised premises unless Owner, by notice to Tenant no later than twenty days prior to the date fixed as the termination of this lease, elects to relinquish Owner's right thereto and to have them removed by Tenant, in which event the same shall be removed from the premises by Tenant prior to the expiration of the lease, at Tenant's expense. Nothing in this Article shall be construed to give Owner title to or to prevent Tenant's removal of trade fixtures, moveable office furniture and equipment, but upon removal of any such from the premises or upon removal of other installations as may be required by Owner, Tenant shall immediately and at its expense, repair and restore the premises to the condition existing prior to installation and repair any damage to the demised premises or the building due to such removal. All property permitted or required to be

GENERAL PRINCIPLES § 1:13

removed, by Tenant at the end of the term remaining in the premises after Tenant's removal shall be deemed abandoned and may, at the election of Owner, either be retained as Owner's property or may be removed from the premises by Owner, at Tenant's expense.

**Maintenance and Repairs:**

4. Tenant shall, throughout the term of this lease, take good care of the demised premises and the fixtures and appurtenances therein. Tenant shall be responsible for all damage or injury to the demised premises or any other part of the building and the systems and equipment thereof, whether requiring structural or nonstructural repairs caused by or resulting from carelessness, omission, neglect or improper conduct of Tenant, Tenant's subtenants, agents, employees, invitees or licensees, or which arise out of any work, labor, service or equipment done for or supplied to Tenant or any subtenant or arising out of the installation, use or operation of the property or equipment of Tenant or any subtenant. Tenant shall also repair all damage to the building and the demised premises caused by the moving of Tenant's fixtures, furniture and equipment. Tenant shall promptly make, at Tenant's expense, all repairs in and to the demised premises for which Tenant is responsible, using only the contractor for the trade or trades in question, selected from a list of at least two contractors per trade submitted by owner. Any other repairs in or to the building or the facilities and systems thereof for which Tenant is responsible shall be performed by Owner at the Tenant's expense. Owner shall maintain in good working order and repair the exterior and the structural portions of the building, including the structural portions of its demised premises, and the public portions of the building interior and the building plumbing, electrical, heating and ventilating systems (to the extent such systems presently exist) serving the demised premises. Tenant agrees to give prompt notice of any defective condition in the premises for which Owner may be responsible hereunder. There shall be no allowance to Tenant for diminution of rental value and no liability on the part of Owner by reason of inconvenience, annoyance or injury to business arising from Owner or others making repairs, alterations,

additions or improvements in or to any portion of the building or the demised premises or in and to the fixtures, appurtenances or equipment thereof. It is specifically agreed that Tenant shall not be entitled to any setoff or reduction of rent by reason of any failure of Owner to comply with the covenants of this or any other article of this Lease. Tenant agrees that Tenant's sole remedy at law in such instance will be by way of an action for damages for breach of contract. The provisions of this Article 4 shall not apply in the case of fire or other casualty which are dealt with in Article 9 hereof.

**Window Cleaning:**

5. Tenant will not clean nor require, permit, suffer or allow any window in the demised premises to be cleaned from the outside in violation of Section 202 of the Labor Law or any other applicable law or of the Rules of the Board of Standards and Appeals, or of any other Board or body having or asserting jurisdiction.

**Requirements of Law, Fire Insurance, Floor Loads:**

6. Prior to the commencement of the lease term, if Tenant is then in possession, and at all times thereafter, Tenant, at Tenant's sole cost and expense, shall promptly comply with all present and future laws, orders and regulations of all state, federal, municipal and local governments, departments, commissions and boards and any direction of any public officer pursuant to law, and all orders, rules and regulations of the New York Board of Fire Underwriters, Insurance Services Office, or any similar body which shall impose any violation, order or duty upon Owner or Tenant with respect to the demised premises, whether or not arising out of Tenant's use or manner of use thereof, (including Tenant's permitted use) or, with respect to the building if arising out of Tenant's use or manner of use of the premises or the building (including the use permitted under the lease). Nothing herein shall require Tenant to make structural repairs or alterations unless Tenant has, by its manner of use of the demised premises or method of operation therein, violated any such laws, ordinances, orders, rules, regulations or requirements with respect thereto. Tenant may, after securing Owner to Owner's satisfaction against all dam-

ages, interest, penalties and expenses, including, but not limited to, reasonable attorney's fees, by cash deposit or by surety bond in an amount and in a company satisfactory to Owner, contest and appeal any such laws, ordinances, orders, rules, regulations or requirements provided same is done with all reasonable promptness and provided such appeal shall not subject Owner to prosecution for a criminal offense or constitute a default under any lease or mortgage under which Owner may be obligated, or cause the demised premises or any part thereof to be condemned or vacated. Tenant shall not do or permit any act or thing to be done in or to the demised premises which is contrary to law, or which will invalidate or be in conflict with public liability, fire or other policies of insurance at any time carried by or for the benefit of Owner with respect to the demised premises or the building of which the demised premises form a part, or which shall or might subject Owner to any liability or responsibility to any person or for property damage. Tenant shall not keep anything in the demised premises except as now or hereafter permitted by the Fire Department, Board of Fire Underwriters, Fire Insurance Rating Organization or other authority having jurisdiction, and then only in such manner and such quantity so as not to increase the rate for fire insurance applicable to the building, nor use the premises in a manner which will increase the insurance rate for the building or any property located therein over that in effect prior to the commencement of Tenant's occupancy. Tenant shall pay all costs, expenses, fines, penalties, or damages, which may be imposed upon Owner by reason of Tenant's failure to comply with the provisions of this article and if by reason of such failure the fire insurance rate shall, at the beginning of this lease or at any time thereafter, be higher than it otherwise would be, then Tenant shall reimburse Owner as additional rent hereunder, for that portion of all fire insurance premiums thereafter paid by Owner which shall have been charged because of such failure by Tenant. In any action or proceeding wherein Owner and Tenant are parties, a schedule or "make-up" of rate for the building or demised premises issued by the New York Fire Insurance Exchange, or other body making fire insurance rates applicable to said premises shall be conclusive evidence of the facts therein stated and of the several items and charges in the fire insurance rates then applicable to said premises. Tenant shall not place a load upon any floor of the demised premises exceeding the floor load per square foot area which it was designed to carry and which is allowed by law. Owner reserves the right to prescribe the weight and position of all safes, business machines and mechanical equipment. Such installations shall be placed and maintained by Tenant, at Tenant's expense, in settings sufficient, in Owner's judgement, to absorb and prevent vibration, noise and annoyance.

**Subordination:**

7. This lease is subject and subordinate to all ground or underlying leases and to all mortgages which may now or hereafter affect such leases or the real property of which demised premises are a part and to all renewals, modifications, consolidations, replacements and extensions of any such underlying leases and mortgages. This clause shall be self-operative and no further instrument of subordination shall be required by any ground or underlying lessor or by any mortgagee, affecting any lease or the real property of which the demised premises are a part. In confirmation of such subordination, Tenant shall execute promptly any certificate that Owner may request.

**Property—Loss, Damage, Reimbursement, Indemnity:**

8. Owner or its agents shall not be liable for any damage to property of Tenant or of others entrusted to employees of the building, nor for loss of or damage to any property of Tenant by theft or otherwise, nor for any injury or damage to persons or property resulting from any cause of whatsoever nature, unless caused by or due to the negligence of Owner, its agents, servants or employees. Owner or its agents will not be liable for any such damage caused by other tenants or persons in, upon or about said building or caused by operations in construction of any private, public or quasi public work.

If at any time any windows of the demised premises are temporarily closed, darkened or bricked up (or perma-

# GENERAL PRINCIPLES § 1:13

nently closed, darkened or bricked up, if required by law) for any reason whatsoever including, but not limited to Owner's own acts, Owner shall not be liable for any damage Tenant may sustain thereby and Tenant shall not be entitled to any compensation therefor nor abatement or diminution of rent nor shall the same release Tenant from its obligations hereunder nor constitute an eviction. Tenant shall indemnify and save harmless Owner against and from all liabilities, obligations, damages, penalties, claims, costs and expenses for which Owner shall not be reimbursed by insurance, including reasonable attorneys fees, paid, suffered or incurred as a result of any breach by Tenant, Tenant's agents, contractors, employees, invitees, or licensees, of any covenant or condition of this lease, or the carelessness, negligence or improper conduct of the Tenant, Tenant's agents, contractors, employees, invitees or licensees. Tenant's liability under this lease extends to the acts and omissions of any sub-tenant, and any agent, contractor, employee, invitee or licensee of any sub-tenant. In case any action or proceeding is brought against Owner by reason of any such claim, Tenant, upon written notice from Owner, will, at Tenant's expense, resist or defend such action or proceeding by counsel approved by Owner in writing, such approval not to be unreasonably withheld.

**Destruction, Fire and Other Casualty:**

9. (a) If the demised premises or any part thereof shall be damaged by fire or other casualty, Tenant shall give immediate notice thereof to Owner and this lease shall continue in full force and effect except as hereinafter set forth. (b) If the demised premises are partially damaged or rendered partially unusable by fire or other casualty, the damages thereto shall be repaired by and at the expense of Owner and the rent, until such repair shall be substantially completed, shall be apportioned from the day following the casualty according to the part of the premises which is usable. (c) If the demised premises are totally damaged or rendered wholly unusable by fire or other casualty, then the rent shall be proportionately paid up to the time of the casualty and thenceforth shall cease until the date when the premises shall have been repaired and restored by Owner, subject to Owner's right

to elect not to restore the same as hereinafter provided. (d) If the demised premises are rendered wholly unusable or (whether or not the demised premises are damaged in whole or in part) if the building shall be so damaged that Owner shall decide to demolish it or to rebuild it, then, in any of such events, Owner may elect to terminate this lease by written notice to Tenant, given within 90 days after such fire or casualty, specifying a date for the expiration of the lease, which date shall not be more than 60 days after the giving of such notice, and upon the date specified in such notice the term of this lease shall expire as fully and completely as if such date were the date set forth above for the termination of this lease and Tenant shall forthwith quit, surrender and vacate the premises without prejudice however, to Landlord's rights and remedies against Tenant under the lease provisions in effect prior to such termination, and any rent owing shall be paid up to such date and any payments of rent made by Tenant which were on account of any period subsequent to such date shall be returned to Tenant. Unless Owner shall serve a termination notice as provided for herein, Owner shall make the repairs and restorations under the conditions of (b) and (c) hereof, with all reasonable expedition, subject to delays due to adjustment of insurance claims, labor troubles and causes beyond Owner's control. After any such casualty, Tenant shall cooperate with Owner's restoration by removing from the premises as promptly as reasonably possible, all of Tenant's salvageable inventory and movable equipment, furniture, and other property. Tenant's liability for rent shall resume five (5) days after written notice from Owner that the premises are substantially ready for Tenant's occupancy. (e) Nothing contained hereinabove shall relieve Tenant from liability that may exist as a result of damage from fire or other casualty. Notwithstanding the foregoing, each party shall look first to any insurance in its favor before making any claim against the other party for recovery for loss or damage resulting from fire or other casualty, and to the extent that such insurance is in force and collectible and to the extent permitted by law, Owner and Tenant each hereby releases and waives all right of recovery against the other or any one claiming through

# GENERAL PRINCIPLES § 1:13

or under each of them by way of subrogation or otherwise. The foregoing release and waiver shall be in force only if both releasors' insurance policies contain a clause providing that such a release or waiver shall not invalidate the insurance. If, and to the extent, that such waiver can be obtained only by the payment of additional premiums, then the party benefitting from the waiver shall pay such premium within ten days after written demand or shall be deemed to have agreed that the party obtaining insurance coverage shall be free of any further obligation under the provisions herof with respect to waiver of subrogation. Tenant acknowledges that Owner will not carry insurance on Tenant's furniture and/or furnishings or any fixtures or equipment, improvements, or appurtenances removable by Tenant and agrees that Owner will not be obligated to repair any damage thereto or replace the same. (f) Tenant hereby waives the provisions of Section 227 of the Real Property Law and agrees that the provisions of this article shall govern and control in lieu thereof.

**Eminent Domain:**

10. If the whole or any part of the demised premises shall be acquired or condemned by Eminent Domain for any public or quasi public use or purpose, then and in that event, the term of this lease shall cease and terminate from the date of title vesting in such proceeding and Tenant shall have no claim for the value of any unexpired term of said lease and assigns to Owner, Tenant's entire interest in any such award.

**Assignment, Mortgage, Etc.:**

11. Tenant, for itself, its heirs, distributees, executors, administrators, legal representatives, successors and assigns, expressly covenants that it shall not assign, mortgage or encumber this agreement, nor underlet, or suffer or permit the demised premises or any part thereof to be used by others, without the prior written consent of Owner in each instance. Transfer of the majority of the stock of a corporate Tenant shall be deemed an assignment. If this lease be assigned, or if the demised premises or any part thereof be underlet or occupied by anybody other than Tenant, Owner may, after default by Tenant,

§ 1:13                    LANDLORD AND TENANT

collect rent from the assignee, under-tenant or occupant, and apply the net amount collected to the rent herein reserved, but no such assignment, underletting, occupancy or collection shall be deemed a waiver of this covenant, or the acceptance of the assignee, under-tenant or occupant as tenant, or a release of Tenant from the further performance by Tenant of covenants on the part of Tenant herein contained. The consent by Owner to an assignment or underletting shall not in any wise be construed to relieve Tenant from obtaining the express consent in writing of Owner to any further assignment or underletting.

**Electric Current:**

12. Rates and conditions in respect to submetering or rent inclusion, as the case may be, to be added in RIDER attached hereto. Tenant covenants and agrees that at all times its use of electric current shall not exceed the capacity of existing feeders to the building or the risers or wiring installation and Tenant may not use any electrical equipment which, in Owner's opinion, reasonably exercised, will overload such installations or interfere with the use thereof by other tenants of the building. The change at any time of the character of electric service shall in no wise make Owner liable or responsible to Tenant, for any loss, damages or expenses which Tenant may sustain.

**Access to Premises:**

13. Owner or Owner's agents shall have the right (but shall not be obligated) to enter the demised premises in any emergency at any time, and, at other reasonable times, to examine the same and to make such repairs, replacements and improvements as Owner may deem necessary and reasonably desirable to the demised premises or to any other portion of the building or which Owner may elect to perform. Tenant shall permit Owner to use and maintain and replace pipes and conduits in and through the demised premises and to erect new pipes and conduits therein provided they are concealed within the walls, floor, or ceiling. Owner may, during the progress of any work in the demised premises, take all necessary materials and equipment into said premises without

the same constituting an eviction nor shall the Tenant be entitled to any abatement of rent while such work is in progress nor to any damages by reason of loss or interruption of business or otherwise. Throughout the term hereof Owner shall have the right to enter the demised premises at reasonable hours for the purpose of showing the same to prospective purchasers or mortgagees of the building, and during the last six months of the term for the purpose of showing the same to prospective tenants. If Tenant is not present to open and permit an entry into the premises, Owner or Owner's agents may enter the same whenever such entry may be necessary or permissible by master key or forcibly and provided reasonable care is exercised to safeguard Tenant's property, such entry shall not render Owner or its agents liable therefor, nor in any event shall the obligations of Tenant hereunder be affected. If during the last month of the term Tenant shall have removed all or substantially all of Tenant's property therefrom. Owner may immediately enter, alter, renovate or redecorate the demised premises without limitation or abatement of rent, or incurring liability to Tenant for any compensation and such act shall have no effect on this lease or Tenant's obligations hereunder.

**Vault, Vault Space, Area:**

14. No Vaults, vault space or area, whether or not enclosed or covered, not within the property line of the building is leased hereunder, anything contained in or indicated on any sketch, blue print or plan, or anything contained elsewhere in this lease to the contrary notwithstanding. Owner makes no representation as to the location of the property line of the building. All vaults and vault space and all such areas not within the property line of the building, which Tenant may be permitted to use and/or occupy, is to be used and/or occupied under a revocable license, and if any such license be revoked, or if the amount of such space or area be diminished or required by any federal, state or municipal authority or public utility, Owner shall not be subject to any liability nor shall Tenant be entitled to any compensation or diminution or abatement of rent, nor shall such revocation, diminution or requisition be deemed constructive or

actual eviction. Any tax, fee or charge of municipal authorities for such vault or area shall be paid by Tenant.

**Occupancy:**

15. Tenant will not at any time use or occupy the demised premises in violation of the certificate of occupancy issued for the building of which the demised premises are a part. Tenant has inspected the premises and accepts them as is, subject to the riders annexed hereto with respect to Owner's work, if any. In any event, Owner makes no representation as to the condition of the premises and Tenant agrees to accept the same subject to violations, whether or not of record.

*[Provision 16 of this lease is a bankruptcy termination clause, which no longer is enforceable, and therefore is omitted. See Chapter 22, infra.]*

**Default:**

17. (1) If Tenant defaults in fulfilling any of the covenants of this lease other than the covenants for the payment of rent or additional rent; or if the demised premises becomes vacant or deserted; or if any execution or attachment shall be issued against Tenant or any of Tenant's property whereupon the demised premises shall be taken or occupied by someone other than Tenant; or if this lease be rejected under 11 USCS § 365 (bankruptcy code); or if Tenant shall fail to move into or take possession of the premises within fifteen (15) days after the commencement of the term of this lease, then, in any one or more of such events, upon Owner serving a written five (5) days notice upon Tenant specifying the nature of said default and upon the expiration of said five (5) days, if Tenant shall have failed to comply with or remedy such default, or if the said default or omission complained of shall be of a nature that the same cannot be completely cured or remedied within said five (5) day period, and if Tenant shall not have diligently commenced during such default within such five (5) day period, and shall not thereafter with reasonable diligence and in good faith, proceed to remedy or cure such default, then Owner may serve a written three (3) days' notice of cancellation of this lease upon Tenant, and upon the expiration of said

three (3) days this lease and the term thereunder shall end and expire as fully and completely as if the expiration of such three (3) day period were the day herein definitely fixed for the end and expiration of this lease and the term thereof and Tenant shall then quit and surrender the demised premises to Owner but Tenant shall remain liable as hereinafter provided.

(2) If the notice provided for in (1) hereof shall have been given, and the term shall expire as aforesaid: or if Tenant shall make default in the payment of the rent reserved herein or any item of additional rent herein mentioned or any part of either or in making any other payment herein required: then and in any of such events Owner may without notice, re-enter the demised premises either by force or otherwise, and dispossess Tenant by summary proceedings or otherwise, and the legal representative of Tenant or other occupant of demised premises and remove their effects and hold the premises as if this lease had not been made, and Tenant hereby waives the service of notice of intention to re-enter or to institute legal proceedings to that end. If Tenant shall make default hereunder prior to the date fixed as the commencement of any renewal or extension of this lease, Owner may cancel and terminate such renewal or extension agreement by written notice.

**Remedies of Owner and Waiver of Redemption:**

18. In case of any such default, re-entry, expiration and/ or dispossess by summary proceedings or otherwise, (a) the rent shall become due thereupon and be paid up to the time of such re-entry, dispossess and/or expiration, (b) Owner may re-let the premises or any part or parts thereof, either in the name of Owner or otherwise, for a term or terms, which may at Owner's option be less than or exceed the period which would otherwise have constituted the balance of the term of this lease and may grant concessions or free rent or charge a higher rental than that in this lease, and/or (c) Tenant or the legal representatives of Tenant shall also pay Owner as liquidated damages for the failure of Tenant to observe and perform said Tenant's convenants herein contained, any deficiency between the rent hereby reserved and/or covenanted to be paid and the net amount, if any, of the rents collected

on account of the lease or leases of the demised premises for each month of the period which would otherwise have constituted the balance of the term of this lease. The failure of Owner to re-let the premises or any part or parts thereof shall not release or affect Tenant's liability for damages. In computing such liquidated damages there shall be added to the said deficiency such expenses as Owner may incur in connection with re-letting, such as legal expenses, attorneys' fees, brokerage, advertising and for keeping the demised premises in good order or for preparing the same for re-letting. Any such liquidated damages shall be paid in monthly installments by Tenant on the rent day specified in this lease and any suit brought to collect the amount of the deficiency for any month shall not prejudice in any way the rights of Owner to collect the deficiency for any month shall not prejudice in any way the rights of Owner to collect the deficiency of any subsequent month by a similar proceeding. Owner, in putting the demised premises in good order or preparing the same for re-rental may, at Owner's option, make such alterations, repairs, replacements, and/or decorations in the demised premises as Owner, in Owner's sole judgment, considers advisable and necessary for the purpose of re-letting the demised premises, and the making of such alterations, repairs, replacements, and/or decorations shall not operate or be construed to release Tenant from liability hereunder as aforesaid. Owner shall in no event be liable in any way whatsoever for failure to re-let the demised premises, or in the event that the demised premises are re-let, for failure to collect the rent thereof under such re-letting, and in no event shall Tenant be entitled to receive any excess, if any, of such net rents collected over the sums payable by Tenant to Owner hereunder. In the event of a breach or threatened breach by Tenant of any of the covenants or provisions hereof, Owner shall have the right of injunction and the right to invoke any remedy allowed at law or in equity as if re-entry, summary proceedings and other remedies were not herein provided for. Mention in this lease of any particular remedy, shall not preclude Owner from any other remedy, in law or in equity. Tenant hereby expressly waives any and all rights of redemption granted by or under any present or future laws in the event of Tenant being evicted or dispossessed for any cause, or in the event of Owner obtaining possession of demised premises, by reason of the violation by Tenant of any of the covenants and conditions of this lease, or otherwise.

**Fees and Expenses:**

**19.** If Tenant shall default in the observance or performance of any term or covenant on Tenant's part to be observed or performed under or by virtue of any of the terms or provisions in any article of this lease, then, unless otherwise provided elsewhere in this lease, Owner may immediately or at any time thereafter and without notice perform the obligation of Tenant thereunder. If Owner, in connection with the foregoing or in connection with any default by Tenant in the covenant to pay rent hereunder, makes any expenditures or incurs any obligations for the payment of money, including but not limited to attorney's fees, in instituting, prosecuting or defending any action or proceeding, then Tenant will reimburse Owner for such sums so paid or obligations incurred with interest and costs. The foregoing expenses incurred by reason of Tenant's default shall be deemed to be additional rent hereunder and shall be paid by Tenant to Owner within five (5) days of rendition of any bill or statement to Tenant therefor. If Tenant's lease term shall have expired at the time of making of such expenditures or incurring of such obligations, such sums shall be recoverable by Owner as damages.

**Building Alterations and Management:**

**20.** Owner shall have the right at any time without the same constituting an eviction and without incurring liability to Tenant therefor to change the arrangement and/or location of public entrances, passageways, doors, doorways, corridors, elevators, stairs, toilets or other public parts of the building and to change the name, number or designation by which the building may be known. There shall be no allowance to Tenant for diminution of rental value and no liability on the part of Owner by reason of inconvenience, annoyance or injury to business arising from Owner or other Tenants making any repairs in the building or any such alterations, additions and improvements. Furthermore, Tenant shall not have any claim against Owner by reason of Owner's imposition of such controls of the manner of access to the building by Tenant's social or business visitors as the Owner may deem necessary for the security of the building and its occupants.

**No Representations by Owner:**

**21.** Neither Owner nor Owner's agents have made any representations or promises with respect to the physical condition of the building, the land upon which it is erected or the demised premises, the rents, leases, expenses of operation or any other matter or thing affecting or related to the premises except as herein expressly set forth and no rights, easements or licenses are acquired by Tenant by implication or otherwise except as expressly set forth in the provisions of this lease. Tenant has inspected the building and the demised premises and is thoroughly acquainted with their condition and agrees to take the same "as is" and acknowledges that the taking of possesion of the demised premises by Tenant shall be conclusive evidence that the said premises and the building of which the same form a part were in good and satisfactory condition at the time such possession was so taken, except as to latent defects. All understandings and agreements heretofore made between the parties hereto are merged in this contract, which alone fully and completely expresses the agreement between Owner and Tenant and any executory agreement hereafter made shall be ineffective to change, modify, discharge or effect an abandonment of it in whole or in part, unless such executory agreement is in writing and signed by the party against whom enforcement of the change, modification, discharge or abandonment is sought.

**End of Term:**

**22.** Upon the expiration or other termination of the term of this lease, Tenant shall quit and surrender to Owner the demised premises, broom clean, in good order and condition, ordinary wear and damages which Tenant is not required to repair as provided elsewhere in this lease excepted, and Tenant shall remove all its property. Tenant's obligation to observe or perform this covenant shall survive the expiration or other termination of this lease. If the last day of the term of this Lease or any renewal thereof, falls on Sunday, this lease shall expire at noon on the preceding Saturday unless it be a legal holiday in which case it shall expire at noon on the preceding business day.

**Quiet Enjoyment:**

23. Owner covenants and agrees with Tenant that upon Tenant paying the rent and additional rent and observing and performing all the terms, covenants and conditions, on Tenant's part to be observed and performed, Tenant may peaceably and quietly enjoy the premises hereby demised, subject, nevertheless, to the terms and conditions of this lease including, but not limited to, Article 31 hereof and to the ground leases, underlying leases and mortgages hereinbefore mentioned.

**Failure to Give Possession:**

24. If Owner is unable to give possession of the demised premises on the date of the commencement of the term hereof, because of the holding-over or retention of possession of any tenant, undertenant or occupants or if the demised premises are located in a building being constructed, because such building has not been sufficiently completed to make the premises ready for occupancy or because of the fact that a certificate of occupancy has not been procured or for any other reason, Owner shall not be subject to any liability for failure to give possession on said date and the validity of the lease shall not be impaired under such circumstances, nor shall the same be construed in any wise to extend the term of this lease, but the rent payable hereunder shall be abated (provided Tenant is not responsible for Owner's inability to obtain possession) until after Owner shall have given Tenant written notice that the premises are substantially ready for Tenant's occupancy. If permission is given to Tenant to enter into the possession of the demised premises or to occupy premises other than the demised premises prior to the date specified as the commencement of the term of this lease, Tenant covenants and agrees that such occupancy shall be deemed to be under all the terms, covenants, conditions and provisions of this lease, except as to

the covenant to pay rent. The provisions of this article are intended to constitute "an express provision to the contrary" within the meaning of Section 223-a of the New York Real Property Law.

**No Waiver:**
   25. The failure of Owner to seek redress for violation of, or to insist upon the strict performance of any covenant or condition of this lease or of any of the Rules or Regulations, set forth or hereafter adopted by Owner, shall not prevent a subsequent act which would have originally constituted a violation from having all the force and effect of an original violation. The receipt by Owner of rent with knowledge of the breach of any covenant of this lease shall not be deemed a waiver of such breach and no provision of this lease shall be deemed to have been waived by Owner unless such waiver be in writing signed by Owner. No payment by Tenant or receipt by Owner of a lesser amount than the monthly rent herein stipulated shall be deemed to be other than on account of the earliest stipulated rent, nor shall any endorsement or statement of any check or any letter accompanying any check or payment as rent be deemed an accord and satisfaction, and Owner may accept such check or payment without prejudice to Owner's right to recover the balance of such rent or pursue any other remedy in this lease provided. No act or thing done by Owner or Owner's agents during the term hereby demised shall be deemed an acceptance of a surrender of said premises, and no agreement to accept such surrender shall be valid unless in writing signed by Owner. No employee of Owner or Owner's agent shall have any power to accept the keys of said premises prior to the termination of the lease and the delivery of keys to any such agent or employee shall not operate as a termination of the lease or a surrender of the premises.

**Waiver of Trial by Jury:**
   26. It is mutually agreed by and between Owner and Tenant that the respective parties hereto shall and they hereby do waive trial by jury in any action, proceeding or counterclaim brought by either of the parties hereto against the other (except for personal injury or

GENERAL PRINCIPLES § 1:13

property damage) on any matters whatsoever arising out of or in any way connected with this lease, the relationship of Owner and Tenant, Tenant's use of or occupancy of said premises, and any emergency statutory or any other statutory remedy. It is further mutually agreed that in the event Owner commences any summary proceeding for possession of the premises, Tenant will not interpose any counterclaim of whatever nature or description in any such proceeding including a counterclaim under Article 4.

**Inability to Perform:**
**27.** This Lease and the obligation of Tenant to pay rent hereunder and perform all of the other covenants and agreements hereunder on part of Tenant to be performed shall in no wise be affected, impaired or excused because Owner is unable to fulfill any of its obligations under this lease or to supply or is delayed in supplying any service expressly or impliedly to be supplied or is unable to make, or is delayed in making any repair, additions, alterations or decorations or is unable to supply or is delayed in supplying any equipment or fixtures if Owner is prevented or delayed from so doing by reason of strike or labor troubles or any cause whatsoever including, but not limited to, government preemption in connection with a National Emergency or by reason of any rule, order or regulation of any department or subdivision thereof of any government agency or by reason of the conditions of supply and demand which have been or are affected by war or other emergency.

**Bills and Notices:**
**28.** Except as otherwise in this lease provided, a bill, statement, notice or communication which Owner may desire or be required to give to Tenant, shall be deemed sufficiently given or rendered if, in writing, delivered to Tenant personally or sent by registered or certified mail addressed to Tenant at the building of which the demised premises form a part or at the last known residence address or business address of Tenant or left at any of the aforesaid premises addressed to Tenant, and the time of the rendition of such bill or statement and of the giving of such notice of communication shall be deemed to be

§ 1:13  LANDLORD AND TENANT

the time when the same is delivered to Tenant, mailed, or left at the premises as herein provided. Any notice by Tenant to Owner must be served by registered or certified mail addressed to Owner at the address first hereinabove given or at such other address as Owner shall designate by written notice.

**Services Provided by Owners:**

**29.** As long as Tenant is not in default under any of the covenants of this lease, Owners shall provide: (a) necessary elevator facilities on business days from 8 a.m. to 6 p.m. and on Saturdays from 8 a.m. to 1 p.m. and have one elevator subject to call at all other times; (b) heat to the demised premises when and as required by law, on business days from 8 a.m. to 6 p.m. and on Saturdays from 8 a.m. to 1 p.m.; (c) water for ordinary lavatory purposes, but if Tenant uses or consumes water for any other purposes or in unusual quantities (of which fact Owner shall be the sole judge), Owner may install a water meter at Tenant's expense which Tenant shall thereafter maintain at Tenant's expense in good working order and repair to register such water consumption and Tenant shall pay for water consumed as shown on said meter as additional rent as and when bills are rendered; (d) cleaning service for the demised premises on business days at Owner's expense provided that the same are kept in order by Tenant. If, however, said premises are to be kept clean by Tenant, it shall be done at Tenant's sole expense, in a manner satisfactory to Owner and no one other than persons approved by Owner shall be permitted to enter said premises or the building of which they are a part for such purpose. Tenant shall pay Owner the cost of removal of any of Tenant's refuse and rubbish from the building; (e) If the demised premises is serviced by Owner's air conditioning/cooling and ventilating system, air conditioning/cooling will be furnished to tenant from May 15th through September 30th on business days (Mondays through Fridays, holidays excepted) from 8:00 a.m. to 6:00 p.m., and ventilation will be furnished on business days during the aforesaid hours except when air conditioning/cooling is being furnished as aforesaid. If Tenant requires air conditioning/cooling or ventilation for more extended hours or on Saturdays, Sundays or on

GENERAL PRINCIPLES § 1:13

holidays, as defined under Owner's contract with Operating Engineers Local 94-94A, Owner will furnish the same at Tenant's expense. RIDER to be added in respect to rates and conditions for such additional service; (f) Owner reserves the right to stop services of the heating, elevators, plumbing, air-conditioning, power systems or cleaning or other services, if any, when necessary by reason of accident or for repairs, alterations, replacements or improvements necessary or desirable in the judgment of Owner for as long as may be reasonably required by reason thereof. If the building of which the demised premises are a part supplies manually-operated elevator service, Owner at any time may substitute automatic-control elevator service and upon ten days' written notice to Tenant, proceed with alterations necessary therefor without in any wise affecting this lease or the obligation of Tenant hereunder. The same shall be done with a minimum of inconvenience to Tenant and Owner shall pursue the alteration with due diligence.

**Captions:**

30. The Captions are inserted only as a matter of convenience and for reference and in no way define, limit or describe the scope of this lease nor the intent of any provisions thereof.

**Definitions:**

31. The term "office", or "offices", wherever used in this lease, shall not be construed to mean premises used as astore or stores, for the sale or display, at any time, of goods, wares or merchandise, of any kind, or as a restaurant, shop, booth, bootblack or other stand, barber shop, or for other similar purposes or for manufacturing. The term "Owner" means a landlord or lessor, and as used in this lease means only the owner, or the mortgagee in possession, for the time being of the land and building (or the owner of a lease of the building or of the land and building) of which the demised premises form a part, so that in the event of any sale or sales of said land and building or of said lease, or in the event of a lease of said building, or of the land and building, the said Owner shall be and hereby is entirely freed and relieved of all covenants and obligations of Owner hereunder, and it

shall be deemed and construed without further agreement between the parties or their successors in interest, or between the parties and the purchaser, at any such sale, or the said lessee of the building, or of the land and building, that the purchaser or the lessee of the building has assumed and agreed to carry out any and all covenants and obligations of Owner, hereunder. The words "re-enter" and "re-entry" as used in this lease are not restricted to their technical legal meaning. The term "business days" as used in this lease shall exclude Saturdays (except such portion thereof as is covered by specific hours in Article 29 hereof), Sundays and all days observed by the State or Federal Government as legal holidays and those designated as holidays by the applicable building service union employees service contract or by the applicable Operating Engineers contract with respect to HVAC service.

**Adjacent Excavation and Shoring:**

32. If an excavation shall be made upon land adjacent to the demised premises, or shall be authorized to be made, Tenant shall afford to the person causing or authorized to cause such excavation, license to enter upon the demised premises for the purpose of doing such work as said person shall deem necessary to preserve the wall or the building of which demised premises form a part from injury or damage and to support the same by proper foundations without any claim for damages or indemnity against Owner, or diminution or abatement of rent.

**Rules and Regulations**

33. Tenant and Tenant's servants, employees, agents, visitors, and licensees shall observe faithfully, and comply strictly with, the Rules and Regulations and such other and further reasonable Rules and Regulations as Owner or Owner's agents may from time to time adopt. Notice of any additional rules or regulations shall be given in such manner as Owner may elect. In case Tenant disputes the reasonableness of any additional Rule or Regulation hereafter made or adopted by Owner or Owner's agents, the parties hereto agree to submit the question of the reasonableness of such Rule or Regulation for decision to the New York office of the American Arbitration Association,

whose determination shall be final and conclusive upon the parties hereto. The right to dispute the reasonableness of any additional Rule or Regulation upon Tenant's part shall be deemed waived unless the same shall be asserted by service of a notice, in writing upon Owner within ten (10) days after the giving of notice thereof. Nothing in this lease contained shall be construed to impose upon Owner any duty or obligation to enforce the Rules and Regulations or terms, covenants or conditions in any other lease, as against any other tenant and Owner shall not be liable to Tenant for violation of the same by any other tenant, its servants, employees, agents, visitors or licensees.

**Security:**

**34.** Tenant has deposited with Owner the sum of $_____ as security for the faithful performance and observance by Tenant of the terms, provisions and conditions of this lease; it is agreed that in the event Tenant defaults in respect of any of the terms, provisions and conditions of this lease, including, but not limited to, the payment of rent and additional rent, Owner may use, apply or retain the whole or any part of the security so deposited to the extent required for the payment of any rent and additional rent or any other sum as to which Tenant is in default or for any sum which Owner may expend or may be required to expend by reason of Tenant's default in respect of any of the terms, covenants and conditions of this lease, including but not limited to, any damages or deficiency in the re-letting of the premises, whether such damages or deficiency accrued before or after summary proceedings or other re-entry by Owner. In the event that Tenant shall fully and faithfully comply with all of the terms, provisions, covenants and conditions of this lease, the security shall be returned to Tenant after the date fixed as the end of the Lease and after delivery of entire possession of the demised premises to Owner. In the event of a sale of the land and building or leasing of the building, of which the demised premises form a part, Owner shall have the right to transfer the security to the vendee or lessee and Owner shall thereupon be released by Tenant from all liability for the return of such security; and Tenant agrees to look to the new Owner solely for the return of said security, and it is agreed that the provisions hereof shall apply to every transfer or assignment made of the security to a new Owner. Tenant further convenants that it will not assign or encumber or attempt to assign or encumber the monies deposited herein as security and that neither Owner nor its successors or assigns shall be bound by any such assignment, encumbrance, attempted assignment or attempted encumbrance.

**Estoppel Certificate:**

**35.** Tenant, at any time, and from time to time, upon at least 10 days' prior notice by Owner, shall execute, acknowledge and deliver to Owner, and/or to any other person, firm or corporation specified by Owner, a statement certifying that this Lease is unmodified and in full force and effect (or, if there have been modifications, that the same is in full force and effect as modified and stating the modifications), stating the dates to which the rent and additional rent have been paid, and stating whether or not there exists any default by Owner under this Lease, and, if so, specifying each such default.

**Successors and Assigns:**

**36.** The covenants, conditions and agreements contained in this lease shall bind and inure to the benefit of Owner and Tenant and their respective heirs, distributees, executors, administrators, successors, and except as otherwise provided in this lease, their assigns.

**In Witness Whereof,** Owner and Tenant have respectively signed and sealed this lease as of the day and year first above written.

Witness for Owner:  ........................
........................   .................... [L.S.]
Witness for Tenant:   ........................
........................   .................... [L.S.]

## ACKNOWLEDGMENTS

CORPORATE OWNER
STATE OF NEW YORK, ss.:
County of
   On this        day of        ,

19 , before me personally came        to me known, who being by me duly sworn, did depose and say that he resides

## GENERAL PRINCIPLES § 1:13

in        : that he is the        of the corporation described in and which executed the foregoing instrument, as OWNER: that he knows the seal of said corporation; that the seal affixed to said instrument is such corporate seal; that it was so affixed by order of the Board of Directors of said corporation, and that he signed his name thereto by like order.

..........................

**INDIVIDUAL OWNER**
STATE OF NEW YORK, ss.:
County of

On this        day of        , 19  , before me personally came        , to me known and known to me to be the individual        described in and who, as OWNER, executed the foregoing instrument and acknowledged to me that        he executed the same.

..........................

**CORPORATE TENANT**
STATE OF NEW YORK, ss.:
County of

On this        day of        , 19  , before me personaly came        , to me known, who being by me duly sworn, did depose and say that he resides in        ; that he is the        of the corporation described in and which executed the foregoing instrument, as TENANT; that he knows the seal of said corporation; that the seal affixed to said instrument is such corporate seal; that it was so affixed by order of the Board of Directors of said corporation, and that he signed his name thereto by like order.

..........................

**INDIVIDUAL TENANT**
STATE OF NEW YORK, ss.:
County of

On this        day of        , 19  , before me personally came        , to me known and known to me to be the individual described in and who, as TENANT, executed the foregoing instrument and acknowledged to me that        he executed the same.

..........................

## GUARANTY

FOR VALUE RECEIVED, and in consideration for, and as an inducement to Owner making the within lease with Tenant, the undersigned guarantees to Owner, Owner's successors and assigns, the full performance and observance of all the covenants, conditions and agreements, therein provided to be performed and observed by Tenant, including the "Rules and Regulations" as therein provided, without requiring any notice of non-payment, non-performance, or non-observance, or proof, or notice, or demand, whereby to charge the undersigned therefor, all of which the undersigned hereby expressly waives and expressly agrees that the validity of this agreement and the obligations of the guarantor hereunder shall in no wise be terminated, affected or impaired by reason of the assertion by Owner against Tenant of

Dated New York City ... 19....
WITNESS:

..............................
STATE OF NEW YORK, ) ss.:
  County of                 )

On this        day of        , 19  , before me personally came        , to me known and known to me to be the individual described in, and who executed

71

§ 1:13                        LANDLORD AND TENANT

any of the rights or remedies reserved to Owner pursuant to the provisions of the within lease. The undersigned further covenants and agrees that this guaranty shall remain and continue in full force and effect as to any renewal, modification or extension of this lease and during any period when Tenant is occupying the premises as a "statutory tenant." As a further inducement to Owner to make this lease and in consideration thereof, Owner and the undersigned covenant and agree that in any action or proceeding brought by either Owner or the undersigned against the other on any matters whatsoever arising out of, under, or by virtue of the terms of this lease or of this guaranty that Owner and the undersigned shall and do hereby waive trial by jury.

the foregoing Guaranty and acknowledged to me that he executed the same.

.................................
           Notary
........................ [L. S.]
Residence .......................
Business Address ................
Firm Name .....................

## IMPORTANT - PLEASE READ

**RULES AND REGULATIONS ATTACHED TO AND MADE A PART OF THIS LEASE IN ACCORDANCE WITH ARTICLE 33.**

1. The sidewalks, entrances, driveways, passages, courts, elevators, vestibules, stairways, corridors or halls shall not be obstructed or encumbered by any Tenant or used for any purpose other than for ingress or egress from the demised premises and for delivery of merchandise and equipment in a prompt and efficient manner using elevators and passageways designated for such delivery by Owner. There shall not be used in any space, or in the public hall of the building, either by any Tenant or by jobbers or others in the delivery or receipt of merchandise, any hand trucks, except those equipped with rubber tires and sideguards. If said premises are situated on the ground floor of the building, Tenant thereof shall further, at Tenant's expense, keep the sidewalk and curb in front of said premises clean and free from ice, snow, dirt and rubbish.

2. The water and wash closets and plumbing fixtures shall not be used for any purposes other than those for which they were designed or constructed and no sweepings, rubbish, rags, acids or other substances shall be deposited therein, and the expense of any breakage, stoppage, or damage resulting from the violation of this rule shall be borne by the Tenant who, or whose clerks, agents, employees or visitors, shall have caused it.

3. No carpet, rug or other article shall be hung or shaken out of any window of the building; and no Tenant shall sweep or throw or permit to be swept or thrown from the demised premises any dirt or other substances into any of the corridors or halls, elevators, or out of the doors or windows or stairways of the building and Tenant shall not use, keep or permit to be used or kept any foul or noxious gas or substance in the demised premises, or permit or suffer the demised premises to be occupied or used in a manner offensive or objectionable to Owner or other occupants of the buildings by reason of noise,

# GENERAL PRINCIPLES § 1:13

odors, and/or vibrations, or interfere in any way with other Tenants or those having business therein, nor shall any animals or birds be kept in or about the building. Smoking or carrying lighted cigars or cigarettes in the elevators of the building is prohibited.

**4.** No awnings or other projections shall be attached to the outside walls of the building without the prior written consent of Owner.

**5.** No sign, advertisement, notice or other lettering shall be exhibited, inscribed, painted or affixed by any Tenant on any part of the outside of the demised premises or the building or on the inside of the demised premises if the same is visible from the outside of the premises without the prior written consent of Owner, except that the name of Tenant may appear on the entrance door of the premises. In the event of the violation of the foregoing by any Tenant, Owner may remove same without any liability, and may charge the expense incurred by such removal to Tenant or Tenants violating this rule. Interior signs on doors and directory tablet shall be inscribed, painted or affixed for each Tenant by Owner at the expense of such Tenant, and shall be of a size, color and style acceptable to Owner.

**6.** No Tenant shall mark, paint, drill into, or in any way deface any part of the demised premises or the building of which they form a part. No boring, cutting or stringing of wires shall be permitted, except with the prior written consent of Owner, and as Owner may direct. No Tenant shall lay linoleum, or other similar floor covering, so that the same shall come in direct contact with the floor of the demised premises, and, if linoleum or other similar floor covering is desired to be used an interlining of builder's deadening felt shall be first affixed to the floor, by a paste or other material, soluble in water, the use of cement or other similar adhesive material being expressly prohibited.

**7.** No additional locks or bolts of any kind shall be placed upon any of the doors or windows by any Tenant, nor shall any changes be made in existing locks or mechanism thereof. Each Tenant must, upon the termination of his Tenancy, restore to Owner all keys of stores, offices and toilet rooms, either furnished to, or otherwise procured by, such Tenant, and in the event of the loss of any keys, so furnished, such Tenant shall pay to Owner the cost thereof.

**8.** Freight, furniture, business equipment, merchandise and bulky matter of any description shall be delivered to and removed from the premises only on the freight elevators and through the service entrances and corridors, and only during hours and in a manner approved by Owner. Owner reserves the right to inspect all freight to be brought into the building and to exclude from the building all freight which violates any of these Rules and Regulations of the lease or which these Rules and Regulations are a part.

**9.** Canvassing, soliciting and peddling in the building is prohibited and each Tenant shall cooperate to prevent the same.

**10.** Owner reserves the right to exclude from the building between the hours of 6 P.M. and 8 A.M. and at all hours on Sundays, and legal holidays all persons who do not present a pass to the building signed by Owner. Owner will furnish passes to persons for whom any Tenant requests same in writing. Each Tenant shall be responsible for all persons for whom he requests such pass and shall be liable to Owner for all acts of such persons.

11. Owner shall have the right to prohibit any advertising by any Tenant which in Owner's opinion, tends to impair the reputation of the building or its desirability as a as a building for offices, and upon written notice from Owner, Tenant shall refrain from or discontinue such advertising.

12. Tenant shall not bring or permit to be brought or kept in or on the demised premises, any inflammable, combustible or explosive fluid, material, chemical or substance, or cause or permit any odors of cooking or other processes, or any unusual or other objectionable odors to permeate in or emanate from the demised premises.

13. If the building contains central air conditioning and ventilation, Tenant agrees to keep all windows closed at all times and to abide by all rules and regulations issued by the Owner with respect to such services. If Tenant requires air conditioning or ventilation after the usual hours, Tenant shall give notice in writing to the building superintendent prior to 3:00 P.M. in the case of services required on week days, and prior to 3:00 P.M. on the day prior in the case of after hours service required on weekends or on holidays.

14. Tenant shall not move any safe, heavy machinery, heavy equipment, bulky matter, or fixtures into or out of the building without Landlord's prior written consent. If such safe, machinery, equipment, bulky matter or fixtures requires special handling, all work in connection therewith shall comply with the Administrative Code of the City of New York and all other laws and regulations applicable thereto and shall be done during such hours as Owner may designate.

### § 1:14. Store Lease

## FORM NO 1.3
## STORE LEASE WITH*
## FORM OF GUARANTY

**Agreement of Lease,** made as of this      day of      19 , between      party of the first part, hereinafter referred to as OWNER, and party of the second part, hereinafter referred to as TENANT,

**Witnesseth:** Owner hereby leases to Tenant and Tenant hereby hires from Owner in the building known as      in the Borough of      , City of New York, for the term of      (or until such term shall sooner cease and expire as hereinafter provided) to commence on the      day of      nineteen hundred and      ,

* This store lease is adopted and copyrighted by The Real Estate Board of New York Inc and reprinted with its permission. Reproduction in whole or in part is prohibited, and all rights are reserved by The Real Estate Board of New York Inc.

GENERAL PRINCIPLES § 1:14

and to end on the          day of          nineteen hundred and          both dates inclusive, at an annual rental rate of          which Tenant agrees to pay in lawful money of the United States which shall be legal tender in payment of all debts and dues, public and private, at the time of payment, in equal monthly installments in advance on the first day of each month during said term, at the office of Owner or such other place as Owner may designate, without any set off or deduction whatsoever, except that Tenant shall pay the first          monthly installment(s) on the execution hereof (unless this lease be a renewal).

The parties hereto, for themselves, their heirs, distributees, executors, administrators, legal representatives, successors and assigns, hereby convenant as follows:

**Rent**

1. Tenant shall pay the rent as above and as hereinafter provided.

**Occupancy**

2. Tenant shall use and occupy demised premises for          and for no other purpose. Tenant shall at all times conduct its business in a high grade and reputable manner, shall not violate Article 37 hereof, and shall keep show windows and signs in a neat and clean condition.

**Alterations:**

3. Tenant shall make no changes in or to the demised premises of any nature without Owner's prior written consent. Subject to the prior written consent of Owner, and to the provisions of this article, Tenant at Tenant's expense, may make alterations, installations, additions or improvements which are non-structural and which do not affect utility services or plumbing and electrical lines, in or to the interior of the demised premises by using contractors or mechanics first approved by Owner. Tenant shall, before making any alterations, additions, installations or improvements, at its expense, obtain all permits, approvals and certificates required by any governmental or quasi-governmental bodies and (upon completion) certificates of final approval thereof and shall de-

§ 1:14   LANDLORD AND TENANT

liver promptly duplicates of all such permits, approvals and certificates to Owner and Tenant agrees to carry and will cause Tenant's contractors and sub-contractors to carry such workman's compensation, general liability, personal and property damage insurance as Owner may require. If any mechanic's lien is filed against the demised premises, or the building of which the same forms a part, for work claimed to have done for, or materials furnished to, Tenant, whether or not done pursuant to this article, the same shall be discharged by Tenant within ten days thereafter, at Tenant's expense, by filing the bond required by law. All fixtures and all paneling, partitions, railings and like installations, installed in the premises at any time, either by Tenant or by Owner in Tenant's behalf, shall, upon installation, become the property of Owner and shall remain upon and be surrendered with the demised premises unless Owner, by notice to Tenant no later than twenty days prior to the date fixed as the termination of this lease, elects to relinquish Owner's rights thereto and to have them removed by Tenant, in which event, the same shall be removed from the premises by Tenant prior to the expiration of the lease, at Tenant's expense. Nothing in this article shall be construed to give Owner title to or to prevent Tenant's removal of trade fixtures, moveable office furniture and equipment, but upon removal of any such from the premises or upon removal of other installations as may be required by Owner, Tenant shall immediately and at its expense, repair and restore the premises to the condition existing prior to installation and repair any damage to the demised premises or the building due to such removal. All property permitted or required to be removed by Tenant at the end of the term remaining in the premises after Tenant's removal shall be deemed abandoned and may, at the election of Owner, either be retained as Owner's property or may be removed from the premises by Owner at Tenant's expense.

**Repairs:**

**4.** Owner shall maintain and repair the public portions of the building, both exterior and interior, except that if Owner allows Tenant to erect on the outside of the building a sign or signs, or a hoist, lift or sidewalk

# GENERAL PRINCIPLES § 1:14

elevator for the exclusive use of Tenant, Tenant shall maintain such exterior installations in good appearance and shall cause the same to be operated in a good and workmanlike manner and shall make all repairs thereto necessary to keep same in good order and condition, at Tenant's own cost and expense, and shall cause the same to be covered by the insurance provided for hereafter in Article 8. Tenant shall, throughout the term of this lease, take good care of the demised premises and the fixtures and appurtenances therein, and the sidewalks adjacent thereto, and at its sole cost and expense, make all nonstructural repairs thereto as and when needed to preserve them in good working order and condition, reasonable wear and tear, obsolescence and damage from the elements, fire or other casualty, excepted. If the demised premises be or become infested with vermin, Tenant shall at Tenant's expense, cause the same to be exterminated from time to time to the satisfaction of Owner. Except as specifically provided in Article 9 or elsewhere in this lease, there shall be no allowance to the Tenant for the diminuation of rental value and no liability on the part of Owner by reason of inconvenience, annoyance or injury to business arising from Owner, Tenant or others making or failing to make any repairs, alterations, additions or improvements in or to any portion of the building including the erection or operation of any crane, derrick or sidewalk shed, or in or to the demised premises or the fixtures, appurtenances or equipment thereof. The provisions of this article 4 with respect to the making of repairs shall not apply in the case of fire or other casualty which are dealt with in article 9 hereof.

**Window Cleaning:**

5. Tenant will not clean nor require, permit, suffer or allow any window in the demised premises to be cleaned from the outside in violation of Section 202 of the New York State Labor Law or any other applicable law or of the Rules of the Board of Standards and Appeals, or of any other Board or body having or asserting jurisdiction.

**Requirements of Law, Fire Insurance:**

6. Prior to the commencement of the lease term, if Tenant is then in possession, and at all times thereafter,

§ 1:14

Tenant at Tenant's sole cost and expense, shall promptly comply with all present and future laws, orders and regulations of all state, federal, municipal and local governments, departments, commissions and boards and any direction of any public officer pursuant to law, and all orders, rules and regulations of the New York Board of Fire Underwriters or the Insurance Services Office, or any similar body which shall impose any violation, order or duty upon Owner or Tenant with respect to the demised premises, and with respect to the portion of the sidewalk adjacent to the premises, if the premises are on the street level, whether or not arising out of Tenant's use or manner of use thereof, or with respect to the building if arising out of Tenant's use or manner of use of the premises or the building (including the use permitted under the lease). Except as provided in Article 29 hereof, nothing herein shall require Tenant to make structural repairs or alterations unless Tenant has by its manner of use of the demised premises or method of operation therein, violated any such laws, ordinances, orders, rules, regulations or requirements with respect thereto. Tenant shall not do or permit any act or thing to be done in or to the demised premises which is contrary to law, or which will invalidate or be in conflict with public liability, fire or other policies of insurance at any time carried by or for the benefit of Owner. Tenant shall pay all costs, expenses, fines, penalties or damages, which may be imposed upon Owner by reason of Tenant's failure to comply with the provisions of this article. If the fire insurance rate shall, at the beginning of the lease or at any time thereafter, be higher than it otherwise would be, then Tenant shall reimburse Owner, as additional rent hereunder, for that portion of all fire insurance premiums thereafter paid by Owner which shall have been charged because of such failure by Tenant, to comply with the terms of this article. In any action or proceeding wherein Owner and Tenant are parties, a schedule or "make-up" of rate for the building or demised premises issued by a body making fire insurance rates applicable to said premises shall be conclusive evidence of the facts therein stated and of the several items and charges in the fire insurance rate then applicable to said premises.

GENERAL PRINCIPLES § 1:14

**Subordination:**

7. This lease is subject and subordinate to all ground or underlying leases and to all mortgages which may now or hereafter affect such leases or the real property of which demised premises are a part and to all renewals, modifications, consolidations, replacements and extensions of any such underlying leases and mortgages. This clause shall be selfoperative and no further instrument of subordination shall be required by any ground or underlying lessor or by any mortgagee, affecting any lease or the real property of which the demised premises are a part. In confirmation of such subordination, Tenant shall execute promptly any certificate that Owner may request.

**Tenant's Liability Insurance Property Loss, Damage, Indemnity:**

8. Owner or its agents shall not be liable for any damage to property of Tenant or of others entrusted to employees of the building, nor for loss of or damage to any property of Tenant by theft or otherwise, nor for any injury or damage to persons or property resulting from any cause of whatsoever nature, unless caused by or due to the negligence of Owner, its agents, servants or employees. Owner or its agents will not be liable for any such damage caused by other tenants or persons in, upon or about said building or caused by operations in construction of any private, public or quasi public work. Tenant agrees, at Tenant's sole cost and expense, to maintain general public liability insurance in standard form in favor of Owner and Tenant against claims for bodily injury or death or property damage occurring in or upon the demised premises, effective from the date Tenant enters into possession and during the term of this lease. Such insurance shall be in an amount and with carriers acceptable to the Owner. Such policy or policies shall be delivered to the Owner. On Tenant's default in obtaining or delivering any such policy or policies or failure to pay the charges therefor, Owner may secure or pay the charges for any such policy or policies and charge the Tenant as additional rent therefor. Tenant shall indemnify and save harmless Owner against and from all liabilities, obligations, damages, penalties, claims, costs

and expenses for which Owner shall not be reimbursed by insurance, including reasonable attorneys fees, paid, suffered or incurred as a result of any breach by Tenant, Tenant's agent, contractors, employees, invitees, or licensees, of any covenant on condition of this lease, or the carelessness, negligence or improper conduct of the Tenant, Tenant's agents, contractors, employees, invitees or licensees. Tenant's liability under this lease extends to the acts and omissions of any subtenant, and any agent, contractor, employee, invitee or licensee of any subtenant. In case any action or proceeding is brought against Owner by reason of any such claim, Tenant, upon written notice from Owner, will, at Tenant's expense, resist or defend such action or proceeding by Counsel approved by Owner in writing, such approval not to be unreasonably withheld.

**Destruction, Fire and Other Casualty:**

**9.** (a) If the demised premises or any part thereof shall be damaged by fire or other casualty, Tenant shall give immediate notice thereof to Owner and this lease shall continue in full force and effect except as hereinafter set forth. (b) If the demised premises are partially damaged or rendered partially unusable by fire or other casualty, the damages thereto shall be repaired by and at the expense of Owner and the rent, until such repair shall be substantially completed, shall be apportioned from the day following the casualty according to the part of the premises which is usable. (c) If the demised premises are totally damaged or rendered wholly unusable by fire or other casualty, then the rent shall be proportionately paid up to the time of the casualty and thenceforth shall cease until the date when the premises shall have been repaired and restored by Owner, subject to Owner's right to elect not to restore the same as hereinafter provided. (d) If the demised premises are rendered wholly unusable or (whether or not the demised premises are damaged in whole or in part) if the building shall be so damaged that Owner shall decide to demolish it or to rebuild it, then, in any of such events, Owner may elect to terminate this lease by written notice to Tenant given within 90 days after such fire or casualty specifying a date for the expiration of the lease, which date shall not be more than

## GENERAL PRINCIPLES § 1:14

60 days after the giving of such notice, and upon the date specified in such notice the term of this lease shall expire as fully and completely as if such date were the date set forth above for the termination of this lease and Tenant shall forthwith quit, surrender and vacate the premises without prejudice however, to Owner's rights and remedies against Tenant under the lease provisions in effect prior to such termination, and any rent owing shall be paid up to such date and any payments of rent made by Tenant which were on account of any period subsequent to such date shall be returned to Tenant. Unless Owner shall serve a termination notice as provided for herein, Owner shall make the repairs and restorations under the conditions of (b) and (c) hereof, with all reasonable expedition subject to delays due to adjustment of insurance claims, labor troubles and causes beyond Owner's control. After any such casualty, Tenant shall cooperate with Owner's restoration by removing from the premises as promptly as reasonably possible, all of Tenant's salvageable inventory and movable equipment, furniture, and other property. Tenant's liability for rent shall resume five (5) days after written notice from Owner that the premises are substantially ready for Tenant's occupancy.
(e) Nothing contained hereinabove shall relieve Tenant from liability that may exist as a result of damage from fire or other casualty. Notwithstanding the foregoing, each party shall look first to any insurance in its favor before making any claim against the other party for recovery for loss or damage resulting from fire or other casualty, and to the extent that such insurance is in force and collectible and to the extent permitted by law, Owner and Tenant each hereby releases and waives all right of recovery against the other or any one claiming through or under each of them by way of subrogation or otherwise. The foregoing release and waiver shall be in force only if both releasors' insurance policies contain a clause providing that such a release or waiver shall not invalidate the insurance and also, provided that such a policy can be obtained without additional premiums. Tenant acknowledges that Owner will not carry insurance on Tenant's furniture and/or furnishings or any fixtures or equipment, improvements, or appurtenances removable

by Tenant and agrees that Owner will not be obligated to repair any damage thereto or replace the same. (f) Tenant hereby waives the provisions of Section 227 of the Real Property Law and agrees that the provisions of this article shall govern and control in lieu thereof.

**Eminent Domain:**

10. If the whole or any part of the demised premises shall be acquired or condemned by Eminent Domain for any public or quasi public use or purpose, then and in that event, the term of this lease shall cease and terminate from the date of title vesting in such proceeding and Tenant shall have no claim for the value of any unexpired term of said lease.

**Assignment, Mortgage, Etc.:**

11. Tenant, for itself, its heirs, distributees, executors, administrators, legal representatives, successors and assigns expressly covenants that it shall not assign, mortgage or encumber this agreement, nor underlet, or suffer or permit the demised premises or any part thereof to be used by others, without the prior written consent of Owner in each instance. If this lease be assigned, or if the demised premises or any part thereof be underlet or occupied by anybody other than Tenant, Owner may, after default by Tenant, collect rent from the assignee, under-tenant or occupant, and apply the net amount collected to the rent herein reserved, but no such assignment, underletting, occupancy or collection shall be deemed a waiver of the covenant, or the acceptance of the assignee, under-tenant or occupant as tenant, or a release of Tenant from the further performance by Tenant of covenants on the part of Tenant herein contained. The consent by Owner to an assignment or underletting shall not in any wise be construed to relieve Tenant from obtaining the express consent in writing of Owner to any further assignment or underletting.

**Electric Current:**

12. Rates and conditions in respect to submetering or rent inclusion, as the case may be, to be added in RIDER attached hereto. Tenant convenants and agrees that at all times its use of electric current shall not exceed the capacity of existing feeders to the building or the risers or

# GENERAL PRINCIPLES § 1:14

wiring installation and Tenant may not use any electrical equipment which, in Owner's opinion, reasonably exercised, will overload such installations or interfere with the use thereof by other tenants of the building. The change at any time of the character of electric service shall in no wise make Owner liable or responsible to Tenant, for any loss, damages or expenses which Tenant may sustain.

**Access to Premises:**

13. Owner or Owner's agents shall have the right (but shall not be obligated) to enter the demised premises in any emergency at any time, and, at other reasonable times, to examine the same and to make such repairs, replacements and improvements as Owner may deem necessary and reasonably desirable to any portion of the building or which Owner may elect to perform, in the premises, following Tenant's failure to make repairs or perform any work which Tenant is obligated to perform under this lease, or for the purpose of complying with laws, regulations and other directions of governmental authorities. Tenant shall permit Owner to use and maintain and replace pipes and conduits in and through the demised premises and to erect new pipes and conduits therein, provided they are within the walls, Owner may, during the progress of any work in the demised premises, take all necessary materials and equipment into said premises without the same constituting an eviction nor shall the Tenant be entitled to any abatement of rent while such work is in progress nor to any damages by reason of loss or interruption of business or otherwise. Throughout the term hereof Owner shall have the right to enter the demised premises at reasonable hours for the purpose of showing the same to prospective purchasers or mortgages of the building, and during the last six months of the term for the purpose of showing the same to prospective tenants and may, during said six months period, place upon the premises the usual notice "To Let" and "For Sale" which notices Tenant shall permit to remain thereon without molestation. If Tenant is not present to open and permit an entry into the premises, Owner or Owner's agents may enter the same whenever such entry may be necessary or permissible by master

key or forcibly and provided reasonable care is exercised to safeguard Tenant's property and such entry shall not render Owner or its agents liable therefor, nor in any event shall the obligations of Tenant hereunder be affected. If during the last month of term Tenant shall have removed all or substantially all of Tenant's property therefrom, Owner may immediately enter, alter, renovate or redecorate the demised premises without limitation or abatement of rent, or incurring liability to Tenant for any compensation and such act shall have no effect on this lease or Tenant's obligations hereunder. Owner shall have the right at any time, without the same constituting an eviction and without incurring liability to Tenant therefor to change the arrangement and/or location of public entrances, passageways, doors, doorways, corridors, elevators, stairs, toilets, or other public parts of the building and to change the name, number or designation by which the building may be known.

**Vault, Vault Space, Area:**

**14.** No vaults, vault space or area, whether or not enclosed or covered, not within the property line of the building is leased hereunder, anything contained in or indicated on any sketch, blue print or plan, or anything contained elsewhere in this lease to the contrary notwithstanding. Owner makes no representation as to the location of the property line of the building. All vaults and vault space and all such areas not within the property line of the building, which Tenant may be permitted to use and/or occupy, is to be used and/or occupied under a revocable license, and if any such license be revoked, or if the amount of such space or area be diminished or required by any federal, state or municipal authority or public utility, Owner shall not be subject to any liability nor shall Tenant be entitled to any compensation or diminution or abatement of rent, nor shall such revocation, diminution or requisition be deemed constructive or actual eviction. Any tax, fee or charge of municipal authorities for such vault or area shall be paid by Tenant.

**Occupancy:**

**15.** Tenant will not at any time use or occupy the

demised premises in violation of, Articles 2 or 37 hereof, or of, the certificate of occupancy issued for the building of which the demised premises are a part. Tenant has inspected the premises and accepts them as is, subject to the riders annexed hereto with respect to Owner's work, if any. In any event, Owner makes no representation as to the condition of the premises and Tenant agrees to accept the same subject to violations whether or not of record.

*[Provision 16 of this lease is a bankruptcy termination clause, which no longer is enforceable, and therefore is omitted. See Chapter 22, infra.]*

**Default:**

**17.** (1) If Tenant defaults in fulfilling any of the covenants of this lease other than the covenants for the payment of rent or additional rent; or if the demised premises become vacant or deserted; or if any execution or attachment shall be issued against Tenant or any of Tenant's property whereupon the demised premises shall be taken or occupied by someone other than Tenant; or if this lease be rejected under 11 USCS § 365 (Bankruptcy Code); or if Tenant shall fail to move into or take possession of the premises within fifteen (15) days after the commencement of the term of this lease, of which fact Owner shall be the sole judge; then, in any one or more of such events, upon Owner serving a written five (5) days notice upon Tenant specifying the nature of said default and upon the expiration of said five (5) days, if Tenant shall have failed to comply with or remedy such default, or if the said default or omission complained of shall be of a nature that the same cannot be completely cured or remedied within said five (5) day period, and if Tenant shall not have diligently commenced curing such default within such five (5) day period, and shall not thereafter with reasonable diligence and in good faith proceed to remedy or cure such default, then Owner may serve a written three (3) days notice of cancellation of this lease upon Tenant, and upon the expiration of said three (3) days, this lease and the term thereunder shall end and expire as fully and completely as if the expiration of such three (3) day period were the day herein definitely fixed for the end and expiration of this lease and the term thereof and Tenant shall then quit and surrender the demised premises to Owner but Tenant shall remain liable as hereinafter provided.

(2) If the notice provided for in (1) hereof shall have been given, and the term shall expire as aforesaid; or if Tenant shall make default on the payment of the rent reserved herein or any item of additional rent herein mentioned or any part of either or in making any other payment herein required; then and in any of such events Owner may without notice, re-enter the demised premises either by force or otherwise, and dispossess Tenant by summary proceedings or otherwise, and the legal representative of Tenant or other occupant of demised premises and remove their effects and hold the premises as if this lease had not been made, and Tenant hereby waives the service of notice of intention to re-enter or to institute legal proceedings to that end.

**Remedies of Owner and Waiver of Redemption:**

**18.** In case of any such default, re-entry, expiration and/or dispossess by summary proceedings or otherwise, (a) the rent, and additional rent, shall become due thereupon and be paid up to the time of such reentry, dispossess and/or expiration. (b) Owner may re-let the premises or any part or parts thereof, either in the name of Owner or otherwise, for a term or terms, which may at Owner's option be less than or exceed the period which would otherwise have constituted the balance of the term of this lease and may grant concessions or free rent or charge a higher rental than that in this lease, and/or (c) Tenant or the legal representatives of Tenant shall also pay Owner as liquidated damages for the failure of Tenant to observe and perform said Tenant's covenants herein contained, any deficiency between the rent hereby reserved and/or convenanted to be paid and the net amount, if any, of the rents collected on account of the subsequent lease or leases of the demised premises for each month of the period which would otherwise have constituted the balance of the term of this lease. The failure of Owner to re-let the premises or any part or parts thereof shall not release or affect Tenant's liability for damages. In computing such liquidated damages there shall be added to the said deficiency such expenses as Owner may incur in connection with re-letting, such as legal expenses, attorneys' fees, brokerage, advertising and for keeping the demised premises in good order or for preparing the same for re-letting. Any such liquidated damages shall be paid in monthly installments by Tenant on the rent day specified in this lease. Owner, in putting the demised premises in good order or preparing the same for re-rental may, at Owner's option, make such alterations, repairs, replacements, and/or decorations in the demised premises as Owner, in Owner's sole judgment, considers advisable and necessary for the purpose of re-letting the demised premises, and the making of such alterations, repairs, replacements, and/or decorations shall not operate or be construed to release Tenant from liability. Owner shall in no event be liable in any way whatsoever for failure to re-let the demised premises, or in the event that the demised premises are re-let, for failure to collect the rent thereof under such re-letting, and in no event shall Tenant be entitled to receive any excess, if any, of such net rent collected over the sums payable by Tenant to Owner hereunder. In the event of a breach or threatened breach by Tenant or any of the covenants or provisions hereof, Owner shall have the right of injunction and the right to invoke any remedy allowed at law or in equity as if re-entry, summary proceedings and other remedies were not herein provided for. Mention in this lease of any particular remedy, shall not preclude Owner from any other remedy, in law or in equity. Tenant hereby expressly waives any and all rights of redemption granted by or under any present or future laws.

**Fees and Expenses:**

19. If Tenant shall default in the observance or performance of any term or covenant on Tenant's part to be observed or performed under or by virtue of any of the terms or provisions in any article of this lease, then, unless otherwise provided elsewhere in this lease, Owner may immediately or at any time thereafter and without notice perform the obligation of Tenant thereunder, and if Owner, in connection therewith or in connection with any default by Tenant in the covenant to pay rent hereunder, makes any expenditures or incurs any obligations for the payment of money, including but not limited

to attorney's fees, in instituting, prosecuting or defending any actions or proceeding, such sums so paid or obligations incurred with interest and costs shall be deemed to be additional rent hereunder and shall be paid by Tenant to Owner within five (5) days of rendition of any bill or statement to Tenant therefor, and if Tenant's lease term shall have expired at the time of making of such expenditures or incurring of such obligations, such sums shall be recoverable by Owner as damages.

**No Representations by Owner:**

20. Neither Owner nor Owner's agents have made any representations or promises with respect to the physical condition of the building, the land upon which it is erected or the demised premises, the rents, leases, expenses of operation, or any other matter or thing affecting or related to the premises except as herein expressly set forth and no rights, easements or licenses are acquired by Tenant by implication or otherwise except as expressly set forth in the provisions of this lease. Tenant has inspected the building and the demised premises and is thoroughly acquainted with their condition, and agrees to take the same "as is" and acknowledges that the taking of possession of the demised premises by Tenant shall be conclusive evidence that the said premises and the building of which the same form a part were in good and satisfactory condition at the time such possession was so taken, except as to latent defects. All understandings and agreements heretofore made between the parties hereto are merged in this contract, which alone fully and completely expresses the agreement between Owner and Tenant and any executory agreement hereafter made shall be ineffective to change, modify, discharge or effect an abandonment of it in whole or in part, unless such executory agreement is in writing and signed by the party against whom enforcement of the change, modification, discharge or abandonment is sought.

**End of Term:**

21. Upon the expiration or other termination of the term of this lease, Tenant shall quit and surrender to Owner the demised premises, broom clean, in good order and condition, ordinary wear excepted, and Tenant shall

remove all its property. Tenant's obligation to observe or perform this covenant shall survive the expiration or other termination of this lease. If the last day of the term of this lease or any renewal thereof, falls on Sunday, this lease shall expire at noon on the preceding Saturday unless it be a legal holdiay in which case it shall expire at noon on the preceding business day.

**Quiet Enjoyment:**

22. Owner covenants and agrees with Tenant that upon Tenant paying the rent and additional rent and observing and performing all the terms, covenants and conditions, on Tenant's part to be observed and performed. Tenant may peaceably and quietly enjoy the premises hereby demised, subject, nevertheless, to the terms and conditions of this lease including, but not limited to, Article 33 hereof and to the ground leases, underlying leases and mortgages hereinbefore mentioned.

**Failure to Give Possession:**

23. If Owner is unable to give possession of the demised premises on the date of the commencement of the term hereof, because of the holding-over or retention of possession of any tenant, undertenant or occupants, or if the premises are located in a building being constructed, because such building has not been sufficiently completed to make the premises ready for occupancy or because of the fact that a certificate of occupancy has not been procured or for any other reason, Owner shall not be subject to any liability for failure to give possession on said date and the validity of the lease shall not be impaired under such circumstances, nor shall the same be construed in any wise to extend the term of this lease, but the rent payable hereunder shall be abated (provided Tenant is not responsible for the inability to obtain possession) until after Owner shall have given Tenant written notice that the premises are substantially ready for Tenant's occupancy. If permission is given to Tenant to enter into the possession of the demised premises or to occupy premises other than the demised premises prior to the date specified as the commencement of the term of this lease. Tenant covenants and agrees that such occupancy shall be deemed to be under all the terms, cove-

nants, conditions and provisions of this lease, except as to the covenant to pay rent. The provisions of this article are intended to constitute "an express provision to the contrary" within the meaning of Section 223-a of the New York Real Property Law.

**No Waiver:**

**24.** The failure of Owner to seek redress for violation of, or to insist upon the strict performance of any covenant or condition of this lease or of any of the Rules or Regulations set forth or hereafter adopted by Owner, shall not prevent a subsequent act which would have originally constituted a violation from having all the force and effect of an original violation. The receipt by owner of rent with knowledge of the breach of any covenant of this lease shall not be deemed a waiver of such breach and no provision of this lease shall be deemed to have been waived by Owner unless such waiver be in writing signed by Owner. No payment by Tenant or receipt by Owner of a lesser amount than the monthly rent herein stipulated shall be deemed to be other than on account of the earliest stipulated rent, nor shall any endorsement or statement of any check or any letter accompanying any check or payment as rent be deemed an accord and satisfaction, and Owner may accept such check or payment without prejudice to Owner's right to recover the balance of such rent or pursue any other remedy in this lease provided. No act or thing done by Owner or Owner's agents during the term hereby demised shall be deemed in acceptance of a surrender of said premises and no agreement to accept such surrender shall be valid unless in writing signed by Owner. No employee of Owner or Owner's agent shall have any power to accept the keys of said premises prior to the termination of the lease and the delivery of keys to any such agent or employee shall not operate as a termination of the lease or a surrender of the premises.

**Waiver of Trial by Jury:**

**25.** It is mutually agreed by and between Owner and Tenant that the respective parties hereto shall and they hereby do waive trial by jury in any action, proceeding or counterclaim brought by either of the parties hereto against the other (except for personal injury or property damage) on any matters whatsoever arising out of or in any way connected with this lease, the relationship of Owner and Tenant, Tenant's use of or occupancy of said premises, and any emergency statutory or any other statutory remedy. It is further mutually agreed that in the event Owner commences any summary proceeding for possession of the premises, Tenant will not interpose any counterclaim of whatever nature or description in any such proceeding.

**Inability to Perform:**

**26.** This lease and the obligation of Tenant to pay rent hereunder and perform all of the other covenants and agreements hereunder on part of Tenant to be performed shall in no wise be affected, impaired or excused because Owner is unable to fulfill any of its obligations under this lease or to supply or is delayed in supplying any service expressly or impliedly to be supplied or is unable to make, or is delayed in making any repair, additions, alterations or decorations or is unable to supply or is delayed in supplying any equipment or fixtures if Owner is prevented or delayed from so doing by reason of strike or labor troubles, government preemption in connection with a National Emergency or by reason of any rule, order or regulation of any department or subdivision thereof of any government agency or by reason of the conditions of supply and demand which have been or are affected by war or other emergency, or when, in the judgment of Owner, temporary interruption of such services is necessary by reason of accident, mechanical breakdown, or to make repairs, alterations or improvements.

**Bills and Notices:**

**27.** Except as otherwise in this lease provided, a bill, statement, notice or communication which Owner may desire or be required to give to Tenant, shall be deemed sufficiently given or rendered if, in writing, delivered to Tenant personally or sent by registered or certified mail addressed to Tenant at the building of which the demised premises form a part or at the last known residence address or business address of Tenant or left at any of the

§ 1:14　　　　　　　　LANDLORD AND TENANT

aforesaid premises addressed to Tenant, and the time of the rendition of such bill or statement and of the giving of such notice or communication shall be deemed to be the time when the same is delivered to Tenant, mailed, or left at the premises as herein provided. Any notice by Tenant to Owner must be served by registered or certified mail addressed to Owner at the address first hereinabove given or at such other address as Owner shall designate by written notice.

**Water Charges:**

28. If Tenant requires, uses or consumes water for any purpose in addition to ordinary lavatory purposes (of which fact Tenant constitutes Owner to be the sole judge) Owner may install a water meter and thereby measures Tenant's water comsumption for all purposes. Tenant shall pay Owner for the cost of the meter and the cost of the installation thereof and throughout the duration of Tenant's occupancy Tenant shall keep said meter and installation equipment in good working order and repair at Tenant's own cost and expense. Tenant agrees to pay for water consumed, as shown on said meter as and when bills are rendered. Tenant covenants and agrees to pay the sewer rent, charge or any other tax, rent, levy or charge which now or hereafter is assessed, imposed or a lien upon the demised premises or the realty of which they are part pursuant to law, order or regulation made or issued in connection with the use, consumption, maintenance or supply of water, water system or sewage or sewage connection or system. The bill rendered by Owner shall be payable by Tenant as additional rent. If the building or the demised premises or any part thereof be supplied with water through a meter through which water is also supplied to other premises Tenant shall pay to Owner as additional rent, on the first day of each month, _____% ($\_\_\_) of the total meter charges, as Tenant's portion. Independently of and in addition to any of the remedies reserved to Owner hereinabove or elsewhere in this lease. Owner may sue for and collect any monies to be paid by Tenant or paid by Owner for any of the reasons or purposes hereinabove set forth.

**Sprinklers:**

29. Anything elsewhere in this lease to the contrary

notwithstanding, if the New York Board of Fire Underwriters or the Insurance Services Office or any bureau, department or official of the federal, state or city government require or recommend the installation of a sprinkler system or that any changes, modifications, alterations, or additional sprinkler heads or other equipment be made or supplied in an existing sprinkler system by reason of Tenant's business, or the location of partitions, trade fixtures, or other contents of the demised premises, or for any other reason, or if any such sprinkler system installations, changes, modifications, alterations, additional sprinkler heads or other such equipment, become necessary to prevent the imposition of a penalty or charge against the full allowance for a sprinkler system in the fire insurance rate set by any said Exchange or by any fire insurance company. Tenant shall, at Tenant's expense, promptly make such sprinkler system installations, changes, modifications, alterations, and supply additional sprinkler heads or other equipment as required whether the work involved shall be structural or nonstructural in nature. Tenant shall pay to Owner as additional rent the sum of $_____, on the first day of each month during the term of this lease, as Tenant's portion of the contract price for sprinkler supervisory service.

**Heat, Cleaning:**

30. As long as Tenant is not in default under any of the covenants of this lease Owner shall, if and insofar as existing facilities permit furnish heat to the demised premises, when and as required by law, on business days from 8:00 a.m. to 6:00 p.m. and on Saturdays from 8:00 a.m. to 1:00 p.m. Tenant shall at Tenant's expense, keep demised premises clean and in order, to the satisfaction to Owner, and if demised premises are situated on the street floor, Tenant shall, at Tenant's own expense, make all repairs and replacements to the sidewalks and curbs adjacent thereto, and keep said sidewalks and curbs free from snow, ice, dirt and rubbish. Tenant shall pay to Owner the cost of removal of any of Tenant's refuse and rubbish from the building. Bills for the same shall be rendered by Owner to Tenant at such times as Owner may elect and shall be due and payable when rendered,

and the amount of such bills shall be deemed to be, and be paid as, additional rent. Tenant shall, however, have the option of independently contracting for the removal of such rubbish and refuse in the event that Tenant does not wish to have same done by employees of Owner. Under such circumstances, however, the removal of such refuse and rubbish by others shall be subject to such rules and regulations as, in the judgment of Owner, are necessary for the proper operation of the building.

**Security:**

31. Tenant has deposited with Owner the sum of $_____ as security for the faithful performance and observance by Tenant of the terms, provisions and conditions of this lease; it is agreed that in the event Tenant defaults in respect of any of the terms, provisions and conditions of this lease, including, but not limited to, the payment of rent and additional rent. Owner may use, apply or retain the whole or any part of the security so deposited to the extent required for the payment of any rent and additional rent or any other sum as to which Tenant is in default or for any sum which Owner may expend or may be required to expend by reason of Tenant's default in respect of any of the terms, covenants and conditions of this lease, including but not limited to, any damages or deficiency in the re-letting of the premises, whether such damages or deficiency accrued before or after summary proceedings or other re-entry by Owner. In the event that Tenant shall fully and faithfully comply with all of the terms, provisions, covenants and conditions of this lease, the security shall be returned to Tenant after the date fixed as the end of the Lease and after delivery of entire possession of the demised premises to Owner. In the event of a sale of the land and building or leasing of the building, of which the demised premises form a part, Owner shall have the right to transfer the security to the vendee or lessee and Owner shall thereupon be released by Tenant from all liability for the return of such security, and Tenant agrees to look to the new Owner solely for the return of said security; and it is agreed that the provisions hereof shall apply to every transfer or assignment made of the security to a new Owner. Tenant further covenants that it will not assign

# GENERAL PRINCIPLES § 1:14

or encumber or attempt to assign or encumber the monies deposited herein as security and that neither Owner nor its successors or assigns shall be bound by any such assignment, encumbrance, attempted assignment or attempted encumbrance.

**Captions:**

32. The Captions are inserted only as a matter of convenience and for reference and in no way define, limit or describe the scope of this lease nor the intent of any provision thereof.

**Definitions:**

33. The term "Owner" as used in this lease means only the Owner, or the mortgagee in possession, for the time being of the land and building (or the Owner of a lease of the building or of the land and building) of which the demised premises form a part, so that in the event of any sale or sales of said land and building or of said lease, or in the event of a lease of said building, or of the land and building, the said Owner shall be and hereby is entirely freed and relieved of all covenants and obligations of Owner hereunder, and it shall be deemed and construed without further agreement between the parties of their successors in interest, or between the parties and the purchaser, at any such sale, or the said lessee of the building, or of the land and building, that the purchaser or the lessee of the building has assumed and agreed to carry out any and all covenants and obligations of Owner hereunder. The words "re-enter" and "re-entry" as used in this lease are not restricted to their technical legal meaning. The term "business days" as used in this lease shall exclude Saturdays (except such portion thereof as is covered by specific hours in Article 30 hereof), Sundays and all days designated as holidays by the applicable building service union employees service contract or by the applicable Operating Engineers contract with respect to H V A C service.

**Adjacent Excavation and Shoring:**

34. If an excavation shall be made upon land adjacent to the demised premises, or shall be authorized to be made, Tenant shall afford to the person causing or authorized to cause such excavation, license to enter upon the

demised premises for the purpose of doing such work as said person shall deem necessary to preserve the wall or the building of which demised premises form a part from injury or damage and to support the same by proper foundations without any claim for damages or indemnity against Owner, or diminution or abatement of rent.

**Rules and Regulations:**

35. Tenant and Tenant's servants, employees, agents, visitors, and licensees shall observe faithfully, and comply strictly with the Rules and Regulations and such other and further reasonable Rules and Regulations as Owner or Owner's agents may from time to time adopt. Notice of any additional rules or regulations shall be given in such manner as Owner may elect. In case Tenant disputes the reasonableness of any additional Rule or Regulation hereafter made or adopted by Owner or Owner's agents, the parties hereto agree to submit the question of the reasonableness of such Rule or Regulation for decision to the New York office of the American Arbitration Association, whose determination shall be final and conclusive upon the parties hereto. The right to dispute the reasonableness of any additional Rule or Regulation upon Tenant's part shall be deemed waived unless the same shall be asserted by service of a notice, in writing upon Owner within ten (10) days after the giving of notice thereof. Nothing in this lease contained shall be construed to impose upon Owner any duty or obligation to enforce the Rules and Regulations or terms, covenants or conditions in any other lease, as against any other tenant and Owner shall not be liable to Tenant for violation of the same by any other tenant, its servants, employees, agents, visitors or licensees.

**Glass:**

36. Owner shall replace, at the expense of Tenant, any and all plate and other glass damaged or broken from any cause whatsoever in and about the demised premises. Owner may insure, and keep insured, at Tenant's expense, all plate and other glass in the demised premises for and in the name of Owner. Bills for the premiums therefor shall be rendered by Owner to Tenant at such times as Owner may elect, and shall be due from, and

payable by, Tenant when rendered, and the amount thereof shall be deemed to be, and be paid as, additional rent.

**Pornographic Uses Prohibited:**

**37.** Tenant agrees that the value of the demised premises and the reputation of the Owner will be seriously injured if the premises are used for any obscene or pornographic purposes or any sort of commercial sex establishment. Tenant agrees that Tenant will not bring or permit any obscene or pornographic material on the premises, and shall not permit or conduct any obscene, nude, or semi-nude live performances on the premises, nor permit use of the premises for nude modeling, rap sessions, or as a so-called rubber goods shops, or as a sex club of any sort, or as a "massage parlor." Tenant agrees further that Tenant will not permit any of these uses by any sublessee or assignee of the premises. This Article shall directly bind any successors in interest to the Tenant. Tenant agrees that if at any time Tenant violates any of the provisions of this Article, such violation shall be deemed a breach of a substantial obligation of the terms of this lease and objectionable conduct. Pornographic material is defined for purposes of this Article as any written or pictorial matter with prurient appeal or any objects of instrument that are primarily concerned with lewd or prurient sexual activity. Obscene material is defined here as it is in Penal law § 235.00.

**Estoppel Certificate:**

**38.** Tenant, at any time, and from time to time, upon at least 10 days prior notice by Owner, shall execute, acknowledge and deliver to Owner, and/or to any other person, firm or corporation specified by Owner, a statement certifying that this lease is unmodified and in full force and effect (or, if there have been modifications, that the same is in full force and effect as modified and stating the modifications), stating the dates which the rent and additional rent have been paid, and stating whether or not there exists any defaults by Owner under this lease, and, if so, specifying each such default.

**Successors and Assigns:**

**39.** The covenants, conditions and agreements contained in this lease shall bind and inure to the benefit of Owner and Tenant and their respective heirs, distributees, executors, administrators, successors, and except as otherwise provided in this lease, their assigns.

**In Witness Whereof,** Owner and Tenant have respectively signed and sealed this lease as of the day and year first above written.

Witness for Owner:

........................

.......................... .................. [L.S.]

Witness for Tenant: ........................

.......................... .................. [L.S.]

## ACKNOWLEDGMENTS

**CORPORATE OWNER**
STATE OF NEW YORK, ss.:
County of

On this    day of    , 19 , before me personaly came    to me known, who being by me duly sworn, did depose and say that he resides in    : that he is the    of the corporation described in and which executed the foregoing instrument, as OWNER: that he knows the seal of said corporation; that the seal affixed to said instrument is such corporate seal; that it was so affixed by order of the Board of Directors of said corporation, and that he signed his name thereto by like order.

........................

**INDIVIDUAL OWNER**
STATE OF NEW YORK, ss.:
County of

On this    day of    , 19 , before me personally came    , to me known and known to me to be the individual described in and who, as OWNER, executed the foregoing instrument and acknowledged to me that    he executed the same.

........................

**CORPORATE TENANT**
STATE OF NEW YORK, ss.:
County of

On this    day of    , 19 , before me personaly came    , to me known, who being by me duly sworn, did depose and say that he resides in    ; that he is the    of the corporation described in and which executed the foregoing instrument, as TENANT; that he knows the seal of said corporation; that the seal affixed to said instrument is such corporate seal; that it was so affixed by order of the Board of Directors of said corporation, and that he signed his name thereto by like order.

........................

**INDIVIDUAL TENANT**
STATE OF NEW YORK, ss.:
County of

On this    day of    , 19 , before me personally came    , to me known and known to me to be the individual described in and who, as TENANT, executed the foregoing instrument and acknowledged to me that    he executed the same.

........................

# GENERAL PRINCIPLES § 1:14

**RULES AND REGULATIONS ATTACHED TO AND MADE A PART OF THIS LEASE IN ACCORDANCE WITH ARTICLE 35.**

1. The sidewalks, entrances, driveways, passages, courts, elevators, vestibules, stairways, corridors or halls shall not be obstructed or encumbered by any Tenant or used for any purpose other than for ingress to and egress from the demised premises and for delivery of merchandise and equipment in a prompt and efficient manner using elevators and passageways designated for such delivery by Owner. There shall not be used in any space, or in the public hall of the building, either by any tenant or by jobbers, or others in the delivery or receipt of merchandise, any hand trucks except those equipped with rubber tires and safeguards.

2. If the premises are situated on the ground floor of the building, Tenant thereof shall further, at Tenant's expense, keep the sidewalks and curb in front of said premises clean and free from ice, snow, etc.

3. The water and wash closets and plumbing fixtures shall not be used for any purposes other than those for which they were designed or constructed.

4. Tenant shall not use, keep or permit to be used or kept any foul or noxious gas or substance in the demised premises, or permit or suffer the demised premises to be occupied or used in a manner offensive or objectionable to Owner or other occupants of the building by reason of noise, odors and/or vibrations or interfere in any way with other Tenants or those having business therein.

5. No sign, advertisement, notice or other lettering shall be exhibited, inscribed, painted or affixed by any Tenant on any part of the outside of the demised premises or the building or on the inside of the demised premises if the same is visible from the outside of the premises without the prior written consent of Owner, except that the name of Tenant may appear on the entrance door of the premises. In the event of the violation of the foregoing by any Tenant, Owner may remove same without any liability and may charge the expense incurred by such removal to Tenant or Tenants violating this rule. Signs on interior doors and directory tablet shall be inscribed, painted or affixed for each Tenant by Owner at the expense of such Tenant, and shall be of a size, color and style acceptable to Owner.

6. No Tenant shall mark, paint, drill into, or in any way deface any part of the demised premises or the building of which they form a part. No boring, cutting or stringing of wires shall be permitted, except with the prior written consent of Owner, and as Owner may direct. No Tenant shall lay linoleum, or other similar floor covering, so that the same shall come in direct contact with the floor of the demised premises, and, if linoleum or other similar floor covering is desired to be used an interlining of builder's deadening felt shall be first affixed to the floor, by a paste or other material, soluble in water, the use of cement or other similar adhesive material being expressly prohibited.

7. Freight, furniture, business equipment, merchandise and bulky matter of any description shall be delivered to and removed from the premises only on the freight elevators and through the service entrances and corridors, and only during hours and in a

manner approved by Owner. Owner reserves the right to inspect all freight to be brought into the building and to exclude from the building all freight which violates any of these Rules and Regulatiohs or the lease of which these Rules and Regulations are a part.

8. Owner reserves the right to exclude from the building between the hours of 6 P.M. and 8 A.M. and at all hours on Sundays, and holidays all persons who do not present a pass to the building signed by Owner. Owner will furnish passes to persons for whom any Tenant requests same in writing. Each Tenant shall be responsible for all persons for whom he requests such pass and shall be liable to Owner for all acts of such person.

9. Owner shall have the right to prohibit any advertising by any Tenant which, in Owner's opinion, tends to impair the reputation of Owner or its desirability as a building for stores or offices, and upon written notice from Owner, Tenant shall refrain from or discontinue such advertising.

10. Tenant shall not bring or permit to be brought or kept in or on the demised premises, any inflammable, combustible or explosive fluid, material, chemical or substance, or cause or permit any odors of cooking or other processes, or any unusual or other objectionable odors to permeate in or emanate from the demised premises.

11. Tenant shall not place a load on any floor of the demised premises exceeding the floor load per square foot area which it was designed to carry and which is allowed by law. Owner reserves the right to prescribe the weight and position of all safes, business machines and mechanical equipment. Such installations shall be placed and maintained by Tenant at Tenant's expense in setting sufficient in Owner's judgement to absorb and prevent vibration, noise and annoyance.

## GUARANTY

The undersigned Guarantor guarantees to Owner, Owner's successors and assigns, the full performance and observance of all the agreements to be performed and observed by Tenant in the attached Lease, including the "Rules and Regulations" as therein provided, without requiring any notice to Guarantor of nonpayment or, nonperformance, or proof, or notice of demand, to hold the undersigned responsible under this guaranty, all of which the undersigned hereby expressly waives and expressly agrees that the legality of this agreement and the agreements of the Guarantor under this agreement shall not be ended, or changed by reason of the claims to Owner against Tenant of any of the rights or remedies given to Owner as agreed in the attached Lease. The Guarantor further agrees that this guaranty shall remain and continue in full force and effect as to any renewal, change or extension of the Lease. As a further inducement to Owner to make the Lease Owner and Guarantor agree that in any action or proceeding brought by either Owner or the Guarantor against the other on any matters concerning the Lease or of this guaranty that Owner and the undersigned shall and do waive trial by jury.

..................... Guarantor

GENERAL PRINCIPLES § 1:15

## D. RESEARCH REFERENCES

### § 1:15. Generally

In addition to the preceding text, the reader is also referred to the following:

49 Am Jur 2d, Landlord and Tenant §§ 1-17

11 Am Jur Legal Forms 2d, Leases of Real Property §§ 161:31-161:36.

New York Jur 2d, Landlord and Tenant (1st ed §§ 1-13).

New York Forms, Leases, Forms 8:1-8:5.

Index to Annotations, Landlord and Tenant.

**VERALEX®:** Cases and annotations referred to herein can be further researched through the VERALEX electronic retrieval system's two services, **Auto-Cite®** and **SHOWME®**. Use Auto-Cite to check citations for form, parallel references, prior and later history, and annotation references. Use SHOWME to display the full text of cases and annotations.

# CHAPTER 2

# REQUISITES AND VALIDITY OF LEASES

A. IN GENERAL
- § 2:1. Necessity for Contract, Express or Implied
- § 2:2. Necessity of Privities of Contract and of Estate
- § 2:3. Necessity of Attornment
- § 2:4. Creation of Landlord-Tenant Relationship by Attornment to Title Paramount
- § 2:5. —By Attornment to Purchaser at Mortgage Foreclosure Sale
- § 2:6. —By Attornment to Stranger
- § 2:7. Necessity for a Valid Contract
- § 2:8. Lease Must Not be Unconscionable
- § 2:9. Delivery and Acceptance of Written Lease
- § 2:10. Necessity for Acknowledgment
- § 2:11. Fraud; Effect and Remedies
- § 2:12. Illegal Use; Effect
- § 2:13. Use in Violation of Subsequently Enacted Laws
- § 2:14. Subsequently Enacted Laws Prohibiting Principal Use
- § 2:15. Subsequently Enacted Laws Limiting Use
- § 2:16. Inability to Comply with Requirements of Law; Tenant at Fault
- § 2:17. —Landlord at Fault
- § 2:18. Violation of Departmental Orders
- § 2:19. Violation of Certificate of Occupancy
- § 2:20. Landlord's Failure to Obtain Certificate of Occupancy
- § 2:21. Zoning Violation
- § 2:22. Conditioning Lease to Protect Tenant in Event of Illegal Use
- § 2:23. Perpetual Leases
- § 2:24. Non-technical Language for Residential Lease (Plain English Law)

B. PARTIES TO A LEASE
- § 2:25. Generally
- § 2:26. The State of New York
- § 2:27. Aliens
- § 2:28. Tenants in Common or Joint Tenants
- § 2:29. Infants
- § 2:30. Insane Persons

§ 2:31. Life Tenant
§ 2:32. Trustees

C. DESCRIPTION OF PREMISES
§ 2:33. Generally
§ 2:34. Form of Description

D. STATUTE OF FRAUDS
§ 2:35. Generally
§ 2:36. Necessity for Pleading Statute
§ 2:37. Effect of Part Performance

E. RESEARCH REFERENCES
§ 2:38. Generally

## A. IN GENERAL

### § 2:1. Necessity for Contract, Express or Implied

The relationship of landlord and tenant, whereby an estate or interest in real property is transferred to a tenant giving him exclusive possession and control of such estate or interest, or the right to such exclusive possession and control,[1] is always created by contract, express or implied,[2] except in the case of a statutory tenancy, which is an exception to this rule.[3]

Although the reservation of rent is not essential to the creation of the landlord-tenant relationship,[4] yet an agreement to pay rent, or its payment and acceptance by the owner of land from one in possession, even though the possession may have been originally that of a trespasser, is deemed a recognition of the right of the occupant as a tenant, and sufficient to warrant the implication of the relation of landlord and tenant.[5] Where an alleged tenant paid the rent, took an assignment of the lease, and paid back rent and water meter rents to procure a discontinuance of a summary proceeding, and left his property in the leased premises and retained possession of the key, it was held that the conventional relationship of landlord and tenant arose by implication.[6] In other words, although the reservation of rent in a lease is not essential to create the relation of landlord

---

1. § 1:2, supra.
2. Stern v Equitable Trust Co. (1924) 238 NY 267, 144 NE 578; Lyddy v Ayling (NYC Civ Ct NY Co 1981) 111 Misc 2d 449, 444 NYS2d 823 (citing text).
3. §§ 10:11, et seq., infra.
4. See § 12:1, infra.
5. Re Bunshaft (AD4 1923) 207 AD 884, 202 NYS 177.
6. Sommer v James Everard's Breweries (1909, Sup App T) 117 NYS 972.

REQUISITES OF LEASES § 2:1

and tenant, yet it is a usual incident of a tenancy, and when it is doubtful whether or not a lease was intended, the fact that rent was not reserved is nomine or substantially becomes a very important circumstance.

The mere consent of an owner of land to the occupation thereof by another in and of itself does not necessarily imply consent to such occupation as tenant.[7] Thus, it has been held that the lawful possession of another's property in and of itself is not sufficient to create a landlord-tenant relationship.[8]

A contract creating the relation of landlord and tenant may be implied from the conduct of the parties.[9] No particular words are necessary to constitute a lease, it has been said,[10] where it appears that it was the intention of one party to dispossess himself of the premises, and of the other to enter and occupy as the former himself had the right to do. But, a contract creating the relation of landlord and tenant will not be implied where the acts and conduct of the parties negate its existence.[11] The test is the intention of the parties, to be derived from the whole instrument, if there is one, or if not, from the transaction.

The execution of a guaranty of the performance of a lease does not create the relation of landlord and tenant between the landlord and the guarantor.[12]

The relationship of landlord and tenant, it has been

---

**7.** Roberts v Eastman (Tioga Co Ct 1929) 134 Misc 677, 236 NYS 353.

**8.** United Secur. Corp. v Suchman (1954) 307 NY 48, 119 NE2d 881, reh den 307 NY 840, 122 NE2d 332; Lyddy v Ayling (NYC Civ Ct 1981) 111 Misc 2d 449, 444 NYS2d 823.

An agreement to pay rent or the reasonable value of use and occupation is not implied from mere occupation of the premises. New York v Fink (S Ct NY Co 1927) 130 Misc 620, 224 NYS 404.

One who purchases the stock of a bankrupt tenant, and who refuses to remove it on demand of the landlord, becomes liable for the reasonable value of the use and occupation of the premises; and such obligation does not rest on trespass or on contract, express or implied in fact, but is one imposed by law for the purpose of bringing about justice without reference to the intention of the parties. Rand Products Co. v Mintz (AD1 1973) 72 Misc 2d 621, 340 NYS2d 444.

**9.** Hershkopf v Engel (1913, Sup App T) 142 NYS 344.

**10.** Canton Steel Ceiling Co. v Duffy Malt Whiskey Co. (AD1 1922) 200 AD 306, 192 NYS 792.

**11.** Stern v Equitable Trust Co. (1924) 238 NY 267, 144 NE 578; Collyer v Collyer (1889) 113 NY 442, 21 NE 114; Geist v State (Ct Cls 1956) 3 Misc 2d 714, 156 NYS2d 183; Hershkopf v Engel (1913, Sup App T) 142 NYS 344.

**12.** Marburt Holding Corp. v Picto Corp. (1958, 1st Dept) 5 AD2d 617, 173 NYS2d 762, app gr (1st Dept) 6 AD2d 791, 175 NYS2d 582.

held, may be created by estoppel, in which case the relationship is created not by operation of law, but by acts of the parties, which estop the tenant from denying the existence of the relation.[13]

## § 2:2. Necessity of Privities of Contract and of Estate

When a landlord enters into a lease with his tenant, a twofold privity arises between them, to wit, a privity of contract, and a privity of estate. Privity of contract rests upon the terms of the agreement between the parties; privity of estate rests upon the interest in the real property leased.[14] The term "privity of estate" is usually defined as a mutual or successive relationship to the same rights of property.[15]

It is firmly established that it is essential to the existence of the relation of landlord and tenant that there be this twofold privity of contract and of estate between the parties.[16]

## § 2:3. Necessity of Attornment

Attornment is the act or agreement of a tenant accepting one person in the place of another as his landlord. At common law the consent or attornment of the tenant was essential to a grant of the reversion; that is, of the landlord's estate. It "signified only the consent of the tenant to the grant of the seigniory, whereby he agreed to become the tenant of the new lord.[17] This consent is no longer necessary; for, the Real Property Law expressly provides,[18] that an attornment to a grantee is not requisite to the validity of a conveyance of real property

---

13. De Vita v Pianisani (AT1 1926) 127 Misc 611, 217 NYS 438.

As to tenancies implied by entry under a void lease, see § 30:43, infra; and by holding over, see §§ 10:1, et seq., infra.

As to creation of landlord-tenant relationship by tenant's exercising option to purchase, see §§ 20:28, et seq., infra.

14. New Amsterdam Casualty Co. v National Union Fire Ins. Co. (1935) 266 NY 254, 194 NE 745, 99 ALR 216.

15. Re Shea's Will (1956) 309 NY 605, 132 NE2d 864; Mygatt v Coe (1891) 124 NY 212, 219, 26 NE 611, later app 142 NY 78, 36 NE 870.

16. New Amsterdam Casualty Co. v National Union Fire Ins. Co. (1935) 266 NY 254, 259, 194 NE 745, 99 ALR 216.

17. Re O'Donnell (1925) 240 NY 99, 147 NE 541.

18. Real Prop L § 248.

occupied by a tenant, or of the rents or profits thereof, or any other interest therein.[19]

Thus, attornment in its primary sense, as it was understood at common law, is an idle ceremony. The transfer of the reversion, whether with the consent of the tenant or without it, is a transfer of the lease and of its rights and obligations.[20]

## § 2:4. Creation of Landlord-Tenant Relationship by Attornment to Title Paramount

Although attornment by a tenant to the grantee of the reversion is not necessary to a transfer of the lease to the grantee, and thereby to create the relationship of landlord and tenant between the tenant and the grantee,[1] there remains, however, said the Court of Appeals,[2] "a secondary sense in which the act of attornment is still significant today. . . . Attornment may also mean the acknowledgment by a tenant that he holds under a new lord who claims by title paramount, and not by grant of the reversion or as privy to the reversioner. In such a situation, 'the new tenancy thus constituted, though popularly spoken of as a continuing tenancy,' is 'in fact a new contract and a new demise'. . . . Ratification of the old demise, at least in any proper sense, there obviously is none, for he who made the demise has not assumed to act for any one except himself, and least of all for one whose claim is paramount and hostile. . . . It is possible of course, to incorporate in the new demise, expressly or by implication, the provisions of the old one, including the term of its duration."

In other words, then, if nothing more is shown in this situation than the payment of rent to, and the acceptance thereof by, the owner of a paramount title, the result will be the creation either of a tenancy at will, or at most of one from year to year.[3]

Since, it is possible to incorporate in the new lease,

---

19. Real Prop L § 248 also provides that the payment of rent to the grantor by his tenant before notice of the conveyance will bind the grantee, and the tenant is not liable to the grantee, before such notice, for the breach of any condition of the lease.

20. Re O'Donnell (1925) 240 NY 99, 105, 147 NE 541.

1. § 2:3, supra.

2. Re O'Donnell (1925) 240 NY 99, 105, 147 NE 541.

3. Re O'Donnell (1925) 240 NY 99, 106, 147 NE 541.

expressly or by implication, the provisions of the old lease including the term of its duration, the question will be whether the payment and receipt of rent are supplemented by declarations and circumstances sufficient to justify a finding that the new lease incorporates the provisions of the old lease. However, if the unexpired term of the old lease be for a period longer than one year, it would seem that the requirements of the statute of frauds would have to be complied with.[4]

### § 2:5. —By Attornment to Purchaser at Mortgage Foreclosure Sale

As has been seen, attornment to a title paramount creates a new tenancy. The provisions of the old lease, including the term of its duration, may be incorporated in the new demise either expressly or by implication, provided, however, that if the remaining unexpired term of the old lease exceeds one year, the statute of frauds must be complied with.[5]

When a tenant holds under an unexpired lease subject to a mortgage, which is subsequently foreclosed, and after the sale in foreclosure free of the lease pays rent to the purchaser, there is an attornment. Under these circumstances the tenant will be deemed to hold from the new owner upon the same terms as he previously held from the landlord.[6] In other words, the courts have incorporated in the new lease by implication the provisions of the old lease. "The act of attornment," said the Appellate Division,[7] "evidenced by the payment of rent to the new owner and its acceptance by him, amounts to an acceptance of the new landlord by the tenant, and an acceptance of the tenancy by the landlord."

Accordingly, it has been held, that where, after a foreclosure sale, a tenant attorns to the purchaser, and thereby creates a new lease, which by implication incorporates the terms of the old lease, the tenant cannot

---

4. General Obligations L § 5-703.
Also, see, Re O'Donnell (1925) 240 NY 99, 106-107, 147 NE 541. See § 2:55, infra, as to effect of attornment after foreclosure sale.

5. See § 2:35, infra.

6. Jacob Reich, Inc. v Fordon (AD1 1931) 234 AD 110, 254 NYS 453; Kelley v Osborn (AD1 1916) 172 AD 6, 157 NYS 1100.

7. Kelley v Osborn (AD1 1916) 172 AD 6, 157 NYS 1100.

avoid liability for the rent for the remainder of the term by subsequently abandoning possession of the premises.[8]

### § 2:6. —By Attornment to Stranger

The Real Property Law provides[9] that the attornment of a tenant to a stranger is absolutely void, and does not in any way affect the possession of the landlord, unless such attornment is made with the consent of the landlord, or pursuant to or in consequence of a judgment, order, or decree of a court of competent jurisdiction,[10] or to a purchaser at a foreclosure sale. Therefore, although the relation of landlord and tenant can be created by attornment,[11] if the attornment is void, it is, as an attornment, inoperative for that or any other purpose.[12] Accordingly, if the attornment to a third person is void, it will not enable the tenant to set up the title of such third person in opposition to the title of his landlord,[13] and the tenant may, notwithstanding such attornment, dispute the title of the party to whom such attornment was made.[14]

Since a purchaser of land for nonpayment of taxes is a grantee of the state, he is not in privity with the former owner, and cannot be deemed to be an assignee of the reversion, but is a stranger, and an attornment by the tenant to him is void.[15]

### § 2:7. Necessity for a Valid Contract

The relationship of landlord and tenant must be created by contract, express or implied.[16] Fundamentally,

---

8. Jacob Reich, Inc. v Fordon (AD1 1931) 234 AD 110, 254 NYS 453; Kelley v Osborn (AD1 1916) 172 AD 6, 157 NYS 1100.

9. Real Prop L § 224.

10. Reversal of the judgment invalidates the attornment. Goldberg v Levine (AD1 1922) 199 AD 292, 192 NYS 124, where a subtenant attorned to a paramount landlord who had obtained a final order ousting the main tenant. This final order was thereafter reversed as a nullity for want of jurisdiction. The attornment was held to have been made to a stranger, and therefore was void and a nullity.

11. §§ 2:3, et seq, supra.

12. Maxrice Realty Corp. v B/G Sandwich Shops, Inc. (AD1 1933) 239 AD 472, 267 NYS 863; Goldberg v Levine (AD1 1922) 199 AD 292, 192 NYS 124; Donnelly v O'Day (Com Pl GT 1892) 1 Misc 165, 20 NYS 688.

13. Jackson ex dem Livingston v De Lancy, 13 Johns 537.

14. Maxrice Realty Corp. v B/G Sandwich Shops, Inc. (AD1 1933) 239 AD 472, 267 NYS 863 (action for rent); Donnelly v O'Day (Com Pl GT 1892) 1 Misc 165, 20 NYS 688 (summary proceedings).

Estoppel to deny landlord's title, see §§ 5:9, et seq, infra.

15. O'Donnel v McIntyre (1890) 118 NY 156, 23 NE 455.

16. § 2:1, supra.

then, the primary question is whether or not a valid contract has been made; for, if no valid contract has been entered into, then there is no agreement of any kind enforceable at law.[17] It is necessary to the formation of a lease that all the essentials of a contract be present.[18] The first requisite is a mutual assent or a meeting of the minds on all the essential elements or terms of the lease,[19] without the reservation of any such element for future negotiations. If a material element of a contemplated agreement is left open for future negotiation and agreement, there is no contract enforceable at all.[20] An agreement to agree is not enforceable.[1] In such a situation, the Court of Appeals said,[2] "The legal effect, or lack of effect, is the same as if the parties had left blanks in the writing, to be filled in later when their minds should meet."

Clearly, the mutual assent of the parties to a lease must be manifested by one party to the other.[3] Such mutual assent is manifested by an offer and an acceptance in the terms of that offer. That is to say, the acceptance of an offer to create a lease must be unconditional, and identical with the offer in order to create a valid lease. Thus, the signing of a form of lease by either the lessor or the lessee, and submitting the same to the other party thereto, constitutes a unilateral offer to lease.[4] If this offer is rejected, or met with a counteroffer, which is the equivalent of a rejection, no lease has been made.[5] Accordingly, if a lessor sends a proposed lease to

17. Foster v Clifford (AT 1904) 42 Misc 496, 86 NYS 28.
18. Israelson v Wollenberg (AT 1909) 63 Misc 293, 116 NYS 626.
19. Malone v Hirsch (AD3 1917) 181 AD 914, 167 NYS 723; Hennessy Realty Co. v Bernstein (AT1 1920) 110 Misc 331, 180 NYS 540.
20. 1130 President Street Corp. v Bolton Realty Corp. (1949) 300 NY 63, 89 NE2d 16, 16 ALR2d 617; Ansorge v Kane (1927) 244 NY 395, 155 NE 683, reh den 245 NY 530, 157 NE 845; Gordon v Siegel (S Ct Schenectady Co 1953) 125 NYS2d 862, mod on other grounds 284 AD 821, 132 NYS2d 437, reh den 284 AD 910, 134 NYS2d 193, vacated 284 AD 994, 136 NYS2d 377.

1. Per Pound J., St Regis Paper Co. v Hubbs & Hastings Paper Co. (1923) 235 NY 30, 36, 138 NE 495.
2. May Metropolitan Corp. v May Oil Burner Corp. (1943) 290 NY 260, 264, 49 NE2d 13.
3. Assent in the sense of the law is a matter of overt acts and expressions, not of inward unanimity in motives, design, or the interpretation of words. Porter v Commercial Casualty Ins. Co. (1944) 292 NY 176, 54 NE2d 353, reh den 292 NY 717, 56 NE2d 122.
4. Friedman v Washington Square Management Corp. (M Ct 1959) 19 Misc 2d 46, 187 NYS2d 888 (affd AT1, April, 1960).
5. Lex-56th Corp. v Morgan (M Ct 1960) 24 Misc 2d 48, 203 NYS2d 59,

## REQUISITES OF LEASES § 2:7

the lessee who alters it, signs it, and returns it to the lessor who refuses to consent to the alteration, no binding lease has been made.[6]

The duration of the term of a lease must be certain, either by the express limitation of the parties at the time the lease is made, or ascertainable by reference to some collateral fact which may with equal certainty measure the continuance of the term; otherwise the lease will be void.[7] That a lease contains a provision for the earlier termination of the term does not render the term uncertain, and thereby prevent the creation of a valid term.[8]

As in the case of contracts generally, a lease to be enforceable must be supported by a valid consideration, or there must exist at the time of its inception mutuality of obligation.[9] Ordinarily the payment of rent is the consideration for a lease.[10] Although at common law a sealed instrument carried with it the presumption that it was given for a valid consideration,[11] it is now provided by

app den (1st Dept) 13 AD2d 912, 217 NYS2d 1020.

**6.** Israelson v Wollenberg (AT 1909) 63 Misc 293, 116 NYS 626.

Where a lessee rejects the offer, he cannot thereafter accept it. Westwitt Realty Corp. v Burger (AD1 1925) 212 AD 622, 209 NYS 486. In this case, after the lessee had inserted a one-year term in a proffered lease for two years, which the lessor rejected, it was held that the lessee could not thereafter accept the original offer.

Whether commercial or residential, and if residential, rent stabilized or free from statutory controls, a written lease agreement requires the formalities of signature by both parties for its proper execution. East 56th Plaza, Inc. v New York City Concilliation & Appeals Bd. (1981, 1st Dept) 80 AD2d 389, 439 NYS2d 361, revd on other grounds 56 NY2d 544, 449 NYS2d 959, 434 NE2d 1337.

**7.** Western Transp. Co. v Lansing (1872) 49 NY 499; Gaswell Service, Inc. v Sinclair Refining Co. (AD2 1934) 240 AD 240, 269 NYS 195, affd 266 NY 539, 195 NE 190; Levy v Amelias (S Ct Cayuga Co 1955) 207 Misc 880, 141 NYS2d 101, affd (4th Dept) 1 AD2d 755, 148 NYS2d 921.

Lease for as long a period as tenant remains an active club is void for indefiniteness; what constitutes an active club, and whether tenant remains one, are subjective, and incapable of measurement. Genesee Conservation Foundation, Inc. v Oatka Fish & Game Club, Inc. (1978, 4th Dept) 63 AD2d 1115, 405 NYS2d 869.

A lease is not void although no specific commencement date is set forth, if it provides for a definitely ascertainable commencement date; e.g., tenant understands that the leased premises are presently occupied by the prior tenant, who has indicated that he will vacate on or about a specified date, and landlord shall give notice to tenant promptly after being advised by the prior tenant of the date on which he will actually vacate. 67 Wall Street Co. v Franklin Nat. Bank (1972, 1st Dept) 38 AD2d 460, 330 NYS2d 670.

**8.** Kavanaugh v Cohoes Power & Light Corp. (S Ct Albany Co 1921) 114 Misc 590, 187 NYS 216.

**9.** Dennis Realty Corp. v Twersky (M Ct 1947) 190 Misc 936, 76 NYS2d 798.

**10.** Kavanaugh v Cohoes Power & Light Corp. (S Ct Albany Co 1921) 114 Misc 590, 187 NYS 216.

**11.** Crocker v Page (AD3 1924) 210

111

statute that except as otherwise expressly provided by statute, the presence or absence of a seal upon a written instrument shall be without legal effect.[12]

### § 2:8. Lease Must Not Be Unconscionable

Leases are subject to judicial scrutiny under the concept of unconscionability,[13] and if the lease or any provision thereof is found to have been unconscionable when made, the court may refuse to enforce the lease or the unconscionable provision.[14]

### § 2:9. Delivery and Acceptance of Written Lease

Before a written lease becomes effective, there must be both a delivery and acceptance with the intent of making the lease an effective conveyance. "The law is too well settled to require the citation of many authorities," said Merrell, J.,[15] "that any deed or instrument, although fully executed, is without force or effect, until delivered."[16] A lease is deemed a grant,[17] and takes effect, so as to vest the estate or interest intended to be conveyed, only from its delivery.[18] However, a delivery of a lease so as to give it effect, requires acts or words, or both acts and words, which clearly manifest that it is the intent of the parties that an interest in the land is, in fact, being conveyed to the lessee.[19]

Of course, a contract may be delivered conditionally, in

AD 735, 206 NYS 481, affd 240 NY 638, 148 NE 738.

12. Gen Constr L § 44-a.

13. State v Wolowitz (1983, 2d Dept) 96 AD2d 47, 468 NYS2d 131.

14. See § 6:13, infra.

15. Ross v Ross (AD1 1931) 233 AD 626, 253 NYS 871, affd 262 NY 381, 187 NE 65, 89 ALR 1007, reh den 262 NY 643, 188 NE 102, 89 ALR 1023.

16. 219 Broadway Corp. v Alexander's, Inc. (1979) 46 NY2d 506, 414 NYS2d 889, 387 NE2d 1205 (citing text); Beck v New York News, Inc. (1983, 1st Dept) 92 AD2d 823, 460 NYS2d 326, affd 61 NY2d 620, 471 NYS2d 850, 459 NE2d 1287.

17. Real Prop L § 246.

18. Real Prop L § 244.

Section 2502.5(c)(9) of the State Tenant Protection Regulations, adopted and promulgated under the Emergency Tenant Protection Act of 1974, provides: "Each owner shall furnish to each tenant signing a new or renewal lease, a copy of the fully executed new or renewal lease bearing the signature of owner and tenant, and the beginning and ending dates of the lease term, within thirty days from the owner's receipt of the new or renewal lease signed by the tenant. The failure to do so will result in the noncollectibility of the guidelines increase otherwise authorized for such lease, until the first rent payment date following the receipt by the tenant of the fully executed lease. For renewal of leases, use of the form prescribed under Section 2503.5 (a) of these Regulations shall be deemed as compliance herewith."

19. 219 Broadway Corp. v Alexander's, Inc. (1979) 46 NY2d 506, 414 NYS2d 889, 387 NE2d 1205 (citing text).

which case it will not be valid until the condition is fulfilled.[20] Thus, where it is mutually agreed between the parties to leave a lease with a person to obtain the signatures thereto of other parties named therein, and thereafter to deliver the lease, a delivery by such person before the signatures of the specified parties are obtained is ineffective to give validity to the lease.[1]

But, it must be observed, in order to complete the delivery of a lease, and to make the instrument operate as a conveyance, an acceptance on the part of the lessee is essential.[2] The delivery of a lease without acceptance is nugatory.[3] Even a lease by way of gift which imposes no obligations on the lessee other than those necessarily incident to the ownership of a leasehold requires acceptance to be operative, for an estate cannot be thrust upon a person against his will.[4] If a lease is executed and delivered to the lessee, and it is beneficial to him, the law may imply an acceptance thereof from his actions or conduct.[5] Although there may be a presumption of acceptance from the beneficial nature of the transaction, there still must be acceptance, and acceptance must be found as a fact.[6]

## § 2:10. Necessity for Acknowledgment

A lease, although a conveyance,[7] does not involve a grant of either a fee or a freehold, and therefore is not required either to be acknowledged or attested in order to be valid.[8] However, a lease of real property for a term exceeding three years, being a conveyance for recording purposes,[9] must be acknowledged, if it is to be recorded, since acknowledgment is necessary as a condition for the recording thereof.[10]

20. First Nat. Bank & Trust Co. v Conzo (S Ct Chemung Co 1938) 169 Misc 268, 7 NYS2d 334.
1. Whitford v Laidler (1883) 94 NY 145.
2. Flommerfelt v Englander (AT 1889) 29 Misc 655, 61 NYS 187.
3. Koehler v Hughes (1896) 148 NY 507, 42 NE 1051.
4. Jackson ex dem McRea v Dunlap, 1 Johns Cas 114.
5. William Wicke Co. v Kaldenberg Manuf'g Co. (AT 1897) 21 Misc 79, 46 NYS 937; M. H. Harris, Inc. v Massry (1941, Sup App T) 27 NYS2d 694.
6. Buszozak v Wolo (S Ct Jefferson Co 1925) 125 Misc 546, 211 NYS 557.
7. § 1:2, supra.
8. Herubin v Malackowski (Oneida Co Ct 1920) 113 Misc 100, 184 NYS 829; Real Prop L § 243 requires acknowledgment or attestation of a grant of a fee or a freehold.
9. § 1:2, supra.
10. Real Prop L § 291.

### § 2:11. Fraud; Effect and Remedies

Since a lease is a contract,[11] the rules of contract law with respect to the reality of the assent of the parties thereto, including matters of mistake, fraud, undue influence, and duress, are equally applicable to leases.

As to what constitutes fraud, the general rule that fraud may be predicated on promises made with an intention not to perform them is also applicable to leases, as in the case of a promise to occupy premises and pay rent therefor,[12] or a promise by the owner of real property to execute a lease to a purchaser of the promisee's business if he finds one.[13] However, the landlord's failure to comply with a promise to make repairs does not constitute a fraudulent representation voiding the lease, in the absence of proof that there was an intent not to keep the promise.[14]

Similarly, the general rule that the affirmation of what one does not know or believe to be true is equally unjustifiable as the affirmation of what is known to be positively false, is applicable to leases. Thus, where a landlord falsely warrants that a specified use of the leased premises by the lessee is permissible and does not violate any statute, ordinance, or restriction, he is guilty of fraud, and liable in damages therefor, even though such use is illegal, since the action to recover damages is not predicated upon the illegal contract.[1] Such a misrepresentation on the part of the landlord as to the legality of use of leased premises will not, as to the tenant, be treated as an opinion of law, and, therefore, fraud will lie for such a misrepresentation.[2]

Whether or not a fraudulent misrepresentation is sufficiently material to warrant relief, if relied on by the tenant, depends upon the facts of the case. The question

---

11. § 1:2, supra.
12. Scaroon Manor Operating Corp. v W. P. & L. Realty Corp. (S Ct NY Co 1930) 136 Misc 910, 241 NYS 229.
13. Rosenwald v Goldfein (1957, 1st Dept) 3 AD2d 206, 159 NYS2d 333, reh and app den (1st Dept) 3 AD2d 744, 161 NYS2d 568.
14. Hone v Burr (Oneida Co Ct 1915) 91 Misc 520, 155 NYS 377.
1. National Conversion Corp. v Cedar Bldg. Corp. (1969) 23 NY2d 621, 298 NYS2d 499 246 NE2d 351; Municipal Metallic Bed Mfg. Corp. v Dobbs (1930) 253 NY 313, 171 NE 75, 68 ALR 1376; Feinsilver v Conrad (1959, 2d Dept) 9 AD2d 769, 192 NYS2d 673.
2. National Conversion Corp. v Cedar Bldg. Corp. (1969) 23 NY2d 621, 298 NYS2d 499, 246 NE2d 351; Municipal Metallic Bed Mfg. Corp. v Dobbs (1930) 253 NY 313, 171 NE 75, 68 ALR 1376.

whether or not facts are material is, from its very nature, not susceptible of abstract determination, but depends upon the factual situation involved in each case.[3] Immaterial representations, generally, are those relating to collateral matters, that is, matters which do not constitute an essential element of the lease,[4] and those inducing one to do what he is bound to do.[5] Where a landlord falsely represented, as an inducement to a tenant to enter into the lease sued upon, that he was paying a certain rental for the premises, such misrepresentation was not material. But, a representation that his lease was not restricted except that the premises were not to be used as a restaurant or saloon, was material.[6] A false representation to a prospective tenant of part of a building that the rents paid by the tenants are the same throughout the building, which induces the prospective tenant to enter into a lease at a higher rental than he otherwise might have done is material.[7] A lessee is not entitled to relief based upon an alleged false representation of the lessor that a provision orally agreed upon was contained in the lease, where the lessee failed to read the lease, although having the opportunity to do so, and continued to occupy the premises for some time without objection.[8]

A tenant who has been induced to enter into a lease by fraudulent misrepresentations has a choice of remedies. He may disaffirm or rescind the lease. Upon rescission, he ceases to be obligated to pay any rent accruing after the rescission.[9] He also may recover such moneys as he may have paid under the lease, such as deposit moneys, rents, and the like, as a consequence of the fraudulent acts of the landlord, as moneys had and received.[10] But a tenant cannot rescind the lease upon the ground of fraud, where

3. Chiodo v Garramone (S Ct Onondaga Co 1958) 11 Misc 2d 743, 175 NYS2d 490.

4. Metropolitan Life Ins. Co. v Union Trust Co. (AD4 1944) 268 AD 474, 51 NYS2d 318, reh den 268 AD 958, 52 NYS2d 567 and affd 294 NY 254, 62 NE2d 59, reh den 294 NY 962, 63 NE2d 187.

5. Herrmann v Glens Falls Indem. Co. (AD2 1938) 255 AD 854, 7 NYS2d 392.

6. Humphreys v Roberts (AT 1908) 61 Misc 284, 113 NYS 792.

7. Greene v O'Leary (1921, Sup App T) 191 NYS 338.

8. Moloughney v White (1918, Sup App T) 168 NYS 532.

9. National Conversion Corp. v Cedar Bldg. Corp. (1969) 23 NY2d 621, 298 NYS2d 499, 246 NE2d 351; Daly v Wise (1892) 132 NY 306, 30 NE 837.

10. Fileman v Mooney (AD2 1918) 184 AD 535, 172 NYS 554. Also, see National Conversion Corp. v Cedar Bldg. Corp. (1969) 23 NY2d 621, 298 NYS2d 499, 246 NE2d 351.

he fails to promptly surrender possession of the property upon the discovery of the fraud.[11] If he continues the use and occupancy of the premises received under the lease, he will be deemed to have elected to affirm the lease. His remedy thereafter, if any, is to recover damages suffered as a result of the fraud.[12]

One who has been induced to execute a lease by fraud may waive the alleged fraud, affirm the lease, and claim damages by reason of the fraud. A lease induced by fraud is merely voidable, not void, and may be ratified by the defrauded party.[13]

It is fundamental that a court of equity has the power to compel the surrender and cancellation of deeds and other written instruments obtained by fraud or held for inequitable and unconscionable purposes.[14] Therefore, if proper grounds exist, a court exercising equitable jurisdiction may direct the recission or cancellation of a lease.[15] Thus, where a prospective tenant was presented with a "typical floor plan" of the apartment he was about to lease, and was not given much of an opportunity to inspect the rooms, a discrepancy of nine and one-half per cent between the actual floor space and that shown by the floor plan was held to have justified him in repudiating the lease before taking possession, and entitled him to a cancellation of it.[16]

Under the general principles of equity relating to the reformation of instruments, it is well established that if a lease, through fraud or mutual mistake, fails to express the intention of the parties thereto, it may be reformed, in equity, upon parol testimony, to effect such intention, when the proof of the fraud or mistake, and what the real agreement was, is clear, satisfactory, and convincing.[17] Similarly, where it is established that because of the

11. Barr v New York, L. E. & W. R. Co. (1891) 125 NY 263, 26 NE 145, reh den (NY) 27 NE 411; Stayton Realty Corp. v Rhodes (AD1 1922) 200 AD 108, 192 NYS 683, affd 234 NY 515, 138 NE 428; Cochran v Scherer (M Ct 1922) 117 Misc 765, 192 NYS 199.

12. Pryor v Foster (1891) 130 NY 171, 179, 29 NE 123.

13. Barr v New York, L. E. & W. R. Co. (1891) 125 NY 263, 26 NE 145, reh den (NY) 27 NE 411.

14. McHenry v Hazard (1871) 45 NY 580, 583.

15. Whitcombe, McGeachin & Co. v Schulte Real Estate Co. (AD1 1933) 238 AD 58, 263 NYS 369 (cancellation for fraud).

16. Shale v Butler (S Ct NY Co 1912) 136 NYS 252.

17. Zimmerman v Goodman Mortg. & Realty Co. (S Ct Kings Co 1921) 191 NYS 698. See also C. L. Holding Corp. v Schutt Court Homes, Inc. (AD1

fraud of the landlord plus the unilateral mistake of the tenant, an agreement intended to be part of the written lease was omitted, reformation of such lease is warranted by a court of equity.[18]

Although a defrauded party has a choice of remedies, the common law doctrine of election of remedies by the mere institution of an action has been nullified by the adoption of former CPA § 112-e,[19] and which has been re-enacted as CPLR 3002(e).[20] This statute permits damages for fraud or misrepresentation to be recovered when joined with a claim for rescission. A claim for damages sustained as a result of fraud is not to be deemed inconsistent with a claim for rescission or based upon rescission. The aggrieved party may obtain complete relief in the one action, but such complete relief shall not include duplication of items of recovery.[1] Thus, a lessee in the one action may sue for rescission of a lease for fraud, and for the resulting damages.[2]

### § 2:12. Illegal Use; Effect

It is fundamental that an illegal contract is void, and will not be enforced by the courts in favor of either party thereto.[3] Therefore, if premises are let to be used for an illegal purpose, the lease is illegal, void, and unenforceable by either party to the lease against the other.[4] Where a lease on its face, whether or not so intended by the parties, offends against statutes intended to promote public safety, the courts will not enforce it.[5]

---

1952) 280 AD 341, 113 NYS2d 610, affd 307 NY 648, 120 NE2d 837.

18. Barash v Pennsylvania Terminal Real Estate Corp. (1970) 26 NY2d 77, 308 NYS2d 649, 256 NE2d 707.

19. L 1941, ch 315.

20. Riviera Congress Associates v Yassky (S Ct NY Co 1965) 48 Misc 2d 282, 264 NYS2d 624, mod on other grounds (1st Dept) 25 AD2d 291, 268 NYS2d 854, affd 18 NY2d 540, 277 NYS2d 386, 223 NE2d 876.

1. CPLR 3002(e).

2. Looney v Smith (S Ct Queens Co 1950) 198 Misc 99, 96 NYS2d 607.

3. Hart v City Theatres Co. (1915) 215 NY 322, 325, 330, 109 NE 497; Ernst v Crosby (1893) 140 NY 364, 367, 35 NE 603.

4. Ernst v Crosby (1893) 140 NY 364, 35 NE 603, premises leased for use as a house of prostitution; Ober v Metropolitan Life Ins. Co. (City Ct NY Co 1935) 157 Misc 869, 284 NYS 966, motion den 157 Misc 872, 284 NYS 969, lease of apartment for valet shop in a restricted residential district; Hartsin Const. Corp. v Millhauser (AT1 1930) 136 Misc 646, 241 NYS 428, lease for haberdashery store in a restricted residential district; Railroad Stores, Inc. v Fabyan & Co. (City Ct NY Co 1922) 120 Misc 142, 197 NYS 815, lease for use as wholesale drug business, city ordinance prohibited such use because building not fireproof.

5. Hart v City Theatres Co. (1915) 215 NY 322, 109 NE 497.

§ 2:12  LANDLORD AND TENANT

By statute, it is provided that whenever the lessee or occupant other than the owner of any building or premises shall use or occupy the same, or any part thereof, for any illegal trade, manufacture, or other business, the lease or agreement for the letting or occupancy of such building or premises or any part thereof shall thereupon become void, and the landlord of such lessee or occupant may enter upon the premises so let or occupied.[6] The statute further provides that the owner of real property, knowingly leasing or giving possession of the same to be used or occupied, wholly or partly, for any unlawful trade, manufacture or business, or knowingly permitting the same to be so used, is liable severally, and also jointly with one or more of the tenants or occupants thereof, for any damage resulting from such unlawful use, occupancy, trade, manufacture or business.[7]

However, where a lease contemplates a correctly and lawfully occupied premises, and it is understood that alterations may have to be made to accomplish such purpose, the lease is not void for illegality merely because the alterations are required by the authorities. The lease will fail as a valid contract only if the contemplated correction becomes impossible, and the legal bar to the sole use within the terms of the lease remains in force. Thus, where premises were leased for a specified use only, and the parties clearly indicated that alterations might have to be made to permit the lawful conduct of such use; for example, reinforce the floors, which tenant undertook to make at its own expense, the lease was held to be a

---

6. Real Prop L § 231, subd 1.
See Chapter 34 infra, in which this subject is discussed, in connection with proceedings to recover possession because of illegal use.

7. Real Prop L § 231, subd 2.
Penal L § 230.40 (derived from former Penal L § 1146) provides that a person is guilty of permitting prostitution when, having possession or control of premises which he knows are being used for prostitution purposes, he fails to make reasonable effort to halt or abate such use.

Real Prop L § 231, subd 3 (added L 1976, ch 495, eff July 6, 1976), provides, "For the purposes of this section, two or more convictions of any person or persons had, within a period of one year, for any of the offenses described in section 230.00, 230.05, 230.20, 230.25, 230.30, or 230.40 of the penal law arising out of conduct engaged in at the same premises consisting of a dwelling as that term is defined in subdivision four of section four of the multiple dwelling law shall be presumptive evidence of unlawful use of such premises and of the owners knowledge of the same."

Under Real Prop L § 231, subds 4 and 5 (added L 1980, ch 206, eff June 9, 1980) the same presumptions apply to gambling.

# REQUISITES OF LEASES § 2:13

valid lease. But, where it became impossible to make such alterations because another tenant in the building refused to give his consent (beams had to be installed in the other tenant's premises), the contract then failed. Thereupon, it was held, the tenant could disavow the lease and recover back the security moneys. Nevertheless, since the lease was valid, the tenant was liable for all rent accruing for the period he remained in possession.[8] Similarly, a lease providing for a use of leased premises which is prohibited by the zoning law is not necessarily illegal where it appears that an appeal board has the authority to permit a variance.[9]

## § 2:13. Use in Violation of Subsequently Enacted Laws

A lease is not saved from the taint of illegality because the use of the premises becomes unlawful after the execution and operation of the lease, but during the term thereof.[10] There is no distinction in principle between a contract the execution of which is unlawful at the time it is made, and therefore void, and one the further performance of which becomes unlawful because of some subsequent change in the law.[11] Where a lease restricts and limits the use of the leased premises to a particular specified purpose, and thereafter, because of the enactment of statutes, governmental decrees or regulations, such use becomes unlawful, the subject matter of the contract is destroyed, and the covenants of such lease will not thereafter be enforced against either party thereto.[12]

---

**8.** Elkar Realty Corp. v Mitsuye T. Kamada (1958, 1st Dept) 6 AD2d 155, 175 NYS2d 669, reh and app den (1st Dept) 6 AD2d 1007, 178 NYS2d 212 and reh den (1st Dept) 6 AD2d 1007, 179 NYS2d 840 and app dismd 5 NY2d 844, 181 NYS2d 786, 155 NE2d 669.

**9.** Verschell v Pike (1981, 2d Dept) 85 AD2d 690, 445 NYS2d 489.

**10.** O'Neill v Derderian (M Ct 1930) 138 Misc 488, 246 NYS 341.

**11.** Doherty v Monroe Eckstein Brewing Co. (AD1 1921) 198 AD 708, 191 NYS 59; Railroad Stores, Inc. v Fabyan & Co. (City Ct NY Co 1922) 120 Misc 142, 197 NYS 815.

**12.** Byrnes v Balcom (AD3 1942) 265 AD 268, 38 NYS2d 801, affd 290 NY 730, 49 NE2d 1004; Hizington v Eldred Refining Co. (AD4 1932) 235 AD 486, 257 NYS 464, regulations adopted by commissioner of public safety prohibited use of premises for specified use; H. B. Shontz Co. v Laffay (AD1 1929) 225 AD 263, 232 NYS 614, fire department ordered business discontinued; O'Neill v Derderian (M Ct 1930) 138 Misc 488, 246 NYS 341, apartment house leased for furnished rooms only, prohibited by subsequently enacted Multiple Dwelling Laws.

As the Appellate Term said,[13] "The parties to the lease contracted to do a thing which at the time the lease was made was lawful. Public authority, in accordance with law, has provided that the very thing which the parties in their lease contemplated should not be done. To carry out the lease according to its terms has now become unlawful. It follows, therefore, that the lease cannot be performed according to its terms, and under such circumstances the obligation of the lessee to pay rent is discharged."

### § 2:14. Subsequently Enacted Laws Prohibiting Principal Use

If after a lease is executed, statutes, governmental decrees, or regulations prohibit the tenant from using the premises for the primary or principal use for which the premises were leased, that is, they deprive the tenant of the beneficial use of the property, the lease is terminated even though other incidental uses might still be made of the premises.[14] Thus, where national emergency regulations had the effect of prohibiting indefinitely the construction of a theatre, required under the terms of a 99-year lease to be erected by a specified time, it was held that the purpose of the lease would fail entirely, and therefore, under the doctrine of complete frustration, the lease was voided by operation of law.[15]

### § 2:15. Subsequently Enacted Laws Limiting Use

Where the use to which leased premises may be put is expressly limited, the subsequent passage of laws prohibiting such limited use terminates the lease.[16] However, a change in the law during the term which merely restricts the specified use of the premises, but does not wholly prohibit the conduct of the business carried on, does not release the tenant from his obligation to pay rent.[17] A lease provided that the premises were to be used for the sale of automobiles, automobile parts, or any accessories

---

13. Adler v Miles (AT 1910) 69 Misc 601, 126 NYS 135.
14. Doherty v Monroe Eckstein Brewing Co. (AD1 1921) 198 AD 708, 191 NYS 59; Kaiser v Zeigler (AT2 1921) 115 Misc 281, 187 NYS 638.
15. Gardiner Properties, Inc. v Samuel Leider & Son, Inc. (AD1 1952) 279 AD 470, 111 NYS2d 88, reh and app den 279 AD 1046, 113 NYS2d 254.
16. § 2:13, supra.
17. Byrnes v Balcom (AD3 1942) 265 AD 268, 38 NYS2d 801, affd 290 NY 730, 49 NE2d 1004.

REQUISITES OF LEASES § 2:15

pertaining to the sale of automobiles. By permission of the landlord, the tenant also used the premises for servicing and repairing cars. Thereafter the government restricted the sale of new cars. The tenant vacated the premises, and defended an action brought to recover rent by contending that the primary and principal use or purpose of the rental of premises within the contemplation of the parties was the sale of new cars; that the government prohibited this, and therefore the primary use had been rendered illegal, and the lease void. In overruling the tenant's contention, the court[18] pointed out that the lease did not limit the use of the premises only to the sale of new cars. It is quite apparent that the lease was made to conduct a general automobile business. True, the lease contemplated the sale of new cars, but the tenant is not restricted to the exclusive sale of such cars, but may devote the property to other legal uses specified in the lease. Furthermore, the tenant's right to sell new cars is not entirely prohibited, but merely restricted. Therefore, this is not a case where a use, which was not illegal when made, was made illegal by subsequent statutes. The tenant's use of the demised premises is merely restricted. Accordingly, the lease was held to be in full force and effect, and the tenant held liable for the rent.

In another case involving a gasoline service station, where federal orders restricted the sale of gasoline and tires, the Appellate Division said[19] "The governmental orders do not regulate the use of the premises but merely control transactions in gasoline, tires, casings and tubes without regard to any particular parcel of property . . . . Were we to accept defendant's interpretation of the agreement any rule, order or regulation of public authority, even of temporary duration, which might affect defendant's business and restrict its profits would allow the defendant to cancel the lease. . . . The federal regulations in question do not restrict the use of the land demised, but they control the business of the defendant. A business

---

18. Byrnes v Balcom (AD3 1942) 265 AD 268, 38 NYS2d 801, affd 290 NY 730, 49 NE2d 1004. Also, see, Colonial Operating Corp. v Hannan Sales & Service (AD2 1943) 265 AD 411, 39 NYS2d 217, app gr 266 AD 742, 41 NYS2d 953.

19. Robitzek Investing Co. v Colonial Beacon Oil Co. (AD1 1943) 265 AD 749, 40 NYS2d 819, app den 266 AD 775, 42 NYS2d 922.

§ 2:15            LANDLORD AND TENANT

enterprise of the type involved is subject to regulation by public agencies, but here that risk must be borne by defendant and not plaintiff."

In other words, where there is complete frustration of performance of a contract by statute or act of government, cancellation of the lease is permissible. Where, however, there is not complete frustration, and the tenant can continue to utilize the leased premises within the terms of the lease, though the volume of his business might suffer substantial diminution because of the statute or regulatory measures, then the tenant is bound by the lease which continues in full force and effect.[20]

### § 2:16. Inability to Comply with Requirements of Law; Tenant at Fault

A distinction is made between a lease which contemplates a use which is unlawful under all circumstances, and one which contemplates a lawful use, but whether or not the premises can be so used depends upon compliance with certain requirements of law, or the exercise of legal discretion by governmental authority in favor of such use.[1]

If a tenant is unable to obtain a license, which is required by statute to enable him to conduct his proposed business, and he therefore is unable to use the leased premises for the use specified in the lease, the tenant will not thereby be relieved of his obligations under the lease.[2]

---

20. Gardiner Properties, Inc. v Samuel Leider & Son, Inc. (AD1 1952) 279 AD 470, 111 NYS2d 88, reh and app den 279 AD 1046, 113 NYS2d 254, where court held that if national emergency regulation had effect of prohibiting indefinitely the construction of a theatre, required under the terms of a 99-year lease to be erected by a time certain, purpose of lease would fail entirely, and lease would be void under doctrine of complete frustration.

Also, see Coffin v United Mfg. Trimming Co. (AT1 1914) 85 Misc 402, 147 NYS 463, where, because of an order of the fire commissioner the tenant had to discontinue one of the purposes permitted by the lease, the tenant was denied the right to abandon the premises. The court said, "Hardships resulting from acts of sovereignty, or the exercise of police power, must be borne by those affected thereby, whether tenants or landlords, and must be deemed to have been in contemplation of the contracting parties at the time they entered into the contract of hiring."

1. 56-70 58th Street Holding Corp. v Fedders-Quigan Corp. (1959) 5 NY2d 557, 186 NYS2d 583, 159 NE2d 150, adhered to 7 NY2d 752, 193 NYS2d 665, 162 NE2d 747.

See *Annotation:* Inability to obtain license, permit, or charter required for tenant's business as defense to enforcement of lease. 89 ALR3d 329.

2. Raner v Goldberg (1927) 244 NY 438, 155 NE 733; Louis Friedman Realty Co. v De Stefan (AD1 1927) 220 AD 661, 222 NYS 371; Kerley v

## REQUISITES OF LEASES § 2:16

The rules discussed in the preceding sections applied to instances where the leases provided for a use which provisions of law then existing or thereafter enacted made unlawful under all possible circumstances. Such rules have no application to the instant situation where a lease provides for a use which the tenant knows, or should know, will be lawful only if a governmental authority exercises legal discretion in favor of such use. In one case, in which this rule was applied, the lease provided that the premises were to be used as a dance hall. To conduct a dance hall it was necessary to procure a license, the granting of which rested in the discretion of the licensing board. The court found that the tenant and landlord were cognizant of this fact. After entering into possession, the tenant was unable to obtain the license, and thereupon brought suit for the return of the deposit money and the first month's rent he had paid in advance. The court refused to grant the tenant any recovery;[3] for, as the court said, "The parties in making the contract of lease did not intend that the premises should be used for an illegal purpose. They intended that the demised premises should be used as a dance hall only when the lessee had obtained a license. A contract so made is not unlawful." They knew, the court held, that the granting of the necessary license was within the discretion of the public officer, and therefore they could have conditioned the lease on the license being granted. "We may not now imply a condition," the court said, "which the parties chose not to insert in their contract, nor hold that the anticipated grant of a license constituted the foundation of the contract, when both parties knew that the grant of a license depended on the discretion of a public officer." Since the tenant had failed to condition the lease on the procuring of the license, the lease was not thereby voided. Similarly, where the weight-bearing capacity of a floor leased to be used for a "tea room and restaurant and for no other purpose" was 75 pounds "live load" per square foot, and the statutory requirement for a restaurant was 100 pounds per square foot, and the lease expressly

---

Mayer (Com Pl GT 1895) 10 Misc 718, 31 NYS 818, affd 155 NY 636, 49 NE 1099.

3. Raner v Goldberg (1927) 244 NY 438, 155 NE 733.

required the tenant to occupy the premises in such a way as not to place upon the floor a load per square foot in excess of that "allowed by law," and to make alterations required to comply with the law, it was held that the lease was not void for illegality. The lease contemplated a correctly, and lawfully, occupied premises. It would fail as a valid contract only if the contemplated correction became impossible through no fault of the tenant, and the legal bar to the sole use within the terms of the lease remained in force. The parties by their very language showed that they intended that the correction was to be made, and that the bar to legal use was readily correctible.[4]

### § 2:17. —Landlord at Fault

Where the inability to obtain the necessary license is not due to the discretionary act of the licensing official, but due solely to the landlord's fault, the lease is voidable at the election of the tenant. Thus, where a lease stipulated that the premises should be used as a cabaret only, and such use was illegal in the building leased because the building was not fireproof, and a license was refused by the authorities on this ground, the lease was held to be voidable at the tenant's election.[5] In distinguishing this situation from the situation discussed in the preceding section,[6] the Appellate Term said, "There, as here, the parties knew that the right to use the premises for the purpose contemplated depended upon the procurement of a license, but in that case the granting or withholding of the license rested in the discretion of the licensing official. If the tenant chose to take a lease without conditions

---

4. Elkar Realty Corp. v Mitsuye T. Kamada (1958, 1st Dept) 6 AD2d 155, 175 NYS2d 669, reh and app den (1st Dept) 6 AD2d 1007, 178 NYS2d 212 and reh den (1st Dept) 6 AD2d 1007, 179 NYS2d 840 and app dismd 5 NY2d 844, 181 NYS2d 786, 155 NE2d 669, where the court said, "On the other hand it would be contemplated in such a leasing that the necessary changes would take some time to negotiate and carry out; and it would be expected certainly that while this was going on the rent should be paid. If, however, it became impossible to make the changes through no fault of the tenant, the lease would be deemed to terminate. It would thereupon have become demonstrated that the intended correction of the unlawful condition could not be effected; and the termination of the lease could be found to have resulted by the implied agreement of the parties flowing consequently from the language of the lease."

5. Economy v S. B. & L. Bldg. Corp. (AT1 1930) 138 Misc 296, 245 NYS 352.

6. § 2:16, supra.

under such circumstances, and so to bind himself absolutely for the payment of rent, the court could not relieve him from the contract. In the present case the right to a license did not depend on the exercise of discretion. The ordinance absolutely forbade the use of the premises for the single purpose to which their use was expressly restricted." (The building was not fireproof.) "The licensing officer had no power to dispense with the statutory prohibition. Use of the premises for the purpose specified in the lease would have been unlawful, with or without a license, and their use for any other purpose was forbidden by the lease. The contract, therefore, was incapable of lawful performance when it was made, . . . ." In other words, when the parties know that the right to use the premises for the purpose contemplated depends upon obtaining a license, which rests in the discretion of the authorities, and the tenant chooses to take a lease without conditions under such circumstances, and so, to bind himself absolutely for the payment of rent, the court cannot relieve him from his contract. But where the license does not depend upon anyone's discretion, and the use of the premises for the single purpose to which their use is expressly restricted is forbidden by law, as, for example, a building is not fireproof, so that the authorities have no power to dispense with the statutory prohibition, and the use of the premises will be unlawful with or without a license, the contract is incapable of lawful performance when made, and therefore is voidable at the tenant's election.

### § 2:18. Violation of Departmental Orders

A distinction is to be drawn between a use of leased premises in violation of a statutory prohibition, and a use in violation of the rules, regulations, or orders of a governmental department or bureau. As the Court of Appeals observed in making this distinction,[7] "In other words, where the legislature in the exercise of the police power enacts a regulation defining the duty of citizens, either in respect to their personal conduct or the use of the property, the reasonableness of the thing enjoined or

---

7. Fire Dept. of New York v Gilmour (1896) 149 NY 453, 458, 44 NE 177.

§ 2:18   LANDLORD AND TENANT

prohibited is not an open question, because the supreme legislative power has determined it by enacting the rule . . . . But where the legislature, as in the present case, enacts no general rule of conduct, but invests a subordinate board with the power to investigate and determine the fact whether in any special case any use is made of property for purposes of storage, dangerous on account of its liability to originate or extend a conflagration, not prescribing the uses which it permits or disallows, then we are of opinion that in such cases the reasonableness of the determination of the board of the order prohibiting a particular use in accordance with such determination, is open to contestation by the party affected thereby, and that he is entitled, when sued for a disobedience of the order, to show that it was unreasonable, unnecessary and oppressive. The general rule in respect to the validity of ordinances of a municipal corporation, passed under a general or implied authority to enact ordinances to secure the welfare of the people of the municipality, is that they must be reasonable, and are void if not so. The courts do and doubtless should exercise caution in interfering with the exercise of police regulations enacted under general powers conferred upon municipal corporations or subordinate public agents. But the public interests are also subserved in protecting citizens against unnecessary, unreasonable and oppressive regulations, interfering with a reasonable use of their property or their freedom of action."

Thus, it had been held that the mere fact that a tenant is carrying on a business on the leased premises without complying with orders of a municipal fire department does not conclusively show an illegal use of the premises as to warrant his removal on that ground under the statute.[8] And, the failure to obey all the orders of municipal officers or departments, the court observed in so holding, is not among the grounds for the removal of a tenant specified in said provision of the statute.[9] In other words, the question is, whether the acts of a tenant alleged to constitute an illegal use are acts which the statute has expressly prohibited, or acts the legality or

---

8. Real Prop Actions and Proceedings Law § 711 (5).

9. Davis Bros. Realty Corp. v Harte (AD1 1921) 195 AD 403, 186 NYS 324.

illegality of which are in the first instance to be passed upon by a subordinate board. In the latter case, when a subordinate board states that the act is illegal, that does not conclude the matter and prove that the tenant is guilty of an illegal use. The owner of the premises in question is entitled to contest in court, whether as a defense to an action for a penalty, or to a prosecution for a misdemeanor, the question of the legality of the acts.[10] However, if the alleged acts constitute a violation of a statutory prohibition, then there is no question but that the tenant is using the leased premises for an illegal purpose.[11]

### § 2:19. Violation of Certificate of Occupancy

A lease is not void for illegality merely because the use of part of it for the purpose specified in the lease is not authorized under the then existing certificate of occupancy, if the lease contemplates a correctly, and lawfully, occupied premises, and the bar to its legal use is readily correctible.[12] A lease so made is not unlawful. Use of the premises in the manner contemplated by the lease is unlawful only because the requirements of law have not been met.[13]

### § 2:20. Landlord's Failure to Obtain Certificate of Occupancy

A lease may not be avoided by a tenant in possession solely because the landlord has failed to obtain a certifi-

---

10. Lazarowitz v Kazan (M Ct Man 1923) 122 Misc 202, 203 NYS 610.

11. Since the violation of, or the failure to comply with, the rules, regulations, or orders of a governmental department or bureau may not give a landlord the necessary grounds for maintaining a summary proceeding as for an illegal use; it would seem prudent for the landlord to exact a proper covenant from the tenant to comply with such rules, regulations, or orders, and to limit the term upon a violation thereof or a failure to comply therewith. (See Form No. 44, § 19:25, infra.) Then, the landlord will be enabled to bring a holdover proceeding without the difficulties of proving illegal use.

12. 56-70 58th Street Holding Corp. v Fedders-Quigan Corp. (1959) 5 NY2d 557, 186 NYS2d 583, 159 NE2d 150, adhered to 7 NY2d 752, 193 NYS2d 665, 162 NE2d 747; Schwalben v Cholowaczuk (S Ct Kings Co 1973) 75 Misc 2d 98, 347 NYS2d 402 (citing text).

13. Raner v Goldberg (1927) 244 NY 438, 155 NE 733.

Whether or not the tenant is liable for rent will depend upon whether there is such failure of consideration as will excuse the payment of rent; that is, whether there is a substantial impairment of possession and a real frustration of the lease. 56-70 58th Street Holding Corp. v Fedders-Quigan Corp. (1959) 5 NY2d 557, 186 NYS2d 583, 159 NE2d 150, adhered to 7 NY2d 752, 193 NYS2d 665, 162 NE2d 747.

§ 2:20   LANDLORD AND TENANT

cate of occupancy. Something more must be shown. It must be shown that the landlord has violated some provision of law which directly and substantially concerns the public health, safety, and welfare, or that the use of the premises are thereby precluded or restricted.[14]

### § 2:21. Zoning Violation

Since the zoning board has power to vary zoning laws, or even to sanction continuance of a prior non-conforming use, a lease for use prohibited by zoning laws is not necessarily illegal. The issue is whether or not there is failure of consideration, which in turn depends upon what the parties had in contemplation at time of lease.[15] However, if there is an incurable zoning proscription against the prescribed use of the premises, so that it may be said to be impossible for the lessee lawfully to use the premises for the prescribed use, the lease is illegal and void.[16]

In other words, the issue is whether or not there is failure of consideration, which in turn depends upon what the parties had in contemplation at the time they entered into the lease.[17]

However, where a lease limits the use of demised premises, and expressly makes the lease subject to the zoning laws, that clearly indicates, it has been held,[18] that

---

14. Robitzek Investing Co. v Colonial Beacon Oil Co. (AD1 1943) 265 AD 749, 40 NYS2d 819, app den 266 AD 775, 42 NYS2d 922; Euclid Holding Co. v Schulte (AT1 1934) 153 Misc 832, 276 NYS 533; Mesfree Realty Corp. v Huyler's (AT1 1934) 153 Misc 667, 275 NYS 816; Salmon v D. A. Schulte, Inc. (M Ct 1934) 154 Misc 139, 276 NYS 535; Minton v D. A. Schulte, Inc. (S Ct NY Co 1934) 153 Misc 195, 274 NYS 641, where tenant, in possession for 12 years without certificate of occupancy ever having been issued, was denied right to recover 12 years' back rent as well as to avoid future rent.

15. Louis Friedman Realty Co. v De Stefan (AD1 1927) 220 AD 661, 222 NYS 371; Elk Realty Co. v Yardney Electric Corp. (1956, Sup App T) 153 NYS2d 730; Say-Phil Realty Corp. v De Lignemare (M Ct 1928) 131 Misc 827, 228 NYS 365.

16. Hartsin Const. Corp. v Millhauser (AT1 1930) 136 Misc 646, 241 NYS 428, lease for haberdashery store in a restricted residential district; Ober v Metropolitan Life Ins. Co. (City Ct NY Co 1935) 157 Misc 869, 284 NYS 966, affd NYLJ Oct 22, 1935, p 1412 (not otherwise reported), lease of apartment for valet shop in a restricted residential district.

17. Elk Realty Co. v Yardney Electric Corp. (1956, Sup App T) 153 NYS2d 730, where no failure of consideration was held to have been shown, since the parties had specified that the lease might be terminated in the event the board finally decided that the demised use was in violation of zoning resolution, but no notice or order of violation had ever been issued.

18. Say-Phil Realty Corp. v De Lignemare (M Ct 1928) 131 Misc 827, 228 NYS 365.

it was the intent of the parties that the risk of failure to secure a variation of the zoning law from the board of appeals was assumed by the tenant. Therefore, if, because the use is prohibited by the zoning laws, the tenant cannot use the premises, the tenant is precluded form asserting the illegality of the lease. "It cannot be claimed here," said Genung, J.,[19] "that the inability of the tenant to use the premises for a drug store was not within the contemplation of the parties at the time of the execution of the lease, for the lease provides, by its very terms in a rider attached to the lease and made a part thereof, that 'this lease is made by the landlord and accepted by the tenant subject to . . . Zoning Law.' It is urged by the tenant that this clause adds nothing to the lease, because the tenant would have been subject to the Zoning Law even if no provision were inserted in the lease. It follows nonetheless that the insertion indicates clearly that it was the intent of the parties that the risk of failure to secure a variation of the Zoning Law from the board of appeals was assumed by the tenant." Therefore, if the inability to use the premises is due to the inability of the tenant to comply with the law, which he undertook to do, then the tenant cannot be relieved from his obligations under the lease.[20]

## § 2:22. Conditioning Lease to Protect Tenant in Event of Illegal Use

In view of the principles discussed in the preceding sections,[1] a tenant is well advised to reserve the right to cancel the lease in the event his business is prohibited or curtailed by reason of inability to get a license, or by reason of governmental regulation, or for any of the reasons discussed in the preceding sections.[2]

---

19. Say-Phil Realty Corp. v De Lignemare (M Ct 1928) 131 Misc 827, 228 NYS 365.

20. Where lease provided that if the Town should officially declare that the use for which the tenant was putting the premises under the lease was illegal, and in violation of the zoning ordinances, the lease should ipso facto terminate, the unilateral act of the tenant of pleading guilty to a zoning violation by the tenant's use of the premises did not automatically terminate the lease, since, if timely notice had been given to landlord, the alleged violation could have been contested. Del Vecchio v Bay Shore Chrysler Plymouth, Inc. (1976, 2d Dept) 53 AD2d 657, 384 NYS2d 874.

1. See §§ 2:13, et seq, supra.

2. See, Teti v West End Brewing Co. (AD4 1910) 140 AD 16, 124 NYS 1, if liquor tax certificate cannot be obtained, lease void at tenant's option; Shear v Healy (AD3 1924) 208 AD 269, 203 NYS 387, if any law

§ 2:22 LANDLORD AND TENANT

However, the reservation of a right to cancel only for a real property restriction will not entitle a cancellation for regulation or curtailment by the authorities of the business to be operated on the premises. Thus, a cancellation clause provided: "It is understood and agreed that if for reason of any law, ordinance, injunction or regulation of properly constituted authority, Lessee is prevented from using all or any part of the property herein leased as a service station for the storage, handling, advertising or sale of gasoline or other petroleum products or for the conduct of any of the business usually conducted in connection with gasoline service stations, or if the use of the premises herein demised shall be in any manner restricted for any of the purposes above stated, . . . the Lessee may, at its option, surrender and cancel this lease, . . . ." During World War II, the government by decree limited the sale of gasoline and tires, whereupon the tenant sought to cancel the lease basing its right, among other reasons, upon this cancellation clause. In overruling the tenant's right to rely on this clause, the Appellate Division said,[3]

"The clause of the lease relied upon by defendant contemplates a cancellation only (1) if the lessee is prevented from using the property for a gasoline service station and the business ordinarily connected therewith, or (2) if the premises have been restricted against such use. The language employed shows that the clause has reference to a law or order regulating not the defendant's business but the use of the premises as such; it refers to a real property restriction. The governmental orders do not regulate the use of the premises but merely control transactions in gasoline, tires, casings and tubes without regard to any particular parcel of property. If it were the intention of the parties to do so, they could readily have provided for cancellation of the lease in the event of a regulation of defendant's business by employing language to that effect. . . . The federal regulations do not restrict the use of the land demised but they control the business of the defendant. . . . Defendant could have continued to

interferes with traffic in liquors, tenant shall have right to terminate lease.
**3.** Robitzek Investing Co. v Colonial Beacon Oil Co. (AD1 1943) 265 AD 749, 40 NYS2d 819, app den 266 AD 775, 42 NYS2d 922.

# REQUISITES OF LEASES § 2:23

operate the gasoline station at the demised premises within the terms of the lease though the volume of its business might have suffered substantial diminution because of the federal regulatory measures." Since the tenant did not claim that performance of the lease had been rendered impossible by governmental authority, but relied exclusively upon the cancellation clause, it was held that the tenant had no right to cancel the lease.[4]

## § 2:23. Perpetual Leases

A lease may be created in perpetuity.[5] A conveyance in fee with the reservation of rent and the right of re-entry for nonpayment is a perpetual lease, is valid and enforceable, and creates the relation of landlord and tenant.[6] However, leases in perpetuity are not favored, and in the absence of language in the lease clearly and unequivocally indicating that such is the intent of the parties, the court will not construe a lease as being in perpetuity.[7] The estate created, however, is not in fee simple absolute, but, by reason of reservation of the rent and right of re-entry for nonpayment, is an estate upon condition.[8]

---

4. Where lease required tenant to obtain all necessary licenses and permits, and then construct a restaurant on the premises, and the lessor warranted that the use by tenant of the premises for restaurant purposes would be a permitted use under the zoning and local laws and ordinances applicable to the premises, and the premises could not be used as a restaurant until 2 years and 9 months later, upon the completion of a public sewer, tenant was entitled to cancel the lease, even though tenant knew that difficulties might be encountered in obtaining the necessary permits. Benderson Dev. Co. v Commenco Corp. (1974, 4th Dept) 44 AD2d 889, 355 NYS2d 859, affd 37 NY2d 728, 374 NYS2d 618, 337 NE2d 130.

5. Genesee Conservation Foundation, Inc. v Oatka Fish & Game Club, Inc. (1978, 4th Dept) 63 AD2d 1115, 405 NYS2d 869; Gleason v Tompkins (S Ct Steuben Co 1975) 84 Misc 2d 174, 375 NYS2d 247.

6. Munro v Syracuse, L. & N. R. Co. (1910) 200 NY 224, 232-233, 93 NE 516; First Religious Soc. v Socony Mobil Oil Co. (S Ct Oneida Co 1964) 44 Misc 2d 415, 253 NYS2d 839; Kavanaugh v Cohoes Power & Light Corp. (S Ct Albany Co 1921) 114 Misc 590, 187 NYS 216, reviewing the authorities on the subject.

Leases in fee are recognized by statute: Real Property Law § 223 provides that the statutory rights of lessees which inure upon the transfer of the reversion also inure to a lessee of a "lease in fee, reserving rent."

Moreover, Real Prop Act & Proc L § 1901 (replacing Real Prop L § 72) prescribes the method whereby any person interested in lands held under a lease in perpetuity, upon which no rent has been paid for at least 20 years, may obtain an order declaring that the rents and reversion have been released to the owner in fee.

7. Gleason v Tompkins (S Ct Steuben Co 1975) 84 Misc 2d 174, 375 NYS2d 247; Levy v Amelias (S Ct Cayuga Co 1955) 207 Misc 880, 141 NYS 101, affd (4th Dept) 1 AD2d 755, 148 NYS2d 921.

8. Van Rensselaer v Ball (1859) 19 NY 100; Kavanaugh v Cohoes Power & Light Corp. (S Ct Albany Co 1921) 114 Misc 590, 187 NYS 216.

## § 2:24. Non-technical Language for Residential Lease (Plain English Law)

General Obligations Law § 5-702 provides,

a. Every written agreement entered into after November first, 1978, for the lease of space to be occupied for residential purposes, or to which a consumer is a party, and the money, property or service which is the subject of the transaction is primarily for personal, family or household purposes must be:

1. Written in a clear and coherent manner using words with common and every day meanings;

2. Appropriately divided and captioned by its various sections.

Any creditor, sellor or lessor who fails to comply with this subdivision shall be liable to a consumer who is a party to a written agreement governed by this subdivision in an amount equal to any actual damages sustained plus a penalty of fifty dollars. The total class action penalty against any such creditor, seller or lessor shall not exceed ten thousand dollars in any class action or series of class actions arising out of the use by a creditor, seller or lessor of an agreement which fails to comply with this subdivision. No action under this subdivision may be brought after both parties to the agreement have fully performed their obligation under such agreement, nor shall any creditor, seller or lessor who attempts in good faith to comply with this subdivision be liable for such penalties. This subdivision shall not apply to agreements involving amounts in excess of fifty thousand dollars nor prohibit the use of words or phrases or forms of agreement required by state or federal law, rule or regulation or by a governmental instrumentality.

b. A violation of the provisions of subdivision a of this section shall not render any such agreement void or voidable nor shall it constitute:

1. A defense to any action or proceeding to enforce such agreement; or

2. A defense to any action or proceeding for breach of such agreement.

c. In addition to the above, whenever the attorney general finds that there has been a violation of this section, he may proceed as provided in subdivision 12 of Executive Law § 63.[9]

## B. PARTIES TO A LEASE

### § 2:25 Generally

A lease, being a contract as well as a conveyance,[10] requires the participation of at least two parties,[11] a lessor and a lessee, with the added requirements that a lessor must be capable of alienating real property,[12] and that a lessee must not be rendered incompetent by some legal disability from entering into a contract or from acquiring real property.

### § 2:26. The State of New York

When the State of New York undertakes to act as a landlord, it drops in that relationship its immunities and privileges, and conducts its real property operation with the usual risks. All this, of course, is with its sovereign consent.[13] However, any lease with the state must be for a term not exceeding 10 years. But, it may provide for optional renewals on the part of the state, for terms of 10 years or less. Moreover, each lease with the state must

---

9. Renewal leases of stabilized tenants come under the mandate of the plain English law, and landlord must comply, if tenant so demands. Francis Apts v McKittrick (NYC Civ Ct Queens Co 1979) 104 Misc 2d 693, 429 NYS2d 516; Newport Apartments Co. v Collins (AT2 & 11 1980) 103 Misc 2d 994, 431 NYS2d 231.

10. § 1:2, supra.

11. Persky v Bank of America Nat. Ass'n (1933) 261 NY 212, 185 NE 77. It is essential to the validity of a grant that the parties be named in the deed, or so plainly designated as to distinguish them with certainty. Heath v Hewitt (1891) 127 NY 166, 27 NE 959.

12. An Indian may take, hold, and convey real property the same as a citizen, but this right extends only to lands outside of tribal lands, and does not apply to any lands owned or occupied as the common property of any nation, tribe, or band of Indians. Indian L § 2.

An executor or administrator, in the absence of contrary or limiting provisions in the order or decree appointing him, or the will, deed or other instrument, or a subsequent court order or decree, is empowered with respect to any property or any estate therein owned by an estate, except where such property or any estate therein is specifically disposed of, to lease the same for a term not exceeding three years. EPTL 11-1.1(b)(5)(C). However, this section further provides that any power to lease so granted, which is prohibited by the terms of the will, deed or other instrument, or by the provisions of this subparagraph, shall, nonetheless, exist upon the approval of the Surrogate's Court where such power is necessary for the purposes set forth in SCPA 1902 (to enable the fiduciary to pay debts, expenses, legacies or distributive shares). EPTL 11-1.1(b)(5)(E).

As to trustees, as parties to leases, see § 2:31, infra.

13. Cosgrove v State (AD3 1951) 277 AD 596, 102 NYS2d 353.

contain a clause that the contract of the state thereunder shall be deemed executory only to the extent of the moneys available, and no liability shall be incurred by the state beyond the money available for the purpose.[14]

### § 2:27. Aliens

All aliens, including alien enemies, if otherwise competent to contract, can either give or take a lease in the same manner as native-born citizens.[15]

Control of the property of alien enemies is left solely to the federal government, which in time of war takes the necessary steps to protect the nation.[16]

### § 2:28. Tenants in Common or Joint Tenants

Joint tenants or tenants in common can make leases of their respective shares in the commonly owned real property, or they can all join in one lease of the whole of the commonly owned real property. However, one tenant in common, or one of several joint tenants, cannot make a valid lease of the whole of the commonly owned real property without the consent of the other owners.[17]

### § 2:29. Infants

As a general rule, leases made to or by an infant are voidable.[18] An infant or minor is a person who has not attained the age of 18 years.[19]

---

14. State Finance L § 161-a, subd 2. Also, see Starling Realty Corp. v State (1941) 286 NY 272, 36 NE2d 201, reh den 286 NY 696, 37 NE2d 138; Drislane v State (1958, 3d Dept) 7 AD2d 141, 181 NYS2d 38; Adson Industries, Inc. v State (Ct Claims 1966) 51 Misc 2d 718, 273 NYS2d 812, mod (3d Dept) 28 AD2d 1183, 284 NYS2d 765.

15. Real Prop L § 10, subd 2.
Prior to 1944 this section limited this power only to "alien friends." However, by the laws of 1944 (Chapter 272, in effect March 22, 1944), the word "friends" was omitted from the section, thus leaving the word "aliens" unqualified.

16. For example, The Trading With The Enemy Act (50 USCS App §§ 1-31), and the various proclamations and executive orders of the Second World War.

17. Valentine v Healey (1899) 158 NY 369, 374, 52 NE 1097; Harrison v L. A. De Luke Co. (Schenectady Co Ct 1962) 35 Misc 2d 39, 229 NYS2d 945; De Lancey v Robbin (1910, Sup App T) 123 NYS 946; See *Annotation:* Effect of lease given by part of cotenants. 49 ALR2d 797.

If a tenant enters and occupies the whole of jointly owned property under a lease thereto made by only one of several joint tenants, the non-joinder of the remaining owners of the property to the lease is no defense to an action for the agreed rent, since a tenant cannot dispute the title of his landlord. See § 5:9 infra.

18. International Text-Book Co. v Connelly (1912) 206 NY 188, 99 NE 722. However, see General Oblig L § 3-101 (superseding Debtor & Creditor L § 260).

19. RPAPL § 111, subd 4 (added L1974, ch 912, § 1).

## § 2:29 REQUISITES OF LEASES

Where an infant lessee disaffirms a lease, the lessor is entitled to the possession of the leased premises, and is entitled to recover the fair and reasonable value of the use and occupation of the premises, but not the rent reserved in the lease.[1]

A guardian of an infant has the power to grant leases of real property belonging to his ward. However, such leases cannot extend beyond the minority of the infant. An infant on coming of age can disaffirm a lease made by his guardian. Nor can such leases made by a guardian for an infant extend beyond the period of the guardianship. Applying these principles, it has been held that a guardian in socage[2] can lease real property belonging to his infant ward, but upon the appointment of a testamentary or general guardian such lease will be subject to disaffirmance by the newly appointed guardian. As the Court of Appeals pointed out in this connection,[3] "As an original question, and in analogy to the authorities, there would seem to be a propriety in holding that the guardian" (in socage) "could have no power to grant any more than his own title. It is probably as well for the interests of the infant, as it seems sound in law, under the principles declared, to hold that the guardian may lease for a time as long as he continues guardian, or for any number of years within the minority of the infant, subject to being defeated by another guardian being appointed pursuant to the statute. It is urged here that one of these infants was under fourteen years of age, when this action was commenced. Under our statute, the age of fourteen has nothing to do with the rights of guardians. They continue only until another guardian is appointed, without any reference to the ward's age of fourteen. Another guardian may be appointed, as well before as after that age, under our statutes (2 R.S., 151, § 5). The title and interest of a guardian in socage are superseded, under our statute, unlike any other guardian, without any fault on his part, by the appointment of another guardian, at any time. I see no necessity for holding this lease void. It was voidable by the new guardian, and he properly signified his intention to avoid it at the end of the year."

1. 9302 Broadwalk Corp. v Littman (M Ct 1927) 164 Misc 124, 298 NYS 320.
2. See Dom Rel L§§ 80, et seq.
3. Emerson v Spicer (1871) 46 NY 594, 597.

### § 2:30. Insane Persons

As a general rule, the contracts of a person of unsound mind, who has not been judicially declared incompetent, are voidable, and not void. A person of unsound mind, before he has been declared incompetent, may convey a good title, and while his deed is ordinarily voidable, it will not be voidable as against bona fide purchasers for value without notice of the incompetency.[4] After lunacy has been judicially determined, a lunatic, for whom a committee has been appointed, is legally incapable of entering into any contract.[5]

A committee of a lunatic cannot convey, mortgage or otherwise dispose of real property, except to lease it for a term not exceeding five years, without the special direction of the court, obtained upon proceedings taken for that purpose, as prescribed in the Mental Hygiene Law § 78.15(d) of which provides, "A committee of the property may not alien, (so in original) mortgage, lease or otherwise dispose of real property without the special direction of the court obtained upon proceedings taken for that purpose as prescribed in the real property actions and proceedings law, provided, however, that without instituting such proceedings, a committee may with the authorization of the court, lease real property for a term not exceeding five years." Mental Hygiene Law § 78.15(f) provides, "The committee shall file with the recording officer of the county wherein the incompetent or patient is possessed of real property, an acknowledged statement to be recorded and indexed under the name of the incompetent or patient identifying the real property possessed by the incompetent or patient and stating the date of adjudication of incompetency or of inability of the patient adequately to conduct his personal or business affairs, and the name, address and surety of the committee."

In other words court approval of a lease made by the committee of an incompetent is required if the termination date is more than five years from the date of the execution of the lease. Therefore, a five-year lease exe-

---

4. Goldberg v McCord (1929) 251 NY 28, 166 NE 793; Finch v Goldstein (1927) 245 NY 300, 157 NE 146.

5. Carter v Beckwith (1891) 128 NY 312, 316, 20 NE 582.

cuted without judicial approval 35 days before the commencement of the lease term is unenforceable.[6]

## § 2:31. Life Tenant

A life tenant has the power to grant a lease to real property.[7] Of course, any lease made by a tenant for life will come to an end upon his death, there being no power ordinarily incidental to a life estate to extend it beyond the period of his life.[8] The fact that the lessee was unaware that his landlord was a life tenant does not change the rule.[9]

Upon the death of the life tenant, if the lessee continues in possession without the express consent of the person then immediately entitled to possession, he is a trespasser, and an action may be maintained against him, or his representative, to recover the full value of the profits received during the wrongful occupation.[10]

The statute provides that a power to make a lease for a term of not more than twenty-one years, which is to commence in possession during his lifetime, can be conferred on a tenant for life with respect to described real property. If the power authorizes, or the life tenant makes, a lease for a term in excess of twenty-one years, such power or lease is valid for twenty-one years, but is void as to the excess.[11] The statute further provides that the power of a life tenant to make leases is not assignable as a separate interest, but is annexed to his estate, and passes by a disposition of such estate unless specially excepted. If so excepted, it is extinguished. Such a power may be released by the life tenant to a person entitled to

---

6. Vernon v Sarra, Inc. (1961) 9 NY2d 94, 211 NYS2d 180, 172 NE2d 559; Rooney v People's Trust Co. (S Ct Kings Co 1908) 61 Misc 159, 114 NYS 612, wherein the Court said, that under § 2339, Code of Civil Procedure (now Mental Hygiene Law § 106), a committee has the power, without leave of the court, to give a lease for a term not exceeding five years.

7. Wechsler v Drey (AD1 1922) 203 AD 692, 197 NYS 453.

8. Re O'Donnell (1925) 240 NY 99, 147 NE 541; Williams v Alt (1919) 226 NY 283, 123 NE 499; Barson v Mulligan (1910) 198 NY 23, 90 NE 1127; Hinton v Bogart (AD1 1915) 166 AD 155, 151 NYS 796; Levy v Amelias (S Ct Cayuga Co 1955) 207 Misc 880, 141 NYS2d 101, affd (4th Dept) 1 AD2d 755, 148 NYS2d 921.

9. Re O'Donnell (1925) 240 NY 99, 147 NE 541; Nesbitt v Thompson (S Ct Franklin Co 1916) 93 Misc 251, 157 NYS 166.

10. Real Prop Act & Proc L § 851. See Re O'Donnell (1925) 240 NY 99, 147 NE 541; Williams v Alt (1919) 226 NY 283, 123 NE 499.

11. EPTL 10-10.2, re-enacting without substantive change former Real Prop L § 160.

an expectant estate in the property, and shall thereupon be extinguished.[12] "Disposition" in this context means a transfer of property by a person during his lifetime or by will.[13]

### § 2:32. Trustees

It is a well recognized principle that in the absence of some form of specific authorization, as by the provisions of the trust instrument or a controlling statute, or by action of the court to whom the trustee is amenable, a trustee has no authority to execute a lease to real property with a term of such length that it will extend, or in all probability will extend, beyond the duration of the trust.[14] "In the absence of a statute," said the Court of Appeals,[15] "a lease for a definite term by a trustee conferred no estate upon the tenant which would continue after the expiration of the trust though the term of the lease had not then expired." However, the statute provides,[16] that a trustee in the absence of contrary or limiting provisions in the order or decree appointing him, or the will, deed or other instrument, or a subsequent court order or decree, is empowered with respect to any property or any estate therein owned by a trust, except where such property or any estate therein is specifically disposed of, to lease the same for a term not exceeding ten years although such term extends beyond the duration of the trust. However, this statute further provides that any power to lease so granted which is prohibited by the terms of the will, deed or other instrument, or by the provisions of this subparagraph, shall, nonetheless, exist upon the approval of the Surrogate's Court where such

---

12. EPTL 10-10.3, re-enacting without change former Real Prop L § 161.

EPTL 10-10.4, re-enacting former Real Prop L § 162, without substantive change, provides "The power of a tenant for life to make leases is neither extinguished nor suspended when such tenant executes a mortgage. The power is bound by the mortgage in the same manner as the real property embraced therein, and the lien of the mortgage on such power: (1) Entitles the mortgagee to an exercise of the power so far as the satisfaction of the debt requires; and (2) causes any subsequent interest, created by the tenant for life by an exercise of such power, to become subject to the mortgage as if in terms embraced therein."

13. EPTL 1-2.4.

14. Raynolds v Browning, King & Co. (AD1 1926) 217 AD 443, 217 NYS 15, affd 245 NY 623, 157 NE 884; Hastings v Black (S Ct Livingston Co 1940) 24 NYS2d 190.

15. City Bank Farmers' Trust Co. v Smith (1934) 264 NY 396, 191 NE 217, 93 ALR 601.

16. EPTL 11-1.1(b)(5)(C).

power is necessary for the purposes set forth in Surrogate's Court Procedure Act 1902 (to enable the trustee to pay debts, expenses, legacies or distributive shares).[17] Real Property Actions and Proceedings Law § 1601 provides for an application by a trustee to the appropriate court "to confirm a lease for a term longer than ten years made by a trustee of such real property without obtaining prior authorization by a court." In other words, unless the instrument creating the trust gives the trustee additional powers, he has no authority without court authorization to grant a valid lease for more than ten years. If he grants a lease for ten years or less, the lessee's terms will not be defeated should the trust expire before the end of the demised term.[18] The statute, said the Court of Appeals,[19] was not intended to restrict the power of the trustee without the approval of the court to enter into a lease for a term exceeding the statutory ten years, which would be valid so long as the trust endures. But, if the trustee grants a lease for more than ten years, without court authorization then the lessee's term will expire whenever the trust expires. This is the chance a lessee will take when he takes a lease from a trustee who exceeds his limited authority.[20]

## C. DESCRIPTION OF PREMISES

### § 2:33. Generally

Just as it is essential for a deed to be operative as a legal conveyance that the land itself, the subject of the conveyance, be described with such certainty and definiteness as to be capable of identification,[1] so too, it is essential for a lease, which also is a conveyance,[2] to be definite and explicit as to the estate granted, or leased.[3] However, the maxim, that "that is sufficiently certain which can be made certain," also applies to leases. In other words a written lease is not void for uncertainty in

---

17. EPTL 11-1.1(b)(5)(D).
18. Re Will of McCormack (Surr Ct Westchester Co 1955) 4 Misc 2d 646, 147 NYS2d 728; Hastings v Black (S Ct Livingston Co 1940) 24 NYS2d 190.
19. City Bank Farmers' Trust Co. v Smith (1934) 264 NY 396, 398, 191 NE 217, 93 ALR 601.
20. Victory Lunch v Carll (S Ct NY Co 1949) 198 Misc 227, 101 NYS2d 194.
1. People ex rel. Buffalo Burial Park Ass'n v Sitwell (1907) 190 NY 284, 293, 83 NE 56.
2. § 1:2, supra.
3. Shepard Warehouses, Inc. v Scherman (S Ct NY Co 1946) 63 NYS2d 421.

the description of the leased premises if, from the words employed, the description can be made certain by extrinsic facts, physical conditons, measurements or monuments referred to in the lease.

Where the description of the leased premises in a written lease is ambiguous, parol evidence or extrinsic circumstances are admissible to enable the court to ascertain the property the parties intended to lease.[4] Thus, where there is an entry into possession of leased premises under a lease, occupancy of a certain space not previously definitely and explicitly described, and payment of the rent therefor under the lease and acquiesced in by the landlord, the objection of uncertainty is removed as to the premises intended to be leased.[5] But, it is well established that parol evidence is not admissible to vary a plain description of the premises in a written lease.[6]

§ 2:34. Form of Description.

Form No. 2

Description of Leased Premises

AGREEMENT OF LEASE made this 1st day of February, 1986, between Lessor Corp., a domestic corporation, having its principal place of business at 1200 East 29th

---

4. Myers v Sea B. R. Co. (AD2 1899) 43 AD 573, 60 NYS 284, affd 167 NY 581, 60 NE 1117; Curcio v Lounsbury (S Ct Westchester Co 1946) 64 NYS2d 128.

Where a lease designated the demised premises as an "apartment, first floor", parol evidence to show that there was no such apartment in the building was admissible. Fifth Ave. & Sixty-Sixth St. Corp. v Delaney (S Ct NY Co 1953) 124 NYS2d 89.

In Mittler v Herter (City Ct 1902) 39 Misc 843, 81 NYS 494, where a written lease provided that plaintiff agreed to hire and defendant agreed to let "the northerly half store of Nos. 7 and 8 Chatham Square", the building being in process of construction, it was held proper to permit plaintiff to introduce into evidence a letter written before the execution of the lease, and to prove conversations between the parties, for the purpose of showing that the premises demised were to be 25 feet wide and 132 feet deep, and that the store offered by defendant was only 19 feet wide and 132 feet deep, as the description was ambiguous and vague.

In Freund v Kearney (AT 1898) 23 Misc 685, 52 NYS 149, where the leased premises were described as the "westerly half" of a certain store, it was held that the lessee might show that during the negotiations preceding the making of the lease, the lessor had pointed out the part the lessee was to occupy, as the description was vague and indefinite.

5. Shepard Warehouses, Inc. v Scherman (S Ct NY Co 1946) 63 NYS2d 421.

6. Cohen v Simon Strauss, Inc. (1913, Sup App T) 139 NYS 929; American Tract Soc. v Jones (AT 1912) 76 Misc 236, 134 NYS 611; Michaels v Studnitz (1907, Sup App T) 103 NYS 817 (proof of oral agreement including more premises than described in written lease, held inadmissible).

Street, Borough of Manhattan, City and State of New York, party of the first part, hereinafter referred to as LANDLORD, and John Lessee, residing at 14 Oak Street, Albany, New York, party of the second part, hereinafter referred to as TENANT,

WITNESSETH: Landlord hereby leases to Tenant and Tenant hereby hires from Landlord the fourth floor, as shown on the attached plan, in the building known as No. 14 Platt Street, in the Borough of Manhattan, City and State of New York.

## D. STATUTE OF FRAUDS

### § 2:35. Generally

A lease to be effective must be executed according to the statutory requirements.[7] General Obligations Law § 5-703(1), derived from, and replacing former Real Property Law § 242, provides that an estate or interest in real property, other than a lease for a term not exceeding one year, cannot be created, granted, assigned, surrendered or declared, unless by act or operation of law, or by a deed or conveyance in writing, subscribed[8] by the person creating, granting, assigning, surrendering or declaring the same, or *by his lawful agent, thereunto authorized by writing*. By the very terms of the statute, therefore, a written lease for a term of more than one year subscribed by the landlord only, is valid. But, a written lease for a term of more than one year subscribed by the lessee only, is not valid. A written lease for more than one year, subscribed by the lawful agent of the landlord, but without the written authority of the landlord to do so, is not valid.[9]

---

7. Herubin v Malackowski (Oneida Co Ct 1920) 113 Misc 100, 184 NYS 829.

8. "Subscribed" means signing at the end of a written instrument. James v Patten (1851) 6 NY 9.

**Annotation:** Statute of frauds: validity of lease or sublease subscribed by one of the parties only. 46 ALR3d 619.

9. Geraci v Jenrette (1977) 41 NY2d 660, 394 NYS2d 853, 363 NE2d 559; Genesee Management, Inc. v Del Bello (1977, 4th Dept) 60 AD2d 779,

400 NYS2d 642; Siemers v Heuchel (S Ct Kings Co 1919) 109 Misc 323, 178 NYS 649.

A managing agent of landlord-corporation, who is not an officer or a director thereof, requires written authorization to execute an enforceable lease or renewal for a term exceeding one year. Commission on Ecumenical Mission & Relations of United Presbyterian Church v Roger Gray, Ltd. (1971) 27 NY2d 457, 318 NYS2d 726, 267 NE2d 467.

A corporate officer or director is not

§ 2:35   LANDLORD AND TENANT

An oral lease for a term of exactly one year or less is valid,[10] but oral leases for a period exceeding one year are void, unless taken out of the statute by part performance,[11] or some other equitable doctrine, such as estoppel. A written one-year lease cannot be increased to a two-year lease by parol authority.[12]

The statute of frauds also provides that a contract which by its terms is not to be performed within one year from the making thereof is void unless it or some note or memorandum thereof be in writing and subscribed by the party to be charged therewith or by his lawful agent.[13] It has been held that agreements concerning land or interests in land are not within the purview of this provision of the statute of frauds, and therefore that a lease for one year to take effect in the future need not be in writing.[14]

### § 2:36. Necessity for Pleading Statute

Although under the statute of frauds an oral lease for more than one year is void; yet, such an oral lease may be enforced by either party thereto against the other unless the statute of frauds is properly pleaded as a defense in any action brought upon such lease,[15] or asserted by a motion to dismiss under CPLR 3211 (a).[16]

The courts have held that the statute of frauds apply-

an "agent" for purposes of the requirement of the statute of frauds that the agent's authority be in writing. Scientific Holding Co. v Plessey, Inc. (1974, CA2 NY) 510 F2d 15.

10. 150 Central Park South, Inc. v Ritz Carlton Valet Service, Inc. (1949) 276 AD 214, 93 NYS2d 478, reh and app den 276 AD 894, 94 NYS2d 197; Pier v Margulies (S Ct Kings Co 1947) 73 NYS2d 309; Messinger v Great Hudson Fur Co. (S Ct NY Co 1946) 62 NYS2d 420, affd 271 AD 820, 66 NYS2d 614.

11. Rosen v 250 West 50 Street Corp. (AD1 1945) 270 AD 171, 59 NYS2d 33, affd 296 NY 567, 68 NE2d 868; Goldpac Holdings, Inc. v Spetsas Realty Corp. (S Ct Kings Co 1956) 156 NYS2d 573.

See § 2:37, infra.

12. Westwitt Realty Corp. v Burger (AD1 1925) 212 AD 622, 209 NYS 486, revg 122 Misc 653, 203 NYS 430.

Effect of entry into possession under a lease void under the statute of frauds, see § 30:44, infra.

13. General Oblig L § 5-701, derived from and replacing former Per Prop L § 31, subd 1.

14. Ward v Hasbrouck (1902) 169 NY 407, 62 NE 434; 150 Central Park South, Inc. v Ritz Carlton Valet Service, Inc. (AD1 1949) 276 AD 214, 93 NYS2d 478, reh and app den 276 AD 894, 94 NYS2d 197. It has been held that a contract for board and room for a year to commence in the future was not a lease of real property, and was within the statute of frauds as a contract not to be performed within a year. Wilson v Martin (1845) 1 Denio 602; Spencer v Halstead (1845) 1 Denio 606, affd 3 Denio 610, How App Cas 319. As to nature of contracts for board and room, see § 4:3, infra.

15. CPLR 3018 (b) requires that the defense of statute of frauds be pleaded affirmatively.

16. CPLR 3211 (e).

ing to leases does not prohibit the making of a lease in any way that the parties may see fit, nor does it render it illegal if not made in some particular way. This statute, it is held, simply requires that a lease for a term exceeding one year must be proved by a writing subscribed by the lessor or by his lawful agent, thereunto authorized by writing. Therefore, it is well settled that the statute merely introduces and enacts a rule of evidence in such cases without condemning as illegal any contract that was legal in the absence of such statute.[17] The effect of this rule is, that where a lease is void by reason of the provisions of the statute, that does not render the contract an illegal or unlawful one if the parties choose to perform it. If the lease is oral, and the term is for a longer period than one year, it is void in the limited sense that neither party can compel the other to perform it, if the party against whom it is sought to enforce the contract either pleads the statute as a defense, or raises the question by making a motion to dismiss. If the statute is not properly raised, the benefit of the statute is not available as an objection to the contract.[18]

### § 2:37. Effect of Part Performance

In order to prevent fraud, equity has always assumed jurisdiction to decree specific performance of contracts unenforceable at law by reason of the statute of frauds.[19] This power has been expressly preserved by statute. General Obligations Law § 5-703 (4), derived from former Real Property Law § 270, provides, "Nothing contained in this article (Article 5, dealing with creation, definition and enforcement of contractual obligations) abridges the power of courts of equity to compel the specific performance of agreements in case of part performance."

The doctrine of part performance, which is permitted in equity to take a lease out of the statute of frauds, is applied on the theory that where a contract is so far performed that the parties cannot be restored to their

17. McKenna v Meehan (1928) 248 NY 206, 212, 161 NE 472; Bayles v Strong (AD2 1905) 104 AD 153, 93 NYS 346, affd 185 NY 582, 78 NE 1099.

18. CPLR 3211 (e). Matthews v Matthews (1897) 154 NY 288, 48 NE 531; Brune v Vom Lehn (S Ct Kings Co 1920) 112 Misc 342, 183 NYS 360, affd 196 AD 907, 187 NYS 928.

19. Wood v Rabe (1884) 96 NY 414, 424.

original position except by equitable aid, equity will extend its aid in order to prevent a fraud upon the performing party.[20] But, said the Court of Appeals,[1] "the part performance must be substantial, and nothing will be considered as part performance which does not put the party into a situation which is a fraud upon him unless the agreement be fully performed; and the acts of part performance should clearly appear to be done solely with a view to the agreement being performed. Generally if they are acts which might have been done with other views, they will not take the case out of the statute, since they cannot properly be said to be done by way of part performance of the agreement. The acts should be so clear, certain and definite in their object and design as to refer exclusively to a complete and perfect agreement, of which they are a part execution."[2]

The mere failure, then, to live up to an oral promise does not amount to a fraud in law or in equity to afford equitable relief.[3] But, it would be inequitable, and a fraud on the part of one insisting upon the statute of frauds, to rely upon it after having, by his acts, induced someone else to do acts in part performance of an oral agreement and upon the faith of its full performance by both parties, and for which the performing party cannot well be compensated in any manner except by a specific performance of the agreement.

Mere payment of money; for example, the payment of rent in advance, it has been held, does not constitute such part performance as to call for equitable relief. Complete restoration may be obtained by an action at law for its recovery.[4]

The method of approach in these situations is first to look to the facts relied on to constitute part performance; and if these facts are unusual, unintelligible, and extraor-

20. Rosen v Rose (Super Ct NYC 1895) 13 Misc 565, 34 NYS 467.

1. Wheeler v Reynolds (1876) 66 NY 227, 231.

2. Also, see, Gracie Square Realty Corp. v Choice Realty Corp. (1953) 305 NY 271, 113 NE2d 416; Burns v McCormick (1922) 233 NY 230, 135 NE 273.

3. Blumenfeld v Aronson (AD1 1921) 196 AD 189, 187 NYS 585.

4. Mulford v Borg-Warner Acceptance Corp. (1985, 3d Dept) 115 AD2d 163, 495 NYS2d 493; Neild v Wolfe (S Ct NY Co 1981) 111 Misc 2d 994, 445 NYS2d 934; Carlyle Record Warehouses Corp. v Scherlo (NYC Civ Ct NY Co 1978) 94 Misc 2d 226, 404 NYS2d 530; Rosen v Rose (Super Ct NYC 1895) 13 Misc 565, 34 NYS 467.

dinary unless accounted for by a contract such as is sought to be established, then the oral promise may be relied on and enforced; otherwise the statute applies, and it may not be enforced.[5] Where a contract has been partly performed by acts which are not only exclusively referable to the contract, but are of such a nature that, if the contract should not be performed, the person who performed these acts would be practically defrauded, equity may decree specific performance.[6] Thus, it has been held, that the making of valuable repairs or improvements of a permanent character, and such as would not ordinarily be required of a tenant, may constitute sufficient part performance to warrant a court of equity to grant relief from the statute of frauds.[7]

The doctrine of part performance is confined to courts of equity, and will not in a court of law save a contract which violates the provisions of the statute of frauds.[8]

## E. RESEARCH REFERENCES

### § 2:38. Generally

In addition to the preceding text, the reader is also referred to the following:

49 Am Jur 2d, Landlord and Tenant §§ 25-40.

5. Hallenbeck v Griffith (S Ct Rensselaer Co 1930) 139 Misc 796, 248 NYS 281, affd 232 AD 785, 249 NYS 838, app dismd 257 NY 622, 178 NE 821.
See, Carlyle Record Warehouses Corp. v Scherlo (NYC Civ Ct NY Co 1978) 94 Misc 2d 226, 404 NYS2d 530, where defense was sustained.
6. Veeder v Horstmann (AD3 1903) 85 AD 154, 83 NYS 99.
7. Veeder v Horstmann (AD3 1903) 85 AD 154, 83 NYS 99; Gibbs v J. M. Horton Ice-Cream Co. (AD2 1901) 61 AD 621, 71 NYS 193.
8. Spota v Hayes (AT 1901) 36 Misc 532, 73 NYS 959; Nasanowitz v Hanf (AT1 1896) 17 Misc 157, 39 NYS 327.
But see, Roedman v Hertel (AT2 1912) 78 Misc 55, 138 NYS 375, where part performance was successfully set up as an equitable defense by a tenant in a holdover summary proceeding.

It may be observed that CPLR 103, like its predecessor, former CPA § 8, provides that there is only one form of civil action, and that the distinction between actions at law and suits in equity, and the forms of those actions and suits have been abolished. But, notwithstanding this abolition, such distinction still exists as part of the framework within which civil legal proceedings are brought. All that has been accomplished is to abolish only the forms of actions at law and suits in equity. In other words although actions will no longer be dismissed because not brought in the proper form (CPLR 103(c)), the characterization of the action as legal or equitable still is of importance; e.g., rights to jury trial; statute of limitations; power of courts of inferior jurisdiction to grant equitable relief. See Weiser v Burdick (Westchester Co Ct 1965) 47 Misc 2d 962, 263 NYS2d 506.

§ 2:38

11 Am Jur Legal Forms 2d, Leasors of Real Property §§ 161:31-161:99

New York Jur 2d, Landlord and Tenant (1st ed. §§ 76-110).

New York Forms, Leases, Forms 8:31-8:55.

Index to Annotations, Landlord and Tenant.

**VERALEX®:** Cases and annotations referred to herein can be further researched through the VERALEX electronic retrieval system's two services, **Auto-Cite®** and **SHOWME®**. Use Auto-Cite to check citations for form, parallel references, prior and later history, and annotation references. Use SHOWME to display the full text of cases and annotations.

# CHAPTER 3

# AGREEMENT FOR A LEASE

A. IN GENERAL
- § 3:1. Nature and Effect
- § 3:2. Distinguished from Option for Lease
- § 3:3. Provision for Execution of Formal Lease
- § 3:4. Necessity for Valid Contract
- § 3:5. Immateriality of Acts Done in Anticipation of Lease
- § 3:6. Certainty of Terms Essential
- § 3:7. Provision for Attorney's Approval of Lease

B. STATUTE OF FRAUDS
- § 3:8. Generally
- § 3:9. Requirements for Note or Memorandum
- § 3:10. Effect of Part Performance

C. DEPOSIT
- § 3:11. Stipulated as Liquidated Damages
- § 3:12. No Purpose Specified for Deposit
- § 3:13. Effect on Deposit Where Lease Not Consummated

D. BREACH
- § 3:14. Action for Damages
- § 3:15. Rescission
- § 3:16. Specific Performance
- § 3:17. First Option to Lease; Damages for Breach

E. RESEARCH REFERENCES
- § 3:18. Generally

## A. IN GENERAL

### § 3:1. Nature and Effect

There is a marked distinction in both the rights and liabilities of the parties between a lease and a mere agreement for a lease.

An agreement for a lease, that is, an agreement to execute a lease, is an executory contract which vests no estate or interest in the lessee. It does not create the relationship of landlord and tenant as does a lease.[1] Accordingly, it is important to distinguish between an agreement for a lease and a lease, because the rights and liabilities of the parties under each are different. The rights and remedies of the parties under an agreement for a lease are not governed by the law of landlord and tenant, but rather by the law of contracts. For example, if there is an agreement for a lease, and the lessee refuses to take a lease pursuant to the agreement, the lessor cannot sue for the rent reserved in the proposed lease, but is limited to an action for damages for breach of contract, or possibly for specific performance.[2] On the other hand, if the lessor refuses to execute a lease, the other party to the agreement has no possessory remedies, but is limited to an action for breach of contract.[3]

### § 3:2. Distinguished from Option for Lease

An option for a lease is to be distinguished from an agreement for a lease. An option is a continuing offer, binding for the time specified, on the one who makes it, but not on the one to whom it is made, unless he accepts it, when for the first time it becomes binding upon both,[4] and brings into existence an agreement for the transfer of an interest in the subject matter.[5] An option for a lease neither transfers, nor agrees to transfer title to property, but confers the bare right to accept an offer within the time limited, and upon the terms provided.[6]

It has been held that since an agreement to sell or convey an interest in land, other than a lease for a term

---

1. Galante v Hathaway Bakeries, Inc. (1958, 4th Dept) 6 AD2d 142, 176 NYS2d 87; Ettinger v Christian Schuck & Co. (AT1 1913) 81 Misc 196, 142 NYS 481.

2. Richman v Robinson (AD2 1911) 148 AD 703, 132 NYS 986; Arnold v R. Rothchild's Sons Co. (AD1 1899) 37 AD 564, 56 NYS 161, affd 164 NY 562, 58 NE 1085; Ettinger v Christian Schuck & Co. (AT1 1913) 81 Misc 196, 142 NYS 481; Goldberg v Wood (AT 1904) 45 Misc 327, 90 NYS 427.

Unless plaintiff demonstrates any exceptional circumstances so as to warrant the equity relief of specific performance, plaintiff is only entitled to compensatory damages. Kalker v Columbus Properties, Inc. (1985, 1st Dept) 111 AD2d 117, 489 NYS2d 495.

3. Taylor v Bradley (1868) 39 NY 129; Jackson ex dem Bulkley v Delacroix (1829) 2 Wend 433.

4. Benedict v Pincus (1908) 191 NY 377, 84 NE 284.

5. Loft, Inc. v Glen Ridge Realty Corp. (S Ct Queens Co 1939) 12 NYS2d 577.

6. Benedict v Pincus (1908) 191 NY 377, 84 NE 284; Loft, Inc. v Glen Ridge Realty Corp. (S Ct Queens Co 1939) 12 NYS2d 577.

# AGREEMENT FOR A LEASE § 3:3

not exceeding one year, must be in writing,[7] an acceptance or an extension of an option to lease for a term exceeding one year must also be in writing to be valid and effective.[8]

## § 3:3. Provision for Execution of Formal Lease

No particular words are necessary to constitute a lease; for, any words which indicate an intention to lease premises in praesenti will generally be held sufficient to constitute a lease, rather than an agreement for a lease.[9] However, instruments are sometimes so drawn as to create a doubt as to whether they are leases or agreements for a lease. For example, a provision may be inserted in such instruments calling for the subsequent execution of a formal lease. In cases of doubt, whether or not an agreement shall be construed as a lease, or as an agreement for a lease, depends, as a general rule, upon the intention of the parties, to be gathered from the entire agreement, the negotiations leading up to it, as well as the conduct of the parties.[10] When the question is one of intent, the courts have held that where an agreement contains words of present demise, and there are circumstances from which it appears that the parties intended that the tenant should have an immediate legal interest in the term, such an agreement will be construed to constitute an actual lease.[11] Where a letter sent by landlord to prospective tenant sets forth all the essential terms of a lease, leaving no material issues on the lease open for discussion, and landlord does not articulate any intent to be bound only by a formal lease, such offer, when accepted by tenant, constitutes a lease, even though the letter provides for the preparation of a formal lease.[12]

However, even though words of present demise are used, if it appears that no legal interest in the term was intended to pass until the execution of a formal lease,

---

7. Gen Obligations L § 5-703.
8. Loft, Inc. v Glen Ridge Realty Corp. (S Ct Queens Co 1939) 12 NYS2d 577. Also, see 1130 President Street Corp. v Bolton Realty Corp. (1949) 300 NY 63, 89 NE2d 16, 16 ALR2d 617.
9. People v St. Nicholas Bank (AD1 1896) 3 AD 544, 38 NYS 379, affd 151 NY 592, 45 NE 1129.
10. Arnold v R. Rothchild's Sons Co. (AD1 1899) 37 AD 564, 56 NYS 161, affd 164 NY 562, 58 NE 1085.
11. People v St. Nicholas Bank (AD1 1896) 3 AD 544, 38 NYS 379, affd 151 NY 592, 45 NE 1129.
12. Kalker v Columbus Properties, Inc. (1985, 1st Dept) 111 AD2d 117, 489 NYS2d 495.

§ 3:3                               LANDLORD AND TENANT

and that the agreement was only preparatory to a formal lease to be entered into thereafter, then such an agreement will be construed to constitute an agreement for a lease, and not a lease.[1] An agreement providing for the giving of a lease of certain premises in all respects similar to another lease, except as to the term thereof, and providing that all the other terms, covenants and conditions of such lease "are hereby made part of this agreement and specifically referred to," is an agreement to give a lease, and not a lease itself.[2] even though a payment is made by the proposed lessee under the preliminary agreement.[3]

Although a provision for the subsequent execution of a formal lease tends to show that the parties intended an agreement for a lease, there may be other factors which may override this provision. Thus, where a lessee entered into possession, and paid the agreed rental prior to the execution of the formal lease provided for in the agreement, such facts were held to justify a construction that the agreement was a lease,[4] and not an agreement for a lease, especially where the agreement contained words of present demise.[5]

A parol lease of premises for one year to commence in futuro is not an agreement for a lease, but is a lease, since it vests a present interest in the term.[6]

---

1. Franke v Hewitt (AD1 1900) 56 AD 497, 68 NYS 968; Mathews v Hogan (1915, Sup App T) 155 NYS 234; Fleming v Ryan (Com Pl GT 1894) 10 Misc 420, 31 NYS 129.

2. Raisin v Shoemaker (1924) 238 NY 630, 144 NE 921, affg 206 AD 122, 200 NYS 615.

3. Jenkelson v Ruff (AT 1900) 31 Misc 276, 64 NYS 40.

4. Galante v Hathaway Bakeries, Inc. (1958, 4th Dept) 6 AD2d 142, 176 NYS2d 87; New York Produce Exchange Safe Deposit & Storage Co. v New York Produce Exch. (AD1 1924) 208 AD 421, 203 NYS 648, affd 238 NY 582, 144 NE 901; People v St. Nicholas Bank (AD1 1896) 3 AD 544, 38 NYS 379, affd 151 NY 592, 45 NE 1129; Herb v Day (1913, Sup App T) 139 NYS 931; Feust v Craig (1907, Sup App T) 107 NYS 637; Marcus v Collins Bldg. & Constr. Co. (AT 1899) 27 Misc 784, 57 NYS 737.

5. An agreement for a lease reciting the payment of a deposit, the amount of rent, and the manner of payment thereof, making a note of the repairs and improvements to be made, giving references, and manner of service, and reciting that the tenant, in consideration of the deposit and the holding of the premises for him, "agrees to take and does take" the same, and to execute further leases, is, after the expiration of the 10 days in which the landlord had an option to return the deposit and cancel the agreement if the references were not found to be satisfactory, binding on both landlord and tenant, and the formal lease provided for is not necessary to create the tenancy. Schneider v Ogden (1917, Sup App T) 167 NYS 352.

6. Becar v Flues (1876) 64 NY 518.

## § 3:4. Necessity for Valid Contract

The primary question is whether or not a valid contract has been made. If no contract has been entered into, then there is no agreement of any kind enforceable at law. After it has been determined that a valid contract has been made, then the secondary question will be whether it is a lease, or an agreement for a lease, in order to determine the rules of law applicable to the resulting relationship.[7]

As in all contracts, the fundamental requirement for a valid agreement for a lease is that there shall be an actual meeting of the minds, or mutuality of assent, on all the material elements of the agreement, without the reservation of any such element for future negotiations. If a material element of a contemplated agreement is left open for future negotiations, there is no contract enforceable at all.[8] In the preceding section it was pointed out that a factor in determining whether or not an agreement constituted a lease, or merely an agreement for a lease, was a provision for the subsequent execution of a formal lease. However, this factor should not be misunderstood. The formal lease thus intended is one merely to embody in a more formal form what has actually been agreed upon. It is not intended to be one which will incorporate new terms agreed upon thereafter. It must be emphasized that it is essential that the minds of the parties should have met upon all the terms as well as the subject matter of the agreement. If anything has been left open for future consideration, or if the subject matter does not appear to have been understood alike between the parties, then there is no agreement whatsoever. Considerable confusion will be avoided if this fundamental principle be kept in mind. As was pointed out in an early case,[9] "Although expressions are found in decisions and textbooks differentiating between an agreement for a lease and a lease, it would seem that the real test to be

---

7. See § 3:1, supra.

8. Ansorge v Kane (1927) 244 NY 395, 155 NE 683, reh den 245 NY 530, 157 NE 845.

A promise to negotiate the making of a lease at a future time is not a contract; it means nothing more than a contemplated discussion in arranging the terms of a contemplated contract which might never take place. Royce Haulage Corp. v Bronx Terminal Garage, Inc. (AT1 1945) 185 Misc 892, 57 NYS2d 760.

Also, see § 2:7, supra.

9. Foster v Clifford (AT 1904) 42 Misc 496, 86 NYS 28.

observed in cases of this character is to determine whether there was any agreement in fact made. If there was no valid contract entered into between the parties, then there was, strictly, no agreement enforceable in law."

In other words, it must first be ascertained whether or not a valid agreement has been made. Then it becomes a question of interpretation to determine whether or not a lease has been entered into, or merely an agreement for a lease. If there is a provision for the subsequent execution of a formal lease because the parties have not yet come to an agreement, there then is no enforceable contract, whether it be called a lease or an agreement for a lease, until the parties do so. However, if the parties provide for the subsequent execution of a formal lease merely for the purpose of embodying in a more formal instrument the provisions agreed on or assented to, then there is a valid agreement which will either be a lease, or an agreement for a lease, depending upon the application of the pertinent principles, discussed in the preceding section. As was aptly said by the Court of Appeals in an early case,[10] "A contract to make and execute a certain written agreement, the terms of which are specific, and materially understood, is, in all respects, as valid and obligatory, where no statutory objection interposes, as the written contract itself would be, if executed. If, therefore, it should appear from the evidence, that the minds of the parties had met; that a proposition for a contract had been made by one party and accepted by the other; that the terms of this contract, were, in all respects, definitely understood and agreed upon, and that a part of the mutual understanding, was, that a written contract, embodying those terms, should be drawn and executed by the respective parties, this is an obligatory contract, which neither party is at liberty to refuse to perform. Such a case cannot be distinguished from that of an agreement to execute a lease. If two parties negotiate for a lease of certain premises, and they agree upon the terms and conditions of the lease, and that a written lease shall be drawn and executed, embracing those terms, this is not a lease, but it is a contract, which,

---

10. Pratt v Hudson R. R. Co. (1860) 21 NY 305, 308.

whenever the statute of frauds does not interfere to prevent, can be enforced; and which the courts will compel the parties specifically to perform."[11]

### § 3:5. Immateriality of Acts Done in Anticipation of Lease

Where no enforceable contract has been entered into, because the minds of the parties have not met on the terms thereof,[12] any acts done by a proposed tenant on the premises in anticipation of a lease thereto being ultimately agreed upon, will be immaterial to the determination of whether or not an enforceable agreement for a lease has been made.

In one case, no completed agreement for a lease had been mutually arrived at, but the proposed tenant, feeling reasonably certain that all difficulties would be ironed out, and that a lease would be executed, made expenditures on the premises in anticipation of getting the lease. He made repairs, laid in a supply of fuel and the like. In holding that these acts on the part of the proposed tenant were immaterial to a determination of whether or not an enforceable agreement for a lease had been executed, Referee Daly, in an opinion adopted by the Appellate Division, said,[13] "It is urged that the plaintiff, in reliance upon the oral agreement to which he testifies, and considering the letting as definitely settled, went on to make certain expenditures upon the premises as lessee. But this consideration, if warranted by the evidence, may also be disposed of upon authority. The contract being for a written lease, the terms of which were left undetermined, the plaintiff assumed the risk of expenditures made in expectation of its being eventually carried out. The circumstances can have no significance in determining the legal relation of the parties. If advanced on any theory of estoppel, the proposition 'is without shadow of support either in principle or authority.'"

Similarly, the payment of part of the proposed rent, or the deposit of money to secure the execution of the

11. Also see 1130 President Street Corp. v Bolton Realty Corp. (1949) 300 NY 63, 89 NE2d 16, 16 ALR2d 617; Kolodny v Schwartz (S Ct Queens Co 1949) 90 NYS2d 48, revd on other grounds 276 AD 930, 94 NYS2d 713.

12. See § 2:7, supra.

13. Franke v Hewitt (AD1 1900) 56 AD 497, 68 NYS 968.

proposed lease will be disregarded in determining whether or not a valid agreement for a lease has been made.[14]

In other words, whereas these acts may be of importance in determining whether or not a valid contract shall be construed as a lease, or as merely an agreement for a lease; yet, if there is no valid contract, then these acts will be of no legal significance.

### § 3:6. Certainty of Terms Essential

An agreement for a lease, to be binding, must be certain as to the terms of the future lease; if it shows on its face that other details are to be settled between the parties, it is not binding. Thus, an agreement for a lease for a specified term of years, which fails to state when the term is to begin or to end, is too uncertain to be enforced.[15] Similarly, it has been held that an agreement which provides for the incorporation into a lease thereafter to be executed, of the "usual" clauses contained in long term leases with respect to certain specified matters, such as repairs and the like, "and such other usual and appropriate clauses as may be agreed upon," is too indefinite and uncertain to be enforced.[16]

### § 3:7. Provision for Attorney's Approval of Lease

The mere fact that an agreement for a lease contains a provision that the lease, when drawn, shall be "subject to the approval of the attorneys to the parties of this agreement," will not prevent the agreement from being binding and enforceable as a valid contract.[17] Under such a provision the attorney for either party has no right to

14. Aquelina v Provident Realty Co. (1903, Sup App T) 84 NYS 1014; Jenkelson v Ruff (AT 1900) 31 Misc 276, 64 NYS 40.

15. Sayles v Lienhardt (M Ct 1922) 119 Misc 851, 198 NYS 337.

**Annotation:** Requirements as to certainty and completeness of terms of lease in agreement to lease. 85 ALR3d 414.

16. Noonan v Mott (S Ct NY Co 1921) 194 NYS 502, affd 202 AD 744, 194 NYS 962.

However, a provision for the making of a lease containing the "usual clauses" used by rental brokers in the vicinity, was held not to render the agreement too indefinite for enforcement, where no essential term had been omitted or left in doubt, and a formal document embodying them could readily be drawn and executed with the addition of the "usual clauses" found in the "stereotyped form" of lease well understood by real estate brokers in that vicinity. 1240 Third Ave., Inc. v Birns (AD1 1931) 232 AD 522, 250 NYS 331.

17. Pittsburgh Amusement Co. v Ferguson (AD1 1905) 100 AD 453, 91 NYS 666.

withhold arbitrarily his approval of a proposed lease. Such disapproval will be effective only if based upon some reasonable ground. If a lease in accordance with the terms of the agreement is presented for execution, an attorney's disapproval thereof would be arbitrary and ineffective.[18] Therefore, if all the terms of an agreement for a lease have been agreed upon, the insertion of a provision for attorney's approval, to insure that the lease presented for execution shall conform to such agreement, will not indicate that no valid contract has been made; that is, that the minds of the parties have not met on all the material elements of the agreement.

## B. STATUTE OF FRAUDS

### § 3:8. Generally

General Obligations Law § 5-703 subd 2 (derived without change from former Real Property Law § 259) provides, "A contract for the leasing for a longer period than one year, or for the sale, of any real property, or an interest therein, is void, unless the contract or some note or memorandum thereof, expressing the consideration, is in writing, subscribed[19] by the party to be charged, or by his lawful agent thereunto authorized by writing."[20] Therefore, an oral agreement for a lease for a term exceeding one year is void.[1]

An oral agreement for the renewal of a lease for a further period of two years has been held void under this statute; for, it is an agreement for the leasing of real property for a longer period than one year.[2]

Under the statute of frauds as presently phrased, it is clear that an agent's authority to execute an agreement for a lease, for a term exceeding one year, must be in writing.[3]

---

18. Pittsburgh Amusement Co. v Ferguson (AD1 1905) 100 AD 453, 91 NYS 666.

19. "Subscribed" means signing at the end of a written instrument. James v Patten (1851) 6 NY 9.

20. Real Prop L § 259 (the predecessor of Gen Oblig L § 5-703), prior to its amendment in 1944 (L 1944 ch 798, eff Sept 1, 1944) merely required that the written contract, note, or memorandum, be subscribed by the lessor, or by his lawfully authorized agent. Cases decided prior to this amendment, such as 300 West End Ave. Co. v Warner (1929) 250 NY 221, 165 NE 271, are no longer controlling.

1. Thomas v Nelson (1877) 69 NY 118.

2. Nassoit v Huber (1911, Sup App T) 130 NYS 143.

3. Prior to 1934 Real Property Law

Although under the statute of frauds an oral agreement for a lease for more than one year is void; yet, such oral agreement may be enforced by either party thereto against the other unless the statute of frauds is properly pleaded as a defense in any action brought thereon,[4] or asserted by a motion to dismiss under CPLR 3211 (a).[5] The courts have held that the statute of frauds, applying to leases and agreements for a lease, does not prohibit the making of such agreements in any way that the parties may see fit, nor renders them illegal if not made in some particular way. This statute, it is held, simply requires that a lease, or an agreement for a lease, for a term exceeding one year must be proved by a writing. Therefore, it is well settled that the statute merely introduces and enacts a rule of evidence in such cases without condemning as illegal any contract that was legal in the absence of such statute.[6]

## § 3:9. Requirements for Note or Memorandum

The rule is well established that a note or memorandum sufficient to take an agreement for a lease out of the operation of the statute of frauds must state with reasonable certainty the entire agreement which the parties made, so that the substance thereof may be made to appear from the instrument itself without recourse to parol evidence.[7] Such essentials must appear without the aid of parol proof, either from the memorandum itself, or from a reference therein to some other writing, and such essentials, to make a complete agreement, must consist of a proper description of the subject matter of the lease,[8]

---

§ 259 (the predecessor of Gen Oblig L § 5-703) did not require an agent's authority to execute an agreement for a lease for a term exceeding one year to be in writing. Cases decided prior to that date holding that an agent acting under parol authority could bind his principal by a contract for a lease for a term exceeding one year are no longer controlling.

A corporate officer or director is not an "agent" for purposes of the requirement of the statute of frauds that the agent's authority be in writing. Scientific Holding Co. v Plessey, Inc. (1974, CA2 NY) 510 F2d 15.

4. CPLR 3018(b).
5. CPLR 3211(e).
6. McKenna v Meehan (1928) 248 NY 206, 212, 161 NE 472; Bayles v Strong (AD2 1905) 104 AD 153, 93 NYS 346, affd 185 NY 582, 78 NE 1099.
7. Mentz v Newwitter (1890) 122 NY 491, 25 NE 1044, reh den (NY) 26 NE 758.
8. Antoville v Bernard (AD1 1927) 220 AD 210, 221 NYS 187; Nasanowitz v Hanf (AT1 1896) 17 Misc 157, 39 NYS 327.

the terms,[9] and the names, or a description, of the parties.[10] As was said by the Court of Appeals,[11] "The requirements which this agreement must meet—that it may be enforced as a contract and satisfy the Statute of Frauds—are clear in theory and not peculiar to a contract for the lease of real property. The parties must have reached final agreement upon all essential terms of a valid contract, without reservation of any such term for future negotiation, and those terms must be embodied in a writing. . . . And such contracts have been held enforcible although a number of customary provisions were omitted. . . . The absence of provisions 'usually found' in commercial leases might have been of crucial significance here if defendant had attempted to prove that the written contract did not set forth a complete agreement. Absent such proof, judicial notice may provide us with the customary terms of such a lease, but it cannot furnish evidence as to the actual agreement between these parties." Thus, a receipt signed by one party, which recited the receipt from another party of a sum of money "for one month's rent in advance from May 1, 1895, to June 1, 1895. Lease to be given at $1600 for one year, and $1800 for next two years," was held to be an insufficient memorandum to comply with the statute of frauds. As McAdam, J., pointed out, in so holding,[12] "In this instance the memorandum does not describe or even refer to the premises, the subject matter and most material part of the contract. . . . It does not specify whether the subject-matter is a whole house or part of one; while the lease offered describes parts of two adjoining houses as the

9. Lawrence v Goodstein (AT1 1915) 91 Misc 19, 154 NYS 229.

10. Gordon v Siegel (S Ct Schenectady Co 1953) 125 NYS2d 862, mod on other grounds (AD3) 284 AD 821, 132 NYS2d 437, reh den 284 AD 910, 134 NYS2d 193, vacated 284 AD 994, 136 NYS2d 377; Dawson v Margolies (S Ct NY Co 1925) 126 Misc 39, 212 NYS 471, affd 218 AD 755, 218 NYS 729.

Memorandum initialed and agreed to by both parties, providing for a basic monthly rental, plus expenses and escalation on the same terms as in a prior sublease; setting forth total space to be covered by sublease; rent required to be paid, and term agreed upon; and requiring payment of 2 months security, and necessity for obtaining consent of the owner; contained all the essential terms of a binding sublease of the premises. Harlow Apparel, Inc. v David Pik International, Inc. (1984, 1st Dept) 106 AD2d 345, 483 NYS2d 258, app dismd, app den 64 NY2d 1013, 489 NYS2d 63, 478 NE2d 204.

11. 1130 President Street Corp. v Bolton Realty Corp. (1949) 300 NY 63, 89 NE2d 16, 16 ALR2d 617.

12. Nasanowitz v Hanf (AT1 1896) 17 Misc 157, 39 NYS 327.

property." Similarly, it has been held that a memorandum which merely recites an agreement to give a lease for five years, without stating when the term begins or ends, or how the rent is to be paid, fails to set forth "the terms," which is an essential prerequisite to an enforceable contract.[13]

As has been seen,[14] the memorandum of the agreement for a lease must be subscribed by the party to be charged, or by his lawful agent thereunto authorized by writing.

### § 3:10. Effect of Part Performance

As has been seen,[15] courts of equity are empowered to compel the specific performance of agreements in case of part performance. But, as in the case of leases,[16] the acts of part performance which will be sufficient to take an agreement for a lease out of the statute of frauds must be substantial, and must be so clear, certain, and definite in their object and design as to refer exclusively to a complete and perfect agreement, of which they are a part execution. Where a contract has been partly performed by acts which are not only exclusively referable to the contract, but are of such a nature that, if the contract should not be performed, the person who performed these acts would be practically defrauded, equity may decree specific performance.[17] Thus, it has been held, that the making of valuable repairs or improvements of a permanent character, and such as would not ordinarily be required of a tenant, may constitute sufficient part performance to warrant a court of equity to grant relief from the statute of frauds.

The method of approach in these situations is first to look to the facts relied on to constitute part performance; and if these facts are unusual, unintelligible, and extraordinary unless accounted for by a contract such as is sought to be established, then the oral promise may be relied on and enforced; otherwise the statute applies, and it may not be enforced. As a general rule, the mere payment of money; for example, the payment of rent in

---

13. Antoville v Bernard (AD1 1927) 220 AD 210, 221 NYS 187; Lawrence v Goodstein (AT1 1915) 91 Misc 19, 154 NYS 229.
14. § 3:8, supra.
15. § 2:37, supra.
16. § 2:37, supra.
17. Veeder v Horstmann (AD3 1903) 85 AD 154, 83 NYS 99.

advance, or the payment of a deposit, does not constitute such an act of part performance as to warrant equitable relief.[18] Thus, where plaintiff alleged that he had paid defendants money on the strength of their oral fraudulent representations that they would permit him to occupy the premises for the purpose of obtaining a buyer of his luncheonette, in which event they would give such purchaser a six-year lease, it was held that the contract to give the lease was by reason of the Statute of Frauds, and that the payment of the money, the execution of a lease, entry into possession and obtaining a purchaser did not constitute sufficient part performance to relieve plaintiff from the production of a writing.[19] Similarly, a tenant's entry into possession, payment of rent, and painting and repairing the premises were held not to be "unequivocally referable" to an alleged oral agreement for a three-year lease, and therefore did not constitute part performance removing the bar of the statute of frauds to its enforcement.[20]

## C. DEPOSIT

### § 3:11. Stipulated as Liquidated Damages

Where a deposit is made by a proposed lessee as security for his agreement to take a lease, the proposed lessor is not necessarily entitled to retain the entire deposit as liquidated damages for breach of the agreement to take the lease.[1] Such deposit will be held as liquidating the damages sustained by such refusal, provided the amount of the deposit is not disproportionate to the actual damages which may result from such refusal. Therefore, if the party making such deposit, without legal excuse, refuses to take the lease, such deposit will be forfeited.[2]

### § 3:12. No Purpose Specified for Deposit

Where a deposit is made in connection with an agreement for a lease, and the parties do not specify the

---

18. Blumenfeld v Aronson (AD1 1921) 196 AD 189, 187 NYS 585; Rosen v Rose (Super Ct NYC 1895) 13 Misc 565, 34 NYS 467.
19. Rosenwald v Goldfein (1957, 1st Dept) 3 AD2d 206, 159 NYS2d 333, reh and app den (1st Dept) 3 AD2d 744, 161 NYS2d 568.
20. Taylor v Creary (1958, 2d Dept) 5 AD2d 876, 171 NYS2d 560.
1. Weber v Williams & Morford Co. (1913, Sup App T) 144 NYS 619.
2. Phillips v New York (AD1 1908) 124 AD 307, 108 NYS 1059.

purpose for which the deposit is given, a problem arises as to the nature of the deposit. Such a deposit may have been given in part performance of the lease. In other words, it may have been given as an advance payment of the rent, or on account of the rent, reserved in the lease to be executed pursuant to the agreement. Or, the deposit may have been given to attest the good faith of the depositor that he will carry out the agreement, and enter into the lease. In other words, it may have been given as security for the fulfillment of the agreement for the lease.

When a deposit is made in connection with an agreement for a lease, and the parties do not specify the purpose of the deposit, in the absence of factors clearly evidencing a different conclusion, the deposit as a general rule will be deemed to be security for the fulfillment of the agreement for a lease.[3] If the depositor enters into the lease, there is no default, and he will be entitled to its return. In other words, where a deposit is made as security for the acceptance of the lease; that is, it is given to secure performance of the agreement for a lease, as distinguished from a deposit given to secure performance of the lease to be executed, the lessee after the execution of the lease is entitled to return of the deposit.[4] However, if there is a default, the recipient will be entitled to retain only that portion of the deposit as will equal the actual damage suffered by reason of the depositor's default.[5] The depositor's default under the agreement for a lease will not preclude his recovery of the deposit, or that part thereof which exceeds the actual damage.[6] But, in any litigation involving the deposit the recipient thereof will have the burden of alleging and proving his actual damages.[7] In one case a tenant gave a landlord a check as a deposit in connection with an agreement for a lease, and thereafter stopped payment on the check, and wrongfully refused to consummate the transaction. The land-

---

**3.** De Salvo v Faerber, Silberman & Co. (1921, Sup App T) 189 NYS 147; Broadway Renting Co. v Wolpin (AT1 1908) 59 Misc 199, 110 NYS 151; Weinberg v Greenberger (AT 1905) 47 Misc 117, 93 NYS 530.

**4.** Rosenfeld v Silver (AT 1905) 49 Misc 117, 96 NYS 1027.

**5.** Lichtenstein v De Peyster Realty Co. (1921, Sup App T) 187 NYS 70; Weinberg v Greenberger (AT 1905) 47 Misc 117, 93 NYS 530.

**6.** De Salvo v Faerber, Silberman & Co. (1921, Sup App T) 189 NYS 147; Weinberg v Greenberger (AT 1905) 47 Misc 117, 93 NYS 530.

**7.** De Salvo v Faerber, Silberman & Co. (1921, Sup App T) 189 NYS 147.

lord brought an action on the check. The court found that there was nothing in the case to indicate that the deposit had been given for any purpose other than to secure the landlord for the fulfillment of the agreement of a lease. Therefore, it was held, the landlord was in the same position as if he had received cash, and could only recover such actual damages as he alleged and proved.[8]

If no purpose is specified for a deposit given in connection with an agreement for a lease, and the circumstances indicate that the deposit was not given to secure performance of the agreement, but rather was given as an advance payment of the rent reserved under the lease to be executed, then a breach of the agreement to take the lease will preclude the depositor from recovering any part of the deposit so made.[9] In one case a deposit equalled the amount of the first month's rent, and the court inferred from that circumstance that the deposit was an advance payment of the rent, although not specifically referred to as such. Therefore, it was held, the depositor who wrongfully refused to execute a lease submitted in conformity with the agreement for the lease was not entitled to its return.[10]

### § 3:13. Effect on Deposit Where Lease Not Consummated

Where an agreement for a lease is not consummated because the parties cannot agree upon the terms of the proposed lease, and therefore there is no binding contract, then the deposit given in connection with the agreement for a lease can be recovered by the depositor.[11]

---

8. Weber v Williams & Morford Co (AT1 1913) 144 NYS 619.

9. Ritter v Berkley House, Inc. (M Ct Man 1942) 37 NYS2d 183, Also, see, Chaude v Shepard (1890) 122 NY 397, 402, 25 NE 358.

10. Ritter v Berkley House, Inc. (M Ct Man 1942) 37 NYS2d 183, affd AT1 June 30, 1942, not reported. See, Weinberg v R. H. T. Bldg. Corp. (M Ct Man 1952) 111 NYS2d 790 (prospective tenant who notified landlord that he would not take lease before lease had been accepted by landlord was entitled to return of his deposit).

11. Smith v Geoghegan (1909, Sup App T) 114 NYS 29; McIntosh v Kilpatrick (1904, Sup App T) 94 NYS 1095; Aquelina v Provident Realty Co. (1903, Sup App T) 84 NYS 1014.

See, Weinberg v R. H. T. Bldg. Corp. (M Ct Man 1952) 111 NYS2d 790 (prospective tenant who notified landlord that he would not take lease before lease had been accepted by landlord was entitled to return of his deposit).

## D. BREACH

### § 3:14. Action for Damages

Where a valid, binding agreement for a lease exists, a cause of action for breach of contract arises when either the prospective lessor[12] or the prospective lessee[13] fails or refuses to enter into the lease. Where one party refuses to perform, the other party, provided he is not himself in default, may maintain the action at once without waiting for the time agreed upon for the termination of the lease.[14]

Where an owner of real property refuses to execute a lease in accordance with a prior agreement, the general rule is that the measure of damages recoverable is the difference between the agreed rent and the rental value of the premises, multiplied by the number of years the lease has to run.[15] However, where the lease is to run for a long term of years, then this general rule will not be applied. In the case of a long term of years, proper allowance is to be made so as to arrive at the present value of the yearly difference between the agreed rent and the rental value of the premises. As the Appellate Division said, in enunciating this rule of measuring damages for breach of an agreement for a long term lease,[16] "It is obvious the correct rule that such damage as the plaintiff suffered by reason of not securing the lease, and losing the benefit of the difference between its value and the rent reserved, is the present value of such sum, arrived at by making such proper abatement as would give the present value of such difference for the period specified in the lease." This present value can be ascertained by using annuity tables.

As has been seen, where the prospective lessee refuses

---

12. Taylor v Bradley (1868) 39 NY 129.

13. Schneider v Ogden (1917, Sup App T) 167 NYS 352; Bacon v Combes (AT 1900) 32 Misc 704, 65 NYS 510.

14. Taylor v Bradley (1868) 39 NY 129.

An unqualified refusal of the prospective lessor to execute the lease as agreed and to give possession to the prospective lessee is a breach without any further demand by the prospective lessee or tender by him of a lease for execution by the prospective lessor, since this would be a vain and idle ceremony. Driggs v Dwight (1837) 17 Wend 71.

15. Bondy v Harvey (AD1 1926) 218 AD 126, 217 NYS 877.

**Annotation:** Measure of damages for lessor's breach of contract to lease or to put lessee into possession. 88 ALR2d 1024.

16. Bondy v Harvey (AD1 1926) 218 AD 126, 217 NYS 877. Also, see, Admae Enterprises, Ltd. v 1000 Northern Blvd. Corp. (1984, 2d Dept) 104 AD2d 919, 480 NYS2d 537.

## AGREEMENT FOR A LEASE § 3:14

to take a lease pursuant to his agreement to do so, an action will not lie against him to recover the rent that he was to pay, since the agreement for a lease does not create the relation of landlord and tenant, and vests no estate in the proposed lessee.[17] The measure of damages recoverable for the breach by a prospective lessee of his agreement to lease property is governed by the same general rules of damages as are applicable where the breach is by the owner of the property.[18] The general rule as to the measure of damages recoverable for such prospective lessee's breach of his agreement is the excess, if any, of the agreed rent over the actual rental value of the premises,[19] together with such special damages as the prospective lessor may plead, and prove to have resulted from the breach.

The extent of the prospective lessee's right of recovery is not necessarily limited to the foregoing rules. Under special circumstances, damages may also be recovered for losses that are the natural, direct and necessary consequences of the breach, where they are capable of being estimated by reliable data, and are such as should reasonably have been contemplated by the parties.[20] Whether special damages will be allowed for a prospective lessor's breach of his agreement to lease depends upon the particular facts in each case. Thus, where the agreement for a lease of a hall indicated that it was for the purpose of an "entertainment and ball," the prospective lessee was held entitled to recover the expense of printing and mailing tickets and circulars explaining the function, since these were within the contemplation of the parties, and therefore were proper items of damages for the prospective lessor's breach of the agreement for a lease.[1] As a general rule, however, the prospective tenant will not be permitted to recover as damages prospective profits which it allegedly would have earned from the operation of the prospective business during the term of the lease.[2] The

17. § 3:1, supra.
18. Dickerson v Menschel (AD1 1919) 188 AD 547, 177 NYS 376.
19. Dickerson v Menschel (AD1 1919) 188 AD 547, 177 NYS 376; Ettinger v Christian Schuck & Co. (AT1 1913) 81 Misc 196, 142 NYS 481.
20. Taylor v Bradley (1868) 39 NY 129.

1. Beth David Hospital v Terrace Garden, Inc. (AT1 1919) 175 NYS 498.
2. Shopwell Foods, Inc. v Parkway Village, Inc. (AD2 1951) 278 AD 671, 102 NYS2d 653; Selmar Garage Corp. v Rink Realty Corp. (AD2 1950) 276 AD 1019, 95 NYS2d 615.

value of the time spent by a prospective lessee in looking for other premises is similarly not recoverable as damages for the prospective lessor's breach of his agreement to lease.[3]

A provision for liquidated damages will be upheld and enforced.[4]

### § 3:15. Rescission

If a prospective lessor refuses to perform his agreement for a lease, the prospective lessee may rescind, and recover back whatever moneys he may have paid pursuant to such agreement.[5]

However, a delay in performance where time is not of the essence, or where the delay was acquiesced in by the other party, will not be a valid ground for rescission.[6]

### § 3:16. Specific Performance

A written agreement for a lease may be specifically enforced as a contract, provided it comes within the general rules governing specific performance of contracts.[7] Courts do not grant specific performance of an agreement for a lease as a matter of course, it has been said,[8] as they do in the case of agreements to buy or sell land. Generally, in the absence of special circumstances, equity insists on a showing of the inadequacy of the remedy at law.

Clearly, however, if the agreement for a lease is not a valid contract,[9] a suit to compel specific performance thereof will not lie.[10]

---

3. Schultz v Brenner (Oneida Co Ct 1898) 24 Misc 522, 53 NYS 972.

4. See § 3:11, supra.

5. Friedlander v Fleischhauer (AT 1911) 132 NYS 508.

6. Porto v O'Reilly (1911, Sup App T) 129 NYS 69; Also see, Taylor v Goelet (1913) 208 NY 253, 101 NE 867.

7. Newburger v American Surety Co. (1926) 242 NY 134, 151 NE 155; New York Produce Exchange Safe Deposit & Storage Co. v New York Produce Exch. (AD1 1924) 208 AD 421, 203 NYS 648, affd 238 NY 582, 144 NE 901.

Equity has the power to specifically enforce an executory agreement to lease property. Shea v Keeney (AD1 1913) 155 AD 628, 140 NYS 912; Brune v Vom Lehn (S Ct Kings Co 1920) 112 Misc 342, 183 NYS 360, affd 196 AD 907, 187 NYS 928.

8. Schwartz v Church & Commerce Corp (S Ct NY Co 1945) 184 Misc 200, 53 NYS2d 666.

9. §§ 3:4 et seq, supra.

10. Ginsberg v Oltarsh (S Ct NY Co 1927) 130 Misc 891, 224 NYS 622; Noonan v Mott (S Ct NY Co 1921) 194 NYS 502, affd 202 AD 744, 194 NYS 962, where the agreement for a lease sought to be enforced provided for the incorporation in the lease of the "usual clauses contained in long-term leases with respect to defaults, insur-

## § 3:17. First Option to Lease; Damages for Breach

The damages for breach of an agreement to give a prospective tenant the first option of leasing the premises on the same terms landlord is willing to accept from anyone else, is measured by the difference between the actual rental value of the premises for the full term of the lease, and the rent reserved in the lease. If the actual rental value is equal to or less than the rent reserved, no damages are recoverable.[11]

## E. RESEARCH REFERENCES

### § 3:18. Generally

In addition to the preceding text, the reader is also referred to the following:

49 Am Jur 2d, Landlord and Tenant §§ 18-24.

11 Am Jur Legal Forms 2d, Leases of Real Property §§ 161:11-161:23.

New York Jur 2d, Landlord and Tenant (1st ed §§ 16-23)

New York Forms, Leases, Forms 8:11-8:18.

Index to Annotations, Landlord and Tenant.

**VERALEX®:** Cases and annotations referred to herein can be further researched through the VERALEX electronic retrieval system's two services, **Auto-Cite®** and **SHOWME®**. Use Auto-Cite to check citations for form, parallel references, prior and later history, and annotation references. Use SHOWME to display the full text of cases and annotations.

---

ance, public ordinances, etc., and covenant against nuisances, and appropriate clauses requiring the tenant to keep the premises in proper repair during the continuance of the lease, and such other usual and appropriate clauses as shall be agreed upon", and the court held such agreement too indefinite to be specifically enforced. Summary proceedings may not be brought by lessee to obtain possession by virtue of an oral lease, which proceeding in effect is an alternative to an action for specific performance. Gardens Nursery School v Columbia University of New York (NYC Civ Ct NY Co 1978) 94 Misc 2d 376, 404 NYS2d 833 (citing text).

11. Selmar Garage Corp. v Rink Realty Corp. (S Ct Kings Co 1952) 114 NYS2d 412, revd on other grounds (AD2 1953) 282 AD 780, 122 NYS2d 658, affd 309 NY 717, 128 NE2d 419. (On appeal from retrial, see 284 AD 1064, 136 NYS2d 229).

Where lease gave tenant first option to rent space occupied by another tenant when it "becomes available," such space did not become available when the occupant assigned his lease to another, and the occupant's lease contained no prohibition against assignment. John Stuart, Inc. v Diriro, Inc. (1978, 1st Dept) 66 AD2d 682, 411 NYS2d 30, affd 48 NY2d 686, 421 NYS2d 882, 397 NE2d 393.

## CHAPTER 4

## LEASES AND OTHER INTERESTS IN REAL PROPERTY DISTINGUISHED

A. IN GENERAL
- § 4:1. Test of Distinction
- § 4:2. Board and Lodging Agreement
- § 4:3. Occupation by Purchaser of Premises
- § 4:4. Occupation by Grantor After Conveyance
- § 4:5. Occupation by Mortgagor or Mortgagee
- § 4:6. Contract to Cultivate Land or Farm on Shares
- § 4:7. Occupation of Premises by Employee
- § 4:8. Effect of Deduction from wages of Employee for Occupancy of Employer's Premises
- § 4:9. Effect on Nature of Occupancy Where Tenant Becomes Employee
- § 4:10. Expense Sharing Arrangement

B. DISTINGUISHING BETWEEN LEASE AND LICENSE
- § 4:11. Test
- § 4:12. Effect of Owner's Right to Regulate Use of Property
- § 4:13. Effect of Cancellation Clause
- § 4:14. Use of Wall or Roof for Advertising Purposes
- § 4:15. Business Concession
- § 4:16. Washing Machine Concession
- § 4:17. Storage of Automobile in Public Garage
- § 4:18. Importance of Distinguishing Between Lease and License
- § 4:19. Non-assignability of License
- § 4:20. Effect of Grantor's Conveyance on License
- § 4:21. Revocability of License

C. PROPRIETARY LEASE (CO-OPERATIVE OWNERSHIP)
- § 4:22. Generally
- § 4:23. Form of Proprietary Lease

D. RESEARCH REFERENCES
- § 4:24. Generally

## A. IN GENERAL

### § 4:1. Test of Distinction

A lease, it has been seen,[1] is the present transfer of an estate in a designated portion of real property, whereby

§ 4:1　　　　　　　　LANDLORD AND TENANT

the lessor yields up to the lessee exclusive possession of such designated portion of real property for a specified term. It is the transfer of absolute control and possession of property which differentiates a lease from other arrangements dealing with property rights.[2] Whether an agreement constitutes a lease, and creates the relation of landlord and tenant, depends upon the intent of the parties,[3] and not on the characterization of the agreement.[4] As the Court of Appeals said,[5] " 'We must look to the rights it [the agreement] confers and the obligation it imposes' in order to determine the true nature of the transaction and the relationship of the parties."[6] No particular words are necessary to constitute a lease, the Appellate Division said,[7] if it appears that it was the intention of one party "to dispossess himself of the premises and of the other to enter and occupy as the former himself had to right to do." Thus the fact that the agreement refers to one of the parties as "lessee,"[8] or that the parties are described therein as landlord and tenant,[9]

1. § 1:2, supra.

2. Feder v Caliguira (1960) 8 NY2d 400, 208 NYS2d 970, 171 NE2d 316; The Statement, Inc. v Pilgrim's Landing, Inc. (1975, 4th Dept) 49 AD2d 28, 370 NYS2d 970; Riverview Apartments Co. v Golos (1983, 3d Dept) 97 AD2d 917, 470 NYS2d 758, app dismd 62 NY2d 976, 479 NYS2d 342, 468 NE2d 297.

3. Feder v Caliguira (1960) 8 NY2d 400, 208 NYS2d 970, 171 NE2d 316.

4. Equitable Life Assur. Soc. v Winter Leasing Corp. (1934) 265 NY 398, 193 NE 246 ("To say that Winter retained an interest or estate in the premises, seems to us to disregard the substance of the agreement and to give effect to mere characterizations"); The Statement, Inc. v Pilgrim's Landing, Inc. (1975, 4th Dept) 49 AD2d 28, 370 NYS2d 970; Riverview Apartments Co. v Golos (1983, 3d Dept) 97 AD2d 917, 470 NYS2d 758, app dismd 62 NY2d 976, 479 NYS2d 342, 468 NE2d 297.

5. Feder v Caliguira (1960) 8 NY2d 400, 404, 208 NYS2d 970, 171 NE2d 316.

6. People v Horowitz (1956) 309 NY 426, 131 NE2d 715; New York World-Telegram Corp. v McGoldrick (1948) 298 NY 11, 80 NE2d 61; Muller v Concourse Investors, Inc. (S Ct NY Co 1952) 201 Misc 340, 111 NYS2d 678; Kaypar Corp. v Fosterport Realty Corp. (S Ct Bx Co 1947) 1 Misc 2d 469, 69 NYS2d 313, affd 272 AD 878, 72 NYS2d 405; Williams v Hylan (S Ct NY Co (1928)) 223 AD 48, 227 NYS 392, affd 248 NY 616, 162 NE 547.

7. Potter v New York, O. & W. R. Co. (AD4 1931) 233 AD 578, 253 NYS 394, affd 261 NY 489, 185 NE 708; Canton Steel Ceiling Co. v Duffy Malt Whiskey Co. (AD1 1922) 200 AD 306, 192 NYS 792.

8. Feder v Caliguira (1960) 8 NY2d 400, 208 NYS2d 970, 171 NE2d 316.

9. People v Horowitz (1956) 309 NY 426, 131 NE2d 715.

"The use of the words 'relationship of landlord and tenant' in the contract of purchase does not necessarily establish such relationship where all the circumstances indicate to the contrary." Vogel v Finkelstein (S Ct Kings Co 1948) 82 NYS2d 861.

## INTERESTS IN REAL PROPERTY § 4:1

or that the agreement is called a lease, does not transform the agreement into a lease if exclusive possession of a specified portion of real property is not granted.[1] As the Court of Appeals said, "While this paper is called a lease, it is manifestly nothing more than a license. . . . It conveys no estate or interest whatever in the realty and no possession or right of possession to the building or any part of it."[2] Although such characterization of the agreement may be indicative of intent, it is not conclusive. The court must also inquire into the nature of the privilege granted in order to determine the true nature of the agreement.[3] Conversely, an agreement may be a lease even though the word "lease" is not used.[4] Moreover, although the reservation of rent is one of the classic indicia of the relationship of landlord and tenant,[5] and is "high evidence of such relation,"[6] it is by itself not conclusive of the relationship. As a matter of fact, the reservation of rent is not essential to the relation.[7]

Therefore, the test to distinguish a lease from other rights or interests in real property is not the characterization of the instrument, or the language used, but whether it is the manifest intent of the parties, gleaned

1. Feder v Caliguira (1960) 8 NY2d 400, 208 NYS2d 970, 171 NE2d 316; People v Horowitz (1956) 309 NY 426, 131 NE2d 715; United Merchants' Realty & Improv. Co. v New York Hippodrome (AD1 1909) 133 AD 582, 118 NYS 128, affd 201 NY 601, 95 NE 1140; Hess v Roberts (AD1 1908) 124 AD 328, 108 NYS 894; Muller v Concourse Investors, Inc. (S Ct NY Co 1952) 201 Misc 340, 111 NYS2d 678.

2. Reynolds v Van Beuren (1898) 155 NY 120, 123, 49 NE 763.

3. New York v Pennsylvania R. Co. (1975) 37 NY2d 298, 372 NYS2d 56, 333 NE2d 361; People v Horowitz (1956) 309 NY 426, 131 NE2d 715; Muller v Concourse Investors, Inc. (S Ct NY Co 1952) 201 Misc 340, 111 NYS2d 678; Planetary Recreations, Inc. v Kerns, Inc. (City Ct NY Co 1945) 184 Misc 340, 54 NYS2d 418.

4. Rochester Poster Advertising Co. v State (Ct Cls 1961) 27 Misc 2d 99, 213 NYS2d 812, affd (4th Dept) 15 AD2d 632, 222 NYS2d 688, affd 11 NY2d 1036, 230 NYS2d 30, 183 NE2d 911.

5. Coffman v Gale (AD3 1936) 248 AD 25, 289 NYS 713.

6. Peer v O'Leary (Super Ct Buffalo 1894) 8 Misc 350, 28 NYS 687.

7. Peerless Sugar Co. v 35 Steuben St. Realty Corp. (S Ct Kings Co 1946) 66 NYS2d 839, app dismd (AD) 69 NYS2d 922; Pfalzgraf v Voso (S Ct Kings Co 1945) 184 Misc 575, 55 NYS2d 171; Manhattan Co. v Nieberg (M Ct Man 1936) 164 Misc 618, 298 NYS 539; 791 Corp. v Engel (M Ct Man 1934) 152 Misc 107, 273 NYS 322.

Where one was in possession, holding for no particular time, paying no rent, making no compensation for the use of the land, but under an agreement to surrender the premises whenever the owner should require the possession, such occupant was held to be a tenant at will, the facts establishing the relation of landlord and tenant. Burns v Bryant (1865) 31 NY 453.

Also, see Harris v Frink (1872) 49 NY 24, 32.

§ 4:1   LANDLORD AND TENANT

from a consideration of the entire agreement involved, that exclusive control and possession, subject to reserved rights, of specified space of real property for a specified term have been granted. The burden of proving the relation of landlord and tenant, as a general rule, rests on the party asserting it.[8]

### § 4:2. Board and Lodging Agreement

Generally, a contract for lodging, or for board and lodging, does not create the relationship of landlord and tenant.[9] In contracts of this type the necessary element to constitute a lease; to wit, dominion over the premises to be occupied,[10] generally is not surrendered to the lodger.[11]

However, if exclusive possession and dominion over the occupied premises are granted to the occupant, and the letting of rooms is the principal thing, and the furnishing of board or services is merely incidental thereto, then the occupant is a tenant, and not a boarder or lodger.[12]

### § 4:3. Occupation by Purchaser of Premises

If a purchaser of real property is permitted or given the right to take possession thereof prior to the delivery of the deed, it has been held that this in and of itself generally is insufficient to create the relation of landlord and tenant between him and the vendor.[13] Absent an

---

8. Kumro v Slattery (City Ct Tonawanda Co 1933) 150 Misc 269, 268 NYS 61.

9. Farose Realty Corp. v Shaff (M Ct Bk 1952) 117 NYS2d 375; Wise v Vaughner (M Ct Bx 1951) 105 NYS2d 338; Ashton v Margolies (AT 1911) 72 Misc 70, 129 NYS 617.

10. § 4:1, supra.

11. Thus, where the owner of a house agreed that her daughter and son-in-law should make the house their home, and should take it upon themselves to board her, and to make the necessary repairs to the house, such agreement to continue during her pleasure, it was held that the conventional relation of landlord and tenant did not exist between the owner and said occupants. It was apparent from the nature of the occupancy and of the duties assumed by the alleged tenants, said the court, that there had been no intention to create such relation. Schreiber v Goldsmith (AT 1901) 35 Misc 45, 70 NYS 236.

12. Oliver v Moore (GT1 1889) 53 Hun 472, 6 NYS 413, affd 131 NY 589, 30 NE 67, where an agreement by which the owner of a dwelling engaged in renting rooms and furnishing board let "all those certain two rooms situated in the third story . . . for the term of 8½ months", from a specified date to a specified date for a specified sum, payable in weekly installments, was held to be a lease, although the landlord also agreed to furnish board for the rent reserved, the provision for board being deemed collateral to the principal undertaking, namely, the leasing of the rooms.

Also, see Shearman v Iroquois Hotel & Apartment Co. (AT 1903) 42 Misc 217, 85 NYS 365.

13. Preston v Hawley (1886) 101 NY 586, 5 NE 770; Pinmor Realty

# INTERESTS IN REAL PROPERTY § 4:4

agreement to create a landlord-tenant relationship, a vendor of real property cannot recover an award for a contract-vendee's use and occupancy of the property.[14] Where a prospective purchaser utilized part of the premises with the acquiescense of one of the tenants by the entirety who was in possession, this in and of itself was held insufficient to establish the relation of landlord and tenant warranting recovery for use and occupation.[15]

However, the parties to a contract for the sale of land can by express agreement create the relation of landlord and tenant pending the closing of title.[16]

## § 4:4. Occupation by Grantor after Conveyance

When a grantor wrongfully continues in possession of real property after a conveyance thereof, the relation between him and his grantee is not, as a general rule, that of landlord and tenant. Thus, where a vendor as part of his contract to sell real property agrees to vacate the premises at a specified time, and to deliver possession thereof to the purchaser, the relation of landlord and tenant generally is not created between the parties.[17] This principle has been held to apply to the State when it appropriates land, because in such situation it stands toward the owner as a vendor toward a purchaser.[18]

In the absence of an express agreement establishing

Corp. v Baris Hotel Corp. (1981, 2d Dept) 83 AD2d 847, 441 NYS2d 751; Stevens v Nye (AD2 1954) 283 AD 666, 127 NYS2d 4, amd 283 AD 671, 127 NYS2d 844; Castle v Armstead (AD2 1915) 168 AD 466, 153 NYS 266, affd 219 NY 615, 114 NE 1062; Smith v Keech (Yates Co Ct 1952) 112 NYS2d 803; Burkhart v Tucker (Lewis Co Ct 1899) 27 Misc 724, 59 NYS 711.

14. Greenbriar-Somers Corp. v Petrone (1986, 2d Dept) 124 AD2d 705, 508 NYS2d 465.

15. Petriski v Ward (1958, 4th Dept) 5 AD2d 950, 171 NYS2d 165, reh den (4th Dept) 7 AD2d 619, 179 NYS2d 677.

16. Stevens v Nye (AD2 1954) 283 AD 666, 127 NYS2d 4, amd 283 AD 671, 127 NYS2d 844, where contract provided that possession was given to the purchaser as a "tenant at sufferance", and that the purchaser shall not be deemed "a vendee in possession".

Millbrook Co. v Gambier (AD1 1917) 176 AD 870, 163 NYS 1025, affd 266 NY 661, 123 NE 878; New York Bldg. Loan Banking Co. v Keeney (AD2 1900) 56 AD 538, 67 NYS 505.

17. Raguso v Ferreira (S Ct Queens Co 1946) 60 NYS2d 418, where grantee was awarded judgment decreeing specific performance of grantor's agreement to vacate, the court holding that there was no conventional relation of landlord-tenant between them which would enable grantee to bring summary proceedings. (However, see Real Property Actions and Proceedings Law § 713(8) which now permits summary proceedings in this situation.)

18. Walker v State (Ct Claims 1958) 15 Misc 2d 4, 178 NYS2d 507; Geist v State (Ct Claims 1956) 3 Misc 2d 714, 156 NYS2d 183.

the relation of landlord and tenant, there must be proof of some circumstances authorizing an inference that the parties intend to assume such relation toward each other. The mere continuance in possession by a grantor after delivery of the deed continues to be of the same character as that which preceded it, unless changed by some contract entered into in the interim.[19] As the Court of Appeals said, in referring to this situation,[20] the purchaser "cannot change the relation existing between himself as a purchaser of real property, and the vendor unlawfully remaining in possession at his option, and impose upon such vendor the character of a tenant, by stating to him that he should thereafter require him to pay rent. It requires the assent of both parties, manifested in some intelligible manner, to make such a contract, and it is not like the case of a tenant continuing in possession after the expiration of his term under an announcement by the landlord of a change in the lease. There the assent of the tenant is implied, from his voluntary continuance of the term after a change in the conditions is stated, and the further occupation by the tenant is rightfully presumed to be under the lease as thus modified by the landlord. In this case there were never any contract relations between the parties except those stated in the deed, and no evidence showing authority in the plaintiff to impose terms upon his vendor, or of assent by him to hold as tenant under his vendee." It is not controlling, said the Appellate Division[1] more recently, that the words "relationship of landlord and tenant" were used in the contract. The contract concerned primarily the purchase and sale of the building, and the reserved right of defendant as vendor to occupy the premises for a limited period of time at a specified monthly sum was incidental to the main object of the transaction which was to sell the property.[2]

### § 4:5. Occupation by Mortgagor or Mortgagee

In New York the common law theory of a mortgage on real property as a conveyance of the legal estate does not

---

**19.** Preston v Hawley (1886) 101 NY 586, 590, 5 NE 770.

**20.** Preston v Hawley (1886) 101 NY 586, 591, 5 NE 770.

**1.** Scheir v Leifer (AD1 1947) 272 AD 789, 69 NYS2d 701.

**2.** Also, see Vogel v Finkelstein (S Ct Kings Co 1948) 82 NYS2d 861.

prevail. A mortgage covering the fee of real property constitutes merely a lien thereon, and vests no legal title thereto in the mortgagee.[3] Clearly, then, there is no relation of landlord and tenant between the mortgagee and mortgagor merely by virtue of the mortgage covering the fee, either before or after a default under the mortgage,[4] or even if the mortgagee enters into possession. The mere possession of the premises cannot change the mortgagor's title, or in any way diminish the estate of the mortgagor, or enlarge the estate of the mortgagee.[5] As the Court of Appeals said,[6] "How can the mere possession change the title from the mortgagor to the mortgagee, or in any way diminish the estate of the one or enlarge the estate of the other? Before taking possession the mortgagee had a mere lien upon the real estate pledged for the security of his debt. After possession he has in his possession the property pledged as his security, the title remaining as it was before. The mortgagor's title is still a legal one, with all the incidents of a legal title subject to the pledge, and the mortgagee's interest is still a mere debt secured by the pledge."

## § 4:6. Contract to Cultivate Land or Farm on Shares

When a landowner permits another person to work his land for a specified period of time, under an agreement whereby the landowner is to receive as compensation for the use of the land a share of the crops or products therefrom, and such other person is to receive the balance of the crops or products as compensation for his services, the courts have found it difficult to determine the resulting relationship between the parties. The relationship may be that of landlord and tenant, or of master and servant, or of owner and cropper.[7] One may be employed for the purpose of raising crops without there

3. Barson v Mulligan (1908) 191 NY 306, 315, 84 NE 75.

4. Roach v Cosine (Super Ct Albany 1832) 9 Wend 227.

See Steigman v Singer Tobacco & Confectionery Co. (1947, Sup App T) 72 NYS2d 560, affd 272 AD 1029, 74 NYS2d 831, holding that a mortgagor in possession is not a "tenant" within the meaning of the emergency rent laws.

5. Lawyers' Title Guaranty Co. v Tausig (M Ct Bk 1933) 149 Misc 594, 268 NYS 815.

6. Trimm v Marsh (1874) 54 NY 599, 606.

7. Harrison v McClellan (AD3 1910) 137 AD 508, 121 NYS 822; Millspaugh v Paduch (City Ct Middletown 1940) 174 Misc 365, 20 NYS2d 756.

§ 4:6            LANDLORD AND TENANT

having been created the relationship of landlord and tenant.[8]

In the absence of express intention, such contracts are ordinarily held not to constitute the parties partners, or joint adventurers.[9] However, the rule is that the relationship in any particular situation is to be determined by an interpretation of the agreement between the parties. As the Court of Appeals said in an early case on the subject,[10]

"Parties are certainly at liberty to define and establish their legal relations by the use of terms legally appropriate to the object; and it is not clear to my mind that courts should not give effect thereto, according to their understood legal meaning. Hence, when A agrees with B that he will employ B, with his team, etc. upon his farm, whether for one year or five, leaving B at liberty to cultivate such fields, and plant such crops as he shall see fit, with just regard to what good husbandry requires, and to pay B, for his work, labor and services, one half of the crops raised,—it is obvious that the parties intend an agreement for work, labor and services, to be paid for by A in a share of the results. On the other hand, if A should demise, lease and let the farm to B, to have and to hold for the term of one or five years, to be cultivated in a husband-like manner, rendering and paying to A an annual rent for the use of the farm, to wit, one-half of the crops raised,—I perceive no sensible reason why the parties should not be deemed to intend an actual and technical lease, which would entitle the lessee to possession, give him a term in the land, make his payment rent in the technical sense. It may well be inferred from this language, contradistinguished from the other, that here it was intended that the tenant should have exclusive possession and the whole ownership for the term, subject only to his duty to pay the rent as it accrued. While in the other case it would be equally plain that the owner did not intend to divest himself of possession or of title to

---

**8.** Millspaugh v Paduch (City Ct Middletown 1940) 174 Misc 365, 20 NYS2d 756.

**9.** Taylor v Bradley (1868) 39 NY 129; Pestlin v Haxton Canning Co. (AD3 1948) 274 AD 144, 80 NYS2d 869, affd 299 NY 477, 87 NE2d 522; Harrison v McClellan (AD3 1910) 137 AD 508, 121 NYS 822.

**10.** Taylor v Bradley (1868) 39 NY 129.

the crops, but to come under an obligation and duty to compensate for the services by paying therefor out of and according to the quantity of the products. In each case the result at the end of the term, if both performed, would be precisely the same; and yet it may be deemed by parties contemplating such arrangements with an owner of land, very important to their security that they should have all the rights of tenants, and when they obtain an instrument in the form of a lease, in very terms, giving them a term, and reserving rent as such, there would seem to me no legal reason for saying the parties did not intend just what such terms express."

Essentially the difference between a cropper and a tenant is that a tenant has an estate in the land for his term and, consequently, a right of property in the crop which he grows, unless the parties expressly agree otherwise.[11] If the transaction, however, is not a lease but a cropping agreement, that is, a contract to work a farm or land on shares, the relationship is that of owner and cropper, and they are deemed to be tenants in common of the crops, the quantum of their interest being dependent upon their agreement.[12] Basically, then, as has been pointed out,[13] if dominion over the premises to be occupied has been surrendered, a lease is created, no matter what phraseology is used. If the owner of a farm agrees with another that he will employ him with his team, for a specified term, leaving the employee to cultivate such fields, and to plant such crops as he shall see fit, with just regard to what good husbandry requires, and the owner further agrees to pay such employee for his work, labor and services, one half of the crops raised, it has been held that it is clear that the parties intend an agreement for

---

11. Taylor v Bradley (1868) 39 NY 129; Putnam v Wise (1841) 1 Hill 234.

12. Hudson v Glens Falls Ins. Co. (1916) 218 NY 133, 138, 112 NE 728; Banta v Merchant (1903) 173 NY 292, 66 NE 13.

Some authorities state that every contract, whether or not a lease, whereby the use of land is given to a person to cultivate and return to the owner a specified portion of the crop produced creates a tenancy in common in the crop until it is divided.

Millspaugh v Paduch (City Ct Middletown 1940) 174 Misc 365, 20 NYS2d 756; Putnam v Wise (1841) 1 Hill 234.

If the parties are regarded as tenants in common of the crop, a cropper may unite with the landowner in an action for trespass de bonis asportatis for cutting and carrying away the crop. Harris v Frink (1872) 49 NY 24.

As to rights of landlord and tenant with respect to crops, see §§ 7:26 et seq, infra.

13. § 4:1, supra.

work, labor and services, to be paid for by the owner in a share of the results. There is nothing to show that the owner intended to divest himself of possession or of title to the crops.[14] However, if the owner should "demise, lease and let" the farm to such employee to have and to hold for a specified term, to be cultivated in a husbandlike manner, rendering and paying to the owner an annual rent for the use of the farm, say, one half of the crops raised, it has been held that such an agreement clearly manifests an intention to create a landlord-tenant relationship, an intention that the tenant shall have exclusive possession and the whole ownership for the term, subject only to his duty to pay the rent as it accrues, even though such rent is to be paid in a share of the crops raised.[15]

The proposed duration of the agreement is to be considered in arriving at the intention of the parties as to the character of the relation created.[16] Thus, it has been held that an agreement to allow one to work land on shares for a single crop is no lease of the land.[17]

The death of a landowner,[18] or cropper,[19] before the time fixed for the expiration of a contract for farming on shares, which does not create the relation of landlord and tenant, has been held not to put an end to the contract.

### § 4:7. Occupation of Premises by Employee

It is important to determine the nature of the relationship created by the occupation by an employee of his employer's premises as part of the employee's compensation. If a tenancy is created, then upon the termination of the employment, the right of the employer to retake possession of the premises is determined solely by the application of the law of landlord and tenant. However, if the relationship created is solely that of employer and

---

14. Taylor v Bradley (1868) 39 NY 129.

15. Taylor v Bradley (1868) 39 NY 129; Putnam v Wise (1841) 1 Hill 234; Jackson ex dem Colden v Brownell (1806) 1 Johns 267.

Where a landlord leases land together with the livestock thereon, the relationship created between the parties is that of landlord and tenant.

Atwater v Lowe (GT1 1886) 39 Hun 150.

16. Putnam v Wise (1841) 1 Hill 234.

17. Harris v Frink (1872) 49 NY 24.

18. Re Strickland (Surr Ct Cattaraugus Co 1894) 10 Misc 486, 32 NYS 171.

19. Re Ballou (Orleans Co Ct 1909) 62 Misc 513, 116 NYS 1118.

# INTERESTS IN REAL PROPERTY § 4:7

employee, then the law of landlord and tenant is not applicable, and, unless the contract of employment contains some provision giving the employee the right to continue in possession, the employer may take immediate possession.[20]

There is no inconsistency between the two relationships of landlord and tenant, and of employer and employee. Both relationships can coexist at the same time. That is, an occupant of premises can be an employee of the owner of the premises, and at the same time, for all legal purposes, can be his tenant as well.[1] However, a tenant, as such, is neither the agent nor the employee of the landlord.[2]

In the absence of an express agreement on the subject clearly defining the relationship, whether the relationship of landlord and tenant exists between an employer and an employee who occupies the employer's premises depends upon this test: If an employee's occupation of his employer's premises is exclusive and independent of and not directly connected with the service rendered by the employee, the employee will be held to be a tenant of the premises.[3] In other words, in order that an employee's occupancy of premises is to be in the dual capacity of employee as well as tenant, it must appear either that the parties themselves did not treat the occupancy as an incident of the employment, or that it was expressly agreed that both relationships should coexist simultaneously.[4] But if the occupation of the employer's premises by the employee as part of the employee's compensation is incidental to and connected with the services rendered

---

20. See Chapter 31, where this subject is discussed.

1. Kerrains v People (1875) 60 NY 221; Marsar Gardens v Guevara (NY C Civ Ct Queens Co 1981) 108 Misc 2d 817, 439 NYS2d 77.

Also, see 344 East 110th Street, Inc. v Doe (AT1 1925) 125 Misc 917, 212 NYS 315; Ofschlager v Surveck (S Ct Onondaga Co 1898) 22 Misc 595, 50 NYS 862.

2. Kerrains v People (1875) 60 NY 221.

A lease creates rights and liabilities as between the parties thereto entirely inconsistent with any theory of agency in so far as liability for torts is concerned. In the absence of an express stipulation in the lease or a statutory provision, a lesee is not the agent of the owner for the purpose of receiving actual notice of a dangerous condition. Becker v Manufacturers Trust Co. (AD1 1941) 262 AD 525, 30 NYS2d 542, reh den 263 AD 810, 32 NYS2d 126.

3. Kerrains v People (1875) 60 NY 221; Maio v Borrelli (City Ct Mt Vernon 1948) 194 Misc 735, 83 NYS2d 532.

4. Tursi v Esposito (M Ct Bk 1949) 194 Misc 498, 86 NYS2d 702.

by the employee, or if the occupation of the employer's premises is required, either expressly or impliedly, by the employer for the necessary or better performance of the services to be rendered by the occupant, then such occupation is deemed to be for the employer's benefit. In such circumstances, the courts have held that the relationship of employer and employee, and not that of landlord and tenant, will arise.[5] In such situation there is no intent that the exclusive possession and control of the premises should pass to the employee during the term of the service,[6] which is the essential element of a lease.[7] Thus, caretakers, janitors, renting agents, and the like, who occupy their employer's premises as such, and as an incident of their employment, are not generally tenants, but employees.[8] Generally, in these types of employments, the occupancy of the premises arises only because of the relationship of employer and employee, and as an incident of such employment. As Beckinella, J., pointed out in a recent case,[9] "It is crystal clear from the evidence that when the owner sought out Esposito, and made him the proposition that he did, he was seeking to acquire a janitor rather than a tenant. The very first question that was asked of him was, 'Do you want to be a janitor?' The offering to him of the apartment was undoubtedly not only as an inducement to have him accept the post of janitor, but also that he would be more accessible and thus the better perform his duties. Under these circumstances it cannot be said that Esposito's occupancy was in the dual capacity of servant and tenant."

If the employee's occupancy is to be in the dual capacity of an employee as well as a tenant, it must clearly appear either that the parties themselves did not treat the occupancy as an incident of the employment, or that

---

**5.** Kerrains v People (1875) 60 NY 221; Maio v Borrelli (City Ct Mt Vernon 1948) 194 Misc 735, 83 NYS2d 532.

**6.** Kerrains v People (1875) 60 NY 221, 224.

**7.** § 4:1, supra.

**8.** Presby v Benjamin (1902) 169 NY 377, 62 NE 430 (caretakers); Bristor v Burr (1890) 120 NY 427, 24 NE 937 (clergyman); Kerrains v People (1875) 60 NY 221 (mill hand); H. L. Judd & Co. v Cushing (GT1 1888) 50 Hun 181, 2 NYS 836 (renting agent); Tursi v Esposito (M Ct Bk 1949) 194 Misc 498, 86 NYS2d 702 (janitor); Maio v Borrelli (City Ct Mt Vernon 1948) 194 Misc 735, 83 NYS2d 532 (superintendent of apartment house); Anderson v Steinrich (AT 1900) 32 Misc 680, 66 NYS 498 (janitor), later app 36 Misc 845, 74 NYS 920.

**9.** Tursi v Esposito (M Ct Bk 1949) 194 Misc 498, 86 NYS2d 702.

# INTERESTS IN REAL PROPERTY § 4:9

the parties expressly agreed for the co-existence of the dual relationship.[10]

## § 4:8. Effect of Deduction from Wages of Employee for Occupancy of Employer's Premises

While the deduction from the wages of an occupant of a specified sum for the use and occupation of the premises, or the absence of such an arrangement, may be a material circumstance in determining the nature of the relationship between an employer, and an employee occupying the employer's premises; yet, it will not be conclusive either way in all cases. Therefore, it has been held, either the deduction, or the absence of such a deduction, from the wages of an occupant is not the determinative factor in establishing the nature of the relationship.[11]

## § 4:9. Effect of Nature of Occupancy Where Tenant Becomes Employee

Where a tenant enters into possession of premises under a lease, and thereafter agrees with the landlord to perform services in connection with the premises, such as janitor's services, for a specific compensation to be deducted from the rent, it has been held that the agreement to perform such services will not, as a general rule, effect a change in the conventional relationship of landlord and tenant already in existence. In other words, in the absence of proof that the parties terminated, or intended to terminate, the pre-existing relationship of landlord and tenant, it will be held that the tenancy continues independently of the agreement to perform services, and the two relationships will coexist at the same time.[12]

Where tenant accepted job of superintendent for a

---

10. Kerrains v People (1875) 60 NY 221; Tursi v Esposito (M Ct Bk 1949) 194 Misc 498, 86 NYS2d 702.

11. Kerrains v People (1875) 60 NY 221; Tursi v Esposito (M Ct Bk 1949) 194 Misc 498, 86 NYS2d 702.

12. Filmat Realty Corp. v Carleo (AT2 1946) 186 Misc 717, 65 NYS2d 805; Marsar Gardens v Guevara (NYC Civ Ct Queens Co 1981) 108 Misc 2d 817, 439 NYS2d 77; Hartman v Sykes (NYC Civ Ct NY Co 1971) 66 Misc 2d 764, 322 NYS2d 158; Cosvira Realty Corp. v Hertelendy (M Ct Bx 1946) 61 NYS2d 283.

But, see Chirico v Kings County Sav. Bank (S Ct Kings Co 1938) 168 Misc 207, 4 NYS2d 723, where the court found that the original relationship of landlord and tenant was later changed by the agreement of the parties to that of master and servant, and that the parties treated the occupancy as incident to the relationship of master and servant, thereby destroying the relationship of landlord and tenant which had existed between them.

salary and right to live rent free, and moved into another apartment in the same building, a dual relationship of landlord and tenant, and employer and employee, existed, and landlord was not entitled to recover possession of apartment upon terminating the employment, irrespective of whether tenant had moved into new apartment at time she was given job, or moved into it after she had assumed the job. Dobson Factors, Inc. v Dattory (NYC Civ Ct NY Co 1975) 80 Misc 2d 1054, 364 NYS2d 723.

### § 4:10. Expense Sharing Arrangement

Where a lease to an apartment is made between landlord and two named lessees, and they occupy the apartment together with a third party under an expense-sharing arrangement for 5 years, the third party has been held not to be a tenant at will subject to removal at the will of the named lessees, nor to be a party to any tenancy relationship, but he is a party to a partnership relationship with the named lessees.[13]

Where lessee of an office agreed with a third party to share occupancy of the office, the third party agreeing to pay two-thirds of the monthly rent and utility charges, it was held that the third party was not a subtenant, but was a "roommate" with the lessee under an agreement to share the stipulated expenses of the office.[14]

## B. DISTINGUISHING BETWEEN LEASE AND LICENSE

### § 4:11. Test

"A license," said the Court of Appeals in a leading case on the subject,[15] "is a personal, revocable and non-assignable privilege, conferred either by writing or parol, to do one or more acts upon land without possessing any interest therein." In other words, a license is the "authority to do a particular act or series of acts upon another's land, which would

---

13. Halbruber v O'Daly (NYC Civ Ct Queens Co 1971) 67 Misc 2d 219, 323 NYS2d 797 (proceeding dismissed).

14. Hispano Americano Advertising, Inc. v Dryer (NYC Civ Ct NY Co 1982) 112 Misc 2d 936, 448 NYS2d 128.

15. Greenwood L. & P. J. R. Co. v New York & G. L. R. Co. (1892) 134 NY 435, 31 NE 874; also see, Mendenhall v Klinck (1872) 51 NY 246, 250; Mammy's Inc. & Pappy's, Inc. v All Continent Corp. (S Ct NY Co 1951) 106 NYS2d 635.

## INTERESTS IN REAL PROPERTY § 4:11

amount to a trespass without such permission."[16] However, as has been seen,[17] a lease is the transfer of an estate or interest in a designated portion of real estate, whereby the landlord yields up to the tenant exclusive possession of such designated portion of real estate for a specified term.

The test of the distinction between a lease and a license depends, substantially, upon the question whether or not the contract or authority granting the right to enter upon the land of another confers upon the person so entering an interest in the land, so as to affect the other in the use of his land. If the instrument purports to yield up exclusive possession of premises against the world, including the owner, it is not a license, but creates an irrevocable estate or interest in the land.[18] As was said by the Court of Appeals, "A lease of property in which the lessee has no right either to use the property or to control its use is an unheard of legal conception."[19] If the agreement conveys no estate or interest whatever in the real estate, and no exclusive possession, or right of exclusive possession, to any specified part of real estate, then the agreement is nothing more than a license to enter upon someone else's land.[20]

A license is not an interest or estate in the land corporeal or incorporeal.[1]

To constitute a lease, therefore, the agreement must yield up to a tenant exclusive possession of a designated space, and not merely permit the use or occupancy of the grantor's real property.[2]

---

**16.** Meers v Munsch-Protzmann Co. (AD1 1926) 217 AD 541, 217 NYS 256.
**17.** § 4:1, supra.
**18.** Williams v Hylan (AD1 1928) 233 AD 48, 227 NYS 392, affd 248 NY 616, 162 NE 547; Mehlman v Atlantic Amusement Co. (AT 1909) 65 Misc 25, 119 NYS 222.
**19.** Feder v Caliguira (1960) 8 NY2d 400, 208 NYS2d 970, 171 NE2d 316.
**20.** Reynolds v Van Beuren (1898) 155 NY 120, 123, 49 NE 763; United Merchants' Realty & Improv. Co. v New York Hippodrome (AD1 1909) 133 AD 582, 118 NYS 128, affd 201 NY 601, 95 NE 1140; Coney Island & B. R. Co. v Brooklyn Cable Co. (S Ct GT2 1889) 53 Hun 169, 6 NYS 108; Rochester Poster Advertising Co. v State (Ct Cls 1961) 27 Misc 2d 99, 213 NYS2d 812, affd (4th Dept) 15 AD2d 632, 222 NYS2d 688, affd 11 NY2d 1036, 230 NYS2d 30, 183 NE2d 911; Bagg v Robinson (Super Ct Buffalo 1895) 12 Misc 299, 34 NYS 37.
**1.** Senrow Concessions, Inc. v Skelton Properties, Inc. (1961) 10 NY2d 320, 222 NYS2d 329, 178 NE2d 726.
**2.** Muller v Concourse Investors, Inc. (S Ct NY Co 1952) 201 Misc 340, 111 NYS2d 678; Polner v Arling Realty, Inc. (S Ct Kings Co 1949) 194 Misc 831, 88 NYS2d 348, and 194

§ 4:11 LANDLORD AND TENANT

It has been seen that what the parties call the instrument, or that the parties refer to each other as landlord and tenant, respectively, is immaterial. The court still must inquire into the nature of the privileges granted in the instrument in order to determine its true character.[3]

**§ 4:12. Effect of Owner's Right to Regulate Use of Property**

When an owner of real property grants another the exclusive right to possession of his property, such right is nonetheless exclusive even if the owner reserves the right to prescribe regulations for the use of the property.[4] This right is very often reserved in many leases in commercial and other realty situations.

Therefore, the reservation of a right to prescribe regulations for the use of the property is not determinative of the nature of the agreement as a lease or as a license.

**§ 4:13. Effect of Cancellation Clause**

If exclusive possession of specified real estate is granted, the instrument generally will be held to be a lease. The mere fact that the instrument contains a cancellation clause will not affect the nature of the instrument if it is otherwise a lease. As was pointed out by the Court, in so holding,[5] exclusive possession is not affected by the fact that the instrument contains a cancellation clause; for, "so do many leases in commercial and other realty situations."

In interpreting an agreement involving this problem, the Appellate Division said,[6] "Every element of a lease is here present. By its terms there is an attempted alienation of the property of the city for 10 years, which lease provided that it can be revoked only in the event that the city needs this property for a public purpose. This lease is

Misc 598, 86 NYS2d 891; Shepard Warehouses, Inc. v Scherman (S Ct NY Co 1946) 63 NYS2d 421.

One who hires desk space in an office has no estate or interest in real property, and therefore is no tenant. Eaton v Hall (S Ct Kings Co 1904) 43 Misc 153, 88 NYS 260.

3. § 4:1, supra.

4. Williams v Hylan (S Ct NY Co 1926) 126 Misc 807, 215 NYS 101, affd 217 AD 727, 216 NYS 936, later app 223 AD 48, 227 NYS 392, affd 248 NY 616, 162 NE 547.

5. Williams v Hylan (S Ct NY Co 1926) 126 Misc 807, 215 NYS 101, affd 217 AD 727, 216 NYS 936, later app 223 AD 48, 227 NYS 392, affd 248 NY 616, 162 NE 547.

6. Williams v Hylan (AD1 1928) 223 AD 48, 227 NYS 392, affd 248 NY 616, 162 NE 547.

similar in many respects to the ordinary 10-year lease, which contains a cancellation clause in case the property should be sold."

Therefore, the reservation of a right to cancel an agreement is not determinative of the nature of the agreement as a lease or as a license.

## § 4:14. Use of Wall or Roof for Advertising Purposes

The grant or "lease" of the exclusive right to place signs on the roof or wall of a building, or on a lot of land, with the right of access to the signs to maintain them, but without granting to the "lessee" some estate or interest in the realty, and the exclusive possession of some specified part thereof, is not a lease, but a license,[7] or, as one court preferred to term it, an easement in gross.[8]

Where an advertising firm was given the right only to use a wall of a building to display advertising material, the Appellate Term said,[9]

"It could do nothing else to or with the wall; it could exercise no act of dominion over it. So far from having exclusive possession, it did not even have exclusive occupation of that part of the plaintiff's premises."[10]

In an early case, a tenant of an entire building gave a defendant the right to use a sign that was situated on the roof. The agreement conferring such right provided that in consideration of a monthly rental, payable in advance, the tenant "leased" to the defendant the roof of the building to be used for advertising purposes. The tenant agreed to keep the roof in repair, and the defendant agreed that if the property were sold, or "improved upon," he would vacate on 30 days' notice. In passing upon the nature of this agreement, the Court of Appeals

---

**7.** Reynolds v Van Beuren (1898) 155 NY 120, 123, 49 NE 763; Realty Advertising & Supply Co. v Hickson (AD1 1918) 184 AD 168, 171 NYS 455; Reeve v Duryee (AD2 1911) 144 AD 647, 129 NYS 748; Stockham v Borough Bill Posting Co. (AD2 1911) 144 AD 642, 129 NYS 745; Goldman v New York Advertising Co. (AT 1899) 29 Misc 133, 60 NYS 275; Manheimer v Gudat (S Ct NY Co 1907) 55 Misc 330, 106 NYS 461.

**8.** Whitmier & Ferris Co. v State (1961, 4th Dept) 12 AD2d 165, 209 NYS2d 247.

**9.** Goldman v New York Advertising Co. (AT 1899) 29 Misc 133, 60 NYS 275.

**10.** Reynolds v Van Beuren (1898) 155 NY 120, 123, 49 NE 763.

§ 4:14   LANDLORD AND TENANT

said, "While this paper is called a lease it is manifestly nothing more than a license by the tenant in possession to the defendants to go upon the roof of the building and place advertisements upon the sign. It conveys no estate or interest whatever in the realty and no possession or right of possession to the building or any part of it."

In a leading case on the subject,[11] the facts were these. Plaintiff "let" to defendant at a monthly rental the roof of a building for two years, to be used for erecting thereon a bulletin board for advertising. Defendant was to have access to the roof during business hours for the purpose of erecting, improving, and maintaining the bulletin board. Plaintiff, however, reserved the right to enter upon the roof at any time to make any improvements it might require, or to place skylights thereon. This agreement was held to be a license, and not a lease. In so holding, the Appellate Division said, "Whether or not this agreement constituted a lease of the roof of this building is a question not free from doubt; but I am inclined to think that the conventional relation of landlord and tenant did not exist. The fact that the parties used the words "let" and "landlord" is not conclusive. . . . There was no specific property leased, but what seems to have been intended was a right to use the roof to erect upon it an advertising sign. The use to which the roof was to be put was strictly limited, and the plaintiff reserved the right of access to the roof at all times. The plaintiff agreed to give the defendant access to the roof during business hours; but such right of access was restricted to the purpose of erecting and maintaining said sign, or changing said sign or the equipment thereof from time to time. There was no right of re-entry reserved, and none was necessary, as the plaintiff had the right of access to the roof at all times. There was no covenant to deliver possession of the premises at the expiration of the agreement, and no possession of the premises was given, except for the purpose of maintaining the sign. It is quite clear that the defendant was not given exclusive possession of the premises at any time."

Thus, the essential element of the lease of real property

---

11. United Merchants' Realty & Improv. Co. v New York Hippodrome (AD1 1909) 133 AD 582, 118 NYS 128, affd 201 NY 601, 95 NE 1140.

# INTERESTS IN REAL PROPERTY § 4:15

is generally lacking in the usual advertising privilege agreement. The advertiser gets no exclusive right of possession of any designated premises, but simply a right to erect or use a sign on real estate, with a right of access thereto merely to maintain the sign.

However, an agreement for the use of a roof for advertising purposes which involved possession and dominion over a substantial part of it for the purpose of constructing and maintaining signs, was a lease and not a mere license.[12]

## § 4:15. Business Concession

It is not uncommon for a drug store to agree to let someone operate a luncheonette concession, or for a theatre or restaurant to grant checkroom and washroom concessions. In construing such agreements, the courts have always applied the fundamental test: Has the real property owner yielded up to the concessionaire exclusive possession of a specified or designated portion of the real property, or has he merely given the concessionaire a license to occupy the premises for the specified purpose?

Thus, where a real property owner gave a concessionaire the privilege of selling drinks and checking clothes in his establishment for a specified period of time, for a stipulated payment, without designating which specified portion of the real property the concessionaire was to occupy, the court held that such an agreement constituted a license, and not a lease. In so ruling, the Supreme Court said,[13] "There was nothing in the agreement to show that the defendant was to be the landlord of plaintiff or that plaintiff was to have exclusive possession of any particular portion of the real estate, which is an indispensable attribute of a leasing."

In an early case a hotel agreed to give a stenographer the exclusive privilege of the public stenographer's office in the hotel for a stipulated monthly rental. The stenographer agreed to do the private correspondence for the hotel management, and to furnish competent stenographers for such service. If the services were not satisfacto-

---

12. Pocher v Hall (AT 1906) 50 Misc 639, 98 NYS 754.
13. Criterion Concessions, Inc. v Jelin Productions, Inc. (S Ct NY Co 1946) 61 NYS2d 239.

§ 4:15                               LANDLORD AND TENANT

rily performed, the hotel reserved the right to revoke the agreement. If the stenographer found that the arrangement was not sufficiently remunerative, she could likewise revoke the agreement. The Appellate Division[14] said, "This instrument is called a lease, although it is nothing of the kind. It is a mere agreement to allow a stenographer and typewriter to carry on business in a hotel. . . . Under such a contract it is quite clear that neither party could insist upon maintaining the agreement against the opposition of the other."

A more recent example of a license-concession arrangement is the one where a night club gives a concessionaire the right to visit the tables in the night club to sell cigars and cigarettes; to take, and to sell photographs to be developed on the premises; and to maintain service in the washrooms and coatrooms. In discussing such an agreement the Court said,[15] "The terms 'lease of concession,' 'landlord,' and 'tenant' are used. These words, however, although highly indicative of intent, are not conclusive in establishing a landlord and tenant relationship. The court must also inquire into the nature of the privileges granted in the instrument in order to determine its true character, regardless of the terms the parties have applied to it. With exception of vague provisions to supply unspecified space for a coatroom and a darkroom, the agreement does not purport to yield up exclusive possession of any particular part of the premises against anyone, including the owner, and does not otherwise create an interest or estate in the property. It is more in the nature of a license than a lease. Under this agreement, there was no demise of specific property. . . ."[16] Similarly, an agreement whereby a concessionaire contracted to install and maintain stands and vending machinery in theatres for the sale of cigarettes, beverages, and candy, was held to be a license, because, as the court pointed out, exclusive possession of a defined portion of the theatre had not been given to the concessionaire under this

14. Hess v Roberts (AD1 1908) 124 AD 328, 108 NYS 894.
15. Planetary Recreations, Inc. v Kerns, Inc. (City Ct NY Co 1945) 184 Misc 340, 54 NYS2d 418.
16. Also, see Schusterman v C. & F. Caterers, Inc. (City Ct Bx Co 1948) 192 Misc 564, 77 NYS2d 718 (coatroom concession, held license).

## INTERESTS IN REAL PROPERTY § 4:15

agreement, nor did the agreement so much as specify where the stands or machines were to be located.[17]

However, an agreement granting concession privileges may constitute a lease. But, then, the concessionaire must be given exclusive possession of a designated space. Thus, the following agreement was held to be a lease because of the presence of this element. A drug store owner gave a concessionaire "permission" to operate a soda fountain and luncheonette counter in the drug store. The size and location of the fountain were to be in accordance with a certain drawing annexed to the agreement, initialled and approved by both parties. The term of the agreement was five years. The rental was a stipulated percentage of the gross receipts. The drug store owner also agreed that in the event he obtained a renewal of his lease, he would grant the concessionaire a renewal of the agreement for a similar term. It is manifest, said the Appellate Division,[18] that it was intended by this agreement to confer upon the concessionaire something more than a bare license. This agreement contained all the essential elements of a lease. The space to be occupied by the concessionaire was specified in the agreement. As long as the concessionaire paid his rental therefor, he was entitled to the exclusive possession thereof. This was more than a grant of authority to do a series of acts upon another's land which, without such permission, would amount to a trespass. Nevertheless, even though the space to be occupied may be defined, diagrammed and apportioned, yet where it is clearly manifest that exclusive possession of such space has not been granted, and that the realty owner has such control that the concessionaire in reality has no more than the privilege of conducting his business on the premises, the agreement is not a lease. Thus, where the space to be occupied was defined, diagrammed and apportioned by the parties but the realty owner reserved the right to remove the concession to another area, the concessionaire agreed to pay the realty owner a percentage of his gross receipts; sales were to be made in the name of the realty owner; the receipts thereof were to go through the regular channels of the realty owner's busi-

---

17. People v Horowitz (1956) 309 NY 426, 131 NE2d 715.

18. Meers v Munsch-Protzmann Co. (AD1 1926) 217 AD 541, 217 NYS 256.

ness after deducting therefrom the realty owner's percentage, were to be retained by him in trust for the concessionaire; the realty owner was to select and engage the employees of the concessionaire, and also to regulate the concessionaire's prices, the agreement was held to be a license, and not a lease.[19]

It has been held that where an agreement is a license for a concession, even though it is a grant of an exclusive right to operate certain specified concessions on someone else's property, such exclusive right is not a lease.[20]

### § 4:16. Washing Machine Concession

With the advent of the electric washing machine, a modern type of concession has arisen. An owner of an apartment house grants permission to another to install and operate coin metered washing machines in the basement of the building for the accommodation of the tenants. Here, again, the basic question determinative of the nature of the agreement as a lease or license is: has the owner granted the machine operator exclusive possession of any designated portion of the basement?

In one case[1] the owner of a building entered into an agreement with a washing machine owner, which agreement was designated "an agreement of lease." The building owner, as "landlord," granted permission to the machine owner to install and maintain a coin metered washing machine, for a period of three years from the date of installation. The machine owner was to retain ownership of the machine, and was granted access to the machine. The building owner agreed to furnish the

---

**19.** Layton v A. I. Namm & Sons, Inc. (AD1 1949) 275 AD 246, 89 NYS2d 72, affd 302 NY 720, 98 NE2d 590.

Similarly an agreement between a drug store owner and an individual, which gave the individual permission to use the soda fountain, belonging to the drug store owner, and regulating the manner of operating the fountain not only as to hours but as to purchases, was held to be a license, and not a lease. Isaacson v Ken Drug Corp. (S Ct NY Co 1948) 195 Misc 246, 85 NYS2d 253. "Management agreement" was held a sublease where manager was to manage restaurant under landlord's liquor permit for a specified period, under the same terms and conditions as were contained in landlord's lease, and at a specified rental, because manager was thereby granted right to absolute control of the premises at an agreed rental. The Statement, Inc. v Pilgrim's Landing, Inc. (1975, 4th Dept) 49 AD2d 28, 370 NYS2d 970.

**20.** Senrow Concessions, Inc. v Skelton Properties, Inc. (1961) 10 NYS2d 320, 222 NYS2d 329, 178 NE2d 726.

**1.** Halpern v Silver (City Ct Bx Co 1946) 187 Misc 1023, 65 NYS2d 336.

## INTERESTS IN REAL PROPERTY § 4:16

"space, power and facilities for the operation" of the machine. The rental was fixed at $4 per month. After the agreement had been made, the building was sold. The new owner of the building thereupon disconnected the machine, and refused to comply further with the agreement. The machine owner, contending that the agreement was a lease, sued to recover damages for an alleged wrongful eviction from his "demised" premises. The court held that this agreement merely had granted a license, which was revoked by the subsequent conveyance of the premises. Manifestly, the agreement did not lease any specific premises; and no exclusive possession thereof was given, except for the limited purpose of maintaining the machine. It is quite clear that the machine owner was not given exclusive possession of the premises at any time. Therefore, the agreement was held not to be a lease, but merely a license.

In another case,[2] a building owner "leased all of that certain real estate consisting of that certain laundry space" in a certain building for the purpose of installing, maintaining, and servicing a washing machine for the term of three years. The machine owner was given free and unobstructed access to, and egress from the machine during reasonable hours of the day to service and maintain the machine. In deciding that this agreement was a license, and not a lease, the Court said, "The main object of the agreement is to procure for the tenants of defendant a laundering service. The plaintiff agrees to furnish the service. The plaintiff, through its installations, is granted a license or privilege to occupy the land for the purpose of performing its contract of furnishing this laundry service to the tenants. The plaintiff has no ownership of the space allotted to its equipment in the sense that usually obtains in the relationship of landlord and tenant. In a lease the tenant is the owner of the premises for the term therein specified. The rent is the purchase price for outright ownership for the duration of the term. In the instant matter, all that is granted by the terms of the contract, properly read, is a license to use the designated space for the installation and maintenance of the

---

2. Kaypar Corp. v Fosterport Realty Corp. (S Ct Bx Co 1947) 1 Misc 2d 469, 69 NYS2d 313, affd 272 AD 878, 72 NYS2d 405.

§ 4:16    LANDLORD AND TENANT

machines. If the occupation of the land is in connection with a service to be rendered to the landlord, then the possession continues to be that of the landlord."[3]

In other words, to constitute a lease or a tenancy, there must be a definite, certain space demised or rented. And, to avoid the difficulties encountered in the cases discussed here, it was suggested[4] that the parties could have by a proper instrument, in plain language, created rights which would constitute a lease yielding up exclusive possession to definite, certain space. Thus, where a washing machine agreement contained a description of the specific space to be occupied exclusively by the machine owner, the agreement was held to be a lease.[5]

### § 4:17. Storage of Automobile in Public Garage

Whether or not parking a car in an open parking lot, or a public garage, for a stipulated fee, without being allotted any specific space, is a license or a bailment, is a question of fact to be determined by the place, condition, and nature of the transaction,[6] but it is not a lease.[7]

Where the tenant of an apartment leases an assigned space in his apartment house garage under a "garage space rider" to his apartment lease, and the monthly rent for the garage space is termed "additional rent," and no keys to the car are delivered to the garage, the relationship is that of landlord and tenant.[8] However, where the car owner is not assigned any specific space, and the car is delivered into the possession of the garage; that is, the car keys are delivered to the garage, or the garage

---

3. Also, see Greenbro Coin Meter Corp. v Basch (S Ct NY Co 1954) 205 Misc 853, 132 NYS2d 876 (license); Muller v Concourse Investors, Inc. (S Ct NY Co 1952) 201 Misc 340, 111 NYS2d 678 (license).

4. Halpern v Silver (City Ct Bx Co 1946) 187 Misc 1023, 65 NYS2d 336.

5. Polner v Arling Realty, Inc. (S Ct Kings Co 1949) 194 Misc 831, 88 NYS2d 348, and 194 Misc 598, 86 NYS2d 891.

6. Osborn v Cline (1934) 263 NY 434, 189 NE 483.

7. Rauch v Mossberg Garage Corp. (M Ct Man 1947) 191 Misc 220, 77 NYS2d 162, affd (AT1) 191 Misc 551, 80 NYS2d 684, affd (AD1) 275 AD 1030, 91 NYS2d 834, affd 301 NY 38, 92 NE2d 871; Esposito v 285 St. Johns Place, Inc. (S Ct Kings Co 1946) 68 NYS2d 18.

In view of the affirmance by the Court of Appeals in the Rauch case, Shepard Warehouses, Inc. v Scherman (S Ct NY Co 1946) 63 NYS2d 421, holding to the contrary, must be deemed no longer controlling.

8. Horowitz v Ambassador Associates, Inc. (NYC Civ Ct Bx Co 1981) 108 Misc 2d 412, 437 NYS2d 608 (exculpatory clause in rider or lease void; but, car owner obligated to prove negligence to recover for loss of car); Rudolph v Riverdale Management, Inc. (M Ct Bx 1952) 202 Misc 586, 113 NYS2d 524.

## INTERESTS IN REAL PROPERTY § 4:19

attendant parks the car, it has been held that there is a bailment.[9]

### § 4:18. Importance of Distinguishing Between Lease and License

It is important to determine whether an agreement is a lease or a license. If a lease is entered into, then a relationship of landlord and tenant is created. If a license has been granted, then no such relationship results, and the law of landlord and tenant will not apply thereto. The rights and obligations of the parties, then, will be governed by the law of contracts.

Aside from the importance of determining the respective rights and obligations of the parties under a particular agreement, the nature thereof will also have an important effect on the grantor's own lease or rights, if the grantor himself is a tenant. If a tenant is restricted by the terms of his lease from granting any subleases, then the nature of the agreement he has entered into must be determined. If it is a lease, then he has violated the restriction against subletting. If, however, it is a license, then he has not. Therefore, the determination of the nature of the agreement is of paramount importance to a tenant; for, he may inadvertently forfeit his own lease by entering into the agreement.[10]

### § 4:19. Non-assignability of License

A license does not create the relationship of landlord and tenant. Therefore, the right of assignment, which a tenant has under a lease in the absence of express restriction,[11] is not a right which inheres in a license agreement. It is the rule, said the Court of Appeals,[12] that "a mere license is personal to the licensee, and is not salable or transferable." Therefore a licensee has no right of assignment.

---

9. Motors Ins. Corp. v American Garages, Inc. (AT1 1979) 98 Misc 2d 887, 414 NYS2d 841.
   **Annotations:**
   Liability for loss of automobile left at parking lot or garage. 13 ALR4th 362.
   Liability for damage to automobile left in parking lot or garage. 13 ALR4th 442.

10. A tenant's right to grant a license may also depend upon whether or not his lease contains any restrictions on the use of the premises. See §§ 415:1, 46 et seq, infra.

11. See, §§ 9:75 et seq, infra.

12. Mendenhall v Klinck (1872) 51 NY 246, 250.

### § 4:20. Effect of Grantor's Conveyance on License

Under a landlord-tenant relationship, a lease is not affected by the conveyance of the fee by the landlord.[13] However, a conveyance of land by a licensor terminates the license.[14]

A license, not being an interest or estate in real property, does not bind the successors in interest of the owner of the real property, even if they have actual knowledge of the license.[15]

### § 4:21. Revocability of License

A license to do certain acts upon the land of a licensor, is revocable at the option of the licensor.[16]

It is revocable, even though a consideration has been paid for the license; and even where it was the intention to confer a continuing right, and money has been expended on the faith of the license.[17]

It does not follow, however, that where a license is given in pursuance of a contract for a definite term, and upon a valuable consideration, a breach of the contract by revoking the authority does not give rise to a personal action upon the contract. While the contract creates no right in the property itself, yet where the parties have made a valid agreement for a license for a definite period, the revocation of that license may give rise to an action for breach of contract.[18]

---

13. See §§ 5:17 et seq, infra.

14. Panama Realty Co. v New York (AD1 1913) 158 AD 726, 143 NYS 893; Wash-O-Matic Laundry Co. v 621 Lefferts Ave. Corp. (S Ct Kings Co 1948) 191 Misc 884, 82 NYS2d 572; Halpern v Silver (City Ct Bx Co 1946) 187 Misc 1023, 65 NYS2d 336.

15. Senrow Concessions, Inc. v Shelton Properties, Inc. (1961) 10 NY2d 320, 222 NYS2d 329, 178 NE2d 726.

16. Harmatz v Glickman (S Ct Kings Co 1958) 13 Misc 2d 271, 176 NYS2d 454.

17. Hartzler v Westair, Inc. (1977, 2d Dept) 55 AD2d 905, 390 NYS2d 630; Eldora Realty Corp. v Nicholson (AD1 1952) 280 AD 324, 113 NYS2d 429, holding that permission to install television aerial, if given by landlord to tenant, constituted a license, and was revocable at will; Tanenbaum v Unger (AT2 1950) 198 Misc 612, 103 NYS2d 260; Caldwell v Mitchell (M Ct Bx 1957) 158 NYS2d 868; Maffetone v Micari (M Ct Queens 1954) 205 Misc 459, 127 NYS2d 756; People ex rel. McGoldrick v Regency Park, Inc. (S Ct Queens Co 1952) 201 Misc 109, 110 NYS2d 163, affd 280 AD 804, 113 NYS2d 172, affd 305 NY 650, 112 NE2d 425; 5411 Realty Corp. v Morse (S Ct Kings Co 1951) 200 Misc 961, 109 NYS2d 758 (television aerial); Mammy's, Inc. & Pappy's, Inc. v All Continent Corp. (S Ct NY Co 1951) 106 NYS2d 635; Schusterman v C. & F. Caterers, Inc. (City Ct Bx Co 1948) 192 Misc 564, 77 NYS2d 718.

18. Schusterman v C. & F. Caterers, Inc (City Ct of NY Bx Co 1948) 192 Misc 564, 77 NYS2d 718.

## C. PROPRIETARY LEASE (CO-OPERATIVE OWNERSHIP)

### § 4:22. Generally

A co-operative is a form of group ownership of multi-unit property.[19]

It appears that the co-operative plan, of Finnish origin, started in New York City, during the nineteenth century,[20] had limited expansion in the nineteen-twenties, and then burgeoned thereafter to a degree far beyond the most optimistic prognostications of enthusiastic real estate experts.[1]

In general, a co-operative ownership plan consists of the vesting of title to the entire property in a corporation,[2] and the issuance to a purchaser of a "proprietary" lease to a specific apartment therein, and shares of stock

---

19. 1165 Fifth Ave. Corp. v Alger (1942) 288 NY 67, 41 NE2d 461, 141 ALR 1157.

20. For an early case involving co-operative apartments, see Barrington Apartment Asso. v Watson (GT1 1886) 38 Hun 545.

1. Per diss op M. M. Frank, J., Weisner v 791 Park Ave. Corp. (1958, 1st Dept) 7 AD2d 75, 180 NYS2d 734, revd 6 NY2d 426, 190 NYS2d 70, 160 NE2d 720.

There are conflicting views as to the desirability of co-operatives. The advantages are said to be the ability to own a home in a desirable neighborhood, where land may not be available or rentals prohibitive, without taking on the onerous responsibilities of home-ownership, and at the same time to gain benefits of tax deductions similar to those of a homeowner. Moreover, the proponents contend, a tenant-owner can make permanent improvements in "his own home," which he would not make in a rented apartment; he has no landlord problems; he has a voice in management and choice of neighbors; and finally he has a relatively easy method of selling his "home."

The opponents of co-operatives contend that each "home owner" is dependent upon the financial stability of his neighbors, so that if any one or more neighbors fall behind in payments, the deficit must be taken up and paid by the remaining solvent ones. Moreover, poor management, or the wishes of a majority, may impose extra assessments upon the "owners," which may become quite onerous. In addition the majority may impose restrictions or adopt regulations which may not always be palatable. Insofar as selling, the required consent of the majority may not always be obtained as easily as one may expect.

2. The corporation is generally organized as a business corporation. To take advantage of the allowance by IRC § 216 of deductions from income tax, the co-operative housing corporation must have one and only one class of stock outstanding; each of the stockholders must be entitled, solely by reason of his ownership of stock in the corporation, to occupy for dwelling purposes a house, or an apartment in a building owned or leased by such corporation; no stockholder shall be entitled, either conditionally or unconditionally, to receive any distribution not out of earnings and profits of the corporation except on a complete or partial liquidation of the corporation, and 80% or more of the gross income of which for the taxable year in which the taxes and interest sought to be deducted are paid or incurred must be derived from tenant-stockholders. IRC § 216.

The title-holding and stock-issuing corporation is not a "co-operative"

proportionate to the investment and reasonably related to the value of the equity.[3] The stockholder-tenant, in monthly installments, pays his commensurate part of the carrying charges for the entire property, such as taxes, interest, amortization of mortgage, and maintenance costs for labor, heating, repairs and other items. The tenant-stockholder, of course, has the right to vote his stock to elect directors of his choice. The board either manages the building directly, or selects the managing agent.[4]

The co-operative plan is sui generis. There are elements of ownership, as well as stock and leasehold rights. The relationship between the co-operative and the shareholders is that of landlord and tenant, each governed by the occupancy agreement or lease.

The occupants are primarily interested in the purchase of homes, and there is a common relationship different from that which exists among individual tenants living under the same roof. While it is true that they pay monthly maintenance charges in much the same manner as tenants pay rent, they have a substantial capital investment, and a direct interest in the financial stability, character, reputation, and personal conduct of the other stockholder-occupants of the premises.[5]

The rights of the various parties in a co-operative ownership plan are determined by the original plan of organization, the subscription agreement, the certificate of incorporation, the by-laws, the proprietary lease, and the rules and regulations adopted by the corporation-owner. All of these instruments together could very well be called the contract. Such a contract is entered into with a view of restricting the ownership, the control, as well as the management of the property. Each tenant-

within the meaning of the Cooperative Corporations Law. Payson v Caputa (1959, 1st Dept) 9 AD2d 226, 193 NYS2d 166.

3. A person desiring to become a resident of a co-operative dwelling must acquire such shares of stock in the corporation as are apportioned to the apartment which he desires to occupy before he can secure a proprietary lease. In addition, such acquisition and occupancy must first be approved by a requisite percentage of the board of directors or stockholders of that corporation. Curtis v Le May (M Ct Man 1945) 186 Misc 853, 60 NYS2d 768.

4. Per diss op M. M. Frank, J., Weisner v 791 Park Ave. Corp. (1958, 1st Dept) 7 AD2d 75, 180 NYS2d 734, revd 6 NY2d 426, 190 NYS2d 70, 160 NE2d 720.

5. Per diss op M. M. Frank, J., Weisner v 791 Park Ave. Corp. (1958, 1st Dept) 7 AD2d 75, 180 NYS2d 734, revd 6 NY2d 426, 190 NYS2d 70, 160 NE2d 720; Carden Hall, Inc. v George (S Ct Kings Co 1968) 56 Misc 2d 865, 290 NYS2d 430.

owner is entitled to strict compliance with the terms of such a contract.[6]

The relation between the corporation-owner and its tenant-members is fiduciary in nature, and the board of directors are bound to manage the affairs thereof so as to carry out its purposes to house its members in a comfortable and efficient manner, and to treat its individual members fairly and equally. The tenant-stockholders have the correlative duty to recognize that the co-operative enterprise must be conducted with the objective of securing the greatest good for the benefit of the entire membership.[7]

A proprietary lease is no different from any other type of lease, and co-operative apartment shares of stock are like any other shares of stock in a corporation owning real property.[8]

The relationship between a shareholder-tenant and the cooperative is that of landlord and tenant.[9]

Shares of stock and proprietary lease in a cooperative apartment are personal property.[10]

## § 4:23. Form of Proprietary Lease

### Form No. 3
### PROPRIETARY LEASE [CO-OPERATIVE APARTMENT LEASE]

Agreement made. . . . . . . . ., 19. . . . between . . . . . . . .

---

[6]. Tompkins v Hale (S Ct NY Co 1939) 172 Misc 1071, 15 NYS2d 854, affd 259 AD 860, 20 NYS2d 398, affd 284 NY 675, 30 NE2d 721.

[7]. Vernon Manor Co-operative Apartments Section 1, Inc. v Salatino (Westchester Co Ct 1958) 15 Misc 2d 491, 178 NYS2d 895.

[8]. Where buyer defaults after making deposit under contract to buy co-op apartment stock and proprietary lease, seller was not entitled to retain deposit, as if contract were for sale of realty, but only was entitled to damages sustained, as provided for under UCC2-718, where subject matter of sale is "goods". Silverman v Alcoa Plaza Associates (1971, 1st Dept) 37 AD2d 166, 323 NYS2d 39.

[9]. Hauptman v 222 East 80th Street Corp. (1979) 100 Misc 2d 153, 418 NYS2d 728; Earl W. Jimerson Housing Co. v Butler (AT 2 & 11, 1979) 102 Misc 2d 423, 425 NYS2d 924; Suarez v Rivercross Tenants' Corp. (AT1 1981) 107 Misc 2d 135, 438 NYS2d 164.

[10]. State Tax Com. v Shor (S Ct NY Co 1975) 84 Misc 2d 161, 378 NYS2d 222, affd (AD1 1976) 53 AD2d 814, 385 NYS2d 290, affd 43 NY2d 151, 400 NYS2d 805, 371 NE2d 523, where the Court of Appeals said that for some special purposes the real property aspect may predominate, but where priorities of judgement creditors are involved, the stock certificate and lease involved in a co-op apartment transaction fit better legally and pragmatically, although with imperfect linguistic formulation, into the statutory framework governing personal property. (A judgment creditor does not obtain a lien on the ownership interest of the tenant merely upon docketing his judgment.)

Apartments, Inc., a New York Corporation, having an office at ........, New York, N. Y., (hereinafter called the Lessor) and ........ presently residing at ........ (hereinafter called the Lessee).

Witnesseth:

Whereas the Lessor is the owner of the land and building at ........, Borough of ........, New York City (hereinafter called the Building); and

Whereas the Lessor, consistent with a plan to provide co-operative ownership of apartments in the Building, has entered into or proposes to enter into agreements with the several owners of its capital stock by instruments known as proprietary leases; and

*[Shares of Stock]*

Whereas the Lessee is the owner of ........ shares of capital stock of the Lessor which have been allocated to the apartment and are appurtenant to this lease,

*[Leased Premises]*

Now, Therefore, in consideration of the premises and of the rents, covenants and agreements herein, the Lessor hereby leases to the Lessee, subject to the terms and conditions hereof, and the Lessee hires from the Lessor all the rooms as presently partitioned on the ........ floor of the Building, known as apartment ........ (and herein referred to as the apartment)

*[Term]*

To Have and to Hold the apartment with the appurtenances unto the Lessee, his legal representatives and authorized assigns from ........, 19... until September 30, 20... (unless the term shall sooner expire as hereinafter provided)

*[Rent]*

At a rent, for each year, or portion of year, during said term, equal to that proportion of the Lessor's cash requirements (as determined by its Board of Directors and as hereinafter defined) which the number of shares of stock specified in the recitals of this lease bears to the total number of shares of stock of the Lessor issued and outstanding on the date of the determination of such cash requirements, together with the additional rent hereinafter provided. Such rent shall be payable monthly in advance or in such installments and at such times as shall be determined by resolution of the Board of Directors of the Lessor, and the additional rent shall be payable as herein provided.

*[Failure to Fix Cash Requirements]*

The omission of the Board of Directors of the Lessor to determine the Lessor's cash requirements for any year or portion thereof shall not be deemed a waiver or modification in any respect of the covenants and provisions hereof, or a release of the Lessee from the obligation to pay the rent or any installment thereof, but the rent last determined for any year or portion thereof shall thereafter continue to be the rent until the cash requirements shall be redetermined.

The power and authority to determine and establish the amount of, and to require payment of, the rent above provided for, shall be possessed only by the Board of Directors of the Lessor. Every such determination by the Board of Directors, within the bounds of this agreement of lease, shall be final and conclusive as to all lessees, and any expenditures made by the Lessor's officers or Managing Agent, under the direction or with the approval of the Lessor's Board of Directors, within the bounds of this agreement of lease, shall, as against the Lessee, be deemed necessarily and properly made.

*[Co-operation]*

1. The Lessor and Lessee shall always in good faith endeavor to observe and promote the co-operative purposes for the accomplishment of which the Lessor is incorporated.

*[Appurtenant Stock to be Specified in Proprietary Leases]*

2. In every proprietary lease heretofore executed by the Lessor there has been specified, and in every proprietary lease hereafter executed by it there shall be specified, the number of shares of the capital stock of the Lessor appurtenant thereto, which number, in relation to the

total number of shares of stock of the Lessor then issued and outstanding, shall constitute the basis for fixing, as hereinbefore provided, the proportionate share of the aggregate amount of the cash requirements of the Lessor, as hereinafter defined, which shall be payable as rent by the Lessee. In the event that, after the fixing of the amounts payable as rent by lessees under proprietary leases for any period of time, one or more additional proprietary leases be made, thus increasing the aggregate number of shares specified in all proprietary leases, the rent to be paid under such additional lease or leases, unless and until the Board of Directors shall otherwise fix the rent to be paid under all proprietary leases, shall be at the same rate per share of stock specified in such additional lease or leases as is applicable to the shares of stock specified in all other proprietary leases in effect at the time of the fixing and determination of such cash requirements, and the rent payable for such peiod of time by lessees under such other proprietary leases shall not be modified or affected by any increase in the aggregate number of shares specified in all proprietary leases.

*[Payment of Rent]*

3. The Lessee shall pay the rent to the Lessor, or to its Managing Agent, upon the terms, at the times and in the manner herein provided, without any deduction on account of any set-off or claim which the Lessee may have against the Lessor.

*[Occupancy and Use of Premises]*

4. The Lessee shall not, without the consent provided for in paragraph 5 hereof, occupy or use the apartment, or permit the same or any part thereof to be occupied or used, for any purpose other than as a private dwelling apartment for the Lessee, members of the Lessee's family, his employees and servants, except that (a) ground floor apartments in their entirety may, subject to applicable zoning and other laws, be used as doctors' offices by the lessees thereof, their employees, and other doctors, who shall be associates or licensees of such lessees and (b) in cases where, on ........, 19..., Lessee was occupying his apartment and was using his apartment for residential and other purposes, such other use may be continued,

provided the use is lawful under all zoning and other applicable laws and provided further that such other use may be continued only so long as Lessee is the lessee of the apartment.

*[Subletting]*

5. The Lessee shall not sublet the whole or any part of the apartment for any term to any person or persons nor, except as provided in paragraph 4 hereof, permit the same to be occupied by any persons other than members of the Lessee's family, his employees and servants, unless consent thereto shall have been duly given by an instrument in writing which is to be signed either (a) by a majority of the then authorized total number of directors of the Lessor, or (b) when duly authorized either by a resolution of the Lessor's Board of Directors or by a resolution adopted at any annual or special meeting of the Lessor's stockholders, by the Managing Agent of the Lessor or an officer of the Lessor. Whenever the Lessee applies to the Lessor for a consent to a subletting, the Lessor may require that the Lessee shall deliver to the Lessor a copy of the sublease to which consent is requested. No such consent shall be required to any subletting (a) by the Lessee to a subtenant in possession on ........, 19..., or (b) by the Sponsors referred to in a Plan of Cooperative Organization for the Building dated ........, 19..., as amended, or their designees, nominees, or representatives, if the Sponsors, before consummating any subletting, consult with a committee of or members of the Board of Directors provided such committee or members are promptly available for such consultation.

*[Assignment]*

6. The Lessee shall not assign this lease or transfer the stock appurtenant thereto or any interest therein, and no such assignment or transfer shall take effect as against the Lessor for any purpose, until

a. an instrument of assignment executed by the assignor shall have been delivered to the Lessor; and

b. an agreement by the assignee assuming and agreeing to perform and comply with all the covenants and conditions of this lease to be performed or complied with by the Lessee on and after the effective date of said assignment shall have been executed and acknowledged by the assignee and delivered to the Lessor, but no such assumption agreement shall be required if the assignee surrenders the assigned lease and enters into a new proprietary lease for the remainder of the term, as hereinafter provided; and

c. all shares of stock of the Lessor appurtenant to this lease shall have been transferred to the assignee, with proper transfer stamps affixed; and

d. all sums due from the Lessee, together with a sum to be fixed by the Board of Directors or the President or a Vice-President of the Lessor to cover reasonable legal and other expenses of the Lessor in connection with such assignment and transfer of stock, shall have been paid to the Lessor; and

e. consent to such assignment shall have been duly given by an instrument in writing which is to be signed either (i) by a majority of the then authorized total number of directors of the Lessor or (ii) when duly authorized either by a resolution of the Lessor's Board of Directors or by a resolution adopted at any annual or special meeting of the Lessor's stockholders, by the Managing Agent of the Lessor, or any officer of the Lessor. No such consent shall be required in the case of an assignment, transfer or bequest of this lease to the Lessee's spouse, or in the case of an assignment by the Sponsors referred to in a Plan of Cooperative Organization for the Building dated . . . . . . . ., 19. . ., as amended, or their designees, nominees or representatives, if the Sponsors, before consummating any assignment, consult with a committee of or members of the Board of Directors provided such committee or members are promptly available for such consultation, or, if the Lessee be more than one person, in the case of an assignment or transfer by one such Lessee to another.

*[Death of Lessee]*

In the event the Lessee shall die during the term of this lease, consent shall not be unreasonably withheld to any assignment or transfer of this lease and the appurtenant stock by bequest or by assignment by the administrator or executor of the Lessee, provided that such

## INTERESTS IN REAL PROPERTY § 4:23

legatee or assignee shall be a financially responsible member of the Lessee's family (other than the Lessee's spouse as to whom no consent is required).

### [Release of Lessee Upon Assignment]

Whenever the Lessee shall, under the provisions of this lease, be permitted to assign and shall so assign the same, and the assignee shall assume all of the unfulfilled obligations of the assignor hereunder, either by an instrument in writing delivered to the Lessor or by surrendering assigned lease and entering into a new lease for the remainder of the term, the assignor shall have no further liability on any of the covenants of this lease to be thereafter performed. At the option and election of the Lessor any assigned lease shall be surrendered and cancelled, and a new proprietary lease for the remainder of the term of this lease, shall in such case be entered into between the Lessor and the assignee.

### [Specific Consent Required]

Regardless of any prior consent theretofore given, neither the Lessee nor his executor, administrator or personal representative, nor any trustee or receiver of the property of the Lessee, nor anyone to whom the interest of the Lessee shall pass by law, shall be entitled to assign this lease, or to sublet to use the apartment, or any part thereof, except upon compliance with the requirements of this lease. The restrictions on the subletting and the occupancy of the apartment and on the assignment of this lease, as hereinbefore set forth, are an especial consideration and inducement for the granting of this lease by the Lessor to the Lessee.

No demand or acceptance of rent from any assignee hereof, or from any subtenant, or other person in possession, shall constitute or be deemed to constitute a consent to or approval of any assignment, sublease or occupancy.

### [Pledge of Stock]

A pledge of stock and/or an assignment of this lease as collateral security, shall not be deemed a violation of any covenant or condition of this lease relating to transfer of stock or assignment of this lease, but neither the pledgee nor any transferee of the pledgee shall have the right to vote or to acquire a proprietary lease of the apartment, by assignment or otherwise, except on compliance with all of the provisions of this paragraph 6.

*[Collection of Rent from Subtenants]*

7. If the Lessee shall at any time sublet the apartment, with or without the Lessor's consent, and shall default in the payment of any rent, the Lessor may, at its option, so long as such default shall continue, demand and receive the rent due or becoming due from such subtenant to the Lessee, up to an amount sufficient to pay all sums due from the Lessee to the Lessor, and any such payment of such subrent to the Lessor shall be sufficient payment and discharge of such subtenant as between such subtenant and the Lessee, to the extent of the amount so paid.

*[Repairs by Lessor]*

8. The Lessor shall keep in good repair the foundations, sidewalks, walls (except interior walls of apartments unless repairs thereto are necessitated by the act or negligence of the Lessor or the failure of the Lessor to make repairs for which it is otherwise responsible), supports, beams, roofs, gutters, fences, cellars, chimneys, entrances and street and court doorways, public halls, public stairways, windows, elevators, pumps and tanks, and all pipes for carrying water, gas or steam through the Building, and the drain pipes and electrical conduits, together with all plumbing, heating and other apparatus intended for the general service of the Building, except those portions of any of the foregoing which it is the duty of the Lessee to maintain and keep in good repair as hereinafter provided, it being agreed that the Lessee shall give the Lessor prompt notice of any accident or defect known to the Lessee and requiring repairs to be made and that the Lessor's obligations are subject to the provisions of paragraph 15 hereof. All such repairs required to be made by the Lessor shall be at the expense of the Lessor, unless the same shall have been rendered necessary by the act or neglect or carelessness of the Lessee, or any of the family, guests, employees or subtenants of the Lessee, in which case the expense is to be borne by the Lessee.

*[Maintenance]*

9. Subject to the provisions of paragraph 15 hereof, the

Lessor shall maintain and manage the Building as a first-class apartment building, and shall keep the elevators and the public halls, cellars and stairways clean and properly lighted and heated, and shall provide the number of attendants requisite, in the judgment of its Board of Directors, for the proper care and service of the Building, and shall, without extra cost to the Lessee, provide the apartment with a proper and sufficient supply of hot and cold water and of heat. The covenants by the Lessor herein contained are subject, however, to the discretionary power of the Board of Directors of the Lessor to determine from time to time what services and what attendants shall be proper and the manner of maintaining and operating the Building, and also what existing services shall be increased, reduced, changed or modified.

*[Interior Repairs]*

10. The Lessee shall keep the interior of the apartment in good repair, and the Lessor shall not be held answerable for any repairs in or to the same, unless such repairs shall be made necessary by the act or negligence of the Lessor. The Lessee shall not permit or suffer anything to be done or kept in the apartment or in any other space occupied or used by the Lessee in the Building, which will increase the rate of fire insurance on the Building or the contents thereof, and shall not interfere with the rights of other lessees or annoy other lessees by unreasonable noises or otherwise, or obstruct the public halls or stairways of the Building. The Lessee will comply with all the requirements of the Board of Health and other governmental authorities and with all laws, ordinances, rules and regulations with respect to the occupancy or use of the apartment by the Lessee, the rate of fire insurance on the Building or its contents shall be increased, the Lessee shall become personally liable for the additional insurance premiums upon all policies covering the Building or any apartment therein, and the Lessor shall have the right to collect the same, as additional rent, for its own account and the account of other lessees. In addition to decorating and keeping the interior of the apartment in good repair the Lessee shall be responsible for the maintenance or replacement of any plumbing fixtures, lighting

fixtures, refrigerators, ranges or other equipment that may at any time be in the apartment.

No upstairs elevator lobby adjoining the apartment shall be deemed a part of the apartment, but the Lessee shall be obligated to paint and decorate the same. If more than one apartment adjoins the same elevator lobby and if the several lessees sharing the use of same cannot agree with respect to the painting and decorating thereof, the Lessor shall determine how and when such lobby shall be painted and decorated and shall determine the portion of the cost thereof to be charged to each lessee. Any such charge paid by the Lessor shall be collected from the Lessee as additional rent.

*[Alterations and Additions
Removal of Fixtures Installed by Lessee]*

11. The Lessee shall not, without first obtaining the written consent of the Lessor (which consent shall not be unreasonably withheld), make in the apartment, or on any terrace appurtenant thereto, any structural alteration or any alteration of the water, gas or steam pipes, electrical conduits or plumbing, or hereafter install any electrical or other equipment which shall impose an excessive load on existing electric or water supplies, or hereafter install any air conditioning equipment, or except as hereinafter authorized, remove any additions, improvements or fixtures from the apartment. If the Lessee, or any prior lessee shall have heretofore placed or shall hereafter place in the apartment any special additions, improvements or fixtures, such as mantels, lighting fixtures, refrigerators, air-conditioning equipment, ranges, woodwork, panelling, ceilings, doors or decorations, then the Lessee shall have the right, during the term of this lease, to remove the same at the Lessee's own expense, provided: (a) that the Lessee at the time of such removal shall not be in default in the payment of rent or in the performance of any other provision or condition of this lease; (b) that prior to any such removal, the Lessee shall give written notice thereof to the Lessor; (c) that the Lessee shall pay the cost of any such removal and shall repair any damage resulting therefrom; and (d) that the Lessee shall replace and re-install at the Lessee's own expense any equipment that was in the apartment at the

INTERESTS IN REAL PROPERTY § 4:23

beginning of the term or, at the Lessee's option, shall put the apartment in tenantable condition by installing standard equipment of a kind and quality customary in buildings of this type and satisfactory to the Lessor.

If the Lessee shall have heretofore, at the Lessee's own expense, placed in the apartment any such additions, improvements or fixtures which the Lessee has the right to remove under the provisions of any lease in effect immediately prior to the commencement of the term of this proprietary lease then the Lessee shall have the right to remove the same upon observing and complying with the provisions of this proprietary lease relating to the removal of the additions, improvements or fixtures hereafter placed in the apartment and the repair of damage resulting from such removal.

*[Surrender of Possession]*

On the expiration of the term hereby granted, or upon a sooner termination of this lease, the Lessee shall surrender to the Lessor possession of the apartment with all additions, improvements and fixtures then included therein, except as hereinabove provided. Any additions, improvements or fixtures not removed by the Lessee at or prior to the termination of this lease shall be deemed abandoned and shall become the property of the Lessor. Any other personal property not removed by the Lessee at or prior to the termination of this lease, may be removed by the Lessor to any place of storage and stored for the account of the Lessee without the Lessor in any way being liable for trespass, conversion or negligence by reason of any acts of the Lessor or of the Lessor's agents, or of any carrier employed in transporting such property to the place of storage, or by reason of the negligence of any person in caring for such property while in storage.

*[Mechanics' Liens]*

12. In case there shall be filed a notice of mechanic's lien against the Building, for, or purporting to be for, labor or material alleged to have been furnished or delivered at the Building or the apartment to or for the Lessee, or any one claiming under the Lessee, the Lessee shall forthwith cause such lien to be discharged by payment, bonding or otherwise; and if the Lessee shall fail to

cause such lien to be discharged within five days after notice from the Lessor, then the Lessor may cause such lien to be discharged by payment, bonding or otherwise, without investigation as to the validity thereof or of any offsets or defenses thereto, and shall have the right to collect, as additional rent, all amounts so paid and all costs and expenses paid or incurred in connection therewith, including reasonable attorneys' fees and disbursements, together with interest thereon from the time or times of payment.

*[Lessor's Right of Entry]*

13. The Lessor and its agents shall be permitted to visit and examine the apartment at any reasonable hour of the day, and workmen may enter at any time, when authorized by the Lessor or the Lessor's agents, to make or facilitate repairs in any part of the Building and to remove such portions of the walls, floors and ceilings of the apartment as may be required for the purpose of making such repairs, but the Lessor shall at its own cost and expense thereafter restore the premises to proper condition. If the Lessee shall not be personally present to permit entry into the apartment, at any time when an entry shall be necessary or permissible hereunder, the Lessor or the Lessor's agents may forcibly enter the apartment without rendering the Lessor or such agent liable to any claim or cause of action for damages by reason thereof (if during such entry the Lessor shall accord reasonable care to the Lessee's property), and without in any manner affecting the obligations and covenants of this lease; and the right and authority hereby reserved do not impose, nor does the Lessor assume by reason thereof, any responsibility or liability whatsoever for the care or supervision of the apartment, or any of the pipes, fixtures, appliances or appurtenances therein contained or therewith in any manner connected, except as may be herein specifically provided.

*[Lessor's Right to Repair at Lessee's Expense]*

14. a. If the Lessee shall fail to make repairs as herein required, or shall fail to comply with any other covenant or condition of this lease on his part to be performed, the Lessor may, after ten days notice to the Lessee (or if the

Lessee or any person dwelling in the apartment shall expressly request the Lessor, its agents or servants, to perform any act not hereby required to be performed by the Lessor, the Lessor may, without such notice) make such repairs, comply with such covenant or condition, or perform such act or arrange for others to do the same, without liability on the Lessor; and, in such event, the Lessor, its agents, servants, and contractors shall, as between the Lessor and Lessee, be conclusively deemed to be acting as agents of the Lessee and all contracts therefor made by the Lessor shall be so construed whether or not made in the name of the Lessee.

*[Lessee's Indemnity of Lessor]*

b. The Lessee agrees to save the Lessor harmless from all liability, loss, damage and expense arising from injury to person or property occasioned by the failure of the Lessee to comply with any provision hereof, or due wholly or in part to any act, default or omission of the Lessee or of any person dwelling or visiting in the apartment, or by the Lessor, its agents, servants and contractors when acting as agent for the Lessee as in this lease provided.

*[Lessor's Additional Remedies]*

c. In addition to other legal remedies hereinbefore or hereinafter provided for, in case of violation of any covenants by the Lessee, the same shall be restrainable by injunction and neither the mention herein nor the election hereafter of one or more of the remedies provided, shall preclude the Lessor from enforcing any other right, remedy, option, election, or priority allowed by law, whether or not herein specifically set forth.

*[Requirement of Notice]*

d. The giving of written notification by the Lessee to the Lessor in the manner provided in paragraph 31 hereof, in the event of (a) any default by the Lessor or (b) any breach by the Lessor of any covenant of this lease, or (c) any failure by the Lessor to comply with any law, ordinance or governmental regulation, shall be a condition precedent to the bringing of any action by the Lessee against the Lessor or the assertion by the Lessee against the Lessor of any defense based thereon.

§ 4:23                    LANDLORD AND TENANT

*[Lessor's Immunities]*

15. The Lessor shall not be liable for, nor shall there be any abatement of rent or other compensation or claim of eviction by reason of: (a) any interference with light, air, view or other interests of the Lessee; or (b) space taken to comply with any law, ordinance or governmental regulation; or (c) unless due to the negligence of the Lessor,

(i) any failure, curtailment or interruption of heat, water supply, electric current, gas, telephone or elevator service, or other service to be supplied by the Lessor hereunder, or

(ii) failure to make, delay in making, or inconvenience involved in making any repairs, alterations or decorations to the Building or to any fixtures or appurtenances therein, or

(iii) injury or damage to person or property caused by the elements or by another lessee or by another person in the Building; or

(iv) steam, gas, electricity, water, rain or snow which may leak or overflow from any part of the Building, or from any of its pipes, drains, conduits, radiators, boilers, tanks, appliances or equipment, or from any other place.

*[Storage Room, Laundry]*

If the Lessor shall furnish to the Lessee any storage space, laundry space or facility, or any other space or facility outside the apartment, the same shall be deemed to have been furnished by the Lessor under a revocable license. The Lessee shall not use such space for the storage of valuable or perishable property or for the storage of rugs or carpets and shall, at his own expense, adequately protect himself and the Lessor by insurance against damage or theft or loss. If washing machines or other equipment are made available to the Lessee or his servants or employees, the same shall be used on condition that the Lessor is not responsible for such equipment, nor for any damage caused to the property of the Lessee resulting from the use thereof, and that any use that may be made of such equipment shall be at the Lessee's own cost, risk and expense.

*[Cars and Packages]*

The Lessor shall not be responsible for any damage to

INTERESTS IN REAL PROPERTY § 4:23

any automobile or other vehicle left in the care of any employee of the Lessor by the Lessee, and the Lessee hereby agrees to hold the Lessor harmless from any liability arising from any injury to person or property caused by or with such automobile or other vehicle while in the care of such employee. The Lessor shall not be responsible for any package or article left with or entrusted to any employee of the Lessor, or for the loss of any property within or without the apartment by theft or otherwise.

*[Window Cleaning]*

16. The Lessee will not clean, nor require, permit, suffer or allow any window in the apartment to be cleaned, from the outside in violation of Section 202 of the Labor Law or of the rules of the Board of Standards and Appeals, or of any other board or body having or asserting jurisdiction.

*[Damage to Building]*

17. If the Building shall be partly damaged by fire or other cause, it shall be repaired as speedily as is reasonably possible, by and at the expense of the Lessor, so as to conform substantially to the condition immediately preceding such damage, but this obligation to restore shall not apply to any additions, improvements or fixtures in the apartment which, under the terms of this lease, the Lessee has the right to remove, and, in case the damage shall be so extensive as to render the apartment untenantable, the rent hereunder shall cease until the apartment shall again be rendered tenantable, but if said damage shall be caused by the act or negligence of the Lessee, or the agents, servants, guests or members of the family of the Lessee, such rental shall abate only to the extent of the rental value insurance, if any, collected with respect to the apartment. In case of the total destruction of the Building by fire or otherwise, the rent shall be paid up to the time of such destruction, and thereupon this lease, and all rights and obligations of the parties hereunder, and the tenancy hereby created, shall wholly cease and expire.

*[Expiration of Lease]*

18. If upon, or at any time after, the happening of any

of the events mentioned in subdivisions (a) to (h) inclusive of this paragraph, the Lessor shall give to the Lessee a notice stating that the term hereof will expire on a date at least five days thereafter, the term of this lease shall expire on the date so fixed, as if that were the date originally fixed for its expiration, and all right, title and interest of the Lessee hereunder shall thereupon cease and expire, and the Lessee shall thereupon quit and surrender the apartment to the Lessor, it being the intention of the parties hereto to create hereby a conditional limitation, and thereupon the Lessor shall have the right to re-enter the apartment and to remove all persons and personal property therefrom, either by summary dispossess proceedings, or by any suitable action or proceeding at law or in equity, or by force or otherwise, and to repossess the apartment in its former estate as if this lease had not been made, and no liability whatsoever shall attach to the Lessor by reason of the exercise of the right of re-entry, re-possession and removal herein granted and reserved.

*[Lessee Ceasing to Own Accompanying Stock]*

(a) If at any time during the term of this lease the Lessee shall cease to be the owner of all of the shares of stock which are hereinbefore stated to be owned by the Lessee and appurtenant to this lease, or if this lease shall pass or be assigned to anyone who is not then the owner of all of said shares.

*[Assignment or Subletting]*

(b) If at any time there be an assignment or purported assignment of this lease without full compliance with the requirements of paragraph 6 hereof, or if at any time there be any subletting hereunder without full compliance with the requirements of paragraph 5 hereof, or if any unauthorized person shall be permitted to use or occupy the apartment, and, in the case of any such subletting or unauthorized use or occupancy, the Lessee shall fail to cure such condition within ten days after written notice from the Lessor.

*[Default in Payment of Rent]*

(c) If the Lessee shall be in default for a period of one month in the payment of any rent or additional rent, or

## INTERESTS IN REAL PROPERTY § 4:23

of any installment thereof herein provided for, and shall then fail to cure such default within 10 days after written notice thereof shall have been given by the Lessor.

*[Default in Other Covenants]*

(d) If the Lessee shall default in the performance of any covenant or provision hereof, other than the covenant to pay rent or covenants otherwise provided for in this paragraph 18, and shall fail to cure any such default within thirty days after written notice thereof shall have been given by the Lessor, provided, however, that if said default consists in failure to perform any act the performance of which requires any substantial period of time, then if within said period of thirty days such performance is commenced and thereafter diligently prosecuted without delay and interruption, the Lessee shall be deemed to have cured said default.

*[Lessee's Objectionable Conduct]*

(e) If at any time the Lessor shall determine, upon the affirmative vote of the holders of record of two-thirds or more of the capital stock of the Lessor then issued and outstanding, at a meeting of such stockholders duly called to take action on the subject, that because of objectionable conduct on the part of the Lessee, or of a person dwelling in or visiting the apartment, the tenancy of the Lessee is undesirable (it being understood, without limiting the generality of the foregoing, that repeatedly to violate or disregard the house rules hereto attached or hereafter established in accordance with the provisions of this lease, or to permit or tolerate a person of dissolute, loose or immoral character to enter or remain in the Building or the apartment, shall be deemed to be objectionable conduct).

*[Termination of All Proprietary Leases]*

(f) If at any time the Lessor shall determine, by action of its Board of Directors concurred in by the affirmative vote of two thirds of the then authorized total number of directors, and upon the affirmative vote of the record holders of at least 80% in amount of its capital stock then issued and outstanding, at a stockholders' meeting duly called for that purpose, to terminate all proprietary leases.

§ 4:23                LANDLORD AND TENANT

*[Condemnation]*

(g) If at any time the Building or a substantial portion thereof shall be taken by condemnation proceedings.

*[Rights Upon Default]*

19. A. In the event of the Lessor's resuming possession of the apartment either by summary proceedings, action of ejectment or otherwise because of default by the Lessee in the payment of rent or additional rent, or any part thereof, or on the expiration of the term under the provisions of subsections (a), (b), (c), (d), (e) or (f) of paragraph 18 hereof, the Lessee shall continue to remain liable for payment of the rent which would have become due hereunder from time to time. No suit brought to recover any installment of such rent shall prejudice the right of the Lessor to recover any subsequent installment. After resuming possession, the Lessor may, at its option, from time to time (a) relet the apartment for its own account, or (b) relet the apartment as the agent of the Lessee, in the name of the Lessee or in its own name, for a term or terms which may be less than or greater than the period which would otherwise have constituted the balance of the term of this lease, and may grant concessions or free rent, in its discretion. Within ten days after reletting the apartment, as aforesaid, the Lessor shall notify the Lessee as to whether the apartment has been relet for the account of the Lessee or for the Lessor's own account. The fact that the Lessor may have relet as agent for the Lessee shall not prevent the Lessor from thereafter notifying the Lessee that it proposes to relet for its own account, and will no longer relet the apartment as agent for the Lessee. If the Lessor relets the apartment as agent for the Lessee, it shall, after reimbursing itself for its expenses in connection therewith, including a reasonable amount for decorations, alterations and repairs in and to the apartment, apply the remaining avails of such reletting against the Lessee's continuing obligations hereunder. There shall be a final accounting between the Lessor and the Lessee upon the earliest of the four following dates: (a) ........, 20...; (b) the date as of which a new proprietary lease covering the apartment shall have become effective; (c) the date the Lessor gives written notice to the Lessee that it has relet the apart-

INTERESTS IN REAL PROPERTY § 4:23

ment for its own account or that it will no longer relet the apartment as agent for the Lessee; (d) the date upon which all proprietary leases of the Lessor terminate. From and after the date upon which the Lessor becomes obligated to account to the Lessee as above provided, the Lessor shall have no further duty to account to the Lessee for any avails of reletting and the Lessee shall have no further liability for sums thereafter accruing hereunder, but such termination of the Lessee's liability shall not affect any liabilities theretofore accrued.

*[Surrender of Stock and Resale thereof by Lessor]*

B. On the termination of this lease under subdivisions (a), (b), (c), (d), (e) or (f) of paragraph 18, or otherwise because of default by the Lessee, the Lessee shall surrender to the Lessor the certificate for the shares of stock of the Lessor owned by the Lessee and appurtenant to this lease. Whether or not said certificate is surrendered, the Lessor may issue a new proprietary lease for the apartment and issue a new stock certificate for the shares of stock of the Lessor owned by the Lessee and allocated thereto, when a purchaser therefor is found, provided that the issuance of such stock and such lease to such purchaser is authorized in the manner provided in paragraph 6 (e) hereof. Upon such issuance the stock certificate owned or held by the Lessee shall be automatically cancelled and rendered null and void. Upon the issuance of any such new proprietary lease and stock certificate, the Lessee's continuing liability hereunder, if not theretofore terminated, shall cease and the Lessee shall only be liable for rent and expenses accrued to that time. The Lessor shall apply the proceeds received from the issuance of such stock towards the payment of the Lessee's indebtedness hereunder, including interest, attorney's fees and other expenses incurred by the Lessor, and if the proceeds are sufficient to pay the same, the Lessor shall pay over any surplus to the Lessee, but if insufficient the Lessee shall remain liable for the balance of the indebtedness.

*[Lessee's Option to Cancel]*

20. This lease may be cancelled by the Lessee on September 30, 19. . ., or on any September 30 thereafter,

upon complying with all the provisions of this paragraph. Irrevocable written notice of intention to cancel must be mailed by the Lessee to the Lessor on or before April 1 in the calendar year in which such cancellation is to occur.

*[Documents Required]*

A. At the time of the mailing of such notice of intention to cancel there must also be mailed or delivered to the Lessor:

(1) the Lessee's counterpart of this lease, with a proper assignment thereof, whereby the full and absolute right, title and interest of the Lessee in and to this lease is assigned in blank, as of August 31 of the year of cancellation, free from all subleases, liens, encumbrances and charges whatsoever (except rights of occupancy of third parties existing on the date the Lessor acquired title to the Building);

(2) the Lessee's certificate for the shares of stock of the Lessor appurtenant to this lease, duly endorsed in blank for transfer with proper transfer stamps thereto affixed;

(3) a written statement setting forth in detail those additions, improvements and fixtures, such as mantels, lighting fixtures, refrigerators, air-conditioning equipment, ranges, woodwork, panelling, ceiling, doors and decorations, in the apartment which the Lessee has, under the terms of this lease, the right to remove, and which the Lessee desires to remove.

*[Removal of Fixtures and Restoration of Premises]*

B. All additions, improvements and fixtures which are removable under the terms of this lease and which are enumerated in the statement made as provided in subparagraph A (3) hereof, shall be removed by the Lessee and the premises restored as provided in paragraph 11 hereof, prior to the 31st day of August next preceding the date fixed in said notice as the date for the cancellation of this lease, and on or before said 31st day of August the Lessee shall deliver possession of the apartment to the Lessor free from all subleases, liens, encumbrances or other charges (except rights of occupancy of third parties existing on the date the Lessor acquired title to the Building) and pay to the Lessor all rent, additional rent and other charges which shall be payable under this lease up to and including the 30th of September succeeding such 31st day of August.

*[Permission to Show and Occupy Premises]*

C. The Lessor and its agents may show the apartment to prospective lessees or purchasers at any time and from time to time after the giving of notice of the Lessee's intention to cancel this lease, and after the 31st day of August next succeeding the date on which such notice of intention to cancel is given, the Lessor and its agents, employees, lessees and purchasers may enter the apartment, occupy the same, and make such alterations, additions and repairs therein as may be necessary or desirable, without diminution or abatement of the rent due hereunder.

*[Cancellation of Lease]*
*[Rights on Lessee's Default]*

D. On the date fixed in said notice as the date for the cancellation of this lease, this lease shall be cancelled and all rights, duties and obligations of the parties hereunder shall cease, terminate and expire as of said date and said shares of stock of the Lessor shall become the absolute property of the Lessor, provided, however, that the Lessee shall not be released or discharged from any indebtedness owing from the Lessee to the Lessor on said last mentioned date, and provided further, that if the Lessee shall fail to do any of the things or make any of the payments at the time, in the amounts and in the manner required by this paragraph 20, or shall otherwise be in default under this lease, the Lessor shall have the option (1) of returning to the Lessee this lease, the certificate of stock and other documents deposited, and thereupon the Lessee shall be deemed to have withdrawn the notice of intention to cancel this lease, or (2) of treating this lease as cancelled as of the 30th day of September named in said notice, and bringing such proceedings and actions as it deems best to evict the Lessee, and to enforce the obligations of the Lessee contained in this paragraph 20.

*[Extension of Option to Cancel]*

E. If on or before April 1st in any year proprietary leases have theretofore been cancelled, or are to be cancelled, in accordance with notices of intention to cancel, on the 30th day of September next succeeding, in such amounts so that it appears, in the opinion of counsel for the Lessor, that the Lessor will not receive 80% or more of its gross income (or such other minimum percentage of gross income as may be then required to qualify the Lessor as a cooperative housing corporation under provisions of the Internal Revenue Code then applicable) for the Lessor's fiscal year next succeeding said April 1st from tenant-stockholders, and sufficient capital stock representing such leases has not been reissued or contracted to be sold by the Lessor to new lessees so as to overcome such deficiency by April 15th of said year, then, in such event, the Lessor shall, prior to May 1st in such year, mail a written notice to the holders of the remaining shares of stock of the Lessor then issued and outstanding stating the total number of shares of such stock then in its treasury, and the total number of shares of stock owned by lessees holding proprietary leases who have given notice of intention to cancel, and stating that (if such is the case) unless the Lessor shall, prior to said next succeeding fiscal year, cure the deficiency by reissuance of cancelled leases to new lessees, the Lessor may cease to qualify under the Internal Revenue Code, as the same may be amended from time to time, as a cooperative housing corporation, and that proprietary lessees may no longer be entitled to their pro rata shares of deductions, for income tax purposes, on account of real estate taxes and interest paid by the Lessor. In such case the proprietary lessees to whom such notice shall have been given, shall have the right to cancel their leases on compliance with the provisions of this paragraph 20, provided only that written notice of intention to cancel such leases may be mailed on or before June 1st instead of April 1st.

*[Exercise of Option by 80% of Stockholders]*

F. If lessees owning at least 80% of the then issued and outstanding stock of the Lessor shall exercise the option to cancel their leases, then this and all other proprietary leases shall thereupon terminate on the 30th of September of the year in which such options shall have been exercised, as though every lessee had exercised such option. In such event none of the lessees shall be required

# INTERESTS IN REAL PROPERTY § 4:23

to surrender his stock to the Lessor and all stock certificates delivered to the Lessor by those who have, during that year, served notice of intention to cancel their leases under the provisions of this paragraph, shall be returned to such lessees.

*[Penthouses and Terraces]*

21. Subject to all the applicable provisions of this lease and to the use of such terrace by the Lessor to enable it to fulfill its obligations hereunder, a lessee of an apartment embracing a penthouse or a portion thereof shall have and enjoy the exclusive use of the terrace appurtenant to such apartment and a lessee of an apartment having direct access to a terrace shall have and enjoy the exclusive use of the portion of such terrace which immediately adjoins the apartment. It is understood and agreed that it shall be the Lessee's duty to keep any such terrace clean, and free from ice, snow and debris, to repair the same and to provide proper drainage therefor and that the Lessor shall have no duties or obligations with respect to any of such matters, except that if the Lessee has fulfilled his obligations hereunder the Lessor shall repair the tile and masonry on such terrace. The Lessor shall have the right to erect, on the roof above a penthouse, for its use and for the use of other lessees, radio or television aerials and antennae or other necessary or desirable improvements and the Lessor and/or other lessees, as the case may be, shall have the right of access thereto for such installations and for the repair and use thereof.

*[Electric Current]*

22. So long as electric current is furnished by a public service corporation directly to the Lessee, the Lessee shall pay for all electric current consumed in and for the apartment. If the Lessor shall contract for the furnishing of electric current to the building by a public service corporation, the Lessee shall purchase from the Lessor all such electric current as the Lessee shall require and shall pay the Lessor for the amount consumed as indicated by the meter furnished therefor. The rates for said current payable by the Lessee shall be the same as those charged by said public service corporation for a consumption

similar to that of the Lessee and the Lessee shall comply with rules and regulations similar to those prescribed by said public service corporation. Payments for such electric current shall be due monthly as and when bills therefor are rendered and if at any time such payments are in default, they shall be deemed to be additional rent due and payable on the first day of the next following month after such bills are rendered or at the option of the Lessor on the first day of any succeeding month.

*[House Rules]*

23. The Lessor hereby establishes the house rules appended to this lease for the management and control of the Building, and may also from time to time alter, amend and repeal such rules, and this lease shall be in all respects subject to the appended rules and to all changes and modifications therein of which notice has been given to the Lessee, and the Lessee shall obey all such rules and see that they are faithfully observed by his family, guests, employees and subtenants, but the Lessor shall not be responsible to the Lessee for the non-observance or violation of such rules by any other lessee or person other than employees of the Lessor.

*[Lease Subordinate to Mortgage]*

24. This lease is and shall be subject and subordinate to any mortgages now a lien upon the Building and to any and all extensions, modifications, renewals and replacements thereof and this lease shall be subject and subordinate to the lien of any other mortgage or mortgages which shall at any time be placed on the Building. The Lessee shall at any time, and from time to time, on demand, execute any instruments that may be required by any mortgagee, or by the Lessor, for the purpose of more formally subjecting this lease to the lien of any such mortgage or mortgages, and the duly elected officers, for the time being, of the Lessor are and each of them is hereby irrevocably appointed the attorney-in-fact and agent of the Lessee to execute the same upon such demand, and the Lessee hereby ratifies any such instrument hereafter executed by virtue of the power of attorney hereby given.

INTERESTS IN REAL PROPERTY § 4:23

*[Books of Account]*

25. The Lessor shall keep full and correct books of account at its principal office or at such other place as the Board of Directors may from time to time determine, and the same shall be open during all reasonable hours to inspection by the Lessee or his representatives. Within three (3) months after the close of each fiscal year of the Lessor, the Lessor will furnish to all Lessees a statement of the amount of rent per share of the Lessor's stock paid by all Lessees during such year and a statement of the separate portions of such rent per share which have been used by the Lessor for the payment of (a) real estate taxes and (b) interest on its mortgage or other indebtedness, together with a financial statement of the operations of the Lessor for such year.

*[Assignment of Lessor's Rights]*

26. In the event that as of the date of the commencement of this lease, any third party should be in possession or have a right to possession of the apartment pursuant to any lease or rental agreement or as a statutory tenant or otherwise, then the Lessor does hereby assign to the Lessee any and all of the Lessor's rights therein or against said third party, including the right to collect rent pursuant to any such lease, rental agreement, statutory tenancy or other arrangement, and the Lessor shall deliver to the Lessee any and all leases and other documents in its possession relating thereto.

*[Cancellation of Prior Agreements]*

27. In the event that as of the date of the commencement of this lease, the Lessee has the right to possession of the apartment under any lease or rental agreement or as a statutory tenant or otherwise, then this lease shall supersede such prior lease, rental agreement, statutory tenancy or other arrangement, and such prior lease, rental agreement, statutory tenancy or other arrangement shall be null and void and of no force and effect after the date of commencement of this lease, except for tenant's obligations which have theretofore arisen thereunder.

*[Changes in Terms and Conditions of Proprietary Leases]*

28. All proprietary leases of apartments in the Building

heretofore executed are, and all such leases hereafter executed shall be, in the form of this lease, except with respect to the statement as to the number of shares of stock owned by the Lessee, unless the variation is approved by lessees owning at least two-thirds in amount of the Lessor's capital stock then issued and outstanding. The Lessor will not make or consent to any change or alteration in the terms or conditions of any proprietary lease which shall have been executed by the Lessor unless such change or alteration shall be similarly approved. Any such approval shall be evidenced by written consent or affirmative vote taken at a meeting called for such purpose.

*[Waivers]*

29. A. The failure of the Lessor to insist, in any one or more instances, upon a strict performance of any of the covenants or conditions hereof, or to exercise any right or option herein contained, or to serve any notice, or to institute any action or proceeding, shall not be construed as a waiver of such default or a relinquishment for the future of the right to enforce such covenant or exercise such option or right thereafter but such covenant or option or right shall continue and remain in full force and effect. The receipt by the Lessor of rent, with knowledge of the breach of any covenant hereof, shall not be deemed a waiver of such breach, and no waiver by the Lessor of any provision hereof shall be deemed to have been made unless in writing and signed by an officer of the Lessor pursuant to authority contained in a resolution of its Board of Directors.

*[Waiver of Right of Redemption]*

B. The Lessee hereby expressly waives any and all right of redemption in case the Lessee shall be dispossessed. The words "enter", "re-enter" and "re-entry" as used in this lease are not restricted to their technical legal meaning.

*[Waiver of Trial by Jury]*

C. The respective parties hereto shall and they hereby do waive trial by jury in any action, proceeding or counterclaim brought by either of the parties hereto against the other on any matters whatsoever arising out of or in

# INTERESTS IN REAL PROPERTY § 4:23

any way connected with this lease, the Lessee's use or occupancy of the apartment, or any claim of damage resulting from any act or omission of the parties in any way connected with this lease or the apartment.

*[Reimbursement of Attorney's Fees and other Expenses]*

30. If the Lessee shall at any time be in default hereunder and the Lessor shall incur any expense (whether paid or not) in performing acts which the Lessee is required to perform, or in instituting any action or proceeding based on such default, the expense thereof to the Lessor, including reasonable attorneys' fees and disbursements, shall be paid by the Lessee to the Lessor, on demand, as additional rent.

*[Notices]*

31. Any notice by the Lessor to the Lessee or by the Lessee to the Lessor shall be deemed to have been duly given, and any demand by the Lessor on the Lessee or by the Lessee on the Lessor shall be deemed to have been duly made, only if in writing and delivered personally or sent by registered mail addressed to the Lessor, at ........, New York, N.Y., or to the Lessee at ........, New York, N.Y., or such other address as may be designated by the Lessor or the Lessee, as the case may be, in the manner herein set forth for the giving of notices.

*[Quiet Enjoyment]*

32. The Lessee upon paying the rent and performing the covenants and complying with the conditions on the part of the Lessee to be performed and complied with as herein set forth, shall, at all times during the term hereby granted, quietly have, hold and enjoy the demised premises without any let, suit, trouble or hindrance from the Lessor.

*[Transfer of Stock]*

33. The shares of stock of the Lessor held by the Lessee and appurtenant to this lease have been acquired and are owned subject to the following conditions agreed upon with the Lessor and with each of the other proprietary lessees for their mutual benefit;

(1) The shares represented by each certificate are transferable only as an entirety;

(2) The shares shall not be sold except to the Lessor, or to an assignee of this lease after compliance with all of the provisions of paragraph 6 of this lease relating to assignments.

*[To Whom Covenants Apply]*

34. Except as otherwise in this lease provided, the references herein to the Lessor shall be deemed to include its successors and assigns, and the references herein to the Lessee or to a stockholder of the Lessor shall be deemed to include the executors, administrators, legal representatives, legatees, distributees and assigns of the Lessee or of such stockholder; and the covenants herein contained shall apply to, bind and enure to the benefit of the Lessor and its successors and assigns, and the Lessee and the executors, administrators, legal representatives, legatees, distributees and assigns of the Lessee.

*[Changes to be in Writing]*

35. The provisions of this lease cannot be changed orally.

*[Lessee More Than One Person]*

36. If more than one person is named as Lessee hereunder, the Lessor may require the signatures of all such persons in connection with any notice to be given or action to be taken by the Lessee hereunder, including, without limiting the generality of the foregoing, the surrender or assignment of this lease, or any request for consent to assignment or subletting. Each person named as Lessee shall be fully liable for all of the Lessee's obligations hereunder. Any notice by the Lessor to any person named as Lessee shall be sufficient, and shall have the same force and effect as though given to all persons named as Lessee.

*[Effect of Partial Invalidity]*

37. If any clause or provision herein contained shall be adjudged invalid, such fact shall not affect the validity of any other clause or provision of this lease, or give rise to any cause of action in favor of either party as against the other.

*[Definitions]*

38. A. *"Cash requirements"* whenever used herein shall

mean the amount in cash which the Board of Directors of the Lessor by resolution duly adopted shall in its judgment estimate to be necessary or proper (1) for the operation, maintenance, care and improvement of the corporate property during the year or portion of the year for which such estimate is made; (2) the creation of such reserve for contingencies as may seem proper; and (3) the payment of, or establishment of reserve for, any obligations, liabilities or expenses incurred (even though incurred during a prior period) or to be incurred—after giving consideration to (a) income reasonably expected to be received during such period (other than rents under proprietary leases) and (b) surplus which the Board of Directors in its discretion may deem applicable. While the Board of Directors of the Lessor may, from time to time, by resolution duly adopted, modify its prior estimates and increase or diminish the amount previously determined as cash requirements of the corporation for a year or portion thereof, no such determination shall have any retroactive effect on the amount of the rent payable by the Lessee for any period elapsed prior to the date of such determination.

Any sums which the Lessee may pay hereunder, but which are used or to be used to meet the cash requirements of the Lessor for mortgage amortization payments or any other mortgage principal payments, shall not be deemed income to the Lessor but shall be deemed contributions to the capital of the Lessor, and shall be credited by the Lessor upon its books to an account entitled "Paid-in Surplus".

B. *"Members of the Lessee's Family"* as used herein, shall be deemed to mean the Lessee's spouse, parents, parents-in-law, brothers and sisters, children, grandchildren, children-in-law and stepchildren, nieces, nephews, or if the Lessee be more than one person, of any of the Lessees.

C. *"Issued and outstanding"* wherever used herein as relating to the shares of stock of the Lessor shall be deemed to include only the shares of stock of the Lessor issued to and outstanding in the names of persons holding proprietary leases on apartments in the Building, and shall not include any stock authorized but unissued, nor any stock previously issued, but returned to the treasury on cancellation of proprietary leases.

*[Marginal Headings]*

39. The marginal headings next to the several paragraphs of this lease shall not be deemed a part of this lease, nor used as evidence of the intent of the parties.

*[Termination of Cooperative Ownership]*

40. On the termination of all proprietary leases, whether by expiration of their terms, or otherwise, the Building and the other assets of the Lessor shall be operated and managed and disposed of in such manner as shall seem proper to the Board of Directors, provided, however, that a meeting of stockholders shall be held not later than one month after such termination, at which the directors shall be instructed by the stockholders as to the future management and operation of the corporate property.

In witness whereof, the Lessor has caused its corporate seal to be hereto affixed and this instrument to be signed by its ........ President, and the Lessee has executed this instrument under seal, the day and year first above written.

## HOUSE RULES

1. The public halls and stairways of the Building shall not be obstructed or used for any purpose other than ingress to and egress from the apartments in the Building, and the fire towers shall not be obstructed in any way.

2. Children shall not play in the public halls, stairways, fire towers or elevators, and shall not be permitted in the service elevators of the Building.

3. No lessee shall make or permit any disturbing noises in the Building or do or permit anything to be done therein which will interfere with the rights, comfort or convenience of other lessees. No lessee shall play upon or suffer to be played upon any musical instrument or permit to be operated a phonograph or a radio or television loud speaker in such lessee's apartment between the hours of eleven o'clock P.M. and the following nine o'clock A.M. if the same shall disturb or annoy other

occupants of the building, and in no event shall any lessee practice or suffer to be practiced either vocal or instrumental music for more than two hours in any day or between the hours of six o'clock P.M. and the following nine o'clock A.M. No lessee shall give vocal or instrumental instruction at any time. In order to reduce sound emanating from an apartment Lessor may require a lessee to cover the floors of any living room, dining room and bedroom, with carpet.

4. Each lessee shall keep such lessee's apartment in a good state of preservation and cleanliness and shall not sweep or throw or permit to be swept or thrown therefrom, or from the doors, windows, terraces or balconies thereof, any dirt or other substance.

5. No article shall be placed in the halls or on the staircase landings, or fire towers, nor shall anything be hung or shaken from the doors, windows, terraces or balconies or placed upon the window sills of the Building. No fences or partitions shall be placed on or affixed to any terrace without the prior approval of the Lessor.

6. No shades, awnings, window guards, ventilators or air conditioning devices shall be used in or about the Building except such as shall have been approved by the Lessor.

7. No sign, notice or advertisement shall be inscribed or exposed on or at any window or other part of the Building, except such as shall have been approved by the Lessor; nor shall anything be projected out of any window of the Building without similar approval.

8. The passenger and service elevators in the Building, unless of the automatic type to be operated by the passenger, shall be operated only by employees of the Lessor and there shall be no interference whatever with the same by lessees or members of their families or their guests, employees or subtenants.

9. No velocipedes, bicycles, scooters, shopping carts, or similar vehicles shall be allowed in the passenger elevators and no baby carriages or any of the above-mentioned vehicles shall be allowed to stand in the public halls, passageways, areas or courts of the Building.

10. Servants, messengers and tradespeople shall use the

service elevators in the Building for ingress and egress and shall not use the passenger elevators for any purpose, except that nurses in the employ of lessees and nurses in the employ of guests or under-tenants of lessees may use the passenger elevators when accompanying children of said lessees, their guests or sub-tenants.

11. Kitchen supplies, market goods and packages of every kind are to be delivered only at the service entrance of the Building and through the service elevators to the apartments.

12. Trunks and heavy baggage shall be taken in or out of the building through the service entrance.

13. Water-closets and other water apparatus in the Building shall not be used for any purposes other than those for which they were constructed, nor shall any sweepings, rubbish, rags or any other article be thrown into the same. Any damage resulting from misuse of any water-closets or other apparatus shall be paid for by the lessee in whose apartment it shall have been caused.

14. No lessee shall send any employee of the Lessor out of the Building on any private business of a lessee.

15. No bird or animal shall be kept or harbored in the Building without the approval of the Lessor. In no event shall dogs be permitted on elevators or in any of the public portions of the Building unless carried or on leash.

16. No radio or television aerial shall be attached to or hung from the exterior of the Building without the approval of the Lessor.

17. The agents of the Lessor, and any contractor or workman authorized by the Lessor, may enter any apartment at any reasonable hour of the day for the purpose of inspecting such apartment to ascertain whether measures are necessary or desirable to control or exterminate any vermin, insects or other pests and for the purpose of taking such measures as may be necessary to control or exterminate any such vermin, insects or other pests. If the Lessor takes measures to control or exterminate carpet beetles within the Lessee's apartment or in any storage or other space in the Building occupied by the Lessee, the cost thereof shall be payable by the Lessee upon demand as additional rent.

INTERESTS IN REAL PROPERTY § 4:24

18. The Lessor shall have the right from time to time to curtail or re-locate any space devoted to storage or laundry purposes.

19. Garbage and refuse from the apartments shall be deposited in such place only in the Building, and at such times and in such manner as the superintendent of the Building may direct.

20. No vehicle belonging to a lessee or to a member of the family or guest, sub-tenant or employee of a lessee shall be parked in such manner as to impede or prevent ready access to the entrance of the Building by another vehicle.

21. Except where the Lessee has been granted the exclusive use of a laundry, the Lessee shall use the laundry facilities available only upon such days and during such hours as may be designated by the Lessor.

22. Complaints, if any, regarding service in the Building shall be made in writing to the managing agent of the Lessor.

23. The Lessor may retain a passkey to each apartment. No lessee shall alter any lock or install a new lock on any door leading into his apartment without the prior approval of the Lessor. If such approval is given, the Lessee shall provide the Lessor with a key for Lessor's use.

24. Any consent or approval given under these house rules by the Lessor (a) may be given by the Lessor's Managing Agent, (b) must be in writing, and (c) shall be revocable at any time.

25. These house rules may be added to, amended or repealed at any time by resolution of the Board of Directors of the Lessor.

26. Patients of doctors having offices in the Building shall enter such offices through private entrances, if available, and not through the public lobby.[11]

## D. RESEARCH REFERENCES

### § 4:24. Generally

In addition to the preceding text, the reader is also referred to the following:

---

11. For form of agreement to assign proprietary lease, see Form No. 12, § 9:81, infra.

**§ 4:24**

49 Am Jur 2d, Landlord and Tenant §§ 5, 7, 8.

New York Jur 2d, Landlord and Tenant (1st ed §§ 6-13).

Index to Annotations, Landlord and Tenant.

**VERALEX®:** Cases and annotations referred to herein can be further researched through the VERALEX electronic retrieval system's two services, **Auto-Cite®** and **SHOWME®**. Use Auto-Cite to check citations for form, parallel references, prior and later history, and annotation references. Use SHOWME to display the full text of cases and annotations.

# CHAPTER 5
# TITLE AND REVERSION OF LANDLORD

### A. IN GENERAL
§ 5:1. Reversion Defined
§ 5:2. Title of Landlord Implied
§ 5:3. Necessity of Title and Possession
§ 5:4. After-acquired Title
§ 5:5. Possession of Tenant as Possession of Landlord
§ 5:6. Acquisition of Appurtenances by Tenant as Property of Landlord
§ 5:7. Possession of Persons Holding Under Tenant as Possession of Landlord

### B. ESTOPPEL TO DENY LANDLORD'S TITLE
§ 5:8. Generally
§ 5:9. Where Attornment Void
§ 5:10. Duration of Estoppel
§ 5:11. Effect of Expiration of Landlord's Title
§ 5:12. Effect of Fraud or Mistake
§ 5:13. Tenant's Acquisition of Title to Attack Landlord's Title
§ 5:14. Where Landlord a Grantee

### C. TRANSFER OF REVERSION
§ 5:15. Generally
§ 5:16. Rights and Obligations of Grantor
§ 5:17. Rights and Obligations of Grantee
§ 5:18. Rights or Transfer of Reversion to Tent Due or to Become Due
§ 5:19. Waiver of Grantor Binding on Grantee
§ 5:20. Concurrent Lease as Transfer of Reversion
§ 5:21. Death of Landlord
§ 5:22. Injury to Reversion by Third Person
§ 5:23. —Particular Injuries

### D. RESEARCH REFERENCES
§ 5:24. Generally

---

## A. IN GENERAL
### § 5:1. Reversion Defined
The estate of a landlord during the existence of an outstanding leasehold estate is called the reversion. The

Estates, Powers and Trusts Law defines a reversion as the future estate, other than a possibility of reverter and a right of reacquisition, left in the creator or his successors in interest upon the simultaneous creation of one or more lesser estates than the creator originally owned.[1] When the owner of real property carves out of his fee a term of years, he does not thereby divest himself of his inheritance. He still has an inheritance in the land, technically a reversion. His prior absolute and unqualified estate has been divided into two estates, one in the termor or lessee, the nature and quality of which is determined by the lease, and the other in himself.[2] Similarly when a lessee having a term of fifteen years sublets the premises for a term of five years, he retains a reversion in a term of years.[3] In other words the estate or interest which the lessor passes by the lease must be less than the lessor has therein, since, if it is for the entire interest of the lessor, it is an assignment rather than a lease.[4]

### § 5:2. Title of Landlord Implied

It is a settled rule of property that a covenant for quiet enjoyment is implied in every lease, whether created by parol or in writing.[5] Such a covenant, in effect, is an agreement on the part of the landlord that for the period of the leased term the tenant shall not be disturbed in his quiet enjoyment of the leased premises by any wrongful act of the landlord, or of his successors in interest, or by the enforcement of any title superior to that of the landlord. Therefore, this covenant comprehends by implication a covenant that the landlord has title or power to grant a valid lease. Otherwise a tenant would have no assurance against the enforcement of a title superior to that of his landlord.[6]

1. EPTL 6-4.4.
2. Kernochan v New York E. R. Co. (1891) 128 NY 559, 564, 29 NE 65.
3. Stewart v Long I. R. Co. (1886) 102 NY 601, 8 NE 200.
4. Kavanaugh v Cohoes Power & Light Corp. (S Ct Albany Co 1921) 114 Misc 590, 187 NYS 216.
5. Fifth Ave. Bldg. Co. v Kernochan (1917) 221 NY 370, 117 NE 579, reh den 222 NY 525, 118 NE 1057; Leventhal v Straus (M Ct 1950) 197 Misc 798, 95 NYS2d 883.

As has been seen, the implication in a lease of a covenant for quiet enjoyment is not prohibited by Real Prop L § 251, since a lease is not a conveyance within the meaning of this section. § 1:2, supra.

6. Mayor, etc., of New York v Mabie (1855) 13 NY 151.

## § 5:3. Necessity of Title and Possession

One may be a lessor, although one is not the owner in fee of the leased premises. For example, a tenant can sublet his leased premises, and thereupon become a lessor.[7] However, the lessor must, at the time of giving the lease, have an estate out of which the term may be carved.[8]

Actual possession is not necessary to enable one to give a valid lease; all that is necessary is the right to the possession of the premises.[9] Where a landlord purports to lease property over which he has no control, or right to lease, there is a failure of consideration, and constructive eviction, and entitles the tenant to vacate immediately upon discovery thereof.[1]

## § 5:4. After-acquired Title

If a landlord has no title at the time of the execution of the lease, but thereafter acquires title, such title will inure to the benefit of the lessee by way of estoppel to bind the lessor's interest, and support the lease from the time of its execution.[2] A lease made without words of restriction as to the lessor's interest or title must be regarded as embracing whatever interest he has at the time or may in the future acquire.[3]

## § 5:5. Possession of Tenant as Possession of Landlord

The statute provides[4] that where the relation of landlord and tenant has existed between any persons, the possession of the tenant is deemed the possession of the landlord until the expiration of ten years after the termination of the tenancy; or, where there has been no

---

7. A lease by one tenant in common is valid as between the parties, and as against the other cotenants, to the extent of the lessor's individual interest. Austin v Ahearne (1874) 61 NY 6.

8. Burr v Stenton (1871) 43 NY 462, 465. As to subsequently acquired title, see § 5:4, infra.

9. Russell v Doty (1825) 4 Cow 576.
Real Prop L § 260 provides that no grant, conveyance or mortgage of real property or interest therein shall be void for the reason that at the time of the delivery thereof such real property is in the actual possession of a person claiming under a title adverse to that of the grantor.

1. H.B.A. Realty Co. v Miller (1961, 3d Dept) 14 AD2d 607, 218 NYS2d 152.

2. Austin v Ahearne (1874) 61 NY 6; Van Horne v Crain (1829) 1 Paige 455.

3. Geneva Mineral Springs Co. v Coursey (AD4 1899) 45 AD 268, 61 NYS 98.

4. Real Prop Act & Proc L § 531.

written lease, until the expiration of ten years after the last payment of rent; notwithstanding that the tenant has acquired another title or has claimed to hold adversely to his landlord. But, this presumption cannot be made after these prescribed periods, and the tenant may then commence to hold adversely to the landlord.

This statutory rule is founded upon the acknowledgment of title in the lessor, which is implied from the acceptance of the lease and the payment of rent, and the confidence reposed by the lessor in the lessee to whom the possession is entrusted. It does not apply where the relation of landlord and tenant arises by mere operation of law, and no grant or return is in fact reserved to the landlord.[5] Of course, the statute does not apply where the relationship of landlord and tenant does not exist with respect to the property in question.[6]

It has been held that the presumption that the possession of the tenant is the possession of the landlord until the expiration of the statutory period after the termination of the tenancy may be rebutted, but to do so effectively, and initiate an adverse holding, the tenant must surrender possession to the landlord or do something equivalent to that, so as to bring home to him knowledge of the adverse claim.[7]

§ 5:6. Acquisition of Appurtenances by Tenant as Property of Landlord

It is a general principle of law that adverse possession of a third person's land by a tenant inures to the benefit of his landlord so as to support the landlord's title to such land by adverse possession. Thus, a tenant may acquire a permanent interest in adjacent lands belonging to a third

---

5. Jackson ex dem Webber v Harsen (1827) 7 Cow 323.

This rule applies only where some rent or return is in fact reserved, and therefore it is not applicable to a person holding under an assessment or tax lease. Bedell v Shaw (1874) 59 NY 46.

6. Lewis v Idones (AD2 1952) 280 AD 980, 116 NYS2d 382, holding that where an adverse claimant seeks to establish title to a strip of neighboring land on which his building encroaches, his possession is not affected by the fact that he and his predecessor in title may have been the tenants of a gasoline station on the adjoining property, for it was not intended that the lease of the adjoining property include the encroaching wall; thus, the relationship of landlord and tenant did not exist with respect thereto and consequently the statute (former CPA § 41, now Real Prop Act & Proc L § 531) does not apply.

7. Whiting v Edmunds (1884) 94 NY 309.

person for the use of the leased property, either by agreement or by prescription, which shall enure to his own benefit while the tenancy continues, and in the absence of agreement, will be presumed to appertain to the landlord on the expiration of the lease. A tenant in making such acquisitions is presumed by law to have acted with a view to adding to the interest of his landlord. However, such presumption is, of course, always subject to rebuttal. The tenant's intent is the main subject of inquiry.[8] On the other hand, where a lessee holds adjoining buildings under separate leases from separate owners, he cannot create an easement in favor of one building burdening the other building as against its owner, by the manner in which he uses the two separate buildings, since any such use is under his lease, and is not adverse to the owner whose property is sought to be burdened with the easement.[9]

## § 5:7. Possession of Persons Holding Under Tenant as Possession of Landlord

The possession of one entering under a tenant is, as a general rule, regarded as subservient and not adverse to the landlord to the same extent as that of the tenant. Having placed himself in the shoes of the tenant, he is bound by the allegiance a tenant owes his landlord, and cannot throw it off at will without notice to the landlord.[10]

The rule that one taking possession of premises under a lease cannot dispute the title of his landlord while that possession continues[11] applies to every person who succeeds to the tenant's possession, by his permission and consent. Therefore the possession of an assignee of the tenant cannot be adverse, and cannot ripen into a title as against the landlord by any mere lapse of time.[12]

---

8. Dempsey v Kipp (1875) 61 NY 462; Baird v Erie R. Co. (S Ct Erie Co 1911) 72 Misc 162, 129 NYS 329, affd 148 AD 452, 132 NYS 971, affd 210 NY 225, 104 NE 614.

See, also, Bedlow v New York Floating Dry Dock Co (1889) 112 NY 263, 19 NE 800, where a tenant of water front property acquired from the authorities the right to extend a pier into the navigable waters, and such right was deemed to have been acquired for the benefit of the leased premises, and on the termination of the lease reverted to the landlord.

9. Olin v Kingsbury (AD1 1918) 181 AD 348, 168 NYS 766.

10. Jackson ex dem Webber v Harsen (1827) 7 Cow 323.

11. § 5:10, infra.

12. Tompkins v Snow (Sup Ct 1872) 63 Barb 525; Tyler v Heidorn (Sup Ct Albany 1866) 46 Barb 439.

## B. ESTOPPEL TO DENY LANDLORD'S TITLE

### § 5:8. Generally

It is well settled that a tenant who has once acknowledged his landlord's title, and taken and held possession under him, and who has not surrendered his lease, nor been evicted from the premises, and who can prove no fraud against the landlord nor any transfer of the latter's title after the lease began, is precluded from denying that the landlord, under whom he has so held and claimed, is the owner of the property.[13] The fact that the lease on its face may show want of title in the landlord does not affect the estoppel.[14] As the Court of Appeals said in this connection, "It is well settled that if a party enters as lessee of another, and the right of the lessor is in no way altered, the lessee is estopped from denying that relation, or that the legal estate and reversion are in the lessor. The title he then acknowledges and accepts he must abide by while the relation lasts. The result is the same, although on the face of the lease it should appear that the landlord had no legal estate. If the parties agree that the relation of landlord and tenant shall be created, and this agreement is carried out by one being let into possession, then, as between them, the relation of landlord and tenant is created, and they are just as much estopped as if there had been no such statement. The foundation of the estoppel is the fact of the one obtaining possession and enjoying possession by the permission of the other. And so long as one has this enjoyment he is prevented by this rule of law from turning round and saying his landlord had no right or title to keep him in possession."[15]

---

13. Tilyou v Reynolds (1888) 108 NY 558, 15 NE 534; Metropolitan Fuel Distributors v Coogan (AD1 1950) 277 AD 138, 97 NYS2d 851; Fergus Motors, Inc. v Kramer (1947, Sup App T) 72 NYS2d 439, affd 273 AD 760, 75 NYS2d 536; Wernick v Mehl Realty Co. (S Ct Kings Co 1947) 190 Misc 400, 71 NYS2d 228.

14. Tilyou v Reynolds (1888) 108 NY 558, 563, 15 NE 534.

15. Tilyou v Reynolds (1888) 108 NY 558, 15 NE 534; Mason v Foxcroft Village, Inc. (1979, 3d Dept) 67 AD2d 1012, 413 NYS2d 255 (citing text), app dismd 46 NY2d 1073, 416 NYS2d 796, 390 NE2d 303.

Tilyou v Reynolds (1888) 108 NY 558, 15 NE 534; Mason v Foxcroft Village Inc (AD3 1979) 67 AD2d 1012, 413 NYS2d 255 (citing text).

This rule has been applied in actions or proceedings to recover possession, People by Long Island State Park Com. v Savage (AD2 1932) 236 AD 745, 258 NYS 624; Haskel v 60 West Fifty-Third Street Corp. (M Ct 1929) 138 Misc 595, 246 NYS 698, affd 231 AD 800, 246 NYS 875; to actions to recover rent, Jones v Reilly (1903) 174 NY 97, 105, 66 NE 649; Vernam v Smith (1857) 15 NY 327; Millbrook

Thus, the making of a lease, under which the tenant enters into possession and pays rent, is sufficient to establish the relation of landlord and tenant, and estops the latter from disputing the former's title, although the landlord is the committee appointed for an incompetent person who is a tenant in common of the land.[16] Similarly, where a tenant has accepted a lease from an executor, it has been held that he is estopped from denying the executor's title and authority to give the lease.[17] In other words, to give rise to the estoppel, the conventional relation of landlord and tenant[18] must exist. As was aptly said in an early case, "It is only in cases where the relation of landlord and tenant exists that the tenant is deemed to be estopped to allege against the landlord his own right of possession under a title adverse to the former. The principle finds its origin in the fact that the lessee conclusively acknowledges title in his landlord when he accepts a lease of the property, with an agreement to pay rent therefor; but it does not exist where such conventional relation of landlord and tenant does not exist as is the case now before us."[19]

### § 5:9. Where Attornment Void

To give rise to the estoppel to deny the title of one's landlord, the conventional relation of landlord and tenant must exist.[20] If a tenant attorns to a new landlord, a new contract and a new letting results.[1] However, if the attornment is void because it is made to a stranger, it is void and inoperative for all purposes.[2] Therefore, the new lease is likewise void, and the necessary conventional relation of landlord and tenant does not exist. Accordingly, if there be a void attornment, a tenant may, notwithstanding such attornment, dispute the title of the party to whom such attornment was made.[3] In other

---

Co. v Gambier (AD1 1917) 176 AD 870, 163 NYS 1025, affd 226 NY 661, 123 NE 878, and to actions to recover for waste, Purton v Watson (City Ct GT 1888) 2 NYS 661.

**16.** Seibert v Mowbray (AT 1910) 123 NYS 128.

**17.** Rowland v Dillingham (AD2 1903) 83 AD 156, 82 NYS 470; Re Goldburg's Estate (Surr Ct Bx Co 1933) 148 Misc 607, 266 NYS 106.

**18.** For discussion of the meaning of conventional relation of landlord and tenant, see §§ 38:5 et seq, infra.

**19.** Hoffman v Hoffman (1892, Sup) 18 NYS 387.

**20.** See § 5:8, supra.

**1.** § 2:4, supra.

**2.** § 2:6, supra.

**3.** Maxrice Realty Corp. v B/G Sandwich Shops, Inc. (AD1 1933) 239 AD 472, 267 NYS 863.

words where a new landlord cannot rely upon a lease with a tenant in possession, but must rely solely upon an attornment to create the relationship of landlord and tenant with such tenant, the rule of estoppel to dispute the landlord's title will not apply. Such tenant can show that the relationship of landlord and tenant did not arise, because under the Real Property Law the attornment was void, and a nullity.[4]

### § 5:10. Duration of Estoppel

It is the general rule that a tenant is estopped to deny his landlord's title while he remains in possession, and until he surrenders the possession to the landlord. Thus, a tenant cannot, in an action involving the possession of the leased premises, controvert the title of his landlord or assert any rights adverse to that title, or set up any inconsistent right to change the relation existing between himself and his landlord, without first delivering up to the landlord the premises acquired by virtue of the agreement between themselves.[5] The estoppel of a tenant in possession continues at least until his term expires, but if he continues in such possession after the expiration of the term, the estoppel continues.[6]

After the tenant surrenders possession, he is no longer estopped to deny his landlord's title. While the protection of landlords is reasonably insured by the rule as to the estoppel of a tenant in possession, the rule has never been carried so far in disregard of the rights of the tenant as to operate as an absolute estoppel against his claim of title. The object of the rule being accomplished by the tenant's restoration of the possession to the landlord on the expiration of the term, the relation between them is functus officio, and the former tenant may controvert the title under which he held without any embarrassment,

---

4. Maxrice Realty Corp. v B/G Sandwich Shops, Inc. (AD1 1933) 239 AD 472, 267 NYS 863 (action for rent); Donelly v O'Day (Com Pl GT 1892) 1 Misc 165, 20 NYS 688 (summary proceeding).

5. Utica Bank v Mersereau (1848) 3 Barb Ch 528.

6. Child v Chappell (1853) 9 NY 246.

But, in McKownville Fire Dist. v Bryn Mawr Bookshop (1976, 3d Dept) 54 AD2d 371, 388 NYS2d 699, it was held that tenant was not estopped to deny landlord's title where tenancy was month to month, and tenant had not paid any rent for 4 years, although he had continued in possession.

## § 5:11. Effect of Expiration of Landlord's Title

The estoppel to deny a landlord's title extends only to a denial of the title which the landlord had at the time of the granting of the lease. Therefore, a tenant can show that since making the lease, the landlord's title has expired, or has been defeated or extinguished, either by its original limitation, or by conveyance, or by the judgment and operation of law.[8] The estoppel rests upon the permissive possession of the tenant under the landlord. If, therefore, the landlord's title, good and recognized at the beginning of the lease, has terminated since the granting of the lease, then the tenant is no longer there by his permissive possession, and may be heard to prove such termination.[9] Thus, where a landlord at the time of a lease held under a lease from a life tenant, his tenant may show that the landlord's estate has expired by the death of the life tenant.[10] Similarly, a subtenant in a summary proceeding brought by his sublessor may show that the estate of the sublessor has been terminated by a reentry of the paramount landlord. As the court said, in so holding,[11] "Assuming that Carpenter" (the subtenant) "attorned by the payment of the rent for November, 1907, to the petitioner, the rule that a tenant cannot dispute his landlord's title does not apply, for the estoppel of the tenant simply exists so long as the title exists as when the tenancy began, and hence the rule does not prevent the tenant from showing the expiry of the title."

except so far as a presumption may be derived from his implied recognition of such title.[7]

Where the reversion of the landlord has been sold under execution, and title has become vested in the

---

7. Baker v Citizens' Trust Co. (S Ct Kings Co 1910) 66 Misc 622; 121 NYS 767, affd 137 AD 888, 121 NYS 767; Utica Bank v Mersereau (1848) 3 Barb Ch 528.

8. Hoag v Hoag (1866) 35 NY 469, 471; Despard v Walbridge (1857) 15 NY 374, 378; Shapiro v Shapiro (1916, Sup App T) 158 NYS 154.

9. Wernick v Mehl Realty Co. (S Ct Kings Co 1947) 190 Misc 400, 71 NYS2d 228.

Also, see Shapiro v Shapiro (1916, Sup App T) 158 NYS 154, holding that a tenant is not estopped to show that the landlord conveyed his reversion after creation of tenancy; Boyd v Auchterlonie (Dist Ct NYC 1896) 17 Misc 728, 40 NYS 1070, holding that in a summary proceeding a defense that petitioner after making the lease conveyed the premises to a third person, is a good defense.

10. Hoag v Hoag (1866) 35 NY 469; Mulligan v Cox (AT 1898) 23 Misc 695, 52 NYS 111.

11. Cohen v Carpenter (AD2 1908) 128 AD 862, 113 NYS 168.

purchaser, who may be a third person or the tenant,[12] the tenant may set up this title as a bar to an action by his landlord for rents subsequently accruing, or to a proceeding to recover possession of the leased premises.[13] Similarly, where the landlord's estate is extinguished by condemnation in eminent domain proceedings, the tenant can set this up as a bar to a claim by his landlord for rent accruing thereafter.[14]

It should be observed that a tenant need not allege and prove that he attorned to the new title in order to be able to urge as a defense that his landlord's title has expired or been extinguished.[15] Therefore, it is not necessary for the tenant to first show a surrender of the premises under these circumstances.

### § 5:12. Effect of Fraud or Mistake

Since the estoppel of a tenant to deny his landlord's title is based on his admission or acknowledgment of such title by his having taken possession thereunder,[16] it has been held that such an estoppel does not obtain where the tenant has been induced to take the lease by force, fraud, misrepresentation, or mistake; for, the tenant should not be estopped to deny what he would not have admitted but for these misdeeds.[17] And, in such circumstances, it is not necessary for the tenant to first surrender possession to be in a position to raise this defense.[18]

### § 5:13. Tenant's Acquisition of Title to Attack Landlord's Title

In considering the question of a tenant's acquisition of a title adverse to his landlord's title, a distinction should be drawn between his right to buy up an adverse title, and his right to assert such a title against his landlord. It

---

12. Hetzel v Barber (1877) 69 NY 1, 15.

13. Hetzel v Barber (1877) 69 NY 1, 15.

14. Lodge v Martin (AD1 1898) 31 AD 13, 52 NYS 385.

15. Hoag v Hoag (1866) 35 NY 469, 471.

16. § 5:8, supra.

17. Jones v Reilly (1903) 174 NY 97, 107, 66 NE 649; People ex rel. Ainslee v Howlett (1879) 76 NY 574, 580, where a tenant was permitted to show that the lease was a mere cover for a usurious agreement for a loan of money to him by the alleged lessor; Fergus Motors, Inc. v Kramer (1947, Sup App T) 72 NYS2d 439, affd 273 AD 760, 75 NYS2d 536; Wernick v Mehl Realty Co. (S Ct Kings Co 1947) 190 Misc 400, 71 NYS2d 228.

18. Wernick v Mehl Realty Co. (S Ct Kings Co 1947) 190 Misc 400, 71 NYS2d 228.

As to necessity for surrender of possession, see § 5:10, supra.

has been held that a tenant is not precluded by the relation of landlord and tenant from purchasing a title adverse to his landlord's.[19] But, he cannot assert such title acquired during his tenancy against his landlord until he surrenders the possession which he acquired under the lease, or does some equivalent act.[20]

It has been held that a tenant cannot acquire a valid title as against his landlord by virtue of a tax sale during the tenancy, for taxes which the tenant had agreed to pay.[1] But, if the tenant was not obligated to pay the taxes, then his acquisition of title at a tax sale, as in the case of an acquisition of title at a judicial sale, can be set up as a defense without first surrendering possession.[2]

### § 5:14. Where Landlord a Grantee

The estoppel to deny a landlord's title is operative in favor of those who succeed to the landlord's title.[3] However, it has been held that until a tenant has attorned, and paid rent, to the new landlord, and thus has recognized the title and the holding of possession thereunder,[4] a tenant is not estopped to deny the validity of the transfer of title, and of the transferee's title as landlord. Any other rule would put the tenant at the mercy of both his landlord and the transferee.[5]

## C. TRANSFER OF REVERSION

### § 5:15. Generally

The owner of leased property may convey such property, and if there is no reservation in the grant, the grant

---

19. Willis v McKinnon (1900) 165 NY 612, 59 NE 1132.

20. Kavanaugh v Cohoes Power & Light Corp. (S Ct Albany Co 1921) 114 Misc 590, 187 NYS 216; Willis v McKinnon (S Ct Delaware Co 1902) 37 Misc 386, 75 NYS 770, affd 79 AD 249, 79 NYS 936, affd 178 NY 451, 70 NE 962; McKeefry v O'Hara (Mun Ct 1920) 113 Misc 159, 184 NYS 700.

1. Wernick v Mehl Realty Co. (S Ct Kings Co 1947) 190 Misc 400, 71 NYS2d 228.

2. Sharpe v Kelley (Super Ct 1848) 5 Denio 431; Senior v Marcinkowski, 1 How Pr NS 331.

3. Drake v Cunningham (AD2 1908) 127 AD 79, 111 NYS 199.

4. Whalin v White (1862) 25 NY 462; Sturges v Van Orden (AT 1902) 37 Misc 499, 75 NYS 1007; Baker v Citizens' Trust Co (S Ct Kings Co 1910) 66 Misc 622, 121 NYS 767, affd 137 AD 888, 121 NYS 769.

5. Despard v Walbridge (1857) 15 NY 374, 377; Sturges v Van Orden (AT 1902) 37 Misc 499, 75 NYS 1007.

See Copperfretti v Shephard (AD2 1934) 241 AD 872, 271 NYS 284, where a tenant, in a summary proceeding instituted by a purchaser at an execution sale on a judgment against the former owner of the property, was permitted to dispute the petitioner-purchaser's title by showing that the judgment was void.

§ 5:15   LANDLORD AND TENANT

conveys the lessor's interest in the lease.[6] In other words, the transfer of the reversion is a transfer of the lease, and of its rights and obligations,[7] even though there is no formal assignment of the lease.[8]

The Real Property Law provides that a grant or devise of real property passes all the estate or interest of the grantor or testator unless the intent to pass a less estate or interest appears by the express terms of such grant or devise or by necessary implication therefrom.[9] If the grantee has notice of the lease, he takes his conveyance subject thereto; and where the lessee is in possession, the grantee takes subject to the lease, and every condition and covenant it contains, even though he has no actual knowledge thereof.[10] As has been seen, attornment of the tenant to the grantee is unnecessary;[11] because the transfer of the reversion, whether with the consent of the

---

**6.** Reltron Corp. v Voxakis Enterprises, Inc. (1977, 4th Dept) 57 AD2d 134, 395 NYS2d 276; Grover v Norton (S Ct Monroe Co 1920) 113 Misc 3, 183 NYS 731.

**7.** Real Prop L § 223 provides, "The grantee of leased real property, or of a reversion thereof, or of any rent, the devisee or assignee of the lessor of such a lease, or the heir or personal representative of either of them, has the same remedies, by entry, action or otherwise, for the nonperformance of any agreement contained in the assigned lease for the recovery of rent, for the doing of any waste, or for other cause of forfeiture as his grantor or lessor had, or would have had, if the reversion had remained in him. A lessee of real property, his assignee or personal representative, has the same remedy against the lessor, his grantee or assignee, or the representative of either, for the breach of an agreement contained in the lease, that the lessee might have had against his immediate lessor, except a covenant against incumbrances or relating to the title or possession of the premises leased. This section applies as well to a grant or lease in fee, reserving rent, as to a lease for life or for years; but not to a deed of conveyance in fee, made before the ninth day of April, eighteen hundred and five, or after the fourteenth day of April, eighteen hundred and sixty."

This section creates no new right, and does not, as between lessor and lessee or their assigns, enlarge the rights and obligations imposed upon either party by the terms of the lease. Morehouse v Woodruff (1916) 218 NY 494, 504, 113 NE 512.

Real Prop L § 223, sweeps away all learning on the subject of attornment where the reversion of leased real property is granted. Metropolitan Life Ins. Co. v Childs Co. (1921) 230 NY 285, 130 NE 295, 14 ALR 685, reh den 231 NY 551, 132 NE 885.

**8.** Stogop Realty Co. v Marie Antoinette Hotel Co. (AD1 1926) 217 AD 555, 217 NYS 106.

**9.** Real Prop L § 245, which further provides, "A greater estate or interest does not pass by any grant or conveyance, than the grantor possessed or could lawfully convey, at the time of the delivery of the deed; except that every grant is conclusive against the grantor and his heirs claiming from him by descent, and as against a subsequent purchaser or incumbrancer from such grantor, or from such heirs claiming as such, other than a subsequent purchaser or incumbrancer in good faith and for a valuable consideration, who acquires a superior title by a conveyance that has been first duly recorded."

**10.** § 1:10, supra.

**11.** § 2:3, supra.

tenant or without it, is a transfer of the lease and of its rights and obligations,[12] and notice to the tenant of the transfer of the reversion is unnecessary to effect the transfer of the lease to the grantee.[13]

### § 5:16. Rights and Obligations of Grantor

A landlord who enters into a lease with a tenant creates both privity of contract as well as privity of estate between them.[14] When the landlord voluntarily conveys the fee to real property encumbered by a lease, he terminates thereby all privity of estate between him and his tenant. However, he does not terminate the privity of contract merely by conveying the fee. In other words, all he has done is to assign the lease. That does not terminate the agreement. Therefore, the grantor-landlord continues to remain liable on all the express covenants on his part contained in the lease, whether or not they run with the land,[15] even after the conveyance of the fee. Liability therefor rests on the privity of contract which continues.

However, as to those covenants running iwth the land which are not expressed in the lease, but implied by law, liability therefor rests on privity of estate. Since this privity has been destroyed by the conveyance, the landlord after the conveyance is not liable for breach of implied covenants running with the land.[16]

With respect to the tenant it has been held that the landlord-grantor's right to enforce agreements on the part of the tenant, which run with the land, and which have not been breached at the time of the conveyance of the fee, ceases with the conveyance. The landlord-grantor by the conveyance is deemed to have discharged the tenant of any and all liability to him upon those covenants in the lease which run with the land accruing after the date of the conveyance.[17]

---

12. Re O'Donnell (1925) 240 NY 99, 147 NE 541.

13. Kilmer v White (1930) 254 NY 64, 171 NE 908.

14. § 2:2, supra.

15. Real Property Law § 223 (for text of this section, see Appendix B, volume 3, infra).

For discussion of real and personal covenants, that is covenants which do, and which do not, run with the land, see §§ 23:6 et seq, infra.

16. Kilmer v White (1930) 254 NY 64, 171 NE 908.

17. Seidlitz v Auerbach (1920) 230 NY 167, 175, 129 NE 461; Richards v Browning (AD1 1925) 214 AD 665, 212

### § 5:17. Rights and Obligations of Grantee

A grantee of real property encumbered by an unexpired lease becomes entitled to all of the rights which the grantor thereof had in the premises and in the lease.[18] Therefore, when a landlord conveys the fee, and makes no reservation as to any unexpired leases, even though he does not formally assign these leases, nevertheless he transfers these leases to the grantee together with all of the grantor's rights in and under them. The conveyance does not terminate the lease.[19] From the time of the conveyance of the fee to the grantee, the grantee becomes bound by, and entitled to the benefits of, all the covenants in the lease which run with the land. A privity of estate has been created between the grantee and the tenant by virtue of the conveyance, and the covenants that run with the land fix and define the tenure by which the parties hold the leased property. If it is a covenant running with the land, it will inure to the benefit of the original landlord's grantee, notwithstanding that the original agreement did not provide that it would be binding on or inure to the benefit of the assigns of the original parties.[20]

A covenant by a tenant to surrender the premises at the end of the term in as good condition as received, is a covenant running with the land.[1] Therefore, a grantee of the fee has a right to enforce this covenant against the tenant.[2]

NYS 738, app dismd (NY) 152 NE 418.

18. 507 Madison Ave. Realty Co. v Martin (AD1 1922) 200 AD 46, 192 NYS 762, affd 233 NY 683, 135 NE 969; Knutsen v Cinque (AD2 1906) 113 AD 677, 99 NYS 911.

19. Stogop Realty Co. v Marie Antoinette Hotel Co. (AD1 1926) 217 AD 555, 217 NYS 106.

20. St. Regis Restaurant, Inc. v Powers (AD1 1927) 219 AD 321, 219 NYS 684; Bank of New York v Hirschfeld (1973) 76 Misc 2d 415, 350 NYS2d 943 (covenant to provide parking space runs with the land, and binds grantee).

See Real Prop L § 223 (in volume 3, Appendix. B.)

For discussion of real and personal covenants, that is, covenants which do, and which do not, run with the land, see §§ 23:6 et seq, infra.

1. Thurber v Losee (AD2 1920) 192 AD 148, 182 NYS 623; Knutsen v Cinque (AD2 1906) 113 AD 677, 99 NYS 911.

2. Thurber v Losee (AD2 1920) 192 AD 148, 182 NYS 623; Knutsen v Cinque (AD2 1906) 113 AD 677, 99 NYS 911.

A covenant by lessee to remove the buildings, structures and fixtures at expiration of lease runs with the land, and inures to the benefit of a grantee of the land even without an assignment of the lease. Clemente Bros., Inc. v Peterson-Ashton Fuels, Inc. (1968, 3d Dept) 29 AD2d 908, 287 NYS2d 955.

# TITLE AND REVERSION OF LANDLORD § 5:18

In other words, the position of a grantee who takes a fee "subject to a lease" is similar to that of a non-assuming assignee of a tenant.[3] The grantee, absent an affirmative assumption of the lease, is not personally liable for the performance of each and every covenant in the lease. The grantee is only liable for those covenants which run with the land.[4] The privity of estate between the grantee and the tenant creates a liability on those covenants in the lease which run with the land, but not on those covenants which are purely personal or collateral.[5] The foundation for liability on collateral covenants that do not run with the land rests on privity of contract. And, there is no such privity in this situation.[6]

Since the basis of the rights and liabilities of the grantee and the tenant depends upon the continued existence of privity of estate, the grantee can sue the tenant for breaches of covenants running with the land that are committed after the conveyance to him, but not for breaches of those covenants that occurred prior to the conveyance of the fee to him.[7]

## § 5:18. Rights on Transfer of Reversion to Rent Due or to Become Due

Rent is an incident to the reversion, and unless specifically reserved by the grantor, follows the estate in reversion upon a transfer thereof.[8] Therefore, by a general grant of the reversion, without more, the rent thereafter to accrue from the realty will pass with it as incident thereto to the grantee, and not as by an assignment of a

---

3. See § 9:25, infra.

4. A brokerage agreement is not a covenant running with the land, and, therefore, a grantee is not liable for payment of brokerage commissions which the grantor had agreed to pay on tenant's exercise of a renewal option, unless the grantee expressly assumed such obligation. Longley-Jones Associates, Inc. v Ircon Realty Co. (1986) 67 NY2d 346, 502 NYS2d 706, 493 NE2d 930; Gurney, Becker & Bourne, Inc. v Bradley (1984, 4th Dept) 101 AD2d 1012, 476 NYS2d 677.

5. See Joseph Fallert Brewing Co. v Blass (AD2 1907) 119 AD 53, 103 NYS 865, where a covenant to return a security deposit was held to be a personal covenant, and not enforceable against a grantee of the fee.

Covenant to reimburse tenant for monies expended in renovating premises,—a one-time only obligation, becoming due and payable within a reasonable time after the work is completed—is not a continuing obligation binding on landlord's successor. Bank of New York v Hirschfeld (1978, 3d Dept) 63 AD2d 794, 404 NYS2d 916.

6. See § 5:16, supra.

7. 810 West End Ave., Inc. v Frankel (AT1 1920) 113 Misc 338, 184 NYS 554.

8. Marshall v Moseley (1860) 21 NY 280; Bernstein v Koch (AT 1907) 52 Misc 550, 102 NYS 524.

chose in action.[9] The grantor cannot after the transfer of the reversion recover of the lessee rents falling due after such transfer in the absence of any showing of such a right retained by him, or assigned to him by his grantee.[10] However, the statute provides that payment of rent to a grantor by his tenant, before notice of the conveyance, binds the grantee; and the tenant is not liable to such grantee, before such notice, for the breach of any condition of the lease.[11]

A grantee, as grantee, takes no cause of action against the tenant in at the time of the grant for any rent then past due. A transfer of the reversion does not carry with it the right to rent accrued at the time of the transfer.[12] Such past due rent must be specifically assigned to the grantee to give him any rights thereto. Rent that has accrued may be assigned like any other chose in action, and rent to accrue is severable from the reversion, and may be assigned independent of the reversion so as to enable the assignee to recover thereon when due.[13]

As is the general rule applicable to assignments, notice to the tenant-debtor of the assignment of rent is not

---

**9.** Marshall v Mosely (1860) 21 NY 280; Van Wicklen v Paulson, 14 Barb 654.

**10.** Re Whitney (1911) 144 AD 117, 128 NYS 1034, app dismd 202 NY 580, 96 NE 1134.

**11.** Real Prop L § 248.
Also, see F. F. Proctor Troy Properties Co. v Dugan Store, Inc. (AD3 1920) 191 AD 685, 181 NYS 786.

**12.** Getty Realty Corp. v 2 East Sixty-First Street Corp. (AT1 1939) 171 Misc 101, 11 NYS2d 730; 810 West End Ave., Inc. v Frankel (AT1 1920) 113 Misc 338, 184 NYS 554; Application of Long Acre Properties, Inc. (S Ct NY Co 1948) 191 Misc 429, 77 NYS2d 831, revd on other grounds 275 AD 691, 86 NYS2d 922.

**13.** Sullivan v Rosson (1918) 223 NY 217, 119 NE 405, 4 ALR 1400.
Also, see, Swan v Inderlied (1907) 187 NY 372, 80 NE 195.

Real Prop L § 294-a provides that an assignment of rent to accrue from "tenancies, subtenancies, leases or subleases of real property," made, subscribed and acknowledged or proved, and certified in a manner to entitle a conveyance to be recorded, may be recorded. If not so recorded, it shall be void as against subsequent purchasers in good faith and for a valuable consideration of either the same realty or of an assignment of rent to accrue therefrom, whose conveyances or assignments are first duly recorded. However, the recording of the assignment shall not be in itself a notice of the assignment to a lessee or tenant, his distributees or devisees, to the assignor or a prior assignee of the rent.

Conley v Fine (AD1 1918) 181 AD 675, 169 NYS 162, and Rolandelli v Stanton (M Ct 1927) 129 Misc 270, 220 NYS 502, holding that assignments of rents need not be recorded, were decided prior to the enactment of Real Prop L § 294-a, and no longer represent the law. This section of the Real Property Law was designed to bring assignments of rent to accrue from a tenancy existing at the time of the assignment within the recording statutes applicable to conveyances of real property. 1944 Leg Doc 65(I).

necessary for its validity as between the assignor and assignee.[14]

Upon a conveyance of the fee, a tenant cannot, on his own initiative, and without the landlord's consent, apportion the rent due between the landlord and the grantee, even though the landlord agreed with the grantee to apportion such rent.[15]

### § 5:19. Waiver of Grantor Binding on Grantee

The transferee of the reversion, subject to a lease, takes the premises under the conditions as to the tenancy that his predecessor in title has established.[16] It is plainly competent for a landlord to waive any rights he may have, as for example, to insist that the premises should be used only for the purposes specified in the lease, and to re-enter when there is a breach thereof. If he waives such rights, his transferee is bound by such waiver.[17] An oral waiver is equally effective, it has been held, even though a written consent is required and provided for in the lease.[18]

Of course, a landlord cannot waive a use of leased premises in violation of the law, and therefore such a waiver is not binding on the grantee.[19]

### § 5:20. Concurrent Lease as Transfer of Reversion

A concurrent lease is one granted for a term which is to commence before the expiration or other determination of a previous lease of the same premises made to

---

**14.** Fisher v Seltzer (1938, Sup App T) 9 NYS2d 240; Fisher v Ball (1938, Sup App T) 9 NYS2d 173; Fisher v Binder (1938, Sup App T) 9 NYS2d 47.

**15.** Mohr v Quigley (AT 1900) 30 Misc 753, 63 NYS 149.

**16.** Radcliffe Associates, Inc. v Greenstein (AD1 1948) 274 AD 277, 82 NYS2d 680, reh and app den 274 AD 984, 85 NYS2d 302; F. F. Proctor Troy Properties Co. v Dugan Store, Inc. (AD3 1920) 191 AD 685, 181 NYS 786; Vendramis v Frankfurt (S Ct NY Co 1949) 86 NYS2d 715, affd 276 AD 903, 94 NYS2d 903.

**17.** Adams-Flanigan Co. v Kling (AD1 1921) 198 AD 717, 191 NYS 32, affd 234 NY 497, 138 NE 421, cert den 260 US 741, 67 L Ed 491, 43 S Ct 98; 215 West 34th Street, Inc. v Feldman (1951, Sup App T) 105 NYS2d 209; 440 West 34th Street Corp. v Rosoff (1948, Mun Ct) 84 NYS2d 16, landlord's waiver of prohibition against subletting binding on grantee; Anderson v Conner (AT 1904) 43 Misc 384, 87 NYS 449, landlord ratified a voidable lease, and bound his transferee.

**18.** Sol Apfel, Inc. v Kocher (S Ct NY Co 1946) 61 NYS2d 508, affd 272 AD 758, 70 NYS2d 138 and affd 272 AD 758, 70 NYS2d 139.

**19.** 47 East 74th Street Corp. v Simon (AT1 1947) 188 Misc 885, 69 NYS2d 746 (rooming house in violation of Multiple Dwelling Law).

another person, the terms of the two leases including at least some time in common. When a landlord grants a concurrent lease, without the reservation of any rights in the existing leasehold, he in effect transfers or assigns a part of the reversion, entitling the concurrent tenant to recover all the rents accruing on the previous lease after the commencement of the concurrent lease.[20]

### § 5:21. Death of Landlord

Death does not terminate a lease,[1] except in the case of a tenancy created by a life tenant,[2] or a tenancy at will.[3]

If the decedent-landlord only owned a leasehold, it passes to his personal representatives; that is, the person who receives letters to administer his estate,[4] for the purposes of the administration of the estate.[5] If the decedent-landlord owned the fee, it passes either to the devisees,[6] or to the distributees in accordance with the statutes regulating the descent and distribution of property.[7] Whoever succeeds to the property occupies the same position as any transferee of the reversion, with corresponding rights and obligations.[8]

### § 5:22. Injury to Reversion by Third Person

Lessor and lessee have separate estates, and each, if injured therein, may have redress; the one for injury to the reversion, the other for the injury inflicted in diminishing his enjoyment of the premises.[9] However, neither can in his separate action recover damages to the estate of the other.[10] Thus, a tenant is entitled to recover dam-

---

20. Burnee Corp. v Uneeda Pure Orange Drink Co. (AT1 1928) 132 Misc 435, 230 NYS 239; Russo v Yuzolino (AT1 1896) 19 Misc 28, 42 NYS 482.

1. Walker v Bradley (S Ct Cayuga Co 1915) 89 Misc 516, 153 NYS 686 (death of lessee).
Also, see Beatty v Rosenberg (AD1 1916) 173 AD 645, 160 NYS 135.
2. § 2:31 supra.
3. § 30:30, infra.
4. EPTL 1-2.13.
5. EPTL 13-1.1(a)(1).
6. See Real Prop L § 245.
7. EPTL 4-1.1.

8. §§ 5:15 et seq, supra.
9. Baumann v New York (1919) 227 NY 25, 124 NE 141, 8 ALR 595; Miller v Edison Electric Illuminating Co. (1906) 184 NY 17, 22, 76 NE 734; Kernochan v Manhattan R. Co. (1900) 161 NY 339, 345, 55 NE 906; Kernochan v New York E. R. Co. (1891) 128 NY 559, 29 NE 65.
10. Miller v Edison Electric Illuminating Co (1906) 184 NY 17, 76 NE 734 (operation of electric light and power plant held to have affected possession, and lessor not entitled to recover therefor as an injury to reversion).

ages for any injury inflicted by a wrongdoer resulting in a diminution of his enjoyment of the premises,[11] and, except as otherwise provided by the statute,[12] only the landlord has a right to recover for permanent injuries to the reversion caused by the same wrongful acts.[13] In order for the lessor to recover, the injury complained of must be of a permanent character to the reversion; a mere disturbance of the tenant's possession or right to possession, even though done in the assertion of a right, will not as a general rule, entitle the lessor to an action.[14] If the injury is of a temporary character which affects the possession only, and the comfortable enjoyment of the premises by the tenant without injuring the reversion, the lessor has no right of action.[15] Thus, it has been held that a landlord is not entitled to recover for injuries to the enjoyment and occupation of the premises while they are in the possession of a tenant, by the maintenance on adjourning premises of a nuisance which is not of a permanent character, although during such maintenance the lease has expired, and been renewed at a reduced rental because of the nuisance.[16]

11. Baumann v New York (1919) 227 NY 25, 124 NE 141, 8 ALR 595.

12. Real Prop Act & Proc L § 833 provides, "When the ownership of land is divided into a possessory estate for life or for years and one or more future interests, and a person having none of these interests causes damage to such land, the damages recoverable by the owner of such possessory interest from the wrongdoing third person may include damages caused to interests in the affected land other than those owned by parties to the action or proceeding when, but only when, all living persons who have either a possessory or a future interest in the affected land are parties thereto. The court in which any such recovery of damages occurs shall make such direction for the distribution of the damages recovered among the persons who are parties to the action or proceeding and for the protection of the interests of persons who are not parties thereto, as justice may require.

"A tenant for life or for years in the land damaged is entitled to receive from the recovery, in satisfaction of the damage to his estate or interest, either a sum in gross or the earnings of a sum invested for his benefit. The determination as to whether a sum in gross or the earnings of a sum invested shall be awarded to the owner of such particular estate shall be governed by the provisions with respect to the proceeds of a sale in partition."

13. Baumann v New York (1919) 227 NY 25, 124 NE 141, 8 ALR 595; Kernochan v Manhattan R. Co. (1900) 161 NY 339, 55 NE 906.

14. Baumann v New York (1919) 227 NY 25, 124 NE 141, 8 ALR 595; Brass v Rathbone (1897) 153 NY 435, 47 NE 905; Tobias v Cohn (1867) 36 NY 363 (lessor not permitted recovery for injury to possession); Taylor v Wright (AD3 1900) 51 AD 97, 64 NYS 344 (injuries to a line fence and the closing of a right of way).

15. Miller v Edison Electric Illuminating Co. (1906) 184 NY 17, 76 NE 734.

16. Miller v Edison Electric Illuminating Co. (1906) 184 NY 17, 76 NE 734.

### § 5:23. —Particular Injuries

To entitle a lessor to maintain an action for an injury to the reversion, the injury must be necessarily of a permanent character.[17] Unless a nuisance is of a permanent character, it will not generally be regarded as an injury to the reversion, but as an injury in diminution of the tenant's enjoyment of his premises.[18] For example, the maintenance and operation of an electric plant was held to be a nuisance to the tenant, for such operation did not crack the walls or injure the structure on the premises, and was of a temporary character.[19] Similarly, a temporary trench obstructing access to the leased premises was deemed an injury to the lessee, and not to the lessor.[20] A presumed intention to continue the nuisance is not sufficient to constitute it an injury to the reversion, even where there is evidence that the premises would sell for less if the nuisance were continued.[1]

An injury to the trees or timber on the leased premises has been held to be an injury to the reversion for which the landlord may sue.[2]

## D. RESEARCH REFERENCES

### § 5:24. Generally

In addition to the preceding text, the reader is also referred to the following:

49 Am Jur 2d, Landlord and Tenant §§ 82-108.

New York Jur 2d, Landlord and Tenant (1st ed §§ 60-75).

Index to Annotations, Landlord and Tenant.

**VERALEX®:** Cases and annotations referred to herein can be further researched through the VERALEX

---

17. § 5:22, supra.
18. Miller v Edison Electric Illuminating Co. (1906) 184 NY 17, 22, 76 NE 734.
19. Miller v Edison Electric Illuminating Co. (1906) 184 NY 17, 22, 76 NE 734.
Also, see Sherman v Levingston (S Ct Oneida Co 1910) 128 NYS 581, denying a lessor an injunction to restrain the maintenance of a public garage near the demised premises, where it was shown that the anticipated injuries from noise and odors would be of a temporary nature, and would damage the lessee's estate and not the lessor's estate.
20. Van Siclen v New York (AD2 1901) 64 AD 437, 72 NYS 209, mod on other grounds 172 NY 504, 65 NE 257.
1. Miller v Edison Electric Illuminating Co. (1906) 184 NY 17, 22, 76 NE 734.
2. Allen v Oscar G. Murray Railroad Employes' Ben. Fund (S Ct Yates Co 1920) 112 Misc 156, 182 NYS 369.

electronic retrieval system's two services, **Auto-Cite®** and **SHOWME®**. Use Auto-Cite to check citations for form, parallel references, prior and later history, and annotation references. Use SHOWME to display the full text of cases and annotations.

# CHAPTER 6

# CONSTRUCTION OF LEASES

A. IN GENERAL
- § 6:1. General Rule
- § 6:2. Ascertaining Intent
- § 6:3. Practical Construction by the Parties
- § 6:4. Statutes as Part of a Lease
- § 6:5. Meaning of Words
- § 6:6. Surrounding Circumstances
- § 6:7. Reconciling Inconsistencies
- § 6:8. Construction Against Draftsman of Lease
- § 6:9. Construction in Favor of Tenant
- § 6:10. Repugnancy Between Printed and Typewritten Matter
- § 6:11. Reasonable Construction
- § 6:12. Additional Liability to be Avoided
- § 6:13. Unconscionable Lease or Clause

B. PAROL EVIDENCE RULE
- § 6:14. Generally
- § 6:15. Exceptions to the Parol Evidence Rule
- § 6:16. Merger Clause and the Parol Evidence Rule
- § 6:17. Form of Provision Against Oral Misrepresentation or Promises
- § 6:18. Ambiguity or Uncertainty in Instrument
- § 6:19. Incomplete Instrument
- § 6:20. Independent Collateral Agreements
- § 6:21. Condition Precedent to Lease Rule

C. MODIFICATION OF LEASE
- § 6:22. Generally
- § 6:23. Necessity of Consideration
- § 6:24. Necessity of Recording
- § 6:25. Oral Modification
- § 6:26. —Provision Against Oral Modification
- § 6:27. Form of Provision Against Oral Modification

D. RESEARCH REFERENCES
- § 6:28. Generally

---

## A. IN GENERAL

### § 6:1. General Rule

A lease like any other contract is to be enforced in accordance with the expressed intention of the parties to the lease.[1] An agreement of lease possesses no peculiar sanctity requiring the application of rules of construction different from those applicable to an ordinary contract.[2] If the interpretation of its language is necessary, the proper and established rules of construction of contracts are to be applied.[3] But, fundamentally the court will so construe a lease as to carry out the intention of the parties if possible;[4] for, the intent of the parties must be considered, and govern.[5]

§ 6:2. Ascertaining Intent

The courts attempt to carry out the intention of the parties to a lease,[6] and to the extent that such intent is demonstrated by the expression of the parties in the lease, such expressed intent will control. The search must be for the intention of the parties, but only to the extent that the parties evidenced what they intended by what they wrote;[7] for the intention of the parties to a lease is to be found in the language used to express such intention.[8] As has been so often stated, in construing a lease the court must search out the intent of the parties, and give life and vigor to all of the provisions of the lease in

1. Orr v Doubleday, Page & Co. (1918) 223 NY 334, 119 NE 552, 1 ALR 338, reh den 223 NY 700, 119 NE 1064.

2. A. Z. A. Realty Corp. v Harrigan's Cafe, Inc. (M Ct 1920) 113 Misc 141, 185 NYS 212.

3. Orr v Doubleday, Page & Co. (1918) 223 NY 334, 341, 119 NE 552, 1 ALR 338, reh den 223 NY 700, 119 NE 1064.

4. Buchanan v Whitman (1896) 151 NY 253, 45 NE 556.

5. Farrell Lines, Inc. v New York (1972) 30 NY2d 76, 330 NYS2d 358, 281 NE2d 162; Re Loew's Buffalo Theatres, Inc. (1922) 233 NY 495, 135 NE 862, remittitur den 234 NY 533, 138 NE 435, remittitur den 234 NY 607, 138 NE 465; County of Erie v Buffalo Bills Div. of Highwood Services, Inc. (1973, 4th Dept) 42 AD2d 922, 348 NYS2d 260.

6. Farrell Lines, Inc. v New York (1972) 30 NY2d 76, 330 NYS2d 358, 281 NE2d 162; Re Loew's Buffalo Theatres, Inc. (1922) 233 NY 495, 135 NE 862, remittitur den 234 NY 533, 138 NE 435, remittitur den 234 NY 607, 138 NE 465; Orr v Doubleday, Page & Co. (1918) 223 NY 334, 119 NE 552, 1 ALR 338, reh den 223 NY 700, 119 NE 1064; Buchanan v Whitman (1896) 151 NY 253, 45 NE 556.

7. Raleigh Associates, Inc. v Henry (1951) 302 NY 467, 99 NE2d 289, reh den 302 NY 940, 100 NE2d 191; Nottingham Realty Co. v Swan Cleaners Syracuse Corp. (S Ct Onondaga Co 1960) 28 Misc 2d 397, 214 NYS2d 776, affd (4th Dept) 13 AD2d 721, 215 NYS2d 735; 37-01-31st. Street Realty Corp. v Young (S Ct Queens Co 1954) 134 NYS2d 250.

8. Wendel Foundation v Moredall Realty Corp. (1940) 282 NY 239, 26 NE2d 241; Brainard v New York C. R. Co. (1926) 242 NY 125, 133, 151 NE 152, 45 ALR 751; Schulte Leasing Corp. v L. & C. Mayers Co. (AD1 1933) 238 AD 403, 264 NYS 664, affd 263 NY 554, 189 NE 694; H. B. Shontz Co. v Laffay (AD1 1929) 225 AD 263, 232 NYS 614; Pyramid Investors Co. v Medina—Maple, Inc. (S Ct Onondaga Co 1973) 72 Misc 2d 893, 339 NYS2d 612.

## CONSTRUCTION OF LEASES § 6:2

order to ascertain that intent.[9] The agreement of the parties to a written lease is to be ascertained from the language of the instrument, and there can be no intendment or implication inconsistent with the express terms thereof. In other words, the intention of the parties must be gathered from the entire instrument, and not from a single clause or part of the lease.[10] Courts cannot be expected to guess at what the parties meant, or order that to be done which the parties were able to do for themselves, and probably would have done, had it been thought of.[11] Nor may the courts under the guise of interpretation, make a new contract for the parties, or change the words of a written contract so as to make it express the real intention of the parties, if to do so would contradict the clearly expressed language of the contract.[12]

The construction of a plain, unambiguous contract is for the court.[13] If the court finds as a matter of law that the contract is unambiguous, evidence of the intention and acts of the parties is irrelevant, and will play no part in ascertaining intention;[14] for, the intent of the parties must be deduced only from the expressed terms of the agreement.[15] If there is no ambiguity in the terms used by

---

9. R. I. Realty Co. v Terrell (1930) 254 NY 121, 172 NE 262; Bovin v Galitzka (1929) 250 NY 228, 165 NE 273.

10. County of Erie v Buffalo Bills Div. of Highwood Services, Inc. (1973, 4th Dept) 42 AD2d 922, 348 NYS2d 260; Nassau Hotel Co. v Barnett & Barse Corp. (AD1 1914) 162 AD 381, 147 NYS 283, affd 212 NY 568, 106 NE 1036 and later app 164 AD 203, 149 NYS 645; 30-88 Steinway Street, Inc. v H. C. Bohack Co. (Civ Ct Queens Co 1971) 65 Misc 2d 1076, 319 NYS2d 679, reinstated (2d Dept) 42 AD2d 577, 344 NYS2d 205, app dismd 33 NY2d 692, 349 NYS2d 672, 304 NE2d 369.

11. Per Crane, Ch. J., Spoor-Lasher Co. v Newburgh Gas & Oil Co. (1936) 269 NY 447, 451, 199 NE 656.

12. Rodolitz v Neptune Paper Products, Inc. (1968) 22 NY2d 383, 292 NYS2d 878, 239 NE2d 628.

13. County of Erie v Buffalo Bills Div. of Highwood Services, Inc. (1973, 4th Dept) 42 AD2d 922, 348 NYS2d 260.

If a lease is clear and unambiguous, it should be interpreted as a matter of law by the trial court, and should not be left to the jury for interpretation as a question of fact. Leotta v Plessinger (1959, 4th Dept) 8 AD2d 502, 188 NYS2d 737, revd 8 NY2d 449, 209 NYS2d 304, 171 NE2d 454, remittitur amd 9 NY2d 686, 212 NYS2d 421, 173 NE2d 241; Park Sheraton Corp. v Grasso (1958, 1st Dept) 6 AD2d 492, 179 NYS2d 697.

14. Wendel Foundation v Moredall Realty Corp. (1940) 282 NY 239, 26 NE2d 241; Brainard v New York C. R. Co. (1926) 242 NY 125, 133, 151 NE 152, 45 ALR 751; Daniel Holding Corp. v Two Thirty Four West Forty Second Street Corp. (AD1 1938) 255 AD 8, 5 NYS2d 391.

15. Martin v Glenzan Associates, Inc. (1980, 3d Dept) 75 AD2d 660, 426 NYS2d 347.

## § 6:2

the parties, and the meaning is plain and direct, it is well established that courts will not give to the lease a meaning which they prefer, or which they think the parties intended.[16] "Intention," said the Court of Appeals, "is to be found in the language used. It is the only sure guide."[17] And, no matter how much the plight in which the parties may find themselves may appeal to sympathy, the courts will not undertake to rewrite the agreement of the parties.[18] Thus, the court has no authority to write into a lease an agreement to furnish live steam after hours simply because the lease contains an agreement to furnish belt power after hours.[1] Even though more apt language might have been used, if the intent is clear, it must prevail.[2] In such case there just is no room for construction.[3] In other words, plain meanings will not be changed by parol, and the courts will not make leases for the parties under the guise of interpretation.[4]

### § 6:3. Practical Construction by the Parties

The general rule of contracts is that in the determination of the meaning of an indefinite or ambiguous contract, the interpretation or construction placed upon the contract by the parties themselves is to be considered by the courts.[5] This general rule of contracts applies to leases:[6] If a lease contains ambiguous and uncertain

---

16. Re Loew's Buffalo Theatres, Inc. (1922) 233 NY 495, 501, 135 NE 862, remittitur den 234 NY 533, 138 NE 435, remittitur den 234 NY 607, 138 NE 465; Blacharsh v Cue Variety Stores, Inc. (NYC Civ Ct 1972) 71 Misc 2d 913, 337 NYS2d 456.

17. Re Loew's Buffalo Theatres, Inc. (1922) 233 NY 495, 499, 135 NE 862, remittitur den 234 NY 533, 138 NE 435, remittitur den 234 NY 607, 138 NE 465.

18. Freehold Invest. v Richstone (AT 1973) 72 Misc 2d 624, 340 NYS2d 362, revd (1st Dept) 42 AD2d 696, 346 NYS2d 718, revd 34 NY2d 612, 355 NYS2d 363, 311 NE2d 500, reinstating order of Appellate Term.

1. East Forty-Sixth St. Realty Corp. v Gutschneider (AD1 1919) 186 AD 503, 174 NYS 518.

2. Burgener v O'Halloran (1920) 111 Misc 203, 181 NYS 235.

3. Christopher & T. S. R. Co. v Twenty-Third S. R. Co. (1896) 149 NY 51, 57, 43 NE 538.

4. Wendel Foundation v Moredall Realty Corp. (1940) 282 NY 239, 26 NE2d 241; Heller v Pope (1928) 250 NY 132, 135, 164 NE 881; Brainard v New York C. R. Co. (1926) 242 NY 125, 133, 151 NE 152, 45 ALR 751; Daniel Holding Corp. v Two Thirty Four West Forty Second Street Corp. (AD1 1938) 255 AD 8, 5 NYS2d 391.

5. Michaels v Fishel (1902) 169 NY 381, 62 NE 425; Mudge v West End Brewing Co. (AD3 1911) 145 AD 28, 130 NYS 350, affd 207 NY 696, 101 NE 1112.

6. Morehouse v Woodruff (1916) 218 NY 494, 502, 113 NE 512; Times Square Improv. Co. v Fleischmann's Vienna Model Bakery (AD1 1916) 173 AD 633, 160 NYS 346; Burgener v O'Halloran (AT2 1920) 111 Misc 203, 181 NYS 235; Smith v Taranto (S Ct

# CONSTRUCTION OF LEASES § 6:4

provisions, the court may, in construing it and in ascertaining its true meaning, look to the practical construction or interpretation that the parties, in the performance of the lease, have placed on such provisions.[7] Thus, where, although vault space was not specifically mentioned as part of the letting, it was deemed included because of the conduct of the parties in having treated it as part of the letting.[8] It has been held that the practical construction of a lease by the parties thereto is an important consideration, and sometimes almost conclusive, in interpreting an indefinite or ambiguous lease.[9] However, it must be emphasized that although the conduct of the parties may fix a meaning to words of doubtful importance, it may not change the clear terms of an unambiguous contract.[10] The practical construction of a lease between the parties thereto is always significant, and sometimes furnishes the only clue to the obligations the parties intended to assume. But, resort to this method of discovering contractual requirements is not to be had when the language of the agreement is plain, unambiguous, and its legal effect unquestionably settled.[11]

## § 6:4. Statutes as Part of a Lease

As is the general rule in the law of contracts, a statute relating to the subject matter of a lease is to be deemed to be read into the lease, and the parties are deemed to have contracted with reference thereto.[12] In attempting to

---

Kings Co 1913) 140 NYS 794, affd 158 AD 912, 143 NYS 1144; Bryant Park Bldg., Inc. v Acunto (M Ct 1928) 133 Misc 225, 231 NYS 451.

7. Zolezzi v Bruce-Brown (1926) 243 NY 490, 154 NE 535, 49 ALR 1414.

8. Berger Properties, Inc. v Kay Jewelry Co. (S Ct Erie Co 1933) 147 Misc 173, 263 NYS 576, where the court said, "For upwards of seven years of the life of the lease the premises have been used by the parties in the way and manner described without any objections or word of protest on the part of the defendant [tenant]. If the defendant claimed greater rights in the basement than those actually exercised, it seems it should have been at least so indicated."

9. Islip v Smith (1957, 2d Dept) 3 AD2d 726, 159 NYS2d 763 (practical construction relied on to interpret "gross receipts derived from all operations of lessee"); Halperin v McCrory Stores Corp. (AD2 1923) 207 AD 448, 202 NYS 385, affd 239 NY 547, 147 NE 189; 507 Madison Ave. Realty Co. v Martin (AD1 1922) 200 AD 146, 192 NYS 762, affd 233 NY 683, 135 NE 969.

10. Brainard v New York C. R. Co. (1926) 242 NY 125, 133, 151 NE 152, 45 ALR 751; East Forty-Sixth St. Realty Corp. v Gutschneider (AD1 1919) 186 AD 503, 174 NYS 518.

11. Allen v Oscar G Murray R Employees' Ben Fund (S Ct Yates Co 1921) 189 NYS 201.

12. Moller v People's Nat. Bank (1932) 258 NY 373, 180 NE 87; Ward v Union Trust Co. (1918) 224 NY 73, 120 NE 81, 3 ALR 1154.

§ 6:4    LANDLORD AND TENANT

discern the intent of the parties by the language which they used, they may also be presumed to have had primary reference to the state of the law as it existed at the date of execution.[13] A material change in the law does not automatically entitle an aggrieved contracting party to reformation. Thus, a landlord is not entitled to the reformation of a lease because the city, for the first time, imposes sewer rents on property owners, creating an additional burden on the landlord which, if foreseen, might have been shifted to the tenant.[14] The law is well settled, said the Court of Appeals, "that changes in a lease are not to be presumed or implied; and no additional liability will be imposed upon a tenant unless it is clearly within the provisions of the instrument under which it is claimed."[15] But, in any event, the parties cannot be deemed to have contracted with reference to a statute which did not then exist.[16]

### § 6:5. Meaning of Words

The general rule of contracts that words will be given their ordinary meaning where nothing appears to show that they are used in a different sense,[17] or where it appears that they were not used in their established legal or strictly technical meaning,[18] applies equally to leases.[19] In other words, the court must give all the words and phrases used in a lease their plain meaning in order to

---

13. Moller v People's Nat. Bank (1932) 258 NY 373, 180 NE 87.

14. Gimbel Bros., Inc. v Brook Shopping Centers, Inc. (1986, 2d Dept) 118 AD2d 532, 499 NYS2d 435.

15. 455 Seventh Ave., Inc. v Frederick Hussey Realty Corp. (1946) 295 NY 166, 65 NE2d 761, reh den 295 NY 827, 66 NE2d 595.

16. Brooklyn Public Library v New York (1929) 250 NY 495, 166 NE 179, remittitur den 251 NY 589, 168 NE 438; Clark v Carolina & Y. R. R. Co. (1919) 225 NY 589, 122 NE 453; Minister, etc., Reformed Protestant Dutch Church v Madison Ave. Bldg. Co. (1915) 214 NY 268, 108 NE 444; Sattler v Hallock (1899) 160 NY 291, 54 NE 667; Clausen v Title Guaranty & Surety Co. (AD1 1915) 168 AD 569, 153 NYS 835, affd 222 NY 675, 119 NE 1035; Mudge v West End Brewing Co. (AD3 1911) 145 AD 28, 130 NYS 350, affd 207 NY 696, 101 NE 1112.

17. Darrow v Family Fund Soc. (1889) 116 NY 537, 22 NE 1093.

18. Nau v Vulcan Rail & Constr. Co. (1941) 286 NY 188, 36 NE2d 106, 50 USPQ 484, reh den 287 NY 630, 39 NE2d 267; Middleworth v Ordway (1908) 191 NY 404, 84 NE 291.

19. Michaels v Fishel (1902) 169 NY 381, 389, 62 NE 425 (re-entry interpreted in its common law meaning); Granada Terrace Constr. Corp. v Roberts (M Ct 1958) 13 Misc 2d 903, 173 NYS2d 769 (tenant shall not expose any sign, advertisement, illumination or projection in or out of the windows, was held not to prohibit placing air conditioner on window sill); Gerry v Siebrecht (1904, Sup App T) 88 NYS 1034 ("ready for occupancy," did not mean ready for use for the conduct of tenant's business).

determine the rights of the parties.[20] Words in a lease are never to be rejected as meaningless or void if they can be made significant by any reasonable construction.[1]

## § 6:6. Surrounding Circumstances

Where there is need for interpretation, because there is ambiguity, it then is a question of ascertaining the intent of the parties by an examination of the lease in the context of the surrounding circumstances at the time of the letting.[2] In these circumstances, it is the duty of the court to place itself in the situation of the parties at the time of the letting, and to consider the accompanying circumstances at the time it was entered into; not for the purpose of modifying or enlarging or curtailing the terms, but to aid in determining the meaning to be given to the ambiguous agreement.[3]

## § 6:7. Reconciling Inconsistencies

The intent of the parties to a lease is to be gathered from the entire instrument, and not from one clause.[4] Effect must be given to every part of the lease so far as practicable.[5] If there are inconsistent clauses, they must be reconciled if possible, and effect given to the intent of

---

**20.** Martin v Glenzan Associates, Inc. (1980, 3d Dept) 75 AD2d 660, 426 NYS2d 347.

**1.** Graziano v Tortora Agency, Inc. (NYC Civ Ct Queens Co (1974) 78 Misc 2d 1094, 359 NYS2d 489.

**2.** United Equities, Inc. v Mardordic Realty Co. (S Ct NY Co 1959) 16 Misc 2d 996, 182 NYS2d 901, mod on other grounds (1st Dept) 8 AD2d 398, 187 NYS2d 714, and as mod affd 7 NY2d 911, 197 NYS2d 478, 165 NE2d 426.

**3.** Levinson v Shapiro (AD1 1933) 238 AD 158, 263 NYS 585, reh den app den 239 AD 816, 263 NYS 976 and affd 263 NY 591, 189 NE 713; Pangburn v Stanley Mark Strand Corp. (S Ct Albany Co 1940) 24 NYS2d 97; Bryant Park Bldg., Inc. v Acunto (M Ct 1928) 133 Misc 225, 231 NYS 451.

When a lease is ambiguous and susceptible of differing interpretations, the court may look to the surrounding facts and circumstances to determine the intent of the parties. 67 Wall Street Co. v Franklin Nat. Bank (1975) 37 NY2d 245, 371 NYS2d 915, 333 NE2d 184.

**4.** R. I. Realty Co. v Terrell (1930) 254 NY 121, 172 NE 262; Bovin v Galitzka (1929) 250 NY 228, 165 NE 273; Nassau Hotel Co. v Barnett & Barse Corp. (AD1 1914) 162 AD 381, 147 NYS 283, affd 212 NY 568, 106 NE 1036 and later app 164 AD 203, 149 NYS 645; Buell v S. S. Kresge Co. (S Ct Monroe Co. 1941) 177 Misc 686, 31 NYS2d 405, affd 263 AD 931, 33 NYS2d 391; Pangburn v Stanley Mark Strand Corp. (S Ct Albany Co 1940) 24 NYS2d 97.

**5.** R. I. Realty Co. v Terrell (1930) 254 NY 121, 124, 172 NE 262; 164 East Seventy-Second Street Corp. v Hesse (AD1 1939) 256 AD 666, 11 NYS2d 1; Bado Realty Co. v Oetjen (S Ct Westchester Co 1957) 5 Misc 2d 914, 161 NYS2d 780; Buell v S. S. Kresge Co. (S Ct Monroe Co 1941) 177 Misc 686, 31 NYS2d 405, affd 263 AD 931, 33 NYS2d 391.

the parties as gathered from the four corners of the instrument.[6]

An inconsistency between a general and a specific clause must be resolved in favor of the specific. Thus, a general clause that all of the covenants of the lease shall bind the respective successors and assigns of the parties will not make a specific clause, which resulted from negotiations, and which provided that it bind the landlord personally as long as he retained ownership of the premises, binding on landlord's successors.[7]

That construction should be given to the lease which gives life and vitality as far as possible to each and every provision thereof, for it is to be presumed that no provision is uselessly inserted in a lease.[8] Thus, the court must read the entire lease, including that which is incorporated therein by reference, and attempt to construe it in a manner which gives harmonious meaning to all the parts thereof.[9] Words written in the margin must be read as part of the clause or provision to which they evidently form a part, so as to make an intelligible whole.[10]

## § 6:8. Construction Against Draftsman of Lease

The rule of contracts that in case of doubt or ambiguity it must be construed most strongly against the party who prepared it,[11] has been applied to leases. Thus, it is well settled that a lease drawn by the landlord is to be construed most strongly against him.[12] One who prepares

---

6. National Conversion Corp. v Cedar Bldg. Corp. (1969) 23 NY2d 621, 298 NYS2d 499, 246 NE2d 351; Daniel Holding Corp. v Two Thirty Four West Forty Second Street Corp. (AD1 1938) 255 AD 8, 5 NYS2d 391; Raynolds v Browning, King & Co. (AD1 1926) 217 AD 443, 217 NYS 15, affd 245 NY 623, 157 NE 884; 37-01-31st. Street Realty Corp. v Young (S Ct Queens Co 1954) 134 NYS2d 250; Buell v S. S. Kresge Co. (S Ct Monroe Co 1941) 177 Misc 686, 31 NYS2d 405, affd 263 AD 931, 33 NYS2d 391.

7. Square Lex 48 Corp. v Shelton Towers Associates (1978) 98 Misc 2d 1039, 415 NYS2d 325.

8. Burgener v O'Halloran (AT2 1920) 111 Misc 203, 181 NY 235; Allen v Forsyth (S Ct Livingston Co 1941) 25 NYS2d 822.

9. Kirschenbaum v M-T-S Franchise Corp. (NYC Civ Ct NY Co 1974) 77 Misc 2d 1012, 355 NYS2d 256.

10. Moskowitz v Diringen (AT 1905) 48 Misc 543, 96 NYS 173.

11. Evelyn Bldg. Corp. v New York (1931) 257 NY 501, 178 NE 771; Reliable Press, Inc. v Bristol Carpet Cleaning Co. (AD1 1941) 261 AD 256, 25 NYS2d 70, reh den 261 AD 899, 26 NYS2d 315 and app den 261 AD 943, 26 NYS2d 496.

12. 67 Wall Street Co. v Franklin Nat. Bank (1975) 37 NY2d 245, 371 NYS2d 915, 333 NE2d 184; Wasservogel v Meyerowitz (1949) 300 NY 125, 89 NE2d 712; Robinson v Beard (1893) 140 NY 107, 114, 35 NE 441; De Cillis v E. G. & B., Inc., Mfrs. & Traders Trust Co. (1977, 4th Dept) 55 AD2d

## CONSTRUCTION OF LEASES § 6:10

a lease is responsible for the language he used, and should not be allowed to demand an interpretation different from the language he used, or different from that of the plain and ordinary meaning of the words he used. But, it must be emphasized, this rule of construction that a lease is to be construed most strongly against its draftsman is to be resorted to only when the words of the instrument are doubtful in meaning or susceptible of more than one construction.

### § 6:9. Construction in Favor of Tenant

As a general rule, if a lease contains any ambiguity, it has been held that it must be resolved in favor of the tenant, and against the landlord, as to the rights transferred to the tenant or reserved by the landlord,[13] especially where the provision to be construed is one which may destroy or defeat the estate of the lessee.[14]

### § 6:10. Repugnancy Between Printed and Typewritten Matter

Where written and printed portions of a lease are in conflict, the typewritten or written portion will control the interpretation of the lease, and will prevail over that which is printed, as it is presumed to convey with more

---

1031, 391 NYS2d 261; Fabulous Stationers, Inc. v Regency Joint Venture (1974, 1st Dept) 44 AD2d 547, 353 NYS2d 766; 164 East Seventy-Second Street Corp. v Hesse (AD1 1939) 256 AD 666, 11 NYS2d 1; Eighteenth St. Realty Corp. v Maxthan Realty Co. (AD2 1931) 233 AD 687, 249 NYS 405; Burgener v O'Halloran (AT2 1920) 111 Misc 203, 181 NYS 235; Granada Terrace Constr. Corp. v Roberts (M Ct 1958) 13 Misc 2d 903, 173 NYS2d 769; Fifth Ave. & Sixty-Sixth St. Corp. v Delaney (S Ct NY Co 1953) 124 NYS2d 89; Bryant Park Bldg., Inc. v Jane Ardsley Frocks Inc. (S Ct NY Co 1951) 108 NYS2d 748; 747 So. Blvd. Realty Corp. v Wein-Rose, Inc. (M Ct 1951) 201 Misc 552, 106 NYS2d 139; Syroma Realty Corp. v Finkelstein (S Ct Queens Co 1950) 98 NYS2d 908; Pangburn v Stanley Mark Strand Corp. (S Ct Albany Co 1940) 24 NYS2d 97; Getty v Fitch, Cornell & Co. (M Ct 1919) 107 Misc 404, 177 NYS 691.

13. 455 Seventh Ave., Inc. v Frederick Hussey Realty Corp. (1946) 295 NY 166, 65 NE2d 761, reh den 295 NY 827, 66 NE2d 595; Broad Properties, Inc. v Wheels, Inc. (1974, 2d Dept) 43 AD2d 276, 351 NYS2d 15, affd 35 NY2d 821, 362 NYS2d 859, 321 NE2d 781; Valenti v Tepper Fields Corp. (AD1 1953) 282 AD 212, 122 NYS2d 599; Foreman v Ruth Elaine Realty Corp. (AD2 1934) 240 AD 490, 270 NYS 625; Moskowitz v Diringen (AT 1905) 48 Misc 543, 96 NYS 173; Pangburn v Stanley Mark Strand Corp. (S Ct Albany Co 1940) 24 NYS2d 97; Kozodoy v Hindy (M Ct 1946) 187 Misc 34, 60 NYS2d 695.

14. Moskowitz v Diringen (AT 1905) 48 Misc 543, 96 NYS 173; Kirschenbaum v M-T-S Franchise Corp. (NYC Civ Ct NY Co 1974) 77 Misc 2d 1012, 355 NYS2d 256.

§ 6:10 LANDLORD AND TENANT

accuracy the latest intention of the parties,[15] or, as one court phrased it, is the clause the tenant would be more apt to read.[16] However, this is the general rule, and is resorted to only from necessity where the printed and written or typewritten clauses cannot be reconciled. Where they may be reconciled by any reasonable construction, as by regarding one as the qualification of the other, that construction must be given, because it cannot be assumed that the parties intended to insert inconsistent provisions.[17]

## § 6:11. Reasonable Construction

Reasonableness is the rule for construing contracts, and determining their implications.[18] The same rule applies to leases.[19] An interpretation which leads to "harsh and unreasonable,"[1] or "impractical and unreal" results,[2] or which will give either party an unreasonable advantage over the other,[3] or which will place one at the mercy of the other,[4] must be avoided.

## § 6:12. Additional Liability to be Avoided

It is well settled that no additional liability will be imposed on a tenant by interpretation unless it is clearly within the provisions of the instrument under which it is claimed.[5] Thus, where a lease provided that the tenant

---

15. Hendrickson v Lexington Oil Co. (1973, 2d Dept) 41 AD2d 672, 340 NYS2d 963; Cammann v Krane (AT1 1931) 142 Misc 10, 253 NYS 761; 180 E. 79th St. Corp. v Barba (M Ct 1957) 5 Misc 2d 588, 159 NYS2d 593; Green v Dalal (1953, Mun Ct) 121 NYS2d 249; Kozodoy v Hindy (M Ct 1946) 187 Misc 34, 60 NYS2d 695.

16. Jamaica Builders Supply Corp v Buttelman (M Ct 1960) 25 Misc 2d 326, 205 NYS2d 303.

17. Von Der Horst v Wolinsky (M Ct 1930) 137 Misc 182, 243 NYS 526.

18. Carns v Bassick (AD1 1919) 187 AD 280, 175 NYS 670.

19. Farrell Lines, Inc. v New York (1972) 30 NY2d 76, 330 NYS2d 358, 281 NE2d 162; Cohen v E. & J. Bass, Inc. (1927) 246 NY 270, 277, 158 NE 618.

1. 10 Suf Realty, Inc. v Fins (M Ct 1951) 202 Misc 944, 116 NYS2d 415, affd 202 Misc 950, 120 NYS2d 60; Fraser v Carton (S Ct Oneida Co 1931) 140 Misc 881, 252 NYS 163, affd 235 AD 651, 254 NYS 1042.

2. Wendel Foundation v Moredall Realty Corp. (1940) 282 NY 239, 246, 26 NE2d 241.

3. Rose v Schumer (AD1 1952) 280 AD 966, 116 NYS2d 505; Columbus Spa, Inc. v Star Co. (AD1 1926) 216 AD 218, 214 NYS 653.

4. Park Sheraton Corp. v Grasso (1958, 1st Dept) 6 AD2d 492, 179 NYS2d 697.

5. Black v General Wiper Supply Co. (1953) 305 NY 386, 390, 113 NE2d 528; 455 Seventh Ave., Inc. v Frederick Hussey Realty Corp. (1946) 295 NY 166, 172, 65 NE2d 761, reh den 295 NY 827, 66 NE2d 595; Ayer v Bonwit (AD1 1914) 161 AD 122, 146 NYS 301; Blacharsh v Cue Variety Stores, Inc. (NYC Civ Ct 1972) 71 Misc 2d 913, 337 NYS2d 456; Broad Properties, Inc. v Wheels, Inc. (1974,

CONSTRUCTION OF LEASES § 6:13

should pay water rent and charges, and after the execution of the lease the city of New York enacted a provision requiring the owners of real property to pay sewer rent, it was held that since changes in a lease are not to be presumed or implied, and no additional liability will be imposed upon a tenant unless it is clearly within the provisions of the instrument under which it is claimed, the tenant should not be saddled with the payment of such sewer rent as part of his obligation to pay water rents or charges.[6]

Where a lease provided that the landlord should have the option to purchase or produce electric current and sell it to the tenant, and that the landlord should have the right to discontinue the supply of electric current upon 30 days' written notice, whereupon the tenant would have to obtain his own current, it was held this provision governed completely the landlord's obligation with respect to current, so that upon giving the required notice there was no further obligation on his part either to supply electric current, or to provide risers by which the tenant could obtain current.[7]

### § 6:13. Unconscionable Lease or Clause

The Real Property Law provides,[8] that if the court as a matter of law finds a lease or any clause of the lease to have been unconscionable at the time it was made the court may refuse to enforce the lease, or it may enforce the remainder of the lease without the unconscionable clause, or it may so limit the application of any unconscionable clause as to avoid any unconscionable result. When it is claimed or appears to the court that a lease or any clause thereof may be unconscionable, the parties shall be afforded a reasonable opportunity to present evidence as to its setting, purpose and effect to aid the

2d Dept) 43 AD2d 276, 351 NYS2d 15, affd 35 NY2d 821, 362 NYS2d 859, 321 NE2d 781; 67 Wall Street Co. v Franklin Nat. Bank (1975) 37 NY2d 245, 371 NYS2d 915, 333 NE2d 184. See Centre Properties Co. v Arnold Constable Corp. (1975, 1st Dept) 50 AD2d 16, 375 NYS2d 874, construing provision of lease relating to tenant's contribution for fixtures.

6. Valenti v Tepper Fields Corp. (AD1 1953) 282 AD 212, 122 NYS2d 599.

7. Joffe v Gramercy Park Bldg. Corp. (S Ct NY Co 1953) 121 NYS2d 521.

8. Real Prop L § 235-c, add L 1976, ch 828, eff July 26, 1976. This provision is substantially similar to UCC § 2-302.

261

court in making the determination.[9] A plenary hearing is required before a lease provision may be found unconscionable.[10] This provision of the Real Property Law applies to all leases, regardless of when executed.[11] However, this provision of the Real Property Law does not apply to an oral lease.[12]

"Unconscionability" means an absence of meaningful choice on the right of one of the parties, together with contract terms which are unreasonably favorable to the other party.[13] Some factors tending to demonstrate an absence of meaningful choice, include, inter alia: a gross inequality of bargaining power; a disparity in the intelligence, education, experience or language ability of the parties; lack of clarity of the language of the lease, deception, fine print or other techniques for obfuscating the intended effect of a provision; and a lack of choice on the part of one of the parties. Reasonableness or fairness of the provisions must also be viewed in terms of the circumstances existing at the time of the execution of the

9. Prior to the enactment of this statute, it had been held that where a lease provision is unreasonably weighted in favor of landlord, it may be subject to the defense of unconscionability, and denied enforcement. Thus, a provision that interruption or curtailment of any service shall not be an eviction, nor entitle tenant to any compensation or to any diminution or abatement of rent, nor subject landlord to any liability for damages or otherwise, is unconscionable and unenforceable, and tenant is entitled to recover for breach of covenant to furnish air conditioning for six of summer's hot weeks. Harwood v Lincoln Square Apartments Section 5, Inc. (NYC Civ Ct NY Co 1974) 78 Misc 2d 1097, 359 NYS2d 387.

10. Ardrey v 12 West 27th Street Associates (1986, 1st Dept) 117 AD2d 538, 498 NYS2d 814.

11. Laws of 1976, ch 828, § 2, adding Real Prop L § 235-c.

12. Valley Forge Village v Anthony (1978) 92 Misc 2d 1007, 401 NYS2d 978, affd 96 Misc 2d 62, 409 NYS2d 957.

13. Rodriguez v Nachamie (1977, 2d Dept) 57 AD2d 920, 395 NYS2d 51, which held that clause providing,

"Neither the partial nor total destruction of any building on the premises, by fire, elements, or any other cause, shall in any manner affect this lease or the rights and obligations of the Tenant hereunder, and the rent shall not abate, diminish or cease. The Tenant expressly waives the provisions of any and all provisions of law now existing or which may hereafter be enacted which provides otherwise", was not unconscionable.

Landlord may not claim relief on the ground of unconscionability because the lease does not contain a provision that tenant pay its share of utility costs—a substantive unconscionability not protected by the statute. Long Island Ophthalmologic Associates, P. C. v West Broadway Professional Bldg., Inc. (1982, 2d Dept) 88 AD2d 585, 449 NYS2d 793.

A landlord cannot have a lease made by his predecessor in title invalidated as unconscionable on the ground that because of the relationship between the predecessor in title and the tenant the lease reserved a low rental. Harold Properties Corp. v Frankel (1983, 1st Dept) 93 AD2d 720, 461 NYS2d 9, mod 60 NY2d 977, 471 NYS2d 268, 459 NE2d 493.

## CONSTRUCTION OF LEASES § 6:13

lease. The test as to this element is far from simple, but the more absolute and unnecessarily one-sided the benefit is to one party to the transaction, the more likely it is that the court will find it to be unconscionably unfair and unreasonable.

The following provisions in a lease have been held not to be unconscionable: Waiver of jury trial;[14] labor rate escalation clause;[15] a rent escalation clause based upon increase in employee wage rates (nor is it violative of public policy);[16] a tax escalation clause negotiated by parties represented by experienced counsel;[17] provision that delivery or acceptance of keys, acceptance of rent, re-renting or resumption of possession, "or any other acts" shall not be deemed a surrender;[18] provision for the forfeiture of a security deposit upon the voluntary surrender of the premises by the tenant prior to the expiration of the term of the lease;[19] provision for legal fees.[20]

The following provisions have been held to be unconscionable: provision whereby tenant agrees not to assert or interpose any offset, defense, or counterclaim to any action or proceeding commenced by landlord against tenant by reason of the failure or omission of tenant to pay a sum of money required by the lease,[1] provision in residential lease for additional rent of $50 of monthly rent of $405 was over 10 days late.[2]

---

**14.** Koslowski v Palmieri (NYC Civ Ct Kings Co. 1978) 94 Misc 2d 555, 404 NYS2d 799, revd 98 Misc 2d 885, 414 NYS2d 599 (reversed because jury waiver claise was in type size less than eight points in depth, see CPLR 4544).

**15.** Graff v Transitube, Inc. (NYC Civ Ct NY Co 1977) 90 Misc 2d 879, 396 NYS2d 313.

**16.** George Backer Management Corp. v Acme Quilting Co. (1978) 46 NY2d 211, 413 NYS2d 135, 385 NE2d 1062.

Tenant's agreement to be bound by any hardship increase for his rent-stabilized apartment, and to pay it in manner set forth by Conciliation and Appeals Board was not unconscionable. Halprin v 2 Fifth Ave. Co. (1982) 55 NY2d 937, 449 NYS2d 175, 434 NE2d 244.

**17.** 75 Henry Street Garage, Inc. v Whitman Owner Corp. (1981, 2d Dept) 79 AD2d 1001, 435 NYS2d 26.

**18.** Schnee v Jonas Equities, Inc. (AT 2 & 11 1981) 109 Misc 2d 221, 442 NYS2d 342.

**19.** Patel v St. Andrews Associates (City Ct Yonkers 1987) 134 Misc 2d 745, 512 NYS2d 758.

**20.** Bay Park One Co. v Crosby (AT 2 & 11 1981) 109 Misc 2d 47, 442 NYS2d 837; N.V. Madison, Inc. v Saurwein (AT1 1980) 103 Misc 2d 996, 431 NYS2d 251; East 55th St. Joint Venture v Litchman (NYC Civ Ct NY Co 1983) 122 Misc 2d 81, 469 NYS2d 1013, affd 126 Misc 2d 1049, 487 NYS2d 256. Also, see McMahon v Schwartz (NYC Civ Ct Bx Co 1981) 109 Misc 2d 80, 438 NYS2d 215 (attorney representing himself entitled to attorney's fees).

**1.** Ultrashmere House, Ltd. v 38 Town Associates (S Ct NY Co 1984) 123 Misc 2d 102, 473 NYS2d 120.

**2.** Spring Valley Gardens Associ-

§ 6:13 LANDLORD AND TENANT

An action to rescind an unconscionable lease must be brought within 6 years after its execution.[3] Real Property Law § 235-c, empowering a court to grant relief from an unconscionable lease, does not revive a claim already barred, and, therefore, cannot be relied on for relief after the statute of limitations has run.[4]

## B. PAROL EVIDENCE RULE

### § 6:14. Generally

The rules governing the admissibility of parol or extrinsic evidence to affect writings, apply to leases. The general rule, variously stated, is, that in the absence of fraud or mistake, conversations, negotiations, and agreements made by the parties either prior to or contemporaneously with the execution of a written lease are considered as having been merged in the final written instrument, and that, therefore, parol or extrinsic evidence in relation to such conversations, negotiations, and antecedent or contemporaneous agreements cannot be admitted in evidence for the purpose of attempting to vary or contradict an unambiguous written lease.[5] When a lease has been re-

---

ates v Earle (Rockland Co Ct 1982) 112 Misc 2d 786, 447 NYS2d 629. But, in Maplewood Mgmt. v Jackson (Dist Ct Nassau Co 1982) 113 Misc 2d 142, 448 NYS2d 966, it was held that $20 late fee if rent not paid by 10th of month, was not unconscionable, nor a penalty.

3. 35 Park Ave. Corp. v Campagna (1979) 48 NY2d 813, 424 NYS2d 123, 399 NE2d 1144.

4. Enactment of RPL 235-c in 1976, after action for rescission of a lease commenced, did not revive a claim already time barred. 35 Park Ave. Corp. v Campagna (1979) 48 NY2d 813, 424 NYS2d 123, 399 NE2d 1144 (An unconscionable lease does not constitute a continuing wrong; cause of action for rescission of unconscionable lease accrues at the execution of the lease.)

5. Pollack v J. A. Green Constr. Corp. (1972, 2d Dept) 40 AD2d 996, 338 NYS2d 486, affd 32 NY2d 720, 344 NYS2d 363, 297 NE2d 99; Geide's Inn, Inc. v Pappas & Janis Realty Corp. (1969, 2d Dept) 32 AD2d 931, 303 NYS2d 6; Danish Maid, Inc. v South Bay Center, Inc. (1960, 2d Dept) 11 AD2d 768, 205 NYS2d 358; Sardone v Joseph Diamond Holding Co. (AD1 1935) 244 AD 300, 279 NYS 659, app dismd 268 NY 631, 198 NE 528; David v Holland (1943, Sup App T) 41 NYS2d 821; Rakover v Blum (1939, Sup App T) 13 NYS2d 464; Direct Realty Co. v Fergang (1938, Sup App T) 9 NYS2d 776; Nottingham Realty Co. v Swan Cleaners Syracuse Corp. (S Ct Onondaga Co 1960) 28 Misc 2d 397, 214 NYS2d 776, affd (4th Dept) 13 AD2d 721, 215 NYS2d 735; Marshak v Loewe (S Ct Nassau Co 1959) 20 Misc 2d 552, 195 NYS2d 695; Rho Realty Corp. v H-M-C Corp. (S Ct Albany Co 1959) 17 Misc 2d 795, 191 NYS2d 668, app dismd (3d Dept) 8 AD2d 915, 187 NYS2d 1011; Hewitt Shopping Center, Inc. v Cooper (S Ct Suffolk Co 1959) 187 NYS2d 814.

Where a lessee alleged that the lease had been executed in furtherance of primary and principal purposes which were frustrated by governmental orders, proof of circumstances showing such primary and principal purposes would be compe-

duced to writing, the laws presumes that the writing contains the whole agreement. To permit terms to be engrafted upon the written agreement by extrinsic evidence would be attended with all the danger, laxity, and inconvenience which the general rule is calculated to exclude; for an agreement might, by such additional terms, be as effectually altered as if the very terms of the agreement had been changed by parol evidence.[6] The parol evidence rule thus renders inadmissible to vary or contradict the terms of a written lease, where there is no ambiguity, proof of an oral agreement by the lessor to make repairs or improvements not contained in the written lease,[7] to give the lessee the exclusive privilege of selling ice to other tenants in the building, to furnish free bus service to the tenant,[8] to release a tenant upon assignment of the lease,[9] to accept on account of rent the value of fixtures installed by tenant,[10] to renew the lease,[11] to permit subletting, where the lease restricts subletting without consent,[12] to continue the maintenance of a restaurant in the building,[13] to bear the legal burden of enforcing a restrictive covenant, where the written lease contained a covenant by the lessor not to rent to competing businesses,[14] not to erect a building on an adjoining lot which will cut off light and air to the demised premises,[15] and not to enforce the tenant's covenant to pay water charges.[16]

tent if such proof would not contradict written provisions of the lease. Farlou Realty Corp. v Woodsam Associates, Inc. (AD1 1943) 266 AD 989, 44 NYS2d 540. Padded Accessories Corp. v Five Herriot Street Corp. (S Ct Westchester Co 1959) 16 Misc 2d 1060, 184 NYS2d 244.

**6.** Fogelson v Rackfay Const. Co. (1950) 300 NY 334, 90 NE2d 881, reh den 301 NY 552, 93 NE2d 349.

**7.** Eisert v Adelson (AD2 1910) 136 AD 741, 121 NYS 446; Hall v Beston (AD1 1898) 26 AD 105, 49 NYS 811, affd 165 NY 632, 59 NE 1123; David v Holland (1943, Sup App T) 41 NYS2d 821.

**8.** Halloran v N. & C. Contracting Co. (1928) 249 NY 381, 164 NE 324. Oral testimony that at time of entering into written lease landlord had orally agreed to furnish free bus service to tenant, but for which agreement tenant would not have entered into lease, held, inadmissible and unenforceable. Fogelson v Rackfay Const. Co. (1950) 300 NY 334, 90 NE2d 881, reh den 301 NY 552, 93 NE2d 349.

**9.** Halbe v Adams (AD1 1917) 176 AD 588, 163 NYS 895.

**10.** Collamer v Farrington (S Ct GT3 1891) 61 Hun 620, 15 NYS 452.

**11.** Fifth Ave. Bond & Mortg. Co. v Ehrlich (1919, Sup App T) 173 NYS 740.

**12.** Smith v Smull (AD2 1902) 69 AD 452, 74 NYS 1061.

**13.** Gale v Heckman (AT1 1896) 16 Misc 376, 38 NYS 85.

**14.** Stonemor Realty Co. v Beyda (AD1 1923) 206 AD 476, 201 NYS 418.

**15.** Cochran v Scherer (M Ct 1922) 117 Misc 765, 192 NYS 199.

§ 6:14            LANDLORD AND TENANT

However, evidence of a supplemental oral agreement made after the execution of a written lease on a subject not covered therein is admissible, since a supplemental agreement is not a modification or variation of the terms of the lease. Thus, where there was no express provision in a written lease forbidding the tenant's use of the elevator, evidence of an oral agreement made after the execution of the lease authorizing elevator-use by the lessee after hours specified in lease, was held not to be violative of the parol evidence rule, nor of provisions of the lease prohibiting oral waiver or modification thereof.[17]

The general rule of contracts, that the parol evidence rule applies only to actions between the parties to the written lease or their privies,[18] applies to leases.[19]

### § 6:15. Exceptions to the Parol Evidence Rule

The rule that parol evidence is inadmissible to contradict or vary a written contract applies only to a written contract which is in force as a binding obligation.[20] Oral testimony which goes directly to the question whether or not because of fraud, accident, or mistake the writing fails to express the actual agreement of the parties, is admissible.[1] It never has been the purpose of the parol evidence rule to exclude evidence negativing the existence of a binding contract[2] by showing want of consideration,[3] fraud,[4] mistake,[5] duress,[6] illegality,[7] or any other

---

**16.** Goerlitz v Schwartz (1908, Sup App T) 112 NYS 1119.

**17.** Brandwein v Croydon Furniture, Inc. (1956, 1st Dept) 2 AD2d 969, 157 NYS2d 764.

**18.** "Although it is sometimes broadly observed that the parol evidence rule has no application to any except parties to the instrument" (cases cited), "it is clear that in the case of a fully integrated agreement, where parol evidence is offered to vary its terms, the rule operates to protect all whose rights depend upon the instrument even though they were not parties to it. Oxford Commercial Corp v Landau (1963) 12 NY2d 362, 239 NYS2d 865, 190 NE2d 230, 13 ALR3d 309.

**19.** Dumois v Mayor, etc., of New York (S Ct NY Co 1902) 37 Misc 614, 76 NYS 161.

**20.** Richards v Day (1893) 137 NY 183, 33 NE 146.

**1.** Smith v Dotterweich (1911) 200 NY 299, 93 NE 985; Kalb v Hoffman (S Ct Queens Co 1960) 24 Misc 2d 996, 205 NYS2d 720.

**2.** Jamestown Business College Ass'n v Allen (1902) 172 NY 291, 64 NE 952; Richards v Day (1893) 137 NY 183, 33 NE 146.

**3.** Baird v Baird (1895) 145 NY 659, 40 NE 222; Re Derrico (S Ct Westchester Co 1949) 90 NYS2d 889, affd 279 AD 615, 107 NYS2d 815.

**4.** Newburger v American Surety Co. (1926) 242 NY 134, 151 NE 155; Marcus Brown Const. Co. v Schlivek (1981, Sup App T) 170 NYS 430 (evidence admissible of misrepresentation as to size of bedroom to be constructed in premises leased); Kulerban Holding Corp. v Blauner (1921, Mun

CONSTRUCTION OF LEASES § 6:16

matter affecting the validity of the writing.[8] In other words, the parol evidence rule does not forbid the use of parol evidence to establish any fact that does not vary, alter, or contradict the terms of the lease, or the legal effect of the terms used therein. In the following sections[9] certain exceptions to the parol evidence rule are discussed. But in dealing with these so-called exceptions to the rule, it should be observed that while they are quite numerous, neither singly nor taken together do they tend to nullify or abrogate the rule itself. On the contrary, in applying such exceptions the courts are quite consistent in stating that the evidence in question is not admissible where its effect is to vary or contradict a complete and unambiguous written lease; but, rather, that such proof does not recognize the lease as ever existing as a valid agreement, and is received from the necessity of the case to show that what appears to be, is not, and never was, a contract.[10] The exceptions and qualifications to the rule are, on the whole, applied with care and discretion, and most of the courts appear to be alert to the ever-present danger that the party seeking to avail himself of an exception is merely using its terminology as a subterfuge to violate the rule itself.

## § 6:16. Merger Clause and the Parol Evidence Rule

Where a written lease provides that it contains all promises, warranties, conditions, representations, and the like, and that no others have been made or shall be binding, such a provision being known as a merger clause, extrinsic facts and evidence cannot be resorted to for the purpose of contradicting or varying the terms of the written lease, in the absence of fraud, accident or

Ct) 190 NYS 484 (evidence admissible of misrepresentation that rent was no greater than other tenants' rent in building); Meyers v Rosenback (City Ct 1893) 5 Misc 337, 25 NYS 521 (evidence admissible of misrepresentation as to suitability of premises for intended use and strength to sustain the contemplated engine power).

5. Newburger v American Surety Co. (1926) 242 NY 134, 142, 151 NE 155.

6. Berg v Hoffman (1937) 275 NY 132, 9 NE2d 806; Jules E. Brulatour, Inc. v Garsson (AD1 1930) 229 AD 466, 242 NYS 583.

7. Thomas v Scutt (1891) 127 NY 133, 27 NE 961; Pink v L. Kaplan, Inc. (AD2 1937) 252 AD 490, 300 NYS 45; Liberty Pipe & Boiler Covering Co. v Zichlin & Fischer, Inc. (1953, Sup App T) 127 NYS2d 83.

8. Newburger v American Surety Co (1926) 242 NY 134, 142, 151 NE 155.

9. §§ 6:18 et seq., infra.

10. Thomas v Scutt (1891) 127 NY 133, 27 NE 961.

§ 6:16

mistake. In other words, if a lease, complete on its face, and drafted designedly and explicitly to prevent reliance upon any promise or agreement not included, could be varied and undermined by parol evidence, written instruments would be unsafe and insecure.[11]

But, as pointed out above, this is the rule in the absence of fraud or mistake. It is well settled that one cannot insulate himself from a charge of fraud by so-called "merger" or "integration" clauses in a lease or contract.[12] A general merger clause does not bar the introduction of parol evidence of fraudulent representations in actions to rescind a lease, nor does it bar an action to reform a lease which by reason of the fraud of one party and the unilateral mistake of the other does not contain the agreement of the parties.[13] A rogue cannot protect himself from liability for his fraud by inserting a printed clause in his contract.[14] However, where a lease or contract contains a specific disclaimer of any representation as to a particular subject, as distinguished from a general merger clause; that is, one which is a general disclaimer as to representations, such specific disclaimer will destroy the allegation of a complaining party that the agreement was entered into in reliance upon a contrary oral representation as to this very subject, and therefore will destroy the foundation of his action.[15]

11. Barash v Pennsylvania Terminal Real Estate Corp. (1970) 26 NY2d 77, 308 NYS2d 649, 256 NE2d 707; Sabo v Delman (1957) 3 NY2d 155, 164 NYS2d 714, 143 NE2d 906; Fogelson v Rackfay Const. Co. (1950) 300 NY 334, 90 NE2d 881, reh den 301 NY 552, 93 NE2d 349.

12. Mosler Holding Corp v Bell (S Ct NY Co 1957) 10 Misc 2d 681, 170 NYS2d 157.

13. Barash v Pennsylvania Terminal Real Estate Corp. (1970) 26 NY2d 77, 308 NYS2d 649, 256 NE2d 707; Sabo v Delman (1957) 3 NY2d 155, 164 NYS2d 714, 143 NE2d 906.

14. Ernst Iron Works, Inc. v Duralith Corp. (1936) 270 NY 165, 169, 200 NE 683.

15. Barash v Pennsylvania Terminal Real Estate Corp. (1970) 26 NY2d 77, 308 NYS2d 649, 256 NE2d 707; Danann Realty Corp. v Harris (1959) 5 NY2d 317, 184 NYS2d 599, 157 NE2d 597; Wittenberg v Robinov (1961) 9 NY2d 261, 213 NYS2d 430, 173 NE2d 868; Carlinger v Carlinger (1964, 1st Dept) 21 AD2d 656, 249 NYS2d 761; Zamzok v 650 Park Ave. Corp. (S Ct NY Co 1974) 80 Misc 2d 573, 363 NYS2d 868.

## § 6:17. Form of Provision Against Oral Misrepresentations or Promises

### FORM NO. 4
### No Representations by Landlord (Merger Clause)

Neither Owner nor Owner's agents have made any representations or promises with respect to the physical condition of the building, the land upon which it is erected or the leased premises, the rents, leases, expenses of operation or any other matter or thing affecting or related to the leased premises or the building of which the same form a part, except as herein expressly set forth, and no rights, easements or licenses are acquired by Tenant by implication or otherwise except as expressly set forth in the provisions of this lease. Tenant has inspected the building and the leased premises, and is thoroughly acquainted with their condition, and agrees to take the same "as is" on the date possession is tendered, and acknowledges that the taking of possession of the leased premises by Tenant shall be conclusive evidence that the said premises and the building of which the same form a part were in good and satisfactory condition at the time such possession was so taken, except as to latent defects. All understandings and agreements heretofore made between the parties hereto are merged in this contract which alone fully and completely expresses the agreement between Owner and Tenant and any executory agreement hereafter made shall be ineffective to change, modify, discharge or effect an abandonment of it in whole or in part, unless such executory agreement is in writing and signed by the party against whom enforcement of the change, modification, discharge or abandonment is sought.

## § 6:18. Ambiguity or Uncertainty in Instrument

As a so-called exception to the parol evidence rule, it is held that parol and extrinsic evidence is generally admissible to explain ambiguities in a written lease. If the lease which expresses the complete agreement is unambiguous, extrinsic evidence to show that the parties attached a meaning different from the ordinary meaning of the

## § 6:18 LANDLORD AND TENANT

language used is excluded by the parol evidence rule.[16] If, however, the lease is ambiguous as to the meaning of the language employed, or is ambiguous by reason of unexpressed terms, extrinsic evidence is admissible to show the meaning intended by the parties.[17] Thus, parol evidence of earlier or contemporaneous matters in relation to the extent of the premises demised by the written lease has been admitted where the evidence has been largely, if not entirely, in "translation" of indefinite language, or in explanation of the description by the aid of the surrounding circumstances. Where the description of the premises was not sufficiently definite to enable the court to say what premises were included, parol evidence, largely, if not entirely, of surrounding circumstances, was admitted to explain the terms of the lease.[18] Where a lease provided that the lessee should have the option of purchasing said premises "and the land of the said lessor adjoining on the east," it was held that extrinsic evidence was admissible to make such description definite and certain.[19]

---

**16.** Raleigh Associates, Inc. v Henry (1951) 302 NY 467, 99 NE2d 289, reh den 302 NY 940, 100 NE2d 191.

**17.** Balkum v Marino (1949) 299 NY 590, 86 NE2d 109; Cordua v Guggenheim (1937) 274 NY 51, 8 NE2d 274.

**18.** Myers v Sea B. R. Co. (AD2 1899) 43 AD 573, 60 NYS 284, affd 167 NY 581, 60 NE 1117.

Where a lease designated the demised premises as "apartment first floor," parol evidence to show that there was no such apartment in the building was admissible. Fifth Ave. & Sixty-Sixth St. Corp. v Delaney (S Ct NY Co 1953) 124 NYS2d 89.

Mittler v Herter (City Ct 1902) 39 Misc 843, 81 NYS 494, where a written lease entered into by the parties provided that the plaintiff agreed to hire and the defendant agreed to let "the northerly half store of Nos. 7 and 8 Chatham Square," the building being then not completed, it was held proper to permit the plaintiff to introduce in evidence a letter written before the execution of the lease, and to prove conversations between the parties, for the purpose of showing that the premises demised were to be 25 feet wide and 132 feet deep, and that the store offered by the defendant was only 19 feet wide and 132 feet deep, as the description was ambiguous and vague.

Freud v Kearney (AT 1898) 23 Misc 685, 52 NYS 149, where the leased premises were described as the "westerly half" of a certain store, it was held that the lessee might show that, during the negotiations preceding the making of the lease, the lessor pointed out the part the lessee was to occupy, as the description was vague and indefinite.

**19.** Heyward v Willmarth (AD2 1903) 87 AD 125, 84 NYS 75, where the court said, "The demised premises and the land adjoining on the east comprised together a single plot of ground of the uniform depth of 125 feet, acquired by the appellant by deed from her husband. The leased part was a little less than half of the lot, and the circumstances left no room for doubt about the identity of the land 'adjoining on the east.' The language used clearly indicates the intention of the parties to include all the land of the lessor adjoining the

## CONSTRUCTION OF LEASES § 6:19

But where the lease provisions are found to be clear and unambiguous, parol evidence is inadmissible, since no explanation is necessary in order for the court to arrive at the intention of the parties. Thus, where a lease contained covenants that there could be only one "dairy and vegetarian restaurant" in the building, the language was held not ambiguous, and hence oral testimony concerning the meaning of the language was inadmissible.[20]

In other words, one does not create an ambiguity by calling something uncertain which is actually quite certain. Where the terms of a lease are plain and unambiguous, there is no room for construction, and it must be given effect according to its language.[1]

### § 6:19. Incomplete Instrument

Another so-called exception to the parol evidence rule, which has been the cause of difficulty, is the one dealing with written instruments claimed to be incomplete, or which are silent in respect to some material particular. It is well established that where a written instrument does

---

demised premises on the east, and the extrinsic evidence showing the unity of the plot necessarily served to render the description definite and certain. Such evidence was competent."

**20.** Hunts Point Restaurant, Inc. v Oval Foods, Inc. (S Ct Bx Co 1934) 153 Misc 451, 274 NYS 450.

Also, see Doherty v Monroe Eckstein Brewing Co. (AD1 1921) 198 AD 708, 191 NYS 59; Direct Realty Co. v Fergang (1938, Sup App T) 9 NYS2d 776 (parol evidence inadmissible to contradict or vary the terms of an unambiguous written lease with respect to the term of the tenancy); Knickerbocker Metallic Bed Co. v Newman (1919, Sup App T) 174 NYS 651.

Where the lease is clear as to the total amount of rent for a period of several years, the lessor may not show that the intent of the parties was that the amount stated for the entire term should be the rent for each year of the term. Liebeskind v Moore Co. (1903, Sup App T) 84 NYS 850.

In Marrotto v McCotter (1903, Sup App T) 85 NYS 431, where it appeared from the written lease that at the time of its execution the plaintiff paid an amount equal to three monthly installments of the yearly rent reserved, but nowhere did it appear that of this amount any part thereof was to be applied in payment of, or to be reserved as security for the payment of, any subsequently accruing rent, it was held that parol evidence was incompetent to show that such had been the actual understanding of the parties.

**1.** A somewhat unusual situation was involved in Raslo Realty Co v Schwartz (M Ct 1936) 161 Misc 467, 292 NYS 311, where it appeared that after the original lease had been made, a new corporation purchased the property, and a sublease was taken by a corporation of which the landlord was the sole owner, and their offices were in the same place. Thereafter the under-tenant paid the tenant only the difference in the rentals, and the court held that the arrangement for the offset of rents due the landlord by the tenant against the amount due the tenant by the under-tenant "was not an attempt to vary the terms of the lease but merely provided for a method of payment."

§ 6:19 LANDLORD AND TENANT

not contain the entire agreement between the parties, parol evidence is admissible for the purpose of establishing the entire agreement. This is not for the purpose of contradicting the writing, but rather for the purpose of establishing the real agreement between the parties, and preventing fraud or injustice.[2] However, before a given case of this character can be held to be within this exception to the parol evidence rule, rather than the rule itself, it must clearly appear first, that the writing on its face is not complete, and second, that the parol evidence offered is consistent with, and not contradictory of, the written instrument.[3]

The courts will not permit the general rule to be circumvented on the theory of incompleteness of a written lease when obviously it is as complete as the parties intended it to be. Thus, in one case a written lease covered only a room in an apartment house to be used for the storage of ice, giving plaintiff access to the premises to deliver ice, and expressly negatived any guaranty of freedom from competition. No other obligations were assumed by the lessor. It was contended that the lessor had breached the lease by the removal of iceboxes and installation of refrigerators. The court, however, held that there was no such obligation provided for in the

---

2. Frasca v Metropolitan Life Ins. Co. (AD2 1936) 248 AD 588, 287 NYS 375, affd 272 NY 588, 4 NE2d 816; Lynch v Harrer (City Ct Tonawanda 1933) 263 NYS 640. Apparel & Accessories Associates, Inc. v New York World's Fair 1939 Inc. (S Ct NY Co 1940) 176 Misc 26, 26 NYS2d 522, affd 261 AD 944, 26 NYS2d 528, reh den 261 AD 1074, 27 NYS2d 469, involved an action to recover the amount paid under a written contract for the remodeling and renting of a World's Fair building. It appeared that the written instrument was incomplete, and that the building and rental plan showed three staircases, but failed to show their point of upper termination; therefore, parol evidence was admissible to show the execution of a supplementary oral agreement made simultaneously with the written contract, by which the defendant undertook to construct a mezzanine floor. The court, in receiving parol evidence to clarify the ambiguity, observed that, "considering the circumstances surrounding the execution of the contract, it cannot be said that the contracting parties should have been expected to embody in the written contract all the details pertaining to the alteration. Evidence of the supplementary oral agreement does not violate the parol evidence rule."

3. Lynch v Harrer (City Ct Tonawanda 1933) 263 NYS 640.

In Fogelson v Rackfay Const. Co. (1950) 300 NY 334, 90 NE2d 881, reh den 301 NY 552, 93 NE2d 349, oral testimony was held inadmissible to show that at the time of executing the written lease the landlord had orally agreed to furnish free bus service to tenant, but for which agreement tenant would not have entered into the lease, especially where the lease expressly provided that it embodied all prior agreements and negotiations.

CONSTRUCTION OF LEASES § 6:20

lease, and any attempt on the part of the lessee to read into the lease some foreign agreement not to be found within the terms of the lease would clearly violate the parol evidence rule.[4] Similarly it was held that a lease is not incomplete on its face because it contains no provision as to repairs, and therefore parol evidence of a prior agreement to make repairs was inadmissible.[5]

### § 6:20. Independent Collateral Agreements

Oral agreements which relate to subject matter not covered in the written lease, and which may be characterized as independent collateral agreements thereto, are generally admitted into evidence, as an exception to the parol evidence rule. The question of what constitutes an agreement collateral to and independent of a written agreement, is a close one, and has given the courts considerable difficulty. Where a landlord orally agreed to construct a storehouse for a tenant for the storage of roofing slate, which should have sufficient capacity and strength to hold at least three carloads of roofing slate, on condition that tenant lease the same for a specified term, such oral agreement was held admissible as collateral to the written lease subsequently made, where the written lease contained no provision inconsistent with the oral agreement.[6] Where, at the time of the making of a lease for a term of years, "paid receipts" for rent for certain months were given to the lessee by the lessor, and also a letter stating that the tenant had "paid receipts" or concessions in rent for specified months, in an action for rent brought by the lessor's grantee it was held that the letter and receipts were admissible as writings which supplemented the lease, rather than superseded or substituted it.[7]

In another case the lease contained no provision as to

---

4. Sardone v Joseph Diamond Holding Co. (AD1 1935) 244 AD 300, 279 NYS 659, app dismd 268 NY 631, 198 NE 528.

5. Ernest Tribelhorn, Inc. v Hanavan (AT 1909) 65 Misc 22, 119 NYS 262.

But, in Herschmann-Tucker Furniture Co. v Barth (AT 1909) 64 Misc 77, 117 NYS 962, it was held that the lessee might show that because the landlord was unable to give possession, he had surrendered the lease and took a new one, beginning a year later, on the oral agreement of the lessor to make certain alterations and repairs, since only part of the contract was in the new lease.

6. Brown v De Graff (AD3 1918) 183 AD 177, 170 NYS 445.

7. Merly Realty Corp v Wallack (M Ct 1929) 134 Misc 96, 234 NYS 491.

fixtures, and provided that tenant should make all "improvements and repairs" necessary to be made on the premises during the continuance of her term, and that she should, at the end of the term, leave on the premises all the repairs and improvements that might have been made or put on the same. The lessee was permitted to give evidence that the lessor had orally agreed that certain specified fixtures then on the premises should be retained and remain there, so that the lessee might enjoy the benefit of them if she took the lease, and that for such oral promise, together with the sale of the good will of the business conducted on the premises, she had paid the lessor a consideration entirely aside from rent or anything stipulated in the lease to be paid by her. Observing that this case was "undoubtedly very near the line," the court upheld the admission of this evidence as a previous distinct collateral agreement upon a collateral and independent consideration which did not merge in the subsequent written lease.[8]

### § 6:21. Condition Precedent to Lease Rule

As an exception to the parol evidence rule,[9] it has been held that in a proper case, parol evidence may be used for the purpose of showing that although the written lease was duly executed and delivered, it was actually delivered upon an oral condition precedent that the instrument was not to become effective unless and until certain events had occurred.[10] Where the lease had never been delivered to the lessee, and the lessee had never taken possession of the premises, it was held that he was properly permitted to prove an oral agreement that the duplicate leases were signed conditionally, and that their delivery was to be postponed until certain repairs had been made.[11] Such a condition may be shown, it has been held, where there is no attempt to contradict or vary a written instrument, but to destroy the same, and to show that the written

---

8. Lewis v Seabury (1878) 74 NY 409.

9. See § 6:15, supra.

10. Frasca v Metropolitan Life Ins. Co. (AD2 1936) 248 AD 588, 287 NYS 375, affd 272 NY 588, 4 NE2d 816.

11. Flommerfelt v Englander (AT 1889) 29 Misc 655, 61 NYS 187.

*Contra:* See American Bill Posting Co. v Geiger (AT2 1912) 76 Misc 571, 137 NYS 148.

CONSTRUCTION OF LEASES § 6:22

lease never had any validity because of an existing condition precedent.[12]

## C. MODIFICATION OF LEASE

### § 6:22. Generally

It is perfectly competent for parties to make a contract which will supersede the lease in whole or in part.[13] They may by mutual consent alter, change, discharge, cancel, or modify its terms. Thus, parties frequently modify the original lease to provide for a reduction of rent,[14] or to work a surrender of the unexpired term.[15]

The intention of the parties to an agreement modifying the original lease is to be determined from what they wrote.[16] Where a lease is subsequently modified, the lease and its modifications must be taken together and construed as one contract to effect the intention of the parties, and that construction of the lease has to be preferred which will make it a just, fair and equitable contract mutually obligatory in its essential provisions.[17] Changes in the lease are not to be presumed or implied; and no additional liability will be imposed upon a tenant unless it is clearly within the provisions of the instrument under which it is claimed.[18] In determining whether a new agreement constitutes a new lease or a modification of an existing lease, it is substance rather than form that is important.[19]

Where the provisions of a modification agreement reducing the rent reserved in the original lease are unambiguous, parol evidence is inadmissible to show what the parties may have had in mind as to the amount of rent to

---

12. Well Financed Investing Co. v Binder (1920, Sup App T) 181 NYS 737. Also, see Saltzman v Barson (1925) 239 NY 332, 146 NE 618.

13. Haight v Cohen (AD2 1908) 123 AD 707, 108 NYS 502.

14. McKenzie v Harrison (1890) 120 NY 260, 24 NE 458; 86 Near Second Ave. Corp. v Fennekohl (Mun Ct 1946) 186 Misc 726, 61 NYS2d 167.

15. Douglaston Realty Co. v Hess (AD2 1908) 124 AD 508, 108 NYS 1036.

16. Raleigh Associates, Inc. v Henry (1951) 302 NY 467, 99 NE2d 289, reh den 302 NY 940, 100 NE2d 191.

17. Ireland Real Estate Co v New York, N H & H R Co (City Ct 1911) 72 Misc 530, 131 NYS 978.

18. 455 Seventh Ave., Inc. v Frederick Hussey Realty Corp. (1946) 295 NY 166, 65 NE2d 761, reh den 295 NY 827, 66 NE2d 595.

19. Winter v Ajax Auto Service Co. (S Ct NY Co 1948) 81 NYS2d 17.

be paid upon renewal of the lease.[20] On the other hand, evidence of a subsequent, supplemental oral agreement, which does not in fact modify or vary the terms of the original lease, does not violate the parol evidence rule or a lease provision prohibiting oral modification.[1]

### § 6:23. Necessity of Consideration

The General Obligations Law provides[2] that an agreement, promise or undertaking to change or modify, or to discharge in whole or in part, any contract, obligation, or lease, or any mortgage or other security interest in personal or real property, shall not be invalid because of the absence of consideration, provided that the agreement, promise or undertaking changing, modifying, or discharging such contract, obligation, lease, mortgage or security interest, shall be in writing and signed by the party against whom it is sought to enforce the change, modification or discharge, or by his agent. By virtue of this statute no consideration is necessary to make a formal written modification of a lease legally enforceable, and either party may enforce it against the other.[3] But, consideration of some sort is necessary to support any promise by either landlord or tenant which substantially modifies the terms of the existing tenancy, where such modification agreement is oral, and has not been executed.[4] Thus, an oral modification reducing the rent reserved in the lease is without consideration, and the lease provision for the payment of rent in stated amounts remains unaffected by the lessor's acceptance of lesser amounts, insofar as the modification agreement remains executory.[5] On the other hand, the parties to a lease cannot escape from their modifying agreement on the ground of want of consideration, where it has been fully executed, nor, if partially executed on both sides, can they repudiate that part which has been executed, although the unexecuted part may be repudiated, unless

---

**20.** Raleigh Associates, Inc. v Henry (1951) 302 NY 467, 99 NE2d 289, reh den 302 NY 940, 100 NE2d 191.

**1.** Brandwein v Croydon Furniture, Inc. (1956, 1st Dept) 2 AD2d 969, 157 NYS2d 764 (oral agreement authorizing use of elevator by tenant after hours specified in lease).

**2.** General Oblig L § 5-1103.

**3.** 86 Near Second Ave Corp v Fennekohl (Mun Ct 1946) 186 Misc 726, 61 NYS2d 167.

**4.** McKenzie v Harrison (1890) 120 NY 260, 24 NE 458; Coe v Hobby (1878) 72 NY 141.

**5.** Auswin Realty Corp. v Kirschbaum (AD2 1946) 270 AD 334, 59 NYS2d 824.

## CONSTRUCTION OF LEASES § 6:25

grounds of equitable estoppel exist.[6] With respect to a modification providing for the reduction of rent, it has been held that the rule, that the acceptance of a sum less than that due cannot operate as a full satisfaction, has no application where the agreement to accept in full satisfaction a sum less than that due as rent has been fully executed on both sides.[7]

### § 6:24. Necessity of Recording

The Real Property Law provides,[8] that where a lease or memorandum of such lease has been recorded, an unrecorded agreement modifying such lease or memorandum is void as against a subsequent purchaser in good faith and for a valuable consideration, and the possession of the tenant shall not be deemed notice of the modification, unless the agreement of modification or a memorandum thereof is recorded prior to the recording of the instrument by which the subsequent purchaser acquires his estate or interest. The statute further provides[9] that a memorandum of an agreement modifying a lease shall contain at least the following information with respect to the agreement: the names of the parties and the addresses if any, set forth in the agreement; a reference to the agreement with its date of execution; a brief description of the leased premises in form sufficient to identify the same; any changes made by the agreement in the term of the lease and the date of the termination of the lease as modified, and any changes in the provisions of the lease as to the rights of extension or renewal. For the purpose of this statute the word "purchaser" includes a person who purchases or acquires by exchange or contracts to purchase or acquire by exchange the leased premises or real property of which the leased premises are part or any estate or interest therein, or acquires by assignment the rent to accrue from tenancies or subtenancies thereof in existence at the time of the assignment.[10]

### § 6:25. Oral Modification

As a general rule, a lease for a term exceeding one

---

6. McKenzie v Harrison (1890) 120 NY 260, 24 NE 458.
7. McKenzie v Harrison (1890) 120 NY 260, 24 NE 458.
8. Real Prop L § 291-cc, subd 1.
9. Real Prop L § 291-cc, subd 2.
10. Real Prop L § 291-cc, subd 3.

year, required by the statute of frauds to be in writing and subscribed by the person creating or granting the same,[11] cannot be effectively modified by a subsequent oral agreement, at least insofar as the oral modification remains unexecuted.[12] Thus, an oral agreement to change the rent in a lease that has more than one year to run needs a written memorandum signed by the landlord.[13] An agreement eliminating the tenant's obligation to pay taxes and other charges for the duration of the term, and providing for a reduction in the rent reserved under the original lease, satisfies the statute of frauds where the agreement is in writing and signed by the landlord, and adequately describes and identifies the parties as landlord and tenant.[14]

However, if a parol modification is fully executed or acted upon, it is valid and enforceable.[15] Thus, for example, an oral agreement of the parties reducing the rent reserved in a written lease is binding so far as it has been executed.[16]

### § 6:26. —Provision Against Oral Modification

The lease may contain a provision that any modification of the lease must be in writing, or may contain a provision which prohibits any modification thereof except in writing. Such a provision is valid and enforceable. The statute provides,[17] that a written agreement or other written instrument which contains a provision to the effect that it cannot be changed orally, cannot be changed by an executory agreement unless such executory agreement is in writing, and signed by the party against whom enforcement of the change is sought or by his agent. Thus, where a lease prohibited subletting without the lessor's consent, and further provided that no part of the

---

11. See § 2:35, supra.
12. Auswin Realty Corp. v Kirschbaum (AD2 1946) 270 AD 334, 59 NYS2d 824.
13. McMeekan v B/G Sandwich Shops, Inc. (AT1 1938) 168 Misc 355, 6 NYS2d 66; Pearlstein Realty Co. v Collins (1921, Sup App T) 187 NYS 191; Seymour v Hughes (AT 1907) 55 Misc 248, 105 NYS 249; Jewell v Irvmac Shoe Shops, Inc. (S Ct Nassau Co 1959) 19 Misc 2d 815, 187 NYS2d 412.

14. Raleigh Associates, Inc. v Henry (1951) 302 NY 467, 99 NE2d 289, reh den 302 NY 940, 100 NE2d 191.
15. Kaiser v Zeigler (AT2 1921) 115 Misc 281, 187 NYS 638.
16. McKenzie v Harrison (1890) 120 NY 260, 24 NE 458; Auswin Realty Corp. v Kirschbaum (AD2 1946) 270 AD 334, 59 NYS2d 824.
17. General Oblig L § 15-301(1).

## CONSTRUCTION OF LEASES § 6:27

lease could be changed or waived orally, it was held that the statute clearly invalidated a fully executory oral consent to subletting given by the lessor's agent.[18]

The statute nullifies only executory oral modification. The statute does not apply to an oral agreement which is not executory, but has been executed, or acted upon by the parties.[19] Once executed, the oral modification may be proved. Where there is partial performance of the oral modification, if the partial performance is unequivocally referable to the oral modification, the requirement for a writing is avoided.[20] Accordingly, despite an express stipulation against oral modifications, a written agreement may be effectively modified by a subsequent oral agreement which is not executory, but has been acted upon by the parties.[1]

### § 6:27. —Form of Provision Against Oral Modification

### FORM NO. 5

#### Prohibition against Oral Modification*

This lease contains the entire agreement between the parties, and any executory agreement hereafter made shall be ineffective to change, modify, discharge or effect an abandonment of it in whole or in part unless such executory agreement is in writing and signed by the party against whom enforcement of the change, modification, discharge or abandonment is sought.

---

18. Dress Shirt Sales, Inc. v Hotel Martinique Associat (1963) 12 NY2d 339, 239 NYS2d 660, 190 NE2d 10.

19. Compton Advertising, Inc. v Madison-59th Street Corp. (S Ct NY Co 1977) 91 Misc 2d 768, 398 NYS2d 607, affd (1st Dept) 63 AD2d 942, 407 NYS2d 436.

20. Rose v Spa Realty Associates (1977) 42 NY2d 338, 397 NYS2d 922, 366 NE2d 1279.

1. Alcon v Kinton Realty, Inc. (1956, 3d Dept) 2 AD2d 454, 156 NYS2d 439, app dismd 2 NY2d 836, 159 NYS2d 974, 140 NE2d 869; Buchholz v Luckner (Mun Ct 1960) 23 Misc 2d 19, 205 NYS2d 737 (referring to former Real Prop L § 282, the substance of which has been transferred to General Oblig L § 15-301(1)); Jewell v Irvmac Shoe Shops, Inc. (S Ct Nassau Co 1959) 19 Misc 2d 815, 187 NYS2d 412.

If a party to a written agreement has induced another's significant and substantial reliance upon an oral modification, the first party may be estopped from invoking the statute to bar proof of that oral modification. The conduct relied upon to establish estoppel must also be unequivocally referable to the oral modification. Rose v Spa Realty Associates (1977) 42 NY2d 338, 397 NYS2d 922, 366 NE2d 1279.

* For complete form of lease see Chapter 28, infra.

## D. RESEARCH REFERENCES

### § 6:28. Generally

In addition to the preceding text, the reader is also referred to the following:

49 Am Jur 2d, Landlord and Tenant §§ 141-190.

New York Jur 2d, Landlord and Tenant (1st ed §§ 76-110).

Index to Annotations, Landlord and Tenant.

**VERALEX®:** Cases and annotations referred to herein can be further researched through the VERALEX electronic retrieval system's two services, **Auto-Cite®** and **SHOWME®**. Use Auto-Cite to check citations for form, parallel references, prior and later history, and annotation references. Use SHOWME to display the full text of cases and annotations.

# PART TWO

# THE RESPECTIVE RIGHTS AND OBLIGATIONS OF LANDLORD AND TENANT

# CHAPTER 7

# PREMISES LEASED; EASEMENTS AND APPURTENANCES

A. IN GENERAL
- § 7:1. What is Included in a Lease?
- § 7:2. Lease of Entire Building as Including Land
- § 7:3. Lease of Dwelling as Including Land, Garden and Curtilage
- § 7:4. Lease of Building as Including Roofs and Walls
- § 7:5. Appurtenances Defined
- § 7:6. Appurtenances Necessary to Enjoyment of Premises as Included in Lease
- § 7:7. Illustrations of Appurtenances Included in a Lease
- § 7:8. Conveniences Not Included in a Lease
- § 7:9. Other Land Not Included in a Lease

B. WHAT IS INCLUDED IN LEASE OF PART OF BUILDING
- § 7:10. Generally
- § 7:11. Basement
- § 7:12. Means of Access and Exit
- § 7:13. Land Not Included
- § 7:14. Roofs and Walls for Common Use
- § 7:15. Roof for Tenant's Sole Use
- § 7:16. Services
- § 7:17. Lobby Attendant Services

C. RIGHT TO LIGHT, AIR, UTILITIES, ETC.
- § 7:18. Light and Air from Adjoining Premises
- § 7:19. —From Lot on Which Leased Premises are Situated
- § 7:20. Heat and Hot Water; Absent Covenant
- § 7:21. Extent of Obligation Under Covenant to Furnish Heat or Hot Water
- § 7:22. Elevator Service
- § 7:23. Water
- § 7:24. Air Space Rights

D. FARM LANDS LEASE
- § 7:25. Generally
- § 7:26. Right to Crops
- § 7:27. Rights With Respect to Hay, Straw, and Manure
- § 7:28. Right to Emblements
- § 7:29. —Special Agreements

§ 7:30. —Effect of Custom or Usage
§ 7:31. —Right of Subtenant

E. RESEARCH REFERENCES
§ 7:32. Generally

## A. IN GENERAL

### § 7:1. What is Included in a Lease?

It has been seen that a lease, to be valid, must describe the premises leased with sufficient certainty so as to indicate what is intended to be conveyed thereby,[1] and only such premises as are described or properly identified in the lease will pass to the lessee. In accordance with the general rules of construction of leases,[2] the court will determine what passes under the lease by ascertaining the intent of the parties as expressed by the terms of the lease. However, where the language used in the lease is ambiguous or obscure, then parol evidence is admissible to determine the premises leased, and the court may resort to the declarations and acts of the parties, as well as all the attending circumstances to ascertain their intent.[3] However, parol evidence is not admissible to vary a plain and unambiguous description of the premises in a written lease

As a general rule, easements, rights, and privileges in other parts of the premises may be implied under certain circumstances.[4] However, the parties may provide that the tenant shall acquire no rights, easements, or licenses by implication or otherwise except as expressly set forth in the provisions of the lease between the parties.[5] Moreover, the term "premises" may include not only land, but personal property, if that is the intent of the parties from the language used in the lease.[6]

### § 7:2. Lease of Entire Building as Including Land

A lease of an entire building, without further descrip-

1. § 2:33, supra.
2. §§ 6:1, et seq, supra.
3. Smith v Finkelstein (AD1 1914) 162 AD 128, 147 NYS 324.
4. §§ 7:6, et seq, infra.
5. See § 6:17, supra.
6. Warner Bros. Pictures, Inc. v Southern Tier Theatre Co. (AD3 1952) 279 AD 309, 109 NYS2d 781, stating that, while the term "premises" is customarily used to refer to land or its appurtenances, this is not because the word itself is thus limited definitively, but because it is usually the intention of the parties that it have this direction or reference; if used in a context showing a wider intent, it may have a meaning which will include personal property in an integral use with the land.

tion, carries with it as part of the leased premises the land on which the building stands, as well as that part of the land in the same lot, not covered by the building, which adjoins it, and which has been appropriated to its use.[7] Therefore, if adjoining a building, and on the same lot with it, there is a yard which has been appropriated to the use of the building, such yard passes with a lease of the building without being specifically mentioned.[8] Similarly, if adjoining a building, and on the same lot with it, there is an alleyway giving necessary access to the yard in the rear of the building, such alleyway passes as part of the leased premises without specific mention thereof in the lease.[9]

### § 7:3. Lease of Dwelling as Including Land, Garden and Curtilage

A lease of a dwelling house, without further description, carries with it as part of the leased premises, the garden, curtilage (courtyard), and close (an exclusive area) adjoining the house, and on which the house is built. Other lands, although occupied with the house, will not pass unless they are specifically described; and it is immaterial that they are necessary to the leased dwelling.[10] Thus, under a lease of premises described as "all that certain dwelling, known, and designated as No. 327 W. Thirtieth Street, in the city of New York, Borough of Manhattan," which contains no reference to any appurtenances, the tenant is not given the use of the yard, nor the landlord precluded from building therein, if the yard be not inclosed, and there be access thereto otherwise than through the house.[11] This rule does not result from the necessity of a garden or curtilage to the reasonable occupation and enjoyment of the house, but from the fact that they are regarded as in fact and in law parcel of it, and as technically within the grant and the description of the thing granted. If a grant is made of a house and there is no garden, curtilage or close annexed to and a part of it, the grantee cannot claim, as incident to the grant, a garden and curtilage such as twelve men may say is

---

7. Doyle v Lord (1876) 64 NY 432.
8. Doyle v Lord (1876) 64 NY 432.
9. People ex rel. Murphy v Gedney (GT 1877, NY) 10 Hun 151.
10. Ogden v Jennings (1875) 62 NY 526, 530.
11. Rural Pub. Co. v Katzman (AD1 1921) 197 AD 295, 188 NYS 537.

reasonably necessary to the proper occupation and enjoyment of the house as a dwelling. Whether a garden is or is not necessary to a dwelling is wholly immaterial in interpreting and giving effect to a grant of the dwelling house, and determining what lands pass by the conveyance.[12]

By the curtilage which passes with the lease of a dwelling house is meant the courtyard in the front or rear, or at the side thereof, or any piece of ground lying near, and included and used with the same, and necessary for its convenient occupation.[13] It has been observed that the term "courtyard" is a corrupted form of "curtilage," and means the same thing.[14] Although curtilage goes with a dwelling house, it does not go with the rental of a cottage by a club member from a club which maintains a club house with recreational features, and in connection therewith maintains a number of small cottages to provide additional rooms for its members. This rental is not a rental of a dwelling, but rather a rental of a suite in a club.[15]

### § 7:4. Lease of Building as Including Roofs and Walls

A lease of a building includes the entire building unless some part thereof is expressly reserved by the landlord.[16] The lease, therefore, will carry the walls of the building to their exterior surface,[17] and the roof thereon.[18] Thus, if the walls of a leased building do not constitute a party wall, a landlord of such building, who also owns an adjoining lot, may not, in building on his adjoining lot, bore holes in the walls of the leased building to insert beams for the new structure.[19]

Where a lease describes the premises by metes and

12. Ogden v Jennings (1875) 62 NY 526, 530.
13. Powelson v Lake Placid Co. (AD3 1953) 281 AD 1054, 121 NYS2d 139; People ex rel. Murphy v Gedney (GT 1877, NY) 10 Hun 151.
14. In Re Lafayette Ave (S Ct Kings Co 1922) 118 Misc 161, 193 NYS 802.
15. Powelson v Lake Placid Co. (AD3 1953) 281 AD 1054, 121 NYS2d 139.
16. For example, see, Grauel v Soeller (GT 1889) 52 Hun 375, 5 NYS 254.
17. Lafayette Forwarding Co. v Rothbart Garage Operators, Inc. (AD1 1923) 205 AD 624, 200 NYS 184.
18. Valentine v Woods (AT 1908) 59 Misc 471, 110 NYS 990.

See, also, Mammy's, Inc. & Pappy's Inc. v All Continent Corp. (S Ct NY Co 1951) 106 NYS2d 635.

19. Lafayette Forwarding Co. v Rothbart Garage Operators, Inc. (AD1 1923) 205 AD 624, 200 NYS 184.

RIGHTS OF LANDLORD AND TENANT § 7:6

bounds, the lessee is entitled to the exclusive use and possession of the entire premises, including the roof and basement, and even though the subject of signs is not mentioned in the lease, the lessee, as an incident of the lease, acquires the right to use the roof and side walls of the building for the purpose of placing appropriate signs thereon to advertise any business which might be lawfully carried on in the building under the terms of the lease.[1]

### § 7:5. Appurtenances Defined

Appurtenances are incorporeal easements or rights and privileges which are essential or reasonably necessary to the full beneficial use and enjoyment of the property conveyed or leased.[2]

### § 7:6. Appurtenances Necessary to Enjoyment of Premises as Included in Lease

A tenant by his lease, even without the specific mention of the word "appurtenances" in the lease,[3] acquires as an appurtenance thereto such incorporeal easements or rights and privileges as are directly and materially essential to the proper and beneficial enjoyment and use of the premises leased to him, unless specifically excepted.[4] Such rights exist, as appurtenant to a grant of lands, and as arising by implication, only by reason of a necessity to the full enjoyment of the property granted. Nothing passes by implication, or as incident or appurtenant to the lands granted or leased, except such rights, privileges and easements as are directly necessary to the proper enjoyment of the granted estate or leased premises,[5] or are intended for the use or benefit of the part of the leased premises.[6]

1. Lyon v Bethlehem Engineering Corp (1930) 253 NY 111, 170 NE 512.
2. Ogden v Jennings (1875) 62 NY 526, 531; Broadway-Spring Street Corp. v Jack Berens Export Corp. (M Ct 1958) 12 Misc 2d 460, 171 NYS2d 342.
3. Kingsway Realty & Mortg. Corp. v Kingsway Repair Corp. (AD3 1928) 223 AD 281, 228 NYS 265; Bauer v Schwartz (S Ct Kings Co 1924) 122 Misc 630, 203 NYS 507, affd 209 AD 827, 204 NYS 893 and affd 211 AD 812, 206 NYS 883.

4. Ogden v Jennings (1875) 62 NY 526; Sturner v Delaware Properties, Inc. (S Ct Erie Co 1930) 135 Misc 514, 239 NYS 52, affd 234 AD 815, 253 NYS 912; Telesca v Bruenn Co. (City Ct New Rochelle 1972) 71 Misc 2d 208, 335 NYS2d 875.
5. Ogden v Jennings (1875) 62 NY 526, 531; Henry A. Fabrycky, Inc. v Nad Realty Corp. (AD2 1941) 261 AD 268, 25 NYS2d 347 (reasonably essential), reh and app den 261 AD 987, 27 NYS2d 440; Keesey v O'Reilly (AD1 1918) 181 AD 665, 168 NYS 844; Ber-

Therefore, although a tenant may have an implied right to all that goes necessarily with a beneficial use of the leasehold even in the absence of the word "appurtenances" from the lease, an appurtenance, to be availed of as such, must be a material and integral part of the leased premises.[7]

### § 7:7. Illustrations of Appurtenances Included in a Lease

A tenant acquires with his lease a right to all that goes necessarily and essentially with a beneficial use of the leased premises, even without specific mention thereof. Thus, a tenant of an apartment has necessarily as appurtenant thereto an implied easement of way in the common halls or passages which afford access to the apartment from the street.[8] Similarly, it has been held that the use of toilets contiguous to rooms rented in an office building, and of the wash basins therein, and of the elevators, hallways, stairs, and entrances to the building, is included in the lease to such rooms, even without mention thereof in the lease.[9] A tenant, as an incident of his lease to an apartment in a multiple dwelling was held to have an easement in common with the other tenants to an area which formed a part of the plot of the building, and which was set aside by the landlord for park purposes, notwithstanding the absence from his lease of the word appurtenances.[10]

If subleases by a tenant are authorized by the landlord, the landlord is obliged to list the names of the sublessees on the directory tablet in the lobby of the building. Such listing is an indispensable appurtenance to the right to use the space leased in the landlord's building, and deprivation of this right would substantially reduce, if not

lin v Yachnin (AT2 1926) 128 Misc 24, 217 NYS 190; Mammy's, Inc. & Pappy's, Inc. v All Continent Corp. (S Ct NY Co 1951) 106 NYS2d 635; Anixter v Bangor Realty Co. (S Ct NY Co 1918) 104 Misc 613, 172 NYS 732 (reasonably necessary and essential).

**6.** Dollard v Roberts (1891) 130 NY 269, 29 NE 104; Grynbaum v Metropolitan Life Ins. Co. (AD1 1947) 27 AD 216, 70 NYS2d 534.

**7.** Kingsway Realty & Mortg. Corp. v Kingsway Repair Corp. (AD2 1928) 223 AD 281, 228 NYS 265, holding that a lease does not include an interest in adjoining land even though owned by a common owner.

**8.** Presby v Benjamin (1902) 169 NY 377, 379, 62 NE 430.

**9.** Hall v Irwin (AD1 1903) 78 AD 107, 79 NYS 614.

**10.** Lemkin v Gulde (S Ct Nassau Co 1960) 25 Misc 2d 144, 205 NYS2d 658.

destroy, the value of the premises leased.[11] In one case, a building contained a basement, a store on the street floor with an extension in the rear thereof, and apartments on the upper floors. The basement contained bins in which the tenants of the building stored coal for heating purposes. The store was leased "with the appurtenances," to be used as a restaurant. The court held that the store tenant acquired, as an appurtenance to his lease, the right to use a bin in the basement for the storage of necessary coal. Laughlin, J., writing for the court,[12] said, "The term 'appurtenances' in a lease includes everything 'which is necessary and essential to the beneficial use and enjoyment of the thing leased or granted'. . . . It was essential to the enjoyment of the lease that the tenant should have a suitable and convenient place for storing coal. It appears that the business required the consumption of about two tons of coal each month. It would be absolutely unreasonable to expect the tenant to store the coal in the restaurant or in the yard or to buy it daily by the sack at a much higher rate than by the ton. It was evidently contemplated that he should store it where it had been stored."

### § 7:8. Conveniences Not Included in a Lease

A mere convenience is insufficient to create or to convey a right or an easement as an incident to a grant or lease, or to impose burdens on land other than those specifically granted.[13] Thus, where a landlord conducted a restaurant in a building in which he rented apartments, the continuance of the restaurant has been held not to be an implied appurtenance to the lease of an apartment in that building. The maintenance of the restaurant is merely a convenience, even though the tenant may be forbidden by the terms of his lease to cook in his apartment.[14] Where a tenant of premises used as a restaurant had two means available on the leased premises to dispose of garbage, neither of which crossed adjoining undemised property of landlord, the tenant could not claim

11. 92 Liberty Street Corp. v Dooney (1952, Sup App T) 116 NYS2d 44.
12. Greenblatt v Zimmerman (AD1 1909) 132 AD 283, 117 NYS 18.
13. Ogden v Jennings (1875) 62 NY 526, 531; Gale v Heckman (AT 1896) 16 Misc 376, 38 NYS 85; Mammy's, Inc. & Pappy's, Inc. v All Continent Corp. (S Ct NY Co 1951) 106 NYS2d 635.
14. Gale v Heckman (AT 1896) 16 Misc 376, 38 NYS 85.

§ 7:8 LANDLORD AND TENANT

the right to cross such landlord's adjoining property to dispose of garbage merely because it would be more convenient. Necessity, it was said, not convenience, must be shown.[15] Similarly, it has been held that where the roof of an apartment house was not equipped for or adapted to use for drying clothes, a lease of an apartment in such building will not carry as an implied easement or appurtenance thereto any right to the use of the roof for such purpose.[16]

A parking area is not an appurtenance to the lease of a building for an insurance agency.[17] Based on this principle it has been held that "appurtenances" in a proprietary lease of a co-operative apartment does not import additional storage room in the storage area of the building in the absence of an established practice to that effect in the particular cooperative or of necessity therefor, as distinguished from convenience.[18]

### § 7:9. Other Land Not Included in a Lease

Since appurtenances are incorporeal easements, or rights and privileges,[19] land cannot pass as appurtenant to land.[20] Therefore, even if the word "appurtenances" is added to a lease, the use of such word will not vary the effect of the lease and extend it so as to include other land not parcel of the premises specifically leased.[1] And, it is immaterial that such other land is owned by the landlord of the leased premises.[2] Thus, it has been held, the word "appurtenances" in a lease will not include a garden or curtilage not annexed to and part of the leased building.[3]

## B. WHAT IS INCLUDED IN LEASE OF PART OF BUILDING

### § 7:10. Generally

A lease of a specified portion of a building gives the

---

15. Mammy's, Inc. & Pappy's, Inc. v All Continent Corp. (S Ct NY Co 1951) 106 NYS2d 635.
16. Keesey v O'Reilly (AD1 1918) 181 AD 665, 168 NYS 844.
17. Telesca v Bruenn Co. (City Ct New Rochelle 1972) 71 Misc 2d 208, 335 NYS2d 875.
18. Oberfest v 300 East End Ave Associates Corp (S Ct NY Co 1962) 34 Misc 2d 963, 231 NYS2d 863.
19. See § 7:5, supra.
20. Doyle v Lord (1876) 64 NY 432.

1. Doyle v Lord (1876) 64 NY 432; Ogden v Jennings (1875) 62 NY 526.
2. Per diss op Maddox, J., in Cohen v Newman (AT2 1915) 91 Misc 561, 155 NYS 30, revd on such diss op 173 AD 976, 158 NYS 1111. Also, see Mammy's, Inc. & Pappy's, Inc. v All Continent Corp. (S Ct NY Co 1951) 106 NYS2d 635, discussed in § 7:8, supra.
3. Ogden v Jennings (1875) 62 NY 526, 531.

# RIGHTS OF LANDLORD AND TENANT § 7:11

tenant no rights outside of such specified part, except such as were intended to be included as appurtenant to the beneficial enjoyment thereof, or such as it is manifest were designed and appropriated for the benefit of the premises leased.[4] This principle will be illustrated by specific instances in the following sections.

### § 7:11. Basement

As a general rule a lease of a store on the first floor of a building does not include the basement underneath.[5] However, where a landlord of a store delivers the keys to the basement at the time of the lease, and the occupancy of the basement is essential to the use and enjoyment of the store, the basement is part of the lease as an appurtenance thereto, even though not specifically mentioned.[6]

A lessee of a store, "with appurtenances," was held to have the right to use the cellar in the building in which the store was located for the storage of coal, where it appeared that other tenants of the building were allowed to use the cellar for storage of coal; that the lessor or her husband had been operating a restaurant in the store part of the premises; that the purpose of the lessee in obtaining the lease was to continue such business, which he had purchased from the lessor or her husband; that the lessor or her husband used a particular part or bin in the cellar for conducting the business in which large quantities of coal were necessarily consumed; that there was on hand at the time the lease was made about one ton of coal which the lessee purchased; and that the lessee continued to use such bin for coal used in connection with the restaurant for the greater part of the four-year term of the lease. The court, after pointing out that the practical construction which the parties placed on the

---

4. Florgus Realty Corp. v Reynolds (1921, Sup App T) 187 NYS 188; Haskins v George A. Fuller Co. (S Ct NY Co 1901) 36 Misc 38, 72 NYS 440.
Also, see, Lubelsky v Haimowitz (AT 1910, Sup) 123 NYS 974, holding that a lease of a "basement bakery" includes the ovens and chimney connected with the basement, even though not specifically mentioned in the lease as part of the grant.

5. Kraus v Smolen (AT 1905) 46 Misc 463, 92 NYS 329.

6. Florgus Realty Corp. v Reynolds (1921, Sup App T) 187 NYS 188; 18th Ave. Pharmacy, Inc. v Wilmant Realty Corp. (S Ct Kings Co 1950) 95 NYS2d 534.

lease during nearly four years of the term was entitled to great weight, stated that the term "appurtenances" in a lease included everything which was necessary and essential to the beneficial use and enjoyment of the thing leased, and that it was essential to the enjoyment of the lease that the tenant should have a suitable and convenient place for storing coal.[7]

### § 7:12. Means of Access and Exit

The right to use the apparent, usual, and proper means of access to the leased premises is one of these appurtenances which is included in the lease as a matter of right.[8] Where a stairway furnishes the means of access to the leased premises, and to no other part of the building in which the leased premises are located, then such stairway is appurtenant to the leased premises, and will be included in the lease without specific mention.[9] However, if a stairway furnishes access to other parts of the building, as well as to the leased premises, then such stairway is not appurtenant to the lease, and will not be included in the lease unless specifically mentioned as part thereof.[10]

A mere convenience is not an appurtenance.[11] Therefore, if such right of ingress and egress extends over other property of the landlord not included in the leased premises, such right will only pass as an appurtenance to the leased premises if it is reasonably necessary to the enjoyment thereof. Thus, a tenant of an apartment has necessarily as appurtenant thereto an easement of way in the common halls, which are not part of the leased apartment, and which afford access to the apartment from the street.[12]

---

7. Greenblatt v Zimmerman (AD1 1909) 132 AD 283, 117 NYS 18.

8. Presby v Benjamin (1902) 169 NY 377, 62 NE 430; Hall v Irwin (AD1 1903) 78 AD 107, 79 NYS 614 (office building); Jones & Brindisi, Inc. v Bernstein (AT1 1922) 119 Misc 697, 197 NYS 263 (loft building hallway); Also, see Brendlin v Beers (AD1 1911) 144 AD 403, 129 NYS 222; Watchtower Bible & Tract Soc. v Metropolitan Life Ins. Co. (S Ct NY Co 1947) 188 Misc 978, 69 NYS2d 385, affd 272 AD 1039, 75 NYS2d 81, affd 297 NY 339, 79 NE2d 433, 3 ALR2d 1423, cert den 335 US 886, 93 L Ed 425, 69 S Ct 232, reh den 335 US 912, 93 L Ed 445, 69 S Ct 479; Anixter v Bangor Realty Co. (S Ct NY Co 1918) 104 Misc 613, 172 NYS 732.

9. Finkelstein v Schlanowsky (AT 1912) 76 Misc 500, 135 NYS 783, later app 79 Misc 47, 140 NYS 624.

10. Hamersmith v Cohn (1911, Sup App T) 132 NYS 323.

11. See § 7:8, supra.

12. Presby v Benjamin (1902) 169 NY 377, 62 NE 430.

However, where at the time of a lease of a basement of a building there was a direct means of access thereto from the street, and also an additional means of access thereto from the hallway in the building, it was held that the tenant did not acquire as an appurtenance to his lease the hallway entrance. Such additional means of access was merely a convenience, but not a necessity.[13] Similarly, where a tenant of part of the lower floor of a building had two ways of access to the rear yard, one through the landlord's store adjoining the leased premises, and one by a stairway to the basement of the leased building, it was held that no right to use the landlord's store as a means of access to the yard passed as an appurtenance.[14]

In other words, the basis for an easement by implication must be a reasonable necessity as distinguished from a mere convenience. If the only means of access to the leased premises is over adjoining property of the landlord, then a right to use such means of access will be implied. But if such means of access over adjoining premises is merely additional to the tenant's regular means of ingress and egress, then such additional means of access will not pass with the lease as an appurtenance.[15]

If a landlord contracts with his tenant to give elevator service, then, if the elevator service fails, it is the landlord's duty to furnish a reasonable, safe substitute as a means of egress, which requires a lighted stairway.[16]

### § 7:13. Land Not Included

A lease to a specified portion of a building does not carry with it any interest in the land on which the

---

13. Schulte Realty Co. v Pulvino (1919, Sup App T) 179 NYS 371.
14. Sturner v Delaware Properties, Inc. (S Ct Erie Co. 1930) 135 Misc 514, 239 NYS 52, affd 234 AD 815, 253 NYS 912.
15. Siegel v John Street Corp. (AD1 1920) 190 AD 349, 179 NYS 705.
Also, see, Holtz Amusement Co. v Schorr (S Ct Kings Co 1924) 122 Misc 712, 204 NYS 733; Kaiser v Cinberg (AD2 1909) 130 AD 254, 114 NYS 716, where, in both cases, theatres had exits onto adjoining lands of the landlord, which the court found were convenient, but not necessary; held, not appurtenant to the leases of the theatre premises; Mammy's, Inc. & Pappy's, Inc. v All Continent Corp. (S Ct NY Co. 1951) 106 NYS2d 635, holding that tenant was not entitled to cross landlord's property adjoining the leased premises to dispose of garbage, because it would be more convenient for him.
16. Truax v Knox (AD3 1919) 188 AD 61, 175 NYS 772.

building stands.[17] Nor, will such a lease carry with it any part of the courtyard as a part of the leased premises unless specifically granted. The only interest in the curtilage which a tenant of a part of a building acquires by implication under his lease is by way of an easement, appurtenant to the leased premises in common with all the other tenants, for all the purposes for which it can be used in common. As for example, for a playground for children of the tenants, and for light and air for rooms in the rear of the building.[18]

### § 7:14. Roofs and Walls for Common Use

Where part of a building is leased to a tenant, the tenant acquires only an implied easement in the foundation, walls, and roof of the building necessary for the support and protection of the premises leased to him.[19] These parts of the building are used in common by all the tenants, and therefore cannot pass under a lease to a part of the building without specific mention.

Thus, it is well settled that where several tenants in a building are sheltered by a common roof, the roof does not pass by implication with the lease of any part of the building.[20] And, this is so, even where a tenant leases a building "above the first story."[1]

### § 7:15. Roof for Tenant's Sole Use

Where a roof forms as much a part of the leased premises as the side and end walls, and completes the inclosure of the leased premises, then the roof is impliedly part of the lease.[2] Thus, where a tenant leased a

---

17. Rowan v Kelsey (1866) 41 NY 594; Graves v Berdan (1863) 26 NY 498.

18. Doyle v Lord (1876) 64 NY 432.

See Lemkin v Gulde (S Ct Nassau Co 1960) 25 Misc 2d 144, 205 NYS2d 658, where a tenant, as an incident of his lease to an apartment in a building, even though the lease did not mention "appurtenances," was held to have an easement in common with the other tenants to an area which formed a part of the plot of the building, and which was set aside by landlord for park purposes.

19. Snow v Pulitzer (1894) 142 NY 263, 36 NE 1059.

Also, see Quigley v H. W. Johns Mfg. Co. (AD2 1898) 26 AD 434, 50 NYS 98; O. J. Gude Co. v Farley (AT 1899) 28 Misc 184, 58 NYS 1036.

See §§ 15:26, et seq., infra, as to right of a tenant of part of a building to use outer walls for display of signs.

20. Alfred Peats Co. v Bradley (AD1 1915) 166 AD 267, 151 NYS 602; Valentine v Woods (AT 1908) 59 Misc 471, 110 NYS 990.

1. Valentine v Woods (AT 1908) 59 Misc 471, 110 NYS 990.

2. Lichtig v Poundt (AT 1898) 23 Misc 632, 52 NYS 136.

store together with a one story extension in the rear covered by a roof, in the center of which was a skylight, the roof over the extension was held to constitute part of the leased premises, without specific mention thereof. The roof of the extension, the court pointed out, existed for no other purpose whatsoever than as an inclosure of the extension. It formed a part of the extension and was essential to its existence and use for the purpose for which it was constructed, so that in leasing it the roof in question formed as much a part of the leased premises as the side and end walls which completed the inclosure—all equally contributing to the inclosure which gave existence to the subject matter of the lease.[3] But, it has been held that where the roof of an apartment house was not equipped for or adapted for use for drying clothes, a lease of an apartment in such building would not carry as an implied easement or appurtenance thereto any right to the use of the roof for such purpose.[4]

### § 7:16. Services

Where various services, such as bus service, doorman service, manually operated elevator service, and the like are voluntarily supplied by the landlord at the time a lease is made, such voluntary act is not sufficient in aid of itself to establish a contractual obligation by the landlord to continue such services, and absent an express covenant or statute providing otherwise, the landlord may discontinue such service at any time.[5]

Thus, in the absence of an express covenant to furnish doorman service, a tenant may not recover by way of diminution of rent upon the discontinuance of such service which had been voluntarily supplied by the landlord.[6]

However, it must be observed that the Real Property

---

3. Lichtig v Poundt (AT 1898) 23 Misc 632, 52 NYS 136.

As to right to use roof and walls for advertising, see §§ 15:26, et seq, infra.

4. Keesey v O'Reilly (AD1 1918) 181 AD 665, 168 NYS 844.

5. Fogelson v Rackfay Const. Co. (1950) 300 NY 334, 340, 90 NE2d 881, reh den 301 NY 552, 93 NE2d 349; Michaels v Macan Estates (AD1 1951) 278 AD 47, 103 NYS2d 142; Lenox Hill Apartments, Inc. v Coogan (1944, Sup App T) 52 NYS2d 40 (doorman service); Shongut v Leavy (S Ct NY Co 1951) 202 Misc 94, 116 NYS2d 691.

6. Lenox Hill Apartments, Inc. v Coogan (1944, Sup App T) 52 NYS2d 40; New Rochelle Mall v Docktor Pet Centers Realty (S Ct NY Co 1970) 65 Misc 2d 303, 317 NYS2d 404 (discontinuance of security personnel for shopping center upheld).

§ 7:16　　　　　　　　　　　LANDLORD AND TENANT

Law provides,[7] "Any lessor, agent, manager, superintendent or janitor of any building, or part thereof, the lease or rental agreement whereof by its terms, express or implied, requires the furnishing of hot or cold water, heat, light, power, elevator service, telephone service or any other service or facility to any occupant of said building, who wilfully or intentionally fails to furnish such water, heat, light, power, elevator service, or telephone service or other service or facility at any time when the same are necessary to the proper or customary use of such building, or part thereof, or any lessor, agent, manager, superintendent or janitor who wilfully and intentionally interferes with the quiet enjoyment of the leased premises by such occupant, is guilty of a violation."

### § 7:17. Lobby Attendant Services

The statute provides that tenants of every class A multiple dwelling containing eight or more apartments shall be entitled to maintain and operate a lobby attendant service for such multiple dwelling at any time or times when an attendant hired or furnished by the owner thereof shall not be on duty. Such lobby attendants so maintained by such tenants shall be engaged solely for security purposes and shall perform no acts or duties other than those which shall be directly related to the safety and security of occupants and visitors to such building while in and about the public portions thereof and no owner shall unreasonably hinder, interfere with, obstruct or prohibit the maintenance and operation of such service, provided that each attendant so engaged by tenants shall at all times when on duty be stationed at and remain in the entrance halls or public lobbies of the building adjacent to the main entrance thereto, and provided further that no owner of such building shall be in any manner liable or responsible for any injury to any such attendant or for any damage or injury arising out of or resulting from any act or omission of any such attendant or for the payment of any wages or other compensation to such attendants. The lobby attendants furnished,

---

7. Real Prop L § 235, added L 1967, ch 680, eff Sept 1, 1967.

operated or maintained by tenants pursuant to this section may consist of or include tenants or other occupants of the multiple dwelling and may include either volunteer or paid personnel or a combination thereof.[8]

## C. RIGHT TO LIGHT, AIR, UTILITIES, ETC.

### § 7:18. Light and Air from Adjoining Premises

The English common law doctrine of ancient lights, and of the acquisition of easements of light and air by prescription, has never prevailed in New York. Therefore, in this State no implied easements of light and air over premises adjoining the leased premises are recognized,[9] whether such adjoining premises are owned by a third person,[10] or are also owned by the landlord of the leased premises.[11] Such a right must be granted by express terms.[12] Even if the word "appurtenances" is included in a lease, the word "appurtenances" will not include an easement of light and air over adjoining premises, even though such adjoining premises are owned by the landlord of the leased premises.[13] Thus, a lease of a building having windows opening on an adjoining lot, whether owned by the landlord or by a third person, carries no implied right to light and air over such lot, and, in the absence of a provision in the lease to the contrary, a landlord incurs no liability to his tenant by the erection of a building upon other lands belonging to him which results in cutting off light and air from the leased premises.

---

8. Mult Dwell L § 50-c, add L 1972, ch 638, eff Sept 1, 1972. The statute further provides: Any agent, owner or other person who shall unreasonably interfere, hinder, obstruct or prohibit the installation, maintenance and operation of any such lobby attendant or shall unreasonably hinder or interefere with the performance of the duties of such lobby attendant engaged pursuant to this section, shall be guilty of a violation with a maximum fine not to exceed fifty dollars.

9. Kingsway Realty & Mortg. Corp. v Kingsway Repair Corp. (AD2 1928) 223 AD 281, 228 NYS 265; De Baun v Moore (AD2 1898) 32 AD 397, 52 NYS 1092, affd 167 NY 598, 60 NE 1110; Joseph v Lidsky (M Ct 1962) 34 Misc 2d 606, 226 NYS2d 636.

10. De Baun v Moore (AD2 1898) 32 AD 397, 52 NYS 1092, affd 167 NY 598, 60 NE 1110.

11. Kingsway Realty & Mortg. Corp. v Kingsway Repair Corp. (AD2 1928) 223 AD 281, 228 NYS 265; Solomon v Fantozzi (AT 1904) 43 Misc 61, 86 NYS 754.

12. De Baun v Moore (AD2 1898) 32 AD 397, 52 NYS 1092, affd 167 NY 598, 60 NE 1110.

13. Per diss op Maddox, J., Cohen v Newman (AT1 1915) 91 Misc 561, 155 NYS 30, which was revd on diss op, 173 AD 976, 158 NYS 1111. Also, see Doyle v Lord (1876) 64 NY 432, 437.

### § 7:19. —From Lot on Which Leased Premises are Situated

A tenant as part of his lease acquires an implied right to light and air from the land on which the leased premises are situated. Thus, where the windows of leased premises overlook a yard forming part of the lot on which the leased premises stand, the light and air passing through the windows from such yard will be deemed an appurtenance to the leased premises.[14] As the Court of Appeals said,[15] "The light passing into the windows from the yard was essential to the beneficial use of the store, and it was clearly the intention at the time the lease was made that plaintiffs" (tenants) "should have it. To this extent, in any view of the case, the plaintiffs were entitled to enjoy an easement in the yard." Therefore, a landlord has no right to erect structures on other parts of the same premises which results in obstructing the light and air to windows in the leased building.

### § 7:20. Heat and Hot Water; Absent Covenant

At common law, in buildings, whether commercial or residential, where the entire building is heated from a central plant which is within the exclusive control of the landlord, a lease of rooms in such building carries with it, by implication, the right to have the leased premises properly heated.[16] Similarly, where there is no way of obtaining hot water except by means of a plant under the landlord's control, the tenants of a building acquire as

---

**14.** Doyle v Lord (1876) 64 NY 432, 437; Aliber v Remsen Street Co. (S Ct Kings Co 1961) 31 Misc 2d 786, 221 NYS2d 464, holding that the fact that the entire rear vacant area is designated on the tax maps by a separate tax description is of no significance upon the question whether such area was appropriated to use with the buildings for light and air; Leventhal v Straus (M Ct 1950) 197 Misc 798, 95 NYS2d 883; Bauer v Schwartz (S Ct Kings Co 1924) 122 Misc 630, 203 NYS 507, affd 209 AD 827, 204 NYS 893 and affd 211 AD 81 206 NYS 883; Stevens v Salomon (S Ct NY Co 1902) 39 Misc 159, 79 NYS 136.

See O'Neill v Breese (Super Ct 1893) 3 Misc 219, 23 NYS 526, wherein it was held that the tenant of a basement room had a right to have light pass into such room through "floor lights" situated in the floor of the room above, and directly under skylights in such upper room, and therefore that a tenant of the upper room had no right to cover the "floor lights" with carpet or matting in such a way as to exclude the light from the basement room.

**15.** Doyle v Lord (1876) 64 NY 432, 439.

**16.** Berlinger v MacDonald (AD1 1912) 149 AD 5, 133 NYS 522; Jackson v Paterno (AT 1908) 58 Misc 201, 108 NYS 1073, affd 128 AD 474, 112 NYS 924.

Adams v Green (NYC Civ Ct Kings Co 1982) 114 Misc 2d 633, 452 NYS2d 143 (quoting text).

## RIGHTS OF LANDLORD AND TENANT § 7:20

part of their lease, by implication, right to a sufficient supply of hot water.[17]

"In the absence of an express agreement on the part of the lessor to supply heat," it was said by the Appellate Term,[18] "his duty to furnish adequate heat may be implied from the covenant of quiet enjoyment, when the means of supplying heat to an apartment in an apartment house are exclusively under the control of the landlord . . . . This duty of the lessor, in these cases, arises solely by implication from the covenant that the tenant may quietly have, hold, and enjoy the premises."

In other words, then, even though no mention of heat or hot water is contained in the lease, the landlord is under a duty to furnish such heat and hot water as is reasonably necessary for the beneficial enjoyment of the leased premises by the tenants in those buildings where the source of heat and hot water is a central plant for the entire building exclusively under the landlord's control.

Multiple Dwelling Law § 79 provides, that every multiple dwelling exceeding 2 stories in height and erected after April 18, 1929, and every garden-type maisonette dwelling project erected after April 18, 1954, shall be provided with heat. On and after November 1, 1959, every multiple dwelling shall be provided with heat or the equipment or facilities therefor. During the months between October 1 and May 31, such heat and the equipment or facilities shall be sufficient to maintain the minimum temperatures required by local law, ordinance, rule or regulation, in all portions of the dwelling used or occupied for living purposes provided, however, that such minimum temperatures shall be as follows: (a) 68 degrees Fahrenheit during the hours between six o'clock in the morning and ten o'clock in the evening whenever the outdoor temperature falls below 55 degrees Fahrenheit, notwithstanding the provisions of paragraph a of subdivision 4 of § 3 of this chapter, and (b) at least 55 degrees

---

17. Lloyd Constr. Co. v Dudgeon (AT 1912) 76 Misc 246, 134 NYS 888.

Where a landlord has covenanted to furnish heat, and the building has no facilities for providing hot water separate from heat, no obligation to furnish hot water during the months when heat is not furnished will be implied. Tibaldi v Custodian Realty Co. (1972, 1st Dept) 39 AD2d 532, 330 NYS2d 805.

18. Jackson v Paterno (AT 1908) 58 Misc 201, 108 NYS 1073, affd 128 AD 474, 112 NYS 924.

§ 7:20 LANDLORD AND TENANT

Fahrenheit during the hours between ten o'clock in the evening and six o'clock in the morning, whenever the outdoor temperature falls below 40 degrees Fahrenheit. Nothing in this section shall be deemed to relieve any owner of the duty of providing centrally supplied or other approved source of heat prior to November first, 1959 in any case where such heat is required by this chapter or any other law, ordinance, rule or regulation to be supplied in a dwelling prior to said date. The heating system in dwellings used for single room occupancy shall be in conformity with the requirements of section 248.[19]

### § 7:21. Extent of Obligation Under Covenant to Furnish Heat or Hot Water

The extent of a lessor's obligation under an express covenant to furnish heat or hot water depends upon the terms of the covenant. Where there is an ambiguity, the practical construction given thereto by the parties to the lease, as well as the surrounding circumstances at the time of the lease, may be resorted to by the courts in order to ascertain the intention of the parties.[20]

In one case a landlord of premises used for manufacturing purposes covenanted to furnish such heating to the leased premises "as the plant at present installed will provide." Nothing was said as to whether heat would be supplied during the night on cold days. Nevertheless,

---

19. Subdivision 2 of § 79 provides that the provisions of subdivision 1 shall not apply to any dwelling (a) which is located in a resort community and is rented or occupied on a seasonal basis between April 15 and October 14 during any calendar year and is not occupied for living purposes during the remainder of such year, except that occupancy of any such dwelling by the family of a caretaker thereof or by the family of the owner thereof during the remainder of the year shall be permitted; or (b) which the department of city planning certifies is in an area to be acquired for a public improvement or for development or redevelopment and for which (1) a request for acquisition has been submitted to the mayor by a public agency or (2) a plan for a development or redevelopment project has received preliminary or first approval of the city planning commission; or (c) for which a demolition permit has been or shall be issued by the municipality pursuant to local law or ordinance.

Subdivision 3 of § 79 provides that the exemption provided in subdivisions 2 (b) and (c) shall be valid for a period of 6 months after the date of the approval of the slum clearance or urban renewal plan or the date of such certification or the date of the issuance of the demolition permit, as the case may be; but such exemption may be extended from time to time by the department provided, however, that such exemption shall not extend beyond November 1, 1961.

20. Columbus Spa, Inc. v Star Co. (AD1 1926) 216 AD 218, 214 NYS 653; Halperin v McCrory Stores Corp. (AD2 1923) 207 AD 448, 202 NYS 385, affd 239 NY 547, 147 NE 189.

during the term of this lease, the landlord furnished the tenant with heat at night, because the tenant during the winter season had to operate his plant during the night. This lease was renewed several times, and the same heat covenant was incorporated in each renewal. During the last renewal period the landlord sought to discontinue heat during the night. In denying the landlord such right, the Appellate Division said[1] "If this action were brought under the first lease to compel the landlord to furnish heat at night, I think it would then be a question to be determined from the construction of this clause of the lease—whether heat was to be furnished at night or not. But I think the course of dealings of the parties has changed the question, to some extent at least. It is undisputed that when the lease was renewed each time, the landlord knew that the tenant was using the leased premises for night work, that heat was essential to enable him to do so, and that the plant at that time installed was providing it. The lease then made must be construed in the light of the surrounding circumstances. Waiving the question of practical construction and considering only the construction of the lease in view of the surrounding circumstances, was not the lessee justified upon a renewal in believing that under the new lease he would be entitled to receive the same amount of heat and during the same hours he had under the former lease? The heating plant was the same. There was nothing to warn the lessee that any change was anticipated and, in fact, no change was contemplated. . . . When the lease was renewed I think each party was entitled to have and to expect to furnish heat to the same extent and of the same character as had theretofore been furnished. The intent of the parties is the controlling factor, when not illegal, in construing an agreement."

In another case, involving the obligation of the landlord to furnish heat at night to a restaurant, where the covenant was silent as to night heat, the Appellate Division said,[2] "It was evidently well known to the parties that the tenant intended to use the premises as a restau-

---

1. Halperin v McCory Stores Corp (AD2 1923) 207 AD 448, 202 NYS 385, affd 239 NY 547, 147 NE 189.
2. Columbus Spa, Inc. v Star Co. (AD1 1926) 216 AD 218, 214 NYS 653.

rant in a district where night life is predominant, and it would be necessary for the landlord to heat such restaurant. The landlord did not stipulate that it would furnish heat for one hour of the day or night or for twenty-four hours. No limitation upon time is fixed in the lease. A reasonable construction, therefore, is that sufficient heat should be furnished to properly conduct the restaurant. Several rules of construction warrant this conclusion. The first is that the intention of the parties, taking into consideration the surrounding circumstances, should govern. It is reasonable to assume that under all the circumstances the landlord intended to heat these premises so that the tenant might successfully operate a restaurant, bearing in mind the location of the restaurant and the requirements of the neighborhood. . . . Secondly, if there is any ambiguity in the clauses of the lease, although we do not believe there is, the tenant is entitled to the benefit of a construction most favorable to him." (The lease had been prepared by the landlord.)[3] "In addition, however, these parties are bound by a practical construction of the lease, for the reason that during part of the first winter the landlord, recognizing its responsibility, furnished sufficient heat to conduct the restaurant business in conformity with the surrounding circumstances, taking into consideration the neighborhood where the restaurant was located."

These cases indicate the importance of expressing clearly the extent of the landlord's obligation to furnish heat and hot water, rather than inviting litigation to determine the scope of the obligation assumed by the covenant.

### § 7:22. Elevator Service

As a general rule, in the case of the lease of a part of a building, used either for dwelling or commercial purposes, and equipped with passenger or freight elevators for the common use of the tenants of the different parts of the

---

3. The general rule, that an instrument is to be construed against the person by whom it is prepared or drawn, applies to leases. § 6:8, supra. See, also, Application of Moore (S Ct Kings Co 1949) 194 Misc 718, 88 NYS2d 367, affd 275 AD 956, 90 NYS2d 533.

# RIGHTS OF LANDLORD AND TENANT § 7:23

building, the right to use the elevators passes as an incident or appurtenance to the part leased.[4]

Where the owner of a loft building with an elevator therein, which was used both for freight and passenger service, leased the fourth floor loft for use as a printing shop without specially reserving the appurtenance of elevator service, it was held that the tenant was entitled to a reasonable use of the elevator as an appurtenance for ingress and egress to the fourth floor loft, the court applying the general rule that appurtenances reasonably essential to the enjoyment of leased premises pass as an incident to them unless specifically reserved, and stating that the fact that elevator service was not mentioned in the lease under the circumstances herein did not bar the tenant's right to the enjoyment thereof.[5]

Where the lease obligated landlord to provide necessary elevator facilities on business days from 8 A.M. to 5 P.M., and provided that tenant's employees should have access to the leased premises and the building of which they formed a part, tenant was entitled to have his mover use the elevator during business hours to remove his records from the leased premises, and landlord could not compel tenant to limit such removal to evening hours or to landlord's employees, nor demand prepayment of the rent for the remainder of the term as a condition to the removal.[6]

It has been held that where a lease contains no express provision requiring a landlord to continue furnishing manually operated elevators, he is at liberty to change the type of elevator from manually operated to automatically controlled.[7]

## § 7:23. Water

Where a building is so piped that each tenant's premises may receive water through pipes connected with the main water system, the use of such pipes for obtaining

---

4. Hall v Irwin (AD1 1903) 78 AD 107, 79 NYS 614.

5. Henry A. Fabrycky, Inc. v Nad Realty Corp. (AD2 1941) 261 AD 268, 25 NYS2d 347, reh and app den 261 AD 987, 27 NYS2d 440.

6. Gulf & Western Industries Inc v Franklin Record Center Inc (S Ct NY Co) NY Law Journal, August 18, 1976, p. 6, c. 3, Fein, J. (Tenant's application for an order directing sheriff to seize the records was granted.)

7. Hikand v Weller (S Ct NY Co 1946) 64 NYS2d 157.

water is a privilege impliedly passing to the tenant with his lease.[8]

In one case where part of a building was leased "to be used as a bakery," it was held that since a water supply is essential to the use and enjoyment of the premises for a bakery, the right to make the necessary connection with the building water main to get a supply of water for the bakery would be implied as an appurtenance to the lease.[9]

The mere fact that the leased premises are equipped with water pipes connected with plants operated either by the municipality or a private company, and with the necessary fixtures for the utilization thereof, does not impose an obligation on the landlord to pay the charges for the water consumed by the tenant.[10] However, the statute provides[11] that for dwellings 3 or more stories in height erected after April 18, 1929, and for all dwellings erected after January 1, 1951, the landlord must supply hot and cold water at all times of the year during all hours.

### § 7:24. Air Space Rights

A recent case has indicated how important it is for the lessor of a long-term lease to reserve to himself the use of air space rights, including the floor area ratio. In this case, the lessor owned a building which did not fully utilize the floor area ratio for that building, and hence there was surplus air space which was buildable. He gave a long-term lease to this building to a lessee who also happened to own in fee the contiguous building. Under a Zoning Resolution, where several contiguous lots are in single ownership, and under this Resolution "ownership" includes a long-term leasehold interest, these lots may be lumped together and treated as a "zoning lot" for the purpose of computing floor area ratio. Thereupon, the lessee commenced to erect a 45-story building on his fee property, and obtained a building permit, which because of his "ownership" of the two contiguous plots, allowed him to incorporate the unused floor area ratio permissible

---

8. West Side Sav. Bank v Newton (1879) 76 NY 616.

9. Gans v Hughes (City Ct Bklyn GT 1891) 38 NY St R 490, 14 NYS 930.

10. 49 Am Jur 2d, Landlord and Tenant, § 211.

11. Multiple Dwelling Law § 75.

and attributable to the building on the leased property in computing the maximum floor area ratio for the proposed building. The lease permitted such alterations to the building as would suit lessee's convenience and the requirements of its business and the business of its tenants, but prohibited certain types of structural alterations without lessor's consent. The Court agreed that the alteration provision is not to be deemed as a source of power authorizing the lessee's utilization of the building's unused air space. However, since the lessor had failed to reserve air development rights, the Court held that there was no restriction on the lessee's qualifying his contiguous property under the Zoning Ordinance, and thus exploiting the otherwise unused air development rights of the leasehold. Accordingly, although the lessor lost a valuable asset—he lost his right to transfer or use his air development rights by alienation of the reversion to an abutting owner, or by acquiring an abutting property—this loss, the Court ruled, was not due to any wrongful act of the lessee, but rather the result of the operation of the Zoning Ordinance, since the lessor had not reserved to himself this valuable right.[12]

## D. FARM LANDS LEASE

### § 7:25. Generally

Under a lease of farm land with the livestock thereon, without any control over such livestock being retained by the landlord, the tenant is regarded as the owner of the livestock for the term of the lease.[13] While the livestock is in the possession, care, and custody of the lessee under such a lease, he is responsible for properly caring for such stock, and is liable for the death of such stock due to his negligence.[14] Moreover, the lessee of a farm and the livestock thereon, being in full control of the stock, is liable for its trespass on the lands of another.[15] A provision in such a lease that if any cow proved a failure, the

---

12. Newport Associates, Inc. v Solow (1972) 30 NY2d 263, 332 NYS2d 617, 283 NE2d 600, cert den 410 US 931, 35 L Ed 2d 593, 93 S Ct 1372, reh den 411 US 977, 36 L Ed 2d 699, 93 S Ct 2140.

13. Harrison v McClellan (AD3 1910) 137 AD 508, 121 NYS 822; Atwater v Lowe (GT 1886, NY) 39 Hun 150.

14. Scott v Lockwood (AD4 1905) 102 AD 223, 92 NYS 401.

15. Atwater v Lowe (GT 1886, NY) 39 Hun 150; Van Slyck v Snell (GT 1872) 6 Lans 299.

landlord would replace it, does not obligate the landlord to replace a cow that has died, since death is not a failure within the terms of the lease.[16]

As in the case of leases generally, the terms of a contract or agreement leasing farmland ordinarily control the rights and obligations of the parties.[17] Thus, in the absence of provision in the lease imposing upon the lessee the duty to occupy the farm, a lease clause that the lessee shall leave as much hay and straw when he leaves the farm as when he received it, will not justify enjoining the lessee and his family from moving during the term of the lease.[18]

### § 7:26. Right to Crops

As between landlord and tenant, the annual crops raised on the leased premises during the tenancy are no part of the freehold, but are the property of the tenant, in the absence of any agreement between the parties to the contrary.[19] One who sows and harvests a crop upon the land of another is entitled to the crop as against the owner of the land, whether he came into the possession of the land lawfully or not, provided he remains in possession until the crop is harvested.[20] Accordingly, even crops gathered by a tenant at will, or by a tenant by sufferance, during his tenancy belong to him, since even a mere trespasser is entitled, as against the owner of the land, to the crops which he sows and harvests while he continues in possession.[1] Likewise, a tenant wrongfully holding over under a farm lease after the expiration of his term is entitled as against the landlord to any farm produce produced and severed by him during the continuance of his possession.[2] In such case the tenant's right to harvest

---

**16.** Scott v Lockwood (AD4 1905) 102 AD 223, 92 NYS 401.

**17.** Burdick v Fuller (AD3 1921) 199 AD 94, 191 NYS 442.

**18.** Burdick v Fuller (AD3 1921) 199 AD 94, 191 NYS 442.

Generally, as to the duty of the tenant to occupy the premises, see § 175, infra.

**19.** Colville v Miles (1891) 127 NY 159, 27 NE 809.

See also Harris v Frink (1872) 49 NY 24; Smith v Dairymen's League Co-op. Ass'n (S Ct Livingston Co 1945) 186 Misc 82, 58 NYS2d 376, affd 270 AD 1071, 63 NYS2d 691.

**20.** Smith v Dairymen's League Co-op. Ass'n (S Ct Livingston Co 1945) 186 Misc 82, 58 NYS2d 376, affd 270 AD 1071, 63 NYS2d 691.

**1.** Smith v Dairymen's League Co-op. Ass'n (S Ct Livingston Co 1945) 186 Misc 82, 58 NYS2d 376, affd 270 AD 1071, 63 NYS2d 691.

**2.** Smith v Dairymen's League Co-op. Ass'n (S Ct Livingston Co 1945)

# RIGHTS OF LANDLORD AND TENANT § 7:27

the crops is not affected by the terms of the original lease, since all contractual relationship ceases upon expiration of the term provided for in the lease.[3]

However, the tenant may lose his right to growing crops where, in accordance with the terms of the lease, the landlord re-enters and takes possession of the premises upon the tenant's default in the payment of the rent.[4] As between the tenant and one claiming under the foreclosure of a mortgage of the landlord made prior to the lease, crops go with the realty and belong to the purchaser at foreclosure.[5]

## § 7:27. Rights with Respect to Hay, Straw, and Manure

In the absence of a restrictive agreement, the straw from crops raised on the premises belongs to the tenant as much as the grain or other crops, and he may remove it from the premises.[6] Wheat straw is deemed to be part of the crop of wheat, and belongs to those who own the crop, and, therefore, in the absence of any stipulation or custom to the contrary, does not go to the landlord as manure made upon the land.[7] Although a tenant has covenanted to feed the hay and straw raised on the farm to stock and not remove the same, it has been held that the hay and straw are, nevertheless, subject to sale on execution at the instance of the tenant's creditors.[8]

It is the general rule that the tenant of a farm has no right to remove manure made on the farm.[9] Accordingly, an outgoing farm tenant is not entitled to the manure made on the farm during his tenancy, even though it is lying in heaps in the farmyard and notwithstanding it

---

186 Misc 82, 58 NYS2d 376, affd 270 AD 1071, 63 NYS2d 691, holding that the landlord's remedy is to recover the rental value of the land during the unlawful withholding.

3. Smith v Dairymen's League Co-op. Ass'n (S Ct Livingston Co 1945) 186 Misc 82, 58 NYS2d 376, affd 270 AD 1071, 63 NYS2d 691.

4. Gregg v Boyd (GT5 1893) 69 Hun 588, 23 NYS 918.

5. Harris v Frink (1872) 49 NY 24; Lane v King, 8 Wend 584.

But see St. John v Swain (GT5 1891, Sup) 14 NYS 743, holding that where the tenant was not made a party to the foreclosure proceeding, his right to growing crops was unaffected by the mortgage foreclosure sale.

6. Colville v Miles (1891) 127 NY 159, 27 NE 809.

7. Fobes v Shattuck, 22 Barb 568.

8. Colville v Miles (1891) 127 NY 159, 27 NE 809.

9. Elting v Palen (GT3 1891) 60 Hun 306, 14 NYS 607; Middlebrook v Corwin, 15 Wend 169.

was made by the tenant's own cattle and from his own fodder.[10] However, where it is the understanding of the parties that manure shall belong to the tenant, the landlord has no right thereto, and the tenant may remove such manure.[11]

### § 7:28. Right to Emblements

Crops which mature after the termination of the lease are designated as "away-going crops," and whether or not a tenant has the right to re-enter, and take them, depends to a great extent on the character of the lease with respect to the certainty or uncertainty of its duration. A distinct and well-defined doctrine,[12] commonly known as the doctrine of emblements or "away-going crops," has been developed in reference to the ownership of such crops in the event of the termination, under certain conditions, of the tenancy of the person who planted them. "Emblements" are corn, wheat, rye, potatoes, garden vegetables, and other crops which are produced annually, not spontaneously, but by labor and industry.[13]

A tenant who holds by a tenure which is uncertain as to the time at which it will cease, as for example, a tenancy at will, or by sufferance, or a periodic tenancy, is, in the absence of a specific agreement governing the disposition of emblements, entitled to enter upon the premises after the tenancy has ceased, to take off the annual crops or emblements which he has planted prior to such termination in the due course of husbandry, if the termination is brought about without any fault on his part,[14] or by some act of the landlord without fault on the

---

10. Middlebrook v Corwin, 15 Wend 169.

11. Carroll v Newton, 17 How Pr 189, wherein it appeared that the tenant of a house and a barn in which he kept a number of horses had told the landlord that he might have the manure to be made at the barn if he would furnish the straw to be used there, which the landlord had declined, the court holding that under the circumstances the landlord would be deemed to have understood that the manure was not made from the produce of the place and therefore belonged to the tenant.

12. Batterman v Albright (1890) 122 NY 484, 25 NE 856.

13. Heller v Amawalk Nursery, Inc. (AD2 1938) 253 AD 380, 2 NYS2d 196, affd 278 NY 514, 15 NE2d 671; Hamilton v Austin (GT4 1885, NY) 36 Hun 138, 142, affd 107 NY 636, 13 NE 941.

14. Batterman v Albright (1890) 122 NY 484, 25 NE 856; Reeder v Sayre (1877) 70 NY 180, 185; Harris v Frink (1872) 49 NY 24; Ferrucci v McDermott (S Ct Oneida Co 1930) 138 Misc 438, 246 NYS 22.

# RIGHTS OF LANDLORD AND TENANT § 7:28

part of the tenant.[15] The whole law of emblements is derived from a rule of public policy. Its object is to encourage agriculture by giving to such tenants as held a possession terminable upon some uncertain event, a return for the capital and labor laid out and expended upon the land of another. There is no basis, therefore, for giving such right to one who has a fixed term,[16] or who knows that his tenancy will expire before a crop which he sows can mature,[17] or whose estate terminates, though indefinite in its original duration, by his own act,[18] as by surrender or forfeiture because of some default.[19] Moreover, a tenant will not be entitled to emblements if the tenancy is terminated as the result of an entry under a title paramount to the title of his landlord.[20]

The general rule that a tenant for a definite term has no right to unharvested crops maturing after the expiration of his lease may be modified by estoppel arising against the landlord claiming the "away-going" crops.[1] Thus, where the landlord of a farm lease terminating in the spring assented to and recognized the right of the tenant to sow a crop in the fall, the landlord is estopped from claiming ownership of such crop even though it was harvested after the termination of the lease.[2] Moreover,

---

**15.** Hatfield v Lawton (AD3 1905) 108 AD 113, 95 NYS 451; Pfanner v Sturmer, 40 How Pr 401.

**16.** Reeder v Sayre (1877) 70 NY 180; Smith v Dairymen's League Coop. Ass'n (S Ct Livingston Co 1945) 186 Misc 82, 58 NYS2d 376, affd 270 AD 1071, 63 NYS2d 691.

**17.** Where a tenant is given notice of termination before he sows the crop, he then knows that his tenancy will expire before the crop can mature, and he will not have the right to remove the crop. Reeder v Sayre (1877) 70 NY 180, 185.

**18.** Samson v Rose (1875) 65 NY 411, 416; Hatfield v Lawton (AD3 1905) 108 AD 113, 95 NYS 451; Ferrucci v McDermott (S Ct Oneida Co 1930) 138 Misc 438, 246 NYS 22, where a tenant, electing to terminate his tenancy because of fire, lost his right to harvest a crop of corn which matured after he had vacated the premises.

**19.** Hatfield v Lawton (AD3 1905) 108 AD 113, 95 NYS 451 (notice of surrender by tenant before end of term and acceptance of surrender by landlord); Gregg v Boyd (GT5 1893) 69 Hun 588, 23 NYS 918 (tenant's failure to pay rent).

Thus, notwithstanding that certain acts of the landlord amount to an eviction, and justify the tenant in leaving the farm, he cannot re-enter and carry away growing grain where he is in default of payment of accrued rent. Tham v Carroll (AD4 1911) 147 AD 229, 132 NYS 4.

**20.** Banta v Merchant (1903) 173 NY 292, 66 NE 13; Batterman v Albright (1890) 122 NY 484, 25 NE 856; Harris v Frink (1872) 49 NY 24, 30.

**1.** Stewart v Doughty, 9 Johns 108; King v Wilcomb, 7 Barb 263.

**2.** Benson v Morse (S Ct Ontario Co 1951) 109 NYS2d 57.

See also Duffus v Bangs (1890) 122 NY 423, 25 NE 980, applying the rule to a tenant's nursery stock.

§ 7:28      LANDLORD AND TENANT

subsequent lessees claiming under such landlord are also estopped to assert ownership of such crop where they have notice of the facts,[3] and the burden is upon such lessees to allege and prove that notice thereof was lacking, in order to assert ownership of such crops as against the previous lessee.[4]

As a general rule, the right of a tenant to take and carry away unharvested crops at the termination of his tenancy must be exercised within a reasonable time after such termination.[5] A tenant who has a right to "away-going" crops, whether by reservation or otherwise, has the right to free ingress, egress, and regress so far as is necessary to gather and remove the crops.[6]

While the right to crops unharvested at the termination of a lease is generally exercised by a landlord or a tenant, the right may be exercised in some instances by other persons, such as the personal representative of a tenant who dies before the crops are ready to be harvested.[7]

### § 7:29. —Special Agreements

The general rules respecting rights of tenants to unharvested crops at the termination of leases may be rendered inapplicable by special agreements between the parties, who may, if they choose, agree that the landlord shall have the crop which would otherwise belong to the tenant, and vice versa.[8]

In this connection, the form of the agreement is of no

---

**3.** Benson v Morse (S Ct Ontario Co 1951) 109 NYS2d 57.

**4.** Benson v Morse (S Ct Ontario Co 1951) 109 NYS2d 57.

**5.** What constitutes a reasonable time for the removal of emblements after the expiration of the tenancy depends upon the facts of each particular case, such as the weather, reasonable opportunity for removal, and the like, to be determined by the jury.

**6.** Sexton v Breese (1892) 135 NY 387, 32 NE 133.

**7.** Reeder v Sayre (1877) 70 NY 180.

Such right applies not only to the tenant, but to anyone who has succeeded to his interest in the crops sown. Stewart v Doughty, 9 Johns 108.

EPTL 13-1.1 provides that for the purposes of administration of an estate, crops growing on the land of the decedent at the time of his death, and every growing grass and fruit ungathered, are personal property, and pass to the personal representative.

**8.** Reeder v Sayre (1877) 70 NY 180; Wadsworth v Allcott & Smith (1851) 6 NY 64; Beck v McLane (AD4 1909) 129 AD 745, 114 NYS 44, affd 198 NY 567, 92 NE 1078; Gregg v Boyd (GT5 1893) 69 Hun 588, 23 NYS 918.

# RIGHTS OF LANDLORD AND TENANT § 7:32

consequence; it is the substance of the agreement which determines its legal character.[9]

### § 7:30. —Effect of Custom or Usage

While the right of a tenant for a definite term to enter and remove crops which have matured since the expiration of the term has been established by custom and usage in some jurisdictions,[10] it has been held that there is no such general custom or usage in New York.[11]

### § 7:31. —Right of Subtenant

A sublessee is in a better position in respect to emblements than the original lessee. If, for example, a lessee, having made an underlease, terminates his estate by his own act, he will have no emblements, but the sublessee will be allowed them, since, the condition having been broken after the underlease was made, it is only reasonable that emblements should be allowed, as the subtenant has no reason to anticipate the special mode by which the lease is terminated, and to which his own act in no respect contributed.[12]

## E. RESEARCH REFERENCES

### § 7:32. Generally

In addition to the preceding text, the reader is also referred to the following:

49 Am Jur 2d, Landlord and Tenant §§ 197-213.

New York Jur 2d, Landlord and Tenant (1st ed §§ 111-124).

Index to Annotations, Landlord and Tenant.

**VERALEX®:** Cases and annotations referred to herein can be further researched through the VERALEX

---

9. Armstrong v Bicknell, 2 Lans 216.

Thus, for example, a contract provision that in case of the termination of the lease by the lessor there should be compensation to the tenant for preparing the ground for reception of seed or for any other extra labor, has been held not to deprive the tenant of his right to emblements. Stewart v Doughty, 9 Johns 108.

10. *Annotation:* Rights, as between landlord and tenant, in respect of crops unharvested at expiration of tenancy, as affected by custom and usage. 141 ALR 1251.

11. Reeder v Sayre (1877) 70 NY 180.

12. Samson v Rose (1875) 65 NY 411 (recognizing the rule, but holding it inapplicable where the subtenant, under a sublease taken pending an action of ejectment by the landlord, had knowledge of the facts.

§ 7:32    LANDLORD AND TENANT

electronic retrieval system's two services, **Auto-Cite®** and **SHOWME®**. Use Auto-Cite to check citations for form, parallel references, prior and later history, and annotation references. Use SHOWME to display the full text of cases and annotations.

# CHAPTER 8

# OBLIGATIONS TO DELIVER POSSESSION AND TO OCCUPY PREMISES

§ 8:1.  Landlord's Obligation to Deliver Possession
§ 8:2.  Right of Rescission Against Landlord
§ 8:3.  Right to Damages Against Landlord
§ 8:4.  —Measure of Damages
§ 8:5.  —Right to Special Damages
§ 8:6.  —Right to Loss of Profits and Time
§ 8:7.  Action to Recover Possession
§ 8:8.  Equitable Relief Against Landlord
§ 8:9.  Remedies for Inability to Get Full Possession
§ 8:10. Remedies Against Third Persons
§ 8:11. Form of Covenant to Deliver Possession
§ 8:12. Form of Provision to Protect Landlord Against Inability to Deliver Possession
§ 8:13. Tenant's Obligation to Occupy
§ 8:14. Research References

## § 8:1. Landlord's Obligation to Deliver Possession

The Real Property Law provides that in the absence of an express provision to the contrary, there shall be implied in all leases executed on or after September 1, 1962, a "condition that the lessor will deliver possession at the beginning of the term."[1]

Prior to the enactment of this provision, decisional law had made a distinction between an obligation "to deliver possession", that is, to give actual physical possession, and an obligation "to give legal possession," that is, merely to give a right to possession. Under this prior law it had been well established that the law would imply in every lease a covenant on the part of a landlord only to give his tenant legal possession. Unless there was an express covenant in the lease undertaking to deliver possession, the landlord was not liable for the withholding of possession from the tenant either by a prior tenant

---

1. Real Prop L § 223-a, add L 1962, ch 170, eff Sept 1, 1962.
**Annotation:** Implied covenant or obligation to provide lessee with actual possession. 96 ALR3d 1155.

§ 8:1 LANDLORD AND TENANT

wrongfully holding over, or by any other person wrongfully in possession. The tenant's inability to obtain possession under these circumstances did not discharge him from any of his obligations under the lease, and he could neither rescind the lease, nor recover any consideration that he might have paid. Of course, since the landlord was under an obligation to give his tenant legal possession, he would be liable to the tenant if the tenant was kept out of possession by a person holding under a paramount title, by a prior tenant holding over with the landlord's consent, or by the landlord's conduct or lack of good faith.[2] This prior decisional law has been changed, as indicated above, by the Real Property Law, so that now, unless a lease expressly provides otherwise, a condition will be implied therein that the landlord will see to it that the tenant can get into physical possession of the leased premises at the commencement of the term, even if the one already in possession is there wrongfully.[3]

A landlord's refusal to give the tenant a key to the leased premises has been held a failure to deliver possession; for a key is the symbol of possession, and the furnishing a tenant with a key to leased premises is a customary incident to the delivery of possession.[4] Where a tenant is unable to enter into physical possession of the leased premises at the commencement of the term because they are in the process of substantial repairs or are unfinished, and therefore are not ready or fit for occupancy, the landlord has been held to have failed to deliver possession.[5]

2. This was established in 1842, in Gardner v Keteltas (S Ct 1842) 3 Hill 330, and was consistently followed until the enactment of Real Prop L § 223-a. See United Merchants' Realty & Improv. Co. v Roth (1908) 193 NY 570, 86 NE 544; Fong Ling v Nathans (AD2 1922) 204 AD 265, 197 NYS 461; Podalsky v Ireland (AD1 1910) 137 AD 257, 121 NYS 950, later app 146 AD 940, 131 NYS 1138, affd 210 NY 598, 104 NE 1138; Smith v Barber (AD1 1904) 96 AD 236, 89 NYS 317, and Smith v Barber (1906) 112 AD 187, 98 NYS 365; Borrello v Brown (1923, Sup App T) 198 NYS 236; Mirsky v Horowitz (AT 1905) 46 Misc 257, 92 NYS 48; Goerl v Damrauer (AT 1899) 27 Misc 555, 58 NYS 297; Nodine v State (Ct of Claims 1948) 192 Misc 572, 79 NYS2d 834; Du Barry Bags, Inc. v Deane (S Ct NY Co 1945) 58 NYS2d 808; Ward v Edesheimer (1892, CP Ct) 17 NYS 173, app den (CP Ct) 18 NYS 139.

3. See § 8:12, infra, for form of provision to protect lessor against inability to deliver possession.

4. American Tract Soc. v Jones (AT 1912) 76 Misc 236, 134 NYS 611.

Also, see Ocean, Fifth Realty Corp. v Stern (M Ct 1951) 202 Misc 336, 109 NYS2d 92; Davies, Turner & Co. v Schatzen (AT1 1924) 124 Misc 170, 207 NYS 217.

5. 163 East Thirty-Sixth Street

## § 8:2. Right of Rescission Against Landlord

The Real Property Law provides that for breach of the implied condition to deliver possession at the beginning of the term,[6] the lessee shall have the right to rescind the lease, and to recover any rent or other consideration he may have paid in advance.[7]

A tenant who desires to rescind his lease must do so promptly and unequivocally; for, under the authorities, slight facts tending to show a lessee's dealing with the premises are sufficient to prove the taking of possession by him. Thus, entry on the land, the putting up of a notice to rent, or the making of repairs, have been held sufficient to establish the fact of entry and actual occupation.[8]

## § 8:3. Right to Damages Against Landlord

The Real Property Law provides that the right of rescission for breach of the implied covenant to deliver possession shall not be deemed inconsistent with any right he may have to recover damages.[1]

It is well established that the breach or non-occurrence of a condition which is not accompanied by any words importing an undertaking to abide by or to perform it, prevents the covenantor from acquiring a right, or deprives him of one, but subjects him to no liability.[2] Accordingly, unless the lease contains an express covenant on the part of the landlord to deliver possession of leased premises at the commencement of the term, the

---

Corp. v Stockbridge (AT1 1921) 114 Misc 98, 185 NYS 577; Kopelman v Gritman (AT2 1912) 76 Misc 188, 136 NYS 296; Meyers v Liebeskind (AT 1905) 46 Misc 272, 91 NYS 725.

A destruction of the leased premises between the time of the making of the lease, and the commencement of the term, similarly constitutes a failure to deliver possession. Wood v Hubbell (1853) 10 NY 479, 487.

6. See § 8:1, supra.

7. Real Prop L § 223-a.

This was also the rule under prior decisional law: Kopelman v Gritman (AT2 1912) 76 Misc 188, 136 NYS 296; Meyers v Liebeskind (AT 1905) 46 Misc 272, 91 NYS 725.

Where a lessee was deprived of possession of the premises by his lessor for the first two weeks of the term under the lease, he was held entitled to recover the rent paid by him for such two weeks. Frank v Morewood Realty Holding Co (AT1 1915) 89 Misc 425, 151 NYS 930.

However, under prior decisional law where there was no express undertaking by the landlord to deliver possession, the tenant had no right of rescission where he was unable to obtain possession because a prior tenant wrongfully held over, or because someone was in possession wrongfully. This is no longer the law.

8. Smith v Barber (AD1 1904) 96 AD 236, 89 NYS 317.

1. Real Prop L § 223-a.

2. See § 23:11, infra.

landlord will not be liable to respond in damages for failure to do so. Breach of the covenant implied by the Real Property Law will not subject the landlord to liability for damages. Thus, a landlord is not liable in damages, in the absence of an express covenant to deliver possession, where his inability to do so results from the wrongdoing of third persons.

What constitutes an express covenant for delivery of possession presents a question for construction, when these precise words are not used. Where a lease provided for the payment of the rent "before possession of the store is delivered to the tenant," it was held that this language clearly imported an undertaking on the part of the lessors to deliver actual physical possession "at the time when the tenant handed them his check for the rent."[3]

### § 8:4. —Measure of Damages

Generally the measure of damages for the landlord's breach of an express covenant to deliver possession at the beginning of the term is measured by the difference between the rent reserved and the actual rental value of the premises for the stipulated term, or, as it is sometimes expressed, the fair value of the use of the premises.[4] If there is no difference between the rental value of the premises for the term of the lease and the agreed rent, or if the latter exceeds the former, only nominal damages are recoverable by the lessee for a failure to receive possession.[5]

### § 8:5. —Right to Special Damages

Damages other than the difference between the rent reserved and the actual rental value of the leased premises for the term of the lease may be recovered for the landlord's breach of an express covenant to deliver pos-

---

3. Harris v Greenberger (AD2 1900) 50 AD 439, 64 NYS 136 (decided prior to Real Prop L § 223-a).

4. New York v Pike Realty Corp. (1928) 247 NY 245, 249, 160 NE 359; Dodds v Hakes (1889) 114 NY 260, 21 NE 398; Burkhard v Morris (AD4 1923) 206 AD 366, 201 NYS 225; Lieberman v Graf Realty Holding Co. (AD1 1916) 174 AD 774, 161 NYS 567; Schwartz v Minsker Realty Co. (AD1 1915) 166 AD 681, 152 NYS 70; Podalsky v Ireland (AD1 1910) 137 AD 257, 121 NYS 950, later app 146 AD 940, 131 NYS 1138, affd 210 NY 598, 104 NE 1138.

5. Lieberman v Graf Realty Holding Co. (AD1 1916) 174 AD 774, 161 NYS 567.

session at the beginning of the term. Such other damages, called special damages, may also be recovered, provided they are proximate in effect, are not speculative or uncertain in character, and were fairly within the contemplation of the parties when the lease had been made, or might have been foreseen as a consequence of the landlord's default in this regard.[6]

If the property is leased for a special purpose, which is known to the lessor, and possession cannot be delivered because of a prior lease to another party, or because of other fault of the lessor, the lessee may recover as damages his actual and necessary expenses incurred in preparing for the occupation of the property in the manner contemplated by the parties.[7] Thus, the actual expense paid or incurred by a tenant in the construction of the necessary fixtures to render the premises tenantable for the purposes for which they were leased are recoverable.[8] In reaching this conclusion the court pointed out that the loss of these expenditures could fairly be considered as naturally arising from the default of the landlord, because the tenant had been restricted by the lease in the use of the premises, and he could not underlet without the written consent of the landlord. If the tenant had deferred the work of preparing for the occupancy of the property until possession had been obtained, some portion of the term would have been practically lost before the necessary equipment for his business could have been furnished and made available. In other words, these expenses are generally recoverable as damages because they are proximate in effect, are not speculative or uncertain in character, and are fairly within the contemplation of the parties when the lease was made, or might have been foreseen as a consequence of the breach. However, where the reason for the rule does not apply to a particular situation, the rule will not be applied. Thus, in one case the court refused to allow damages for ordinary fixtures which were not particularly designed for the

---

6. Friedland v Myers (1893) 139 NY 432, 436, 34 NE 1055.
7. Friedland v Myers (1893) 139 NY 432, 34 NE 1055.
8. Friedland v Myers (1893) 139 NY 432, 34 NE 1055.

premises, and which could easily be obtained in the open market at any time without a day's delay.[9]

Similarly, where a tenant sought to recoup from his landlord the loss he sustained by being compelled to sell a perishable stock of goods which he had bought in anticipation of getting possession, such damages were disallowed.[10] Such advance purchase, the court held, could not have been within the contemplation of the parties, and was unnecessary in order for the tenant to get the full benefit of the term, as the market therefor was in the same city.[11]

Moving expenses incurred by a tenant are as a general rule recoverable as special damages.[12]

### § 8:6. —Right to Loss of Profits and Time

A tenant not yet in possession of leased premises may not recover profits which allegedly would have been earned from the business he intended to conduct on the leased premises if not for a breach by the landlord of his express covenant to deliver possession.[13] Presumably the courts so hold, because the probable profits of a business not in actual operation depend so much on the capacity of the party proposing to engage in it to conduct it successfully, and on so great a variety of circumstances which make for success or failure, that evidence of that character would be too speculative and remote.[14] Similarly, a tenant generally has been denied recovery for loss of time

---

9. Price v Eisen (AT 1900) 31 Misc 457, 64 NYS 405.

Also, see, Chansky v William Const. Co. (Atl 1913, Sup) 144 NYS 687, where court held that tenant could not recover as damages rent he had paid for an apartment in vicinity of store he rented, in anticipation of getting possession of such store, as not being within the contemplation of the parties.

10. Friedland v Myers (1893) 139 NY 432, 34 NE 1055.

11. However the court pointed out, "The rule might be different if he had been compelled to send to a distant market to make his purchase, and a long time must intervene before they could be delivered." Friedland v Myers (1893) 139 NY 432, 438, 34 NE 1055.

12. Burkhard v Morris (AD4 1923) 206 AD 366, 201 NYS 225.

13. Whitmier & Ferris Co. v Buffalo Structural Steel Corp. (1985) 66 NY2d 1013, 499 NYS2d 386, 489 NE2d 1288; Dodds v Hakes (1889) 114 NY 260, 21 NE 398; Shopwell Foods, Inc. v Parkway Village, Inc. (AD2 1951) 278 AD 671, 102 NYS2d 653; Kolodny v Schwartz (AD2 1950) 276 AD 930, 94 NYS2d 713 (summer rooming house); Williamson v Stevens (AD1 1903) 84 AD 518, 82 NYS 1047.

14. Smith v Feigin (AD1 1950) 276 AD 531, 96 NYS2d 123.

# POSSESSION OF PREMISES § 8:8

and expenses incurred by him in obtaining other premises.[15]

## § 8:7. Action to Recover Possession

Since the purpose of an action to recover possession (ejectment) is to enforce a right of entry, when it exists in real property, by a person who, having the right of possession, is excluded from it by another, a tenant who is being excluded from possession by a wrongful act of the landlord may bring such an action against him to gain possession.[16]

## § 8:8. Equitable Relief Against Landlord

As a general rule, a tenant who is aggrieved by a landlord's breach of covenant to deliver possession at the beginning of the term has full and adequate remedies at law.[17] Therefore, an equitable suit for a mandatory injunction or specific performance to compel a landlord to give him possession may not, as a general rule, be brought by a tenant.[18] But, where a tenant's remedy at law is defective, or its enforcement attended with doubt, or where it is shown that mere damages are not an adequate remedy,[19] a court of equity may intervene.[20] However, it must be emphasized that a mandatory injunction is rarely granted by the courts, and that a very strong case must be presented before a court of equity will grant such a drastic remedy.

---

**15.** Berkowitz v Iorizzo (AT1 1919) 106 Misc 489, 174 NYS 719; Shultz v Brenner (Co Ct 1898) 24 Misc 522, 53 NYS 972.

**16.** Golde Clothes Shop, Inc. v Loew's Buffalo Theatres, Inc. (1923) 236 NY 465, 141 NE 917, 30 ALR 931; Koenig v Eagle Waist Co. (AD1 1917) 176 AD 726, 163 NYS 1019; Smith v Revels (GT 1894) 79 Hun 213, 29 NYS 658; Du Barry Bags, Inc. v Deane (S Ct NY Co 1945) 58 NYS2d 808.

The common-law action for ejectment still survives in New York, and the common-law principles governing the ejectment action are unchanged unless explicitly modified by statute. Alleyne v Townsley (1985, 2d Dept) 110 AD2d 674, 487 NYS2d 600.

**17.** Koenig v Eagle Waist Co. (AD1 1917) 176 AD 726, 163 NYS 1019.

**18.** Rockefeller Purchasing Corp. v Rockefeller Center, Inc. (1936) 270 NY 447, 1 NE2d 842; Koenig v Eagle Waist Co. (AD1 1917) 176 AD 726, 163 NYS 1019.

Also, see Du Barry Bags, Inc. v Deane (S Ct NY Co 1945) 58 NYS2d 808, where a plaintiff-tenant in an action for a declaratory judgment to determine his right to possession, asked, as incidental relief, that the court require the then occupant of the demised premises to deliver possession to plaintiff, such relief was denied by the court.

**19.** See concurring opinion of O'Brien, P.J., in Goldman v Corn (AD1 1906) 111 AD 674, 97 NYS 926.

**20.** See Rein v Robert Metrick Co (S Ct Nassau Co 1951) 200 Misc 231, 105 NYS2d 160, where court granted rescission.

## § 8:9. Remedies for Inability to Get Full Possession

If a landlord wrongfully fails to deliver to his tenant at the beginning of the term possession of all that the letting calls for, the tenant has the right to refuse to take only part of the leased premises. He may rescind the lease, and recover damages for the landlord's breach of his undertaking. If, however, a tenant, knowing he cannot get possession of all the property, accepts possession of a portion of it, he is not put in that position through any wrongful act of the landlord. Having had the right of election to refuse to take a portion of the leased premises or to take the portion of which he can have possession, and having elected to take only a portion of the leased premises, he takes it only under his lease, and so obligates himself to comply with its terms. This makes him liable for the rent called for by the lease.[1] As McLaughlin, J., speaking for the Appellate Division, succinctly phrased it,[2] "A tenant, when called upon to pay rent, must do one of two things,—he must either pay the rent due, or else restore possession of the premises to the landlord. He cannot keep both the rent and the possession." The tenant is not prejudiced by this rule. Under decisional law he has the right to bring an action to have the rent apportioned, or to recover his damages arising from the landlord's failure to give him possession of the whole property as agreed, and if he is sued for nonpayment of the rent, or a proceeding to remove him from the property is based thereon, he may defend on the ground that he is entitled to an apportionment or to damages for the landlord's breach of the agreement. In this way the tenant's rights are fully protected.[3]

---

**1.** Carnegie Hall v Zysman (AD1 1933) 238 AD 515, 264 NYS 312; Smith v Barber (AD1 1904) 96 AD 236, 89 NYS 317; Forshaw v Hathaway (AT2 1920) 112 Misc 112, 115, 182 NYS 646, 648.

The defense of partial eviction is not applicable to such a situation. Webb & Knapp, Inc. v Churchill's Terminal Restaurant, Inc. (1956, 1st Dept) 2 AD2d 332, 155 NYS2d 588.

Where tenant occupied premises and paid rent for 26 months before vacating them, at no time objecting to landlord's failure to make the installations which the lease provided landlord was obligated to make before the lease commenced, and as a condition precedent to duties under said lease, or requesting that they be made, tenant waived the condition and landlord's obligation thereunder, and was liable for the rent. Silverstein v Empire State Shoe Co. (1964, 3d Dept) 20 AD2d 735, 246 NYS2d 832.

**2.** Douglas v Chesebrough Bldg. Co. (AD1 1900) 56 AD 403, 67 NYS 755.

**3.** Duhain v Mermod, Jaccard & King Jewelry Co. (1914) 211 NY 364, 105 NE 657; Carnegie Hall v Zysman

However, if the tenant takes possession of the part offered to him in reliance on the landlord's promise to oust the person in occupation, and promptly vacates from such part as soon as he learns of the landlord's failure or inability to do so, such possession will not be deemed a waiver of the tenant's right to rescind.[4]

### § 8:10. Remedies Against Third Persons

If a tenant cannot enter into physical possession of the leased premises because they are occupied by one who has no title or right thereto, the tenant may bring an action against the wrongdoer to recover possession (ejectment).[5] Notice to quit is unnecessary to maintain an ejectment action against a tenant who wrongfully holds over after expiration of a fixed and definite term.[6] The tenant excluded from possession may sue the wrongdoer for damages.[7] The damages recoverable against a former tenant who fails to vacate at the expiration of his term were held to be limited to items that the parties had reason to foresee. Denied, were loss of income; legal expenses incurred in connection with the holding over; salary of maid, which tenant felt morally obligated to pay; expenses incident to placing cat in a kennel; and taxi fares to the premises to pick up mail. Granted, was money expended for removal of furniture to the warehouse for storage.[8] The excluded tenant also may bring summary proceedings to recover possession.[9] The statute provides,[10] that a tenant may be removed from possession by a special proceeding when he continues in possession of any portion of the premises after the expiration of his term without the permission of the landlord or, in a case where a new lessee is entitled to possession, without the permission of the new lessee. This statute completely

---

(AD1 1933) 238 AD 515, 264 NYS 312; Smith v Barber (AD1 1904) 96 AD 236, 89 NYS 317; Forshaw v Hathaway (AT2 1920) 112 Misc 112, 182 NYS 646.

4. Sullivan v Schmitt (AD2 1904) 93 AD 469, 87 NYS 714.

5. Fong Ling v Nathans (AD2 1922) 204 AD 265, 197 NYS 461; Gardner v Keteltas (1842) 3 Hill 330.

6. Alleyne v Townsley (1985, 2d Dept) 110 AD2d 674, 487 NYS2d 600.

7. Nodine v State (Ct of Claims 1948) 192 Misc 572, 79 NYS2d 834.

8. Schreiber v Kleban (NYC Civ Ct NY Co 1970) 63 Misc 2d 628, 312 NYS2d 1007.

9. Summary proceedings are discussed in Chapters 29, et seq, infra.

10. Real Prop Act & Proc L § 711(1).

abrogates prior decisional law[11] which held that the new tenant in this situation could not bring summary proceedings to oust the holdover tenant from possession.

### § 8:11. Form of Covenant to Deliver Possession

An express covenant to deliver possession is necessary as a foundation for the recovery of damages.[12]

## FORM NO. 6
### Form of Covenant to Deliver Actual Possession*

Landlord hereby agrees to deliver to Tenant actual physical possession of the leased premises at the commencement of the term granted herein.

### § 8:12. Form of Provision to Protect Landlord Against Inability to Deliver Possession

Frequently, when a building is in the process of construction, or when repairs are being made to the leased premises, the landlord is desirous of protecting himself against the results of delay and of the inability to deliver to the tenant possession at the time fixed for the commencement of the term. The following clauses are found in many leases today to protect the landlord in such and like instances.

## FORM NO. 7
### Provision Protecting Landlord against Inability to Deliver Possession

If Landlord is unable to give possession of the leased premises on the date of the commencement of the term hereof, because of the holding-over or retention of possession of any tenant, undertenant or occupants, or if the premises are located in a building being constructed, because such building has not been sufficiently completed to make the premises ready for occupancy or because of the fact that a certificate of occupancy has not been procured or if Landlord has not completed any work required to be performed by Landlord or for any other reason, Landlord shall not be subject to any liability for failure to give possession on said date and the validity of

---

11. Eells v Morse (1913) 208 NY 103, 106, 101 NE 803.

12. See § 8:3, supra.

* For complete form of lease see Chapter 21.

## POSSESSION OF PREMISES  § 8:12

the lease shall not be impaired under such circumstances, nor shall the same be construed in any wise to extend the term of this lease, but the rent payable hereunder shall be abated (provided Tenant is not responsible for the inability to obtain possession) until after Landlord shall have given Tenant written notice that the premises are substantially ready for Tenant's occupancy. If permission is given to Tenant to enter into the possession of the leased premises or to occupy premises other than the leased premises prior to the date specified as the commencement of the term of this lease, Tenant covenants and agrees that such occupancy shall be deemed to be under all the terms, covenants, conditions and provisions of this lease, except as to the covenant to pay rent. The provisions of this article are intended to constitute "an express provision to the contrary" within the meaning of Section 223-a of the New York Real Property Law.[13]

*Tenant may wish to substitute the following clause:*

If possession of the leased premises is not given, or the leased premises are not available for occupancy by Tenant on or before ........, anything in this lease contained to the contrary notwithstanding, this lease and the term and estate hereby granted may be terminated by Tenant by giving written notice of such termination to

---

13. Under a provision exculpating landlord from liability where its failure to give possession is due to the incompletion of a building under construction, and providing that the lease was to remain effective, and postponing payment of rent until possession was actually delivered, it was held that such a provision, if strictly enforced, would cause extreme hardship and the most undesirable results; that the law in such cases properly engrafts a rule of reason upon such provisions so that they do not, contrary to the intention of the parties, become arbitrary and unreasonable, and therefore, that implicit in this exculpation is a promise to deliver possession on the date fixed by the lease or within a reasonable time thereafter unless factors beyond the landlord's control make that event impossible. Therefore, since more than 8 months had elapsed from the occupancy date fixed by the lease (⅛th of the leased term), and the landlord had failed to establish the existence of mitigating circumstance, or that the factors causing the delay were beyond his control, the tenant was entitled to recover the one month's rent and security he had paid upon signing the lease. Hartwig v 6465 Realty Co (AD1 1971) 67 Misc 2d 450, 324 NYS2d 567; Seabrook v Commuter Housing Co. (NYC Civ Ct Queens Co 1972) 72 Misc 2d 6, 338 NYS2d 67, affd (AT2) 79 Misc 2d 168, 363 NYS2d 566.

The provision in these cases did not, as the provision in the text, contain the clause that the provisions of this article are intended to constitute an express provision to the contrary within the meaning of Real Prop L § 223-a. It remains to be seen, therefore, whether or not the courts will decide differently when presented with such a clause.

§ 8:12

Landlord on or before ........, by certified mail addressed to Landlord at its address hereinabove set forth, and thereupon this lease and the term and estate hereby granted shall terminate on the date of the giving of such notice with the same effect as if such date were the date herein specified for the expiration of the term of this lease, and thereupon neither party hereto shall be under any further obligation hereunder to the other, except, however, that Landlord shall return to Tenant the first monthly installment of rent as well as any other moneys paid by Tenant upon the execution of this lease.

### § 8:13. Tenant's Obligation to Occupy

As soon as a lease is made and delivered to the lessee, the lessee thereupon becomes the owner of the leased premises for the term reserved. He thereby acquires the legal right to possession. He may or may not occupy the premises, as he pleases,[14] and he is under no obligation, in the absence of a specific provision therefor, to occupy or use, or continue to use, the leased premises, even though one of the parties, or both, expected and intended that they would be used for the particular purpose to which they seemed to be adapted or constructed.[15] As was said

---

14. Becar v Flues (1876) 64 NY 518; Hellenberg v Schmidt (AT 1913) 81 Misc 157, 142 NYS 330; Dodd v Hart (AT 1910) 30 Misc 459, 62 NYS 484; See, also, P. & R. Realty Corp. v Hagel (M Ct Man 1948) 191 Misc 732, 79 NYS2d 536; Copper v Fretnoransky (1892, CP Ct GT) 16 NYS 866.

Where operator of a food market in a shopping center notified landlord 2½ years after the commencement of a 15-year lease that it intended to vacate the premises, and to continue paying the rent (an annual fixed rent plus 1% of gross annual sales in excess of a specified amount) until landlord relet the premises, landlord was denied specific performance to compel tenant to occupy the premises, even though there would be a loss to the other tenants in the shopping center if the food market were vacant, since specific performance would require judicial supervision over a long period of time. Grossman v Wegman's Food Markets, Inc. (1973, 4th Dept) 43 AD2d 813, 350 NYS2d 484.

The conduct of an execution sale on leased premises of tenant's personal property does not constitute an "occupation" of the premises. Alex & Gregory, Inc. v Nick La Vista's Glen Cove Service Station, Inc. (S Ct Nassau Co 1984) 124 Misc 2d 257, 475 NYS2d 1015.

15. Burdick v Fuller (AD3 1921) 199 AD 94, 191 NYS 442.

Where the leased premises on the commencement of the term were infested with roaches, sufficiently seriously to constitute a constructive eviction, the tenant was not obligated to move in and then immediately move out. He therefore was under no obligation to take possession, Ianacci v Pendis (Civ Ct Queens Co 1970) 64 Misc 2d 178, 315 NYS2d 399 (tenant also was entitled to the return of his security money); Mayers v Kugelman (Dist Ct Suffolk Co 1975) 81 Misc 2d 998, 367 NYS2d 144.

in an early case,[16] "By no express or implied terms of the demise was the tenant obliged to occupy the premises. His engagement was not to occupy them, but to pay rent for them; and the engagement of the landlord was that he might, not must, occupy them. Indisputably the tenant was free to leave the premises at will."[17]

But, whether or not he occupies the leased premises, he must, in any event, pay the rent, which is the purchase price of the estate in the land thus acquired.[18]

However, there is no law which requires a landlord to hunt up his tenant, and ask him to go into possession of the premises, before he can claim the rent which his tenant has agreed to pay. It is the duty of the tenant to demand possession of the premises at the premises.[19]

### § 8:14. Research References

In addition to the preceding text, the reader is also referred to the following:

49 Am Jur 2d, Landlord and Tenant §§ 216-225.

New York Jur 2d, Landlord and Tenant (1st ed §§ 125-130).

New York CLS Real Property Law § 223-a.

New York Forms, Leases, Forms 8:141-8:145.

Index to Annotations, Landlord and Tenant.

16. Copper v Fretnoransky (1892, CP Ct GT) 16 NYS 866.

17. In the absence of a continuous use clause, a provision in a lease, even a shopping center lease, that tenant covenants and agrees to use the leased premises for a specified purpose, does not obligate tenant to remain open for business during the term of the lease. Fay's Drug Co. v Geneva Plaza Associates (1983, 4th Dept) 98 AD2d 978, 470 NYS2d 240, affd 62 NY2d 886, 478 NYS2d 867, 467 NE2d 531 (observing that other jurisdictions have construed continuous use clauses as requiring tenant to remain open for business; however, the lease in this case would not be so construed, since it contained no percentage rental clause; the subject premises were the smallest of the 3 stores in the shopping center; there was no evidence that the tenant's store served as a magnet for the other 2 stores; and landlord suffered no damage as a result of tenant's closing the leased premises).

18. Becar v Flues (1876) 64 NY 518; Darob Holding Co v House of Pile Fabrics, Inc (Civ Ct NY Co 1970) 62 Misc 2d 899, 310 NYS2d 418 (citing text).

See, also, P. & R. Realty Corp. v Hagel (M Ct Man 1948) 191 Misc 732, 79 NYS2d 536; 59 Madison Ave. Corp. v Bauer (M Ct Bronx 1958) 15 Misc 2d 780, 180 NYS2d 1013.

**Annotation:** Liability of lessee who refuses to take possession under executed lease or executory agreement to lease, 85 ALR3d 514.

19. Millie Iron-Min. Co. v Thalman (AD1 1898) 34 AD 281, 54 NYS 276.

§ 8:14 LANDLORD AND TENANT

**VERALEX®:** Cases and annotations referred to herein can be further researched through the VERALEX electronic retrieval system's two services, **Auto-Cite®** and **SHOWME®**. Use Auto-Cite to check citations for form, parallel references, prior and later history, and annotation references. Use SHOWME to display the full text of cases and annotations.

# CHAPTER 9

# ASSIGNMENT AND SUBLETTING

A. IN GENERAL
§ 9:1. Scope of Chapter
§ 9:2. Assignment and Sublease Defined
§ 9:3. Requisites of Assignment

B. DISTINGUISHING BETWEEN ASSIGNMENT AND SUBLEASE
§ 9:4. Fundamental Test
§ 9:5. Pro Tanto Assignment and Sublease
§ 9:6. —Illustrations of Pro Tanto Assignment
§ 9:7. —Determination of Rent Payable Under Pro Tanto Assignment
§ 9:8. Materiality of Name or Form of Instrument
§ 9:9. Effect of Right of Re-entry
§ 9:10. Effect of Different Rental or Terms
§ 9:11. Effect of Transfer for Period Exceeding Tenant's Term
§ 9:12. Effect of Covenant to Surrender at End of Term
§ 9:13. Explanation of Suggestion that Assignment be Treated as Sublease in Certain Situations
§ 9:14. Distinction Between Assignment and Sublease Summarized
§ 9:15. Importance of Distinguishing Between Assignment and Sublease

C. PRESUMPTION OF ASSIGNMENT
§ 9:16. From Possession by Stranger
§ 9:17. From Payment of Rent by Stranger
§ 9:18. Overcoming Presumption

D. ASSIGNOR'S LIABILITY
§ 9:19. Importance of Privity of Contract and Privity of Estate
§ 9:20. Assignor's Liability on Express Covenants
§ 9:21. Ineffective Termination of Assignor's Liability
§ 9:22. Effective Termination of Assignor's Liability
§ 9:23. Form of Clause Consenting to Assignment with Release of Tenant

E. NON-ASSUMING ASSIGNEE'S LIABILITY
§ 9:24. Nature of Problem

## LANDLORD AND TENANT

§ 9:25. Liability on Covenants Running with Land
§ 9:26. Liability on Covenant to Pay Rent
§ 9:27. Liability on Covenant to Pay Taxes
§ 9:28. Liability on Pro Tanto Assignment
§ 9:29. Liability Where Assignment in Violation of Lease Restriction
§ 9:30. Termination of Non-assuming Assignee's Liability
§ 9:31. —Effect of Termination
§ 9:32. —Requisites of Bona Fide Assignment
§ 9:33. —Necessity of Consideration; Motive for Assignment
§ 9:34. Liability as Between Non-assuming Assignee and Assignor

F. ASSUMING ASSIGNEE'S LIABILITY

§ 9:35. Definition of "Assumption"
§ 9:36. Scope and Extent of Liability
§ 9:37. —Illustrations
§ 9:38. Landlord's Right to Enforce Assumption Agreement
§ 9:39. Requirements of Assumption Agreement
§ 9:40. —Illustrations
§ 9:41. Form of Assignment with Assumption Agreement
§ 9:42. Liability as Between Assuming Assignee and Assignor

G. ASSIGNEE'S RIGHTS

§ 9:43. Generally

H. LIABILITY OF TENANT'S ASSIGNEE FOR BENEFIT OF CREDITORS

§ 9:44. Generally
§ 9:45. What Constitutes Acceptance of Lease by Assignee for Benefit of Creditors
§ 9:46. Scope of Liability
§ 9:47. Summary of Liability
§ 9:48. Terminating Liability
§ 9:49. —Illustration
§ 9:50. Liability on Lease Not Accepted
§ 9:51. Valuation of Use and Occupation by Assignee

I. SURVIVAL OF DECEASED TENANT'S LIABILITY

§ 9:52. Generally
§ 9:53. Nature of Liability of Personal Representative
§ 9:54. —Illustration

J. SECURITY DEPOSITS

§ 9:55. Effect of Assignment of Lease on Security Deposit
§ 9:56. Effect of Mortgage on Lease on Security Deposit

K. SUBTENANT'S LIABILITIES AND RIGHTS

§ 9:57. Form of Sublease

ASSIGNMENT AND SUBLETTING

§ 9:58. Liability to Paramount Landlord
§ 9:59. Liability to Sublessor
§ 9:60. Rights Limited by Terms of Paramount Lease
§ 9:61. Right to Perform Paramount Lease
§ 9:62. —Illustration
§ 9:63. Right to Compel Sublessor's Performance of Paramount Lease
§ 9:64. Form of Agreement Permitting Subtenant to Remedy Sublessor's Default
§ 9:65. Right to Contest Summary Proceedings Brought Against Sublessor
§ 9:66. Rights on New Lease to Sublessor

L. SUBTENANT'S RIGHTS ON CANCELLATION OF PARAMOUNT LEASE

§ 9:67. Right to Vacate
§ 9:68. Effect of Subtenant's Failure to Vacate on Cancellation of Paramount Lease
§ 9:69. Right to Possession
§ 9:70. Effect of Assignment of Sublease After Cancellation of Paramount Lease
§ 9:71. Right to Vacate on Threat of Cancellation
§ 9:72. Summary of Rights

M. SUBTENANT'S RIGHTS ON VOLUNTARY SURRENDER OF PARAMOUNT LEASE

§ 9:73. Generally
§ 9:74. Illustrative Cases

N. RIGHT TO ASSIGN AND SUBLET

§ 9:75. Generally
§ 9:76. Effect of Personal Relationship
§ 9:77. Effect of Emergency Rent Laws
§ 9:78. Residential Tenant's Statutory Right to Assign
§ 9:79. Residential Tenant's Statutory Right to Sublet
§ 9:80. Mobile Home Tenant's Statutory Right to Assign and Sublet
§ 9:81. Form of Agreement to Assign Proprietary Lease (Co-operative Ownership)
§ 9:82. Form of Assignment of Proprietary (Co-operative Apartment) Lease

O. RESTRICTIONS ON RIGHT TO ASSIGN AND SUBLET

§ 9:83. Restrictions Not Favored by Courts
§ 9:84. Covenant Restricting Assignment and Subletting in Proprietary Leases (Co-operative Ownership)
§ 9:85. Effect of Consent or Waiver on Covenant Restricting Assignment
§ 9:86. Effect of Consent or Waiver on Covenant Restricting Subletting

§ 9:87. Effect of Emergency Rent Laws on Restrictions
§ 9:88. Statutory Modification of Restrictions Because of Race or Color
§ 9:89. Breach of Restriction; Voluntary Acts of Tenant
§ 9:90. —Operation of Law
§ 9:91. —Sale by Judicial Officer
§ 9:92. —Bankruptcy
§ 9:93. —Assignment for Benefit of Creditors
§ 9:94. —Acts of Personal Representatives of Deceased Tenant
§ 9:95. Form of Clauses Restricting Assignment and Subletting
§ 9:96. Right of Landlord to Withhold Consent
§ 9:97. Contractual Modification of Right to Withhold Consent
§ 9:98. Criteria for Determination of Reasonableness
§ 9:99. Statutory Modification of Right to Withhold Consent in Case of a Deceased Residential Tenant
§ 9:100. Tenant's Remedies for Landlord's Breach of Covenant to Consent
§ 9:101. Landlord's Remedies for Breach of Restriction Against Assignment or Subletting
§ 9:102. —Equitable Relief
§ 9:103. —Damages

P. RESEARCH REFERENCES
§ 9:104. Generally

## A. IN GENERAL

### § 9:1. Scope of Chapter

After a tenant has taken possession, he may desire to permit someone to occupy part of his leased premises; or, he may desire to turn the premises over to someone else. If during the term the tenant dies, or becomes insolvent, someone other than the tenant may take over the possession. Or, the landlord may convey his fee.

All of these supposed events create practical problems of rights and liabilities. These problems rather naturally fall into three divisions. At the outset, the legal nature of the particular transaction must be determined. Having determined this, an analysis of the resulting rights and liabilities of the respective parties to the situation involved must then be made. Finally, having determined the legal nature of the transaction, consideration must be given to the rights of the parties to enter into the transaction.

These problems will be considered in that order in the following sections.

ASSIGNMENT AND SUBLETTING § 9:3

The effect of a transfer of the reversion on the rights and obligations of the grantor and grantee, and on rent due or to become due, has been discussed in an earlier chapter.[1]

### § 9:2. Assignment and Sublease Defined

An assignment of a lease is a transfer by a tenant of his *entire* estate or interest in the whole, or in a part, of the leased premises. However, a sublease is a transfer by a tenant of only *part* of his estate or interest in the whole, or in a part, of the leased premises, with the reservation unto himself of a reversionary interest in the leasehold estate.[2] The essential attribute of an assignment is the yielding of the exclusive possession and control of the leased premises to another without any reversionary provision.[3]

### § 9:3. Requisites of Assignment

To constitute a valid assignment of a lease, no particular form need be followed,[4] and it may be by voluntary act of the parties,[5] or by operation of law.[6] However, an estate or interest in real property, other than a lease for a term not exceeding one year, cannot be assigned, unless by operation of law, or by a deed or conveyance in writing subscribed by the person assigning the interest or by his lawful agent thereunto authorized by writing.[7] In

---

1. Chapter 5, supra.
2. New Amsterdam Casualty Co. v National Union Fire Ins. Co. (1935) 266 NY 254, 194 NE 745, 99 ALR 216; Stewart v Long I. R. Co. (1886) 102 NY 601, 8 NE 200, 203; Lomax Holding Co. v Calitri (AT1 1983) 117 Misc 2d 941, 461 NYS2d 152 (citing text).
3. Mann Theatres Corp. v Mid-Island Shopping Plaza Co. (1983, 2d Dept) 94 AD2d 466, 464 NYS2d 793, affd 62 NY2d 930, 479 NYS2d 213, 468 NE2d 51; Mann Theatres Corp. v Mid-Island Shopping Plaza Co. (1984) 62 NY2d 930, 479 NYS2d 213, 468 NE2d 51.
4. See § 9:4, infra.
5. See § 9:75, infra.
6. See §§ 9:90, et seq., infra.
7. Gen Obligations L § 5-703. See § 2:34, supra.

Gen Oblig L § 5-703, subd 2, provides that a contract for the leasing for a longer period than one year, or for the sale, of any real property, or any interest therein, is void, unless the contract or some note or memorandum thereof, expressing the consideration, is in writing, subscribed by the party to be charged or by his lawful agent thereunto authorized by writing. Therefore, an oral contract involving the sale of a lease having over 7 years to run is void. Lippe v Fink (AD2 1931) 233 AD 754, 250 NYS 763, affd 257 NY 577, 178 NE 802.

An agreement for the sale and transfer of shares in a co-op corporation, and for the assignment and assumption of the apartment lease based thereon, which is signed by the proposed purchaser, but not by the leaseholder-shareholder, nor by the

other words, an oral assignment of a lease with an unexpired term in excess of one year, is invalid;[8] but, if the unexpired term of the lease being assigned does not exceed one year, it may be assigned orally.[9] However, it has been held that an occupant may be held liable, as an assignee, for rent accruing while he was in possession though the assignment was oral, and in violation of the Statute of Frauds.[10]

As is the general rule, part performance may take the transaction out of the operation of the statute of frauds.[11]

If the unexpired term of an assigned leasehold exceeds 3 years, the assignment thereof may be recorded.[12] However, a failure to record will not affect the relationship between the assignor and assignee. But it may be necessary to record the assignment as against third persons.[13]

To make an assignment effective, it is not necessary that the assignee go into actual possession. But, to constitute a complete and valid assignment, a delivery and acceptance of the assignment are essential.[14]

## B. DISTINGUISHING BETWEEN ASSIGNMENT AND SUBLEASE

### § 9:4. Fundamental Test

"The distinction between a sublease and an assignment of the original lease," it was said in a leading case,[15] "has been the cause of much discussion, and of some apparent, rather than real, difference of opinion. It is quite well settled however that it is immaterial what form of instrument is used, or whether on its face it purports to be a sublease or merely the assignment of a lease. The essen-

co-op corporation, is unenforceable as in violation of Gen Oblig L § 5-703, subd 2. Frank v Rubin (S Ct NY Co 1969) 59 Misc 2d 796, 300 NYS2d 273.

8. Klampert v Hirsch (1923, Sup App T) 202 NYS 266; Moskowitz v Eastern Brewing Co. (1909, Sup App T) 117 NYS 1017.

9. Grauer v Rudingsky (1908, Sup App T) 111 NYS 530.

10. Carter & Carter v Hammett & Balch (1851) 12 Barb 253, affd 18 Barb 608.

As Crane, J, said in Mann v Ferdinand Munch Brewery (1919) 225 NY 189, 193, 121 NE 746, in citing this case, "A person in possession who holds himself out to the landlord as assignee is estopped from denying the assignment or objecting that the assignment was not in writing."

11. See § 2:37, supra.

12. Real Prop L §§ 290, subd 3, and 291

13. As to recording, see §§ 1:7 et seq, supra.

14. Lynch v Joseph (AD4 1930) 228 AD 367, 240 NYS 176.

15. Herzig v Blumenkrohn (AD1 1907) 122 AD 756, 107 NYS 570.

# ASSIGNMENT AND SUBLETTING § 9:6

tial distinction between a sublease and an assignment lies in the extent to which the original lessee has parted with his interest. If he has parted with his entire interest, he has made an assignment. If he has retained a reversion in himself, he has made a sublease."[16]

In other words, fundamentally the distinction between an assignment and a sublease depends solely upon the quantity of the interest or estate which passes, and does not depend upon the *physical quantity* of the premises transferred. If the tenant transfers his entire interest in the leased premises, and reserves no reversionary interest therein, he makes an assignment of his lease. If the tenant does not transfer his entire interest, but retains a reversionary interest, however small, he makes a sublease.

### § 9:5. Pro Tanto Assignment and Sublease

When a tenant transfers his entire estate or interest in only part of the leased premises, reserving no reversionary interest in that part, he makes a pro tanto assignment of the lease. It is not a sublease.[17]

The physical quantity of the premises transferred does not affect the nature of the transaction as an assignment if the entire estate of the tenant is transferred.[18] "If a lessee has two houses," said Dwight, C.,[19] "embraced in one lease at an entire rent and sells all his interest in one of the houses, this is an assignment pro tanto, and not a subletting."

### § 9:6. —Illustrations of Pro Tanto Assignment

In a leading case,[20] the owner of a building had leased two floors therein to a tenant. The tenant by a written instrument, in form a sublease, "sublet" part of one of the floors to the defendant for the entire balance of the tenant's term. The tenant did not retain any reversionary

---

16. Also, see, New Amsterdam Casualty Co. v National Union Fire Ins. Co. (1935) 266 NY 254, 258, 194 NE 745, 99 ALR 216; Bokhara Realty Corp. v Barton's Bonbonniere, Inc. (AT1 1959) 19 Misc 2d 1086, 189 NYS2d 255.

17. New Amsterdam Casualty Co. v National Union Fire Ins. Co. (1935) 266 NY 254, 194 NE 745, 99 ALR 216; Woodhull v Rosenthal (1875) 61 NY 382.

18. See § 9:4, supra.

19. Woodhull v Rosenthal (1875) 61 NY 382, 391.

20. New Amsterdam Casualty Co. v National Union Fire Ins. Co. (1935) 266 NY 254, 194 NE 745, 99 ALR 216.

interest in the part of the premises "sublet" to defendant. Thereafter, the tenant vacated from the remaining part of the premises. The owner of the building, contending that the defendant was an assignee pro tanto of the tenant who had vacated, brought suit against defendant to recover the rent reserved in the "sublease" for that portion of the floor rented to him. "The primary question with which we are concerned on this appeal," said Hubbs, J.,[21] "is whether a lessee by transferring a portion of the premises which he holds under an original lease to a third party for the entire balance of his term thereby makes an assignment pro tanto of the original lease or a sublease." After reviewing the cases dealing with the subject, the court affirmed a judgment for the rent in favor of the owner of the building, and squarely held that an assignment by a tenant of a part of the leased premises for the entire remainder of his term, without the retention of any reversionary interest therein, as was the situation in this case, is an assignment pro tanto of his lease, and is not a sublease.

In another case,[1] plaintiffs were tenants of a store. They executed an instrument to defendant which purported to "sublet" for the entire balance of their term the entire store with the exception of a space of 10 feet by 10 feet in the rear of the store. Subsequently they sued defendant for failure to pay the rent reserved, and were met with the defense that the rent had been paid by defendant to the paramount landlord, that is, plaintiffs' landlord. The court upheld this defense, on the ground that the transaction was an assignment pro tanto as between plaintiffs and their landlord, which gave their landlord a right of action against the assignee, the defendant, for rent. "The landlord having demanded the rent of defendant," said the court, "the latter paid it, and thus has a defense to the present action, which is brought by plaintiffs for the same rent."

Where a tenant of a building under a lease expiring April 29, 1944, "leased" part of that building to another under a lease expiring April 30, 1944, this latter "lease"

---

21. 266 NY at p 257.
1. Dreyfuss v Phillips (1910, Sup App T) 121 NYS 378.

# ASSIGNMENT AND SUBLETTING § 9:8

was held to be an assignment pro tanto of the original lease.[2]

## § 9:7. —Determination of Rent Payable Under Pro Tanto Assignment

If no rent is reserved in an assignment pro tanto, the rule laid down by the Court of Appeals[3] applies: "When the demised premises are held by divers assignees of the term in several parts, the rent, which is a common charge upon all the parts, may be apportioned amongst them according to the extent of their several shares."

## § 9:8. Materiality of Name or Form of Instrument

Even though an instrument takes the form of a sublease; even though the parties may call the transaction a sublease and refer to each other as sublessor and sublessee; yet, the fact remains that if the tenant transfers his entire estate without retaining any reversionary interest, the transaction is an assignment of the lease.[4] The importance of looking to the nature of the transaction, instead of relying merely on the form of the instrument, or the names attached to it by the parties thereto, may be illustrated by the following case. In this case, a tenant had executed two irrevocable powers of attorney to a third party; one, to carry on his business; and the other, to "hold, sell, assign or surrender" any interest he might have in his lease to the premises in which his business was located. Thereafter the tenant withdrew from the business and took no part in it whatsoever. The tenant, it is to be noted, had inserted in these powers of attorney a statement that no assignment of the lease was to be deemed made thereby. The court, nevertheless, held that the tenant had assigned his lease, and had used this device merely as a cunning attempt to circumvent the prohibition in his lease against assigning the lease without the landlord's consent. (As a matter of fact it was

---

2. D. A. Schulte, Inc. v Loft, Inc. (1936) 271 NY 420, 3 NE2d 578, reh den 272 NY 535, 4 NE2d 436.

3. Damainville v Mann (1865) 32 NY 197, 205.

4. New Amsterdam Casualty Co. v National Union Fire Ins. Co. (1935) 266 NY 254, 194 NE 745, 99 ALR 216; Stewart v Long I. R. Co. (1886) 102 NY 601, 608, 8 NE 200, 203; Gilbert v Van Kleeck (AD3 1954) 284 AD 611, 132 NYS2d 580, motion to modify den 284 AD 857, 134 NYS2d 193 and app dismd 308 NY 882, 126 NE2d 383, motion den 308 NY 1045, 127 NE2d 873; Bokhara Realty Corp. v Barton's Bonbonniere, Inc. (AT1 1959) 19 Misc 2d 1086, 189 NYS2d 255.

shown at the trial that prior to these transactions the tenant had asked the landlord for consent to an assignment on several occasions, and the landlord refused.) The court pointed out, "Under the power O'Brien (the third party) was not only authorized to sell and assign the lease, but 'to hold' plaintiff's (tenant's) interest therein, and this irrevocably, and possession was surrendered to him. I cannot see that this left any reversion in plaintiff."[5]

### § 9:9. Effect of Right of Re-entry

Under the Estates, Powers and Trusts Law, a right of re-entry, or "right of reacquisition," as it is now termed,[6] is a future estate left in the creator or in his successors in interest upon the simultaneous creation of an estate on a condition subsequent.[7] Since the right of reacquisition is a future estate, it is a reversionary interest, which is descindible, devisable, and alienable, in the same manner as an estate in possession.[8] It would seem, then, when a tenant transfers his lease, and reserves a right to re-enter for breach of a specified condition or covenant, the transfer is a sublease.[9]

### § 9:10. Effect of Different Rental or Terms

When a tenant leases his premises to another for the entire remainder of his term at a rental different from his, or upon terms different from those contained in his original lease, the question arises whether such a transaction should be considered a sublease because of the new terms or the different rental reserved in the new agreement.

It is well settled that neither new terms, nor a different

---

5. Glendening v Western Union Tel. Co. (AD1 1914) 163 AD 489, 148 NYS 552.

6. Since the provision was intended to apply to personal property as well as real property, it was deemed more appropriate to use "reacquisition," instead of "re-entry," to refer thereto.

7. EPTL 6-4.6.

8. EPTL 6-5.1.

9. *Contra:* Gillette Bros., Inc. v Aristocrat Restaurant, Inc. (1924) 239 NY 87, 145 NE 748. Gilbert v Van Kleeck (AD3 1954) 284 AD 611, 132 NYS2d 580, motion to modify den 284 AD 857, 134 NYS2d 193 and app dismd 308 NY 882, 126 NE2d 383, motion den 308 NY 1045, 127 NE2d 873.

But, it must be observed that when these decisions were rendered, a right of re-entry was not a reversionary interest, but merely a chose in action; that is, a right or power to terminate the estate granted, and to retake it. Upington v Corrigan (1896) 151 NY 143, 45 NE 359. These contrary decisions can no longer be accepted as valid precedents.

rental reserved in the new agreement will make the transaction a sublease if the tenant has transferred his entire interest or estate in the leasehold. Neither the new terms, nor the different rental, constitute a reversionary interest.[10]

### § 9:11. Effect of Transfer for Period Exceeding Tenant's Term

If a tenant should lease his premises to another for a period exceeding his own term, such a transaction is an assignment of the lease.[11]

Clearly the tenant has parted with his entire estate or interest in the leasehold. For example, a tenant of a five-year term leases his premises to another for seven years. The tenant has assigned his lease.

Such an assignment is not void because the tenant has conveyed for a period exceeding his own term. Such an assignment will merely pass to the assignee such estate or interest which the tenant can lawfully convey.[12]

### § 9:12. Effect of Covenant to Surrender at End of Term

Many leases provide for a forfeiture thereof should the tenant assign his lease without the landlord's consent. "In the desire to avoid forfeitures," said Scott, J.,[13] "the courts have been astute to discover in instruments asserted to be assignments features which implied some reservation sufficient to justify a finding that the original lessee had reserved to himself some portion of the term. Thus, when the instrument, although it disposed of the whole term, contained a covenant on the part of the second lessee to surrender to the original lessee on the last day of the term, it was considered that there had been reserved a reversion of a part of the last day of the term, and hence the instrument was deemed a sublease, and not an assignment."

In other words by requiring a surrender on the part of

---

10. Stewart v Long I. R. Co. (1886) 102 NY 601, 611, 612, 8 NE 200, 203.

11. Stewart v Long I. R. Co. (1886) 102 NY 601, 608, 8 NE 200, 203.

12. Real Prop L § 247 provides: A conveyance made by a tenant for life or years, of a greater estate than he possesses, or can lawfully convey, does not work a forfeiture of his estate, but passes to the grantee all the title, estate or interest which such tenant can lawfully convey.

13. Herzig v Blumenkrohn (AD1 1907) 122 AD 756, 107 NYS 570.

the new tenant to the old tenant at some time on the last day of the term of the original lease, the old tenant reserved to himself some fragment of the original term, though almost inappreciable in point of duration. This right to possession on the part of the old tenant on the last day of the term leaves a fragment of that last day of the term in him, and is sufficient to constitute the retention of a reversionary interest.[14] And, the retention of a reversionary interest, no matter how small, makes the transaction a sublease.

However, when the instrument provides that the new tenant will at the end of the term quit and surrender the premises in good condition, and further provides that the term shall end simultaneously with the term of the original lease; then, since the original tenant's term ends simultaneously with the term of the new tenant, the latter cannot surrender to the former, but to whoever is entitled thereto, that is, the paramount landlord. Therefore, in this transaction the original tenant has parted with his entire estate in the leasehold; he has reserved no reversionary interest therein; and the transaction constitutes an assignment.[15]

### § 9:13. Explanation of Suggestion that Assignment be Treated as Sublease in Certain Situations

Some confusion, and an anomalous situation have resulted from the suggestion made by the Court of Appeals in an early case[16] that an assignment of a lease should be treated as an assignment whenever the question arises between the paramount landlord and the transferee of the tenant, but that at the same time it should be treated also as a sublease, if the parties so intend, when the question arises between the tenant and his transferee. The court said, by Rapallo, J., "Where a lessee of land leases the same land to a third party, the question has often arisen whether the second lease is in legal effect an assignment of the original lease, or a mere sublease. The question has frequently, and probably most generally,

---

14. Stewart v Long I. R. Co. (1886) 102 NY 601, 611, 8 NE 200, 203; McKinley Realty & Const. Co. v Rosenblum (M Ct 1933) 149 Misc 730, 268 NYS 67.

15. Gillette Bros., Inc. v Aristocrat Restaurant, Inc. (1924) 239 NY 87, 90, 145 NE 748; Herzig v Blumenkrohn (AD1 1907) 122 AD 756, 107 NYS 570.

16. Stewart v Long I. R. Co. (1886) 102 NY 601, 607, 608, 8 NE 200, 203.

## ASSIGNMENT AND SUBLETTING § 9:13

arisen between the lessee and his transferee, and much confusion will be avoided by observing the distinction between those cases, and cases where the question has been between the transferee and the original landlord. In the latter class of cases the rule is well settled that if the lessee parts with his whole term or interest as lessee, or makes a lease for period exceeding his whole term, it will, as to the landlord, amount to an assignment of the lease, and the essence of the instrument as an assignment, so far as the original lessor is concerned, will not be destroyed by its reserving a new rent to the assignor with a power of reentering for nonpayment, nor by its assuming, by the use of the word *demise* or otherwise, the character of a sublease; and the assignee, so long as he continues to hold the estate, is liable directly to the original lessor on all covenants in the original lease which run with the land, including the covenant to pay rent. . . . But as between the *original lessee* and *his lessee* or transferee, even though the original lessee demises his whole term, if the parties intend a lease, the relation of landlord and tenant, as to all but strict reversionary rights, will arise between them. The effect, therefore, of a demise by a lessee for a period equal to or exceeding his whole term is to divest him of any reversionary right and render his lessee liable, as assignee, to the original lessor, but at the same time the relation of landlord and tenant is created between the parties to the second demise, if they so intended."

But the two positions are seemingly so inconsistent that it seems clear that all the court meant and intended was that the assignee—the transferee of the tenant—will be bound by any promises he may have made in connection with the assignment. That is, the transaction is, and remains an assignment. It cannot be both an assignment and a sublease at the same time. But, to protect a tenant who has "demised" his term to another, the courts will, in any dispute between the tenant and his transferee, treat the transaction as though it were a "sublease"; that is, a new lease, and thereby enable him to enforce the obligations of the transferee. Thus, if the transferee has promised to pay a higher rent than that reserved in the tenant's original lease, the transferee, after paying the rent reserved in the original lease, must pay the excess amount agreed upon to the assignor. This, it is suggested, is the purport of what the court intended by its suggestion of treating an assignment as a sublease when the question arises between a tenant and his transferee.[17]

### § 9:14. Distinction Between Assignment and Sublease Summarized

In an early leading case on the subject,[18] the Court of Appeals tersely summarized the distinction between assignments and subleases as follows: "The essential distinction between an assignment and a sub-lease is simply this: If a lessee, by any instrument whatever, whether reserving conditions or not, parts with his entire interest, he has made a complete assignment; if he has transferred his entire interest in a part of the premises, he has made an assignment *pro tanto*. If he retains a reversion in himself, he has made a sub-lease."

### § 9:15. Importance of Distinguishing Between Assignment and Sublease

Since under an assignment the assignor parts with his entire interest or estate in the leasehold, and reserves unto himself no reversionary interest therein, no new leasehold estate is created by the assignment. What in reality occurs is, that the assignee becomes the owner of the leasehold estate, and is substituted in the place of the assignor under the lease.[19]

However, in the case of a sublease a reversionary interest in the leasehold estate has been retained. Therefore, a new estate is created by the transaction, which is carved out of the original leasehold estate, and a new relationship of landlord and tenant is created. The sub-

---

17. Also, see Spencer Operating Corp. v Spencer Hotel Corp. (AT1 1959) 17 Misc 2d 887, 186 NYS2d 923; O'Connell v Sugar Products Co. (AT1 1921) 114 Misc 540, 187 NYS 98. Blitzkrieg Amusement Corp. v Rubenstein Bros. Drinks, Inc. (M Ct Man 1945) 184 Misc 975, 55 NYS2d 379.

18. Woodhull v Rosenthal (1875) 61 NY 382, 391.

19. Lo Russo v Great 110, Inc. (Dist Ct Suffolk Co 1969) 59 Misc 40, 298 NYS2d 61.

See Howard Stores Corp. v Robison Rayon Co. (Civ Ct NY Co 1970) 61 Misc 2d 939, 307 NYS2d 491, affd 64 Misc 2d 913, 315 NYS2d 720, affd (1st Dept) 36 AD2d 911, 320 NYS2d 861, holding that the refusal of the landlord to permit the tenant-assignor to re-enter the premises after the assignee had defaulted in payment of rent, and had been evicted by a nonpayment proceeding, did not relieve the assignor from his rental obligation.

tenant, the tenant of the original tenant, because of the outstanding reversionary interest, cannot be substituted in the place of the original tenant. As the Court of Appeals said,[20] "An assignment creates no new estate; but transfers an existing estate into new hands; an underlease, creates a perfectly new estate."

Accordingly, the distinction between an assignment and a sublease is of considerable practical importance. It will determine the relationship of the parties in the particular transaction involved. Having determined such relationship, problems will then arise as to the scope and extent of their respective rights and liabilities as affected by such new relationships. These problems will be considered in the following sections.

## C. PRESUMPTION OF ASSIGNMENT

### § 9:16. From Possession by Stranger

In a leading case[1] the rule was laid down by Crane, J., that, "Where a person other than the lessee is shown to be in possession of the leasehold premises, the law presumes that the lease has been assigned to him. It further presumes that the assignment was sufficient to transfer the term, and to satisfy the Statute of Frauds."[2]

### § 9:17. From Payment of Rent by Stranger

Payment of rent by one, other than the tenant, who has been let into possession of the leased premises by the tenant, is prima facie evidence of the assignment of the whole term.[3] However, mere payment of rent by one who is not in possession of the leased premises does not by operation of law render such person liable under the lease.[4]

### § 9:18. Overcoming Presumption

The burden of overcoming the presumption of an as-

---

20. Collins v Hasbrouck (1874) 56 NY 157, 162.

1. Mann v Ferdinand Munch Brewing (1919) 225 NY 189, 193, 121 NE 746.

2. Possession and occupancy of leased premises by a purchaser of business under an executed contract of sale raises a presumption of assignment. Risolo v Bruno (S Ct Nassau Co 1962) 36 Misc 2d 247, 232 NYS2d 436.

See also, Ribner v Babyatsky (S Ct Orange Co 1951) 103 NYS2d 599.

3. Mann v Ferdinand Munch Brewing (1919) 225 NY 189, 193, 121 NE 746.

4. Ruthbart Real Estate Corp. v Newtal Corp. (1965, 2d Dept) 23 AD2d 693, 257 NYS2d 623, app dismd 18 NY2d 684, 273 NYS2d 434, 219 NE2d 881 and affd 19 NY2d 777, 279 NYS2d 531, 226 NE2d 318.

signment rests on the third party in possession. In one case[5] it was held, therefore, that the exclusion by the trial court of evidence offered by the third party to explain his possession, and to negative an assignment to him of the lease, constituted reversible error. The court said, "On the trial the plaintiff (landlord) gave no evidence of any assignment, in writing or otherwise, of the lease from the Federal Brewing Company; but it gave evidence showing that the defendant went into possession of the premises and paid to the plaintiff the monthly installments of rent provided for in the lease for a period of considerably over a year. Under these circumstances, the plaintiff made out a prima facie case that there had been a due assignment of the lease to the defendant, and that it held possession of the demised premises by privity of estate under the lease by virtue of an assignment; for under such circumstances the law presumes an assignment. . . . This presumption is not absolute, and it may be rebutted by proof that there was in fact or intent no actual assignment, or no valid assignment, of the lease, under which any privity of estate was acquired by the new occupant of the demised premises. . . . In the case at bar, the defendant gave some evidence showing that no assignment of the lease in question had been made to it, and endeavored to give further proof as to the understanding between it and the original lessee, the Federal Brewing Company, as to the lease in question. This proof was excluded on objection, and an exception was taken. This ruling was error, as the evidence was admissible."

The presumption of assignment arising out of possession of leased premises by one not the tenant thereof may be rebutted by showing that such party is in possession as a subtenant.[6] But, merely claiming to be in possession as a subtenant without offering any evidence showing the terms or scope of the alleged sublease is insufficient to rebut the presumption of assignment.[7]

**5.** Benoliel v New York & Brooklyn Brewing Co. (AD2 1911) 144 AD 651, 129 NYS 606.
**6.** Frank v Erie & G. V. R. Co. (1890) 122 NY 197, 219, 25 NE 332, motion den (NY) 26 NE 755.
**7.** Rohdenburg v Sol Lazarus, Inc (AT1 1933) 148 Misc 583, 266 NYS 153.

## D. ASSIGNOR'S LIABILITY

### § 9:19. Importance of Privity of Contract and Privity of Estate

When a landlord enters into a lease with his tenant, a twofold privity arises between them; to wit, a privity of contract, and a privity of estate. "The first," said Hubbs, J.,[8] "rests upon the terms of the agreement between the parties; the second, upon the interest in the real property leased." "The term privity in estate," said Follett, Ch. J.,[9] "denotes mutual or successive relationship to the same rights of property."

The following sections will demonstrate that the determination of the rights and liabilities of the parties involved in assignments and subleases depends primarily upon the application of this twofold privity of contract and of estate to the particular situation. If each situation will be analyzed to ascertain the presence or absence of these privities, the solution of the problem will be facilitated.

### § 9:20. Assignor's Liability on Express Covenants

The liability of a tenant on his express covenants contained in the lease rests on the privity of contract which arises out of the lease agreement between him and his landlord. When a tenant assigns his lease, he does not affect this privity of contract,—that continues. One cannot rid oneself of a contractual liability merely by abandoning it.

Therefore, when a tenant assigns his lease, he continues to be personally liable on all of the express covenants in the lease on his part, notwithstanding the assignment. This means, then, that a tenant who assigns his lease continues to be personally liable not only for his breaches of the lease committed by him before the assignment, but also for all breaches of the lease committed after the assignment by his immediate, or even by any subsequent, assignee of the lease.[10]

---

8. New Amsterdam Casualty Co. v National Union Fire Ins. Co. (1935) 266 NY 254, 259, 194 NE 745, 99 ALR 216.

9. Mygatt v Coe (1891) 124 NY 212, 219, 26 NE 611, later app 142 NY 78, 36 NE 870; Re Shea's Will (1956) 309 NY 605, 132 NE2d 864.

10. Gillette Bros., Inc. v Aristocrat Restaurant, Inc. (1924) 239 NY 87, 90, 145 NE 748; Verschleiser v Newman (AT 1912) 76 Misc 544, 135 NYS 671; 209-13 West 48th Realty Corp. v Rose Offset Printing Corp. (S Ct NY Co

## § 9:21. Ineffective Termination of Assignor's Liability

An assignment of a lease by a tenant does not destroy the privity of contract which results from the making of the lease agreement. Therefore, it is well established that a tenant who assigns his lease remains liable, nevertheless, on his express covenants in the lease after the assignment thereof, even though the landlord consents to the assignment,[11] accepts rent from the assignee,[12] enters into the lease with the understanding that the tenant will immediately thereafter assign the lease,[13] and even though the assignee expressly assumes the obligations of the assigned lease.[14]

None of these acts destroys the existing privity of contract. Therefore, in each of the instances given, the assignor-tenant continues to remain personally liable on all of the express covenants in the lease on his part notwithstanding the assignment.[15]

---

1947) 74 NYS2d 216, affd 273 AD 754, 75 NYS2d 774; Inip Co. v Bailey, Green & Elger, Inc. (D Ct Nassau Co 1974) 78 Misc 2d 235, 356 NYS2d 436 (citing text).

An assignor, unless he reserves the right, has no right of possession after default by the assignee, and he continues liable for the rent. Howard Stores Corp. v Robison Rayon Co. (AD1 1971) 36 AD2d 911, 320 NYS2d 861. (But, said the court, "Because there is pending another action for the rent during the remainder of the term, it should be emphasized that this determination is not on the merits and without prejudice to consideration by the trial court of the question of whether the landlord acted in good faith in failing to rerent the vacated premises.")

11. Iorio v Superior Sound, Inc. (1975, 4th Dept) 49 AD2d 1008, 374 NYS2d 76; Werfelman v Quick (AD1 1919) 187 AD 732, 176 NYS 58; Zinwell Co. v Ilkovitz (AT1 1913) 83 Misc 42, 144 NYS 815; Manley v Berman (AT 1908) 60 Misc 91, 111 NYS 711.

12. Halbe v Adams (AD1 1916) 172 AD 186, 158 NYS 380, later app 176 AD 588, 163 NYS 895; Hayward v Polisuik (AT1 1914) 84 Misc 79, 145 NYS 924.

13. Halbe v Adams (AD1 1916) 172 AD 186, 158 NYS 380, later app 176 AD 588, 163 NYS 895.

14. Brill v Friedhoff (AD1 1918) 184 AD 673, 172 NYS 544, affd 229 NY 547, 129 NE 909; Piser v Hecht (AD1 1915) 170 AD 668, 156 NYS 601.

15. Brill v Friedhoff (AD1 1918) 184 AD 673, 172 NYS 544, affd 229 NY 547, 129 NE 909; Piser v Hecht (AD1 1915) 170 AD 668, 156 NYS 601.

Where a tenant of premises used as a liquor store assigned his written lease with the understanding that he would remain liable for payment of the minimum guaranteed rental, and for performance of all the other terms of the lease, such tenant was not excused from his continuing liability on the lease upon the default of his assignee merely because he had voluntarily surrendered his own liquor license simultaneously with the assignment of the lease, and therefore was unable thereafter to operate the store. The court, in so holding, also pointed out that even without the reservation of continuing liability, the same result followed. Schine-Oswego Corp v Provato (Mun Ct City of Syracuse 1948) 191 Misc 556, 76 NYS2d 639.

ASSIGNMENT AND SUBLETTING § 9:22

## § 9:22. Effective Termination of Assignor's Liability

In order to relieve the original tenant-assignor from his continuing liability after the assignment of the lease on his express covenants therein, the basis of such liability; to wit, the privity of contract must be destroyed. This may be done by a release from the landlord, or by a surrender and acceptance of the lease.[16]

As was said by McLaughlin, J., speaking for the Appellate Division,[17] "It must appear, . . . that there was an express agreement by which the lessee was released from his covenant to pay the rent, or facts shown from which such agreement can be implied." In this case the lease contained a prohibition against the assignment thereof without the landlord's consent, with this additional clause: "and whereas, the said lessees contemplate the organization of a corporation which shall carry on the business which they design to conduct on the premises hereby demised, the lessor now hereby consents that in that event the lessees may assign this lease to such corporation when formed." The court said, "Here it is not claimed there was any express agreement to release the defendants nor are facts set forth from which, I think, such agreement can be inferred. It may be assumed that Charles Halbe (the landlord) was informed of the defendants' purpose to form a corporation for the purposes stated and that he consented to the assignment of the lease to that end. But, even so, it does not follow that he thereby consented to or did release the defendants from their covenant to pay rent."

The tenant, of course, should have had the lease provide that upon the organization of the corporation and the assignment of the lease to the corporation, the tenant would be released from any further liability under the lease. (See the suggested form of such an agreement,

**16.** Halbe v Adams (AD1 1916) 172 AD 186, 158 NYS 380, later app 176 AD 588, 163 NYS 895; Howard Stores Corp. v Robison Rayon Co. (Cir Ct NY Co 1970) 61 Misc 2d 939, 307 NYS2d 491, affd 64 Misc 2d 913, 315 NYS2d 720, affd (1st Dept) 36 AD2d 911, 320 NYS2d 861, citing text, and further holding that the refusal of the landlord to permit the tenant-assignor to re-enter the premises after the assignee had defaulted in payment of rent, and had been evicted by a nonpayment proceeding, did not relieve the assignor from his rental obligation; Zimmerman v Bonwit (M Ct 1927) 128 Misc 887, 220 NYS 599, affd 223 AD 882, 228 NYS 927.

**17.** Halbe v Adams (AD1 1916) 172 AD 186, 158 NYS 380, later app 176 AD 588, 163 NYS 895.

§ 9:23, infra.) After this appeal was decided, the tenant attempted by an amended answer to show that there had been an oral agreement to this effect, but such afterthought failed in its purpose.[18]

Therefore, neither the consent of the landlord to the assignment, nor his acceptance of the rent from the assignee will release the original tenant. There must be either a surrender and acceptance of the lease, or an agreement to release the tenant-assignor. This release must either be express, or implied from facts other than the mere assent to the assignment, and the acceptance of rent from the assignee.

### § 9:23. Form of Clause Consenting to Assignment with Release of Tenant

#### FORM NO. 8

#### Permission to Assign with Release of Tenant-Assignor

A. Anything in this lease to the contrary notwithstanding, Tenant may assign this lease without the consent of Landlord to any partnership or corporation which is a successor to Tenant either by merger, consolidation, or acquisition of all or substantially all of the assets of Tenant, and the assignment shall be valid only as, if, and when Landlord shall have received personally or by certified mail a duplicate original of the assignment, duly executed by Tenant in form for recording; an agreement duly executed and acknowledged by the assignee assuming from and after the date of the assignment the performance of all of the terms, conditions, and covenants of this lease on the part of Tenant to be performed as if the assignee were originally named herein as Tenant, and agreeing that Landlord's consent to the assignment shall not in any way be construed or deemed to relieve the assignee, or any succeeding assignee, or any person claiming any right, title, or interest by or through or under Tenant or the assignee or any succeeding assignee, from first obtaining Landlord's express consent in writing to any further assignment.

B. Tenant shall, from and after the date of the assign-

---

18. Halbe v Adams (AD1 1917) 176 AD 588, 163 NYS 895.

ment made pursuant to the aforesaid terms and conditions be released from any and all obligations under this lease.

*[Add, if desired:]*

C. Tenant may assign to the assignee all his right, title and interest in and to the security deposited under this lease, subject to the provisions of this lease relating thereto, provided Tenant shall simultaneously with the assignment deliver to Landlord, personally or by certified mail, a duplicate original of the assignment duly executed and acknowledged.

## E. NON-ASSUMING ASSIGNEE'S LIABILITY

### § 9:24. Nature of Problem

Liability on express covenants in a lease rests upon the privity of contract existing by virtue of the lease agreement between a tenant and his landlord.[19] When a tenant assigns his lease, and the assignee accepts such assignment, a mutual or successive relationship to the property results between the assignee and the landlord; that is, privity of estate.[20] But, since there is no agreement between the assignee and the landlord, there is no privity of contract between them.

The problem then arises as to the nature and extent of the liability of a non-assuming assignee. This will be considered in the following sections.

### § 9:25. Liability on Covenants Running with Land

The privity of estate resulting from an assignee's acceptance of a lease imposes on an assignee the obligation to perform all those covenants in the lease on the part of the tenant which run with the land.[1] Such covenants fix and define the tenure by which the assignee holds the leased property.[2]

However, such liability continues only as long as such privity of estate, the foundation for such liability, contin-

---

19. See § 9:20, supra.
20. New Amsterdam Casualty Co. v National Union Fire Ins. Co. (1935) 266 NY 254, 259, 194 NE 745, 99 ALR 216.
1. Gillette Bros., Inc. v Aristocrat Restaurant, Inc. (1924) 239 NY 87, 90, 145 NE 748; Stewart v Long I. R. Co. (1886) 102 NY 601, 8 NE 200, 203.
2. For definition of covenants running with land, see § 23:6, infra.

## § 9:25

ues. This means, then, that a non-assuming assignee of a lease is not liable for any breaches of the lease which occurred prior to the assignment of the lease to him. He is only liable for those breaches of covenants in the lease on the part of the tenant which run with the land, and which he commits during the existence of the privity of estate.[3]

It must be emphasized that it is the acceptance of an assignment by the assignee which results in the creation of privity of estate between him and the landlord. Whether or not such acceptance is followed by his entering into possession of the demised premises is immaterial to the creation of the privity of estate.[4]

The non-assuming assignee of a lease, however, is not liable upon those express covenants in the lease on the part of the tenant which are collateral or merely personal. Such covenants do not run with the land.[5] The basis for liability upon these covenants rests on privity of contract. Since the non-assuming assignee did not assume the lease, that is, did not enter into any agreement with the landlord, there is no privity of contract, and consequently no such liability.

## § 9:26. Liability on Covenant to Pay Rent

"The covenant to pay rent," said the Court of Appeals,[6] "runs with the land." Therefore, as was pointed out by McLaughlin, J.,[7] "When an assignee accepts an assignment of a lease of real property, he thereupon, by virtue of the assignment, becomes liable to the lessor for the rent stipulated to be paid. The acceptance of the assign-

---

**3.** Townsend v Scholey (1870) 42 NY 18, 21; Estate Property Corp. v Hudson Coal Co. (AD1 1940) 259 AD 546, 19 NYS2d 857, affd 284 NY 772, 31 NE2d 762; Dananberg v Reinheimer (AT 1898) 24 Misc 712, 53 NYS 794; Ribner v Babyatsky (S Ct Orange Co 1951) 103 NYS2d 599.

**4.** Stone v Auerbach (AD1 1919) 133 AD 75, 117 NYS 734; 78th St. & Broadway Co. v Purssell Mfg. Co. (AD1 1915) 166 AD 684, 152 NYS 52.

**5.** Dolph v White (1855) 12 NY 296, 301.

See Spivak v Madison-54th Realty Co (S Ct Kings Co 1969) 60 Misc 2d 483, 303 NYS2d 128, where it was held that the purchaser of leasehold was not obligated to pay brokerage on tenant's renewal of the lease, which former owner of leasehold had agreed to pay, but which the purchaser had not assumed, since an agreement to pay broker's commissions is a personal covenant which does not affect title to, or the possession, use or enjoyment of real property.

**6.** Mann v Ferdinand Munch Brewing (1919) 225 NY 189, 195, 121 NE 746.

**7.** 78th St. & Broadway Co. v Purssell Mfg. Co. (AD1 1915) 166 AD 684, 152 NYS 52.

# ASSIGNMENT AND SUBLETTING § 9:29

ment creates a privity of estate between the lessor and the assignee, and it is not material that such acceptance be followed by the assignee's entering into possession of the premises."

### § 9:27. Liability on Covenant to Pay Taxes

In the leading case on this subject,[8] it was held: "The covenant to pay taxes ran with the land. (cases cited) The defendant having accepted the assignment of the entire estate of the plaintiff's lessee, a privity of estate was thereby created between him and the plaintiff, which gave the plaintiff a right of action against the defendant on the covenant for the payment of taxes, upon default in so doing. . . . Moreover, it seems that it is not material whether the defendant entered into possession of the premises or not, since it is alleged, and not denied, that he accepted the assignment of the lease."

### § 9:28. Liability on Pro Tanto Assignment

"Where a covenant, which runs with the land, is divisible in its nature, if the entire interest in different parts or parcels of the land passes by assignment to separate and distinct individuals, the covenant will attach upon each parcel *pro tanto*. In such case, the assignee of each part would be answerable for his proportion of any charge upon the land, which is a common burden, and would be exclusively liable for the breach of any covenant which related to that part alone."[9]

Thus, in the absence of any express reservation of rent in the *pro tanto* assignment, then the covenant to pay rent, which is divisible in its nature and a common charge on the entire leasehold, may be apportioned among the divers assignees of the term according to the extent of their several shares.[10]

### § 9:29. Liability Where Assignment in Violation of Lease Restriction

Where a lease contains a prohibition against assignment without the landlord's consent, the argument is

---

8. Stone v Auerbach (AD1 1909) 133 AD 75, 117 NYS 734.

9. Quoted from Astor v Miller (Ch Ct 1830) 2 Paige 68, by Brown, J, in Damainville v Mann (1865) 32 NY 197, 204.

10. Damainville v Mann (1865) 32 NY 197, 205.

frequently advanced that if an assignment thereof be made in violation of such prohibition, the assignment is void; that no privity of estate is thereby created; and that, therefore, there is no liability on the part of the assignee.

However, it is well settled that an assignment of a lease in violation of the usual restrictive covenant contained in the lease is not void, but voidable. The lease is not thereby ipso facto forfeited without further action on the part of the landlord unless the lease expressly provides otherwise. Therefore, unless the landlord chooses to void the assignment, the assignment is valid; privity of estate results; and the assignee is liable thereunder.[11]

In a leading case on the subject,[12] this rule was discussed, and the court said, "It seems that this lease contained a provision that the lessee should not assign or sublet without the consent of the lessor; and the plaintiff insists that, that covenant being in the lease, no privity arose between himself and the landlord, because the landlord refused to recognize him as tenant, lest that should release the lessors (the original tenants). But that fact is of no importance. The liability to pay rent arose by operation of law, and from the fact of possession as assignee under the lease; and, as long as that existed, the liability to pay rent followed as a necessary incident."[13]

In other words, the restriction on assignments is for the benefit of the landlord, and may be availed of only by him. It affords the assignee no rights whatsoever. If the landlord does not void the assignment, and the assignee has accepted the assignment, the liability of the assignee, as assignee, is complete.

## § 9:30. Termination of Non-assuming Assignee's Liability

Since the liability of an assignee who does not assume

---

11. Agus v Bierman (AD2 1950) 277 AD 1139, 101 NYS2d 405; S. Liebmann's Sons Brewing Co. v Lauter (AD1 1902) 73 AD 183, 76 NYS 748; Long Bldg., Inc. v Buffalo Anthracite Coal Co. (S Ct Kings Co 1947) 190 Misc 97, 74 NYS2d 281; Nipet Realty, Inc. v Melvin's Rest. & Bar, Inc. (NYC Cir Ct NY Co 1971) 67 Misc 2d 790, 327 NYS2d 2.

12. Sayles v Kerr (AD1 1896) 4 AD 150, 38 NYS 880, 74 NY St R 774.

13. Also, see Condit v Manischewitz (AD1 1927) 220 AD 366, 221 NYS 371, where assignment in violation of lease restriction held not to preclude assignee from exercising rights under renewal covenant, which runs with land.

# ASSIGNMENT AND SUBLETTING § 9:32

performance of the covenants of the lease grows out of the privity of estate resulting from the acceptance of the assignment, and that only,[14] such liability, said the Court of Appeals,[15] "ceases when that privity ceases to exist and each successive assignee is liable only for such breaches of covenant as occur while there is privity of estate between him and the lessor."

## § 9:31. —Effect of Termination

An assignee who has not assumed the lease can terminate his liability thereunder by destroying or extinguishing the privity of estate, the foundation for his liability. It is well settled that he can do this by either making a bona fide assignment—not a colorable one—of the lease, or by a surrender and acceptance of the lease.[16] Therefore, when an assignee makes a bona fide reassignment of his lease, or when he surrenders the lease to the landlord who accepts such surrender, the privity of estate is extinguished, and with it the foundation of his liability on covenants in the lease running with the land.

However, it must be emphasized that privity of estate cannot be destroyed or extinguished merely by an abandonment of the premises.[17]

## § 9:32. —Requisites of Bona Fide Assignment

To make the reassignment of a lease by the assignee effective to extinguish the privity of estate, all that is necessary is a delivery and an acceptance of such assignment. It is not essential that the new assignee go into possession of the demised premises; for the test of liability is based not on possession of demised premises, but rather upon ownership of the leasehold estate which arises from the acceptance of the assignment.[18] The entry into posses-

---

14. See § 9:25, supra.
15. Mann v Ferdinand Munch Brewing Co (1919) 225 NY 189, 195, 121 NE 746.
16. Lynch v Joseph (AD4 1930) 228 AD 367, 240 NYS 176; Dassori v Zarek (AD2 1902) 71 AD 538, 75 NYS 841; 78th St. & Broadway Co. v Purssell Mfg. Co. (AT1 1915) 92 Misc 178, 155 NYS 259, affd 173 AD 887, 157 NYS 1145.
17. Romas v Adregna (1957, 3d Dept) 4 AD2d 992, 167 NYS2d 990; Lynch v Joseph (AD4 1930) 228 AD 367, 240 NYS 176; 78th St. & Broadway Co. v Purssell Mfg. Co. (AT1 1915) 92 Misc 178, 155 NYS 259, affd 173 AD 887, 157 NYS 1145.

18. Lynch v Joseph (AD4 1930) 228 AD 367, 240 NYS 176; Stone v Auerbach (AD1 1909) 133 AD 75, 117 NYS 734; 78th St. & Broadway Co. v Purssell Mfg. Co. (AT1 1915) 92 Misc 178, 155 NYS 259, affd 173 AD 887, 157 NYS 1145.

§ 9:32 LANDLORD AND TENANT

sion is material only as an aid in determining whether a bona fide assignment was made, or only a colorable one.[19]

"Colorable assignment," said the Appellate Division,[20] "means, not an assignment to avoid liability for rent under the lease, but that, the assignor retaining possession, the assignment was made to conceal that possession. 'A merely colorable or fictitious assignment of a lease, which does not accomplish an actual transfer of the interest of the assignor in the demised premises, but leaves him in the rightful possession and enjoyment thereof, is a nullity.' (Tate v McCormick, 23 Hun 218.)"

In another case the Appellate Division[1] applied this principle, and in an opinion written by Merrell, J., said of the situation then before it, "If, however, Sudbrink (the assignee of the lease) was the mere agent or dummy of the defendant, and if the defendant intended to remain in possession, keeping control of the property . . ., it certainly cannot be said that there was any bona fide transfer of the lease to Sudbrink, which would relieve defendant from its liability to pay rent to the plaintiff. The circumstances surrounding the transfer of the lease are more than suspicious, and were sufficient to warrant the jury in finding that Sudbrink was a mere agent or dummy of the defendant. If this be true, the defendant could not rid itself of liability by such assignment."

## § 9:33. —Necessity of Consideration; Motive for Assignment

No consideration need be expressed in an assignment of a lease; for, the assignment being subject to the payment of rent reserved in the lease is supported by sufficient consideration.[2] The Court of Appeals said, "It was in its power (assignee's) to escape this liability at any time by assigning the lease and abandoning possession, even if it were done for the express purpose of avoiding further payment of rent. (cases cited) Privity of estate would thus

---

19. Century Holding Co. v Ebling Brewing Co. (AD1 1918) 185 AD 292, 173 NYS 49; Adams v H. Koehler & Co. (AD1 1910) 136 AD 623, 121 NYS 390.

20. Adams v H. Koehler & Co. (AD1 1910) 136 AD 623, 121 NYS 390.

1. Century Holding Co. v Ebling Brewing Co. (AD1 1918) 185 AD 292, 173 NYS 49.

2. Frank v Erie & G. V. R. Co. (1890) 122 NY 197, 221, 25 NE 332, motion den (NY) 26 NE 755.

be destroyed, and with it the foundation of future liability."

Therefore, it has been held that an assignment of a lease can be made to one who cannot be sued, or to a beggar, or even to one to whom a bonus has been given solely for accepting the assignment. None of these facts impeaches the validity of the assignment.[3]

### § 9:34. Liability as Between Non-assuming Assignee and Assignor

When a tenant assigns his lease to a non-assuming assignee, the tenant by the assignment merely destroys privity of estate with the landlord, but not privity of contract. Therefore, notwithstanding the assignment, the tenant remains liable for the performance of the covenants on his part in the lease. However, the non-assuming assignee upon accepting the assignment creates privity of estate with the landlord, and therefore becomes liable for the performance of the covenants on the part of the tenant in the lease which run with the land. Hence, there are now two obligors liable for the performance of the same obligation; that is, the covenants running with the land. Since the assignee is in possession, he really should be primarily liable. Therefore, in this situation the law implies a promise on the part of the assignee to indemnify the tenant against a default in the performance of the obligation. Stated differently, as between the tenant and his non-assuming assignee, the tenant becomes a surety, and the assignee the principal.[4] But, this liability of suretyship on the part of the non-assuming assignee arises from the promise implied by law, and does not rest on privity of estate nor privity of contract, because neither one exists between a tenant and his non-assuming assignee. Therefore such liability exists only as long as the assignee remains liable to perform the covenants of the lease which run with the land.

Accordingly, when the tenant becomes obligated to pay the landlord for the default of the non-assuming assignee,

---

3. Century Holding Co. v Ebling Brewing Co. (AT1 1917) 98 Misc 226, 162 NYS 1061.

4. Crowley v Gormley (AD2 1901) 59 AD 256, 69 NYS 576; McKeon v Wendelken (AT 1899) 25 Misc 711, 55 NYS 626; Schlessel v Sherman (M Ct 1927) 130 Misc 633, 224 NYS 593.

the tenant may sue the assignee for reimbursement of any sums he has to pay out by reason of the default.

If, however, the non-assuming assignee reassigns his lease, then he terminates the privity of estate, and with it, any further liability to the landlord accruing after the reassignment. (But not as to any liability which accrued prior to the reassignment.) Therefore, if a default should occur after the reassignment, the first non-assuming assignee, who dropped out of the situation, incurs no liability to anyone. But, then, the subsequent assignee has become the principal obligor and he now is obligated to indemnify the tenant for any loss occurring by reason of his default. As Genung, J., said,[5] "However, when the assignee assigns to a subsequent assignee, as in the instant case, and the subsequent assignee defaults and the lessee is obliged to pay the landlord for the said default, the lessee has no cause of action against his assignee, as there is no privity of estate between them nor is there privity of contract. Since in such a situation the assignee is not the principal obligor, the lessee may not recover from his assignee on principles of suretyship. In such instance the principal obligor is the subsequent assignee and the lessee would have a cause of action against him."

## F. ASSUMING ASSIGNEE'S LIABILITY

### § 9:35. Definition of "Assumption"

To assume a lease means to assume all of it, and not such part only as might please the assignee according to subsequent events.[6] "The definition of the word 'assume' in matters of law," said the Court of Appeals,[7] "is 'to take upon one's self,' or the agreement of the transferee of property to pay the obligations of the transferer which are chargeable on it."

### § 9:36. Scope and Extent of Liability

When an assignee accepts an assignment of a lease, and in addition expressly agrees to assume performance

---

**5.** Schlessel v Sherman (M Ct 1927) 130 Misc 633, 224 NYS 593.

**6.** Mann v Ferdinand Munch Brewery (1919) 225 NY 189, 195, 196, 121 NE 746.

**7.** Mann v Ferdinand Munch Brewery (1919) 225 NY 189, 196, 121 NE 746.

# ASSIGNMENT AND SUBLETTING § 9:37

of all of the covenants on the part of the tenant contained in the lease, two privities with the landlord then arise: privity of estate, which arises from the mere acceptance of the assignment; and privity of contract, which arises from the assumption contract. The assuming assignee then will be liable from the time of the assignment not only for breaches of covenants in the lease running with the land, but also for all breaches of the express covenants in the lease which are collateral and do not run with the land.[8]

Therefore, an assuming assignee of a lease is in the same position as the original tenant. By the assumption agreement he becomes liable from the time of the assignment till the end of the term for breaches of all the covenants on the tenant's part in the lease, whether committed by him, or by his immediate assignee or by any subsequent assignee.[9] When the assuming assignee reassigns the lease, he merely destroys the privity of estate, but not the privity of contract. Privity of contract can only be destroyed by a release, or by a surrender and acceptance of the lease.[10]

## § 9:37. —Illustrations

The case of Zinwell Co. v Ilkovitz[11] affords an excellent illustration of the application of the principles involved upon an assumption of a lease by an assignee. In this case, the tenant assigned his lease to A and B with the landlord's consent. A and B as part of this transaction executed the following agreement: "For and in consideration of One ($1) dollar and other valuable considerations and the consent to the assignment of the within lease to us, we do hereby jointly and severally, for ourselves, our heirs, executors, and administrators, assume and agree to observe and perform each and every one of the covenants contained in the said lease, and which on the part and behalf of the lessee therein named are to be observed and performed." A and B thereafter assigned the lease to C,

---

8. Hart v Socony-Vacuum Oil Co. (1943) 291 NY 13, 16, 50 NE2d 285, 148 ALR 390; Trustees of Columbia University v Rathbone (1919) 227 NY 560, 124 NE 902; Townsend v Scholey (1870) 42 NY 18.

9. Mann v Ferdinand Munch Brewery (1919) 225 NY 189, 196, 121 NE 746; Zinwell Co. v Ilkovitz (AT1 1913) 83 Misc 42, 144 NYS 815.

10. See § 9:22, supra.

11. (AT1 1913) 83 Misc 42, 144 NYS 815.

who signed a similar agreement. C failed to pay the rent, but the landlord sought to recover the said rent from A and B. The court upheld the landlord's right to recover from A and B, and pointed out: "By the assignment of the lease, together with the agreement on the part of the assignee to assume all the covenants of the lease, not alone did the assignee become obligated to pay the rent by reason of privity of estate, but also by privity of contract with the lessor. When the assignee, therefore, in turn assigned the lease and his assignee went into possession, the privity of estate was broken; but the privity of contract was not thereby destroyed, and the defendants remained liable upon their contract for the rent that might subsequently accrue up to the end of the term."[12]

## § 9:38. Landlord's Right to Enforce Assumption Agreement

An assumption agreement is generally made by the assignee with his assignor upon accepting the lease. However, even though the landlord is not a party to that agreement, the landlord may enforce such assumption agreement, under the doctrine of Lawrence v Fox[13] as a third party beneficiary.[14]

## § 9:39. Requirements of Assumption Agreement

An assignee of a lease can be held to contractual liability only if he in some form clearly and expressly undertakes such liability, thereby creating the necessary privity of contract with his landlord. Therefore, if such contractual liability is sought to be founded upon an assumption agreement, such agreement must be based on a valid consideration, and must specifically and in express terms assume the covenants of the lease.[15]

When an assignee accepts an assignment of a lease "subject to all of its terms, covenants, and conditions," it has been held that such an assignment is insufficient to

---

12. Also, see, Probst v Rochester Steam Laundry Co. (1902) 171 NY 584, 589, 64 NE 504.
13. (1859) 20 NY 268.
14. Kottler v New York Bargain House, Inc. (1926) 242 NY 28, 37, 150 NE 591, remittitur den 242 NY 568, 152 NE 430.
15. 78th St. & Broadway Co. v Purssell Mfg. Co. (AT1 1915) 92 Misc 178, 155 NYS 259, affd 173 AD 887, 157 NYS 1145.

# ASSIGNMENT AND SUBLETTING § 9:40

constitute an assumption of the lease.[16] Such an assignment involves no obligation other than the one which automatically arises from the mere acceptance of the assignment. The assignee by accepting an assignment is by virtue thereof bound to perform the "terms, covenants, and conditions" which run with the land during the existence of the privity of estate. There is nothing to indicate that the assignee has undertaken a contractual obligation to perform. There is no rule of law, said the Court of Appeals in an early case,[17] "which imposes the liability in question, unless the parties have declared it in words appropriate or sufficient to express that meaning."

## § 9:40. —Illustrations

In an early case, which went to the Court of Appeals,[18] the facts indicate that an assignee, who had not expressly assumed the covenants of the lease when he accepted the assignment, was held liable for the rent of the unexpired portion of the term, although before its expiration he had reassigned the lease, and abandoned possession of the premises. But this case upon analysis does not contradict any of the principles discussed in the preceding sections. In this case the lease gave the tenant the privilege of renewing it upon giving to the landlord written notice of such election. Before the end of the original term the tenant assigned this lease to the assignee. At the expiration of the term the assignee continued in possession without having given the landlord notice of its election to renew the lease, and paid the rent as it became due, which the landlord accepted. During the renewed term the assignee then reassigned the lease, and abandoned possession. The assignee contended that its liability arose only from privity of estate, and therefore when it reassigned its lease it terminated any further liability under the lease. However, the Court of Appeals in an opinion by Vann, J., said, "The assignment of the lease in question by the lessee to the defendant conferred upon it all his rights, including the privilege of exercising the option to extend the term. . . . The assignee thereupon became

---

16. Schwartz v Cahill (1917) 220 NY 174, 178, 115 NE 451; Dassori v Zarek (AD2 1902) 71 AD 538, 75 NYS 841.

17. Belmont v Coman (1860) 22 NY 438.

18. Probst v Rochester Steam Laundry Co (1902) 171 NY 584, 64 NE 504.

liable for the rent by privity of estate so long as it remained in possession, but it could have terminated the liability at any time during the first year by assigning the lease and leaving the premises. . . . The act of continuing in possession and paying rent, operating through the option in the lease which then belonged to the assignee, resulted in an implied contract to extend the lease, and thenceforward there was privity of contract between the parties as well as privity of estate. The lessor by accepting the rent accruing after the expiration of the fixed term impliedly waived the notice required by the lease, and the assignee by remaining in possession and continuing to pay rent impliedly exercised the option to extend the term for the further period of two years. . . . We think that from the mutual action of the parties, the one remaining in possession and paying the rent and the other consenting thereto by accepting the rent, a contract arose by implication of law binding upon both, which extended the lease for the period named in the option." Thus, privity of contract between the parties arose not from the acceptance of the assignment, but from the contract of renewal entered into between the assignee and the landlord, and therefore, contractual liability resulted, just as effectively as if the assignee in express terms had specifically assumed the covenants of the lease.

In a more recent case the Court of Appeals[19] had occasion to pass on these problems. In this case the original tenant had assigned his lease to the defendant. Defendant thereafter reassigned the lease to one Stark and surrendered possession. Subsequently Stark, the second assignee, failed to pay his rent, and the landlord instituted this action to recover this rent from the first assignee, that is, Stark's assignor. Plaintiff landlord sued on the theory that the first assignee, although originally an assignee with only the limited liability of a non-assuming assignee, became in 1932, through an agreement then made between plaintiff and the first assignee, contractually liable to perform all the covenants of the lease until its expiration. This agreement came about in this way. The lease required the tenant thereunder to maintain

---

19. Hart v Socony-Vacuum Oil Co (1943) 291 NY 13, 50 NE2d 285, 148 ALR 390.

certain insurance covering the premises. The 1932 agreement between the landlord and the first assignee eliminated this requirement for insurance, and instead bound the first assignee to assume the role of insurer. "There is in that agreement," said Desmond, J., writing the opinion, "no express statement regarding any assumption by defendant of any liability except in relation to insurance. We are told, however, that an all-inclusive assumption by defendant of the original lease's burdens was effected by this language found therein: 'It is further mutually understood and agreed that except as herein expressly modified, all other provisions and covenants contained in said lease shall remain in full force and effect.'" In the courts below the landlord succeeded in convincing the courts that this agreement in itself, without explanation or supporting proof, meant that the parties intended to accomplish a complete assumption by defendant of the whole lease. The Court of Appeals, however, disagreed with this, and held that "it was erroneous to read the 1932 agreement as containing on its face a flat agreement by defendant to assume the lease." In the course of his opinion Desmond, J., said, "On its face that paper shows only an intent to modify the existing arrangements in one particular, that is as to insurance, and the quoted language may well have been added, solely out of caution, to make sure that no other changes resulted. Since that may be all that the parties had in mind, no result so grave as a sweeping assumption of a long-term lease, by one not otherwise liable thereon, should be held to follow automatically and regardless of real intent. Furthermore, it is doubtful whether the 1932 agreement is susceptible of the meaning ascribed to it below. There is strong authority which says that to hold liable an assignee under a lease, after he has given up the lease and vacated the premises, there must be produced an express promise by him to perform the covenants of the lease. (citations) If such an express covenant be made by an assignee, then he is thereafter liable both by privity of estate and by privity of contract with the lessor. But such an express covenant is never assumed to have been made . . . it must always be proven. . . . It is not every reference to, or mention of, the covenants of a lease, by an assignee, that amounts to an assumption by him. Even where he covenants that his assignment is to be 'subject' to the terms of the lease, that language, without more definite words of promise, does not make him liable as by privity of contract. . . . Plaintiff makes some claim also that the provision of the original lease making all its covenants binding upon the parties thereto, 'their respective heirs, executors, successors, and assigns,' has a special meaning in this connection. Ordinarily such language is employed not to impose direct contractual liability on 'assigns' but to make it clear that the lease covenants run with the land (see Mygatt v Coe, 147 NY 456, 467), otherwise some of those covenants, such as the covenants to keep the premises insured, might be held to be personal engagements of the lessee only."

Thus, this case reemphasizes the principle that in order to impose contractual liability on an assignee, it must be proved that the assignee did more than merely accept an assignment. It must be shown that a privity of contract was created between the assignee and the landlord. This should not be left to implication, but must be based on a clear and express undertaking of the covenants of the lease.

### § 9:41. Form of Assignment with Assumption Agreement

#### FORM NO. 9
#### Assignment of Lease with an Assumption Agreement by Assignee

KNOW THAT Richard Roe, assignor, residing at 1116 East 29th Street, New York, New York, in consideration of Ten ($10.00) dollars and other good and valuable consideration paid by John Doe Inc., assignee, a domestic corporation having its principal office at 11 West 29th Street, New York, New York, hereby assigns unto assignee, a certain lease made by and between assignor and 65 Ninth Realty Corp, dated December 1, 1984 (add, if lease was recorded: and recorded on December 3, 1984, in the office of the Register of the County of New York, in Liber 10 of conveyances, at page 5) covering premises described as follows: *[set forth premises described in lease]* together with all right, title, and interest of the

## ASSIGNMENT AND SUBLETTING § 9:41

tenant thereunder in and to the premises described therein *[add if pertinent:* and in and to the buildings thereon] with the appurtenances and all of the rights and benefits under said lease *[add if desired:* together with the security moneys in the sum of $. . . ., deposited thereunder]. *[If lease contains an option to renew, it is important for the lessee-assignee either to reserve unto itself the option to renew, or expressly exclude the renewal option from the assignment. See § 11:52, infra.]*

TO HAVE AND TO HOLD the same unto the assignee, and to the successors and assigns of the assignee from the first day of February, 1984, for all the rest of the term of ten (10) years mentioned in said lease, subject to the rents, covenants, conditions, and provisions therein mentioned on the part of the tenant to be kept, observed, and performed.

AND the assignor hereby covenants that it is not in default under said lease, that said lease is not encumbered by any prior transfer, assignment or any encumbrance, and that assignor has full and lawful authority to assign said lease [and said security moneys].

The assignee hereby assumes the performance of all of the terms, covenants and conditions of the lease herein assigned by the assignor to the assignee as of . . . . . . . ., 19 , and agrees to pay the rent reserved by the said lease on the next rent day, and monthly thereafter until the termination of the said lease, and will well and truly perform and observe all the terms, covenants, and conditions of the said lease herein assigned, as of . . . . . . . ., 19 all with full force and effect as if the assignee had signed the lease originally as tenant named therein.

The assignee hereby agrees that said assignee will well and truly indemnify and hold harmless the assignor from all manners of suit, actions, damages, charges, and expense, including attorney and counsel fees that the assignor may sustain by reason of the assignee's failure to pay the rent reserved in the said lease, or by reason of the assignee's breach of any of the terms, covenants, and conditions of the lease hereby assigned.

The assignee further agrees that the consent of the landlord to this assignment shall not in any way be construed or deemed to relieve the assignee, the assignor, or any succeeding transferee, successor, or assignee of this lease, or any person claiming any right, title, or interest by or through or under the assignor, this assignee, or any succeeding transferee, successor, or assignee of this lease from obtaining the prior written consent of the landlord to an assignment in each and every subsequent instance.

The assignee hereby agrees that the obligations herein assumed by the assignee shall inure jointly and severally to the landlord named in the lease herein assigned, and to the assignor herein.

This agreement may not be changed, modified, discharged or terminated orally or in any other manner than by an agreement in writing signed by the parties hereto or their respective successors and assigns.

IN WITNESS WHEREOF, this assignment has been duly executed by the parties hereto this 31st day of January, 1984.

In presence of

[Signature with name printed underneath]

[Signatures of assignor and assignee with names printed underneath]

Acknowledgments

### § 9:42. Liability as between Assuming Assignee and Assignor

In a preceding section[20] it was shown that when a tenant assigns his lease, he becomes a surety for the non-assuming assignee on such assignee's primary obligation to perform the covenants running with the land. However, if there be an assignment to an assuming assignee, then different results will follow from those in the case of a non-assuming assignee.

For facility of treatment of this difficult subject assume a lease between L and T. T assigns to A, an assuming assignee. A reassigns to A-1, a non-assuming assignee. A-1 fails to pay his rent.

T is, of course, liable to the landlord notwithstanding his assignment; for the assignment merely destroyed the

---

20. See § 9:34, supra.

## ASSIGNMENT AND SUBLETTING  §9:42

privity of estate with the landlord, but not the privity of contract.

A is liable to the landlord, notwithstanding the reassignment, for the same reason. Moreover, A is liable to T for performance of the lease by privity of contract arising out of the assumption agreement. Although as between T and A, T is liable as surety and A is liable as principal for the same obligation, this liability does not arise from any promises implied by law, as in the case of a non-assuming assignee. Here A expressly agreed with T to perform. Therefore the reassignment does not affect A's liability to T.

A-1 is liable to the landlord only by reason of privity of estate, resulting from the acceptance of the assignment. Since he is in possession, the law will imply a promise on his part to indemnify T as well as A against any of his defaults on the lease. T and A, although out of possession, are still liable on the lease, and therefore they are sureties for the primary obligation of A-1 under the lease.

Now, the rule of law is that where there are several sureties for the same obligation, as between them the primary liability will rest upon the last one. Therefore, as between T and A, A is the last surety, and therefore primarily liable. So that if A has to pay the defaulted rent, he cannot look to T for reimbursement, who is only secondarily liable on this obligation with respect to A.[1]

To fully determine the rights and obligations of the parties, one final rule of law must now be considered. "The rule may be definitely drawn from numerous cases," said the Court of Appeals,[2] "that where indemnity only is expressed, damages must be sustained before a recovery can be had; but a positive agreement to do an act which is to prevent damage to the plaintiff will sustain an action where the defendant neglects or refuses to do such act." Therefore, in the situation under discussion, these conclusions follow:

T can sue A-1 for the defaulted rent, but can only

---

1. National Surety Co. v Trilby Realty Corp. (AD1, 1937) 249 AD 566, 293 NYS 219.
2. Rector, etc, Trinity Church in New York v Higgins (1872) 48 NY 532, 537; Pinmor Realty Corp. v Baris Hotel Corp. (1981, 2d Dept) 83 AD2d 847, 441 NYS2d 751.

§ 9:42

recover from him if he proves that he paid it to L. A-1's obligation was only one of indemnity implied by law.

T can sue A for the defaulted rent, and can recover regardless of whether or not he, T, paid the rent to L. A's obligation was not one of indemnity implied by law, but a positive agreement, under his assumption agreement, to perform the covenants of the lease.[3]

A can sue A-1 for the defaulted rent, but can only recover from him if he proves that he, A, paid it to L. A-1's obligation to A was only one of indemnity implied by law. As between T and A, A is primarily liable, and therefore he cannot sue T for reimbursement.

L, however, may sue all three, that is, T, A, and A-1; or, any one of the three. If he sues one, or all three, he can have but one satisfaction. That is, payment by any one of the three will release all of the others of any further obligation to L.[4]

"If payment by the assignee relieves the lessee," said the Appellate Term,[5] "a release of payment for rent due or to become due would also release the lessee." Therefore, if L should release any one of the three, that is, T, A, or A-1, L will thereby release the others. There then would be no obligation left to enforce against the others.

## G. ASSIGNEE'S RIGHTS

### § 9:43. Generally

When an assignee of a lease accepts an assignment

---

3. Beier v Snitzer (1917, Sup App T) 167 NYS 303; 500 Fifth Ave., Inc. v Nielsen (Cir Ct NY Co 1968) 56 Misc 2d 392, 288 NYS2d 970, holding that landlord preserved his rights to recover unpaid rent against tenant-assignor after settlement with assuming assignee by reserving his rights against any other party to the lease in the release delivered. See Buchholz v Luckner (M Ct Brooklyn 1960) 23 Misc 2d 19, 205 NYS2d 737, which involved an action by a tenant-assignor against an assuming assignee on his express agreement to indemnify tenant-assignor, to recover the amount of unpaid rent accruing after assignee had vacated from the premises, although the assignor had settled the landlord's action to recover such unpaid rent for a much lesser amount. It was held that since the settlement had been made without the consent or knowledge of assignee, and without any demand by assignor for performance of his obligation under the lease, the maximum amount of any recovery was the amount of the settlement; moreover, the assignor by reason of these facts ran the risk of being able to prove that he would have been held liable for the rent in the landlord's action, and that there was no good defense to the action. This the assignor was unable to prove and the action was dismissed.

4. Schlesinger v Perper (AT 1911) 70 Misc 250, 126 NYS 731; Zimmermann v Bonwit (M Ct 1927) 128 Misc 887, 220 NYS 599, affd 223 AD 882, 228 NYS 927.

5. Ayen v Schmidt (AT2 1913) 80 Misc 670, 141 NYS 938.

ASSIGNMENT AND SUBLETTING § 9:44

thereof, he creates a privity of estate with the landlord. The tenure by which these parties hold the demised property after the assignment is fixed by the covenants in the lease which run with the land. Therefore, an assignee is liable to the landlord for performance of the covenants in the lease on the part of the tenant that run with the land. Similarly, the landlord is liable to the assignee by virtue of this privity of estate for performance of the covenants in the lease on the part of the landlord that run with the land. Therefore the benefits of covenants in the lease running with the land inure to an assignee of the lease.

This rule is not changed in any way because the assignee may have assumed performance of the lease. The assuming assignee merely has created for himself an additional liability. But the landlord did not create by any act of his a liability to the assuming assignee to perform those covenants in the lease which are personal, and do not run with the land.

For example, it has been held that a covenant in a lease giving the tenant the right to renew it is one running with the land. Therefore, it has been held, such a covenant inures to the benefit of an assignee of the lease, and may be enforced by him against the landlord.[6]

## H. LIABILITY OF TENANT'S ASSIGNEE FOR BENEFIT OF CREDITORS

### § 9:44. Generally

"It is the well settled law," said the Court of Appeals,[7] "that an assignee for the benefit of creditors when receiving, among the assets of his assignor, the unexpired term of a lease, has a reasonable time in which to decide whether he will accept the lease and assume the burdens of its covenants on behalf of the estate, or surrender possession of the premises to the landlord."

---

**6.** 507 Madison Ave. Realty Co. v Martin (AD1 1922) 200 AD 146, 192 NYS 762, affd 233 NY 683, 135 NE 969; Bradley v General Store Equipment Corp. (M Ct 1944) 183 Misc 199, 51 NYS2d 420, affd 268 AD 852, 50 NYS2d 771.

Also, see Goldman v Corn (AD1 1906) 111 AD 674, 97 NYS 926, holding that assignee succeeds to assignor's right to possession.

**7.** Walton v Stafford (1900) 162 NY 558, 561, 57 NE 92. Also, see, Paddell v Janes (S Ct NY Co 1914) 84 Misc 212, 145 NYS 868.

The assignee for benefit of creditors, therefore, is given an opportunity to ascertain whether the lease should be made available for the benefit of the creditors whom he represents. He may find that the term, burdened with the payment of rent and the performance of other conditions is an interest of no value; that instead of being a benefit, it will probably diminish the amount to which the creditors might otherwise be entitled. On the other hand his investigations may lead him to believe that the lease is a valuable asset. For these reasons, the assignee has been given this right of election.

Thus, initially the scope and extent of the liability of an assignee for benefit of creditors is dependent upon the election made by him to either accept or to abandon the lease.

### § 9:45. What Constitutes Acceptance of Lease by Assignee for Benefit of Creditors

When an assignee for benefit of creditors receives among the assets of his assignor the unexpired term of a lease, he may enter into possession of the demised premises, and occupy them for some period of time. He is permitted a reasonable time to remove or otherwise dispose of the assignor's property on the demised premises. If however the assignee remains in occupation for a greater period of time than is judged by the courts to be reasonably necessary to execute his duties, he will be deemed to have elected to accept the lease.[8] Clearly, then, this constitutes a question of fact to be determined by the proper tribunal, and will be decided in the light of all the circumstances, such as difficulty of moving the property, and the like.

The assignee for benefit of creditors may also elect to accept his assignor's lease by doing, as Hooker, J., phrased it,[9] "any other act which is equivalent to signifying the acceptance of the term as assignee of the lease."

### § 9:46. Scope of Liability

If an assignee for benefit of creditors elects to accept

---

8. H. L. Judd & Co. v Bennett (AT 1899) 28 Misc 558, 59 NYS 624, holding six days including a Sunday not to be unreasonable; Draper v Salisbury (Super Ct GT 1895) 11 Misc 573, 32 NYS 757.

9. Mead v Madden (AD2 1903) 85 AD 10, 82 NYS 900.

## ASSIGNMENT AND SUBLETTING § 9:46

the lease, then the lease becomes a part of the assigned estate, held by the assignee in his trust or representative capacity, and subject to the covenants contained therein.[10] However it is important to observe that it is the assigned estate, and not the assignee for benefit of creditors, which then is the owner of the leasehold. The assignee is merely the representative or agent for the assigned estate.

Since the assignee for benefit of creditors did not either personally or as a representative enter into the lease, no privity of contract between the estate and the landlord exists, or results from the mere acceptance of the lease. Therefore the liability of the assigned estate on the lease is not contractual.[11] However, when the assignee for benefit of creditors accepts the lease, he does so merely as the agent or representative of the estate he represents. Pursuant to the power the law vests in him he creates a privity of estate between the landlord and the assigned estate for which he acts. Therefore the liability of the assigned estate on the lease is the same as an ordinary non-assuming assignee of a lease. That is, the assigned estate will then only be liable for the performance of those covenants in the lease which run with the land during the existence of such privity of estate.[12] Stated differently, the assigned estate is liable by privity of estate, and not by privity of contract.[13]

Since the assigned estate, and not the assignee for the benefit of creditors, is the owner of the leasehold, the more recent cases hold that if suit be brought on a lease accepted by an assignee for benefit of creditors, it is properly brought against the assignee in his representative capacity, and should not be brought against him individually.[14]

---

10. Walton v Stafford (AD1 1897) 14 AD 310, 43 NYS 1049, affd 162 NY 558, 57 NE 92.

11. Walton v Stafford (AD1 1897) 14 AD 310, 43 NYS 1049, affd 162 NY 558, 57 NE 92.

12. See § 9:25, supra.

13. Walton v Stafford (AD1 1897) 14 AD 310, 43 NYS 1049, affd 162 NY 558, 57 NE 92; Paddell v Janes (S Ct NY Co 1914) 84 Misc 212, 145 NYS 868.

14. Walton v Stafford (AD1 1897) 14 AD 310, 43 NYS 1049, affd 162 NY 558, 57 NE 92; Oboler v Miller (AT1 1933) 146 Misc 509, 262 NYS 548; Paddell v Janes (S Ct NY Co 1914) 84 Misc 212, 145 NYS 868.

However, the following cases seem to present a contrary view: Re Application of Otis (1886) 101 NY 580, 585, 5 NE 571; Mead v Madden (AD2 1903) 85 AD 10, 82 NYS 900; Smith v Wagner (Com Pl Gen T 1894) 9 Misc 122, 29 NYS 284.

### § 9:47. Summary of Liability

In Paddell v Janes,[15] the subject of liability arising out of the acceptance of a lease by the tenant's assignee for benefit of creditors was exhaustively treated. The court, by Davis, J., said, "The possession of the assignee under his election to take is in effect the possession of the assignor. There has really been no change of possession, no new liability incurred. It is the assigned estate that is liable for the rent, as well as the assignor personally. It is true the assignee gets the legal title to the assignor's property, but the words 'legal title' are misleading when used with reference to a lease. What the assignee really acquires by his election to take the lease is the lessee's right to occupy the leasehold premises and under the same conditions as his agent for the purposes of the trust. The principal's money, the assigned estate, must pay the rent. There is, in fact, no question of lease or of sublease or of assignment of lease. In plain English, free from all legal verbiage, the lessee has simply put his agent, the assignee, in possession of the leased premises for an indefinite time, until the purposes for which the trust was created are satisfied, the lessee continuing to pay the rentals out of the assigned estate until the trust terminates, when the lease reverts to the lessee just as if he had never made the assignment for the benefit of creditors. . . . The assignee has no absolute right to occupy the leasehold through all its term. His naked right of occupation is coextensive with and limited by the life of the trust. The interest of the lessee as absolute owner of the lease never passes to his assignee in an assignment for the benefit of creditors. There is no passing of an existing estate to the assignee, but rather the appointment of a trustee, a representative, an agent to hold the leasehold for certain purposes; a holding in trust until those purposes have been accomplished, and not the absolute transfer of the whole interest and term of the lease."

### § 9:48. Terminating Liability

Since the assigned estate, which accepts the assignor's lease through its representative, the assignee for benefit

---

15. (S Ct NY Co 1914) 84 Misc 212, 145 NYS 868.

of creditors, is liable by reason of privity of estate only, such liability will cease when that privity of estate ceases.

When the purposes for which an assignee for benefit of creditors holds a lease have been accomplished, the assignee for benefit of creditors then may abandon possession, and thereby terminate the further liability of the assigned estate. The privity of estate between the assigned estate and the landlord, the foundation of liability, has been destroyed; because the lease then goes back to the owner thereof, the tenant who made the assignment for benefit of creditors. As Davis, J., in Paddell v Janes[16] said, "The assignee (for benefit of creditors) had no absolute right to occupy the leasehold through all its term. His naked right of occupation is coextensive with and limited by the life of the trust. The interest of the lessee as absolute owner of the lease never passes to his assignee in an assignment for the benefit of creditors. There is no passing of an existing estate to the assignee, but rather the appointment of a trustee, a representative, an agent, to hold the leasehold for certain purposes; a holding in trust until those purposes have been accomplished, and not the absolute transfer of the whole interest and term of the lease."

In other words, when the assignee for benefit of creditors gives up possession, he in effect turns the lease back to the owner of the leasehold, the tenant-assignor. Therefore there is no violation of the rule that privity of estate may not be destroyed by abandonment of possession.[17] What in reality occurs is that the assignee for benefit of creditors destroys privity of estate by reassigning the lease. Of course, as pointed out by the Appellate Division[18] the liability of the assigned estate may also be terminated "upon his eviction by the lessor, or upon his assignment of the lease to a third person, with surrender of possession."

### § 9:49. —Illustration

The following situation is adapted from the facts in the

16. (S Ct NY Co 1914) 84 Misc 212, 145 NYS 868.
17. See § 9:31, supra.
18. Walton v Stafford (AD1 1897) 14 AD 310, 43 NYS 1049, affd 162 NY 558, 57 NE 92.

§ 9:49                          LANDLORD AND TENANT

case of Walton v Stafford,[19] and illustrates how the liability of the assigned estate on an accepted lease may be terminated.

A lease provides that the rent reserved thereunder shall be payable in advance on the first day of each month. The tenant makes an assignment for benefit of creditors on the second day of a month, which the assignee accepts. The assignee thereupon enters into possession on the second day of the month. The assignee for the benefit of creditors vacates from the premises on the 30th day of that month, and before another month's rent falls due. Under these facts the assignee for benefit of creditors as representative of the assigned estate is not liable for any rent. That is, the assigned estate has incurred no liability for rent by reason of the assignee's going into possession and occupying the premises from the 2nd to the 30th day of the month.

This conclusion is based on the following reasons.[20] When the assignee accepted the lease, he created privity of estate. This established liability on those covenants in the lease running with the land which were breached during the existence of such privity of estate. But no liability arose for breaches of those covenants which occurred either prior to the creation of the privity of estate, or subsequent to its destruction.[1] When the lease was accepted on the second day of the month, the covenant to pay rent in advance on the first day of the month had already been breached. Consequently the assignee, as such, was not chargeable with primary liability for that month's rent. That was a debt of the assignor-tenant, already in existence at the time of the assignment, and provable as a claim against the assigned estate. Before any further rent fell due—the first day of the next month—the privity of estate was extinguished. Hence the assignee, as such, was not chargeable with liability for a breach of covenant which occurred subsequent to the destruction of privity of estate.

It should be pointed out that in the situation discussed in this section no recovery can be had for use and

---

19. (AD1 1897) 14 AD 310, 43 NYS 1049, affd 162 NY 558, 57 NE 92.

20. Adapted from the reasoning of the court in Walton v Stafford (AD1 1897) 14 AD 310, 43 NYS 1049, affd 162 NY 558, 57 NE 92.

1. See § 9:25, supra.

occupation, or upon a quantum meruit. There can be no such recovery, pointed out the Court of Appeals,[2] "as the lease was in full force and effect during the period of occupancy." That being so, then the only liability during that period must be measured by the covenants of the lease.

### § 9:50. Liability on Lease Not Accepted

If an assignee for benefit of creditors elects not to accept the lease of his assignor, but occupies the demised premises temporarily; for example, merely to remove or dispose of his assignor's property thereon, the assigned estate then has nothing to do with the lease. In this case the assignee becomes individually liable for the reasonable value of his use and occupation of the demised premises for the period of his occupation. The assignee in turn has a claim for reimbursement for this charge, as an administrative expense, out of the assets of the estate.[3]

It was pointed out in the preceding section that an action for use and occupation cannot be maintained when there is an existing lease in full force and effect. That rule only applies when the assignee accepts the lease. However, when he does not accept the lease, then the lease as to the assignee is not in full force and effect, and the reason for the rule falls. Therefore, it has been held that the assignee for benefit of creditors who has chosen not to accept the lease is liable for the value of his use and occupation of the demised premises. "The statement in Walton v Stafford, 162 New York 558, at p 563", said Callahan, J., in Oboler v Miller,[4] "that there could be no recovery against the assignee for use and occupation 'as the lease was in full force and effect during the period of his occupancy', must be considered in the light of the fact that the possession of the assignee in that case was under an acceptance of the lease, and his liability was accordingly measured solely by its terms."

### § 9:51. Valuation of Use and Occupation by Assignee

When an assignee for benefit of creditors does not

2. Walton v Stafford (1900) 162 NY 558, 563, 57 NE 92.
3. Oboler v Miller (AT1 1933) 146 Misc 509, 262 NYS 548; Re Izrue Corp. (S Ct Richmond Co 1968) 53 Misc 2d 343, 295 NYS2d 204.
4. Oboler v Miller (AT1 1933) 146 Misc 509, 262 NYS 548.

§ 9:51    LANDLORD AND TENANT

accept his assignor's lease, and occupies the premises temporarily, he is individually liable for the reasonable value of his use and occupation of the premises for the period of his occupation. (Of course, as pointed out in the preceding section, the assignee in turn has a claim for reimbursement for this charge, as an administrative expense, out of the assets of the estate.) The rent reserved in the lease is usually held to be the reasonable value of the use and occupation, in the absence of a clear showing of unreasonableness.[5]

## I. SURVIVAL OF DECEASED TENANT'S LIABILITY

### § 9:52. Generally

Death of a lessee does not terminate his lease.[6] Upon the death of the lessee the leasehold, as personal property,[7] passes to his personal representatives; that is, the person who receives letters to administer his estate for the purposes of the administration of his estate.[8] The personal representative of a deceased tenant has the right, until the expiration of the lease, to possession of the leased premises in his capacity as a representative of the deceased tenant's lease.[9]

If the deceased tenant was liable to the lessor by privity of contract, such contractual liability cannot be terminated by the executor's or administrator's merely refusing to accept the lease on behalf of the estate.

### § 9:53. Nature of Liability of Personal Representative

An executor or administrator of a deceased tenant has

---

5. Walton v Stafford (1900) 162 NY 558, 57 NE 92; Oboler v Miller (AT1 1933) 146 Misc 509, 262 NYS 548.

6. Joint Properties Owners, Inc. v Deri (1986, 1st Dept) 113 AD2d 691, 497 NYS2d 658; Walker v Bradley (S Ct Cayuga Co 1915) 89 Misc 516, 153 NYS 686.

7. See § 1:3, supra.

8. EPTL 13-1.1(a)(1).

See, Re Althause's Estate (AD1 1901) 63 AD 252, 71 NYS 445, affd 168 NY 670, 61 NE 1127; Goldberg v Himlyn (Co Ct Kings 1923) 121 Misc 580, 201 NYS 837.

In the absence of a specific bequest the unexpired term of a lease goes to the executor of the deceased lessee, and not to his heirs. Putch v Jacard Realty Co (S Ct NY Co 1964) 44 Misc 2d 177, 253 NYS2d 335.

An executor takes the unexpired term of his decedent's leasehold by operation of law, and not by assignment. Charcowsky v Stahl (AT1 1959) 19 Misc 2d 1096, 189 NYS2d 384.

9. Joint Properties Owners, Inc. v Deri (1986, 1st Dept) 113 AD2d 691, 497 NYS2d 658.

## ASSIGNMENT AND SUBLETTING § 9:53

the election of accepting his decedent's lease, or of abandoning it.

If he abandons the lease, that will not discharge the decedent's estate from the liability on the lease which the decedent had contracted in his lifetime. The landlord in this case will have his rights against the estate.[10]

If, however, a representative of a deceased tenant accepts his decedent's lease, he does so in his representative capacity, and presumably for the best interests of the estate; and whatever rights he may acquire during his term, he acquires in his representative capacity.[11] An estate cannot assume a life of its own, it has been observed,[12] exercising rights the decedent never had. It may not on behalf of the heirs or distributees it represents, inherit an apartment and become a full-fledged tenant. The right of an executor or administrator to manage its decedent's leasehold interest in an apartment should be limited to the life of the lease and to those functions necessary to the winding up of the estate. An estate does not stand in the shoes of a deceased tenant for purposes of exercising a right to purchase his apartment which the decedent did not have when he died.

It is the duty of the fiduciary of a deceased tenant, upon accepting the lease to receive the rents or profits from the leasehold, and to apply them to the payment of the obligations thereof, instead of placing them among the general assets of the estate. To insure that this is done, the law, then, imposes a limited personal liability on a personal representative who accepts his decedent's lease. This personal liability is imposed only to the extent of the rents or profits received by the representative from the decedent's leasehold.

This rule of a limited personal liability was enunciated by the Court of Appeals in an early case,[13] where the Court said, "This lease upon the death of Edward Knox,

---

10. See § 9:52, supra.
11. Remford Corp. v Rosenfeld (AD1 1948) 274 AD 769, 79 NYS2d 756; Charcowsky v Stahl (AT1 1959) 19 Misc 2d 1096, 189 NYS2d 384.

An executor of a tenant's estate may occupy the tenant's leased residential apartment, but only in his representative capacity, and not as a tenant under the lease. Rosefan Constr. Corp. v Salazar (NYC Civ Ct Queens Co 1982) 114 Misc 2d 956, 452 NYS2d 1016.

12. Lomnitz v 61 East 86th Street Equities Group (1985) 129 Misc 2d 157, 492 NYS2d 915.
13. Miller v Knox (1872) 48 NY 232, 237.

passed to his administrators, and became a portion of the assets in their hands. If the lease was worth anything, it was their duty to sell it, or to assume control of the premises and collect the rents, or in some form secure the profits thereof. If they either took possession of the premises or received the profits or collected the rents thereof, they became personally liable for the rent, to the extent of the rents or profits received by them. Administrators do not become personally liable for the full amount of the rent reserved in the lease, unless the rent or profits of the premises are at least equal to the amount of the rent. A landlord, after the death of his tenant, always has these remedies for rent accruing after death: He may collect the same of the estate of the deceased, or he may collect the same of the administrators or executors personally to the extent of the rents or profits received by them of the premises; and he may collect of the executors or administrators so much of the rent as they are personally liable for, and the balance, of the estate. This personal liability of the administrators and executors grows out of the fact that it is their duty to receive the rents or profits, and to the extent of the rent, apply them in payment thereof, instead of placing them among the general assets. That the rents and profits are not sufficient to pay the rent is, however, strictly matter of defence, as the law *prima facie* supposes them to be sufficient."

An executor or administrator may incur a full personal liability. This liability however will arise from the fact that he personally creates it. If, after the liability of his decedent on the lease terminates, the representative enters into a new liability, then the personal representative has created a privity of contract between himself personally and the landlord. This is not the obligation of the decedent or of the estate. Therefore the personal representative must bear this liability personally without reimbursement from the estate. Thus, if a decedent during his lifetime had entered into a lease for one year, at the end of that year all liability of the decedent on the lease should terminate. If the representative by any act of his extends the liability on that lease beyond that year, such

ASSIGNMENT AND SUBLETTING § 9:54

liability is one of his own creation, and should not be saddled onto the estate.[14]

### § 9:54. —Illustration

In Beatty v Rosenberg,[15] a landlord sought to hold the administrator of a deceased tenant liable both individually and as a representative for the payment of rent. In that case the tenant had entered into a lease for one year from October 1, 1913. In November 1913 the tenant died, and the defendant in the action shortly thereafter was appointed the administrator of his estate. The landlord claimed that the administrator immediately after his appointment entered upon and took possession of the demised premises under the lease, and remained in actual possession until October 1, 1914, the end of the lease, and thereafter continued to remain in possession of the premises. The landlord elected to treat this holding over by the administrator as a renewal of the lease for another year. Therefore, the landlord sought to recover from defendant both individually and as a representative of the tenant's estate the unpaid rent from the date the lease started (the decedent had never paid any rent) till the commencement of this action—a total period of seventeen months. The trial court found as a matter of fact that the administrator had not entered upon and taken possession of the premises during any part of the original term, nor had he for any period of time after the term had expired. Therefore the court refused to grant the landlord a judgment against the defendant individually, but granted the landlord a judgment against the defendant in his representative capacity for the rent due from October 1, 1913 till the end of the original term. In affirming this judgment the Appellate Division, by Scott, J., said, "The whole controversy turns upon the question whether or not defendant took possession under the lease and continued in possession thereunder. Legget v Pelletreau, 213 NY 237. In our opinion it is quite clear that he did not. It is true that he demanded admission to the apartment, and that he went there twice, but it is evident that his purpose in so doing was to ascertain what

---

14. Chisholm v Toplitz (AD1 1903) 82 AD 346, 82 NYS 1081, affd 178 NY 599, 70 NE 1096.

15. (AD1 1916) 173 AD 645, 160 NYS 135.

personal property decedent had left, and to look for papers relating to the estate. The second visit was with the transfer tax appraiser, and was apparently for the purpose of making an inventory and appraisal. These visits were within his right and duty as administrator, and cannot properly be construed as an adoption of the lease. He was not bound to do any affirmative act to surrender or disavow the lease. The actual occupant of the premises during the period for which it is sought to hold defendant personally was the widow of the decedent. There is nothing to indicate that defendant put her into possession, or kept her there. She appears to have remained by common consent. Defendant, as administrator, apparently permitted her to use the furniture belonging to the estate; but this falls far short of a personal assumption of her tenancy. As to the period after the lease expired, there is not a scintilla of evidence upon which to hold the defendant."

In other words, here, the representative did not accept the lease. Therefore the court refused to impose the limited personal liability suggested by the Miller v Knox case, discussed in the preceding section. Since the representative did not hold over after the expiration of the term, he did not create any new contract. Therefore there was no personal liability. The only liability left, then, was the liability of the decedent's estate for the lease obligation which had been incurred by the decedent during his lifetime. This liability was not extinguished by death. Therefore this estate liability was imposed on the representative of the estate in his representative capacity.[16]

## J. SECURITY DEPOSITS

### § 9:55. Effect of Assignment of Lease on Security Deposit

An assignment of a lease does not pass title to the security or moneys deposited by a tenant with his landlord to secure performance of the lease, unless they are

---

16. As to the liability of the committee for an incompetent tenant, see Re Application of Otis (1886) 101 NY 580, 5 NE 571; as to the liability of a receiver of a tenant, see Prince v Schlesinger (AD1 1906) 116 AD 500, 101 NYS 1031, affd 190 NY 546, 83 NE 1130; Woodruff v Erie R. Co. (1883) 93 NY 609.

specifically referred to and included in the assignment.[17] In one case, an assignment of lease covered "all rights, privileges, interests, and assets of every name and nature owned by the party of the first part or used in the conduct of his business" including the lease and his interest in the lease. The court held that this assignment did not refer specifically to any security, and that the language of the assignment was not broad enough to convey to the assignee any right in collateral deposited to secure performance of the lease.[18]

### § 9:56. Effect of Mortgage on Lease on Security Deposit

It has been held that a mortgage on a lease which uses the statutory language:[19] "together with the appurtenances and all the estate and rights of the" mortgagor, includes the deposit moneys, although they may not be specifically mentioned in the mortgage.[20] The reason for this difference from the rule applied to assignments of lease was pointed out by the Appellate Division.[1] There the court said, "The substantial claim made by the appellant is that, regardless of the statute, the mortgagee of the lease gets no greater rights under the mortgage than the assignee under an absolute assignment would get to the security, and that it is the law of this state that such an assignee gets no title to the security. (Cases cited.) There is a substantial difference, however, between the purpose sought to be accomplished by an ordinary assignment of a lease and that sought to be accomplished by a mortgage thereof. In the one instance the purpose of the transaction is to transfer the tenancy and right of possession, and in the other the purpose is to transfer all beneficial interest of the tenant under the lease as security for the payment of the mortgage debt. In the case of an assignment, the transfer of the security is not a

---

17. Piser v Hecht (AD1 1915) 170 AD 668, 156 NYS 601; Shattuck v Buek (AD1 1913) 158 AD 709, 143 NYS 1045; Friedman v Isaacs (AT1 1929) 133 Misc 435, 232 NYS 545; Re Izrue Corp. (S Ct Richmond Co 1968) 58 Misc 2d 343, 295 NYS2d 204; Whiteway Books, Inc. v Cohen (NYC Cir Ct NY Co 1972) 70 Misc 2d 940, 335 NYS2d 148 (citing text); Goodale Real Estate Corp. v Subridge Holding Corp. (M Ct 1931) 139 Misc 587, 248 NYS 663.

18. Nemtzoff v Vagnier (1917, Sup App T) 163 NYS 1075.

19. Real Prop L § 272.

20. Keusch v Morrison (AD1 1934) 240 AD 112, 269 NYS 169.

1. Keusch v Morrison (AD1 1934) 240 AD 112, 269 NYS 169.

## K. SUBTENANT'S LIABILITIES AND RIGHTS[2]
### § 9:57. Form of Sublease
#### FORM NO. 10
#### Sublease

AGREEMENT made June 1, 1986, by and between John Doe, residing at 5 North Street, Albany, New York, herein called Sublessor, and Richard Roe, residing at 17 South Street, Albany, New York, herein called Sublessee, WHEREIN IT IS MUTUALLY AGREED AS FOLLOWS:

1. Sublessor hereby represents and warrants that Fort Lee, Inc., by agreement dated December 1, 1985, leased to Sublessor the first floor in the building known as and by #16 West Street, Albany, New York, for a term of 10 years commencing May 1, 1986, and ending at midnight on April 30, 1996, a copy of which lease is annexed hereto as Exhibit "A", and hereby made a part of this agreement.

2. Sublessor hereby represents and warrants that said lease is now in full force and effect, and that Sublessor has full right, power, and authority to sublet the said premises as herein provided.

3. Sublessor hereby sublets to Sublessee, and Sublessee hereby hires from Sublessor the said first floor in the said building #16 West Street, Albany, New York, for a term commencing June 1, 1986, and ending at noon on March 31, 1996, at the annual rental of $12,000, which Sublessee hereby agrees to pay in equal monthly installments in advance on the first day of each and every month during the said term, provided, however, that the first of said monthly installments shall be paid to Sublessor simultaneously with the execution and delivery of this agreement.

4. Said premises shall be used by Sublessee as a show-

---

2. In the case of rent controlled or rent stabilized residential premises, the rental charged to the subtenant is limited by statute; e.g., Emergency Tenant Protection Act.

# ASSIGNMENT AND SUBLETTING § 9:57

room for the display of the women's clothes it manufactures at another location, and for no other purpose or purposes whatsoever.

5. Sublessee shall not, without the prior written consent of Sublessor and of the owner of the fee of said premises first obtained, assign the term hereby leased, nor suffer or permit it to be assigned by operation of law or otherwise, nor shall Sublessee, without the prior written consent of Sublessor and of said owner of the fee, underlet or permit the said premises, or any part thereof, to be used by others.

6. All of the terms, provisions, covenants and conditions contained in the said lease between Sublessor and its lessor, as set forth in Exhibit "A", hereto attached and hereby made a part of this sublease except as herein otherwise expressly provided, and such rights and obligations as are contained in said Exhibit "A" are, during the term of this sublease, hereby imposed upon the respective parties hereto, the Sublessor being substituted for the Lessor in the said agreement, and the Sublessee being substituted for the Lessee in the said agreement [*add, if desired:* provided, however, that the Sublessor shall not be liable for any defaults by its said Lessor, Fort Lee, Inc., or its successors or assigns].

7. If Sublessee shall violate any of the terms, provisions, covenants or conditions of this agreement, then, in any one or more of such events, upon Sublessor's serving a written five days' notice upon Sublessee, in the manner provided in said lease set forth in Exhibit "A", specifying the nature of said default, and upon the expiration of said five days, if Sublessee shall have failed to comply with or remedy said default, or if the said default or omission complained of shall be such as cannot be completely cured or remedied within said five days, and if Sublessee shall not have diligently commenced curing said default within the said five days' period, and shall not thereafter with reasonable diligence, and in good faith have proceeded to remedy or cure said default, then Sublessor may serve Sublessee with a written three days' notice of termination, in the manner provided in said lease set forth in Exhibit "A", and upon the expiration of said three days, this sublease and the term hereunder shall

§ 9:57          LANDLORD AND TENANT

end and expire as fully and completely as if the date of expiration of said three days' period were the day herein definitely fixed for the end and expiration of this sublease, and the term thereof, and Sublessee shall then quit and surrender the leased premises to Sublessor, but Sublessee shall remain liable as provided in the said lease set forth in Exhibit "A".

IN WITNESS WHEREOF, the parties hereto have signed this agreement the day and year first above written.

**JOHN DOE
RICHARD ROE**
*[ANNEX COPY OF PARAMOUNT LEASE]*

### § 9:58. Liability to Paramount Landlord

In the preceding sections of this chapter it is shown that under an assignment the tenant parts with his entire interest or estate in the leasehold, and does not reserve any reversionary interest therein whatsoever. In effect the assignee is substituted in the place of the original tenant. However, in the case of a sublease, the tenant reserves a reversionary interest in the leasehold estate. Therefore, a new estate is created by the sublease, which is carved out of the original leasehold, and a new relationship of landlord and tenant is created. The subtenant because of the outstanding reversionary interest cannot be substituted in the place of the original tenant. As the Court of Appeals said,[3] "An assignment creates no new estate; but transfers an existing estate into new hands; an underlease, creates a perfectly new estate." These fundamental principles determine the liability of a subtenant to the landlord of his sublessor, the paramount landlord.

The sublease creates no privity of contract between the subtenant and the paramount landlord. There is no agreement between the subtenant and the paramount landlord. Therefore no contractual liability arises between the subtenant and the paramount landlord. Because of the reversionary interest remaining in the sublessor, the sublease does not create any privity of estate

---

3. Collins v Hasbrouck (1874) 56 NY 157, 162.

## ASSIGNMENT AND SUBLETTING § 9:60

between the subtenant and the paramount landlord.[4] Therefore there is no liability on the part of a subtenant to the paramount landlord on any of the covenants of the lease between the sublessor and the paramount landlord, whether or not such covenants run with the land.[5]

### § 9:59. Liability to Sublessor

The subtenant receives his estate from the sublessor. He holds his estate from his sublessor alone, and then only by reason of the covenants contained in the sublease. Therefore the subtenant's liability is only to his sublessor, and on all the covenants contained in the sublease. The relationship of landlord and tenant exists between them. Accordingly, as between a subtenant and his sublessor all the incidents of the relationship of landlord and tenant apply.

### § 9:60. Rights Limited by Terms of Paramount Lease

Since a sublease is carved out of the paramount lease between his sublessor and the paramount landlord, the sublease is dependent on the paramount lease for its existence. By necessity, therefore, the rights of the subtenant may be limited by the terms of the paramount lease. "There is no doubt", said the Appellate Division,[6] "that the subtenant is bound in his occupancy of the demised premises by the covenants of the lease to his immediate lessor, who is the tenant under said lease."

Accordingly, when the paramount lease contains a covenant restricting the use of the premises by the tenant, the subtenant will be bound by such a covenant. The paramount landlord, then, may enjoin not only his immediate tenant, but also the subtenant for a violation of the agreement to use the demised premises as restricted by the paramount lease.[7]

---

**4.** Stewart v Long I. R. Co. (1886) 102 NY 601, 607, 8 NE 200, 203.

**5.** Subtenant incurs no liability directly to a paramount lessor for performance of covenants contained in the main lease. Tefft v Apex Pawnbroking & Jewelry Co. (1980, 2d Dept) 75 AD2d 891, 428 NYS2d 52.

A subtenant is not necessary party to primary landlord's action based on breach of terms of primary lease. Joscar Co. v Arlen Realty (1976, 1st Dept) 54 AD2d 541, 387 NYS2d 117.

**6.** Bartholdi Realty Co. v Robard Realty Co. (AD1 1913) 156 AD 528, 141 NYS 353.

**7.** Bartholdi Realty Co. v Robard Realty Co. (AD1 1913) 156 AD 528, 141 NYS 353.

A restriction against the tenant's

When the paramount lease comes to an end by an act done within its very terms, the sublease which was carved out of it falls with it.[8] Therefore, although the subtenant is not directly liable nor personally answerable for the performance of the terms, conditions, and covenants of the paramount lease; yet, he, together with the sublessor, may be dispossessed by the paramount landlord because of a breach of the paramount lease by the sublessor.

In a leading case,[9] the Court of Appeals, by Allen, J., summed up the position of a subtenant in the following language: "The plaintiff, the sublessee, by the contract of hiring, acquired a valid term in and a right to possession of the part of the demised premises let to him for the time agreed upon, subject, only, to be defeated by the expiration of the term of Morrison, (the sublessor) or a reentry by the owner of the fee, and supreme landlord, for some condition of the demise broken. He held the premises subject to the conditions of his own hiring, and, with these limitations, his right to hold for the term granted to him was perfect."

### § 9:61. Right to Perform Paramount Lease

If a tenant-sublessor fails to pay his rent to the paramount landlord, he may be ousted from possession. If the sublessor be ousted and his estate terminated, then the subtenant's estate, which depends on the sublessor's estate for its existence, will likewise terminate.[10] Therefore, when a subtenant is faced with a loss of possession because of the defaults of his sublessor under the paramount lease, the courts have held that the subtenant in self-protection may perform the breached covenant. Thus, he may pay to the paramount landlord, if he so desire, the rent due from the sublessor to the paramount land-

---

assignment or subletting is binding on the tenant's subtenants. Mann Theatres Corp. v Mid-Island Shopping Plaza Co. (1983, 2d Dept) 94 AD2d 466, 464 NYS2d 793, affd 62 NY2d 930, 479 NYS2d 213, 468 NE2d 51.

**8.** Century Paramount Hotel v Rock Land Corp. (NYC Civ Ct NY Co 1971) 68 Misc 2d 603, 327 NYS2d 695; Precision Dynamics Corp. v Retailers Representatives, Inc. (NYC Civ Ct NY Co 1983) 120 Misc 2d 180, 465 NYS2d 684 (citing text); Bove v Coppola (AT 1904) 45 Misc 636, 91 NYS 8.

**9.** Eten v Luyster (1875) 60 NY 252, 258.

Also, see Ashton Holding Co. v Levitt (AD1 1920) 191 AD 91, 180 NYS 700.

**10.** Berman v Seeger (AT1 1929) 133 Misc 849, 234 NYS 339.

ASSIGNMENT AND SUBLETTING § 9:62

lord. Such payment, if made in good faith and under compulsion, will be a good defense to an action brought against him by the tenant-sublessor for the same rent.[11]

In Peck v Ingersoll,[12] the Court of Appeals said, "It has been frequently decided, upon the most obvious principles of justice, that if an under-tenant be compelled to pay rent to the head-landlord he may deduct it from the rent due to his immediate lessor; or, if the sum paid exceeds that due to the lessee, the tenant may, in an action of *assumpsit* for money paid to the use of the lessor, recover the excess. . . . This privilege upon the part of the under-tenant exists, if there be in the head-landlord a legal right, by the exercise of which, the person who pays may be damnified, unless he satisfies it. . . . It is not necessary, that the head-landlord should distrain, or even demand the money, or commence or threaten a suit. The right to enforce his claim in this way will make the payment by the under-tenant compulsory, within the principle of the decisions."

However, it should be pointed out, a paramount landlord is not required to accept performance of the terms of the paramount lease by a subtenant of his tenant, but can insist upon performance by his tenant with whom he is in privity.[13]

### § 9:62. —Illustration

In Sokolow v Meyer[14] the fee owner had instituted summary proceedings against his tenant for non-payment of rent, and had joined the tenant's subtenants as parties to the proceedings. A final order was granted the fee owner, and a warrant was thereafter issued. Prior to the execution of the warrant the subtenant, in order to avoid being evicted from the demised premises, paid the rent in arrears under the paramount lease directly to the fee owner. This payment by the subtenant was held to be a

---

11. Cohen v 515 Broadway Realty Corp. (AT1 1934) 150 Misc 288, 269 NYS 113; Sokolow v Meyer (M Ct 1931) 139 Misc 424, 248 NYS 405.

12. (1852) 7 NY 528.

13. 214 West 39th Street Corp. v Miss France Coats, Inc. (AD1 1948) 274 AD 597, 84 NYS2d 818; Precision Dynamics Corp. v Retailers Representatives, Inc. (NYC Civ Ct NY Co 1983) 120 Misc 2d 180, 465 NYS2d 684; 305 Broadway Co. v Stanpud Operating Corp. (Civ Ct NY Co 1965) 48 Misc 2d 95, 264 NYS2d 327 (paramount landlord refusing tender of rent from subtenant entitled to possession in nonpayment proceeding).

14. (M Ct 1931) 139 Misc 424, 248 NYS 405.

good defense to an action brought against the subtenant to recover rent accruing under the sublease. The court said, "At the time he (subtenant) paid the rent for May and June, 1930, to the owner of the fee, the owner of the fee had a warrant which, if enforced, would oust him from possession. Under these circumstances, it seems to me that the payment made by this defendant (subtenant) was under compulsion, and that he acted in good faith in paying the rent to the owner of the fee. It may be that if there were any reason to suppose that the undertenant acted in bad faith in paying the rent to the owner of the fee, that such a payment would not be a defense, but it would be inequitable to hold that an undertenant would have to submit to actual ouster and be relegated to his action for damages against a lessor, perhaps insolvent. It seems to me that an undertenant in such a position would have his choice of either paying the rent due to the owner of the fee in order to protect his possession, or of giving up possession or submitting to dispossession and then seek to hold his lessor responsible in damages. So long as the undertenant acts in good faith, I am of the opinion that his payment of the rent to the owner of the fee is a valid defense. To hold otherwise would be to violate the most ordinary principles of justice and common sense."

However, in Peck v Ingersoll,[15] the paramount landlord merely threatened to exercise the right of reentry for the sublessor's default. Even though no summary proceedings nor any legal action had been commenced by the paramount landlord; yet, the subtenant was held justified in paying the rent in arrears to the paramount landlord. In other words, the mere right on the part of a paramount landlord to enforce his claim for the sublessor's breach by legal steps will make the performance by the subtenant compulsory within the principle set forth.

### § 9:63. Right to Compel Sublessor's Performance of Paramount Lease

Since a subtenant has the right to perform covenants of the paramount lease breached by his sublessor in order to protect his possession, when threatened because of such

---

15. (1852) 7 NY 528.

## ASSIGNMENT AND SUBLETTING § 9:64

defaults, it has been held that the subtenant then has an adequate remedy at law.[16] Therefore, when a subtenant is in danger of losing possession because of a threatened or possible breach by the sublessor of the paramount lease, the subtenant cannot maintain a suit in equity to require the sublessor to perform the paramount lease, and thus avert the threatened loss of possession. "I am satisfied," said Levy, J., in a case denying the subtenant such equitable relief,[17] "that this is not a case requiring equitable intervention, in that the plaintiffs (subtenants) have an adequate remedy at law." The argument advanced in this case by the subtenants, that the admitted insolvency of the sublessor determines that they have no adequate remedy at law, was held untenable. The court pointed out that it is the ability to bring an action and recover judgment that determines the adequacy of legal remedy, and not the ability to collect that judgment.

### § 9:64. Form of Agreement Permitting Subtenant to Remedy Sublessor's Default

#### FORM NO. 11
#### Agreement by Paramount Landlord to Notify Subtenant of Defaults and to Permit Subtenant to Remedy Same

AGREEMENT made June 1, 1986, among Fort Lee, Inc., a domestic corporation having its principal office at 16 West Street, Albany, New York, herein called Lessor, John Doe, residing at 5 North Street, Albany, New York, herein called Sublessor, and Richard Roe, residing at 17 South Street, Albany, New York, herein called Sublessee, WHEREIN IT IS MUTUALLY AGREED AS FOLLOWS:

1. If during the term of the sublease between Sublessor and Sublessee, dated June 1, 1986, subletting the first floor in the building known as and by #16 West Street, Albany, New York, any default shall occur by reason of which Lessor might, under any of the terms, provisions or conditions of the lease between Lessor and Sublessor, dated December 1, 1985, leasing the said first floor in said building known as and by #16 West Street, Albany, New York, terminate the said lease, and declare the same to

---

16. Blank v La Montagne-Chapman Co. (S Ct NY Co 1924) 123 Misc 238, 205 NYS 45.

17. Blank v La Montagne-Chapman Co. (S Ct NY Co 1924) 123 Misc 238, 205 NYS 45.

be at an end, or might exercise its right of re-entry by force or otherwise, at any time or times, Lessor agrees to give Sublessee thirty days' written notice, in the manner provided in said lease for the giving of notices, of any such default before exercising its right to so terminate the said lease or to re-enter by force or otherwise; and if during the said period of thirty days, the Sublessee shall remedy, or cause to be remedied, the said default, then, and in such event, Lessor shall not terminate the said lease or exercise its right to re-enter by force or otherwise.

2. If Sublessee shall incur any expense in consequence of remedying any such default on the part of Sublessor in respect of which notice shall have been given by Lessor to Sublessee, then, and in such event, Sublessee shall be entitled to deduct such expenditures incurred by Sublessee from the next installment or installments of rent falling due under said sublease.

3. For the purposes of this agreement Sublessee shall not be required to inquire into the invalidity of any claim of any default that may be made by Lessor under said lease, but Sublessee shall be entitled to treat as conclusive evidence of any such default any notice so received by him from Lessor.

IN WITNESS WHEREOF the parties hereto have hereunto signed this agreement the day and year first above written.

> Fort Lee, Inc.,
> by James Lee, President
> John Doe
> Richard Roe.
> [Acknowledgments]

### § 9:65. Right to Contest Summary Proceedings Brought Against Sublessor

When a paramount landlord brings a summary proceeding to evict his tenant, if he wishes to obtain complete possession of the leased premises, he must make all of the subtenants parties to the proceeding. If he fails to join a subtenant, then he will not be able to evict such subtenant pursuant to the warrant he may obtain in the proceeding directing the removal of the paramount tenant. In other words, whatever effect the summary proceeding may have on the sublease, the subtenant's rights to possession, at least, will not be affected by the issuance of a warrant in a summary proceeding to which such subtenant was not made a party.[18]

However, when a summary proceeding has been brought against a sublessor by the paramount landlord, and the subtenant is made a party thereto, to avoid collusion and fraud the subtenant must be permitted to answer and to contest the proceeding, even though the sublessor defaults in appearing or in contesting the proceeding. Thus, it was held to be reversible error to strike out a subtenant's answer in a summary proceeding merely because the sublessor had defaulted in appearing therein.[19] "It is well established," said the Appellate Term,[20] "that undertenants have a right to prevent forfeiture of their estates arising out of default of the lessee in payment of rent . . . a right which would be of little value if the lessor may without compliance with the provisions of the summary statute terminate their estates in the premises."

### § 9:66. Rights on New Lease to Sublessor

Where a tenant-sublessor surrenders his lease for the purpose of getting a new lease, the sublease by virtue of Real Property Law § 226, remains wholly unaffected. This section provides:

> The surrender of an under-lease is not requisite to the validity of the surrender of the original lease, where a new lease is given by the chief landlord. Such a surrender and renewal do not impair any right or interest of the chief landlord, his lessee or the holder of an under-lease, under the original lease; including the chief landlord's remedy by entry, for the rent or duties secured by the new lease, not exceeding the rent and duties reserved in the original lease surrendered.

---

**18.** New York R. Corp. v Savoy Associates, Inc. (AD1 1933) 239 AD 504, 268 NYS 181; Cohen v 515 Broadway Realty Corp. (AT1 1934) 150 Misc 288, 269 NYS 113.

**19.** Neusberger v Prodelefsky (AT1 1900) 31 Misc 749, 64 NYS 131; Teachers College v Wolterding (NYC Civ Ct NY Co 1973) 75 Misc 2d 465, 348 NYS2d 286 (citing text), revd on other grounds 77 Misc 2d 81, 351 NYS2d 587.

**20.** Cohen v 515 Broadway Realty Corp. (AT1 1934) 150 Misc 288, 269 NYS 113.

## L. SUBTENANT'S RIGHTS ON CANCELLATION OF PARAMOUNT LEASE

### § 9:67. Right to Vacate

"The subtenant's rights," said the Appellate Term,[1] "are measured by those of his immediate landlord, the original tenant, and the cancellation of the lease, by its own terms, as to one, cancels it as to both."

As has been seen,[2] whatever effect a summary proceeding brought by a paramount landlord may have on a sublease, the right of a subtenant to possession, at least, will not be affected by the issuance of a warrant in a summary proceeding to which he was not made a party. But, if a warrant be issued in that proceeding for the removal of the paramount tenant, the paramount lease will be terminated.[3]

Upon termination of the paramount lease, the sublease dependent upon the paramount lease for existence, likewise terminates. Therefore, although a subtenant's rights to continue in possession may not be terminated because he was not made a party defendant to the summary proceeding; yet, his rights as a subtenant under the sublease will be extinguished.[4]

As was pointed out by the Appellate Division,[5]

"The rights of the subtenant respondent under its lease were subordinate to and depending on the primary lease . . . . When that lease was terminated by the warrant in the dispossess proceeding, all right of the subtenant under its lease fell with it. . . . The failure to make the subtenant a party to the first dispossess proceeding could not affect the character of its estate after the overlease fell for nonpayment of rent. Its only effect was to prevent the landlord from taking action against it without further proceedings to which it was a party."

Therefore, if a sublease comes to an end because of the cancellation of the paramount lease, by its own terms,

---

1. Bruder v Geisler (AT 1905) 47 Misc 370, 94 NYS 2.
   Also, see, Ashton Holding Co. v Levitt (AD1 1920) 191 AD 91, 180 NYS 700.
2. See § 9:65, supra.
3. Real Prop Act & Proc L § 749, subd 3.
4. New York R. Corp. v Savoy Associates, Inc. (AD1 1933) 239 AD 504, 268 NYS 181.
5. New York R. Corp. v Savoy Associates, Inc. (AD1 1933) 239 AD 504, 268 NYS 181.

# ASSIGNMENT AND SUBLETTING § 9:68

the subtenant may, if he so desires, vacate from the premises, and thereby avoid any further liability under this sublease.[6]

### § 9:68. Effect of Subtenant's Failure to Vacate on Cancellation of Paramount Lease

When a subtenant is faced with loss of possession because of the defaults of his sublessor under the paramount lease, the subtenant in self-protection may perform the breached covenant in his stead.[7] When the paramount lease is cancelled by its own terms, the sublease is similarly cancelled, and the subtenant may thereupon vacate from the premises.[8]

However, if the subtenant does not perform the breached covenant of the paramount lease, and does not vacate when the paramount lease is cancelled therefor, then the subtenant is faced with the unpleasant obligation of having to continue to perform the terms of his sublease. And he must do this, even though loss of possession is imminent,—when the paramount landlord takes the proper steps to oust him. In this situation it was held that the subtenant is under an obligation to pay the rent due under his sublease to the sublessor, even though a warrant for the removal of the sublessor had been issued in a summary proceeding brought to evict the sublessor. In the case so holding, The Assembly v Giller,[9] the paramount landlord had brought summary proceedings against the sublessor for nonpayment of rent. These proceedings resulted in a final order in favor of the paramount landlord. Execution on the warrant was stayed until July 1. In the meantime the sublessor had instituted summary proceedings against his subtenant for nonpayment of the rent reserved in the sublease. These proceedings came on for trial on July 1. The subtenant defended on the ground that the conduct of the sublessor in refusing to perform the obligations of the paramount lease constituted a complete repudiation of the sublessor's obligations under the sublease. Therefore, argued the subtenant, since these acts occurred before the rent ac-

---

6. D. A. Schulte, Inc. v Cross (AT1 1933) 146 Misc 763, 262 NYS 798.
7. See §§ 9:61, 9:62, supra.
8. See § 9:67, supra.

9. (AT1 1930) 135 Misc 542, 239 NYS 280, revg (M Ct) 134 Misc 657, 236 NYS 308.

crued, for which these proceedings were brought, he was relieved from the obligation to pay such rent. In addition, the subtenant demanded the return of the money deposited by him with the sublessor to secure performance of the sublease. The trial court sustained the defense, and awarded a final order in favor of the subtenant, together with a judgment for the amount of the deposit money. However, the Appellate Term reversed the trial court, and dismissed the petition of the sublessor without prejudice to the bringing of an appropriate action against the subtenant to recover the unpaid rent reserved in the sublease. The court said, "In this summary proceeding by sublessor against tenant for nonpayment of rent, it appears that prior to the trial, in a nonpayment proceeding by the owner against the sublessor and subtenants, a final order was made in favor of the owner, with a stay of execution of the warrant until July 1, the date of the trial of this proceeding. The Assembly, Inc v Giller, 134 Misc Rep 657, 236 NYS 308, at pages 314, 315. Under the circumstances, the relation of landlord and tenant between the parties having been terminated by the issuing of the warrant, a final order could not be awarded in favor of the sublessor, landlord herein, and, as no such final order could be granted, this landlord cannot have a judgment for the rent due. It was error for the trial judge to award the tenant herein judgment for the deposit, for as long as the tenant remained in possession, in the absence of an attornment to the senior landlord, or payment by this tenant of the rent due by the sublessor to the owner, respondent (subtenant) was bound to pay rent to his landlord (sublessor), and the amount of the rent exceeded the deposit."

Therefore, since because of the technicalities involved, no judgment for rent could be awarded the sublessor in these particular summary proceedings, the petition was dismissed without prejudice to the bringing of an appropriate action therefor by the sublessor.

Accordingly, even though a subtenant is faced with loss of possession because his sublessor has defaulted under the paramount lease; he must nevertheless continue to perform the terms and conditions of his sublease. True, he has the right to perform the terms of the paramount lease in the place of the sublessor, and offset that against the obligations due under his sublease. True, if the paramount lease be cancelled by its own terms, he may vacate from possession. But if he fails to take advantage of such rights he has no excuse for not carrying out his own contract. Until the subtenant is ousted from possession, or until he attorns to the paramount landlord, and thereby creates a new relationship, he is still obligated under his sublease to his sublessor.

### § 9:69. Right to Possession

If a paramount lease be cancelled by its own terms, the sublease likewise is cancelled. If the subtenant then wishes to vacate, he may do so. If he does not vacate, he must continue to perform the terms of his sublease even though loss of possession is imminent,—when the paramount landlord takes the proper steps to evict him.[10] Therefore, a subtenant, whose sublease has been prematurely cancelled by a cancellation of the paramount lease, must, if he desire to continue in possession, enter into a new agreement with the paramount landlord.

Such a new agreement with the paramount landlord constitutes a new lease, and if for a longer period than one year, must be in writing.[11]

However, if the subtenant cannot, or does not wish to enter into a new agreement with the paramount landlord, the subtenant should not overestimate his position. He merely acquires a temporary right to possession because of the paramount landlord's failure to join him in the summary proceeding against the sublessor. The paramount landlord still has the right to institute a subsequent summary proceeding, making the subtenant a party.[12]

---

10. See §§ 9:67, 9:68, supra.

11. New York R. Corp. v Savoy Associates, Inc. (AD1 1933) 239 AD 504, 268 NYS 181.

12. Christatos v United Cigar Stores Co. (AT1 1932) 144 Misc 322, 258 NYS 586, revg (M Ct) 143 Misc 453, 256 NYS 614. In this case, Untermeyer, J., suggested that the paramount landlord could also recover for use and occupation notwithstanding that the relation of landlord and tenant did not exist. However, since a landlord-tenant relationship is a sine qua non to an action for use and occupation, this suggestion is of doubtful validity, and, as a matter of fact, has been rejected as unsound. Glickman v Glenwood-Syosset Appliances Corp. (AT2 1965) 45 Misc 2d 655, 257 NYS2d 498.

### § 9:70. Effect of Assignment of Sublease After Cancellation of Paramount Lease

Sometimes a clause similar to the following is inserted by a paramount landlord in the tenant's lease, in anticipation that the demised premises will be sublet by the tenant. "In the circumstance hereinafter mentioned, the lessee hereby assigns, transfers and sets over to the lessor, its successors and assigns, such of the subleases now outstanding and those which the lessee may hereafter make of the demised premises, and of all parts thereof, as said lessor may select, as well as all rent and other sums of money which may hereafter become due and payable thereunder to the lessee herein, upon condition, however, that this assignment shall become operative and effective only in the event that this lease and the term hereby granted is cancelled or terminated pursuant to the provisions hereof or in the event of the issuance of a warrant of dispossess or other reentry or repossession by the lessor under the provisions hereof."[13] However, when the paramount lease comes to an end by an act done within its very terms, the sublease which was carved out of it falls with it. Therefore, the quoted clause will be ineffective to transfer any of the subleases, because there is nothing to be assigned. This situation was presented to the courts for decision.[14] In this case, the paramount landlord had dispossessed the sublessor, and relying upon the clause of assignment of the sublease, quoted above, sought to recover rent from the subtenant. The court denied the landlord the right to such recovery, and said, "As the issuing of the warrant in the summary proceeding cancelled the principal lease[15] as of the time of the issuing of the precept the provisions of paragraph nineteenth (the above quoted clause of assignment) relied upon could not after such cancellation effect an assignment of the sublease, which as between the plaintiff and the lessee, at least, depended for its existence upon the principal lease. It is true that the defendant-undertenant, apparently not a party to the summary proceeding, could not have been dispossessed by the warrant if he had

---

13. Quoted from the lease litigated in D. A. Schulte, Inc. v Cross (AT1 1933) 146 Misc 763, 262 NYS 798.

14. D. A. Schulte, Inc. v Cross (AT1 1933) 146 Misc 763, 262 NYS 798.

15. See Real Prop Act & Proc L § 749, subd 3.

chosen to remain in possession; but here he did in fact remove pursuant to the issuance of the warrant. It is evident therefore that the provisions of paragraph nineteenth did not create the relation of landlord and tenant between plaintiff and defendant, and the right of the plaintiff to rent upon the theory of assignment of the sublease cannot be sustained."

In Christatos v United Cigar Stores Co.,[16] the same principles were applied, precluding the landlord from suing the subtenant for rent reserved in the sublease after he had disposed the sublessor. There, the paramount landlord had brought a summary proceeding against the tenant-sublessor for nonpayment of rent, but did not make the subtenant a party defendant. A final judgment was rendered, and a warrant issued therein. Thereafter the tenant-sublessor assigned the sublease to the paramount landlord who then sued the subtenant for rent reserved under the sublease. It was found as a fact that the subtenant had never attorned to the paramount landlord. The court, in denying the landlord the right to recover, said: "It is equally clear that after the issuance of the warrant, the sublessor could not assign the sublease to the plaintiff. Only by virtue of the lease was the lessee enabled to make any sublease of the premises. The lessee's rights as sublessor were dependent upon the continued existence of the lease, and the cancellation of the lease by the dispossess proceeding effectively terminated the lessee's rights as sublessor."

### § 9:71. Right to Vacate on Threat of Cancellation

In a case which went to the Court of Appeals,[17] it was held that after a landlord serves a tenant with a precept in summary proceedings, if the tenant thereupon vacates the premises, such act on the part of the tenant cancels the lease and annuls the relation of landlord and tenant as of the time of the removal. The court, by Collin, J., said, "Judicial decisions have uniformly held that the moving by the tenant from the leased premises, enabling thereby the landlord to take peaceable possession of them, after the issuance and service of the precept in the

---

16. (AT1 1932) 144 Misc 322, 258 NYS 586, revg (M Ct) 143 Misc 453, 256 NYS 614.

17. Cornwell v Sanford (1918) 222 NY 248, 252, 118 NE 620.

§ 9:71    LANDLORD AND TENANT

summary proceedings, cancels the lease and annuls the relation of landlord and tenant as of the time of the removal; the service of the precept is an election and declaration on the part of the landlord that the tenant should remove from the premises and effect the cancellation of the lease at any time thereafter; the removal is the precise act and effect the landlord sought through the service of the precept and the proceeding, and it is entirely immaterial, within the law, whether it is produced through the warrant or the conduct of the tenant in obedience to the precept."

However, a distinction must be made, said the court in Irrose Realty Corp. v Warren-Nash Motor Corp.,[18] "between the case of a landlord requesting or commanding his own tenant to remove from the demised premises and the case of an owner in fee or superior landlord so doing against his tenant, joining the latter's sublessee as an undertenant." The difference is important. In this case the landlord leased certain premises to a tenant, who sublet part thereof to a subtenant. The landlord instituted summary proceedings against the tenant for non-payment of rent, and joined the subtenant as party defendant. Thereupon the subtenant vacated the premises. Before the return day of the precept the landlord and tenant settled their differences, and discontinued the proceedings. The tenant then brought this action against his subtenant for rent. The subtenant defended on the ground that before the rent accrued, the sublease had been terminated by the service on him of the precept and his removal in compliance therewith. The court overruled this defense, and said, "But the mere commencement of a summary proceeding by a superior landlord against his tenant, joining as parties the latter's subtenants, would not produce such a result. The main tenant might very well have a genuine dispute with the superior landlord. The main tenant is not consulted when the superior landlord joins the subtenants as parties to the summary proceeding. The superior landlord properly regards the subtenants as necessary parties, who might choose to pay the rent to the superior landlord and gain the right of

18. (M Ct 1932) 144 Misc 5, 257 NYS 825, affd by Appellate Term 1st Dept, Dec 1932, not reported.

ASSIGNMENT AND SUBLETTING § 9:72

subrogation, or might have a valid objection to some of the landlord's proceedings.[19] The main tenant might compose his differences with the superior landlord, as appears to have been done here, before a final order or a warrant would ever issue. The subtenant's lease would in such case continue unaffected."

Therefore, when the paramount landlord threatens to cancel the paramount lease, and even goes to the extent of instituting summary proceedings to that end; the subtenant may not anticipate the actual cancellation and vacate from the premises. Such a course of conduct is fraught with danger; for, if the sublessor and the paramount landlord should settle their differences, the vacating subtenant will find himself in the unenviable position of being held liable for breach of his sublease, which in such case continues unaffected by all the preceding legal skirmishes.

### § 9:72. Summary of Rights

A subtenant is in a precarious position. He has a lease, but it is dependent for existence upon the continued existence of his landlord's paramount lease.

If the sublessor defaults in the performance of the covenants of the paramount lease, the subtenant is faced with a threatened loss of possession. He can, if he wishes to, perform the sublessor's breached covenant.[20] In this way he can preserve his sublease. But this may be too onerous, and even though he has the right of reimbursement from the sublessor, the cost of performance may be far in excess of the rent he has agreed to pay under the sublease. The likelihood of recovering the excess from the sublessor may be impossible.

If the subtenant does not take advantage of his right to perform the paramount lease, the paramount landlord may then proceed to cancel the paramount lease. If the subtenant is joined as a party to the summary proceeding, then upon the issuance of a warrant therein the subtenant will be evicted. If for some reason the subtenant is not made a party to the summary proceeding, he

---

19. Citing Croft v King, 8 Daly 265; Schlaich v Blum (1903) 42 Misc 225, 85 NYS 335.

20. See §§ 9:61, 9:62, supra.

§ 9:72 LANDLORD AND TENANT

cannot vacate before the warrant is issued for execution, and thereby avoid any further liability on his sublease.[1]

Even though he may soon thereafter be evicted when the paramount landlord takes the proper steps to evict him, he must, nevertheless, continue to perform his sublease.[2]

His only alternative, then, is to succeed in making a new lease with the paramount landlord.[3] If he fails to do this, he can do nothing else to preserve his possession.

These are the disadvantages inherent in a subletting, and should be realistically borne in mind by a prospective subtenant. It is often of no consolation to know that one can protect oneself by being able to perform the terms of the paramount lease. Nor, is it of any greater consolation, then, to get an agreement from the paramount landlord that he will notify the subtenant of any defaults by the sublessor. However, under the circumstances, this is the least the subtenant should get, so that he may learn as soon as possible of the true situation, and thereby be in a position to decide what to do.[4]

## M. SUBTENANT'S RIGHTS ON VOLUNTARY SURRENDER OF PARAMOUNT LEASE

### § 9:73. Generally

When a sublessor voluntarily surrenders his paramount lease, and such surrender is not made pursuant to any provision of the paramount lease, then the rule is, that the sublease is not thereby terminated if the subtenant is not a party to the surrender agreement.

It is now well settled that the effect of a voluntary surrender by a tenant-sublessor to his paramount landlord, which surrender is not made pursuant to any provision of the paramount lease, is the equivalent of a transfer of the reversion, as encumbered by the sublease, to the then owner of the fee, and the subtenant's rights remain unaffected.[5] Thereupon, as was said by the Appel-

1. See § 9:71, supra.
2. See § 9:68, supra.
3. See § 9:68, supra.
4. See Form No 11 (§ 9:64), supra.
5. Kottler v New York Bargain House, Inc. (1926) 242 NY 28, 37, 150 NE 591, remittitur den 242 NY 568, 152 NE 430; Eten v Luyster (1875) 60 NY 252; Harwyn Dress Corp. v International Dress Co. (S Ct NY Co 1955) 147 NYS2d 254; Da Costa's Automotive, Inc. v Birchwood Plaza Shell,

## ASSIGNMENT AND SUBLETTING § 9:73

late Term,[6] "the undertenant 'becomes the immediate tenant of the original lessor' and 'the interest and terms of the subtenant of the lessee continued as if no surrender had been made.'"

In Eten v Luyster,[7] the Court of Appeals pointed out that "it was not competent for the lessor and lessee to affect the rights of third parties by a formal surrender of the lease. The interests and the terms of the subtenant of the lessee continued as if no surrender had been made. The defendants, the surrenderees and owners in fee, became the immediate landlords of the plaintiff, (subtenant) with only such rights as his lessor would have had to the possession of the premises before the expiration of the term. . . . Morrison (the tenant-sublessor) could not sell, give up, or surrender to the defendants anything that did not belong to him; and he could not terminate the lease to the plaintiff, (subtenant) or destroy his rights."

Therefore, if the subtenant, now a paramount tenant, pays the rent reserved in the sublease to the paramount landlord, who accepts it, this will constitute merely an attornment under an existing lease; that is, the sublease.[8] Payment of such rent does not constitute payment of damages for use and occupation, nor a new agreement with the paramount landlord implying an hiring for an indefinite term.[9]

The effect of these principles is important. Upon acceptance by the paramount landlord of the rent reserved in the sublease, a relationship of landlord and tenant between the paramount landlord and the subtenant arises. Such relationship creates a tenancy in the subtenant upon the terms, provisions, and covenants of the sublease then existing. Accordingly, the subtenant can remain in possession as long as he performs the terms of his sub-

---

Inc. (1984, 2d Dept) 106 AD2d 484, 482 NYS2d 832 (citing text); Metropolitan Life Ins. Co. v Hellinger (1935) 246 AD 7, 284 NYS 432, affd 272 NY 24, 3 NE2d 621; Precision Dynamics Corp. v Retailers Representatives, Inc. (NYC Civ Ct NY Co 1983) 120 Misc 2d 180, 465 NYS2d 684.

**6.** Rhinelander Real Estate Co. v Cammeyer (AT1 1921) 117 Misc 67, 190 NYS 516, affd 216 AD 299, 214 NYS 284.

**7.** (1875) 60 NY 252, 259.

**8.** Ashton Holding Co. v Levitt (AD1 1920) 191 AD 91, 180 NYS 700.

**9.** Rhinelander Real Estate Co. v Cammeyer (AD1 1926) 216 AD 229, 214 NYS 284; Ashton Holding Co. v Levitt (AD1 1920) 191 AD 91, 180 NYS 700.

**§ 9:73**  LANDLORD AND TENANT

lease until the expiration thereof.[10] And, the paramount landlord must perform the sublessor's covenants contained in the sublease which run with the land, even though the paramount lease may not have contained such a covenant.

"If such were not the fact," said the Appellate Division,[11] "the benefit of such covenants inserted in the sublease for the benefit of a tenant, in order to enable him to carry on his business, would be lost upon a surrender to another landlord, although he would be still obliged to pay rent and perform other covenants provided in the lease. This cannot be the rule."

### § 9:74 Illustrative Cases

The effect on a sublease of a voluntary surrender of the paramount lease by the sublessor was discussed most instructively in the case of Ashton Holding Co. v Levitt.[12] There, the Appellate Division said, "There can be no doubt that the clause in the lease that, in case of a contract of sale of the property, the landlord could terminate the lease by giving 20 days' written notice, created a conditional limitation upon the term demised. If the landlord had proceeded under this clause of the lease, the term of the lease would have expired at the end of the 20 days, and the landlord could have proceeded against the tenant and those claiming under him as holding over after the expiration of the term. . . . In the case under consideration, however, the parties did not proceed under the clause in the lease; therefore the condition upon which the limitation was predicated never happened. Mollie Levitt, (subtenant) by the contract of hiring, acquired a valid term and a right of possession in the part of the demised premises let to her for the time agreed upon until the expiration of the lease of her immediate landlord, subject only to be defeated by the expiration of the term of her immediate landlord or a re-entry of the owner of the fee for some condition broken. The surrender by the immediate landlord of his case to the owner of

---

10. Rhinelander Real Estate Co. v Cammeyer (AD1 1926) 216 AD 229, 214 NYS 284; Ashton Holding Co. v Levitt (AD1 1920) 191 AD 91, 180 NYS 700.

11. Rhinelander Real Estate Co. v Cammeyer (AD1 1926) 216 AD 229, 214 NYS 284.

12. (AD1 1920) 191 AD 91, 180 NYS 700.

the fee, and the consequent merger of the greater and lesser interest, terminated the lease of Wiegan, (sublessor) and the term created thereby, as between the parties to the lease. But it was not competent for the owner and its lessee to affect the rights of third parties. The interest and term of the subtenant of the lessee continued as if no surrender had been made. The owner of the premises, upon the surrender of the lease, became the immediate landlord of Mollie Levitt, with only such rights as Wiegan would have had to the possession of the premises before the expiration of the term. Weigan could not sell, give up, or surrender anything that did not belong to him. He could not terminate the lease to Mollie Levitt or destroy her right therein. . . . She is in possession under the terms of her lease and entitled to remain in possession so long as she performs the conditions of the lease on her part until the expiration of the demised term."

In Horn & Hardart Co. v 115 East 114th Street Co.,[13] the paramount lease provided that the paramount landlord would grant the tenant, at the expiration of the lease, a renewal for a further term of twenty-one years if the tenant so requested it. During the term the tenant sublet the premises to plaintiff with a similar privilege of renewal. Prior to the expiration of the lease the tenant elected to renew the term by a written notice, and the paramount landlord consented to grant such renewal. Thereafter the tenant made what the court termed as "unwarranted demands" on the subtenant, who refused to comply. In retaliation the tenant thereupon withdrew its election to renew its paramount lease, and refused to grant the subtenant a renewal of the sublease pursuant to the privileges granted him in the sublease. Plaintiff-subtenant thereupon brought this action against the tenant and the paramount landlord to obtain specific performance of the renewal provisions of lease and sublease. In granting judgment for the plaintiff-subtenant, Miller, J., said, "The term of the lease having been extended on October 20, 1936, and the rights of the parties thereto unalterably fixed, the rights of the plaintiff as subtenant, measured by its lessor's estate under the principal lease,

---

13. (S Ct NY Co 1938) 7 NYS2d 688, affd 257 AD 813, 12 NYS2d 784, affd 281 NY 802, 24 NW2d 482.

could not thereafter without its consent be cut down by the withdrawal of the written notice of election given on October 20, 1936, by which the lease had been extended. . . . The plaintiff, having duly elected on April 5, 1937, to renew its sublease, it is entitled to judgment as demanded in the complaint."

In other words, when the tenant-sublessor exercised his election to renew the paramount lease, there was then in existence a paramount lease for a term extending beyond the original term. Neither the sublessor nor the paramount landlord could thereafter terminate the sublease, or destroy the subtenant's rights therein by a voluntary surrender of the paramount lease, before its expiration, without the subtenant's consent.

## N. RIGHT TO ASSIGN AND SUBLET

### § 9:75. Generally

It is well established that in the absence of an express restriction, either by contract or by statute, a tenant has the absolute right to assign his lease, or to sublet the premises leased to him.[14] (However, residential tenant in a dwelling having 4 or more residential units has the right to sublet subject to the written consent of the landlord in advance of the subletting. See § 7:79.)[15] The power of assignment and of subletting, it has been said, is incident to a leasehold estate in the absence of contractual restriction.[16] A monthly tenant may assign his lessee interest.[17]

A tenant at will, and a tenant at sufferance, have no

---

**14.** Fleisch v Schnaier (AD1 1907) 119 AD 815, 104 NYS 921; 18th Ave. Pharmacy, Inc. v Wilmant Realty Corp. (S Ct Kings Co 1950) 95 NYS2d 534; Werber v Weinstein (M Ct Bx 1955) 207 Misc 707, 138 NYS2d 196; Van Walderveen v Martin (City Ct Albany 1949) 195 Misc 91, 91 NYS2d 234; Syracuse Sav. Bank v D'Elia (M Ct City of Syracuse 1945) 185 Misc 928, 56 NYS2d 800.

**15.** A covenant restricting right to assign may be implied, but only when it is clear that a reasonable landlord would not have entered into the lease without such an understanding. The situation must be such that the failure to imply the covenant "would be to deprive a party of the benefit of his bargain." Although a percentage clause is some sign of the implied covenant, its significance varies with the other terms of the lease, the surrounding circumstances, the nature of the business, the identities and expectations of the parties. Rowe v Great Atlantic & Pacific Tea Co. (1978) 46 NY2d 62, 412 NYS2d 827, 385 NE2d 566 (covenant not implied).

**16.** Butterick Pub. Co. v Fulton & Elm Leasing Co. (S Ct NY Co 1928) 132 Misc 366, 229 NYS 86.

**17.** Zeltner v Santora (AT1 1923) 198 NYS 253.

## ASSIGNMENT AND SUBLETTING § 9:75

right either to assign their estate or interest, or to sublet the premises they occupy.[18] If they do either, they will terminate their estate in the premises, and the person to whom they have assigned their estate, or to whom they have sublet the premises, will enter the premises as a trespasser only, if the landlord so chooses to treat him.[19] As the Court of Appeals said, in this connection,[20] "A tenant at will is disqualified from granting a lease available against any one but himself; for the demise would amount to a termination of the will, and it would be optional with the landlord to regard the entry of the lessee of the tenant at will as a disseizin. . . . The same rule holds as to a tenant by sufferance. . . . The yielding of the possession of the premises terminates the original tenancy, and a new tenancy at will of the owner cannot be created except by his or her assent. Every lease at will is at the will of both parties, and a tenant at will has no certain and indefeasible estate; nothing that can be granted by him to a third person. If a tenant at will assigns over his estate to another who enters on the land, he is a disseizor, and the landlord may have an action of trespass against him. . . . A tenancy by sufferance, existing only by the laches of the owner, cannot give the occupant an estate or interest capable of transmission to another."

As has been seen, a tenant under a lease for a term to commence in the future has a right to assign the lease before the term commences.[1]

Although a leasehold interest is part of a deceased tenant's estate, the estate's representative does not have the unrestricted right to sublet the leased premises, or to assign the lease. A lease is not a property right that devolves upon death to be passed from one generation to another. The right of the estate of a deceased tenant to assign or sublet is controlled exclusively by Real Property Law § 236.[2]

**18.** Reckhow v Schanck (1871) 43 NY 448; 18th Ave. Pharmacy, Inc. v Wilmant Realty Corp. (S Ct Kings Co 1950) 95 NYS2d 534.

**19.** Landon v Townshend (1891) 129 NY 166, 178, 29 NE 71; Reckhow v Schanck (1871) 43 NY 448.

**20.** Reckhow v Schanck (1871) 43 NY 448, 450.

**1.** § 1:4, supra.

**2.** Joint Properties Owners, Inc. v Deri (1986, 1st Dept) 113 AD2d 691, 497 NYS2d 658.

See § 9:99, infra.

### § 9:76. Effect of Personal Relationship

"Doubtless, the general rule is," said Cullen, Ch. J.,[3] "that an executory contract not necessarily personal in its character, which can, consistent with the rights and interests of the adverse party, be sufficiently executed by the assignee, is assignable in the absence of agreement in the contract." Ordinarily, then, a lease is assignable under this rule.

However, if it is clear that a lease is made with a particular tenant in sole reliance upon the landlord's personal trust and confidence in that tenant, then the lease will not be assignable even though there be no restriction on assignments in the lease. "The reason which underlies the basis of the rule," said McLaughlin, J.,[4] "is that a party has the right to the benefit contemplated from the character, credit, and substance of him with whom he contracts (case cit) and in such case he is not bound to recognize either an assignment of the contract or an undisclosed principal."

In Nassau Hotel Co. v Barnett & Barse Corp.,[5] a landlord leased a hotel and its furnishings valued at more than one million dollars, and agreed to accept from the tenants as rental a percentage of the gross receipts. The tenants were two individuals who, the court found, were financially responsible and had had a long and successful experience in managing hotels. The court found that these factors were undoubtedly an inducing cause for the landlord's making the lease. Thereafter, the two tenants organized a corporation to carry on the hotel business, and assigned the lease to the corporation. The landlord thereupon brought this action to cancel the lease and to recover possession on the ground that the lease was not assignable. The court upheld the landlord's complaint on the theory that reading the lease in its entirety it clearly appeared that a personal trust or confidence was reposed by the landlord in the two individual tenants when the

---

3. New York Bank Note Co. v Hamilton Bank Note Engraving & Printing Co. (1905) 180 NY 280, 291, 73 NE 48.

4. Nassau Hotel Co. v Barnett & Barse Corp. (AD1 1914) 162 AD 381, 147 NYS 283, affd on opinion below of McLaughlin J., 212 NY 568, 106 NE 1036 and later app 164 AD 203, 149 NYS 645.

5. (AD1 1914) 162 AD 381, 147 NYS 283, affd on opinion below of McLaughlin, J., 212 NY 568, 106 NE 1036, and later app 164 AD 203, 149 NYS 645.

lease was made, and that they were to personally carry out the terms of the lease. Therefore it was not assignable. The court also overruled the contention that because the lease provided that it should "inure to the benefit of and bind the respective parties hereto, their personal representatives and assigns", the two tenants had a right to assign the lease. "But the intention of the parties," said McLaughlin, J., "is to be gathered, not from one clause, but from the entire instrument. . . ."[6]

Therefore, absent a restriction in the lease on the right to assign it, a tenant generally has the right to assign the lease. However, if the rights under the lease "involve a relationship of personal confidence such that the party whose agreement conferred those rights must have intended them to be exercised only by him in whom he actually confided";[7] then the courts will hold the lease to be unassignable notwithstanding the absence of a restrictive covenant, and notwithstanding a general provision in the lease that the lease is to be binding on the respective parties' representatives and assigns. While a percentage clause in a lease is some sign of an implied agreement to limit the lessee's power to assign the lease, its significance will vary with the other terms of the lease, the surrounding circumstances, the nature of the business conducted upon the premises, and the identities and expectations of the parties.[8]

### § 9:77. Effect of Emergency Rent Laws[9]

As a general rule the primary purpose of emergency rent control laws is to protect tenants in their occupancy, and against the extortion of unjust and unreasonable rents. During a period when such emergency rent control laws are in effect, upon the expiration of a term created by agreement, the continuance of the tenant's occupancy

---

6. But, see MacFadden-Deauville Hotel, Inc. v Murrell (1950, CA5) 182 F2d 537, holding that the fact that the rent was computed on the basis of a percentage of income did not make the lease a personal undertaking so as to preclude assignment, where there also was a provision for a substantial, fixed minimum rental payment, and where the term of the lease was 33 years.

7. Arkansas Valley Smelting Co. v Belden Mining Co. (1888) 127 US 379, 32 L Ed 246, 8 S Ct 1308.

8. Rowe v Great Atlantic & Pacific Tea Co. (1978) 46 NY2d 62, 412 NYS2d 827, 385 NE2d 566 (covenant not implied).

9. As to effect of Emergency Rent Laws on the covenant restricting assignments and subleases, see § 9:87, infra.

of the demised premises is by virtue of the emergency statute, and not pursuant to the agreement of the parties. Neither landlord nor tenant obtains rights except those given by such statute. However, unless in contravention of such statute, the obligations of the parties are those of the lease. Under the agreement of lease the tenant is obligated to surrender possession to his landlord, and since his occupancy is that only which is continued by the statute upon the condition therein prescribed; namely, that he pay the emergency rent, it would follow that the statute gives the tenant no right to confer any privilege of occupancy upon a stranger by assignment.[10]

Similarly, it has been held that the right to sublet is not projected into a statutory tenancy.[11] However, where a provision against subletting was waived by the acceptance of rent for many years with knowledge of the breach, the unlimited right to sublet was held to have been projected into the statutory tenancy.[12]

### § 9:78. Residential Tenant's Statutory Right to Assign

The Real Property Law provides,[13] that unless a greater right to assign is conferred by the lease, a tenant renting a *residence* may not assign his lease without the written consent of the owner. The owner may unconditionally withhold his consent without cause, provided that the owner then must release the tenant from the lease if the tenant requests the release on 30 days' notice. Release

---

10. Clason Management Co. v Altman (1972, 1st Dept) 40 AD2d 635, 336 NYS2d 65, affd 34 NY2d 643, 355 NYS2d 378, 311 NE2d 510; Hunt v Gilmore (AT1 1950) 198 Misc 50, 98 NYS2d 322; Greif Realty Corp. v Moroff (1948, Sup App T) 82 NYS2d 396.

Also, see Bisbano v 42-20 Restaurant Corp. (AD2 1952) 280 AD 790, 113 NYS2d 215 (provision in lease giving tenant right to assign without landlord's consent does not survive the expiration of the lease, and is not projected into the ensuing statutory tenancy), app dismd 304 NY 780, 109 NE2d 78; Dyckman v Mackie (1957, Sup App T) 160 NYS2d 903.

11. Emtico Associates v Gabel (S Ct NY Co 1965) 47 Misc 2d 577, 262 NYS2d 885, affd (1st Dept) 25 AD2d 718, 269 NYS2d 675. But see, 18th Ave. Pharamcy, Inc. v Wilmant Realty Corp. (S Ct Kings Co 1950) 95 NYS2d 534; and Van Walderveen v Martin (City Ct Albany 1949) 195 Misc 91, 91 NYS2d 234, wherein it was held that a tenant for a term of years who continued in possession after the expiration of his term as a statutory tenant has a right to sublet a part of the premises in the absence of any restriction in the lease against subletting.

12. 41st. Street Bldg. Corp. v Rothenberg (M Ct 1958) 12 Misc 2d 111, 173 NYS2d 913, affd 17 Misc 2d 620, 184 NYS2d 71.

13. Real Prop L § 226-b, added L 1983, ch 403, § 37, effective June 30, 1983, replacing former Real Prop L § 226-b, enacted in 1975, and repealed L 1983, ch 403, § 37, eff June 30, 1983.

shall be the sole remedy of the tenant.[14] However, if the owner reasonably withholds consent, then there shall be no assignment, and the tenant shall not be released from the lease.[15]

Any assignment which does not comply with the provisions of this section of the Real Property Law constitutes a substantial breach of the lease or tenancy, thus constituting grounds for termination of the lease by the landlord.[16]

Any provision of a lease or rental agreement purporting to waive a provision of Real Prop L § 226-b is null and void.[17]

These provisions of the Real Property Law shall not be deemed to prevent or limit the right of a tenant of a loft to sell improvements to a unit pursuant to Article 7-C of the Multiple Dwelling Law (see § 43:29, infra).[18]

The provisions of this section of the Real Property Law do not apply to public housing and other units for which there are constitutional or statutory criteria covering admission thereto, nor to a proprietary lease, that is, a lease to or held by a tenant entitled thereto by reason of ownership of shares in a corporate owner of premises which operates the same on a cooperative basis.[19]

With respect to units covered by the Emergency Tenant

---

14. Real Prop L § 226-b, subd 1. Vance v Century Apartments Associates (1984) 61 NY2d 716, 472 NYS2d 611, 460 NE2d 1096.

15. Real Prop L 226-b, subd 1. As to what constitutes unreasonable withholding of consent, see § 9:97. Under the 1975 Real Prop L § 226-b, the following reasons for disapproval of a requested assignment were held to be unreasonable: (1) The existence of waiting lists for prospective tenants; (2) inability to obtain a vacancy increase; (3) being compelled to offer the assignee a renewal lease; (4) imposition of security problems from turnover of tenancies resulting in a policy of denying requests for consent; (5) the existence of "switch" lists (renting the apartment to an existing tenant in another apartment; (6) creating a situation whereby transfer of the apartment could take place from one assignee to another ad infinitum. Bragar v Berkeley Associates Co. (S Ct NY Co 1981) 111 Misc 2d 333, 444 NYS2d 355.

16. Real Prop L § 226-b, subd 5.

Where landlord refuses, albeit unreasonably, to consent to tenant's assignment of his rent-stabilized apartment, the attempt to assign is ineffective. Parks v Mengoni (1984, 1st Dept) 100 AD2d 785, 474 NYS2d 487.

17. Real Prop L § 226-b, subd 6.

18. Real Prop L § 226-b, subd 8.

This provision granting a loft tenant the right to sell fixtures is not to be construed as granting an unconditional right to sell a leasehold interest; and, therefore, a loft tenant may not assign the lease in violation of a prohibition contained in the lease. Krax Peripatie Apanu Stu Krokodrilos Tus Platos, Ltd. v Dexter (NYC Civ Ct NY Co 1984) 124 Misc 2d 381, 476 NYS2d 745.

19. Real Prop L § 226-b, subd 3.

Protection Act of 1974, or the Rent Stabilization Law of 1969, the exercise of the rights granted by this section of the Real Property Law shall be subject to the applicable provisions of such laws. Moreover, nothing contained in this section of the Real Property Law shall be deemed to affect the rights, if any, of any tenant subject to Title Y of Chapter 51 of the Administrative Code of the City of New York or the Emergency Housing Rent Control Law.[20]

### § 9:79. Residential Tenant's Statutory Right to Sublet

Real Property Law § 226-b, enacted in 1975, was repealed, and new Real Property Law § 226-b was enacted in its place in 1983.[1] This new section provides that a tenant renting a residence pursuant to an "existing lease" in a dwelling *having 4 or more residential units* shall have the right to sublease his premises subject to the written consent of the landlord "in advance of the subletting." Such consent must not be unreasonably withheld.[2]

The right to sublet is not automatic. In order to be able to sublet, the tenant must inform the landlord of his intent to sublease by mailing a notice of such intent by certified mail, return receipt requested. Such request must be accompanied by the following information: (a) the term of the sublease; (b) the name of the proposed sublessee; (c) the business and permanent home address of the proposed sublessee; (d) the tenant's reason for subletting; (e) the tenant's address for the term of the sublease; (f) the written consent of any cotenant or guarantor of the lease; and (g) a copy of the proposed sublease, to which a copy of the tenant's lease shall be attached if available, acknowledged by the tenant and proposed subtenant as being a true copy of such sublease[3]

Within ten days after the mailing of such request, the

---

20. Real Prop L § 226-b, subd. 4. For text of these laws, see RENT CONTROL AND STABILIZATION, by Joseph Rasch, published by The Lawyers Co-operative Publishing Co., Rochester, New York, 14694.

1. See § 9:78, supra.
2. Real Prop L § 226-b, subd 2(a).
3. Real Prop L § 226-b, subd 2(b).

To invoke the protection of RPL 226-b, the tenant must establish that he notified the landlord in the manner required by RPL 226-b; such notification, if given by his subtenant, is ineffective. Clarkton Estates, Inc. v Chiaro (NYC Civ Ct NY Co 1983) 122 Misc 2d 721, 471 NYS2d 942, affd 124 Misc 2d 691, 480 NYS2d 165.

## ASSIGNMENT AND SUBLETTING § 9:79

landlord may ask the tenant for additional information as will enable the landlord to determine if rejection of such request will be unreasonable. Any such request for additional information shall not be unduly burdensome. Within thirty days after the mailing of the request for consent, or of the additional information reasonably asked for by the landlord, whichever is later, the landlord shall send a notice to the Tenant of his consent, or, if he does not consent, his reasons therefor. Landlord's failure to send such a notice shall be deemed to be a consent to the proposed subletting. If the landlord consents, the premises may be sublet in accordance with the request, but the tenant thereunder, shall nevertheless remain liable for the performance of tenant's obligations under said lease. If the landlord reasonably withholds consent, there shall be no subletting, and the tenant shall not be released from the lease. If the landlord unreasonably withholds consent, the tenant may sublet in accordance with the request and may recover the costs of the proceeding and attorneys fees if it is found that the owner acted in bad faith by withholding consent.[4]

Any subletting which does not comply with the provisions of the 1983 Real Property Law § 226-b constitutes a substantial breach of lease or tenancy,[5] thus constituting grounds for termination of the lease of the tenant.[6] Moreover, any provision of a lease or rental agreement purporting to waive a provision of this statute is null and void.[7]

With respect to units covered by the Emergency Tenant Protection Act of 1974, or the Rent Stabilization Law of 1969, the exercise of the rights granted by the 1983 Real

---

4. Real Prop L § 226-b, subd 2(c).

As to what constitutes unreasonable withholding of consent, see § 9:97.

The remedies provided by Real Property L § 226-b are exclusive and expressly limited. 72nd Street Associates v Pyle (1984, 1st Dept) 105 AD2d 607, 481 NYS2d 341 (tenant cannot recover damages, compensatory or punitive), app dismd 64 NY2d 774, 485 NYS2d 991, 475 NE2d 457.

5. Real Prop L § 226-b, subd 5.

6. Tenant must comply strictly with the provisions of this subdivision of the statute if the sublease is to be upheld, and landlord will not be deemed to have waived his rights arising upon tenant's failure to comply with these provisions by permitting the proposed sublessee to fill out an application at a time when the landlord knew that the sublessee already had entered into possession of the subject apartment. Bleecker Associates v Hayward (NYC Civ Ct NY Co 1983) 121 Misc 2d 174, 467 NYS2d 535.

7. Real Prop L § 226-b, subd 6.

Property Law § 226-b to sublet are subject to the applicable provisions of such laws.[8] Tenants of units subject to these 2 laws have the right to sublet pursuant to Real Property Law § 226-b provided that (a) the rental charged to the subtenant does not exceed the legal regulated rent plus a ten percent surcharge payable to the tenant if the unit sublet was furnished with the tenant's furniture; (b) the tenant can establish that at all times he has maintained the unit as his primary residence and intends to occupy it as such at the expiration of the sublease; (c) an owner may terminate the tenancy of a tenant who sublets or assigns contrary to the terms of this section but no action or proceeding based on the non-primary residence of a tenant may be commenced prior to the expiration date of his lease;[9] (d) where an apartment is sublet, the prime tenant shall retain the right to a renewal lease and the rights and status of a tenant in occupancy as they relate to conversion to condominium or cooperative ownership; (e) where a tenant violates the provisions of subdivision (a) of this section the subtenant shall be entitled to damages of three times the overcharge and may also be awarded attorneys fees and interest from the date of the overcharge at the rate of interest payable on a judgment pursuant to section five thousand four of the

---

8. Real Prop L § 226-b, subd 4. For the text of these statutes, see RENT CONTROL AND RENT STABILIZATION, by Joseph Rasch, published by The Lawyers Co-operative Publishing Co., Rochester, New York, 14694.

9. A tenant who rents an apartment not for his own use, but for the express purpose of subleasing for profit, is not a legitimate prime tenant, but an illusory prime tenant who is not entitled to the protection of the Rent Laws. Hutchins v Conciliation & Appeals Bd. (S Ct NY Co 1984) 125 Misc 2d 809, 480 NYS2d 684.

A distinction must be made between a summary proceeding brought on the ground of non-primary residence, and one brought upon the ground of illegal subletting because the sublessor does not intend to reoccupy the premises at the expiration of the sublease. See Pamela Equities Corp. v Camp (NYC Civ Ct NY Co 1985) 127 Misc 2d 395, 486 NYS2d 149.

In this connection, see § 5(a)(11) of the Emergency Tenant Protection Act, as am L 1983, ch 403, § 55, which provides that the issue of primary residence must be determined by a court of competent jurisdiction, and that no action or proceeding shall be commenced against tenants subject to the ETPA seeking to recover possession on the ground that a housing accommodation is not occupied by the tenant as his primary residence unless the owner or lessor shall have given 30 days' notice to the tenant of his intention to commence such action of proceeding on that ground.

In Lee v Christie (NYC Civ Ct NY Co 1983) 123 Misc 2d 244, 470 NYS2d 86, it was held that where a holdover proceeding is based on an unauthorized subletting as well as on the nonprimary residence of the tenant who had sublet, the proceeding is barred until the expiration of the lease.

## ASSIGNMENT AND SUBLETTING § 9:79

civil practice law and rules; (f) the tenant may not sublet the unit for more than a total of two years, including the term of the proposed sublease, out of the four-year period preceding the termination date of the proposed sublease. The provisions of this subdivision (f) shall only apply to subleases commencing on and after July first, nineteen hundred eight-three; and (g) for the purposes of this section only, the term of the proposed sublease may extend beyond the term of the tenant's lease. In such event, such sublease shall be subject to the tenant's right to a renewal lease. The subtenant shall have no right to a renewal lease. It shall be unreasonable for an owner to refuse to consent to a sublease solely because such sublease extends beyond the tenant's lease.[10]

However, nothing contained in Real Property Law § 226-b shall be deemed to affect the rights, if any, of any tenant subject to the New York City Rent and Rehabilitation Law (Administrative Code of the City of New York, Title 26, Chapter 3) or the Emergency Housing Rent Control Law.[11]

These provisions of the Real Property Law shall not apply to public housing and other units for which there are constitutional or statutory criteria covering admission thereto, nor to a proprietary lease, viz., a lease to, or held by, a tenant entitled thereto by reason of ownership of shares of stock in a corporate owner of premises which operates the same on a cooperative basis.[12]

It must be observed that commercial tenants are not covered by this statute, and are governed by common law rules which permit subletting unless expressly prohibited by the terms of the lease[13]

Subletting in accordance with the statutory requirements is permissible for the limited purpose of allowing a legitimate residential tenant in actual occupancy of the apartment to retain his home when a temporary absence becomes necessary.[14]

---

**10.** Emergency Protection Act § 10-a; Rent Stabilization Law, New York City Administrative Code § 26-511, subd c (12) (superseding New York City Administrative Code § YY51-6.0 subd c (14)).

**11.** Real Prop L § 226-b, subd 4.

**12.** Real Prop L § 226-b, subd 3.

**13.** See § 9:75, supra.

**14.** Landlord's refusal to approve a 2-year sublease was unreasonable where based on ground that tenant had been sentenced to 4 years in prison with possibility of parole that

A landlord's refusal of a subletting request is only reasonable if it is based on objective grounds: the proposed sublessee's financial responsibility, identity, or suitability for the particular apartment or building, legality of the proposed use or nature of the occupancy, or any other sound real estate business, except loss of profit or property control.[15]

### § 9:80. Mobile Home Tenant's Statutory Right to Assign and Sublet

Real Property Law § 233 (t) (added L 1984, ch 910, eff January 1, 1985) provides:

1. Unless a greater right to assign is conferred by the lease, a mobile home tenant may not assign his lease without the written consent of the mobile home park owner or operator, which consent may be unconditionally withheld without cause provided that the mobile home park owner or operator shall release the mobile home tenant from the lease upon request of the mobile home tenant upon thirty days notice if the mobile home park owner or operator unreasonably withholds consent which release shall be the sole remedy of the tenant. If the owner reasonably withholds consent, there shall be no assignment and the mobile home tenant shall not be released from the lease.

2. (a) A mobile home tenant renting space or a mobile home in a mobile home park with four or more mobile homes pursuant to an existing lease shall have a right to sublease his premises subject to the written consent of the park owner in advance of the subletting. Such consent shall not be unreasonably withheld.

(b) The mobile home tenant shall inform the mobile home park owner or operator of his intent to sublease by mailing a notice of such intent by certified mail, return receipt requested. Such request shall be accompanied by

---

may or may not have allowed tenant to return to the apartment as soon as the sublease ended, where tenant established that the apartment was his primary residence, and that he intended to maintain the apartment as his primary residence when he was released from prison. 216-220 East 67th Street Associates v Quinn (NYC Cir Ct NY Co 1987) 136 Misc 2d 188, 518 NYS2d 302.

15. 216-220 East 67th Street Associates v Quinn (NYC Cir Ct NY Co 1987) 136 Misc 2d 188, 518 NYS2d 302.

## ASSIGNMENT AND SUBLETTING § 9:80

the following information: (i) the term of the sublease, (ii) the name of the proposed sublessee, (iii) the business and permanent home address of the proposed sublessee, (iv) the tenant's reason for subletting, (v) the tenant's address for the term of the sublease, (vi) the written consent of any co-tenant or guarantor of the lease, and (vii) a copy of the proposed sublease, to which a copy of the mobile home tenant's lease shall be attached if available, acknowledged by the mobile home tenant and proposed subtenant as being a true copy of such sublease.

(c) Within ten days after the mailing of such request, the mobile home park owner or operator may ask the mobile home tenant for additional information as will enable the mobile home park owner or operator to determine if rejection of such request shall be unreasonable. Any such request for additional information shall not be unduly burdensome. Within thirty days after the mailing of the request for consent, or of the additional information reasonably asked for by the mobile home park owner or operator, whichever is later, the mobile home park owner or operator shall send a notice to the mobile home tenant of his consent or, if he does not consent, his reasons therefor. Mobile home park owner's or operator's failure to send such a notice shall be deemed to be a consent to the proposed subletting. If the mobile home park owner or operator consents, the premises may be sublet in accordance with the request, but the mobile home tenant thereunder, shall nevertheless remain liable for the performance of mobile home tenant's obligations under said lease. If the mobile home park owner or operator reasonably withholds consent, there shall be no subletting and the mobile home tenant shall not be released from the lease. If the mobile home park owner or operator unreasonably withholds consent, the mobile home tenant may sublet in accordance with the request and may recover the costs of the proceeding and attorneys fees if it is found that the mobile home park owner or operator acted in bad faith by withholding consent. The rights and obligations of the mobile home park owner or operator and the mobile home tenant shall be governed by the provisions of this subdivision and subdi-

§ 9:80　　　　　　　　LANDLORD AND TENANT

visions three, five, six, seven and eight of section two hundred twenty-six-b of this article.[16]

**§ 9:81. Form of Agreement to Assign Proprietary Lease (Co-operative Ownership)**

FORM NO. 12

AGREEMENT TO ASSIGN PROPRIETARY LEASE

[Co-operative Apartment Lease]

THIS AGREEMENT, made the　　day of　　　, 19　BETWEEN John Vendor, residing at　　　, New York, hereinafter described as the assignor, and Robert Vendee, residing at　　　, New York, hereinafter described as the assignee, Wherein it is mutually agreed:

1. Assignor hereby agrees to sell, transfer, convey, and assign to assignee, and assignee hereby agrees to purchase from assignor all the right, title and interest of assignor in and to twenty (20) shares of stock of Belle Apartments, Inc., represented by stock certificate number 2346, and in and to the proprietary lease dated February 1, 1980, made by Belle Apartments Inc., as lessor, to assignor for apartment number 4D in premises 12 Beekman Plaza, County of New York, City and State of New York, for the purchase price of Two Hundred and Fifty Thousand ($250,000) Dollars, payable as follow: Fifty Thousand ($50,000) Dollars by check drawn on a New York bank upon the execution of this agreement, the receipt whereof is hereby acknowledged, subject to collection; and Two Hundred Thousand ($200,000) Dollars by certified check of the assignee drawn on a New York bank on the date of closing hereinafter set forth.

2. This agreement is expressly made subject to the provisions of the endorsement on said certificate of stock, and of paragraph "6" of said proprietary lease, copies of which are attached hereto as Exhibits "A", and "B" respectively, and made a part hereof as if fully set forth herein, and assignee agrees to comply promptly upon request of assignor and/or the lessor with the terms thereof insofar as such terms require any performance on his part as "assignee" of the within proprietary lease. In

---

16. See §§ 9:78, 9:79, supra.

the event the necessary consents referred to in said Exhibits "A" and "B" shall not have been given by the date of closing hereinafter set forth, and provided the failure to give such consents shall not be due to the failure or refusal of assignee to execute the instruments, or to furnish the information, reasonably required by the said lessor, then all sums paid hereunder shall be immediately repaid to assignee, without interest, and without any deductions whatsoever, and thereupon this agreement shall be null and void, and none of the parties to this agreement shall have any right or claim whatsoever against the other.

3. This sale includes all right, title, and interest of assignor, subject to the provisions of the proprietary lease, only in and to the following items of personal property in the apartment: The refrigerator, dishwasher, gas range, the built-in library in the maid's room; all hanging chandeliers except the one in the maid's room; the crystal chandelier in the dining room and in the smaller bedroom. Assignor agrees to use due care in removing said excluded chandeliers as well as other excluded fixtures, mirrors, and articles of personal property so as to cause as little damage to the premises as possible.

4. Assignee represents and warrants to assignor to induce assignor to enter into this agreement in reliance thereon, that no broker brought about this sale.

5. Assignor represents and warrants to assignee to induce assignee to enter into this agreement in reliance thereon that (a) assignor is the owner of the said shares of stock and lease being sold hereunder; (b) there are no claims, security interests, or liens against the said lease or the said shares; (c) the said shares are fully paid and nonassessable; (d) assignor has the full right and authority to assign and transfer the said shares and lease, subject only to the consents referred to in said Exhibits "A" and "B"; (e) there are no unsatisfied judgments, tax liens, or undischarged bankruptcy proceedings either of record or outstanding against assignor; (f) there are no filed mechanics' liens for work performed within said apartment or materials supplied on account of such work; (g) the current maintenance charges are as

**§ 9:81**

follows         , and (h) except as in this agreement expressly stated, there are no accrued but unpaid special assessments *(or: there are the following accrued but unpaid special assessments:         )*.

6. The within purchase and sale shall close on         , 19   , at         o'clock in the forenoon at the office of         , at         , New York, or, if so required, at the office of the attorneys for the lessor, 48 hours' advance notice of which will be given to the said attorneys for assignee. At such closing, assignee will pay the balance of the purchase price, as hereinabove provided; all necessary papers will be executed and delivered by the respective parties hereto; assignor will pay for the transfer stamps required for the transfer of the said certificate of stock; the maintenance charges of the said apartment for the month of closing will be apportioned; assignor will pay the charges made by the lessor for its consent, not in excess of $    , and assignor and assignee will divide equally any charges in excess of $    , and thereupon assignor will deliver and surrender to assignee full possession of said apartment, broom clean, and free and clear of any and all occupants. Time of closing is of the essence of this agreement.

a. At such closing assignor shall deliver to assignee his stock certificate number 2346, duly endorsed for transfer, and bearing the required stock transfer stamps; the duplicate original of the proprietary lease assigned hereunder; an assignment of said lease to assignee as in the form attached hereto as "Exhibit C", and made a part hereof as if fully set forth herein *[see § 9:82 for Form of assignment]*, and the consent of the lessor to the transfer of the shares of stock and lease being sold hereunder.

7. This agreement shall bind and inure to the benefit of the parties hereto, and their respective distributees, executors, administrators, legal representatives, and assigns. However, it is expressly agreed that this agreement cannot be assigned, or otherwise transferred, encumbered, or disposed of by assignee, without the prior written consent of assignor first had and obtained in each instance.

IN WITNESS WHEREOF, the parties have executed this agreement the day and year first above written

*[Signatures with printed names underneath]*
*[Attach exhibits]*

Exhibit "A"

The rights of any holder hereof are subject to the provisions of the by-laws of Belle Apartments, Inc. and to all the terms, covenants, conditions and provisions of a certain proprietary lease made between the person in whose name this certificate is issued, as Lessee, and Belle Apartments, Inc., as Lessor, for an apartment in the premises 12 Beekman Plaza, New York, New York, which lease limits and restricts the title and rights of any transferee hereof. The shares represented by this certificate are transferable only as an entirety and only to an approved assignee of such proprietary lease. Copies of the proprietary lease and the by-laws are on file and available for inspection at the office of Belle Apartments, Inc.

Exhibit "B"

*Assignment*

6. The Lessee shall not assign this lease or transfer the stock appurtenant thereto or any interest therein, and no such assignment or transfer shall take effect as against the Lessor for any purpose, until

a. an instrument of assignment executed by the assignor shall have been delivered to the Lessor; and

b. an agreement by the assignee assuming and agreeing to perform and comply with all the covenants and conditions of this lease to be performed or complied with by the Lessee on and after the effective date of said assignment shall have been executed and acknowledged by the assignee and delivered to the Lessor, but no such assumption agreement shall be required if the assignee surrenders the assigned lease and enters into a new proprietary lease for the remainder of the term, as hereinafter provided; and

c. all shares of stock of the Lessor appurtenant to this lease shall have been transferred to the assignee, with proper transfer stamps affixed; and

d. all sums due from the Lessee, together with a sum to be fixed by the Board of Directors or the President or a Vice-President of the Lessor to cover reasonable legal and other expenses of the Lessor in connection with such assignment and transfer of stock, shall have been paid to the Lessor; and

e. consent to such assignment shall have been duly given by an instrument in writing which is to be signed either (i) by a majority of the then authorized total number of directors of the Lessor or (ii) when duly authorized either by a resolution of the Lessor's Board of Directors or by a resolution adopted at any annual or special meeting of the Lessor's stockholders, by the Managing Agent of the Lessor, or any officer of the Lessor. No such consent shall be required in the case of an assignment, transfer or bequest of this lease to the Lessee's spouse, or in the case of an assignment by the Sponsors referred to in a Plan of Cooperative Organization for the Building dated January 16, 1962, as amended, or their designees, nominees or representatives, if the Sponsors, before consummating any assignment, consult with a committee of or members of the Board of Directors provided such committee or members are promptly available for such consultation, or, if the Lessee be more than one person, in the case of an assignment or transfer by one such Lessee to another.

*Death of Lessee*

In the event the Lessee shall die during the term of this lease, consent shall not be unreasonably withheld to any assignment or transfer of this lease and the appurtenant stock by bequest or by assignment by the administrator or executor of the Lessee, provided that such legatee or assignee shall be a financially responsible member of the Lessee's family (other than the Lessee's spouse as to whom no consent is required).

*Release of Lessee Upon Assignment*

Whenever the Lessee shall, under the provisions of this lease, be permitted to assign and shall so assign the same, and the assignee shall assume all of the unfulfilled obligations of the assignor hereunder, either by an instrument in writing delivered to the Lessor or by surrendering the assigned lease and entering into a new lease for the remainder of the term, the assignor shall have no further liability on any of the covenants of this lease to be

### ASSIGNMENT AND SUBLETTING § 9:81

thereafter performed. At the option and election of the Lessor any assigned lease shall be surrendered and cancelled, and a new proprietary lease for the remainder of the term of this lease, shall in such case be entered into between the Lessor and the assignee.

*Specific Consent Required*

Regardless of any prior consent theretofore given, neither the Lessee nor his executor, administrator or personal representative, nor any trustee or receiver of the property of the Lessee, nor anyone to whom the interest of the Lessee shall pass by law, shall be entitled to assign this lease, or to sublet or use the apartment, or any part thereof, except upon compliance with the requirements of this lease. The restrictions on the subletting and the occupancy of the apartment and on the assignment of this lease, as hereinbefore set forth, are an especial consideration and inducement for the granting of this lease by the Lessor to the Lessee.

No demand or acceptance of rent from any assignee hereof, or from any subtenant, or other person in possession, shall constitute or be deemed to constitute a consent to or approval of any assignment, sublease or occupancy.

*Pledge of Stock*

A pledge of stock and/or an assignment of this lease as collateral security, shall not be deemed a violation of any covenant or condition of this lease relating to transfer of stock or assignment of this lease, but neither the pledgee nor any transferee of the pledgee shall have the right to vote or to acquire a proprietary lease of the apartment, by assignment or otherwise, except on compliance with all of the provisions of this paragraph 6.

Exhibit "C" [see § 9:82]

*Note: Since shares of stock and proprietary lease in cooperative apartments are personal property (State Tax Com. v Shor (1977) 43 NY2d 151, 400 NYS2d 805, 371 NE2d 523), General Obligations Law § 5-1311 is not applicable. Therefore, the parties should agree upon some provision covering the consequences of damage to the apartment by fire or other casualty between the date of contract and closing.*

## § 9:82. Form of Assignment of Proprietary (Co-operative Apartment) Lease

### FORM 13

### ASSIGNMENT OF PROPRIETARY (CO-OPERATIVE APARTMENT) LEASE[17]

KNOW that Richard Doe, Assignor, residing at 1 East 29th Street, Borough of Manhattan, City and State of New York, in consideration of one ($1) dollar, and other good and valuable consideration paid by John Doe, Assignee, residing at 2 West 29th Street, Borough of Manhattan, City and State of New York, hereby assigns unto Assignee, a certain lease made by          , as landlord, to Richard Doe, as tenant, dated February 1, 1985 *(add if lease was recorded:* and recorded on          , in the office of the City Register, County of New York, in liber    , of conveyances, at page    ), covering apartment #    in premises known as and by         , Borough of Manhattan, City and State of New York,

TO HAVE AND TO HOLD the same unto Assignee and his personal representatives and assigns from          , 1985, for all the rest of the term of said lease, subject to the rents, terms, covenants, conditions, and provisions therein set forth, and SUBJECT to the trust fund provisions of § 13 of the Lien Law.

AND Assignor hereby covenants that there are no claims, security interests, or liens against the said lease, or the shares of said lessor corporation allocated to said apartment; that there are no unsatisfied judgments, tax liens or undischarged bankruptcy proceedings either of

---

17. The statute of frauds applicable to realty transactions also applies to sales of co-op shares and the proprietary lease based thereon. Silverman v Alcoa Plaza Associates (1971, 1st Dept) 37 AD2d 166, 323 NYS2d 39.

The statute of frauds bars enforcement of an alleged oral contract for the sale of the shares of stock in a co-op and the assignment of the proprietary lease based thereon. Frank v Rubin (S Ct NY Co 1969) 59 Misc 2d 796, 300 NYS2d 273; Sebel v Willismas (NYC Civ Ct Queens Co) NYLJ August 11, 1976, p 11, c 6, Posner, J.

A cooperative corporation may not pursuant to a resolution adopted after a tenant purchased a lease and shares of stock impose a charge for permitting an assignment of the lease and a transfer of the underlying shares, where the lease does not contain any provision for imposing a charge. Jamil v Southridge Cooperative, Section 4, Inc. (NYC Civ Ct Queens Co 1978) 93 Misc 2d 383, 402 NYS2d 292, revd on other grounds 102 Misc 2d 404, 425 NYS2d 905, affd 77 AD2d 822, 429 NYS2d 340, cert den 450 US 919, 67 L Ed 2d 346, 101 S Ct 1366, reh den 450 US 1050, 68 L Ed 2d 247, 101 S Ct 1771.

record or outstanding against Assignor; and that there are no filed mechanics' liens for work performed within said apartment or materials supplied on account of such work.

The assignee hereby assumes the performance of all of the terms, covenants, and conditions of the lease herein assigned by the assignor to the assignee, and agrees to perform and comply with all the covenants and conditions of this lease to be performed or complied with by the lessee, all with full force and effect as if the assignee had signed the lease originally as lessee named therein.

The assignee further agrees that neither the present consent of the lessor to this assignment nor any prior consent of the lessor to an assignment shall in any way be construed or deemed to relieve this assignee, or any succeeding transferee, successor, or assignee of this lease, or any person climing any right, title, or interest by or through or under the assignee herein, or any succeeding transferee, successor, or assignee of this lease from obtaining the prior written consent of the lessor to an assignment in each and every subsequent instance.

IN WITNESS WHEREOF Assignor has executed this assignment on          , 1985.

*[Signature with name printed underneath]*
(L.S.)

**STATE OF NEW YORK,**    ss.:
**County of . . . . . . . . . . .**

On this    day of         , 1985, before me personally came Richard Roe, to me known and known to me to be the individual described in and who executed the foregoing assignment of lease, and duly acknowledged to me that he executed the same.

*[Signature with name printed underneath]*
Notary Public[1]

### O. RESTRICTIONS ON RIGHT TO ASSIGN AND SUBLET

### § 9:83. Restrictions Not Favored by Courts

It is universally recognized that an owner of real property, when leasing such property, may validly impose a restriction against assignment and subletting without

### § 9:83 LANDLORD AND TENANT

his consent. However, covenants restricting assignment or subletting do not run with the land; are deemed to be a restraint on the free alienation of estates in land; and are not favored by the courts.[18] "It is to be observed," said the Court of Appeals,[19] "that 'such covenants are restraints which courts do not favor. They are construed with the utmost jealousy, and very easy modes have always been countenanced for defeating them.'"

### § 9:84. Covenant Restricting Assignment and Subletting in Proprietary Leases (Co-operative Ownership)

Proprietary leases[20] usually provide that the lessee shall not assign the lease, nor sublet the premises, nor shall any assignment or sublease take effect as against the lessor for any purpose, unless and until it shall have been authorized by the written consent thereto of either a majority of the directors of the lessor corporation or by two-thirds of the lessees of the building. Such a provision is valid and enforceable,[1] and the right of the directors to refuse to authorize or consent to an assignment or subletting is not reviewable by the courts.[2] A provision in a proprietary lease requiring such consent to an assignment does not constitute an invalid restraint against the

---

**18.** Rowe v Great Atlantic & Pacific Tea Co. (1978) 46 NY2d 62, 412 NYS2d 827, 385 NE2d 566 (citing text); Francis v Ferguson (1927) 246 NY 516, 159 NE 416, 55 ALR 982; Riggs v Pursell (1876) 66 NY 193; Murdock v Fishel (AT 1910) 67 Misc 122, 121 NYS 624; Paddell v Janes (S Ct NY Co 1914) 84 Misc 212, 145 NYS 868.

**19.** Presby v Benjamin (1902) 169 NY 377, 380, 62 NE 430, quoting from opinion of Earl, J in Riggs v Pursell (1876) 66 NY 193, 201.

**20.** § 82, supra.

**1.** Weisner v 791 Park Ave. Corp. (1959) 6 NY2d 426, 190 NYS2d 70, 160 NE2d 720, holding that the lessee who contracts to assign his proprietary lease, and to transfer his shares of the stock of the lessor corporation, is under no obligation to obtain the necessary consent, absent a provision in the agreement so providing; Goldstone v Constable (1981, 1st Dept) 84 AD2d 519, 443 NYS2d 380; Penthouse Properties, Inc. v 1158 Fifth Ave., Inc. (AD1 1939) 256 AD 685, 11 NYS2d 417; Barrington Apartment Asso. v Watson (GT1 1886, NY) 38 Hun 545 (subletting).

**2.** Weisner v 791 Park Ave. Corp. (1959) 6 NY2d 426, 190 NYS2d 70, 160 NE2d 720, wherein the court said, "The statute which prohibits discrimination in co-operatives because of race, color, religion, national origin or ancestry is not involved in this case. Absent the application of these statutory standards, and under the terms of the agreement between plaintiff and Gilbert, there is no reason why the owners of the co-operative apartment house could not decide for themselves with whom they wish to share their elevators, their common halls and facilities, their stockholders' meetings, their management problems and responsibilities and their homes."

alienation of corporate stock. The special nature of the ownership of co-operative apartment houses by tenant-owners, it has been held, requires that they be not included in the general rule against restraint on the sale of stock in corporations organized for profit.[3]

### § 9:85. Effect of Consent or Waiver on Covenant Restricting Assignment

If a landlord consents to one assignment of the lease, the covenant in the lease restricting assignments is thereafter eliminated from the lease.[4] As the Court of Appeals said in a leading case on the subject,[5] "The condition against assignment was dispensed with by the lessors. A condition against assignment, once dispensed with, is dispensed with forever." Therefore, where a lease provides that a tenant may not assign the lease without the landlord's consent, if the landlord consents to the tenant's assignment thereof, the assignee then may reassign the lease without getting the landlord's consent.

It is also the settled rule that if the landlord once waives a breach of the restrictive covenant against an assignment of the lease, the restrictive covenant is likewise eliminated from the lease, and the assignee of the lease may then reassign the lease without any restriction whatsoever.[6]

Acceptance of rent from an assignee with full knowledge of the assignment constitutes a waiver of the breach.[7] The mere fact that the landlord, on accepting the rent from the assignee, insists on making out the receipt therefor in the name of the original tenant does not nullify the fact that he has waived the breach by taking the rent from the assignee.[8]

3. Penthouse Properties, Inc. v 1158 Fifth Ave., Inc. (AD1 1939) 256 AD 685, 11 NYS2d 417.

4. Lynch v Joseph (AD4 1930) 228 AD 367, 240 NYS 176; Nipet Realty, Inc. v Melvin's Rest. & Bar, Inc. (NYC Civ Ct NY Co 1971) 67 Misc 2d 790, 327 NYS2d 2.

5. Murray v Harway (1874) 56 NY 337, 343.

6. Gillette Bros., Inc. v Aristocrat Restaurant, Inc. (1924) 239 NY 87, 145 NE 748.

7. Conger v Duryee (1882) 90 NY 594, 599; Condit v Manischewitz (AD1 1927) 220 AD 366, 221 NYS 371; Texaco, Inc. v Greenwich-Kinney, Inc. (S Ct NY Co 1971) 68 Misc 2d 817, 328 NYS2d 180, affd in part and mod in part on other grounds (1st Dept) 39 AD2d 877, 333 NYS2d 544, affd 32 NY2d 910, 347 NYS2d 67, 300 NE2d 435.

8. Paterson v University of State (S Ct Nassau Co 1962) 237 NYS2d 845, affd (2d Dept) 18 AD2d 822, 237

A consent to assignment, which a lease requires of the lessor, may be implied from the acts and correspondence of the parties.[9]

Many leases contain clauses similar to these:

> The party of the second part (the lessee) hereby agrees not to assign this lease or sublet said premises or any portion thereof without the written consent of said parties of the first part (the lessors).
>
> It is further agreed and understood that in case said first parties consent, suffer, or permit the doing by said second party of any act or omission which might alter, change or modify any of the covenants or provisions of this agreement, such consent whether express or implied shall not be deemed to and shall not be a waiver of such or of any of the covenants or provisions of this agreement, except for that instance alone, and shall not be construed to and shall not authorize said second party to make any further violation thereof.

It is to be noted, said the Appellate Division,[10] "that both quoted paragraphs are limited to prohibiting acts by the party of the second part, that is, by the lessee itself, the C. H. Wood Company. Nowhere does the language of the lease include a prohibition against the assignees of the C. H. Wood Company. In fact nowhere in the lease are assigns of either lessors or lessee mentioned."

Therefore, the use of a general clause, such as the one quoted, will not be effective to nullify the rule that a single consent to an assignment, or a single waiver of a breach of the covenant restricting assignments eliminates the restriction from the lease. "Very special" language binding the assigns of the tenant must be used, so that the restriction will be made to run with the land. (See form of restrictive covenant binding the tenant's assignees, § 9:95, infra.)[11]

---

NYS2d 990; Clark v Greenfield (GT 1895) 13 Misc 124, 34 NYS 1.

9. Mann v Ferdinand Munch Brewery (1919) 225 NY 189, 121 NE 746.

10. Lynch v Joseph (AD4 1930) 228 AD 367, 240 NYS 176.

11. Where a lease clearly provides that acceptance of rent with knowledge of the breach of any provision of the lease shall not be a waiver of such breach, such non-waiver clause will be enforced to preclude a waiver of the breach of a provision prohibiting assignment or subletting. Monarch Information Services, Inc. v 161 William

## § 9:86. Effect of Consent or Waiver on Covenant Restricting Subletting

Acceptance of rent from a tenant with full knowledge of a violation of a lease restriction against subletting constitutes a waiver of such violation.[12] However, where a landlord objected to the subletting as a violation of the lease, refused to accept further rent from the tenant as soon as the subletting was discovered, and returned the rent paid for the previous month, and thereafter by arrangement of the parties the rent for the said previous month and all succeeding months was accepted "without prejudice" to either party, it was held that the landlord had not waived the breach.[13]

Unlike the rule governing a consent or waiver of the restriction against assignment of a lease,[14] a consent to a particular subletting, or a waiver of the restriction against subletting in any one instance, does not confer on the lessee the right to make further subleases in violation of the restriction to sublet.[15]

Therefore, where a lease contains a covenant against subletting, with a penalty of forfeiture, the waiver by the landlord of a violation thereof on one occasion will not estop the landlord from suing for a subsequent violation of the covenant against subletting. Unlike the covenant against assignment, the covenant not to sublet is a continuing one, and each subsequent breach gives rise to a separate and distinct cause of action for a forfeiture.[16]

Associates (1984, 1st Dept) 103 AD2d 703, 477 NYS2d 650.

12. Melroy Realty Corp. v Siegel (Civ Ct NY Co 1969) 60 Misc 2d 383, 303 NYS2d 198; Burckhardt v Saul (1948, Sup App T) 80 NYS2d 85; Farose Realty Corp. v Shaff (1952, Mun Ct Bk) 117 NYS2d 375; 440 West 34th Street Corp. v Rosoff (1948, Mun Ct Man) 84 NYS2d 16; Westdale Realty Corp. v Labella (Westchester Co Ct 1947) 188 Misc 738, 73 NYS2d 31; Irbar Realty Corp. v Vallins (1946, Mun Ct Bx) 64 NYS2d 843; Syracuse Sav. Bank v D'Elia (M Ct City of Syracuse 1945) 185 Misc 928, 56 NYS2d 800.

13. 18th Ave. Pharmacy, Inc. v Wilmant Realty Corp (S Ct Kings Co 1950) 95 NYS2d 534.

14. See § 9:85, supra.

15. Ireland v Nichols (1871) 46 NY 413, 417; Northerly Corp. v Hermett Realty Corp. (1962, 1st Dept) 15 AD2d 888, 225 NYS2d 327; Fischer v Ginzburg (AD1 1920) 191 AD 418, 181 NYS 516; One University Place, Inc. v Egan (AT1 1956) 6 Misc 2d 212, 158 NYS2d 823; Fifth Ave. Realty Corp. v Lynch (M Ct Man 1957) 10 Misc 2d 391, 166 NYS2d 687; Werber v Weinstein (M Ct Bx 1955) 207 Misc 707, 138 NYS2d 196.

16. McCarter v Davis (AD2 1922) 202 AD 519, 194 NYS 688.

However, there are several cases which have held to the contrary. In Kingdale Realties, Inc. v Sherry (AT1

## § 9:87. Effect of Emergency Rent Laws on Restrictions

Emergency rent laws usually provide that so long as a tenant pays the rent to which the landlord is entitled under such statutes, the tenant may not be removed from possession solely because his lease has expired. Such a tenant becomes what the courts have called "a statutory tenant."[17] It is well settled that the terms and conditions of a statutory tenant's expired lease are deemed to continue in effect during the statutory tenancy except only where they are plainly inconsistent with the emergency rent laws.[18] "It has become the established rule," said one court,[19] "that in such tenancies, all of the provisions of the original agreement, not inconsistent with the statutory restraints, except for the rent reserved and the term, are projected into and become a part of the relationship imposed upon the parties by law." Accordingly, covenants in a lease restricting assignment or subletting continue in effect during the statutory tenancy, and bind the statutory tenant.[20] As Gavagan, J., said,[1] "The covenant

---

1951) 106 NYS2d 796, it was held that where a landlord over a period of years had waived a provision restricting subletting, such waiver would have the effect of nullifying the restriction in the lease, even though the waiver was not in writing as provided by the lease.

In Farose Realty Corp. v Shaff (1952, Mun Ct Bk) 117 NYS2d 375 and Wise v Vaughner (1951, Mun Ct Bx) 105 NYS2d 338, it was held that acceptance of rent with knowledge of breach would be considered not only as a license to the tenant to continue to do so but also as a waiver of condition of lease prohibiting subletting. It must be observed that these cases were decided during a period when the relationship was controlled by emergency rent control principles and may have been influenced by the dictum of the Court of Appeals in Park East Land Corp. v Finkelstein (1949) 299 NY 70, 75, 85 NE2d 869, wherein it said, "mechanical application of common-law rules will not promote reasonable decision in cases controlled by emergency rent legislation." In other words it is difficult to state whether these principles are suspended because of the rent emergency, or abrogated, until the courts will have made their position clearer.

17. See §§ 10:11 et seq., infra.

18. Klipack v Raymar Novelties, Inc. (AD1 1947) 273 AD 54, 75 NYS2d 418, mod 273 AD 1005, 79 NYS2d 881; Barrow Realty Corp. v Village Brewery Restaurant, Inc. (AD1 1947) 272 AD 262, 70 NYS2d 545, app gr 272 AD 873, 72 NYS2d 260; Lewittes & Sons v Spielmann (AT1 1947) 190 Misc 35, 73 NYS2d 552; Shelton Bldg. Corp. v Baggett (AT2 1947) 188 Misc 709, 71 NYS2d 434.

19. Wasservogel v Becker (M Ct Bx 1948) 191 Misc 599, 79 NYS2d 526, affd (Sup App T) 87 NYS2d 237, affd 275 AD 387, 89 NYS2d 290, mod 300 NY 125, 89 NE2d 712.

20. Shelton Bldg. Corp. v Baggett (AT2 1947) 188 Misc 709, 71 NYS2d 434; 130 West 57 Corp. v Hyman (AT1 1946) 188 Misc 92, 66 NYS2d 332; Leventhal v 128 West 30th Street Corp. (S Ct NY Co 1956) 158 NYS2d 398; Leibowitz v 18 East 41st St. Corp. (S Ct NY Co 1949) 89 NYS2d 160, affd 276 AD 759, 93 NYS2d 307.

1. Glauberman v University Place

against assignment or subletting of demised premises *without the written consent* of the landlord has been regarded by the courts as a valued right and courts of equity have been zealous in its protection and enforcement. Any legislative act in repeal of such right should be strictly construed. I find no such legislative intention in the Emergency Rent Control acts and regulations, Federal or State."[2]

### § 9:88. Statutory Modification of Restrictions Because of Race or Color

The General Obligations Law provides,[3]

> Any promise, covenant or restriction in a contract, mortgage, lease, deed or conveyance or in any other agreement affecting real property, heretofore or hereafter made or entered into, which limits, restrains, prohibits or otherwise provides against the sale, grant, gift, transfer, assignment, conveyance, ownership, lease, rental, use or occupancy of real property to or by any person because of race, creed, color, national origin, or ancestry, is hereby declared to be void as against public policy, wholly unenforceable, and shall not constitute a defense in any action, suit or proceeding. No such promise, covenant or restriction shall be listed as a valid provision affecting such property in public notices concerning such property. The invalidity of any such promise, covenant or restriction in any such instrument or agreement shall not affect the validity of any other provision therein, but no reverter shall occur, no possessory estate shall result, nor any right of entry or right to a penalty or forfeiture shall accrue by reason of the disregard of such promise, covenant or restriction. This section shall not apply to conveyances or devises to religious associations or corporations for religious purposes, but, such promise, covenant or restriction shall cease to be enforceable and shall otherwise

---

Apartments, Inc. (S Ct NY Co 1946) 188 Misc 277, 66 NYS2d 335, affd 272 AD 758, 70 NYS2d 139, app dismd 297 NY 587, 74 NE2d 558, referring to former Federal Rent Regulations for Housing, 50 App USCA §§ 901 et seq, and L 1945, chs 3 and 315, Unconsol L §§ 8521, et seq.

2. Also, see Shelton Bldg. Corp. v Baggett (AT2 1947) 188 Misc 709, 71 NYS2d 434.

3. General Obligations Law § 5-331

become subject to the provisions of this section when the real property affected shall cease to be used for such purpose.

The Executive Law makes it unlawful to refuse to sell, rent, or lease a housing accomodation because of the race, creed, color, national origin, sex, age or disability or marital status of the tenant or purchaser, or to discriminate for the same reasons in the terms, conditions, or privileges of the sale, rental, or lease of any such housing accommodation, except in the rental of an owner-occupied one or two family home, or the rental of a room or rooms by the occupant of a housing accommodation, or where all the rooms in a housing accommodation are rented to individuals of the same sex, or the sale, rental or lease of housing accommodations exclusively to persons 55 years of age or older.[4]

### § 9:89. Breach of Restriction; Voluntary Acts of Tenant

Restrictions on the right to assign or sublet are not favored by the courts, and as has been said in a leading case, "very easy modes have always been countenanced for defeating them."[5] Such restrictions are construed strictly against the landlord. Therefore, it has been held, a sublease is not a breach of a covenant prohibiting assignments of a lease, nor is an assignment of a lease a breach of a covenant prohibiting subletting.[6] Similarly it has been held that a prohibition against assignments or subleases "of the premises" is not breached by an assignment pro tanto, nor by a sublease of part of the premises.[7]

A change in the personnel of a partnership-tenant either by an increase or decrease in the number of

---

4. Exec L § 296, subd 5(a).

Executive L § 296, subd 5(b) makes it unlawful to refuse to sell, rent, or lease land or commercial space because of the age, race, creed, color, national origin, sex, or disability, or marital status of the purchaser or tenant. However, with respect to age, the foregoing provision shall not apply to the restriction of the sale, rental, or lease of land or commercial space exclusively to persons 55 years of age or older.

5. Riggs v Pursell (1876) 66 NY 193, 201, where it was held that a restriction against assignments is not breached by a mortgage on the lease.

6. Murdock v Fishel (AT 1910) 67 Misc 122, 121 NYS 624; Wise v Vaughner (1951, Mun Ct Bx) 105 NYS2d 338.

7. Roosevelt v Hopkins (1865) 33 NY 81.

Also, see Presby v Benjamin (1902) 169 NY 377, 380, 62 NE 430; Wise v Vaughner (1951, Mun Ct Bx) 105 NYS2d 338.

## ASSIGNMENT AND SUBLETTING § 9:89

partners, is not a breach of a covenant restricting assignments of a lease.[8] Corporate tenant's transfer of all of the shares of its stock to a third party does not breach a covenant restricting assignment of lease[9]

To constitute a violation of a prohibition against subletting, there must be an attempt to put in possession a new tenant, and not merely a new occupant. It is well settled that an agreement by a lessee with a third person for permissive use by the latter of the leased premises does not constitute a violation of covenants in a lease against assigning or subletting, but amount merely to a license to use the property.[10] Thus, it has been held that as a general rule a letting of a room to a lodger is not a breach of a covenant against subletting.[11] Similarly, a tenant operating a sound studio business was held not to have violated the restriction against assignment or subletting by renting its studios to the trade for a fixed term and rental, where the customers so renting the studios

---

**8.** Roosevelt v Hopkins (1865) 33 NY 81; Twenty-Fifth St. Realty Co. v Wachtel (AD1 1920) 193 AD 76, 183 NYS 332; 244 West 27th Street Corp. v Lieberman (1949, Sup App T) 93 NYS2d 823; Morris Glick, Inc. v Grubman (S Ct NY Co 1945) 56 NYS2d 324; Paul Pleating & Stitching Co. v Levine (M Ct 1930) 137 Misc 82, 242 NYS 729.

**9.** Rubinstein Bros. v Ole of 34th Street, Inc. (NYC Cir Ct NY Co 1979) 101 Misc 2d 563, 421 NYS2d 534.

**10.** Presby v Benjamin (1902) 169 NY 377, 62 NE 430, where it was held that placing a caretaker in charge of demised premises did not violate a covenant prohibiting subletting.

A clause which forbids assignment and subletting only, does not prevent the granting of a license. Mann Theatres Corp. v Mid-Island Shopping Plaza Co. (1983, 2d Dept) 94 AD2d 466, 464 NYS2d 793, affd 62 NY2d 930, 479 NYS2d 213, 468 NE2d 51. *Annotation:* Grazing or pasturage agreement as violation of covenant in lease or provision of statute against assigning or subletting without lessor's consent. 71 ALR3d 780.

**11.** Smith v Rector of St. Philip's Church (1888) 107 NY 610, 619, 14 NE 825; Farose Realty Corp. v Shaff (1952, Mun Ct Bk) 117 NYS2d 375; Wise v Vaughner (1951, Mun Ct Bx) 105 NYS2d 338.

Also, see Application of Bierman (AD2 1948) 274 AD 1003, 84 NYS2d 355; where it was held, apparently on the same theory, that "The renting of a single furnished room in a six-room apartment occupied and maintained by the tenant did not constitute a subletting" in violation of a restriction against subletting. It should be noted that these rulings are presumably based on the premise that generally a contract for lodging, or for board and lodging, does not create the relationship of landlord and tenant. In contracts of this type dominion over the premises to be occupied is not surrendered by the tenant to the lodger. If the tenant retains general control and dominion over the premises,—which, the court pointed out in Smith v Rector, etc, of St. Philip's Church, supra, was the situation there,—then the occupant is merely a lodger, and not a tenant. If, however, possession and dominion is given to the occupant, then he becomes a tenant. (See § 63, supra.) Ashton v Margolies (AT 1911) 72 Misc 70, 129 NYS 617; Shearman v Iroquois Hotel & Apartment Co. (AT 1903) 42 Misc 217, 85 NYS 365; Wilson v Martin (Super Ct 1845) 1 Denio 602.

were not desirous of using the tenant's space as such, but rather its specially built studios.[12]

Thus, to constitute a breach of a restrictive covenant against assignments or sublettings, the act complained of must come clearly within the express terms of the restriction, which will be construed strictly against the landlord.

Where one knowingly takes an assignment of a lease from the lessee in violation of a covenant in the lease requiring the consent of the landlord who subsequently cancels the lease and relets the premises, equity will not grant any relief to such assignee as against his assignor to whom he has paid the consideration for the assignment and advanced a month's rent, since both parties were wagering upon the chances of getting the landlord's consent to the assignment.[13]

### § 9:90. —Operation of Law

As a general rule an involuntary assignment, or an assignment by operation of law, does not constitute a breach of the covenant restricting the tenant's right to assign.[14]

### § 9:91. —Sale by Judicial Officer

A restrictive covenant against assignment is not breached by a transfer of the lease by a referee in execution of a judgment to foreclose a mortgage on the lease.[15] So, too, there is no breach of the restrictive covenant against assignment by the sale of the leasehold estate on execution of a judgment, whether the judgment was confessed or obtained after an action was started, providing the judgment was not fraudulently confessed.[16]

In each of the instances given, the leasehold was assigned through no voluntary act of the tenant, but by operation of law, and therefore did not violate the covenant restricting the tenant from assigning the lease.

---

12. Nina Bujola Realty Corp. v Eastern Sound Studios, Inc. (1954) 206 Misc 329, 131 NYS2d 682.

13. Leo Finkenberg, Inc. v Crompton Bldg. Corp. (AT1 1922) 118 Misc 626, 195 NYS 33.

14. Francis v Ferguson (1927) 246 NY 516, 518, 159 NE 416, 55 ALR 982; Riggs v Pursell (1876) 66 NY 193, 201; Salter v Columbia Concerts, Inc. (S Ct NY Co 1948) 191 Misc 479, 77 NYS2d 703.

15. Riggs v Pursell (1876) 66 NY 193; Dunlop v Mulry (AD1 1903) 85 AD 498, 83 NYS 477; Johnston v Flickinger (S Ct NY Co 1916) 97 Misc 169, 160 NYS 962, affd 183 AD 887, 169 NYS 1098.

16. Jackson ex dem Schuyler v Corliss (Sup Ct 1811) 7 Johns 531.

## § 9:92. —Bankruptcy

Another example of an assignment by operation of law which has been held not to violate a covenant restricting assignment is the transfer of a lease to a trustee caused by the tenant's bankruptcy. Nor is the subsequent sale of the lease by the trustee for the benefit of the bankrupt-tenant's creditors a breach of the restricted covenant. The passage of the tenant's estate from the bankrupt to the trustee as of the date of the adjudication is by operation of law, and not by the act of the bankrupt, nor can it be said to be a sale. A sale by the trustee for the benefit of tenant's creditors is not forbidden by the conditions of the lease, and cannot be in breach thereof. It is not a voluntary assignment by the tenant, nor a sale of the tenant's interest, but of the trustee's interest held under the bankruptcy proceedings for the benefit of creditors.[17]

The Bankruptcy Reform Act of 1978 (Title 11, US Code), effective October 1, 1979, provides that notwithstanding a provision in an unexpired lease, or in applicable law, an unexpired lease of the debtor may not be terminated or modified, and any right or obligation under such lease may not be terminated or modified at any time after the commencement of the case in bankruptcy solely because of a provision in such lease that is conditioned on (a) the insolvency or financial condition of the debtor at any time before the closing of the case in bankruptcy; (b) the commencement of a case under the Bankruptcy Reform Act; or (c) the appointment of or taking possession by a trustee in a case under the Bankruptcy Reform Act or a custodian before such commencement.[18]

The Bankruptcy Reform Act of 1978 further provides that whether or not the lease prohibits or restricts assignment thereof, bankruptcy termination or forfeiture provi-

---

17. Gazlay v Williams (1908) 210 US 41, 47, 52 L Ed 950, 28 S Ct 687.

Also, see Re Prudential Lithograph Co. (1920, CA2 NY) 270 F 469, cert den 256 US 692, 65 L Ed 1174, 41 S Ct 534; 78th St. & Broadway Co. v Purssell Mfg. Co. (AT1 1915) 92 Misc 178, 155 NYS 259, affd 173 AD 887, 157 NYS 1145.

18. 11 USCS § 365(e)(1).

11 USCS § 363(l) provides that bankruptcy termination provisions, or other provisions which would effect, or give an option to effect, a forfeiture, modification, or termination of the debtor's interest in property, where such provisions are contained in a lease, are unenforceable as against the trustee's power to use, sell, or lease property pursuant to the statute, and as against a provision in a Chapter 11, or Chapter 13 plan providing for the use, sale or lease of property.

sion of a lease may be enforceable if applicable non-bankruptcy law excuses a party, other than the debtor, to such lease from accepting performance from or rendering performance to the trustee or to an assignee of such lease, whether or not such lease prohibits or restricts assignment of rights or delegation of duties; and such party does not consent to such assumption or assignment.[19]

### § 9:93. —Assignment for Benefit of Creditors

Where a tenant makes an assignment for the benefit of creditors, and includes his lease as an asset, the assignee has an election either to accept the lease, or surrender possession to the landlord. If he accepts the lease, then, it has been held, there is no violation of a general restrictive covenant in the lease against assignments by the tenant without consent. Whether or not a lease passes under a deed of assignment for the benefit of creditors depends upon the election of the assignee. The transfer of the lease, if it takes place, is rendered effective not by the deed of assignment, but by acts done under the assignment by the assignee in his official capacity.[1] The general restrictive covenant, it has been held, merely forbids only the ordinary out and out transfer of a lease to an outside party as absolute owner without the aid of any additional instrument or deed or statutory proceeding. Therefore without an express provision to that effect such a covenant does not prevent the tenant from taking advantage of the statutory assignment for the benefit of creditors.[2]

### § 9:94. —Acts of Personal Representatives of Deceased Tenant

On the death of a tenant his property, including the unexpired term of a lease he entered into in his lifetime, passes to his personal representatives by operation of

---

[19]. 11 USCS § 365(e)(2).

As to right of a trustee in bankruptcy, under the Bankruptcy Reform Act of 1978, to assume or reject a debtor's unexpired lease, and to assign a debtor's unexpired lease, notwithstanding a provision in the lease restricting or conditioning the assignment of such lease, see §§ 22:1, et seq., infra.

[1]. Paddell v Janes (S Ct NY Co 1914) 84 Misc 212, 145 NYS 868. Also see §§ 9:44, et seq, supra.

[2]. Paddell v Janes (S Ct NY Co 1914) 84 Misc 212, 145 NYS 868.

See Form No. 14 in § 9:82, infra.

law,[3] and not by assignment.[4] Such a transfer of the leasehold does not constitute a breach of the general restrictive covenant against assignments. If the personal representatives, pursuant to their power to take the lease, do so, and thereafter dispose of the lease as an asset of the estate, such transfer likewise will not constitute a breach of the general covenant restricting the tenant's right to assign. "An ordinary covenant against assignment," said the Court of Appeals in a leading case,[5] "does not bind the executors of the tenant, and is not broken by a transfer of the leased premises by operation of law. . . . The covenant may, however, be so drawn as expressly to prohibit such a transfer. To accomplish such a prohibition in case of a devolution to executors, its language must be 'very special.' . . . The use of general language, not specially related to the covenant against assignment—language which the law would imply as a term of the lease—is not the 'very special' prohibition which the cases require." The general clause which the court referred to is the one usually appearing at the end of a lease and reads as follows: "and it is further understood and agreed that the covenants and agreements herein contained are binding on the parties hereto and their legal representatives." Such a clause, the court pointed out, "expresses merely what the law presumes, in the absence of such a clause. 'It is a presumption of law, in the absence of express words, that the parties to a contract intend to bind not only themselves, but their personal representatives.' "[6]

Therefore, without an express provision specifically restraining assignments of leases by operation of law, the general restrictive covenant against assignments will not be breached by a transfer of the lease after the tenant's death to his personal representatives, or by a transfer of the lease by his personal representatives. (See § 9:95,

3. EPTL 13-1.1.
4. Charcowsky v Stahl (AT1 1959) 19 Misc 2d 1096, 189 NYS2d 384.
An executor of a tenant's estate may occupy the tenant's leased residential apartment, but only in his representative capacity, and not as a tenant under the lease. Rosefan Constr. Corp. v Salazar (NYC Civ Ct Queens Co 1982) 114 Misc 2d 956, 452 NYS2d 1016.
5. Francis v Ferguson (1927) 246 NY 516, 159 NE 416, 55 ALR 982.
6. Citing Kernochan v Murray (1888) 111 NY 306, 308, 18 NE 868, 869.

§ 9:94            LANDLORD AND TENANT

infra for a covenant restricting assignments by operation of law.)

The exemption of a personal representative of a deceased tenant from the restriction in the lease against assignment or subletting is shared by a legatee to whom the tenant bequeathed his business.[1] It should be observed that whatever right the legal representatives may acquire during the term of the decedent's lease, they acquire in their representative capacity.[2]

### § 9:95. Form of Clauses Restricting Assignment and Subletting

It has been seen[3] that the restrictions of a tenant's right to assign or sublet are not favored by the courts, and that very easy modes have been devised for defeating them. For example, a covenant restricting an assignment by a tenant, if waived or consented to, will not prohibit an assignee from reassigning the lease. A covenant restricting a tenant from assigning the lease will only prohibit voluntary acts of the tenant, but not involuntary acts, that is, assignments by operation of law. However, in three of the cases referred to in the preceding sections,[4] the courts pointed out that special covenants were necessary to protect a landlord adequately. The following clauses are submitted as the "very special" prohibitions which the cases require to protect the landlord against involuntary assignments and reassignments.

### FORM NO. 14

#### Covenant Restricting Assignments by Operation of Law or Otherwise, and Sublettings.*

a. Tenant, and Tenant's heirs, distributees, executors, administrators, committee, legal representatives, successors, transferees, and assigns, shall not assign, sell, mortgage, pledge or otherwise encumber, transfer, or dispose of this lease, any money or collateral deposited hereun-

---

1. Charcowsky v Stahl (AT1 1959) 19 Misc 2d 1096, 189 NYS2d 384.
2. Remford Corp. v Rosenfeld (AD1 1948) 274 AD 769, 79 NYS2d 756.
3. See §§ 9:83 et seq., supra.
4. Lynch v Joseph (AD4 1930) 228 AD 367, 240 NYS 176, in § 9:85, supra; Paddell v Janes (S Ct NY Co 1914) 84 Misc 212, 145 NYS 868, in § 9:93, supra; and Francis v Ferguson (1927) 246 NY 516, 159 NE 416, 55 ALR 982, in § 9:94, supra.

* For complete form of lease see Chapter 1.

## ASSIGNMENT AND SUBLETTING § 9:95

der, or any of the rights of Tenant therein or thereunder, nor sublet, or use or permit the demised premises or any part thereof to be used by others, nor suffer, permit, or allow any of the foregoing to be done without obtaining the prior written consent of Landlord in each and every instance. If this lease be assigned, or if the leased premises or any part thereof be underlet or occupied by anybody other than Tenant, Landlord may, after default by Tenant, collect rent from the assignee, under-tenant or occupant, and apply the net amount collected to the rent herein reserved, but no such assignment, underletting, occupancy or collection shall be deemed a waiver of this covenant, or the acceptance of the assignee, under-tenant or occupant as tenant, or a release of Tenant from the further performance by Tenant of covenants on the part of Tenant herein contained.

b. The consent or waiver of said consent by Landlord in any instance shall not in any way be construed or deemed to relieve Tenant, or any succeeding transferee, successor, or assignee of this lease, or any person claiming any right, title, or interest by or through or under Tenant, or by or through or under any succeeding transferee, successor or assignee of this lease, or the heirs, distributees, executors, administrators, committee, or legal representatives of Tenant, or of any succeeding transferee, successor, or assignee of this lease, or of any person claiming any right, title, or interest by or through or under Tenant or any succeeding transferee, successor or assignee of this lease from obtaining the prior written consent of Landlord to an assignment or subletting in each and every subsequent instance.

c. If any of the acts prohibited above in subdivision "a" shall be done or threatened to be done, Landlord shall have the right of injunction to restrain the same, and the right to invoke any remedy by law, or in equity, as if specific remedies, indemnity or reimbursement were not provided for in this lease.

d. The rights and remedies given to Landlord herein are distinct, cumulative, and separate, and no one of them whether or not exercised by Landlord shall be deemed to be in exclusion of any of the others.

*(The addition of any of the following subdivisions is optional)*

e. Landlord will not withhold the consent required by the provisions of subdivision "a" unreasonably.

*or*

e. Landlord will consent to assignments of this lease only on condition that the assignee, and each succeeding assignee, shall execute and deliver to Landlord an agreement, duly acknowledged, wherein such assignee shall expressly assume and agree to abide by and to specifically observe, keep, and perform all and each of the agreements, terms, conditions, and covenants of this lease on the part of Tenant to be observed, kept and performed as if said assignee was originally named herein as Tenant. (For form of assumption agreement, see § 9:41, supra.)

f. A change in the majority of the officers or in the board of directors, either by increasing the number thereof, or otherwise, of, or a transfer of stock control by, Tenant or any corporation which may hereafter succeed to any rights of Tenant shall be deemed to be an assignment within the meaning of that term as used herein.[5]

g. Tenant may sublet part of the demised premises or grant concessions or licenses therein for any use similar to or in conjunction with the Tenant's use of the leased premises.

## § 9:96. Right of Landlord to Withhold Consent[6]

When a lease contains a covenant restricting assignment or subletting without the landlord's consent, the landlord can withhold his consent arbitrarily,[7] and no action lies against him therefor.[8]

---

**5.** Form of provision giving tenant right to assign to successor partnership or corporation, see Form No 8, § 9:23, supra.

**6.** See §§ 9:78, 9:79, supra, as to residential tenant's statutory right to assign or sublet.

**7.** Dress Shirt Sales, Inc. v Hotel Martinique Associates (1963) 12 NY2d 339, 239 NYS2d 660, 190 NE2d 10; Conrad v Third Sutton Realty Co. (1981, 1st Dept) 81 AD2d 50, 439 NYS2d 376 (citing text); Singer Sewing Machine Co. v Eastway Plaza, Inc. (S Ct Monroe Co 1957) 5 Misc 2d 509, 158 NYS2d 647; Ogden v Riverview Holding Corp. (S Ct NY Co 1929) 134 Misc 149, 234 NYS 678, affd 226 AD 882, 235 NYS 850 (action for declaratory judgment that withholding of consent was unreasonable, and directing that such consent be given, was dismissed); Sarner v Kantor (S Ct NY Co 1924) 123 Misc 469, 205 NYS 760. Also, see Weisner v 791 Park Ave. Corp. (1959) 6 NY2d 426, 190 NYS2d 70, 160 NE2d 720, holding that specific performance would not be granted where contract called for assignment of lease subject to approval

## § 9:97. Contractual Modification of Right to Withhold Consent

Tenants usually try to get some modification of the arbitrary right to withhold consent to assignments and sublettings, if they cannot eliminate the restriction entirely. One method is by having the landlord agree that he will not unreasonably withhold his consent to any assignment or subletting. However, it must be borne in mind that such modification, to be of real benefit to the tenant, must be in the form of an express agreement on the part of landlord, rather than in the form of a qualification of the tenant's covenant not to assign or sublet. For example, in an early case,[9] the restrictive clause provided: "The tenant agrees that it will not assign, mortgage, or alienate this lease . . . without the written consent of the landlord, but the consent to sublet will not be unreasonably withheld." The court said, in construing the rights of the parties, "Under the clause in the lease now under consideration, as a matter of law, the plaintiff, as lessee, has no action at law for damages for breach of covenant by lessor, as the lessor never covenanted or agreed not to withhold his consent unreasonably. Nor has the plaintiff a legal right to demand that the landlord be compelled to consent in writing to a proposed lease or assignment. The lessor never convenanted or agreed to do so."[10] In another case, another instance is found of a court holding a modification provision ineffective.[11] There the covenant restricting the right of the tenant concluded with "Nothing herein contained shall permit the landlord

by board of directors of co-operative apartment building, and application for such approval had been refused.

**Annotation:** When lessor may withhold consent under unqualified provision in lease prohibiting assignment or subletting of leased premises without lessor's consent. 21 ALR4th 188.

**8.** Dress Shirt Sales, Inc. v Hotel Martinique Associates (1963) 12 NY2d 339, 239 NYS2d 660, 190 NE2d 10.

Landlord's exercise of his right to withhold his consent arbitrarily does not constitute economic duress so as to entitle tenant to damages. Herlou Card Shop, Inc. v Prudential Ins. Co. (1979, 1st Dept) 73 AD2d 562, 422 NYS2d 708.

**9.** Butterick Pub. Co. v Fulton & Elm Leasing Co. (S Ct NY Co 1928) 132 Misc 366, 229 NYS 86.

**10.** Sarner v Kantor (S Ct NY Co 1924) 123 Misc 469, 205 NYS 760.

Also, see Mann v Steinberg (S Ct NY Co 1946) 188 Misc 652, 64 NYS2d 68 (involving clause restricting subletting).

**11.** Sarner v Kantor (S Ct NY Co 1924) 123 Misc 469, 205 NYS 760.

to unreasonably withhold his consent to any sublease." The tenant, alleging an unreasonable refusal by the landlord to consent to a sublease, brought suit to recover damages, and the return of the deposit he had made under the lease. The court in denying the tenant relief, said, "Plaintiff cannot recover unless this fourth clause is a covenant by defendant not unreasonably to withhold his consent to a sublease. The purpose of the provision is to protect the lessee against liability for damages or risk of forfeiture, if consent of the lessor is improperly withheld. . . . Nowhere does the lessor expressly covenant not to withhold his consent, unreasonably. The only covenant is by plaintiff not to sublet, and it is plaintiff's own covenant that is qualified by the condition that the lessor shall not unreasonably withhold his consent."

To state it differently, if a tenant desires an effective covenant from the landlord not to arbitrarily or unreasonably refuse his consent to assignments or subleases, he must get an express covenant from the landlord that he will not withhold his consent unreasonably. (See paragraph e of the form in § 9:95 supra.) A qualification of the tenant's covenant not to assign without consent by the addition of the phrase, "but such consent will not be unreasonably withheld," does not bind the landlord to anything. However, it should be observed that there are some recent decisions which have indicated that the rights of a tenant should not be affected by a mere question of semantics, and that the fact that the modification is not in the form of an express agreement on the part of the landlord is not fatal.[12] Nevertheless, it is better to be safe than to be sorry, especially with such little effort. It is therefore suggested that the draftsman of the lease set forth in simple, yet clear terms that the landlord agrees that he will not unreasonably withhold

---

12. Singer Sewing Machine Co. v Eastway Plaza, Inc. (S Ct Monroe Co 1957) 5 Misc 2d 509, 158 NYS2d 647; Arlu Associates, Inc. v Rosner (1961, 1st Dept) 14 AD2d 272, 220 NYS2d 288, affd 12 NY2d 693, 233 NYS2d 477, 185 NE2d 913, indicating that it is questionable if the rule enunciated in the cases discussed in the text will be followed. However, this was in the form of dicta, since in this case the landlord had expressly agreed not to withhold his consent unreasonably.

**Annotations:** Construction and effect of provision in lease that consent to subletting or assignment will not be arbitrarily or unreasonably withheld. 54 ALR3d 679; Lessor's Consent to Subletting, 59 ALR3d 679.

# ASSIGNMENT AND SUBLETTING § 9:98

his consent, and not rely on litigation to prove himself right.

### § 9:98. Criteria for Determination of Reasonableness

Where a landlord agrees that he will not unreasonably withhold his consent, the landlord's refusal to consent will have to stand on something better than mere caprice or whim. His refusal will have to be, as he agreed, "reasonable." Thus, where the proposed subtenant was unquestionably financially responsible, and the landlord refused to consent to the subletting because of his religious and ideological differences with the proposed subtenant, it was held that his refusal would be held "unreasonable."[13] Similarly, where the sole reason for the landlord's refusal to consent to an assignment was that an officer of the landlord corporation required the leased premises, it was held that the landlord had breached its agreement not to withhold its consent unreasonably.[14] A landlord's refusal to consent to subletting because the tenant was not occupying the subject apartment as his primary residence was reasonable.[15] On the other hand, where a tenant's right to sublet was limited to a sublease of the "entire" premises, without landlord's consent, which landlord agreed not to withhold unreasonably, the landlord's refusal to consent to a sublease of a portion of the leased premises was held not to be unreasonable, since the purpose of the provision was to prevent multiple subtenancies in a "prestige" building, even though the

---

13. American Book Co. v Yeshivah University Development Foundation, Inc. (S Ct NY Co 1969) 59 Misc 2d 31, 297 NYS2d 156.

Where tenant in answer to landlord's objections to a sublease delivered a document binding the proposed subtenant to each and every provision of the prime lease, so that the subtenant could not even arguably be afforded any greater rights vis a vis the landlord than were enjoyed by the prime tenant, the continued objection of the landlord was held to be captious, and his consent to the subletting unreasonably withheld. Filmways, Inc. v 477 Madison Ave., Inc. (1971, 1st Dept) 36 AD2d 609, 318 NYS2d 506, affd 30 NY2d 597, 331 NYS2d 31, 282 NE2d 119.

Refusal of landlord to consent to assignment of lease by surviving partners of partnership-tenant to corporation organized by them, which kept intact all assets and liabilities, and merely changed the form of its organization, was held to be unreasonable. Grossman v S. E. Nichols Co. (1973, 1st Dept) 43 AD2d 674, 349 NYS2d 745, affd 35 NY2d 985, 365 NYS2d 531, 324 NE2d 888.

14. Cedarhurst Park Apartments, Inc. v Milgrim (Dist Ct Nassau Co 1967) 55 Misc 2d 118, 284 NYS2d 330.

15. Cutler v North Shore Towers Associates (1986, 2d Dept) 125 AD2d 532, 509 NYS2d 609.

landlord thereafter entered into a lease with the same proposed subtenant.[16]

In other words, to be reasonable, the landlord's reasons for a refusal should be objective, rather than subjective. The courts have adopted a policy of judicial disapproval of subjective reasons, which have been characterized as mere caprice or whim.[17] By "objective" reasons are meant those standards which are readily measurable criteria or a proposed subtenant's or assignee's acceptability, from the viewpoint of *any* landlord. These criteria are: (a) The financial solvency of the proposed tenant; (b) the nature of his business, its suitability for the premises and general business area, and the necessity of altering the premises to suit the assignee's business; (c) the legality of the proposed use. These categories would form a ready basis upon which to predicate a "reasonable" refusal.[18]

### § 9:99. Statutory Modification of Right to Withhold Consent in Case of a Deceased Residential Tenant

The Real Property Law provides,[19] that notwithstanding any contrary provision contained in any lease made after May 11, 1965, which affects premises demised for residential use, or partly for residential and partly for professional use, the executor, administrator or legal representative of a deceased tenant under such a lease, may request the landlord thereunder to consent to the assignment of such a lease, or to the subletting of the premises demised thereby. Such request shall be accompanied by the written consent thereto of any co-tenant or guarantor of such lease and a statement of the name, business and home addresses of the proposed assignee or sublessee. Within ten days after the mailing of such request, the landlord may ask the sender thereof for additional information as will enable the landlord to determine if rejec-

---

16. Time, Inc. v Tager (Civ Ct NY Co 1965) 46 Misc 2d 658, 200 NYS2d 413.

17. Subjective concerns and personal desires cannot play a role in a landlord's decision to withhold his consent to an assignment. Ontel Corp. v Helasol Realty Corp. (1987, App Div, 2d Dept) 515 NYS2d 567.

18. Restrictions against assignment or subletting provide a landlord with the opportunity to assess the financial responsibility and "business character" of any proposed assignee or subtenant, as well as the legality of the proposed use and the nature of the occupancy. Mann Theatres Corp. v Mid-Island Shopping Plaza Co. (1983, 2d Dept) 94 AD2d 466, 464 NYS2d 793, affd 62 NY2d 930, 479 NYS2d 213, 468 NE2d 51.

19. Real Prop L § 236, add L 1965, Ch 156, eff May 11, 1965.

## ASSIGNMENT AND SUBLETTING § 9:99

tion of such request shall be unreasonable. Within thirty days after the mailing of the request for consent, or of the additional information reasonably asked for by the landlord, whichever is later, the landlord shall send a notice to the sender thereof of his election to terminate said lease or to grant or refuse his consent. Landlord's failure to send such a notice shall be deemed to be a consent to the proposed assignment or subletting. If the landlord consents, said lease may be assigned in accordance with the request provided a written agreement by the assignee assuming the performance of the tenant's obligations under the lease is delivered to the landlord in form reasonably satisfactory to the landlord, or the premises may be sublet in accordance with the request, as the case may be, but the estate of the deceased tenant, and any other tenant thereunder, shall nevertheless remain liable for the performance of tenant's obligations under said lease. If the landlord terminates said lease or unreasonably refuses his consent, said lease shall be deemed terminated, and the estate of the deceased tenant and any other tenant thereunder shall be discharged from further liability thereunder as of the last day of the calendar month during which the landlord was required hereunder to exercise his option. If the landlord reasonably refuses his consent, said lease shall continue in full force and effect, subject to the right to make further requests for consent hereunder. Any request, notice or communication required or authorized to be given hereunder shall be sent by registered or certified mail, return receipt requested. This act shall not apply to a proprietary lease, viz.: a lease to, or held by, a tenant entitled thereto by reason of ownership of stock in a corporate owner of premises which operates the same on a cooperative basis. Any waiver of any part of this section shall be void as against public policy.[20]

The right of an executor of a deceased residential tenant to assign or sublet the decedent's leasehold is specifically delineated in this statute, and the executor is not entitled to the benefit of the more extensive rights

---

20. Executor of estate of deceased residential tenant does not have the unrestricted power to assign the tenant's lease, but is subject to the provisions of Real Prop L § 236. Rosefan Constr. Corp. v Salazar (NYC Civ Ct Queens Co 1982) 114 Misc 2d 956, 452 NYS2d 1016.

granted to a residential tenant to assign or sublet under Real Property Law § 226-b.¹ Thus, it is clear that the sole and exclusive remedy available to the estate of a deceased residential tenant for a landlord's unreasonable withholding of consent to an assignment or sublease is a release from any further rental obligations. There is no authorization, statutory or otherwise, for the executor of an estate, upon a landlord's rejection of a request to assign or sublet, to occupy an apartment in his individual capacity.²

### § 9:100. Tenant's Remedies for Landlord's Breach of Covenant to Consent

Where a landlord has agreed not to withhold his consent unreasonably, and he violates such agreement, the courts have held that the tenant may adopt one of the following courses. First, the tenant may ignore the restrictive covenant and assign lease or sublet the premises.³ However this course of action is fraught with danger. The landlord may still assert his rights alleging a breach of the covenant, and it will then be necessary for the tenant to prove that under all the facts and circumstances the consent was unreasonably withheld. It is difficult to state categorically in advance of litigation whether the tenant's position will be upheld. As an alternative, and by far, more preferable course of action, the tenant may sue for a declaratory judgment[4] to determine whether or not the landlord's consent is being unreasonably withheld.⁵ In addition the tenant has been held entitled to maintain an action to recover damages,⁶ or interpose a counterclaim therefor in the landlord's

1. Wishod v Kibel (1985, 2d Dept) 115 AD2d 735, 496 NYS2d 544. See §§ 9:78, 9:79, supra.
2. Joint Properties Owners, Inc. v Deri (1986, 1st Dept) 113 AD2d 691, 497 NYS2d 658.
3. Butterick Pub. Co. v Fulton & Elm Leasing Co. (S Ct NY Co 1928) 132 Misc 366, 229 NYS 86; Singer Sewing Machine Co. v Eastway Plaza, Inc. (S Ct Monroe Co 1957) 5 Misc 2d 509, 158 NYS2d 647.
4. CPLR 3001.
5. Singer Sewing Machine Co. v Eastway Plaza, Inc. (S Ct Monroe Co 1957) 5 Misc 2d 509, 158 NYS2d 647; Mann v Steinberg (S Ct NY Co 1946) 188 Misc 652, 64 NYS2d 68; Butterick Pub. Co. v Fulton & Elm Leasing Co. (S Ct NY Co 1928) 132 Misc 366, 229 NYS 86; Sarner v Kantor (S Ct NY Co 1924) 123 Misc 469, 205 NYS 760.
6. Arlu Associates, Inc. v Rosner (1961, 1st Dept) 14 AD2d 272, 220 NYS2d 288, affd 12 NY2d 693, 233 NYS2d 477, 185 NE2d 913; Singer Sewing Machine Co. v Eastway Plaza, Inc. (S Ct Monroe Co 1957) 5 Misc 2d 509, 158 NYS2d 647.

# ASSIGNMENT AND SUBLETTING § 9:102

action for rent;[7] or maintain an action for specific performance of the agreement.[8] However, a landlord's breach of his covenant not to unreasonably withhold his consent to a sublease does not justify tenant's abandonment of the leased premises or refusal to pay rent.

## § 9:101. Landlord's Remedies for Breach of Restriction Against Assignment or Subletting

An assignment or a sublease in violation of a restriction in the lease is not void. It is voidable and passes an estate subject to the consequences of the breach.[9] By appropriate provisions in the lease a landlord may reserve unto himself the right to recover possession for a breach of the restriction, and thereby void the assignment. If for example the lease provides that by reason of such a violation of the terms of the lease, the lease is thereby ipso facto forfeited without further action on the part of the landlord, the landlord can thereupon void the assignment by instituting holdover summary proceedings against the tenant to recover possession. If the lease reserves to the landlord the right of re-entry for such a violation of the terms of the lease, then the landlord can likewise void the assignment, and recover possession by a proper exercise of his right of re-entry; that is, either by an ejectment action, or if peaceable re-entry can be effected, by taking possession without action. However, absent the reservation in the lease of possessory rights for a breach of a restriction against assignments or sublettings, a landlord cannot recover possession as a remedy for a tenant's breach of the restriction.[10]

## § 9:102. —Equitable Relief

The covenant against assignment or subletting without the written consent of the landlord has been regarded by

---

7. 601 West 26 Corp. v John Wiley & Sons, Inc. (1969, 1st Dept) 32 AD2d 522, 298 NYS2d 1018; 72nd Street Associates v Pyle (AT1 1984) 124 Misc 2d 1087, 480 NYS2d 160, mod on other grounds (1st Dept) 105 AD2d 607, 481 NYS2d 341, app dismd 64 NY2d 774, 485 NYS2d 991, 475 NE2d 457.

8. Singer Sewing Machine Co v Eastway Plaza Inc (S Ct Monroe Co 1957) 5 Misc 2d 509, 158 NYS2d 647.

9. See § 9:29, supra.

10. Symonds v Hurlbut (1925) 240 NY 96, 98, 147 NE 540 (subletting); Storms v Manhattan R. Co. (AD1 1902) 77 AD 94, 79 NYS 60 (assignment), affd 178 NY 493, 71 NE 3; S. Liebmann's Sons Brewing Co. v Lauter (AD1 1902) 73 AD 183, 76 NYS 748 (assignment); Lane v Spiegel (1909, Sup App T) 117 NYS 262 (assignment).

the courts as a valuable right, and courts of equity have been zealous in its protection and enforcement.[11] Therefore a landlord may bring an action in equity to restrain a violation of covenant restricting assignments or subleases.[12] As Merrell, J., said, speaking for the Appellate Division, "I do not think the defendants should be heard to assert the claim that the plaintiff should be denied injunctive relief, merely because by a continuance of the tenancy of the sublessees he will not have suffered irreparable damages, even though plaintiff had failed to show such damage. . . . Inasmuch as it was made a condition of the granting of the lease to the (tenants) that they should not, without the written consent of the lessor, sublet said premises or any part thereof, the plaintiff was entirely within his rights in asking the court to grant a mandatory injunction summarily ousting the sublessees. The plaintiff was entitled to injunctive relief to restrain occupancy contrary to the terms of the lease. Such relief is in the nature of specific performance, and is not dependent upon the absence of adequate remedy at law. . . . This is not a question as to whether plaintiff has or has not an adequate remedy at law. He is entitled to insist that his lessees obey the terms and conditions of the lease under which they hold."[13]

However it should be noted that such an action will imply a continuance of the lease; not its cancellation and re-entry by the lessor.[14] If a landlord exercises the right of termination granted him under the paramount lease for an unauthorized assignment or subletting, he cannot thereafter bring a suit in equity, but must resort to his other remedies.[15] As Van Brunt, P.J., said, in so holding,[16] "After having elected that the lease should cease he now seeks, by this action, to enforce covenants contained in the instrument which has ended. If the plaintiff had not

**11.** Glauberman v University Place Apartments, Inc. (S Ct NY Co 1946) 188 Misc 277, 66 NYS2d 335, affd 272 AD 758, 70 NYS2d 139, app dismd 297 NY 587, 74 NE2d 558.
**12.** Symonds v Hurlbut (1925) 240 NY 96, 98, 147 NE 540; Boskowitz v Cohn (AD1 1921) 197 AD 776, 189 NYS 419; S. Liebmann's Sons Brewing Co. v Lauter (AD1 1902) 73 AD 183, 76 NYS 748; Morris Glick, Inc. v Grubman (S Ct NY Co 1945) 56 NYS2d 324.
**13.** Boskowitz v Cohn (AD1 1921) 197 AD 776, 189 NYS 419.
**14.** Symonds v Hurlbut (1925) 240 NY 96, 98, 147 NE 540.
**15.** Kramer v Amberg (S Ct GT 1 1899) 53 Hun 427, 6 NYS 303.
**16.** Kramer v Amberg (S Ct GT 1 1899) 53 Hun 427, 6 NYS 303.

elected that the lease should determine and come to an end by reason of the breach of these covenants, he would have had the right, by injunction in a proper suit in equity, to enforce the covenants in the lease, suing upon the lease, but having elected that the lease should terminate, then his right to bring suit to enforce covenants in that lease also terminated, because upon an instrument which has ended no right of action can be based. As already stated, the plaintiff had the right to elect that the lease should end because of the breach of these covenants; and having so elected, the lease terminated, and the only remedy which he had was a right of re-entry which was to be enforced by the ordinary proceedings for the recovery of the possession of real property unjustly withheld from its true owner, viz., by an action in ejectment."

### § 9:103. —Damages

A landlord upon the tenant's breach of the covenant restricting the right to assign or sublet, can sue the tenant for such damages as he sustained by reason of such breach.[17] Such damages however do not include the rentals which the tenant collected from his subtenants.[18]

As a general rule counsel fees paid by a landlord in a suit to restrain a tenant from violating the restriction in a lease against subletting or assignment are not recoverable as damages.[19]

## P. RESEARCH REFERENCES

### § 9:104. Generally

In addition to the preceding text, the reader is also referred to the following:

49 Am Jur 2d, Landlord and Tenant §§ 391-512.

---

**17.** Symonds v Hurlbut (1925) 240 NY 96, 98, 147 NE 540; S. Liebmann's Sons Brewing Co. v Lauter (AD1 1902) 73 AD 183, 76 NYS 748.

**18.** Erwin v Farrington (S Ct Steuben Co 1954) 132 NYS2d 20, revd on other grounds (AD4) 285 AD 1212, 140 NYS2d 379.

**19.** Cuyler Realty Co. v Teneo Co. (AD1 1921) 196 AD 440, 188 NYS 340, reh den 197 AD 934, 188 NYS 917 and affd 233 NY 647, 135 NE 954. In this case it was further held that such counsel fees are not covered by a provision in the lease that the landlord shall add to the next installment of rent money paid because of breaches of covenants on the part of the tenant. As to this, however, see § 359, infra, for a form of clause entitling a landlord to recover such counsel fees.

**§ 9:104** LANDLORD AND TENANT

10 Am Jur Proof of Facts 2d 481, Landlord's Unreasonable Refusal to consent to an Assignment or a Sublease.

11 Am Jur Legal Forms 2d, Leases of Real Property §§ 161:981-161:1036, 161:1071-161:1115.

16 Am Jur Pleading and Practice Forms (Rev ed), Landlord and Tenant, Forms 361-363.

New York Jur 2d, Landlord and Tenant (1st ed §§ 210-270).

New York CLS Real Property Law §§ 226, 226-6, 236.

New York Forms, Leases, Forms 8:261-8:269.

Index to Annotations, Landlord and Tenant.

**VERALEX®:** Cases and annotations referred to herein can be further researched through the VERALEX electronic retrieval system's two services, **Auto-Cite®** and **SHOWME®**. Use Auto-Cite to check citations for form, parallel references, prior and later history, and annotation references. Use SHOWME to display the full text of cases and annotations.

# CHAPTER 10
# EFFECT OF HOLDING OVER

A. IN GENERAL
- § 10:1. Effect of Holding Over by Tenant
- § 10:2. Terms and Conditions of Holdover Tenancy
- § 10:3. Holding Over; Burden of Proof
- § 10:4. Leaving Property on Premises as Holding Over
- § 10:5. Breach of Covenant to Surrender in Good Condition as Holding Over
- § 10:6. Holding Over Where Term Ends on Saturday, Sunday, or Holiday
- § 10:7. Holding Over by Assignee or Subtenant
- § 10:8. Retention of Key as Holding Over
- § 10:9. Measure of Damages for Holding Over
- § 10:10. Double Rent Not Recoverable as Damages

B. STATUTORY TENANCY
- § 10:11. Holding Over by Virtue of Emergency Rent Laws
- § 10:12. Duration of Tenancy
- § 10:13. Expiration of Tenancy on Death of Tenant
- § 10:14. Terms and Conditions of Tenancy
- § 10:15. —Waiver of Jury Trial Clause
- § 10:16. —Security Clause
- § 10:17. —Provision for Attorney's Fees
- § 10:18. —Option to Purchase
- § 10:19. —Automatic Renewal Clause
- § 10:20. Damages on Termination of Tenancy

C. RESEARCH REFERENCES
- § 10:21. Generally

---

## A. IN GENERAL

### § 10:1. Effect of Holding Over by Tenant

Upon the expiration of a lease, it is the obligation of a tenant to vacate from the leased premises. His rights to continue in possession thereof have expired. If, nevertheless, he continues in possession, he then becomes a trespasser on his landlord's property. Prior to September 1, 1959, it had been well established by decisional law that when a tenant wrongfully held over after the expiration of the term of his lease, his landlord had the exclusive

§ 10:1

right of election either to treat him as a trespasser or as a tenant for a new term. If the landlord elected to treat the holding-over tenant as a tenant for a new term, then he thereby created a holdover tenancy.[1] Under this rule the tenant holding over had no option or choice in the matter.[2] So strictly was this rule enforced that even though a tenant prior to the expiration of his lease notified the landlord that he did not intend to stay on for a new term, and then, nevertheless, did stay on, if the landlord elected to treat him as a holdover tenant, the tenant was bound by such election.[3]

The Real Property Law has changed this rule. It now provides,[4] "Where a tenant whose term is longer than one month holds over after the expiration of such term, such holding over shall not give to the landlord the option to hold the tenant for a new term solely by virtue of the tenant's holding over. In the case of such a holding over by the tenant, the landlord may proceed, in any manner permitted by law, to remove the tenant, or, if the landlord shall accept rent for any period subsequent to the expiration of such term, then, unless an agreement either express or implied is made providing otherwise, the tenancy created by the acceptance of such rent shall be a tenancy from month to month commencing on the first day after the expiration of such term."[5]

In other words, under the Real Property Law the mere holding over by a tenant whose term is longer than one month does not allow the landlord to create a holdover tenancy without his acceptance of rent from the holding over tenant. If the tenant does not offer any rent, or if he does offer the rent, but the landlord does not accept it, no holdover tenancy is created by the holding over, and the

---

1. Stern v Equitable Trust Co. (1924) 238 NY 267, 269, 144 NE 578; United Merchants' Realty & Improv. Co. v Roth (1908) 193 NY 570, 86 NE 544; Herter v Mullen (1899) 159 NY 28, 53 NE 700; Schuyler v Smith (1873) 51 NY 309.

2. Foster v Stewart (AD4 1921) 196 AD 814, 188 NYS 151; Farrell v Woodward (AT1 1917) 101 Misc 560, 167 NYS 605.

3. Haynes v Aldrich (1892) 133 NY 287, 31 NE 94; 805 St. Marks Ave. Corp. v Finkelstein (AD2 1931) 234 AD 15, 253 NYS 785.

4. Real Prop L § 232-c, add L 1959, Ch 114, eff September 1, 1959.

5. Where tenant under an indefinite tenancy in New York City continues in possession after October first next after possession commences under the agreement, and continues to pay the rent which the landlord accepts, a month to month tenancy is created. Adina 74 Realty Corp. v Hudson (1980) 104 Misc 2d 634, 428 NYS2d 977.

landlord's remedy is limited to removal of the tenant, and the recovery of damages. The landlord's right to remove the tenant may of course be waived, or it may be postponed by agreement. But, in the absence of such waiver or agreement, or of statutory restriction, such as restrictions provided by emergency rent laws, the right of a landlord, or of his grantee, if he has transferred his reversion during the original term,[6] to remove a holding-over tenant is preserved until his acceptance of the rent.

Accordingly, where a landlord before the expiration of a term notifies his tenant that if he should stay over, he will be deemed a tenant for a new term at an increased rental, and if the tenant ignores this notice, holds over, and tenders the old rent, which the landlord refuses to accept, no holdover tenancy is created, and an action for nonpayment of rent, or a nonpayment summary proceeding, based on such notice purporting to fix a new rent, never agreed upon by the tenant and never paid by him, does not lie, there being no tenancy in fact or at law obligating the tenant for such rent.[7]

### § 10:2. Terms and Conditions of Holdover Tenancy

The duration of a holdover tenancy is now fixed by statute.[1] The Real Property Law provides,[2] that if a

---

**6.** Stewart v Briggs (AD3 1911) 147 AD 386, 132 NYS 89.

**7.** Jaroslow v Lehigh Valley R. Co. (1969) 23 NY2d 991, 298 NYS2d 999, 246 NE2d 757; Farrell Lines, Inc. v New York (S Ct NY Co 1970) 63 Misc 2d 542, 312 NYS2d 260 (tenant by remaining in possession after expiration of lease was not liable for increased rental demanded by landlord, notwithstanding that lease granted tenant option to renew at 10% increase, nor that before expiration of lease landlord had informed tenant that if tenant stayed on, his rental would be at an increased rent), affd (1st Dept) 35 AD2d 788, 315 NYS2d 794, affd 30 NY2d 76, 330 NYS2d 358, 281 NE2d 162; Reimer v Kaslov (NYC Civ Ct King's Co 1970) 61 Misc 2d 960, 307 NYS2d 760; Palagonia v Pappas (D Ct Suffolk Co 1974) 79 Misc 2d 830, 361 NYS2d 236 (citing text).

**1.** Under the common law rule, which has been abrogated by the Real Property Law, the duration of the holdover tenancy was determined as follows: If the lease which expired provided for a term of one year or more, then the duration or term of the holdover tenancy would be for one year from the date of expiration of the expired lease. Kennedy v New York (1909) 196 NY 19, 89 NE 360; Schuyler v Smith (1873) 51 NY 309; Baylies v Ingram (AD1 1903) 84 AD 360, 82 NYS 891, affd 181 NY 518, 73 NE 1119. If, however, the expired lease provided for a term of less than one year, then the duration of the holdover tenancy would be for a period similar to that of the expired lease. Thus, if the expired lease had been for eleven months, the holdover tenancy would be for eleven months. Ketcham v Ochs (S Ct Kings Co 1901) 34 Misc 470, 70 NYS 268, affd 74 AD 626, 77 NYS 1130.

As to effect of Real Prop L § 232-c on a periodic tenancy for periods lon-

§ 10:2                                    LANDLORD AND TENANT

landlord does not proceed to remove a tenant holding over after the expiration of his term, which term was longer than one month, but accepts rent from him, the holding over will create only a month-to-month tenancy, unless the parties agree, either expressly or impliedly, to a longer term. The language in the statute, "unless an agreement either express or implied is made providing otherwise", refers only to the extension of the duration of the holdover tenancy beyond a tenancy from month to month.[3]

However, the statute says nothing about the terms and conditions of the new tenancy. Therefore, it would seem that the rule established by prior decisional law would still be applicable. This rule provides, that where a tenant holds over without any other or new agreement with his landlord, the law will imply a continuance of the tenancy on the same terms, and subject to the same covenants as those contained in the original lease, except as to duration.[4] Thus, a lease provision obligating tenant for attorneys' fees incurred in connection with a dispossess by summary proceedings, is carried forward as a provision of the holdover month-to-month tenancy.[5] Upon expiration of a lease, a provision granting the tenant the right to assign or sublet with landlord's consent, becomes inapplicable to a holdover tenancy, since the tenant no longer has a leasehold to assign or sublet.[6]

Of course, such terms and conditions of the old tenancy may be modified or changed by mutual agreement.[7] Although the law implies that a tenant holding over does so upon the same terms and conditions as under his previ-

ger than month to month, see §§ 30:40, 30:43, infra.

2. Real Prop L § 232-c; see § 10:1, supra.

3. Jaroslow v Lehigh Valley R. Co. (1969) 23 NY2d 991, 298 NYS2d 999, 246 NE2d 757.

4. Baylies v Ingram (AD1 1903) 84 AD 360, 82 NYS 891, affd 181 NY 518, 73 NE 1119; Scully v Roche (AT 1912) 76 Misc 458, 135 NYS 633; Wager v Haberman (S Ct NY Co 1974) 85 Misc 2d 314, 378 NYS2d 837; Tubbs v Hendrickson (S Ct Tioga Co 1976) 88 Misc 2d 917, 390 NYS2d 791.

Annotation: Binding effect on tenant holding over of covenants in expired lease. 49 ALR2d 480.

5. Museum of Modern Art v Kirk (AT1 1981) 111 Misc 2d 1074, 448 NYS2d 93. Contra: Raleigh Co v Society for Avatar Meher Baba (NYC Civ Ct NY Co) NYLJ November 13, 1974, p 18, col 7, Cohen, J.

6. Gavish v Rapp (S Ct NY Co 1984) 127 Misc 2d 255, 485 NYS2d 407.

7. Arol Development Corp. v Goodie Brand Packing Corp. (NYC Civ Ct Bx Co 1975) 83 Misc 2d 477, 372 NYS2d 324 (citing text), affd (AT1) 84 Misc 2d 493, 378 NYS2d 231.

ous tenancy, the implication does not obtain where the acts and conduct of the parties negate the existence of the original contract, or where the implication is inappropriate by reason of changed conditions, or where the circumstances tend to refute any intent to continue the applicability of a particular provision which is not an essential element of the landlord-tenant relationship.[8]

### § 10:3. Holding Over; Burden of Proof

Since a tenant who continues in possession after the term of his lease expires is a trespasser, and subject to damages therefor,[9] it becomes pertinent to discuss what constitutes holding over. The burden of proving a holding over is upon the landlord.[10]

"Holding over," said Ingraham, J., in an early leading case,[11] "is defined to be the act of keeping possession of the premises"; and this "keeping of possession," the same justice said in a later case[12] "must be an actual possession of the property as against the landlord, so that the tenant would by virtue of his possession become a trespasser."

In other words, to constitute a holding over there must be a wrongful retention by the tenant after the term expires of the possession which the tenant acquired under the expired lease.

### § 10:4. Leaving Property on Premises as Holding Over

The question of whether or not the mere leaving by a tenant of property upon the leased premises after the expiration of his lease constitutes a holding over is usually a question of fact. This question of fact is to be determined by taking into consideration the nature of the property leased, the amount paid as rent, the value of the real property, the value of the personal property left on the leased premises, the intent with which it was left,

8. Transit Drive-In Theater, Inc. v Outdoor Theatre Caterers, Inc. (1976, 4th Dept) 53 AD2d 1009, 386 NYS2d 482.

9. See § 10:1, supra.

10. Myers v Beakes Dairy Co. (AD1 1909) 132 AD 710, 117 NYS 569; Frost v Akron Iron Co. (AD1 1896) 1 AD 449, 37 NYS 374.

11. Frost v Akron Iron Co. (AD1 1896) 1 AD 449, 37 NYS 374.

12. Myers v Beakes Dairy Co. (AD1 1909) 132 AD 710, 117 NYS 569. Also, see Canfield v Elmer E. Harris & Co. (AD4 1927) 222 AD 326, 225 NYS 709, affd 248 NY 541, 162 NE 517.

and all the other facts and circumstances surrounding the case.[13]

Although, generally, the question is one of fact; yet, where only rubbish and worthless articles were left behind by the tenant, who, when he vacated, returned the keys to the landlord, the courts have not hesitated to hold that there was no continued possession; that is, no holding over by the tenant.[14]

Similarly, even though generally the question is one of fact; yet, "There can be no doubt," said Hubbs, P. J.,[15] "but what there may be cases where the mere leaving of property on the premises after the expiration of the lease would constitute a holding over and retention of possession of the premises as a matter of law." However, it will be found that such cases are extreme cases where the amount and value of the property are so great as to leave no doubt that there was a holding over. So that, if a tenant in possession of a store should leave his entire stock and fixtures in the store after his lease expired, that fact would require a ruling as a matter of law that the tenant held over.[16]

### § 10:5. Breach of Covenant to Surrender in Good Condition as Holding Over

"The covenant in the lease to surrender the premises in the same condition as in at the commencement of the term," said Hubbs, P. J.,[17] "has no bearing upon the question. If the plaintiff (landlord) suffered damage by the violation of that covenant, she has a remedy." But, the breach of that covenant will not constitute a holding over if the tenant has actually vacated from the premises.

---

**13.** Canfield v Elmer E. Harris & Co. (AD4 1927) 222 AD 326, 225 NYS 709, affd 248 NY 541, 162 NE 517.

**14.** Myers v Beakes Dairy Co. (AD1 1909) 132 AD 710, 117 NYS 569.

Also, see Frankman v Evans (City Ct Utica 1942) 34 NYS2d 95.

**15.** Canfield v Elmer E. Harris & Co. (AD4 1927) 222 AD 326, 225 NYS 709, affd 248 NY 541, 162 NE 517.

**16.** Canfield v Elmer E. Harris & Co. (AD4 1927) 222 AD 326, 225 NYS 709, affd 248 NY 541, 162 NE 517.

Also, see Haynes v Aldrich (1892) 133 NY 287, 31 NE 94; Vosburgh v Corn (AD2 1897) 23 AD 147, 48 NYS 598.

**17.** Canfield v Elmer E. Harris & Co. (AD4 1927) 222 AD 326, 225 NYS 709, affd 248 NY 541, 162 NE 517.

## § 10:6. Holding Over Where Term Ends on Saturday, Sunday, or Holiday

The statute provides,[18] that, where a contract by its terms authorizes or requires the payment of money or the performance of a condition on a Saturday, Sunday or a public holiday, or authorizes or requires the payment of money or the performance of a condition within or before or after a period of time computed from a certain day, and such period of time ends on a Saturday, Sunday or a public holiday, unless the contract expressly or impliedly indicates a different intent, such payment may be made or condition performed on the next succeeding business day, and if the period ends at a specified hour, such payment may be made or condition performed, at or before the same hour of such next succeeding business day, with the same force and effect as if made or performed in accordance with the terms of the contract.[19] It has been held, therefore, that where the last day of a term falls on a Sunday, the tenant may move on the following day without incurring any penalty therefor.[20]

## § 10:7. Holding Over by Assignee or Subtenant

Prior to September 1, 1959, when § 232-c was added to the Real Property Law,[1] it had been well established by decisional law that when a tenant assigned his lease, and the assignee continued in possession after the expiration of the term, such holding over would not be deemed a holding over by the tenant-assignor.[2] So, it was held that where one of several partners held over under a lease made to a partnership, which lease had been assigned to

---

18. Gen Constr L § 25(1), as am L 1965, Ch 848, eff Sept 1, 1965.

19. Also, see Gen Constr L § 25-a (1), as am L 1965, Ch 848, eff Sept 1, 1965, which provides, that when any period of time, computed from a certain day, within which or after which or before which an act is authorized or required to be done, ends on a Saturday, Sunday or a public holiday, such act may be done on the next succeeding business day and if the period ends at a specified hour, such act may be done at or before the same hour of such next succeeding business day, except that where a period of time specified by contract ends on a Saturday, Sunday or a public holiday, the extension of such period is governed by Gen Constr L § 25.

20. Frost v Akron Iron Co. (AD1 1896) 1 AD 449, 37 NYS 374; Terra Firma Corp. v Zinn (1942, Sup) 38 NYS2d 21, both of which cases having been decided prior to the amendment of the statute by the addition of Saturday and public holiday.

1. § 10:1, supra.

2. Probst v Rochester Steam Laundry Co. (1902) 171 NY 584, 586, 64 NE 504; Phelan v Kennedy (AD1 1919) 185 AD 749, 173 NYS 687; Manley v Winkler (AT 1912) 75 Misc 637, 133 NYS 972.

him during the term by his copartners who thereupon retired from the firm, he alone could be held liable as a holdover tenant. But, the retiring partners, who had assigned the lease, could not be held liable because they did not hold over.[3]

This decisional law would seem to be still applicable under the statute governing holdovers. On the other hand, under prior decisional law, if a subtenant continued in possession after the sublessor's lease expired, it was held that such wrongful holding over would be deemed the wrongful holding over of the tenant-sublessor.[4] As the Appellate Division said,[5] "Having entered into an absolute and express agreement to deliver possession of the premises at the expiration of his term, and being charged with that duty, it could not relieve itself from its engagement or duty by subletting the premises, or by any other voluntary act which rendered performance impossible." This rule was held applicable even though the tenant had sublet the premises with the consent of the landlord,[6] and even though the subtenant held over without the tenant's authority and against his wishes.[7] As the Appellate Division[8] observed, "The declaration of the defendant (sublessor) that he would not be responsible for rent thereafter did not operate as a surrender or abandonment of the premises by him, inasmuch as his subtenant remained in possession beyond the term." Nothing in Real Property Law § 232-c indicates that this decisional law is still not applicable. Therefore, when a tenant sublets, the burden is on him to see to it that when his lease expires the subtenant vacates with him from the premises. If the subtenant holds over, although the landlord cannot create a holdover tenancy merely because of that (inasmuch as

3. James v Pope (1859) 19 NY 324.
Also, see, Buchanan v Whiteman (1896) 151 NY 253, 45 NE 556.
4. Stahl Associates Co. v Mapes (1985, 1st Dept) 111 AD2d 626, 490 NYS2d 12; Syracuse Associates v Touchette Corp. (1979, 4th Dept) 73 AD2d 813, 424 NYS2d 72; Goodwin v Humbert (AD1 1926) 216 AD 295, 215 NYS 20, app dismd 244 NY 584, 155 NE 906; Phelan v Kennedy (AD1 1919) 185 AD 749, 173 NYS 687; Hall Steam-Power Co. v Campbell Printing Press & Manuf'g Co. (1893) 5 Misc 264, 25 NYS 106, affd 8 Misc 430, 28 NYS 662.
5. Sullivan v George Ringler & Co. (AD2 1901) 59 AD 184, 69 NYS 38, affd 171 NY 693, 64 NE 1126.
6. Sullivan v George Ringler & Co. (AD2 1901) 59 AD 184, 69 NYS 38, affd 171 NY 693, 64 NE 1126.
7. Manheim v Seitz (AD2 1897) 21 AD 16, 47 NYS 282.
8. Manheim v Seitz (AD2 1897) 21 AD 16, 47 NYS 282.

that can only be done if the tenant proffers the rent, and the landlord accepts such rent), yet, he still can recover damages for the wrongful holding over.[9]

### § 10:8. Retention of Key as Holding Over

"The key," said the court in an early case,[10] "is sometimes looked upon as the symbol through which possession is delivered and returned, but sometimes keys are lost or misplaced, and cannot be returned." In this case the lease expired on May 1. The tenant vacated on that day, but left a stove on the premises. The next day he tendered the keys to the premises to the landlord. The court then added, "Whether the stove was left and key retained until May 2nd willfully or accidentally, or through excusable or unavoidable circumstances, has much to do with the question of intent, of good faith, and of bad faith, and these are all considerations for the jury. The case ought to have gone to the jury to determine whether there was in fact a wrongful holding over by the defendant or not."

Therefore, the mere retention of keys is not in and of itself sufficient to constitute a holding over. This is merely one of the facts to be considered with all the other facts in the case in determining the question of fact as to whether or not there was a holding over after the expiration of the lease.[11]

### § 10:9. Measure of Damages for Holding Over

The measure of damages for wrongfully holding over is the reasonable rental value of the premises for the period possession is withheld, that is, the value of the use and occupation of the premises for the period possession is withheld.[12] Where a tenant wrongfully holds over, he may be relieved of liability for use and occupation by tendering vacant possession of the premises and the keys to the

---

9. Jaroslow v Lehigh Valley R. Co. (1969) 23 NY2d 991, 298 NYS2d 999, 246 NE2d 757.

10. McCabe v Evers (City Ct GT 1890) 9 NYS 541.

11. Also, see Magner v Barrett (AD2 1910) 139 AD 172, 123 NYS 690.

12. Earl v Nalley (AD3 1948) 273 AD 451, 78 NYS2d 92; Land Associates Corp. v Grand Union Stores, Inc. (AD3 1941) 261 AD 1014, 25 NYS2d 986; Vernon v Brown (AD2 1899) 40 AD 204, 58 NYS 11; Marbridge Bldg. Co. v White (AT1 1921) 115 Misc 320, 188 NYS 233.

As to remedies of new lessee against holding-over lessee, see § 8:10, supra.

landlord, from the time of the tender. It is not necessary for the landlord to accept the tender, since a "surrender" is the giving up by a tenant of his term, and a holdover tenant has no term to give up.[13] Where subtenant of part of a building prevents sublessor of the entire building from surrendering the entire building at the expiration of the term, it was held that the damages recoverable must be based on the value of the use and occupation of the entire building during the holdover period, and not on the rental reserved in the sublease.[14]

A landlord is not entitled to recover as damages counsel fees and other expenses incurred by him in obtaining the removal of a tenant who is wrongfully holding over after the expiration of his term,[15] in the absence of any express provision for reimbursement of such attorney's fees and expenses.[16]

Aside from the general damages based on the reasonable rental value of the premises which have been wrongfully held over by the tenant, the landlord may in proper cases recover special damages suffered by him as the result of the tenant's failure to surrender the premises,[17] provided they are not speculative.[18]

---

13. Elliot v Polny (NYC Civ Ct NY Co 1986) 132 Misc 2d 236, 503 NYS2d 673.

14. Syracuse Associates v Touchette Corp. (1979, 4th Dept) 73 AD2d 813, 424 NYS2d 72. But, see Spector v Fine (1922, Sup App T) 196 NYS 545, which held that a tenant who has surrendered all of the rented premises except a part which a subtenant continues to occupy is liable to the landlord for the reasonable rental value of only such part. Also, see Phelan v Kennedy (AD1 1919) 185 AD 749, 173 NYS 687 (measuring damages to lessee for sublessee's holdover at amount for which lessee became obligated to lessor rather than the amount at which premises were sublet).

15. Marbridge Bldg Co v White (AT1 1921) 115 Misc 320, 188 NYS 233.

16. Airways Supermarkets, Inc. v Santone (S Ct Bx Co 1951) 107 NYS2d 187, affd 280 AD 924, 116 NYS2d 128, attorney's fees held recoverable by virtue of a lease provision to the effect that if the lessor incurred any expense, including reasonable attorneys' fees, in any action arising out of any default of the tenant, such sum should become payable to the lessor; London v State (Ct of Claims 1949) 196 Misc 823, 92 NYS2d 756; Printerion Realty Corp. v Mancini (S Ct NY Co 1945) 61 NYS2d 200.

17. Phelan v Kennedy (AD1 1919) 185 AD 749, 173 NYS 687; Vernon v Brown (AD2 1899) 40 AD 204, 58 NYS 11; Nodine v State (Ct of Claims 1948) 192 Misc 572, 79 NYS2d 834; Airways Supermarkets, Inc. v Santone (S Ct Bx Co 1951) 107 NYS2d 187, affd 280 AD 924, 116 NYS2d 128.

18. Nodine v State (Ct of Claims 1948) 192 Misc 572, 79 NYS2d 834.

# EFFECT OF HOLDING OVER § 10:11

## § 10:10. Double Rent Not Recoverable as Damages

The Real Property Law provides,[19] that if a tenant gives notice of his intention to quit the premises held by him, and does not accordingly deliver up the possession thereof, at the time specified in such notice, he or his personal representatives must, so long as he continues in possession, pay to the landlord, his heirs or assigns, double the rent which he should otherwise have paid, to be recovered at the same time, and in the same manner, as the single rent.

It is well settled that this section of the Real Property Law applies only to a tenancy of indefinite duration, and where the tenant has the right, and seeks by notice to terminate the tenancy.[20] However, where the tenancy has a definitely fixed term, then the tenancy will expire automatically by its own terms, whether or not the tenant gives notice of his intention to quit. Hence, the statute is inapplicable to a tenancy with a fixed term.

Accordingly, where a tenant gave his landlord notice of his intention not to renew his lease, and then held over after the term of the original lease had expired, it was held that if the landlord elected to treat the tenant as a trespasser, he could not recover double rent as damages under this statute.[1] As the Appellate Term said,[2] "Where the term is definitely fixed, the tenancy expires ex vi termini, and the giving of notice to quit is a work of supererogation, which furnishes no rights and creates no liabilities."

## B. STATUTORY TENANCY

### § 10:11. Holding Over by Virtue of Emergency Rent Laws

By virtue of emergency rent laws, enacted from time to time, so-called statutory tenancies have been created. The primary, but not the only, purpose of such emergency rent laws is to prevent the wholesale eviction of tenants who are willing to pay a reasonable rent, but who cannot agree with their landlords as to the amount to be paid.

---

19. Real Prop L § 229.
20. Lerner v Wolf (AT1 1923) 121 Misc 114, 200 NYS 368; Regan v Fosdick (AT1 1897) 19 Misc 489, 43 NYS 1102.

1. 805 St. Marks Ave. Corp. v Finkelstein (AD2 1931) 234 AD 15, 253 NYS 785.
2. Regan v Fosdick (AT1 1897) 19 Misc 489, 43 NYS 1102.

§ 10:11  LANDLORD AND TENANT

By suspending possessory remedies under the lease, these laws extend against the will of the landlord the right of the tenant to remain in possession of the leased premises so long as he continues to pay the rent fixed as reasonable by such laws. The tenant thus remains in possession not by virtue of any agreement, express or implied, but by the compulsion of law. In the case of commercial and business rent control laws, generally, the purpose is the protection of those engaged in business against what might be their loss of means of livelihood, the place in which they conduct their business, by being compelled to pay such an amount in rent as would make it impossible profitably to conduct their business.[3] It is well established that a tenant who has a lease which fixes a definite term, and who remains in possession after the expiration of such term by virtue of emergency rent laws becomes a statutory tenant.[4] "The tenant," said the Court of Appeals,[5] "does not offer to remain in possession of the premises. He insists upon doing so. The landlord does not accept his proposition. The law forces it upon him. The tenant does not offer any proposition to the landlord upon which the conventional relation of landlord and tenant, as to length of term and amount of rent, based on offer and acceptance can be inferred. To this extent the landlord is optionless and the tenant stands on his statutory rights, which become the measure of his term and of his liability." More recently, the Appellate Term,[6] said that,

---

**3.** Stern v Equitable Trust Co. (1924) 238 NY 267, 144 NE 578; Kaypar Corp. v Fosterport Realty Corp. (S Ct Bx Co 1947) 1 Misc 2d 469, 69 NYS2d 313, affd 272 AD 878, 72 NYS2d 405.

**4.** Under L 1920, ch 944, as am [now repealed], see Stern v Equitable Trust Co. (1924) 238 NY 267, 144 NE 578; 1239 Madison Ave. Corp. v Neuburger (AD1 1924) 208 AD 87, 203 NYS 137.

Under the emergency commercial rent laws, L 1945, chs 3, 315, as am [now repealed], see Schork v Hayden (AD2 1948) 274 AD 812, 79 NYS2d 856; Graf v Miller (M Ct 1952) 202 Misc 887, 120 NYS2d 154, holding that a monthly or a month-to-month tenant becomes a statutory tenant at the end of the first month of his occupancy; Lewittes & Sons v Spielmann (AT1 1947) 190 Misc 35, 73 NYS2d 552; True-Value Slipper & Sandal Corp. v Quaker Mechanical Corp. (City Ct 1947) 189 Misc 328, 71 NYS2d 221; Royce Haulage Corp. v Bronx Terminal Garage, Inc. (AT1 1945) 185 Misc 892, 57 NYS2d 760.

A lessee who remains in possession at the end of his lease by virtue of the rent stabilization law becomes a statutory tenant, and not a month-to-month tenant. Park Summit Realty Corp. v Frank (AT1 1980) 107 Misc 2d 318, 434 NYS2d 73, affd (1st Dept) 84 AD2d 700, 448 NYS2d 414, affd 56 NY2d 1025, 453 NYS2d 643, 439 NE2d 358.

**5.** Stern v Equitable Trust Co (1924) 238 NY 267, 270, 144 NE 578.

**6.** Royce Haulage Corp v Bronx

# EFFECT OF HOLDING OVER § 10:12

"Chapter 315, Laws 1945,[7] has, for the period therein prescribed, eliminated the holdover tenancy, and after the expiration of the term such tenancy continues as a statutory tenancy under said act."

## § 10:12. Duration of Tenancy

The duration of a statutory tenancy is fixed by the particular emergency rent statute under which the tenant claims his right to possession, and not by the term specified in the expired lease.[8] Whether or not a landlord or a tenant must give the other notice of termination will also depend upon the terms of the emergency rent statute then in force.[1] However, it has been held that statutory tenants are neither tenants at will nor on sufferance, entitled to 30 days' notice under Real Property Law § 228, nor monthly tenants, nor month-to-month tenants entitled to 30 days' notice under Real Property Law § 232-a, or Real Property Law § 232-b.[2]

Although in the absence of statute no notice of termination need be given to a statutory tenant, yet such a tenancy cannot be terminated during a rent-paid period, unless some act of the tenant inconsistent with his tenancy terminates his right of possession. A landlord by accepting a month's rent clearly manifests his intention that the tenancy should continue at least for the balance of that month, and that is the legal effect of such acceptance.[3] In other words, a statutory tenant who pays rent in advance for a month is entitled to possession of the leased premises for that month against his landlord. This principle is not vitiated by the fact that the tenant may

---

Terminal Garage, Inc (AT1 1945) 185 Misc 892, 57 NYS2d 760.

Also, see, Schork v Hayden (AD2 1948) 274 AD 812, 79 NYS2d 856.

7. Unconsol L §§ 8551 et seq.

8. Stern v Equitable Trust Co. (1924) 238 NY 267, 144 NE 578; Lewittes & Sons v Spielmann (AT1 1947) 190 Misc 35, 73 NYS2d 552.

1. For example, Emergency Housing Rent Control Law § 5 (7), and New York City Rent and Rehabilitation Law § 26-408, subd i, each requires a statutory tenant to give 30 days' written notice by registered or certified mail of intent to vacate.

See Landerson, Inc. v Staten (NYC Civ Ct NY Co 1972) 71 Misc 2d 568, 336 NYS2d 710, where landlord was found to have suffered no loss of rent as a result of tenant's failure to give notice of intention to vacate, and court denied landlord recovery of one month's rent.

2. Whitmarsh v Farnell (1949) 298 NY 336, 83 NE 543; Lewittes & Sons v Spielmann (AT1 1947) 190 Misc 35, 73 NYS2d 552.

3. Galluccio v Moscatiello (1947, Sup App T) 74 NYS2d 897; Empire State, Inc. v Graceline Handbags, Inc. (M Ct 1948) 192 Misc 679, 80 NYS2d 266.

§ 10:12

lose his right to possession because of some breach of a covenant by him, or by an illegal use of the premises; for, in these instances it is the act of the tenant contrary to the legal right of possession which deprives him of the possession. The payment of rent in advance, therefore, does not relieve him of his own violation. But, if there is no such violation contrary to the legal right of possession, the landlord, having accepted the stipulated rental for a definite period, cannot arbitrarily terminate that right of possession before it expires by natural limitation.[4]

A month-to-month tenant does not become a statutory tenant during the period of an emergency rent law, since he is not continuing in possession after the expiration of a definite term fixed in an agreement of lease. In this situation a month-to-month tenant continues as such, and is entitled to the statutory thirty-day notice of termination of tenancy.[5]

### § 10:13. Expiration of Tenancy on Death of Tenant

A statutory tenancy expires upon the death of the tenant. If rent is payable in advance on the first day of the month, his estate is liable for that month's rent which accrued before the tenancy expired. The estate will not be liable for any rent thereafter.[6] If the leased prop-

---

4. Empire State Inc v Graceline Handbags Inc (M Ct 1948) 192 Misc 679, 80 NYS2d 266.

5. A. & S. Const. Co. v Brock (AD2 1922) 201 AD 584, 194 NYS 691; Almin Realty Corp. v Livingston (1950, Sup App T) 103 NYS2d 166 (statutory tenant), holding that a statutory tenant is not, and that a month-to-month tenant is, entitled to a thirty days' notice of increase of rent granted by the emergency rent control authorities; Paray Realty Corp. v Goodwine (AT2 1949) 194 Misc 538, 90 NYS2d 181, app den 275 AD 836, 89 NYS2d 232; Cannon v Gordon (AT1 1944) 181 Misc 950, 48 NYS2d 124; Acierno v Kutchuk (M Ct 1949) 196 Misc 514, 92 NYS2d 170 (month-to-month tenancy).

Residential tenant in possession on a month-to-month basis at the time rent control became effective does not become a statutory tenant, but remains a month-to-month tenant, entitled to a 30-day notice of termination.

Stribula v Wien (AT1 1980) 107 Misc 2d 114, 438 NYS2d 52 (citing text).

Although a tenant who remains in possession by virtue of the rent laws is a statutory tenant, and the statutory notice to quit is not required to terminate such a tenancy, nevertheless, housing accommodations not occupied by the tenant as his primary residence are excluded from coverage by the Rent and Rehabilitation Law (New York City Administrative Code § 26-403, subd 2(10)). Such a tenant, therefore, is not to be treated as a statutory tenant but as a month-to-month tenant, and must be served with the 30-day notice terminating the tenancy, as well as the notice of intent to institute a summary proceeding based on nonprimary tenancy. Charlotte Realty Co. v Lubarsky (AT2 § 11 1986) 133 Misc 2d 785, 509 NYS2d 691.

6. Stern v Equitable Trust Co. (1924) 208 AD 13, 203 NYS 91, affd

# EFFECT OF HOLDING OVER § 10:13

erty is residential property, the right of the members of his immediate family to continued occupancy is governed by the prevailing rent laws.[7] However, it has been held that such persons who were not living with the statutory tenant at the time of his death, and seek to take possession thereafter, are not within the protection of emergency rent laws.[8]

New York City Rent Eviction and Rehabilitation Regulations § 2204.6(d) provides: "No occupant of housing accommodations shall be evicted under this section where the occupant is either the surviving spouse of the deceased tenant or some other member of the deceased tenant's family who has been living with the tenant." This provision, it has been ruled, affords protection to those family members of a statutory tenant who have fully, and with a fair degree of permanency, integrated themselves into the family living unit of the statutory tenant.[9] "Section 2204.6(d) is not to be utilized as a mechanism by which a departing statutory tenant may anoint a family member not fully integrated into the former's family living unit as a successor to that tenancy. Nor may a family member of a statutory tenant, who has access to the latter's apartment, but who is not an established member of the statutory tenant's family living unit, utilize such mere access to the apartment as a means by which to succeed to the tenancy upon the death of the statutory tenant."[10]

---

238 NY 267, 144 NE 578; 1239 Madison Ave Corp. v Neuburger (AD1 1924) 208 AD 87, 203 NYS 137.

7. Mitchel Manor No. 1 Corp. v Board of Assessors (1960, 2d Dept) 10 AD2d 854, 199 NYS2d 638; Koppel v Evelyn (M Ct 1955) 208 Misc 667, 145 NYS2d 213; Boman Realty Corp. v Trice (M Ct Man 1954) 205 Misc 588, 131 NYS2d 771.

8. Boman Realty Corp. v Trice (M Ct 1954) 205 Misc 588, 131 NYS2d 771.

Upon the death of a statutory tenant, the rights to possession of his subtenants who are not members of his family terminate. Yates v Kaplan (NYC Civ Ct NY Co 1973) 75 Misc 2d 259, 347 NYS2d 543 (citing text).

It has been held that the Emergency Business Rent Control Law [now repealed] does not protect the surviving spouse of a statutory tenant who first enters possession after the death of the tenant. Rofar Realty Co. v Amos (AT1 1958) 12 Misc 2d 75, 174 NYS2d 485.

As to right of landlord to evict paramour of deceased tenant, see § 38:21.

9. Goodhue House Co v Bernstein (AT1 1981) NYLJ December 7, 1981.

10. There must be evidence of permanence or continuity of occupancy by a relative of a tenant to find that the relative was "living" with the tenant, and would be protected from eviction under New York City Rent and Eviction Regulations. 829 Seventh Avenue Co. v Reider (1986) 67 NY2d 930, 502 NYS2d 715, 493 NE2d

### § 10:14. Terms and Conditions of Tenancy

The amount of rent to be paid by a statutory tenant, continuing in possession of leased premises after the expiration of his lease by virtue of emergency rent laws, is generally fixed by such laws at a "reasonable rental" or "a reasonable rent or price for their use and occupation." Therefore, regardless of what rent was reserved in the expired lease, such rent provisions must be deemed modified by the emergency rent statutes prevailing during the statutory tenancy.[11]

With the exceptions of the duration of the term,[12] and the amount of rent payable, the rule established by the weight of authority is that insofar as the provisions of a lease which has expired are not in conflict with the then prevailing emergency rent statutes, and are not confined to the period of the expired lease, they are projected into the statutory tenancy, and will continue in effect during the term of the statutory tenancy.[13] Thus, it has been held that covenants by a tenant not to drill holes in the walls or permit extensions beyond or upon the building,[14] or to permit projections to be attached to outside walls of the building,[15] are carried over and projected into the statu-

---

939 (granddaughter residing with grandmother-tenant was not "living" with grandmother where granddaughter had never put her name on the mailbox, had not advised landlord of her occupancy, left all her furniture in her own apartment, maintained her telephone number in her own apartment, and kept her bank accounts at a bank near her own apartment, all of which indicated temporary occupancy with grandmother).

**11.** Where lease between landlord's predecessor and tenant, which had provided for a rent less than the maximum emergency rent, expired before present landlord acquired title, present landlord is entitled to the maximum rent without being required to give tenant a 30-day notice. Gabor v Feldman (Civ Ct NYC 1965) 49 Misc 2d 44, 266 NYS2d 880.

**12.** § 10:12, supra.

**13.** Barrow Realty Corp. v Village Brewery Restaurant, Inc. (AD1 1947) 272 AD 262, 70 NYS2d 545, app gr 272 AD 873, 72 NYS2d 260; Cecere v Rosenthal (1949, Sup App T) 90 NYS2d 243; Cecere v Pegler (1949, Sup App T) 90 NYS2d 528; Shelton Bldg. Corp. v Baggett (AT2 1947) 188 Misc 709, 71 NYS2d 434; 130 West 57 Corp. v Hyman (AT1 1946) 188 Misc 92, 66 NYS2d 332; 18th Ave. Pharmacy, Inc. v Wilmant Realty Corp. (S Ct Kings Co 1950) 95 NYS2d 534; Leibowitz v 18 East 41st St. Corp. (S Ct NY Co 1949) 89 NYS2d 160, affd 276 AD 759, 93 NYS2d 307; Girard Holding Corp. v Hollander (S Ct Queens Co 1949) 195 Misc 878, 91 NYS2d 188; Van Walderveen v Martin (City Ct Albany 1949) 195 Misc 91, 91 NYS2d 234.

As to projection of right to assign and sublet into statutory tenancy, see § 9:77, supra; and as to projection of restriction against assignment and subletting, see § 9:87, supra.

**14.** 660 Locust St. Corp. v MacPherson (AD2 1952) 279 AD 927, 111 NYS2d 29.

**15.** Girard Holding Corp. v Hollan-

# EFFECT OF HOLDING OVER § 10:14

tory tenancy. Similarly, a lease provision permitting a landlord to place upon the demised premises a "to let" sign during a specified period prior to the expiration of the lease was held to be carried over into a statutory tenancy.[16] However, it has been held that a provision restricting a landlord from renting other property for competitive businesses,[17] and a fire termination clause in a lease,[18] are not carried over into a statutory tenancy. Provisions in an expired lease for a concession,[19] or for

der (S Ct Queens Co 1949) 195 Misc 878, 91 NYS2d 188.

**16.** M. Adler's Sons, Inc. v Front Line Sweaters, Inc. (S Ct NY Co 1949) 195 Misc 352, 90 NYS2d 255. However, since a statutory tenant's term is co-extensive with the duration of the emergency, as defined by the statute, it was further held, that unless the landlord could show that the period was not in excess of six months, the landlord would have no right to erect and maintain the sign; for, the right so to do would not have materialized. In 11 West 42nd Street, Inc. v Elzee Realty Corp. (AD1 1950) 277 AD 434, 100 NYS2d 529, app den 278 AD 555, 102 NYS2d 431, however, the landlord was held entitled to display a "to let" sign because of different circumstances. Unconsol Laws § 8558(k), as am in 1949 [now repealed], gave a landlord the right to recover possession of business space upon receiving a bona fide offer to rent the store for at least $7,500 a year for a ten year term, subject, however, to the statutory tenant's right of prior refusal to enter into such a lease on the same basis. Therefore, the court held, the contractual right to display a "to let" sign must be held to be enforceable to the extent necessary to further the statutory rights conferred upon the landlord by this statute. (For the final outcome of this case, see, 199 Misc 572, 104 NYS2d 522, where the court found that the landlord in seeking to display "to let" sign was acting in good faith to accomplish the rights conferred upon him by the statute, and therefore was entitled to an injunction restraining the tenant from interfering with this right.) To same effect, Powers v Chambers (S Ct NY Co 1950) 103 NYS2d 762.

**17.** Rappaport v Raylen Corp. (S Ct Bx Co 1953) 204 Misc 729, 124 NYS2d 331; Klein v Ernst (S Ct Bx Co 1951) 106 NYS2d 897; Gansvoort Apartments v Droutman (S Ct NY Co 1950) 198 Misc 872, 101 NYS2d 419; Jacobs v Equitable Life Assur. Soc. (S Ct Bx Co 1950) 106 NYS2d 951. In Nussbaum v Garstaff Realty Co. (S Ct Bx Co 1950) 197 Misc 527, 96 NYS2d 161, it was held that a statutory tenant is not entitled to restrain his landlord from violating provisions of the expired lease prohibiting landlord from leasing vacant stores "now forming part" of premises to competitive businesses.

In Ottavino v Auricchio (S Ct Queens Co 1951) 199 Misc 616, 104 NYS2d 27, a tenant, during the term of his leasehold, had secured an injunction against his landlord restraining him from violating a covenant not to lease property to a competitive business. Upon the expiration of the demised term, the tenant continued as a statutory tenant. Held, since covenant involved did not carry over into statutory tenancy, landlord was entitled to move to have the injunctive provisions of the judgment discharged of record on the ground of performance; that is, the landlord fully performed, since he had not rented to a competitive business during the term of the lease.

**18.** Bing Chung Chan v 60 Eldridge Corp. (NYC Civ Ct NY Co 1985) 129 Misc 2d 787, 494 NYS2d 284 (rent controlled or rent stabilized tenants' leases can be terminated only on grounds specified in the statute).

**19.** Harkap Realty Corp. v Poler (AT2 1950) 198 Misc 473, 102 NYS2d 41.

§ 10:14

the right to accelerate rent on the default of any monthly installment,[20] are not projected into a statutory tenancy.

A provision that if the tenant failed to comply with violations, landlord might do so, and the cost thereof would then be deemed additional rent, was held not to be projected into a statutory tenancy.[1]

### § 10:15. —Waiver of Jury Trial Clause

It has been held that a lease provision waiving a trial by jury of any or all issues arising in any action or proceeding between the landlord and tenant under or connected with the lease or any of its provisions, is not in conflict with emergency rent statutes, unless expressly so provided in such statutes. Therefore, such a provision will be generally carried over and projected into a statutory tenancy so as to apply during its continuance.[2] Accordingly, a waiver by the tenant of trial by jury will be applied to a summary proceeding brought to evict the tenant pursuant to the provisions of emergency rent laws, enacted after the date of the lease.[3] However, such a waiver will not apply to any action brought under the emergency rent laws, enacted after the date of the lease, to collect a penalty imposed on the landlord by such laws for demanding and receiving more than the emergency rent.[4] The reason for this difference in the application of the rule was explained by the Appellate Division[5] thus: "In that case (the summary proceeding), however, the proceeding was one directly relating to the occupancy of

---

**20.** 371 East 137th Street Corp. v Winstead (M Ct 1956) 3 Misc 2d 71, 156 NYS2d 68.

**1.** Brown v Denner (M Ct Man 1961) 30 Misc 2d 229, 218 NYS2d 834.

**2.** Maiden Lane Service Stations, Inc. v Rubin (AT1 1956) 5 Misc 2d 328, 159 NYS2d 268; Cecere v Pegler (1949, Sup App T) 90 NYS2d 528; Cecere v Rosenthal (1949, Sup App T) 90 NYS2d 243; Jamaica Investors, Inc. v Blacharsh (AT2 1949) 193 Misc 949, 87 NYS2d 807, app den 277 AD 951, 99 NYS2d 755; Friedman v Riley Hogan Co. (AT1 1947) 188 Misc 548, 70 NYS2d 625; 130 West 57 Corp. v Hyman (AT1 1946) 188 Misc 92, 66 NYS2d 332; Pierre v Williams (NYC Civ Ct Kings Co. 1980) 106 Misc 2d 81, 431 NYS2d 249; Teitler v Tetenbaum (AT1 1984) 123 Misc 2d 702, 477 NYS2d 544 (citing text).

**3.** Schultz v Wietchner (AD1 1947) 271 AD 971, 69 NYS2d 327 (referring to L 1945, chs 3 and 315, Unconsol L §§ 8521, et seq, now repealed). A memorandum opinion, but the facts of this case are discussed in Klipack v Raymar Novelties, Inc. (AD1 1947) 273 AD 54, 75 NYS2d 418, mod 273 AD 1005, 79 NYS2d 881.

**4.** Klipack v Raymar Novelties, Inc. (AD1 1947) 273 AD 54, 75 NYS2d 418 (referring to L 1945, chs 3 and 315, Unconsol L §§ 8521, et seq, now repealed), mod 273 AD 1005, 79 NYS2d 881.

**5.** Klipack v Raymar Novelties, Inc. (AD1 1947) 273 AD 54, 75 NYS2d 418, mod 273 AD 1005, 79 NYS2d 881.

# EFFECT OF HOLDING OVER § 10:17

the tenant and to the right of the landlord to recover possession after termination of the written lease. In the present case (action to recover penalty) the causes of action are those created entirely by statute. They in no way affect the conventional relationship of landlord and tenant. They exist not by virtue of such relationship but solely because of the statute itself. In that way they differ from the other terms and conditions of the written lease which exist by virtue of the contractual relationship and are carried over into the new statutory tenancy."

### § 10:16. —Security Clause

A lease provided that the tenant had deposited with the landlord the sum of $1,500, "as security for the full and faithful performance by the lessee of all the terms, . . . of this lease. . . . The lessor agrees to apply the security of $1,500 . . . toward the payment of the rent . . . for the last four months of the term hereof. . . ." During the term of the lease emergency rent laws came into effect, and the tenant notified the landlord that he intended to continue in possession after the expiration of the lease as a statutory tenant. The tenant thereupon contended that because of the phraseology of the security clause, he did not have to pay the last four months' rent of the term of his lease which was about to expire. The landlord contended, however, that if the tenant continued in possession, the security clause would be carried over into the statutory tenancy, and that therefore the security would then have to be applied to the last four months of the statutory tenancy. The court in passing on these contentions held that the landlord was right in his contention; for, the security clause was not in conflict with the emergency rent statutes, then in force, and therefore would be projected into and become a part of the statutory tenancy.[6]

### § 10:17. —Provision for Attorney's Fees

"We are of the opinion," said the Appellate Division,[7]

---

6. True-Value Slipper & Sandal Corp. v Quaker Mechanical Corp. (City Ct Bx Co 1947) 189 Misc 328, 71 NYS2d 221, referring to former L 1945 c 3 and c 315, Unconsol L §§ 8521 et seq.

*Contra:* See Edroan Realty Corp. v Barnett (M Ct 1950) 200 Misc 323, 109 NYS2d 511.

7. Barrow Realty Corp. v Village Brewery Restaurant, Inc. (AD1 1947)

"that the clause in a lease, providing that any expense, including reasonable attorney's fees, incurred by the landlord in any proceeding instituted by reason of the tenant's default 'hereunder' shall be deemed to be additional rent 'hereunder,' is carried over, as are other provisions of the lease, to the tenant's occupancy during the period in which he remains in possession under the emergency rent law after the expiration of the term of the lease." Therefore, it was held, the tenant during his statutory tenancy was obligated to pay the counsel fees incurred by the landlord in collecting unpaid rent.[8]

### § 10:18. —Option to Purchase

It is the general rule[9] that an option to purchase granted to the tenant by a provision in the lease does not survive the expiration of the lease. Where a tenant holds over by virtue of emergency rent laws, the option will neither survive the expiration of the lease, nor be carried over into the statutory tenancy.[10] The basic purpose of emergency rent laws is to curb the evils of exorbitant rents and widespread evictions. To effectuate that object, it has been held,[11] it is unnecessary to afford a tenant, holding over by virtue of statutory compulsion the right to enforce an option to purchase contained in a lease the term of which has expired.

### § 10:19. —Automatic Renewal Clause

An automatic renewal clause in a lease is inoperative during the period of a statutory tenancy. Therefore, the rental to be paid during the statutory tenancy is that fixed by the emergency rent laws, and not that stipulated in the automatic renewal clause.[12]

272 AD 262, 70 NYS2d 545, app gr 272 AD 873, 72 NYS2d 260.

**8.** Also, see Minet Realties, Inc. v Prigal (NYC Civ Ct NY Co 1974) 80 Misc 2d 137, 362 NYS2d 780; Feierstein v Moser (S Ct NY Co 1984) 124 Misc 2d 369, 477 NYS2d 545; Scotia Associates v Bond (NYC Civ Ct NY Co 1985) 126 Misc 2d 885, 484 NYS2d 479.

**9.** See § 20:20, infra.

**Annotation:** Holding over under lease, or renewal or extension thereof, as extending time for exercise of option to purchase contained therein. 15 ALR3d 470.

**10.** Rabinovitz v Williamson (1949) 275 AD 841, 88 NYS2d 370, reh and app den 275 AD 938, 89 NYS2d 926. Also, see, Wasservogel v Meyerowitz (1949) 300 NY 125, 131, 89 NE2d 712.

**11.** Rabinovitz v Williamson (AD2 1949) 275 AD 841, 88 NYS2d 370, reh and app den 275 AD 938, 89 NYS2d 926.

See, also, Wasservogel v Meyerowitz (1949) 300 NY 125, 131, 89 NE2d 712.

**12.** Park View Gardens, Inc. v

## § 10:20. Damages on Termination of Tenancy

While emergency rent laws permit tenants to continue in possession after the expiration of their leases, landlords of such leased premises are generally permitted to recover possession under certain specified conditions; as for example, where an owner requires the premises in good faith for his immediate and personal use. A statutory tenant who wrongfully resists a landlord's demand for possession under any of the grounds specified in the statute for recovery of possession will run the risk of being held liable for all the damages resulting from such withholding of possession. Such a statutory tenant will be held to be a trespasser from the moment a final judgment is entered awarding possession to the landlord, and thereby adjudging that the landlord's demand for possession was rightful. After the entry of such final judgment, the statutory tenant is no longer entitled to the protection of the emergency rent laws.[13] The statutory tenant thereupon becomes liable for the attorney fees incurred by the landlord in effecting his removal by the summary proceedings, if the lease so provides;[14] for the reasonable value of the use and occupation of the premises, as

---

Greene (AD2 1949) 274 AD 1062, 85 NYS2d 396; Doniday Estates, Inc. v Fox (1954, Sup App T) 134 NYS2d 633; Harkap Realty Corp. v Poler (AT2 1950) 198 Misc 473, 102 NYS2d 41.

13. Amorose v Price (1956, 1st Dept) 1 AD2d 815, 149 NYS2d 101, affg (Sup App T) 142 NYS2d 922, and app den (1st Dept) 1 AD2d 950, 151 NYS2d 602; 105 Franklin Street Corp v Seratoff (AD1 1954) 284 AD 262, 131 NYS2d 257, affd 308 NY 1025, 127 NE2d 865; Smith v Feigin (AD1 1950) 276 AD 531, 96 NYS2d 123; Self Service Super Market, Inc. v Harris (S Ct Bx Co 1954) 139 NYS2d 52.

*Contra:* See Colonna & Co. v Anthony M. Meyerstein, Inc. (S Ct Queens 1950) 198 Misc 556, 96 NYS2d 316, affd 278 AD 588, 102 NYS2d 920, where it was held that if the court granting the final order stays execution of the warrant, the tenant's possession is "legal", and cannot constitute a trespass until the stay expires; Roseben Knitting Mills, Inc. v Great Atlantic & Pacific Tea Co. (S Ct Queens Co 1950) 104 NYS2d 311, where it was held that until the issuance of the warrant, and pending the running of the stay, the landlord could proceed under the former Emergency Business Rent Control Act to have the rent of the premises fixed.

14. 207-17 West 25th Street Co. v Blu-Strike Safety Razor Blade Co. (1951) 302 NY 624, 97 NE2d 356. Attorney's fees usually are allowed for proceedings based "on any default of the tenant hereunder". In this case attorney's fees under such a clause were allowed because the court found that the tenant in withholding possession acted wrongfully, and this constituted a "default." However, in 105 Franklin Street Corp. v Seratoff (AD1 1954) 284 AD 262, 131 NYS2d 257, affd 308 NY 1025, 127 NE2d 865, attorney's fees were disallowed because the tenant was not in "default" when he resisted in court and in good faith a proceeding by a landlord seeking possession of premises for his own immediate use, even though the court may have ultimately upheld the landlord.

§ 10:20

general damages;[15] and for such special damages as the landlord can prove flowed directly and naturally from the trespass.[16] This liability is measured from the date of the entry of the final judgment until his removal from the premises, even if such removal is delayed by a stay of the execution of the warrant granted either by the court granting the final judgment, or by an appellate court pending an appeal from the judgment.[17]

General damages are measured by the excess of the fair rental value of the premises over the rent actually paid.[18] If the emergency rent paid represents such fair rental value, then the landlord will be entitled only to nominal damages.[19]

---

**15.** Amorose v Price (1956, 1st Dept) 1 AD2d 815, 149 NYS2d 101, app den (1st Dept) 1 AD2d 950, 151 NYS2d 602; 105 Franklin Street Corp. v Seratoff (AD1 1954) 284 AD 262, 131 NYS2d 257, affd 308 NY 1025, 127 NE2d 865; Smith v Feigin (AD1 1950) 276 AD 531, 96 NYS2d 123; Self Service Super Market, Inc. v Harris (S Ct Bx Co 1954) 139 NYS2d 52.

**16.** Amorose v Price (1956, 1st Dept) 1 AD2d 815, 149 NYS2d 101, affg (Sup App T) 142 NYS2d 922, and app den (1st Dept) 1 AD2d 950, 151 NYS2d 602; Smith v Feigin (AD1 1950) 276 AD 531, 96 NYS2d 123 (charges for storage of landlord's equipment from date of final order until he could get possession, allowed).

**17.** Amorose v Price (1956, 1st Dept) 1 AD2d 815, 149 NYS2d 101, app den (1st Dept) 1 AD2d 950, 151 NYS2d 602; 105 Franklin Street Corp. v Seratoff (AD1 1954) 284 AD 262, 131 NYS2d 257, affd 308 NY 1025, 127 NE2d 865; Smith v Feigin (AD1 1948) 273 AD 277, 77 NYS2d 229, affd 298 NY 534, 80 NE2d 668; Self Service Super Market, Inc. v Harris (S Ct Bx Co 1954) 139 NYS2d 52.

*Contra:* See, Colonna & Co Inc v Anthony M Meyerstein Inc (S Ct Queens Co 1950) 198 Misc 556, 96 NYS2d 316, affd 278 AD 588, 102 NYS2d 920.

**18.** Smith v Feigin (AD1 1950) 276 AD 531, 96 NYS2d 123; Self Service Super Market, Inc. v Harris (S Ct Bx Co 1954) 139 NYS2d 52. However, due regard must be given to the contemporaneous existence of emergency rent regulations, and their effect on the fair value of rent in the market. 207-17 West 25th St. Co. v Blu-Strike Safety Razor Blade Co. (AD1 1950) 277 AD 93, 98 NYS2d 62, revd on other grounds 302 NY 624, 97 NE2d 356.

**19.** 207-17 West 25th St. Co. v Blu-Strike Safety Razor Blade Co. (AD1 1950) 277 AD 93, 98 NYS2d 62, revd on other grounds 302 NY 624, 97 NE2d 356. So, when this case came back to Special Term for the assessment of damages on the difference between the emergency rent and the fair rent, the court held that since the landlord would not have been able to increase the rent under the applicable emergency rent laws, and which had been paid by the tenant, no damages existed and landlord was entitled to recover nominal damages only. 207-17 West 25th St. Co. v Blu-Strike Safety Razor Blade Co. (S Ct NY Co 1951) 200 Misc 243, 107 NYS2d 202, affd 279 AD 1071, 113 NYS2d 286, affd 305 NY 683, 112 NE2d 769.

Also, see, 105 Franklin Street Corp. v Seratoff (AD1 1954) 284 AD 262, 131 NYS2d 257, affd 308 NY 1025, 127 NE2d 865.

## C. RESEARCH REFERENCES

### 10:21. Generally

In addition to the preceding text, the reader is also referred to the following:

49 Am Jur 2d, Landlord and Tenant §§ 1115-1153.

16 Am Jur Pleading and Practice Forms (Rev ed), Landlord and Tenant, Forms 31-33.

New York Jur 2d, Landlord and Tenant (1st ed §§ 404-413).

New York CLS Real Property Law § 232-c.

Index to Annotations, Landlord and Tenant.

**VERALEX®:** Cases and annotations referred to herein can be further researched through the VERALEX electronic retrieval system's two services, **Auto-Cite®** and **SHOWME®**. Use Auto-Cite to check citations for form, parallel references, prior and later history, and annotation references. Use SHOWME to display the full text of cases and annotations.

# CHAPTER 11

# RENEWAL OF LEASES

A. RIGHT TO RENEWAL ABSENT COVENANT
 § 11:1. Generally
 § 11:2. Protection of Tenant's Expectancy of Renewal
 § 11:3. —Effect of Landlord's Refusal to Renew
 § 11:4. —Against Persons in Positions of Trust and Confidence
 § 11:5. —As Between Cotenants
 § 11:6. —As Between Tenant and His/Her Assignee
 § 11:7. —As Between Tenant and His/Her Subtenant
 § 11:8. Mobile Home Park Tenancy

B. COVENANT TO RENEW
 § 11:9. Phraseology of Covenant
 § 11:10. —Illustrations
 § 11:11. Necessity of Certainty
 § 11:12. Terms Implied in Renewal Covenant
 § 11:13. Form of Covenant to Renew at Lessee's Election
 § 11:14. Provision for Determination of Renewal Rental
 § 11:15. —Form of Provision
 § 11:16. Rights of Parties Pending Appraisal to Determine Renewal Terms
 § 11:17. Illustrations of Indefinite Renewal Covenants

C. WHO CAN ENFORCE COVENANT TO RENEW
 § 11:18. Right of Renewal at Tenant's Sole Option
 § 11:19. —Landlord's Covenant to Pay for Improvements or Renew
 § 11:20. —Landlord's Covenant to Sell Property or Renew
 § 11:21. —Summary of Rule
 § 11:22. Renewal at Landlord's Sole Option
 § 11:23. "First Privilege of Renewal" Clauses
 § 11:24. Assignee or Sublessee
 § 11:25. —Where Assignor Reserves Right of Renewal
 § 11:26. —Where Assignment is in Violation of Lease Restriction
 § 11:27. Personal Representative of Deceased Tenant
 § 11:28. —Liability of Personal Representative upon Renewal
 § 11:29. Joint Tenants
 § 11:30. Surviving Partner
 § 11:31. Partner Remaining After Dissolution

## D. AGAINST WHOM COVENANT TO RENEW ENFORCEABLE

§ 11:32. Landlord's Grantee
§ 11:33. Trustee or Personal Representative

## E. EXERCISING RIGHT TO RENEW

§ 11:34. Necessity of Strict Performance of Conditions Precedent
§ 11:35. Necessity of Timely Notice to Renew
§ 11:36. When Performance of Other Provisions of Lease Necessary
§ 11:37. Rent Payment as Condition Precedent
§ 11:38. Provision for Renewal "at Expense of Tenant"
§ 11:39. Equitable Relief from Failure to Give Timely Notice of Election to Renew
§ 11:40. Waiver of Performance of Conditions to Renewal
§ 11:41. Effect of Non-waiver of Conditions to Renewal
§ 11:42. Exercising Right of Renewal Where No Notice Required

## F. RENEWAL LEASE

§ 11:43. Necessity for New Lease
§ 11:44. Terms of Renewal Lease Absent Provision Therefor
§ 11:45. Modification of Lease as Projected into Renewal Term
§ 11:46. Modification of Rent as Projected into Renewal Term
§ 11:47. Right to Perpetual Renewals
§ 11:48. Form of Provision for Perpetual Renewals
§ 11:49. Effect of Emergency Rent Laws
§ 11:50. Nature and Effect of Renewed Lease
§ 11:51. —Illustrative Cases
§ 11:52. Tenant-Assignor's Liability Under Renewal Lease

## G. AUTOMATIC RENEWALS

§ 11:53. Form of Automatic Renewal Clause
§ 11:54. Statutory Protection of Tenants Against Automatic Renewal Clauses
§ 11:55. —Effect of Non-compliance with Statute
§ 11:56. —Waiver of Statutory Protection

## H. REMEDIES FOR BREACH OF COVENANT TO RENEW

§ 11:57. Damages Recoverable
§ 11:58. —Measure of Damages
§ 11:59. Specific Performance
§ 11:60. Action for Declaratory Judgment

## I. RESEARCH REFERENCES

§ 11:61. Generally

## A. RIGHT TO RENEWAL ABSENT COVENANT

### § 11:1. Generally

In the absence of a covenant in the lease, or some agreement therefor, there is no way, said the Court of Appeals[1] "legal or equitable, of compelling a renewal." Therefore, when the term of a lease has expired, the Appellate Division pointed out,[2] "the landlord, in the absence of a contract to renew, is at liberty to refuse to do so, and any one with whom he sees fit to deal can become his tenant . . . ."

Accordingly, if a tenant desires an enforceable right to a renewal of his lease, he must have some agreement from his landlord therefor. Such an agreement is customarily inserted in the lease, and is called a renewal covenant.

However, under the New York City Rent Stabilization Law, a one or 2-year renewal lease must be offered to a rent-stabilized tenant.[3]

In East Four-Forty Associates v Ewell (AT1) NY Law Journal, February 2, 1988, p. 11, col 1, it was held that RSC § 2523(b)(2) is invalid and that only the tenant named in the lease is entitled to a renewal.

A landlord may refuse to renew a rent-stabilized tenant's lease because the leased apartment is not being occupied as the tenant's primary residence.[4] A tenant who has moved into a nursing home is no longer occupy-

---

1. Robinson v Jewett (1889) 116 NY 40, 51, 22 NE 224.
2. McDonald v Fiss (AD1 1900) 54 AD 489, 67 NYS 34.
3. New York City Administrative Code § 26-511c(9).
In 1985, the Court of Appeals in Sullivan v Brevard Associates (1985) 66 NY2d 489, 498 NYS2d 96, 488 NE2d 1208, held that under the Rent Stablilization Law a landlord was obligated to offer a renewal lease only to the tenant named in the lease and was not obligated to offer a renewal lease to a member of the named tenant's family who occupied the apartment during a portion of the lease term. However, effective May 1, 1987, the Rent Stabilization Code was adopted which in § 2523.5(b)(2) affords qualified members of the named tenant's family the right to a renewal lease after the death of the tenant. Also, see Soling v Little (NYC Civ Ct NY Co 1987) 135 AD2d 871, 517 NYS2d 686. Rent Stabilization Code § 2520.6(O) defenses "family member".

Gay life partner of named rent-stabilized tenant was not entitled to renewal lease after the death of the named tenant. Two Associates v Brown (1987, 1st Dept) 127 AD2d 173, 513 NYS2d 966.

4. Rent Stabilization Code for Rent Stabilized Apartments in New York City, § 2524.4(c). See § 30.63, infra.

ing the apartment as his primary residence.[5] A tenant who is serving an indeterminate term of 15 years to life is not occupying the apartment as his primary residence.[6] A landlord who refuses to renew a rent-stabilized tenant's lease because the apartment is not the primary residence of the tenant must give notice of such refusal to the tenant during the 120-150 day period before the lease expires in order to raise that issue.[7]

### § 11:2. Protection of Tenant's Expectancy of Renewal

Although as between landlord and tenant the tenant has, independently of contract, no legal or equitable right to a renewal, since it depends upon the mere volition of the landlord,[8] yet, it is well established by decisional law that a court of equity recognizes a tenant's expectancy of renewal as a valuable interest which it will protect as against third persons who defeat such expectancy wrongfully.[9] As the Court of Appeals said,[10] "Those who are in possession of lands under a lease have an interest therein beyond the subsisting term, usually called the tenant's right of renewal. Between the landlord and tenant this interest cannot strictly be denominated a right or estate, but is merely a hope or expectation, there being in the absence of contract, no way, legal or equitable, of compelling a renewal. But, as between third persons, the law recognizes this interest as a valuable property right, and the renewal as a reasonable expectancy of the tenants in possession."[11]

As a general rule, when a person occupies any relationship of trust or confidence to a tenant, and by virtue of such relationship is enabled to get a new lease from the landlord "behind the back" of the tenant, equity will step in and protect the tenant's expectancy of renewal. Such

---

5. Herzog v Joy (1980, 1st Dept) 74 AD2d 372, 428 NYS2d 1, affd 53 NY2d 821, 439 NYS2d 922, 422 NE2d 582.

6. Emay Properties Corp. v Norton (ATI 1987) 136 Misc 2d 127, 519 NYS2d 90.

7. 525 Park Ave. Associates v De Hoyas (1986, 1st Dept) 121 AD2d 908, 504 NYS2d 426, reh den, in part, app gr, in part (1st Dept) 123 AD2d 272, 506 NYS2d 283 and affd 69 NY2d 692, 512 NYS2d 21, 504 NE2d 388.

8. § 11:1, supra.

9. Robinson v Jewett (1889) 116 NY 40, 22 NE 224; Mitchell v Reed (1874) 61 NY 123, 130.

10. Robinson v Jewett (1889) 116 NY 40, 51, 22 NE 224.

11. Also, see Thayer v Leggett (1920) 229 NY 152, 156, 128 NE 133.

person who thus obtains a new lease by taking inequitable advantage of his position or duty will be deemed to have obtained the new lease wrongfully, and in fraud of the tenant.

Equity, as a general rule, will decree that such wrongdoer holds the new lease in trust for the wronged tenant;[12] or, instead, may treat the new lease as a renewal of, or a graft upon, the old lease for the benefit and use of the wronged tenant.[13] This principle, said the Court of Appeals in a leading case on the subject,[14] "springs from the fact that the party obtained the new lease from the position he occupied, being in possession and having the good-will which accompanies that, or being connected with the old lease in some way, and thus enabled to take an inequitable advantage of other parties also interested, to whom he owed some duty."

Of course, if the third person who obtains a lease of the premises at the expiration of the one which is about to expire, has no relation whatever with the tenant then in possession, then clearly such an act is no infringement of any right of the tenant, and no violation of good faith. "It is a thing," said the Appellate Division, "which every person has a right to do if he sees fit. The term having expired, the landlord, in the absence of a contract to renew, is at liberty to refuse to do so, and any one with whom he sees fit to deal can become his tenant, and whoever takes a lease under those circumstances is entitled to the term for his own benefit."[15]

### § 11:3. —Effect of Landlord's Refusal to Renew

Equity, it has been held, will not withhold its protection of a tenant's expectancy of renewal against a wrongdoer merely because the landlord refused, or indicated that he would be unwilling, to renew the lease to the tenant. When the rule is applicable, said the Court of

---

12. Thayer v Leggett (1920) 229 NY 152, 128 NE 133; Mitchell v Reed (1874) 61 NY 123.

13. Thayer v Leggett (1920) 229 NY 152, 128 NE 133. But, see, Meinhard v Salmon (1928) 249 NY 458, 164 NE 545, 62 ALR 1, where a wrongdoer took the new lease in the name of a corporation, and the court decreed that the wrongdoer would have the option of either having the trust attach to the lease, or to a portion of the shares of stock of the corporation.

14. Mitchell v Reed (1874) 61 NY 123, 130.

15. McDonald v Fiss (AD1 1900) 54 AD 489, 67 NYS 34.

Appeals,[16] "it matters not that the new lease is upon different terms from the old one, or for a larger rent, or that the lessor would not have leased" to the old tenant.[17]

### § 11:4. —Against Persons in Positions of Trust and Confidence

He who holds a lease in trust for another, said Andrews, J.,[18] may not deprive the latter of his expectancy of renewal "by taking a renewal or a new lease in his own name (Keech v Sandford, Select Cas. in Ch. 61); nor may an executor or administrator holding the lease as a part of the estate of a deceased (Matter of Morgan, 18 Ch. Div. 93); nor may a guardian as against his ward (Milner v Harewood, 18 Ves 274). A like rule is applied in many situations where because of his position or because of the trust and confidence reposed in him one owes a duty to another. In such cases equity exacts fair dealing and a scrupulous regard for honesty. An officer or director of a corporation in possession of a lease may not secretly for his own benefit take a renewal of it or a new lease to himself (Robinson v Jewett, supra);[19] nor may a partner as against his firm (Mitchell v Reed, 61 NY 123); nor an agent as against his principal (Davis v Hamlin, 108 Ill 39) . . . . In short, as has been said, no one who is in possession of a lease or a particular interest in a lease which is affected with any sort of equity for third persons can renew the same for his own use only, but such renewal must be considered a graft upon the old stock."[20]

In other words courts of equity will protect a tenant in the enjoyment of his mere chance or expectancy of renewal by the landlord, against the clandestine acts of those standing, as to the tenant, in a position of trust and confidence.

---

16. Mitchell v Reed (1874) 61 NY 123, 129.

17. Steinberg v Steinberg (S Ct Bx Co 1924) 123 Misc 764, 206 NYS 134; Bennett v Vansyckel (GT 1855) 11 NY Super Ct 462.

18. Thayer v Leggett (1920) 229 NY 152, 156, 128 NE 133.

19. (1889) 116 NY 40, 22 NE 224.

20. Also, see Meinhard v Salmon (1928) 249 NY 458, 164 NE 545, 62 ALR 1, involving joint adventurers; Struthers v Pearce (1873) 51 NY 357, involving partners; James Everard's Breweries v Wohlstadter (AD1 1917) 177 AD 862, 164 NYS 899, involving a mortgagee of the lease; Steinberg v Steinberg (S Ct Bx Co 1924) 123 Misc 764, 206 NYS 134, involving tenant's brother and sister whom he employed as sales clerks who obtained a lease during tenant's absence from the city.

## § 11:5. —As Between Cotenants

Courts of equity, said Bischoff, J.,[21] "have ever regarded the rights of joint tenants and tenants in common respecting their common estate to be reciprocal, neither being permitted during the continuance of the cotenancy furtively to acquire and hold any advantage which would not also inure to the other's benefit, provided the latter manifests a willingness to assume his just proportion of any burdens attending its acquisition and maintenance."

Therefore, equity will protect the expectancy of renewal in the case of cotenants by preventing one from acquiring furtively a new lease in his own name to premises which he had held in common with another, to the detriment of his cotenant.[1]

## § 11:6. —As Between Tenant and His/Her Assignee

Unless a tenant-assignor is bound by some agreement, or unless some special equity exists between him/her and his/her assignee, no relation of trust and confidence arises between him/her and his/her assignee. And, if no such relation of trust and confidence is created, then they deal at arm's length, and there is no reason why either may not acquire a renewal for himself. "Nor is it material," said Andrews, J.,[2] "whether this renewal was obtained before or after the assignment."

## § 11:7. —As Between Tenant and His/Her Subtenant

It has been held that no relationship of trust and confidence exists between a tenant and his/her subtenant. Therefore, either one may obtain a new lease in his/her own name from the paramount landlord without any legal or equitable obligation resulting to the other.[3]

## § 11:8. Mobile Home Park Tenancy

Real Property Law § 233(e) provides that a mobile home park owner or operator is required to offer the mobile home tenant the opportunity to sign a lease for a

---

**21.** Hackett v Patterson (Com Pl NY GT 1891) 16 NYS 170.

**1.** Thayer v Leggett (1920) 229 NY 152, 128 NE 133; Hackett v Patterson (1891, CP Ct NY GT) 16 NYS 170.

**2.** Thayer v Leggett (1920) 229 NY 152, 158, 128 NE 133.

**3.** Thayer v Leggett (1920) 229 NY 152, 158, 128 NE 133; Barclay v Muller (S Ct NY Co 1959) 16 Misc 2d 964, 189 NYS2d 942; Silvers v Coyne (S Ct NY Co 1946) 64 NYS2d 94.

minimum of one year. The protection for tenants provided under this statutory provision is limited to the prevention of arbitrary expulsions during the first year of park occupancy only.[4] But, this statutory provision does not require the owner or operator to offer a renewal lease. If the mobile home tenant continues in possession after the expiration of his lease, a month-to-month tenancy is created if the landlord accepts the holdover tenant's rent.[5] However, the tenant must be given at least 90 days' notice of any rent increase, and at least 90 days to remove if the tenant objects to the increase.[6]

## B. COVENANT TO RENEW

### § 11:9. Phraseology of Covenant

No particular form of words is necessary to constitute a covenant for the renewal of a lease. It is primarily a question of construction to gather the intent of the parties. As the Court of Appeals said,[7] "The word 'renewal' or the words 'to renew' have not a definite and fixed legal significance to which the parties are bound by the use of them. A lease like any other contract is to be enforced in accordance with the expressed intention of the contracting parties."

The principle of construction in this connection was summarized by the Appellate Term[8] as follows: "That construction should be given to the instrument which gives life and vitality as far as possible to each and every provision thereof; and the legal presumption goes further in holding that no provision is uselessly inserted in a contract, and that so far as renewal provisions in leases are concerned, whether they provide for 'privileges,' 'options,' 'refusals,' or 'notices' of intention or desire to renew, the giving of notice that the tenant desires to

---

4. A.K.A.B.&E. Mobile Home Rentals, Inc. v Marshall (Poughkeepsie Town Ct 1982) 114 Misc 2d 622, 452 NYS2d 144.

5. Comorford v Jones (Tompkins Co Ct 1983) 121 Misc 2d 141, 467 NYS2d 329. Real Prop L § 232-c.

6. Real Prop L § 233(f)(3)(c). Comorford v Jones (Tompkins Co Ct 1983) 121 Misc 2d 141, 467 NYS2d 329.

7. Orr v Doubleday, Page & Co. (1918) 223 NY 334, 119 NE 552, 1 ALR 338, reh den 223 NY 700, 119 NE 1064.

8. Burgener v O'Halloran (AT2 1920) 111 Misc 203, 181 NYS 235.

# RENEWAL OF LEASES § 11:11

avail himself of the privilege obligates the landlord, and the lease becomes thereby extended."[9]

Covenants for renewal, it has been held, are to be construed most favorably to the lessee.[10]

All problems relating to construction of agreements are difficult, but if the intent to grant a renewal of the privilege of a renewal is clear, although more apt language might have been used, such intent will generally prevail.

### § 11:10. —Illustrations

Leases which provide that the tenant shall have "a privilege of one year or more"; or "the privilege of a renewal";[11] or "the privilege of continuing in possession for the further period of five years";[12] or "the refusal of the premises at the expiration of the lease, for three years longer";[13] or that the tenant "reserves the right of renewing the lease";[14] have all been construed as containing a covenant to renew. If they were not so construed, the courts indicated, these clauses would be meaningless. Furthermore, it was clear that these clauses were inserted in the leases with the intent of giving the tenants the privilege of a renewal.

### § 11:11. Necessity of Certainty

To be valid and enforceable, a covenant for renewal must either be reasonably definite and certain as to the term and the rent,[15] or must contain a definite method whereby such term and rent may be determined.

Thus, it has been held that an agreement to renew at a

---

**9.** Also, see, Sisson Realty Corp. v Mathews (S Ct Lawrence Co 1928) 131 Misc 714, 227 NYS 721, revd on other grounds, but approved as to this point, 225 AD 716, 231 NYS 338, affd 250 NY 626, 166 NE 349.

**10.** Joseph Martin, Jr., Delicatessen, Inc. v Schumacher (1979, 2d Dept) 70 AD2d 1, 419 NYS2d 558 (citing text), revd on other grounds 52 NY2d 105, 436 NYS2d 247, 417 NE2d 541.

**11.** Orr v Doubleday, Page & Co. (1918) 223 NY 334, 119 NE 552, 1 ALR 338, reh den 223 NY 700, 119 NE 1064; Kolasky v Michels (1890) 120 NY 635, 24 NE 278; Chretien v Doney (1848) 1 NY 419.

**12.** Western N Y & P R Co v Riecke (AD4 1903) 83 AD 576, 81 NYS 1093.

**13.** Tracy v Albany Exchange Co (1852) 7 NY 472.

**14.** Sisson Realty Corp. v Mathews (S Ct Lawrence Co 1928) 131 Misc 714, 227 NYS 721, revd on other grounds, but approved as to this point, 225 AD 716, 231 NYS 338, affd 250 NY 626, 166 NE 349.

**15.** Letter from tenant to landlord casually referring to a renewal, and making no mention of the amount of rent to be paid, nor the date on which the term is to commence, is void for indefiniteness, and unenforceable as a lease renewal. Rhee v Dahan (AT1 1982) 116 Misc 2d 548, 457 NYS2d 684.

rate to be mutually agreed upon by both landlord and tenant "to be fair and reasonable to both parties involved," is certain and enforceable, for it indicates that the parties intended to bind themselves to an objectively ascertainable fair and reasonable rent fixed either by a court, arbitrator, or other third party.[16] Similarly, where the tenant is given the option of renewing a lease for specified periods upon the same terms and conditions except for the amount of rent, and the renewal clause fixes future rents at a "reasonable market value price," the renewal clause is not unenforceable for indefiniteness.[17] However, if it appears that the parties have expressly left the term and the rent for the renewal period to be agreed upon at some future time, the covenant will be held void for uncertainty and unenforceable.[18]

### § 11:12. Terms Implied in Renewal Covenant

"A bare covenant to renew," said the Appellate Division,[19] "means on the same terms of the original lease."

---

**16.** Merman v The Surrey (S Ct NY Co 1981) 106 Misc 2d 941, 436 NYS2d 690.

**17.** Northrup v Hushard (1987, 4th Dept) 129 AD2d 1005, 514 NYS2d 304.

**18.** Joseph Martin, Jr., Delicatessen, Inc. v Schumacher (1981) 52 NY2d 105, 436 NYS2d 247, 417 NE2d 541; Western Transp. Co. v Lansing (1872) 49 NY 499, 504; Tracy v Albany Exchange Co. (1852) 7 NY 472; Sautkulis v Conklin (S Ct Nassau Co 1955) 208 Misc 903, 145 NYS2d 62, affd (2d Dept) 1 AD2d 962, 150 NYS2d 356, affd 2 NY2d 919, 161 NYS2d 885, 141 NE2d 916; Huber v Ruby (S Ct Nassau Co 1947) 188 Misc 1001, 69 NYS2d 760, affd 272 AD 779, 70 NYS2d 579.

In Moran v Wellington (S Ct Steuben Co 1917) 101 Misc 594, 167 NYS 465, the renewal clause read: "with the privilege to the said lessee to renew this lease for the term of five years upon the expiration of this contract upon terms then to be mutually agreed upon." Such clause was held void and unenforceable, because it failed to make any provision for a fixing of its terms if the parties disagreed.

In 58-59 Realty Corp. v Park Cent. Valet (AD1 1937) 252 AD 72, 297 NYS 40, the renewal clause provided: "this lease is made upon the condition that if it is in effect upon the expiration of the term hereby demised, then and thereupon this lease shall be deemed to be and the same is hereby renewed and extended without further act or deed of the parties for an additional term of . . . years from the expiration date of this lease, upon the same covenants, conditions and agreements as herein contained, excepting that the rent for each year of such additional term shall be at the same rate per year as the rate provided herein for the last year of the term hereby demised, without any concession, and there shall be no obligation on the landlord to repair or redecorate the demised premises". This renewal clause was held too incomplete, indefinite and uncertain to be enforceable. There was no definiteness as to term. The clause called for a renewal for ". . . years." Literally, said the court, there could be no renewal for the same term. If the renewal clause is read as written it calls for a renewal for a period of "years", which would eliminate the seven months of the original term of three years and seven months.

**19.** Hoff v Royal Metal Furniture

# RENEWAL OF LEASES § 11:13

Where a tenant is given a right to renew the lease in general terms, and nothing is said about the term of the renewal period, or about the rent to be paid, such a covenant is not indefinite and uncertain. The terms and conditions of the original lease are definite, and those terms and conditions will govern the renewal term by implication.

Therefore, a general covenant in a lease to renew it, without any provision as to the term to be granted, or the amount of the rent to be paid, is valid and enforceable.[20]

## § 11:13. Form of Covenant to Renew at Lessee's Election

### FORM NO. 15

#### Covenant to Renew at Lessee's Election

If at the expiration of the term of this lease, this lease shall be in full force and effect, and Tenant shall have fully kept, performed and observed all of the terms, provisions, covenants and conditions of this lease on Tenant's part to be kept, observed and performed, Landlord at the option of the Tenant shall grant to Tenant a renewal of this lease for a further period of . . . . years from the expiration of the term of this lease, upon the same terms, covenants, and conditions of this lease, provided Tenant shall have notified Landlord by certified mail at Landlord's address hereinabove set forth on or before . . . . . . . ., 19. . ., of Tenant's election to renew[1] *(add if desired:* provided, however, that this renewal option shall be inoperative in the event Landlord shall sell the

---

Co. (AD2 1907) 117 AD 884, 103 NYS 371, affd 189 NY 555, 82 NE 1128, later app 127 AD 440, 111 NYS 541, affd 194 NY 545, 87 NE 1129.

Also, see Tracy v Albany Exchange Co (1852) 7 NY 472.

**20.** 58-59 Realty Corp. v Park Cent. Valet (AD1 1937) 252 AD 72, 297 NYS 40; Western N. Y. & P. R. Co. v Riecke (AD4 1903) 83 AD 576, 81 NYS 1093.

**1.** The general view is that a conveyance by the lessor does not relieve him from liability on his covenant to renew, and, therefore, after a conveyance, although executed before the time has arrived for a renewal, an action for damages may be maintained against him by the lessee for breach of the covenant. 50 Am Jur 2d, Landlord and Tenant, § 1175. Therefore, where the right to a renewal is made conditional upon the fact that the lessor does not sell the leased premises, a bona fide sale will defeat the right of the lessee to renew. Newberger v Matchak (1906, Sup App T) 99 NYS 470.

For covenant to renew with provision for determination of rental for renewal period, see FORM No. 16, § 11:15, infra.

§ 11:13　　　　　　　　　　　LANDLORD AND TENANT

building in which the leased premises are situated, at or prior to the expiration of this lease).[2]

### § 11:14. Provision for Determination of Renewal Rental

There is a type of renewal covenant which provides that the tenant shall have the privilege of a renewal of the lease, at such rental as may be agreed upon, and in the event that the parties cannot agree, such rental shall be determined by a definite method set forth in the covenant. If the method whereby the terms for the renewal period are to be determined is definite and certain, then such a renewal covenant has been held to be sufficiently definite and certain to be enforceable as a covenant to renew.[3]

### § 11:15. —Form of Provision

### FORM NO. 16

### Covenant to Renew or to Pay for Building on Premises with Provision for Determination of Terms by Appraisal*

If Tenant shall have fully performed on Tenant's part

---

2. For complete form of lease see Chapter 1.

3. Moran v Wellington (S Ct Steuben Co 1917) 101 Misc 594, 167 NYS 465.
A lease provided for a rental of $400 per month, and granted an option to tenant to renew for an additional five-year term "at an annual rental to be determined by the landlord." When tenant exercised his option, landlord informed him that the rental for the renewal term would be $2,000 per month. Tenant refused to pay this, and when his lease expired continued in possession, whereupon landlord brought a holdover proceeding. Tenant interposed the equitable defense that the parties mistakenly had omitted a provision limiting the renewal rent to a sum not in excess of 15% of the original rent. The trial court found that this defense had not been sustained, and granted landlord judgment. The Appellate Term reversed, although concurring with the finding that the defense had not been sustained, and held that the rental fixed appeared arbitrary and unconscionable, and that the case should be remanded for a new trial, to be treated as a nonpayment proceeding, to determine whether or not the rent was in fact arbitrary and unconscionable, and if so, to fix a rent "not unconscionable in the circumstances, upon proof of all relevant factors and not necessarily confined to what may be deemed a reasonable rent." This determination was affirmed by the Appellate Division. Tai on Luck Corp. v Cirota (1970, 1st Dept) 35 AD2d 380, 316 NYS2d 438, app dismd 29 NY2d 747, 326 NYS2d 400, 276 NE2d 234, motion den 29 NY2d 868, 328 NYS2d 173, 278 NE2d 343, where the court said, "Rigid formalism should not present courts from refusing to enforce arbitrary and unconscionable acts."

**Annotation:** Validity and Enforceability of Provision for Renewal of Lease at Rental to Be Fixed by Subsequent Agreement of Parties. 58 ALR3d 500.

* For complete form of lease see Chapter 1.

all of the terms, covenants and conditions of this lease, at the expiration of the term of this lease Landlord either will pay to Tenant the value at that time of the building erected on the leased premises, which shall be ascertained in the manner hereinafter provided, or will grant to Tenant *(add if desired:* at Tenant's expense) a renewal of this lease for a further term of twenty-one years at an annual rent which shall be ascertained as hereinafter provided, and otherwise containing the same terms, covenants and conditions of this lease. The said value of the said building, or the said annual rent shall be such amounts as shall be agreed upon by Landlord and Tenant, but in no event shall the annual rent be less than the rent provided in this lease to be paid as the rent for the period ending ........, regardless of any modifications thereof that may be granted.[4] If said rent or said value cannot be agreed upon or or before ........, then each party shall select one appraiser; such selection shall be made and signified by each party to the other at least three months before the expiration of the term; if the persons so selected or appointed shall differ in judgment as to any determination to be made by them as herein provided, they shall choose a third person; and the decision in writing of any two of such three appraisers under oath shall be final and conclusive. In the case of renewal, said appraisers shall determine the value of the leased premises at its full and fair worth or price at private sale, considering the same as an unencumbered vacant lot of land, and five per cent of the amount of said valuation shall be the annual rent of the leased premises for the renewal term. *(Add if desired:* If Landlord shall elect to pay the value of the building, determined as hereinabove provided, Tenant shall not be compelled to surrender the premises until such payment shall be made or tendered.)

The concluding clause of this form in regard to payment to the tenant of the value of the building before he shall be compelled to surrender the premises, it has been held, is in the nature of an arrangement to secure such payment, and does not serve to extend the relation of

---

4. See § 11:46, infra, as to projection of modifications into renewal term.

§ 11:15  LANDLORD AND TENANT

landlord and tenant beyond the expiration date of the lease. Accordingly, this clause, providing that if at the expiration of the term the landlord should not agree upon a renewal, appraisers should be appointed to determine the payment to be made to tenant for the value of the building before the tenant might be compelled to surrender the premises, merely prescribes a method for ascertaining the value of the building as of the termination of the lease, and requires the landlord who notifies the tenant that he will not renew the lease, to secure an appraisal of the building as of the date of the termination of the lease within a reasonable time antedating the expiration of the term of the lease. The tenant's contention that appraisal proceedings prior to the expiration of the lease are premature, is untenable and was not sustained by the court.[5]

### § 11:16. Rights of Parties Pending Appraisal to Determine Renewal Terms

It will be observed that the renewal covenant set forth in the preceding section (§ 11:15, supra) provides that the landlord has the election of either granting a renewal or buying the buildings on the leased premises erected by the tenant; and that if the landlord does not grant a renewal, then the tenant "shall not be compelled to surrender the premises until" payment of the value of the building "be made or tendered."

If at the time the lease expires the landlord shall not have made his election, or the appraisal shall not have been completed, a problem arises as to whether or not the tenant may nevertheless continue in possession. If he may continue in possession, what rent shall he pay, since the lease is at an end?

In passing on these problems the Court of Appeals said[6] "Where a lease for a term of years contains a covenant on the part of the lessor that at the expiration of the term the lessee shall be paid the appraised value of the building, or a new lease at an appraised rent shall be granted, the lessee at the expiration of the term is

---

[5]. Sheridan Associates Inc v Potasnik (S Ct NY Co 1956) 155 NYS2d 81.
[6]. Van Beuren v Wotherspoon (1900) 164 NY 368, 379, 57 NE 633, reh den 164 NY 585, 58 NE 1093.

entitled to retain the possession until the covenant shall be performed by the lessor. This binds both the lessor and lessee. The lessee is not, however, discharged from the payment of the rent, but in an action for use and occupation the lessor can recover no more than the rent originally reserved.[7] Clearly, such continuance of possession by virtue of this type of renewal covenant will not constitute a holding over so as to give the landlord a right to elect to treat the tenant as a trespasser. For, as pointed out by the Appellate Term,[8] "where from the terms of the original lease or the conduct of the parties it is evident that some continuance of the tenancy beyond the original term has been contemplated, so that the holding over is not wrongful, or other circumstances demonstrate that both parties contemplate something other than an implied continuance of the term, the implication necessarily yields to the actual facts."

### § 11:17. Illustrations of Indefinite Renewal Covenants

Covenants which provide for a renewal of a lease upon such terms as the parties might agree, and fail to make any provision for a definite method by which such terms are to be determined in the event the parties cannot agree, are void and unenforceable.[9] An illustration of an indefinite renewal covenant is the one found in the lease litigated in Moran v Wellington.[10] There, the clause read: "With the privilege to the said lessee to renew this lease for the term of five years upon the expiration of this contract upon terms then to be mutually agreed upon." This clause fails to make any provision for a fixing of its

---

7. Also, see Trustees of Columbia University v Kalvin (1929) 250 NY 469, 473-474, 166 NE 169, 63 ALR 1151, later app 226 AD 775, 235 NYS 4; Doyle v Hamilton Fish Corp. (AD1 1911) 144 AD 131, 128 NYS 898, later app 153 AD 892, 137 NYS 1118.

8. Orville Realty Co v Warnick (AT1 1920) 113 Misc 346, 184 NYS 641.

9. § 11:11, supra.

10. (S Ct Steuben Co 1917) 101 Misc 594, 167 NYS 465.

See, also, Huber v Ruby (S Ct Nassau Co 1947) 188 Misc 1001, 69 NYS2d 760, affd 272 AD 779, 70 NYS2d 579, where the renewal clause read: "It is also understood and agreed that tenant will have the privilege of renewal for the period of one year from the expiration of this lease by giving notice in writing to the landlord, sixty days prior to expiration, at a rental price to be agreed upon." In refusing to enforce the tenant's claim to a renewal, Hill, J., in this case, said, that this "renewal clause in the lease does not bind the landlord to renew until and unless the 'price' can be agreed upon, which, in effect, is no contract at all because of uncertainty."

terms if the parties disagree; as, for example, providing for an appraisal; and specifically negatives any idea that it is to be renewed on the same terms. "It is nothing," said the court, "beyond a consent to make an agreement five years from its date, if the parties can or will. That such contracts are void has been consistently held in this state."

In the more recent case of 58-59 Realty Corp. v Park Cent. Valet,[11] the renewal clause provided: "Twenty-eighth. This lease is made upon the condition that if it is in effect upon the expiration of the term hereby demised then and thereupon this lease shall be deemed to be and the same is hereby renewed and extended without further act or deed of the parties for an additional term of . . . years from the expiration date of this lease, upon the same covenants, conditions and agreements as herein contained, excepting that the rent for each year of such additional term shall be at the same rate per year as the rate provided herein for the last year of the term hereby demised, without any concessions, and there shall be no obligation on the landlord to repair or redecorate the demised premises." The original lease involved provided for a term of three years, and seven months. The court held that this renewal clause was too incomplete, indefinite, and uncertain to be enforceable. There is no definiteness as to term. The clause in question calls for a renewal for ". . . years." "Literally," said Martin, J., for the court, "there could be no renewal for the same term. . . . If the renewal clause is read as written it calls for a renewal for a period of 'years,' which would eliminate the seven months of the original term." Furthermore, the parties used a printed form of lease, and in addition to the blank space in the renewal clause, there were blanks in the "Twenty-fourth" printed clause, covering installation of a sprinkler system, and in the "Twenty-fifth" clause, dealing with security. These blanks were left as they appeared in the printed form. There was attached a typewritten rider covering security; yet, the "Twenty-fifth" printed clause was not stricken out. "It would thus appear," Martin, J., continued, "that the parties intended

---

11. 58-59 Realty Corp. v Park Cent. Valet (AD1 1937) 252 AD 72, 297 NYS 40.

that where clauses in the printed form contained blanks, such clauses should be wholly disregarded. The clause must be regarded as incomplete, indefinite, and uncertain. If any intention is evidenced it is to leave open to future negotiation the duration of the term of the renewal."

Where a lease granted the tenant a further renewal of twenty-one years to be granted after the expiration of the first term "at a reappraisal of five percentum of the value at that time by experts," such a covenant was held to be indefinite and unenforceable. There is no provision whatever, said Shearn, J.,[12] "as to who should select the experts, how many experts there should be, or what should happen if the experts did not agree. Evidence could not be received to show the agreement or intention of the parties as to these matters, for this is not an ambiguity, but is a plain case of supplying an agreement where none was made. . . . We are forced to the conclusion that this memorandum constitutes nothing but an agreement to agree, and is therefore unenforceable by specific performance. To compel the defendant to deliver an instrument containing such vague and uncertain provisions as are called for by this memorandum would be merely to invite years of litigation." This renewal convenant is distinguishable from the one discussed in §§ 11:14, 11:15, supra, in that here no definite method is specified for conducting the appraisal. In the renewal covenant discussed in §§ 11:14, 11:15, supra, there are specific provisions as to who should select the appraisers, how many there should be, and what should happen if they disagree. These are the elements which have formed the basis for determining that that renewal covenant is definite and certain. Because these elements were lacking in the clause discussed by Shearn, J., it was held void for uncertainty.

In other words, as Sawyer, J.,[13] pointed out, courts have no process whereby they can force a meeting of the minds of litigants. "Courts can only enforce contracts which the parties thereto have actually made. This means contracts

12. H. M. Weill Co. v Creveling (AD1 1917) 181 AD 282, 168 NYS 385, affd 223 NY 672, 119 NE 1048.

13. Moran v Wellington (S Ct Steuben Co 1917) 101 Misc 594, 167 NYS 465.

sufficiently definite for the court to determine what was agreed to. All others are beyond its power of interference, and hence void for uncertainty, or as the commonly used phrase is, 'for indefiniteness.'"

Therefore, a covenant which provides that the terms for the renewal period shall be agreed upon at some future time, and fails to provide a specific method by which the terms can be determined in the event the parties disagree, is merely an agreement to agree. Such an uncertain and vague covenant is void, and will not be enforced by the courts.

## C. WHO CAN ENFORCE COVENANT TO RENEW

### § 11:18. Right of Renewal at Tenant's Sole Option

Renewal covenants may be classified according to whether they are operative at the sole option of the tenant, or whether they are operative at the sole option of the landlord.

Where a lease contains only an agreement on the part of the landlord to grant a renewal if the tenant elects to renew the lease, but none on the part of the tenant to accept or take a renewal, then such a covenant is operative at the sole option of the tenant. In other words the only acts called for to effect a renewal are on the part of the tenant. In Orr v Doubleday, Page & Co.[14] the lease contained the following provision: "with the privilege to said tenant of a renewal for another term of 10 years, upon the same terms as are contained herein. But should said tenant elect to renew the within lease for said term of 10 years, then and in that event it will, by a notice in writing notify said landlord, his heirs or assigns, at least 90 days prior to the expiration of the term hereby created, of such intention to renew said lease." The court, in construing this renewal clause ruled that this covenant was operative at the sole option of the tenant. The landlord had no choice or decision in the matter. "The only acts called for to effect the renewal," said the court, "are on the part of the defendant (tenant)."

14. (1918) 223 NY 334, 119 NE 552, 1 ALR 338, reh den 223 NY 700, 119 NE 1064.

In an early case,[15] the covenant for a renewal provided that if the tenant should pay the rents and perform the covenants of the lease on his part, then the landlord "shall and will at the end or expiration of the term" grant tenant a new lease for a further specified term. The landlord brought an action to compel the tenant to accept a renewal of the lease. The court held that it would not grant such relief. "We find in the agreement," said Danforth, J., "some covenants binding the parties mutually, others only the lessor, and others still the lessee,—expressed in apt words without ambiguity or confusion. . . . It is very plain that here is a covenant by the lessor only, —an agreement by her to give a new lease. There is none by the lessee to accept it. If we consider it in connection with the covenants which have preceded it, we see that it thus expresses the whole intention of the parties, for such is their language. It declares a covenant on the part of one to do an act. If it had been intended to bind both, or to impose a correlative obligation on the other, we should expect a clear statement to that effect, not only that one would give, but that the other would take a lease, or the use of words from which such an agreement must necessarily have been implied. . . . It may be regarded as an offer for the benefit of the lessee, . . . . It would therefore be a perversion of the plain reading of the agreement to impose upon the lessee the obligation which is assumed to lie at the foundation of this action, and it could only be done by a disregard of well settled principles of law."

### § 11:19. —Landlord's Covenant to Pay for Improvements or Renew

Where a landlord covenants that at the expiration of the lease he will either pay the tenant the value of the building or other improvements on the leased premises as appraised by persons selected by the landlord and tenant, or grant a renewal of the lease, such covenant of renewal is operative at the sole option of the tenant. True, the landlord has primarily the sole choice of deciding whether or not to renew, but unless the tenant has

15. Bruce v Fulton Nat. Bank (1979) 79 NY 154, 161-162.

covenanted to accept the renewal offered, he need not, nor can he be compelled to, renew the lease.[16]

If there is no covenant on the part of the tenant to accept either the tender by the landlord of the value of the building, or the renewal of the lease, then, said the Court of Appeals,[17] "When the landlord expresses its choice the only right left in the tenant, under the terms of the lease, is to accept or reject the offer. If the landlord offers a renewal and the tenant rejects it, he loses the building and cannot compel the landlord to pay the value of the building as fixed by the appraisal."

Therefore, this type of renewal covenant is operative at the sole option of the tenant. If he rejects the offer of renewal, he cannot be compelled to accept it. The only effect of his rejection of the offer of renewal is to lose any rights he may have to be compensated for the building or other improvements.

## § 11:20. —Landlord's Covenant to Sell Property or Renew

In Bamman v Binzen[18] the covenant construed by the court provided that the landlord would, at the expiration of the term, renew the lease, or sell the property to the tenant at its then market value. O'Brien, J., said, "We think such a covenant is analogous to the common covenant whereby a landlord agrees to renew the term or pay for the improvements on the property. Both reason and authority favor the view that such a covenant leaves it optional with the landlord as to whether he will renew the lease or purchase the buildings. By parity of reasoning, a similar conclusion, it seems to us, should flow from an optional contract such as this, wherein the landlord agrees to do one of two things, and where the tenant agrees to do neither. It must be remembered that the tenant here assumes no obligation. He neither agrees to renew the term nor to purchase. The covenant is one entirely on the part of the landlord, and it would thus seemingly be necessary that the option should be with

---

**16.** Trustees of Columbia University v Kalvin (1929) 250 NY 469, 166 NE 169, 63 ALR 1151, later app 226 AD 775, 235 NYS 4; Zorkowski v Astor (1898) 156 NY 393, 50 NE 983.

**17.** Trustees of Columbia University v Kalvin (1929) 250 NY 469, 475, 166 NE 169, 63 ALR 1151, later app 226 AD 775, 235 NYS 4.

**18.** (GT3 1892) 65 Hun 39, 19 NYS 627, affd 142 NY 636, 37 NE 566.

RENEWAL OF LEASES § 11:22

her. By the terms of this covenant, the landlord bound herself to the tenant, but the tenant did not bind himself at all. While, therefore, it was compulsory upon the landlord either to offer to renew the lease or to sell the property, the option was with her as to which she should do; and then the right rested with the tenant of rejecting such offer."

Thus while under this type of renewal covenant the landlord has the first option of deciding whether or not to offer a renewal, the renewal, nevertheless, is operative at the tenant's sole option; for, the tenant has not agreed to accept any renewal.

### § 11:21. —Summary of Rule

When a renewal covenant in a lease contains only an agreement on the part of the landlord to give a renewal, and does not contain any agreement by the tenant to take or to accept a renewal, then the tenant is the only one who can exercise the right to renew. Such a renewal covenant, in effect, is merely an offer of renewal which the landlord must tender, and which the tenant is at liberty to accept or reject.

This is true even in the case of those covenants in which the landlord is given the sole choice of either renewing the lease, or buying the buildings on the land, or selling the property to the tenant. Absent a covenant on the part of the tenant to take the renewal, the landlord cannot compel him to do so.

Therefore, a renewal covenant to be mutually binding must contain not only a covenant on the part of the landlord to give, but also a covenant on the part of the tenant to take, a renewal of the lease.

The important thing to be remembered by the draftsman of a lease is, as said by Vann, J.,[19] "When it is apparent that the parties had the subject in mind, and either has withheld an express promise in regard to it, one will not be implied."

### § 11:22. Renewal at Landlord's Sole Option

In contrast to the type of renewal clause which is effective to renew the lease at the sole option of the

---

19. Zorkowski v Astor (1898) 156 NY 393, 50 NE 983.

§ 11:22

tenant,[20] there are renewal clauses which are operative at the landlord's sole option. Under such renewal covenants, the tenant gains no renewal of the lease by giving the landlord notice of a desire or election to renew the lease.[1] In one case,[2] the lease contained this clause: "And the tenant hereby expressly agrees to give formal written notice to the landlord on or before January 15, 1920, of the tenant's wish as to continuance of the tenancy beyond the term hereby granted." The court, holding that this clause was unambiguous and gave the tenant no option or privilege of renewal, said: "It is conceivable that the landlord of said premises would desire to know, several months in advance of the end of the term, whether the tenant intends to stay for another year, and make arrangements accordingly, and there seems no room for doubt that it is just what the language quoted means—an agreement on the part of the tenant to express in writing on or before January 15 whether he wishes to renew his lease."

In Sylvan Mortg. Co. v Astruck[3] the renewal clause read as follows: "The lessee expressly covenants and agrees to give written notice to the lessor or the agent of the said lessor five months before the termination of this lease or any renewal thereof as to whether said lessee desires to surrender the premises or make a new lease therefor, and the lessee covenants and agrees that failure to give such notice when requested to do so in writing shall at the option of the lessor constitute a renewal of this lease or any renewal thereof for one year from the expiration thereof upon the same terms and conditions as herein contained." The court, holding that this clause was for the landlord's benefit, and that the tenant gained no right of renewal by giving the stipulated notice, said: "In the lease at bar, to hold that the provisions entitled the tenant to a renewal of the lease at the tenant's option would, in effect, be making a new contract for the parties, and would practically amount to a holding that, when the

20. §§ 11:18-11:21, supra.

1. Walsh v Ft. Schuyler Brewing Co. (Co Ct Oneida Co 1914) 83 Misc 488, 146 NYS 160; Holloway v Schmidt (AT 1900) 33 Misc 747, 67 NYS 169.

2. Bernstein v Smith (AT1 1922) 119 Misc 34, 194 NYS 789, affd 205 AD 884, 198 NYS 902, revd 236 NY 448, 141 NE 911, 30 ALR 901.

3. (AD1 1923) 205 AD 455, 199 NYS 438.

lessor inserts in his lease a provision expressly for his benefit, a reciprocal provision for the benefit of the tenant may be implied in the lease, although the same is not expressed."

## § 11:23. "First Privilege of Renewal" Clauses

An interesting question of construction arises from the use of the phrase: "with the first privilege of a renewal of this lease at the end of said term." (This is to be distinguished from the clause found in the lease in Orr v Doubleday Page & Co., discussed in § 11:18, supra, where the tenant was given "the privilege of renewal.") Such phrase, as construed by the courts, means that the tenant shall have the first privilege; that is, the prior right, of a renewal for the same term and at the same rent as provided in the original lease, provided the landlord leases the premises to anyone. Therefore, in this type of renewal clause, the mere service upon the landlord of a demand or notice of the tenant's desire to renew will not automatically give the tenant a renewal of the lease. In other words, the tenant is not given an absolute right of renewal; rather, the question of renewal depends upon the landlord's desire to lease the premises again after the original term expires.[4]

Recently the Court of Appeals[5] had occasion to construe a similar type of covenant: the tenant is given "first privilege to buy said property for the sum of $14,000." The tenant contended, said the court, that the "legal effect of the words is to give the lessee an absolute right to purchase the premises at the price named." "If that position is correct," said Hubbs, J., writing for the court, "the lessor was deprived of the right to determine whether or not he wished to sell. The use of the words 'first privilege' indicates that the parties must have had in mind some other opportunity of the lessor to sell and that the lessor was not prevented from selling to another if he desired. It bound the lessor, however, not to sell to another for that price without first giving the lessee the opportunity or privilege to purchase the property at the

---

4. Forma v Moran (AD2 1948) 273 AD 818, 76 NYS2d 232; Walsh v Ft. Schuyler Brewing Co. (Co Ct Oneida Co 1914) 83 Misc 488, 146 NYS 160; Holloway v Schmidt (AT 1900) 33 Misc 747, 67 NYS 169.

5. R I Realty Co v Terrell (1930) 254 NY 121, 124, 172 NE 262.

price specified, and, if the lessee did not exercise the privilege to purchase, the lessor was free to sell to anyone else. The words 'first privilege' did not grant an absolute option to the lessee to purchase the premises at any time during the term of the lease. The right of the lessee to purchase depended upon the lessor's desire to sell. If the lessor desired to sell at the price named, then the lessee was to have the 'first privilege to buy' at the figure specified. In construing the clause in question, the court is required to give some meaning to all the words used. To construe the clause in accordance with the contention of the respondent (tenant) would require that the word 'first' be eliminated. With that word eliminated the privilege would be absolute and enforceable. (case cit.) Therefore, it must have been used to prevent the agreement from constituting an absolute option to sell. The phrase 'first privilege to buy' and the words 'privilege to buy' have an entirely different meaning; one is conditional and the other absolute."

In other words a "first privilege" of renewal does not give a tenant an absolute right of renewal. Under such a provision the landlord has the sole option of deciding whether or not to offer the tenant a renewal.

### § 11:24. Assignee or Sublessee

"A covenant in a lease providing for a renewal of the lease by the tenant," said the Appellate Division,[6] "is a covenant running with the land inuring to the benefit of the assignee of the lease." Therefore, as said by Vann, J.,[7] "The assignment of the lease in question by the lessee to the defendant conferred upon it all his rights, including the privilege of exercising the option to extend the term."[8]

A renewal covenant, however, does not pass to a sublessee.[9] As between the lessee and his sublessee, the lessee ordinarily has the right of renewal of the prime lease,

---

**6.** 507 Madison Ave. Realty Co. v Martin (AD1 1922) 200 AD 146, 192 NYS 762, affd 233 NY 683, 135 NE 969.

Also, see Loudave Estates, Inc. v Cross Roads Improv. Co. (S Ct NY Co 1961) 28 Misc 2d 54, 214 NYS2d 72, affd (1st Dept) 20 AD2d 864, 251 NYS2d 408.

**7.** Probst v Rochester Steam Laundry Co. (1902) 171 NY 584, 64 NE 504.

**8.** Michael's Distributors Inc v New York Soc of Methodist Church (S Ct NY Co 1950) 101 NYS2d 85, affd 278 AD 819, 105 NYS2d 407.

**9.** Loudave Estates, Inc. v Cross Roads Improv. Co. (S Ct NY Co 1961) 28 Misc 2d 54, 214 NYS2d 72, affd (1st Dept) 20 AD2d 864, 251 NYS2d 408.

and the sublessee's right to renewal of his sublease is conditioned on the lessee's obtaining a renewal of the prime lease, in which event the sublessee acquires no right unless the lessee obtains such renewal.[10] Where a sublease was expressly made subject to the terms of the prime lease, the subtenant was held to have no legal right to compel the tenant to exercise an option granted the tenant for renewal of the prime lease of the entire premises with a 12-story building in order to enable the subtenant to exercise an option granted it for the renewal of its sublease of the ground floor and a part of the basement only, in the absence of either proof of an agreement on the part of the tenant to exercise its option, or proof of special circumstances entitling the subtenant to such relief.[11]

## § 11:25. —Where Assignor Reserves Right of Renewal

If a tenant-assignor expressly reserves to himself the right to renew the lease, when he assigns the lease, such right of renewal contained in the lease will not pass to the assignee of the lease. The assignee, then, will have no right of renewal under the renewal covenant; but, such right will remain in the tenant-assignor.[12] As Daly, J.,[13] said, "An assignment of the lease, or of the whole term, passes with it all covenants that run with the land, including covenants of renewal. . . . There must be, therefore, express reservation to prevent every right and interest of the lessee passing under such an assignment."

## § 11:26. —Where Assignment is in Violation of Lease Restriction

An interesting problem arises as to the right of an

---

10. Loudave Estates, Inc. v Cross Roads Improv. Co. (S Ct NY Co 1961) 28 Misc 2d 54, 214 NYS2d 72, affd (1st Dept) 20 AD2d 864, 251 NYS2d 408.

11. Minister, Elders & Deacons of the Reformed Protestant Dutch Church v 198 Broadway, Inc. (1983) 59 NY2d 170, 464 NYS2d 406, 451 NE2d 164, 39 ALR4th 818, later proceeding (1st Dept) 114 AD2d 751, 494 NYS2d 594, app gr 67 NY2d 609, 494 NE2d 114 and affd 68 NY2d 456, 510 NYS2d 63, 502 NE2d 978, motion den, reh den 69 NY2d 741, 512 NYS2d 369, 504 NE2d 696, motion den 69 NY2d 897, 515 NYS2d 231, 507 NE2d 1087.

12. New York Business Bldgs. Corp. v James McCutcheon & Co. (AD1 1930) 229 AD 681, 243 NYS 255, affd 257 NY 554, 178 NE 792; Michael's Distributors, Inc. v New York City Soc. of Methodist Church (S Ct NY Co 1950) 101 NYS2d 85, affd 278 App Div 819, 105 NYS2d 407.

13. Downing v Jones (Com Pl NYGT 1882) 11 Daly 245.

§ 11:26 LANDLORD AND TENANT

assignee to exercise the right of renewal when the assignment of the lease is made in violation of a covenant by the tenant not to assign the lease without the landlord's consent. On principle such an assignee, despite the assignment in violation of the lease restriction, would still have the right to exercise the right of renewal if the landlord did not previously void the assignment by some affirmative act. An assignment in violation of a restrictive covenant is not void, but voidable; and if the landlord does not choose to avail himself of the breach by voiding the assignment, the acceptance of the assignment by the assignee then will result in creating a privity of estate between the assignee and the landlord. This being so, then such an assignee can avail himself of the covenant to renew, which runs with the land.[14] This situation was presented to the courts in the case of Condit v Manischewitz.[15] There the lease provided that the lease could not be assigned without the landlord's consent. However the tenant disregarded this restriction, and assigned the lease to the defendant. Simultaneously with the assignment, the tenant covenanted with his assignee "to exercise his option for the renewal of his original lease with the landlord pursuant to the terms of his lease." When the original term of the lease expired, the tenant—not the assignee—gave the landlord notice of his election to renew the lease. The landlord by a submission to the court on an agreed statement of facts sought to obtain an adjudication that the lease had not been renewed, and that the landlord was entitled to the possession of the premises at the expiration of the original term. The Appellate Division in a per curiam opinion (Merrell, J. dissenting in a separate opinion) said, "Plaintiff (landlord) would have been justified in demanding possession of the premises by reason of this breach." (The assignment without landlord's consent.) "But she clearly waived this right, and adopted and ratified the assignments by the acceptance of rent with full knowledge. . . . This ratification is not impaired by the provision in the lease that the failure of the landlord to insist upon strict performance 'shall not be construed as a waiver or relinquishment for

[14]. § 11:24, supra. Also, see § 9:29, supra.
[15]. (AD1 1927) 220 AD 366, 221 NYS 371.

the future of any such covenant, condition or option.' That provision relates only to the right of the landlord to demand future performance of any covenant of the tenant's despite any waiver of past performance thereof. Plaintiff (landlord) contends, however, that, inasmuch as the lease was assigned, the right of renewal rested in the assignee and not in the defendant, (the tenant-assignor) and that the defendant's notice of exercise of the option was therefore inoperative. . . . Here the lessee exercised the option as agent for his assignee pursuant to his covenant so to do. It would be inequitable in the extreme to permit the plaintiff to avoid the consequences of her covenant to renew, merely because the lessee omitted to state in the notice that he was acting for the assignee. . . . We conclude, therefore, that the option to renew the lease was validly exercised for the benefit of the defendant's assignee."

### § 11:27. Personal Representative of Deceased Tenant

The death of a tenant does not render a renewal covenant in a lease inoperative. Such a covenant has been held to constitute personal property, and as such passes to the personal representatives of the deceased tenant.[16] If a notice of election to renew is required to be given by the tenant, upon his death his personal representatives must give such notice; they cannot delegate this power to anyone else.[17]

In an action to compel specific performance of a covenant to renew, a motion was made to substitute the heirs at law of the deceased tenant as parties in the tenant's place. The court held that this motion could not be granted; for, the covenant is personal property, and passed to the personal representatives, who should be substituted as parties, rather than the heirs at law.[18]

### § 11:28. —Liability of Personal Representative upon Renewal

When a personal representative of a deceased tenant

---

16. Schmitt v Stoss (1913) 207 NY 731, 100 NE 1119; Kolasky v Michels (1890) 120 NY 635, 24 NY 278.

17. Goldberg v Himlyn (Co Ct Kings Co 1923) 121 Misc 580, 201 NYS 837.

18. Schmitt v Stoss (1913) 207 NY 731, 100 NE 1119.

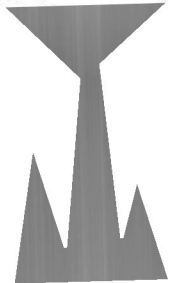

§ 11:28  LANDLORD AND TENANT

exercises the election to renew contained in the lease made by the deceased tenant, he is liable individually, and not in his representative capacity, on such renewed lease.[19] This is so, even where the renewal lease is made with him in his representative capacity.[20] In Chisholm v Toplitz,[1] the defendant was an administrator with the will annexed, but was being sued personally for rent. His decedent had been a tenant of a term which by its terms did not expire until one year after the death of decedent. The lease, only of the land, provided for perpetual renewals at the tenant's option, but made no provision for payment for any structures on the land in the event that the option for renewal was not exercised. The defendant-administrator did exercise the option, and the renewal lease was made to him "as administrator with the will annexed of the estate of Lippman Toplitz, deceased." It was held that the action was properly brought against the defendant-administrator personally. The Appellate Division affirmed on the opinion of Scott, J., in the court below, who said, "It is well settled in this state by a long line of decisions that, as a general rule, executors or trustees cannot, by their executory contracts, although made in the interest and for the benefit of the estate they represent, if made upon a new and independent consideration, bind the estate, and thus create a liability not founded upon the contract or obligation of the testator. (case cited.) The defendant insists that this case falls within the exception to the general rule, because the lease upon which suit is brought is founded upon a lease made by the testator in his lifetime. It is founded upon it, however, only in the sense that the fact that the testator had entered upon the prior lease afforded an opportunity to the defendant to make the present lease. It did not create any obligation so to do. If the option to renew had been vested in the lessor and not the lessee, so that the defendant in consequence of the testator's agreement had been obliged to accept a new lease, the case would have

---

**19.** Chisholm v Toplitz (AD1 1903) 82 AD 346, 82 NYS 1081, affd 178 NY 599, 70 NE 1096; Durand v Lipman (M Ct 1937) 165 Misc 615, 1 NYS2d 468.

**20.** Chisholm v Toplitz (AD1 1903) 82 AD 346, 82 NYS 1081, affd 178 NY 599, 70 NE 1096; Durand v Lipman (M Ct 1937) 165 Misc 615, 1 NYS2d 468.

**1.** (AD1 1903) 82 AD 346, 82 NYS 1081, affd 178 NY 599, 70 NE 1096.

been brought within the exception. But it is said that the fact that, if the lease had not been renewed, the testator's estate would have forfeited the building on the lot, justified and practically compelled the administrator, in the interest of the estate, to renew the lease. That is precisely the question that cannot be litigated in an action against the defendant as administrator. Whether it was a judicious act to renew the lease in order to save the building is a question in which the legatees or distributees of the estate are interested, and upon which they are entitled to be heard. They could not be so heard if the landlord had sued the administrator, as such, in an action at law. In my opinion, the action is properly brought against the defendant personally. . . ."

### § 11:29. Joint Tenants

It is well settled, said McLaughlin, J.,[2] "that where a lease is made to two or more tenants jointly, with covenant for a renewal or a privilege for an additional term, it cannot be exercised by one of them alone." "The legal question presented," said the Appellate Division,[3] "is whether one tenant may, by his act in holding over after his term, exercise the option of renewing the lease and thereby bind his cotenant for a new term without his consent." The court answered this question by ruling that one tenant cannot bind his cotenant to the renewal of a term by any unauthorized agreement or act in respect to the common property; for, said Davis, J., "Where there are two tenants, in order that they may make a new contract by exercising an option, it must be done by their united action, either by giving such notice or by jointly holding over, and thus raising the implication that they have made such election."

### § 11:30. Surviving Partner

Where a lease to a partnership gives the partnership-tenant the privilege of renewing the lease upon giving a specified notice, when one partner dies, the survivor, as such, can give the required notice to enforce a fulfillment

---

2. Goldberg v Himlyn (Co Ct Kings Co 1923) 121 Misc 580, 201 NYS 837. Also, see Zazzara v Cassata (AD4 1949) 275 AD 615, 92 NYS2d 62.

3. Foster v Stewart (AD4 1921) 196 AD 814, 188 NYS 151.

of the renewal covenant.[4] As the Court of Appeals said,[5] "Upon the death of one of two partners, the survivor takes the partnership property for the purpose of holding and administering it until it can be converted into money and the partnership debts paid. . . . This lease was partnership property. The right to renew a lease is frequently a very valuable property, and as such when it belongs to a firm, is part of the partnership assets. . . . It is true that the partnership was dissolved by the death of Place, and, thereafter, the plaintiff (surviving partner) had no power to incur any new liabilities on account thereof. After the death of his partner he could bind no one but himself; and all the liabilities of the firm fell upon his individually. He took this lease as survivor, with all the covenants pertaining to it. He had the same power and control over it, and the same right to enforce the covenants contained in it, as he would have had if he had been the sole lessee named in it. He had the power and the right to give the notice, and thus extend the lease. By so doing he undoubtedly made himself liable for the rent." But, the court pointed out, that is a matter of no concern to the landlord. Therefore, the court concluded, "The plaintiff (surviving partner) was the only person who could enforce this covenant or sue for its breach. By operation of law he became the sole lessee, and the only person legally interested in this covenant."

### § 11:31. Partner Remaining After Dissolution

Where a lease is given to a partnership, and the partnership is dissolved by the withdrawal of some of the partners prior to the expiration of the original term, but the remaining partners continue in possession, it has been held that those partners who do continue in possession of the demised premises cannot renew the lease by exercising the renewal option contained therein without the consent of the other partners who were the tenants in the original lease. The dissolution placed it out of the power of any one of the partners to bind the others by an election to renew. Nor, is the landlord bound to grant a renewal of the lease to those of the partners continuing

---

4. Betts v June (1873) 51 NY 274, 278.

5. Betts v June (1873) 51 NY 274, 278.

an executor or administrator is empowered to make a lease for a term not exceeding three years, and a trustee is empowered to make a lease for a term not exceeding ten years, although such term extends beyond the duration of the trust.[14]

The Real Property Actions and Proceedings Law provides,[15] that when the assets of a trust estate include an interest in real property, the trustee may apply for an order authorizing the trustee to lease such property, or to confirm a lease for a term longer than ten years which he made without obtaining prior court authorization. Accordingly, when a tenant takes a lease from a trustee, unless the instrument creating the trust or the court decree appointing the trustee gives the trustee additional powers, he has no authority without the court's permission to grant a valid lease for more than ten years. If the trustee grants a lease for ten years or less, the tenant's term will not be defeated should the trust expire before the end of the term. But, if the trust grants a lease for more than ten years without court approval, then the tenant's term will expire whenever the trust expires. That is the chance the tenant will take when he gets a lease from a trustee who exceeds his limited authority. If a tenant takes a lease from a personal representative, the lease cannot exceed more than three years without court approval or authority.

The importance of these principles to renewal of leases arises, because when a tenant exercises a right to renew, the lease becomes one for the entire period covered by the original term and the renewal term combined.[16]

Therefore, when a tenant receives a lease from a trustee, even though the lease may provide for a term of less than ten years, yet, if by exercising an option to renew, granted therein, the term of the lease will then exceed ten years, the tenant should assure himself that the trustee is authorized to make such a lease. If the instrument creating the trust does not authorize the

---

**14.** Under former Real Prop L § 106, which is superseded by EPTL 11-1.1(b)(5)(C), trustees were empowered to make a lease for a term not exceeding 5 years. Prior to the EPTL no statutory power existed with respect to the power of executors or administrators to lease estate real property.

**15.** Real Prop Act & Proc L § 1601, superseding former Real Prop L § 107.

**16.** See §§ 11:50, 11:51, infra.

trustee to make such a lease, then the tenant should insist that the trustee obtain the court's approval of the lease.

## E. EXERCISING RIGHT TO RENEW

### § 11:34. Necessity of Strict Performance of Conditions Precedent

If a lease provides that as a condition precedent to obtaining a renewal the tenant must perform certain acts, then the strict performance of such conditions precedent is absolutely necessary at law to the right of renewal.[17]

Once a tenant exercises his option to renew, he is bound thereby and cannot withdraw his acceptance.[18]

### § 11:35. Necessity of Timely Notice to Renew

If a lease provides that as a condition to obtaining a renewal the tenant shall notify the landlord in writing on or before a certain date of his intention to exercise the right to renew, failure to give such notice on or before that date will forfeit the right to renew at law.[19] Absent a waiver or special circumstances which warrant equitable

---

17. J. N. A. Realty Corp. v Cross Bay Chelsea, Inc. (1977) 42 NY2d 392, 397 NYS2d 958, 366 NE2d 1313; People's Bank of New York v Mitchell (1878) 73 NY 406, 410; Joyous Holdings, Inc. v Volkswagen of Oneonta, Inc. (1987, 3d Dept) 128 AD2d 1002, 513 NYS2d 841; Niagara Frontier Services, Inc. v Thress (1985, 4th Dept) 109 AD2d 1089, 487 NYS2d 228; McVey v Simone (1980, 2d Dept) 73 AD2d 959, 424 NYS2d 265; Raleigh Associates, Inc. v Henry (AD1 1950) 277 AD 978, 100 NYS2d 184, reh den 277 AD 1037, 100 NYS2d 1019 and mod on other grounds 302 NY 467, 99 NE2d 289, reh den 302 NY 940, 100 NE2d 191; Fidelity & Columbia Trust Co. v Levin (S Ct Erie Co 1927) 128 Misc 838, 221 NYS 269, affd 221 AD 786, 223 NYS 866, affd 248 NY 551, 162 NE 521; Doepfner v Bowers (S Ct NY Co 1907) 55 Misc 561, 106 NYS 932.

18. 1020 Park Ave., Inc. v Raynor (1978) 97 Misc 2d 288, 411 NYS2d 172.

**Annotations:** Sufficiency as to method of giving oral or written notice exercising option to renew or extend lease. 29 ALR4th 903.

Sufficiency of provision of lease to effect second or perpetual right of renewal. 29 ALR4th 172.

What constitutes timely notice of exercise of option to renew or extend lease. 29 ALR4th 956.

19. J. N. A. Realty Corp. v Cross Bay Chelsea, Inc. (1977) 42 NY2d 392, 397 NYS2d 958, 366 NE2d 1313; Sy Jack Realty Co. v Pergament Syosset Corp. (1971) 27 NY2d 449, 318 NYS2d 720, 267 NE2d 462; Ocumpaugh v Engel (AD4 1907) 121 AD 9, 105 NYS 510; Application of Topp (S Ct Queens Co 1948) 81 NYS2d 344; Doepfner v Bowers (S Ct NY Co 1907) 55 Misc 561, 106 NYS 932.

Notice of renewal given to receiver for landlord to whom tenant had paid rent, and before termination of receivership, was proper, and effected renewal. Court Tower Corp. v Miss Silver Co. (S Ct NY Co 1980) 106 Misc 2d 451, 431 NYS2d 946.

§ 11:35 LANDLORD AND TENANT

relief, the right to renew is lost upon a tenant's failure to give timely, definite, and unequivocal notice of his intention to renew.[20] It is well settled, said the Court of Appeals, that when a contract requires that written notice be given within a specified time, the notice is ineffective unless the notice is actually received within the time prescribed.[1] Time is of the essence in such a covenant, and the giving of timely notice is a condition precedent upon the performance of which the tenant's right to a renewal is dependent.[2] As has been said, "The notice of election to renew must be unequivocal and unqualified, and strictly according to the terms of the original lease."[3] If it is unqualified and unequivocal, it is self-operative, and the acknowledgement thereof by the landlord is not essential to the inception and operation of the renewal.[4]

However, where a lease provides for notice to be given by registered mail, and the receipt of a letter by ordinary mail is not disputed, then strict compliance will be held to be unessential; for, "The obvious purpose of providing for notice by registered mail," said the Appellate Division,[5] "was to insure the delivery of the notice, and to settle any dispute that might arise between the parties as to whether or not the notice was duly received." In this connection, it has been held that where the agreement provides a method for giving notice, the use of that method suffices, and receipt is not necessary; but if any

**20.** Schoen v Scudder (1976, 4th Dept) 51 AD2d 666, 378 NYS2d 178.

**1.** Maxton Builders, Inc. v Lo Galbo (1986) 68 NY2d 373, 509 NYS2d 507, 502 NE2d 184.

**2.** Doepfner v Bowers (S Ct NY Co 1907) 55 Misc 561, 106 NYS 932.

See § 11:39, infra, relative to obtaining equitable relief from failure to perform conditions precedent to a right to exercise an option to renew.

**Annotation:** Timely notice: what constitutes timely notice of exercise of option to renew or extend lease. 29 ALR4th 956.

Sufficiency as to parties giving or receiving notice of exercise of option to renew or extend lease. 34 ALR4th 857.

**3.** Goldberg v Himlyn (Kings Co Ct 1923) 121 Misc 580, 201 NYS 837.

**4.** Orr v Doubleday, Page & Co. (1918) 223 NY 334, 340, 119 NE 552, 1 ALR 338, reh den 223 NY 700, 119 NE 1064.

Also, see, Chamberlain v Dunlop, 126 NY 45, 26 NE 966. In this case the court held that a notice of election to renew was not to be deemed insufficient because the tenant had made a suggestion in the letter containing the notice of election that if the landlord would choose to grant him a longer lease than called for by the option he, the tenant, would take it.

**5.** East Eighty-Second St. Corp. v Rogers (AD1 1920) 192 AD 633, 183 NYS 297.

other method than the one stipulated is used, then the tenant must prove actual receipt of the notice.[6]

## § 11:36. When Performance of Other Provisions of Lease Necessary

It is important to determine whether or not the privilege of renewal is dependent upon the performance of other covenants in the lease. The Court of Appeals in an instructive opinion by Collin, J., said,[7] "In Kingston v Preston, cited at the bar in Jones v Barkley (2 Douglas 684), Lord Mansfield expressed himself to the following effect: 'There are three kinds of covenants: 1. Such as are called mutual and independent, where either party may recover damages from the other, for the injury he may have received by a breach of the covenants in his favour, and where it is no excuse for the defendant, to allege a breach of the covenants on the part of the plaintiff. 2. There are covenants which are conditions and dependent, in which the performance of one depends on the prior performance of another, and, therefore, till this prior condition is performed, the other party is not liable to an action on his covenant. 3. There is also a third sort of covenants, which are mutual conditions to be performed at the same time; and, in these, if one party was ready, and offered, to perform his part, and the other neglected, or refused, to perform his, he who was ready, and offered, has fulfilled his engagement, and may maintain an action for the default of the other; though it is not certain that either is obliged to do the first act.' The complexities of modern industrial and commercial transactions have not rendered the classification inaccurate or inadequate. By a long series of decisions, the rule has been established that the question whether covenants are to be held dependent or independent of each other is to be determined by the intention and meaning of the parties, as expressed by them, and by the application of common sense to each case submitted for adjudication. (cases cit.) The efforts put forth in judicial opinions and by text writers to define or

---

**6.** Peabody v Satterlee (1901) 166 NY 174, 59 NE 818; Sasmor v V. Vivaudou, Inc. (S Ct NY Co 1951) 200 Misc 1020, 103 NYS2d 640; Kelcon Constr. Corp. v Marvin (Civ Ct NY Co 1967) 53 Misc 2d 194, 278 NYS2d 117 (notice given by certified mail, as required by lease, sufficed without proof of receipt).

**7.** Rosenthal Paper Co. v National Folding Box & Paper Co. (1919) 226 NY 313, 319-320, 123 NE 766.

§ 11:36

formulate the distinctions of dependence and independence of promises or covenants have revealed their comparative futility and served, in the main, to strengthen the rule. Parties have the right to contract as they will for any lawful purpose and the problem for the courts is to ascertain, in accordance with established rules of interpretation, the real contract or agreement. If they make their promises dependent or independent throughout, or dependent in part and independent in part, it is not for the courts to thwart them. Their expressed intention and meaning, ascertained from the whole instrument, rather than from technical or conventional expressions, are the guides in determining the character and force of their respective covenants."

As a general rule, unless there is evidence of different intention, "dependence or independence of covenants may be determined by the order of time in which, by the terms and meaning of the contract, their performance is required."[8]

Therefore, if a lease provides that a tenant may have the right to renew provided he shall have fully performed all the terms and conditions of the lease on his part to be performed, failure to perform all of such terms and conditions will forfeit the right to renew.[9] However, if the lease does not so provide, then a question of construction will arise as to whether or not the parties intended to make the right to renew dependent upon the performance of any of the other conditions in the lease.

Where a burden is imposed on the tenant which is not susceptible of precisely defined content, the tenant's right to renew will be governed by the standard of substantial compliance, where there is no evidence of injury to the landlord. For example, in the case of a covenant by the tenant to keep the premises in good repair, the intention of the parties is fairly inferable that the tenant, in

---

8. Clark v West (AD2 1910) 137 AD 23, 122 NYS 380, affd 201 NY 569, 95 NE 1125, reh den 201 NY 600, 95 NE 1126.

Also, see, Glenn v Rossler (1898) 156 NY 161, 50 NE 785; Delaware Trust Co. v Calm (1909) 195 NY 231, 88 NE 53.

9. People's Bank of New York v Mitchell (1878) 73 NY 406, 410. See § 11:13, supra.

**Annotation:** Right to exercise option to renew or extend lease as affected by tenant's breach of other covenants or conditions. 23 ALR4th 908.

# RENEWAL OF LEASES § 11:37

possession, of the premises should protect the landlord from loss in the value of the property from deterioration. So, too, with the covenant to comply with governmental orders and regulations, the landlord has required the tenant to immunize him from the property standards of health and safety. Where these covenants are substantially performed by the tenant, and there is no evidence of injury to the landlord, the tenant should not lose all rights of renewal because of the variance from total satisfaction of the covenant. This exception to the strict compliance rule recognizes the sound distinction between general covenants, and these particular covenants. Covenants requiring the tenant to comply with governmental regulations or to keep the premises in good repair rests upon an intention ancillary to the major consideration inherent in the lease. These covenants suggest a continuing performance during the term of the lease, and imply a quality of performance which is not immediately ascertainable as being full or partial within the framework of compliance under the circumstances present at the time of demand to perform.[10] In other words, although a tenant may be in default under his lease, he may exercise an option to renew his lease, but his being in good standing may be made a condition precedent to his right to renew.

## § 11:37. Rent Payment as Condition Precedent

Unless otherwise expressly provided, the payment of rent is not a condition precedent to the right of a tenant to a renewal.[11] In an early case, the Court of Appeals[12] by Jewett, J., said "As to the objection made by the defendant, that there was rent in arrear, and, therefore, the plaintiff was not entitled to a further lease, the covenant being independent, the liability of the defendant for the breach of the covenant in question remained. The payment of the rent was not a condition precedent to the right of the plaintiff to a renewal of the lease under the covenant, and he might bring his action for a breach of it,

---

10. Vanguard Diversified, Inc. v Review Co. (1970, 2d Dept) 35 AD2d 102, 313 NYS2d 269.

11. Gruen v Patterson (1981, 1st Dept) 79 AD2d 915, 434 NYS2d 420 (citing text) (chronic late payment of rent is not a ground for refusing to offer a lease renewal required by NYC Rent Stabilization Code $50), affd 55 NY2d 631, 446 NYS2d 253, 430 NE2d 1306.

12. Tracy v Albany Exchange Co (1852) 7 NY 472.

although he was guilty of a default in the payment of his rent or performance of his covenant." More recently the Appellate Division,[13] after analyzing the provisions of the lease before it, found that there was nothing in the lease which made the covenant to renew dependent upon payment by the tenant of the rent reserved in the lease. "The two covenants," said Townley, J., "are wholly separate and distinct. Under well established rules when the covenants are independent, the fact that the tenant was in default in the payment of rent constitutes no answer to the tenant's claim under the covenant providing for a renewal or payment for the building upon the leased premises."

### § 11:38. Provision for Renewal "at Expense of Tenant"

Where a lease provides that if landlord elects to grant a renewal it shall be "at the expense of the tenant," and in case of failure to agree on the rent for the renewed term each party shall appoint an appraiser to determine such rent, it has been held that payment of this "expense" is not a condition precedent to the granting of a new lease. "It is not provided," said Scott, J.,[14] "that the payment of this expense should be a condition precedent to such a grant, and the only provision on the subject amounts to creating, if a new grant be made, a single debt from the tenant to the landlord."

Incidentally, the court held that the statutory notary's fees for taking the acknowledgment to the lease, and a reasonable attorney's fee for preparing the lease were covered by the word "expenses," but, not the fee paid by the landlord to his appraiser.

### § 11:39. Equitable Relief from Failure to Give Timely Notice of Election to Renew

The modern rule is,[15] a court of equity may grant

---

13. Berry v Stuyvesant (AD1 1935) 245 AD 516, 283 NYS 191.

14. Doyle v Hamilton Fish Corp. (AD1 1911) 144 AD 131, 128 NYS 898, later app 153 AD 892, 137 NYS 1118.

15. Under the early cases, it was held that equity would not relieve a tenant from the failure to perform conditions precedent to the right of a renewal. For example, the failure to give timely notice of renewal precluded any equitable relief: Fidelity & Columbia Trust Co v Levin (S Ct Erie Co 1927) 128 Misc 838, 221 NYS 269, affd 221 AD 786, 223 NYS 866, affd 248 NY 551, 162 NE 521; Doepfner v

equitable relief against the consequences of a lessee's failure to notify the lessor within the stipulated time of an intention to exercise the option to renew, where such delay results from an honest mistake or excusable default; where such delay results from an ambiguity in the terms of the renewal option; where the lessee has made substantial improvements on the premises and has a valuable interest in the leasehold and would suffer a "forfeiture"; or where the delay results from fraud or other special circumstances warranting equitable relief; and the lessor is not prejudiced thereby. However, if there were no penalty or forfeiture resulting from the tenant's default, equity will not grant relief.[16] "Forfeiture" in this context has been held to mean a resulting loss of the value of tenant's substantial improvements to the premises, the loss of tenant's good will established at the location during the initial term, or disruption of tenant's professional practice.[17]

The matter is largely one of discretion. The gravity of the fault must be compared to the gravity of the hardship which results. Thus, where a notice was sent by ordinary mail, although certified mail was required, it was held that the tenant should be granted equitable relief.[18] But, it should be emphasized, substantial noncompliance with the terms of an option clause may not be rewarded by judicial forgiveness which redounds to the detriment of the other party to the contract.[19]

Bowers (S Ct NY Co 1907) 55 Misc 561, 106 NYS 932.

**16.** J. N. A. Realty Corp. v Cross Bay Chelsea, Inc. (1977) 42 NY2d 392, 397 NYS2d 958, 366 NE2d 1313; Soho Dev. Corp. v Dean & De Luca, Inc. (1987, 1st Dept) 131 AD2d 385, 517 NYS2d 498; Godnig v Belmont Realty Co. (1986, 2d Dept) 124 AD2d 701, 508 NYS2d 213; Bank of New York v Ulster Heights Properties, Inc. (1985, 2d Dept) 114 AD2d 431, 494 NYS2d 345; Rizzo v Morrison Motors, Inc. (1968, 4th Dept) 29 AD2d 912, 289 NYS2d 903; Jones v Gianferante (AD3 1952) 280 AD 856, 113 NYS2d 703, affd 305 NY 135, 111 NE2d 419; Ringelheim v Karsch (S Ct Kings Co 1952) 112 NYS2d 130; Application of Topp (S Ct Queens Co 1948) 81 NYS2d 344.

Where failure to give timely notice was due to fact that when tenant purchased the business operated on the leased premises he had been told by the attorney for the seller that the renewal option was being exercised, tenant was relieved of his default. Eva Donut Shop, Inc. v Pace (1976, 2d Dept) 54 AD2d 575, 387 NYS2d 139.

**17.** Home of Histadruth Ivrith, Inc. v State Facilities Dev. Corp. (1986, 3d Dept) 114 AD2d 200, 498 NYS2d 883; Blumenthal v 162 East 80th Tenants, Inc. (1982, 1st Dept) 88 AD2d 871, 451 NYS2d 771.

**18.** Joseph Steier, Inc. v New York (S Ct NY Co 1970) 65 Misc 2d 296, 317 NYS2d 455.

**19.** McVey v Simone (1980, 2d Dept) 73 AD2d 959, 424 NYS2d 265.

Where the renewal notice was to be

§ 11:39                    LANDLORD AND TENANT

To illustrate the application of these rules: Where a tenant has negligently or inadvertently failed to give notice, but has made in good faith improvements of such nature that he would sustain a substantial loss if the lease were not renewed, equity will intervene to prevent a forfeiture if the landlord has not materially changed his position to his prejudice in reliance on the tenant's failure to exercise the option.[20] Similarly, where a tenant had mailed its notice of election to renew within the stipulated time, which notice miscarried in the mail and was never delivered, but landlord actually received notice of the tenant's election, although after the stipulated time, and before he took any steps to find another tenant or to lease the space, the tenant was relieved of his default which neither harmed nor prejudiced the landlord, and was not due to bad faith, and tenant stood to lose a substantial and valuable leasehold.[1]

In sum, the consensus of the modern cases is, that at least the following elements must be established in order to obtain equitable relief: (1) That no harm or prejudice to the landlord has resulted from the default or delay in giving the notice; and (2) that the default or delay was due to an honest mistake or similar excusable default. These would seem to be the minimum requirements in order to excuse a tenant. In addition, the courts have looked at other factors such as ambiguity in the terms of the lease as to when such notice was to be given; substan-

sent by November 30, 1968, the lease expired February 28, 1969, and the tenant's attorney sent the notice February 27, 1969, the court refused to grant the tenant relief, because it felt that the renewal clause was clear and well understood by the tenant; the landlord had already granted a new lease to another tenant, and the excuse for the delay, that it had been due to a misunderstanding between the tenant and his attorney as to who was to send the notice, is not the sort of mistake envisioned by the courts as entitling the tenant to relief. Galloway v Scaraggi (Yonkers City Ct 1969) 59 Misc 2d 984, 302 NYS2d 10.

**20.** Niagara Frontier Services, Inc. v Thress (1985, 4th Dept) 109 AD2d 1089, 487 NYS2d 228; Geo. W. Millar & Co. v Wolf Sales & Service Corp. (NYC Civ Ct NY Co 1971) 65 Misc 2d 585, 318 NYS2d 24.

In the case of a lease option, a tenant's equitable interest is recognized and protected against forfeiture in some cases where the tenant has, in good faith, made improvements of a substantial character, intending to renew the lease, if the landlord is not harmed by the delay in the giving of the notice, and the lessee would sustain substantial loss in case the lease were not renewed. Grunberg v George Associates (1984, 1st Dept) 104 AD2d 745, 480 NYS2d 217.

**1.** Sy Jack Realty Co. v Pergament Syosset Corp. (1971) 27 NY2d 449, 318 NYS2d 720, 267 NE2d 462 (citing text).

tial improvements to the premises made by the tenant at some cost to him; substantial loss to the tenant if the default prohibition is enforced; and no prejudice results to the landlord from the delay.[2]

### § 11:40. Waiver of Performance of Conditions to Renewal

Even though strict performance of the prescribed conditions precedent is generally necessary to obtain the privilege of renewal; yet, it is quite competent for the parties to waive such performance, and such waiver may even be implied from their conduct.[3] Thus, where the landlord permitted 5 to 6 weeks to elapse before rejecting tenant's 14-day late notice of lease renewal, and landlord and tenant occupied adjoining premises in same building and saw each other casually a number of times during this period, landlord was deemed to have waived tenant's default.[4]

However, whether or not a landlord has waived a failure to perform the conditions to a renewal is a question of fact.[5] Although acceptance of rent with knowledge of tenant's violation of the terms of the lease generally results in a waiver of the violation,[6] there is no necessary inconsistency in treating a party as a tenant by accepting the rent with knowledge of a violation of the lease, but in also refusing to extend the lease for a further term.[7]

---

2. Gallagher v Marconi (Dist Ct Suffolk Co 1971) 68 Misc 2d 319, 326 NYS2d 697 (equitable relief granted); Siesel Co. v Steve Werner, Inc. (NYC Civ Ct NY Co 1981) 109 Misc 2d 653, 440 NYS2d 530; Pepe's Shamrock, Inc. v Vecchio (1987, 2d Dept) 128 AD2d 599, 512 NYS2d 858.

**Annotation:** Circumstances excusing lessee's failure to give timely notice of exercise of option to renew or extend lease. 27 ALR4th 266.

3. Long v Stafford (1886) 103 NY 274, 283, 8 NE 522.

Also, see Probst v Rochester Steam Laundry Co. (1902) 171 NY 584, 64 NE 504; Feldman v Sheridan Warehouse Cooperative Corp. (AD4 1936) 247 AD 82, 285 NYS 1033; Northmann v Hass (AT1 1921) 114 Misc 384, 186 NYS 609.

4. Modlin v Town & Country Tux, Inc. (1973, 2d Dept) 42 AD2d 586, 344 NYS2d 703 (citing text).

5. Jefpaul Garage Corp. v Presbyterian Hospital in New York (1984) 61 NY2d 442, 474 NYS2d 458, 462 NE2d 1176.

6. See § 23:16, infra.

7. Jefpaul Garage Corp. v Presbyterian Hospital in New York (1984) 61 NY2d 442, 474 NYS2d 458, 462 NE2d 1176, where the court said, "The landlord may desire that the tenant complete the term but not wish to extend it for a variety of reasons. The refusal to extend results not in a forfeiture for the tenant but only in the loss of the privilege, because the conditions precedent to enjoyment of the privilege have not been met. In the absence of some prejudice to the tenant, therefore, a waiver of the right to terminate the tenancy will not auto-

Acceptance of rent without a re-entry for tenant's default in performing the lease does not necessarily waive the right to reject tenant's exercise of the option to renew.[8] The rent was due whether or not the tenant had met the conditions precedent to renewal.

Where a lease provides that "the receipt by landlord of rent with knowledge of the breach of any covenant of the lease shall not be deemed a waiver of such breach and no provision of this lease shall be deemed to have been waived by landlord unless such waiver be in writing signed by the landlord," this clause will be enforced to preclude a finding of waiver of the conditions precedent to renewal by acceptance of rent.[9]

In other words, the mere failure to assert a forfeiture of a lease for breach of covenants or conditions therein does not, as a general rule, prevent the lessor from asserting a forfeiture of the right of renewal for the breach of said covenants and conditions.

### § 11:41. Effect of Non-waiver of Conditions to Renewal

If a tenant fails to perform the condition precedent to a renewal, and the landlord refuses to waive such non-performance, then the tenant, by continuing in possession after the expiration of his term, simply becomes a holdover, removable at the will of the landlord.[10]

### § 11:42. Exercising Right of Renewal Where No Notice Required

If no particular method for exercising a right to renew

matically result in a waiver of the conditions precedent to renewal."

8. Jefpaul Garage Corp. v Presbyterian Hospital in New York (1984) 61 NY2d 442, 474 NYS2d 458, 462 NE2d 1176, where the Court pointed out that Atkin's Waste Materials, Inc. v May (1974) 34 NY2d 422, 358 NYS2d 129, 314 NE2d 871, does not require a contrary holding, because although the tenant in the Atkins case had failed to perform the covenants in the lease, which was a condition precedent to the right of renewal, the landlord kept the notice of renewal for 4 months before it rejected it, and during the period of the alleged defaults and until the end of the lease, about 11 months after the notice of renewal, it continued to accept rent payments. "Inasmuch as it had accepted rental payments with knowledge of the default and without attempting to terminate the lease in the method provided by its terms, we held that the city had waived the default and that tenant had properly exercised its option to renew."

9. Jefpaul Garage Corp. v Presbyterian Hospital in New York (1984) 61 NY2d 442, 474 NYS2d 458, 462 NE2d 1176.

Waiver or estoppel as to notice requirement for exercising option to renew or extend lease. 32 ALR4th 452.

10. Ocumpaugh v Engel (AD4 1907) 121 AD 9, 105 NYS 510.

is prescribed in the lease, a tenant may adopt any reasonable method at the end of his term to indicate that he elects to renew the lease. He may give the notice orally or in writing, or his election may even be implied from his continuing in possession after the expiration of the lease.[11] It has been held repeatedly that when a renewal covenant gives a tenant the right to renew the lease at his option, without requiring that the tenant give notice of his election to renew, if the tenant continues in possession after his lease expires, he will be deemed to have elected to renew the lease under the renewal covenant.[12] There can be no stronger evidence of an election to renew, it has been said,[13] than remaining in possession after the expiration of the term and paying the stipulated rent.

## F. RENEWAL LEASE

### § 11:43. Necessity for New Lease

If a lease be renewed pursuant to a renewal covenant contained therein, no new lease need be entered into unless it is so expressly provided for.[14] In one case, the lease provided that the tenant "may have a further lease of the premises" at an increased rental for a further specified term provided the tenant gives the landlord written notice of "his desire to have such lease on or before December 1, 1902." The tenant prior to the specified date gave the landlord notice of his desire to renew, and the landlord acknowledged receipt thereof. The tenant continued in possession for three of the six years of

---

11. Foster v Stewart (AD4 1921) 196 AD 814, 188 NYS 151; Schwalben v Cholowaczuk (S Ct Kings Co 1973) 75 Misc 2d 98, 347 NYS2d 402 (citing text).

12. Miller v Knox (1872) 48 NY 232, 237; Kelly v Varnes (AD4 1900) 52 AD 100, 64 NYS 1040; Fritz v City of New York (M Ct 1925) 125 Misc 296, 210 NYS 717.

It should be observed that during a period of emergency rent control laws, since a tenant has the right to holdover as a statutory tenant (see § 10:11, supra), continuance in possession upon the expiration of a lease therefore will not necessarily demonstrate an intention to exercise a renewal option. An issue of fact will thereby be raised. Koss Holding Corp v Liquori (S Ct Bronx Co 1950) 99 NYS2d 482.

13. Voege v Ronalds (S Ct GT2 1894) 83 Hun 114, 31 NYS 353.

14. Jones & Brindisi, Inc. v Breslaw (1928) 250 NY 147, 151, 164 NE 887; Orr v Doubleday, Page & Co. (1918) 223 NY 334, 340, 119 NE 552, 1 ALR 338, reh den 223 NY 700, 119 NE 1064.

the renewal period and then abandoned possession. He sought to avoid liability for rent thereafter falling due during the renewal term by contending that the covenant for renewal specifically called for the execution of a new lease and that therefore a renewal term could be created only by a written lease. In overruling this contention and awarding the landlord a judgment for the rent, the court said, "It is clearly established that the defendant (tenant) did desire the lease for the further period, that he duly gave notice to that effect, and that both parties considered that everything necessary had been done to extend the lease for the renewal period, because they continued on for almost three years of such renewal period; the defendant holding possession of the premises and paying the rent to the plaintiff at the increased rate. One of the definitions of the word 'lease' is 'any tenure by grant or permission; the term of duration of such tenure; any period of time allotted for possession' Standard Dictionary. The indenture or writing is the evidence of the lease, although the term 'lease' is sometimes used to designate the writing or instrument. When the defendant served due notice upon the plaintiff of his desire to have such further lease, and remained in possession and paid the rent at the rate fixed for the renewal period, an extension of the term for the additional six years was effectuated, and such extension constituted the 'further lease' mentioned in the covenant."[15]

However, the renewal clause discussed in Goldberg v Himlyn[16] presents an instance when the execution of a new lease is necessary. In this case the lease provided that if the tenant gave notice of his election to renew three months prior to the expiration of the term, the landlord would "execute and deliver" to the tenant "a further lease of said premises" for a period of seven years upon a rental to be determined in a manner therein stipulated. The court held that this provision for the execution and delivery of a further lease necessitated the execution of a new lease, and, therefore, that the tenant's contention that merely by giving notice of this election to renew he automatically extended the term could not be

---

**15.** Mattlage v McGuire (City Ct 1908) 59 Misc 28, 111 NYS 1083.
Also, see, Finn v Krieger Shoe Co (AT2 1915) 93 Misc 83, 156 NYS 424.
**16.** (Kings Co Ct 1923) 121 Misc 580, 201 NYS 837.

sustained. "A new lease," said the court, "was both necessary and proper."

In other words, where a renewal covenant provides that a tenant may have a further lease, or provides in general terms for a renewal of the lease, the execution of a new lease is not necessary. The performance by the tenant of the prescribed conditions precedent to obtaining a renewal will automatically renew the lease. Such a general renewal clause will be self-operative. If, however, the parties intend that a renewal clause shall not be self-operative, but that the execution of a new lease is intended, then, such intention must be clearly expressed. Merely using the phrase "further lease," or the word "lease" without more, will be insufficient; for, such words will be construed, as a general rule, to refer to a term or an estate for years, rather than to the written evidence of a term or an estate for years. That is, to the indenture of lease.

### § 11:44. Terms of Renewal Lease Absent Provision Therefor

When a covenant to renew a lease makes no mention of, or provision for, the terms of the renewal lease, then the renewal will be on the same terms and conditions as are contained in the original lease. "A bare covenant to renew,"[17] "means on the same terms of the original lease."[18] Of course, where the lease expressly provides that a particular provision shall be inserted in the renewal lease, the tenant is entitled to have such provision inserted in the renewal, regardless of the reason advanced by the landlord for its omission.[19]

### § 11:45. Modification of Lease as Projected into Renewal Term

When a lease is to be renewed on the same terms and conditions, if during the original term any of the terms or conditions of the original lease have been modified, then

17. Hoff v Royal Metal Furniture Co. (AD2 1907) 117 AD 884, 103 NYS 371, affd 189 NY 555, 82 NE 1128, later app 127 AD 440, 111 NYS 541, affd 194 NY 545, 87 NE 1129.

18. Also, see, Tracy v Albany Exchange Co (1852) 7 NY 472; Western N. Y. & P. R. Co. v Riecke (AD4 1903) 83 AD 576, 81 NYS 1093; Zimmermann v Bonwit (M Ct 1927) 128 Misc 887, 220 NYS 599, affd 223 AD 882, 228 NYS 927.

19. Martin v Babcock & Wilcox Co (1906) 186 NY 451, 79 NE 726.

the lease as modified will be renewed.[20] In other words, if a provision in a lease has been removed therefrom by agreement of the parties, a renewal of the lease upon the same terms, conditions and covenants of the "present" lease does not revive the provision so removed.[1] Thus, where a landlord and tenant mutually agreed to eliminate a cancellation clause from the lease, and thereafter agreed to renew the lease "at the present rental price under the terms of the present lease," it was held that after the parties had agreed to eliminate the cancellation clause it was no longer a part of the lease. Therefore, when the parties extended "the present lease," the "present lease" did not contain a cancellation clause, and such clause would not be a term of the renewed lease.[2]

### § 11:46. Modification of Rent as Projected into Renewal Term

When drafting a lease containing a renewal clause, with the rental for the renewal period to be determined in a definite manner should the parties be unable to agree thereon, but such renewal rent in no event to be less than a fixed minimum rental, some thought should be given to the possibility of rent modifications during the original term. Likewise, the draftsman of such a modification agreement should make it clear whether or not the parties intend to carry over the rent modification into the renewal period. This problem has vexed the courts in two recent cases. In the first case,[3] a twenty-one year lease contained an option to renew at a rental to be agreed upon by the parties, "but not less than the rent herein reserved." If the parties could not agree on the renewal rental, such rental was to be fixed by appraisers in a specified manner, but in no event was said rental "to be fixed at a less sum than herein provided to be paid as the rental for the period ending February 1, 1945" (the end of the original term). During the original term a modification agreement was entered into which provided that the tenant should pay additional yearly rents in addition to

---

**20.** Woolsey v Donnelly (GT2 1889, Sup) 5 NYS 238.
**1.** Brown v Mulliken (AD2 1921) 195 AD 907, 186 NYS 935.
**2.** Brown v Mulliken (AD2 1921) 195 AD 907, 186 NYS 935.

**3.** 455 Seventh Ave., Inc. v Frederick Hussey Realty Corp. (1946) 295 NY 166, 65 NE2d 761, reh den 295 NY 827, 66 NE2d 595.

the annual rent reserved in the original lease. All of said additional yearly rents, it was further provided, were to be paid on specified dates "with the same force and effect as if said yearly original rent were the yearly rent originally reserved in said lease." Quaere, what was the rental for the renewal period: Were the additional rents to apply only to the balance of the original term, or were they to be carried over into the renewal period? (The parties conceded that a rental fixed by an appraisal in the manner specified by the lease would be futile, for, such a rental would not equal the rental formula contained in the original lease.) The Appellate Division in this case held,[4] that the total of the original and additional rents was incorporated in the original lease as if this new total "were the yearly rents originally reserved in said lease." Therefore, concluded the Appellate Division, since the lease provided that in no event was the rental for the renewal period to be less than the rent provided in the lease "to be paid as the rental for the period ending February 1, 1945," the renewal rental could not be less than this total. However, the Court of Appeals disagreed with this interpretation, and reversed the Appellate Division. Dye, J., writing for the court, said,[5] "The law is well settled that changes in a lease are not to be presumed or implied; and no additional liability will be imposed upon a tenant unless it is clearly within the provisions of the instrument under which it is claimed." Since the modification agreement contained no words indicating an intention to increase the base rent,— all modified rental amounts were described as "additional yearly rents,"—the basic formula for determining the renewal rental contained in the original lease remains unaltered. "Had the parties so desired," continued Dye, J., "they could have easily stated in so many words that the additional rental in the modification agreement was to be deemed the rent reserved in the original lease for the purposes of renewal."

4. 455 Seventh Ave., Inc. v Frederick Hussey Realty Corp. (AD1 1945) 269 AD 81, 53 NYS2d 809 (two justices dissented), revd 295 NY 166, 65 NE2d 761, reh den 295 NY 827, 66 NE2d 595.

5. 455 Seventh Ave., Inc. v Frederick Hussey Realty Corp. (1946) 295 NY 166, 172, 65 NE2d 761, reh den 295 NY 827, 66 NE2d 595.

§ 11:46   LANDLORD AND TENANT

In the second case[6] a twenty-one year lease provided for a fixed annual rent, with a provision that the tenant pay taxes as additional rent. The tenant was given an option to renew for two further twenty-one year terms. As to the rental for the renewal terms, the lease provided that if the parties could not agree thereon, then the annual rent was to be determined by an appraisal, but in no event was the net annual rent for the renewal term to be less than "the net annual rent reserved for the last year in the then current term." In all cases, the lease continued, the tenant under the renewal lease was to pay taxes. During the original term a modification agreement was entered into, which eliminated the tenant's obligation to pay taxes, and reduced the originally reserved net annual rental. This agreement provided that the provision for the payment of the fixed annual rent in the lease "shall be and hereby is modified so as to provide the rent at the rate of $12,000, per year during the said term instead of $25,000, per year, effective as of July 1, 1942; "otherwise the lease was to remain in full force and effect." Nothing was said about renewals. Quaere, in renewing the lease was the rental for the renewal period to be $12,000, per year, or $25,000? Was the tenant freed from paying taxes during the renewal period? (An appraisal was held which determined the rental to be $12,000.) Special Term[7] ruled that the tenant had to pay $25,000 per year, as well as the taxes during the renewal period. In other words, it held that the base rent in the original lease was unaffected by the modification agreement. The Appellate Division agreed with the reasoning of Special Term.[8] The Court of Appeals disagreed[9] and held that the renewal

6. Raleigh Associates, Inc. v Henry (1951) 302 NY 467, 99 NE2d 289, reh den 302 NY 940, 100 NE2d 191.

7. Sub nom Raleigh Associates, Inc v Jackson (S Ct NY Co 1949) 96 NYS2d 524, as supplemented by (Sup) 96 NYS2d 528, mod 277 App Div 978, 100 NYS2d 184, reh den 277 App Div 1037, 100 NYS2d 1019 and mod 302 NY 467, 99 NE2d 289, reh den 302 NY 940, 100 NE2d 191.

8. Raleigh Associates, Inc. v Henry (AD1 1950) 277 AD 978, 100 NYS2d 184, reh den 277 AD 1037, 100 NYS2d 1019 and mod 302 NY 467, 99 NE2d 289, reh den 302 NY 940, 100 NE2d 191. However, the judgment of the court below was modified because the Appellate Division felt that the tenant had sought to renew on the basis of $12,000 per year, and therefore that the tenant would not be deemed to have committed himself to a renewal at $25,000 per year. Accordingly, it was held that the option to renew was not exercised, and that the tenant would be held to be a statutory tenant.

9. Three judges dissented, among whom was Dye, J., who had written

rent was $12,000, which was the "net annual rent reserved for the last year of the then current term," and that the tenant was obligated to pay taxes during the renewal period. The parties by their modification, the court said, converted the base rent originally reserved to the lesser rent. When the renewal option came to be exercised there was to be carried forward into the new term a sum not less than the substituted rental base of $12,000, since that amount was unquestionably the fixed "annual rent reserved for the last year of the then current term." In this respect this case differed from the first case discussed. In the first case discussed the original lease had carefully specified that in no event was the renewal rent "to be fixed at a less sum than herein provided to be paid as the rent for the (lease) period ending February 1, 1945," and the modification agreement there left unaltered that basic rental. In this case, however, the base rent was effectively modified, and the lease provided that the annual rental for the renewal period was to be the "annual rent reserved for the last year of the then current term." With respect to taxes, the tenant was clearly obligated to pay them during the renewal period; for the lease specifically provided that "in all cases" the tenant was to pay them; that is, regardless of who might be paying taxes at the end of the current rental period, the tenant was under the necessity of paying them during the renewal term. If the landlord in the second case discussed had desired to assure himself of a renewal rent not less than $25,000, he could have done one of three things.[10] He could have provided in the original lease that the net annual rent would be at least $25,000 upon the first renewal; or he could have provided in the original lease, as was done in the first case discussed, that the renewal rent would in no event be fixed at a less sum than "herein provided" to be paid; or he could have signified in the modification agreement itself that the reduced rental was not to be used in measuring or determining the minimum rent for the renewal term.

the opinion for the court in the 455 Seventh Ave, Inc v Hussey case.
**10.** Per opinion of Fuld, J., in Raleigh Associates, Inc. v Henry (1951) 302 NY 467, 474, 99 NE2d 289, reh den 302 NY 940, 100 NE2d 191.

§ 11:46 LANDLORD AND TENANT

The burden of providing against later applicability of the decrease to a renewal term falls on the landlord.[11]

### § 11:47. Right to Perpetual Renewals

A provision for a renewal of a lease is exhausted by one renewal. Therefore, the renewed lease will not be deemed to contain the renewal covenant in the absence of express words evidencing clearly an intention that the renewed tenancy is also to contain a renewal provision.[12] As said by the Appellate Term,[13] "The exercise of the option (to renew) renewed all of the terms of the old lease, except that of the option itself." "Renewal clauses in a lease," said Chilvers, J.,[14] "will not be construed to mean that a renewed tenancy is also to contain a renewal provision in the absence of express words evidencing such intention clearly. If renewals are to go on ad infinitum, a species of perpetuity would be created that the courts could not countenance in the absence of express intention. A provision for renewal in a lease gives the right of one renewal, unless as otherwise expressed. A further renewal cannot be allowed by implication."[15] The intention to grant renewals in perpetuity is not shown by a general covenant to renew upon the same terms, conditions, and agreements contained in the original lease.[16]

However, where the lease clearly expresses the intention that the renewed lease shall contain a covenant for a further renewal, or renewals, such a provision for successive or perpetual renewals is not void. "Such covenants," said the Appellate Division,[17] "are lawful and in general

---

11. Charason Realty Corp v Bank of New York (AD1 1953) 282 AD 134, 121 NYS2d 621, affd 306 NY 902, 119 NE2d 595.

12. Burns v New York (1915) 213 NY 516, 108 NE 77, remittitur amd 214 NY 658, 108 NE 1090; Pflum v Spencer (AD2 1908) 123 AD 742, 108 NYS 344; Levy v Amelias (S Ct Cayuga Co 1955) 207 Misc 880, 141 NYS2d 101, affd (4th Dept) 1 AD2d 755, 148 NYS2d 921; Huber v Ruby (S Ct Nassau Co 1947) 188 Misc 1001, 69 NYS2d 760, affd 272 AD 779, 70 NYS2d 579.

**Annotation:** Sufficiency of provision of lease to effect second or perpetual right of renewal. 29 ALR4th 172.

13. Finn v Krieger Shoe Co (AT2 1915) 93 Misc 83, 156 NYS 424.

14. Brown, Wheelock, Harris, Vought & Co v One Park Ave Corp (M Ct 1929) 134 Misc 313, 235 NYS 297.

15. Also, see, Syms v New York (1887) 105 NY 153, 157, 11 NE 369; Levy v Amelias (S Ct Cayuga Co 1955) 207 Misc 880, 141 NYS2d 101, affd (4th Dept) 1 AD2d 755, 148 NYS2d 921.

16. Gleason v Tompkins (S Ct Steuben Co 1975) 84 Misc 2d 174, 375 NYS2d 247.

17. Hoff v Royal Metal Furniture Co. (AD2 1907) 117 AD 884, 103 NYS

use." Furthermore, they are not indefinite, and are therefore enforceable.[18]

The renewal clause construed by the court in Burns v New York,[19] presents an excellent illustration of a provision for perpetual renewals. The renewal clause there provided that the landlord would "at the expiration of the term hereby demised, again demise and to farm let the above premises in pursuance of this present lease unto the said John Dixey, his executors, administrators or assigns for and during the term of twenty-one years thereafter, with a like covenant for future renewals of the lease as is contained in this present indenture, and upon such rents and other terms and conditions as shall be agreed upon between the parties, or as shall be determined by two sworn appraisers. . . ." "But one question of law," said Chase, J., "is presented on this appeal and that is involved in the construction of that part of the lease quoted relating to the renewals thereof. Was it the intention of the parties to the lease to provide for perpetual renewals? Covenants by a landlord for continued renewals are not favored for they tend to create a perpetuity. When they are explicit the more established weight of authority is in favor of their validity. . . . Reading the provisions of the leases in question in the light of the settled law upon the subject of the construction of covenants for renewal, it is difficult to avoid the conclusion that the parties to the original lease in preparing the same had the established rule of law in mind and intended to bind the city to grant future renewals in perpetuity. Such intention is not left to conjecture or to be implied. It is clearly and specifically provided by the lease that it shall run for a term of twenty-one years and that at the expiration of the term it will be renewed 'with a like covenant for future renewals of the lease as is

371, affd 189 NY 555, 82 NE 1128, later app 127 AD 440, 111 NYS 541, affd 194 NY 545, 87 NE 1129.

**18.** Van Beuren & New York Bill Post Co. v Sarah S. Kenney & C. J. Sullivan Advertising Co. (S Ct NY Co 1908) 60 Misc 338, 113 NYS 450.

De Santis v Kessler (1981, 4th Dept) 83 AD2d 766, 443 NYS2d 485 (provisions in lease granting tenant option each year after initial 5-year period of renewing lease, and option of purchasing leased premises in event they were for sale at any terminal date of lease, gave tenant option to renew lease yearly so long as landlord remained owner of premises).

**19.** (1915) 213 NY 516, 108 NE 77, remittitur amd 214 NY 658, 108 NE 1090.

§ 11:47  LANDLORD AND TENANT

contained in this present indenture.' As the language in regard to future renewals is clear, it should be enforced. . . . The intention to grant renewals in perpetuity is not shown by a general covenant to renew upon the same covenants, conditions and agreements as contained in the original lease. There must be some language in the covenant which shows an intention to include in the renewal leases a particular covenant in regard to future renewals (cases cited). The lease under consideration expressly provides that the renewal leases shall contain a covenant in regard to renewals the same as in the original lease. This agreement the parties are entitled to have carried out."

A covenant providing that the tenant shall have "the privilege of renewing this lease from year to year upon notice to that effect in writing, given on or before the day of the date of the expiration of each and every year," was also held to provide for perpetual renewals.[20] In these cases the parties clearly expressed their intention to provide for successive renewals, and therefore the covenant to renew contained in the original lease was not exhausted by the first renewal.

### § 11:48. Form of Provision for Perpetual Renewals

#### FORM NO. 17

#### Covenant to Renew with Provision for Perpetual Renewals

If Tenant shall have fully performed on its part all of the terms, covenants, and conditions of this lease, Landlord shall grant to Tenant a renewal of this lease for a further period of five years from the expiration of the term of this lease, upon the same terms, covenants, and conditions of this lease with a like covenant for future renewals of this lease as is contained herein, provided Tenant shall have notified Landlord by certified mail at Landlord's address hereinabove set forth on or before ........, 19..., of Tenant's election to renew *(add if desired:* provided, however, that this renewal option shall

---

20. Hoff v Royal Metal Furniture Co. (AD2 1907) 117 AD 884, 103 NYS 371, affd 189 NY 555, 82 NE 1128, later app 127 AD 440, 111 NYS 541, affd 194 NY 545, 87 NE 1129. Also, see, Van Beuren & New York Bill Post Co. v Sarah S. Kenney & C. J. Sullivan Advertising Co. (S Ct NY Co 1908) 60 Misc 338, 113 NYS 450.

RENEWAL OF LEASES § 11:50

be inoperative in the event Landlord shall sell the building in which the leased premises are situated at or prior to the expiration of this lease).*

* For complete form of lease see Chapter 1.

### § 11:49. Effect of Emergency Rent Laws

Emergency rent laws generally establish a maximum rent, the payment of which entitles a tenant to remain in possession even though the term of his lease may have expired. Although rents may be frozen to a statutory maximum, it has been held that renewal covenants contained in leases made prior to the enactment of the emergency statutes, providing for a rental during the renewal period which may be higher than the statutory maximum, is nevertheless enforceable in so far as the tenant has a right to exercise the privilege of renewal. But, while the rent control statutes do no abrogate the right of the tenant to exercise his option to renew, the landlord may not demand during the renewal period a rent in excess of the emergency rent or seek a reasonable rent in excess of the amount agreed in the lease.[1] However, it has been suggested that if during the renewed term the emergency rent statutes are repealed or expire, then the tenant from the repeal or expiration date will have to pay the rent as reserved in the renewal option.[2]

### § 11:50. Nature and Effect of Renewed Lease

The tenant's exercise of an option to renew his lease does not create a new lease, but simply prolongs the original lease for a further period. Once the option is exercised, the original lease is deemed to be one for the entire term.[3] It is as if the original lease had contained a term for the renewal period as well as the original term, and the parties hold, not under any contract by virtue of the renewal, but by virtue of the original lease.[4]

1. United States Trust Co. v Nedab Holding Corp. (S Ct NY Co 1949) 197 Misc 310, 93 NYS2d 376, affd 277 AD 853, 98 NYS2d 196; Plessdore Realty Corp. v Fasano (S Ct Queens Co 1947) 188 Misc 975, 69 NYS2d 435; Warfield v Belanca Robe Corp. (M Ct 1946) 186 Misc 910, 64 NYS2d 66, affd 187 Misc 731, 68 NYS2d 87, affd 271 AD 781, 66 NYS2d 407.

2. Lewittes & Sons v Spielmann (AT1 1947) 190 Misc 35, 73 NYS2d 552.

3. Harvey Holding Corp. v Satter (1947) 297 NY 113, 75 NE2d 619.

4. Atkin's Waste Materials, Inc. v May (1974) 34 NY2d 422, 358 NYS2d 129, 314 NE2d 871; Orr v Doubleday, Page & Co. (1918) 223 NY 334, 119 NE 552, 1 ALR 338, reh den 223 NY

### § 11:51. —Illustrative Cases

The importance of the rule that a renewed tenancy pursuant to an option to renew is merely a prolongation, or continuation of the lease, and not a new term separate from the term which preceded it, may be illustrated by the following cases.[5]

In a case that went to the Court of Appeals,[6] the lease gave the tenant an option to renew, and also an option to purchase the premises for a stipulated sum "at any time during the term and existence of the lease." The tenant exercised his right to renew the lease. During the renewal period the tenant sought to exercise the option to purchase. The landlord disputed this right; because, he contended, the lease had expired, and therefore the option to purchase was not being exercised during "the term and existence of the lease." This contention was overruled. When the tenant exercised his right to renew the lease, the court pointed out, he thereupon extended the term as a present lease for a term measured by the original as well as the renewal period. Since the option to purchase "could be exercised at any time during the term and existence of the lease," the tenant could avail himself of this option at any time during the renewal period.

In a more recent case[7] the lease provided for a term of five years commencing June 1, 1925, with an option on the part of the tenant to renew for another five years at a stipulated rental "plus any increase in the local taxes which may occur during the term of the lease." It was held that the tenant, who had renewed the lease, was liable for the payment of the increase in the taxes for the year 1930 over the amount of the taxes for the year 1925. The tenant urged that the original lease had expired, and therefore that he was liable only for the excess taxes which might accrue in subsequent years over the amount

---

700, 119 NE 1064; Swan v Inderlied (1907) 187 NY 372, 80 NE 195; New York Business Bldgs. Corp. v James McCutcheon & Co. (AD1 1930) 229 AD 681, 243 NYS 255, affd 257 NY 554, 178 NE 792; Sun Rock Bldg. Corp. v Abrams (S Ct Nassau Co 1963) 38 Misc 2d 192, 238 NYS2d 143; Horn & Hardart Co. v 115 East 14th Street Co. (S Ct NY Co 1938) 7 NYS2d 688, affd 257 AD 813, 12 NYS2d 784, affd 281 NY 802, 24 NE2d 482.

5. Also, see § 11:33, supra for another illustration of the importance of the principle discussed in the text relating to the nature of a renewed lease.

6. Masset v Ruh (1923) 235 NY 462, 139 NE 574.

7. Bribitzer v Wahlig (AD2 1932) 235 AD 702, 256 NYS 45.

of the taxes for the year 1930, the commencement of the new term. However, the court overruled the tenant's contention, and held that since "the lease as renewed must be construed as containing a single term," therefore, the increase must be measured from the beginning of the term; to wit, 1925.

In Jones & Brindisi, Inc. v Breslaw[8] the lease in question provided for a term of two years and four months with the following renewal clause: "It is further understood and agreed by and between the parties hereto that six (6) months before the termination of the present lease, the Landlord will give the tenant the option of renewing present lease for two (2) years upon the same terms and conditions and at the same rental." Below the tenant's signature on the lease appeared the following:

We hereby guarantee the payment of the rent as stipulated in the above lease.
Bernstein & Kaplan
by L. Kaplan.

The tenant exercised the option to renew. During the renewal period he vacated from the premises. The landlord thereupon sued the tenant for rent, recovered judgment, but failed to collect thereon. He then sued the guarantors. They disclaimed liability on the ground that their guaranty only extended and applied to the first two years and four months, and not to the next two years. However the court ruled in favor of the landlord, and said, in an opinion written by Crane, J., "The rent stipulated in the above lease was for four years and two months if the tenants exercised the privilege of extension. They exercised the option and became bound to pay the rent stipulated in the lease. There was no new lease; none was required; all the stipulations and agreements were contained in the one instrument, which by the election of the tenant continued for four years and two months. . . ." The guarantors knew what a renewal clause in a lease meant, continued the opinion. "Had they intended merely to be bound by a term of two years and four months or any other period less than the full term, the contract of guaranty would have so stated. It is evident

---

8. (1928) 250 NY 147, 164 NE 887.

§ 11:51          LANDLORD AND TENANT

they had nothing of this kind in mind." Therefore, the court held, the guarantors having guaranteed "the payment of the rent as stipulated in the above lease," they were clearly liable for the rent for the renewal period.

### § 11:52. Tenant-Assignor's Liability Under Renewal Lease

Where a tenant assigns his lease which contains a privilege of renewal, and the assignee exercises the privilege and renews the lease, the tenant-assignor remains liable for breaches of the lease committed by the assignee during the renewed term.[9]

As has been seen,[10] when a tenant assigns his lease he destroys the privity of estate existing between him and his landlord, but not the privity of contract. Therefore, the tenant-assignor continues to be liable, notwithstanding the assignment, for his breaches of the lease committed by him before the assignment, as well as for all breaches of the lease, committed after the assignment by his immediate, or even by any subsequent assignee of the lease. When the assigned lease is renewed by the option contained therein, the effect is as if the original lease had contained a term for the renewal period as well as the original term. After the renewal there is no new lease, but merely the original lease prolonged for the renewed period. Therefore, the tenant-assignor is still liable on the lease as renewed even though out of possession.

The tenant-assignor could have protected himself against the happening of this event, said the Appellate Division,[11] by reserving to himself, or by not assigning to his assignee, the right to renew the lease. But failing to do this, he will be held liable during the renewal period as if he were personally in possession. As Daly, J.,[12] said, "An assignment of the lease, or of the whole term, passes with it all covenants that run with the land, including covenants of renewal. . . . There must be, therefore, express reservation to prevent every right and interest of the lessee passing under such an assignment."

9. New York Business Bldgs. Corp. v James McCutcheon & Co. (AD1 1930) 229 AD 681, 243 NYS 255, affd 257 NY 554, 178 NE 792.
10. § 9:20, supra.
11. New York Business Bldgs. Corp. v James McCutcheon & Co. (AD1 1930) 229 AD 681, 243 NYS 255, affd 257 NY 554, 178 NE 792.
12. Downing v Jones (Com P1 NY GT 1882) 11 Daly 245.

Therefore, it must be emphasized, when a tenant has a renewal covenant in his lease, he must remember that when he assigns the lease, he will remain liable during the renewed period for all breaches of the lease committed by his assignee, or by a subsequent assignee, who may exercise the option to renew. Failing to get a release from his landlord,[13] he must, then, upon assignment expressly reserve to himself the right to renew the lease, or he must expressly exclude the renewal covenant from the assignment.

## G. AUTOMATIC RENEWALS

### § 11:53. Form of Automatic Renewal Clause

### FORM NO. 18

#### Automatic Renewal Clause*

At the expiration of the term specified in this lease, such term shall be extended and renewed by and against the parties hereto for the further term of one year from the expiration of the term granted hereby, at the same rental without any deduction or concession, and upon all the above terms, conditions, and covenants, unless either party on or before the first day of ........ next preceding the termination of any term granted hereby, shall give notice to the other of an intention to surrender or have possession of the premises as the case may be. Notice by either party to the other must be given by sending the same by U. S. Certified mail.[14]

[Add if so desired: This clause shall be and continue operative likewise with respect to any renewals or extensions of this lease.] Such clauses are valid, and are enforceable.[15] In effect they provide that the failure to give the specified notice automatically will renew the lease for the new period agreed upon.

However, an automatic renewal clause in a lease is

---

13. § 9:22, supra.
14. Adapted from the lease discussed in Simon Ginsberg Realty Co v Greenstein (AT1 1936) 158 Misc 473, 286 NYS 33.

15. J. H. Holding Co. v Wooten (1943) 291 NY 427, 52 NE2d 934; Manhattan Realty Appraisers v Marchbank (AT1 1914) 87 Misc 336, 149 NYS 834.

* For complete form of lease see Chapter 1.

inoperative during a period controlled by emergency rent legislation.[16]

### § 11:54. Statutory Protection of Tenants Against Automatic Renewal Clauses

Many harsh results ensued from the inadvertent failure of the tenant to give the requisite notice under automatic renewal clauses, and as a result, in 1934, a new section was added to the Real Property Law,[17] to take effect September 1, 1935, and which has been transferred to the General Obligations Law, without change.[18]

This statute provides:

No provision of a lease of any real property or premises which states that the term thereof shall be deemed renewed for a specified additional period of time unless the tenant gives notice to the lessor of his intention to quit the premises at the expiration of such term shall be operative unless the lessor, at least fifteen days and not more than thirty days previous to the time specified for the furnishing of such notice to him, shall give to the tenant written notice, served personally or by registered or certified mail, calling the attention of the tenant to the existence of such provision in the lease.

"This statute," it has been said, "was designed to prevent the existing practice of incorporating automatic renewal clauses in leases, a practice deemed iniquitous, in consequence of which tenants found themselves bound for an extended term solely through their omission or forgetfulness to notify their landlords several months anterior to the expiration of the lease, of their intention not to renew. This provision was, indubitably, a trap for the unwary or forgetful tenant, and was deliberately inserted in the lease by the landlord for that very purpose. This provision led to much protest and bitter complaint that thereby the landlord took an unfair and unconscionable advantage of the tenant, and to remedy this condition,

---

**16.** Park View Gardens, Inc. v Greene (AD2 1949) 274 AD 1062, 85 NYS2d 396; Doniday Estates, Inc. v Fox (1954, Sup App T) 134 NYS2d 633; Harkap Realty Corp. v Poler (AT2 1950) 198 Misc 473, 102 NYS2d 41.

**17.** Former Real Prop L § 230, added L 1934 c 576, am L 1936 c 702. The original Real Prop L § 230 was repealed by L 1920 c 138.

**18.** General Oblig L § 5-905.

the Legislature, by the enactment of the statute in question, made it the affirmative duty of the landlord, if he contemplated and intended to avail himself of such automatic renewal clause, to specifically call the tenant's attention to its existence in the lease, so that the tenant would be fully apprised thereof, and, forewarned with such notice and knowledge, govern himself accordingly. The burden, the obligation, the duty to give such notice are cast exclusively upon the landlord. Nowhere in the statute is the tenant required to do or perform any act under it in order to receive the benefit of its provisions."[19]

It must be noted, however, that the statute in no way destroys the contractual rights of the parties to agree upon automatic renewal convenants. Their rights to do so remain unimpaired. The statute merely imposes upon the landlord a condition with which he must comply before he may proceed to invoke this particular provision of the lease. That is, he must warn the tenant at the appropriate time that such a clause exists. Then the tenant must give notice of intention to surrender if he does not wish to have the lease automatically renew itself.

### § 11:55. —Effect of Non-compliance with Statute

The statute relating to automatic renewal clauses in leases[20] was enacted solely for the protection of the tenant, and only affects the lease insofar as it provides for automatic renewal "unless the tenant gives notice to the lessor of his intention to quit the premises at the expiration of such term." Only this provision is affected by the statute, the purpose of the statutory notice being simply to warn the tenant that if notice of intention "to surrender" is not given, the term will be renewed. By refraining from giving the statutory notice a landlord is not excused from complying with the provision of the lease that unless it gives notice or intention to have possession, the tenant will be entitled to remain in possession for another term, as expressly provided in the renewal clause.[1]

Accordingly, the operation of an automatic renewal clause may be defeated either by a notice from the

19. Simon Ginsberg Realty Co v Greenstein (M Ct Man 1935) 157 Misc 148, 283 NYS 100, affd 158 Misc 473, 286 NYS 33.

20. Gen Obligations L § 5-905; see § 11:54, supra.

1. J H Holding Co v Wooten (1943) 291 NY 427, 52 NE2d 934.

§ 11:55            LANDLORD AND TENANT

landlord that he desires to have possession of the premises, or by a notice from the tenant that he desires to surrender possession. The only effect of the statute is that if a landlord wishes to renew the lease, he must first give the statutory warning to the tenant of the existence of the clause. Then, if the tenant fails to give the landlord notice of his intention to surrender the premises, the lease will automatically renew itself.

However, if the landlord does not serve the statutory warning, and also fails to serve the tenant with a notice that the landlord desires possession, then the tenant has the sole option of deciding whether or not to renew the lease. In such case if the tenant wishes to renew, he need do nothing but continue in possession. If he wishes not to renew, all he need do is serve notice of his intention to surrender. The landlord, by failing to serve both the statutory warning and the notice of termination, places himself in the position of abiding by the tenant's choice of what he wishes to do.[2]

It must be observed that the tenant is under no duty to serve upon the landlord any warning or notice of the existence of the automatic renewal clause. This duty rests on the landlord only.

### § 11:56. —Waiver of Statutory Protection

The statute governing automatic renewal clauses was designed to protect tenants.[3] A waiver of this statutory protection has been held to be void as against public policy.[4]

## H. REMEDIES FOR BREACH OF COVENANT TO RENEW

### § 11:57. Damages Recoverable

A tenant may recover damages from his landlord for the landlord's breach of covenant to renew the lease.[5] Similarly, if a landlord is given the option to renew the

---

2. Green v Goldberg (NYC Civ Ct 1962) 37 Misc 2d 192, 234 NYS2d 441.

3. J. H. Holding Co. v Wooten (1943) 291 NY 427, 52 NE2d 934; Boyd H. Wood Co. v Horgan (1943) 291 NY 422, 52 NE2d 932, 152 ALR 1392.

4. Boyd H Wood Co v Horgan (1943) 291 NY 422, 52 NE2d 932, 152 ALR 1392.

5. Tracy v Albany Exchange Co (1852) 7 NY 472.

# RENEWAL OF LEASES § 11:58

lease, he may, where the tenant refuses to accept a renewal, maintain an action for damages.[6]

### § 11:58. —Measure of Damages

Generally, the measure of damages for breach of a covenant to renew is the value of the leasehold for the renewal period less the rent reserved at the time of the breach.[7] However, the tenant's damages may be measured differently, depending on the circumstances. Where a landlord in violation of the renewal covenant refuses to grant a renewal unless the tenant signs a new lease at an increased rental, and the tenant complies; the general measure of damages will not be applied. Nor, will the tenant waive his right to recover damages by acquiescing in the landlord's wrongful demands in order to save himself from losing possession. As was said by the Court of Appeals in an early case,[8] "The plaintiff (tenant) was not restricted to the time when the term granted by the lease expired, to make his election for a renewal for the further term; and if made, and a renewal demanded, the defendant was bound to comply with his covenant in that respect. The plaintiff, in February 1849, made his election and demanded a performance; the defendant refused, unless he would consent to take a renewal at an enhanced rent, and gave him notice that unless he would do so, the defendant would rent the premises to another; this, I think, constituted a breach of the covenant by the defendant. The taking of the lease by the plaintiff for a different term, under the circumstances, could not operate as a surrender of the first, or as a performance of the covenant by the defendant. The term of this second lease did not commence until the expiration of the first; and besides, the evidence shows that it was not intended by the plaintiff to relinquish or surrender, or by the parties that it should be accepted as a performance of the covenant, and that should be regarded as decisive of the question. . . . The measure of damages was correct. It was confined to the difference between what the plaintiff

---

**6.** Ryder v Jenny (GT 1864) 25 NY Super Ct 56.

**7.** Neiderstein v Cusick (AD2 1908) 126 AD 409, 110 NYS 287, affd 195 NY 594, 89 NE 1106.

**8.** Tracy v Albany Exchange Co (1852) 7 NY 472, 474.

was to have paid for the rent for the term, and what he was compelled to pay under the new lease."

### § 11:59. Specific Performance

A tenant is not restricted to an action at law to recover damages for a breach by the landlord of his agreement to renew a lease. He may sue in equity for specific performance of the renewal covenant, where he has acted on faith of the renewal covenant, and placed himself in such position that he cannot be adequately compensated except by a renewal of the lease.[9]

Where a lessee has duly exercised his right to renew his lease, it has been held that the lessor may be enjoined from leasing the premises to someone else.[10]

### § 11:60. Action for Declaratory Judgment

Where the right to a renewal is in dispute, in order to determine in advance of the expiration of a lease the respective rights and obligations of the landlord and the tenant under a renewal covenant, an action under CPLR 3001 for a declaratory judgment, will lie, and should be instituted.[11]

## I. RESEARCH REFERENCES

### § 11:61. Generally

In addition to the preceding text, the reader is also referred to the following:

50 Am Jur 2d, Landlord and Tenant §§ 1154-1204.

11 Am Jur Legal Forms 2d, Leases of Real Property §§ 161:721-161:748.

New York Jur 2d, Landlord and Tenant (1st ed §§ 414-435)

---

[9.] Robinson v Beard (1893) 140 NY 107, 35 NE 441; Loughman v Lilliendahl (AD1 1921) 195 AD 867, 187 NYS 401; Horn & Hardart Co. v 115 East 14th Street Co. (S Ct NY Co 1938) 7 NYS2d 688, affd 257 AD 813, 12 NYS2d 784, affd 281 NY 802, 24 NE2d 482.

[10.] Van Beuren & New York Bill Post Co. v Sarah S. Kenney & C. J. Sullivan Advertising Co. (S Ct NY Co 1908) 60 Misc 338, 113 NYS 450.

[11.] Leibowitz v Bickford's Lunch System (1926) 241 NY 489, 150 NE 525; Morlee Sales Corp. v Manufacturers Trust Co. (S Ct Kings Co 1959) 16 Misc 2d 599, 185 NYS2d 679, affd (2d Dept) 11 AD2d 796, 205 NYS2d 979, but revd on other grounds 9 NY2d 16, 210 NYS2d 516, 172 NE2d 280; Fidelity & Columbia Trust Co. v Levin (S Ct Erie Co 1927) 128 Misc 838, 221 NYS 269, affd 221 AD 786, 223 NYS 866, affd 248 NY 551, 162 NE 521.

# RENEWAL OF LEASES § 11:61

New York CLS Real Property Law § 226.

New York Forms, Leases, Forms 8:231-8:234.

Index to Annotations, Landlord and Tenant.

**VERALEX®:** Cases and annotations referred to herein can be further researched through the VERALEX electronic retrieval system's two services, **Auto-Cite®** and **SHOWME®**. Use Auto-Cite to check citations for form, parallel references, prior and later history, and annotation references. Use SHOWME to display the full text of cases and annotations.

# CHAPTER 12
# RENT

A. IN GENERAL
- § 12:1. Nature and Definition
- § 12:2. Distinguished from Other Payments to be Made by Tenant
- § 12:3. When Other Payments to be Made by Tenant Constitute Rent
- § 12:4. Cost of Repairs as Rent
- § 12:5. Mortgage Interest and Taxes as Rent
- § 12:6. Attorney's Fees as Rent
- § 12:7. Attorney's Fees as Rent; Mobile Homes
- § 12:8. Forms of Clauses Making Other Payments Rent
- § 12:9. Importance of Ascertaining when Other Payments to be Made by Tenant Constitute Rent
- § 12:10. Express Covenant to Pay Rent
- § 12:11. Interest on Rent
- § 12:12. Implied Agreement to Pay Rent
- § 12:13. Percentage Rentals
- § 12:14. When Percentage Rent Payable
- § 12:15. Tenant's Obligation Under a Percentage Rental Provision
- § 12:16. Executory Modification of Rent
- § 12:17. Executed Modification of Rent

B. PAYMENT OF RENT
- § 12:18. To Whom Payable
- § 12:19. Duty of Landlord to Provide Written Receipt
- § 12:20. When and Where Payable
- § 12:21. —Sunday or Public Holiday
- § 12:22. Application of Rent Payments
- § 12:23. When Payable in Advance
- § 12:24. —Form
- § 12:25. Course of Conduct Establishing Mode of Payment
- § 12:26. Provision for Acceleration
- § 12:27. —Form
- § 12:28. Recovery by Tenant of Rent Paid
- § 12:29. Separate Actions for Installments
- § 12:30. Liability for Rent upon Death of Tenant

C. RESEARCH REFERENCES
- § 12:31. Generally

## A. IN GENERAL

### § 12:1. Nature and Definition[1]

Although the reservation of rent is not essential to the relationship of landlord and tenant,[2] it is a normal incident of the relationship. It is one of the classic indicia of the relationship, although not conclusive.[3]

Rent is the compensation to be paid by a tenant for the use and occupation of land, or for the right thereto,[4] and as such, comes only from the land leased, and only out of the relationship of landlord and tenant.[5] It is the return made by the tenant for the land which he occupies.[6]

### § 12:2. Distinguished from Other Payments to be Made by Tenant

Upon first impression it might seem that rent should be regarded as the entire consideration which a tenant pays to a landlord for the use of the leased premises, whether directly as rent proper, or indirectly and for his benefit in the form of taxes, assessments, insurance, and the like. But the word "rent" must be interpreted in the light of its context, and means something different from "insurance premiums," "taxes," "repairs," "removal of snow and ice," and the like, which the tenant may also covenant to do or pay under the terms of a lease.[7] As was said in an early case,[8] "It is said that the payment of taxes is part of the return made by the defendant to his landlord

---

1. As to rights on transfer of reversion to rent due or to become due, see § 5:18, supra.
2. Pfalzgraf v Voso (S Ct Kings Co 1945) 184 Misc 575, 55 NYS2d 171.
3. Coffman v Gale (AD3 1936) 248 AD 25, 289 NYS 713.
4. Munro v Syracuse, L. & N. R. Co. (1910) 200 NY 224, 93 NE 516; Andrus v Lehigh V. R. Co. (AD2 1924) 209 AD 368, 204 NYS 810.
"Rent" implies a fixed sum to be paid at certain times for the use of property. 140 West 69th Street Corp. v Simis (M Ct 1945) 186 Misc 342, 61 NYS2d 548.
5. Jacob Ruppert Realty Corp. v Bank of United States (S Ct NY Co 1935) 156 Misc 93, 281 NYS 761, affd 249 AD 721, 292 NYS 997, affd 276 NY 629, 12 NE2d 611.
6. Gasoff Realty Corp. v Berger (AT1 1947) 188 Misc 622, 69 NYS2d 46.

Penal L § 180.55 provides that a person is guilty of rent gouging when, in connection with the leasing, rental or use of real property, he solicits, accepts or agrees to accept from a person some consideration of value, in addition to lawful rental and other lawful charges, upon an agreement or understanding that the furnishing of such consideration will increase the possibility that some person may obtain the lease, rental or use of such property, or that a failure to furnish it will decrease the possibility that some person may obtain the same. (Rent gouging is a class B misdemeanor.)

7. Arcangel v Holling (AD4 1939) 258 AD 180, 15 NYS2d 975, reh and app den 258 AD 1031, 16 NYS2d 954; Bixby v Casino Co. (GT 1895) 14 Misc 346, 35 NYS 677.
8. Garner v Hannah (Com Pl GT 1857) 13 NY Super Ct 262.

for the use of the property, and, therefore, properly comes under the definition of rent. But in one sense the performance of every covenant on the part of the lessee is a return made by the tenant for the use of the land. Yet it would hardly be contended that money stipulated to be expended in repairs or for insurance, or in the way of improvements, was any portion of the rent. Taxes, being payable annually, approach, it is true, to the idea and character of rent, which is a certain yearly return reserved to the landlord in money, or kind, or service for the enjoyment of the freehold; but they are distinguishable from rent in this, that they are uncertain both as to amount and time of payment, and are payable not to the landlord but to the government, and are imposed for the benefit of the public, and the landlord may, by the terms of his agreement with the tenant, be relieved from their payment; taxes are not, on that account, any more rent than the expenditure of money for insurance, under a covenant to that effect on the part of the lessee." Therefore, when a lease provides that a tenant shall pay taxes, insurance, the cost of repairs, and other payments of a similar nature, such payments do not constitute rent.

### § 12:3. When Other Payments to be Made by Tenant Constitute Rent

"Rent is a term," said Watson, J.,[9] "which is peculiarly applicable to income to be derived only from real estate, and is a certain profit issuing out of lands or tenements. Whether all payments which a tenant is bound to make under the terms of a lease are a part of the rent depends upon the contract of the parties, which is the lease." Therefore, when additional payments are covenanted to be made by a tenant under a lease, such as taxes, assessments, the cost of repairs, insurance premiums, and the like, such payments will constitute rent only if the parties so agree. The term "rent" will not be deemed to include any other payments which the tenant has covenanted to make, unless the parties expressly provide that such other payments shall constitute rent.[1]

9. 140 West 69th Street Corp. v Simis (M Ct 1945) 186 Misc 342, 61 NYS2d 548.

1. Petrakakis v Crown Hotels, Inc. (1956, 3d Dept) 3 AD2d 635, 158 NYS2d 15; Charles F. Noyes Co. v Standard Industries, Inc. (AT1 1976) 85 Misc 2d 853, 381 NYS2d 185;

If the parties intend, and they express such intention clearly, that the amount of the other payments to be made by the tenant under the terms of his lease shall be part of the rent for the use of the leased premises, and, as such, added, when liquidated, to the constant, liquidated rent originally reserved, then such other payments will be treated as rent, and will be enforceable as such;[2] for, a lease may provide for payment of rent in any manner or at any time that the parties elect.[3]

### § 12:4. Cost of Repairs as Rent

Where parties to a lease agreed that the cost of repairs made by a landlord, on the tenant's default so to do, should be added to the stipulated monthly rent, "and same should be and constitute rent together with rent hereinabove provided for," such cost of repairs was held to be rent, and enforceable as such. As the Appellate Term pointed out, additional payments are rent when the parties expressly agree that the landlord can enforce payment thereof as part of the rent reserved by the lease.[4]

### § 12:5. Mortgage Interest and Taxes as Rent

Where a lease provided for rent "at the yearly rent or sum as follows: the payment of the fixed sum of $2600, and in addition the interest on the first mortgage on said property for the sum of $100,000; together with taxes, water rates, and assessments against the said property, to be paid semiannually or as said obligations may accrue . . . and the said parties of the second part do covenant to pay unto the said party of the first part the said yearly rent as herein specified." Here, the court said, the parties had expressly reserved the payment of other items as rent. Therefore the landlord could enforce payment thereof as rent.[5]

Knepper v Rothbaum (AT1 1918) 104 Misc 554, 172 NYS 109; Mulligan v Kraus (AT1 1915) 88 Misc 538, 151 NYS 401; Cochran v Reich (AT1 1897) 20 Misc 623, 46 NYS 443.

2. Knepper v Rothbaum (AT1 1918) 104 Misc 554, 172 NYS 109; Mulligan v Kraus (AT1 1915) 88 Misc 538, 151 NYS 401.

3. 34 West 34th Street Corp. v Nehama Realty Corp. (S Ct NY Co 1956) 7 Misc 2d 532, 153 NYS2d 427.

4. Knepper v Rothbaum (AT1 1918) 104 Misc 554, 172 NYS 109.

5. Mulligan v Kraus (AT1 1915) 88 Misc 538, 151 NYS 401.

## § 12:6. Attorney's Fees as Rent

A covenant by a tenant to reimburse his landlord for attorney's fees expended in connection with proceedings either to compel compliance by the tenant of his obligations, or to recover damages resulting from non-compliance, is not contrary to public policy, is not per se unconscionable,[6] and is enforceable.[7]

Absent a statute or a provision in a lease for attorneys' fees, neither landlord nor tenant has a right to attorneys' fees.[8] A covenant providing that if by reason of tenant's default the landlord pays, or does any act which requires the payment of money, such sums so paid or required to be paid shall be deemed to be and shall constitute rent, and be collectible as if originally reserved as rent, will not include attorney's fees. To include attorneys' fees in such a provision, attorneys' fees must be expressly named as included.[9]

---

6. See § 6:13, supra.

7. Trump Village Section 3, Inc. v Moore (1981, 2d Dept) 84 AD2d 812, 444 NYS2d 134; 379 Madison Ave. v Stuyvesant Co. (AD1 1934) 242 AD 567, 275 NYS 953, affd 268 NY 576, 198 NE 412.

Attorney's fees were denied landlord in a nonpayment proceeding despite lease provision therefor, where tenant had been represented by legal aid society. Republic Co. v Medina (Dist Ct Nassau Co 1973) 75 Misc 2d 279, 347 NYS2d 785. But in Fairhaven Apartments v James (Dist Ct Nassau Co 1974) 79 Misc 2d 569, 360 NYS2d 389, and McClelland-Metz Mgt., Inc. v Faulk (Dist Ct Nassau Co 1976) 86 Misc 2d 778, 384 NYS2d 919, it was held that the mere fact that a tenant receives welfare is not sufficient to negate, cancel out, or cause to be null and void a written provision in a lease requiring the tenant to pay attorneys' fees because of the tenant's default, and this notwithstanding the fact that the tenant is indigent, and must look to the County for the meeting of his obligations.

Where the premises are subject to the Residential Rent Control Law, a landlord may not collect expenses and attorneys' fees in a nonpayment proceeding, notwithstanding landlord's designation of same as additional rent, since to this would subvert the public policy of this law. Perry Gault Management Co. v Perhaes (NYC Civ Ct NY Co 1972) 71 Misc 2d 162, 335 NYS2d 744.

8. Enright v Mintz (NYC Civ Ct NY Co 1982) 116 Misc 2d 1084, 457 NYS2d 180.

9. Cuyler Realty Co. v Teneo Co. (AD1 1921) 196 AD 440, 188 NYS 340, reh den 197 AD 934, 188 NYS 917 and affd 233 NY 647, 135 NE 954.

If the parties expressly include attorney's fees in the tenant's covenant for reimbursement as rent, liability will be imposed on a tenant for the payment of the attorney's fees incurred as a result of tenant's breach of covenant to surrender possession at the expiration of his term. 207-17 West 25th Street Co. v Blu-Strike Safety Razor Blade Co. (1951) 320 NY 624, 97 NE2d 356; Airways Supermarkets, Inc. v Santone (1951, Sup) 107 NYS2d 187, affd 280 AD 924, 116 NYS2d 128. Printerion Realty Corp. v Mancini (S Ct NY Co 1945) 61 NYS2d 200, holding contra, must be deemed to be no longer a valid precedent.

See 105 Franklin Street Corp. v Seratoff (AD1 1954) 284 AD 262, 131 NYS2d 257, affd 308 NY 1025, 127 NE2d 865, which held that a tenant

§ 12:6                                  LANDLORD AND TENANT

Attorneys' fees incurred in a proceeding to collect attorneys' fees are not recoverable.[10]

The obligation to pay attorneys' fees being made an additional rent obligation, it can only be recovered in the same action or proceeding in which the claim for rent for the applicable period results in judgment on the merits. The claim for attorneys' fees is interrelated with the claim for a breach of the lease provision and constitutes one single cause of action.[11] Such claim for attorneys' fees, therefore, cannot be asserted in subsequent litigation, because to do so would be an improper splitting of a cause of action.[12]

With respect to residential property in the state of New

was not in "default," and therefore not liable for attorney's fees, when he resisted in court and in good faith a proceeding by landlord seeking possession of premises for his own immediate use, under the emergency rent control laws, even though the court ultimately upheld the landlord.

Under lease provision requiring tenant to indemnify landlord for reasonable attorneys' fees incurred as a result of any breach of covenant or condition of the lease, or any negligence or any improper conduct on part of tenant, the "improper conduct" must relate to tenant's conduct as tenant, so that landlord was not entitled to attorneys' fees incurred to defend a derivative stockholders' action brought by tenant against landlord. Paliotto v Tensor Corp. (1976, 2d Dept) 54 AD2d 709, 387 NYS2d 454.

Attorneys' fees incurred by landlord in defending action brought by tenant against him for a declaratory judgment may not be recovered under provision in lease that if tenant shall default in the performance of the lease, landlord may perform in tenant's place, and may recover any expenditures, including attorneys' fees, incurred in connection therewith. Landlord's attorneys' fees were not incurred in connection with performing an obligation for the account of the tenant. Frank B. Hall & Co. v Orient Overseas Associates (1982, 1st Dept) 84 AD2d 338, 446 NYS2d 59, affd 56 NY2d 965, 453 NYS2d 680, 439 NE2d 395.

Attorneys' fees may not be awarded to the landlord in connection with his success at an administrative hearing. East 55th St. Joint Venture v Litchman (NYC Civ Ct NY Co 1983) 122 Misc 2d 81, 469 NYS2d 1013, affd 126 Misc 2d 1049, 487 NYS2d 256.

Provision for reimbursement of landlord's attorneys' fees based on tenant's default does not apply to defense of action based on landlord's refusal to pay over proceeds from sale of tenant's property. Sayers v 510 Park Ave. Corp. (1975, 1st Dept) 49 AD2d 818, 373 NYS2d 150 (sale of condominium).

See § 12:8, infra, for illustrative forms.

10. Zauderer v Barcellona (NYC Civ Ct NY Co 1985) 130 Misc 2d 234, 495 NYS2d 881.

11. Zauderer v Barcellona (NYC Civ Ct NY Co 1985) 130 Misc 2d 234, 495 NYS2d 881.

12. Emery Roth & Sons v National Kinney Corp. (1978) 44 NY2d 912, 407 NYS2d 640, 379 NE2d 168; 930 Fifth Corp. v King (1977) 42 NY2d 886, 397 NYS2d 788, 366 NE2d 875; Syracuse Associates v Touchette Corp. (1979, 4th Dept) 73 AD2d 813, 424 NYS2d 72. Helmsley v Anderson Clayton & Co. (1978, 1st Dept) 60 AD2d 808, 400 NYS2d 544; Columbia Corrugated Container Corp v Skyway Container Corp (AD2 1971) 37 AD2d 845, 326 NYS2d 208, app dismd 31 NY2d 903, 340 NYS2d 639, 292 NE2d 783; Seventy-Second Street Properties, Inc. v Woods (NYC Civ Ct NY Co 1971) 67 Misc 2d 539, 324 NYS2d 339.

York, the statute provides[13] "Whenever a lease of residential property shall provide that in any action or summary proceeding the landlord may recover attorneys' fees and/or expenses incurred as the result of the failure of the tenant to perform any covenant or agreement contained in such lease, or that amounts paid by the landlord therefor shall be paid by the tenant as additional rent, there shall be implied in such lease a covenant by the landlord to pay to the tenant the reasonable attorney's fees and/or expenses incurred by the tenant as the result of the failure of the landlord to perform any covenant or agreement on its part to be performed under the lease or in the successful defense of any action or summary proceeding commenced by the landlord against the tenant arising out of the lease, and an agreement that such fees and expenses may be recovered as provided by law in an action commenced against the landlord or by way of counterclaim in any action or summary proceeding commenced by the landlord against the tenant. Any waiver of this section shall be void as against public policy."[14]

This statute confers upon a residential tenant a reciprocal right to recover reasonable legal fees "incurred" if the lease permits the landlord to recover legal fees as against the tenant. But, it must be observed that this statute expressly limits its provisions to residential tenants. Accordingly, if a lease to commercial premises contains a provision for attorneys' fees, a commercial tenant does not have a reciprocal right thereto unless he expressly provides for them in the lease.

The term "legal fees incurred" means that the party is liable for the expense.[15] It has been held, therefore, that

---

**13.** Real Prop L § 234, added L 1966, ch 286, eff July 1, 1966, as am L 1969, ch 297, eff July 1, 1969. Prior to its amendment in 1969 this section was only applicable to leases of residential property in the city of New York. Now it is applicable to leases of residential property throughout the state.

**14.** Real Prop L § 234 encompasses legal services rendered in an administrative proceeding before the Loft Board. 119 Fifth Ave. Corp. v Berkhout (NYC Civil Ct NY Co 1987) 134 Misc 2d 963, 513 NYS2d 642, amd, on reconsideration 135 Misc 2d 773, 516 NYS2d 877. Contra: East 55th St. Joint Venture v Litchman (NYC Civ Ct NY Co 1983) 122 Misc 2d 81, 469 NYS2d 1013, affd 126 Misc 2d 1049, 487 NYS2d 256.

**15.** Where landlord wrongfully withheld security moneys, requiring tenant to bring an action therefor, tenant was held entitled to recover attorneys' fees incurred in the action, under a lease provision that if landlord shall institute an action or summary proceeding against tenant based upon a failure to perform the lease,

§ 12:6                    LANDLORD AND TENANT

where the tenant was represented by a publicly funded legal services organization, and was not required to pay for the legal services rendered, the tenant did not "incur" legal fees within the meaning of the statute.[16] A prevailing landlord in a non-primary residence proceeding may not recover attorneys' fees under a lease provision which speaks to a default under the terms of the lease. Similarly, the prevailing tenant in such a proceeding may not recover attorneys' fees.[17]

Where landlord's first summary proceeding was dismissed without prejudice because of his nonappearance, and his second proceeding was dismissed because of defective verification of the petition, and landlord's third proceeding was still pending, tenant could not bring an action to recover his attorney's fees in the 2 dismissed proceedings, but had to await the outcome of the third proceeding, since the award of fees under the statute is intended to be based on the ultimate outcome of the controversy between the landlord and tenant, and not on the outcome of each separate step of the controversy.[18]

he shall be entitled to attorneys' fees since a similar provision is implied in favor of tenant. Conforti v Alston (Dist Ct Suffolk Co 1972) 71 M2d 900, 337 NYS2d 17.

Where tenant establishes that landlord breached the warranty of habitability, and therefore was entitled to set off against the rent due the damages he sustained, landlord is not entitled to recover his attorney's fees under the lease provision therefor in the event an action is initated to recover rent. However, tenant under Real Prop L § 234 was entitled to attorney's fees. Concord Village Management Co. v Rubin (Dist Ct Suffolk Co 1979) 101 Misc 2d 625, 421 NYS2d 811; Parker 72nd Associates v Isaacs (NYC Civ Ct NY Co 1980) 109 Misc 2d 57, 436 NYS2d 542.

See, Rubin v Empire Mut. Ins. Co. (1969) 25 NY2d 426, 306 NYS2d 914, 255 NE2d 154, 40 ALR3d 1008.

**16.** Maplewood Management, Inc. v Best (AT 9's, 10 1986) 133 Misc 2d 769, 509 NYS2d 449.

But, see William Manor Management Associates v Deutsch (City Ct Mt Vernon 1984) 126 Misc 2d 1006, 481 NYS2d 937, holding that where lease provided that tenant shall have the right to collect reasonable legal fees "incurred" in a successful disposition of a lawsuit brought by landlord against tenant or by tenant against landlord to the extent provided by RPL 234, tenant may assert the claim for legal fees as soon as the fees have been incurred, whether or not payment has been made, and within the same lawsuit, and even though tenant's attorney informed tenant that he had no intention of charging him for his services but would look only to the landlord for payment.

In Scotia Associates v Bond (NYC Civ Ct NY Co 1985) 126 Misc 2d 885, 484 NYS2d 479, it was held that attorney's fees may be awarded to attorney who undertook case with understanding that he would not receive a fee unless fees were recovered from landlord.

**17.** Eleven Waverly Associates v Waering (AT1 1987) 134 Misc 2d 1093, 515 NYS2d 381.

**18.** Elkins v Cinera Realty, Inc. (1978, 2d Dept) 61 AD2d 828, 402 NYS2d 432. But, in McMahon v Schwartz (NYC Civ Ct Bx Co 1981) 109 Misc 2d 80, 438 NYS2d 215, a

The general criterion for determining whether a dismissal warrants a tenant's being entitled to attorneys' fees under this statute, said the court in a recent case,[19] is whether the dismissal is a victory in a "battle" in a "continuing war" on the issue between the parties, or an end of the "war."[20]

In determining the amount of reasonable attorneys' fees to be considered are the complexity of the case, experience of the attorney, the skill exercised in handling the case, and the results obtained.[1] The affirmation of an attorney, it has been held, is an inadequate basis for awarding legal fees. There should be a hearing at which the parties will have an opportunity to establish and refute the value of the legal services rendered.[2]

An attorney appearing pro se is entitled to recover attorneys' fees[3]

### § 12:7. Attorney's Fees as Rent; Mobile Homes

Real Prop L § 233, subd o (added by L 1984, ch 910), effective January 1, 1985, provides:

Whenever a lease shall provide that in any action or

different result was reached because the 2 summary proceedings which had been dismissed on procedural grounds were holdovers, seeking a termination of the lease, and the third proceeding, which was pending at the time of the application for legal fees, was nonpayment, thus affirming that the lease was in existence, and therefore the claim that the lease had been terminated culminated favorably to the tenant. In N.V. Madison, Inc. v Saurwein (AT1 1980) 103 Misc 2d 996, 431 NYS2d 251, tenant was held entitled to attorneys' fees where the summary proceeding was disposed of without prejudice on procedural grounds, unrelated to the merits of landlord's claim, even though the previous proceeding was not disposed of on the merits, because landlord contemplated no further proceeding to determine the underlying merits.

19. Scotia Associates v Bond (NYC Civ Ct NY Co 1985) 126 Misc 2d 885, 484 NYS2d 479.

20. Tenant who prevailed in holdover proceeding is not barred from recovery of attorney's fees in the proceeding because of the pendency of landlord's second holdover proceeding based on different grounds. Dowling v Yamoshiro (NYC Civ Ct NY Co 1982) 116 Misc 2d 86, 455 NYS2d 231 ($890 awarded for attorney's fees).

Where landlord's holdover summary proceeding was dismissed because of defective notice to cure a default, and landlord did nothing for 2 years, apparently abandoning his claim, tenant was entitled to reasonable attorneys' fees. Park South Associates v Essebag (AT1 1984) 126 Misc 2d 994, 487 NYS2d 252.

1. Zauderer v Barcellona (NYC Civ Ct NY Co 1985) 130 Misc 2d 234, 495 NYS2d 881; N.V. Madison, Inc. v Saurwein (AT1 1980) 103 Misc 2d 996, 431 NYS2d 251.

2. N.V. Madison, Inc. v Saurwein (AT1 1980) 103 Misc 2d 996, 431 NYS2d 251.

3. McMahon v Schwartz (NYC Civ Ct Bx Co 1981) 109 Misc 2d 80, 438 NYS2d 215; Parker 72nd Associates v Isaacs (NYC Civ Ct NY Co 1980) 109 Misc 2d 57, 436 NYS2d 542.

§ 12:7                           LANDLORD AND TENANT

summary proceeding the mobile home park owner or operator may recover attorney's fees and/or expenses incurred as the result of the failure of the tenant to perform any covenant or agreement contained in such lease, or that amounts paid by the mobile home park owner or operator therefor shall be paid by the tenant as additional rent, there shall be implied in such lease a covenant by the mobile home park owner or operator, to pay to the tenant the reasonable attorney's fees and/or expenses incurred by the tenant to the same extent as is provided in section two hundred thirty-four of this article which section shall apply in its entirety. (See § 12:6)

### § 12:8. Forms of Clauses Making Other Payments Rent

#### FORM NO. 19

#### PROVISION FOR ADDITIONAL RENT*

If tenant shall default in the observance or performance of any term or covenant on tenant's part to be observed or performed under or by virtue of any of the terms or provisions in any article of this lease, then, unless otherwise provided elsewhere in this lease, landlord may immediately or at any time thereafter and without notice perform the obligation of tenant thereunder, and if landlord, in connection therewith or in connection with any default by tenant in the covenant to pay rent hereunder, makes any expenditures or incurs any obligations for the payment of money, including but not limited to attorney's fees, in instituting, prosecuting or defending any action or proceeding, such sums so paid or obligations incurred with interest and costs shall be deemed to be and shall constitute additional rent hereunder and shall be paid by tenant to landlord within five (5) days of rendition of any bill or statement to tenant therefor, and if tenant's lease term shall have expired at the time of making of such expenditures or incurring of such obligations, such sums shall be recoverable by landlord as damages.

When using this provision in a lease of residential

\* For complete form of lease, see Chapter 1, supra.

property, counsel should bear in mind the provisions of Real Property Law § 234, with respect to attorney's fees.[4]

Some clauses for attorney's fees provide that the tenant will be obligated to pay as additional rent, to be added to the following month's rent, expenses incurred if the landlord is "compelled" to incur any such expenses by reason of the breach of the lease by the tenant. The use of the word "compel" creates unnecessary problems. In a recent case,[5] the court said, "What, therefore, is the landlord's right to recovery of expenses under the subject lease? The landlord by his own authorship has selected the specific words 'If . . . *landlord is compelled to incur any expenses* . . . .' (Emphasis supplied.) Such a compulsion must be judicially examined in the atmosphere of affording reasonable protection to a landlord against the apparent dangers of a defaulting tenant. In such event, a landlord must satisfy the trial court that a reasonable course of conduct would command the institution of summary proceedings. As a matter of pure logic, if it was a landlord's intention to gain for himself the absolute right to recover expenses incurred by the mere bringing of a prior action, *compulsion* notwithstanding, he could have endowed himself with such a right by an expression in the lease of clear and unequivocal language, which the landlord failed to do."

## FORM NO. 20
### PROVISION FOR INCREASE OR DECREASE IN FIXED RENT KEYED TO OPERATING EXPENSES
### [ESCALATION CLAUSE]*

A. If in any lease year following the base year, operating costs shall be increased above or decreased below the operating costs for the base year, the annual rent hereinabove reserved shall be increased or decreased by . . .% of the amount of such increase or decrease.

B. "Operating costs" shall mean the following described expenses of normal operation, maintenance and repair of the building in which the demised premises are situated:

---

4. See § 12:6, supra.
5. Village Leasing Corp. v Arnold (Civ Ct Queens Co 1969) 58 Misc 2d 958, 296 NYS2d 894.

* For complete form of lease see Chapter 1, supra.

(1) Wages and salaries; taxes imposed upon employers in respect to wages and salaries, including social security, unemployment insurance, and disability insurance; fringe benefits, including vacation, holiday and other proper allowances, hospitalization, medical, surgical, welfare, retirement, pension and profit sharing plans under collective bargaining agreements; and workmen's compensation insurance payable by Lessor with respect to such wages and salaries; of all persons directly employed by Lessor for, and rendering services in, the normal operation, maintenance and repair of the said building, and the sidewalks and curbs adjoining the same, such as, superintendents, clerks, engineers, electricians, mechanics, helpers, handymen, floor directors, security officers, caretakers, freight and passenger elevator operators, matrons, porters, cleaners, and window washers. Overtime wages and salaries shall not be included in "expenses" unless the overtime is for a service that is furnished on a regular, recurrent basis as part of normal operation or maintenance of the said building.

(2) Full contract costs of the following when regularly performed and furnished by independent contractors in the normal operation, maintenance, and repair of the said building and the sidewalks and curbs adjoining the same; cleaning, including window washing, rubbish removal and other services which may be rendered by cleaning contractors; elevator inspection and maintenance; air conditioning inspection and maintenance, including water treatment, filter replacement, inspection and maintenance of tower and turbine equipment, and pumps and piping; supply and cleaning of uniforms and work clothes; and directory service.

(3) Costs of fuel or other energy for heating the said building and operating the air conditioning system, and for electricity, steam or other power in connection with the operation of the said building.

(4) Water rates and sewer rents for water used in the operation of the said building.

(5) Actual cost of insurance, including fire and extended coverage, elevator, boiler including piping, sprinkler leakage, water damage, water damage legal liability, public liability and property damage, but excluding rental value

and plate glass, insurance carried by Lessor with respect to the said building or with respect to any accident or casualty occurring therein or with respect thereto. No charge for insurance shall be included that reflects any increase in premiums due to an act or omission of any of the tenants of the said building for which Lessor would be entitled to reimbursement from such tenants.

(6) "Expenses" shall not, in any event, be deemed to include the cost of painting, repainting, decorating or redecorating for any occupant of the said building, or of providing for any such occupant special cleaning services; any administrative wages and salaries, management fees or renting commissions; the cost of any unusual or extraordinary work or service, or of any other work or service not normally performed or rendered without additional charge by a reasonably prudent operator of a comparable first class office building in the Borough of Manhattan in the city of New York; legal fees and expenses in enforcing the terms of any leases; and the cost of any repair or replacement item which is, or by sound accounting practice should be, capitalized on the books of Lessor.

(7) All expenses to be taken into account pursuant to this Article shall be net only, and for such purpose shall be deemed reduced by the amounts of any insurance or other reimbursement, recoupment, discount, credit reduction or allowance received or receivable by Lessor in connection with such expenses.

C. "Base year" shall mean the twelve-month period from ........, 19..., to ........, 19...; and "lease year" shall mean each twelve-month period commencing ........, 19..., during the term of this lease.

D. Within ninety days after the expiration of the lease year immediately following the base year, and within ninety days after the expiration of each subsequent lease year, Lessor shall furnish to Lessee a statement showing a comparison of the operating costs applicable to the base year and to the lease year covered by the said statement, and setting forth the amount, if any, of the increase or decrease in rent. Within thirty days after the rendition of such statement, Lessee shall pay to Lessor, or Lessor shall credit Lessee on account of the rent next becoming due, as the case may be, an amount equal to such increase or decrease.

(1) Lessee may, within thirty days from the rendition of any statement, question any item thereon, and any item not so questioned shall be deemed to have been approved by Lessee.

(2) In the event Lessor and Lessee cannot agree as to any item so questioned, each then shall select one arbitrator, and the two arbitrators so selected shall select a third arbitrator, and the three arbitrators so selected shall fix and determine the item in dispute. Each arbitrator must be a qualified realtor with at least ten years' experience in the leasing or management of premises comparable to the said building. Pending such determination, however, the nonpayment by Lessee of so much of the amount as is in dispute shall not constitute a default under this lease. The expenses involved in such determination shall be borne by the party against whom a decision is rendered, provided that if more than one item is disputed, and the decision shall be against each party in respect to any item or number of items so disputed, then the expenses shall be apportioned according to the number of items decided against each party.

E. If the term of this lease shall expire on any day other than ........, any payment due by reason of any increase or decrease in operating costs shall be prorated for the fractional portion of the lease year in which the term expires, and subject to the determination of any item in dispute, Lessee shall pay to Lessor the amount of any such increase, or Lessor shall pay to Lessee the amount of any such decrease, within thirty days after the rendition of the final statement.

F. Lessee or Lessee's representative shall have the right to inspect the books of Lessor during business hours for the purpose of verifying the information in the last statement served by Lessor, provided written request for such inspection shall be made by Lessee within five business days after receipt of such statement.

G. In the event that as a result of condemnation, fire or other casualty, the rentable area of Lessee or the rentable area of the said building shall be changed, and this lease shall not have been cancelled, the percentage of increase or decrease in operating costs shall be equitably adjusted, and in the event the parties cannot agree, the matter shall be determined by . . . . . . . ., or by such impartial person as he may designate, whose determination shall be final and conclusive upon the parties hereto.

*Lessee may wish to add a noncumulative or cumulative limit on escalation:*

H. Anything in this Article to the contrary notwithstanding, Lessee shall not be obligated to pay any increase in rent under the provisions of this Article in any one lease year, an amount greater than . . .% of the annual rent reserved hereinabove, nor shall Lessee for any lease year be entitled to any payment in an amount greater than . . .% of the annual rent reserved hereinabove.

*or*

H. Anything in this Article to the contrary notwithstanding, Lessee shall not be required to pay any increase in rent under the provisions of this Article, or be entitled to any credit against the fixed rent, for any lease year in excess of a sum equal to . . .% of the fixed annual rent, multiplied by the number of years which have elapsed since the commencement of the term.

## FORM NO. 21

### ESCALATION CLAUSE-RIDER FOR USE WITH THE REAL ESTATE BOARD OF NEW YORK, INC., LOFT LEASE FORMS*

Rider No. _____, attached to and made a part of Lease dated _____ between _____ as Landlord and _____ as Tenant.

**A. TAXES**

Tenant agrees to pay as additional rent __% of any and all increases in Real Estate Taxes above the Real Estate Taxes for the 19__-19__ New York City fiscal year (hereinafter referred to as the "Base Tax Year") imposed on the Property with respect to every Tax Year or part thereof during the term of this lease, whether any such increase results from a higher tax rate or an increase in the assessed valuation of the property, or both. "Property" shall mean the land and

---

* This form is copyrighted by the Real Estate Board of New York, Inc., and reprinted by its permission. Reproduction in whole or in parts is prohibited, and all rights are reserved by the said Real Estate Board of New York, Inc. The loft lease form is reprinted in Chapter 1, supra.

building, including any "air rights", of which the demised premises are a part. "Real Estate Taxes" shall mean taxes and assessments imposed upon the Property including any special assessment imposed thereon for any purpose whatsoever and also including taxes payable by Landlord to a ground lessor with respect thereto. If due to a change in the method of taxation any franchise, income, profit, or other tax, however designated, shall be levied against Landlord's interest in the property in whole or in part for or in lieu of any tax which would otherwise constitute Real Estate Taxes, such change in method of taxation shall be included in the term "Real Estate Taxes" for purposes hereof. "Tax Year" shall mean each period of twelve months commencing on the first day of July subsequent to the Base Tax Year, in which occurs any part of the term of this lease or such other period of twelve months occurring during the term of this lease as hereafter may be duly adopted as the fiscal year for real estate tax purposes of the City of New York. All such payments shall be appropriately pro-rated for any partial Tax Years occurring during the first and last years of the term of this lease. A copy of the Tax Bill of the City of New York shall be sufficient evidence of the amount of Real Estate Taxes and for calculation of the amount to be paid by Tenant.

Only Landlord shall be eligible to institute tax reduction or other proceedings to reduce the assessed valuation. Should Landlord be successful in any such reduction proceedings and obtain a rebate for periods during which Tenant has paid Tenant's share of increases, Landlord shall, after deducting Landlord's expenses in connection therewith including without limitation attorney's fees and disbursements, return to Tenant Tenant's pro-rata share of such rebate except that Tenant may not obtain any portion of the benefits which may accrue to Landlord from any reduction in Real Estate Taxes for any Tax Year below those imposed in the Base Tax Year.

B. WAGES

I. For purposes of this article only, the following words and terms shall have the following meaning:

(1) "WAGE RATE" shall mean the minimum hourly rate of wages in effect from time to time (whether paid by Landlord or any contractor employed by Landlord) computed as paid over a forty hour week to Porters in Class A office buildings pursuant to an Agreement between Realty Advisory Board on Labor Relations, Incorporated, or any successor thereto, and Local 32B of the Building Service Employees International Union, AFL-CIO, or any successor thereto or if such agreement is not applicable to the building, then pursuant to the wage agreement in force covering porters and elevator operators; and provided, however, that if there is no such agreement in effect prescribing a wage rate for Porters, computations and payments shall thereupon be made upon the basis of the regular hourly wage rate actually payable to Porters by Landlord or by Landlord's service contractors over a forty hour week.

(2) "BASE WAGE RATE" shall mean the Wage Rate in effect as of January 1, 19___

(3) "RENTABLE AREA OF THE DEMISED PREMISES" as measured by the Standard Method of Floor Measurement approved by The Real Estate Board of New York, Inc. shall mean ___ square feet.

(4) The term "PORTERS" shall

mean that classification of non-supervisory employees employed in and about the structure who devote a major portion of their time to general cleaning, maintenance and miscellaneous services essentially of a non-technical and non-mechanical nature and are the type of employees who are now included in the classification of "Class A-Others" in the Commercial Building Agreement between the Realty Advisory Board and the aforesaid Union.

(5) "OPERATION YEAR" shall mean each calendar year in which occurs any part of the term of this lease.

II. If the Wage Rate in any Operation Year shall be increased above the Base Wage Rate, then Tenant shall pay, as additional rent for such Operation Year, an amount equal to the product obtained by multiplying the Rentable Area of the Demised Premises by ____ cent(s) (including any fraction of a cent) for each cent by which the Wage Rate is greater than the Base Wage Rate. Such amounts will be pro-rated for any partial calendar years during the term. Landlord shall give Tenant written notice of each change in Wage Rate which will be effective to create or change Tenant's obligation to pay additional rent pursuant to the provisions of this Article and such notice shall contain Landlord's calculation of the annual rate of additional rent payable resulting from such increase in Wage Rate.

Every notice given by Landlord pursuant to subdivision B II shall be conclusive and binding upon Tenant unless within thirty (30) days after the receipt of such notice Tenant shall notify Landlord that Tenant disputes the correctness of the notice, specifying the particular respects in which the notice is claimed to be incorrect and, pending the determination of such dispute, Tenant shall pay additional rent in accordance with Landlord's notice and such payment or acceptance shall be without prejudice to Tenant's position.

The amounts due under subdivisions A. "TAXES" and B. "WAGES" hereunder shall be collected as additional rent without set off or deduction, and shall be paid in the following manner:

A) Any adjustment in rent occurring by reason of subdivision A "TAXES" shall be effective as of the first day of the Tax Year concerned and, after Landlord shall have furnished Tenant with a statement setting forth the Real Estate Taxes for the Base Tax Year and the Real Estate Taxes for the Tax Year concerned, all monthly installments of rent shall reflect 1/12th of the annual amount of such adjustment until a new adjustment becomes effective pursuant to the provisions of said subdivision A. Any adjustments in rent payable pursuant to this Rider by reason of changes in the Real Estate Taxes for the Base Year or any Tax Year prior to the then current Tax Year, if any, shall be paid by Tenant to Landlord within thirty (30) days after the statement covering such period is delivered to Tenant or a credit given by Landlord towards the next ensuing rent installments until the credit is exhausted, as the case may be.

B) Landlord, after the effective date of any change in the "Wage Rate", shall furnish Tenant with a statement thereof, and all monthly installments of Fixed Rent thereafter due shall reflect one-twelfth (1/12th) of the annual amount of such adjustment until a new adjustment becomes effective, pursuant to the provisions of Subdivision B.

If any such Tax or Wage Rate statement is furnished to Tenant after the commencement of the effective date of any such adjustment, there shall be promptly paid by Tenant to Landlord an amount equal to the portion of such adjustment allocable to that part of the Operation or Tax Year, as the case may be, which shall have elapsed prior to the first day of the calendar month next succeeding the calendar month in which said statement was furnished to Tenant.

Landlord's failure during the lease term to prepare and deliver any of the foregoing tax bills, statements or bills, or Landlord's failure to make a demand, shall not in any way waive or cause Landlord to forfeit or surrender its rights to collect any of the foregoing items of additional rent which may have become due during the term of this lease. Tenant's liability for the amounts due under this article shall survive the expiration of the term.

In no event shall any rent adjustment hereunder result in a decrease in the fixed annual rent.

INITIAL HERE _____

## FORM NO. 22

## STANDARD ESCALATION CLAUSE-RIDER FOR USE WITH THE REAL ESTATE BOARD OF NEW YORK, INC. OFFICE AND STORE LEASE FORMS*

Rider No. _____, attached to and made a part of Lease dated _____, between _____ as Owner and _____ as Tenant.

### A. TAXES

Tenant agrees to pay as additional rent __% of any and all increases in Real Estate Taxes above the Real Estate Taxes for the 19__-19__ New York City fiscal year (hereinafter referred to as the "Base Tax Year") imposed on the Property with respect to every Tax Year or part thereof during the term of this lease, whether any such increase results from a higher tax rate or an increase in the assessed valuation of the property, or both. "Property" shall mean the land and building including any "air rights", of which the demised premises are a part. "Real Estate Taxes" shall mean taxes and assessments imposed upon the Property including any special assessment imposed thereon for any purpose whatsoever and also including taxes payable by Owner to a ground lessor with respect thereto, and unmetered water taxes and sewer rents. If due to a change in the method of taxation

---

* This form is copyrighted by The Real Estate Board of New York, Inc., and reprinted by its permission. Reproduction in whole or in parts is prohibited, and all rights are reserved by the said Real Estate Board of New York, Inc. The office and store lease forms are reprinted in Chapter 1, supra.

any franchise, income, profit, or other tax, however designated, shall be levied against Owner's interest in the property in whole or in part for or in lieu of any tax which would otherwise constitute Real Estate Taxes, such change in method of taxation shall be included in the term "Real Estate Taxes" for purposes hereof. "Tax Year" shall mean each period of twelve months commencing on the first day of July subsequent to the Base Tax Year, in which occurs any part of the term of this lease or such other period of twelve months occurring during the term of this lease as hereafter may be duly adopted as the fiscal year for real estate tax purposes of the City of New York. All such payments shall be appropriately pro-rated for any partial Tax Years occurring during the first and last years of the term of this lease. A copy of the Tax Bill of the City of New York shall be sufficient evidence of the amount of Real Estate Taxes and for calculation of the amount to be paid by Tenant.

Only Owner shall be eligible to institute tax reduction or other proceedings to reduce the assessed valuation. Should Owner be successful in any such reduction proceedings and obtain a rebate for periods during which Tenant has paid Tenant's share of increases, Owner shall, after deducting Owner's expenses in connection therewith including without limitation attorney's fees and disbursements, return to Tenant Tenant's pro-rata share of such rebate except that Tenant may not obtain any portion of the benefits which may accrue to Owner from any reduction in Real Estate Taxes for any Tax Year below those imposed in the Base Tax Year.

**B. OPERATING EXPENSES**

For purposes of this article only, the following words and terms have the following meaning:

(1) "BASE OPERATION YEAR"—shall mean the calendar year 19__.

(2) "OPERATION YEAR"—shall mean each calendar year in which occurs any part of the term of this lease. If the lease term shall commence or terminate on a date other than January 1, or December 31 of an Operation Year, any increase or decrease in additional rent by reason hereof shall be apportioned.

(3) "OPERATING EXPENSES"—shall mean any or all of the following incurred by Owner with respect to the building of which the demised premises form a part: salaries, wages, hospitalization, medical, surgical and general welfare benefits (including group insurance) and pension payments of employees of Owner engaged in the operation and maintenance of the building of which the demised premises are a part, payroll taxes, workmen's compensation insurance, gas, oil, or other fuel, electricity, steam, together with any taxes thereon, utility taxes, water, (including sewer rental), rent, casualty and liability and other insurance covering Owner, Owner's agent, mortgagee and any portion of Owner's property, repairs and maintenance, building and cleaning supplies, uniforms and dry cleaning, window cleaning, management fees, service contracts with independent contractors, telephone, telegraph, stationery, advertising, and all other expenses paid in connection with the operation of said premises properly chargeable against income, including but not limited to accounting expenses for all statements with respect to Owner's Property, including statements required under this Article and any work in connection with any

governmental entity, and attorney's fees and fees to professionals for services rendered in connection with the maintenance, repair and operation of Owner's Property and in respect of real estate taxes payable on Owner's Property; dues and fees for trade and industry associations and costs of their related activities, all relating to Owner's Property; and home office administration costs for the proportionate share of any salaries of Owner's employees engaged in Property management and for bookkeeping and telephone. Owner's Operating Expenses shall not include any item otherwise properly constituting an operating expense to the extent payment of reimbursement therefore is actually received by Owner from space occupants for services rendered or performed directly for the account of such space occupants and for which Owner makes a separate charge, or for electrical energy for which Tenants pay under an electrical rent inclusion or submetering plans provided, however, that the foregoing exclusion shall be only to the extent of the actual cost to Owner of the service rendered to each space occupant, nor real estate taxes, mortgage interest and amortization, brokerage or other costs in connection with leasing or mortgages, rent under a superior lease, depreciation, nor the cost of any item required under good accounting and tax practice to be capitalized (Other than those which under generally applied real estate practice are expense or regarded as deferred expenses and other than capital expenditures made by reason of legal requirements or insurance requirements, in any of which cases the cost thereof shall be included in Operating Expenses for the Operational Year in which the costs are incurred and subsequent Operational Years, amortized on a straight-line basis over an appropriate period not exceeding fifteen years, including interest at the prime interest rate changed by Owner's first institutional mortgagee at the time of Owner's having made such expenditure or in the absense thereof by Citibank N.A.) If Owner shall eliminate the payment of any of the salaries, wages, benefits or other payments to employees and the payroll taxes and workmen's compensation insurance premiums relating thereto as the result of the installation of labor-saving devices or by other means, in computing the additional rent payable under this paragraph (B), the corresponding items of said salaries, wages, benefits and other payments to employees and of said taxes and premiums relating thereto in the base year shall be deducted from the operating expenses for the base year and there shall be included in Operating Costs the cost and expense of such labor-saving device as amortized over the useful life thereof, or the amount of the reduction in Operating costs, whichever is the lesser.

(4) In the event that the Operating Expenses incurred by Owner during any Operation Year shall be greater than the Operating Expenses incurred by Owner during the Base Operation Year, Tenant shall pay to Owner as additional rent for the Operation Year in question an amount equal to __% of the increase.

The amounts due under subdivision A. "TAXES" and B. "OPERATING EXPENSE" hereunder shall be collected as additional rent without set off or deduction, and shall be paid in the following manner.

(A) Any adjustment in rent occurring by reason of subdivision A "TAXES" shall be effective as of the first day of the Tax Year concerned and, after Owner shall have furnished Tenant with a statement setting forth the Real Estate Taxes for the Base Tax Year and the Real Estate Taxes for the Tax Year concerned, all monthly installments of rent shall reflect 1/12th of the annual amount of such adjustment until a new adjustment becomes effective pursuant to the provisions of said subdivision A. Any adjustments in rent payable pursuant to this Rider by reason of changes in the Real Estate Taxes for the Base Year or any Tax Year prior to the then current Tax Year, if any, shall be paid by Tenant to Owner within thirty (30) days after the statement covering such period is delivered to Tenant or a credit given by Owner towards the next ensuing rent installments until the credit is exhausted, as the case may be.

B) For the first Operation Year and each subsequent Operation Year Owner shall furnish Tenant with an operating expense statement. Tenant shall pay the amount of additional rent shown thereon, if any, within thirty days (30) after rendition of such statement. Tenant shall be given a credit on such statement for payments made during the Operating Year on account of the amount due and in case of an overpayment Tenant shall receive a credit. In order to provide for current payment of additional rent which may be payable upon the rendering of the next Operating Expense Statement, all monthly installments of rent following the rendition of any such statement shall reflect one-twelfth of the annualized amount of the additional rent shown on the most recent statement and 1/12th of the amount, if any, by which the amount due under such most recent statement increased over the most previous statement without respect to credits for advanced payments. In all events Tenant's tax escalation payments shall be made so that they are due and payable at least thirty (30) days prior to the date payments are due either to the taxing authority or to any first institutional mortgagee under a real estate tax escrow requirement.

The statements of Operating Expenses to be furnished by Owner hereunder shall be prepared in reasonable detail by a Certified Public Accountant (who may be a CPA employed by Owner for the audit of Owner's accounts). Said CPA may rely on Owner's allocations and estimates provided such CPA determines that there is a reasonable basis for such allocations and estimates. The statements thus furnished to Tenant shall constitute the final determination as between Owner and Tenant of the Operating Expenses for the period covered thereby. If any such Tax or Operating Expenses statement is furnished to Tenant after the commencement of the effective date of any such adjustment, there shall be promptly paid by Tenant to Owner an amount equal to the portion of such adjustment allocable to that part of the Operation of Tax Year, as the case may be, which shall have elapsed prior to the first day of the calendar month next succeeding the calendar month in which said statement was furnished to Tenant.

Owner's failure during the lease term to prepare and deliver any of the foregoing tax bills, statements or bills, or Owner's failure to make a demand, shall not in any way waive or cause Owner to forfeit or surrender Owner's rights to collect any of the foregoing items of additional rent which may have become due during the term of this lease. Tenant's liability for the amounts

§ 12:8

due under this article shall survive the expiration of the term.

In no event shall any rent adjustment hereunder result in a decrease in the fixed annual rent.

INITIAL HERE _____

An escalation clause is entitled to be enforced if it is not ambiguous, illegal, against public policy, unreasonable, or created by fraud or mutual mistake. An escalation clause is neither unconscionable nor ambiguous which provides that tenant shall pay the total of a specified share of landlord's increase in taxes within 10 days after demand, although landlord could pay such taxes in quarterly installments. Nor is it unconscionable when it provides that tenant shall pay a specified share of increased labor costs, even though if all the tenants in the building were subject to the same clause, landlord would receive as additional rent an amount equal to several times the actual increased labor costs incurred.[6]

### § 12:9. Importance of Ascertaining When Other Payments to be Made by Tenant Constitute Rent

Fundamentally, an assignee of a lease who does not assume performance thereof, is liable only for the performance of all those covenants in the lease on the part of the tenant which run with the land. But he is not liable upon those express covenants in the lease on the part of the tenant which are collateral, or merely personal, and which do not run with the land.[7] A covenant running with the land, said Rhodes, J.,[8] "relates to some condition or thing to be done by him to entitle him to use and possession of the premises; an obligation arising out of or growing out of, the use or possession of the property."

A covenant to pay rent is a covenant running with the land. "An assignee of the term is always liable to the lessor for rent reserved," said the Court of Appeals,[9] "in the same manner and to the same extent that the lessee was."

Therefore, if a lease provides that a payment which a tenant is to make shall be rent, then the covenant to make such payment will run with the land, and will bind a nonassuming assignee. However, if such payment is not rent, and is not agreed to be rent, then it is necessary to ascertain, by construction of the lease, whether or not the

---

6. Rich v Don-Ron Trousers Corp. (NYC Civ Ct NY Co 1973) 74 Misc 2d 259, 343 NYS2d 684.
7. § 9:25, supra.
8. Beach v Deyo Oil Co. (S Ct Broome Co 1928) 131 Misc 765, 228 NYS 702, affd 224 AD 772, 230 NYS 800.
9. Dolph v White (1855) 12 NY 296, 300.

Also, see § 9:26, supra.

covenant to make such payment is one which by its very nature runs with the land, or is one which is purely personal or collateral. Thus, a lease provided that a tenant of part of a building should pay any increase over the prevailing insurance on the entire building as well as on the landlord's stock of merchandise kept in the building. The court held[10] that this covenant was personal, and did not run with the land. However, since the parties further provided in the lease that such increase should, when paid by the landlord, be added to the rent to be paid by the tenant, then the obligation to pay such increase was held to be a covenant to pay rent which, regardless of the fact that otherwise it was a personal covenant, thereupon became one which ran with the land, and would bind a non-assuming assignee of the lease. As James O'Malley, J., said in this case, "It is to be observed that the covenant in question is wholly unlike an obligation on the part of the lessee to insure or a covenant on the part of the lessor to devote the proceeds of an insurance loss to a reconstruction of the building. Our conclusion is that, in so far as the covenant was one to pay increased cost of insurance, as such, either on the building or the stock, it was personal to the original lessor and for its benefit only. As a covenant to pay additional rent, however, it would clearly run with the land. The clause in question must be considered in connection with all the facts and surrounding circumstances. We think, that what the lessor had in mind was to assure to itself the net rental reserved in the lease. To accomplish this, provision was made that, in the event there resulted increased cost of insurance, by reason of the nature of the occupancy of the premises, such cost, if not paid by the lessee, might be added as rent to the amount reserved. The covenant provided specifically that, in the event the tenant should omit to pay such increased insurance rates, the landlord 'shall be entitled to pay the same, and the amount so paid shall be added to the rent then or next to become due hereunder.' By this provision it was intended that the amount of increased premium

---

10. St. Regis Restaurant, Inc. v Powers (AD1 1927) 219 AD 321, 219 NYS 684; Beach v Deyo Oil Co. (S Ct Broome Co 1928) 131 Misc 765, 228 NYS 702, affd 224 AD 772, 230 NYS 800.

was to be considered as rent and as such added when liquidated to the constant liquidated rent reserved."

In another case a lease provided that the tenant should pay the landlord the excess which the tenant might receive upon his assignment of the lease. This was held to be a personal covenant.[11] Since the payment to be made by the tenant was not rent, nor agreed to be so, it did not run with the land and would not be binding on the tenant's non-assuming assignee if he should assign the lease.

Therefore, to determine whether a non-assuming assignee is obligated to carry out his assignor's covenant in the lease to make a stipulated payment, in addition to the rent reserved, it must be ascertained whether or not such covenant runs with the land or is merely personal. To avoid such an issue the landlord should provide that such stipulated payment shall be deemed to be rent.[12]

### § 12:10. Express Covenant to Pay Rent

"At common law an action of assumpsit would not lie for rent," said Maynard, J.,[13] "except on an express promise made at the time of the demise, . . . ."

Rent is reserved in a letting, it was pointed out in an early case,[14] by such words as "reserving," "rendering," "yielding," "paying," and the like. However, leases today invariably contain an express covenant to pay rent. Therefore there is no point in reviewing many of the old cases on the subject. All that is necessary to note is that any words which indicate an agreement to pay rent will be sufficient. In the absence of some statutory[15] or contractual limitation, the right to fix the charge which is to be paid for the occupancy of property is in the owner of the property, and is a matter for his sole determination.[16] However, the law cannot imply a contract to pay rent

---

11. Beach v Deyo Oil Co. (S Ct Broome Co 1928) 131 Misc 765, 228 NYS 702, affd 224 AD 772, 230 NYS 800.

12. Also, see, Summary Proceedings, Chap 32, infra where this question arises to determine whether a default in making such other payments by a tenant will entitle a landlord to bring summary proceedings for non-payment of rent.

13. Preston v Hawley (1893) 139 NY 296, 300, 34 NE 906.

14. Dolph v White (1855) 12 NY 296, 300.

15. See statutory tenancies under emergency rent laws, §§ 10:11, et seq, supra.

16. Tropp v Knickerbocker Village (S Ct NY Co 1953) 205 Misc 200, 122 NYS2d 350, affd 284 AD 935, 135 NYS2d 618.

contrary to the intention of the parties, or in the face of the contract provisions that the property may be used "free of charge."[17]

A covenant to pay rent is one which runs with the land.[18]

## § 12:11. Interest on Rent

A tenant is bound to pay interest on installments of rent from the time they become due.[19] Therefore, when rent is not payable in advance[20] interest on rent due for the month of January, for example, is only allowable from February 1.[1]

However, it has been held that a landlord is not entitled to interest on respective installments of rent increased retroactively by the court in a proceeding to fix rent under emergency rent statutes.[2]

## § 12:12. Implied Agreement to Pay Rent

When one enters possession of land under a lease which is invalid because it violates the statute of frauds, or without any agreement as to the amount of rent to be paid, the law implies an agreement to pay a reasonable rent, which may be enforced in an action for use and occupation. The Real Property Law provides,[3] that the landlord may recover a reasonable compensation for the use and occupation of real property by any person, under an agreement, not made by deed; and a parol lease or other agreement may be used as evidence of the amount

---

17. Northern New York Power Corp. v State (Ct of Claims 1937) 183 Misc 306, 298 NYS 688, affd 265 AD 908, 38 NYS2d 893, affd 293 NY 756, 57 NE2d 837.

An obligation to pay rent will not be implied from mere occupancy; there must be an agreement between the parties, or at least circumstances from which the inference of an agreement can be drawn. Marrano v State (Ct Cl 1975) 80 Misc 2d 768, 364 NYS2d 751.

18. § 9:26, supra.

19. Bryant Park Bldg., Inc. v Richmond (S Ct NY Co 1948) 85 NYS2d 531.

Residential lease provision for $50 additional rent if monthly rent of $405 was over 10 days late constituted a penalty, and was unconscionable, and void. Spring Valley Gardens Associates v Earle (Rockland Co Ct 1982) 112 Misc 2d 786, 447 NYS2d 629.

But, in Maplewood Mgmt. v Jackson (Dist Ct Nassau Co 1982) 113 Misc 2d 142, 448 NYS2d 966, it was held that $20 late fee if rent not paid by 10th of month, was not unconscionable, nor a penalty.

20. See § 12:23, infra.

1. Hanfeld v A Broido, Inc. (M Ct 1938) 167 Misc 85, 3 NYS2d 463.

2. 23 West Street Corp. v Gibbs & Cox, Inc. (AD1 1953) 282 AD 362, 123 NYS2d 386, affd 307 NY 723, 121 NE2d 543.

3. Real Prop L § 220.

to which he is entitled. This statutory enactment was necessary, the Court of Appeals observed,[4] because, at common law an action of assumpsit would not lie for rent, except on an express promise made at the time of the letting. However, before a recovery can be had under this statute it must be made to appear that the conventional relation of landlord and tenant existed between the parties.[5] Liability for rent depends upon the existence of the conventional relationship of landlord and tenant;[6] and "conventional" means, by agreement of the parties, and not by operation of law.[7] Thus, where a grantor wrongfully remains in possession after the conveyance, the relation of landlord and tenant does not arise between them, and the grantee cannot maintain an action for use and occupation.[8]

Although possession and beneficial enjoyment of real property with the owner's permission is ordinarily sufficient to sustain an action upon an implied agreement for use and occupation; where such use and occupation, however, are under such circumstances as to show that there was no expectation of rent by either party, a contract to pay rent will not be implied.[9]

The burden of proving the reasonable value of the use and occupation is on the landlord seeking its recovery.[10]

---

4. Preston v Hawley (1893) 139 NY 296, 300, 34 NE 906.

5. Preston v Hawley (1893) 139 NY 296, 34 NE 906.

Complaint alleging plaintiff's ownership in fee of subject premises; defendant's continuous use and occupancy thereof as tenant, and with plaintiff's consent and permission; the value of the reasonable use and occupancy; and defendant's refusal to pay this sum on demand; is sufficient to state a cause of action under Real Prop L § 220. (AD3 1975) 48 AD2d 741, 368 NYS2d 305. New York State Teachers' Retirement System v Huberty (1975, 3d Dept) 48 AD2d 741, 368 NYS2d 305.

6. Deickler v Abrams (1956, Co Ct Westchester) 159 NYS2d 449, affd (2d Dept) 4 AD2d 779, 164 NYS2d 756.

7. Manhattan Co. v Nieberg (M Ct 1936) 164 Misc 618, 298 NYS 539.

8. Preston v Hawley (1886) 101 NY 586, 5 NE 770.

Also, see Raguso v Ferreira (S Ct Queens Co 1946) 60 NYS2d 418.

9. Collyer v Collyer (1889) 113 NY 442, 448, 21 NE 114.

Where one of several tenants in common of real property occupies the property without having entered into any agreement in respect to its use, and without having ousted or denied the right of any of his cotenants, the law will not imply any agreement by the occupant to pay rent to his cotenants for such use and occupation. Le Barron v House (1890) 122 NY 153, 25 NE 253; Zapp v Miller (1888) 109 NY 51, 57, 15 NE 889.

10. Kornblum v Schell (AT2 1921) 117 Misc 325, 191 NYS 188.

In discharging the burden of proving reasonable value of use and occupancy, landlord may rely upon the testimony of an expert witness. Beacway Operating Corp. v Concert Arts

# RENT § 12:13

In the absence of other proof as to the value of the use and occupation, the agreed rent is some evidence thereof.[11]

### § 12:13. Percentage Rentals

Leases which provide that the rent is to be based in whole or in part on a percentage of the lessee's profits, sales, income, or receipts have come into widespread use in recent years. A provision for a rental to be measured by a stipulated percentage of the gross receipts of the tenant's business, either with or without a guaranteed minimum monthly rental, is valid and enforceable.[12]

Since the construction and application of the percentage provision of a lease depend largely upon the particular phraseology used therein, it is impractical to formulate a rule of general application to such provisions.[13] In calculating rentals under percentage provisions, the courts have had occasion to construe such particular terms as gross income, gross sales, and the like,[14] and whether such terms include amounts received by the

Soc. (NYC Civ Ct NY Co 1984) 123 Misc 2d 452, 474 NYS2d 227 (where court held that impact of landmark designation was a factor to be considered in determining reasonable value of use and occupancy, rather than the opinion of an expert based on a commercial use of the premises).

11. Real Prop L § 220.
Lucina Realty Co. v Flachner (1920, Sup App T) 180 NYS 732.
Where landlord having the right to terminate a lease fails to do so, and permits tenant to continue in possession, tenant becomes a tenant at will, and the rental agreed upon in the lease is evidence of the rental to which landlord is entitled. The Statement, Inc. v Pilgrim's Landing, Inc. (1975, 4th Dept) 49 AD2d 28, 370 NYS2d 970.

12. Goldberg, 168-05 Corp. v Levy (AD2 1939) 256 AD 1086, 11 NYS2d 315; Orkin's Fashion Stores, Inc. v S. H. Kress & Co. (S Ct NY Co 1947) 68 NYS2d 766; Levy v Forma (S Ct NY Co 1946) 65 NYS2d 505, affd 271 AD 970, 69 NYS2d 324, affd 297 NY 848, 78 NE2d 865; Carlson v D. A. Schulte, Inc. (AT1 1925) 124 Misc 880, 209 NYS 631.

13. *Annotation:* Calculation of Rental Under Commercial Percentage Lease. 58 ALR3d 384; Construction and application of provision in lease under which landlord is to receive percentage of lessee's profits or receipts, 38 ALR2d 1113.

**Law Review:** Shopping Center Lease Negotiations. 49 NY State Bar Journal, p 28 (January 1977); A Guide to Problems in Shopping Center Leases, 29 Brooklyn L Rev 56 (1962); Problems in drafting percentage leases. Landis, 36 Boston U. Law Review 190.

14. Chemung Canal Trust Co. v Montgomery Ward & Co. (1957, 3d Dept) 4 AD2d 95, 163 NYS2d 332, affd 4 NY2d 1017, 177 NYS2d 525, 152 NE2d 542; Mutual Life Ins. Co. v Tailored Woman, Inc. (AD1 1953) 283 AD 173, 126 NYS2d 573, affd 309 NY 248, 128 NE2d 401; Levy v Forma (S Ct NY Co 1946) 65 NYS2d 505, affd 271 AD 970, 69 NYS2d 324, affd 297 NY 848, 78 NE2d 865.

§ 12:13  LANDLORD AND TENANT

tenant for taxes,[15] income of a sublessee,[16] income from transactions taking place in part on premises other than the leased premises,[17] or income from incidental or subsidiary operations.[18]

In providing for percentage rentals it is important to express clearly whether it is intended that such percentage be based on gross receipts or net income, that is, receipts less costs.[19] In other words the term "gross in-

15. Excise taxes that are passed on to the consumer by way of increase or addition to the purchase price are included in "gross sales." Excise taxes being levied on the manufacturer, processor, or vendor, it is clear that excluding them from gross sales would be deducting an item of expense from actual sales. V. R. O. K. Co. v Turin Theatre Corp. (S Ct Bx Co 1949) 195 Misc 569, 92 NYS2d 104. However "gross box office receipts", defined by parties to a lease as "the actual cash paid admissions collected at the box office," will not include sums received for Federal Admissions Tax. Admission taxes are levied upon the consumer, and are merely collected by the theatre operator for the Government and held as a special fund for the United States. 26 USC §§ 1700, 3661; 26 C F R Cum Supp 101.4 & 101.31. Therefore, they cannot be regarded as any part of the "paid admission." V. R. O. K. Co. v Turin Theatre Corp. (S Ct Bx Co 1949) 195 Misc 569, 92 NYS2d 104.

When a lease provides for a computation of additional rent upon a stated percentage of "gross sales" exclusive of "sales taxes," it has been held that "gross sales" has no relationship to profit, and means actual sales without deducting expenses. Levy v Forma (S Ct NY Co 1946) 65 NYS2d 505, affd 271 AD 970, 69 NYS2d 324, affd 297 NY 848, 78 NE2d 865.

16. Hempstead Theatre Corp. v Metropolitan Playhouses, Inc. (1954) 308 NY 712, 124 NE2d 332. Where the lease of an airport provided for a fixed rent plus a specified percentage of "gross receipts derived from all operations of the lessee, direct or indirect," and also defined "gross income" as "total income received by sublessees derived from all sources by reason of the operation of the sublessee," it was held in Islip v Smith (1957, 2d Dept) 3 AD2d 726, 159 NYS2d 763, that the percentage rentals were to be calculated only upon the sums actually received by the lessee under the terms of the sublease which provided for a fixed rent, and which was approved by the lessor, and should not be calculated on the basis of any percentage of the receipts of sublessees from their own operations.

17. § 12:15, infra.

18. In 277 Park Ave. Corp. v New York C. R. Co. (S Ct NY Co 1951) 106 NYS2d 338, wherein the lessee of an apartment building collected from its tenants charges for valet services rendered by one who occupies a portion of the premises, retaining 25 per cent of such collections as the latter's rent, it was held that the collections, over and above 25 per cent, were not "gross earnings" inter alia as revenues "accruing to the lessee from the use of the demised premises, including but not limited to all rentals from tenants, concessionaries and other occupants of space in the demised premises and all accruals for privileges therein granted." This interpretation of the lease was held not to be affected by the fact that the tenant had, for a number of years previously, included the collections in its earnings reports to the landlord, the court pointing out that in the absence of ambiguity, no extrinsic evidence, including that of practical construction, was available to vary the terms of a written agreement.

19. See Hempstead Theatre Corp. v Metropolitan Playhouses, Inc. (1959) 6 NY2d 311, 189 NYS2d 837, 160 NE2d 604, where a lease provision reached the Court of Appeals, and even there received a disputed interpretation (four to three decision). The lease was between an operator of a movie and

come" does not carry a definite and inflexible meaning under all circumstances. It will be defined by the courts in such a way as to ascertain the sense in which it was used by the parties when they drew the lease involved in the litigation.[20]

## § 12:14. When Percentage Rent Payable

A lease provided for a rental based on eight percentum of the gross sales with a minimum guaranteed monthly rental. The tenant agreed to pay the guaranteed monthly rental in advance on the first of every month. He further agreed to pay the excess rental, if any, over the guaranteed rental, on the first of every month. "It is quite clear therefore," said the Appellate Term,[1] "that in any month

the owner thereof and provided for a rental based on a percentage of (a) "all box office receipts excluding taxes on admissions," (b) all rentals and/or income derived from rental space, and (c) all income derived from concessions and advertising. The court held that the parties had intended to differentiate between "receipts" and "income." Therefore the first two items meant receipts or gross income, and that the last item meant income and not receipts. Accordingly, the operator was entitled to deduct from the gross receipts of the candy and refreshment concession the costs of the candy sold.

In Marlton Operating Corp. v Local Textile Mills, Inc. (S Ct NY Co 1954) 137 NYS2d 438, it was held that payments from hotel guests for telephone services were not to be included in determining hotel rental under lease in which part of rental was based on gross income from operation of premises, primarily because the parties had acted as if this were the case for eight years.

20. Marlton Operating Corp. v Local Textile Mills, Inc. (S Ct NY Co 1954) 137 NYS2d 438.

A lease required tenant to pay as additional rent 27½% of its net profits over a stated amount, and defined "net profits" as the net profit in a given lease year derived from the operation by the tenant of the leased premises, as ascertained through the use of standard accounting practices, but before deducting the fixed net rent and the additional rent reserved "in this lease" for that lease year. The lease also required the payment as additional rent of certain taxes, insurance, utility charges and licenses. Landlord contended that in computing net profits, tenant could not deduct from its annual income any of these items included in the provision for additional rent (i.e., taxes, insurance, utility charges, etc.). Tenant argued that this interpretation converted its obligation to pay a percentage of its net profits to a percentage of its gross income, and that by providing for the nondeductability of "additional rent reserved in this lease," it was intended to preclude the deduction of "overage rent" in arriving at the amount of overage rent due; i.e., tenant could not determine its overage rent in the first instance, and then deduct that sum from its net profit to arrive at a lower base for average rent purposes. Both the Appellate Division and the Court of Appeals (with dissents) agreed with the tenant, and held that real estate, gross receipt, and water taxes, utility charges, and licenses were not "additional rent" within the meaning of that term as used in arriving at net profits. River View Associates v Sheraton Corp of America (1970) 27 NY2d 718, 314 NYS2d 181, 262 NE2d 416, affg (1st Dept) 33 AD2d 187, 306 NYS2d 153.

1. Carlson v D. A. Schulte, Inc. (AT1 1925) 124 Misc 880, 209 NYS 631.

where the 8 per cent of the total gross sales actually exceeded the guaranteed rental the landlord was entitled to receive from the tenant the so-called excess rental on the 1st day of the month immediately following."[2]

### § 12:15. Tenant's Obligation Under a Percentage Rental Provision

When a lease provides for rent to be computed wholly or partly by a percentage of the tenant's gross sales, a covenant by the tenant will be implied that he will not do anything that will bring about, or that will contribute to bring about, a reduction of the gross value of the sales made in the leased premises.[3] For, there is in every contract an implied covenant of fair dealing.[4] Thus, where a lease provided for a rental measured partly by a percentage of the gross receipts of the tenant's business, and authorized a cancellation of the lease if the tenant's gross sales for any year should not equal a fixed sum, it was held that the tenant could not avoid liability under the lease by diverting business to another store for the sole purpose of reducing his gross sales to the cancellation point.[5] Similarly, applying this principle, it was held under a quite similar percentage rental provision that a tenant could not defeat the landlord's right to a percentage rental by vacating five and one half months before the end of the lease.[6]

However, it is a question of fact whether the facts warrant an implication of an obligation on the part of a tenant not to do anything to bring about a reduction of the gross sales to be made in the leased premises.[7] Thus,

---

2. See Chemung Canal Trust Co. v Montgomery Ward & Co. (1957, 3d Dept) 4 AD2d 95, 163 NYS2d 332, affd 4 NY2d 1017, 177 NYS2d 525, 152 NE2d 542, for construction of clause providing for payment of percentage rental.

3. Goldberg, 168-05 Corp. v Levy (AD2 1939) 256 AD 1086, 11 NYS2d 315; Orkin's Fashion Stores, Inc. v S. H. Kress & Co. (S Ct NY Co 1947) 68 NYS2d 766.

See Mutual Life Ins. Co. v Tailored Woman, Inc. (AD1 1953) 283 AD 173, 126 NYS2d 573, affd 309 NY 248, 128 NE2d 401, where the court, although conceding the principle stated in the text to be valid, refused to apply it in the instant case because the facts did not warrant it.

4. Mutual Life Ins. Co. v Tailored Woman, Inc. (1955) 309 NY 248, 128 NE2d 401.

5. Goldberg, 168-05 Corp. v Levy (AD2 1939) 256 AD 1086, 11 NYS2d 315.

6. Orkin's Fashion Stores v S H Kress, Inc. & Co (S Ct NY Co 1947) 68 NYS2d 766.

7. Mutual Life Ins. Co. v Tailored Woman, Inc. (AD1 1953) 283 AD 173, 126 NYS2d 573, affd 309 NY 248, 128

in an action to recover percentage rent under a lease providing for a fixed rent, and an additional percentage rental based on tenant's sales, where tenant paid the fixed rental, but vacated from the premises and operated its business elsewhere (across the street), so that there were no sales on which to pay a percentage, landlord was denied summary judgment because, issues were presented as to whether tenant had impliedly convenanted to keep its business in operation to the expiration of lease, and whether tenant had acted in bad faith.[8]

A percentage rental clause may be some sign of an implied covenant not to assign the lease, but its significance varies with the other lease terms, the surrounding circumstances, the nature of the business, and the identities and expectations of the parties. The situation must be such that the failure to imply the covenant would be to deprive a party of the benefit of his bargain. When a landlord, relying on tenant's reputation as a large volume merchandiser, agrees to a fixed rent, which is not substantial, and depends upon an additional percentage of sales to provide a fair and adequate return, such a lease involves personal credit and confidence, and therefore there is an implied covenant not to assign the lease, so as to insure that the landlord will have the benefit of the specific risk sharing venture for which he bargained.[9]

## § 12:16. Executory Modification of Rent

It is perfectly competent for parties to make a contract which will supersede the lease either in whole or in part.[10] Therefore, rent may be increased or reduced by a written agreement made subsequently to the lease.

The statute provides,[11] that the absence of consideration no longer vitiates an executory agreement modifying the rent if such modification agreement is in writing, and signed by the landlord or his agent. This statute declares:

An agreement, promise or undertaking to change

---

NE2d 401, where no obligation was implied.

8. Tuttle v W. T. Grant Co. (1959) 6 NY2d 754, 186 NYS2d 655, 159 NE2d 202 (see dissenting opinion of Halpern, J in court below, 5 AD2d 370, 171 NYS2d 954).

9. Rowe v Great Atlantic & Pacific Tea Co. (1978, 2d Dept) 61 AD2d 473, 402 NYS2d 593 (covenant not implied), revd 46 NY2d 62, 412 NYS2d 827, 385 NE2d 566.

See § 9:76, supra, for effect of personal relationship or right to assign.

10. §§ 6:22 et seq, supra.

11. Gen Obligations L § 5-1103.

or modify, or to discharge in whole or in part, any contract, obligation, or lease, or any mortgage or other security interest in personal or real property, shall not be invalid because of the absence of consideration, provided that the agreement, promise or undertaking changing, modifying or discharging such contract, obligation, lease, mortgage or security interest, shall be in writing and signed by the party against whom it is sought to enforce the change, modification or discharge, or by his agent.[12]

Moreover, an agreement modifying the rent payable under a lease which has more than one year to run must comply with the statute of frauds.[13] Thus, it was held that an agreement to change the rent reserved in a lease which had six years to run needed a written memorandum signed by the landlord to be valid and enforceable.[14]

It should also be observed that recorded mortgage-restrictions on the right of a mortgagor-landlord to modify a lease or to receive pre-payment of rent may be binding on the tenant.[15]

### § 12:17. Executed Modification of Rent

Insofar as an agreement for the modification of the rent to be paid under a lease has been executed, whether or not it is supported by any consideration, such modification agreement is binding on both parties. The courts have treated the difference between the rent originally reserved and the modified rent, paid by the tenant and accepted by the landlord pursuant to the modification agreement, as a gift from the landlord to the tenant.[16] Thus, an oral agreement by a landlord to accept reduced rent payments in full satisfaction of the rental payments called for by the lease, when carried out by payment by the tenant and acceptance by the landlord, will preclude the landlord from suing thereafter to recover the differ-

---

**12.** A corporate officer or director is not an "agent" for purposes of the requirement of the statute that the agent's authority be in writing. Scientific Holding Co. v Plessey, Inc. (1974, CA2 NY) 510 F2d 15. (See Gen Obligations L § 5-1111).

**13.** § 6:25, supra.

**14.** Jewell v Irvac Shoe Shops, Inc.
(S Ct Nassau Co 1959) 19 Misc 2d 815, 187 NYS2d 412.

**15.** See, Real Prop L § 291-f, quoted in § 27:75, infra.

**16.** McKenzie v Harrison (1890) 120 NY 260, 24 NE 458; Concourse & 181st Street Corp. v Freiman (AD1 1949) 276 AD 131, 93 NYS2d 13; Auswin Realty Corp. v Kirschbaum (AD2 1946) 270 AD 334, 59 NYS2d 824.

ence for those months for which he accepted the agreed reduction.[17]

However, the tenant must show that his payment, and that the landlord's acceptance, of the reduced rent were made pursuant to the landlord's agreement to reduce the rent. Thus, it has been held that the tenant's payment and the landlord's acceptance, of a sum less than the rent originally reserved without showing that the landlord had agreed to reduce the rent, and that the lesser amount was accepted by the landlord in full discharge of the tenant's liability for the whole rent, will be ineffective to discharge the tenant from liability for such difference.[18]

## B. PAYMENT OF RENT

### § 12:18. To Whom Payable

Unless assigned to someone else, rent is payable only to the one who is landlord at the time the rent accrues or becomes due and payable.[19] Where one other than the landlord seeks to recover the rent reserved in a lease, it is incumbent upon him to show his right and title to the rent involved.[20]

The Real Property Law provides, that where a tenant for life, who shall have leased the real property, dies before the first rent day, or between two rent days, his personal representative may recover the proportion of rent which accrued to him before his death.[1]

### § 12:19. Duty of Landlord to Provide Written Receipt

Real Property Law § 235-e provides, that upon the receipt of cash rent for *residential premises,* in the form of cash or any instrument other than the personal check of the tenant it shall be the duty of the landlord to

---

17. Greenberg v Furrer (AT1 1945) 56 NYS2d 340.
18. Pape v Rudolph Bros., Inc. (AD4 1939) 257 AD 1032, 13 NYS2d 781, reh and app den 257 AD 1100, 14 NYS2d 1007 and affd 282 NY 692, 26 NE2d 817.
19. 810 West End Ave., Inc. v Frankel (AT1 1920) 113 Misc 338, 184 NYS 554; Tufor Realty Corp. v Equity Express, Inc. (1953, City Ct NY Co) 120 NYS2d 693.

As to the rights to rent due or to become due on the transfer of the reversion by the landlord, see § 5:18, supra; as to rights of receiver in mortgage foreclosure action, see § 27:75, infra.

20. Drexler v Cohen (1908, Sup App T) 108 NYS 679; Gibbons v Hellwig (AT1 1899) 27 Misc 787, 58 NYS 291.

1. Real Prop L § 222.

## § 12:19     LANDLORD AND TENANT

provide the payor with a written receipt containing (1) the date, (2) the amount, (3) the identity of the premises and period for which paid, and (4) the signature and title of the person receiving the rent. Where a tenant, in writing, requests that a landlord provide a receipt for rent paid by personal check, it shall be the duty of the landlord to provide the payor with the receipt described above for each such written request.[2]

With respect to mobile home parks, Real Prop L § 233(q) provides:

Upon receipt of rent, fees, charges or other assessments, in the form of cash or any instrument other than the personal check of the tenant, it shall be the duty of the mobile home park owner or operator to provide the payor with a written receipt containing the following:

1. the date;

2. the amount;

3. the identity of the premises and the period for which paid;

4. the signature and title of the person receiving rent.

---

2. Section 27-2105 of the Administrative Code of the City of New York provides that at the time of each rental payment, either a rent bill or receipt for such payment shall be issued to the tenant of an apartment or rooming unit, stating the name and New York City address of the managing agent as recorded in the current registration statement on file in the Department. The registered name and address of the owner may be substituted for that of the managing agent if the owner resides or maintains an office where he or she customarily transacts business within New York City.

§ 2500.11 of the Tenant Protection Regulations of the Emergency Tenant Protection Act of 1974 provides, that no payment of rent need be made unless the landlord tenders a receipt for the amount to be paid when so requested by a tenant. (For full text of these Regulations, see New York RENT CONTROL AND RENT STABILIZATION by Joseph Rasch, published by The Lawyers Co-operative Publishing Co., Rochester, New York, 14694.

The owner of a multiple dwelling in the city of New York must issue to every residential tenant either a rent bill or rent receipt at the time of each rental payment as required by Housing Maintenance Code Section D26-41.17. The receipt may be imprinted on the tenant's check or money order rendered in payment of rent. All statements on such bill or receipt shall be legible and there shall be printed in ink or stamped thereon: (1) the name and address of the licensed real estate broker or firm in charge of the dwelling, stating that he or the firm is so licensed, or the name and address of the managing agent as recorded in the registration on file with the Office of Code Enforcement; (2) at the owner's option, a telephone listing at which he or someone acting in his behalf may be reached by the tenant for repairs and service; (3) at the owner's option, a statement, if rent is paid by check or money order, that such payment is received subject to collection.

Real Prop L § 233(r) provides for a limitation on late charges:

A late charge on any rental payment by a mobile home owner which has become due and remains unpaid shall not exceed and shall be enforced to the extent of five percent of such delinquent payment; provided, however, that no charge shall be imposed on any rental payment by a mobile home owner received within ten days after the due date. In the absence of a specific provision in the lease or the mobile home park's rules and regulations, no late charge on any delinquent rental payment shall be assessed or collected.

### § 12:20. When and Where Payable

The question where rent is payable usually becomes material in cases where a demand therefor is necessary as incident to an attempt by a landlord to work a forfeiture. It was said in a very early case that "rent issuing out of the land savors so far of the realty that it is payable on the leased premises."[3] Whether this is the reason, or whether it is reasonable to suppose that the parties intended that the rent should be paid on the leased premises, when a lease is silent as to the place of payment, the law fixes the place of payment at the leased premises.[4] Of course, if by the terms of the lease, the place where the tenant should pay the rent is fixed, the rent is payable at that place,[5] since, a lease may provide for payment of rent in any manner, or at any time that the parties elect.[6]

A covenant to pay rent creates no debt until the time stipulated for the payment thereof arrives.[7]

---

3. Walter v Dewey (1819) 16 Johns 222.

4. M. & E. Design Co., Inc. v Whitney's Cadillac Rental, Inc. (S Ct Queens Co 1947) 75 NYS2d 924.

5. Van Rensselaer v Jewett (1849) 2 NY 141, also holding that if there is a building on the land, the demand should be made at the front door thereof.

6. 34 West 34th Street Corp. v Nehama Realty Corp. (S Ct NY Co 1956) 7 Misc 2d 532, 153 NYS2d 427.

7. Re Ryan's Estate (1945) 294 NY 85, 60 NE2d 817.

Even though lease agreement of partnership is executed prior to a partner's entry into the partnership, rent as a debt arises only when it becomes due, and accordingly only those who were partners at the time of the default may be held personally liable therefor. Barbro Realty Co. v Newburger (1976, 1st Dept) 53 AD2d 34, 385 NYS2d 68.

§ 12:20      LANDLORD AND TENANT

Since the law takes no account of fractions of days,[8] rent which is due on a day certain is due at any and every hour of that day.[9] Therefore a tenant has until midnight of the day on which rent is due by the terms of a lease to pay it.[10]

### § 12:21. —Sunday or Public Holiday

It has been held that if the day on which the rent falls due is a Sunday,[11] or a public holiday, then it becomes due the next business day.[12] The statute now provides,[13] that where a contract by its terms authorizes or requires the payment of money or the performance of a condition on a Saturday, Sunday or a public holiday, or authorizes or requires the payment of money or the performance of a condition within or before or after a period of time computed from a certain day, and such period of time ends on a Saturday, Sunday or a public holiday, unless the contract expressly or impliedly indicates a different intent, such payment may be made or condition performed on the next succeeding business day, and if the period ends at a specified hour, such payment may be made or condition performed, at or before the same hour of such next succeeding business day, with the same force and effect as if made or performed in accordance with the terms of the contract.[14]

---

8. Craig v Butler (GT 1894) 83 Hun 286, 31 NYS 963, affd 156 NY 672, 50 NE 962.

9. Craig v Butler (GT 1894) 83 Hun 286, 31 NYS 963, affd 156 NY 672, 50 NE 962.

10. McDonald v Ruggiero (AD2 1910) 136 AD 699, 121 NYS 417, later app 144 AD 230, 129 NYS 77; Henninger v Clay (AT2 1956) 4 Misc 2d 795, 162 NYS2d 230; Wingood Realty Co. v Von Bayer (1918, Sup App T) 169 NYS 241; McCahill v Megs Palace Amusement Co. (1917, Sup App T) 167 NYS 373.

11. Pugh v Kraft (AT 1910) 126 NYS 162.

12. Where rent became due on January 1, 1959, a legal holiday, the tenant was held entitled to make payment on the next business day. Udell Estate, Inc. v Standard Handkerchief Co. (AT1 1959) 17 Misc 2d 879, 186 NYS2d 882; Walton v Stafford (1900) 162 NY 558, 561, 57 NE 92, holding contra, is no longer a valid precedent.

13. Gen Constr L § 25(1).

14. Gen Constr L § 20 provides, a number of days, specified as a period from a certain day within which or after or before which an act is authorized or required to be done means such number of calendar days exclusive of the calendar day from which the reckoning is made. If such period is a period of two days, Saturday, Sunday or a public holiday must be excluded from the reckoning if it is in an intervening day between the day from which the reckoning is made and the last day of the period. In computing any specified period of time from a specified event, the day upon which the event happens is deemed the day from which the reckoning is made. The day from which any specified period of time is reck-

## § 12:22. Application of Rent Payments

In the absence of any agreement to the contrary, the landlord can apply the moneys received from the tenant either to arrears in rent which theretofore accrued, or to the current rent.[15] However, in the absence of proof as to how the landlord credited rent payments, it will be presumed that the payments were credited against the oldest items due.[16]

## § 12:23. When Payable in Advance

Rent is not payable until after it has been earned. Therefore, when a lease provides that the rent shall be paid monthly, such rent is payable at the end of each month, and not in advance, in the absence of an express agreement to the contrary.[17] Thus, where a tenant agreed to pay an annual rent of $1500, payable in equal monthly payments on the first day of each and every month during the term, Ingraham, J., said,[18] "There was no provision in the lease that the rent was payable in advance. The defendant agreed to pay an annual rent of $1,500, payable in equal monthly payments on the 1st day of each and every month during the term, but this is not stated to be in advance. The payment was to be made on the 1st day of each month for the rent that had accrued for the preceding month."

A two-year lease provided "That the tenant shall pay the rent, nine hundred dollars ($900.00) per annum, from September 1, 1919, to August 31, 1921." "Under the terms of the lease," said Guy, J.,[19] "the rent was payable at the end of the first year, and evidence varying the terms of the written contract was incompetent, and should have been excluded." But, as to a monthly or month to month tenancy, it has been held that the rent is payable in advance on the first day of the month without the necessity of any agreement to that effect.[20]

Where parties during negotiations for a lease agreed to

oned shall be excluded in making the reckoning.

**15.** 2765 Ocean Ave. v Roth (1942, Sup App T) 33 NYS2d 418.

**16.** Hughes v Wagner (1957, 3d Dept) 4 AD2d 980, 167 NYS2d 869.

**17.** Smathers v Standard Oil Co. (AD1 1922) 199 AD 368, 191 NYS 843, affd 233 NY 617, 135 NE 942.

**18.** Goldsmith v Schroeder (AD1 1904) 93 AD 206, 87 NYS 558.

**19.** Hayes v Rosenblatt (AT1 1920) 111 Misc 370, 181 NYS 241.

**20.** Cohen v Rhoades (1942, Sup App T) 36 NYS2d 320.

incorporate in the formal lease the "usual convenants and conditions," it was held that such an agreement would not include a covenant to pay rent in advance, since, as the court in so holding said, the covenant to pay rent in advance is not "a usual one."[1]

However, the parties to a lease may make provision for the payment of rent in advance. "A contract to pay rent in advance," said Taylor, J.,[2] is not illegal or void." Accordingly, even though the tenant may occupy the leased premises only for a few days during a particular month, if the rent is payable monthly in advance on the first day of the month, the tenant is obligated to pay the entire month's rent.[3]

Therefore, unless a lease expressly provides for the payment of the rent in advance, it is payable at the end of the term, or at the end of the stipulated period.[4]

## § 12:24. —Form

### FORM NO. 23

### Provision for Payment of Rent in Advance*

Landlord hereby leases to Tenant, and Tenant hereby hires from Landlord ........, for the term of ........ (or until such term shall sooner cease and expire as hereinafter provided) to commence on ........ and to end on ........, both dates inclusive, at an annual rental rate of ........ which Tenant agrees to pay in equal monthly installments in advance on the first day of each month during said term at the office of Landlord or such other place as Landlord may designate, without any setoff or deduction whatsoever, except that Tenant shall pay the first ........ monthly installment(s) on the execution hereof (unless this lease is a renewal).

---

1. Arcade Realty Co. v Tunney (AT 1906) 52 Misc 148, 101 NYS 593.
2. Giles v Comstock (1850) 4 NY 270, 272.
3. Bernstein v Englander (AT1) 25 NYS2d 319.
4. De Simone v Canzonieri (AD2 1935) 246 AD 735, 283 NYS 860; Smathers v Standard Oil Co. (AD1 1922) 199 AD 368, 191 NYS 843, affd 233 NY 617, 135 NE 942; McCahill v Megs Palace Amusement Co. (1917, Sup App T) 167 NYS 373.

No suit may be brought for future rent in the absence of a clause permitting acceleration. Utility Garage Corp. v National Biscuit Co. (1979, 1st Dept) 71 AD2d 578, 418 NYS2d 87.

* For complete form of lease see Chapter 1.

## § 12:25. Course of Conduct Establishing Mode of Payment

Although a lease may stipulate the times when, and the places where, rents are payable, yet the parties may by their course of conduct establish another method,[5] or place[6] for the payment of rent.

In order to re-establish the method of payment required by the terms of the lease, after a modification thereof by the course of conduct of the parties, the landlord must notify the tenant that the custom created by the tenant will not be permitted, nor should be continued, in the future, and that payment of rent will be required upon the days stipulated in the lease. Otherwise, so long as the tenant complies with the customary method of payment, he will not be regarded as in default in performing his covenant to pay rent as originally provided.[7]

Although a lease may contain a non-waiver provision, nevertheless, if a course of conduct has been established of accepting tardy rent payments, the tenant will not be regarded as in default. Thus, in one case a lease provided that the rent was to be paid in advance on the first day of each and every month during the term. The tenant paid March rent on the 28th of March, and paid April rent on the 18th of April. On May 6 the tenant tendered May's rent, but the landlord rejected it as too late, and sought to terminate the lease under a provision therein allowing the landlord to terminate the lease on five days' notice for tenant's breach thereof. The tenant contended that a course of conduct had been established of accepting rent after the first, and that as long as he complied with this method of payment he could not be regarded as in default. The landlord sought to overcome the application of this rule by relying on this provision in the lease: "The failure of the landlord to insist upon a strict performance of any of the terms, conditions and covenants herein shall

---

5. McCutcheon Realty Corp. v Kilb (M Ct 1927) 129 Misc 637, 222 NYS 244.
Also, see Montant v Moore (AD1 1909) 135 AD 334, 120 NYS 556; Paul Pleating & Stitching Co. v Levine (M Ct 1930) 137 Misc 82, 242 NYS 729.

6. Stratford Leasing Corporation v Meyerson (AT1 1959) 21 Misc 2d 291, 199 NYS2d 782, app den (1st Dept) 10 AD2d 614, 197 NYS2d 421.

7. Montant v Moore (AD1 1909) 135 AD 334, 120 NYS 556; Small v De Bruyn (M Ct 1946) 187 Misc 1045, 65 NYS2d 591; Paul Pleating & Stitching Co. v Levine (M Ct 1930) 137 Misc 82, 242 NYS 729; McCutcheon Realty Corp. v Kilb (M Ct 1927) 129 Misc 637, 222 NYS 241, 244.

not be deemed a waiver of any rights or remedies that the landlord may have and shall not be deemed a waiver of any subsequent breach or default in the terms, conditions and covenants herein contained." Lauer, J.,[8] in ruling that the tenant was not in default notwithstanding this provision of non-waiver, said, "It is true that the lease provides that a previous waiver shall not be deemed a waiver of any subsequent breach or default, but where a course of conduct has been established of the acceptance of rent by the landlord after the 1st of the month, when, according to the terms of the lease, the rent was payable, something must be done to indicate to the tenant that the landlord intends to live up to the strict letter of the lease. Here the landlord accepted on a day much later than the due date the rents for the two previous months, thus leading the tenant to the belief that a strict performance according to the terms of the lease so far as the date of payment of the rent is concerned was not insisted upon. Had the landlord sought to advise the tenant that it proposed to have him live up to the strict terms of the agreement by making the payment of rent on the 1st of the month, as therein provided, I think a proper construction of the waiver clause of the lease would be that the landlord had not waived his right to insist on payments according to the terms of the lease. In other words, he would not have waived his right of insistence upon strict performance by any earlier waiver such as the acceptance of rent for two previous months at a later date than the due date."

Therefore, a party to whom a sum of money is payable at a specific time can, if he wishes, waive the right to receive it at such a time, or waive the right to enforce any penalty or forfeiture because of a failure of payment at the specified time. Such waiver will result from the parties' having established a custom by which a particular method has been adopted for making such payments, and, so long as such custom is complied with, the person who is obligated to make the payments is not in default. This customary method of payment will prevail over the method stipulated in the lease until, as the Appellate

---

8. Paul Pleating & Stitching Co. v Levine (M Ct 1930) 137 Misc 82, 242 NYS 729.

Division said,[9] "the lessee has notice of the fact that such a custom will not in the future be continued and payment is required upon the day named in the contract."[10]

### § 12:26. Provision for Acceleration

A lease may provide that upon default in the payment of the rent in installments as therein provided, the whole of the rent reserved for the balance of the term shall at once become due and payable without any notice or demand. Such an acceleration clause is valid and enforceable.[11]

The argument has been advanced, that such a clause in its operation upon a default in paying one installment of rent exacts a penalty, which the courts will refuse to enforce no matter in what form the exaction is framed, nor in what disguise it is dressed. But, such argument is untenable; for there is no other basis in such a clause for exacting the payment of the whole rent, other than that provided for in the clause; to wit, the default in the payment of an installment of rent. As the Appellate Division said,[12] "That an agreement for the payment of rent in advance for the whole duration of any term would be a condition which might be imposed unrelated to any other condition of the lease seems to be conceded, as indeed it must, if parties are to have their liberty of contract preserved. The mere fact, then, that another clause permits the payment of the rent in monthly in-

---

9. Montant v Moore (AD1 1909) 135 AD 334, 120 NYS 556.

10. See Lester Taylor, Inc. v Teller (AD1 1960) 28 Misc 2d 508, 208 NYS2d 142, where the court pointed out that while late rent-payments may have been acquiesced in by the landlord for a lengthy period, the issuance of nine precepts within 16 months shows conclusively that he did not condone the late payments for this last period of the tenancy.

11. Belnord Realty Co. v Levison (AD1 1923) 204 AD 415, 198 NYS 184; Engelberg v Morris (City Ct Long Beach 1960) 25 Misc 2d 409, 202 NYS2d 670; Myer v Garlock, (S Ct NY Co 1944) 183 Misc 547, 49 NYS 437.

Fifty States Management Corp. v Pioneer Auto Parks, Inc. (1979) 46 NY2d 573, 415 NYS2d 800, 389 NE2d 113 (citing text) ("Absent some element of fraud, exploitive overreaching or unconscionable conduct on the part of the landlord to exploit a technical breach, there is no warrant, either in law or equity, for a court to refuse enforcement of the agreement of the parties.")

However, it has been observed that a lessor who elects to accelerate future rentals may be acting unconscionably if the lessee's default was the result of a mistake of a trifling nature, the lessee had attempted to cure the default immediately upon learning of it, and the default did not prejudice the lessor. Di Matteo v North Tonawanda Auto Wash, Inc. (1984, 4th Dept) 101 AD2d 692, 476 NYS2d 40. Also, see § 23:53.

12. Belnord Realty Co. v Levison (AD1 1923) 204 AD 415, 198 NYS 184.

§ 12:26 LANDLORD AND TENANT

stallments for convenience cannot render that which was otherwise permissible a violation of the legal rule against the enforcement of a provision exacting a penalty. . . . Nothing is found in this lease but an acceleration of payments, so as to make the full sum at once due based on a default in a single payment, a familiar and recognized form of agreement in bonds secured by mortgage, in promissory notes, in sales of chattels on installment payments, and in contracts for services, hitherto never contended as unenforceable because of penal attribute."

An acceleration clause providing that the rent for the balance of the term shall become due prior to an assignee's entry into possession of the leased premises has been held to be valid and enforceable.[13]

But the draftsman of an acceleration clause must be careful to avoid providing for an acceleration as a penalty. In a leading case in the Court of Appeals,[14] Andrews, J., said, that "where a contract contains a number of covenants of different degrees of importance, and the loss resulting from the breach of some of them will be clearly disproportionate to the sum sought to be fixed as liquidated damages, especially where the loss in some cases is readily ascertainable, the sum so fixed will be treated as a penalty." If the clause is a penalty, it will not be enforced.

If the acceleration clause, then, provides that the basis for the acceleration is not only a default in paying an installment of rent, but may become operative upon the breach of many trivial and inconsequential conditions of the lease, then the court will treat such clause as a penalty, and will not enforce it. The following clause is of that type:

> The tenant hereby agrees to pay the rent as above stipulated without any deduction, fraud or delay, and the tenant also agrees that if said rent is not paid at the time and in the manner above provided, or if default shall be made in any cove-

---

13. Conditioner Leasing Corp. v Sternmor Realty Corp. (1966) 17 NY2d 1, 266 NYS2d 801, 213 NE2d 884.

14. Seidlitz v Auerbach (1920) 230 NY 167, 173, 129 NE 461.

Also, see, Fifty States Management Corp. v Pioneer Auto Parks, Inc. (1979) 46 NY2d 573, 415 NYS2d 800, 389 NE2d 113.

nant or agreement herein contained, or if the said premises or any part thereof shall become vacant during the term hereby demised, or if the lease is terminated by the landlord in article 15 hereof, the landlord may resume possession of said premises by summary proceedings to dispossess or otherwise, without notice to the tenant, which notice is hereby expressly waived, and in the event of the landlord so resuming possession, an amount equal to the whole of the rent herein reserved for the balance of the term as herein originally demised shall thereupon become immediately due and payable by the tenant to the landlord, and the tenant expressly agrees that he will forthwith pay the same to the landlord, . . . .

In analyzing this clause, Dowling, J., speaking for the Appellate Division[15] observed that this clause was so unconscionable as to amount to a forfeiture or penalty, and would not be enforced. Under the terms of the clause the landlord will become entitled to payment of an amount equal to the whole of the rent therein reserved ($22,500) less any rent that may have been paid, upon (a) failure to pay any monthly installment of rent when due; (b) default in any covenant or agreement of the lease,—these number sixteen, some important, many trivial, such as not driving picture or other nails into the walls, or making disturbing noises or singing after 10 p.m.; (c) if the premises or any part shall become vacant during the term, even if the tenant is willing to continue his monthly installments; (d) if the lease be terminated as provided by another article of the lease. "It will be seen," Dowling, J., said, "that this lease, most exhaustive in the restrictions and burdens placed upon the tenant, leaves him at the mercy of the landlord, who for breach of the most trivial requirement has the right to declare a default, and to call for payment of the rent for the remainder of the term. Some of the conditions under which this may happen are so insignificant and trivial, involving either no damage whatever or a nominal amount, as to show that the provision for the payment of the whole

---

**15.** 884 West End Ave. Corp. v Pearlman (AD1 1922) 201 AD 12, 193 NYS 670, affd 234 NY 589, 138 NE 458.

§ 12:26     LANDLORD AND TENANT

rent reserved is in reality a penalty entirely disproportionate to any damage that could possibly ensue for the tenant's acts. Nor is this case comparable to those where an acceleration of the date for payment of the principal of a mortgage is provided in case of failure to meet interest due. There the obligation to pay the entire principal is fixed and certain, and the whole amount is payable in any event. . . . the acceleration of payment in the case is not effected by default in the payment of rent only, but may be enforced for breach of many trivial and inconsequential conditions."

Accordingly, although an acceleration clause may be used, it should be made operative only in the event of a default in the payment of an installment of rent. Otherwise, it may be construed to constitute a penalty, and will be unenforceable.

It is a well established that no action can be brought for future rent in the absence of a provision permitting acceleration,[16] since the breach of an agreement to pay money in installments is not a breach of the entire agreement, and will not permit a recovery of all the damages in advance.[17]

### § 12:27. —Form

## FORM NO. 24

### Acceleration Clause

It is hereby mutually agreed that, notwithstanding anything herein to the contrary, the said premises are leased for a rental of *[Fifteen Thousand ($15,000) Dollars]* for the entire said term, payable at the time of the making of this lease, and that the provisions herein contained for the payment of said rent in installments are for the convenience of Tenant only, and that, upon default in payment of the rent in installments as herein allowed, then the whole of the rent hereby reserved for the whole of the said term and then remaining unpaid shall at once become due and payable, without any notice or demand.[18]

---

16. Maflo Holding Corp. v S. J. Blume, Inc. (1955) 308 NY 570, 127 NE2d 558, remittitur amd 309 NY 751, 128 NE2d 798.

17. McCready v Lindenborn (1902) 172 NY 400, 65 NE 208.

18. Adapted from the clause held valid and enforceable in Belnord

## § 12:28. Recovery by Tenant of Rent Paid

It is universally recognized that money voluntarily paid with full knowledge of the facts cannot be recovered.[19] This rule has been applied to voluntary payments of rent in excess of the amount owing.[20]

Similarly, the general principle of contract law that recovery may be had of payments made as the consequence of duress, fraud, mistake, or failure of consideration, are also applicable to the right of a tenant to recover back rent payments made by him under these circumstances.[1] However, where there was simply a mistake as to the ownership of the rented property, not induced by the fraud of the lessor, and the tenant paying rental under such mistaken belief had possession of the rented premises without interference for the term for which the rent had been paid, and was not required to pay the true owner of the property for such occupancy, it was held that he could not recover the rentals paid to the lessor-recipient, even though the latter was not the owner of the property for which rent had been paid.[2]

The right of a tenant to recover back rent which he has paid has been adjudicated in a number of specific situations. Thus, where the lease stipulated that the building could be used only for cabaret purposes, but a license was refused by the public authorities because the building was not fireproof, it was held that the tenant could recover the rent which he had paid, the court stating that where parties, in good faith, make an agreement under which one has paid money and promises to make further payments over a long period, the consideration must be deemed to have failed where the contract was incapable of lawful performance when it was made.[3] However, it has been held that a tenant cannot recover back rent

---

Realty Co. v Levison (AD1 1923) 204 AD 415, 198 NYS 184.

For complete form of lease see Chapter 1.

**19.** Adrico Realty Corp. v New York (1928) 250 NY 29, 164 NE 732, 64 ALR 1.

**20.** Kienle v Fred Gretsch Realty Co. (AD2 1909) 133 AD 391, 117 NYS 500; Gerry v Siebrecht (1904, Sup App T) 88 NYS 1034.

**1.** § 2:11, supra.

**2.** Metropolitan Fuel Distributors v Coogan (AD1 1950) 277 AD 138, 97 NYS2d 851.

**3.** Economy v S. B. & L. Bldg. Corp. (AT1 1930) 138 Misc 296, 245 NYS 352.

paid during his unlawful occupancy of the premises.[4] Similarly, where the contemplated reinforcement of the floor of the leased premises, which was to be done in order to comply with the requirements of law, is prevented because of the refusal of a tenant on a lower floor to grant permission to alter the premises, the tenant is not entitled to a return of the rent paid during the period of his occupancy.[5]

If there are no circumstances surrounding the payment which constitute coercion or compulsion in the eyes of the law, the fact that the payment is made under the most solemn protest does not render it any the less voluntary, and the payment cannot be recovered.[6] The payment should be made "without prejudice to tenant's right to contest landlord's demand."[7]

### § 12:29. Separate Actions for Installments

The general rule that in the case of contracts to pay money in installments, each default in payment of an installment may be the subject of an independent action, provided it is brought before the next installment is due,[8] applies to actions to recover installments of rent.[9] Accord-

---

4. Thus, where occupation of leased premises was unlawful because of violation of zoning and building regulations, the tenant who thereupon abandoned possession was not permitted to recover back the rent he had paid during such unlawful occupation. Schotz-Powers Co. v Treidler (AT1 1926) 128 Misc 466, 219 NYS 4.

The fact that a tenant's occupancy was unlawful, because of the lack of a certificate of occupancy as required by law, would not permit him to recover back rent paid during such unlawful occupancy. Wokal v Sequin (M Ct Queens 1938) 167 Misc 463, 4 NYS2d 86, referring to Multiple Dwelling L § 302, subd 1, and holding that the provision prohibiting the recovery of rent by the landlord during the period of violation did not, however, extend any right of recovery back to the tenant.

A tenant may not, because of a subsequent violation of the requirement of a certificate of occupancy, recover rents paid previously to such violation. Bridge Hardware Co. v Mayer (AT1 1954) 131 NYS2d 823.

5. Elkar Realty Corp. v Mitsuye T. Kamada (1958, 1st Dept) 6 AD2d 155, 175 NYS2d 669, reh and app den (1st Dept) 6 AD2d 1007, 178 NYS2d 212 and reh den (1st Dept) 6 AD2d 1007, 179 NYS2d 840 and app dismd 5 NY2d 844, 181 NYS2d 786, 155 NE2d 669.

For additional examples, see § 8:2, supra, where landlord cannot deliver possession; §§ 2:12, et seq, supra, dealing with tenant's remedies where the occupancy of the leased premises is illegal or becomes illegal; §§ 25:3, et seq, infra, where the premises are destroyed during the term.

6. Gerry v Siebrecht (1904, Sup App T) 88 NYS 1034; Castano v Gabriel (Civ Ct NY Co 1969) 60 Misc 2d 218, 302 NYS2d 943.

7. Castano v Gabriel (Civ Ct NY Co 1969) 60 Misc 2d 218, 302 NYS2d 943.

8. McCready v Lindenborn (1902) 172 NY 400, 65 NE 208.

9. Lorillard v Clyde (1890) 122 NY 41, 25 NE 292; Pearlbroad Realty

ingly, if rent is payable periodically under a lease for a definite term, the landlord may maintain an action for each installment as it becomes due, without violating the rule against splitting causes of action, or prejudicing his right to sue for subsequent installments as they become due.[10] An action for rent due on a single contract must include all installments due at the time of its commencement, since if there are several installments due, the claim therefor cannot be split up into several actions;[11] and all installments due when the action is brought for rent due and unpaid, which are not included in the action, are thereafter barred if there is a recovery in the action.[12]

### § 12:30. Liability for Rent upon Death of Tenant

As has been seen,[13] the death of the tenant does not terminate a lease. The leasehold passes as personal property to the executor or administrator of the deceased tenant. Accordingly, the contract of the tenant to pay rent is not discharged by his death, but survives as a claim against the tenant's estate, not only for rent accrued at the time of the tenant's death, but also for rents subsequently accruing.[14]

The executor or administrator of the deceased tenant is not personally liable as an assignee of the decedent's lease unless he enters and holds possession.[15]

## C. RESEARCH REFERENCES

### § 12:31. Generally

In addition to the preceding text, the reader is also referred to the following:

49 Am Jur 2d, Landlord and Tenant §§ 513-650.

11 Am Jur Legal Forms 2d, Leases of Real Property §§ 161:121-161:237.

16 Am Jur Pleading and Practice Forms (Rev ed), Landlord and Tenant, Forms 1-112.

---

Corp. v Broadstreet Stationers, Inc. (1945, Sup App T) 56 NYS2d 289.

**10.** Kennedy v New York (1909) 196 NY 19, 89 NE 360.

**11.** Kennedy v New York (1909) 196 NY 19, 89 NE 360.

**12.** Kennedy v New York (1909) 196 NY 19, 89 NE 360. Solow v Avon Products, Inc. (1977, 1st Dept) 56 AD2d 785, 392 NYS2d 618, affd 44 NY2d 711, 405 NYS2d 449, 376 NE2d 921.

**13.** See § 9:52, supra.

**14.** MacDonald v Rosenblum (1934) 150 Misc 556, 269 NYS 562.

**15.** See § 9:53, supra.

§ 12:31                 LANDLORD AND TENANT

New York Jur 2d, Landlord and Tenant (1st ed §§ 271-326).

New York CLS Real Property Law §§ 221, 222.

New York Forms, Leases, Forms 8:101-8:121.

Index to Annotations, Landlord and Tenant.

**VERALEX®:** Cases and annotations referred to herein can be further researched through the VERALEX electronic retrieval system's two services, **Auto-Cite®** and **SHOWME®**. Use Auto-Cite to check citations for form, parallel references, prior and later history, and annotation references. Use SHOWME to display the full text of cases and annotations.

## CHAPTER 13

## DEPOSIT TO SECURE PERFORMANCE OF LEASE

A. IN GENERAL
§ 13:1. Provision for Security Deposit; Form
§ 13:2. Importance of Determining Nature of Deposit
§ 13:3. Difficulty of Ascertaining Nature of Deposit
§ 13:4. Nature of Deposit Determined as of Execution of Lease
§ 13:5. Immateriality of Names Used, in Determining Nature of Deposit
§ 13:6. Criteria for Determining Nature of Deposit
§ 13:7. Effect of Agreement to Apply Deposit to Rent
§ 13:8. Penalty Construction Favored
§ 13:9. Construction Where Performance of Several Covenant Secured
§ 13:10. Construction Where Deposit Limited to Breach of a Material Covenant
§ 13:11. Rent Security Deposit by Social Service Officials
§ 13:12. Exempt from Satisfaction of Judgment
§ 13:13. Determination of Nature of Deposit Binding on Both Parties

B. RIGHTS TO DEPOSIT
§ 13:14. On Renewal of Lease
§ 13:15. On Creation of Holdover Tenancy
§ 13:16. On Conveyance of Fee
§ 13:17. On Assignment of Lease by Tenant
§ 13:18. Assignability of Deposit
§ 13:19. Rights of Assignee of Lease
§ 13:20. Rights to Deposit Assigned in Violation of Lease

C. DUTY WITH RESPECT TO DEPOSIT ON CONVEYANCE OF LEASED PROPERTY
§ 13:21. Landlord's Statutory Duty on Conveyance
§ 13:22. Liability of Grantee or Assignee for Deposits Made by Tenant on Conveyance of Rent Stabilized Dwelling Units
§ 13:23. Liability of Grantee or Assignee for Deposits Made by Tenant on Conveyance of Non-Rent Stabilized Dwelling Units
§ 13:24. Form of Clause for Landlord-Grantor's Protection on Conveyance

§ 13:1            LANDLORD AND TENANT

    § 13:25. Liability for Interest
    § 13:26. Federal Income Tax on Security Deposit Interest

D. CONVERSION OF DEPOSIT
    § 13:27. Deposit as Trust Fund
    § 13:28. —Mobile Home Park Lease
    § 13:29. Conversion of Deposit
    § 13:30. —As Bar to Summary Proceeding

E. AGREEMENT TO APPLY DEPOSIT TO RENT
    § 13:31. How Applied
    § 13:32. Agreement Binding on Grantee

F. RESEARCH REFERENCES
    § 13:33. Generally

## A. IN GENERAL

### § 13:1. Provision for Security Deposit; Form

It is quite usual for a landlord to require a tenant to deposit with him a sum of money or other security, such as a bond,[1] to secure payment of rent, or performance of the covenants and conditions of the lease on the tenant's part to be performed.[2] Failure to give a required security

---

1. Piser v Hecht (AD1 1915) 170 AD 668, 156 NYS 601. Deposit under agreement for lease, see §§ 3:11 et seq, supra.

2. NY City Rent Eviction and Rehabilitation Regulations § 2205.4 provides, with respect to security deposits: "Regardless of any contract, agreement, lease or other obligation heretofore or hereafter entered into, no person shall demand, receive or retain a security deposit for or in connection with the use and occupancy of housing accommodations, except: (a) if the demand, collection, or retention of such security deposit was permitted under the Rent Regulations promulgated pursuant to the Federal Act, the State Rent Law or the local laws of the City of New York, and said security deposit does not exceed the rent for one month in addition to the authorized collection of rent; or (b) if the demand, collection, or retention of such security deposit was pursuant to a rental agreement with the tenant and said security deposit does not exceed the rent for one month (or for one week where the rental payment period is for a term of less than one month) in addition to the authorized collection of rent, provided in all cases (1) that said security deposit shall be deposited in a banking organization no later than July 15, 1960, or within 15 days after receipt thereof, whichever is later, which shall be placed in an interest bearing account on or before October 1, 1974, or the date of any deposit made thereafter; (2) the person depositing such security money shall be entitled to receive as reimbursement for administrative expenses a sum equivalent to one percent per annum upon the security money so deposited; (3) the balance of the interest paid by the banking organization shall be held in trust until applied for the rental of the housing accommodations, or until paid to the tenant not less often than annually by check or cash; and provided further, with respect to properties or buildings containing six or more family dwelling units, nothing set forth in this section shall be construed to relieve any person receiving or retaining any rent security deposit for or in connection with the use or occupancy of any dwelling unit therein from complying and continuing to comply with the requirements

deposit constitutes a breach of a substantial obligation of a tenancy.[3] and if the security deposit is not kept whole, the landlord may maintain a suit in equity to compel the tenant to restore the deposit.[4]

## FORM NO. 25
### Provision for Security Deposit*

Tenant has deposited with Landlord by check, subject to collection, the sum of $    as security for the faithful performance and observance by Tenant of the terms, provisions and conditions of this lease; it is agreed that in the event Tenant defaults in respect of any of the terms, provisions and conditions of this lease, including, but not limited to, the payment of rent and additional rent, Landlord may use, apply or retain the whole or any part of the security so deposited to the extent required for the payment of any rent and additional rent or any other sum as to which Tenant is in default or for any sum which Landlord may expend or may be required to expend by reason of Tenant's default in respect of any of the terms, covenants and conditions of this lease, including but not limited to, any damages or deficiency in the re-letting of the premises, whether such damages or deficiency accrued before or after summary proceedings or other re-entry by Landlord. In the event that Tenant shall fully and faithfully comply with all of the terms, provisions, covenants and conditions of this lease, the security shall be returned to Tenant after the date fixed as the end of the Lease and after delivery of entire possession of the leased premises to Landlord. In the event of a sale of the land and building or leasing of the building, of which the leased premises form a part, Landlord shall have the right to transfer the security to the vendee or lessee and Landlord shall thereupon be released by Tenant from all liability for the return of such security; and Tenant agrees to look to the new Landlord

of Article 7 of the General Obligations Law.

3. Park Holding Co. v Johnson (NYC Civ Ct NY Co 1980) 106 Misc 2d 834, 435 NYS2d 479 (tenant's check for security dishonored; landlord rightfully terminated lease).

4. Atlas v Moritz (1926) 217 AD 38, 216 NYS 490; Turquoise Realty Corp. v Burke (M Ct 1938) 168 Misc 670, 6 NYS2d 125.

* For complete form of lease, see Chapter 1, supra.

§ 13:1  LANDLORD AND TENANT

solely for the return of said security; and it is agreed that the provisions hereof shall apply to every transfer or assignment made of the security to a new Landlord. Tenant further covenants that it will not assign or encumber or attempt to assign or encumber the monies deposited herein as security and that neither Landlord nor its successors or assigns shall be bound by any such assignment, encumbrance, attempted assignment or attempted encumbrance.[5]

### § 13:2. Importance of Determining Nature of Deposit

A deposit of money or other security to secure payment of rent or performance of the conditions and covenants of the lease on the tenant's part to be performed may constitute a penalty, or, as it is sometimes called, security; or, the deposit may constitute liquidated damages. It is important to ascertain the nature of the deposit.

If a deposit is determined to be liquidated damages for a stipulated breach or breaches of a lease, then, upon the occurrence of such breach or breaches, the deposit is immediately forfeited to the landlord as the full measure of the tenant's liability for such breach. Thereupon, any further claims of the landlord for damages by reason of such breach or breaches are extinguished and no action can be brought for the return of the deposit.[1] Where there is a provision in a lease as to the amount of damages that is to be paid by either party for a stipulated breach, then, said the Appellate Division, [2] "in the absence of fraud or mistake, the only question which arises is as to the breach. In that case the actual damage is not involved. One cannot recover both. The recovery of one precludes the recovery of the other. . . . To permit a recovery of actual damage, where liquidated damages have been provided for, is to nullify the statute or destroy a contract with reference thereto. The sole purpose of providing for liquidated damages is to prevent, in case of a breach, any

---

5. See § 13:9, infra. This provision constitutes a penalty.

1. Seidlitz v Auerbach (1920) 230 NY 167, 129 NE 461; Caesar v Rubinson (1903) 174 NY 492, 67 NE 58; Downtown Harvard Lunch Club v Rasco, Inc. (S Ct NY Co 1951) 201 Misc 1087, 107 NYS2d 918.

2. New York v Seely-Taylor Co. (AD1 1912) 149 AD 98, 133 NYS 808, affd 208 NY 548, 101 NE 1098.

question being raised as to the amount that shall be paid or recovered therefor."[3]

However, if a deposit is determined to be a penalty, rather than liquidated damages, then it is merely security, or indemnity, for performance. If the tenant breaches his agreement, the landlord is not confined to the deposit for his remedy. But, if he does resort to it, he will be entitled to retain no more of it than will make him whole, that is, indemnify him, for the actual damages he may have sustained by the breach.[4] As the Court of Appeals said,[5] "Nonperformance by the depositor, in the case of a security deposit, does not vest title in the secured party. It merely gives the secured party the right to resort to the security, but only to the extent of actual indemnification for his loss or damage."

### § 13:3. Difficulty of Ascertaining Nature of Deposit

As early as 1877, the Court of Appeals said,[6] "The question whether a sum named in a contract, to be paid for a failure to perform, shall be regarded as stipulated damages, or a penalty, has been frequently before the courts, and has given them much trouble. The cases cannot all be harmonized, and they furnish conspicuous examples of judicial efforts to make for parties wise and more prudent contracts than they had made for themselves."

In 1891 the same Court said,[7] "The result of an examination of cases is to confirm the idea that it is difficult, if it is even possible, to lay down a general rule applicable to all the cases which arise, where parties have undertaken to provide against a loss consequent upon a breach of an agreement."[8]

---

3. Also, see Kreiger v Nusbaum (AT1 1917) 100 Misc 673, 166 NYS 729.

Where parties have provided for a liquidated damage clause, there is no necessity for plaintiff to show affirmatively that he has sustained actual damages in any specific amount. Alwan v Ayoub (1970, 2d Dept) 35 AD2d 1006, 318 NYS2d 387.

4. Seidlitz v Auerbach (1920) 230 NY 167, 174, 129 NE 461; Chaude v Shepard (1890) 122 NY 397, 25 NE 358; Scott v Montells (1888) 109 NY 1, 3, 15 NE 729; Downtown Harvard Lunch Club v Rasco, Inc (S Ct NY Co 1951) 201 Misc 1087, 107 NYS2d 918.

5. Peirson v Lloyds First Mortg. Co. (1932) 260 NY 214, 222, 183 NE 368.

6. Kemp v Knickerbocker Ice Co. (1877) 69 NY 45.

7. Ward v Hudson River Bldg. Co. (1891) 125 NY 230, 235, 26 NE 256.

8. Also, see Realworth Properties, Inc. v Bachler (S Ct Monroe Co 1962) 33 Misc 2d 39, 223 NYS2d 910.

## § 13:3

Apparently the situation had not improved as late as 1920; for, then, Andrews, J., speaking for the Court of Appeals,[9] said, "There is little satisfactory discussion on this question in the higher courts of the state."

The difficulty arises from the fact that fundamentally it is a question of construction which depends upon the intent of the parties, as evidenced by the entire agreement construed in the light of the circumstances under which it was made.[10]

An analysis of the cases dealing with this subject indicates that certain guides or rules of construction have been regularly followed by the courts. A knowledge of these rules will be helpful in drafting a deposit clause, so that the intent of the parties may be clearly expressed.

### § 13:4. Nature of Deposit Determined as of Execution of Lease

In determining whether, a deposit is to be treated as liquidated damages, or as a penalty, the courts will invariably interpret the lease as of its date, and not as of its breach.[11] The reason for this rule of interpretation, it has been observed,[12] is that if this question were to be determined by events subsequent to the making of the agreement, the greater the neglect of the defaulting party, the better position he would occupy.

### § 13:5. Immateriality of Names Used, in Determining Nature of Deposit

"Whether the sum agreed between parties," said the Court of Appeals,[13] "to be paid, in the event of a breach of some agreement is termed by them a 'penalty' or 'liquidated damages,' is not controlling upon the question of construction. Their use of such words is not always conclusive as to their legal meaning. To get at that we must consider the subject matter and nature of the agreement and understand clearly the intention of the

---

9. Seidlitz v Auerbach (1920) 230 NY 167, 173, 129 NE 461.

10. Ward v Hudson River Bldg. Co. (1891) 125 NY 230, 235, 26 NE 256.

11. Seidlitz v Auerbach (1920) 230 NY 167, 172, 129 NE 461; Realworth Properties, Inc. v Bachler (S Ct Monroe Co 1962) 33 Misc 2d 39, 223 NYS2d 910; Downtown Harvard Lunch Club v Racso, Inc. (S Ct NY Co 1951) 201 Misc 1087, 107 NYS2d 918.

12. Dunn v Morgenthau (AD1 1902) 73 AD 147, 76 NYS 827, affd 175 NY 518, 67 NE 1081.

13. Ward v Hudson River Bldg. Co. (1891) 125 NY 230, 234, 26 NE 256.

parties."[14] Thus, where a stipulation in a lease providing for a deposit as security for the faithful performance by the lessee, the deposit to be retained as liquidated damages in case the landlord should bring summary proceedings, was held to be a provision for a penalty, the court explained this holding by saying, "It is, of course, well established that parties have a right to agree that, in case of a breach of covenant, a certain sum shall be fixed in advance as the damages for that breach. If they have actually agreed that the sum to be paid on a breach represents an estimate of the damages sustained, the party in default must pay these damages, even though the agreement uses words such as 'forfeit' or 'penalty.' On the other hand, though the parties, in their agreement, have used words such as 'liquidated damages,' the courts will regard the clause for the payment of a fixed sum upon the happening of a breach as a penalty or forfeiture, if it appears that the parties did in fact regard the sum fixed as a penalty, and not as an estimate of probable damages fixed in advance."[15]

No rule of law forbids parties from agreeing between themselves with respect to the anticipatory loss which shall be occasioned by a failure to carry out an obligation. When they have done so, however, "their declaration, in the event anticipated, that the sum fixed is a liquidation of the damages, or a penalty, is not conclusive and its interpretation is for the court; having regard to the nature of the contract and the circumstances."[16]

### § 13:6. Criteria for Determining Nature of Deposit

In order for a provision for a deposit to constitute a stipulation for liquidated damages, it is essential that the actual damages contemplated be uncertain or difficult to ascertain. This requirement is fundamental, since the purpose of provisions for liquidated damages is to enable the parties to fix in advance of a breach the amount to be paid therefor, where the exact amount of damages would

---

**14.** Also, see Caesar v Rubinson (1903) 174 NY 492, 496, 67 NE 58.

**15.** Feinsot v Burstein (AT1 1912) 78 Misc 259, 138 NYS 185 (this case was again before the court in 161 AD 651, 146 NYS 939, affd 213 NY 703, 108 NE 1093, where it was again held that the stipulation provided for a penalty).

**16.** Mosler Safe Co. v Maiden Lane Safe Deposit Co. (1910) 199 NY 479, 485, 93 NE 81.

be uncertain, and thereby to protect themselves against the difficulty, uncertainty, and expense which necessarily is a consequence of judicial proceedings for the ascertainment of damages.[17]

In addition, for a provision for a deposit to constitute liquidated damages, there must be some attempt to proportion the amount of the deposit to the possible or foreseeable loss consequent upon a breach.[18] The parties must not lose sight of the principle of compensation if they wish to have the deposit constitute liquidated damages.[19] Where a sum has been stipulated as a payment by a defaulting party, which is disproportionate to the presumable or probable damages, or to a readily ascertainable loss, the courts will treat it as a penalty and will relieve, on the principle that the precise sum was not of the essence of the agreement, but was in the nature of a security for performance.[20]

In other words, in order to construe an agreement concerning a deposit as liquidated damages, such agreement must not be, as the Appellate Division said,[1] "but a cloak of language to attempt to hide a sum which is out of proportion to, and differs greatly from, the actual damages which would in the ordinary course be suffered."[2]

### § 13:7. Effect of Agreement to Apply Deposit to Rent

A lease, in addition to the usual provision that the tenant's deposit shall secure performance by him of his covenants under the lease, may further provide that if the tenant shall perform the obligations of the lease on his part, the deposit then will be applied to the payment of rent during certain specified months of the term.

Such a deposit will not lose its character merely be-

---

17. Ward v Hudson River Bldg. Co. (1891) 125 NY 230, 235, 26 NE 256.

18. Seidlitz v Auerbach (1920) 230 NY 167, 174, 129 NE 461; Mosler Safe Co. v Maiden Lane Safe Deposit Co. (1910) 199 NY 479, 485, 93 NE 81; Caesar v Rubinson (1903) 174 NY 492, 496, 67 NE 58.

19. Seidlitz v Auerbach (1920) 230 NY 167, 174, 129 NE 461.

20. Ward v Hudson River Bldg. Co. (1891) 125 NY 230, 26 NE 256.

1. I. & H. Garage, Inc. v H. Flow Corp. (AD1 1928) 225 AD 65, 232 NYS 24 affd 251 NY 553, 168 NE 424.

2. Also, see Realworth Properties, Inc. v Bachler (S Ct Monroe Co 1962) 33 Misc 2d 39, 223 NYS2d 910.

cause it may also be applied to rent. It is either a penalty or liquidated damages, and is to be held as such until the stipulated time arrives for its application to the rent. The tenant, however, cannot insist that the deposit be applied to any unpaid rent prior to such time; otherwise the landlord will have no deposit left to secure himself against the tenant's defaults.[3]

The landlord, on the other hand, cannot keep the deposit as prepayment of rent, that is, attempt to treat it as liquidated damages, if it is not such, in advance of the stipulated time to apply it to the rent.

In one case a deposit had been made to secure the tenant's performance of the lease. The parties further agreed that if the lease was not terminated before its expiration date by reason of the tenant's default, then the deposit would be applied as payment of the rent for the last three months of the term. During the term the tenant failed to pay one month's rent, which in amount was less than the deposit. After the landlord had dispossessed the tenant for such default, the landlord insisted that he had the right to retain the entire deposit, even though it exceeded the unpaid installment of rent. The court, after analyzing the lease, construed the deposit to be a penalty. Therefore, the court held[4] that the landlord could not retain the entire deposit. It was a penalty, and continued to be so, notwithstanding the provision that it might be applied to rent during the last months of the term. Such a provision did not change the character of the deposit. Accordingly, after the dispossess of the tenant, the landlord could only retain such part of the deposit-penalty as would satisfy his claim against the tenant, and the tenant was entitled to any surplus remaining.

### § 13:8. Penalty Construction Favored

The tendency of the courts in doubtful cases is to favor the construction which makes the sum payable for breach of contract a penalty rather than liquidated damages, even where the parties have styled it liquidated damages

---

[3]. Brill v Schlosser (AT 1903) 40 Misc 247, 81 NYS 678.

[4]. Chaude v Shepard (1890) 122 NY 397, 25 NE 358.

§ 13:8      LANDLORD AND TENANT

rather than a penalty, because then such sum may be apportioned according to the loss actually sustained.[5]

### § 13:9. Construction Where Performance of Several Covenants Secured

The great weight of authority is to the effect that, where a contract contains a number of covenants of different degrees of importance, and the loss resulting from the breach of some of them will be clearly disproportionate to the sum sought to be fixed as liquidated damages, especially where the loss in some cases is readily ascertainable, the entire sum, so fixed, will be treated as a penalty.[6] In other words, as said by the Court of Appeals,[7] "The strength of a chain is that of its weakest link."[8]

A lease provided for a deposit of $7,500, "as security for the faithful performance by the tenant of all the covenants and agreements herein contained and to indemnify the landlord against loss by reason of any such default; and, as the damages which the landlord would sustain in the event of a default by the tenant hereunder would not be susceptible of ascertainment, it is hereby covenanted and agreed between the landlord and tenant that in the event of any such default the damages sustained by the said landlord be and they are hereby fixed and liquidated at the amount of seven thousand five hundred dollars, in payment of which the landlord shall retain the said sum of seven thousand five hundred dollars so deposited as aforesaid, without any deduction or offset whatever." The lease contained numerous express conditions. Some of them were comparatively of slight importance; as for instance, that requiring the tenant to keep the sidewalks free from ice and snow, and not to allow waste to accumulate. Others were much more vital. Again, the damages caused by the breach of certain conditions were

---

5. New York v Brooklyn & Manhattan Ferry Co. (1924) 238 NY 52, 143 NE 788; Vernitron Corp. v CF 48 Associates (1984, 2d Dept) 104 AD2d 409, 478 NYS2d 933; Realworth Properties, Inc. v Bachler (S Ct Monroe Co 1962) 33 Misc 2d 39, 223 NYS2d 910.

6. Hackenheimer v Kurtzmann (1923) 235 NY 57, 66, 138 NE 735; Seidlitz v Auerbach (1920) 230 NY 167, 173, 129 NE 461; Vernitron Corp. v CF 48 Associates (1984, 2d Dept) 104 AD2d 409, 478 NYS2d 933.

7. Seidlitz v Auerbach (1920) 230 NY 167, 173, 129 NE 461.

8. Also, see 884 West End Ave. Corp. v Pearlman (AD1 1922) 201 AD 12, 193 NYS 670, affd 234 NY 589, 138 NE 458.

susceptible of accurate valuation, such as that the tenants should obtain a liability insurance policy of $10,000, and pay the premiums. In this case the tenant failed to pay one month's rent, about $500, and was dispossessed. The landlord retained the entire deposit. The tenant thereupon brought suit to recover the deposit less the one month's rent. The Court of Appeals[9] held that this deposit was a penalty, and that therefore the tenant was entitled to its return less such damages as the landlord could show he sustained by virtue of any breaches of the lease committed by the tenant. "It is impossible to believe", said the court, "that the lessor and the lessee here intended that the sum of $7,500 should be treated alike as liquidated damages for the breach of a covenant involving the payment of many thousand dollars of rent and of a covenant involving the payment of an insurance premium of $17."

In other words, if a lease contains a number of covenants of different degrees of importance, and the loss resulting from the breach of any of them will be clearly disproportionate to the sum deposited, then such deposit will be treated as a penalty. The fact that the parties have stated that the deposit is to be liquidated damages will not change the result.[10]

## § 13:10. Construction Where Deposit Limited to Breach of a Material Covenant

In commenting on the rule discussed in the preceding section, the Court of Appeals has observed[11] that such a rule may be pressed to so extreme a conclusion as to make it impossible to draw any contract providing for liquidated damages. Therefore, an exception has been grafted on to the rule. Where a lease contains a number of covenants of different degrees of importance, but it clearly appears that it is the intent of the parties to forfeit the deposit only in the event of a breach of a material covenant, rather than in the event of a breach of any one of the covenants regardless of the nature of

---

9. Seidlitz v Auerbach (1920) 230 NY 167, 129 NE 461.

10. Hackenheimer v Kurtzmann (1923) 235 NY 57, 138 NE 735; 884 West End Ave. Corp. v Pearlman (AD1 1922) 201 AD 12, 193 NYS 670, affd 234 NY 589, 138 NE 458.

11. Hackenheimer v Kurtzmann (1923) 235 NY 57, 138 NE 735.

**§ 13:10**  LANDLORD AND TENANT

their importance; then, the deposit will be treated as liquidated damages, if the deposit is not out of proportion to, or does not differ greatly from, the damages which would be suffered from such breach in the ordinary course of events.[12]

A lease provided, "The parties of the second part have this day deposited with the party of the first part the sum of $10,000 . . . to be held by the party of the first part as security for the faithful performance of all the terms, covenants and conditions in this lease contained, it being expressly understood and agreed that if the parties of the second part surrender said premises or are dispossessed therefrom prior to the expiration of this term, then in that event said sum of Ten Thousand Dollars ($10,000) shall belong to said party of the first part as liquidated damages, and the parties hereto stipulate to treat said deposit as such liquidated damages because they cannot ascertain the exact amount of damage which the party of the first part would sustain in the event of any breach or violation hereunder. . . ." "It is to be noted," the court said in construing this provision,[13] "that the lease provides that this sum shall be treated as liquidated damages only if the premises are surrendered or the tenant is dispossessed prior to the expiration of the lease. In the case at bar, the plaintiff was dispossessed for nonpayment of rent. . . . The total rent was $19,000 a year, or at the rate of $1,583 a month. The vacating of the premises would, in the ordinary course, entail several months' loss of rent. Also there would be the necessity, as in the ordinary case, of making repairs to the premises when a tenant leaves and as demanded by a new tenant. It follows that the sum of $10,000 provided as liquidated damages, in accordance with the terms of the lease, cannot be said to differ so greatly from the damages suffered in the ordinary course as to require the court to disregard the express stipulation of the parties and to hold the sum recoverable as a penalty."

In other words, if the lease is so drafted that a breach of any covenant, however minute or unimportant, is to

12. Hackenheimer v Kurtzmann (1923) 235 NY 57, 138 NE 735.
13. J. & H. Garage, Inc. v H. Flow Corp. (AD1 1928) 225 AD 65, 232 NYS 242, affd 251 NY 553, 168 NE 424.

bring down upon the tenant the loss of the entire security, then the deposit will be treated as a penalty. However, if the parties agree to accept the deposit as the liquidated measure of the damages flowing from a material breach of a lease, such as the loss of future rents, then the deposit will be treated as liquidated damages.[14]

### § 13:11. Rent Security Deposit by Social Service Officials

The Social Services Law provides that where a landlord rents a housing accomodation to a recipient of public assistance, and requires security against nonpayment of rent or for damages, a local social services official may provide such security by means of an agreement or by depositing money in an escrow account. However, where housing accommodations available in a particular area are especially scarce, he may make the deposit in cash.[15]

### § 13:12. Exempt from Satisfaction of Judgment

Moneys deposited as security for the rental of real property to be used as the residence of a judgment debtor or judgment debtor's family are exempt from application to the satisfaction of a money judgment.[16]

The Real Property Law provides that any lease of real property to be used by the lessee as a residence, which contains therein a provision pledging personal property exempt by law from levy and sale by virtue of an execution, as security for the payment of rent due or to become due thereunder, is void as to such provision.[17]

### § 13:13. Determination of Nature of Deposit Binding on Both Parties

A lease provided that the tenant should deposit one month's rent "as liquidated and stipulated damages for the faithful performance of the term and covenants of this lease." During the term of the lease the tenant failed to pay two months' rent, and the landlord brought on action to recover such rent. The tenant contended that the deposit he had made constituted liquidated damages,

---

14. Lenco, Inc. v Hirschfeld (1928) 247 NY 44, 51, 159 NE 718.

15. Social Services L § 143-c. This statute "shall apply to federally-aided categories of public assistance except to the extent prohibited by applicable federal laws and regulations."

16. CPLR 5205(g).

17. Real Prop L § 231, subd 4.

§ 13:13                    LANDLORD AND TENANT

and that therefore the deposit was the full measure of the landlord's recovery regardless of the number of months' rent remaining unpaid. Seabury, J., in overruling the tenant's contention, said,[18] "To hold that this sum should constitute liquidated damages for any breach of the covenant to pay rent on the part of the lessees, even if the lessees were to fail to pay the rent during the whole term of the lease, is to arbitrarily fix a given sum as damages which is entirely out of proportion to the amount of damage sustained. The damages which the landlord sustained were easily ascertainable, and were obviously the amount of the rent reserved for each month for which the tenant failed to pay rent. . . . Here the amount of the sum deposited is out of all proportion to the actual loss suffered by the landlord, which loss is easily ascertainable, and the sum deposited should be treated as security only and not as liquidated damages. As in the case of a lease which in terms provides that the landlord shall keep the amount of the tenant's deposit, which amount is out of proportion to the damages sustained by the landlord, which are easily ascertainable, the courts refuse to enforce a penalty; so in the case of a lease which in terms provides that the tenant shall treat the sum deposited, which is equal to one month's rent, as liquidated damages regardless of the number of months' rent unpaid by the tenant, the courts will refuse to construe such provision so as to work a forfeiture of the landlord's rights under the lease."

Therefore, if a deposit be a penalty, or liquidated damages, it is such as to both the landlord as well as the tenant in any lawsuit brought by either against the other.

## B. RIGHTS TO DEPOSIT

### § 13:14. On Renewal of Lease

When a covenant to renew a lease makes no mention of, or provision for, the terms of the renewal lease, then the renewal will be on the same terms and conditions as are contained in the original lease.[19] Therefore, a renewal of a lease, in the absence of any provision in the lease to

---

18. Emsheimer v Thorner (AT1 1913) 83 Misc 432, 145 NYS 42.

19. See § 11:44, supra.

the contrary, will operate as a renewal of the deposit clause in the lease. As the Appellate Term said,[20] "Although the deposit was made as security for the term ending May 1, 1896, the renewal of the lease operated as a renewal of the agreement regarding such deposit."

Accordingly, in the absence of any provision in a lease to the contrary, a tenant must continue his deposit for the renewed term.

### § 13:15. On Creation of Holdover Tenancy

Prior to the enactment of Real Property Law § 232-c, governing the creation of holdover tenancies,[1] it had been held that upon the creation of a holdover tenancy the landlord could retain the tenant's deposit during the new term so created.[2] Since this statute has made no change in the decisional law that the terms and conditions of the new tenancy continue, in the absence of an agreement providing otherwise,[3] it would seem that this holding is still applicable.

### § 13:16. On Conveyance of Fee

If the time stipulated for the return of a deposit has not arrived, then the conveyance of the fee, or the assignment of the lease, by the landlord will not in and of itself entitle the tenant to its immediate return. This is so whether the landlord retains the deposit, or turns it over to the grantee.[4] A deposit need not be returned to the tenant merely because leased premises have been conveyed. The deposit may be retained until the right to hold it as security has terminated.[5]

A transferee of a fee, who takes subject to a lease, cannot compel his grantor-landlord, who has received a deposit from a tenant, to turn such deposit over to him.[6]

A covenant to return a deposit is a personal one, and the burden of a covenant to return a deposit does not run

---

20. Bernstein v Heinemann (AT 1898) 23 Misc 464, 51 NYS 467.

1. See Chapter 10, supra.

2. Earlington Realty Corp. v Neschis (City Ct NY 1925) 124 Misc 603, 208 NYS 756.

3. § 10:2, supra.

Also, see § 10:16, supra, as to effect of Emergency Rent Laws on application of deposit clause during statutory tenancy.

4. Mauro v Alvino (AT1 1915) 90 Misc 328, 152 NYS 963.

5. Rosenfeld v Aaron (1928) 248 NY 437, 441, 162 NE 478, remittitur amd 249 NY 512, 164 NE 565.

6. Mauro v Alvino (AT1 1915) 90 Misc 328, 152 NYS 963; Pollack v Jackson (City Ct NY 1925) 124 Misc 608, 209 NYS 120.

§ 13:16   LANDLORD AND TENANT

with the land.[7] Therefore, if a grantee of a fee does not receive from his grantor the deposit made by a tenant, he will incur no liability for its return.[8]

However, it is well settled that the benefits of the deposit do run with the land. As the Court of Appeals has said, "The benefit of a covenant of a surety for the rent runs with the land, and, in the absence of a stipulation to the contrary, the grantee who takes subject to a lease obtains the benefit of securities deposited for the due performance of the lease,"[9] Therefore, it has been held that a grantee of real estate, subject to a lease, is entitled to the benefits of a deposit made with the grantor by a tenant, and may sue whoever holds such deposit for such damages caused by the tenant's default under the lease up to the amount of such deposit.[10] A tenant deposited $125 as security with his landlord. The landlord sold the premises to a grantee subject to the lease, but did not turn over the deposit. Subsequently the grantee dispossessed the tenant for nonpayment of rent which amounted to $136.44. The grantee thereupon sued his grantor, the original landlord, to recover $125, the amount of the deposit. It was held,[11] that the grantee could recover. The original landlord's rights were transferred to the grantee, the deed operating as an assignment of such rights. One of these rights is the right to indemnity from the funds held by the landlord-grantor as security. And, the benefit of a deposit runs with the land.

In a case where the grantor had not turned over the

---

**7.** Mallory Associates, Inc. v Barving Realty Co. (1949) 300 NY 297, 90 NE2d 468, 15 ALR2d 1193, reh den 300 NY 680, 91 NE2d 331, 15 ALR2d 1193; Joseph Fallert Brewing Co. v Blass (AD2 1907) 119 AD 53, 103 NYS 865; Mauro v Alvino (AT1 1915) 90 Misc 328, 152 NYS 963; Re Walter's Will (Surr Ct Westchester Co 1948) 79 NYS2d 17 (executor of landlord who had received deposit was obligated for its return after the landlord's death); Pollack v Jackson (City Ct 1925) 124 Misc 608, 209 NYS 120.

**8.** Halsted v Globe Indem. Co. (1932) 258 NY 176, 180, 179 NE 376, reh den 259 NY 663, 182 NE 225; Joseph Fallert Brewing Co. v Blass (AD2 1907) 119 AD 53, 103 NYS 865; Rybre Realty Co. v Wolff (AT1 1924) 122 Misc 672, 203 NYS 409; Mauro v Alvino (AT1 1915) 90 Misc 328, 152 NYS 963; Sanford v Zimmern (AT 1912) 76 Misc 434, 134 NYS 1116.

**9.** Halsted v Globe Indem. Co. (1932) 258 NY 176, 180, 179 NE 376, reh den 259 NY 663, 182 NE 225.

**10.** Metropolitan Life Ins. Co. v Stephen Realty Co. (City Ct 1942) 178 Misc 53, 33 NYS2d 146; Donnelly v Rosoff (M Ct 1937) 164 Misc 384, 298 NYS 946, affd no op AT1 January 14, 1938 (not reported).

**11.** Donnelly v Rosoff (M Ct 1937) 164 Misc 384, 298 NYS 946, affd no op AT1 January 14, 1938 (not reported).

## DEPOSIT  § 13:16

deposit to the grantee, the Appellate Term, by Lehman, J., said, "The original landlord, by his assignment of the reversion, without reserving the rents, has parted with all the benefits of the lease though he remains under the obligation to repay the deposit, for this is a collateral covenant. It does not, in my opinion, however, follow that at the present time he must return the deposit. While the privity of estate between the tenant and himself has ceased, the privity of contract still exists. The term of the lease has not expired and the lease is in full existence, yet by the terms of the lease he has agreed to return the deposit only at the expiration of the lease, and that time has not yet arrived. . . . Moreover, while the grantee cannot claim the deposit because he is not under any obligation to return it, yet the tenant has expressly agreed that this deposit shall be held as security for the lease. The benefit of a covenant of a surety for the rent does run with the land. . . . The grantee who takes subject to a lease should also, on principle, obtain the benefit of security deposited for the due performance of the lease. While he cannot compel his grantor to transfer the deposit to him because the grantor is bound by his covenant with the lessee personally to return it to him at the expiration of the lease, yet so far as the circumstances permit he should receive the benefit of this security. If his grantor is permitted to hold the security exactly as the parties have themselves provided, then upon the expiration of the lease, while the grantor could not counterclaim in his own right for any damages which may have accrued by reason of any breach on the part of the tenants, yet the grantee in whom such right of action rests could assign his chose in action to his grantor, and the grantor could, by virtue of such assignment, set up the counterclaim."[12]

"In other words," said Lehman, J., "not only has the time not yet arrived at which the landlord agreed to return the deposit, but the landlord and his grantee acting together are still in a position to obtain a benefit from holding the deposit in accordance with the terms upon which it was made."[13]

---

[12]. Mauro v Alvino (AT1 1915) 90 Misc 328, 152 NYS 963.

[13]. Mauro v Alvino (AT1 1915) 90 Misc 328, 152 NYS 963.

### § 13:17. On Assignment of Lease by Tenant

The substitution of one tenant in place of another, as is the case when a tenant assigns his lease, does not operate to discharge, as a matter of law, the first tenant from further performance of his covenants under the lease.[14] Therefore, unless the liability of a tenant-assignor has been effectively terminated, the tenant continues liable for any breach of the lease committed after the assignment by the immediate or any subsequent assignee.[15] This being so, the landlord is entitled to retain any deposit given to him to secure performance of the lease, notwithstanding the assignment of the lease by his tenant, unless the landlord discharges the tenant from any further liability on the lease after the assignment.[16]

### § 13:18. Assignability of Deposit

If a lease contains a restriction on the tenant's right to assign the lease, such restriction does not prevent a tenant from assigning any deposit he made under the lease to secure performance thereof.[17] In holding that an assignment of a deposit by a tenant was not a violation of a restriction in the lease that "the lessee shall not assign, transfer or set over this lease or any part thereof . . ." without the landlord's written consent, Coleman, J.,[18] said, "But this provision is inapplicable. The assignment is not of an interest in the leasehold but of a claim to money deposited—a personal claim; there is no reason why the claim could not be assigned independently of other interests under the lease and without the consent of the landlord."

However, the parties to a lease may stipulate that a tenant cannot assign his deposit.[19] There is no legal objection to such an agreement.[20]

### § 13:19. Rights of Assignee of Lease

It has been seen that an assignment of a lease in and of

---

14. Piser v Hecht (AD1 1915) 170 AD 668, 156 NYS 601.
15. See §§ 9:20, et seq, supra.
16. Piser v Hecht (AD1 1915) 170 AD 668, 156 NYS 601.
17. Manhattan Shirt Co. v Cisternino (City Ct NY Co 1945) 184 Misc 986, 55 NYS2d 174.

18. Manhattan Shirt Co. v Cisternino (City Ct NY Co 1945) 184 Misc 986, 55 NYS2d 174.
19. Wertheimer v Marks (AT1 1913) 81 Misc 137, 142 NYS 331.
For form of restriction on right to assign security, see § 9:95, supra.
20. Wertheimer v Marks (AT1 1913) 81 Misc 137, 142 NYS 331.

itself will not pass to the assignee any right or title to any deposit made by the tenant-assignor to secure performance of the lease.[1] The deposit must be specifically assigned to give the assignee any right or title to it.[2]

A lease provided that a deposit was to be applied to the last two months' rent. The tenant assigned the lease, and the assignee paid rent for the last two months of the term. The assignee thereupon sued the landlord to recover the deposit on the theory that since the deposit constituted payment of the last two months' rent, in paying such rent he had overpaid the landlord. The assignee was denied any recovery because he could not prove that the deposit had been assigned to him.[3]

## § 13:20. Rights to Deposit Assigned in Violation of Lease

As has been seen, a tenant may assign his deposit, even though he is restricted from assigning the lease without the landlord's consent. To bar a tenant from assigning the deposit, there must be a specific restriction on the right to assign the deposit.[4]

An assignment of a deposit in violation of a stipulation that a tenant shall not assign his interest in the deposit, and that the claim thereto shall remain personal with the tenant, will pass no title to the deposit to the assignee.[5] And this is so even though the landlord has consented to an assignment of the lease.[6]

However, after the term of a lease expires, the provision of a lease that the tenant's deposit shall not be assigned without the landlord's consent will not bar an action brought by an assignee to recover the deposit. After the term expires the tenant has a cause of action to recover the deposit. Such cause of action may be assigned, like any other cause of action, and is not affected by the restriction on an assignment of the deposit itself during the term.[7]

1. § 9:55, supra.
2. Shattuck v Buek (AD1 1913) 158 AD 709, 143 NYS 1045; Wertheimer v Marks (AT1 1913) 81 Misc 137, 142 NYS 331.
3. Shattuck v Buek (AD1 1913) 158 AD 709, 143 NYS 1045.
4. See § 13:18, supra.
5. Wertheimer v Marks (AT1 1913) 81 Misc 137, 142 NYS 331.
6. Wertheimer v Marks (AT1 1913) 81 Misc 137, 142 NYS 331.
7. Hodge v 177-10 Corp. (AT1 1946) 186 Misc 233, 59 NYS2d 876.

## C. DUTY WITH RESPECT TO DEPOSIT ON CONVEYANCE OF LEASED PROPERTY

### § 13:21. Landlord's Statutory Duty on Conveyance

General Obligations Law § 7-105 provides that *unless the agreement between the landlord and tenant or licensee is inconsistent with the following provisions,* any person, firm, or corporation, and the employers, officers or agents thereof, whether the owner or lessee of the property leased, who or which has or hereafter shall have received from a tenant or licensee a sum of money or any other thing of value as a deposit or advance of rental as security for the full performance by such tenant or licensee of the terms of his lease or license agreement, or who or which has or shall have received the same from a former owner or lessee, shall

1. upon conveying such property or assigning his or its lease to another, or

2. upon the judicial appointment and qualifying of a receiver in an action to foreclose a mortgage or other lien of record affecting the property leased, or

3. upon the conveyance of such property to another person, firm or corporation by a referee in an action to foreclose a mortgage or other lien of record affecting the property leased if a receiver shall not have been appointed and qualified in such action at the time of the delivery of the deed or instrument or assignment or within 5 days thereafter, or within 5 days after the receiver shall have qualified, deal with the security deposit as follows:

1. turn over to his or its grantee or assignee, or to the receiver in the foreclosure action, or to the purchaser at the foreclosure sale if a receiver shall not have been appointed and qualified, the sum so deposited, *and*

2. notify the tenant or licensee by registered or certified mail of such turning over, and the name and address of such grantee, assignee, purchaser or receiver.

Any owner or lessee turning over to his or its grantee, assignee, to a purchaser of the leased premises at a foreclosure sale, or to the receiver in the foreclosure action the amount of such security deposit is thereby relieved of and from liability to the tenant or licensee for the repayment thereof; and the transferee of such security deposit is thereby made responsible for the return thereof to the tenant or licensee, unless he or it shall thereafter and before the expiration of the term of the tenant's lease or licensee's agreement, transfer such security deposit to another, and give the requisite notice in connection therewith as provided thereby.

A receiver shall hold the security subject to such disposition thereof as shall be provided in an order of the court to be made and entered in the foreclosure action.

Any failure to comply with this statute is a misdemeanor.[8]

General Obligations Law § 7-109 provides, that if it appears to the Attorney General that any person, association, or corporation has violated or is violating any of the provisions of the foregoing statute dealing with money deposited as security to be held in trust, an action or proceeding may be instituted by the Attorney General in the name of the people of the state of New York to compel compliance with such provisions, and may enjoin any violation or threatened violation thereof.

## § 13:22 Liability of Grantee or Assignee for Deposits Made by Tenant on Conveyance of Rent Stabilized Dwelling Units.

General Obligations Law § 7-107 provides, with respect to all written contracts for the transfer of dwelling units subject to the New York City Rent Stabilization Law of 1969 or the Emergency Tenant Protection Act of 1974, that any grantee of assignee of any such dwelling unit shall be liable to a tenant for any sum of money or any other thing of value deposited as security for the full performance by such tenant of the terms of his lease, plus any accrued interest, if his or its predecessor in interest was liable for such funds. Such liability shall attach

---

[8]. To establish a prima facie case under this section of the General Obligations Law, the People must show only that the landlord, in his capacity as landlord, collected security deposits from the tenants; that a receiver was judicially appointed; and that the receiver made a demand for the security deposits that was not complied with by the landlord. The landlord may nonetheless raise as a defense that he no longer possessed the funds at the time the demand was made, and that the funds were used in a manner provided for in the lease, albeit inconsistently with the statute. People v Elliott (1985) 65 NY2d 446, 492 NYS2d 581, 482 NE2d 60.

§ 13:22　　　　　　　LANDLORD AND TENANT

whether or not the successor in interest has, upon the conveyance of such dwelling unit, received the sum as deposited.

The liability of a receiver for payment of any security deposit plus accrued interest pursuant to this provision of the General Obligations Law shall be limited to the amount of such deposit actually turned over to him or it pursuant to the provisions of General Obligations Law § 7-105 (see § 13:21, supra) and to the operating income in excess of expenses generated during his or its period of receivership.[9]

Any agreement by a lessee or tenant of a dwelling unit waiving or modifying his rights as set forth in this statute shall be void.[10]

### § 13:23. Liability of Grantee or Assignee for Deposits Made by Tenant on Conveyance of Non-Rent Stabilized Dwelling Units

General Obligations Law § 7-108 provides, with respect to all written contracts for the transfer of dwelling units with written leases in residential premises containing 6 or more dwelling units, and dwelling units subject to the New York City Rent and Rehabilitation Law or the Emergency Housing Rent Control Law, unless such dwelling unit is specifically referred to in General Obligations Law § 7-107 (see § 13:22 supra), as follows: Where any sum of money or any other thing of value deposited as security for the full performance by a tenant of the terms of his lease is not turned over to a successor in interest pursuant to General Obligations Law § 7-105 (see § 13:21, supra), the grantee or assignee of the leased premises shall also be liable to such tenant, upon conveyance of such leased premises, for the repayment of any such security deposit, plus accrued interest, as to which such grantee or assignee has actual knowledge. A grantee or assignee of such leased premises shall be deemed to have actual knowledge of any security deposit which is (a) deposited at any time during the 6 months immediately prior to closing or other transfer of title in any banking organization pursuant to subdivision 2-a of General Obligations Law § 7-103, or (b) acknowledged in any lease in

---

9. Gen Oblig L § 7-107, subd 2(b).
10. Gen Oblig L § 7-107, subd 3.

effect at the time of closing or other transfer of title, or (c) supported by "documentary evidence," defined below, provided by the tenant or lessee.[11]

With respect to any such leased premises for which there is no record of security deposit pursuant to (a) or (b) hereinabove set forth, the grantee or assignee of the leased premises shall be obligated to notify the tenant thereof in writing, no later than 30 days following the closing or other transfer of title, to the fact that there is no record of a security deposit for said leased premises, and that unless the tenant within 30 days after receiving notice provides him or it with "documentary evidence" of deposit, the tenant shall have no further recourse against him or it for said security deposit.[12]

"Documentary evidence" shall be limited to any cancelled check drawn to the order of, a receipt from, or a lease signed, by any predecessor in interest, if such predecessor's interest in the leased premises existed on or after September 30, 1984. Except as otherwise provided in (a) and (b) hereinabove set forth, the grantee or assignee of the leased premises shall not be charged with actual knowledge of the security deposit where the tenant fails within the 30-day period to provide said documentary evidence. Where the grantee or assignee of the leased premises fails to notify the tenant as hereinabove set forth within 30 days following the closing or other transfer of title, the tenant shall be entitled to produce documentary evidence at any time.[13]

The grantee or assignee of the leased premises shall have the right to demand that the grantor or assignor thereof establish an escrow account equal to one month's rent for any leased premises for which there is no record of a security deposit to be used for the purpose of holding harmless the grantee or assignee in any case where, at a date subsequent to the closing or other transfer of title, the tenant furnishes documentary evidence of a deposit.[14]

The liability of a receiver for payment of any security deposit plus accrued interest shall be limited to the amount of such deposit actually turned over to him or it pursuant to General Obligations Law § 7-105 (see § 13:21,

---

11. Gen Oblig L § 7-108, subd 2(b).
12. Gen Oblig L § 7-108, subd 2(c).
13. Gen Oblig L § 7-108, subd 2(c).
14. Gen Oblig L § 7-108, subd 2(d).

§ 13:23

supra) and to the operating income in excess of expenses generated during his or its period of receivership.[15]

Any agreement by a lessee or tenant of a dwelling waiving or modifying his rights as set forth in this statute shall be absolutely void.[16]

## § 13:24. Form of Clause for Landlord-Grantor's Protection on Conveyance

Notwithstanding the exculpatory provisions of the statute governing security deposits on the conveyance of the fee,[17] the following clause is in general use as a precautionary measure to protect a landlord who, on conveying the fee, desires to turn over the deposit to the grantee, and to be relieved of any further questions as to his liability therefor.

### FORM NO. 26
### Right to Turn Over Deposit

In the event of a sale of the land and building, or a leasing of the building of which the leased premises form a part, Landlord shall have the right to transfer the deposit made by Tenant hereunder to the grantee or lessee, and Landlord, his successors and assigns shall thereupon be released by Tenant from any and all claims or liability for the return of said deposit, and Tenant agrees to look to the transferee of said deposit solely for the return thereof. It is agreed that the provisions hereof shall apply to each and every transfer of said deposit to a new Landlord.*

* For complete form of lease see Chapter 1.

## § 13:25. Liability for Interest

It has been held that in the absence of an express agreement to pay interest on a deposit, none is chargeable thereon.[18] An obligation to pay interest must be expressed or implied in fact, or else it does not exist. It is not implied as a matter of law under general principles of law.[19] However, as will be discussed below, the statute has provided an exception to this rule.

15. Gen Oblig L § 7-108, subd 2(d).
16. Gen Oblig L § 7-108, subd 3.
17. See § 13:21, supra.
18. Re Cromwell's Estate (Surr Ct NY Co 1918) 102 Misc 503, 169 NYS 204.
19. New York State Thruway Authority v Hurd (1969) 25 NY2d 150, 303 NYS2d 51, 250 NE2d 335.

## § 13:25

If there is an agreement to pay interest and the amount of interest is not agreed upon, or if the parties merely agree to "legal interest," the landlord is liable to pay the legal statutory interest rate.[20] However, although the obligation of a landlord to pay interest on the deposit is a matter for agreement, with the one exception discussed below, if the deposit does bear interest, either because the nature of the deposit is such that it bears interest (interest-bearing securities), or the depositary pays interest (a savings bank), or the landlord agrees to pay interest, such interest, less statutory administration expenses,[1] together with the deposit must be held in trust as the tenant's property.[2] However, the landlord must dispose of the interest, less the administrative expenses, in one of 2 ways: hold the interest in trust, or make annual payments to the tenant.[3]

Mention was made herein that there is a statutory exception to the rule that there is no obligation to pay interest on a deposit unless it has been expressly undertaken to do so. General Obligations Law § 7-103, subd 2-a, provides that where security money is deposited or advanced on a contract or license agreement "for the rental of property containing six or more family dwelling units, the person receiving such money must deposit it in an interest bearing account in a banking organization within the state of New York, which account must earn interest at a rate which shall be the prevailing rate earned by

---

20. Levy v Shellsey (AT1 1900) 30 Misc 789, 63 NYS 150.

1. Gen Obligations L § 7-103, subd 2, which provides, that if the person depositing such security money in a banking organization shall deposit the same in an interest-bearing account, he shall be entitled to receive, as administration expenses, a sum equivalent to one percent per annum upon the security money so deposited, which shall be in lieu of all other administrative and custodial expenses.

2. General Obligations Law § 7-103, subd 1. Also, see Stuarco, Inc. v Slafbro Realty Corp. (1968, 2d Dept) 30 AD2d 80, 289 NYS2d 883.

Where the deposit need not be placed in an interest bearing account, but interest is earned thereon, the interest beyond the administrative expense of 1% per annum also constitutes trust money. Purfield v Kathrane (NYC Civ Ct NY Co 1973) 73 Misc 2d 194, 341 NYS2d 376; Parmaki v Levine (NYC Civ Ct Queens Co 1973) 75 Misc 2d 900, 349 NYS2d 979.

3. General Obligations Law § 7-103, subd 2.

McKee v Wellington Estates, Ltd. (1983) 60 NY2d 853, 470 NYS2d 139, 458 NE2d 380 (neither the statutory language nor the legislative history mandates that a landlord apply the accrued interest to a subsequent increase in the security deposit when new leases are entered into at higher rentals).

other such deposits made with banking organizations in such area."[4]

Any waiver by a tenant of any of the foregoing provisions of the General Obligations Law is "absolutely" void.[5]

### § 13:26. Federal Income Tax on Security Deposit Interest

When a landlord deposits a tenant's security deposit into an interest-bearing bank account, under federal income tax law, a "grantor-trust" is considered to have been created, for which the landlord acts as trustee of the trust, and the tenant, or if more than one tenant's security deposit is deposited in the one account, each tenant, is treated as the owner of his or her security deposit which is an asset of the grantor-trust. The tenant must report on his or her individual income tax return the gross amount of interest earned on his or her security deposit during the calendar year, even though he or she may not receive that interest because of the restrictions placed on it by the applicable statute. The tenant is entitled to deduct as an itemized expense for the production of income, the amount of the administrative fee granted to the landlord-trustee (to wit, a sum equivalent to one percent per annum upon the security money so deposited).[6] (But, the tenant cannot deduct this amount if the tenant uses the standard deduction.)

The landlord must file an income tax return for the trust in accordance with the instructions on Treasury Form 1041 for a grantor trust if the trust income is $600 or more, or if there is any taxable income. The trustee may use a copy of Schedule K-1 (Form 1041) to show each

---

4. It should be observed that whereas the purpose of this provision is, in the words of the Governor accompanying the bill, to "require the landlord of every apartment house with six or more apartments to place any security deposits made by his tenants in an interest bearing account"; yet, the language of the law applies only to security deposited for the rental of "property containing" six or more family units.

The Attorney General may institute an action or proceeding to compel compliance with rent-security deposit interest laws where "any person, association, or corporation has violated or is violating any of the provisions" of such laws. Gen Oblig L § 7-107; People by Lefkowitz v Parker (1975) 38 NY2d 743, 381 NYS2d 43, 343 NE2d 761.

5. General Obligations Law § 7-103, subd 3.

6. See § 13:25, supra.

tenant-grantor the gross amount of money earned on the security deposit, and the amount of the deduction under Internal Revenue Code § 212 to which he or she is entitled. Each bank paying interest of $10, or more, on security deposits to a landlord-tenant trust must file Forms 1099 and 1096 with the Internal Revenue Service, and furnish a statement to the trustee-landlord.[7]

As indicated above, Form 1041 must be filed if the trust income for the year is $600 or more, or if there is any taxable income. Even though the income of a grantor trust is viewed as the grantor's direct income, that income must be taken into account by the trust in determining whether the trust meets the $600 test for filing the return. But, as to the alternative "taxable income" requirement, "any taxable income" refers only to any taxable income of the trust itself, not income taxable to the tenant-grantor. Therefore, unless the trust has income other than the interest taxable to the tenant-grantors, the taxable income test will not be met. For example, suppose a sole tenant receives $100 interest on his security deposit account. The landlord does not have to file Form 1041 because there is no taxable income to the trust, and the trust's gross income is under $600.

## D. CONVERSION OF DEPOSIT

### § 13:27. Deposit as Trust Fund

The statute provides,[8] that whenever money shall be deposited or advanced on a contract or license agreement for the use or rental of real property as security for performance of the contract or agreement or to be applied to payments upon such contract or agreement when due, such money, with interest accruing thereon, if any, until repaid or so applied, shall continue to be the money of the person making such deposit or advance and shall be held in trust by the person with whom such deposit or advance shall be made and shall not be mingled with the personal moneys or become an asset of the person receiving the same, but may be disposed of as provided in the General Obligations Law in the case of a conveyance of

---

7. Revenue Ruling 75-363, IRB 1975-34, 19.

8. Gen Obligations L § 7-103.

§ 13:27 LANDLORD AND TENANT

the property.[9] This provision of the General Obligations Law requiring security deposits to be placed in a trust account is part of a lease contract as if it had been actually written into it.[10]

Prior to the enactment of the General Obligations Law, the courts had determined that the relation in which a deposit was to be held was a matter of agreement between the parties.[11] If the lease did not contain an express provision that the deposit was to be held in trust or in some other fiduciary relationship, or did not contain any provision which necessarily justified the inference that the landlord was to be restricted in the use of deposit money, the relationship as to the deposit was generally deemed to be that of debtor and creditor.[12] However, this has been changed by the General Obligations Law: A landlord who receives a deposit from his tenant to secure performance of the lease is now a trustee with respect to the deposit. He may not mingle such deposit with his own funds, nor use them for his own purposes. He must segregate such funds and keep them intact.[13]

The Court of Appeals has held[14] that this provision of the General Obligations Law is not expressly limited to deposits made under a contract for the use or rental of real property situated in New York, and that, therefore, the protection afforded thereunder applies to funds deposited in New York as security under a contract to a lease made in New York between corporations created by New York, even though the real property which is the subject matter of the contract is located elsewhere. In so holding,

---

9. Gen Obligations L § 7-105 deals with the statutory requirements upon the transfer of a deposit in the case of a conveyance. See § 13:21, supra.

10. Hartzell v Burdick (City Ct Albany 1977) 91 Misc 2d 758, 398 NYS2d 649.

11. Mendelson-Silverman, Inc. v Malco Trading Corp. (AT2 1932) 146 Misc 215, 260 NYS 881, affd 238 AD 852, 262 NYS 991, affd 262 NY 621, 188 NE 92.

12. Jahmes Co. v Propper (AD1 1933) 238 AD 326, 264 NYS 219; Levinson v Shapiro (AD1 1933) 238 AD 158, 263 NYS 585, reh and app den 239 AD 816, 263 NYS 976 and affd 263 NY 591, 189 NE 713; Mendelson-Silverman, Inc. v Malco Trading Corp. (AT2 1932) 146 Misc 215, 260 NYS 881, affd 238 AD 852, 262 NYS 991, affd 262 NY 621, 188 NE 92.

13. People v Horowitz (1956) 309 NY 426, 131 NE2d 715.

Placing the deposit moneys in the name of another living person is not a "holding" within the requirements of the statute. Ferguson v Vaughan Imported Cars, Inc. (AT1 1957) 9 Misc 2d 188, 163 NYS2d 884.

14. Mallory Associates, Inc. v Barving Realty Co. (1949) 300 NY 297, 90 NE2d 468, 15 ALR2d 1193, reh den 300 NY 680, 91 NE2d 331, 15 ALR2d 1193.

# DEPOSIT § 13:27

said Conway, J., for the court, "we are not giving extraterritorial operation to the statute, but, on the contrary, in accordance with the evident legislative intent, we are permitting it to govern the rights and liabilities of corporations created by New York, under a New York contract, with respect to a New York subject matter, viz: the security deposit."[15]

It has been held that the fact that the language of the lease nowhere describes money paid as a "security deposit" is not determinative of the character of the payment; if it is in fact security, the statute according trust status applies.[16] But, where a lease provided for prepayment of rent, and did not further provide that the amount thereof either was to be security or was to be applied to rental payments when due, it was held that the statute had no application to such prepayment of rent; and the landlord could mingle such money with his own funds without being guilty of conversion.[17] In other words the statute does not bar, nor undertake to bring within its operative reach other relationships, such as debtor-creditor arrangements. A bona fide loan arrangement between a landlord and tenant, which relates to the leased premises, does not violate the statute when the

---

15. Where a lease to Florida property was executed in New York (although reciting it was made in Florida), and security moneys deposited in New York in escrow with lessor's attorney, but lessor was a resident of Florida, lease had been negotiated in Florida, delivery of security pursuant to escrow to lessor in Florida, and his commingling of it with his funds there, did not entitle lessee to return of deposit pursuant to New York statute. Alachua Inn Corp. v Cooper (S Ct NY Co 1971) 66 Misc 2d 479, 321 NYS2d 222, affd (1st Dept) 38 AD2d 796, 327 NYS2d 1006.

16. Prudential Westchester Corp. v Tomasino (AD1 1958, 1st Dept) 5 AD2d 489, 172 NYS2d 652, affd 6 NY2d 824, 188 NYS2d 214, 159 NE2d 699, where the court refused to be bound by the labels which the parties had applied to a payment of money, and after examining the true nature of the transaction, held the transaction to be a sale of furniture, and that payments made in connection therewith were "not" advances on account of rent or security; Purfield v Kathrane (NYC Civ Ct NY Co 1973) 73 Misc 2d 194, 341 NYS2d 376.

17. 34 West 34th Street Corp. v Nehama Realty Corp (S Ct NY Co 1956) 7 Misc 2d 532, 153 NYS2d 427, where the rental for the term was $1,575,000, and the lease provided that it was payable $50,000, upon execution, and $12,500, on the first day of the second month, and a like sum of $12,500, every second month thereafter until the whole rent was paid.

The payment of a sum of money at the time of execution of a lease of the same amount as the specified monthly rent will be assumed to be the payment of the first month's rent, and not a deposit of security within the ordinary meaning of that word as used in leases. Wolff v Donohue (AT 1917) 164 NYS 33, revd oth gds 180 AD 438, 167 NYS 1047.

§ 13:27   LANDLORD AND TENANT

money is used to acquire title to or benefit the leased premises.[18]

The General Obligations Law provides,[19] that whenever the person receiving security money deposits is in a banking organization, he shall thereupon notify in writing each of the persons making such security deposit or advance, giving the name and address of the banking organization in which the deposit of security money is made, and the amount of such deposit.[20] Deposits in a banking organization must be made in a banking organization having a place of business within the state of New York. If the person depositing such security money in a banking organization shall deposit same in an interest bearing account, he shall be entitled to receive, as administration expenses, a sum equivalent to one percent per annum upon the security money so deposited, which shall be in lieu of all other administrative and custodial expenses. The balance of the interest paid by the banking organization shall be the money of the person making the deposit or advance and shall either be held in trust by the person with whom such deposit or advance shall be made, until repaid or applied for the use or rental of the leased premises, or annually paid to the person making the deposit of security money.[1]

Whenever the security deposit is for the rental of property containing *6 or more family dwelling units,* the person receiving such security deposit must deposit it in an interest bearing account in a banking organization

---

18. Re Amphitheatre, Inc. (1968, CA2 NY) 405 F2d 309, cert den 395 US 908, 23 L Ed 2d 221, 89 S Ct 1750; Ja-Mo Associates, Inc. v 56 Fulton St. Garage Corp. (1968, 1st Dept) 30 AD2d 287, 291 NYS2d 62; Barrow Associates v South Broad Realty Corp. (AD1 1949) 275 AD 914, 90 NYS2d 499; Land v Gladol Realty Corp. (S Ct Kings Co 1959) 18 Misc 2d 103, 187 NYS2d 216.

19. General Obligations Law § 7-103, subd 2.

20. Failure to give the required notice does not entitle the tenant to a return of his deposit. Purfield v Kathrane (NYC Civ Ct NY Co 1973) 71 Misc 2d 194, 341 NYS2d 376.

1. Banking Law § 237, subd 4, provides: "Notwithstanding any inconsistent provision of law, a savings bank may accept deposits of moneys paid under and as security for the performance of any lease or leases, or to be applied to payments under such lease or leases when due, although the person depositing such moneys is held accountable therefor as a trustee of trust funds. Moneys received from or held for persons under more than one lease may be deposited in one or more accounts.

"Notwithstanding any inconsistent provision of law, the word 'person' as used in this subdivision shall include an individual, municipal corporation, partnership, corporation, association or any other organization operated for profit."

DEPOSIT § 13:28

having a place of business in the state of New York, which account shall earn interest at a rate which is the prevailing rate earned by other such deposits made with banking organizations in such area.

Gen Obli L § 7-103, subd 2-a.

Any provision of a lease whereby a person who deposits or advances money as a security deposit waives any of the provisions of the General Obligations Law is "absolutely void."[2]

The statute provides that if it appears to the Attorney General that any person, association, or corporation has violated or is violating any of the provisions of the statutes dealing with money deposited as security to be held in trust (General Obligations L §§ 7-103 to 7-107), an action or proceeding may be instituted by the Attorney General in the name of the people of the state of New York to compel compliance with such provisions, and enjoin any violation or threatened violation thereof.[3]

### § 13:28. —Mobile Home Park Lease

The Real Property Law provides,[4] that whenever money shall be deposited or advanced on a contract or license agreement for the use or rental of premises and the mobile home, if rented, in a mobile home park as security for performance of the contract or agreement or to be applied to payments upon such contract or agreement when due, such money with interest accruing thereon, if any, until repaid or so applied, shall continue to be the money of the person making such deposit or advance and shall be a trust fund in the possession of the person with whom such deposit or advance shall be made and shall not be mingled with other funds or become an asset of the park owner, operator or his agent.

Whenever the person receiving money so deposited or advanced shall deposit such money in a banking organization, such person shall thereupon notify in writing each of the persons making such security deposit or advance,

2. General Obligations Law § 7-103, subd 3.
3. General Obligations Law § 7-109.
The Attorney General has no standing to bring a proceeding for violation of Gen Obl L §§ 7-103 to 7-107 under Exec L § 63, subd 12; this proceeding can only be brought under Gen Obl L § 7-109. People by Lefkowitz v Parker (1975) 38 NY2d 743, 381 NYS2d 43, 343 NE2d 761.
4. Real Prop L § 233, subd g 4(a).

giving the name and address of the banking organization in which the deposit of security money is made, and the amount of such deposit. Deposits in a banking organization shall be made in a banking organization having a place of business within the State of New York. If the person depositing such security money in a banking organization shall deposit same in an interest bearing account, he shall be entitled to receive, as administration expenses, a sum equivalent to one percent per annum upon the security money so deposited, which shall be in lieu of all other administrative and custodial expenses. The balances of the interest paid by the banking organization shall be the money of the person making the deposit or advance and shall either be held in trust by the person with whom such deposit or advance shall be made, until repaid or applied for the use or rental of the leased premises, or annually paid to the person making the deposit of security money.[5]

Whenever the money so deposited or advanced is for the rental of a mobile home park lot on property on which are located *six or more mobile home park lots*, the person receiving such money shall, subject to the provisions of this section, deposit it in an interest bearing account in a banking organization within the state which account shall earn interest at a rate which shall be the prevailing rate earned by other such deposits made with the banking organizations in such area.[6]

In the event that a lease terminates other than at the time that a banking organization in such area regularly pays interest, the person depositing such security money shall pay over to his mobile home tenant such interest as he is able to collect at the date of such lease termination.[7]

Any provision of such a contract or agreement whereby a person who deposits or advances money waives any of these provisions is void.[8]

### § 13:29. Conversion of Deposit

A landlord who receives from his tenant a deposit to

---

5. Real Property Law § 233, subd g 4(b).

6. Real Property Law § 233, subd g 4(c).

7. Real Property Law § 233, subd g 4(d).

8. Real Property Law § 233, subd g 4(e).

# DEPOSIT § 13:29

secure performance of the lease may not mingle the deposit with his own funds, or use them for his own purposes, but must segregate the deposit and keep it intact; that is, he must hold such deposit in trust.[9] If he mingles the deposit with his own funds, or uses them for his own purposes, he will be liable in tort for a conversion thereof.[10]

When a landlord extends credit for the amount of the tenant's security to the purchaser of the premises, and the purchaser acknowledges that he holds such amount as the tenant's security, there is no depletion of the deposit, and, therefore, no conversion thereof.[11]

If a landlord has converted the trust fund, that is, the deposit, the tenant may either sue for such conversion, or counterclaim therefor in any action brought by the landlord for the recovery of rent.[12] But, the landlord's duty to keep the deposit as a trust fund, and the tenant's obligation to pay rent are independent, and accordingly the conversion of the trust fund is not a defense to the claim for rent.[13]

In an action by a tenant against his landlord for a conversion of the deposit moneys, the breach of the terms of the lease by the tenant is not a defense.[14]

Similarly, it has been held that in an action by a tenant's assignee for the benefit of creditors for the return of converted security, a landlord will not be permitted to set-off his creditor's claim against the tenant based upon a judgment for arrears of rent.[15]

---

**9.** § 13:27, supra.

**10.** Levinson v Shapiro (AD1 1933) 238 AD 158, 263 NYS 585, reh and app den 239 AD 816, 263 NYS 976 and affd 263 NY 591, 189 NE 713; Atlas v Moritz (AD4 1926) 217 AD 38, 216 NYS 490; 2300 Concourse Realty Corp. v Klug (M Ct 1952) 201 Misc 179, 111 NYS2d 168.

**11.** Tow v Maidman (S Ct Nassau Co 1968) 56 Misc 2d 468, 288 NYS2d 837.

**12.** Mercantile Exchange Leasing Corp. v Astor-Broadway Holding Corp. (1957, 1st Dept) 3 AD2d 833, 161 NYS2d 677, affd 4 NY2d 910, 174 NYS2d 661, 151 NE2d 92; Atlas v Moritz AD4 1926) 217 AD 38, 216 NYS 490; 2710 Eighth Ave., Inc. v Frank Forman Pharmacy, Inc. (AT1 1943) 180 Misc 376, 42 NYS2d 887; 2300 Concourse Realty Corp. v Klug (M Ct 1952) 201 Misc 179, 111 NYS2d 168.

**13.** Turquoise Realty Corp. v Burke (M Ct 1938) 168 Misc 670, 6 NYS2d 125.

**14.** Pollack v Springer (City Ct 1949) 195 Misc 523, 91 NYS 847, mod on other grounds 196 Misc 1015, 95 NYS2d 527.

**15.** Re Perfection Technical Services Press, Inc. (1965, 2d Dept) 22 AD2d 352, 256 NYS2d 166, app dismd 16 NY2d 958, 265 NYS2d 105, 212 NE2d 539 and affd 18 NY2d 644, 273

While a lease is still in force, and the tenant is still in possession, the fact that the landlord on one occasion commingled deposit moneys does not effect a forfeiture thereof, especially where the deposit moneys are thereafter deposited in a special account, and no damage is shown to have been suffered.[16] But, if the depositor is no longer in possession of the leased premises, commingling of the security deposit constitutes a conversion entitling him to a return thereof.[17]

### § 13:30. —As Bar to Summary Proceeding

A tenant who has agreed to make a deposit with his landlord, to secure the performance of the lease, must keep good the amount of such deposit as long as he continues in possession of the demised premises under the lease.[18]

If such deposit be reduced by reason of the tenant's defaults, the tenant cannot demand the right to continue in possession without replenishing the amount of the deposit. Therefore, when a landlord brings a summary proceeding to evict the tenant for non-payment of rent, the tenant will not be permitted to interpose as a bar to such proceeding, either by way of defense or by way of counterclaim, the alleged conversion by the landlord of the deposit. For, if the tenant be permitted any recovery on such counterclaim, he would be thus permitted to

---

NYS2d 71, 219 NE2d 424; Re General Assignment for Ben. of Creditors of John Holst Co. (S Ct Kings Co 1961) 213 NYS2d 952.

Landlord who has not improperly commingled the tenant's security deposit with its own funds may, as against assignee for benefit of creditors of a tenant who breached its lease, retain the security deposit. Glass v Janbach Properties, Inc (1980, 2d Dept) 73 AD2d 106, 425 NYS2d 343. Re Perfection Technical Services Press Inc., supra, is not contra, because in the Perfection case the landlord had improperly commingled the deposit, and thereby had forfeited the right to retain the deposit as against the assignee for benefit of creditors.

16. Bridge Hardware Co. v Mayer (1954, Sup App T) 131 NYS2d 823 (moneys segregated after action started); Stern Juvenile Furniture Co. v Rochman (S Ct Nassau Co 1960) 203 NYS2d 360, motion den (2d Dept) 12 AD2d 624, 210 NYS2d 757 and app dismd (2d Dept) 13 AD2d 531, 214 NYS2d 708; 19 North Village Realty Corp. v Kominos (S Ct Queens Co 1956) 3 Misc 2d 768, 155 NYS2d 318 (money segregated after action started), affd (2d Dept) 3 AD2d 754, 160 NYS2d 825; 160 Realty Corp. v 162 Realty Corp. (S Ct NY Co 1952) 113 NYS2d 618 (money segregated before action started) affd 280 AD 762, 113 NYS2d 678.

17. Purfield v Kathrane (NYC Civ Ct NY Co 1973) 73 Misc 2d 194, 341 NYS2d 376.

18. Atlas v Moritz (AD4 1926) 217 AD 38, 216 NYS 490; Turquoise Realty Corp. v Burke (M Ct 1983) 168 Misc 670, 6 NYS2d 125; Euclid Holding Co. v Kermacoe Realty Co. (M Ct 1928) 131 Misc 466, 227 NYS 103.

# DEPOSIT § 13:31

reduce the amount of his deposit. Thereupon the landlord could maintain a suit in equity to compel the tenant to restore the amount of the deposit.[19] To avoid such circuity of procedure the courts have held that the landlord has a good equitable defense to any such counterclaim, and have, therefore, dismissed the counterclaim.[20]

Of course, if the counterclaim is dismissed, it should be dismissed without prejudice to an action for the conversion of the deposit at such time as the tenant by the provisions of the lease becomes entitled to its return.[1]

The fact that the statute creates a trust relationship as to the deposit is immaterial. The statute merely commands that the deposit be kept in a certain manner. The contract between the parties, which is not abrogated by the statute, fixes the time for its return. Until that time arrives the tenant remains under the duty to keep the deposit good.[2]

## E. AGREEMENT TO APPLY DEPOSIT TO RENT

### § 13:31. How Applied

When parties to a lease agree that a deposit, in addition to securing performance thereof, shall be applied to the payment of rent for certain designated months, when the stipulated time arrives, and the tenant has performed the conditions entitling him to the benefit of the application of the deposit, then the tenant need not make any further payment of rent. As the Appellate Division said,[3] "The rule thus enuciated appears to be that a clause in a lease providing that a deposit is to be applied by the

---

**19.** Atlas v Moritz (AD4 1926) 217 AD 38, 216 NYS 490; Truquoise Realty Corp. v Burke (M Ct 1938) 168 Misc 670, 6 NYS2d 125.

**20.** Turquoise Realty Corp. v Burke (M Ct 1938) 168 Misc 670, 6 NYS2d 125; Euclid Holding Co. v Kermacoe Realty Co. (M Ct 1928) 131 Misc 446, 227 NYS 103; Alumor Garage, Inc. v George L. Stivers, Inc. (M Ct 1926) 128 Misc 400, 218 NYS 683; Contra, see 2710 Eighth Ave. Inc. v Frank Forman Pharmacy, Inc. (AT1 1943) 180 Misc 376, 42 NYS2d 887; 2300 Concourse Realty Corp. v Klug (M Ct 1952) 201 Misc 179, 111 NYS2d 168; Wasserman v Johnroy Properties, Inc. (M Ct 1951) 201 Misc 744, 109 NYS2d 750, revd on other grounds 202 Misc 83, 116 NYS2d 474, app gr 283 AD 660, 127 NYS2d 820.

**1.** Turquoise Realty Corp. v Burke (M Ct 1938) 168 Misc 670, 6 NYS2d 125.

**2.** Turquoise Realty Corp. v Burke (M Ct 1938) 168 Misc 670, 6 NYS2d 125.

**3.** Walker v 18th Street Holding Corp. (AD1 1943) 267 AD 141, 44 NYS2d 866.

landlord to payment of rent during the last months of the term is one that effects payment of the rent without further action by the tenant, provided the tenant has kept the other agreements by him to be performed."

A deposit clause provided that a sum of $7,000 "shall be held by the landlord as security for the full and faithful performance by the tenant of all the terms and conditions of this lease upon its part to be performed, which said sum shall be applied by the tenant as hereinafter provided, provided the tenant has fully and faithfully carried out all of the terms, covenants and conditions on its part to be performed. . . . Said security to be applied to payment of last 12 months' rent in monthly installments." This clause means, continued the court,[4] "that the difference between the rent reserved, and a sum measured by one-twelfth of the security, plus interest, will be the rent for each month during the last year of the term. There was to be no obligation on the part of the tenant to make any further payment if he kept his other agreements. In other words, his rent was the difference between the full rent and the deposit, on the performance of the other conditions."

In other words a deposit made by a tenant to secure his performance of the lease, with a provision that if he does perform, the deposit shall be applied to the payment of the last month's rent, will continue either as a penalty or as liquidated damages—whichever it may be, until the stipulated time arrives for its application to the rent. If at that time the tenant shall have performed, then the deposit automatically pays the designated rent without further action on the part of the tenant. The tenant need do nothing; the rent will have been paid by virtue of this clause.[5] However, it has been held, under such a provision

---

4. Walker v 18th Street Holding Corp. (AD1 1943) 267 AD 141, 44 NYS2d 866.

5. See, also, Flatbush Sav. Bank v Levy (S Ct Kings Co 1951) 109 NYS2d 247; Edroan Realty Corp. v Barnett (M Ct Man 1950) 200 Misc 323, 109 NYS2d 511, holding that where security deposit was used to pay rent, and the tenant held over as a statutory tenant, the tenant would not be compelled to replace the security deposit which had thus been depleted by its application to rent.

the tenant cannot insist that the deposit be applied to any unpaid rent prior to the time specified; otherwise the landlord will have no deposit left to secure himself against the tenant's defaults.[6]

### § 13:32. Agreement Binding on Grantee

It has been seen[7] that a covenant to repay a deposit is a personal one, and that the burden of such covenant does not run with the land. Unless, therefore, a grantee receives a security deposit from the landlord-grantor, the grantee will incur no liability to the tenant for its return.

But, such rule does not apply to an agreement to apply the security deposit to rent. A covenant to apply the security deposit to rent runs with the land and is binding on the grantee of the fee even if he does not receive the deposit.[8] The right of application of a security deposit to rent under such agreement is an unqualified one, and unless the lease provides otherwise, the deposit need not be transferred to any successor in interest of the landlord in order that the tenant may have the right of applying the deposit to rent available to him.

Therefore, even though a landlord's grantee receives no part of the tenant's deposit, the grantee will be bound by such a deposit clause. The grantee, then, will not be entitled to any rent for the period stipulated to be paid by the application of the deposit; for, the tenant is under no obligation to pay such rent, providing, of course, that he will have duly performed the covenants of the lease on his part to be performed.

A grantee, who takes a fee subject to leases, should, therefore, make some provision with his grantor about the deposit if the lease contains a provision for its application to rent.

6. § 13:7, supra.
7. § 13:16, supra.
8. Walker v 18th Street Holding Corp. (AD1 1943) 267 AD 141, 44 NYS2d 866. Also, see Shenk v Brewster (AD1 1919) 189 AD 608, 179 NYS 147, holding that such clause was binding on the heirs of a landlord, who had died intestate, even though they had not received the deposit, which as personal property, went to the administrators of the landlord; Flatbush Sav. Bank v Levy (S Ct Kings Co 1951) 109 NYS2d 247, holding that such a clause is binding upon receiver in foreclosure seeking to compel tenant to pay rent for period covered by deposit moneys; Maldon Bldgs, Inc. v Allied Health Careers Jamaica, Inc. (NYC Civ Ct Queens Co 1974) 78 Misc 2d 337, 356 NYS2d 531 (citing text).

§ 13:33　　　　　　　　　LANDLORD AND TENANT

## F. RESEARCH REFERENCES

### § 13:33. Generally

In addition to the preceding text, the reader is also referred to the following:

49 Am Jur 2d, Landlord and Tenant §§ 651-657.

11 Am Jur Legal Forms 2d, Leases of Real Property §§ 161:241-161:263.

16 Am Jur Pleading and Practice Forms (Rev ed), Landlord and Tenant, Forms 371-376.

New York Jur 2d, Landlord and Tenant (1st ed §§ 327-343).

New York Forms, Leases, Forms 8:191, 8:192.

Index to Annotations, Landlord and Tenant.

**VERALEX®:** Cases and annotations referred to herein can be further researched through the VERALEX electronic retrieval system's two services, **Auto-Cite®** and **SHOWME®**. Use Auto-Cite to check citations for form, parallel references, prior and later history, and annotation references. Use SHOWME to display the full text of cases and annotations.

## CHAPTER 14

## TENANT'S OBLIGATION TO PAY TAXES AND WATER CHARGES

A. TENANT'S OBLIGATION ABSENT COVENANT
 § 14:1. Generally
 § 14:2. On Buildings Erected by Tenant
 § 14:3. On Buildings Owned by Tenant
 § 14:4. —Effect of Landlord's Agreement to Pay All Taxes "Assessed Against Premises"
 § 14:5. Water Taxes and Water Rents Distinguished
 § 14:6. Tenant's Obligation to Pay for Water Absent Covenant

B. COVENANT TO PAY TAXES
 § 14:7. Problems Raised by Covenant
 § 14:8. Rule of Practical Construction Not Applicable
 § 14:9. Special Assessments
 § 14:10. —Effect of Covenant to Comply with Laws
 § 14:11. Landlord's Income Tax on Rentals
 § 14:12. —When Landlord Exempt
 § 14:13. Covenant to Pay Increase in Taxes
 § 14:14. Covenant to Pay Tax on Amount of Increase in Assessed Valuation
 § 14:15. Obligation to Protest Increase Where Tenant to Pay Increase
 § 14:16. Covenant to Pay Increase in Taxes Caused by Tenant's Improvements
 § 14:17. Covenant to Pay Increase in Taxes Caused by Landlord's Improvements
 § 14:18. Effect of Renewal of Lease on Covenant to Pay Increase in Taxes
 § 14:19. Form of Covenant to Pay Increase in Taxes
 § 14:20. Effect of Change in the Law
 § 14:21. Liability to Pay Taxes as of Due Date or Date of Imposition
 § 14:22. Covenant to Pay Taxes as of Date of Imposition of Tax
 § 14:23. Covenant to Pay Taxes "Levied or Imposed During Term"
 § 14:24. Covenant to Pay Taxes "Imposed in Any and Every Year During the Term"
 § 14:25. Covenant to Pay Taxes "Assessed During Term"

619

§ 14:26. Covenant to Pay Taxes as of Date of Imposition of Tax; Rule Summarized
§ 14:27. Form of Covenant to Pay Taxes as of Date of Imposition of Tax
§ 14:28. Covenant to Pay Taxes as of Due Date of Tax
§ 14:29. Covenant to "Keep Premises Free, Clear, Discharged and Unincumbered from All Taxes"
§ 14:30. Covenant to Pay Taxes "So That Landlord Shall Receive a Net Rental"
§ 14:31. Covenant to "Pay Carrying and Maintenance Charges"
§ 14:32. Covenant to Pay Taxes "Charged During Term"
§ 14:33. Covenant to Pay Taxes as of Due Date of Tax; Rule Summarized
§ 14:34. Liability of Assignee on Covenant to Pay Taxes
§ 14:35. Right of Grantee to Enforce Covenant to Pay Taxes
§ 14:36. Remedies of Landlord for Breach of Covenant
§ 14:37. Remedy of Tenant for Taxes Paid by him

C. COVENANT TO PAY FOR WATER AND SEWER RENTS
§ 14:38. Remedies of Landlord for Breach of Covenant
§ 14:39. Obligation to Install Water Meter
§ 14:40. Tenant's Obligation to Pay Sewer Rents
§ 14:41. Form of Covenant to Pay for Water and Sewer Rents

D. RESEARCH REFERENCES
§ 14:42. Generally

## A. TENANT'S OBLIGATION ABSENT COVENANT

### § 14:1. Generally

It is well settled that the obligation of a tenant to pay taxes on leased premises rests solely upon the terms of the lease, and does not arise merely by reason of the relation of landlord and tenant.[1] In the absence of a clear and express agreement by the tenant to pay taxes, they must be borne by the landlord,[2] since, as has been seen,[3] no additional liability will be imposed on a tenant by interpretation, unless it is clearly within the provisions of the instrument under which it is claimed.

1. Rensselaer & S. R. Co. v Delaware & Hudson Co. (AD3 1915) 168 AD 699, 154 NYS 739, affd 217 NY 692, 112 NE 1072.
2. Black v General Wiper Supply Co. (1953) 305 NY 386, 113 NE2d 528; New York University v American Book Co. (1910) 197 NY 294, 296, 90 NE 819; People ex rel. International Nav. Co. v Barker (1897) 153 NY 98, 101, 47 NE 46.
3. § 6:12, supra.

## § 14:2. On Buildings Erected by Tenant

It is the well settled rule in the law of real property that permanent structures, erected by persons who are not owners of the land on which they are erected, become part of the realty, and, as such, the property of the landowner.[4] Therefore, if a tenant erects a building on the leased premises, in the absence of any agreement on the part of the tenant to pay taxes, the landlord is obligated to pay the taxes assessed against the leased premises including the building. For, the building belongs to the landlord, and therefore is not assessable against the tenant.[5]

The fact that a tenant erects a building on the leased premises for the purpose of the tenant's business will not change the rule; for, if the building be a permanent structure, it still becomes a part of the realty, and therefore, belongs to the landowner.[6]

Where a lease provided that permanent structures erected by a tenant "shall become the property" of the landlord "on the expiration of the lease," it was contended that the phrase "shall become the property" of the landlord meant that until the expiration of the lease the structures were to remain the tenant's property. Therefore, the landlord argued that he was not liable for the taxes assessed thereon. However, in overruling this contention, and deciding that the landlord was liable for the taxes assessed against the structures erected by the tenant, the Court of Appeals said,[7] "When the lease in question provides that the sheds are to become the property of the city" (landlord) "at its expiration, the language does not warrant the inference of an intermediate ownership; unless we attach an undue significance to the word 'become.' Such a meaning we do not think should be attached to that word; whether we regard the purpose that it apparently subserves; or whether we regard the

---

**4.** Spoor-Lasher Co. v Newburgh Gas & Oil Co. (1936) 269 NY 447, 199 NE 656; People ex rel. Muller v Board of Assessors (1883) 93 NY 308, 311; Re Long Beach Land Co. (AD2 1905) 101 AD 159, 91 NYS 503.

**5.** Spoor-Lasher Co. v Newburgh Gas & Oil Co. (1936) 269 NY 447, 199 NE 656; People ex rel. International Nav. Co. v Barker (1897) 153 NY 98, 101, 47 NE 46; Re Long Beach Land Co. (AD2 1905) 101 AD 159, 91 NYS 503.

**6.** Re Long Beach Land Co. (AD2 1905) 101 AD 159, 91 NYS 503.

**7.** People ex rel. International Nav. Co. v Barker (1897) 153 NY 98, 47 NE 46.

confusion of ideas which would follow, if it had the meaning claimed for it. Its use was, evidently, to prevent any misunderstanding as to a right of removal, whether under a general claim of property in the erections, or under a claim to them as trade fixtures. It was to make the city's ownership definite. The provisions followed naturally, and not without some degree of pertinence, upon the obligation imposed upon the lessee to erect a shed. Its presence had the effect of negativing any inference from the requirement that the lessor had waived its ownership. The obligation resting upon the lessee to erect a shed was one of the conditions of the letting by the city and formed a part of its consideration. As the learned counsel for the respondent justly observed, it is not legally conceivable that the relator could be an owner until the termination of the lease and that then a new ownership should spring up in the city; for 'ownership necessarily implies perpetuity, or at least the possibility of perpetuity.'"

### § 14:3. On Buildings Owned by Tenant

Although the title and ownership of permanent structures erected by one person upon the land of another, in the absence of contract provisions regulating the interests of the respective parties, generally follow and accrue to the holder of the title to the land; yet, it is perfectly competent for parties by contract to so regulate their respective interests that one may be the owner of the buildings and another of the land.[8] Therefore, a landlord and a tenant may agree between themselves that the tenant, who shall erect permanent structures on the land, shall remain the owner of such structures. In such case the structures erected by the tenant will, for tax purposes, be real estate assessable to the tenant, and the tenant will have to pay the taxes thereon.[9] The Tax Law, said the Court of Appeals,[10] "defines 'land,' 'real estate,' and 'real property' to include 'all buildings and other articles and structures,' as well as 'all wharves and piers'

---

8. People ex rel. Muller v Board of Assessors (1883) 93 NY 308, 311.

9. People ex rel. Muller v Board of Assessors (1883) 93 NY 308; Re Long Beach Land Co. (AD2 1905) 101 AD 159, 91 NYS 503.

10. People ex rel Hudson River Day Line v Franck (1931) 257 NY 69, 71; 177 NE 312. The definitions cited by the Court as being in the Tax Law have been transferred to Real Property Tax Law § 102.

erected upon land above or under water. In cases involving tax assessments, therefore, it matters not that, at the common law, a building erected upon the lands of another, pursuant to an agreement with the landowner that at the end of a term the builder may remove it, is sometimes classified as personal property belonging to the builder. . . . The building is real estate assessable as such to the builder as its owner, while the land upon which it stands remains subject to assessment against the landowner."

However, such retention of ownership by the tenant presents an exception, by force of the statute, to the general rule that permanent structures, erected by persons not owners of the land, become part of the realty, and as such are taxable as the property of the landowner. To establish this exception, clear and explicit language must be employed, indicating with precision that the builder retains the right of removal and remains the owner.[11] The fact that the landlord reserves the right to re-enter in case of a breach by the tenant of his covenants will not change an agreement of the parties that the building erected by the tenant shall belong to the tenant.[12] Nor, will the reservation by the landlord of an option to pay the tenant the value of the building instead of granting him renewal of the lease.[1]

Accordingly, if the parties clearly and expressly provide that the tenant shall remain the owner of any building or other permanent structure he erects on the leased premises, such structure will, for tax purposes, be real estate, assessable to the tenant. The tenant, then, must pay the taxes assessed on the structure, even though the lease contains no covenant on his part to pay taxes.

### § 14:4. —Effect of Landlord's Agreement to Pay All Taxes "Assessed Against Premises."

Where a landlord permits a tenant to erect structures on the premises, and provides that they shall belong to the tenant, if the landlord covenants to pay all the taxes "assessed against the premises" during the term, then the

11. People ex rel. Hudson River Day Line v Franck (1931) 257 NY 69, 71, 177 NE 312.

12. People ex rel. Muller v Board of Assessors (1883) 93 NY 308.

1. People ex rel. Muller v Board of Assessors (1883) 93 NY 308.

§ 14:4  LANDLORD AND TENANT

landlord will have to pay the taxes which are assessed against the land as well as against such structures. Without such a covenant to pay all the taxes, the duty to pay the taxes assessed against the structures belonging to the tenant, as was shown in the preceding section, devolves upon the tenant.

A landlord leased vacant land to a tenant, and granted the tenant the privilege of erecting buildings and oil tanks on the land. It was agreed between them that all improvements, except oil tanks and personal equipment, were to become the landlord's property. It was further agreed that upon the landlord's default in paying "any taxes assessed against the premises," the tenant could pay such taxes, and deduct the amount thereof from the rent. The tenant erected oil tanks on the land. The landlord's estate tax was assessed on the value of the land and of the tanks. The landlord demanded that the tenant should pay that part of the tax assessed against the tenant's tanks. It was held that the landlord had to pay the entire tax assessed. In so holding, The Court of Appeals said,[2] "Here we have a case where land is leased with permission given the lessee to erect oil tanks on the property, title to which shall not pass to the landlord. . . . The lessor agrees that if it defaults in the payment of taxes against the premises, the tenant may pay and deduct the amount for the rent due. This would indicate that the lessor was to pay all the taxes assessed against the premises, as they then existed or would exist after the tenant had exercised its privilege of erecting buildings or tanks. If buildings, they become the property of the lessor; if tanks, they were to belong to the lessee; but in either case the lessor was to pay the taxes. If the parties had anything else in mind, or the word 'premises' was not to include all the premises or all the real estate as it existed at the time of the assessment, the lease should have so stated. Courts cannot be expected to guess at what the parties meant, or order that to be done which the parties were able to do for themselves and probably would have done had it been thought of."

Therefore, although the tanks became part of the

---

2. Spoor-Lasher Co. v Newburgh Gas & Oil Co. (1936) 269 NY 447, 199 NE 656.

realty for the purposes of taxation, and since they belonged to the tenant, the tenant should have paid the taxes thereon; yet, since the landlord agreed to pay all the taxes assessed "against the premises," the landlord was obligated to pay them. The tanks were clearly part of the "premises."[3]

## § 14:5. Water Taxes and Water Rents Distinguished

A municipality usually adopts one of two methods of compensating itself for furnishing water to its inhabitants. The first method is by exercising the power of taxation. By this method the municipality establishes a uniform scale of rates and charges for supplying water to different classes of buildings. These charges are not dependent upon the quantity of water used, but on the class or type of building to which water is supplied. Therefore, such charges must be paid regardless of the quantity used. Such charges or rates are water taxes.[4]

The second method is by selling the water. By this method the municipality installs a water meter, and makes a charge only for the amount of water actually used. Such charges are water rents, and are not, properly speaking, taxes.[5]

## § 14:6. Tenant's Obligation to Pay for Water Absent Covenant

When a lease is silent as to who shall pay for water used on the leased premises, in order to determine who is obligated to pay therefor it is first necessary to ascertain whether the charge involved is a water tax or a water rent.[6] If the water supplied to the leased premises is not metered, so that the charge therefor is a water tax, then unless the tenant has agreed to pay such water tax, the

---

3. Also, see People ex rel. International Nav. Co. v Barker (1897) 153 NY 98, 47 NE 46.

But, see Witschger v Kamages (AD2 1949) 275 AD 1053, 92 NYS2d 165, app den 276 AD 784, 93 NYS2d 304, where upon apparently similar facts the court arrived at a different conclusion, and imposed the obligation upon the tenant to pay the taxes assessed upon the improvements erected by the tenant, and which, under the lease, the tenant had the right to remove at the termination of the lease.

4. New York University v American Book Co (1910) 197 NY 294, 297, 90 NE 819.

5. New York University v American Book Co. (1910) 197 NY 294, 297, 90 NE 819; Silkman v Board of Water Com'rs (1897) 152 NY 327, 331, 46 NE 612.

6. See § 14:5, supra.

landlord must pay it. As has been seen, in the absence of an agreement relative to taxes, the landlord must bear all taxes imposed on the property.[7] This will include water taxes.[8]

However, if the water supplied to the leased premises is measured by a water meter, then the tenant must pay such water rent, even though the lease is silent as to who shall pay taxes imposed on the property, or as to who shall pay for the water consumed.[9] Here, there is merely a voluntary purchase by a consumer from the municipality of such quantity of water as he chooses to buy, and the obligation to pay therefor must primarily rest upon him who buys and consumes the article.[10]

## B. COVENANT TO PAY TAXES

### § 14:7. Problems Raised by Covenant

The parties to a lease may be provisions therein regulate as between themselves their respective liability for taxes and assessments upon the leased premises. In the absence of a covenant on the part of a tenant to pay taxes upon leased premises, it has been seen, a tenant is under no obligation to pay them.[11] However, if a tenant does covenant to pay taxes, then such covenant will present the usual difficulties of construction. As Hofstadter, J., said,[12] "The difficulty presented by provisions of this character arises from the fact that the event which has occurred was probably not in the contemplation of the parties when the instrument was drawn." And, of course, as Crane, Ch. J., pointed out, "Courts cannot be expected to guess at what the parties meant, or order that to be done which the parties were able to do for themselves and probably would have done had it been thought of."[13] It must always be remembered that the court may not, under the guise of interpretation, make a new contract

---

7. See § 14:1, supra.
8. Miller v Wilke (AD3 1913) 158 AD 208, 143 NYS 154; Brandt v Stadler (AT1 1913) 139 NYS 884; Darcey v Steger (AT 1898) 23 Misc 145, 50 NYS 638.
9. New York University v American Book Co. (1910) 197 NY 294, 297, 90 NE 819; Butler Estates v Simon (AT1 1917) 165 NYS 376; Brandt v Stadler (AT1 1913) 139 NYS 884.

10. New York University v American Book Co. (1910) 197 NY 294, 297, 90 NE 819; Brandt v Stadler (AT1 1913) 139 NYS 884.
11. See § 14:1, supra.
12. Huyler v Huyler's (S Ct NY Co 1943) 44 NYS2d 255.
13. Spoor-Lasher Co. v Newburgh Gas & Oil Co. (1936) 269 NY 447, 451, 199 NE 656.

## TENANT'S OBLIGATIONS § 14:8

for the parties, or change the words of a written contract so as to make it express the real intention of the parties if to do so would contradict the clearly expressed language of the contract.[14]

An analysis of the cases shows that the majority of problems arising under a tenant's tax covenant can be classified under three general headings: First, as to what charges imposed by the authorities the tenant is obligated to pay under his covenant. Second, as to what effect changes in the tax laws, occurring after the inception of the lease, will have on the tenant's obligation under his tax covenant. Third, as to whether the date of the assessment of the taxes governs, or the date when the taxes become due and payable governs, under the tenant's tax covenant.

These are the problems which will be treated in the following sections.

It may observed that allocation of tax liability between landlord and tenant is a proper subject of agreement between landlord and tenant, and will be enforced.[15]

### § 14:8. Rule of Practical Construction Not Applicable

It is familiar contract law that in the event of ambiguity, the practical construction placed upon an instrument by the parties is a potent factor in interpretation. However, that the language of a contract may be difficult to interpret, does not make it ambiguous in a legal sense.[16] "If the court finds," said the Court of Appeals,[17] "as matter of law that the contract in unambiguous, evidence of the intention and acts of the parties plays no part in the decision of the case. Plain and unambiguous words, undisputed facts, leave no question of construction except for the court. The conduct of the parties may fix a meaning to words of doubtful import. It may not change the terms of a contract."

Therefore, if a tax covenant clearly imposes a duty on a

---

**14.** Rodolitz v Neptune Paper Products, Inc. (1968) 22 NY2d 383, 292 NYS2d 878, 239 NE2d 628.

**15.** J. C. Penney Co. v 1700 Broadway Co. (S Ct NY Co 1980) 104 Misc 2d 787, 429 NYS2d 369.

**16.** Farmers' Loan & Trust Co. v Park & Tilford (S Ct NY Co 1925) 127 Misc 59, 215 NYS 244.

**17.** Brainard v New York C. R. Co. (1926) 242 NY 125, 133, 151 NE 152, 45 ALR 751.

§ 14:8    LANDLORD AND TENANT

tenant to pay taxes, the fact that the landlord may mistakenly or inadvertently pay such taxes is not an admission binding on the courts that under a proper construction of the tax covenant the landlord is obligated to pay such taxes. "When the instrument is clear in the eye of the law," said Pound, J.,[18] "the error of the parties cannot control its effect. The mere fact that the landlord chooses to relieve a tenant of a duty tends in no way to create a duty not imposed by the contract."[19]

However, the rule that in construing ambiguous language there is no better evidence of the parties' intent than their practical construction of an agreement, applies to the construction of an ambiguous tax provision in a lease.[20]

### § 14:9. Special Assessments

A covenant to pay taxes does not include special assessments for public improvements;[1] for a special assessment is not a tax.[2] Although in a broad sense taxes undoubtedly include special assessments, yet in practise the courts repeatedly have distinguished between them.[3] Therefore, in the absence of an express covenant to pay special assessments, a tenant is not obligated to pay them under a general covenant to pay taxes.[4] Generally, a

18. Brainard v New York C. R. Co. (1926) 242 NY 125, 134, 151 NE 152, 45 ALR 751.

19. Citing Elefante v Pizitz (AD1 1918) 182 AD 819, 169 NYS 910, affd 230 NY 567, 130 NE 896.

Also, see Western Union Tel. Co. v Pacific & Atlantic Tel. Co. (1947) 297 NY 124, 134, 75 NE2d 843; Wendel Foundation v Moredall Realty Corp. (1940) 282 NY 239, 247, 26 NE2d 241; Northwestern Tel. Co. v Western Union Tel. Co. (S Ct NY Co 1949) 194 Misc 352, 85 NYS2d 263, affd 275 AD 914, 90 NYS2d 685; Farmers' Loan & Trust Co. v Park & Tilford (S Ct NY Co 1925) 127 Misc 59, 215 NYS 244.

20. Refrigeration for Science, Inc. v Deacon Realty Corp. (S Ct Nassau Co 1972) 70 Misc 2d 500, 334 NYS2d 418, affd (2d Dept) 42 AD2d 691, 344 NYS2d 1018.

1. McVickar Gaillard Realty Co. v Garth (AD1 1906) 111 AD 924, 97 NYS 640.

2. Hassan v Rochester (1876) 67 NY 528, 533.

3. Re Hun (1895) 144 NY 472, 39 NE 376; Roosevelt Hospital v New York (1881) 84 NY 108.

Real Prop Tax L § 102, subd 15, defines "special assessment" as a charge imposed upon benefited real property in proportion to the benefit received by such property to defray the cost, including operation and maintenance, of a special district improvement or service or of a special improvement or service.

Real Prop Tax L § 102, subd 20, defines "tax" or "taxation" as a charge imposed upon real property by or on behalf of a county, city, town, village or school district purposes, including a service charge, but does not include a special ad valorem levy or a special assessment.

4. McVickar Gaillard Realty Co. v Garth (AD1 1906) 111 AD 924, 97 NYS 640.

## TENANT'S OBLIGATIONS § 14:11

covenant in a lease, binding the lessee to pay "taxes and assessments," or broader terms to that effect, includes the payments by lessee of special assessments.[5]

Requirement to pay "real estate taxes" which may be payable with respect to the leased premises, includes school taxes assessed upon leased premises.[6]

### § 14:10. —Effect of Covenant to Comply with Laws

The contention has been advanced that where a tenant covenants to comply with and execute all laws, orders, and regulations of the authorities, he thereby obligates himself to pay special assessments, since they are imposed by order of the authorities. This contention has been rejected by the courts as untenable.[7] Such a covenant refers to building, sanitary and police orders, laws and regulations; and it would be a violent stretch of language, it has been held, to apply those words to the payment of a special assessment for a public improvement decided to be a benefit to the property. Therefore, it has been held that the covenant to comply with the law or other orders of the authorities does not impose an obligation to pay either taxes or special assessments.[8]

### § 14:11. Landlord's Income Tax on Rentals

A distinction must be made between taxes on the income of property, and taxes on the property itself. "With monotonous frequency," said the Court of Appeals,[9] "the courts have held in this connection that a tax on the rents or income of real property is not a tax on the property itself. When the lessee is to pay all taxes, ordinary and extraordinary, which shall be imposed in the demised premises or 'in respect thereof,' the tax on rent is a tax not in relation to the property demised, but in relation to the income thereof."

---

**5.** Post v Kearney (1848) 2 NY 394 (covenant "to discharge all such rates, taxes and assessments" for which the premises shall be liable, held to include an assessment for opening a street); Arthur v Harty (S Ct NY Co 1896) 17 Misc 641, 40 NYS 1091 ("all taxes, assessments, or water rents that may be levied upon the demised premises").

**6.** Fitzpatrick v Mister Donut of America, Inc. (1980, 2d Dept) 78 AD2d 647, 432 NYS2d 242.

**7.** McVickar Gaillard Realty Co. v Garth (AD1 1906) 111 AD 924, 97 NYS 640, which affd on the opinion of the court below, rendered by Clarke, J.

**8.** McVickar Gaillard Realty Co. v Garth (AD1 1906) 111 AD 924, 97 NYS 640.

**9.** Brainard v New York C. R. Co. (1926) 242 NY 125, 131, 151 NE 152, 45 ALR 751.

§ 14:11    LANDLORD AND TENANT

Therefore, the general rule (sometimes called the Brainard rule, because it was enunciated in a case bearing that name)[10] is: unless a lease expressly provides for the payment of taxes on the income from rentals received under the lease, the imposition of such a burden on a tenant is not justified; for, words which are commonly used only to describe property taxes will not be construed to include income taxes.

Thus, a covenant "to pay, bear, and discharge all taxes and assessments of every description, assessed, imposed, levied, and accruing" upon the leased premises, does not include an obligation to pay the income taxes which a landlord must pay on the rental received under the lease. "An income tax," said John M. Kellogg, J., in so ruling,[11] "is not a tax upon specific property, but is a tax upon the annual net gain of the individual or corporation received from its business, the use of its property, or otherwise." Therefore, the tenant should not be required to pay such a tax. He only covenanted to pay taxes on specific property,—the leased premises. A covenant to "pay all taxes and assessments which may be levied or become chargeable on the said road or property, or upon the said (lessor) by reason of its ownership thereof," describes property taxes only, and neither includes nor has reference to income taxes.[12] Similarly, a covenant to pay all annual rentals "without any deduction or abatement for or on account of taxes or assessments or for any purpose whatsoever," or "without any deduction or abatement for or on account of taxes or assessments on the aforesaid leased property, or for any other purpose whatsoever," has been held to describe property taxes, and to impose no obligation on the tenant to pay the landlord's income taxes on the rental of the property.[13]

In other words, then, landlords must pay their own income taxes on the rentals from their property unless

---

10. Brainard v New York C. R. Co. (1926) 242 NY 125, 132, 151 NE 152, 45 ALR 751. Also, see Western Union Tel. Co. v Pacific & Atlantic Tel. Co. (1947) 297 NY 124, 132, 75 NE2d 843, where the court said, "The Brainard rule is still the law."

11. Rensselaer & S. R. Co. v Delaware & Hudson Co. (AD3 1915) 168 AD 699, 154 NYS 739, affd 217 NY 692, 112 NE 1072.

12. Brainard v New York C. R. Co. (1926) 242 NY 125, 151 NE 152, 45 ALR 751.

13. Western Union Tel. Co. v Pacific & Atlantic Tel. Co. (1947) 297 NY 124, 75 NE2d 843.

there be found express language in the lease whereby the tenant expressly assumes such an obligation.[14]

However, the draftsman of a lease should bear the following case in mind. In this case, a company leased its properties and business to a tenant for 99 years, with rentals payable directly to the landlord's shareholders. The tenant covenanted to keep the whole property and business of the landlord "clear from all incumbrances arising from tax, assessment or judgment liens," and to surrender the leased property at the end of the term "as free from . . . encumbrance thereon as they were, when received." The words "income taxes" were not used. Nevertheless, the Court of Appeals held[15] that the tenant's covenant included an obligation to pay the Federal income taxes imposed on the landlord on the rental received. The basis for this construction was that the failure of the tenant to pay the income taxes would result in liens upon the leased property. Unless the tenant paid such taxes, therefore, he could not perform his promise to keep and return the leased property free and clear of tax liens, and as free from encumbrances thereon as they were, when received.[16]

This case is not to be misinterpreted as overruling the Brainard rule. This case merely indicates that income taxes need not be mentioned by name to impose this obligation on a tenant. Desmond, J., who wrote the opinion in this case, said in a later case,[17] that the Brainard rule is still the law, and that it was not overruled by this case, but rather was reaffirmed by it. Express language whereby a tenant assumes an obligation to pay a landlord's income tax on the rentals is still necessary. Words which are commonly used only to describe property taxes will not be construed to include income taxes, and to impose such a burden on a tenant. All this case holds,

14. Northwestern Tel. Co. v Western Union Tel. Co. (S Ct NY Co 1949) 194 Misc 352, 85 NYS2d 263, affd 275 AD 914, 90 NYS2d 685; New York C. R. Co. v New York & H. R. Co. (S Ct NY Co 1945) 185 Misc 420, 56 NYS2d 712, affd 272 AD 870, 72 NYS2d 404, affd 297 NY 820, 78 NE2d 612.

15. Johnson v Western Union Tel. Co. (1944) 293 NY 379, 385, 57 NE2d 721, reh den 293 NY 859, 59 NE2d 446. But, see, strong dissenting opinion of Conway, J.

16. But, see Northwestern Tel. Co. v Western Union Tel. Co. (S Ct NY Co 1949) 194 Misc 352, 85 NYS2d 263, affd 275 AD 914, 90 NYS2d 685, where tenant held not obligated to pay income taxes.

17. Western Union Tel. Co. v Pacific & Atlantic Tel. Co. (1947) 297 NY 124, 132, 133, 75 NE2d 843.

therefore, is that the tax covenant in this case sufficiently expressed an obligation on the part of the tenant to bear such a burden. But it also points up the importance of careful draftsmanship. In view of the difficulties encountered in leaving the subject open to construction by the courts, it would seem more prudent for the draftsman to comply with what a plain reading of the Brainard rule indicates should be done: Expressly provide for the payment of taxes on the income from rentals received under the lease.

### § 14:12. —When Landlord Exempt

A lease contained this tax covenant: The tenant shall pay in each year a sum equal to "all the income, excise and license taxes or duties of every kind, additional and super as well as normal, extraordinary as well as ordinary, unforeseen as well as foreseen, that shall be imposed, levied or assessed in any such year upon the rent reserved by this lease or the income secured hereby from the leased premises, by any present or future law of the United States of America, or of the State of New York, or of any other public or governmental body whatsoever, . . . without the benefit to the Tenant, its successors and assigns of any deductions or exemptions to which the Landlord, their heirs, successors or assigns may be entitled, . . . ." The landlord, a charitable organization, was exempt under the law from payment of all income, excise, and license taxes or duties of every kind. Nevertheless, the landlord sued the tenant to recover a sum equal to the amount of annual income taxes which it would have been required to pay on the rental, had it been subject to the payment of an income tax.

"It is argued," said Rippey, J., speaking for the Court of Appeals,[18] "that the expression that the additional rent is payable 'without the benefit to the Tenant, its successors or assigns of any deductions or exemptions to which the Landlords . . . may be entitled' indicates a purpose to make the hypothetical taxes payable as additional rent regardless of any requirement on the part of the landlords to pay. It is safe to stand upon the wording of the

---

18. Wendel Foundation v Moredall Realty Corp. (1940) 282 NY 239, 245, 26 NE2d 241.

written lease. If we take the words of the instrument to mean what they clearly say, it follows that the so-called exemption clause above quoted is consistent only with the requirement on the part of the landlords to pay taxes. It was immaterial who the landlords were, whether individuals or corporations, or what deductions or exemptions he or they might properly have in connection with income taxes to be paid. Unless such taxes were properly imposed and required to be paid, deductions and exemptions referred to are meaningless. But if and when income taxes were imposed, levied and assessed, then and then only did the parties remove from the realm of quibble and litigation the question of the amount to be paid as additional rent."

In other words the intention of the parties must be found in the words used to express such intention. If the parties intend that the tenant shall pay a fixed minimum rental, and in addition is to pay as indemnity to the landlord such sums as the landlord is required to pay, as they arise out of and are incidental to the ownership and leasing of the property, the tenant will not have to pay more than that. If the landlord does not have to pay any particular tax, then there is nothing to indemnify, and the tenant will not have to pay that tax.

### § 14:13. Covenant to Pay Increase in Taxes

Covenants to pay taxes sometimes provide that the tenant shall pay any increase in the amount of the taxes imposed on the property over those imposed on the property at the time of the execution of the lease. Such covenants are valid, and are enforceable. However, the primary difficulty in their enforcement has been the fact that the parties have not always expressed their intention clearly, thus creating problems of construction as to whether the tenant must pay the entire amount of the increase in the taxes over the amount of taxes imposed on the property when the lease started, or only the tax on the amount of the increase in the assessed valuation.[19]

A lease provided that the tenant shall pay any taxes and assessments in excess of the present "tax rate" for

---

19. Annotation: Landlord and tenant: construction of provision of lease providing for escalation of rental in event of tax increases. 48 ALR3d 287.

the year 1925, but in the event that the amount of additional taxes shall exceed the sum of $500 in any one year, then the tenant shall be obligated only up to said $500 yearly. During the term of the lease the tax rate went up .0002; the assessed valuation went up from $82,000 to $95,000; and the tax was increased by $368.70. The landlord contended that the tenant was obligated to pay the increase in tax; to wit, $368.70. However, the tenant contended that all he had to pay was $19; that is .0002 times the new assessment of $95,000. The court held[20] that a proper construction of this tax covenant required the tenant to pay the entire increase in taxes, arising either from an increase in assessed valuation or from an increase in the tax rate, providing such increase did not exceed $500 in any one year. Therefore, the landlord was entitled to recover $368.70. "Assessment," said the court, "means the determination of the liability of the property to taxation, and its valuation for that purpose." "Tax" means the sum of money imposed or assessed on the person or property by the government.[1] "Tax" and "rate" are synonymous terms. However, interpreting the covenant as phrased by the parties, said the court, "the words 'tax rate,' as used here, merely limit and point out what taxes and assessments the lessee is to pay, for without this word 'tax-rate' the covenant would read that the lessee agrees to pay any taxes and assessments in excess of the year 1925, and by the inclusion of the word 'tax-rate,' it connotes that the only taxes and assessments that the lessee was to pay were those assessed against the real property. . . . The very fact that the parties fixed in this provision a maximum amount for which the lessee shall be liable in case of additional taxes proves most cogently that the intention of the contracting parties was that the lessee should pay all increases of taxes levied upon the real property up to a maximum amount of $500 per year, and not an increased rate of the

---

20. Auerbach v Mr. & Mrs. Foster's Place, Inc. (M Ct 1927) 128 Misc 875, 220 NYS 281.

1. Real Property Tax L § 102, subd 2, insofar as pertinent here, provides that "assessment" means a determination made by assessors of the valuation of real property, including the valuation of exempt real property. Real Property Tax L § 102, subd 20, provides that "tax" means the charge imposed upon real property by or on behalf of the taxing authority.

## TENANT'S OBLIGATIONS § 14:13

percentage of levy as contended by the defendant." (tenant)

In another case the lease provided that the tenant shall pay as additional rent, commencing July 1, 1949, "one-half of the excess of real estate taxes affecting the real property of which the demised premises form a part over and above the amount of such taxes for the fiscal year 1947-1948." The lease was executed June 16, 1948, at which time the assessed valuation of the property for the fiscal year 1947-1948 was $815,000, and the taxes based on this valuation amounted to $24,531.50. The landlord had protested this valuation, and on June 17, 1948, one day after the execution of the lease, succeeded in having the assessed valuation reduced. This resulted in a tax reduction for the fiscal year 1947-1948. But, the tenant at the time he entered into the lease did not know that proceedings were pending to reduce the assessed valuation. The question posed was whether the lease contemplated taxes as reduced for the base year, or taxes as imposed for the base year. The lower court[2] held that the tenant was obligated to pay one-half of the excess of the taxes over and above the reduced amount, which was actually paid, and not over and above the original imposition. In other words, the lower court felt that the taxes as reduced for the base year had been contemplated by the parties. The Appellate Division, however, disagreed.[3] It held that on the facts in this case the parties had contracted on the basis of the known levy at the time of entering into the lease, and not some unknown figure resulting from legal proceedings of which they had no knowledge when they entered into the lease. The amount of taxes which would result from the known assessment is what they understood and meant by "taxes for the fiscal year 1947-48." In other words, the Appellate Division held that the taxes as imposed for the base year had been contemplated by the parties. The Court of Appeals affirmed the Appellate Division.[4]

---

[2]. City Bank Farmers Trust Co. v J & J. Slater, Inc. (S Ct NY Co 1950) 101 NYS2d 617, mod 278 AD 366, 105 NYS2d 146, affd 303 NY 971, 106 NE2d 58.

[3]. City Bank Farmers Trust Co. v J & J Slater, Inc. (AD1 1951) 278 AD 366, 105 NYS2d 146, affd 303 NY 971, 106 NE2d 58.

[4]. City Bank Farmers Trust Co. v J. & J. Slater, Inc. (1952) 303 NY 971, 106 NE2d 58.

§ 14:13    LANDLORD AND TENANT

Since tax escalation clause as written was meant to provide relief for landlord when "assessed" tax required actual payment, where real estate taxes increased, but actual bill decreased due to exemptions, no payment was due landlord, especially where escalation clause further provided, "the submission of a duplicate tax bill of the landlord shall be deemed to be conclusive evidence of the payment of real estate taxes payable by the landlord and should be the basis for computation of any additional rent to be paid hereunder by tenant."[5]

Where lease provided that tax escalation should commence when temporary or permanent certificate of occupancy for the building of which leased premises formed a part was issued permitting tenant to enter the occupancy of the leased premises, the issuance of a temporary certificate will trigger tax escalation even though tenant was unable to occupy the building in accordance with the terms of the lease.[6]

Where lease provided that tenant would pay as additional rent any increase in land and building taxes levied by the Town on the premises leased, occurring on and after the first assessment by the Town of said premises as improved property, and that landlord should have the Town designate the leased premises as a separate tax lot as soon as practicable, and landlord failed to have the Town designate the leased premises as a separate tax lot, landlord could not recover after the expiration of the lease a proportionate part of the increased property taxes paid upon such property, since landlord's failure substantially impaired tenant's rights, and cancelled tenant's obligation to pay the increase. Broad Properties, Inc. v Wheels, Inc. (1974, 2d Dept) 43 AD2d 276, 351 NYS2d 15, affd 35 NY2d 821, 362 NYS2d 859, 321 NE2d 781. (In absence of any covenant in a lease to contrary, where an apportionment is necessary to determine the extent of tenant's obligation under a tax covenant, primary obligation of apportionment is on landlord. See § 14:36.)

Where lease drawn by landlord provided that tenant should pay any increase in real estate taxes over "the year 1972", the court construed this ambiguity against the landlord, and held that the base year was the fiscal year 1972–1973. Graziano v Tortora Agency, Inc. (NYC Civ Ct Queens Co 1974) 78 Misc 2d 1094, 359 NYS2d 489.

Under lease providing that if real estate taxes on leased premises vary upward in excess of 5% of the amount of taxes levied for the full tax year 1965, then the monthly rental therein reserved for any month falling within such tax year is to be increased by one-twelfth of the amount of such excess, but in no event is the rental fixed under this clause to vary from the rental fixed under this lease by more than $1006.50 per year, tenant is obligated to pay no more than $1006.50 in any one year over the amount of the base rental. Bensons Plaza v Great Atlantic & Pacific Tea Co. (1978) 44 NY2d 791, 406 NYS2d 33, 377 NE2d 477.

5. Fairfax Co. v Whelan Drug Co. (1984, 1st Dept) 105 AD2d 647, 481 NYS2d 366.

6. Frank B. Hall & Co. v Orient Overseas Associates (1979) 48 NY2d 958, 425 NYS2d 66, 401 NE2d 189.

# TENANT'S OBLIGATIONS § 14:14

A tax escalation clause in a lease negotiated by parties with experienced counsel is not unconscionable.[7]

## § 14:14. Covenant to Pay Tax on Amount of Increase in Assessed Valuation

In the preceding section, the covenant discussed was interpreted to mean that the tenant had to pay the entire amount of the increase in taxes over the amount of taxes imposed on the property when the lease started. However, the following covenant was interpreted to mean that the tenant only had to pay the tax upon the amount of the increase in the assessed valuation. The lease provided that if at any time after the inception of the lease the building, of which the leased premises formed a part, "be assessed for the purpose of taxation in excess of the assessment in the year 1914, the tenant will pay an amount equal to one-half of the tax on such excess." The court held[8] that the tenant was liable only for one-half of the taxes on the increased assessed valuation, and not on one-half of the increase in the amount of the taxes. Assessment and taxes, the court pointed out, were not being used synonymously. The tenant only had agreed to pay one-half of the taxes upon the increased assessed valuation.

Under a provision that lessor shall construct a building, and that tenant shall pay any increase in taxes above the taxes which shall be due and payable for the tax years during which the premises as improved shall be first assessed, the base was arrived at as follows. The lease commenced June 1, 1959. The building was erected in the summer of 1959. For the 1959-1960 tax year the assessment was $155,950 for the building and $15,000 for the land, the land assessment being the same as the previous year although the land was no longer unimproved. In 1961-1962, the building was assessed without increase, but the land was increased to $39,200. This, the court held, was the first assessment of the premises as improved, and therefore was the tax base within the

7. 75 Henry Street Garage, Inc. v Whitman Owner Corp. (AD2 1981) 79 AD2d 1001, 435 NYS2d 26.

8. Bernstein v Bernstein (AD2 1923) 205 AD 741, 200 NYS 1.

contemplation of the parties.[9] Similarly, under a provision requiring the tenant to pay an increase in realty taxes imposed over and above the realty taxes levied against the leased premises for the first year after completion of the building, where the building was completed in December 1959, the base period was held to be the calendar year 1961 for town taxes, and the fiscal year commencing July 1, 1961 for school taxes, it having been established that an assessment for the completed building was for the first time made on June 1, 1960 for the year 1961, and that the assessment made on June 1, 1959 for the year 1960 had been based on an incomplete building.[10] However, in the following situation, a different conclusion was reached. In this case a lease of property on which a building was being constructed provided that the assessment upon which the taxes are based, and applying to the first three (3) years of the term of this lease "as herein defined," shall be averaged, that the average shall be deemed the limit of the lessor's obligation, who shall pay the taxes based on such average assessed valuation, and that the excess above such ceiling shall be payable by the lessee. A preceding provision in the lease provided that the obtaining of either a permanent or temporary certificate of occupancy shall be deemed the commencement of the term. It was held that the three-year period accordingly began when a temporary certificate of occupancy was issued.[11] In the Klion case, hereinabove discussed,[12] the base tax year referred to was that in which the premises were first assessed as improved, and not the entire year during which the tenant had taken possession, but in which the assessment was not based upon the property as improved. In this case, however,[13] the lease provided that the first three years from the "commencement of the term" should be averaged, and the com-

9. H. L. Klion, Inc. v Venimore Bldg. Corp. (1964) 15 NY2d 601, 255 NYS2d 264, 203 NE2d 651.

10. Wister Corp. v Safeway Stores, Inc. (S Ct NY Co 1963) 40 Misc 2d 320, 243 NYS2d 107.

11. Rodolitz v Neptune Products, Inc. (1968) 22 NY2d 383, 292 NYS2d 878, 239 NE2d 628, revg (2d Dept) 28 AD2d 859, 281 NYS2d 381, which had held that the three years which would be averaged were to be the first three years for which as assessment was made on the basis of the land and the completed building.

12. H. L. Klion, Inc. v Venimore Bldg. Corp. (1964) 15 NY2d 601, 255 NYS2d 264, 203 NE2d 651.

13. Rodolitz v Neptune Paper Products, Inc. (1968) 22 NY2d 383, 292 NYS2d 878, 239 NE2d 628.

mencement of the term should be deemed to have taken place upon occupancy.

### § 14:15. Obligation to Protest Increase Where Tenant to Pay Increase

It has been held that absent a specific undertaking to that effect, a landlord is under no obligation to initiate any proceeding to reduce an assessment or the taxes levied thereon.[14]

### § 14:16. Covenant to Pay Increase in Taxes Caused by Tenant's Improvements

A lease provided that the tenant was to pay all increases in taxes above the tax based on the assessed valuation for the year preceding the execution of the lease. The tenant was also authorized by another provision in the lease to make improvements on the property. The court held[15] that the undertaking of the tenant to pay all increases in taxes was clear, and was an absolute undertaking. Therefore, the tenant's obligation was not conditioned upon the fact that the increase only should be caused by the tenant's improvements. Whether or not the tenant made improvements, the obligation was that if there were an increase in taxes, the tenant would have to pay them. Where a lease provided that tenant is authorized to make improvements to the leased premises, and shall pay any increased taxes resulting from an increase in the assessed valuation of the property, or increase in taxes resulting from such improvements, it was held that the tenant is obligated to pay any increase in the taxes.[16]

### § 14:17. Covenant to Pay Increase in Taxes Caused by Landlord's Improvements

In contrast to the tax covenant discussed in the preceding section, is the following covenant. A tenant agreed to pay a stipulated percentage of the increase in taxation on

14. City Bank Farmers Trust Co. v J. & J. Slater, Inc. (S Ct NY Co 1950) 101 NYS2d 617, mod on other grounds 278 AD 366, 105 NYS2d 146, and affd 303 NY 971, 106 NE2d 58.

15. Gridley v Einbigler (AD1 1904) 98 AD 160, 90 NYS 721, affd 182 NY 566, 75 NE 1130.

16. King v Cardamone (S Ct Queens Co 1975) 86 Misc 2d 625, 383 NYS2d 123, affd (2d Dept) 52 AD2d 633, 383 NYS2d 548.

**Annotation:** Clause of lease providing for payment of taxes by lessor as applicable to increase in real-estate taxes occasioned by lessee's improvements. 68 ALR2d 1289.

the premises in which he had leased space. Subsequently the landlord increased the height of the building on the premises. As a result the assessed valuation of the building was increased resulting in an increase in taxes. The court held,[17] that the tenant's obligation to pay taxes was founded on the basis of the valuation of the structure as it had existed at the time of signing of the lease, and not on the basis of an increase in valuation caused by acts of the landlord. The court refused to construe the clause as obligating the tenant to pay any portion of an increase in tax due to an increase in the assessed valuation of a building, when such assessed valuation was increased wholly by extraordinary and unforeseen building alterations made on the landlord's own initiative.

### § 14:18. Effect of Renewal of Lease on Covenant to Pay Increase in Taxes

When a lease is renewed by virtue of a renewal clause, the effect is as if the original lease had contained a single term for the renewal period as well as the original term.[18] Therefore, when a tenant covenants to pay an increase in taxes, in the event the lease is renewed pursuant to a renewal clause, the increase in taxes for which the tenant will be liable will be the increase over the taxes imposed at the inception of the tenancy, and not the increase over the taxes imposed at the inception of the renewal period.

Thus, a tenant entered into a lease in 1925, and was given the option to renew it at a stipulated yearly rental "plus any increase in the local taxes which may occur during the term of the lease." The lease was renewed in 1930. The tenant contended that he was only liable for an increase in taxes over the taxes imposed in 1930. However, the landlord contended that the year 1925, the inception of the lease, was to be the basis for determining whether or not there was any increase in taxes in any year during the renewal period. The court held[19] that the landlord's position was correct; and that since the lease as renewed must be construed as containing a single term, the increase must be measured from 1925, the beginning of the term of the lease.

17. Bryant Park Bldg., Inc. v Acunto (M Ct 1928) 133 Misc 225, 231 NYS 451.

18. See § 11:50, supra.

19. Bribitzer v Wahlig (AD2 1932) 235 AD 702, 256 NYS 45.

## § 14:19. Form of Covenant to Pay Increase in Taxes
### FORM NO. 27
### Covenant to Pay Increase in Taxes and Special Assessments

Tenant agrees to pay to Landlord in any and every year during the term of this lease or any renewal thereof, on demand, 10% *(or any other percentage agreed on)* of the amount by which the annual real estate taxes which are imposed or levied during the term of this lease and any renewal thereof upon the land and building thereon at ........, of which the leased premises form a part, exceed the amount of the real estate taxes actually paid by the landlord thereon for the fiscal real estate tax year for the period July 1, .... to June 30, .... *(or, set forth any other fiscal tax period)* whether any such increase results from a higher tax rate or from an increase in the assessed valuation of the property, or both, and 10% *(or any other percentage agreed on)* of any special assessment imposed for any purpose whatsoever upon any or all of the aforesaid property of Landlord including the sidewalks or streets in front of or adjoining the said property or any vault or vaults thereunder, provided, however, that any real estate tax increase for the fiscal real estate tax year in which the term of this lease or of any renewal thereof shall expire shall be apportioned, so that Tenant shall be obligated to pay only Tenant's said percentage of that portion of such increase for such fiscal real estate tax year which corresponds with that portion of the fiscal real estate tax year as falls within the term. In the case of special assessments Tenant shall only be obligated to pay such installments as fall due during the term or any renewal thereof, on condition that Tenant shall take such steps as may be prescribed by law to convert the payment of the special assessment into installment payments.

If Tenant shall fail to pay on demand Tenant's said percentage of any increase in real estate taxes or of any special assessment, as hereinabove provided, in addition to any other remedy available to Landlord for the collection thereof, Landlord may at Landlord's option, if the term of this lease shall not have expired or been terminated, add the amounts thereof with all interest and

§ 14:19   LANDLORD AND TENANT

penalties which may be accrued and become due and payable thereon, to the next succeeding monthly installment of rent payable hereunder, and such amounts shall be deemed to be and shall constitute rent hereunder, and shall be collectible in the same manner and with the same remedies as if such amounts had been originally reserved herein as rent.*

* For complete form of lease see Chapter 1.

A tax bill shall be sufficient evidence of the amount of the real estate taxes or special assessment imposed, and for the calculation of the amount to be paid by Tenant hereunder.

## § 14:20. Effect of Change in the Law

Unless the parties clearly express a contrary intent, when a tenant covenants to pay all taxes which shall be levied or imposed against the property during the term of the lease, the tenant is obligated to pay not only the taxes imposed by the laws in force at the time the lease was executed, but also such taxes as may be imposed by laws enacted thereafter during the term.[20] The Court of Appeals said,[1] "We should not let the tenant out of his promise because the change in the charter increases his burdens in this regard." And, this seems to be the principle guiding the courts in imposing liability on a tenant who has covenanted to pay taxes. The court will take the language in the lease as it finds it. A seemingly harsh result due to subsequent developments, it has been held,[2] does not justify the court in altering a clear contract by reading into it something that might work out a seemingly fairer result.

Taxes, like death, are certain; but no one knows, when the lease is drawn, what forms of taxation will be imposed from time to time. However, there is no legal impediment to an assumption by the parties of all the risks of changes in the tax laws.[3] When the tenant undertakes to pay all taxes imposed during his term, if he

20. Ward v Union Trust Co. (1918) 224 NY 73, 120 NE 81, 3 ALR 1154; Post v Kearney (1849) 2 NY 394.
1. Wall v Hess (1922) 232 NY 472, 476, 134 NE 536, 20 ALR 1497.
2. Cohen v Jonathan Levi Co. (S Ct Schenectady Co 1933) 151 Misc 156, 269 NYS 865.
3. Johnson v Western Union Tel. Co. (1944) 293 NY 379, 386, 57 NE2d 721, reh den 293 NY 859, 59 NE2d 446.

does not wish to be burdened by new and larger taxes, he must expressly limit his undertaking so as to exclude an additional burden.

It has been held that a tax covenant in a lease contemplates payment of legal taxes, and therefore does not obligate a tenant to pay taxes which may be illegal and void.[4]

## § 14:21. Liability to Pay Taxes as of Due Date or Date of Imposition

A covenant to pay taxes frequently raises the problem as to whether a tenant is obligated to pay those taxes which are imposed during the term, but which do not become due and payable until after the term has ended. For example:[5] A tenant agrees to "pay and discharge when due and payable or within sixty days thereafter, all and every tax and taxes, Croton water or other water rates . . . charges, assessments, duties, and other impositions whatsoever, as well ordinary as extraordinary, which shall be assessed, levied, or imposed upon the said premises, or any part thereof during the said term." The lease expires April 30, 1917. The taxes for that year by the statute then in force are fixed and levied on March 28, 1917. However, the taxes are payable in two equal installments; one-half on May 1, 1917, and one-half on November 1, 1917. Under the tax covenant, then, must the tenant pay any part or all of the taxes for the year 1917, even though they become due, and are payable after the expiration of the term?

"It would," said Hofstadter, J.,[6] "of course, have been perfectly possible to phrase the obligation of the tenant in such language so as to make it absolutely clear whether the date of the imposition of the taxes governs or the date when the taxes become due and payable governs. Having used somewhat ambiguous language, the court must naturally draw such inferences as it can from the meaning of the words and the surrounding circumstances. It is not surprising, therefore, that similar provisions have received differing interpretations by the courts."

---

4. Erwin v Farrington (AD4 1955) 285 AD 1212, 140 NYS2d 379.

5. This was the factual situation presented for decision in Wall v Hess (1922) 232 NY 472, 134 NE 536, 20 ALR 1497.

6. Huyler v Huyler's (S Ct NY Co 1943) 44 NYS2d 255.

§ 14:21

The problem presented by such a covenant to pay taxes, then, is whether or not under the terms of the covenant, and the intention of the parties to be gathered from the entire lease, the tenant is to be deemed to have undertaken to pay all taxes assessed on the demised premises during the term, or only those taxes as become due and payable during the term. In other words, as the Appellate Division said,[7] the problem is "whether the assessment of the tax fixes the liability, if it is made during the term of the agreement, or whether the fact that the tax is payable while the term subsists fixes the liability."

The problem is a simple one. The difficulty, as presented by the many seemingly conflicting decisions, is the ascertainment of the intent of the parties from the terms of ambiguous covenants. Hence, although as said by Lehman, J.,[8] "It must be remembered that the courts always attempt to construe leases in accordance with the intention of the parties, and a construction by the court of the language in one lease may be a very dangerous guide to the ascertainment of the intention of the parties in using similar, but not identical language in another lease, perhaps made under different circumstances"; yet, a discussion and an analysis of the cases will prove helpful to indicate what the tax covenant should provide, and how the covenant should be drawn so as to eliminate any ambiguity as to what the parties intend.

### § 14:22. Covenant to Pay Taxes as of Date of Imposition of Tax

As indicated in the preceding section, it is difficult to reconcile the many cases dealing with the construction of tax covenants. It is more difficult to formulate any one rule that can categorically be applied to all situations. However, an analysis of the cases indicates that there are two general rules which have been applied in the solution of the problem.

The first general rule is: if it appears from the terms of the lease that the parties intended that the tenant is to

---

7. Walker v Stein (AD1 1928) 222 AD 22, 225 NYS 209.
8. R A Manning Realty Corp. v Topping Bros. (AT1 1923) 120 Misc 592, 199 NYS 241, affd 207 AD 852, 201 NYS 939.

pay all the taxes which shall be imposed or levied during the term, then the tenant must pay them even though they may become due and payable after the expiration of the term. But,—and this is the important additional thought, the fact that the parties may have added to the tax covenant a provision as to when or how the tenant shall pay such taxes will not change the primary liability to pay all the taxes that have been levied or imposed during the term.

The cases in which this first general rule has been applied, will be discussed in the following section, and will help to clarify it.

### § 14:23. Covenant to Pay Taxes "Levied or Imposed During Term"

A tax covenant provided that the tenant should "pay and discharge when due and payable or within sixty days thereafter, all and every tax and taxes, Croton water or other water rates, . . . charges, assessments, duties and other impositions whatsoever, as well ordinary as extraordinary, which shall be assessed, levied or imposed upon the said premises, or any part thereof, . . . during said term, . . . ." The lease by its terms expired April 30, 1917 at midnight. The taxes for 1917, under the statutes then in force were fixed and levied on March 28, 1917, and the first half thereof became due and payable May 1, 1917, and the second half on November 1, 1937. Thus, both parts of the taxes became payable after the term had expired. The court held[9] that under this covenant the tenant had obligated himself to pay all the taxes that might be levied, or imposed against the premises during the term, regardless of when they became due and payable. That is precisely what he said he was to do. As Pound, J., said in this case, "No escape is possible from the conclusion that the taxes for the year 1917 were finally and unalterably fixed and imposed against the demised premises during the term of the lease, although not payable until after the expiration of such term."

The mere fact that the landlord consented that the tenant could pay the taxes either when they were due to the city authorities, or sixty days thereafter, did not

---

9. Wall v Hess (1922) 232 NY 472, 134 NE 536, 20 ALR 1497.

change the obligation of the tenant to pay those taxes which were imposed during the term, but which might become payable after the term expired. Thus, the tenant in this case was held liable for the taxes for the year 1917.[10]

In other words, the fact that the lease provides for payment of the obligation in installments, some of which fall due beyond the lease term, does not operate to diminish the tenant's obligation.[11]

### § 14:24. Covenant to Pay Taxes "Imposed in Any and Every Year During the Term"

A lease provided that the tenant was to pay as rent six per centum of the increase in the amount of real estate taxes over and above $36,200, which might be imposed upon the property of which the premises demised were a part in any and every year during the term of the lease. The parties further agreed that a tax bill should be sufficient evidence of the amount of the taxes. The lease expired April 30, 1921 at midnight. The taxes for that year were imposed by the statute then in force, in March, 1921, but were made payable in two installments, on May 1, and on November 1, 1921, respectively. There being an increase in the taxes over the stipulated sum, the landlord demanded that the tenant pay his share thereof. The

---

10. Also, see Gainsborough Real Estate Corp. v George Kemp Real Estate Co. (S Ct NY Co 1955) 207 Misc 156, 137 NYS2d 531.

*Contra*, R. A. Manning Realty Corp. v Topping Bros. (AT1 1923) 120 Misc 592, 199 NYS 241, affd 207 AD 852, 201 NYS 939. In this case the tenant had agreed to pay all the taxes imposed on the premises during the term as soon as they became due and payable. The lease commenced May 1, 1917, and ended April 30, 1922. The tenant paid the taxes for the year 1917, which had been imposed prior to the commencement of the term, but which fell due during the term. The tenant also paid the taxes for the years 1918 to 1921, inclusive. The court refused to follow Wall v Hess, although the tax covenants in the two cases cannot be distinguished. The court held that because of the practical construction placed on the lease by the parties, in the case of the 1917 taxes, the tenant would not be compelled to pay the tax for 1922, which had been imposed before the term expired, but which did not become due and payable until after the term expired. The court also indicated that it felt that a tenant for a five-year term could not have intended to pay taxes for six years. It is quite apparent that but for the practical construction placed on the clause by the parties themselves, the court would have been constrained to follow the doctrine enunciated in Wall v Hess; for the clause clearly calls for the application of the first rule. It is doubtful whether the court was justified in relying on the practical construction theory. See § 14:8, supra.

11. Credit Exchange, Inc. v 461 Eighth Ave. Associates (1987) 69 NY2d 994, 517 NYS2d 903, 511 NE2d 47 (citing text), reconsideration den 70 NY2d 748, 514 NE2d 392.

## TENANT'S OBLIGATIONS § 14:25

landlord contended that since the entire amount of the taxes for the year 1921 was imposed during the term, the tenant was liable notwithstanding that no part of the taxes became due and payable, or a lien, until the day after the lease expired, and that one-half thereof did not become due or payable, or a lien, until 6 months thereafter. The tenant however contended that in view of the provision requiring him to pay the taxes as rent, he should be held liable only for a proportionate part of the 1921 taxes; to wit, the four months of the tax year during which he occupied the premises. The court[12] held that the tax covenant plainly obligated the tenant to pay the specified percentage of the increase over the taxes of $36,200, for the entire year 1921, regardless of the fact that such a construction would render the tenant liable for taxes for a period longer than that of his occupancy of the premises. And, the court added, the provisions obligating the tenant to make this payment as rent, and providing that it shall be collectible as rent, and that a tax bill should be sufficient evidence for the calculation of the amount to be paid by the tenant, are insufficient to change the obligation. These are merely additional remedies provided for the benefit of the landlord to collect the taxes. This case followed the rule enunciated in Wall v Hess.[13]

### § 14:25. Covenant to Pay Taxes "Assessed During Term"

A lease contained the following covenant: the tenants "shall for and during the term of this agreement, and during the period of any subsequent renewal of this agreement, pay all the taxes which shall be assessed upon said demised premises by the state or municipal authority, and such taxes shall be paid" by said tenants "within 30 days after such taxes shall become due and payable," and should "the tenants make default in any such payment, the landlord shall pay the same, and the amount so paid shall be added to and paid with the next installment of rent in each case falling due, after such charges shall have become due and payable." Taxes for the year 1919

---

12. Apex Leasing Co. v White Enamel Refrigerator Co. (AD1 1922) 202 AD 354, 195 NYS 259.

13. (1922) 232 NY 472, 134 NE 536, 20 ALR 1497, discussed in § 427, supra.

were assessed by the city in March, 1919. Under the law then in force one-half of all taxes became due and payable on May 1, and the second half became due and payable on November 1. Taxes became liens on the property when they became due and payable, and not earlier. The tenant paid the first half of the tax bill, but refused to pay the second half becoming due on November 1, after his lease had expired. The court held[14] the tenant liable for the second half of the tax bill, due after the lease had expired. The language of the agreement, pointed out McAvoy, J., writing for the court, "indicates that the tenants are liable to pay all the taxes which are assessed upon the premises, and that the terms of the covenant reciting the time of such payment are not controlling upon liability. The context of the clause indicates that the terms, 'Such taxes shall be paid . . . after such taxes shall become due and payable,' are intended to prescribe the time when payment shall be made, but not to limit the liability to a time when such payment is required to be made to the city authorities. The words, 'Said parties of the second part shall for and during the term of this agreement, and during the period of any subsequent renewals, . . . pay all the taxes, which shall be assessed upon said demised premises,' indicate the nature of the obligation."

In other words, the court found that under the terms of the lease, and the intention of the parties to be gathered therefrom, the parties intended that the imposition of the tax during the term fixed liability, and not the date when the tax became payable.[15]

### § 14:26. Covenant to Pay Taxes as of Date of Imposition of Tax; Rule Summarized

Thus, the rulings of the courts in the cases discussed in

14. Walker v Stein (AD1 1927) 222 AD 22, 225 NYS 209.

15. Also, see, to the same effect, Big Four Realty Corp. v Belnord Garage (AT1 1931) 141 Misc 472, 252 NYS 742, affd 235 AD 672, 255 NYS 906; Ogden v Getty (AD1 1905) 100 AD 430, 91 NYS 664.

In Gokey v Gokey (AD4 1930) 230 AD 563, 234 NYS 518, it was held that under a lease which expired November 12, 1925, in which the tenant agreed to pay all taxes which were "levied or assessed upon said property, or any part thereof, during the said term," he was not liable for taxes for the year 1925 where the assessment roll was not adopted by the city council until December 4, 1925, although it had been completed on or about May 29, 1925, but had been left open for review and correction, and was not finally filed until November 18, 1925.

the preceding sections[16] demonstrate that if the tenant has agreed, or has evidenced an intention, to pay any and all taxes that are levied or imposed during the term, the obligation of the tenant to pay such taxes thereupon becomes a fixed and definite debt, collectible even after the term has expired. The taxes become a debt owing to the landlord from the date they are levied or imposed by the taxing authorities. True, the debt may not be due at the time they are levied or imposed. But, the fact remains that the tenant has a fixed obligation to pay an already existing debt as and when it does become due and payable. This fixed obligation to pay an already existing debt as and when it becomes due cannot be changed by the mere fact that the landlord may grant an extension of time to pay it; as, for example, thirty days after the taxing authorities require the taxes to be paid. Nor, is this fixed obligation changed by the fact that the parties provide an additional method for enforcing payment of the debt; as, for example, adding the amount of the taxes to the rent.

## § 14:27. Form of Covenant to Pay Taxes as of Date of Imposition of Tax

The following tax covenant provides for the payment by a tenant of all taxes levied or imposed during the term, even though they may become due and payable after the expiration of the term.

### FORM NO. 28

### Covenant to Pay Taxes as Determined by the Date of Imposition, and Not by the Date They Are Payable to the Authorities*

Tenant shall promptly pay and discharge when and as same shall become due and payable all taxes and special assessments which may during the term hereby granted be imposed or levied upon the building and land, of which the leased premises form a part. If Tenant shall fail to pay any such tax or special assessment or any part thereof as the same shall become due and payable, the amount thereof with all interest and penalties which may

---

16. See §§ 14:23, 14:25, supra.

* For complete form of lease see Chapter 1.

§ 14:27 LANDLORD AND TENANT

be accrued and become due and payable thereon may, at landlord's option if the term of this lease shall not have terminated or expired, be added to the next succeeding monthly installment of rent payable hereunder, and shall be deemed to be and shall constitute rent hereunder, and shall be collectible in the same manner and with the same remedies as if such amounts had been originally reserved herein.

### § 14:28. Covenant to Pay Taxes as of Due Date of Tax

The second general rule is:[17] if the intent of the parties is, as indicated by the terms of the lease and the tax covenant, that the landlord is to get a net rental for the exact term leased freed from taxes; then, the tenant will only be obligated to pay those taxes that become due and payable during the term. In other words, the fact that the tax is payable while the term subsists fixes the liability; whereas, under the first rule the levy or imposition of the tax while the term subsists fixes the liability.

The cases in which this second general rule has been applied will be discussed in the following section, and will help to clarify it.

### § 14:29. Covenant to "Keep Premises Free, Clear, Discharged and Unincumbered from All Taxes"

A tenant agreed "to pay and discharge all annual taxes as shall during said term be imposed on said premises hereby leased, as soon as they become due and payable, . . . and to keep said demised premises free, clear, discharged and unincumbered from all such taxes . . . during the said term, . . . ." The lease expired at noon, May 1, 1914. Under the tax statute then in force the taxes for 1914 were assessed in March, 1914, and were payable in two halves: one half on May 1, and the remaining half on November 1. The landlord contended that the tenant should pay the entire tax for the year 1914. The tenant refused to pay any part of the tax, contending that his term had ended; and, that since he had had a five year term, there was no reason why he should have to pay taxes for six years. It will be observed that one half of the

---

17. See §§ 14:22-14:26, supra, for a discussion of the first rule.

TENANT'S OBLIGATIONS § 14:29

tax became a lien on the demised premises on May 1, a few hours before the lease expired. The court held[18] that the tenant was liable, not for all the taxes for the year 1914 which had been levied against the premises during the term of the lease, but only for the one-half thereof which became due and payable and a lien on the demised premises on May 1, 1914, a few hours before the expiration of the term of the lease. Said Chase, J., writing the opinion for the court in this case, "Reading the covenant as a whole, the promise of the tenant includes the general taxes imposed and becoming due and payable within the term. The demised premises became incumbered with one-half of the tax of 1914 on May 1, 1914. The lessee could not leave the leased premises free, clear, discharged and unincumbered from taxes during said term if the taxes so actually due and payable on the date of the expiration of the lease were left unpaid. . . . If the lessee desired to restrict its obligation to the payment of taxes for the five fiscal years ending January 1, 1914, it should have so stipulated in the lease. Its term extended into the sixth fiscal year, as we have seen, and the lease as written required the lessee to pay annual taxes becoming due and payable in that term."

In other words, the expression of the intention of the parties that the first half of the year's taxes, falling due before the lease expired, should be paid was found entirely in the words, "keep said demised premises free, clear, discharged, and unincumbered from all such taxes during said term." In commenting on this case Pound, J., speaking for the Court of Appeals, said,[19] "The gist of the decision plainly is the clause as to incumbrances, which is treated as evidencing the intention of the parties to the lease, and not as making a general rule. The landlord was to receive his rent during the term and was to be subject to no expense on account of the demised premises for taxes which became due and payable and liens during said term. The landlord covenanted to receive the premises unincumbered and the duty of the tenant was discharged when it so delivered them."

---

**18.** Ward v Union Trust Co. (1918) 224 NY 73, 120 NE 81, 3 ALR 1154.
**19.** Wall v Hess (1922) 232 NY 472, 134 NE 536, 20 ALR 1497, discussed in § 14:23 supra.

### § 14:30. Covenant to Pay Taxes "So That Landlord Shall Receive a Net Rental"

A tenant agreed to pay in addition to the rent all taxes levied against the property so that the "said rental above referred to shall yield a net rental to the" landlord. The lease expired May 1, 1912. The landlord demanded that the tenant pay one third of the taxes for the year 1912, since the tenant had occupied the premises for one third of that year. The tenant refused to pay any portion of the taxes imposed for that year. The first half of the taxes for that year became a lien, and were payable on May 1. The court[20] sustained the tenant in his refusal to pay any portion of the 1912 taxes, and said, "By the lease the defendant did not undertake to pay the taxes which should be assessed against the property during the term demised, nor did he agree to pay any particular tax which should become a lien during the term or any other time; what the defendant agreed to do was to pay, in addition to the rent reserved, 'all taxes, assessments and Croton water rates as may be assessed against said property so that the said rental above referred to shall yield a net rental to Charles F. Ayer.' (landlord) . . . What it seems to the parties clearly intended was that the tenant would pay any tax, assessment, or Croton water rates that became a lien upon the property, and which the landlord would be required to pay, which would reduce the rental that he would receive below the rent reserved by the lease, and it was not important when a tax was assessed or when it became payable. . . . Where, as in this case, the obligation of the tenant depends entirely upon a covenant that he would pay, not a particular tax or lien, but all taxes that may be assessed against the property, so that a certain net rental should be received by the landlord, and where he has paid all taxes or charges assessed against the property which insures the landlord the rental reserved without any deduction or obligation, the tenant has complied with this covenant, and an additional liability cannot be imposed."

Here, again, the court decided as it did only because it

---

[20]. Ayer v Bonwit (AD1 1914) 161 AD 122, 146 NYS 301.

found that the parties had intended to give the landlord a net rental for the term leased freed from taxes.

### § 14:31. Covenant to "Pay Carrying and Maintenance Charges"

A tenant agreed to "pay all carrying and maintenance charges on said premises, including taxes, assessments, water rents, insurance, upkeep, heating, lighting, etc." The lease expired in 1929, and in 1927, $4561 was assessed by the municipality for widening the streets. This assessment, however, was by special agreement with the municipality made payable in ten annual installments. The tenant paid the three annual installments falling due during her term, but refused to pay the remaining seven payable after the expiration of the lease. The court sustained the tenant's contention.[1] Taylor, J., writing the opinion for the court, said, "The question here, narrows down to the precise obligation assumed by the tenant under the lease; in other words, to the meaning of the word 'assessments' as used and understood by the parties. If the lease had provided that the tenant should deliver back the premises at the end of the term free and clear of incumbrances, there would be no doubt that the tenant would be liable to pay this assessment. Or, if the lease had stipulated that the tenant was to pay all taxes and assessments without qualification, judgment would go for the landlord. . . . But this tenant did not agree to pay all taxes and assessments. She agreed to pay all carrying and maintenance charges. The word 'including' in the lease immediately after the words 'carrying and maintenance charges,' was evidently intended to specify some of the 'charges' contemplated and to limit the liability of the tenant to such assessments as were in the nature of the carrying and maintenance charges." Thus, the second rule was applied here because the tenant had agreed to give the landlord a net rental, freed from taxes, for the exact term demised.[2]

---

1. Baker v Schleyer (AD4 1931) 233 AD 584, 253 NYS 351, affd 260 NY 673, 184 NE 140.

2. Clause in contract for purchase of real property requiring purchaser, as consideration for possession under lease until closing of title, to pay all expenses of property, obligates purchaser to pay taxes, water, and sewer charges. Pinmor Realty Corp. v Buris Hotel Corp. (1981, 2d Dept) 83 AD2d 847, 441 NYS2d 751.

## § 14:32. Covenant to Pay Taxes "Charged During Term"

In a recent case decided by the Court of Appeals,[3] a tenant covenanted to "discharge in each and every year all such taxes, water rates, and assessments as may be imposed or charged upon the demised premises herein described, and if the same shall not be so paid and discharged within three months after the same shall have been imposed, then to yield, render and pay unto the said party of the first part, his legal representatives or assigns, within one month after such default, as and for additional rent whatever sums may be necessary to pay and discharge the said taxes, water rates, and assessments for such year, or either of the same remaining unpaid, with all penalties and interest accrued thereon." At the time the lease was executed taxes were due and payable on the first Monday of October in each year. That statute also provided that all taxes should be and become liens on the real estate affected on the day when they become due and payable, and should remain liens thereon until paid. During the term of the lease, however, the law was changed. The new statute provided that one half of the taxes shall be paid on May 1, and the second half on November 1. The new statute also provided "All taxes shall be and become liens on the real estate affected thereby and shall be construed as and deemed to be charges thereon on the respective days when they become due and payable as hereinbefore provided and not earlier, and shall remain such liens until paid."

Thus, it will be noted, the lease uses the words "imposed or charged." The statute in force at the time the lease was executed used neither word. O'Brien, J., pointed out, that in Wall v Hess[4] where a tenant had covenanted to pay taxes which shall be "assessed, levied or imposed" during the term, on the date prescribed for the delivery of assessment rolls to the tax collector the taxes were held to be finally and unalterably fixed and imposed on the premises, although not then payable. So, if we take "charged" to mean "imposed," we would be obliged to decide here that on March 27, (when, under the new

---

3. Moller v People's Nat. Bank (1932) 258 NY 373, 180 NE 87.

4. (1922) 232 NY 472, 134 NE 536, 20 ALR 1497.

statute, the assessment rolls were to be delivered to the tax collector) the taxes were imposed, and the tenant must pay them although they were not to become payable, and no lien was to attach to the realty until the following May 1. If, however "imposed" is explained and defined by the word "charged" then the tenant is not liable until the taxes become liens or charges.

The court finally concluded that the purpose of this clause must fairly be read as intending to protect the landlord from the imposition only of such liens, charges, penalties, and interest on unpaid taxes as might become payable during the term. The word "imposed" must have been intended to mean the same as "charged" and to signify an assessment which has ripened into a due payment. Otherwise the parties would not have provided for a three months' grace period which would start running from a date prior to the date the tax was payable. "Yet," said the court, "that would be the result of holding that it ran from the date when the tax was imposed if 'imposed' is interpreted as meaning something different from 'charged.'" Therefore, it was held that the tenant whose lease expired April 30, was not liable to pay taxes assessed in the preceding March, but due and payable on May 1.

### § 14:33. Covenant to Pay Taxes as of Due Date of Tax; Rule Summarized

Thus, the rulings of the courts in the cases discussed in the preceding sections[5] demonstrate that if the tenant has agreed, or has evidenced an intention, to pay to the landlord a net rental for the exact term demised, freed from taxes which may become payable during the term, then the tenant will only be obligated to pay such taxes as fall due during the term. Such an intent will be found by the use of such phrases as: "keep the premises free, clear, discharged and unincumbered from all taxes"; "pay all taxes assessed against the property so that said rental shall yield a net rental"; or "pay all carrying and maintenance charges." Once such intent has been found, then, it is immaterial when the taxes are imposed or levied; if they fall due during the term, the tenant must pay them.

---

5. §§ 14:28-14:32, supra.

§ 14:33     LANDLORD AND TENANT

If they fall due after the term expires, the tenant will be under no obligation to pay them.

### § 14:34. Liability of Assignee on Covenant to Pay Taxes

It has been shown earlier in this volume[6] that the privity of estate resulting from an assignee's acceptance of a lease imposes on an assignee the obligation to perform all those covenants in the lease on the part of the tenant which run with the land. It is well established that a covenant to pay taxes runs with the land.[7] Therefore, an assignee of the tenant, upon acceptance of the assignment, becomes obligated to pay the taxes under the tax covenant.[8] However such liability exists only during the period the privity of estate exists between the assignee and the landlord.[9] Of course, if the assignee upon accepting the assignment assumed performance of the lease, then his liability on the tax covenant exists as long as the privity of contract with the landlord continues.[10]

### § 14:35. Right of Grantee to Enforce Covenant to Pay Taxes

A covenant to pay taxes runs with the land.[11] Therefore it inures to the benefit of the grantee of the fee the moment such grantee succeeds to the title.[12]

### § 14:36. Remedies of Landlord for Breach of Covenant

A covenant requiring the lessee to pay taxes and special assessments during the term is breached when he neglects to pay a tax or special assessment duly imposed.[13] Upon a breach of the lessee's covenant to pay taxes and special assessments imposed upon the leased premises during the term, the lessor is entitled, as damages, to recover the amount of such tax or special assess-

---

6. See § 9:25, supra.
7. Stone v Auerbach (AD1 1909) 133 AD 75, 117 NYS 734; Lehmaier v Jones (AD1 1905) 100 AD 495, 91 NYS 687.
8. Dunlop v James (1903) 174 NY 411, 414, 67 NE 60.
9. McKeon v Wendelken (AT 1899) 25 Misc 711, 55 NYS 626.

Also, see §§ 9:25, et seq, supra.
10. See § 9:36, supra.
11. § 14:34, supra.
12. Lehmaier v Jones (AD1 1905) 100 AD 495, 91 NYS 687.
13. Rector, etc, of Trinity Church in New York v Higgins (1872) 48 NY 532.

ment.[14] Moreover, the landlord may maintain an action against the tenant to recover the taxes or special assessments which the tenant failed to pay in breach of his covenant to do so, without first paying them himself,[15] even though the lease provides that he may pay such taxes upon the lessee's default, and add them to subsequent rent.[16] As the Court of Appeals said in an early case,[17] "The covenant of the defendant is affirmative and positive, not collateral or secondary, in its terms. He covenants to 'bear, pay and discharge all taxes and assessments,' etc., as an obligation or debt of his own, and the language conveys no idea that the plaintiffs are first to bear and pay, before the demand becomes obligatory upon the defendant for payment. The covenant is broken when the defendant neglects to pay taxes or assessments duly imposed. The defendant is not at liberty to say that it is the debt of the plaintiffs; let them first pay it, and I will pay them. It is his own debt, made so by the terms of his covenant."

In other words a distinction is to be made between a covenant whereby a tenant makes the amount to be paid his own debt, and a covenant of indemnity, whereby the covenant is not broken until the amount has been paid. If the covenant to pay the taxes is affirmative and positive, then the landlord may recover the amount of taxes when the tenant neglects or refuses to pay them; and, the landlord need not show, in order to sustain his right of recovery, that he, the landlord, paid the taxes.[18]

In the absence of any covenant in a lease to the contrary, where an apportionment is necessary to deter-

---

14. Rector, etc, of Trinity Church in New York v Higgins (1872) 48 NY 532; Surprise Bldg. Co. v Rosenblatt (AD1 1934) 240 AD 424, 279 NYS 109.

15. Rector, etc, of Trinity Church in New York v Higgins (1872) 48 NY 532; Erwin v Farrington (S Ct Steuben Co 1954) 132 NYS2d 20, revd on other grounds 285 AD 1212, 140 NYS2d 379.

16. Under a covenant requiring the tenant to pay all taxes levied on the demised premises, and further providing that if the tenant did not pay them, the landlord might pay them and add the amount thereof with interest to the next month's rent, upon a breach of this covenant the landlord is not limited to paying the taxes and adding them to the next month's rent, but may sue for the breach of the covenant. Jamaica Sav Bank v Carsons Jamaica, Inc (S Ct Queens Co 1959) 18 Misc 2d 877, 190 NYS2d 866.

17. Rector, etc, of Trinity Church in New York v. Higgins (1872) 48 NY 532, 535.

18. Erwin v Farrington (S Ct Steuben Co 1954) 132 NYS2d 20, revd on other grounds 285 AD 1212, 140 NYS2d 379.

mine the extent of a tenant's obligation under a tax covenant, the primary obligation of apportionment rests upon the landlord.[19] A lease covered part of a tract upon which taxes were assessed as a whole. The lease provided that the tenant shall pay all taxes assessed against the "demised premises." It was held,[20] that since the lease obligates the tenant to pay an apportioned amount of the whole tax without specifying upon whom the duty rests to have the tax allocated to the "demised premises," such primary obligation of apportionment devolves upon the landlord. An additional liability, said the court in this case, will not be imposed upon a tenant unless it is clearly within the provisions of the lease. And, until the taxes have been apportioned, there will be no liability on the part of the tenant to pay any taxes.

A landlord may also bring a summary proceeding to remove the tenant for failure to pay taxes and special assessments covenanted to be paid by the tenant.[1] However, under the statute authorizing a summary proceeding for nonpayment of taxes, the landlord is required to wait 60 days after the tenant's default before commencing the proceeding.[2] To avoid this waiting period, landlords frequently provide that if the tenant fails to pay taxes, then upon such default the amount of unpaid taxes shall be added to the rent, and shall be deemed and constitute rent, and shall be collectible as such. In this way the landlord may then institute a summary proceeding for nonpayment of rent, immediately upon a default in the payment of taxes.

As has been discussed hereinabove, if a tenant affirmatively and positively agrees to pay taxes, then the landlord is not required to first pay the taxes to sue the tenant for failure so to do.

However, if the tax covenant provides that the landlord must first pay the taxes before they can be added to the rent, and be deemed rent, then the landlord must comply with such a covenant before he can bring a summary

---

**19.** Wisser Oil Co. v Ganfrank Holding Corp. (S Ct Nassau Co 1937) 163 Misc 357, 296 NYS 806.

**20.** Wisser Oil Co. v Ganfrank Holding Corp. (S Ct Nassau Co 1937) 163 Misc 357, 296 NYS 806.

**1.** Real Prop Act & Proc L § 711, subd 3, discussed in Chapter 33, infra.

**2.** Real Prop Act & Proc L § 711, subd 3. See Chapter 33, infra.

## TENANT'S OBLIGATIONS § 14:36

proceeding as for nonpayment of rent upon the tenant's failure to pay taxes.[3]

A tax covenant provided that if the tenant failed to pay the taxes when payable, and if such default continued for twenty days after notice and demand by the landlord, the landlord at his option could pay such unpaid taxes whereupon the tenant would reimburse him on demand, with interest. However, on failure to make such reimbursement, "the sum or sums so paid by the Lessor together with interest as aforesaid and all costs and charges shall be and hereby are declared to be rent payable on the first day of the next succeeding month." "Unless the landlord brings himself within the provisions of his lease," said Watson, J.,[4] "he cannot base this proceeding (summary proceeding for nonpayment of rent) upon the nonpayment of the taxes by the tenant. The lease provided that after taxes became due, the landlord should serve a notice upon the tenant demanding the payment of the same from him. Only in the event of the tenant's default in payment for twenty days after such notice, then, and in such instance, upon the payment by the landlord of such taxes, the sum or sums so paid by the landlord were to constitute rent payable under the lease. The landlord has not paid the taxes, the twenty days' notice and demand was not given, and hence the amount of the unpaid taxes cannot be considered as rent for the purpose of this proceeding."

In other words in drafting the tax covenant so as to give the landlord the right to treat unpaid taxes as rent, the landlord must be careful in drafting such a covenant. If the language provides that to constitute unpaid taxes as rent they must first be paid by the landlord, then the landlord will have to first pay the taxes before he can base a summary proceeding as for nonpayment of rent upon the tenant's default in paying taxes.

In another case[5] the tax covenant provided that the

---

3. Addoms' Estate v Citarella (M Ct 1932) 143 Misc 428, 256 NYS 669.
4. Addoms' Estate v Citarella (M Ct 1932) 143 Misc 428, 256 NYS 669.
5. Haskel v 60 West Fifty-Third Street Corp. (M Ct 1929) 138 Misc 595, 246 NYS 698, affd no op 231 AD 800, 246 NYS 875.

§ 14:36 LANDLORD AND TENANT

landlord might pay unpaid taxes which the tenant should have paid, and that the amount so paid should become due from the tenant as additional rent. The tenant, therefore, contended that the landlord could not maintain summary proceedings as for nonpayment of rent until after the landlord had paid the taxes. However, another provision of the lease required that, in the event of the tenant's default in payment of installments of rent or additional or augmented rent, or "any other payments herein provided for to be made by the tenant, . . . the landlord shall be entitled to remove the tenant from the premises by summary proceedings or in any other lawful manner, . . . anything to the contrary thereof herein contained notwithstanding." Under this provision, Genung, J., said in this case, "the landlord had the option either to pay the taxes and water charges and later demand payment thereof as additional or augmented rent, or make demand on the tenant for the payment thereof, and, if he refused, to institute summary proceedings. The landlord has made such demand for payment by the tenant, and the tenant has failed or refused to pay the taxes and water charges."

However, this case but emphasizes the necessity for using care in drafting a tax covenant. If the tenant wishes to make the landlord first pay unpaid taxes before being able to proceed against him, such a provision should be inserted. Absent such a provision it is clear that the landlord may proceed against the tenant upon default in paying taxes without first paying them himself.

### § 14:37. Remedy of Tenant for Taxes Paid by him

The statute provides,[6] "If a tax upon real property has been collected from any occupant, and any other person by agreement or otherwise is liable to pay such tax or any part thereof, such occupant shall be entitled to recover the amount which such person should have paid or to retain the same from any rent due or accruing from him to such person for the land on which the tax was paid."

---

6. Real Prop Tax L § 988.

## C. COVENANT TO PAY FOR WATER AND SEWER RENTS

### § 14:38. Remedies of Landlord for Breach of Covenant

A distinction is made between a water tax and a water rent.[7] If the charge for water be a tax, then there is no liability on the part of the tenant to pay it unless he has expressly covenanted to pay water taxes.[8] If, however, the charge for water is a water rent, then, the tenant is under an obligation to pay the water rent whether or not he has covenanted to do so. If he fails to pay it, then the landlord may pay and recover the amount thereof from the tenant. The landlord, upon such payment, will be subrogated to the city's rights against the defaulting tenant.[9] As the Court of Appeals said,[10] "In this class of cases there is merely a voluntary purchase by the consumer from the city of such quantity of water as he chooses to buy . . . and the obligation to pay therefor must primarily rest upon him who buys and consumes the article. As the sale by the city is necessarily on credit, as security for the payment of the debt a lien is imposed on the property itself for any unpaid charge. The plaintiff's property being thus pledged for the security of the defendant's debt, the plaintiff occupied the position of a surety, and on payment of the city's claim was subrogated to its rights against the defendant."

Therefore, if a tenant fails to pay water rents for the water he has consumed, whether or not he has agreed with the landlord to pay it, the landlord may pay such water rents, and recover the amount thereof from the tenant.

When a tenant agrees to pay a pro rata share of all the water rents which may be assessed during the term upon a building in which a tenant rents space, the tenant's share, then, will be computed by the means at hand. That is, the share of the tenant's space will be proportionate to those of all the other occupants' premises. As the court said in so holding,[11] "But the language of the covenant indicates that the share of their loft was to be proportion-

---

7. See § 14:5, supra.
8. See § 14:6, supra.
9. New York University v American Book Co. (1910) 197 NY 294, 90 NE 819.
10. New York University v American Book Co. (1910) 197 NY 294, 297, 90 NE 819.
11. Goerlitz v Schwartz (AT 1908) 112 NYS 1119.

ate to those of all the lofts. They undertook their share, and it needs be computed by the means at hand, unless they put in, as they might under the regulations of the water department, a meter for themselves and procured a change of the lease." After all, the court pointed out, when the tenant signed the lease he knew the only means of arriving at the indebtedness, and accepted it. He, therefore, should have no cause for complaint. If he desired to pay only for what he consumed he should have had a water meter installed. However, the landlord may not assess a tenant with a proportionate part of the gross water charge for a building, measured either by the amount of space occupied by a tenant or by the number of tenants in the building, under a covenant by the tenant to pay such charge for the use of water as may be "imposed according to law upon the demised premises," where there is only a single meter in the building, and separate meters are authorized by law. In so holding, the court said,[12] "In the case at bar the clause in the lease contains an express covenant. It is plain and certain in its provisions, and contains neither patent nor latent ambiguity, and no extrinsic testimony is necessary to determine its meaning. It obligates the defendants to pay only such charges for the use of water as might be "imposed according to law" upon the demised premises. It is evident that there could be no liability on the part of the defendants, under that covenant in the lease, until such water rent was lawfully assessed upon that portion of the premises occupied by them under the lease. This could have been ascertained by the plaintiff by the placing of a water meter, so that the actual amount of water used by the defendants could have been determined, and they be lawfully charged therewith . . . . In that way the defendants could have been lawfully charged with the amount of water used by them, and their liability fixed under their covenant in the lease. Under the facts and circumstances of this case it would be unjust and inequitable to allow the plaintiff to recover one-third of the total water rent charged against the whole premises . . . ."

12. Bristol v Hammacher (AT 1900) 30 Misc 426, 62 NYS 517.

# TENANT'S OBLIGATIONS § 14:40

If the charge for water be a water rent, and not a water tax[13] then summary proceedings will not lie to evict the tenant for nonpayment thereof.[14]

Of course, if a lease provides that if water rents are not paid by the tenant when due and payable they shall be added to the rent reserved, and shall be deemed to be and shall constitute rent, then a summary proceeding as for nonpayment of rent may be instituted upon the tenant's default in so paying them.

### § 14:39. Obligation to Install Water Meter

Unless a tenant expressly covenants to install a water meter, he is under no obligation so to do. As was said by the court, in so holding,[15] "Had the parties contemplated the payment by the tenant for a new water meter . . . it should have been specifically mentioned in the lease, and such an addition to the premises cannot be properly termed repairs nor deemed to be included within a clause in the lease requiring the tenant to put in good order and keep in repair the demised premises."

### § 14:40. Tenant's Obligation to Pay Sewer Rents

A covenant by a tenant to pay water charges will not include sewer rents payable by a landlord under any local law. Such a sewer rent is payable by the landlord because it is a charge levied on owners of property for the use of the sewer system owned, operated, and maintained by the city, and therefore cannot be deemed a water rent or charge within the intendment of a covenant to pay water charges.[16]

---

13. See § 14:5, supra.
14. Kleinstein v Gonsky (AD2 1909) 134 AD 266, 118 NYS 949.
15. Epstein v Saviano (AT 1906) 51 Misc 28, 99 NYS 910.
16. Rubber Corp. of America v Chalfin (AD2 1954) 284 AD 991, 135 NYS2d 483, app den 285 AD 814, 137 NYS2d 837; Valenti v Tepper Fields Corp. (AD1 1953) 282 AD 212, 122 NYS2d 599; Black v General Wiper Supply Co. (M Ct 1951) 200 Misc 516, 109 NYS2d 810, affd 200 Misc 834, 111 NYS2d 259, revd on other grounds 280 AD 807, 113 NYS2d 493, affd 305 NY 386, 113 NE2d 528.

§ 14:41. Form of Covenant to Pay for Water and Sewer Rents

## FORM NO. 29

### Covenant to Pay for Water and Sewer Rents with Provisions for Apportionment of for Installation of Meter*

If Tenant requires, uses or consumes water for any purpose in addition to ordinary lavatory purposes (of which fact Tenant constitutes Landlord to be the sole judge) Landlord may install a water meter and thereby measure Tenant's water consumption for all purposes. Tenant shall pay Landlord for the cost of the meter and the cost of the installation thereof and throughout the duration of Tenant's occupancy Tenant shall keep said meter and installation equipment in good working order and repair at Tenant's own cost and expense in default of which Landlord may cause such meter and equipment to be replaced or repaired and collect the cost thereof from Tenant. Tenant agrees to pay for water consumed, as shown on said meter as and when bills are rendered, and on default in making such payment Landlord may pay such charges and collect the same from Tenant as additional rent. Tenant covenants and agrees to pay as additional rent the sewer rent, charge or any other tax, rent, levy or charge which now or hereafter is assessed, imposed or a lien upon the leased premises or the realty of which they are part pursuant to law, order or regulation made or issued in connection with the use, consumption, maintenance or supply of water, water system or sewage or sewage connection or system. The bill rendered by Landlord for the above shall be based upon Tenant's consumption and shall be payable by Tenant as additional rent within five (5) days of rendition.

If the building or the leased premises or any part thereof be supplied with water through a meter through

---

* This is Paragraph 29 of the Standard Form of Loft Lease copyright by the Real Estate Board of New York, Inc., and reprinted by its permission. Reproduction in whole or in parts prohibited and all rights reserved by the Real Estate Board of New York, Inc. For complete form of lease see Chapter 1.

# TENANT'S OBLIGATIONS § 14:42

which water is also supplied to other premises, Tenant shall pay to Landlord as additional rent, on the first day of each month, . . .% of the total meter charges, as Tenant's portion. Any such costs or expenses incurred or payments made by Landlord for any of the reasons or purposes hereinabove stated shall be deemed to be, and shall constitute, additional rent hereunder, and shall be collectible as rent in the same manner and with the same remedies as if it had been rent originally reserved herein, and shall be due and payable by Tenant to Landlord on the first day of the month following the rendition of such bill either of the public authorities or of Landlord. Independently of and in addition to any of the remedies hereinabove reserved to Landlord, or elsewhere in this lease, Landlord may sue for and collect any monies to be paid by Tenant or paid by Landlord for any of the reasons or purposes hereinabove set forth.

## D. RESEARCH REFERENCES

### § 14:42. Generally

In addition to the preceding text, the reader is also referred to the following:

49 Am Jur 2d, Landlord and Tenant §§ 354-366.

11 Am Jur Legal Forms 2d, Leases of Real Property §§ 161:521-161:558.

16 Am Jur Pleading and Practice Forms (Rev Ed), Landlord and Tenant, Form 303.

New York Jur 2d, Landlord and Tenant (1st ed §§ 185-195).

New York Forms, Leases, Forms 8:201-8:205.

RIA Federal Tax Coordinator 2d, ¶ K-4303.

Index to Annotations, Landlord and Tenant.

**VERALEX®:** Cases and annotations referred to herein can be further researched through the VERALEX electronic retrieval system's two services, **Auto-Cite®** and **SHOWME®**. Use Auto-Cite to check citations for form, parallel references, prior and later history, and annotation references. Use SHOWME to display the full text of cases and annotations.

# CHAPTER 15

# TENANT'S RIGHTS IN THE USE OF THE LEASED PREMISES

A. IN GENERAL
- § 15:1. General Rule
- § 15:2. Where Lease is of Portion of Building
- § 15:3. Right of Tenant to Permit or Invite Persons upon Leased Premises
- § 15:4. Sharing of Apartment
- § 15:5. Landlord's Right to Waive Tenant's Unlawful Use of Lease Premises

B. WASTE
- § 15:6. Tenant's Obligation Not to Commit Waste; Definitions
- § 15:7. Structural Alterations as Waste
- § 15:8. Structural Alterations Made in Good Faith
- § 15:9. Ability to Restore Premises as Justification for Structural Alterations
- § 15:10. Structural Alterations Beneficial to Landlord

C. WHEN TENANT MAY MAKE ALTERATIONS
- § 15:11. Generally
- § 15:12. Necessity for Written Consent to Make Structural Alterations
- § 15:13. Consent Granted by Lease "To Make Inside Alterations Provided Premises Not Injured"
- § 15:14. Form of Provision Consenting to Tenant-Alterations
- § 15:15. Tenant May Not Go Beyond Consent Granted to Make Alterations
- § 15:16. Consent to Alterations Required by Lease; as Affecting Structural Alterations
- § 15:17. —As Affecting Non-structural Alterations Necessary to Carry on Business
- § 15:18. Form of Provision Requiring Landlord's Consent to Alterations and Improvements
- § 15:19. When Landlord May Withhold Lease-required Consent to Alterations
- § 15:20. Right of Tenant in Multiple Dwellings to Install Locks
- § 15:21. Statutory Authorization to Make Alterations

## LANDLORD AND TENANT

§ 15:22. Forms for Obtaining Statutory Authorization to Make Alterations

D. REMEDIES FOR UNAUTHORIZED ALTERATIONS
§ 15:23. Right of Injunction to Restrain Unauthorized Alterations
§ 15:24. Injunction to Compel Restoration of Premises Altered without Authorization
§ 15:25. Right to Damages for Unauthorized Alterations

E. RIGHT TO DISPLAY SIGNS
§ 15:26. Where Entire Building Leased
§ 15:27. —Limitations
§ 15:28. Where Part of Building Leased
§ 15:29. —Limitations

F. MISCELLANEOUS RIGHTS
§ 15:30. Erect Television Aerials
§ 15:31. Cut Trees and Timber
§ 15:32. Tenant's Right to Form, Join, or Participate in Tenants' Groups
§ 15:33. Protection from Harassment of Landlord

G. EXPRESS RESTRICTIONS ON USE OF PREMISES BY TENANT
§ 15:34. General Rule
§ 15:35. Binding on Tenant's Assignee
§ 15:36. Binding on Subtenants
§ 15:37. Enforceable by Landlord's Grantee
§ 15:38. Rule of Construction
§ 15:39. Specification of Purpose as Description or Limitation of Use of Premises; Forms
§ 15:40. No Implied Covenant or Warranty that Premises Fit for Restricted Use
§ 15:41. Includability of Covenant of No Legal Impediments
§ 15:42. Display of Signs
§ 15:43. —Where Entire Building Leased
§ 15:44. Restriction by Rules and Regulations of Landlord
§ 15:45. —Form of Clause
§ 15:46. —Rules and Regulations Must be Reasonable
§ 15:47. Mobile Home Parks
§ 15:48. Form of Rules and Regulations
§ 15:49. Projections from Window of Lease Apartment
§ 15:50. Racial Discriminatory Restrictions Under Statute
§ 15:51. Statutory Restrictions Against Children in Dwellings

H. WAIVER OF EXPRESS RESTRICTION
§ 15:52. Generally
§ 15:53. Parol Waiver
§ 15:54. By Acceptance of Rent with Knowledge of Breach
§ 15:55. Waiver Binding on Grantee

# TENANT'S RIGHTS § 15:1

## I. INJUNCTION TO RESTRAIN IMPROPER USE OF PREMISES
§ 15:56. Against Tenant
§ 15:57. Against Tenant's Assignee
§ 15:58. Against Subtenant

## J. RESTRICTION ON LESSOR'S USE OF OTHER PREMISES
§ 15:59. Generally
§ 15:60. Restriction of "Same or Similar Business"; Form
§ 15:61. Restriction of Sale of Specified Articles
§ 15:62. Remedies at Law Against Lessor for Breach
§ 15:63. Paying Rent as Waiver of Breach
§ 15:64. Measure of Damages for Breach
§ 15:65. Equitable Relief Against Lessor
§ 15:66. Remedies at Law Against Competing Tenant
§ 15:67. Equitable Relief Against Competing Tenant

## K. RESEARCH REFERENCES
§ 15:68. Generally

---

## A. IN GENERAL

### § 15:1. General Rule

As a general rule, when premises are leased, the right to use them during the term is transferred from the landlord to the tenant,[1] and in the absence of a contrary provision in the lease, the tenant has the sole and exclusive right to the occupation and control of the leased premises during the term.[2] The right to exclusive occupation granted to a tenant by a lease entitles him to use the premises in the same manner that the owner might have used them, subject, however, to the qualification that he must not do anything that injures the inheritance or which constitutes waste.[3]

In the absence of any restriction contained in a lease, a tenant may occupy and use the leased premises in any lawful way not materially different from the way in which they are usually employed, to which they are

---

1. Bedlow v New York Floating Dry-Dock Co. (1889) 112 NY 263, 19 NE 800.
2. Baumann v New York (1919) 227 NY 25, 124 NE 141, 8 ALR 595.
3. People v Scott (1970) 26 NY2d 286, 309 NYS2d 919, 258 NE2d 206; Lyon v Bethlehem Engineering Corp. (1930) 253 NY 111, 113, 170 NE 512; Bovin v Galitzka (1929) 250 NY 228, 231, 165 NE 273; Presby v Benjamin (1902) 169 NY 377, 379, 62 NE 430; A & B Cabrini Realty Co. v Newman (1963, Civ Ct) 237 NYS2d 970; Sigsbee Holding Corp. v Canavan (Civ Ct 1963) 39 Misc 2d 465, 240 NYS2d 900, holding that a tenant is not guilty of waste in replacing with new ones, old, used cabinets which hung only on two nails; Syracuse Sav. Bank v D'Elia (M Ct Syracuse 1945) 185 Misc 928, 56 NYS2d 800.

See §§ 15:6, et seq, infra, as to discussion of what constitutes waste between landlord and tenant.

§ 15:1

adapted, and for which they were constructed.[4] Even in the absence of any covenant in the lease on the part of a lessee to comply with the laws, a lessor, said the court,[5] is "entitled to anticipate and assume as an implied provision in the letting and hiring that the lessee would not affront the statutes or violate ordinances having the force of statutes."[6] Moreover, the statute provides,[7] "Whenever the lessee or occupant other than the owner of any building or premises, shall use or occupy the same, or any part thereof, for any illegal trade, manufacture or other business, the lease or agreement for the letting or occupancy of such building or premises shall thereupon become void, and the landlord of such lessee or occupant may enter upon the premises so let or occupied."

It has been held that a violation of the Sabbath law by a tenant is not such a breach of a lease provision requiring the tenant to comply with statutes imposing any violation, order, or duty on landlord and tenant with respect to use or occupation of premises as to entitle a landlord to terminate the lease, since, as a result of such violation, the landlord suffered no exposure, penal or civil; his property rights were in no way affected or imperiled; and no financial burden was imposed on him.[8]

### § 15:2. Where Lease is of Portion of Building

Where property is leased to different tenants, and the landlord retains control of passageways, hallways, and other parts of the property for the use of the different tenants in common, it is well settled that each tenant has the right to make reasonable use of that portion of the property retained for the use of the different tenants in common.[9]

### § 15:3. Right of Tenant to Permit or Invite Persons upon Leased Premises

As a general rule, in the absence of any restrictions in

---

4. Bovin v Galitzka (1929) 250 NY 228, 165 NE 273; Presby v Benjamin (1902) 169 NY 377, 379, 62 NE 430.

5. Wineburgh Advertising Co. v Faust Co. (AT 1908) 113 NYS 709.

6. As to illegal use of leased premises, see §§ 2:12, et seq, supra.

7. Real Prop L § 231, subd 1.

8. Kearns v Barney's Clothes, Inc. (S Ct NY Co 1963) 38 Misc 2d 787, 239 NYS2d 318.

9. Brendlen v Beers (AD1 1911) 144 AD 403, 129 NYS 222.

As to right of landlord to regulate use of such parts of the property as are to be used in common, see § 15:44, infra.

the lease, a tenant has the right, even against his landlord's wishes, to have any invitee of his choice enter his leased premises. As has been said, in a recent case,[10] "Unless otherwise restricted by the leases between the owner and the tenants, third persons who are invited by a tenant in a matter incidental to the tenant's business have the right to make reasonable use of the tenant's usual means of ingress and egress. . . . Defendant's (landlord's) contention is in effect that the owner of a loft building may exclude persons who are invitees of its tenants or under agreements with them in matters relating to their business use of the premises, without proof that such invitees have conducted themselves improperly or unlawfully or imposed any unreasonable burden on the owner. This amounts to a claim that the owner has the unrestricted right to select the tenant's visitors and trades people. If that follows from the mere fact of ownership, then it would seem the owner of an apartment house would have the right to select the laundress, grocer, butcher, or milkman of his tenants and compel them to deal with such trades people of the owner's selection to the exclusion of those the tenant himself has invited. We think the mere statement of such claim, based on ownership alone, without proof of any special restrictions, regulations or agreements, carries its own refutation."[11]

This principle has also been applied to situations where a landlord owns a development, such as a colony of cottages, and seeks to prevent the tenants from obtaining their supplies by purchase from others than the landlord, or from those to whom the landlord has granted the exclusive privilege of dealing in such supplies. Absent a restriction in the tenant's lease to that effect, the landlord cannot bar the tenant's invitee, that is, his grocer, or butcher, or milkman, from coming on the land and from using the same means of ingress and egress as the tenant has the right to use, to make his deliveries. As Cullen, J.,

---

10. Federal Waste Paper Corp. v Garment Center Capitol, Inc. (AD1 1944) 268 AD 230, 51 NYS2d 26, affd 294 NY 714, 61 NE2d 451.

11. Also, see Brendlin v Beers (AD1 1911) 144 AD 403, 129 NYS 222; Todisco v Tishman Realty & Constr. Co. (S Ct Kings Co 1946) 62 NYS2d 458.

As to right of landlord to regulate the use of the premises by tenant and his invitees, see § 15:44, infra.

said,[12] "But to impose such a restriction on the tenant, some condition or covenant to that effect must be found in the lease. Otherwise the dominion of the tenant is as absolute during the demised term as that of the owner previous to the demise." In another case, in which these principles were applied, the owner of a building in its lease to a tenant for the conduct of a restaurant business, covenanted that such tenant should have the exclusive outgoing order business in the building insofar as it lay within the power and legal right of the owner to control. But, it was held, the landlord could not give such tenant or, for that matter, third persons the right to prohibit other tenants and their employees from purchasing in their own premises food, beverages, or other supplies from whomsoever they choose to invite to their leased space in the building for such purpose. Accordingly, a business visitor cannot be enjoined from entering a building when he does so at the request of a tenant, even though such request may constitute a breach of contractual arrangements which the landlord may have with someone else.[13]

## § 15:4. Sharing of Apartment

Real Property Law § 235-f, enacted in 1983,[14] entitled "Unlawful Restrictions on Occupancy" (known as the roommate law), provides that it shall be unlawful for a landlord to restrict occupancy of residential premises, by express lease terms or otherwise, to a tenant or tenants or to such tenants and immediate family. Any such restriction in a lease or rental agreement entered into or renewed "before or after" June 30, 1983, shall be unenforceable as against public policy.[15] Under this statute a "tenant" means a person occupying or entitled to occupy

---

12. Thousand Island Park Ass'n v Tucker (1903) 173 NY 203, 212, 65 NE 975.

13. Colbee 52nd Street Corp. v Madison 52nd Corp. (S Ct NY Co 1957) 8 Misc 2d 175, 169 NYS2d 175, 169 NYS2d 716 (tenant allowed coffee-wagon service to enter premises for its employees), affd 5 AD2d 97, 173 NYS2d 243.

14. L 1983, Ch 403, § 39, eff June 30, 1983.

15. Real Prop L § 235-f, subd 2.

Real Prop L § 235-f applies to cooperative apartments. Sherwood Village Cooperative A, Inc. v Slovik (NYC Civ Ct Queens Co 1986) 513 NYS2d 577.

Cases decided prior to June 30, 1983, which held that landlord could restrict occupancy to tenants only or to tenant's immediate family, are no longer valid precedents; for example, Hudson View Properties v Weiss (1983) 59 NY2d 733, 463 NYS2d 428, 450 NE2d 234.

## TENANT'S RIGHTS § 15:4

a residential rental premises who is either a party to the lease or rental agreement for such premises, or is a statutory tenant pursuant to the Emergency Housing Rent Control Law, or the City Rent and Rehabilitation Law, or Article 7-c of the Multiple Dwelling Law. "Occupant" means a person, other than a tenant or a member of a tenant's immediate family, occupying a premises with the consent of the tenant or tenants.[16] However, the statute does not define "immediate family," thus leaving this term to be defined by case law.[17]

Any lease or rental agreement for residential premises entered into by one tenant shall be construed to permit occupancy by (a) the tenant, (b) the immediate family of the tenant, (c) one additional occupant, and (d) dependent children of the occupant provided that the tenant or the tenant's spouse occupies the premises as his primary residence.[18] Thus, a lease entered into by one tenant permits such tenant to take in one occupant and the occupant's dependent children in addition to the tenant's immediate family. The situation is different where a residential lease is entered into by two or more tenants.[19]

Any lease or rental agreement for residential premises entered into by 2 or more tenants shall be construed to permit occupancy by (a) the tenants, (b) the immediate family of the tenants, (c) occupants, and (d) dependent children of occupants. However, there are 2 limitations imposed by the statute on apartment sharing when 2 or

---

**16.** Real Prop L § 235-f, subd 1(a) and (b).

**17.** Grandnephew does not constitute a member of tenant's immediate family. 301 East 69th Street Corp. v Vasser (NYC Civ Ct NY Co 1982) 118 Misc 2d 896, 461 NYS2d 932.

Siblings qualify as immediate family members. Avrum Realty Corp. v Talgon (AT1 1983) 120 Misc 2d 534, 467 NYS2d 489.

Section 2500.2(m) of the Tenant Protection Regulations, adopted and promulgated under the Emergency Tenant Protection Act of 1974, defines "immediate family" as "Husband, wife, son, daughter, grandson, granddaughter, stepson, stepdaughter, father, mother, father-in-law, mother-in-law, grandfather, grandmother, stepfather, or stepmother." Rent Stabilization Code § 2520.6(n) and (o) contains a similar definition. (For full text of these Regulations, see "New York Rent Control and Rent Stabilization," by Joseph Rasch, and published by The Lawyer's Co-operative Publishing Co., Rochester, New York 14694.)

**18.** Real Prop L § 235-f, subd 3.

**19.** Although the statute limits the number of additional occupants who may share the apartment, these limitations are not applicable to members of the tenant's immediately family; and, accordingly, tenant can permit his mother to reside in the apartment even if thereby the number of occupants who may share the apartment is exceeded. 38th Astoria Associates v Chavez (NYC Civ Ct Queens Co 1985) 126 Misc 2d 811, 484 NYS2d 467.

## § 15:4 LANDLORD AND TENANT

more tenants enter into the lease or rental agreement. First, the total number of tenants and occupants, not counting occupants' dependent children, may not exceed the number of tenants specified in the current lease or rental agreement. Second, at least one tenant or a tenant's spouse must occupy the premises as his primary residence.[20] In other words, when 2 or more individuals sign a residential lease, the lease can prohibit them from bringing in any additional occupants except for immediate family members and dependent children. However, if a lease-signer moves out, the remaining lease-signers may then bring in an occupant (or occupants, if 2 or more tenants remain) so long as the total number of tenants and occupants, not counting immediate family of tenants or dependent children of occupants, does not exceed the total number of tenants specified in the lease.

A tenant must inform the landlord of the name of any occupant within 30 days following the commencement of occupancy by such person, or within 30 days following a request by the landlord.[21]

No occupant nor occupant's dependent child shall, without express written permission of the landlord, acquire any right to continued occupancy in the event that the tenant vacates the premises or acquire any other rights of tenancy; provided that nothing in this section shall be construed to reduce or impair any right or remedy otherwise available to any person residing in any housing accommodation on the effective date of this section which accrued prior to such date.[22] Thus, this section of the Real Property Law permits a tenant the right to add an additional occupant to his household, but makes it clear that the additional occupant acquires no right to remain once the tenant vacates. When the tenant dies, the occupant does not acquire any rights to the continued occupancy of the leased premises and may be evicted as a licensee who no longer is entitled to possession.[23]

A provision in a residential lease permitting tenant and the members of his immediate family to occupy the

20. Real Prop L § 235-f, subd 4.
21. Real Prop L § 235-f(5).
22. Real Prop L § 235-f, subd 6.
23. Park South Associates v Daniels (NYC Civ Ct NY Co 1983) 121 Misc 2d 933, 469 NYS2d 319 (the live-in lover of deceased tenant of record not entitled to continued occupancy after death of tenant).

apartment contemplates concurrent occupancy by the tenant and his family members, so that tenant's son who did not reside in the apartment with his father at the time of the father's departure from the apartment was not entitled to move into the apartment.[24]

Any provision of a lease or rental agreement purporting to waive any provision of this section of the Real Property Law is null and void.[1]

However, nothing in this section of the Real Property Law shall be construed as invalidating or impairing the operation of, or the right of a landlord to restrict occupancy in order to comply with federal, state, or local laws, regulations, ordinances, or codes.[2]

Any person aggrieved by a violation of Real Prop L § 235-f may (1) obtain an injunction to enjoin and restrain such unlawful practice, (2) obtain actual damages sustained as a result of such unlawful practice; and (3) obtain court costs.[3]

### § 15:5. Landlord's Right to Waive Tenant's Unlawful Use of Leased Premises

A landlord cannot waive a use of the leased premises in violation of the law by the tenant. Therefore, a landlord, it has been held, cannot waive his right to evict the tenant for an occupancy in violation of the law.[4]

## B. WASTE

### § 15:6. Tenant's Obligation Not to Commit Waste; Definitions

A tenant, it has been seen,[5] must not do anything which constitutes waste. It is the duty of a tenant to exercise ordinary care in the use of the demised property,

---

24. Tagert v 211 East 70th Street Co. (1984) 63 NY2d 818, 482 NYS2d 246, 472 NE2d 22.

Also, see M & L Jacobs, Inc. v Del Grosso (NYC Civ Ct Queens Co 1985) 128 Misc 2d 725, 490 NYS2d 963, affd 133 Misc 2d 542, 509 NYS2d 237, where daughter of named rent-controlled tenant, who had resided in the apartment her entire life, continuously and without interruption prior to time tenant moved out, was held entitled to remain in possession.

1. Real Prop L § 235-f, subd 7.
2. Real Prop Law § 235-f, subd 8.
3. Real Prop L § 235-f, subd 9.
4. 47 East 74th Street Corp. v Simon (AT1 1947) 188 Misc 885, 69 NYS2d 746, rooming house in violation of Multiple Dwelling Law. Also, see, Mult Dwell L § 304.

A landlord cannot permit an unlawful condition to persist with impunity. People v Scott (1970) 26 NY2d 286, 309 NYS2d 919, 258 NE2d 206.

5. § 15:1, supra.

§ 15:6    LANDLORD AND TENANT

and not to cause any material and permanent injury thereto over and above ordinary wear and tear. For any injury resulting from his wrongful acts or his failure to exercise such care, a tenant is liable to the landlord in damages.[6]

"'Waste,' in its simplest definition," said Patterson, J.,[7] "is whatever does a lasting damage to the freehold or inheritance. It is either voluntary or permissive . . ."

"Permissive waste consists in the negligent or willful omission to do what is required to prevent an injury to demised premises,—as to suffer the demised premises or a part thereof to go to decay for the want of repairs."[8]

Since a tenant must not do anything which constitutes waste, a tenant will be held liable for his acts of permissive waste. But to constitute this particular kind of waste, there must have been neglect, omission, sufferance, or permission of the tenant. The most ordinary kind of permissive waste is suffering a building to fall into decay from neglect. But, since the very essence of liability of a tenant for permissive waste is negligence, all that is required from a tenant is that he be diligent to prevent delapidation of, or injury to, the demised premises.[9]

Voluntary waste, or, as it is sometimes called, commis-

---

**6.** Agate v Lowenbein (1874) 57 NY 604; Robinson v Wheeler (1862) 25 NY 252; Charles A. Luisi, Inc. v Richard Lumber Co. (City Ct Kings Co 1948) 80 NYS2d 536; 711 Corp. v Cavadi (1947, Sup App T) 71 NYS2d 887; Weadock v Jewett (1943, City Ct) 39 NYS2d 891; Spring-Mercer Corp. v Goodman (AT1 1926) 126 Misc 371, 213 NYS 500.

**7.** Beekman v Van Dolsen (S Ct GT1 1892) 63 Hun 487, 18 NYS 376.

**8.** Per Bischoff, J., in Regan v Luthy (Com Pl GT 1890) 11 NYS 709.

Also, see Rogers v Atlantic, G. & P. Co. (1915) 213 NY 246, 250, 107 NE 661.

**9.** Rogers v Atlantic, G. & P. Co. (1915) 213 NY 246, 250, 107 NE 661; Beekman v Van Dolsen (S Ct GT1 1892) 63 Hun 487, 18 NYS 376.

Also, see, Robinson v Wheeler (1862) 25 NY 252, 259, where court held that a tenant was liable as for waste, where the demised premises were damaged or destroyed by fire caused by the tenant's negligence; Haas v Brown (AT 1897) 21 Misc 434, 47 NYS 606, where court held that where a floor gives way through overloading, it is a question for the jury to determine whether such overloading is negligent, or arises out of a reasonable use of the premises, in which latter event tenant would not be liable for damage to the premises; Galante v Hathaway Bakeries, Inc. (S Ct Ontario Co 1957) 9 Misc 2d 19, 167 NYS2d 277, affd (4th Dept) 6 AD2d 142, 176 NYS2d 87, where the court held tenant liable for cost of repairs necessitated by fire caused by tenant's negligence; Second United Cities Realty Corp. v Price & Schumacher Co. (1926) 242 NY 120, 124, 151 NE 150, where Crane, J., said, "If it were a fact that the floor, reasonably safe, collapsed because of the tenant's negligence in overloading it, he would be bound to repay the cost of restoring it to its original condition."

sive waste, said Bischoff, J.,[10] "consists of injury to the demised premises or some part thereof, when occasioned by some deliberate or voluntary act, as, for instance, the pulling down of a house, or the removal of wainscots, floors, benches, furnaces, windows, doors, shelves, or other things fixed to and constituting a material part of the freehold."

In the popular sense, probably any injury may be waste. But it is not waste in the legal sense, unless caused in such manner as to be within the legal definition of either voluntary or permissive waste.[11]

The issue in any waste claim is, whether or not the tenant at the time of the wrongful act was done, caused an injury which then affected the landlord as to his reversion.[12]

## § 15:7. Structural Alterations as Waste

A structural change or alteration is such a change as affects a vital and substantial portion of the premises, as changes its characteristic appearance, the fundamental purpose of its erection, or the uses contemplated, or, a change of such a nature as affects the very realty itself—extraordinary in scope and effect, or unusual in expenditure.[13]

A lease gives a tenant the right to make use of leased premises, but not the right to exercise acts of ownership. The power of making structural alterations, or alterations which injure the reversion, does not arise out of a mere right of user. Such acts constitute acts of ownership.

---

10. Regan v Luthy (Com Pl GT 1890) 11 NYS 709.

Also, see, Rogers v Atlantic, G. & P. Co. (1915) 213 NY 246, 250, 107 NE 661.

11. Per Miller, J., in Rogers v Atlantic, G. & P. Co. (1915) 213 NY 246, 251, 107 NE 661.

Waste is to be distinguished from trespass in that the wasteful or injurious act is committed in the former case by one who is, and in the latter case by one who is not, in lawful possession of the premises involved. Van Deusen v Young (1864) 29 NY 9.

12. PBN Associates v Xerox Corp. (S Ct Rockland Co 1987) 136 Misc 2d 205, 517 NYS2d 1015.

13. Wall Nut Products, Inc. v Radar Cent. Corp. (1963, 1st Dept) 20 AD2d 125, 244 NYS2d 827; Refrigeration for Science, Inc. v Deacon Realty Corp. (S Ct Nassau Co 1972) 70 Misc 2d 500, 334 NYS2d 418, affd (2d Dept) 42 AD2d 691, 344 NYS2d 1018.

The installation by a tenant in premises leased for a restaurant of three air conditioning units, which weighed 750 pounds each, and which were not attached to the floor or walls, but which stood on their own support, was held not to constitute the making of an alteration in violation of the terms of the lease. Leong Won v Snyder (S Ct Kings Co 1949) 94 NYS2d 247.

As the Court of Appeals said,[14] "By a lease the use, not the dominion of the property demised, is conferred. If a tenant exercises an act of ownership, he is no longer protected by his tenancy." Thus, tearing down partitions between rooms,[15] tearing up a marble platform adjoining the building on the outside,[16] or changing an apartment or residential building to a store building, where the alteration would be the taking out of the front and putting in a storefront,[17] constitutes a change in the nature or character of the building itself, and therefore is waste. No right to do so can be claimed from the mere relation of landlord and tenant. If such right exists at all, it must depend on agreement.[18] Tenant's removal of old painted kitchen cabinets, and replacement with new oak veneer cabinets; and installation of metallic wallcovering material and imbedded ceiling and lighting arrangements in living room and bedroom, it was held, constituted such a misuse of the leased premises, which resulted in prejudice to the present and prospective interest of the owner, and substantial injury to the freehold, as entitled the landlord to terminate the lease.[19]

### § 15:8. Structural Alterations Made in Good Faith

The real inquiry in all cases involving alterations made by a tenant is, as to whether there is damage done which injuries the reversion,[20] and good faith on the tenant's part is no defense where the act, on general principles of law, amounts to waste.[1]

14. Agate v Lowenbein (1874) 57 NY 604, 607.
15. McDonald v O'Hara (S Ct NY Co 1921) 117 Misc 517, 192 NYS 545.
16. Satzman v Barry (AT1 1918) 170 NYS 929.
17. Brown v Broadway & Seventy-Second Street Realty Co. (AD1 1909) 131 AD 780, 116 NYS 306.
18. Agate v Lowenbein (1874) 57 NY 604, 607.
19. Freehold Invest. v Richstone (AT1 1973) 72 Misc 2d 624, 340 NYS2d 362 (citing text), revd (1st Dept) 42 AD2d 696, 346 NYS2d 718, revd 34 NY2d 612, 355 NYS2d 363, 311 NE2d 500, which reinstated order of Appellate Term.
Replacement of ceiling, installation of new ceiling light fixtures, and attachment of wooden closet to wall and wooden frame around window by tenant of rent controlled apartment could not be characterized as causing permanent and lasting injury to the premises, was not waste, and therefore, it was held, did not constitute violation of a substantial obligation of tenancy inflicting serious and substantial injury upon the landlord within meaning of § 52(a) of the New York City Rent and Eviction Regulations. Rumiche Corp. v Eisenreich (1976, 1st Dept) 40 NY2d 174, 386 NYS2d 208, 352 NE2d 125.

20. See § 15:7, supra, for definition of structural alteration.

1. Agate v Lowenbein (1874) 57 NY

## § 15:9. Ability to Restore Premises as Justification for Structural Alterations

"It is, in general, no justification for an act of waste," said the Court of Appeals,[2] "that a party will, at some future time, put the premises in the same condition as they were when the lease was made. The question is, whether the tenant, at the time the wrongful act was done, caused an injury which then affected the plaintiff as to his reversion. How can it be known, as matter of law, that a tenant will retrace his steps and repair an injury which he has deliberately caused? The landlord has a right to a continuance of the state of things as they existed when the injury was done. The tenant has no right to exercise an act of ownership."[3]

## § 15:10. Structural Alterations Beneficial to Landlord

It is well settled that an owner of property is entitled to have his property remain as it is, without material change in its structure, form, and character. Therefore, an alteration which materially injures the reversion, or materially changes the nature and character of the leased premises, is waste even though the value of the property may be enhanced by the alteration,[4] and even though in its consequences it may not be prejudicial to the landlord.[5]

It is the impingement upon the ultimate estate of the landlord which is the keynote to the definition of waste.[6]

### C. WHEN TENANT MAY MAKE ALTERATIONS

### § 15:11. Generally

It does not follow that a tenant, by virtue of his obligation to commit no waste, may make no alterations

---

604, 614; Purton v Watson (1888, City Ct GT) 2 NYS 661.

2. Agate v Lowenbein (1874) 57 NY 604, 614.

3. See, also, Charles A. Luisi, Inc. v Richard Lumber Co. (1948, City Ct) 80 NYS2d 536.

4. Freehold Invest. v Richstone (AT1 1973) 72 Misc 2d 624, 340 NYS2d 362 (citing text), revd (1st Dept) 42 AD2d 696, 346 NYS2d 718, revd 34 NY2d 612, 355 NYS2d 363, 311 NE2d 500, which reinstated order of Appellate Term; McDonald v O'Hara (S Ct NY Co 1921) 117 Misc 517, 192 NYS 545.

See § 15:7, supra, for definition of structural alterations.

5. Andrews v Day Button Co. (1892) 132 NY 348, 353, 30 NE 831.

6. Rumiche Corp. v Eisenreich (1976, 1st Dept) 40 NY2d 174, 386 NYS2d 208, 352 NE2d 125 (citing text).

§ 15:11　　　　　LANDLORD AND TENANT

whatsoever. Except as the tenant's rights may be limited by the terms of the lease, the tenant is at liberty to erect structures, or to make non-structural alterations, for the purpose of carrying on his legitimate business on the leased premises, and to remove them within the term, provided such structures or alterations will not do any serious injury to the realty.[7] In other words, as the Appellate Term said,[8] "There can be, however, little question but what the lessee would have the right to make such changes as could be readily restored or replaced."

### § 15:12. Necessity for Written Consent to Make Structural Alterations

When a tenant wishes to make structural alterations, in order to avoid the possibility of an action for waste he should obtain the written consent of the landlord.[9] The statute provides[10] an action for waste lies against a tenant by the curtesy, in dower, for life, or for years, or the assignee of such a tenant, who, during his estate or term, commits waste upon the real property held by him, without a special and lawful written license so to do; or against such a tenant who lets or grants his estate and still retaining possession thereof commits waste without a like license.

### § 15:13. Consent Granted by Lease "To Make Inside Alterations Provided Premises Not Injured"

Where the lease contains an express provision regarding alterations by the tenant, such provision will control the rights of the parties in this respect, and the question becomes one of construction whether the changes made

---

7. Rumiche Corp. v Eisenreich (1976, 1st Dept) 40 NY2d 174, 386 NYS2d 208, 352 NE2d 125 (quoting text); Andrews v Day Button Co. (1892) 132 NY 348, 353, 30 NE 831; Agate v Lowenbein (1874) 57 NY 604, 609; Gabin v Goldstein (NYC Civ Ct Kings Co 1986) 131 Misc 2d 153, 497 NYS2d 984 (citing text).

Frequency Electronics, Inc. v We're Associates Co. (1986, 2d Dept) 120 AD2d 489, 501 NYS2d 693 (premises to be used for manufacture, distribution, and sale of electronic products: installation of exhaust systems, partitioning and air conditioning units without landlord's consent, permitted).

For definition of structural alteration, see § 15:7, supra.

8. Ayen v Schmidt (AT2 1913) 80 Misc 670, 141 NYS 938.

9. Purton v Watson (City Ct GT 1888) 2 NYS 661.

For definition of structural alteration, see § 15:7, supra.

10. Real Prop Act & Proc L § 801.

or contemplated by the tenant are with the meaning of the provision.

A lease provided that the tenant shall have the right to make any inside alterations to the leased premises as he may think proper, provided the same do not injure the premises. The tenant thereupon made extensive alterations by taking down partitions, removing doors and fixtures, and destroying some of the plumbing work. Clearly, without a license to do these acts, such acts amounted to waste. In construing this clause the Court of Appeals held[11] that "the clause in the lease in question confers upon the lessee more power to make alterations than he would have had if it had not been inserted; it may be supposed to allow acts which, in point of law, and technically are waste, and yet are not accompanied by actual injury to the premises. It plainly gives only a qualified right to make alterations. The lessee's will is limited by the fact that the alterations are to cause no injury to the premises. A further reasonable limitation is, that the acts of alteration are not to be wanton or capricious, but must be made with a purpose to facilitate the transaction of the lessee's business. . . . The clause concerning the right to make alterations must be supposed to have been inserted with the view of enabling the lessee to adapt the premises to such business as might happen to be carried on there." The court then held that whether the acts committed by the tenant constituted waste, therefore, should be submitted to a jury to determine whether they did really cause injury to the property, and whether they were reasonably required for the enjoyment of the premises according to the business which the tenant carried on.

## § 15:14. Form of Provision Consenting to Tenant-Alterations

### FORM 30

### Provision Consenting to Tenant-Alterations

Tenant may from time to time during the term make such changes, alterations, additions, substitutions or improvements (herein collectively called Tenant-Alterations)

---

11. Agate v Lowenbein (1874) 57 NY 604.

in and to the leased premises as Tenant may reasonably consider necessary and desirable to adapt or equip the premises for Tenant's occupancy. Prior to the making of any Tenant-Alterations which will cost in excess of *[$25,-000]*, or involve structural work or changes, Tenant shall deliver plans and specifications thereof to Landlord, and obtain Landlord's written approval thereof, which approval Landlord agrees it will not unreasonably withhold or delay. If Landlord shall not have signified its disapproval of such plans and specifications within fifteen (15) days after delivery thereof to Landlord, such plans and specifications shall be deemed to have been approved by Landlord. Tenant shall have the right to change and amend said plans and specifications so approved by Landlord, and without Landlord's consent, provided the change or amendment made shall not substantially affect the character or value of the work so to be done.[12]

### § 15:15. Tenant May Not Go Beyond Consent Granted to Make Alterations

A tenant was granted by the terms of his lease the right to make alterations so as to make the leased premises more desirable for his business. The tenant thereupon sought to lower the floor of his space three feet at one end, and by a gradual slope, bring it to the former floor level at the entrance. However, in so doing the tenant would be appropriating a portion of space from the basement, which had been leased to another tenant. The tenant contended that, as this alteration would make the leased premises more desirable for his business, he had the right to do so. The court overruled this contention,[13] and held that a right to make alterations "on leased premises" did not give the tenant a right to extend the alterations "off the leased premises"; for a tenant may not exceed the permission given him to make alterations.

Where a lease required the tenant to make repairs, and expressly prohibited the making of any alterations without the prior written consent of the landlord, it was held that the tenant could not make structural changes in the

---

12. Adapted from lease litigated in Times Square Stores Corp. v Bernice Realty Co. (1985, 2d Dept) 107 AD2d 677, 484 NYS2d 591.

13. Cohen v Simon Strauss, Inc. (AT1 1913) 139 NYS 929.

# TENANT'S RIGHTS § 15:17

building without consent, since such changes were not repairs, but were alterations.[14]

It has been held that a provision in a lease granting express permission to make certain alterations implicitly prohibits all other alterations.[15]

The violation of an express covenant not to make alterations is a substantial violation.[16]

## § 15:16. Consent to Alterations Required by Lease; as Affecting Structural Alterations

A tenant's covenant that he will not make any alterations in the leased premises without the landlord's consent, is nothing more than an undertaking imposed by law, to the effect that any material and substantial change or alteration in the nature of the property is waste, and may not be done without such consent.[17]

## § 15:17. —As Affecting Non-structural Alterations Necessary to Carry on Business

Non-structural alterations necessary to carry on a tenant's business may be made without the landlord's consent.[18] This is true even where the lease requires that no alterations may be made without the landlord's consent, provided, however, that such alterations will not injure the reversion, and provided, further, that they are reasonably necessary to enable the tenant to use the leased premises in the manner set forth in the lease.[19]

---

**14.** Margold Residence Corp. v Younger (AD1 1955) 286 AD 244, 142 NYS2d 46, affd 2 NY2d 937, 162 NYS2d 34, 142 NE2d 209.

Where tenant without first getting landlord's consent, required by lease, removed a sink and stove from his apartment and placed them intact in the basement of the building, and then had his own sink and stove installed, it was held that this substitution did not constitute an alteration in violation of the lease, warranting a termination of the lease, and a holdover summary proceeding. Lansis v Meklinsky (1960, 2d Dept) 10 AD2d 649, 198 NYS 247. Also, to same effect, involving removal of refrigerator and substitution of new one, see Parker v Johnson (M Ct 1960) 26 Misc 2d 31, 206 NYS2d 594.

**15.** Two Guys from Harrison N. Y., Inc. v S. F. R. Realty Associates (1984) 63 NY2d 396, 482 NYS2d 465, 472 NE2d 315.

**16.** Rumiche Corp. v Eisenreich (1976, 1st Dept) 40 NY2d 174, 386 NYS2d 208, 352 NE2d 125.

**17.** Andrews v Day Button Co. (1892) 132 NY 348, 353, 30 NE 831; Brooklyn Properties, Inc. v Cargo Packers, Inc. (1956, 2d Dept) 1 AD2d 1040, 152 NYS2d 359.

**18.** See § 15:11, supra.

**19.** C. Wayne Motors, Inc. v Somers (1981, 3d Dept) 81 AD2d 964, 439 NYS2d 746; Diener v Burghart (1921, Sup App T) 186 NYS 565; Klein's Rapid Shoe Repair Co. v Sheppardel Realty Co. (S Ct NY Co 1929) 136 Misc 332, 241 NYS 153, affd 228 AD 688, 239 NYS 790; Rubinstein Bros. v

§ 15:17    LANDLORD AND TENANT

A provision in a lease restricting a tenant in the use he may make of the leased premises, it has been held, will be construed as carrying with it the privilege of making such non-structural alterations as will enable the tenant to use the premises in the manner provided by the terms of the lease.[20] A tenant, under the terms of his lease, was given the right to sublet. The lease further provided that the tenant should not make any alterations without the landlord's written consent. The tenant desired to erect a temporary partition from the front to the rear of the premises so as to enable him to sublet the premises. The court held,[1] that the right to sublet should be construed to carry with it the privilege of making any reasonable alterations necessary to exercise such right to sublet without the necessity of obtaining the landlord's written consent, as required by the terms of the lease; and that the erection of the temporary partition was such a reasonable alteration.[2]

## § 15:18. Form of Provision Requiring Landlord's Consent to Alterations and Improvements

### FORM NO. 31

### Covenant to Make No Alterations or Improvements Without Landlord's Consent*

Tenant shall make no changes of any nature in or to

---

Ole of 34th Street, Inc. (NYC Civ Ct NY Co 1979) 101 Misc 2d 563, 421 NYS2d 534, citing texts (pegs added to the walls for purpose of hanging merchandise, are trade fixtures and not alterations, violative of lease).

20. Diener v Burghart (AT1 1921) 186 NYS 565.

Restaurant tenant may make such nonstructural alterations in basement of restaurant as are reasonably necessary for the efficient use of the leased premises, without obtaining landlord's prior written consent required for alterations or improvements. Williams v Ron-Jay Enterprises, Inc. (1978, 4th Dept) 65 AD2d 213, 411 NYS2d 86.

Metal frame rack trade fixture, installation of which without landlord's consent not violative of provision against making alterations without landlord's consent. N. & S. Decor Fixture Co. v V. J. Enterprises, Inc. (1977, 2d Dept) 57 AD2d 890, 394 NYS2d 278 (quoting text).

1. Klein's Rapid Shoe Repair Co. v Sheppardel Realty Co. (S Ct NY Co 1929) 136 Misc 332, 241 NYS 153, affd 228 AD 688, 239 NYS 790. Also, see Two Guys from Harrison-N.Y., Inc. v S.F.R. Realty Associates (1984) 63 NY2d 396, 482 NYS2d 465, 472 NE2d 315.

2. In this case the landlord had agreed not to withhold his consent unreasonably, and the court further held that on the facts recited in the text the landlord was withholding his consent unreasonably.

* This is Article 3 of the Standard Form of Loft Lease, copyrighted by The Real Estate Board of New York Inc., and reprinted by its permission. Reproduction in whole or in parts is prohibited, and all rights are reserved by The Real Estate Board of New York. For complete form of lease, see Chapter 1.

the leased premises without Landlord's prior written consent. Subject to the prior written consent of Landlord and to the provisions of this article, Tenant at Tenant's expense, may make alterations, installations, additions or improvements which are non-structural and which do not affect utility services or plumbing and electrical lines, in or to the interior of the leased premises by using contractors or mechanics first approved by Landlord. Tenant shall, before making any alterations, additions, installations or improvements, at its expense, obtain all permits, approvals and certificates required by any governmental or quasi-governmental bodies and (upon completion) certificates of final approval thereof and shall deliver promptly duplicates of all such permits, approval and certificates to Landlord and Tenant agrees to carry and will cause Tenant's contractors and sub-contractors to carry such workman's compensation, general liability, personal and property damage insurance as Landlord may require. If any mechanic's lien is filed against the leased premises, or the building of which the same forms a part, for work claimed to have been done for, or materials furnished to, Tenant, whether or not done pursuant to this article the same shall be discharged by Tenant within 30 days thereafter, at Tenant's expense, by filing the bond required by law. All fixtures and all panelling, partitions, railings and like installations, installed in the premises at any time, either by Tenant or by Landlord on Tenant's behalf, shall upon installation become the property of Landlord and shall remain upon and be surrendered with the leased premises unless Landlord, by notice to Tenant no later than twenty days prior to the date fixed as the termination of this lease, elects to have them removed by Tenant, in which event, the same shall be removed from the premises by Tenant forthwith, at Tenant's expense. Nothing in this article shall be construed to prevent Tenant's removal of trade fixtures, moveable office furniture and equipment but upon removal of any such from the premises or upon removal of other installations as may be required by Landlord, Tenant shall immediately and at its expense, repair and restore the premises to the condition existing prior to installation and repair any damage to the leased premises or the building due to such removal. All property permitted or required to be removed by Tenant at the end of the term remaining in the premises after Tenant's removal shall be deemed abandoned and may, at the election of Landlord, either be retained as Landlord's property or may be removed from the premises by Landlord at Tenant's expense.

### § 15:19. When Landlord May Withhold Lease-required Consent to Alterations

If the alterations desired to be made by a tenant are structural,[3] and the lease provides that they may not be made without the landlord's consent, such consent may be withheld, even arbitrarily.[4]

A lease provided that the premises were to be used only for executive offices, showrooms, and sales rooms, and that no structural alterations should be made without the landlord's consent. The tenant without permission used part of the premises as a restaurant. This was in violation of the terms of the lease. In order to continue such use, it became necessary to make certain structural alterations to the leased premises, as well as to the adjoining premises. The landlord refused to grant such permission, and the tenant brought suit for a declaratory judgment determining that the tenant had the right to make such alterations. The tenant contended that the landlord had waived his right to withhold his consent, since he had acquiesced in the wrongful use of the premises as a restaurant. The court, however, denied the tenant the right to make the proposed alterations, and said,[5]

"The defendant's (landlord's) acquiescence in plaintiff's operation of the restaurant may estop it from asserting that this constituted a breach of the lease, but I cannot subscribe to the view that the defendant is also precluded thereby from insisting upon its right to forbid the making of structural alterations or improvements. . . . If the plaintiff were employing the premises for the purposes

---

3. For definition of structural alteration, see § 15:7, supra.

4. Wall Nut Products, Inc. v Radar Cent. Corp. (1963, 1st Dept) 20 AD2d 125, 244 NYS2d 827.

5. Sanka Coffee Corp. v Ramcadis Realty Corp. (S Ct NY Co 1930) 136 Misc 919, 242 NYS 630, affd 233 AD 653, 249 NYS 867.

permitted by its lease, no alterations would appear to be necessary to render its occupancy legal and proper. The failure of the defendant, or its predecessor in interest, to object to the restaurant use would seem to be nothing more than an act of grace and certainly should not subject it to penalties and burdens that it never assumed." Furthermore, the court pointed out, even if the alterations proposed were non-structural in nature, and therefore could be made without consent, nevertheless, the permission to make such alterations would have to be confined to the leased premises, and could not be extended to cover other premises even if such other premises were owned or controlled by the same landlord.[6]

### § 15:20. Right of Tenants in Multiple Dwellings to Install Locks

The Multiple Dwelling Law provides that every tenant of a multiple dwelling, except a tenant of a multiple dwelling under the supervision and control of a municipal housing authority, occupied by him, except as a hotel or motel, or college or school dormitory, shall have the right to install and maintain or cause to be installed and maintained in the entrance door of his particular housing unit in such multiple dwelling, a lock, separate and apart from any lock installed and maintained by the owner of such multiple dwelling, not more than three inches in circumference, as an ordinary incident to his tenancy, provided that a duplicate key to such lock shall be supplied to the landlord or his agent upon his request; and every provision of any lease hereafter made or entered into which reserves or provides for the payment by such tenant of any additional rent, bonus, fee or other charge or any other thing of value for the right or privilege of installing and/or maintaining any such lock, shall be deemed to be void as against public policy and wholly unenforceable.[7]

Tenant's violation of this statute, as well as the explicit provision of the lease requiring him to deliver a duplicate key to the landlord upon request, is a violation of a substantial obligation of the lease.[8]

---

6. As to this, see also, § 15:15, supra.
7. Multiple Dwelling Law § 51-c.
8. Lavanant v Lovelace (AT1 1972)

### § 15:21. Statutory Authorization to Make Alterations

When a person having an estate for life or for years in land, proposes to make an alteration in, or a replacement of a structure or structures located thereon, the statute provides that the owner of a future interest in such land can neither recover damages for, nor enjoin the alteration or replacement, if the person proposing to make such alteration or replacement complies with certain specified requirements, with respect to security, and establishes the following facts: (a) that the proposed alteration or replacement is one which a prudent owner of an estate in fee simple absolute in the affected land would be likely to make in view of the conditions existing on or in the neighborhood of the affected land; (b) that the proposed alteration or replacement, when completed, will not reduce the market value of the interests in such land subsequent to the estate for life or for years; (c) that the proposed alteration or replacement is not in violation of the terms of any agreement or other instrument regulating the conduct of the owner of the estate for life or for years or restricting the land in question; (d) that the life expectancy of the owner of the estate for life or the unexpired term of the estate for years is not less than five years; and (e) that the person proposing to make such alteration or replacement, not less than thirty days prior to commencement thereof, served upon each owner of a future interest, who is in being and ascertained, a written notice of his intention to make such alteration or replacement specifying the nature thereof, which notice was served personally or by registered mail sent to the last known address of each such owner of a future interest.[9]

When the owner of a future interest in the affected land demands security that the proposed alteration or replacement, if begun, will be completed, and that he be protected against responsibility for expenditures incident to the making of the proposed alteration or replacement,

---

71 M2d 974, 337 NYS2d 962 (issuance of warrant permanently stayed if within 10 days after service of copy of order, tenant furnishes landlord with duplicate key), affd (1st Dept) 41 AD2d 905, 343 NYS2d 559.

9. Real Prop Act & Proc L § 803. This statute only applies to estates for life or for years created on or after September 1, 1937. Real Prop Act & Proc L § 803, subd 3.

the court in which the action to recover damages or to enjoin the alteration or replacement is pending, or if no such action is pending, the supreme court, on application thereto, on such notice to the interested parties as the court may direct, shall fix the amount and terms of the security reasonably necessary to satisfy such demand. The furnishing of the security so fixed shall be a condition precedent to the making of the proposed alteration or replacement.[10]

In other words, this statute sets forth certain conditions under which a tenant for life or for years may alter the property over the objections of any owner of a future interest. In brief, the tenant must establish that a prudent owner would make the same change, which will not reduce the market value of the future interest, and does not violate any contract regulating the tenant's conduct. In addition, the tenancy must be expected to continue for more than 5 years, and written notice of the intention to make the alterations must be given. Finally, the owner of a future interest may obtain security that the proposed alteration will be completed.

### § 15:22. Forms for Obtaining Statutory Authorization to Make Alterations

#### FORM NO. 32

#### Notice of Intention to Make Alterations or Replacements

To ........ [Name and Address of Owner of a future interest]

PLEASE TAKE NOTICE, that pursuant to section 803 of the Real Property Actions and Proceedings Law of the State of New York the undersigned, a life tenant [or a tenant for years] of the following property: ........ [describe property] hereby intends, not less than thirty days from the service of this notice to alter [or replace] the structure [or structures] thereon in the following manner and particulars: ........ [specify nature and extent of alterations or replacements]. The estimated cost of the aforesaid alterations [or replacements] is ........ dollars.

---

10. Real Prop Act & Proc L § 803. This statute only applies to estates for life or for years created on or after September 1, 1937. Real Prop Act & Proc L § 803, subd 3.

Dated, New York, .........., 19. ...
[Signature with name printed underneath]

## FORM NO. 33

### Notice of Motion for Security for Completion of Proposed Alterations

Supreme Court
County of ........

|  |  |
|---|---|
| ........, Plaintiff<br>against<br>........, Defendant | Notice of Motion<br><br>Index No. ... |

PLEASE TAKE NOTICE that upon the annexed affidavit of ........, sworn to on the ... day of ........, 19..., a motion pursuant to Real Property Actions and Proceedings Law, § 803, subdivision 2, will be made at a Special Term of this court, to be held at the court house thereof at ..., on the ........ day of ..., 19..., at ... o'clock in the ... noon of that day, or as soon thereafter as counsel can be heard, for an order directing ........, the life tenant [or the tenant for years] of the property described in the said annexed affidavit, to give security to ........, as the owner of the future interest in said property, to insure that the alterations or replacements proposed by said ........ if begun, will be completed, and to protect said ........ against responsibility for expenditures incident to the making of the proposed alterations [or replacements] and granting such other and further relief as may be just.

Dated, New York, ........, 19...

........
Attorney for ........
[Office address and telephone number]

To. .......

## FORM NO. 34

### Affidavit in Support of Motion for Security

[Title of Court and Cause]    Affidavit in Support of
Motion For Security
Index No. ...

TENANT'S RIGHTS                                    § 15:23

State of New York
                         ss:
County of ........

........, being duly sworn deposes and says:

1. At all the times hereinafter mentioned I was and still am the owner in fee of the following described premises situate in the County of ........, State of New York: ........ *[set forth description]*.

2. On the ... day of ........, 19..., I entered into a written agreement with ........, whereby I, as owner, leased to ........, as lessee, the above described premises for a term of ... years. A copy of said lease is annexed hereto as Exhibit "A".

3. Said ........ has been in possession of said premises as lessee from ........, 19..., and still occupies the same.

4. On the ... day of ........, 19..., said ........ served me with a written notice of intention to make alterations *[or* replacements] upon, or of the structures located on, the said premises. A copy of said notice is annexed hereto as Exhibit "B".

5. Upon information and belief the estimated cost of such alterations *[or* replacements] will be ... dollars.

6. I respectfully pray for an order directing that said ........ file an undertaking in the amount of ... dollars, or in such amount as the court may direct, as security to insure that the proposed alterations *[or* replacements] if begun, will be completed, and that I will not be held responsible for expenditures incident to the proposed alterations *[or* replacements], and further directing that the furnishing of said security as fixed by this court shall be a condition precedent to the making of the proposed alterations *[or* replacements].

[Jurat]

[Signature with name printed underneath]

### D. REMEDIES FOR UNAUTHORIZED ALTERATIONS

**§ 15:23. Right of Injunction to Restrain Unauthorized Alterations**

A landlord is entitled to an injunction to prevent a

tenant from making unauthorized alterations, or alterations which constitute waste.[11]

In an action by a landlord to enjoin violation by tenant of a provision of a lease forbidding tenant from making any alterations, that the contemplated alterations were for the purpose of satisfying the requirements of the public authorities constitutes no defense where the alterations were necessitated by overloading of the floors in the leased premises in violation of the lease.[12]

## § 15:24. Injunction to Compel Restoration of Premises Altered Without Authorization

When a tenant has gone beyond the powers conceded to him by the lease, and has made unauthorized alterations, the Court of Appeals said,[13] "he has either been restrained by injunction or compelled at once to make satisfaction or to restore the premises to the condition in which he found them. There has been no case in which the landlord was required to wait until the end of the lease to see whether the premises might be restored by the tenant to their original condition. If the waste committed went beyond the license an immediate wrong was done, which was at once the subject of redress in a court either of law or equity."

In such case, then, a landlord is entitled to a mandatory injunction before the expiration of the term for the restoration of the premises to the condition they were in before the work of destruction took place.[14] However, it must be observed that the injunction generally will be withheld as oppressive if the injury is not serious or substantial. It is only when the injury caused by the wilful act is indeed serious and irreparable that the injunction will issue.[15]

---

**11.** Agate v Lowenbein (1874) 57 NY 604, 612; Brooklyn Properties, Inc. v Cargo Packers, Inc. (1956, 2d Dept) 1 AD2d 1040, 152 NYS2d 359; Chamberlain v Childs' Unique Dairy Co. (S Ct NY Co 1907) 53 Misc 371, 104 NYS 912.

**12.** 209-13 West 48th Realty Corp. v Rose Offset Printing Corp. (S Ct NY Co 1947) 74 NYS2d 216, affd 273 AD 754, 75 NYS2d 774.

**13.** Agate v Lowenbein (1874) 57 NY 604, 612.

**14.** Agate v Lowenbein (1874) 57 NY 604, 613; McDonald v O'Hara (AT1 1921) 117 Misc 517, 192 NYS 545; Chamberlain v Childs' Unique Dairy Co. (S Ct NY Co 1907) 53 Misc 371, 104 NYS 912.

**15.** Brooklyn Properties, Inc. v Cargo Packers, Inc. (1956, 2d Dept) 1 AD2d 1040, 152 NYS2d 359, denying mandatory injunction and awarding damages, as constituting adequate re-

## § 15:25. Right to Damages for Unauthorized Alterations

The statute provides,[16] that if the plaintiff recovers in an action for waste, other than an action brought as prescribed in Real Property Actions and Proceedings Law, § 817,[17] the final judgment must award to him compensatory damages. Where the action is brought by the person next entitled to the reversion, and it appears, in like manner, that the injury to the estate in reversion is equal to the value of the tenant's estate or unexpired term, the final judgment must also award to the plaintiff the forfeiture of the defendant's estate, and the possession of the place wasted.[18] The measure of damages for impermissible structural alterations is what it would cost to put the premises in the required state of repair,[19] regardless of whether or not the landlord has actually expended money in making such repairs.[20]

## E. RIGHT TO DISPLAY SIGNS

### § 15:26. Where Entire Building Leased

Under a lease of an entire building, in the absence of any restrictions in the lease, a tenant has the right to use the roof and side walls, or to sublet or license their use, for the erection and maintenance of signs to advertise any business which might be lawfully carried on in the building under the terms of the lease.[1]

Under this principle where a tenant hires a building for residential purposes, it would seem that he would have no implied right to use the roof and side walls, nor

---

lief under the circumstances proven; Sussman Volk Co. v 88 Delicatessen, Inc. (S Ct NY Co 1950) 100 NYS2d 303.

**16.** Real Prop Act & Proc L § 815, derived from former Real Prop L § 524, added L 1920, ch 930, § 1, am L 1935, ch 797, § 1, eff Sept 1, 1935.

**17.** Real Prop Act & Proc L § 817 provides for actions for waste brought by joint tenants or tenants in common against their co-tenant.

**18.** Also, see Agate v Lowenbein (1874) 57 NY 604.

**19.** Farrell Lines, Inc. v New York (1972) 30 NY2d 76, 330 NYS2d 358, 281 NE2d 162; Mudge v West End Brewing Co. (AD3 1911) 145 AD 28, 130 NYS 350, affd 207 NY 696, 101 NE 1112; Gabin v Goldstein (NYC Civ Ct Kings Co 1986) 131 Misc 2d 153, 497 NYS2d 984.

**20.** Niles v Iroquois Realty Co. (AD1 1909) 130 AD 744, 115 NYS 602; Gabin v Goldstein (NYC Civ Ct Kings Co 1986) 131 Misc 2d 153, 497 NYS2d 984.

**1.** Lyon v Bethlehem Engineering Corp. (1930) 253 NY 111, 170 NE 512; Brown v Broadway & Seventy-Second Street Realty Co. (AD1 1909) 131 AD 780, 116 NYS 306; Schmidt v Louis, Inc. (S Ct Erie Co 1924) 122 Misc 249, 203 NYS 515.

to sublet or license their use, for the erection and maintenance of signs to advertise any business. For, no business may be lawfully carried on in the building under the terms of the lease.

A tenant of an entire building erected upon the roof a sign which was used for general advertising purposes. The landlord sought to enjoin such use, and contended that this was not permissible under the lease. The lease, however, contained no restrictions on the use of the building, nor made mention of the subject of signs. Ingraham, J., in upholding the tenant's right to use the roof of the building for general advertising purpose, said,[2] "There is nothing in this lease that applies to the use of signs upon the leasehold premises. . . . It is quite clear that the lessee of this property has the right to use the property in any way consistent with the purpose for which it was erected and not restricted by the lease. If the landlord wishes to restrict the tenant in his use of the property, he must depend upon an express covenant in the lease preventing a use to which he objects."

### § 15:27. —Limitations

Where a tenant has the implied right to display signs for advertising purposes, as in the case of a lease of an entire building without any restrictions on the use thereof, then the tenant, in exercising this right, may not injure the building, obstruct the public passageways, offend public taste, or otherwise violate any prevailing law.[3]

### § 15:28. Where Part of Building Leased

In the case of a lease covering less than the entire building, the tenant, in the absence of any restriction in the lease, has the right to paint or affix an appropriate sign relating to his own business on the walls enclosing his leased premises.[4] Thus, where a lease covers a store and basement, and nothing is said in the lease regarding

---

2. Brown v Broadway & Seventy-Second Street Realty Co. (AD1 1909) 131 AD 780, 116 NYS 306.

3. Lyon v Bethlehem Engineering Corp. (1930) 253 NY 111, 170 NE 512; Schmidt v Louis, Inc. (S Ct Erie Co 1924) 122 Misc 249, 203 NYS 515.

4. Blumenthal v Kelsey (AD1 1917) 176 AD 369, 162 NYS 967; Di Marco v Isaac (AT 1911) 74 Misc 459, 132 NYS 363.

the erection of signs, the tenant may hang a sign over the entrance to the store stating his name and business.[5]

### § 15:29. —Limitations

When a tenant leases part of a building, his right to put up a sign is limited by the rights of the other tenants in the same building, who have a similar right.

A tenant rented the entire fourteenth floor in a building. A bookbinder was a tenant of the lower floors in the same building. With the approval of the landlord, the bookbinder painted large signs advertising his business on the easterly and westerly walls of the thirteenth as well as the fourteenth floors of the building. The Court of Appeals held that the fourteenth floor tenant had a right to a judgment directing the removal of such signs, and said, by Cardozo, J.,[6] that where a tenant leases an entire floor in a building, such lease "must carry with it the appurtenant right to exclude signs, advertising the business of persons other than the tenant, from those parts of the walls which form the inclosure of the floor." A different rule would mean, the Judge continued, that "without redress, the space occupied by a lawyer may be advertised by signs as devoted to the promotion of a gold mine, and an institute of learning as a wareroom for a proprietary medicine. We are unwilling to believe that the tenant is so helpless."

Moreover, the right of a tenant to paint or affix signs relating to his own business on the walls enclosing his leased premises must be done in such a way as not to injure or damage the building,[7] nor violate any statute or ordinance, and thereby impose a penalty on the landlord.[8]

## F. MISCELLANEOUS RIGHTS

### § 15:30. Erect Television Aerials

It has been held that a tenant of an apartment in a building has no legal right, without the landlord's express permission to erect, attach or maintain television aerials either on the roof, or to the outside frame of a window in

---

5. Di Marco v Isaac (AT 1911) 74 Misc 459, 132 NYS 363.

6. Stahl & Jaeger v Satenstein (1922) 233 NY 196, 198, 135 NE 242, 22 ALR 798.

7. Schmidt v Louis, Inc. (S Ct Erie Co 1924) 122 Misc 249, 203 NYS 515.

8. Wineburgh Advertising Co. v Faust Co. (AT 1908) 113 NYS 709.

the landlord's building, or along the wall of the landlord's building.[9]

Executive Law § 828 provides, "1. No landlord shall

a. interfere with the installation of cable television facilities upon his property or premises, except that a landlord may require: i. that the installation of cable television facilities conform to such reasonable conditions as are necessary to protect the safety, functioning and appearance of the premises, and the convenience and well-being of other tenants, ii. that the cable television company or the tenant or a combination thereof bear the entire cost of the installation, operation or removal of such facilities, and iii. that the cable television company agree to indemnify the landlord for any damage caused by the installation, operation or removal of such facilities.

b. demand or accept payment from any tenant, in any form, in exchange for permitting cable television service on or within his property or premises, or from any cable television company in exchange therefor in excess of any amount which the commission [the commission on cable television created by Article 28 of the Executive Law] shall, by regulation, determine to be reasonable; or

c. discriminate in rental charges, or otherwise, between tenants who receive cable television service and those who do not.

2. "Cable television system" shall mean any system which operates for hire the service of receiving and amplifying programs broadcast by one or more television or radio stations or any other programs originated by a

---

9. West Holding Corp. v Cordero (S Ct Kings Co 1952) 114 NYS2d 668 (television aerial attached to window frame enjoined and ordered removed); Kaplan v Ladimer (AT2 1950) 197 Misc 270, 97 NYS2d 642; Goldstein v Alweiss (AT2 1949) 196 Misc 513, 93 NYS2d 854; 349 East 19th Street, Inc. v Bernstein (S Ct Kings Co 1950) 99 NYS2d 299 (tenant enjoined).

In People v Stein (AD2 1950) 277 AD 996, 100 NYS2d 41, it was held that a landlord was guilty of malicious mischief when he cut the wires leading from a window television aerial to the apartment of a tenant, and twisted the antenna, when the tenant refused to remove the aerial pursuant to the landlord's demand [former Penal L § 1433, now Penal L § 145:00]. However, in Vassalo v Stakser (AT1 1951) 199 Misc 216, 105 NYS2d 34; Tanenbaum v Unger (AT2 1950) 198 Misc 612, 103 NYS2d 260; and Kolodney v Shapiro (AT1 1950) 100 NYS2d 70; it was held that where a tenant refused to remove a roof antenna after reasonable notice from the landlord to remove it, the landlord was within his legal rights to remove it, and the tenant had no cause of action against the landlord in consequence thereof.

For cases dealing with air conditioning unit, see cases discussed in notes to § 35:13, infra.

## TENANT'S RIGHTS § 15:31

cable television company or by any other party, and distributing such programs by wire, cable, microwave or other means, whether such means are owned or leased, to persons in one or more munipalities who subscribe to such service. Such definition does not include (a) any system which serves fewer than 50 subscribers; or (b) any master antenna television system.

3. No cable television company may enter into any agreement with the owners, lessees or persons controlling or managing buildings served by a cable television, or do or permit any act that would have the effect, directly or indirectly of diminishing or interfering with existing rights of any tenant or other occupant of such building to use or avail himself of master or individual antenna equipment."

This statute which requires a landlord to allow installation of cable television facilities upon his property for the use of his tenants or the tenants of other buildings or both is a taking requiring compensation, notwithstanding that the staute permits the payment by the cable television company for such installation of such amount as the State Commission on Cable Television determines to be reasonable.[10]

### § 15:31. Cut Trees and Timber

Under the English common law, a tenant of farm land has the right to reasonable estovers, that is, the right to take from the leased premises such amount of wood or timber as is sufficient or necessary for fuel, the repair of buildings, of implements of husbandry, and of fences, as well as other agricultural needs. This right of estovers is implied from the mere leasing of farm land, and is recognized in this state.[11] However, a tenant may be guilty of waste if he cuts green trees for fuel where there is dry wood sufficient for the purpose.[12]

A tenant of land leased for agricultural purposes, which is wild and uncleared, has the right to clear timber from such land in order to prepare it for cultivation, and

---

10. Loretto v Teleprompter Manhattan CATV Corp. (1982) 458 US 419, 73 L Ed 2d 868, 102 S Ct 3164.

11. Van Rensselaer v Radcliff (1830) 10 Wend 639; Jackson ex dem Church v Brownson (1810) 7 Johns 227.

12. Jackson ex dem Church v Brownson (1810) 7 Johns 227.

to sell the timber so cut,[13] in the absence of any provision in the lease to the contrary.[14] But, he cannot cut lumber or wood merely to sell or dispose of it for profit, even in the absence of any provision in the lease prohibiting him from doing so. Thus, where a tenant wrongfully cut trees, the landlord was held entitled to recover for damages to his reversion, or, since trees wrongfully felled by a tenant become personal property and belong to the landlord, he could maintain an action for their possession, or for damages for their conversion, in the same manner as if the tenancy did not exist.[15]

### § 15:32. Tenant's Right to Form, Join, or Participate in Tenants' Groups

Real Property Law § 230 provides that no landlord shall interfere with the right of a tenant to form, join, or participate in the lawful activities of any group, committee or other organization formed to protect the rights of tenants; nor shall any landlord harass, punish, penalize, diminish, or withhold any right, benefit or privilege of a tenant under his tenancy for exercising such right. Moreover, tenants' groups, committees, or other tenants' organizations are to have the right to meet in any location on the premises which is devoted to the common use of all tenants in a peaceful manner, at reasonable hours and without obstructing access to the premises or facilities; and no landlord may deny such right.[16]

### § 15:33. Protection from Harassment of Landlord

Real Property Law § 235-d provides,[17]

---

13. McGregor v Brown (1854) 10 NY 114; Jackson ex dem Church v Brownson (1810) 7 Johns 225.

14. Verplanck v Wright (1840) 23 Wend 506.

15. Mooers v Wait (1820) 3 Wend 104.

16. See, Whitby Operating Corp. v Schleissner (1982) 117 Misc 2d 794, 459 NYS2d 203.

17. Section 1 of L 1978, ch 508, enacting Real Prop L § 235-d, provides, The legislature finds and declares that harassment of residential and non-residential tenants in the city of New York causes serious disruption adverse to the health, safety and welfare of such tenants and city residents generally. Harassment of small business concerns, intended to cause them to vacate their rented space, causes great harm to the commercial fabric of the city. Such disruption of orderly business activities often results in the closing of business concerns or their flight to locations outside the state with consequent losses of employment opportunities for city and state residents. Harassment of artists, artisans and other persons, residing in rented premises converted from previous manufacturing uses, produces similar disruptions in cultural and artistic communities within the city.

## TENANT'S RIGHTS § 15:33

1. Notwithstanding any other provision of law, within a city having a population of one million or more, it shall be unlawful and shall constitute harassment for any landlord of a building which at any time was occupied for manufacturing or warehouse purposes, or other person acting on his behalf, to engage in any course of conduct, including, but not limited to intentional interruption or discontinuance or willful failure to restore services customarily provided or required by written lease or other rental agreement, which interferes with or disturbs the comfort, repose, peace or quiet of a tenant in the tenant's use or occupancy of rental space if such conduct is intended to cause the tenant (i) to vacate a building or part thereof; or (ii) to surrender or waive any rights of such tenant under the tenant's written lease or other rental agreement.

2. The lawful termination of a tenancy or lawful refusal to renew or extend a written lease or other rental agreement shall not constitute harassment for purposes of this section.

3. As used in this section the term "tenant" means only a person or business occupying or residing at the premises pursuant to a written lease or other rental agreement, if such premises are located in a building which at any time was occupied for manufacturing or warehouse purposes and a certificate of occupancy for residential use of such building is not in effect at the time of the last alleged acts or incidents upon which the harassment claim is based.

4. A tenant may apply to the supreme court for an order enjoining acts or practices which constitute harassment under subdivision one of this section; and upon sufficient showing, the supreme court may issue a temporary or permanent injunction, restraining order or other order, all of which may, as the court determines in the exercise of its sound discretion, be granted without bond. In the event the court issues a preliminary injunction it shall make provision for an expeditious trial of the underlying action.

The necessity in the public interest for the provisions hereinafter enacted is hereby declared as a matter of legislative determination.

5. The powers and remedies set forth in this section shall be in addition to all other powers and remedies in relation to harassment including the award of damages. Nothing contained herein shall be construed to amend, repeal, modify or affect any existing local law or ordinance, or provision of the charter or administrative code of the city of New York, or to limit or restrict the power of the city to amend or modify any existing local law, ordinance or provision of the charter or administrative code, or to restrict or limit any power otherwise conferred by law with respect to harassment.

6. Any agreement by a tenant in a written lease or other rental agreement waiving or modifying his rights as set forth in this section shall be void as contrary to public policy.

## G. EXPRESS RESTRICTIONS ON USE OF PREMISES BY TENANT

### § 15:34. General Rule

Parties to a lease have the right to impose any restrictions upon the mode of using the leased premises which they may agree upon, provided such restrictions are not contrary to law or public policy.[18] "It is a well established rule," said Norton, J.,[19] "that a lessor may by covenants in the lease restrict the use of the demised premises as he please. 'The owner of land selling or leasing it, may insist on just such conditions as he pleases touching the use and mode of enjoyment of land. He has a right to define the injury for himself, and a party contracting with him must abide the definition.' "[20]

---

18. Lyon v Bethlehem Engineering Corp. (1930) 253 NY 111, 170 NE 512; Bovin v Galitzka (1929) 250 NY 228, 165 NE 273; Presby v Benjamin (1902) 169 NY 377, 62 NE 430; 30-88 Steinway Street, Inc. v H. C. Bohack Co. (Civ Ct Queens Co 1971) 65 Misc 2d 1076, 319 NYS2d 679, reinstated (2d Dept) 42 AD2d 577, 344 NYS2d 205, app dismd 33 NY2d 692, 349 NYS2d 672, 304 NE2d 369.

19. Schmidt v Louis, Inc. (S Ct Erie Co 1924) 122 Misc 249, 203 NYS 515.

20. Also, see Lyon v Bethlehem Engineering Corp. (1930) 253 NY 111, 170 NE 512; Bovin v Galitzka (1929) 250 NY 228, 165 NE 273; Presby v Benjamin (1902) 169 NY 377, 62 NE 430.

Shopping center leases often provide that "during the term of the lease, tenant shall not directly or indirectly engage in any similar or competing business within a radius of 3 miles from the outside boundary of the shopping center." See Cale-Glens Falls Inc v Mack Drug Co. (S Ct NY Co) NY Law Journal Nov 14, 1975, p. 6, col 1, Helman, J.

**Annotation:** Shopping center lease restrictions on type of business conducted by tenant, 1 ALR4th 942.

## TENANT'S RIGHTS § 15:38

Where the use and occupation of lease premises are restricted by express provision to the purpose therein specified, any material departure from the specified use constitutes a violation of the express terms of the lease.[1]

### § 15:35. Binding on Tenant's Assignee

The burden of restrictions on the use of leased premises by a tenant runs with the land, and is binding on the tenant's assignee.[2]

### § 15:36. Binding on Subtenants

It is well established that there is neither privity of contract nor privity of estate between a subtenant and the paramount landlord.[3] Therefore, a subtenant is not personally liable to the paramount landlord for the breach of any restrictive covenants contained in the paramount lease.

However, a subtenant is bound in his occupancy of the leased premises by the covenants contained in the paramount lease; for, the sublease is carved out of, and dependent for its existence on, the paramount lease. A subtenant cannot have any greater rights as to the use of the leased premises than his own landlord, the paramount tenant, can have.[4] Therefore, a restriction on the use of the leased premises is binding on a subtenant. To what extent the paramount landlord may enforce such restriction as against a subtenant will be discussed under remedies.[5]

### § 15:37. Enforceable by Landlord's Grantee

The benefit of restrictions on the use of leased premises runs with the land, and therefore, inures to the benefit of, and may be enforced by, the landlord's grantee.[6]

### § 15:38. Rule of Construction

The general rule for construing restrictive covenants in

1. Lyon v Bethlehem Engineering Corp. (1930) 253 NY 111, 170 NE 512; Schmidt v Louis, Inc. (S Ct Erie Co 1924) 122 Misc 249, 203 NYS 515. Also, see discussion of what constitutes an objectionable tenant in §§ 30:59, et seq, infra.

2. Lyon v Bethlehem Engineering Corp. (1930) 253 NY 111, 170 NE 512; Round Lake Ass'n v Kellogg (1894) 141 NY 348, 36 NE 326.

3. See §§ 9:58, et seq, supra.

4. Bartholdi Realty Co. v Robard Realty Co. (AD1 1913) 156 AD 528, 141 NYS 353. See §§ 9:58, et seq, supra.

5. See § 15:58, infra.

6. F. F. Proctor Troy Properties Co. v Dugan Store, Inc. (AD3 1920) 191 AD 685, 181 NYS 786.

a lease is to so construe them as to carry out the intent of the parties, and this is to be ascertained from an examination of the entire lease, and not from the particular clause alone.[7] However, it is well established that such covenants, being restrictive, are not favored by the courts, and will not be extended by implication beyond the terms of the restriction,[8] since parties who wish to impose restrictions on the use of property can readily and expressly do so by apt words.[9] As has so often been said by the courts, the intention to restrict should not be one of inference, but should be unmistakably expressed in the lease.[10] Accordingly, restrictive covenants, as a general rule, are to be construed strictly against those who formulate and impose them, and the one who seeks to enforce them carries the burden of demonstrating that his version of the restriction is sustained by a plain and natural interpretation of its language.[11] It is not necessary for a tenant to show any particular provision to justify his unlimited right to the use and occupation of the leased premises; the landlord who denies it will be required to point out the covenant which expressly restricts the tenant's rights.[12]

## § 15:39. Specification of Purpose as Description or Limitation of Use of Premises; Forms

Since a landlord has the legal right to control the uses to which his property may be put, and may do so by appropriate provisions in a lease, he may by express provisions limit and restrain the use of a building to specific purposes.[13] In such case, however, the question

---

7. Bovin v Galitzka (1929) 250 NY 228, 232, 165 NE 273; 30-88 Steinway Street, Inc. v H. C. Bohack Co. (Civ Ct Queens Co 1971) 65 Misc 2d 1076, 319 NYS2d 679, reinstated (2d Dept) 42 AD2d 577, 344 NYS2d 205, app dismd 33 NY2d 692, 349 NYS2d 672, 304 NE2d 369.

**Annotation:** Shopping center lease restrictions on type of business conducted by tenant. 1 ALR4th 942.

8. King Drug Stores, Inc. v Ramsgate Realty Co. (S Ct NY Co 1933) 152 Misc 41, 273 NYS 71, affd 241 AD 806, 270 NYS 936.

9. Bovin v Galitzka (1927) 131 Misc 479, 226 NYS 361, revd 223 AD 737, 227 NYS 775, revd 250 NY 228, 165 NE 273.

10. Bristol Hotel Co. v Pegram (AT 1906) 49 Misc 535, 98 NYS 512.

11. Baumert v Malken (1923) 235 NY 115, 120, 139 NE 210; Card Appeal, Inc. v Deli-Bake, Inc. (S Ct Rockland Co 1986) 131 Misc 2d 724, 501 NYS2d 560 (quoting text).

12. Lyon v Bethlehem Engineering Corp. (1930) 253 NY 111, 113, 170 NE 512; Thousand Island Park Ass'n v Tucker (1903) 173 NY 203, 212, 65 NE 975; Presby v Benjamin (1902) 169 NY 377, 379, 62 NE 430.

13. Lyon v Bethlehem Engineering Corp. (1930) 253 NY 111, 170 NE 512.

## TENANT'S RIGHTS § 15:39

arises as to whether the specification in the lease as to use is merely descriptive of the use the tenant intends to make of the premises, or is actually a restriction upon the use the tenant may make of the premises.

The rule is, that unless the language of a lease clearly shows that no other use than that specified is intended, the statement in a lease as to use will be construed merely as descriptive of the use intended to be made of the premises by the tenant, and not as a limitation to the purpose therein stated.[14] This rule may be illustrated by the following case. A lease to a corner store and part of the cellar underneath provided that the premises were "to be used and occupied—real estate office." The tenant was given the right to sublet without the landlord's consent. The tenant sublet the premises, and the subtenant used the premises for a grocery and dairy store. The landlord thereupon brought an action to enjoin the tenant and subtenant from using the premises for any business other than a real estate office, and to have the sublease declared void. In denying the landlord the relief requested, the Court of Appeals said,[15] "It is not charged that the defendants have used the premises in an improper or untenantlike manner, or put them to a use different from that for which they had usually been used, or for which they were adapted and constructed. In view of the description of the premises contained in the lease—'the corner store and part of the cellar'—it could hardly be urged that their use as grocery and dairy store constituted a violation of any implied obligation on the part of the tenant and his sublessees. There is no express covenant in the lease restraining the defendants from using the premises for a store. It is urged, however, by the landlord that the words in the lease 'to be used and occupied as a real estate office' have the effect of a restrictive covenant, and prevent the use of the premises by the tenant and his sublessees for any other purpose. . . . When the lease is examined as a whole, it seems reasonably clear that the words in question were used to express the intended purpose of the lessee in

---

14. Bovin v Galitzka (1929) 250 NY 228, 165 NE 273; 57th Street Luce Corp. v General Motors Corp. (S Ct NY Co 1944) 182 Misc 164, 46 NYS2d 730, affd 267 AD 978, 48 NYS2d 557, affd 293 NY 717, 56 NE2d 732.

15. Bovin v Galitzka (1929) 250 NY 228, 231, 165 NE 273.

regard to the use of the premises, and not as a restriction upon the use of the premises to the one purpose stated."

In a recent case,[16] the lease provided that the leased premises were "to be used for an automobile showroom, and/or service station, and/or warehouse, and/or garage, and/or general automobile, tractor, implement, airplane, and/or truck business, and/or accessories thereto, and/or any line of business allied to or connected with any of the above, or any type of business conducted or controlled by General Motors Corporation, for which said premises may be now or hereafter at the time of such occupancy lawfully occupied." The tenant sublet one floor in the building to be occupied only for manufacturing and printing of folding paper cartons, and necessary office purposes. The court held that the tenant did not violate the provisions of his lease by so subletting the premises. The provision in the lease as to the use to be made thereof was not a limitation thereon, but merely descriptive of the uses to which the tenant contemplated putting the building. Therefore, it was held, the tenant could use the building for any lawful purpose. As Eder, J., said, in so holding, "The building here in concern is a business structure and there is no claim or proof that its value has in any manner been impaired by the nature of the business of the sublessee, or in any way damaged, or that there is any likelihood thereof, and, as said in the Lyon case, supra[17] in the absence of restrictions contained in a lease a tenant may utilize the demised premises in any lawful manner, not materially different from that to which it is adapted, and for which it was constructed."

In other words, as Greenbaum, J., said,[18] "under the familiar rules of construction applicable to the restrictive covenants, the intention so to restrict should not be one of inference, but unmistakably expressed in the contract of leasing." Unless, therefore, a landlord expressly shows that no other use than that specified is intended, the statement of purpose will be construed as merely descrip-

---

**16.** 57th Street Luce Corp. v General Motors Corp. (S Ct NY Co 1944) 182 Misc 164, 46 NYS2d 730, affd 267 AD 978, 48 NYS2d 557, affd 293 NY 717, 56 NE2d 732.

**17.** Lyon v Bethlehem Engineering Corp. (1930) 253 NY 111, 170 NE 512.

**18.** Bristol Hotel Co. v Pegram (AT1 1906) 49 Misc 535, 98 NYS 512.

tive of the intended use to be made of the leased premises by the tenant.

On the other hand, if the language of a lease clearly shows that no other use than that specified is intended, then the tenant will be precluded from using the premises for any other purpose than that specified. Such a limitation on the use of the premises is deemed equivalent to an express covenant not to put the premises to any other use, and will preclude the use of the premises for any other purpose than that specified.[19] To effectively restrict a tenant in the use of the leased premises, the landlord must expressly and clearly state the intention that no other use than the one specified is intended. Where a lease provides that the building is "to be used for the following purposes, and those only," and then specifies what those purposes are, the courts have held that this language constitutes an enforceable restriction on the use of the premises by the tenant, and limits him to the purposes specified.[20]

A limitation on the use of the leased premises for a specified purpose and "for no other purpose" is a restrictive covenant which is not converted to a description of use by an agreement of landlord to be reasonable in consenting to a variance.[1]

However, it is not essential to use the word "only," and no other word or expression. So long as the language clearly shows that no other use than that specified is intended, the intent of the parties will be carried out.[2] Nevertheless, the draftsman of a lease will find that it is preferable to use the word "only", or the phrase "not for any other purpose." An examination of the cases indicate that the use of such word or phrase has proved to be the best, and avoids the difficulties of a construction of the language used.

Thus, a lease which provides that the leased premises are to be used for a cabaret and "for no other purpose,"

**19.** Doherty v Monroe Eckstein Brewing Co. (AD1 1921) 198 AD 708, 191 NYS 59.

**20.** Lyon v Bethlehem Engineering Corp. (1930) 253 NY 111, 170 NE 512; 18th Ave. Pharmacy, Inc. v Wilmant Realty Corp. (S Ct Kings Co 1950) 95 NYS2d 534.

**1.** Rubinstein Bros. v Ole of 34th Street, Inc. (NYC Civ Ct NY Co 1979) 101 Misc 2d 563, 421 NYS2d 534 (citing text).

**2.** Kaiser v Zeigler (AT2 1921) 115 Misc 281, 187 NYS 638.

**§ 15:39**  LANDLORD AND TENANT

will restrict the use of the premises to this single purpose, and no other.[3] Similarly, it was held that a lease which provided that it was "expressly agreed that the only business to be carried on in said premises is the saloon business," restricted the tenant's use of the premises to that business, and to no other.[4]

A "Burger King" restaurant may not be conducted where lease limits use of the premises for a service restaurant, Automat restaurant, cafeteria, counter and stool restaurant, or a retail shop for the sale of baked goods and other items usually sold in Horn & Hardart retail stores, there being a difference between cafeterias and shortorder, limited menu food service primarily for off-premises consumption.[5]

In drafting a limitation of use covenant, it is important to note that the use of a general term, e.g., "foodmarket," "private dwelling place," may raise questions as to whether the tenant's activities are those usually connected with, or incidental to, the expressed limited use, or whether the tenant is carrying on an entirely different business by such activities. Thus, where a lease provided that premises were to be used only for a foodmarket, it was held that the tenant would be permitted to sell certain hardware and allied houseware items customarily sold at supermarkets, because the court found such had been the intention of the parties, deduced from the facts that such items are customarily sold in present day food markets, that the landlord was aware of the sale of such items by tenant and did not demur, and that in modifying the lease the tenant was referred to in the modification agreement as "supermarket."[6]

Provision restricting use of premises as a supermarket is violated by a retail store whose sales volume consists

**3.** Economy v S. B. & L. Bldg. Corp. (AT1 1930) 138 Misc 296, 245 NYS 352.
**4.** Doherty v Monroe Eckstein Brewing Co. (AD1 1921) 198 AD 708, 191 NYS 59.
See, 18th Ave. Pharmacy, Inc. v Wilmant Realty Corp. (S Ct Kings Co 1950) 95 NYS2d 534, "to be used and occupied only for drug store and luncheonette" precludes tenant's selling diamonds, platinum, and gold mountings, and tenant's repairing of watches and jewelry.
**5.** Horn & Hardart Co. v Junior Bldg., Inc. (1976) 40 NY2d 927, 389 NYS2d 831, 358 NE2d 514.
**6.** Rosen v Pustilnik (S Ct Queens Co 1960) 204 NYS2d 221.

overwhelmingly of men's and boys' shirts, pants, socks and shoes.[7]

Tenant's sale of "grocery items" which amounts to less than 10 percent and closer to 5 percent of the tenant's gross sales constituted a material breach of a restrictive covenant for use of the premises as a "butcher store."[8]

The sale and rental of video cassettes is prohibited by a provision restricting the use of the leased premises solely to the sale of comic books, toys, posters, books.[9]

Under a covenant to use the leased premises only for the parking of automobiles of the general public "and any lawful purpose incidental to such use," the operation of a car wash is not a purpose incidental to the use as a parking lot.[10]

The sale and rental of video tapes, not being incidental to the use of the premises as a gasoline station, is prohibited by a provision permitting the premises to be used solely as a gasoline station.[11]

Where a residential lease provided that the tenant shall not use or occupy the apartment for any purpose other than as and for a private dwelling place, and landlord "hereby advises tenant that the character of the occupancy of the apartment and the use thereof, as in this case restricted, is a special consideration and inducement for the making of the lease by the landlord," the use by the tenant of the apartment as a counseling office where she conducted her entire professional psychotherapy practice, constituted a violation of a substantial obligation of the lease.[12]

A tenant in an apartment house who agrees to a lease limiting his occupancy to that of a private dwelling apartment may not use his apartment for his profession

---

7. 30—88 Steinway Street, Inc. v H. C. Bohack Co. (1973, 2d Dept) 42 AD2d 577, 344 NYS2d 205, app dismd 33 NY2d 692, 349 NYS2d 672, 304 NE2d 369.

8. Burber v Jilamb Prime Meat, Inc. (NYC Civ Ct 1982) 115 Misc 2d 976, 455 NYS2d 44.

9. Qwakazi, Ltd. v 107 West 86th Street Owners Corp. (1986, 1st Dept) 123 AD2d 253, 506 NYS2d 162.

10. Texaco, Inc. v Greenwich-Kinney, Inc. (S Ct NY Co 1971) 68 Misc 2d 817, 328 NYS2d 180, affd in part and mod in part on other grounds (1st Dept) 39 AD2d 877, 333 NYS2d 544, affd 32 NY2d 910, 347 NYS2d 67, 300 NE2d 435.

11. Rodking Service Station, Inc. v Gribin (1985, 2d Dept) 109 AD2d 873, 486 NYS2d 786.

12. Park West Village v Lewis (1984) 62 NY2d 431, 477 NYS2d 124, 465 NE2d 844, 46 ALR4th 489.

§ 15:39 LANDLORD AND TENANT

or business. But, a casual and intermittent connection with some patient in his apartment does not constitute using the apartment for his profession.[13]

Sale of lottery tickets is consistent with the use of the premises as a "card, gift, and stationery store," since this use is a customary and usual activity for stores of the same character in the same commercial setting.[14] A lease provision restricting the premises to be "used" only for a convenience food market is not violated by the tenant's sale of lottery tickets.[15]

## FORM NO. 35

### Restrictions on Tenant's Use of the Premises

The parties hereto, for themselves, their heirs, distributees, executors, administrators, legal representatives, successor and assigns, hereby covenant as follows:

Tenant during the term of this lease and any renewal or extension thereof will use and occupy the leased premises only for ........, and for no other purpose.

## FORM NO. 36

### Provision for Frustrated Use of Premises by Tenant

It is agreed that the use of the leased premises intended by the Tenant, as hereinabove provided, is a major consideration for Tenant's entering into this lease. In the event that after the making of this lease, a permit for such use is denied, or if such use is prohibited by any legislation or by a competent authority *[add if desired:* or in the event substantial repairs, renovations, or alterations are required by such competent authority to be made by Tenant which would involve a cost exceeding $........,] Tenant shall have the option to terminate this lease by written notice, as herein provided for the giving of notices, of at least ........ days *[add if desired:* provided however, that if Landlord undertakes to make such substantial repairs, renovations or alterations at Land-

---

**13.** Galloway v Ortega (City Ct Yonkers 1969) 61 Misc 2d 539, 305 NYS2d 546.

**14.** Card Appeal, Inc. v Deli-Bake, Inc. (S Ct Rockland Co 1986) 131 Misc 2d 724, 501 NYS2d 560.

**15.** Sky Four Realty Co. v C.F.M. Enterprises, Inc. (1987, 3d Dept) 128 AD2d 1011, 513 NYS2d 546.

lord's own cost and expense, Tenant shall not have such option to terminate this lease].

### § 15:40. No Implied Covenant or Warranty that Premises Fit for Restricted Use

When a lease contains a restriction on the use of the premises by the tenant, such restriction is neither an express or implied covenant or warranty that the leased premises are fit for the specified or restricted use.[16] It must be remembered that a restriction on the use of the leased premises is a restriction on the tenant, but imposes no obligation on the landlord. As Earl, J., said[17] "There is an implied warranty upon an executory sale of merchandise that the property is in a merchantable condition, and upon the sale of a chattel by the manufacturer thereof, that the chattel is fit and suitable for the purpose for which it was intended and is purchased, and upon the sale of provisions for consumption, that they are wholesome and proper for use as food; but upon the demise of real estate, there are no such implied warranties. It is a universal rule, to which no exception can be found in any case now regarded as authority, that upon the demise of real estate there is no implied warranty that the property is fit for occupation, or suitable for the use or purpose for which it is hired.[18] Thus, where a lease recited that the premises were to be used and occupied for a printing business, such provision, it was held, would not be construed as implying a warranty that the premises had a floor load capacity suitable for the establishment therein of twelve printing presses.[19]

### § 15:41. Includability of Covenant of No Legal Impediments

A distinction must be made between physical defects, and legal impediments which may prevent the specified use of leased premises. When a landlord restricts the use of leased premises to a specified purpose he impliedly covenants that there is no legal impediment in his title to

16. 140 West Thirty-Fourth Street Corp. v Davis (AT1 1936) 158 Misc 470, 285 NYS 957; Lyons v Gavin (AT1 1904) 43 Misc 659, 88 NYS 252.

17. Edwards v New York & H. R. Co. (1885) 98 NY 245, 247.

18. Also, see Franklin v Brown (1889) 118 NY 110, 115, 23 NE 126.

19. Mulligan v Fioravera (AD1 1930) 228 AD 270, 239 NYS 438, affd 255 NY 539, 175 NE 304.

§ 15:41    LANDLORD AND TENANT

prevent such use.[20] A landlord rented premises to be used only for a saloon. It was subsequently discovered that the premises could not be used for a saloon because the landlord's title to the fee was encumbered by a restrictive covenant prohibiting the sale of any beer, ale, malt or intoxicating liquors of any kind on that parcel of land. The tenant was held entitled to recover the damages suffered because the landlord in limiting the use to the specified purpose covenanted, in effect, that there was no legal defect in his own title which would prevent such use.[1]

### § 15:42. Display of Signs

The right of a tenant to display signs where the lease contains no restrictions on such a right has been discussed in preceding sections.[2] However, a landlord may restrict the right of a tenant to display signs, and such a restriction is enforceable.[3] Thus, where a lease contained a covenant that the tenant would "neither place, nor cause or allow to be placed, any sign or signs of any kind whatsoever, at, in or about the entrance to said store, except in or at such place or places as may be indicated by the said landlords and consented to them in writing," it was held that displaying without consent an auctioneer's flag from the premises was a violation of such restriction, and an injunction restraining such display was granted.[4]

### § 15:43. —Where Entire Building Leased

Where the use and occupation of a building are restricted by express provision to the purposes therein

20. Fenning v Laskas (AD2 1920) 191 AD 374, 181 NYS 567.

1. Fenning v Laskas (AD2 1920) 191 AD 374, 181 NYS 567. However, it should be noted that in the opinion of the court, per Rich, J., appears this statement: "The appellant's (landlord's) agreement amounted to an express covenant against such a defect in their title, and even if it had not, the covenant for quiet enjoyment would have been implied." Therefore, the principle discussed in the text may be based either on a covenant implied from the landlord's restricting covenant, or on the implied covenant of quiet enjoyment which is implied in every lease.

2. See §§ 15:26-15:29, supra.

3. Lyon v Bethlehem Engineering Corp. (1930) 253 NY 111, 170 NE 512; Bernstein v Bernstein (AD2 1925) 214 AD 790, 210 NYS 539, affd 243 NY 559, 154 NE 604; Bartholdi Realty Co. v Robard Realty Co. (AD1 1913) 156 AD 528, 141 NYS 353; Schmidt v Louis, Inc. (S Ct Erie Co 1924) 122 Misc 249, 203 NYS 515.

4. Weil v Abrahams (AD1 1900) 53 AD 313, 66 NYS 244.

specified, "Any material departure," said the Court of Appeals,[5] "in the use of the building from the purposes specified would constitute a violation of the express terms of the lease." Accordingly, even though the subject of signs may not be mentioned in a lease, yet the right to display signs may be restricted because of the restriction imposed on the use of the building.[6]

A landlord leased vacant land, and the tenant covenanted to erect a building thereon. It was agreed that the building would "be used for the following purposes, and those only: Restaurant, stores, store-rooms and offices in the first floor and basement; and for offices, showrooms, and salesrooms for the remaining upper floors, such use of all parts of said premises, however, to conform at all times to the provisions of all laws." The lease was assigned, and the assignee leased to Roxy Theatre Corporation the right to attach to the roof of the building and to maintain thereon an electric sign built of steel, forty feet in height and sixty feet long. The landlord deemed the erection of such a structure on the roof to be a violation of the terms of the lease, and sought an injunction to restrain the erection and maintenance of such a structure. In upholding the landlord's contention the Court of Appeals in an opinion by Hubbs, J., said[7] "In the case at bar, the use and occupation of the building is restricted by express provision of the lease to the purposes therein specified. Any material departure in the use of the building from the purposes specified would constitute a violation of the express terms of the lease. The construction of the sign on the roof of the building advertising a theatre was in violation of the terms of the lease. If that sign could be lawfully constructed by the tenant, a sign advertising any other lawful business could be erected, no matter how distasteful it might be to the landlord, or how much it might cheapen and detract from the appearance of the building. . . . It would be strange indeed, if the landlord, who, by express terms, has limited the tenant's rights as to the use and occupancy of the building in question, should be held to be powerless to prevent its use

5. Lyon v Bethlehem Engineering Corp. (1930) 253 NY 111, 170 NE 512.
6. Lyon v Bethlehem Engineering Corp. (1930) 253 NY 111, 170 NE 512; Schmidt v Louis, Inc. (S Ct Erie Co 1924) 122 Misc 249, 203 NYS 515.
7. Lyon v Bethlehem Engineering Corp. (1930) 253 NY 111, 170 NE 512.

§ 15:43  LANDLORD AND TENANT

for the purpose to which the defendants have attempted to put it."

In other words, where the use to which a building may be put is expressly restricted, the use of the roof or the side walls for the display of general advertising, not relating to any business which may be conducted on the premises, is a violation of the lease, even though the lease may be silent on the subject of signs or advertising displays.[8]

## § 15:44. Restriction by Rules and Regulations of Landlord

A landlord, to maintain a certain standard for his property, may wish to establish appropriate rules and regulations for the use of the property by the tenant, and the tenant's invitees. If such rules and regulations are expressly set forth in the lease, and if the tenant covenants to abide by them, then the landlord can enforce compliance with them by the tenant as well as by the tenant's invitees.[9] As has been pointed out by the Court of Appeals,[10] when a landlord leases his property he has the right to subject the leases to such conditions, and the tenants to such covenants as he sees fit to impose.

## § 15:45. —Form of Clause

### FORM NO. 37

### Covenant to Abide by Rules and Regulations Then in Force or Thereafter Established*

Tenant and Tenant's *(in an apartment lease add:* family) servants, employees, agents, visitors, licensees, and invitees, shall observe faithfully and comply strictly with the rules and regulations annexed to this lease, and made a part hereof, and with such other and further reasonable rules and regulations as Landlord may from time to time

---

8. Schmidt v Louis, Inc. (S Ct Erie Co 1924) 122 Misc 249, 203 NYS 515.

9. Luna Park Housing Corp. v Besser (1972, 2d Dept) 38 AD2d 713, 329 NYS2d 332; Brendlin v Beers (AD1 1911) 144 AD 403, 129 NYS 222. Also, see, Federal Waste Paper Corp. v Garment Center Capitol, Inc. (AD1 1944) 268 AD 230, 51 NYS2d 26, affd 294 NY 714, 61 NE2d 451, wherein it was held that, absent regulations contained in the lease, a tenant's invitees have the same right as the tenant to make use of the tenant's usual means of ingress and egress.

10. Thousand Island Park Ass'n v Tucker (1903) 173 NY 203, 212, 65 NE 975.

* For complete form of lease see Chapter 1.

adopt. It is mutually agreed that Landlord shall not be liable to Tenant for the violation of any of said rules or regulations by any other tenant in the building.

## FORM NO. 38
### Another Form of Covenant to Abide by Rules and Regulations Then in Force or Thereafter Established

Tenant and Tenant's servants, employees, agents, visitors and licensees shall observe faithfully, and comply strictly with, the Rules and Regulations and such other and further reasonable Rules and Regulations as Landlord or Landlord's agents may from time to time adopt. Notice of any additional rules or regulations shall be given in such manner as Landlord may elect. In case Tenant disputes the reasonableness of any additional Rule or Regulation hereafter made or adopted by Landlord or Landlord's agents, the parties hereto agree to submit the question of the reasonableness of such Rule or Regulation for decision to the New York office of the American Arbitration Association whose determination shall be final and conclusive upon the parties hereto. The right to dispute the reasonableness of any additional Rule or Regulation upon Tenant's part shall be deemed waived unless the same shall be asserted by service of a notice, in writing upon Landlord within ten (10) days after the giving of notice thereof. Nothing in this lease contained shall be construed to impose upon Landlord any duty or obligation to enforce the Rules and Regulations or terms, covenants or conditions in any other lease, as against any other tenant and Landlord shall not be liable to Tenant for violation of the same by any other tenant, its servants, employees, agents, visitors or licensees.

### § 15:46. —Rules and Regulations Must Be Reasonable

It will be observed that the covenant set forth in the preceding section provides that the tenant will keep and perform subsequently imposed "reasonable" rules. This is in accordance with the well settled rule that rules and regulations, imposed during the term pursuant to the reserved right so to do, to be valid and enforceable must be reasonable, and have some direct relationship to the

§ 15:46 LANDLORD AND TENANT

use of the property by the tenants thereof.[11] The following illustrations taken from cases on the subject may be helpful in determining what the courts may hold to be reasonable or unreasonable.

A resolution adopted by a co-operative apartment building providing in substance that the community room in the building could be used until 11:30 P.M. from Monday through Thursday, on Friday and Saturday nights until 2 A.M. the following morning, music to end at 1 A.M. the following morning, was held to be reasonable.[12] However, regulations by a co-operative housing corporation prohibiting the playing of musical instruments in excess of an hour and a half per day by one person, and the playing of musical instruments after 8:00 P.M., have been held to be arbitrary and unreasonable.[13]

A regulation requiring that all goods be delivered, and that all bills be collected, through the dumbwaiter in the basement of the building, was held to be a reasonable rule, and one which the landlord could impose. It was, therefore, binding on the tenant as well as on third persons wishing to enter the building.[14]

A summer bungalow colony operator reserved the right in his leases to impose rules and regulations "not inconsistent with the terms of this lease, and which in (his) judgment, is for the best interests of all, and which, in (his) opinion, will best carry out the spirit of this lease and preserve its right." The landlord then passed a rule which required all incoming cars to be parked in designated areas, for which a charge was to be made. The only road available for automobile use in the colony was a 12-foot wide cinder road running through the colony. Access

---

11. Thousand Island Park Ass'n v Tucker (1903) 173 NY 203, 212-213, 65 NE 975.

If a rule bears a relationship to the legitimate purpose of the cooperative or condominium, the Board's discretion in promulgating the rule will not be deemed arbitrary and capricious, and will be upheld. Lenox Manor, Inc. v Gianni (NYC Civ Ct 1983) 120 Misc 2d 202, 465 NYS2d 809.

12. Baum v Ryerson Towers (S Ct Kings Co 1968) 55 Misc 2d 1045, 287 NYS2d 791.

Rule prohibiting any person to remain in tenant's apartment overnight without the presence of tenant is invalid as unreasonably restricting the use and occupation of the apartment for dwelling purposes. La Coquille of Westhampton Beach, Inc. v Robinson (1975, 1st Dept) 48 AD2d 633, 368 NYS2d 195.

13. Justice Court Mut. Housing Co-operative, Inc. v Sandow (S Ct Queens Co 1966) 50 Misc 2d 541, 270 NYS2d 829.

14. Brendlin v Beers (AD1 1911) 144 AD 403, 129 NYS 222.

## TENANT'S RIGHTS § 15:46

to the bungalows was afforded by miles of cement walk intended for and adapted to the use of pedestrians only. One tenant contended that the rule imposed was unreasonable in that he, as well as his invitees and tradesmen were denied access to his demised premises. After pointing out that the tenant was not deprived of access on foot, May, J., said,[15] "From the proof adduced herein, I do not find that the regulations adopted by the defendant with reference to the use of its parking spaces, and incidentally its cinder roads, and the charge therefor, was an unreasonable modification of the lease. Concededly, parking in the twelve-foot wide roadway was impracticable. The cinder-surfaced roads are pathways clearly designed only to meet the necessities of the colony. They were evidently never intended as highways in the ordinary sense. The testimony showed that during the season the population of the colony was from 9,000 to 12,000 persons, exclusive of visitors, of which number about 4,000 were children. The reasons advanced by the defendant for the regulations, to wit, increasing congestion of traffic, the danger to children therefrom, and the heavy wear and tear on the road, and the necessity of keeping the roads open and unobstructed for the use of fire apparatus, ambulances, and the like emergency and service use, are reasonable arguments which cannot fairly be refuted, although plaintiffs contend that such reasons are a mere subterfuge."[16]

A regulation, passed by a religious corporation organized for camp meeting purposes, prohibiting the use of any demised premises for the sale of merchandise without a license was held to be reasonable in view of the purposes of the landlord corporation. As the Court of Appeals said, in so deciding,[17] "As the principal and primary use

---

**15.** Dougherty v Rockaway Operating Co. (S Ct Queens Co 1937) 163 Misc 806, 298 NYS 242.

**16.** The court added this pertinent thought: "It is undoubtedly true that if plaintiff had a vested right to use the road without charge, such right might not be taken from him under the guise of an addition to or modification of the rules. It may be that such charge as exacted from the individual plaintiff and his invitees other than the corporate plaintiff and similar tradesmen would be in violation of a vested right inasmuch as no such charge was made or agreed to when the lease was entered upon. The difficulty with the individual plaintiff's position in this respect is that he seeks no specific relief on this score . . . ."

**17.** Round Lake Ass'n v Kellogg (1894) 141 NY 348, 36 NE 326.

of the grounds of the association was for religious purposes, it is manifest that the plaintiff must necessarily maintain the strictest supervision of its property. The regulation of the vending of goods in a store or from house to house falls within the limits of this reasonable power."

A landlord of a colony of cottages, pursuant to the reservation in his leases of a general and unrestricted right to impose regulations from time to time, had established a rule which in effect prevented any of his tenants from obtaining their supplies by purchase from others than the landlord, or from those to whom the landlord granted the exclusive privilege of dealing in such supplies. In refusing to enforce such rule, the court said,[18] "In the leases granted by the plaintiff, certain regulations adopted by it were expressly recited. None of these restricted the right of the tenant to purchase stores and merchandise for consumption in the park where and from whom he pleased. The lease contained the further condition that the tenant should keep and perform all such conditions or rules and regulations as the landlord should from time to time impose. Thus there was reserved to the landlord the power to subsequently make new regulations. Such power, however, though general in form, is not absolute or unqualified. A new regulation established under this reservation, to be valid, must be reasonable." And, the court held, this regulation was arbitrary and unreasonable in that it did not regulate the use of the land, but rather attempted to regulate the tenant's mode of living.

In this connection it may be observed that the statute provides that a contract, agreement or arrangement entered into or executed by and between the owner or prospective owner of an apartment house, tenement, or what is commonly known as a bungalow colony, and a dealer in or seller of fuel, ice or food, for the purpose of giving to such dealer or seller the privilege of selling or delivering fuel, ice, or food, to the occupants of the apartment house, tenement or bungalow colony is against public policy and void.[19]

18. Thousand Island Park Ass'n v Tucker (1903) 173 NY 203, 212-213, 65 NE 975.

19. Real Prop L § 238. This section is derived from former Penal L § 861, under which it was held that said

# TENANT'S RIGHTS § 15:47

### § 15:47. —Mobile Home Parks

Real Prop L § 233(f) provides:

1. A mobile home park owner or operator may promulgate rules and regulations governing the rental or occupancy of a mobile home lot provided such rules and regulations shall not be unreasonable, arbitrary or capricious. A copy of all rules and regulations shall be delivered by the mobile home park owner or operator to all mobile home tenants at the commencement of occupancy. A copy of the rules and regulations shall be posted in a conspicuous place upon the mobile home park grounds.

2. If a rule or regulation is not applied uniformly to all mobile home tenants of the mobile home park there shall be a rebuttal presumption that such rule or regulation is unreasonable, arbitrary and capricious, provided, however, that an inconsistency between a rule or regulation and a lease term contained in a lease signed before the date the rule or regulation is effective shall not raise a rebuttable presumption that such rule is unreasonable, arbitrary or capricious.

3. Any rule or regulation which does not conform to the requirements of this section or which has not been supplied or posted as required by paragraph one of this subdivision shall be unenforceable and may be raised by the mobile home tenant as an affirmative defense in any action to evict on the basis of a violation of such rule or regulation.

4. No rules or regulations may be changed by the mobile home park owner or operator without specifying the date of implementation of said changed rules and regulations, which date shall be no fewer than thirty days after written notice to all tenants.

Real Prop L § 233(g) provides:

1. No tenant shall be charged a fee for other than rent, utilities and charges for facilities and services available

section was inapplicable to a situation where lessee covenanted that he would purchase all his supplies from lessor, or from such shops or markets as lessor should establish or permit within the colony, so far as such supplies were sold by lessor or such shops or markets, though lessee and members of his family could bring supplies from outside the colony. Dougherty v Rockaway Operating Co. (1937) 163 Misc 806, 298 NYS 242.

to the tenant. All fees, charges or assessments must be reasonably related to services actually rendered.

2. A mobile home park owner or operator shall be required to fully disclose in writing all fees, charges, assessments, including rental fees, rules and regulations prior to a mobile home tenant assuming occupancy in the mobile home park.

3. No fees, charges, assessments or rental fees may be increased by mobile home park owner or operator without specifying the date of implementation of said fees, charges, assessments or rental fees which date shall be no less than ninety days after written notice to all mobile home tenants. Failure on the part of the mobile home park owner or operator to fully disclose all fees, charges or assessments shall prevent the mobile home park owner or operator from collecting said fees, charges or assessments, and refusal by the mobile home tenant to pay any undisclosed charges shall not be used by the mobile home park[20] owner or operator as a cause for eviction in any court of law.

Real Prop L § 233(h) provides:

No mobile home park owner shall:

1. Require a mobile home tenant therein to purchase from said mobile home park owner or operator skirting or equipment for tying down mobile homes, or any other equipment. However, the mobile home park owner or operator may determine by rule or regulation the style or quality of such equipment to be purchased by the mobile home tenant from the vendor of the mobile home tenant's choosing, providing such equipment is readily available.

2. Charge any mobile home tenant who chooses to install an electric or gas appliance in his mobile home an additional fee solely on the basis of such installation unless such installation is performed by the mobile home park owner or operator at the request of the mobile home tenant, nor shall the mobile home park owner or operator restrict the installation, service or maintenance of any such appliance, restrict the ingress or egress of repairers to enter the mobile home park for the purpose of installa-

---

20. Real Prop L § 233(g) subd 4 relates to the rights and liabilities as to moneys deposited as security. See § 13:28, supra.

tion, service or maintenance of any such appliance, or restrict the making of any interior improvement in such mobile home, so long as such an installation or improvement is in compliance with applicable building codes and other provisions of law and further provided that adequate utilities are available for such installation or improvement.

3. Require, by contract, rule, regulation or otherwise, a mobile home dweller to purchase from the mobile home park owner or any person acting directly or indirectly on behalf of the park owner, commodities or services incidental to placement or rental within such park; nor shall the park owner restrict access to the mobile home park to any person employed, retained or requested by the mobile home dweller to provide such commodity or service, unless the mobile home park owner establishes that such requirement or restriction is necessary to protect the property of such park owner from substantial harm or impairment.

Real Prop L § 233(i) provides:

1. No mobile home park owner or operator shall deny any mobile home tenant the right to sell his mobile home within the mobile home park provided the mobile home tenant shall give to the mobile home park owner or operator twenty days' written notice of his intention to sell, or require the mobile home owner or subsequent purchaser to remove the mobile home from the mobile home park solely on the basis of the sale thereof. The mobile home park owner or operator may reserve the right to approve the purchaser of said mobile home as a mobile home tenant for the remainder of the seller's term but such permission may not be unreasonably withheld. If the mobile home park owner or operator unreasonably withholds his permission, the mobile home tenant may recover the costs of the proceedings and attorneys' fees if it is found that the mobile home park owner or operator acted in bad faith by withholding permission.

2. The mobile home park owner or operator shall not exact a commission or fee with respect to the price realized by the seller unless the mobile home park owner or operator has acted as agent for the mobile home owner in the sale pursuant to a written contract.

3. If the ownership of management rejects a purchaser as a prospective tenant, the selling tenant must be informed in writing of the reasons therefor.

### § 15:48. Form of Rules and Regulations

#### FORM NO. 39
#### RULES AND REGULATIONS[1]
#### RULES AND REGULATIONS ATTACHED TO AND MADE A PART OF THIS LEASE IN ACCORDANCE WITH ARTICLE 36

1. The sidewalks, entrances, driveways, passages, courts, elevators, vestibules, stairways, corridors or halls shall not be obstructed or encumbered by any Tenant or used for any purpose other than for ingress to and egress from the leased premises and for delivery of merchandise and equipment in a prompt and efficient manner using elevators and passageways designated for such delivery by Landlord. There shall not be used in any space, or in the public hall of the building, either by any Tenant or by jobbers or others in the delivery or receipt of merchandise, any hand trucks, except those equipped with rubber tires and sideguards. If said premises are situate on the ground floor of the building Tenant thereof shall further, at Tenant's expense, keep the sidewalks and curb in front of said premises clean and free from ice, snow, dirt and rubbish.

2. The water and wash closets and plumbing fixtures shall not be used for any purposes other than those for which they were designed or constructed and no sweepings, rubbish, rags, acids or other substances shall be deposited therein, and the expense of any breakage, stoppage, or damage resulting from the violation of this rule shall be borne by the tenant who, or whose clerks, agents, employees or visitors, shall have caused it.

3. No carpet, rug or other article shall be hung or shaken out of any window of the building; and no Tenant shall sweep or throw or permit to be swept or thrown

---

1. These Rules and Regulations are part of the Standard Form of Loft Lease, prepared and copyrighted by The Real Estate Board of New York, Inc, and are reprinted with its permission. Reproduction in whole or in parts prohibited and all rights reserved by the Real Estate Board of New York, Inc.

from the leased premises any dirt or other substances into any of the corridors or halls, elevators, or out of the doors or windows or stairways of the building, and Tenant shall not use, keep or permit to be used or kept any foul or noxious gas or substance in the leased premises, or permit or suffer the leased premises to be occupied or used in a manner offensive or objectionable to Landlord or other occupants of the building by reason of noise, odors and/or vibrations, or interfere in any way with other Tenants or those having business therein, nor shall any animals or birds be kept in or about the building. Smoking or carrying lighted cigars or cigarettes in the elevators of the building is prohibited.

4. No awnings or other projections shall be attached to the outside walls of the building without the prior written consent of Landlord.

5. No sign, advertisement, notice or other lettering shall be exhibited, inscribed, painted or affixed by any Tenant on any part of the outside of the leased premises or the building or on the inside of the leased premises if the same is visible from the outside of the premises without the prior written consent of Landlord, except that the name of Tenant may appear on the entrance door of the premises. In the event of the violation of the foregoing by any Tenant, Landlord may remove same without any liability, and may charge the expense incurred by such removal to Tenant or Tenants violating this rule. Interior signs on doors and directory tablet shall be inscribed, painted or affixed for each Tenant by Landlord at the expense of such Tenant, and shall be of a size, color and style acceptable to Landlord.

6. No Tenant shall mark, paint, drill into, or in any way deface any part of the leased premises or the building of which they form a part. No boring, cutting or stringing of wires shall be permitted, except with the prior written consent of Landlord, and as Landlord may direct. No Tenant shall lay linoleum, or other similar floor covering, so that the same shall come in direct contact with the floor of the leased premises, and, if linoleum or other similar floor covering is desired to be used an interlining of builder's deadening felt shall be first affixed to the floor, by a paste or other material,

soluble in water, the use of cement or other similar adhesive material being expressly prohibited.

7. No additional locks or bolts of any kind shall be placed upon any of the doors or windows by any Tenant, nor shall any changes by made in existing locks or mechanism thereof. Each Tenant must, upon the termination of his Tenancy, restore to Landlord all keys of stores, offices and toilet rooms, either furnished to, or otherwise procured by, such Tenant, and in the event of the loss of any keys, so furnished, such Tenant shall pay to Landlord the cost thereof.

8. Freight, furniture, business equipment, merchandise and bulky matter of any description shall be delivered to and removed from the premises only on the freight elevators and through the service entrances and corridors, and only during hours and in a manner approved by Landlord. Landlord reserves the right to inspect all freight to be brought into the building and to exclude from the building all freight which violates any of these Rules and Regulations or the lease of which these Rules and Regulations are a part.

9. No Tenant shall obtain for use upon the leased premises ice, drinking water, towel and other similar services, or accept barbering or bootblacking services in the leased premises, except from persons authorized by Landlord, and at hours and under regulations fixed by Landlord. Canvassing, soliciting and peddling in the building is prohibited and each Tenant shall co-operate to prevent the same.

10. Landlord reserves the right to exclude from the building between the hours of 6 P.M. and 8 A.M. and at all hours on Sundays, and legal holidays all persons who do not present a pass to the building signed by Landlord. Landlord will furnish passes to persons for whom any Tenant requests same in writing. Each Tenant shall be responsible for all persons for whom he requests such pass and shall be liable to Landlord for all acts of such persons.

11. Landlord shall have the right to prohibit any advertising by any Tenant which, in Landlord's opinion, tends to impair the reputation of the building or its desirability as a building for offices, and upon written notice from

# TENANT'S RIGHTS § 15:50

Landlord, Tenant shall refrain from or discontinue such advertising.

12. Tenant shall not bring or permit to be brought or kept in or on the leased premises, any inflammable, combustible or explosive fluid, material, chemical or substance, or cause or permit any odors of cooking or other processes, or any unusual or other objectionable odors to permeate in or emanate from the leased premises.

13. Tenant shall not use the leased premises in a manner which disturbs or interferes with other Tenants in the beneficial use of their premises.

## § 15:49. Projections from Windows of Leased Apartment

Many leases provide that the tenant "shall not expose any sign, advertisement, illumination or projection in or out of the windows or exterior, or from the said building or upon it any place, except as shall be approved and permitted in writing by the landlord." Such a provision, it has been held, is violated by the erection and maintenance of a television aerial leading from the window of a leased apartment and along the wall to the roof of the building in which such apartment is located.[2] and by the maintenance of an air conditioning unit on window sill, which projects beyond the exterior wall of the building.[3]

## § 15:50. Racial Discriminatory Restrictions Under Statute

The General Obligations Law provides,[4]

"Any promise, covenant, or restriction in a contract, mortgage, lease, deed or conveyance or in any other agreement affecting real property, heretofore or hereafter made or entered into, which limits, restrains, prohibits or otherwise provides against the sale, grant, gift, transfer, assignment, conveyance, ownership, lease, rental, use or occupancy of real property to or by any person because of race, creed, color, national origin, or ancestry, is hereby

---

2. Joan Bldg. Corp. v Gould (AD2 1949) 276 AD 765, 92 NYS2d 925, affg (S Ct Queens Co) 93 NYS2d 870; Scroll Realty Corp. v Mandell (S Ct Kings Co 1949) 195 Misc 972, 92 NYS2d 813; Kaplan v Ladimer (AT2 1950) 197 Misc 270, 97 NYS2d 642.

3. Girard Holding Corp. v Hollander (S Ct Queens Co 1949) 195 Misc 878, 91 NYS2d 188.

4. Gen Obligations L § 5-331.

declared to be void as against public policy, wholly unenforceable, and shall not constitute a defense in any action, suit or proceeding. No such promise, covenant or restriction shall be listed as a valid provision affecting such property in public notices concerning such property. The invalidity of any such promise, covenant or restriction in any such instrument or agreement shall not affect the validity of any other provision therein, but no reverter shall occur, no possessory estate shall result, nor any right of entry or right to a penalty of forfeiture shall accrue by reason of the disregard of such promise, covenant or restriction. This section shall not apply to conveyances or devises to religious associations or corporations for religious purposes, but, such promise, covenant or restriction shall cease to be enforceable and shall otherwise become subject to the provisions of this section when the real property affected shall cease to be used for such purpose."[5]

## § 15:51. Statutory Restrictions Against Children in Dwellings

Real Property L § 236 entitled: "Discrimination against children in dwelling houses and mobile home parks," provides:

a. Any person, firm or corporation owning or having in charge any apartment house, or mobile home park, tenement house or other building used for dwelling purposes who shall refuse to rent any part of any such building or mobile home park to any person or family, or who discriminates in the terms, conditions, or privileges of any

---

[5]. Executive L § 296, subd 5(a), makes it unlawful to refuse to sell, rent, or lease a housing accommodation because of the race, creed, color, national origin, sex, age or disability or marital status of the tenant or purchaser, or to discriminate for the same reasons in the terms, conditions, or privileges of the sale, rental, or lease of any such housing accommodation, except in the rental of an owner-occupied one- or two-family home, or the rental of a room or rooms by the occupant of a housing accommodation, or where all the rooms in a housing accommodation are rented to individuals of the same sex, or the sale, rental or lease of housing accommodations exclusively to persons 55 years of age or older.

Executive L § 296, subd 5(b) makes it unlawful to refuse to sell, rent, or lease land or commercial space because of the age, race, creed, color, national origin, sex, or disability, or marital status of the purchaser or tenant. However, with respect to age, the foregoing provision shall not apply to the restriction of the sale, rental, or lease of land or commercial space exclusively to persons 55 years of age or older.

# TENANT'S RIGHTS § 15:53

such rental, solely on the ground that such person or family has or have a child or children shall be guilty of a misdemeanor and on conviction thereof shall be punished by a fine of not less than fifty nor more than one hundred dollars for each offense; provided, however, the prohibition against discrimination against children in dwelling houses and mobile home parks contained in this section shall not apply to: (1) housing units for senior citizens subsidized, insured, or guaranteed by the federal government; or (2) one or two family owner occupied dwelling houses or mobile homes; or (3) mobile home parks exclusively for persons fifty-five years of age or older.

b. Civil liability: (1) where discriminatory conduct prohibited by this section has occurred, an aggrieved individual shall have a cause of action in any court of appropriate jurisdiction for damages, declaratory and injunctive relief; (2) in all actions brought under this section, reasonable attorney's fees as determined by the court may be awarded to a prevailing plaintiff.

Real Property L § 237 provides, any person, firm or corporation owning or having in charge any apartment house, tenement house or other building or mobile home park used for dwelling purposes who shall, in any lease of any or part of any such building or mobile home park, have a clause therein providing that during the term thereof the tenants shall remain childless or shall not bear children, shall be guilty of a violation.

## H. WAIVER OF EXPRESS RESTRICTION

### § 15:52. Generally

A landlord may waive any right he may have to insist that the premises shall be used only for the purposes specified in the lease,[6] except in the case of an illegal use.[7]

### § 15:53. Parol Waiver

Even though a lease may provide for the landlord's written consent to any change in the restrictions on the

---

**6.** Adams-Flanigan Co. v Kling (AD1 1921) 198 AD 717, 191 NYS 32, affd 234 NY 497, 138 NE 421, cert den 260 US 741, 67 L Ed 491, 43 S Ct 98; Sol Apfel, Inc. v Kocher (S Ct NY Co 1946) 61 NYS2d 508, affd 272 AD 758, 70 NYS2d 138 and affd 272 AD 758, 70 NYS2d 139; Weisbrod v Dembosky (AT 1898) 25 Misc 485, 55 NYS 1.

**7.** But, see § 15:5, supra, as to waiver of an illegal use.

tenant's use of the leased premises, nevertheless, an oral waiver is good, and will be binding on the landlord.[8]

## § 15:54. By Acceptance of Rent with Knowledge of Breach

See § 23:16 as to effect of lease provision that acceptance of rent with knowledge of breach shall not constitute a waiver.

When a landlord knows that the tenant is violating the restrictions he has imposed on the use of the premises, and does not object thereto, and accepts rent from the tenant thereafter, the landlord will be held to have waived his right to enforce the restrictions he has imposed on the use of the leased premises.[9] Thus, the collection of rent for two years with knowledge that the tenant had installed, and was using a movable washing machine, was held to constitute a waiver of the right to terminate the lease, even though it contained a provision that the installation or use of a laundry machine should constitute a violation of a substantial obligation of the lease entitling the landlord to terminate.[10] Similarly, where a tenant had been using the apartment for piano instruction for eight years with landlord's knowledge, and without objection, it was held that the restrictive provision of the lease as to the use of the apartment was waived, and landlord would be thereafter estopped from contending that such occupancy and use violated the terms of the lease.[11] However, it has been held that a landlord's acceptance of rent during a period which the landlord has demanded that tenant cure a breach of the

---

8. Adams-Flanigan Co. v Kling (AD1 1921) 198 AD 717, 191 NYS 32, affd 234 NY 497, 138 NE 421, cert den 260 US 741, 67 L Ed 491, 43 S Ct 98; Sol Apfel, Inc. v Kocher (S Ct NY Co 1946) 61 NYS2d 508, affd 272 AD 758, 70 NYS2d 138 and affd 272 AD 758, 70 NYS2d 139; Weisbrod v Dembosky (AT 1898) 25 Misc 485, 55 NYS 1.

9. Radcliffe Associates, Inc. v Greenstein (AD1 1948) 274 AD 277, 82 NYS2d 680, reh and app den 274 AD 984, 85 NYS2d 302; Adams-Flanigan Co. v Kling (AD1 1921) 198 AD 717, 191 NYS 32, affd 234 NY 497, 138 NE 421, cert den 260 US 741, 67 L Ed 491, 43 S Ct 98; 215 West 34th Street, Inc. v Feldman (AT1 1951) 105 NYS2d 209 (open and notorious possession in breach of restriction for long periods of time, as well as rent collections with knowledge of breach, held, waiver).

10. Fanchild Investors, Inc. v Cohen (Civ Ct 1964) 43 Misc 2d 39, 250 NYS2d 446.

11. Vendramis v Frankfurt (S Ct NY Co 1949) 86 NYS2d 715, affd 276 AD 903, 94 NYS2d 903.

# TENANT'S RIGHTS § 15:56

lease, or during the period when a restraining order or injunction is in effect, does not result in a waiver.[12]

## § 15:55. Waiver Binding on Grantee

If a landlord waives any right he may have to insist that the premises shall be used only for the purposes specified in the lease, such waiver will be binding on the landlord's grantee, or assignee. A grantee takes the premises under the conditions as to tenancy that his predecessor-grantor established.[13] Accordingly, it has been held that a waiver by a landlord of a violation of a lease restriction against assignment or subletting is binding on the landlord's grantee.[14]

## I. INJUNCTION TO RESTRAIN IMPROPER USE OF PREMISES

### § 15:56. Against Tenant

It is well settled that a court of equity may, by injunction, prevent or restrain a tenant from using the leased premises for a purpose which violates the restrictive covenants of the lease.[15]

---

12. S. E. Nichols, Inc. v American Shopping Centers, Inc. (1985, 3d Dept) 115 AD2d 856, 495 NYS2d 810, later proceeding (App Div, 3d Dept) 515 NYS2d 638.

13. Radcliffe Associates, Inc. v Greenstein (AD1 1948) 274 AD 277, 82 NYS2d 680, reh and app den 274 AD 984, 85 NYS2d 302; Adams-Flanigan Co. v Kling (AD1 1921) 198 AD 717, 191 NYS 32, affd 234 NY 497, 138 NE 421, cert den 260 US 741, 67 L Ed 491, 43 S Ct 98; F. F. Proctor Troy Properties Co. v Dugan Store, Inc. (AD3 1920) 191 AD 685, 181 NYS 786; 215 West 34th Street, Inc. v Feldman (AT1 1951) 105 NYS2d 209; Ditmas Apartments v Coster (S Ct Kings Co 1949) 196 Misc 728, 94 NYS2d 634; Vendramis v Frankfurt (S Ct NY Co 1949) 86 NYS2d 715, affd 276 AD 903, 94 NYS2d 903.

14. Natanson v Gavaert Co. of America, Inc (M Ct 1949) 96 NYS2d 774 (subletting waived); 440 West 34th Street Corp. v Rosoff (M Ct 1948) 84 NYS2d 16 (subletting waived); Irbar Realty Corp. v Vallins (M Ct 1946) 64 NYS2d 843.

15. Lyon v Bethlehem Engineering Corp. (1930) 253 NY 111, 115, 170 NE 512; Bovin v Galitzka (1929) 250 NY 228, 165 NE 273. Also, see Bartholdi Realty Co. v Robard Realty Co. (AD1 1913) 156 AD 528, 141 NYS 353, enjoining signs; Weil v Abrahams (AD1 1900) 53 AD 313, 66 NYS 244, enjoining signs.

Maintenance of television aerial enjoined: Eldora Realty Corp. v Nicholson (AD1 1952) 280 AD 324, 113 NYS2d 429 (permission granted to tenant to install aerial held a revocable license and upon landlord's demand, tenant was obliged to remove aerial); Joan Bldg. Corp. v Gould (AD2 1949) 276 AD 765, 92 NYS2d 925; 5411 Realty Corp. v Morse (S Ct Kings Co 1951) 200 Misc 961, 109 NYS2d 758; Scroll Realty Corp. v Mandell (S Ct Kings Co 1949) 195 Misc 972, 92 NYS2d 813; West Holding Corp. v Cordero (S Ct Kings Co 1952) 114 NYS2d 668.

However, see Piankay Realties, Inc. v Romano (AD1 1946) 271 AD 104, 62 NYS2d 533, affd 296 NY 920, 73 NE2d 39, where the court held that

### § 15:57. Against Tenant's Assignee

Restrictions on the use of leased premises, contained in a lease, run with the land, and bind the tenant's assignees.[16] Therefore, it has been held, a court of equity may by injunction prevent or restrain a tenant's assignee from violating the restrictions on use contained in the lease.[17]

### § 15:58. Against Subtenant

True, there is no privity of estate or contract between a subtenant and the paramount landlord. Therefore, there is no liability of the subtenant to the paramount landlord for the breach by the sublessor of any of the covenants contained in the paramount lease.[18]

However, a sublease is dependent for its existence on the paramount lease. The subtenant can have no greater rights to the use of the premises than his sublessor has[19] Therefore, it has been held, that a restrictive covenant contained in the paramount lease on the use of the leased premises will be binding on the subtenant.[20] Although then, a subtenant is not liable for a breach of the sublessor's restrictive covenant; yet, it is well settled, a court of equity may, by injunction, prevent or restrain the tenant

---

the landlord would not be granted an injunction against the tenant's use of demised loft space for manufacturing picture and pocketbook frames and lucite objects, instead of custom made furniture as provided by the lease in view of the acute shortage of available commercial space, prejudice to the tenant for having to give up his only business, and absence of evidence that landlord was prejudiced by such added use. (See strong diss op which sought to apply rule stated in text.)

It should be observed, however, that if prior to the "freeze date" of the emergency rent statutes, to wit, March 1, 1950, permission had been given by the landlord to the erection of an antenna on the roof the use of the roof on the "freeze date" constituted a service furnished by the landlord to the tenant on that date which the landlord was obliged to continue until a contrary order of the rent administrator. 660 Locust St. Corp. v MacPherson (AD2 1952) 279 AD 927, 111 NYS2d 29.

But, see People ex rel. McGoldrick v Regency Park, Inc. (AD2 1952) 280 AD 804, 113 NYS2d 172, affd 305 NY 650, 112 NE2d 425, where tenant relied on oral consent of landlord, which court refused to consider because of the parol evidence rule and the expressly contrary provisions of the written lease, therefore the court held that the landlord was in this case under no obligation as of the freeze date to provide the space for the tenant.

As to right of landlord to evict a tenant for an illegal use of the leased premises, see Chapter 34, infra; as to right of eviction of objectionable tenant, and what constitutes "objectionable," see Chapter 30, infra.

16. See § 15:35, supra.

17. Lyon v Bethlehem Engineering Corp. (1930) 253 NY 111, 115, 170 NE 512; Round Lake Ass'n v Kellogg (1894) 141 NY 348, 356, 36 NE 326.

18. See §§ 9:58 et seq. supra.

19. See §§ 9:58, et seq, supra.

20. Bartholdi Realty Co. v Robard Realty Co. (AD1 1913) 156 AD 528, 141 NYS 353.

# TENANT'S RIGHTS § 15:59

as well as his subtenant from using the premises in violation of any restrictive covenants contained in the paramount lease.[1]

## J. RESTRICTION ON LESSOR'S USE OF OTHER PREMISES

### § 15:59. Generally

When an owner of a building leases part of it to one type of business, the tenant may desire to protect his business by having the landlord refrain from leasing any other part of the landlord's property to another tenant who might sell the same merchandise.

However, it is well settled that in the absence of any covenant restricting the landlord's right so to do, the landlord may use the remaining portions of his property in any lawful way he sees fit, provided that such use will not interfere with the tenant's reasonable use and enjoyment of the premises leased to him.[2] As has been seen,[3] an intention to restrict the use of property should not be one of inference, but unmistakably expressed in the contract of leasing.[4] Accordingly, if a tenant desires to restrict the landlord in the use of the property remaining in his possession, the tenant must exact an express covenant from him which will express precisely his intent; for, such restrictive covenants will not be extended by implication beyond their clearly expressed meaning, and will be construed strictly against those who formulate and seek to impose them.[5]

---

1. Lyon v Bethlehem Engineering Corp. (1930) 253 NY 111, 115, 170 NE 512; Bovin v Galitzka (1929) 250 NY 228, 231, 165 NE 273.

2. Bristol Hotel Co. v Pegram (AT 1906) 49 Misc 535, 98 NYS 512; Mam Restaurant, Inc. v Rector Street Properties Associates (S Ct NY Co 1963) 41 Misc 2d 487, 245 NYS2d 653, affd (1st Dept) 21 AD2d 751, 251 NYS2d 909, affd 16 NY2d 623, 261 NYS2d 70, 209 NE2d 113; Hunts Point Restaurant, Inc. v Oval Foods, Inc. (1934) 153 Misc 451, 274 NYS 450.

3. See § 15:38, supra.

4. Bristol Hotel Co. v Pegram (AT 1906) 49 Misc 535, 98 NYS 512. Also, see, Schoonmaker v Heckscher (AD1 1916) 171 AD 148, 157 NYS 75, affd 218 NY 722, 113 NE 1066.

5. Val-Kill Co. v Cities Service Oil Co. (1951) 278 AD 164, 103 NYS2d 681, affd 303 NY 823, 104 NE2d 370; Mam Restaurant, Inc. v Rector Street Properties Associates (S Ct NY Co 1963) 41 Misc 2d 487, 245 NYS2d 653, affd (1st Dept) 21 AD2d 751, 251 NYS2d 909, affd 16 NY2d 623, 261 NYS2d 70, 209 NE2d 113; Weinberg v Edelstein (S Ct NY Co 1952) 201 Misc 343, 110 NYS2d 806; King Drug Stores, Inc. v Ramsgate Realty Co. (S Ct NY Co 1933) 152 Misc 41, 273 NYS 71, affd 241 AD 806, 270 NYS 936.

But, see Daitch Crystal Dairies, Inc. v Neisloss (1959, 2d Dept) 8 AD2d 965, 190 NYS2d 737, affd 8 NY2d 723, 201 NYS2d 101, 167 NE2d 643, hold-

§ 15:59   LANDLORD AND TENANT

It should be observed that in all the cases discussed in connection with this subject, the courts have apparently assumed without discussion the validity of a covenant by the lessor in a lease of premises to a particular lessee, that he will not lease other property of his for a business similar to that of the covenantee.

Undertakings, whether written or oral, express or implied, constituting or contained in a contract entered into between a banking organization and the owner of an interest in real property located within this state, which bars such owner from leasing, selling, or otherwise disposing of any interest in such real property to any other banking organization is rendered null and void by statute.[6] Thus, banking institutions desiring to acquire space in a shopping center or other real estate complex may not seek or receive promises from landlords to exclude by oral or written agreement any competing financial institution from acquiring space in the same complex.[7] Anyone injured by reason of such undertaking may sue on

ing that where a landlord covenants with tenant of a store in a building containing seventeen stores, not to permit building to be used as supermarket, and such tenant's rental is to be computed on a percentage of his gross business, a covenant on the part of landlord will be implied not to erect additional stores on the landlord's vacant land adjoining that building and to permit a supermarket thereon, entitling the tenant to an injunction against landlord.

However, such a restriction, as a general rule, is not projected into a statutory tenancy. Gansvoort Apartments v Droutman (S Ct NY Co 1950) 198 Misc 872, 101 NYS2d 419; Nussbaum v Garstaff Realty Co. (S Ct Bx Co 1950) 197 Misc 527, 96 NYS2d 161; Jacobs v Equitable Life Assur. Soc. (S Ct Bx Co 1950) 106 NYS2d 951; Klein v Ernst (S Ct Bx Co 1951) 106 NYS2d 897; Rappaport v Raylen Realty Corp. (S Ct Bx Co 1953) 204 Misc 729, 124 NYS2d 331.

In Ottavino v Auricchio (S Ct Queens Co 1951) 199 Misc 616, 104 NYS2d 27, a tenant, during the term of his leasehold, had secured an injunction against his landlord restraining him from violating a covenant not to lease property to a competitive business. Upon the expiration of the demised term, the tenant continued as a statutory tenant. Held, since covenant involved did not carry over into statutory tenancy, landlord was entitled to move to have the injunctive provisions of the judgment discharged of record on the ground of performance; that is, the landlord fully performed, since he had not rented to a competitive business during the term of the lease.

**Annotation:** Validity, construction, and effect of lessor's covenant against use of his other property in competition with the lessee-covenantee. 97 ALR2d 4.

**6.** Banking L § 674-1, subd 1. The statute applies to banking organizations, bank holding companies, national banking associations, federal savings and loan associations, and foreign banking corporations.

**7.** This statute does not apply retroactively to restrictive covenants entered into prior to its effective date; to wit, September 1, 1973. Peoples Sav. Bank v County Dollar Corp. (1974, 2d Dept) 43 AD2d 327, 351 NYS2d 157, affd 35 NY2d 836, 362 NYS2d 864, 321 NE2d 784.

account thereof, and recover three times the amount of the damages sustained plus costs, including reasonable attorneys' fees.[8]

### § 15:60. Restriction of "Same or Similar Business"; Form

What constitutes the violation of a covenant or restriction in a lease that the lessor will not rent other premises to anyone having "the same or a similar business," has been the subject of much controversy, since the question depends upon the wording of the particular covenant or restriction, and the facts of the particular case. Moreover, under present business conditions, most types of business have lost their identity, and now sell almost anything. A tenant in exacting a restrictive covenant from his landlord must bear in mind the dangers of overlapping of businesses. One need only visit the modern "drug store" to appreciate that it is in reality a vest pocket department store.

A study of the cases dealing with the question indicates that where a restrictive covenant is directed against a business of the "same or similar nature" to the tenant's, a question of fact will be deemed to arise to determine whether or not the competing goods sold by the competitors are merely incidental to the competitors' business, or whether or not they constitute a distinct branch of the competitors' business. If incidental, there will be no breach. If, however, a distinct branch, whether on a large or small scale, there will be a breach.[9] The determination of the question does not depend upon names, but upon substance.[10] The following illustrations taken from the

---

8. Banking L § 674-a, subd 2. This subd. applies only to contracts entered into after Sept 1, 1973. L 1973, Ch 279, § 2.

9. Weiss v Mayfolwer Doughnut Corp. (1956) 1 NY2d 310, 152 NYS2d 471; 135 NE2d 208; People's Trust Co. v Schultz Novelty & Sporting Goods Co. (1926) 244 NY 14, 154 NE 649; Gross v Flagreen Realty Corp. (S Ct Kings Co 1949) 94 NYS2d 804.

10. People's Trust Co. v Schultz Novelty & Sporting Goods Co. (1926) 244 NY 14, 154 NE 649; Arista Luncheonette, Inc. v Harann Operating Corp. (1955, 2d Dept) 1 AD2d 681, 147 NYS2d 144, affd 1 NY2d 724, 151 NYS2d 934, 134 NE2d 682 (holding that lease of adjoining premises for use as a grocery and delicatessen, in which packaged and canned foods, cold cuts and dairy products were sold for off-premises consumption, did not violate covenant not to lease adjoining premises for a line of business similar to that for which tenant was authorized to use demised premises, where lease containing covenant au-

§ 15:60

cases on the subject may be helpful in determining how the courts apply this principle of construction.

A tenant was engaged in the business of "toys, sporting goods, and kindred articles." The restrictive covenant was not to let any portion of the building for the use of any business "of the same or similar nature conducted" by the tenant. A new tenant opened a haberdashery and sold bathing suits, belts, sweaters, and other articles which come under the classification of "sporting goods and kindred articles." It was shown that the value of the overlapping articles which the haberdasher sold amounted to about five per centum of his business, and to about ten per centum of the tenant's business. In deciding that these facts presented a jury question, the Court of Appeals said,[11] "The question is whether the business of the subtenants (haberdasher) is the same or similar to that of defendant (tenant). . . . The business of haberdashery and the business of selling toys, sporting goods, and like articles are not similar, although they may in some respects overlap. The same things might be sold in both stores to some extent. The purely incidental and occasional sale thereof would not be a breach of the agreement not to carry on a competing business. . . . Names do not count. The substance must be considered. Who can delimit and classify the articles which belong exclusively to one business and may not be carried by another without destroying its character? Drug stores and candy stores both sell soda water and similar innocuous and lawful drinks. They also sometimes sell light lunches. The sales are of similar articles, but are the businesses similar? Is a drug store or a candy store carrying on a business similar to a restaurant because they all serve and sell soft drinks and light lunches? Possibly if the drug or candy business were a mere incident to the restaurant feature, but not necessarily. If the sale of sporting goods is a distinct branch of the competing business, the subtenants are, to that extent, carrying on the same business whether on a large or small scale. . . . The question is whether the business of the subtenants,

thorized use of demised premises only for luncheonette, confectionery store, ice cream parlor, and for sale of stationery, tobacco, tobacco products and supplies, greeting cards, newspapers, periodicals, toys, games and drug store items).

11. People's Trust Co. v Schultz Novelty & Sporting Goods Co. (1926) 244 NY 14, 154 NE 649.

taken as a whole, was of the same or similar nature as that conducted by the defendant. While the subtenants were carrying on what would be generally known as a haberdashery, and were also selling sporting goods, such sale of sporting goods did not, as matter of law, transform their business from that of a haberdashery to that of a house for the sale of sporting goods. To a certain extent, the business overlapped, but the haberdashery did not lose its characteristics as such, because it also incidentally carried and sold some articles similar to some of those sold by the defendant. The question of distinct branch or incidental sales was for the jury."

A tenant conducted a Nedick's orange juice stand, and the landlord covenanted not to rent for any "line of business" similar to the tenant's business. The court held[12] that it was a question for the jury whether or not a doughnut shop, which conducted a luncheonette, was so similar to the orange stand as to constitute a violation of the landlord's covenant.

It has been held to be a jury question whether or not an A & P store, which sells candy, cigarettes and bottled soda, violates a restrictive covenant against renting for the same line of business as a "modern confectionery, toys, stationery, and cigar store."[13]

In another case the tenant operated a store for the retail sale of cigars, stationery, candy, and soda. The landlord covenanted not to rent for purposes similar to the tenant's business. The landlord rented a store for the retail sale of dairy items, groceries, fruits, and vegetables, and non-kosher delicatessen. The new tenant sold bottled soda for off-premises consumption. Callahan, J., said,[14] "Renting a second store as a grocery and delicatessen was not a rental for a purpose similar to 'cigars, stationery, candy and sodas.' The distinction between these types of stores is well recognized in the City of New York. That there might be an overlapping in a single item commonly carried in both stores would not make the defendant's use inconsistent with the landlord's covenant. . . . Bottled

---

12. Supreme Finance Corp. v Burnee Corp. (AT1 1933) 146 Misc 374, 262 NYS 147.

13. Schmukler v Raynes Realty Corp. (S Ct NY Co 1930) 137 Misc 320, 242 NYS 514.

14. Topol v Smoleroff Dev. Corp. (AD1 1942) 264 AD 164, 34 NYS2d 653.

§ 15:60   LANDLORD AND TENANT

soda-water for off-premises consumption is one of the customary articles dealt with by a grocer and delicatessen. A different situation might exist if Kane (the new tenant) had set up a sodawater fountain, or sold soft drinks for consumption in his store."

A "wet and dry stationery store" complained of a violation of a restrictive covenant against a "similar business" because a grocery and delicatessen sold after-dinner mints, bottled soda and cigarettes. The court held[15] that neither the grocer nor the delicatessen can be said to be doing a "similar business" to the stationery store merely because they sold some overlapping items. As Wenzel, J., said, in writing the opinion, "Our so-called 'stationery' store of today is no more true to its name and genus than most of our 'drug' stores. It might be termed a vest pocket department store and it is hard to think of a store which does not sell some item which may also be purchased in a 'wet and dry stationery store.' Surely it was never within the contemplation of these parties that the landlord was to be compelled to rent the balance of his property to dyeing and cleaning establishments."[16]

A luncheonette has been defined to be a place where sandwiches, salads, quickly prepared hot food and non-alcoholic beverages are served. It serves a light meal or snack in contradistinction to a full meal supplied or furnished in a restaurant.[17] An eating place wherein tenant proposes to provide only counter service, with food prepared and served from a service back-bar and from cooking grills in window exposed to customers, is a luncheonette, rather than a restaurant, within terms of a covenant prohibiting use of premises for the operation or a soda fountain of soda fountain-luncheonette.[18] The sale of doughnuts and coffee and soft drinks for on- and off-

15. Bloom v Apico Realty Co. (S Ct Queens Co 1938) 167 Misc 236, 2 NYS2d 847.

16. Also, see, Rialto Luncheonette, Inc. v 1481 Broadway Corp. (S Ct NY Co 1939) 170 Misc 754, 11 NYS2d 39, where it was held that a drink stand for sale of soft drinks and ice cream was not a violation of a restriction not to rent for a "luncheonette or restaurant" merely because of overlapping of items.

17. Weiss v Mayflower Doughnut Corp. (1956) 1 NY2d 310, 152 NYS2d 471, 135 NE2d 208, wherein the court concluded that an eating establishment, though called a restaurant, did not compete with plaintiff's drugstore luncheonette in violation of the lease restriction.

18. Fulway Corp. v Liggett Drug Co. (S Ct NY Co 1956) 1 Misc 2d 527, 148 NYS2d 222.

# TENANT'S RIGHTS § 15:60

premises consumption, even though there are twenty counter stools for customers to sit on while consuming their purchases, is neither a luncheonette nor a restaurant.[19]

Where a landlord agreed with his drugstore tenant that he would not rent any other store in the building for a drugstore, fountain or luncheonette, it was held that this agreement was breached by the landlord when he rented another store in the building for the sale of ice cream, candy, and gift novelties, and the new tenant served ice cream sodas and carbonated drinks. The landlord contended that there was no breach of his agreement because the new tenant served only at tables, and not at the counter. However, the court held that the parties intended by the use of the words "fountain and luncheonette" to restrain the landlord from renting any other store in the building for the sale, in whole or in part, of fountain products, whether served at the fountain itself or at tables a few feet from the fountain.[20]

A restriction against renting space for restaurant, luncheonette and soda fountain is not violated by permitting tenant of space rented for general office use to have incoming cart service, canteen service, automatic vending machine service, or outside order service for the benefit of its employees.[1]

## FORM NO. 40

### Restrictions on Landlord's Use of Other Premises

Landlord covenants and agrees that during the term of this lease or any renewal or extension thereof, as long as Tenant is not in default in the payment of rent or the performance of any of the covenants of this lease on the Tenant's part to be performed, Landlord will not, either directly or by or through any subsidiary or affiliated corporation, operate, use, engage in, or carry on a ........ within the building of which the leased premises

---

[19]. Harper Successors, Inc. v Sandab Realty Corp. (S Ct Kings Co 1963) 40 Misc 2d 6, 242 NYS2d 503.

[20]. Larchmont Drug Store, Inc. v 4915 Realty Corp. (AD2 1951) 278 AD 954, 105 NYS2d 266, affd 303 NY 845, 104 NE2d 380.

[1]. Mam Restaurant, Inc. v Rector Street Properties Associates (S Ct NY Co 1963) 41 Misc 2d 487, 245 NYS2d 653, affd (1st Dept) 21 AD2d 751, 251 NYS2d 909, affd 16 NY2d 623, 261 NYS2d 70, 209 NE2d 113.

forms a part, or in any other building presently owned or hereafter acquired by Landlord within a radius of . . . . miles from the leased premises; lease to any third person within the building of which the leased premises forms a part, or any land or building, whether presently owned or hereafter acquired within a radius of . . . . from the leased premises, for use as a . . . . . . . . This agreement shall be binding on Landlord and its officers, directors, managers, or major shareholders. Landlord agrees to deliver to Tenant a representation and warranty signed by the officers, directors, managers, and major shareholders of Landlord, warranting and representing that they and each of them are bound by the restrictive covenant contained in this Paragraph, and that they, and each of them will adhere thereto, and comply therewith. In the event that the Landlord shall breach the covenant in this Paragraph, Tenant's remedy shall be limited to the securing of an injunction against Landlord for the violation of this covenant, without any right on the part of Tenant to cancel this lease, or to withhold or deduct rentals or to institute an action for damages.

### § 15:61. Restriction of Sale of Specified Articles

The difficulties arising under a restrictive covenant against renting to a "similar business" have been discussed in the preceding sections. The main difficulty is due to the fact that under present conditions most businesses sell goods which are traditionally not associated with that type of business. The question raised is whether or not the sale of an overlapping item is an integral part of a business, or merely an incident thereof.

However, where a landlord agrees that he will not rent to any business which will sell enumerated articles, such questions are eliminated.

A landlord agreed that he would not enter into a new lease without a restriction prohibiting the "display, exhibition, or sale of furniture or floor covering; it being the intention of the parties that the landlord shall not suffer or permit the ground floor to be used for the display, exhibition or sale of furniture or home furnishings." Permitting the sale by a new tenant of table and floor

## TENANT'S RIGHTS § 15:61

lamps, and shades was held to be a violation of such a covenant.[2]

In another case a landlord agreed "not to rent any portion of the building and premises of which the store hereby leased is a part to anyone for the purposes of wholesaling and retailing cigars and tobacco," nor "to consent to other tenants subletting" for the same purposes. The landlord rented an adjoining store as a grocery store, which, with the landlord's knowledge, sold cigars as a regular part of its business. (In this case the grocer executed an agreement to indemnify the landlord for any expenses he might incur in the event the tenant sued to restrain such sales.) In deciding that the sale of cigars by the grocer violated the covenant, the Appellate Division said,[3] "This covenant was not against renting the store for the tobacco business, or to a tenant who would conduct a tobacco business there, but that the landlord would not lease the store for the purposes of wholesaling or retailing cigars and tobacco. . . . It seems to me that it would be a clear violation of the defendants' covenant if they leased an adjoining store to a tenant for the purpose of carrying on the business of wholesaling and retailing tobacco and cigars, although it was in connection with some other business, like the grocery business. It is clear that these reciprocal covenants were intended to prevent . . . the landlord from renting the premises to any one for the purpose of carrying on a cigar and tobacco business, whether alone or in connection with another business."

"A different question," the judge concluded, "would be presented if the defendants had simply agreed not to lease the building for a cigar and tobacco business." Thus, by specifying the particular articles in the restrictive covenant, rather than a "similar business," the tenant avoided the troublesome question of overlapping items as being a distinct branch of the competing business, or as being only incidental thereto.[4]

2. C. Ludwig Baumann & Co. v Manwit Corp. (AD2 1925) 213 AD 300, 207 NYS 437.

3. Waldorf-Astoria Segar Co. v Salomon (AD1 1905) 109 AD 65, 95 NYS 1053, affd 184 NY 584, 77 NE 1197.

4. Discussed in § 15:60, supra.

However, see Weinberg v Edelstein (S Ct NY Co 1952) 201 Misc 343, 110 NYS2d 806, where it was held that a restrictive covenant which prohibited sale by competing tenant of "dresses"

### § 15:62. Remedies at Law against Lessor for Breach

Unless restricted by a provision of the lease,[5] tenant may bring an action at law against his landlord to recover damages for breach of covenant not to rent other property retained by the landlord for specified uses.[6] The fact that a landlord, instead of renting the premises retained by him, uses such premises himself in violation of the covenant is no escape from the prohibitions of the covenant. To tolerate such an avoidance of the effects of plain language, said the court in so holding, would be to write nullification of honest agreements made among men. A covenant not to rent is the equivalent of a covenant not to use.[7] However, where a restrictive covenant in lease of realty for use as automobile parking lot and for gasoline service station provided that landlord would not permit other property owned by it in the vicinity to be used in competition with tenant's business, it was held that it was not violated by the landlord when he permitted residents on other realty belonging to him to park their automobiles adjacent to their residences or to keep them in private garages attached to their residences.[8]

---

would not preclude sale of "blouse-skirt combinations" which when worn together, looked like dresses but could be worn separately with other garments; L. & S. Delicatessen, Inc v Carawana (S Ct Nassau Co 1955) 143 NYS2d 350, holding, cold cuts, including sausage, liverwurst, and bolognas, are "prepared and cooked meat products" within meaning of lease giving first tenant exclusive right to sell "prepared and cooked meat products."

**5.** See, for example, FORM No. 40, in § 15:60, supra.

**6.** Deepdale Cleaners, Inc. v Friedman (1959, 2d Dept) 7 AD2d 926, 183 NYS2d 411; Humphrey v Trustees of Columbia University (AD1 1930) 228 AD 168, 239 NYS 461; Stearns v Lichternstein (AD2 1900) 48 AD 498, 62 NYS 949, app den 49 AD 636, 63 NYS 1117; Supreme Finance Corp. v Burnee Corp. (AT1 1933) 146 Misc 374, 262 NYS 147, breach of landlord's covenant set up as a counterclaim in a non-payment of rent summary proceeding.

Whether lessor's covenant is in the form of a covenant not to lease the restricted premises for a particular use, or a covenant not to permit a particular use of the premises, or in the form of a grant of an exclusive right, lessor is under the duty not to lease the restricted premises for the prohibited use or purpose, and furthermore he is under the duty to insure that under the terms of the subsequent lease the restricted premises cannot lawfully be used by the subsequent lessee for the purpose or use prohibited by the lessor's covenant. Five Towns Card & Gift Shop, Inc. v Lawrence Drug Co. (1975, 2d Dept) 49 AD2d 568, 370 NYS2d 623.

**7.** Goldberg v Siegel (S Ct Queens Co 1944) 182 Misc 1068, 47 NYS2d 678. Also, see, Banos v Winkelstein (S Ct Onondaga Co 1948) 192 Misc 130, 78 NYS2d 832.

**8.** Val-Kill Co. v Cities Service Oil Co. (AD1 1951) 278 AD 164, 103 NYS2d 681, affd 303 NY 823, 104 NE2d 370.

### § 15:63. Paying Rent as Waiver of Breach

A tenant by remaining in possession and paying rent with knowledge that his landlord has breached a covenant not to rent to a competing business, does not preclude himself from claiming damages for such breach.[9]

### § 15:64. Measure of Damages for Breach

The proper measure of damages for a breach by the landlord of the covenant restricting his use of other premises retained by him is the difference between the rental value of the leased premises with and without the competing business.[10]

In the absence of proof of substantial damages, the tenant is entitled to at least nominal damages.[11] But, if the tenant fails to establish that competition results in either a loss of profits of a reduction in rental value, he is not entitled to any damages.[12]

However, a tenant is not limited to a recovery of the difference between the rental value of the demised premises with and without the competing business. As Finch, J., said in a leading case on the subject,[13] "There exists no such limitation. It is true that courts have excluded profits where the source was vague and the income of the business uncertain either because the business had just started or for other reasons. Here, however, the testimony making out a prima facie case of loss of business was certain and direct and presented more vital proof than the usual proof of difference in rental value. The plaintiff was entitled to have this testimony admitted, submitted to, and considered by the jury. The testimony

---

9. Stearns v Lichtenstein (AD2 1900) 48 AD 498, 62 NYS 949.

10. Fairview Hardware, Inc. v Strausman (1959, 2d Dept) 9 AD2d 944, 195 NYS2d 816; Kennedy v Abarno (AD2 1950) 277 AD 883, 97 NYS2d 907; Humphrey v Trustees of Columbia University (AD1 1930) 228 AD 168, 239 NYS 461; Supreme Finance Corp. v Burnee Corp. (AT1 1933) 146 Misc 374, 262 NYS 147; Friedman v Celfan Bldg. Corp. (S Ct Kings Co 1958) 13 Misc 2d 192, 176 NYS2d 723; L. & S. Delicatessen, Inc. v Carawana (S Ct Nassau Co 1955) 143 NYS2d 350.

11. Stearns v Lichtenstein (AD2 1900) 48 AD 498, 62 NYS 949.

12. C. L. Holding Corp. v Schutt Court Homes, Inc. (1954) 307 NY 648, 120 NE2d 837.

13. Humphrey v Trustees of Columbia University (AD1 1930) 228 AD 168, 239 NYS 461.

§ 15:64 LANDLORD AND TENANT

tended directly to establish a measure by which the plaintiff's damage could be ascertained."[14]

### § 15:65. Equitable Relief Against Lessor

It is well settled that a court of equity will enforce by injunction a covenant on the part of a landlord not to rent his remaining property for specified purposes.[15] However, where a landlord convenanted in his lease to a dealer in certain supplies and materials that he would not rent any part of the building to anyone handling a similar line of goods, an injunction for a violation of the covenant was held to be too broad which enjoined the making of a lease to anyone who, in connection with some other business, should happen to deal in any one of a large list of specified articles, as it would serve no useful purpose to adopt or paraphrase the language of the covenant, and a general restraining order so vague that no one could be punished for violating it would not be efficacious to prevent future violations.[16]

### § 15:66. Remedies at Law Against Competing Tenant

A landlord agreed with a tenant not to rent his remaining property for a restaurant. Pursuant to this covenant the landlord, in renting another store, inserted a prohibition in the new lease against the use of the new store for a restaurant. The new tenant, knowing of the landlord's restrictive covenant, nevertheless, violated his own restrictive covenant as to use, and used the new store for a

---

**14.** Fairview Hardware, Inc. v Strausman (1959, 2d Dept) 9 AD2d 944, 195 NYS2d 816 (loss of profits disallowed because plaintiff's business was new); Kennedy v Abarno (AD2 1950) 277 AD 883, 97 NYS2d 907, where court pointed out that although loss of net profits is usually a more accurate measure of damages than the mere opinion evidence of real estate experts as to difference in rental value before and after the breach, yet there must be some basis in the record for such award. The tenant in this case was denied such recovery because of insufficient proof; Supreme Finance Corp. v Burnee Corp. (AT1 1933) 146 Misc 374, 262 NYS 147, which found proof of profits insufficient to warrant their recovery.

**15.** C. Ludwig Baumann & Co. v Manwit Corp. (AD2 1925) 213 AD 300, 207 NYS 437; Waldorf-Astoria Segar Co. v Salomon (AD1 1905) 109 AD 65, 95 NYS 1053, affd 184 NY 584, 77 NE 1197; Colbee 52nd Street Corp. v Madison 52nd Corp. (S Ct NY Co 1957) 8 Misc 2d 175, 169 NYS2d 716, affd (1st Dept) 5 AD2d 971, 173 NYS2d 243, where injunction against landlord was denied; Gross v Flagreen Realty Corp. (S Ct Kings Co 1949) 94 NYS2d 804; Staff v Bemis Realty Co. (S Ct NY Co 1920) 111 Misc 635, 183 NYS 886, affd 233 NY 643, 135 NE 952.

**16.** Harry Angelo Co. v Improved Property Holding Co. (AD1 1910) 137 AD 308, 122 NYS 199.

# TENANT'S RIGHTS § 15:67

restaurant. It was held that the old tenant could not sue the new tenant at law for a violation by him of the covenant made by the landlord; for, such covenant was personal to the landlord, and did not run at law.[17]

It was further held that the old tenant could not sue the new tenant at law for the latter's violation of the latter's covenant against using the new store for a restaurant. A compliance with such covenant by the new tenant, it is true, would have been beneficial to the old tenant, inasmuch as it would eliminate competition. But this benefit was incidental; for, its primary purpose was to protect the landlord under his restrictive covenant. "The doctrine of Lawrence v Fox, 20 NY 268," said Cropsey, J.,[18] "does not seem to have been extended to cover such a case." Therefore, no legal action, it was held, is vested in the old tenant against the competing tenant.[19]

### § 15:67. Equitable Relief Against Competing Tenant

If a landlord covenants with his tenant not to rent his remaining property for specified purposes, such tenant can enforce this covenant in equity against a subsequent tenant who rents such remaining property with notice or knowledge of the restrictive covenant. The original tenant will, as a general rule, be given injunctive relief restraining the subsequent tenant from violating the restrictive covenant.[20] The theory on which the subsequent tenant will be subject to injunction, pointed out Callahan, J.,[1] is that equity will not permit him to use his leased premises inconsistently with a covenant entered into by his landlord with another tenant for the benefit of the leased premises, if he took his premises with notice of that covenant. However, as Wheeler, J., said,[2] "Notice or knowledge of the covenant is the gravamen of the ac-

---

17. Safran v Westrich (S Ct Queens Co 1930) 136 Misc 81, 240 NYS 238.
18. Safran v Westrich (S Ct Queens Co 1930) 136 Misc 81, 240 NYS 238.
19. Safran v Westrich (S Ct Queens Co 1930) 136 Misc 81, 240 NYS 238.
20. Topol v Smoleroff Dev. Corp. (AD1 1942) 264 AD 164, 34 NYS2d 653; Waldorf-Astoria Segar Co. v Salomon (AD1 1905) 109 AD 65, 95 NYS 1053, affd 184 NY 584, 77 NE 1197; Rappaport v Raylen Realty Corp. (S Ct Bx Co 1953) 204 Misc 729, 124 NYS2d 331; Weinberg v Edelstein (S Ct NY Co 1952) 201 Misc 343, 110 NYS2d 806; Gross v Flagreen Realty Corp. (S Ct Kings Co 1949) 94 NYS2d 804.

1. Topol v Smoleroff Dev. Corp. (AD1 1942) 264 AD 164, 34 NYS2d 653.
2. Senn v Ladd (S Ct Monroe Co 1942) 179 Misc 306, 38 NYS2d 820.

§ 15:67 LANDLORD AND TENANT

tion."[3] Thus, where at time tenant entered into lease containing covenant prohibiting landlord from renting other space to a competing tenant, landlord had already rented other space for similar purposes, and tenant not only actually knew it, but such other lease was on record, tenant was held to have executed its lease subject to the use-provision of the other lease.[4] However, a tenant was denied injunctive relief against a competing tenant where the first tenant's lease had not been recorded, and there was no proof that the competing tenant had actual or constructive notice of the restrictive covenant until nearly two months after it had executed its lease, and after it had taken possession and had spent a considerable sum in improving its leased premises.[5] The recording of a lease containing a restrictive covenant will constitute notice thereof to the competing tenant.[6]

In other words, one who rents premises with knowledge of a prior restrictive covenant agreed to by his lessor in favor of another tenant is bound by the restriction and the construction placed on it, even though he did not believe it would be so construed, and relied on the advice of counsel that it would not be so construed.[7]

Essentially, the defense of laches consists of an unreasonable delay by a plaintiff to the prejudice of a defendant. But, mere delay, however long, without the neces-

[3]. Also, see, Greenspan v 4201 Ave. D Realty Corp. (AD2 1942) 265 AD 967, 38 NYS2d 915; Metzger v Gardencorner, Inc. (AD2 1931) 233 AD 689, 249 NYS 409; Waldorf-Astoria Segar Co. v Salomon (AD1 1905) 109 AD 65, 95 NYS 1053, affd 184 NY 584, 77 NE 1197; L. & S. Delicatessen, Inc. v Carawana (S Ct Nassau Co 1955) 143 NYS2d 350.

[4]. Danish Maid, Inc. v South Bay Center, Inc. (1960, 2d Dept) 11 AD2d 768, 205 NYS2d 358.

Necessity of recording lease, see §§ 1:7, et seq, supra.

[5]. Fox v Congel (1980, 3d Dept) 75 AD2d 681, 426 NYS2d 878 (terms of restrictive covenant not binding on competing tenant who did not know of, and was not chargeable with knowledge of, the covenant when he entered into his lease, even though he was subsequently notified thereof);

Metzger v Gardencorner, Inc. (AD2 1931) 233 AD 689, 249 NYS 409.

[6]. Deepdale Cleaners, Inc. v Friedman (1959, 2d Dept) 7 AD2d 926, 183 NYS2d 411; Hill Top Toys, Inc. v Great Atlantic & Pacific Tea Co. (1957, 2d Dept) 4 AD2d 691, 164 NYS2d 269; Cromwell Hardware Long Island Corp. v Great Atlantic & Pacific Tea Co. (1957, 2d Dept) 4 AD2d 690, 163 NYS2d 761; Fulway Corp. v Liggett Drug Co. (S Ct NY Co 1956) 1 Misc 2d 527, 148 NYS2d 222.

[7]. Weiss v Mayflower Doughnut Corp. (1956) 1 NY2d 310, 152 NYS2d 471, 135 NE2d 208. (The court indicated that evidence of the violation by plaintiff tenant of the restriction on use contained in his own lease was admissible and in issue under competing tenant's defense of unclean hands.)

# TENANT'S RIGHTS § 15:68

sary elements to create an equitable estoppel, does not preclude the granting of equitable relief. Where the facts show that the delay in instituting the action was not unreasonable, and that plaintiff's conduct did not cause the competing tenant to change its position to its detriment, relief will not be withheld.[8]

## K. RESEARCH REFERENCES

### § 15:68. Generally

In addition to the preceding text, the reader is also referred to the following:

49 Am Jur 2d, Landlord and Tenant §§ 191-276.

11 Am Jur Legal Forms 2d, Leases of Real Property §§ 161:321-161:397.

16 Am Jur Pleading and Practice Forms (Rev ed), Landlord and Tenant, Forms 341-348.

New York Jur 2d, Landlord and Tenant (1st ed §§ 131-147).

New York CLS Real Property Law § 220.

New York Forms, Leases, Forms 8:131-8:134.

Index to Annotations, Landlord and Tenant.

**VERALEX®:** Cases and annotations referred to herein can be further researched through the VERALEX electronic retrieval system's two services, **Auto-Cite®** and **SHOWME®**. Use Auto-Cite to check citations for form, parallel references, prior and Auto-Cite to check citations for form, paralles references, prior and later history, and annotation references. Use SHOWME to display the full text of cases and annotations.

---

[8]. Weiss v Mayflower Doughnut Corp. (1956) 1 NY2d 310, 152 NYS2d 471, 135 NE2d 208.

# CHAPTER 16

# FIXTURES

A. IN GENERAL
　§ 16:1.　Fixture Defined
　§ 16:2.　Trade and Domestic Fixtures Defined

B. REMOVAL OF FIXTURES
　§ 16:3.　Tenant's Right to Remove Trade and Domestic Fixtures
　§ 16:4.　—Limitation on Tenant's Right
　§ 16:5.　—Duty on Removal
　§ 16:6.　—Illustrative Cases
　§ 16:7.　Agreement Restricting Tenant's Right to Remove Fixtures
　§ 16:8.　Effect of Provision that "Tenant's Fixtures Shall Belong to Landlord"
　§ 16:9.　Effect of Provision that "Alterations Except Movable Fixtures Shall Belong to Landlord"
　§ 16:10.　Effect of Provision that "Alterations, Additions, Etc. Except Movable Office Furniture Shall Belong to Landlord"
　§ 16:11.　Tenant's Right to Remove Fixtures as Against Grantee of Fee
　§ 16:12.　When Tenant May Remove Fixtures
　§ 16:13.　When Tenant Holding Over May Remove Fixtures
　§ 16:14.　Tenant's Right to Remove Fixtures Where He Takes New Lease
　§ 16:15.　Tenant's Right to Remove Fixtures upon Abandonment of Possession
　§ 16:16.　Tenant's Reservation of Right to Remove Fixtures
　§ 16:17.　Right of Removal of Substitutions or Replacements of Fixtures Made by Tenant
　§ 16:18.　Tenant's Right to Personal Property Left on Premises After His/Her Removal or Eviction
　§ 16:19.　Landlord's Obligation as to Tenant's Personal Property Left on Premises After His/Her Removal or Eviction
　§ 16:20.　Form of Provision for Removal of Fixtures

C. RESEARCH REFERENCES
　§ 16:21.　Generally

## A. IN GENERAL

### § 16:1. Fixture Defined

It is familiar law that, generally speaking, a fixture is a chattel which, although movable in its original state or condition, has been so affixed to real property as to become a part of the real property, and no longer removable by the original owner of the chattel without the consent of the owner of the fee.

However, there are certain chattels which have such a determinate character as movables that they remain personal property even after their annexation to the real property. For example, carpets, window shades, and gas fixtures. These are "movables," and not fixtures.[1] There are other chattels, such as the brick, stone, and plaster placed in the walls of a building which conclusively become real property after their annexation thereto. None of these is a fixture.[2]

Where there is a unity of all these three elements: actual annexation of a permanent nature to the real property, or something appurtenant thereto; adaptability to the use or purpose to which that part of the real property with which it is connected is appropriated; and intention to make thereby a permanent accession to the freehold,[3] the law uniformly recognizes the object so affixed to the real property as part thereof.[4]

There is no inflexible and universal rule by which to determine under all circumstances whether that which was originally personal property has become part of the realty through being affixed thereto and used in connection therewith. The rule differs in different relationships. It is broader and stricter, for instance, in transforming personalty into realty as between an ordinary vendor and vendee than as between a landlord and tenant in the case of improvements made by the tenant.[5] The courts accordingly recognize that the relationship of the disputing

---

1. Cosgrove v Troescher (AD1 1901) 62 AD 123, 70 NYS 764.
2. Madfes v Beverly Development Corp. (1929) 251 NY 12, 166 NE 787, remittitur amd 251 NY 589, 168 NE 438.
3. Voorhees v McGinnis (1872) 48 NY 278, 282; Potter v Cromwell (1869) 40 NY 287, 296.
4. East Side Car Wash, Inc. v K.R.K. Capitol, Inc. (1984, 1st Dept) 102 AD2d 157, 476 NYS2d 837; Phipps v State (CT Cl 1910) 69 Misc 295, 127 NYS 261.
5. People ex rel. Interborough Rapid Transit Co. v O'Donnel (1911) 202 NY 313, 95 NE 762; Foureal Co. v National Molding Corp. (Dist Ct Suffolk Co 1973) 74 Misc 2d 316, 344 NYS2d 598 (citing text).

parties is an important factor in determining the character of objects as fixtures, and sanction the application of rules of law differing as the relationship of the parties varies. This approach to the problem, it must be emphasized, does not abrogate the general tests and criteria for making the determination whether the object is a fixture, but merely furnishes a guideline for their application. That is to say, while an intention to make a permanent accession to the freehold may legitimately be presumed where the annexer is, for example, the owner of the fee, no such presumption necessarily arises where he is a lessee. So, a given object may be a fixture as between vendor and vendee, but a chattel as between lessor and lessee.[6] "It is undoubtedly the general rule as between landlord and tenant," it has been said,[7] "fixtures cease to be personal property, when they are firmly attached to the real estate, so that they cannot be removed without material injury to the realty; and when they are adapted to the use of the realty, and it was the intention of the parties that they should be permanently annexed."

"The old theory," said the Court of Appeals,[8] "which made physical annexation the sole test has been expanded so as to include intention, use and adaptability."

It is apparent, then, that the determination of what is a fixture is a difficult one, and has perplexed the courts. It has been held, however, that the question is usually a mixed one of fact and law.[9]

### § 16:2. Trade and Domestic Fixtures Defined

Trade and domestic fixtures are those articles of personal property which a tenant annexes to the leased premises for the purposes of the trade or business carried on by him, or for the ornamentation of the premises, or for the convenience of his occupation.[10] For example,

---

6. Re Allen St. (1931) 256 NY 236, 176 NE 377.

7. Crater's Wharf, Inc. v Valvoline Oil Co. (AD2 1922) 204 AD 840, 196 NYS 815, which aff'd on opinion below of Sears, J.

8. Gould v Springer (1912) 206 NY 641, 646, 99 NE 149.

9. Gould v Springer (1912) 206 NY 641, 646, 99 NE 149.

10. J.K.S.P. Restaurant, Inc. v County of Nassau (1987, 2d Dept) 127 AD2d 121, 513 NYS2d 716; Webber v Franklin Brewing Co. (AD1 1908) 123 AD 465, 108 NYS 251, affd 198 NY 509, 92 NE 1103; Foureal Co. v National Molding Corp. (Dist Ct Suffolk Co 1973) 74 Misc 2d 316, 344 NYS2d 598.

Trade fixtures are fixtures installed by a tenant during its lease term to carry on its business; they are the

exhaust fans installed in circular holes made in ceiling of discotheque are trade fixtures.[11]

However, it must be noted that such fixtures do not include those chattels "where the subject or mode of annexation is such that the attributes of personal property cannot be predicated of the thing in controversy"; "as where the property could not be removed without practically destroying it, or where it or part of it, is essential to the support of that to which it is attached." Nor those chattels which have a determinate character as movables.[12]

## B. REMOVAL OF FIXTURES

### § 16:3. Tenant's Right to Remove Trade and Domestic Fixtures

A tenant as a general rule has the right to remove his trade and domestic fixtures,[1] even though the lease may not contain any provision with respect to the right of removal.[2] In other words, as between a landlord and tenant, a tenant is allowed to remove certain types of fixtures annexed to the freehold. But, it must be emphasized, it is only as between landlord and tenant that the rule of the common law, that anything that was annexed to the freehold by a substantial connection becomes a part of the real property, has been relaxed.[3] As the Court of Appeals has said in a leading case,[4] "All the cases upon this branch of the law of fixtures proceed upon the idea that erections which would clearly be a part of the realty under ordinary circumstances, are personal chattels as regards the rights of a tenant who has put them up for the purpose of trade or manufacture."

In other words, trade and domestic fixtures do not lose

---

fixtures which the lessee has supplied at its own expense, and has the right under the lease to remove. East Side Car Wash, Inc. v K.R.K. Capitol, Inc. (1984, 1st Dept) 102 AD2d 157, 476 NYS2d 837.

11. Malloy v Club Marakesh, Inc. (1979, 2d Dept) 71 AD2d 614, 418 NYS2d 135.

12. Madfes v Beverly Development Corp. (1929) 251 NY 12, 166 NE 787, remittitur amd 251 NY 589, 168 NE 438.

1. See § 16:2, supra.

2. Globe Marble Mills Co. v Quinn (1879) 76 NY 23; Cohen v Wittemann (AD1 1905) 100 AD 338, 91 NYS 493; Van Vleck v White (AD2 1901) 66 AD 14, 72 NYS 1026.

3. Re Acquiring Certain Property (North River) (AD1 1907) 118 AD 865, 103 NYS 908, affd 189 NY 508, 81 NE 1162.

4. Ford v Cobb (1859) 20 NY 344.

# FIXTURES § 16:4

their character as fixtures. But, because the common law rule has been relaxed as between landlord and tenant, trade and domestic fixtures "remain personal property in the eye of the law, so far as the right of removal is concerned."[5] This is so even with respect to structures as substantial as entire buildings, which have been held to constitute trade fixtures, and thus are removable by the tenant.[6] In addition to buildings, among the types of property that have been held to constitute trade fixtures are bank vaults,[7] brick chimneys,[8] docks,[9] gasoline service station greasing pits,[10] and restaurant units.[11]

However, it is important to consider the limitations on this general rule, which will be discussed in the succeeding sections.

## § 16:4. —Limitation on Tenant's Right

Upon the termination of a lease, a tenant may leave his trade fixtures on the leased premises only with the landlord's consent; otherwise, they must be removed and the premises restored to their original condition.[12]

A tenant has the right to remove his trade and domestic fixtures provided that they can be removed without seriously damaging the freehold.[13] "The familiar limitation upon the right to remove such fixtures," said the Court of Appeals,[14] "is that the removal must be accomplished without substantial injury to the freehold. The further condition has not been adopted so far as we are aware in the broad language used in this proceeding that the property must be susceptible of removal 'without injury to said property.'"

---

5. Massachusetts Nat. Bank v Shinn (AD2 1897) 18 AD 276, 46 NYS 329, affd 163 NY 360, 57 NE 611. Also, see Crater's Wharf, Inc. v Valvoline Oil Co. (AD2 1922) 204 AD 840, 196 NYS 815, which affd on opinion below of Sears, J.

6. J.K.S.P. Restaurant, Inc. v County of Nassau (1987, 2d Dept) 127 AD2d 121, 513 NYS2d 716.

7. Manhattan Co. v Mosler Safe Co. (1937) 252 AD 863, 299 NYS 417.

8. Moore v Wood, 12 Abb Prac 393.

9. Crater's Wharf, Inc. v Valvoline Oil Co. (1922) 204 AD 840, 196 NYS 815.

10. Marnall Steel Products, Inc. v Bernard (1933) 147 Misc 314, 263 NYS 485, affd 241 AD 616, 269 NYS 907.

11. Mine Realty Corp. v 2131 Broadway Corp. (1938) 253 AD 299, 1 NYS2d 979, reh den 254 AD 655, 4 NYS2d 185.

12. Malloy v Club Marakeesh, Inc. (1979, 2d Dept) 71 AD2d 614, 418 NYS2d 135; Farber v Wards Co. (CA2 1987) 825 F2d 684.

13. Re Water Front on North River (1908) 192 NY 295, 84 NE 1105.

14. Re Water Front on North River (1908) 192 NY 295, 84 NE 1105.

§ 16:4 LANDLORD AND TENANT

Because the interest of a tenant in the land is temporary, the law presumes that he affixes trade and domestic fixtures to the realty with a view to his own enjoyment during the term, and not to enhance the value of the realty. Hence, the law permits him to remove such fixtures "if done," as the Court of Appeals said,[15] "without injury to the freehold, and in agreement with known usages."[16] Thus, in one case it was held that the tenant was not permitted to remove lighting fixtures, which were not the plug-in type, but on removal would seriously damage the premises; but, he was permitted to remove air-conditioning units, which could be detached from the plumbing, and unbolted from the floor without damage to the building.[17]

§ 16:5. —Duty on Removal

In all cases where a tenant has the right to, and does, remove domestic or trade fixtures, he must do so with as little injury as possible to the freehold. Where the injury done is more than insignificant, he must repair and restore the freehold to its original condition.[18]

§ 16:6. —Illustrative Cases

The following cases will illustrate how the courts have applied the principles discussed in the preceding sections to specific situations.

A steam heating plant was installed by a tenant in a building leased to him. Its removal would virtually destroy the building. Applying the rules discussed, it was held that the tenant would not be permitted to remove the plant as his personal property. "The great preponderance of the evidence," said the court, in so holding,[19] "clearly shows that the plant was permanently annexed to the realty, and that its removal would cause serious injury thereto, and that it was peculiarly adapted to the use of the freehold; . . . It is true that there is a presumption that, when articles are trade fixtures, which can be

15. Tifft v Horton (1873) 53 NY 377, 382.
16. Also see, Smusch v Kohn (AT 1898) 22 Misc 344, 49 NYS 176.
17. Re General Assignment for Ben. of Creditors, etc. (Suffolk Co Ct 1954) 205 Misc 852, 133 NYS2d 734.

18. Schwelger Realty Co. v Audubon Nat. Bank (AT1 1914) 88 Misc 14, 150 NYS 171.
19. Jacob v Kellogg (AT 1907) 56 Misc 661, 107 NYS 713. Also, see McOwen v Zimmerman (AT 1912) 133 NYS 461.

removed from place to place for use in a particular business, there is an intention on the part of the landlord and tenant that the attachment to the realty shall not be permanent. But this steam-heating plant can scarcely be regarded as such a trade fixture, under the circumstances presented in the case at bar. It was a proper and usual part of the building for practically any purpose to which the building might be put, and had no peculiar use in" the tenant's particular business. Thus, since the plant was a fixture, and was not a trade fixture, the tenant was not permitted to remove it. The general rule as to fixtures[20] was held determinative of the rights of the parties.

Permanent buildings and cottages of a substantial character do not come within the rule permitting a tenant to remove those trade and domestic fixtures which are removable without substantial injury to the freehold.[1] However, if the building erected by a tenant is a trade fixture, and is removable without substantial injury to the land, then the tenant may remove it.[2] Thus, a tenant of an inn erected a ballroom, 60 feet by 30 feet, made of wood, resting on stone posts slightly imbedded in the soil, and removable without injury to the land. In holding that such building was removable by the tenant as a trade fixture, the Court of Appeals said,[3] "The rule to be gathered from the cases I think is that a tenant may remove, during his term, all erections made by him for the purpose of trade that can be removed without injury to the land or something permanently attached thereto. Where the foundation upon which a building rests is imbedded in the earth he cannot remove the foundation. When the building rests upon such foundation and is confined by its weight only, he may remove the building. Such a rule promotes the interest of the tenant. It enables him to obtain the greatest advantage from the use of the land. It works no injury to the landlord. He obtains his land at the end of the term in as good condition as

---

20. See, § 16:1, supra.

1. Re Long Beach Land Co. (AD2 1905) 101 AD 159, 91 NYS 503.

2. Lewis v Ocean Nav. & Pier Co. (1891) 125 NY 341, 26 NE 301, building so constructed as to be easily removable: built on blocks, buried about 3 feet in sand, upon these blocks posts were set, sills were then placed on the posts and the building superimposed thereon; Debobes v Butterly (AD1 1924) 210 AD 50, 205 NYS 104, refreshment stand.

3. Ombony & Dain v Jones (1859) 19 NY 234, 243.

though no erections had been made. There is no reason why he should appropriate to himself the fruit of the tenant's outlay without compensation. The building in question was not in any manner affixed to the freehold save by its weight. Barmore, therefore, had a right to remove it."

### § 16:7. Agreement Restricting Tenant's Right to Remove Fixtures

It is entirely competent for a landlord and a tenant to contract that any or all of the property placed upon or attached to the leased premises shall belong to the landlord upon the expiration or termination of the lease.[4] "In the absence of an agreement to the contrary," said the Appellate Division,[5] "a tenant may remove trade fixtures before the termination of his tenancy, provided the removal will not materially injure the freehold. But this rule has for its basis the intention of the parties, and it always yields to an agreement to the contrary."

In other words, the presumption of law, that because of the temporary interest of a tenant in the land the fixtures he annexes to the real estate are for his own enjoyment, and not to enhance the value of the estate, may be done away with entirely by an agreement to the contrary.[6] Thus, a lease required the tenant to erect a commercial building to cost a certain amount, and further provided that, at the expiration of the term the landlord would pay one half of the appraised value of the building or renew the lease, the building on the payment of said value or renewal of the lease to belong to the landlord. The tenant constructed the building, and installed therein an elevator, and an engine and boiler to operate it and to heat the building. In holding that the elevator, engine, and boiler belonged to the landlord, and

---

4. Niagara Falls Hydraulic Power & Mfg. Co. v Schermerhorn (AD4 1909) 132 AD 442, 117 NYS 10, affd 197 NY 542, 91 NE 1118. It was contended that since the lease provided that buildings erected by tenant shall become property of landlord on termination of the lease for failure to pay rent, a forfeiture was created which was so unconscionable that it should not be enforced. The court overruled this contention, and said, "It is not unconscionable, and its enforcement does no injustice to the lessee . . . since it was only necessary to pay the rent within the time after service of notice as provided by the lease, to avoid the effect of the provision."

5. Shiels v Byrd (AD1 1915) 168 AD 112, 153 NYS 728.

6. Tifft v Horton (1873) 53 NY 377, 382.

could not be removed by the tenant, the Court of Appeals said,[7] "We think that as between lessor and lessee, under the peculiar contract to which they were parties, the elevator, engine and boiler were a part of the building and of the real estate. They were supplied for its use; were fairly included in the description of a first-class commercial building; could not be removed without substantial injury to the structure; were within the reasonable contemplation of the contract; and were a part of the very expenditure which the lessee was bound to make, and the lessor was entitled to receive. If there be doubt whether as between vendor and vendee of a first-class commercial building an elevator and the machinery necessary to operate it are to be treated as part of the realty, it is dissipated in the present case by the peculiar character of the contract, and the nature of its conditions. If the proof had shown that these appurtenances had been supplied by the tenant in excess of the $30,000 he was bound to expend, and so for his own convenience, and not in part performance of his contract obligation, the question would have been purely one of fixtures. Upon the evidence as it stands, we do not doubt that the articles in question must be deemed a part and parcel of the building . . . ."

In other words, in the law of fixtures, general and otherwise controlling principles may be avoided by agreement, and the rights of the parties determined as they may desire.[8]

### § 16:8. Effect of Provision that "Tenant's Fixtures Shall Belong to Landlord"

A provision in a lease to the effect that any alterations or improvements made by a tenant, or all fixtures attached to the realty, shall belong to the landlord at the expiration of the term, has been construed to include trade fixtures.[9]

7. Finkelmeier v Bates (1883) 92 NY 172, 180.
8. People ex rel. Interborough Rapid Transit Co. v O'Donnel (1911) 202 NY 313, 95 NE 762.
9. Estate Property Corp. v Hudson Coal Co. (S Ct NY Co 1931) 139 Misc 808, 249 NYS 418, affd 237 AD 878, 261 NYS 978. Also, see Levin v Improved Property Holding Co. (AD2 1910) 141 AD 106, 125 NYS 963, where it was held to include long partition, placed in a room from which shorter ones were carried to the wall, which was bolted to plugs set in the concrete floor and secured to the wall by bolts, comprising 58 feet of partition, 7 feet high, made of

"Improvements," said Davies, J.,[10] "clearly, in the lease here used, embrace every addition, alteration, erection or annexation made by the lessees during the demised term, to render the premises more available and profitable, or useful and convenient to them. It is a more comprehensive word than 'fixtures', and necessarily includes it, and such additions as the law might not regard as fixtures. It would be difficult to select a more comprehensive word; and where the parties say that all improvements which may be placed on the premises shall belong to the lessors, it is difficult to say what, if anything, would be excluded."

A lease provided that "all fixtures attached to the realty shall belong to the" landlord. It was found that all of the fixtures in controversy were attached to the realty but not in any substantial manner. In ruling that nevertheless such fixtures belonged to the landlord the Appellate Division said,[11] "But the clause of the lease, it will be observed, did not require them to be so attached in order to prevent their removal. They were to belong to the landlord, if they were in fact attached to the realty, and the proof clearly established that they were. In the absence of an agreement to the contrary, a tenant may remove trade fixtures . . . . It must be assumed, therefore that the parties, when they inserted in the lease the words 'all fixtures attached to the realty', did so for the purpose of giving to the landlord something which he otherwise would not have had. Such words are meaningless, unless that is what the parties intended."

---

oak with glass panels and doors; Lesser v Rayner (AT 1897) 21 Misc 666, 47 NYS 1102, where it was held to include stalls or partitions to improve sheds, affixed by screws, cleats, and slides.

However, see Webber v Franklin Brewing Co. (AD1 1908) 123 AD 465, 108 NYS 251, affd 198 NY 509, 92 NE 1103, which held, that "all improvements and alterations which may be put, placed or made in or upon said premises shall belong to and become the property (of landlord) when so made, and treated as fixtures to the freehold," should not be deemed to include such trade fixtures as a bar and back bar, three mirrors, one hand and foot rail, two screens, four summer doors, one ice box, three large and three small radiators, three partition doors, two window screens, six chandeliers, two window chandeliers, with gas and electric fixtures, some chairs and bottles, on the ground that none of these was so affixed to the realty that they could not be easily and readily removed.

10. French v Mayor etc of New York (S Ct GT 1959) 29 Barb 363, 16 How Pr 220.

11. Shiels v Byrd (AD1 1915) 168 AD 112, 153 NYS 728.

## § 16:9. Effect of Provision that "Alterations Except Movable Fixtures Shall Belong to Landlord"

A lease provided that all alterations made by either the landlord or tenant, except movable fixtures, shall be landlord's property. It was held[12] that by such a provision in a lease the tenant gave up his right to remove even trade fixtures. Said the court, "We may not regard this provision of the lease as being without meaning. We are bound to assume that it was placed in the lease for some purpose, and was designed to give the defendant some right that he would not have in its absence. If the lease was silent upon the question of the rights of the parties with reference to trade fixtures placed upon the property by the tenant for the accommodation of his patrons, Rathkamp (tenant) would have the right to remove them at the termination of the lease. It seems to me plainly apparent that the use of the words limiting his right of removal to 'movable fixtures' . . . establishes the intent of the parties to be that the legal right of removal of trade fixtures, which the law gave the lessee without reservation, was to be limited and restricted to such fixtures and alterations as were movable and could be taken out of the building without interference with or detriment to the building itself, including its walls, ceiling, and floors. There is no other meaning that can be given to the words used in this lease. They are either without meaning and wholly purposeless, or they operated as a limitation of such rights as the lessee would have had, and an enlargement of the rights which the landlord would have had, in their absence."

## § 16:10. Effect of Provision that "Alterations, Additions, Etc. Except Movable Office Furniture Shall Belong to Landlord"

A lease provided that all alterations, additions, or improvements which may be made by either landlord or tenant, except movable office furniture put in at expense of tenant, shall be the property of landlord. The subject of controversy was partitions "commonly known as sectional, movable, and interchangeable partitions," which can be removed without injury or damage to the building.

---

12. Excelsior Brewing Co. v Smith (AD2 1908) 125 AD 668, 110 NYS 8, affd 198 NY 519, 92 NE 1084.

In holding that such partitions were removable by the tenant as his movable office furniture, the Appellate Division said,[13] "If the words 'movable office furniture,' in the lease, were intended to be limited to such furniture as chairs, desks, tables, or other personal property, which is not any wise affixed to the building, it is difficult to understand why any reference to such furniture should have been made in a lease. It seems to us that the word 'furniture' must be given a meaning broad enough to embrace any movable equipment installed in the office to facilitate the transaction of the tenant's business, and that the words 'movable office furniture' shall be deemed as synonymous with the words 'movable fixtures,' as distinguished from fixtures which are so affixed to the realty that their removal would deface or injure the walls, ceilings, or floors."

### § 16:11. Tenant's Right to Remove Fixtures as Against Grantee of Fee

A tenant's right of removal of his fixtures is not affected by the transfer of the landlord's reversion after the annexation of the fixtures by the tenant.[14] This is true, even though the new owner derived his title through a foreclosure of the mortgage on the fee.[15] The new owner of the fee occupies the position of the original landlord, and unless the tenant by some act or omission after the mortgage on the fee was executed, or before the fee was conveyed, lost the right to treat the fixtures as his property, so that they passed with the conveyance of the fee as part of the realty, the tenant's rights are preserved notwithstanding the conveyance.[16]

### § 16:12. When Tenant May Remove Fixtures

The well settled rule is that whatever fixtures a tenant

---

**13.** Century Holding Co. v Pathe Exchange, Inc. (AD1 1922) 200 AD 62, 192 NYS 380. Also, see, United Booking Offices v Pittsburgh Life & Trust Co. (AT1 1909) 65 Misc 31, 119 NYS 216. But, in Bigalke & Ecker Co. v Wm. Knabe & Mfg. Co. (AT1 1909) 65 Misc 29, 119 NYS 1114, a contrary result was reached because the partitions involved there had been erected in a substantial manner, and were of such a nature as not includible in the term "movable fixtures." (See opinion of Greenbaum, J., in the United Booking Offices case.)

**14.** Globe Marble Mills Co. v Quinn (1879) 76 NY 23, 25.

**15.** Globe Marble Mills Co. v Quinn (1879) 76 NY 23, 25; Robinson v Pratt (AD3 1912) 151 AD 738, 136 NYS 98.

**16.** Globe Marble Mills Co. v Quinn (1879) 76 NY 23, 25.

FIXTURES § 16:14

has the right to remove must be removed before his term expires, or within the period limited to do so by the provisions of the lease, or at all events, before quitting possession of the leased premises.[17] "The right of a tenant to remove fixtures erected for trade," said the Court of Appeals,[18] "is conceded to him for reasons of public policy and, being in the nature of a privilege, it must be exercised before the expiration of the term, or before he quits possession. If the right to remove other fixtures exists by virtue of some agreement, then it must be exercised in like manner."

However, where the tenancy is of uncertain duration, depending upon a contingency which may be determined unexpectedly to the tenant, the courts have held that the tenant may be entitled to a reasonable time for removing fixtures after the expiration of such a tenancy.[19]

## § 16:13. When Tenant Holding Over May Remove Fixtures

It is generally held that when a tenant holds over after the expiration of his term, he retains the right to remove his fixtures before he quits possession. In other words, a tenant may remove his fixtures during the period of his possession of leased premises, although the term may have expired.[20]

## § 16:14. Tenant's Right to Remove Fixtures Where He Takes New Lease

In 1959, the Real Property Law was amended to provide[1] that unless the parties expressly agree otherwise, where a tenant has a right to remove fixtures or improvements, such right shall not be lost or impaired by reason of his acceptance of a new lease of the same premises without any surrender of possession between terms. This expressly abrogated the contrary rule which had been

17. Loughran v Ross (1871) 45 NY 792, 794.
18. Talbot v Cruger (1896) 151 NY 117, 120, 45 NE 364.
19. Loughran v Ross (1871) 45 NY 792, 794; Ombony & Dain v Jones (1859) 19 NY 234, 239.

20. Lewis v Ocean Navi. & Pier Co. (1891) 125 NY 341, 351, 26 NE 301; Sigrol Realty Corp. v Valcich (1961, 2d Dept) 12 AD2d 430, 212 NYS2d 224, affd 11 NY2d 668, 225 NYS2d 748, 180 NE2d 904.
1. Real Prop L § 226-a.

757

established by decisional law prior to the enactment of this amendment.[2]

### § 16:15. Tenant's Right to Remove Fixtures upon Abandonment of Possession

When a tenant surrenders possession, or abandons possession, of leased premises, without removing his fixtures, by operation of law, title to all fixtures remaining on the premises is vested in the landlord.[3]

### § 16:16. Tenant's Reservation of Right to Remove Fixtures

Basically, a landlord has been given title to fixtures left on the leased premises by the tenant after abandoning possession on the theory of an implied gift or of an abandonment of the fixtures. When, however, the facts and circumstances negative such theory of gift or abandonment, the tenant's right of removal will be observed. Thus, where a tenant leaves his fixtures on the premises after the termination of his lease, relying on a promise of the landlord that they may be removed at a later date, the tenant will not thereby lose his right of removal.[4]

Where a tenant was induced to surrender his lease and possession of the premises with his fixtures thereon, under an agreement with his landlord that in the event of a sale of the premises or a new lease, the landlord would either purchase or procure the new owner or tenant to purchase the fixtures, it was held that the tenant did not forfeit his right to the fixtures. "Leaving the property on the premises after the expiration of their

---

2. Prior to the amendment the law was well settled that when a tenant had the right of removal, he lost such right upon taking a new lease to the premises without mention of the fixtures or of his right of removal. Upon continuing in possession under such new lease he was not permitted to remove such fixtures either during or at the expiration of the new term. Loughran v Ross (1871) 45 NY 792; Precht v Howard (1907) 187 NY 136, 79 NE 847; Stephens v Ely (1900) 162 NY 79, 56 NE 499; Talbot v Cruger (1896) 151 NY 117, 45 NE 364.

This statute, however, is not applicable to leases entered into prior to September 1, 1959, its effective date. Wedtke Realty Corp. v Karanas (1961, 4th Dept) 13 AD2d 615, 213 NYS2d 757, aff'd 10 NY2d 949, 224 NYS2d 273, 180 NE2d 56.

3. Bedlow v New York Floating Dry-Dock Co. (1889) 112 NY 263, 283, 19 NE 800; Mott Pipe & Supply Corp. v Blue Ridge Coal Corp. (M Ct Bx 1955) 208 Misc 601, 146 NYS2d 607; Metzger v Price (S Ct Suffolk Co 1911) 73 Misc 294, 132 NYS 411.

4. Duffus v Bangs (1890) 122 NY 423, 25 NE 980.

# FIXTURES § 16:18

term, under such circumstances," said the Court of Appeals,[5] "did not work a forfeiture of its ownership."

## § 16:17. Right of Removal of Substitutions or Replacements of Fixtures Made by Tenant

A fixture substituted by a tenant for another fixture which was upon the premises at the time of the making of the lease cannot ordinarily be removed by him if the original fixture has been injured or permanently removed, or there is no evidence of what disposition was made of the replaced fixture.[6] But, it has been held that if the original fixture has been preserved and can be replaced, the tenant may then remove the new fixture, if, of course, it is a trade or domestic fixture which he can remove.[7]

## § 16:18. Tenant's Right to Personal Property Left on Premises After His/Her Removal or Eviction

The doctrine of abandonment of fixtures upon surrender or abandonment of possession by a tenant[8] does not apply to movable personal property belonging to the tenant.[9] As to ordinary chattels belonging to a tenant, and left by him on the premises after his removal or eviction, the tenant does not abandon his title thereto by leaving them there.[10] As Bosworth, J., said[11] in an early case, "Such articles, when placed by a tenant in a demised building during his term, are his property. If not removed by him during the term, they do not, for that reason, cease to be his property. He may remove them after his term expires without subjecting himself to any damage for such removal, even though he be liable to an action of trespass for an entry on the demised premises."

---

**5.** Thorn v Sutherland (1890) 123 NY 236, 241, 25 NE 362. Also, see, Yorkshire Ice Co. v Flanagan (AD1 1917) 176 AD 536, 163 NYS 212; Stone v National Surgical Stores Co. (AT1 1922) 193 NYS 684, where it was held that a new tenant could not object to the removal by a previous tenant of the latter's fixtures, where the landlord did not object and made no claim thereto.

**6.** Bartholomay Brewery Co. v Davenport (AD3 1913) 158 AD 47, 142 NYS 960.

**7.** Andrews v Day Button Co. (1892) 132 NY 348, 30 NE 831; Bartholomay Brewery Co. v Davenport (AD3 1913) 158 AD 47, 142 NYS 960.

**8.** See § 16:15, supra.

**9.** Sears v Sovie (AD3 1913) 158 AD 102, 143 NYS 317; Reich v Cochran (AD1 1906) 114 AD 141, 99 NYS 755.

**10.** Congregation Anshe Sefard, Inc. v Title Guarantee & Trust Co. (1943) 291 NY 35, 50 NE2d 534, 148 ALR 647, reh den 291 NY 669, 51 NE2d 939; Reich v Cochran (AD1 1906) 114 AD 141, 99 NYS 755.

**11.** Lawrence v Kemp (S Ct GT 1852) 8 NY Super Ct 363, 365.

### § 16:19. Landlord's Obligation as to Tenant's Personal Property Left on Premises After His/Her Removal or Eviction

As to ordinary chattels left upon the premises on removal or after eviction of a tenant, it is the duty of the landlord to notify the tenant to remove them, and, in case he does not, to himself cause their removal;[12] and the law will imply an obligation on the part of the tenant to reimburse the landlord for the reasonable cost of removal.[13] But, if the landlord, his grantee, or succeeding tenant appropriates such property to his own use, or refuses to allow such property to be removed, he will be guilty of a conversion.[14]

### § 16:20. Form of Provision for Removal of Fixtures

#### Form No. 41

#### Tenant's Right of Removal of Fixtures

Tenant shall make no changes in or to the leased premises of any nature without Landlord's prior written consent. Subject to the prior written consent of Landlord, and to the provisions of this article, Tenant at Tenant's expense, may make alterations, installations, additions or improvements which are non-structural and which do not affect utility services or plumbing and electrical lines, in or to the interior of the leased premises by using contractors or mechanics first approved by Landlord. All fixtures

---

12. Congregation Anshe Sefard, Inc. v Title Guarantee & Trust Co. (1943) 291 NY 35, 50 NE2d 534, 148 ALR 647, reh den 291 NY 669, 51 NE2d 939; Reich v Cochran (AD1 1906) 114 AD 141, 99 NYS 755.

Also, see Abandoned Prop L § 1310.

13. Ide v Finn (AD1 1921) 196 AD 304, 187 NYS 202; Wilk Enterprises, Inc. v J. I. B. Realty Corp. (NYC Civ Ct Queens Co 1972) 72 Misc 2d 507, 339 NYS2d 75.

14. Yorkshire Ice Co. v Flanagan (AD1 1917) 176 AD 536, 163 NYS 212; Marder v Heinemann (AD1 1906) 114 AD 794, 100 NYS 250; Price v Hoyle (Rockland Co Ct 1975) 82 Misc 2d 174, 368 NYS2d 126.

A landlord has no absolute right to retain or destroy personal property belonging to a tenant. Even where a tenant is legally dispossessed, the landlord's rights extend only to the real property. He acquires no concomitant right to use or retain the tenant's personal property. Glass v Weiner (1984, 2d Dept) 104 AD2d 967, 480 NYS2d 760.

Whether tenant abandons leased premises, or is locked out therefrom, landlord has no right whatsoever to tenant's personal property. If landlord seizes it because of allegedly accrued rent, it is distress for rent, which has been abolished (see § 993, main volume). Price v Hoyle (Rockland Co Ct 1975) 82 Misc 2d 174, 368 NYS2d 126.

The reletting of the premises, and the removal of the property by the new tenant is not a conversion of the property by the landlord. Huntington v Herrman (AD1 1906) 111 AD 875, 98 NYS 48, affd 188 NY 622, 81 NE 1166.

and all paneling, partitions, railings and like installations, installed in the premises at any time, either by Tenant or by Landlord in Tenant's behalf, shall, upon installation, become the property of Landlord and shall remain upon and be surrendered with the leased premises unless Landlord, by notice to Tenant no later than twenty days prior to the date fixed as the termination of this lease, elects to relinquish Landlord's right thereto and to have them removed by Tenant, in which event, the same shall be removed from the premises by Tenant prior to the expiration of the lease, at Tenant's expense. Nothing in this article shall be construed to give Landlord title to or to prevent Tenant's removal of trade fixtures, moveable office furniture and equipment, but upon removal of any such from the premises or upon removal of other installations as may be required by Landlord, Tenant shall immediately and at its expense, repair and restore the premises to the condition existing prior to installation and repair any damage to the leased premises or the building due to such removal. All property permitted or required to be removed by Tenant at the end of the term remaining in the premises after Tenant's removal shall be deemed abandoned and may, at the election of Landlord, either be retained as Landlord's property or may be removed from the premises by Landlord at Tenant's expense. Tenant shall, before making any alterations, additions, installations or improvements, at its expense, obtain all permits, approvals and certificates required by any governmental or quasi-governmental bodies and (upon completion) certificates of final approval thereof and shall deliver promptly duplicates of all such permits, approvals and certificates to Landlord and Tenant agrees to carry and will cause Tenant's contractors and sub-contractors to carry such workman's compensation, general liability, personal and property damage insurance as Landlord may require. If any mechanic's lien is filed against the leased premises, or the building of which the same forms a part, for work claimed to have been done for, or materials furnished to, Tenant, whether or not done pursuant to this article, the same shall be discharged by Tenant within ten days thereafter, at Tenant's expense, by filing the bond required by law.

**§ 16:20**  LANDLORD AND TENANT

*[Add, if desired:* All electric light fixtures that may be installed by Tenant, together with all wiring and other equipment pertaining thereto, shall continue to be the property of Tenant, and may be removed by Tenant at the expiration or other termination of the lease.][15]

## C. RESEARCH REFERENCES

### § 16:21. Generally

In addition to the preceding text, the reader is also referred to the following:

35 Am Jur 2d, Fixtures §§ 35 et seq.;

49 Am Jur 2d, Landlord and Tenant §§ 25, 35, 342, 703, 742, 929, 994, 1015, 1053, 1079.

11 Am Jur Legal Forms 2d, Leases of Real Property §§ 161:451-161:462.

New York CLS Real Property Law § 226-a.

New York Forms, Leases, Forms 8:221-8:224.

Index to Annotations, Landlord and Tenant.

**VERALEX®:** Cases and annotations referred to herein can be further researched through the VERALEX electronic retrieval system's two services, **Auto-Cite®** and **SHOWME®**. Use Auto-Cite to check citations for form, parallel references, prior and later history, and annotation references. Use SHOWME to display the full text of cases and annotations.

---

15. For form of complete lease, see Chaper 1, supra.

# NEW YORK PRACTICE LIBRARY

## New York Landlord and Tenant

including
**Summary Proceedings**
Third Edition

by

**Joseph Rasch**
of the New York Bar

> INSERT this new cumulative supplement into the pocket located on the inside back cover of your volume. DISCARD the previously issued cumulative supplement at this time.

**Cumulative Supplement to Volume 1**

Prepared by
**Robert F. Dolan**
former Nassau County District Court Judge

Issued June 1997

**Lawyers Cooperative Publishing™**
Aqueduct Building, Rochester, New York 14694

Copyright © 1990, 1991
by
The Lawyers Co-operative Publishing Company

Copyright © 1992-1997
by
Lawyers Cooperative Publishing,
a division of Thomson Information Services, Inc.

Authorization to photocopy items for internal, educational, or personal use, or for the internal or personal use of specific clients, may be obtained from Lawyers Cooperative Publishing, a division of Thomson Information Services, Inc., by contacting the **Copyright Clearance Center,** 222 Rosewood Drive, Danvers, MA 01923, USA (508) 750-8400; fax (508) 750-4470; and by paying the appropriate fee. For authorization to reprint items for inclusion in a publication for sale only, please contact an LCP Client Services representative at 1-800-527-0430, in lieu of contacting the CCC.

"This publication is designed to provide accurate and authoritative information in regard to the Subject Matter covered. It is sold with the understanding that the publisher is not engaged in rendering legal, accounting, or other professional service. If legal advice or other expert assistance is required, the services of a competent professional person should be sought." From a Declaration of Principles jointly adopted by a Committee of the American Bar Association and a Committee of Publishers and Associations.

*Library of Congress Catalog Card Number 88-81921*

# PREFACE

This treatise was first published in 1950 and over the years became the "Bible" of summary proceedings and landlord-tenant law in New York State. It was written, revised and updated for almost 40 years by one author, Joseph Rasch, until his death in 1990.

I am very pleased and flattered to have been selected by Lawyers Cooperative Publishing to author the supplements of this distinguished work.

My objective will be not only to keep the practitioner (by that I mean lawyer and trial judge) apprised of new case law but to continually review older case law and assess how it applies to current trends in legal thinking on the subject of landlord-tenant law.

I will be referring to more Law Journal cases than the present work. It is my belief that although these cases are not always officially reported they set forth a trend of thought of the judiciary and therefore are a guide to the practitioner.

I will also comment cases and trends setting forth my opinion.

I welcome comments and suggestions from both the bench and bar to make this work responsive to the landlord-tenant practitioner.

ROBERT F. DOLAN

# TABLE OF CONTENTS

## VOLUME 1

### PART ONE

### THE COMMENCEMENT OF THE LANDLORD-TENANT RELATIONSHIP

#### CHAPTER 1

#### GENERAL PRINCIPLES

A. IN GENERAL
- § 1:1. Definitions of Fundamental Terms
- § 1:2. Nature of a Lease
- § 1:4. Interest of Tenant in Term to Commence in Future
- § 1:5. Possession of Tenant as Possession of Landlord

B. NOTICE OF TENANT'S RIGHTS
- § 1:7. Notice of Tenant's Rights by Recording Lease
- § 1:10. Notice of Tenant's Rights from Possession

#### CHAPTER 2

#### REQUISITES AND VALIDITY OF LEASES

A. IN GENERAL
- § 2:1. Necessity for Contract, Express or Implied
- § 2:4. Creation of Landlord-Tenant Relationship by Attornment to Title Paramount
- § 2:7. Necessity for a Valid Contract
- § 2:8. Lease Must Not Be Unconscionable
- § 2:11. Fraud; Effect and Remedies
- § 2:19. Violation of Certificate of Occupancy
- § 2:20. Landlord's Failure to Obtain Certificate of Occupancy
- § 2:21. Zoning Violation

D. STATUTE OF FRAUDS
- § 2:35. Generally

# TABLE OF CONTENTS

## CHAPTER 3
### AGREEMENT FOR LEASE

A. IN GENERAL
  § 3:1.  Nature and Effect

C. DEPOSIT
  § 3:11. Stipulated or Liquidated Damages
  § 3:13. Effect on Deposit Where Lease Not Consummated

D. BREACH
  § 3:14. Action for Damages
  § 3:16. Specific Performance

## CHAPTER 4
### LEASES AND OTHER INTERESTS IN REAL PROPERTY DISTINGUISHED

A. IN GENERAL
  § 4:1.  Test of Distinction
  § 4:9.  Effect of Nature of Occupancy Where Tenant Becomes Employee

B. DISTINGUISHING BETWEEN LEASE AND LICENSE
  § 4:11. Test
  § 4:21. Revocability of License

C. PROPRIETARY LEASE (CO-OPERATIVE OWNERSHIP)
  § 4:22. Generally

E. CONDOMINIUM OWNERSHIP *(NEW)*
  § 4:25. Generally
  § 4:26. Defined
  § 4:27. Distinguished From Other Forms of Co-ownership
  § 4:28. Ownership of Unit
  § 4:29. Common Interest
  § 4:30. Required Documents of Ownership
  § 4:31. Floor Plan
  § 4:32. Bylaws
  § 4:33. Recording of Declaration
  § 4:34. Rights of Unit Owners
  § 4:35. Obligations of Unit Owners
  § 4:36. Separate Taxation of Units
  § 4:37. Type of Work by Unit Owners Prohibited
  § 4:38. Lien for Common Charges
  § 4:39. Insurance of Building
  § 4:40. Repair or Reconstruction of the Building

# TABLE OF CONTENTS

§ 4:41. Waiver of Use of Common Elements
§ 4:42. Common Profits and Expenses
§ 4:43. Satisfaction of Blanket Liens on Units on Conveyance
§ 4:44. Liens against Common Elements
§ 4:45. Actions against Unit Owners
§ 4:46. Withdrawal From Provisions of Condominium Act

## CHAPTER 5

## TITLE AND REVERSION OF LANDLORD

A. IN GENERAL
  § 5:5. Possession of Tenant as Possession of Landlord

B. ESTOPPEL TO DENY LANDLORD'S TITLE
  § 5:8. Generally

C. TRANSFER OF REVERSION
  § 5:15. Generally
  § 5:17. Rights and Obligations of Grantee
  § 5:18. Rights on Transfer of Reversion to Rent Due or to Become Due
  § 5:19. Waiver of Grantor Binding on Grantee

## CHAPTER 6

## CONSTRUCTION OF LEASES

A. IN GENERAL
  § 6:2. Ascertaining Intent
  § 6:3. Practical Construction by the Parties
  § 6:4. Statutes as Part of a Lease
  § 6:7. Reconciling Inconsistencies
  § 6:13. Unconscionable Lease or Clause

B. PAROL EVIDENCE RULE
  § 6:14. Generally
  § 6:15. Exceptions to the Parol Evidence Rule
  § 6:18. Ambiguity or Uncertainty in Instrument

C. MODIFICATION OF LEASE
  § 6:22. Generally
  § 6:25. Oral Modification
  § 6:26. —Provision Against Oral Modification
  § 6:27. —Form of Provision Against Oral Modification

# TABLE OF CONTENTS

## PART TWO

## THE RESPECTIVE RIGHTS AND OBLIGATIONS OF LANDLORD AND TENANT

### CHAPTER 7

### PREMISES LEASED: EASEMENTS AND APPURTENANCES

A. IN GENERAL
- § 7:1. What is Included in a Lease?
- § 7:5. Appurtenances Defined
- § 7:7. Illustrations of Appurtenances Included in a Lease

B. WHAT IS INCLUDED IN LEASE OF PART OF BUILDING
- § 7:10. Generally
- § 7:17. Lobby Attendant Services

C. RIGHT TO LIGHT, AIR, UTILITIES, ETC.
- § 7:24. Air Space Rights

D. FARM LANDS LEASE
- § 7:26. Right to Crops
- § 7:28. Right to Emblements

### CHAPTER 8

### OBLIGATIONS TO DELIVER POSSESSION AND TO OCCUPY PREMISES

- § 8:3. Right to Damages Against Landlord
- § 8:6. —Right to Loss of Profits and Time
- § 8:7. Action to Recover Possession
- § 8:11. Form of Covenant to Deliver Possession
- § 8:12. Form of Provision to Protect Landlord Against Inability to Deliver Possession
- § 8:13. Tenant's Obligation to Occupy

### CHAPTER 9

### ASSIGNMENT AND SUBLETTING

A. IN GENERAL
- § 9:2. Assignment and Sublease Defined

B. DISTINGUISHING BETWEEN ASSIGNMENT AND SUBLEASE
- § 9:4. Fundamental Test
- § 9:5. Pro Tanto Assignment and Sublease

# TABLE OF CONTENTS

§ 9:14. Distinction Between Assignment and Sublease Summarized

I. SURVIVAL OF DECEASED TENANT'S LIABILITY
§ 9:52. Generally
§ 9:53. Nature of Liability of Personal Representative

K. SUBTENANT'S LIABILITIES AND RIGHTS
§ 9:60. Rights Limited by Terms of Paramount Lease

L. SUBTENANT'S RIGHTS ON CANCELLATION OF PARAMOUNT LEASE
§ 9:67. Right to Vacate
§ 9:69. Right to Possession

M. SUBTENANT'S RIGHTS ON VOLUNTARY SURRENDER OF PARAMOUNT LEASE
§ 9:73. Generally

N. RIGHT TO ASSIGN AND SUBLET
§ 9:75. Generally
§ 9:77. Effect of Emergency Rent Laws
§ 9:78. Residential Tenant's Statutory Right to Assign
§ 9:79. Residential Tenant's Statutory Right to Sublet

O. RESTRICTIONS ON RIGHT TO ASSIGN AND SUBLET
§ 9:89. Breach of Restriction; Voluntary Acts of Tenant
§ 9:94. —Acts of Personal Representatives of Deceased Tenant
§ 9:96. Right of Landlord to Withhold Consent
§ 9:98. Criteria for Determination of Reasonableness
§ 9:99. Statutory Modification of Right to Withhold Consent in Case of a Deceased Residential Tenant
§ 9:101. Landlord's Remedies for Breach of Restriction Against Assignment or Subletting

## CHAPTER 10

### EFFECT OF HOLDING OVER

A. IN GENERAL
§ 10:7. Holding Over by Assignee or Subtenant
§ 10:9. Measure of Damages for Holding Over

B. STATUTORY TENANCY
§ 10:13. Expiration of Tenancy on Death of Tenant
§ 10:14. Terms and Conditions of Tenancy

## TABLE OF CONTENTS

### CHAPTER 11

### RENEWAL OF LEASES

A. RIGHT OF RENEWAL ABSENT COVENANT
- § 11:1. Generally
- § 11:8. Mobile Home Park Tenancy

B. COVENANT TO RENEW
- § 11:11. Necessity of Certainty

E. EXERCISING RIGHT TO RENEW
- § 11:34. Necessity of Strict Performance of Conditions Precedent
- § 11:35. Necessity of Timely Notice to Renew
- § 11:36. When Performance of Other Provision of Lease Necessary
- § 11:39. Equitable Relief from Failure to Give Timely Notice of Election to Renew
- § 11:40. Waiver of Performance of Conditions to Renewal

H. REMEDIES FOR BREACH OF COVENANT TO RENEW
- § 11:59. Specific Performance
- § 11:60. Action for Declaratory Judgment

### CHAPTER 12

### RENT

A. IN GENERAL
- § 12:1. Nature and Definition
- § 12:6. Attorney's Fees as Rent
- § 12:7. Attorney's Fees as Rent; Mobile Homes
- § 12:12. Implied Agreement to Pay Rent

B. PAYMENT OF RENT
- § 12:26. Provision for Acceleration

### CHAPTER 13

### DEPOSIT TO SECURE PERFORMANCE OF LEASE

A. IN GENERAL
- § 13:2. Importance of Determining Nature of Deposit
- § 13:5. Immateriality of Names Used in Determining Nature of Deposit
- § 13:6. Criteria for Determining Nature of Deposit

# TABLE OF CONTENTS

C. DUTY WITH RESPECT TO DEPOSIT ON CONVEYANCE OF LEASED PROPERTY
 § 13:22. Liability of Grantee or Assignee for Deposits Made by Tenant on Conveyance of Rent Stabilized Dwelling Units

D. CONVERSION OF DEPOSIT
 § 13:27. Deposit as Trust Fund

## CHAPTER 14

## TENANT'S OBLIGATION TO PAY TAXES AND WATER CHARGES

B. COVENANT TO PAY TAXES
 § 14:9. Special Assessments
 § 14:13. Covenant to Pay Increase in Taxes
 § 14:23. Covenant to Pay Taxes "Levied or Imposed During Term"

## CHAPTER 15

## TENANT'S RIGHTS IN THE USE OF THE LEASED PREMISES

A. IN GENERAL
 § 15:4. Sharing of Apartment

B. WASTE
 § 15:7. Structural Alterations as Waste

C. WHEN TENANT MAY MAKE ALTERATIONS
 § 15:11. Generally
 § 15:13. Consent Granted by Lease "To Make Inside Alterations Provided Premises Not Injured"
 § 15:20. Right of Tenants in Multiple Dwellings to Install Locks

F. MISCELLANEOUS
 § 15:33. Protection from Harassment of Landlord

G. EXPRESS RESTRICTIONS ON USE OF PREMISES BY TENANT
 § 15:39. Specification of Purpose as Description or Limitation of Use of Premises; Forms
 § 15:44. Restriction by Rules and Regulations of Landlord
 § 15:47. Mobile Home Parks

# TABLE OF CONTENTS

**H. WAIVER OF EXPRESS RESTRICTION**
§ 15:55. Waiver Binding on Grantee

**J. RESTRICTION ON LESSOR'S USE OF OTHER PREMISES**
§ 15:59. Generally
§ 15:62. Remedies at Law Against Lessor for Breach
§ 15:64. Measure of Damages for Breach
§ 15:67. Equitable Relief Against Competing Tenant

## CHAPTER 16
## FIXTURES

**A. IN GENERAL**
§ 16:1. Fixture Defined
§ 16:2. Trade and Domestic Fixtures Defined

---

## TOTAL CLIENT-SERVICE LIBRARY® REFERENCES

**Am Jur Proof of Facts:**

2 Am Jur Proof of Facts 3d 393, Landlord's Liability for Inquiry by Tenant's Dog

3 Am Jur Proof of Facts 3d 581, Sexual Harassment by Landlord

7 Am Jur Proof of Facts 3d 655, Material Breach of Commercial Lease

**Am Jur Trials:**

27 Am Jur Trials 621, Resolving Real Estate Disputes Through Arbitration

28 Am Jur Trials 1, Housing Discrimination Litigation

35 Am Jur Trials 1, Landlord Liability for Criminal Attack on Tenant

**ALR Index:** Landlord and Tenant

# PART ONE
## THE COMMENCEMENT OF THE LANDLORD-TENANT RELATIONSHIP

### CHAPTER 1
### GENERAL PRINCIPLES

A. IN GENERAL
 § 1:1. Definitions of Fundamental Terms
 § 1:2. Nature of a Lease
 § 1:4. Interest of Tenant in Term to Commence in Future
 § 1:5. Possession of Tenant as Possession of Landlord

B. NOTICE OF TENANT'S RIGHTS
 § 1:7. Notice of Tenant's Rights by Recording Lease
 § 1:10. Notice of Tenant's Rights from Possession

---

### A. IN GENERAL
### § 1:1. Definitions of Fundamental Terms

p. 4, n. 3—Whether a document is a lease must be determined by its terms. In Miller v New York (1964) 15 NY2d 34, 255 NYS2d 78, 203 NE2d 478, the Court of Appeals held that a document calling itself a license was in actuality a lease where it granted an exclusive right to use and occupy the land.

In Skolnik v Utica Shell Service Center, Ltd. (1975) 81 Misc 2d 417, 366 NYS2d 301, the court reviewed an alleged franchise agreement and determined it contained all the essential elements of a lease.

A court is empowered to construe the true nature of an instrument and is not bound by the terms employed by the parties. Jobco-Mitchel Field, Inc. v Lazarus (1989, 2d Dept) 156 App Div 2d 426, 548 NYS2d 700, app den 75 NY2d 711, 557 NYS2d 310, 556 NE2d 1117, reconsideration den 76 NY2d 889.

Davis v Dinkins (1994, 2d Dept) 206 AD2d 365, 613 NYS2d 933, app den 85 NY2d 804, 626 NYS2d 756, 650 NE2d 415. The distinguishing characteristic of a lease, the court held, is the surrender of absolute possession and control of property to another party for an agreed-upon rental.

In Mur-Mil Caterers, Inc. v Werner (1990, 2d Dept) 166 AD2d 565, 560 NYS2d 849 the court determined that in order "[t]o constitute a valid agreement for the lease of real property, the parties must have reached final agreement upon all its essential terms, without reservation of any terms for future negotiations."

### § 1:2. Nature of a Lease

p. 5, n. 17—The court emphasized the established rule that "the primary

13

§ 1:2

LANDLORD AND TENANT

characteristics of a lease are that it be a bilateral agreement which divests the party owning the property of possession, dominion, and control and vests those rights in a second party," and also that "there must be a provision for rent which is either specifically stated in the agreement or ascertainable from other facts in accordance with a formula or agreement contained within the agreement." Kay Management Group, Inc. v Hill (1989) 145 Misc 2d 161, 545 NYS2d 1015.

A lease governs the rights and duties of the landlord to the tenant and the rights and duties of the tenants to the landlord but does not govern the rights and obligations of the cotenants to each other. Marks v Macchiarola (1994, 1st Dept) 204 App Div 2d 221, 612 NYS2d 405.

23 Realty Assocs. v Teigman (1995, 1st Dept) 213 AD2d 306, 624 NYS2d 155. The residential lease is a purchase of services from the landlord.

p. 6, n. 20—A letter may constitute a lease when it 1) sets forth the area to be leased, 2) the duration of the lease, and 3) the price to be paid. Bernstein v 1995 Assoc. (1992, 1st Dept) 185 AD2d 160, 586 NYS2d 115. However, a memorandum which designates the parties and identities and describes the subject matter does not represent a contract to convey an interest in real property when it does not state all of the essential terms of a complete agreement, such as the consideration. Spirt v Spirt (1994, 2d Dept) 209 AD2d 688, 619 NYS2d 316.

p. 7, n. 5—Since a residential lease is now effectively deemed a sale of shelter and services by the landlord, those provisions of General Business Law § 349, dealing with deceptive acts and practices apply to a residential lease. Frazier v Priest (City Ct Jefferson Co 1988) 141 Misc 2d 775, 534 NYS2d 846. ("The days of caveat emptor, caveat lessee, and the deceptions of the Simon Legree are over as a matter of law for tenants," per Harberson, J.)

COMMENT: Although the

14

section provides for a private right of action for persons injured by a violation of the statute, it is not clear that § 349 was intended to become a factor in the *defense* of a summary proceeding. See § 43:21.

§ 1:4. Interest of Tenant in Term to Commence in Future

p. 8, n. 13—Jobco-Mitchel Field, Inc. v Lazarus (1989, 2d Dept) 156 App Div 2d 426, 548 NYS2d 700, app den 75 NY2d 711, 557 NYS2d 310, 556 NE2d 1117, reconsideration den 76 NY2d 889.

§ 1:5. Possession of Tenant as Possession of Landlord

p. 9, n. 17—See Rasch, New York Law and Practice of Real Property § 30:23.

B. NOTICE OF TENANT'S RIGHTS

§ 1:7. Notice of Tenant's Rights by Recording Lease

p. 11, n. 8—See Rasch, New York Law and Practice of Real Property § 28:6.

§ 1:10. Notice of Tenant's Rights from Possession

p. 14, n. 18—Relying on Phelan v Brady (1890) 119 NY 587, 23 NE 1109, the court, in 52 Riverside Realty Co. v Ebenhart (1986, 1st Dept) 119 AD2d 452, 500 NYS2d 259, held that possession of the premises constitutes constructive notice to a purchaser of the rights of the possessor.

## GENERAL PRINCIPLES § 1:10

In Fekishazy v Thomson (1994, 3d Dept) 204 AD2d 959, 612 NYS2d 276, app dismd 84 NY2d 844, 617 NYS2d 130, 641 NE2d 151 and app den 84 NY2d 812, 622 NYS2d 915, 647 NE2d 121 the prior record owner's actual possession of the premises as tenant did not provide notice of lease.

**p. 15, n. 3**—Majestic Farms Supply, Ltd. v Surowiec (1990, 2d Dept) 160 AD2d 777, 553 NYS2d 856.

# CHAPTER 2
# REQUISITES AND VALIDITY OF LEASES

A. IN GENERAL
  § 2:1. Necessity for Contract, Express or Implied
  § 2:4. Creation of Landlord-Tenant Relationship by Attornment to Title Paramount
  § 2:7. Necessity for a Valid Contract
  § 2:8. Lease Must Not Be Unconscionable
  § 2:11. Fraud; Effect and Remedies
  § 2:19. Violation of Certificate of Occupancy
  § 2:20. Landlord's Failure to Obtain Certificate of Occupancy
  § 2:21. Zoning Violation

D. STATUTE OF FRAUDS
  § 2:35. Generally

## A. IN GENERAL

### § 2:1. Necessity for Contract, Express or Implied

p. 104, n. 2—Oppenheimer & Co. v Oppenheim, Appel, Dixon & Co. (1995) 86 NY2d 685. In this case, where the parties had entered into a conditional sublease providing that it would be executed only upon the satisfaction of certain conditions, the court set forth its understanding of the principles of "condition precedent," "express conditions" and "implied or constructive conditions" in contracts for the lease or sale of real property.

A "conditional precedent," the court held, is an act or event, other than a lapse of time, which, unless the condition is excused, must occur before a duty to perform a promise in the agreement arises and therefore no contract arises "unless and until the condition occurs."

The court stated that conditions can be express or implied. Express conditions, it held, are those agreed to and imposed by the parties themselves, whereas implied or constructive conditions are those "imposed by law to do justice." Express conditions must be literally performed, whereas constructive conditions, which ordinarily arise from language of promise, are subject to the principle that "substantial compliance is sufficient."

In determining whether a particular agreement makes an event a "condition" a court will interpret doubtful language as embodying a promise or "constructive condition" rather than an "express condition." This interpretive preference by the courts, it stated, is especially strong when a finding of "express condition" would increase the risk of forfeiture by the obligee.

The court further emphasized that

# REQUISITES AND VALIDITY OF LEASES § 2:8

interpretation as a means of reducing the risk of forfeiture cannot be employed "if the occurrence of the event as a condition is expressed in unmistakable language." Stating that where the language is clear, the policy favoring freedom of contract requires that, within broad limits, the agreement of the parties should be honored even though it results in a forfeiture, the court nonetheless held that the occurrence of the condition may yet be excused by waiver, breach or forfeiture. If the non-occurrence of a condition would cause disproportionate forfeiture, it held that a court may excuse the non-performance of the condition unless its occurrence was a "material part of the agreed exchange."

p. 105, n. 8—Loren v Marry (1993, 3d Dept) 195 App Div 2d 776, 600 NYS2d 369, app dismd 82 NY2d 800, 604 NYS2d 554, 624 NE2d 692 and app dismd, in part, app den, in part 83 NY2d 824, 612 NYS2d 103, 634 NE2d 598, reconsideration den 83 NY2d 954, 615 NYS2d 878, 639 NE2d 419, amd 84 NY2d 846, 617 NYS2d 132, 641 NE2d 152. See § 4:11, infra.

## § 2:4. Creation of Landlord-Tenant Relationship by Attornment to Title Paramount

p. 107, n. 3—Boyar v Goodman (1994, 2d Dept) 202 AD2d 541, 609 NYS2d 279. Upon the death of the life tenant, the landlord, the tenant's lease and right to possession of the premises terminated and he became a tenant at sufferance. Upon the receipt of a notice to quit, his tenancy was terminated. By paying rent directly to the remaindermen, the subtenants attorned to the landlord which, in effect, ousted the plaintiff-tenant and reinstated possession under the remaindermen.

## § 2:7. Necessity for a Valid Contract

p. 110, n. 18—The court held that the provision in a lease which stated that rent was to be "predicated upon a normal increase," was not a figure ascertainable by an objective standard and therefore the purported lease failed for indefiniteness Mur-Mil Caterers, Inc. v Werner (1990, 2d Dept) 166 AD2d 565, 560 NYS2d 849.

p. 110, n. 1—The "doctrine of definiteness or certainty" means that a court cannot enforce a contract unless it is able to determine what in fact the parties have agreed to. 166 Mamaroneck Ave. Corp. v 151 East Post Rd. Corp. (1991) 78 NY2d 88, 571 NYS2d 686, 575 NE2d 104. Therefore, if an agreement is not reasonably certain in its material terms, there can be no legally enforceable contract. While the principle of "definiteness" is often stated, its application may be difficult and the concept cannot be reduced to a precise universal measurement. Cobble Hill Nursing Home, Inc. v Henry & Warren Corp. (1988, 2d Dept) 144 AD2d 518, 534 NYS2d 399, app dismd without op 74 NY2d 791, 545 NYS2d 105, 543 NE2d 748, reh gr, app gr, stay gr, reh den 74 NY2d 803, 545 NYS2d 691, 544 NE2d 610 and revd, remanded 74 NY2d 475, 548 NYS2d 920, 548 NE2d 203, reh den, motion den 75 NY2d 863, 552 NYS2d 925, 552 NE2d 173 and cert den 498 US 816, 112 L Ed 2d 33, 111 S Ct 58, appeal after remand (2d Dept) 196 AD2d 564, 601 NYS2d 334, app den 83 NY2d 756, 614 NYS2d 386, 637 NE2d 277.

## § 2:8. Lease Must Not Be Unconscionable

p. 112, n. 13—In granting tenant's request for specific performance of an option to purchase real property the court, in Bay Ridge Fed. Sav. & Loan Ass'n v Morano (1993, 2d Dept) 199 AD2d 354, 605 NYS2d 377, app den 84 NY2d 801, 617 NYS2d 135, 641 NE2d 156, held that there was no evidence that the lease was unfair when it was made. Furthermore, the option to purchase was not an unconscionable provision since there was no evidence that the landlord lacked a "meaningful choice" in signing the lease nor

§ 2:8

that the option to purchase was "unreasonably favorable" to the tenant. The fact that an option to purchase may no longer be beneficial to the landlord as a result of changing circumstances or subsequent events, the court held, does not preclude its performance. See also Khayyam v Diplacidi (1990, 1st Dept) 167 AD2d 300, 562 NYS2d 43 which held that equity will not relieve parties from bargains simply because they are unreasonable or unprofitable.

§ 2:11. Fraud; Effect and Remedies

p. 114, n. 11—Jakobs v Gambino (1994, 2d Dept) 204 App Div 2d 397, 614 NYS2d 183. The court dismissed the action to recover damages for a breach of a commercial lease for fraudulent misrepresentation stating that "[i]t is well settled that a cause of action seeking damages for fraud cannot be sustained when the only fraud charged relates to a breach of contract."

§ 2:19. Violation of Certificate of Occupancy

p. 127, n. 12—Kosher Konvenience, Inc. v Ferguson Realty Corp. (1991, 2d Dept) 171 App Div 2d 650, 567 NYS2d 131. Plaintiff's application declaring a commercial lease void due to the absence of a certificate of occupancy was denied since the lease specifically provided that plaintiff would procure the certificate of occupancy at its own expense in the event it was required by any governmental authority. "A commercial lease is not void for illegality merely because the premises is not covered by a certificate of occupancy. The lease will be considered a valid contract and the bar or legal use of the premises is readily correctable and the language used in the leases indicates that the parties intended that the defect be corrected and the premises legally occupied."

See also Turmon v Fantasia Auto, Inc. (1990, Dist Ct) 147 Misc 2d 450, 556 NYS2d 195.

p. 127, n. 13—See § 2:20, infra.

## LANDLORD AND TENANT

§ 2:20. Landlord's Failure to Obtain Certificate of Occupancy

p. 128, n. 14—See also Kosher Konvenience, Inc. v Ferguson Realty Corp. (1991, 2d Dept) 171 App Div 2d 650, 567 NYS2d 131; Turmon v Fantasia Auto, Inc. (1990, Dist Ct) 147 Misc 2d 450, 556 NYS2d 195.

Cromwell v Le Sannom Bldg. Corp. (1991, 1st Dept) 171 App Div 2d 372, 576 NYS2d 125. Since there is no certificate of occupancy for the building plaintiff sought the refund of past use and occupancy and that she should not have to pay future use and occupancy of the premises. The court found that compliance with MDL 284, that the owner take all reasonable and necessary action to obtain a certificate of occupancy, is sufficient to entitle the owner to collect use and occupancy despite the provisions of MDL 302 and despite any possible contrary interpretation of the decision in County Dollar Corp. v Douglas (1990, 1st Dept) 160 App Div 2d 537, 556 NYS2d 533, and (1st Dept) 161 App Div 2d 370.

Phillips & Huyler Assocs. v Flynn (1995, Sup App T) 164 Misc 2d 347, 627 NYS2d 868. In an action where the use of the premises as a medical office violated the certificate of occupancy and zoning law the court held that tenant is required to pay rent for use and occupancy of the premises holding that tenant should not be absolved from his fundamental obligation to pay rent.

§ 2:21. Zoning Violation

p. 128, n. 17—See § 2:20, supra.

## D. STATUTE OF FRAUDS

§ 2:35. Generally

p. 142, n.10—An oral agreement for five years is unenforceable. Farash v Sykes Datatronics, Inc. (1983) 59 NY2d 500, 465 NYS2d 917, 452 NE2d 1245; Otiniano v Magier (1992, 1st Dept) 181 AD2d 438, 580 NYS2d 759.

# CHAPTER 3
# AGREEMENT FOR A LEASE

A. IN GENERAL
§ 3:1. Nature and Effect

C. DEPOSIT
§ 3:11. Stipulated or Liquidated Damages
§ 3:13. Effect on Deposit Where Lease Not Consummated

D. BREACH
§ 3:14. Action for Damages
§ 3:16. Specific Performance

---

## A. IN GENERAL

### § 3:1. Nature and Effect

p. 148, n. 2—In Mur-Mil Caterers, Inc. v Werner (1990, 2d Dept) 166 AD2d 565, 560 NYS2d 849, the court held that to constitute a valid agreement for the lease of real property, the parties must agree upon all its essential terms, without reservation of any term for future negotiation. See § 1:1 and § 2:7, supra.

## C. DEPOSIT

### § 3:11. Stipulated or Liquidated Damages

p. 159, n. 2—Defendant signed a written lease for an apartment in plaintiff's building and paid one month's rent and a security deposit. The lease provided that it shall not bind the owner "unless and until it has been duly executed by the Owner and delivered to the Tenant." Prior to the execution of the lease by the owner, tenant notified the rental agent that he would not proceed with the rental. After receipt of the notice that defendant was unwilling to go forward with the rental the owner executed the lease and delivered it to defendant-tenant. Landlord-Owner thereafter commenced an action for six months rent for premature termination of the tenancy pursuant to a liquidated damage clause in the lease. Defendant-Tenant counterclaimed for return of his deposit. The lower court granted summary judgment in favor of defendant dismissing the complaint but refused to grant him summary judgment for the return of his deposit. The Appellate Division reversed and granted judgment in favor of defendant finding that absent a valid lease, there cannot be a default in the obligation warranting the forfeiture of the deposit and that the obligation to pay rent never occurred. Rivertower Assoc. v Chalfen (1990, 1st Dept) 153 App Div 2d 196, 549 NYS2d 719.

19

## § 3:13. Effect on Deposit Where Lease Not Consummated

p. 161, n. 11—Rivertower Assoc. v Chalfen (1990, 1st Dept) 167 App Div 2d 309, 562 NYS2d 54. Where a proposed lease is never executed and a rental application is no more than an offer to lease the premises subject to acceptance, the landlord must return the security and rent deposit.

## D. BREACH

## § 3:14. Action for Damages

p. 162, n. 16—Ordinarily punitive damages may not be awarded in an action involving a breach of a lease. Ciraolo v Miller (1988, 2d Dept) 138 AD2d 443, 525 NYS2d 861. However, in certain situations punitive damage may be appropriate. In Suffolk Sports Ctr. v Belli Constr. Corp. (1995, 2d Dept) 212 AD2d 241, 628 NYS2d 952, the court granted punitive damages since the landlord intentionally prevented tenant's access to the leased premises.

## § 3:16. Specific Performance

p. 164. n. 8—Straisa Realty Corp. v Woodbury Assoc. (1989, 2d Dept) 154 App Div 2d 453, 546 NYS2d 19.

## CHAPTER 4
## LEASES AND OTHER INTERESTS IN REAL PROPERTY DISTINGUISHED

A. IN GENERAL
  § 4:1. Test of Distinction
  § 4:9. Effect of Nature of Occupancy Where Tenant Becomes Employee

B. DISTINGUISHING BETWEEN LEASE AND LICENSE
  § 4:11. Test
  § 4:21. Revocability of License

C. PROPRIETARY LEASE (CO-OPERATIVE OWNERSHIP)
  § 4:22. Generally

E. CONDOMINIUM OWNERSHIP *(NEW)*
  § 4:25. Generally
  § 4:26. Defined
  § 4:27. Distinguished From Other Forms of Co-ownership
  § 4:28. Ownership of Unit
  § 4:29. Common Interest
  § 4:30. Required Documents of Ownership
  § 4:31. Floor Plan
  § 4:32. Bylaws
  § 4:33. Recording of Declaration
  § 4:34. Rights of Unit Owners
  § 4:35. Obligations of Unit Owners
  § 4:36. Separate Taxation of Units
  § 4:37. Type of Work by Unit Owners Prohibited
  § 4:38. Lien for Common Charges
  § 4:39. Insurance of Building
  § 4:40. Repair or Reconstruction of the Building
  § 4:41. Waiver of Use of Common Elements
  § 4:42. Common Profits and Expenses
  § 4:43. Satisfaction of Blanket Liens on Units on Conveyance
  § 4:44. Liens against Common Elements
  § 4:45. Actions against Unit Owners
  § 4:46. Withdrawal From Provisions of Condominium Act

## A. IN GENERAL

## § 4:1. Test of Distinction

p. 168, n. 1—In overruling the lower court the Appellate Division reaffirmed its statement in Cale Dev. Co. v Conciliation & Appeals Bd. (1983, 1st Dept) 94 AD2d 229, 463 NYS2d 814, affd 461 NY2d 979, 475 NYS2d 278, 463 NE2d 619 that "Lease interpretation is subject to the same rules of construction as are applicable to other agreements. . . . The parties' intention should be determined from the language employed, and where the language is clear and unambiguous, interpretation is a matter of law to be determined solely by the court. . . . In such circumstances resort cannot be had to extrinsic evidence to contradict the express terms of the writing." Louis R. Morandi, P. C. v Charter Management Co. (1990, 1st Dept) 159 AD2d 422, 553 NYS2d 663, amd (1st Dept) 166 AD2d 286.

p 168, n. 2—In American Jewish Theatre v Roundabout Theatre Co. (1994, 1st Dept) 203 App Div 2d 155, 610 NYS2d 256, involving preliminary injunctive relief, the court held "[w]hat defines the proprietary relationship between the parties is not its characterization or the technical language used in the instrument, but rather the manifest intention of the parties. . . . The nature of the transfer of absolute control and possession is what differentiates a lease from a license or any other arrangement dealing with property rights. . . . Whereas a license connotes use or occupancy of the grantor's premises, a lease grants exclusive possession of designated space to a tenant, subject to rights specifically reserved by the lessor. The former is cancellable at will, and without cause. . . . Where one party's interest in another's real property exists for a fixed term, not revocable at will, and terminable only on notice, a landlord-tenant relationship has been created." (citations omitted)

p. 168, n. 4—American Jewish Theatre v Roundabout Theatre Co. (1994, 1st Dept) 203 App Div 2d 155, 610 NYS2d 256.

p. 169, n. 1—American Jewish Theatre v Roundabout Theatre Co. (1994, 1st Dept) 203 App Div 2d 155, 610 NYS2d 256.

Davis v Dinkins (2d Dept) 206 App Div 2d 365, 613 NYS2d 933. This court held that "[t]he central distinguishing characteristic of a lease is the surrender of absolute possession and control of property to another party for an agreed-upon rental."

In Kay Management Group, Inc. v Hill (1989) 145 Misc 2d 161, 545 NYS2d 1015 the court set forth two primary characteristics of a lease 1) that it be a bilateral agreement divesting the party owning the property of possession, dominion, and control and vesting those rights in a second party, and 2) that there be a provision for rent which is either specifically stated in the agreement or ascertainable from other facts in accordance with a formula or arrangement contained within the agreement.

p. 170, n. 8—Universal Motor Lodges, Inc. v Seignious (1990) 146 Misc 2d 395, 550 NYS2d 800. See p. 182, n. 3, infra.

## § 4:9. Effect of Nature of Occupancy Where Tenant Becomes Employee

p. 179, n. 12—Where a landlord-tenant relationship existed prior to the master-servant relationship and tenant does not pay rent after termination of his employment the proper remedy is a non-payment summary proceeding since the landlord-tenant relationship continues after termination of the employment.

Where no landlord-tenant relationship existed prior to the master-servant relationship the proper remedy is to commence a holdover summary proceeding and no notice to quit is required.

Madali, Inc. v Brooms, NYLJ 1-23-90 at 30, col. 3 (Dist. Ct., Nassau Co.). In

# INTERESTS IN REAL PROPERTY § 4:11

this case the respondent had been a tenant prior to the master-servant relationship. During the course of her employment with landlord the local municipality adopted the ETPA. Because of her prior status as a tenant she had the right to a renewal lease when her employment terminated. When she refused to sign the renewal lease and pay rent the petitioner commenced a non-payment proceeding. The lower court held this was the proper procedure. However, the Appellate Term, Madali, Inc. v Brooms (1991, Sup App T) 149 Misc 2d 714, 573 NYS2d 344, reversed the decision and dismissed the proceeding, stating that there was no "agreement" which could serve as an underpinning to the maintenance of a nonpayment proceeding.

Gottlieb v Adames (1994, App Term) NYLJ 9-23-94 p. 21, col. 1. Reversing a decision in favor of the landlord, the court stating that a superintendent who occupies an apartment as an incident of employment must vacate the living quarters upon termination of the employment, however the landlord-tenant relationship survives the termination of employment if a superintendent moved into the premises as a tenant before becoming an employee.

## B. DISTINGUISHING BETWEEN LEASE AND LICENSE

### § 4:11. Test

p. 180, n. 15—Loren v Marry (1993, 3d Dept) 195 App Div 2d 776, 600 NYS2d 369, app dismd 82 NY2d 800, 604 NYS2d 554, 624 NE2d 692 and app dismd, in part, app den, in part 83 NY2d 824, 612 NYS2d 103, 634 NE2d 598, reconsideration den 83 NY2d 954, 615 NYS2d 878, 639 NE2d 419, amd 84 NY2d 846, 617 NYS2d 132, 641 NE2d 152. Although the parties referred to themselves as landlord and tenant in their agreement, the court held that the words used were immaterial. Because the rent was nominal and not payable until the expiration of the agreement, based upon the agreement as a whole, the court could not conclude that the agreement entered into between the parties was intended to grant petitioner exclusive possession of the premises; rather the court determined that "the agreement may be fairly characterized as a license."

p. 181, n. 18—In American Jewish Theatre v Roundabout Theatre Co. (1994, 1st Dept) 203 App Div 2d 155, 610 NYS2d 256, involving preliminary injunctive relief against summary eviction, the court held "[w]hat defines the proprietary relationship between the parties is not its characterization or the technical language used in the instrument, but rather the manifest intention of the parties. . . . The nature of the transfer of absolute control and possession is what differentiates a lease from a license or any other arrangement dealing with property rights. . . . Whereas a license connotes use or occupancy of the grantor's premises, a lease grants exclusive possession of designated space to a tenant, subject to rights specifically reserved by the lessor. The former is cancellable at will, and without cause. . . . Where one party's interest in another's real property exists for a fixed term, not revocable at will, and terminable only on notice, a landlord-tenant relationship has been created." (citations omitted).

p. 182, n. 3—Landlord, owner of a motel, brought a summary proceeding to evict respondent on the basis that she was a licensee. The tenant, an otherwise homeless person, had been a resident of the motel for two (2) years and her rent has been paid by the Department of Social Services. The court held that respondent is not a mere transient or licensee for whom a 10-day notice to quit would be sufficient, but is a month-to-month tenant entitled to a 30-day notice to vacate. Universal Motor Lodges, Inc. v Seignious (1990) 146 Misc 2d 395, 550 NYS2d 800.

## § 4:21. Revocability of License

p. 192, n. 17—American Jewish Theatre v Roundabout Theatre Co. (1994, 1st Dept) 203 App Div 2d 155, 610 NYS2d 256.

## C. PROPRIETARY LEASE (CO-OPERATIVE OWNERSHIP)

## § 4:22. Generally

p. 194, n. 3—"The protection of tenants and dwellings during cooperative conversions has been the subject of several decisions.

The Court of Appeals determined that the Attorney General may properly include the sponsor's apartment in the base-denominator count in determining if the 51% tenants' approval requirements of General Business Law § 352-eeee(2)(d)(i) has been met. (Church Street Apartment Corp. v Abrams (1989) 74 NY2d 728, 544 NYS2d 816, 543 NE2d 81.) (A more detailed explanation on this subject is found in the decision of the lower court. Church Street Apartment Corp. v Abrams (1988, 1st Dept) 139 AD2d 280, 531 NYS2d 540, affd 74 NY2d 728, 544 NYS2d 816, 543 NE2d 81.)

"Only bona fide tenants in occupancy on the date the Attorney General accepts the plan for filing are afforded the exclusive right to purchase their apartments upon the conversion of a residential apartment building to a cooperative status . . . The 'time of the offering,' i.e., the date of acceptance by the Attorney General, is thus considered the 'critical date' to determine who has the right to purchase." Ganson v Goldfader (1990) 148 Misc 2d 608, 561 NYS2d 366.

In De Kovessey v Coronet Properties Co. (1987) 69 NY2d 448, 515 NYS2d 740, 508 NE2d 652, reconsideration den 70 NY2d 694, 518 NYS2d 1030, 512 NE2d 556, the court held that the party who is to be protected by the provisions of General Business Law § 352-eeee must be a "tenant in occupancy" at the time the plan is accepted for filing and the "tenant in occupancy" must be in actual possession and occupying the unit at the time the conversion plan is accepted for filing in order to qualify at the less-than-open-market insider price. (See also, Eight Cooper Equities v Abrams (1989) 143 Misc 2d 52, 539 NYS2d 673; Gratz v Century Apartment Assoc. (1989, Sup) 143 Misc 2d 423, 540 NYS2d 940.)

Before their divorce, husband and wife were cosignatories to a residential lease that served as the couple's marital home. During the term of the lease a cooperative conversion plan was accepted for filing by the Attorney General and both parties sought a declaration of the rights to subscribe to the shares in the apartment. Determining that the "critical date" for determining whether an interested party is a "tenant in occupancy" entitled to participate in a cooperative conversion on the date the offering plan is accepted for filing by the Attorney General, the court found that husband and wife were entitled to purchase the subject apartment on a coequal joint basis as cotenants since husband maintained his landlord-tenant relationship as of the date the plan was accepted for filing. Manolovici v 136 East 64th Street Associates (1987) 70 NY2d 785, 521 NYS2d 414, 515 NE2d 1212.

The Court of Appeals held that "The purpose of rent laws, as they pertain to cooperative conversions, is to protect dwellings for entitled persons or entities" and therefore an estate cannot list among its assets the "insider price" of its decedent's apartment before the apartment was offered for sale under the subsequently accepted cooperative conversion plan, because the apartment here has no "tenant in occupancy" as legally contemplated under the statement. Rubinstein v 160 West End Owners Corp. (1989) 74 NY2d 443, 548 NYS2d 155, 547 NE2d 357.

Russell v Raynes Assoc. Ltd., Partnership (1991, 1st Dept) 166 AD2d 6,

# INTERESTS IN REAL PROPERTY § 4:22

569 NYS2d 409. The lower court dismissed plaintiff's complaint for a request for declaratory judgment seeking his entitlement to purchase the shares allocated to a decedent's apartment and the issuance of a proprietary lease in accordance with the offering plan. The Appellate Division reversed that decision and reinstated the complaint, pointing out that while under the rationale of *DeKovessey* and *Rubinstein,* the Sponsors were not required to extend an offer to plaintiff they were not prohibited from doing so. Giving an estate insider's rights upon a cooperative conversion merely by virtue of the happenstance that an offering plan had been filed prior to the deceased tenant's death, rather than afterwards, would in no way further the purposes of the regulatory scheme designed to protect the rights of rent-stabilized tenants who actually occupy their apartments as residences.

The definition of "tenant in occupancy" for determining who has the right to subscribe to cooperative shares at the "insider" price was held to be "a bona fide tenant of record with an unexpired lease on the date the plan is accepted for filing . . . even though the tenant has sublet his or her dwelling or the dwelling unit is not the tenant's primary residence." Novack v 50 Plaza Co. (1990, 2d Dept) 161 AD2d 565, 555 NYS2d 142.

Luby v Babad (1990, 1st Dept) 166 AD2d 391, 561 NYS2d 194. Plaintiff, a rent-stabilized tenant in a residential apartment building that was converted to cooperative ownership by defendant, was initially given right to purchase the apartment at an insider price pursuant to the first amendment of the offering plan, brought an action for a summary judgment directing specific performance of the delivery of shares of stock and a proprietary lease to a cooperative apartment. Holding in favor of plaintiff the court held that personal service of the amendment of the offering plan had been effected by service upon a woman who, although living in the apartment, was not plaintiff's wife, had never held herself out as his wife, and had never been a tenant of record.

In Neidich v Gottlieb (1991, 1st Dept) 169 AD2d 541, 564 NYS2d 394, the court held that a subtenant has no right to purchase the shares allocable to an apartment upon a conversion nor retain the status of a nonpurchasing tenant who never acquired the status of a tenant.

p. 195, n. 6—Luby v Babad (1990, 1st Dept) 166 App Div 2d 391, 561 NYS2d 194. Plaintiff, a rent-stabilized tenant in a residential apartment building that was converted to cooperative ownership by defendant, was initially given right to purchase the apartment at an insider price pursuant to the first amendment of the offering plan, brought an action for a summary judgment directing specific performance of the delivery of shares of stock and a proprietary lease to a cooperative apartment. Holding in favor of plaintiff the court held that personal service of the amendment of the offering plan had been effected by service upon a woman who, although living in the apartment, was not plaintiff's wife, had never held herself out as his wife, and had never been a tenant of record.

In Neidich v Gottlieb (1991, 1st Dept) 169 App Div 2d 541, 564 NYS2d 394, the court held that a subtenant has no right to purchase the shares allocable to an apartment upon a conversion nor retain the status of a nonpurchasing tenant who never acquired the status of a tenant.

De Santis v White Rose Assoc. (1991, Sup) 152 Misc 2d 567, 578 NYS2d 363. A question was raised in an action where a sponsor defaults and an individual lender (rather than an institution) commences a foreclosure action. What then are the rights of the proprietary lessees in the foreclosure and sale of cooperative ownership property? The proprietary lessees stand in the same position as renters and may not be ousted except in accordance with the New York City Rent Stabilization Law and Rent Stabilization Code, which automatically became applicable as soon as a multiple dwelling is no longer owned as a cooperative.

p. 195, n. 7—Levandusky v One Fifth Ave. Apartment Corp. (1990) 75 NY2d 530, 554 NYS2d 807, 553 NE2d 1317, later proceeding (1st Dept) 171 AD2d 590, 567 NYS2d 662. The Court of Appeals details the legal question of what standard of review should apply when a board of directors of a corporation seeks to enforce a matter of building policy against a tenant-shareholder. The court concludes that the "business judgment rule" furnishes the correct standard of review. The court sets forth guidance on the issue in detail.

The "business judgment rule" established by *Levandusky* permits judicial inquiry into claims of fraud or self-dealing by board members of a cooperative corporation only where such claims have a basis and claimant must submit evidence that the board did not act in the best interest of the shareholders. Simpson v Berkley Owner's Corp. (1995, 1st Dept) 213 App Div 2d 207, 623 NYS2d 583.

Katz v 215 W. 91st St. Corp. (1995, 1st Dept) 215 App Div 2d 265, 626 NYS2d 796. This court held that the reasonableness of decisions of a board of directors may not be questioned without proof of a breach of its fiduciary duty to the cooperative corporation.

In determining the enforceability of house rules regarding the installation of washing machines and dryers in individual cooperatives' apartment the court applied the "business judgment rule" and not the standard of "reasonableness." Cannon Point N. v Abeles (1993, Sup App T) 160 Misc 2d 30, 612 NYS2d 289. However, where the action of a Board of Directors clearly violate the express terms of the proprietary lease, the business judgment rule is inapplicable. Ludwig v 25 Plaza Tenants Corp. (1992, 2d Dept) 184 App Div 2d 623, 584 NYS2d 907.

The court in Oakley v Longview Owners (1995, Sup) 165 Misc 2d 192, 628 NYS2d 468, held that the Board of Directors of a cooperative housing corporation does not have the power by resolution to restrict the transfer of shares of stock by imposing an absolute "floor price" on the sale of shares of the corporation.

Chemical Bank v 635 Park Ave. Corp. (1992, Sup) 155 Misc 2d 433, 588 NYS2d 257. This court held that a condition in a proprietary lease which requires tenants engaged in litigation or administrative proceedings with the cooperative to settle their actions prior to selling their apartments constitutes an unreasonable restraint on alienation and is unlawful as against public policy.

p. 195, n. 9—Southridge Cooperative Section No. 3, Inc. v Menendez (1988) 141 Misc 2d 823, 535 NYS2d 299.

Add text at end of section on p. 195:

Shares of stock and proprietary lease in a cooperative apartment are personal property.

Although the relationship between shareholder-tenant and the cooperative maybe that of landlord-tenant, that may not give the cooperative the opportunity to commence a summary proceedings against the shareholder.

It is common practice for the sponsor of the cooperative to purchase the unsold shares of stock and to sublet the apartments. When the shareholder fails to pay maintenance charges and is not in actual possession of the apartment, the question arises as to whether the courts have jurisdiction to entertain a summary proceeding. This question was answered in the negative in two cases in New York Civil Court (Queens County and New York County, thereby encompassing both the First and Second Departments). In Belgravia Gardens Corp. v Belgravia Properties Co., NYLJ 6-20-90 at 30, col. 1 (Civ. Ct., Queens Co.), and Gracie Gardens Owners, Corp. v Ettinger, NYLJ 8-29-90 at 22, col. 3 (Civ. Ct., NY Co.), the courts held that since respondent-shareholder was not in actual or constructive possession of the apartments and petitioner was not seeking possession of the apartments, the court lacked jurisdiction to entertain the proceeding.

The same problem was handled differently by the cooperative in 160 Bleecker Street Associates v 160 Bleecker Street Owners, Inc., NYLJ 8-22-90 at 22, col. 3 (Sup. Ct. NY Co.). There the cooperative notified the defaulting shareholder (the owner of 106 apartments) that it proposed to sell at public auction the shares of stock allocated to its apartments. The court denied the shareholders' request for a preliminary injunction, holding that the cooperative may seize the stock pursuant to UCC Article 9; further, since the cooperative can cancel the stock certificates and issue new ones it can acquire the collateral without a breach of the peace and therefore need not resort to judicial process.

COMMENT: As of the time of publication these cases were not officially reported and it could not be determined if they had been appealed.

## E. CONDOMINIUM OWNERSHIP (NEW)

### § 4:25. Generally

Ownership of property in condominium form has been used for some time in European and Latin American countries, and is beginning to be used extensively in this country.[12]

In 1964, New York legalized condominium ownership of property by enacting the Condominium Act.[13] The Act is to be liberally construed to effect the purposes thereof.[14]

12. Condominiums are believed to have had their origin in the Roman Law of Condominium in the sixth century B.C. However, a papyrus in the Brooklyn museum indicates that a form of property ownership similar to condominium ownership was used by the ancient Hebrews.

13. Article 9-B (§§ 339-339-ii), which shall be known and may be cited as the Condominium Act (Real Prop L § 339-d).

14. Real Prop L § 339-ii. See § 4:27, n. 1 (Supplement).

## § 4:26. Defined

Condominium ownership of property is a form of co-operative or joint ownership of real property whereby a natural person, corporation, partnership, association, trustee, or other legal entity,[15] owns individually one or more "units"[16] in a multi-unit piece of property voluntarily submitted to the provisions of the Condominium Act,[17] and in addition, owns an undivided interest in the common areas and facilities that serve the property, collectively called the "common elements" of the property.[18] The owners of the units also mutually agree to observe specified rules and regulations governing the administration of the property, their mutual relationships, and their sharing of the cost of operating and maintaining the common elements.

Now that the statute sanctions the division of ownership on a condominium basis, and since title insurance, mortgage financing,[19] and FHA insurance[20] are available for the individually owned units in property subject to the Condominium Act, this form of co-ownership is expected to increase in this state.

15. Real Prop L § 339-e(10).

16. See § 15:11, infra.

17. See § 15:13, infra.

18. Condominium is a system of ownership of real property whereby a parcel of real estate and the building existing thereon are owned by more than one person, each of whom has two separate and distinct property interests: (1) Fee simple ownership of a unit or apartment; and (2) an undivided interest, together with all of the other unit owners in the project, in the common elements. Gerber v Clarkstown (1974) 78 Misc 2d 221, 356 NYS2d 926.

19. Mortgages on units are legal investments for fiduciaries. Real Prop L § 339-ff provides "(a) The following persons: (1) public officers, bodies of the state, municipalities, and municipal subdivisions, (2) persons doing an insurance business (as defined by section forty-one of the insurance law), (3) banking organizations (as defined by section two of the banking law), and (4) executors, administrators, trustees, guardians and other fiduciaries, are authorized to invest in bonds, notes and evidences of indebtedness which are secured by first mortgages or deeds of trust upon units and the appurtenant common interests, wherever such persons may invest, and subject to all of the rules and limitations applicable to such investment, in bonds, notes and evidences of indebtedness which are secured by first mortgages or deeds of trust upon real estate. Where the applicable limitations are dependent upon the type of use of the real estate, only the type of use of the particular unit or units which constitute the security for such investment shall be taken into consideration for the purpose of such limitations. The existence of any prior lien for taxes, assessments or other similar charges not yet delinquent shall be disregarded in determining whether a mortgage or deed of trust is a first mortgage or deed of trust. (b) No person enumerated in subdivision (a) of this section may invest in bonds, notes or evidences of

# INTERESTS IN REAL PROPERTY § 4:27

indebtedness secured by mortgages or deeds of trust upon units and the appurtenant common interests, which are other than first mortgages or deeds of trust thereupon, notwithstanding any other provision of law (including section three hundred thirty-nine-g of this chapter)."

20. National Housing Act § 234 authorizes the FHA to insure mortgages covering an individually owned one-family unit in a multi-family structure and an undivided interest in the common areas and facilities which serve the structure, in States where real property title and ownership are established for such units.

## § 4:27. Distinguished From Other Forms of Co-ownership

Condominium ownership, although a form of co-ownership,[1] is distinguishable from the conventional cooperative apartment house ownership. In condominium ownership the owner of a unit owns his unit in fee simple absolute, or in the case of a condominium devoted exclusively to non-residential purposes, owning a unit held under a lease or sublease,[2] together with an undivided interest in the common elements which are appurtenant thereto.[3] He/she takes title to his/her unit,[4] and receives a recordable deed therefor,[5] exactly as if he/she were purchasing any piece of realty. The owner may, as any owner of realty, sell, rent, exchange or mortgage his/her unit independently of his/her neighbors owning units in the same property.[6]

The owner is taxed separately. The Condominium Act provides, "With respect to all property submitted to the provisions of the article other than property which is the subject of a qualified leasehold condominium, each unit and its common interest, not including any personal property, shall be deemed to be a parcel and shall be subject to separate assessment and taxation by each assessing unit, school district, special district, county or other taxing unit, for all types of taxes authorized by law including but not limited to special ad valorem levies and special assessments, except that the foregoing shall not apply to a unit held under lease or sublease unless the declaration requires the unit owner to pay all taxes attributable to his unit. Neither the building, the property nor any of the common elements shall be deemed to be a parcel. In no event shall the aggregate of the assessment of the units plus their common interests exceed the total valuation of the property were the property assessed as a parcel."[7]

Moreover, owners are re-

29

sponsible only for the mortgage indebtedness and taxes involving their own units.[8]

No specific section of the Internal Revenue Code is applicable to condominiums. Condominium unit owners are permitted to deduct for income tax purposes the real estate taxes and mortgage interest which they pay, just as the owners of other types of real property may do. This is different from a conventional co-operative, in which each individual is merely a shareholder-lessee, not an owner of real property. The individual owns shares in the corporation which owns the property, and acquires thereby the right of occupancy to a specific unit. The shareholder pays his/her portion of the taxes and mortgage on the entire project in the monthly carrying charges, and the amount of this payment may be augmented if other co-operative shareholders default in their payments. Moreover, the right to sell, rent, exchange or mortgage is dependent upon the consent of the others in the co-operative project.[9]

Condominium ownership is distinguishable from a tenancy in common in that the owner of a unit in property subject to the Condominium Act owns a fraction of the property, not as a tenant in common of the entire property, but independently by virtue of his own individual ownership of such fraction.

It should be observed that a unit in condominium-owned property may be owned by the entireties, jointly or in common.[10]

Article 9-A of the Real Property Law, governing subdivided lands, does not apply to property subject to the Condominium Act or any unit therein, and similarly Article 11 of the Tax Law, governing tax on mortgages, does not apply to declarations or any lien for common charges provided for in the Condominium Act.[11]

1. Real Prop L § 339-ee provides that all units of a property which shall be submitted to the provisions of the Condominium Act shall be deemed to be cooperative interests in realty within the meaning of Gen Bus L § 352-e. Therefore condominium sales-offerings are subject to Regulations issued by the Attorney General, just as are co-operatives.

In Frisch v Bellmarc Management, Inc. (1993, 1st Dept) 190 App Div 2d 383, 597 NYS2d 962, condominium ownership is explained as a form of ownership "based on a bipartite scheme whereby participants own space purchased by them, as well as an undivided interest in the land, structures, and facilities held in common with all other owners in fee." It is a form of fee ownership of property

## INTERESTS IN REAL PROPERTY § 4:27

and is not a leasehold interest involving a landlord-tenant relationship and while some superficial aspects of condominium and cooperative ownership are similar, the two forms of interest in real property are fundamentally different by design and as a matter of law.

Abbady v Abbady (1995, App Div, 1st Dept) 629 NYS2d 6. The implied warranty of habitability pursuant to RPL § 235-b does not apply to an individual unit within a condominium. See also Residential Bd. of Managers of the Century Condominium by Simons v Berman (1995, 1st Dept) 213 App Div 2d 206.

2. Real Prop L § 339-e(16) which provides that "unit owner" means the person or persons owning a unit in fee simple absolute or, in the case either of a condominium devoted exclusively to nonresidential purposes, or a qualified leasehold condominium, owning a unit held under a lease or sublease.

3. Real Prop L § 339-i(1).

4. "Each owner shall be entitled to the exclusive ownership and possession of his unit." Real Prop L § 339-h.

5. Real Prop L §§ 339-o, 339-s.

6. It should be observed that the by-lawss of a condominium project may contain provisions governing the alienation, conveyance, sale, leasing, purchase, ownership and occupancy of units, provided, however, that there shall be no provision restricting the alienation, conveyance, sale, leasing, purchase, ownership, and occupancy of units because of race, creed, color or national origin. Real Prop L § 339-v(2).

7. Real Prop L § 339-y(a), (b). "Qualified leasehold condominium" means any leasehold interest in real property intended to be used for either residential purposes, commercial purposes, industrial purposes or any combination of such purposes, together with any fee simple absolute or leasehold interest in the buildings and all other improvements which have been or at any time hereafter may be erected upon such real property, which has been or is intended to be submitted to the provisions of this article, provided that the Battery Park City authority or the Roosevelt Island operating corporation is, on the date of the recording of the declaration, the holder of the tenant's interest in such leasehold interest. Real Prop L § 339-e(12).

8. Real Prop L § 339-g.

9. See §§ 16:2, 16:8.

10. Real Prop L § 339-i(3).

11. Real Prop L § 339-ee, also provides, "Any provision of the multiple dwelling law, the multiple residence law, or any state building construction code as to multiple residences pursuant to the provisions of article eighteen of the executive law, requiring registration by the owner or other person having control of a multiple dwelling shall be deemed satisfied in the case of a property submitted to the provisions of this article by registration of the board of managers, such registration to include the name of each unit owner and the designation of his unit; each unit owner shall be deemed the person in control of the unit owned by him, and the board of managers shall be deemed the person in control of the common elements, for purposes of enforcement of any such law or code, provided, however, that all other provisions of the multiple dwelling law or multiple residence law, otherwise applicable, shall be in full force and effect." Real Prop L § 339-ee, subd 2, provides that in the event the proceeds of a construction mortgage were applied to construction of a unit of a condominium submitted to the provisions of this article, or in the event that a unit submitted to the provisions of this act was subject to a blanket mortgage, and a mortgage recording tax was duly paid on such construction or blanket mortgage in accordance with article eleven of the tax law, then, as each unit is first conveyed, there shall be allowed a credit against the mortgage recording taxes (except the special additional

§ 4:27

mortgage recording tax imposed by subdivision one-a of section two hundred fifty-three of the tax law) that would otherwise be payable on a purchase money mortgage, said credit to be in the amount resulting from the product of the purchaser's pro rata percentage of interest in the common elements and the mortgage tax already paid on the construction or blanket mortgage. No credit shall be allowed under this subdivision on account of the special additional mortgage recording tax imposed by subdivision one-a of section two hundred fifty-three of the tax law.

A condominium is not a subdivision of realty, and hence Gen Mun L § 239-m (authorizing County Planning Bd to review certain subdivision plots) and Town L § 276 (authorizing Planning Board to approve plots showing lots, blocks or sites) are inapplicable thereto. Gerber v Clarkstown (1974) 78 Misc 2d 221, 356 NYS2d 926.

### § 4:28. Ownership of Unit

"Property" which is subject to the Condominium Act means and includes the land, the building and all other improvements thereon, owned in fee simple absolute, or in the case of a condominium devoted exclusively to nonresidential purposes, held under a lease or sublease, or separate unit leases or subleases, the unexpired term or terms of which on the date of recording of the declaration shall not be less than 30 years, or in the case of a qualified leasehold condominium, held under a lease or sublease, or separate unit leases or subleases, the unexpired term or terms of which on the date of recording of the declaration shall not be less than 50 years, and all easements, rights and appurtenances belonging thereto, and all other property, personal or mixed, intended for use in connection therewith.[12] A unit is a part of such property intended for any type of use or uses (so that in New York condominium ownership is not limited to dwelling property), and with an exit to a public street or highway or to a common element or elements leading to a public street or highway, and may include such appurtenances as garage and other parking space, storage room, balcony, terrace and patio.[13] A unit, together with its common interest,[14] shall for all purposes constitute real property.[15] An owner of a unit owns it in fee simple absolute, or in the case of a condominium devoted exclusively to nonresidential purposes, held under a lease or sublease, or separate unit leases or subleases, the unexpired term or terms of which on the date of recording of the declaration shall not be less than thirty years,[16] and is entitled to the exclusive ownership and possession thereof.[17] However, a unit may be owned jointly, in common, or by the entireties.[18]

The ownership of a condominium unit may be thought of as ownership of a cube of space which that particular unit occupies in a structure. Some realtors aptly describe it as an air lot. In addition the owner of the unit acquires ownership, collectively with all the other unit owners in that structure, in all of the common parts of the structure, called the common interest. The fundamental problem is to describe accurately and precisely the location of each unit. This may be done best by dividing, measuring and locating the particular cube of space in three-dimensional terms, so that it cannot possibly be confused with any other unit.

12. Real Prop L § 339-e(11).

13. Real Prop L § 339-e(14).

14. A common interest is the proportionate, undivided interest in fee simple absolute, or proportionate undivided leasehold interest in the common elements appertaining to each unit. Real Prop L § 339-e(5).

15. Real Prop L § 339-g.

16. Real Prop L § 339-e(16) which provides that "unit owner" means the person or persons owning a unit in fee simple absolute or, in the case either of a condominium devoted exclusively to nonresidential purposes, or a qualified leasehold condominium, owning a unit held under a lease or sublease.

17. Real Prop L § 339-h.

**Annotation:** Standing to bring action relating to real property of condominium, 74 ALR4th 165.

18. Real Prop L § 339-i(3).

## § 4:29. Common Interest

A unit owner owns not only the unit, but also a common interest in the common elements. These common elements, unless otherwise provided in the declaration which subjects the property to the Condominium Act,[19] mean and include (a) the land on which the building is located; (b) the foundations, columns, girders, beams, supports, main walls, roofs, halls, corridors, lobbies, stairs, stairways, fire escapes, and entrances and exits of the building; (c) the basements, cellars, yards, gardens, recreational or community facilities, parking areas and storage spaces; (d) the premises for the lodging or use of janitors and other persons employed for the operation of the property; (e) central and appurtenant installations for services such as power, light, gas, hot and cold water, heating, refrigeration, air conditioning and incinerating; (f) the elevators, escalators, tanks, pumps, motors, fans, compressors, ducts and in general all apparatus and installations existing for safety, or normally in common use.[20]

Each unit in a condominium shall have appurtenant thereto a common interest as expressed in the declaration. Such interest shall be (a) in the approximate proportion that the fair value of the unit at the date of the declaration bears to the then aggregate fair value of all the units, or (b) in the approximate proportion that the floor area of the unit at the date of the declaration bears to the then aggregate floor area of all the units, but such proportion shall reflect the substantially exclusive advantages enjoyed by one or more but not all units in a part or parts of the common elements, or (c) the interest of each of the units shall be in equal percentages, one for each unit as of the date of filing the declaration, or in equal percentages within separate classifications of units as of the date of filing the declaration, or (d) upon floor space, subject to the location of such space and the additional factors of relative value to other space in the condominium, the uniqueness of the unit, the availability of common elements for exclusive or shared use, and the overall dimensions of the particular unit.[1]

The common interest appurtenant to each unit, as expressed in the declaration, shall have a permanent character and shall not be altered without the consent of all unit owners affected, expressed in an amended declaration. However, the declaration may contain provisions relating to the appropriation, taking or condemnation by eminent domain by a federal, state or local government, or instrumentality thereof, including, but not limited to, reapportionment or other change of the common interest appurtenant to each unit, or portion thereof, remaining after a partial appropriation, taking or condemnation. The common interest shall not be separated from the unit to which it appertains. Nothing contained in the statute prohibits the division of any unit and common interest appurtenant thereto in a non-residential unit in the manner permitted by the declaration and bylaws, including changes in the number of rooms; in no case may such division result in a greater percentage of common interest for the total of the new units than existed for the original unit before division. Where authorized by the declaration and bylaws, an appropriate amendment to the declaration may be filed by the new unit owners under the same file number and under procedure set forth in Real Property Law § 339-P, and the local tax authorities must provide and certify upon the proposed amendment a conforming tax lot number upon completion of the new units.[2]

The common elements shall remain undivided, and no right shall exist to partition or divide any thereof, except as otherwise provided in the case of withdrawal from the Condominium Act. Any provision to the contrary shall be null and void.[3]

19. See § 16:14, infra.

20. Real Prop L § 339-e(3).

1. Real Prop L § 339-i(1).
In a condominium complex which established five different unit classifications and assigned a percentage of the interest in the common areas to each class which were equal within each classification, the court determined that all units within a particular class have the same percentage allocation of common elements and that the method established complied with the statute (RPL 339-i[1]). Albert v Glick Developers of North Hills, Inc. (1989, 2d Dept) 155 AD2d 569, 547 NYS2d 648.
Annotation: Validity and construction of condominium association's regulations governing members' use of common facilities, 72 ALR3d 308.

2. Real Prop L § 339-i(2).

3. Real Prop L § 339-i(3).

## § 4:30. Required Documents of Ownership

The required basic documents of condominium ownership are the declaration and bylaws, which must be recorded, and the floor plans, which must be filed.[4]

The Condominium Act[5] provides that it shall be applicable only to property the sole owner or all the owners of which submit the same to the provisions thereof by duly executing and recording a declaration.[6] The declaration must contain the following particulars[7] (1) a statement of intention to submit the property to the provisions of Article 9-B of the Real Property Law; (2) description of the land on which the building and improvements are or are to be located; (3) description of the building, stating the number of stories, basements and cellars, the number of units and the principal materials of which it is or is to be constructed; (4) the unit designation of each unit, and a statement of its location, approximate area, number of rooms in residential area, and common element to which it has imme-

§ 4:30 LANDLORD AND TENANT

diate access, and any other data necessary for its proper identification; (5) description of the common elements and a statement of the common interest of each unit owner; (6) statement of the uses for which the building and each of the units are intended; (7) the name of a person to receive service of process in any action relating to the common elements or more than one unit[8] together with the residence or place of business of such person, which shall be within the city, town or village and the county in which the building is located; (8) any further details in connection with the property which the person or persons executing the declarations may deem desirable to set forth; and (9) the method by which the declaration may be amended, consistent with the provisions of the Condominium Act.

4. The filing of a subdivision map (Real Prop L § 335) is not necessary for a condominium. Kaufman & Broad Homes, Inc. v Albertson (1972) 73 Misc 2d 84, 341 NYS2d 321.

5. Real Prop L § 339-f.

6. A declaration means the instrument by which the property is submitted to the provisions of the Condominium Act, and such instrument as from time to time amended, consistent with the provisions of the Act and of the bylaws. Real Prop L § 339-e(7).

Real Prop L § 339-f makes proposals for the development of certain condominiums subject to comprehensive review by (a) county planning boards pursuant to the provisions of Gen Mun Law § 239-n of article 12-B; (b) cities pursuant to article 3 of the Gen City Law; (c) towns pursuant to article sixteen of the Town Law; and (d) villages pursuant to article 7 of the Village Law.

7. Real Prop L § 339-n.

8. Real Prop L § 339-dd.

§ 4:31. Floor Plan

Simultaneously with the recording of the declaration there shall be filed in the office of the recording officer a set of the floor plans of the building showing the layout, locations and approximate dimensions of the units, stating the declarant's names and bearing the verified statement of a registered architect or licensed professional engineer certifying that it is an accurate copy of portions of the plans of the building as filed with and approved by the municipal or other governmental subdivision having jurisdiction over the issuance of permits for the construction of buildings. If such floor plans do not contain unit designations certified by the appropriate local tax authorities as conforming to the official tax lot number, there shall be filed in the office of the recording officer prior to the first conveyance

# INTERESTS IN REAL PROPERTY § 4:32

of a unit a floor plan containing a unit designation certified by the appropriate local tax authority as conforming to the official tax lot number. It shall be the duty of the appropriate local tax authority to provide such number for each unit upon completion of such unit. If such plans do not include a verified statement by such architect or engineer that such plans fully and fairly depict the layout, location, unit designations and approximate dimensions of any particular unit or units as built, there shall be recorded prior to each first conveyance of such particular unit or units an amendment to the declaration to which shall be attached a verified statement of a registered architect or licensed professional engineer certifying that the plans theretofore filed, or being filed simultaneously with such amendment fully and fairly depict the layout, location, unit designations and approximate dimensions of the particular unit or units as built.[9] Such plans shall be designated "condominium," assigned a file number and kept on file by the recording officer. Such plans shall be indexed under the names of the declarants and in the block index if any. The record of the declaration shall contain a reference to the file number of the floor plans of the building affected thereby.[10]

9. Real Prop L § 339-p.

10. Real Prop L § 339-p. True copies of the floor plan, the declaration, the bylaws and any rules and regulations shall be kept on file in the office of the board of managers and shall be available for inspection at convenient hours of weekdays by persons having an interest. Real Prop L § 339-q.

## § 4:32. Bylaws

The operation of the property shall be governed by bylaws, a true copy of which shall be annexed to and recorded with the declaration. No modification of or amendment to the bylaws shall be valid unless set forth in an amendment to the declaration, and such amendment is duly recorded.[11]

The bylaws shall provide, at minimum, for the following: (a) the nomination and election of a board of managers, the number of persons constituting the same, and that the terms of at least one-third of the members of such board shall expire annually; the powers and duties of the board; the compensation, if any, of the members of the board; the method of removal from office of members of the board; and whether or not the board may engage the services of a manager or managing agent or both, and specifying which of the powers and duties granted to the board by this article or otherwise may be delegated by the board to either or both of them; however nothing contained in the statute bars the incorporation of the board of managers under applicable statutes of New York; such incorporation must be consistent with the other provisions of the statute and the nature of the condominium purpose; (b) the method of calling meetings of the unit owners; what percentage of the unit owners, if other than a majority, shall constitute a quorum; and what percentage shall, consistent with the provisions of the statute, be necessary to adopt decisions binding on all unit owners; (c) the election of a president from among the board of managers who shall preside over the meetings of such board and of the unit owners; (d) the election of a secretary who shall keep a record wherein actions of such board and of meetings of the unit owners shall be recorded; (e) the election of a treasurer who shall keep the financial records and books of account; (f) operation of the property, payment of the common expenses and determination and collection of the common charges; (g) the manner of designation and removal of persons employed for the operation of the property; (h) the method of adopting and of amending administrative rules (that is, "house rules"), and regulations governing the details of the operation and use of the common elements;[12] (i) such restrictions on and requirements respecting the use and maintenance of the units and the use of the common elements, not set forth in the declaration, as are designed to prevent unreasonable interference with the use of their respective units and of the common elements by the several unit owners; and (j) the percentage of the unit owners, but not less than sixty-six and two-thirds per cent in number and common interest, which may at any time modify or amend the bylaws.[13]

In addition, the bylaws may also provide for: (a) provisions governing the alienation, conveyance, sale, leasing, purchase, ownership and occupancy of units provided, however, that the bylaws shall con-

## § 4:32

tain no provision restricting such transactions because of race, creed, color or national origin; (b) provisions governing the payment, collection and disbursement of funds, including reserves, to provide for major and minor maintenance, repairs, additions, improvements, replacements, working capital, bad debts and unpaid common expenses, depreciation, obsolescence and similar purposes; (c) the form by which the board of managers, acting on behalf of the unit owners, where authorized by this statute or the declaration, may acquire and hold any unit and lease, mortgage and convey the same; and (d) any other provisions, not inconsistent with the provisions of the Condominium Act, relating to the operation of the property.[14]

The Condominium Act provides that each unit owner must comply strictly with the bylaws and with the rules, regulations, resolutions and decisions adopted pursuant to the bylaws. Failure to comply with any of them shall be grounds for an action to recover sums due, for damages or injunctive relief or both maintainable by the board of managers on behalf of the unit owners, or, in a proper case, by an aggrieved unit owner. In any case of flagrant or repeated violation by a unit owner, he may be required by the board of managers to give sufficient surety for his future compliance with the bylaws, rules, regulations, resolutions, and decisions.[15]

11. Real Prop L § 339-u.

12. Issues typically covered by house rules are: use of laundry facilities and prohibited uses, such as washing machine dyes; pet regulations; use of balconies and decks; use of noise-generating equipment, such as televisions, radios, stereos, and musical instruments; and use of individual units for nonresidential purposes, such as music lessons, or professional offices.

The bylaws should also provide for an easy procedure for amending the house rules, and also for the service of any amended rules on all unit owners.

13. Real Prop L § 339-v(1).

14. Real Prop L § 339-v(2).

Board of Managers at North Hills Condominium v Fairways at North Hills (1989, 2d Dept) 150 AD2d 32, 545 NYS2d 343, later proceeding (2d Dept) 193 AD2d 322, 603 NYS2d 867. The Board of Directors of a condominium commenced an action against the sponsors of the condominium alleging misrepresentation in the offering plan. In dismissing the complaint the court held that the board of managers of a condominium did not have a private cause of action against the sponsor to recover damages for violation of the Martin Act (General Business Law art 23-A). See CPC International Inc. v McKesson Corp. (1987) 70 NY2d 268, 519 NYS2d 804, 514 NE2d 116, CCH Fed Secur L Rep ¶ 93419 and also Vermeer Owners, Inc. v Guterman (1991) 78 NY2d 1114, 578 NYS2d 128 (dismissing a cause of action asserted pursuant to the Martin Act).

In addition, the Fairways at North Hills court held that the First Department's prior holding in East End Owners Corp. v Roc-East End Associates (1987, 1st Dept) 128 AD2d 366, 516 NYS2d 663, namely, that a cooperative's board of directors has a private action to recover damages for a violation of General Business Law 352-e, was impliedly overruled. In any event, the court declined to follow the First Department's holding because it disagreed with the underlying rationale.

In an action for judgment declaring that defendants' election to purchase plaintiff's condominium is unenforceable, and upon review of provisions contained in condominium's bylaws, the court concluded that the board may not rely upon a power of attorney signed by a homeowner to circumvent the explicit provisions in the bylaws. The board acted outside its authority in electing to purchase plaintiff's unit without first obtaining approval of the homeowners. Ng v Bayridge at Bayside Condominium III (1990, 2d Dept) 161 AD2d 688, 555 NYS2d 824.

Whitehall Tenants Corp. v Estate of Olnick (1995, 1st Dept) 213 App Div 2d 200, 623 NYS2d 585, app den 86 NY2d 704, 631 NYS2d 608, 655 NE2d 705.

15. Real Prop L § 339-j.

Keeping a dog in violation of a lawfully adopted regulation constitutes a substantial breach. Trump Village Sec. 4, Inc. v Cooper (1969) 61 Misc 2d 757, 306 NYS2d 759, affd 66 Misc 2d 220, 319 NYS2d 1018; Triangle Management Corp. v Inniss (1970) 62 Misc 2d 1095, 312 NYS2d 745; 1036 Park Corp. v Rubin (1983, 1st Dept) 92 AD2d 452, 458 NYS2d 595, affd 59 NY2d 877, 466 NYS2d 316, 453 NE2d 545 (injunction granted).

A sublease not executed in strict conformity with the bylaws may be enjoined. Board of Managers of Village House v Frazier (1981, 1st Dept) 81 AD2d 760, 439 NYS2d 360, affd 55 NY2d 991, 449 NYS2d 188, 434 NE2d 257.

## § 4:33. Recording of Declaration

The statute authorizes the recording of the declaration. Real Property Law § 339-s provides that the declaration, any amendment or amendments thereof, and every instrument affecting the property[16] or any unit included within the meaning of "conveyance," as used in Article 9 of the Real Property Law dealing with recording instruments affecting real property, shall be entitled to be indexed and recorded pursuant to and with the same effect as provided in said Article dealing with recording. Neither the declaration nor any amendment thereof shall be valid unless duly recorded.[17]

16. Real Prop L § 339-e(11) provides that "property" means and includes the land, the building and all other improvements thereon, owned in fee simple absolute, or in the case of a condominium devoted exclusively to non-residential purposes, held under a lease or sublease, or separate unit leases or subleases, the unexpired term or terms of which on the date of recording of the declaration shall not be less than 30 years, or in the case of a qualified leasehold condominium, held under a lease or sublease, or separate unit leases or subleases, the unexpired term or terms of which on the date of recording of the declaration shall not be less than 50 years, and all easements, right and appurtenances belonging thereto, and all other property, personal or mixed, intended for use in connection there-

with, which have been or are intended to be submitted to the provisions of Article 9-B, Real Property Law.

17. Real Prop L § 339-s.

## § 4:34. Rights of Unit Owners

With respect to all property submitted to the provisions of the Article other than property which is the subject of a qualified leasehold condominium, each unit owner is entitled to the exclusive ownership and possession of his unit.[18] In addition, he may use the common elements in accordance with the purpose for which they are intended, without hindering the exercise of or encroaching upon the rights of the other unit owners.[19] However, the declaration or bylaws may provide that some unit or units may enjoy substantially exclusive advantages in a specified part or parts of the common elements.[20]

The unit owners shall have the irrevocable right, to be exercised by the board of managers, to have access to each unit from time to time during reasonable hours to the extent necessary for the operation of the property, or for making emergency repairs therein necessary to prevent damage to the common elements or to another unit or units, and the bylaws may contain reasonable rules and regulations for the administration of this right as the privacy of the units and the protection of them and their contents from burglary, theft or larceny requires.[1]

18. Real Prop L § 339-h.

19. Real Prop L § 339-i(4).

20. Real Prop L § 339-I(4).

1. Real Prop L § 339-i(5).

North Broadway Estates, Ltd. v Schmoldt (1990) 147 Misc 2d 1098, 559 NYS2d 457. This court found that the board of directors in this cooperation had no authority to adopt a house rule instituting a "flat $30 fee" for the late payment of rent.

## § 4:35. Obligations of Unit Owners

Each unit owner shall comply strictly with the bylaws, and with the rules, regulations, resolutions and decisions adopted pursuant thereto. Failure to comply with any of them shall be ground for an action to recover sums due for damages or for injunctive relief, or both, maintainable by the board of managers on behalf of the unit owners or, in a proper case, by an aggrieved unit owner. In any case of flagrant or repeated violation by a unit owner, he/she may be required by the board of managers to give sufficient surety or sureties for his/her future compliance with the bylaws, rules, regulations, resolutions and decisions.[2]

2. Real Prop L § 339-j.
The Court of Appeals detailed the legal question of what standard of review should apply when a board of directors of a condominium corporation seek to enforce a matter of building policy against a tenant-shareholder. The court determined that a standard of review that is analogous to the business judgment rule applied by courts to resolve challenges to decisions made by corporate directors is the correct one. Levendusky v One Fifth Ave. Apartment Corp. (1990) 75 NY2d 530, 554 NYS2d 807, 553 NE2d 1317, later proceeding (1st Dept) 171 AD2d 590, 567 NYS2d 662.

Katz v 215 W. 91st St. Corp. (1995, 1st Dept) 215 App Div 2d 265, 626 NYS2d 796. See also p. 195, n. 7, supra.

## § 4:36. Separate Taxation of Units

Each unit and its common interest, not including any personal property, shall be deemed to be a parcel and shall be subject to separate assessment and taxation by each assessing unit, school district, special district, county or other taxing unit, for all types of taxes authorized by law including but not limited to special ad valorem levies and special assessments, except that the foregoing shall not apply to a unit held under lease or sublease unless the declaration requires the unit owner to pay all taxes attributable to his unit. Neither the building, the property nor any of the common elements shall be deemed to be a parcel. In no event shall the aggregate of the assessment of the units plus their common interests exceed the total valuation of the property assessed as a parcel.[3]

The Condominium Act provides that "[t]he board of managers may act as an agent of each unit owner who has given his written authorization to complain or apply to the board of assessment review of the assessing agency by filing a single complaint on behalf of all such unit owners pursuant to section five hundred twelve of the real property tax law and to commence and prosecute a special proceeding for the review of assessments of real property as an aggrieved person pursuant to section seven hundred four of the real property tax law. The board of managers may retain legal counsel on behalf of all unit owners for which it is acting as agent and to charge all such unit owners a pro rata share of expenses, disbursements and legal fees for which charges the board of managers shall have a lien pursuant to section three hundred thirty-nine-z."[4]

# INTERESTS IN REAL PROPERTY § 4:38

3. Real Prop L § 339-y, subd (a).

The imposition of a transfer fee (flip tax) when it is validly adopted by the board of directors may be imposed on the sale of a condominium unit. Holt v 45 East 66th Street Owners Corp. (1991, 1st Dept) 161 AD2d 410, 555 NYS2d 340.

**Annotation:** Real-estate taxation of condominiums, 71 ALR3d 952.

4. Real Prop L § 339-y, subd 2.

"Qualified leasehold condominium" means any leasehold interest in real property intended to be used for either residential purposes, commercial purposes, industrial purposes or any combination of such purposes, together with any fee simple absolute or leasehold interest in the buildings and all other improvements which have been or at any time hereafter may be erected upon such real property, which has been or is intended to be submitted to the provisions of this article, provided that the Battery Park City authority is, on the date of the recording of the declaration, the holder of the tenant's interest in such leasehold interest. Real Prop L § 339-e, subd 12.

## § 4:37. Type of Work by Unit Owners Prohibited

No unit owner may do any work which would jeopardize the soundness or safety of the property, reduce the value thereof or impair any easement or hereditament, nor may any unit owner add any material structure or excavate any additional basement or cellar, without first obtaining in every such case the consent of all of the unit owners affected.[5]

5. Real Prop L § 339-k.

## § 4:38. Lien for Common Charges

A "common charge" under the Condominium Act means each unit's proportionate share of the common expenses in accordance with its common interest.[6]

The board of managers, on behalf of the unit owners, has a lien on each unit for the unpaid common charges thereof, together with interest thereon, prior to all other liens, excepting only (a) liens for taxes on the unit in favor of any assessing unit, school district, special district, county or other taxing unit, and (b) all sums unpaid on a first mortgage of record on the unit. In other words the lien of a mortgage on a unit is superior to the lien of the board of managers for common charges. Upon the sale or conveyance of a unit, such unpaid common charges must be paid out of the sale proceeds or by the grantee. Any grantor or grantee of a unit is entitled to a statement from the manager or board of managers, setting forth the amount of the unpaid common charges accrued against the unit, and neither such grantor nor grantee is liable for, nor may the unit conveyed be subject to a lien for, any unpaid common charges against such unit accrued prior to such conveyance in excess of the amount therein set forth. Notwithstanding the above, the declaration of an exclusive nonresidential condominium may provide that the lien for common charges will be superior to any mortgage lien of record.[7]

The lien for common charges is effective from and after the filing in the office of the recording officer in which the declaration is filed a verified notice of lien stating the name (if any) and address of the property, the liber and page of record of the declaration, the name of the record owner of the unit, the unit designation,[8] the amount and purpose for which due, and the date when due; and shall continue in effect until all sums secured thereby, with the interest thereon, is fully paid or until expiration of six years from the date of filing, whichever occurs sooner. Upon such payment, the unit owner is entitled to an instrument duly executed and acknowledged certifying to the fact of payment. Such lien may be foreclosed by suit authorized by and brought in the name of the board of managers, acting on behalf of the unit owners, in like manner as a mortgage of real property, without the necessity, however, of naming as a party defendant any person solely by reason of his owning a common interest with respect to the property. In any such foreclosure the unit owner is required to pay reasonable rental for the unit for any period prior to sale pursuant to judgment of foreclosure and sale, if so provided in the bylaws, and the plaintiff in such foreclosure is entitled to the appointment of a receiver to collect the same. The board of managers, acting on behalf of the unit owners, has power, unless prohibited by the bylaws, to bid in the unit at foreclosure sale, and to acquire and hold, lease, mortgage and convey the same. A suit to recover a money judgment for unpaid common charges is maintainable without foreclosing or waiving the lien securing the same, and foreclosure is maintainable notwithstanding the pendency of suit to recover a money judgment.[9]

If a municipal corporation acquires title to a unit as a result of tax enforcement proceedings, such municipal corporation is not liable for and not subject to suit for recovery of the common charges applicable to such unit during the period while title to such unit is held by the municipal corporation or for the payment of any rental for the unit under the provisions of this section, except to the extent of any rent arising from such unit received by such municipal corporation during such period.[10]

6. Real Prop L § 339-e(2).

7. Real Prop L § 339-z.

8. A "unit designation" means the number, letter or combination thereof or other official designations conforming to the tax lot number, if any, designating the unit in the declaration and on the floor plans. Real Prop L § 339-e(15).

9. Real Prop L § 339-aa.

10. Real Prop L § 339-aa.

## § 4:39. Insurance of Building

The board of managers, if required by the declaration, the bylaws or by a majority of the unit owners, must insure the building against loss or damage by fire and such other hazards as shall be required, and must give written notice of such insurance and of any change therein or termination thereof to each unit owner. In the case of a qualified leasehold condominium, such insurance shall be required in any event, and shall be in an amount equal to full replacement cost of the building. The policy or policies of such insurance shall be updated annually to maintain such insurance in such amount. The right of each unit owner to insure his own unit for his own benefit shall not be prejudiced by such insurance. The premiums for such insurance on the building shall be deemed common expenses, provided, however, that in charging the same to the unit owner'sconsideration may be given to the higher premium rates on some units than on others.[11]

11. Real Prop L § 339-bb.

## § 4:40. Repair or Reconstruction of the Building

Damage to or destruction of the building must be promptly repaired and reconstructed by the board of managers, using the proceeds of insurance, if any, on the building for that purpose, and any deficiency constitutes common expenses. However, if three-fourths or more of the building is destroyed or substantially damaged and seventy-five per cent or more of the unit owners do not duly and promptly re-

§ 4:40

solve to proceed with repair or restoration, then and in that event the property or so much thereof as remains is subject to an action for partition at the suit of any unit owner or lienor as if owned in common, in which event the net proceeds of sale, together with the net proceeds of insurance policies, if any, must be considered as one fund and must be divided among all the unit owners in proportion to their respective common interests, provided, however, that no payment may be made to a unit owner until there has first been paid off out of his share of such funds all liens on his unit.[12]

12. Real Prop L § 339-cc.

### § 4:41. Waiver of Use of Common Elements

No unit owner may exempt himself from liability for his common charges by waiver of the use or enjoyment of any of the common elements or by abandonment of his unit. Subject to such terms and conditions as may be specified in the bylaws, any unit owner may, by conveying his unit and his common interest to the board of managers on behalf of all other unit owners, exempt himself from

common charges thereafter accruing.[13]

13. Real Prop L § 339-x.
Board of Managers of First Ave. Condominium v Shandel (1989) 143 Misc 2d 1084, 542 NYS2d 466. In an action by the Board of Managers of a condominium the court held that defendants, as units owners, are bound by Real Property Law 339-x and the condominium bylaws to pay common charges and monthly assessments.

### § 4:42. Common Profits and Expenses

Common profits of the property subject to the Condominium Act, that is, the excess of all receipts of the rents, profits and revenues from the common elements remaining after the deduction of common expenses,[14] must be distributed among the unit owners according to their respective common interests.[15]

"Common expenses" of such property, that is, expenses of operating the property,[16] which include not only the administration and operation of the property, but also the maintenance, repair, and replacement of, and the making of any additions and improvements to, the common elements,[17] and those sums designated by the Condominium Act, the declaration, or the bylaws as common expenses,[18] must be charged to the unit owners

## INTERESTS IN REAL PROPERTY § 4:44

according to their respective common interests. Notwithstanding any provision of Act, profits and expenses may be specially allocated and apportioned by the board of managers in a manner different from common profits and expenses, to one or more non-residential units where so authorized by the declaration and bylaws. In the case of units in any building, residential or non-residential, or a combination thereof, profits and expenses may be specially allocated and apportioned based on special or exclusive use or availability or exclusive control of particular units or common areas by particular unit owners, if so authorized by the declaration and bylaws, in a manner different from common profits and expenses.[19] However, in charging expenses of insurance, consideration may be given to the higher premium rates on some units than others.[20]

The Condominium Act provides that the manager or board of managers shall keep detailed, accurate records, in chronological order, of the receipts and expenditures arising from the operation of the property. Such records and the vouchers authorizing the payments must be available for examination by the unit owners at convenient hours of weekdays. A written report summarizing such receipts and expenditures must be rendered by the board of managers to all unit owners at least once annually.[1]

14. Real Prop L § 339-e(6).
15. Real Prop L § 339-m.
16. Real Prop L § 339-e(4)(a).
17. Real Prop L § 339-e(9).
18. Real Prop L § 339-e(4)(b).
19. Real Prop L § 339-m.
20. Real Prop l § 339-bb.
1. Real Prop L § 339-w.

### § 4:43. Satisfaction of Blanket Liens on Units on Conveyance

At the time of the first conveyance of each unit, every mortgage and other lien affecting such unit and any other unit must be paid and satisfied of record, or the unit being conveyed and its common interest must be released therefrom by partial release duly recorded.[2]

2. Real Prop L § 339-r.

### § 4:44. Liens Against Common Elements

Subsequent to recording the declaration and while the property remains subject to the Condominium

§ 4:44     LANDLORD AND TENANT

Act, no lien of any nature may thereafter arise or be created against the common elements except with the unanimous consent of the unit owners. During such period, liens may arise or be created only against the several units and their respective common interests.

Labor performed on or materials furnished to a unit may not be the basis for the filing of a lien pursuant to Lien Law, Article 2, against the unit of any unit owner not expressly consenting to or requesting the same, except in the case of emergency repairs. No labor performed on or materials furnished to the common elements may be the basis for a lien thereon, but all common charges received and to be received by the board of managers, and the right to receive such funds, constitute trust funds for the purpose of paying the cost of such labor or materials performed or furnished at the express request or with the consent of the manager, managing agent or board of managers, and the same must be expended first for such purpose before expending any part of the same for any other purpose.[3]

3. Real Prop L § 339-1. A mechanic's lien for labor and materials furnished to condominium with respect to its common elements is invalid. Similarly, such a lien filed against unit owner, who neither hired nor consented to the labor and materials, is invalid. Country Village Heights Condominium (Group I) v Mario Bonito, Inc. (1975) 79 Misc 2d 1088, 363 NYS2d 501.

### § 4:45. Actions Against Unit Owners

Actions may be brought or proceedings instituted by the board of managers in its discretion, on behalf of two or more of the unit owners, as their respective interests may appear, with respect to any cause of action relating to the common elements or more than one unit. Service of process on the unit owners in any action relating to the common elements or more than one unit may be made on the person designated in the declaration to receive service of process.[4]

4. Real Prop L § 339-dd.

### § 4:46. Withdrawal From Provisions of Condominium Act

If withdrawal of the property from the Condominium Act is authorized by at least eighty per cent in number and in common interest of the units, or by at least such larger percentage either in number or in common interest, or in both number and common interest, as may be specified in the bylaws, then

## INTERESTS IN REAL PROPERTY § 4:46

the property is subject to an action for partition by any unit owner or lienor as if owned in common, in which event the net proceeds of sale must be divided among all the unit owners in proportion to their respective common interests, provided, however, that no payment may be made to a unit owner until there has first been paid off out of his share of such net proceeds all liens on his unit. Such withdrawal of the property from this article does not bar its subsequent submission to the provisions of the Condominium Act in accordance with the terms thereof.[5]

5. Real Prop L § 339-t.

# CHAPTER 5
# TITLE AND REVERSION OF LANDLORD

A. IN GENERAL
  § 5:5. Possession of Tenant as Possession of Landlord

B. ESTOPPEL TO DENY LANDLORD'S TITLE
  § 5:8. Generally

C. TRANSFER OF REVERSION
  § 5:15. Generally
  § 5:17. Rights and Obligations of Grantee
  § 5:18. Rights on Transfer of Reversion to Rent Due or to Become Due
  § 5:19. Waiver of Grantor Binding on Grantee

---

## A. IN GENERAL

### § 5:5. Possession of Tenant as Possession of Landlord

p. 231, n. 4—The 10-year statute of limitations only begins to run after the termination of the lease. Ley v Innis (1989, 1st Dept) 149 AD2d 366, 539 NYS2d 942.

## B. ESTOPPEL TO DENY LANDLORD'S TITLE

### § 5:8. Generally

p. 234, n. 13—In light of the rule that a "tenant is estopped to deny the title of his landlord" the court denied tenant's challenge to landlord's proof of ownership. Parkway Associated v Berkoff (1995, 2d Dept, App T) NYLJ 3-7-95, p. 29, col. 2.

## C. TRANSFER OF REVERSION

### § 5:15. Generally

p. 241, n. 12—Boyar v Goodman (1994, 2d Dept) 202 AD2d 541, 609 NYS2d 279. The court held that the lease and the rights of a tenant were terminated upon the death of the landlord who held the premises with a life estate.

### § 5:17. Rights and Obligations of Grantee

p. 242, n. 18—"It is a well established principle that an owner's rights and remedies run with the land and may be assumed by a new owner. Thus, it has been held that a new owner upon taking title may succeed to rights under a notice of termination which has not expired, under a notice of termination which has become effective, and even under a warrant of

# TITLE AND REVERSION OF LANDLORD § 5:19

eviction if the warrant were amended to award possession to the new owner." 815 Park Owners, Inc. v West LB Admin., Inc. (1983, Civ Ct) 119 Misc 2d 671, 463 NYS2d 1015. See also Kohl v Fusco (1994, Civ Ct) 164 Misc 2d 431, 624 NYS2d 509.

## § 5:18. Rights on Transfer of Reversion to Rent Due or to Become Due

p. 244, n. 11—World Challenge v 39 Food (1994, Civ Ct) 163 Misc 2d 1081, 623 NYS2d 498. Since the tenant had not received notice of the assignment of its lease the court held that the landlord, an assignee of the title of the premises, is entitled to a money judgment in a non-payment proceeding for all of the unpaid rent since it obtained title. However, the landlord may not obtain a possessory judgment for the past rent since it had not notified the tenant of the assignment of the past rent from the prior owner.

## § 5:19. Waiver of Grantor Binding on Grantee

p. 245, n. 16—Sharp v Melendez (1988, 1st Dept) 139 AD2d 262, 531 NYS2d 554, app den 73 NY2d 707, 539 NYS2d 300, 536 NE2d 629.

# CHAPTER 6
# CONSTRUCTION OF LEASES

A. IN GENERAL
 § 6:2. Ascertaining Intent
 § 6:3. Practical Construction by the Parties
 § 6:4. Statutes as Part of a Lease
 § 6:7. Reconciling Inconsistencies
 § 6:13. Unconscionable Lease or Clause

B. PAROL EVIDENCE RULE
 § 6:14. Generally
 § 6:15. Exceptions to the Parol Evidence Rule
 § 6:18. Ambiguity or Uncertainty in Instrument

C. MODIFICATION OF LEASE
 § 6:22. Generally
 § 6:25. Oral Modification
 § 6:26. —Provision Against Oral Modification
 § 6:27. —Form of Provision Against Oral Modification

---

## A. IN GENERAL
## § 6:2. Ascertaining Intent

p. 252, n. 8—101 Fleet Place Assocs. v New York Tel. Co. (1994, 1st Dept) 197App Div 2d 27, 609 NYS2d 896, app dismd 83 NY2d 962, 616 NYS2d 13, 639 NE2d 752. Landlord brought action against a tenant to recover the expenses incurred by the landlord to remedy damage to property caused by leakage of gasoline from tenant's underground storage tanks. The court determined that a broad provision of the lease stating that "[t]he landlord at his sole expense shall comply with all laws, orders and regulations of federal, state, county and with any proceeding of any public officer or officers, pursuant to law, which shall impose any violation, order or duty upon landlord or tenant with respect to demised premises or the use or occupation thereof" imposed on the landlord the obligation to remove the gasoline tanks and to perform cleanup at the premises at its own expense in accordance with state requirements.

p. 253, n. 10—In overruling the lower court the Appellate Division reaffirmed its statement in Cale Dev. Co. v Conciliation & Appeals Bd. (1983, 1st Dept) 94 AD2d 229, 463 NYS2d 814, affd 461 NY2d 979, 475 NYS2d 278, 463 NE2d 619 that "Lease interpretation is subject to the same rules of

## CONSTRUCTION OF LEASES § 6:2

construction as are applicable to other agreements. . . . The parties' intention should be determined from the language employed, and where the language is clear and unambiguous, interpretation is a matter of law to be determined solely by the court. . . . In such circumstances resort cannot be had to extrinsic evidence to contradict the express terms of the writing." Cale Dev. Co. v Conciliation & Appeals Bd. (1983, 1st Dept) 94 AD2d 229, 463 NYS2d 814, affd 61 NY2d 976, 475 NYS2d 278, 463 NE2d 619.

p. 253, n. 12—Petrol Assocs. v Amoco Oil Co., NYLJ 11-23-88 at 27, col. 1 (Dist. Ct. Nassau Co.).

Partrick v Guarniere (1994, 2d Dept) 204 App Div 2d 702, 612 NYS2d 630, app den 84 NY2d 810, 621 NYS2d 519, 645 NE2d 1219. In this breach of contract action the court held that in construing contract language the proper aim of the court is to arrive at a construction which will give fair meaning to all of the language employed by the parties, and to reach a practical interpretation of the expressions of the parties to the end that there is a realization of their reasonable expectations. Relying on this case the court in Joseph v Creek & Pines (1995, App Div, 2d Dept) 629 NYS2d 75, app dismd without op 86 NY2d 885, 635 NYS2d 950, 659 NE2d 773 stated that a "contract should not be interpreted in such a way as would leave one of the provisions substantially without force and effect."

*(The first sentence of the text accompanying footnote 13 on page 253 should read as follows)*

p. 253, n. 13—The construction of a plain, unambiguous contract is for the courts, and whether the writing is ambiguous is a question of law to be resolved by the courts.[13]

13. Wallace v 600 Partners Co. (1995) 86 NY2d 543, 634 NYS2d 669, 658 NE2d 715; Van Wagner Advertising Corp. v S & M Enterprises (1986) 67 NY2d 186, 501 NYS2d 628, 492 NE2d 756, ALR4th 2808; Sutton v East River. Sav. Bank (1982) 55 NY2d 550, 450 NYS2d 460, 435 NE2d 1075.

Where the parties rely upon a written agreement, agree that the facts are not in dispute, and do not refer to any parol evidence to shed light upon the meaning of the contract, the interpretation of that written contract presents an issue of law which the court may determine on a motion for summary judgment. Tantleff v Truscelli (1985, 2d Dept) 110 App Div 2d 240, 493 NYS2d 979, affd 69 NY2d 769, 513 NYS2d 113, 505 NE2d 623; Moon v Haeussler (1989, 3d Dept) 153 App Div 2d 1002, 545 NYS2d 623, app dismd without op 76 NY2d 890. See also Boasberg v Weyerhaeuser Co. (1989, 4th Dept) 155 App Div 2d 989, 548 NYS2d 1016, app dismd, in part, app den, in part 75 NY2d 937, 555 NYS2d 688, 554 NE2d 1276; Fox Paper, Ltd. v Schwarzman (1990, 2d Dept) 168 App Div 2d 604, 563 NYS2d 439.

The Court of Appeals in Chimart Associates v Paul (1986) 66 NY2d 570, 498 NYS2d 344, 489 NE2d 231, set forth the reasoning for the determination in the reformation of contracts that there is a "heavy presumption that a deliberately prepared and executed written instrument manifest(s) the true intention of the parties" and a correspondingly high order of evidence is required to overcome that presumption (p. 574). This case has been cited by the Appellate Division, Second Department in cases interpreting commercial leases. Mid-Island Shopping Plaza Co. v Nathan's Famous of Hicksville, Inc. (1989, 2d Dept) 147 App Div 2d 536, 537 NYS2d 836; Mantek Services, Inc. v Rye Office Associates (1989, 2d Dept) 149 App Div 2d 671, 540 NYS2d 311.

New York Overnight Partners, L. P. v Gordon (1995, 1st Dept) 217 App Div 2d 20, 633 NYS2d 288. The question before this court was the interpretation of the word "land" in a lease to determine the value of property involving the Ritz-Carlton Hotel. It held that the lease required the appraiser set the value of the raw land only in

§ 6:2                                        LANDLORD AND TENANT

arriving at the appraised value of the land. Applying the rule that lease interpretation is subject to the same rules of construction that are applicable to other agreements, absent ambiguity, the court held that interpretation is a matter of law to be determined solely by the court.

p. 253, n. 15—In order to determine the rights of the parties in a lease a court is required to give all the words and phrases used their plain meaning. Bermont Operating Corp. v New York (1983, 1st Dept) 95 AD2d 729, 463 NYS2d 830, affd 60 NY2d 901, 470 NYS2d 575, 458 NE2d 1252.

p. 254, n. 4—Parol evidence may be used only where there is an ambiguity in the language used. Papa Gino's of America, Inc. v Plaza at Latham Associates (1988, 3d Dept) 135 AD2d 74, 524 NYS2d 536, later app (3d Dept) 144 AD2d 172, 535 NYS2d 116.

§ 6:3. Practical Construction by the Parties

p. 255, n. 11—The rules governing the construction of ambiguous contracts are not triggered unless the court finds an ambiguity. Wallace v 600 Partners Co. (1995) 86 NY2d 543, 634 NYS2d 669, 658 NE2d 715

§ 6:4. Statutes as Part of a Lease

p. 256, n. 15—Chimart Associates v Paul (1986) 66 NY2d 570, 498 NYS2d 344, 489 NE2d 231. Reformation, the court held, should be limited both substantively and procedurally.

§ 6:7. Reconciling Inconsistencies

p. 258, n. 6—Stage Club Corp. v West Realty Co. (1995, 1st Dept) 212 AD2d 458, 622 NYS2d 948; Bruni v County of Otsego (1993, 3d Dept) 192 AD2d 939, 596 NYS2d 888.

§ 6:13. Unconscionable Lease or Clause

p. 262, n. 13—In re Estate of LoGu-

idice (1992, 2d Dept) 186 AD2d 659, 588 NYS2d 623. The court held that a lease, executed by the nephew of the deceased owner, was unconscionable. The rent provided in the lease was less than one-quarter of the market value of the house, there was no increase in rent for the potential 30-year period of the lease, the estate was to be responsible for all maintenance, taxes, and other expenses of the house, including utilities, and the tenant was given the unqualified right to sublet the house. It also did not give the invalid sister of decedent any right to remain in the house, which had been her home for over 40 years.

B. PAROL EVIDENCE RULE

§ 6:14. Generally

p. 264, n. 5—Chimart Associates v Paul (1986) 66 NY2d 570, 498 NYS2d 344, 489 NE2d 231; Creative Ways v Image Mix (1995, 1st Dept) 211 AD2d 514, 621 NYS2d 339.

p. 265, n. 6—Stage Club Corp. v West Realty Co. (1995, 1st Dept) 212 AD2d 458, 622 NYS2d 948.

p. 265, n. 7—Braten v Bankers Trust Co. (1983) 60 NY2d 155, 468 NYS2d 861, 456 NE2d 802, reconsideration den 61 NY2d 670 and reh den 61 NY2d 670. This court held that evidence of what may have been agreed upon orally between the parties prior to the execution of a written instrument cannot be received to vary the terms of the writing.

§ 6:15. Exceptions to the Parol Evidence Rule

p. 266 n. 20—Parol evidence is inadmissible to contradict, vary, add to, or subtract from the terms of the written agreement between the parties. Smith v Fitzsimmons (1992, 4th Dept) 180 AD2d 177, 584 NYS2d 692.

## CONSTRUCTION OF LEASES § 6:27

### § 6:18. Ambiguity or Uncertainty in Instrument

p. 270, n. 17—67 Wall Street Co. v Franklin Nat'l Bank (1975) 37 NY2d 245, 371 NYS2d 915, 333 NE2d 184.

### C. MODIFICATION OF LEASE

### § 6:22. Generally

p. 275, n. 16—"It is axiomatic that a modification can only occur by mutual assent; it cannot be presumed or implied. . ." Northern Metro. Residential Health Care Facility, Inc. v Ledri Realty Assoc., Inc. (1992, 3d Dept) 179 AD2d 133, 582 NYS2d 521.

### § 6:25. Oral Modification
### § 6:26. —Provision Against Oral Modification

p. 279, n. 20—Stendig, Inc. v Thom Rock Realty Co. (1990, 1st Dept) 163 AD2d 46, 558 NYS2d 917.

Brook Shopping Ctrs. v F.W. Woolworth Co. (1995, 2d Dept) 215 App Div 2d 620, 628 NYS2d 318. Landlord commenced this action to recover rent allegedly due for the use of certain outdoor space adjacent to the store it leased to respondent. Although the written lease between the parties did not authorize defendant to use the outdoor space, it had paid landlord a percentage of its gross sales from both the store and the outdoor space since 1960. Because of tenant's payment and landlord's acceptance of the rent for the outdoor space the court held that it had an agreement with tenant to accept that rent for the remainder of the term of the lease and therefore dismissed landlord's complaint.

### § 6:27. —Form of Provision Against Oral Modification

The reference to Chapter 28 for Forms of complete leases should be to Chapter 1.

# PART TWO
# THE RESPECTIVE RIGHTS AND OBLIGATIONS OF LANDLORD AND TENANT

## CHAPTER 7
## PREMISES LEASED: EASEMENTS AND APPURTENANCES

A. IN GENERAL
   § 7:1. What is Included in a Lease?
   § 7:5. Appurtenances Defined
   § 7:7. Illustrations of Appurtenances Included in a Lease

B. WHAT IS INCLUDED IN LEASE OF PART OF BUILDING
   § 7:10. Generally
   § 7:17. Lobby Attendant Services

C. RIGHT TO LIGHT, AIR, UTILITIES, ETC.
   § 7:24. Air Space Rights

D. FARM LANDS LEASE
   § 7:26. Right to Crops
   § 7:28. Right to Emblements

---

### A. IN GENERAL

### § 7:1. What is Included in a Lease?

p. 284, n. 3—Whether or not a lease provision is ambiguous is a question of law to be resolved by a court. Papa Gino's of America, Inc. v Plaza at Latham Associates (1988, 3d Dept) 135 AD2d 74, 524 NYS2d 536; Van Wagner Advertising Corp. v S & M Enterprises (1986) 67 NY2d 186, 501 NYS2d 628, 492 NE2d 756; 67 Wall Street Co. v Franklin Nat'l Bank (1975) 37 NY2d 245, 371 NYS2d 915, 333 NE2d 184.

### § 7:5. Appurtenances Defined

p. 287, n. 2—See Rasch, New York Law and Practice of Real Property, § 18:8.

## § 7:7. Illustrations of Appurtenances Included in a Lease

*(Add to the last paragraph on page 289 in § 7:7)*

In another case the court held that the construction of a McDonald's hamburger store in the parking lot of a shopping center interfered with the tenant's appurtenant rights and deprived it of a substantial part of the easement that was necessary to the full use of the leased premises. [12.1]

12.1. 487 Elmwood, Inc. v Hassett (1990, 4th Dept) 161 AD2d 1170, 556 NYS2d 425, app den 77 NY2d 803, 568 NYS2d 347, 569 NE2d 1026.

## B. WHAT IS INCLUDED IN LEASE OF PART OF BUILDING

### § 7:10. Generally

p. 291, n. 4—A lease of an entire floor in a multi-tenant building is not intended to include stairs, corridors, landings, and other common areas. Wilfred Laboratories, Inc. v Fifty-Second Street Hotel Associates (1987, 1st Dept) 133 AD2d 320, 519 NYS2d 220, app dismd without op 71 NY2d 994, 529 NYS2d 277, 524 NE2d 878.

### § 7:17. Lobby Attendant Services

p. 297, n. 8—In reversing the lower court's grant of summary judgment to defendant New York City Housing Authority, the Court of Appeals determined there was a question of fact as to whether the New York Housing Authority was liable for damages after a resident was raped inside landlord's building which had not been equipped with locks to the entrance doors. Multiple Dwelling Law § 50-a [3] mandates the installation of self-closing, self-locking doors in buildings constructed before 1968 upon the request or consent of tenants occupying a majority of apartments within the multiple dwelling structure. If tenants do not consent, then no installation is mandated by statute. However, this does not relieve the landlord of all duty to install security devices. The court stated that regardless of the absence of a statutory obligation, a landlord is subject to the common law duty to take minimal precautions to protect tenants from foreseeable harm. Jacqueline S. v City of New York (1993) 81 NY2d 288, 598 NYS2d 160, 614 NE2d 723, reconsideration den 82 NY2d 749, 602 NYS2d 807, 622 NE2d 308.

## C. RIGHT TO LIGHT, AIR, UTILITIES, ETC.

### § 7:24. Air Space Rights

p. 305, n. 12—The Appellate Division held that a tenant of a long-term recorded lease is a "party in interest" that would be "adversely affected" by a planned transfer of the air rights from the building it occupies. Macmillan, Inc. v Cadillac Fairview Corp. (1982, 1st Dept) 86 AD2d 15, 448 NYS2d 668.

In Macmillan, Inc. v CF Lex Associates (1982) 56 NY2d 386, 452 NYS2d 377, 437 NE2d 1134, the Court of Appeals reversed, holding that the tenant was not a party in interest. The court held that air rights have "historically been conceived as one of the bundle of rights associated with ownership of the land rather than ownership of the structures erected thereon."

## D. FARM LANDS LEASE

### § 7:26. Right to Crops

p. 306, n. 19—Triggs v Kahn (1990, 3d Dept) 167 AD2d 680, 563 NYS2d 262.

# RIGHTS OF LANDLORD AND TENANT § 7:28

p. 306, n. 20—Triggs v Kahn (1990, 3d Dept) 167 AD2d 680, 563 NYS2d 262.

p. 306, n. 1—Triggs v Kahn (1990, 3d Dept) 167 AD2d 680, 563 NYS2d 262.

p. 306, n. 2—Triggs v Kahn (1990, 3d Dept) 167 AD2d 680, 563 NYS2d 262.

p. 307, n. 3—Triggs v Kahn (1990, 3d Dept) 167 AD2d 680, 563 NYS2d 262.

## § 7:28. Right to Emblements

p. 308, n. 14—Triggs v Kahn (1990, 3d Dept) 167 AD2d 680, 563 NYS2d 262.

p. 309, n. 16—Triggs v Kahn (1990, 3d Dept) 167 AD2d 680, 563 NYS2d 262. Since the duration of the tenancy was for a certain period the court held that the doctrine of emblements was not applicable.

# CHAPTER 8

## OBLIGATIONS TO DELIVER POSSESSION AND TO OCCUPY PREMISES

§ 8:3. Right to Damages Against Landlord
§ 8:6. —Right to Loss of Profits and Time
§ 8:7. Action to Recover Possession
§ 8:11. Form of Covenant to Deliver Possession
§ 8:12. Form of Provision to Protect Landlord Against Inability to Deliver Possession
§ 8:13. Tenant's Obligation to Occupy

---

### § 8:3. Right to Damages Against Landlord

### —Right to Loss of Profits and Time

p. 318, n. 13—In an action for lost profits, when a tenant is not yet in possession it may not recover profits which allegedly should have been earned if not for a breach by the landlord preventing the tenant from taking possession. Maruki, Inc. v Lefrak Fifth Ave. Corp. (1990, 1st Dept) 161 AD2d 264, 555 NYS2d 293.

### § 8:7. Action to Recover Possession

p. 309, n. 16—See Rasch, New York Law and Practice of Real Property, §§ 39:1 - 39:64.

### § 8:11. Form of Covenant to Deliver Possession

The reference to Chapter 21 for forms of complete leases should be to Chapter 1.

### § 8:12. Form of Provision to Protect Landlord Against Inability to Deliver Possession

p. 323, n. 13—However, in Fox Paper, Ltd. v Schwarzman (1990, 2d Dept) 168 AD2d 604, 563 NYS2d 439, the court denied tenant's action to recover money advanced upon the execution of a lease since a paragraph in the lease absolved the landlord from liability for failure to deliver possession at the commencement of the term of the lease.

### § 8:13. Tenant's Obligation to Occupy

p. 324, n. 15—Buffardi v Parillo (1990, 3rd Dept) 168 App Div 2d 812, 563 NYS2d 948. Plaintiff and defendant entered into a lease agreement which required defendant to obtain all necessary governmental approvals and permits and "no rental shall become due thereunder until and unless such approvals are obtained." Defendant decided not to proceed with the transaction and plaintiff commenced an action to recover rent and taxes allegedly due under the lease. Contrary to

## POSSESSION OF PREMISES § 8:13

defendant's contention that he made a good-faith effort to obtain the necessary governmental approvals the court held that defendant abandoned his effort to obtain the building permit without consulting a state-licensed architect or engineer. In dismissing defendant's counterclaim the court stated that "Although the law does not require a party to fulfill a condition of a contract that is incapable of fulfillment and is not that party's fault, there must be a genuine effort to fulfill the condition."

# CHAPTER 9
## ASSIGNMENT AND SUBLETTING

A. IN GENERAL
　§ 9:2.　Assignment and Sublease Defined

B. DISTINGUISHING BETWEEN ASSIGNMENT AND SUBLEASE
　§ 9:4.　Fundamental Test
　§ 9:5.　Pro Tanto Assignment and Sublease
　§ 9:14. Distinction Between Assignment and Sublease Summarized

I. SURVIVAL OF DECEASED TENANT'S LIABILITY
　§ 9:52. Generally
　§ 9:53. Nature of Liability of Personal Representative

K. SUBTENANT'S LIABILITIES AND RIGHTS
　§ 9:60. Rights Limited by Terms of Paramount Lease

L. SUBTENANT'S RIGHTS ON CANCELLATION OF PARAMOUNT LEASE
　§ 9:67. Right to Vacate
　§ 9:69. Right to Possession

M. SUBTENANT'S RIGHTS ON VOLUNTARY SURRENDER OF PARAMOUNT LEASE
　§ 9:73. Generally

N. RIGHT TO ASSIGN AND SUBLET
　§ 9:75. Generally
　§ 9:77. Effect of Emergency Rent Laws
　§ 9:78. Residential Tenant's Statutory Right to Assign
　§ 9:79. Residential Tenant's Statutory Right to Sublet

O. RESTRICTIONS ON RIGHT TO ASSIGN AND SUBLET
　§ 9:89. Breach of Restriction; Voluntary Acts of Tenant
　§ 9:94. —Acts of Personal Representatives of Deceased Tenant
　§ 9:96. Right of Landlord to Withhold Consent

# ASSIGNMENT AND SUBLETTING § 9:52

§ 9:98. Criteria for Determination of Reasonableness
§ 9:99. Statutory Modification of Right to Withhold Consent in Case of a Deceased Residential Tenant
§ 9:101. Landlord's Remedies for Breach of Restriction Against Assignment or Subletting

## A. IN GENERAL
### § 9:2. Assignment and Sublease Defined

p. 331, n. 3—269 Fulton Corp. v H.A.B. Realty Assoc. (1992, 2d Dept) 179 App Div 2d 752, 579 NYS2d 115, app den 80 NY2d 756, 588 NYS2d 824, 602 NE2d 232. Where a tenant did not convey its entire interest in the lease the court held that it was not required to provide to the landlord an assignment by its assignee of the obligations under the lease.

p. 331, n. 8—The Appellate Term stated that a sublease can confer no greater rights on a subleasee than those afforded to the tenant by its prime lease. Millicom, Inc. v Breed, Abbott & Morgan (1990, 1st Dept) 160 AD2d 496, 554 NYS2d 160, app den 76 NY2d 703, 559 NYS2d 982, 559 NE2d 676.

## B. DISTINGUISHING BETWEEN ASSIGNMENT AND SUBLEASE
### § 9:4. Fundamental Test

p. 333, n. 16—269 Fulton Corp. v H.A.B. Realty Assoc. (1992, 2d Dept) 179 App Div 2d 752, 579 NYS2d 115, app den 80 NY2d 756, 588 NYS2d 824, 602 NE2d 232. Where a tenant did not convey its entire interest in the lease the court held that it was not required to provide to the landlord an assignment by its assignee of the obligations under the lease.

### § 9:5. Pro Tanto Assignment and Sublease

p. 333, n. 17—269 Fulton Corp. v H.A.B. Realty Assoc. (1992, 2d Dept) 179 App Div 2d 752, 579 NYS2d 115, app den 80 NY2d 756, 588 NYS2d 824, 602 NE2d 232. Where a tenant did not convey its entire interest in the lease the court held that it was not required to provide to the landlord an assignment by its assignee of the obligations under the lease.

### § 9:14. Distinction Between Assignment and Sublease Summarized

p. 340, n. 18—269 Fulton Corp. v H.A.B. Realty Assoc. (1992, 2d Dept) 179 App Div 2d 752, 579 NYS2d 115, app den 80 NY2d 756, 588 NYS2d 824, 602 NE2d 232. Where a tenant did not convey its entire interest in the lease the court held that it was not required to provide to the landlord an assignment by its assignee of the obligations under the lease.

## I. SURVIVAL OF DECEASED TENANT'S LIABILITY
### § 9:52. Generally

p. 372, n. 9—Until a will is probated or the administrator distributes the property the estate, not the landlord, is the sole party entitled to possession of the premises for the balance of the lease. East Harlem Pilot Block Bldg. 1 Housing Dev. Fund Corp. v Serrano (1992, Civ Ct) 153 Misc 2d 776, 583 NYS2d 751.

## § 9:53. Nature of Liability of Personal Representative

p. 373, n. 11—East Harlem Pilot Block Bldg. 1 Housing Dev. Fund Corp. v Serrano (1992, Civ Ct) 153 Misc 2d 776, 583 NYS2d 751. A representative of a deceased tenant accepts his decedent's lease in his representative capacity for the best interest of the estate.

## K. SUBTENANT'S LIABILITIES AND RIGHTS

### § 9:60. Rights Limited by Terms of Paramount Lease

p. 381, n. 7—11 Park Place Assocs. v Barnes (1994, 1st Dept) 204 App Div 2d 170, 611 NYS2d 556. Although the jury demand was timely filed the court granted plaintiff's motion to strike the jury demand since the subtenant was bound by the provisions in the paramount lease which provided for a waiver of a jury demand.

## L. SUBTENANT'S RIGHTS ON CANCELLATION OF PARAMOUNT LEASE

### § 9:67. Right to Vacate

p. 388, n. 4—170 West 85th Street Tenants Ass'n v Cruz (1991, 1st Dept) 173 AD2d 338, 569 NYS2d 705; Beacway Operating Corp. v Luski (1996, App T) NYLJ 10-1-96, p. 21, col. 3. Repondent-undertenant's possessory claim was extinguished on cancellation of the paramount lease. (Citing text.).

Ocean Grille v Pell (1996, App Div, 2d Dept) 641 NYS2d 373. Where a subtenant is not made a party to a voluntary termination agreement of a paramount lease, and where the paramount lease makes no provision for termination, it does not terminate the sublease. After the voluntary termination of the paramount lease a subtenant becomes the immediate tenant of the original lessor and the interest of the subtenant and the terms of the sublease continue as if no termination had occurred. Unless the subtenant has already vacated the premises the landlord must commence further proceedings against the subtenant to effect removal.

See also Unionport Shoes v Parkchester S. Condominium (1994, 1st Dept) 205 AD2d 385, 613 NYS2d 605. The voluntary surrender of a lease does not operate to terminate a sublease.

### § 9:69. Right to Possession

p. 391, n. 12—The court held that a subtenant remaining in possession after termination of the paramount lease retained the common-law status of a tenant at sufferance and required a 30-day notice to vacate. Mastas v Extra Closet, Inc. (1990) 146 Misc 2d 698, 553 NYS2d 582.

## M. SUBTENANT'S RIGHTS ON VOLUNTARY SURRENDER OF PARAMOUNT LEASE

### § 9:73. Generally

p. 396, n. 5—Ocean Grille v Pell (1996, App Div, 2d Dept) 641 NYS2d 373 (citing text)

## N. RIGHT TO ASSIGN AND SUBLET

### § 9:75. Generally

p. 401, n. 2—East Harlem Pilot Block Bldg. 1 Housing Dev. Fund Corp. v Serrano (1992, Civ Ct) 153 Misc 2d 776, 583 NYS2d 751.

# ASSIGNMENT AND SUBLETTING § 9:79

## § 9:77. Effect of Emergency Rent Laws

*Add text at end of section on p. 404:*

Both the Emergency Tenant Protection Act and the Rent Stabilization Code have restrictions on the right of a tenant to sublet.[12.1] A violation of these restrictions may not be cured pursuant to RPAPL § 753(4).[12.2]

12.1. 9 NYCRR 2505.7 (ETPA); 9 NYCRR 2525.6 (Rent Stabilization Code). The rights granted by Real Prop Law § 226-b to assign a lease or sublease premises with respect to units covered by the emergency tenant's protection act of 1974 or the rent stabilization code are subject to the provisions of 9 NYCRR 2505.7 (ETPA) and 9 NYCRR 2525.6 (Rent Stabilization Code), [RPL § 226-b(4)].

12.2. Continental Towers Ltd. Partnership v Freuman (1985) 128 Misc 2d 680, 494 NYS2d 595. The court determined that "a cure in these circumstances would not be in furtherance of the public interest." See also, Paulsen Real Estate Corp. v Goldberg, NYLJ 2-10-89 at 26, col. 5 (Dist. Ct., Nassau Co.)

The reasoning of Continental Towers Ltd. Partnership v Freuman, *supra*, was cited with approval by the Appellate Division, Second Department in Avon Furniture Leasing, Inc. v Popolizio (1986, 1st Dept) 116 App Div 2d 280, 500 NYS2d 1019, app den 68 NY2d 610, 508 NYS2d 1028, 501 NE2d 601.

Applying the rationale of Continental Towers, *supra*, the court in Hurst v Miske (1986) 133 Misc 2d 362, 505 NYS2d 984, determined that a rent-controlled tenant can forfeit her rights to an apartment by subletting it for profit.

This rationale has also been applied in a case which involves a rental situation between a tenant and a sublease/roommate, Diamond v Menasche (1988) 141 Misc 2d 899, 535 NYS2d 335. However, in 520 East 81st Street Assoc. v Roughton-Hester (1990, 1st Dept) 157 App Div 2d 199, 555 NYS2d 70, the court determined in a rent stabilized unit where the subtenant is a roommate there is no partial sublet and therefore the prohibitions against profiteering do not apply.

COMMENT: The basic flaw in the Roughton-Hester decision is the idea that a roommate situation is not a sublet arrangement. The purpose of Real Prop. Law § 235-f ("roommate law") was to remove the roommate from the requirements of Real Prop. Law § 226-b (assignments and sublet) and therefore not require the prime tenant to request permission from the landlord. Whether the prime tenant remains in possession or vacates the premises the situation is still a sublet. The appellate court should have realized their mistake when they decided that where a prime tenant vacates the premises then the prohibition against profiteering will apply but if the prime tenant remains in possession the sky is the limit. No contrary decision could be found in any other jurisdiction and therefore this unfortunate decision is the current law. It is the opinion of this author that the determination in Diamond v Menasche, supra, is the correct decision. (Up to December 31, 1991, I could find no court that has used the Roughton-Hester decision.)

## § 9:78. Residential Tenant's Statutory Right to Assign

p. 405, n. 18—577 Broadway Real Estate Partners v Giacinto (1992, 1st Dept) 182 App Div 2d 374, 582 NYS2d 123. See § 43:29, infra.

## § 9:79. Residential Tenant's Statutory Right to Sublet

p. 408, n. 9—Plaintiff commenced an action to obtain relief from its

## § 9:79

obligation to offer a renewal lease to defendant on the ground that it was not occupying the rent-stabilized apartment units as "primary residences," but rather was subletting the units to its employees. Since plaintiff did not give respondent notice of its intention not to offer a renewal lease not more than 150 days and not less than 120 days prior to the expiration of the existing lease term, respondent is entitled to renewal lease. 520 East 81st Street Assoc. v Lenox Hill Hosp. (1991) 77 NY2d 944, 570 NYS2d 479, 573 NE2d 567.

## O. RESTRICTIONS ON RIGHT TO ASSIGN AND SUBLET

### § 9:89. Breach of Restriction; Voluntary Acts of Tenant

### § 9:94. —Acts of Personal Representatives of Deceased Tenant

p. 432, n. 2—East Harlem Pilot Block Bldg. 1 Housing Dev. Fund Corp. v Serrano (1992, Civ Ct) 153 Misc 2d 776, 583 NYS2d 751.

### § 9:96. Right of Landlord to Withhold Consent

p. 435, n. 8—Millicom, Inc. v Breed, Abbott & Morgan (1990, 1st Dept) 160 AD2d 496, 554 NYS2d 160, app den 76 NY2d 703, 559 NYS2d 982, 559 NE2d 676.

*Add text at end of section on p. 434:*

Landlord can refuse consent to assignment where lease restricting assignment without landlord's consent has no clause requiring that consent not be unreasonably withheld.[8.1]

8.1. Caridi v Markey (1989, 2d Dept) 148 AD2d 653, 539 NYS2d 404.

Citing Mann Theatres Corp. v Mid-Island Shopping Plaza Co. (1983, 2d Dept) 94 App Div 2d 466, 464 NYS2d 793, affd 62 NY2d 930, 479 NYS2d 213, 468 NE2d 51 and Dress Shirt Sales, Inc. v Hotel Martinique Associates (1963) 12 NY2d 339, 239 NYS2d 660, 190 NE2d 10, the court held that, *in a commercial lease,* "it is the well established law of this State that in the absence of a clause prohibiting the unreasonable withholding of consent, a landlord may refuse to consent to the assignment of a lease which contains an express restriction against assignment without the Landlord's consent (citations)."

### § 9:98. Criteria for Determination of Reasonableness

p. 438, n. 18—F.H.R. Auto Sales, Inc. v Scutti (1988, 4th Dept) 144 AD2d 956, 534 NYS2d 266 (citing text).

### § 9:99. Statutory Modification of Right to Withhold Consent in Case of a Deceased Residential Tenant

p. 440, n. 2—East Harlem Pilot Block Bldg. 1 Housing Dev. Fund Corp. v Serrano (1992, Civ Ct) 153 Misc 2d 776, 583 NYS2d 751.

### § 9:101. Landlord's Remedies for Breach of Restriction Against Assignment or Subletting

p. 441, n. 10—The statement in the bound volume that ". . . absent the reservation in the lease of possessory rights for a breach of a restriction against assignments or sublettings, a landlord cannot recover possession as a remedy for a tenant's breach of the restriction" is no longer a correct statement of the law. RPL § 226-b now

## ASSIGNMENT AND SUBLETTING § 9:101

provides that a tenant renting a residence may not assign his lease without the written consent of the owner. The provisions of this statute apply to leases entered into or renewed before or after the effective date of this section and any sublet or assignment by the tenant which does not comply with the provisions of this section constitutes a substantial breach of the lease or tenancy. (See §§ 9:78 and 9:79, infra.)

The provisions of RPL § 226-b have been upheld by the Court of Appeals in Vance v Century Apartments Associates (1984) 61 NY2d 716, 472 NYS2d 611, 460 NE2d 1096 (release from the lease is the sole remedy of a tenant where the landlord has unreasonably withheld consent to the tenant's request to assign a lease); Sitomer v Melohn Properties Management (1985) 65 NY2d 881, 493 NYS2d 310, 482 NE2d 1226 (a tenant's sole remedy for a landlord's unreasonable refusal to consent to a proposed sublease or assignment is to be released from the lease); Blum v West End Associates (1985) 64 NY2d 939, 488 NYS2d 635, 477 NE2d 1089 (Landlord's failure to send to a tenant a notice of termination of the leases only entitles the tenant to be released from the lease).

See also Fox v 85th Estates Co. (1984, 1st Dept) 100 App Div 2d 797, 474 NYS2d 521, affd 63 NY2d 1009, 484 NYS2d 536, 473 NE2d 764 (the sole remedy of a tenant whose landlord unreasonably refused to consent to an assignment is to be released from the lease); Parks v Mengoni (1984, 1st Dept) 100 App Div 2d 785, 474 NYS2d 487 (holding that in light of the amendment to RPL ( 226-b an assignment is not legally effective without the consent of the landlord); Bennett v Rockrose Dev. Corp. (1984, 1st Dept) 106 App Div 2d 256, 482 NYS2d 23, affd 64 NY2d 1155, 490 NYS2d 769, 480 NE2d 383 (a landlord may prevent assignment, even by unreasonably withholding consent, and the tenant's sole remedy is to be released from the lease); Levai v Alcoma Corp. (1984, 1st Dept) 106 App Div 2d 292, 483 NYS2d 4 (Citing Vance v Century Apartments Associates, supra, the court held that "release from the lease is the sole remedy of a tenant where the landlord has unreasonably withheld consent to the tenant's request to assign the lease"); Cutler v North Shore Towers Associates (1986, 2d Dept) 125 App Div 2d 532, 509 NYS2d 609 (since the tenant sublet the apartment without the consent of the landlord he committed a substantial breach of the lease entitling the landlord to possession of the premises).

# CHAPTER 10

# EFFECT OF HOLDING OVER

## A. IN GENERAL
§ 10:7. Holding Over by Assignee or Subtenant
§ 10:9. Measure of Damages for Holding Over

## B. STATUTORY TENANCY
§ 10:13. Expiration of Tenancy on Death of Tenant
§ 10:14. Terms and Conditions of Tenancy

## A. IN GENERAL

### § 10:7. Holding Over by Assignee or Subtenant

p. 452, n. 4—Radin v Arthur Holding Co. (1989, 2d Dept) 149 AD2d 576, 540 NYS2d 267. The wrongful holdover by a subtenant is deemed the same as a wrongful holding over of the prime tenant.

1133 Bldg. Corp. v Ketchum Communications (1996, 1st Dept) 224 AD2d 336, 638 NYS2d 450, app dismd without op 88 NY2d 963, 647 NYS2d 716, 670 NE2d 1348. Where a subtenant had agreed to be bound by all of the provisions and restrictions of the main lease and remained in possession of the sublet premises beyond the expiration of both the sublease and the main lease without the permission of the landlord, the subtenant was found liable for the use and occupation of the sublease as well as the main lease.

p. 453, n. 9—A wrongful holdover by a subtenant is deemed the same as a wrongful holdover of the prime tenant-sublessor. Radin v Arthur Holding Co. (1989, 2d Dept) 149 AD2d 576, 540 NYS2d 267.

### § 10:9. Measure of Damages for Holding Over

p. 453, n. 12—1133 Bldg. Corp. v Ketchum Communications (1996, 1st Dept) 224 AD2d 336, 638 NYS2d 450, app dismd without op 88 NY2d 963, 647 NYS2d 716, 670 NE2d 1348. Where a subtenant had agreed to be bound by all of the provisions and restrictions of the main lease and remained in possession of the sublet premises beyond the expiration of both the sublease and the main lease without the permission of the landlord, the subtenant was liable for the use and occupation of the sublease as well as the main lease.

Mitchell & Titus Assoc., Inc. v Mesh Realty Corp. (1990, 1st Dept) 160 AD2d 465, 554 NYS2d 136. In a commercial lease the lessor is not under a duty to mitigate damages. See also 11 Park Place Assocs. v Barnes (1994, 1st Dept) 202 AD2d 292, 608 NYS2d 664, app dismd without op 86 NY2d 887, 635 NYS2d 952, 659 NE2d 775; Sage Realty Corp. v Kenbee Management-New York, Inc. (1992, 1st Dept) 182 AD2d 480, 582 NYS2d 182.

# EFFECT OF HOLDING OVER § 10:13

## B. STATUTORY TENANCY

### § 10:13. Expiration of Tenancy on Death of Tenant

p. 458, n. 6—In a licensee proceeding upon the death of the rent-controlled statutory tenant, the court held that the petition was improperly dismissed on the ground that the landlord failed to first apply to the DHCR for a certificate of eviction. Bromer v Rosensweig (1995, App T) 166 Misc 2d 201, 634 NYS2d 43.

p. 459, n. 9—Nieces and nephews have been held family members of the tenant entitled to protection. Bistany v Williams (Yonkers City Ct 1975) 83 Misc 2d 228, 372 NYS2d 6.

p. 459, n. 10—A "gay life partner" is not deemed either the functional equivalent of a surviving spouse or a de facto family member entitled to remain in occupancy of a rent controlled apartment after the death of the named tenant. Koppelman v O'Keefe (1988) 140 Misc 2d 828, 535 NYS2d 871 (the denial of this right to a gay life partner is not a denial of equal protection).

Where a surviving live-in-lover of a deceased tenant can establish that his relationship with the deceased tenant was longtime, and characterized by an emotional and financial commitment, and interdependence he will be considered a family member of the deceased tenant, and pursuant to New York City Rent and Eviction Regulation § 2204.6(d) will be permitted to remain in occupancy of the tenant's rent-controlled apartment. Braschi v Stahl Associates Co. (1989) 74 NY2d 201, 544 NYS2d 784, 543 NE2d 49.

*[See § 11:1, infra, this supp, for discussion of Rent Stabilization Code § 2523(b)(2), a similar provision for rent stabilized units.]*

East 10th Street Assoc. v Estate of Goldstein (1990, 1st Dept) 154 App Div 2d 142, 552 NYS2d 257, applying *Braschi* to Rent Stabilization Code, § 2520.6(o) which defines a Family Member; see also, 2-4 Realty Associates v Pittman (1989) 144 Misc 2d 311, 547 NYS2d 515; Lerad Realty Co. v Reynolds, NYLJ 8-28-90 at 22, col. 5 (Civ. Ct., NY Co.).

Applying *Braschi* the Appellate Division, Second Department, held that an individual who lived with a family for 22 years and who was considered part of the family although the relationship had not been formalized by an adoption should be granted the protection afforded by New York City's Rent Control Law. Athineos v Thayer (1989, 2d Dept) 153 App Div 2d 825, 545 NYS2d 337.

Cohen v Berger (1989, 2d Dept) 153 App Div 2d 920, 545 NYS2d 728, app dismd without op 75 NY2d 809, 552 NYS2d 111, 551 NE2d 604, applied Braschi to 9 NYCRR 2523.5(b)(2) of the Rent Stabilization Code. As a result of the decision in *Braschi* a new section has been added to 9 NYCRR 2520.6(o) of the Rent Stabilization Code as follows:

"(2) Any other person residing with the tenant or permanent tenant in the housing accommodation as a primary or principal residence, respectively, who can prove emotional and financial commitment, and interdependence between such person and the tenant or permanent tenant. Although no single factor shall be solely determinative, evidence which is to be considered in determining whether such emotional and financial commitment and interdependence existed, may include, without limitation, such factors as listed below. In no event would evidence of a sexual relationship between such persons be required or considered.

(i) longevity of the relationship;

(ii) sharing of or relying upon each other for payment of household or family expenses, and/or other common necessities of life;

(iii) intermingling of finances as evidenced by, among other things, joint

§ 10:13 LANDLORD AND TENANT

ownership of bank accounts, personal and real property, credit cards, loan obligations, sharing a household budget for purposes of receiving government benefits, etc.;

(iv) engaging in family-type activities by jointly attending family functions, holidays and celebrations, social and recreational activities, etc.;

(v) formalizing of legal obligations, intentions, and responsibilities to each other by such means as executing wills naming each other as executor and/or beneficiary, granting each other a power of attorney and/or conferring upon each other authority to make health care decisions each for the other, entering into a personal relationship contract, making a domestic partnership declaration, or serving as a representative payee for purpose of public benefits, etc.;

(vi) holding themselves out as family members to other family members, friends, members of the community or religious institutions, or society in general, through their words or actions;

(vii) regularly performing family functions, such as caring for each other or each other's extended family members, and/or relying upon each other for daily family services;

(viii) engaging in any other pattern of behavior, agreement, or other action which evidences the intention of creating a long term, emotionally-committed relationship."

In Rent Stabilization Assn. v Higgins (1990, 1st Dept) 164 AD2d 283, 562 NYS2d 962, the Appellate Division reversed the lower decision and approved the regulations adopted by the Division of Housing and Community of Renewal amending the Emergency Housing Rent Control and Rent and Eviction Regulations (9 NYCRR 2104.6(d)); New York City Rent Control, New York City Rent and Eviction Regulations (9 NYCRR 2204.6(d)); Rent Stabilization and Rent Stabilization Code (9 NYCRR 2520.6(n) and (o) and (q)); and Emergency Tenant Protection, Emergency Tenant Protection Regulations (9 NYCRR 2500.2(m), (n), (o) and (p)). (The amendments are set forth in detail in the supplement to New York Landlord and Tenant Rent Control and Rent Stabilization.) The DHCR amended the four sets of administrative regulations under its administration, to provide the leasehold succession rights in accordance with the broad definition of the term "family" set out in *Braschi v Stahl Associates Co.* by promulgating an emergency rule applicable to all four sets of regulations. The emergency rule broadened the definition of family member entitled to succession rights to include, in addition to those traditional relations previously named, those individuals residing in the housing accommodation, with the tenant of record, as a primary residence, who can prove emotional and financial commitment and interdependence between themselves and the tenant of record. The court held that the regulations represent a codification of the Court of Appeals decision in *Braschi v Stahl Associates Co.* and the Appellate Division case *East 10th Street Associates v Goldstein Estates,* and are a response to substantially the same public needs as the succession provisions approved in *Feasta v Leshen.*

Reaffirming its earlier decision (164 AD2d 283, 562 NYS2d 562), the Appellate Division, First Department held that the regulations adopted by DHCR were a valid exercise of their administrative power and did not constitute a "taking." Rent Stabilization Ass'n v Higgins (1993, 1st Dept) 189 AD2d 594, 592 NYS2d 255. This decision was affirmed by the Court of Appeals, Rent Stabilization Ass'n v Higgins (1993) 83 NY2d 156, 608 NYS2d 930, 630 NE2d 626, motion gr, cert den (US) 129 L Ed 2d 823, 114 S Ct 2693. In a concurring opinion J. Bellacosa stated that "[i]n the distribution and delegation of governmental powers, it is quite momentous that any administrative agency should possess the potent public policy power to extend the durational and relational sweep of the plurality rationale of Braschi v Stahl Assocs. Co. (74 NY2d 201), including fully into the rent stabilization category and more widely than was allowed even in the rent control field of

## EFFECT OF HOLDING OVER § 10:13

that case. The case-by-case application of this judicially approved regulatory initiative adds layers of great sensitivity and breadth to the implementation of this case. However high-purposed, well-intentioned and possessed of special expertise respondents' agency is, the societal equation is delicately weighted with practical, legal and fiscal consequences on all sides. Thus, while I also agree with the Chief Judge's acknowledgment of the primacy of legislative choices in the field . . . I believe it useful to go farther and urge the Legislature to carefully assess the sweeping power it impliedly invested in this administrative agency in the execution of a unique human sheltering mission."

In Seminole Realty Co. v Greenbaum (1994, App Div, 1st Dept) 619 NYS2d 5, the court found that the relationship of respondent and the deceased tenant was that of a "close friend and roommate" and therefore respondent was not entitled to succession rights. Stating they "never intermingled their finances or jointly owned real or personal property, held themselves out as a family unit, executed documents formalizing legal obligations, jointly celebrated most major holidays or attended important celebrations with each other's families" the court awarded possession in favor of landlord.

In Gottlieb v Licursi (1993, 1st Dept) 191 App Div 2d 256, 595 NYS2d 17, the court granted possession in favor of landlord finding that since respondent had maintained ownership of a house in White Plains, had filed income tax returns from, and registered to vote in Westchester County throughout her claimed 18 month cooccupancy of the apartment, she was not qualified as a family member of the deceased tenant of record.

In order to become a family member the resident must "establish a contemporaneous occupancy with the named tenant and some indication of permanence or continuity." Tener v New York State Div. of Housing & Community Renewal (1990, 1st Dept) 159 App Div 2d 270, 552 NYS2d 271.

333 East 53rd Street Associates v Mann (1986, 1st Dept) 121 App Div 2d 289, 503 NYS2d 752, affd 70 NY2d 660, 518 NYS2d 958, 512 NE2d 541. Under what may be considered a set of unusual facts, the court declared that defendant was the lawful rent-controlled tenant of the apartment in question. In 1970 at the age of 67 defendant moved into the apartment with Blanchard, age 83, who had lived in the apartment since 1940. Defendant resided there continuously until Blanchard died in 1984. On April 15, 1983, the building was converted to cooperative ownership pursuant to a noneviction plan. On April 20, 1983, by order of the Surrogate's Court of New York, Blanchard adopted Mann as his child. Since Mann had become a member of Blanchard's family entitled to continue residing in the apartment, the court decided in favor of the tenant and dismissed landlord's action seeking a declaratory judgment and an order ejecting defendant from the apartment.

Petitioner moved into her grandmother's apartment to care for her and after her grandmother's death sought "remaining family" member status. Her application was denied by the New City Housing Authority. Because petitioner commenced an article 78 proceeding 17 months after the Housing Authority's final determination was mailed to her the Court of Appeals affirmed the Appellate Division decision which had denied her application, holding that "it is well established that an application to reconsider an administrative determination does not extend the four-month Statute of Limitations." Simmons v Popolizio (1991) 78 NY2d 917, 573 NYS2d 464, 577 NE2d 1056.

In Greenberg v Coronet Properties Co. (1990, 1st Dept) 167 AD2d 291, 562 NYS2d 33, an issue arose involving Section 2204.6(d) of the New York City Rent and Eviction Regulations (9 NYCRR 2204.6), which prohibits removal of occupants of rent control apartments who are either the "surviving spouse of the deceased tenant or some other member of the deceased

## § 10:13 LANDLORD AND TENANT

tenant's family who has been living with the tenant." Relying upon the decision in 829 Seventh Ave. Co. v Reider (1986) 67 NY2d 930, 502 NYS2d 715, 493 NE2d 939, the Appellate Division held that the "living with" requirement has been defined to mean "living with such statutory tenant in a family unit, which in turn connotes an arrangement, whatever it duration, bearing some indicia of permanence or continuity." In Louis v Barthelme (1992, 1st Dept) 179 AD2d 604, 579 NYS2d 656, the court relied on *Greenburg* and held that 9 NYCRR 2204.6 prohibits the removal of a person who is either the surviving spouse of the deceased tenant or some other member of the family who has been living with the tenant.

Lepar Realty Corp. v Griffin (1991, Sup App T) 151 Misc 2d 579, 581 NYS2d 521. After respondent Deborah Griffin departed her rent-stabilized apartment, respondent landlord commenced a holdover proceeding against respondent and Larry Rhodes, who had lived with respondent since 1982. In reversing the trial court decision, the appellate court found that the evidence established that Rhodes's relationship with respondent was characterized by the requisite "emotional and financial commitment and interdependence" connoting a family relationship. In addition, the evidence showed that Rhodes had resided in the apartment for approximately six years, shared rent expenses, held himself out as a family member and that a child had been born to respondents.

## § 10:14. Terms and Conditions of Tenancy

p. 460, n. 13—Murphy v Vivian Realty Company (1993, 1st Dept) 199 App Div 2d 192, 605 NYS2d 285. Plaintiff, whose use of the building roof for a garden exceeded the use permitted by the terms of her lease, claimed that she was entitled to greater rights as a rent controlled tenant than under the lease and that the use of the roof for gardening purposes constituted an "essential service." This claim was rejected. A rent controlled tenant, the court held, is only allowed to continue to enjoy the same leasehold rights during the term of its statutory tenancy.

## CHAPTER 11
## RENEWAL OF LEASES

A. RIGHT TO RENEWAL ABSENT COVENANT
    § 11:1. Generally
    § 11:8. Mobile Home Park Tenancy

B. COVENANT TO RENEW
    § 11:11. Necessity of Certainty

E. EXERCISING RIGHT TO RENEW
    § 11:34. Necessity of Strict Performance of Conditions Precedent
    § 11:35. Necessity of Timely Notice to Renew
    § 11:36. When Performance of Other Provisions of Lease Necessary
    § 11:39. Equitable Relief from Failure to Give Timely Notice of Election to Renew
    § 11:40. Waiver of Performance of Conditions to Renewal

H. REMEDIES FOR BREACH OF COVENANT TO RENEW
    § 11:59. Specific Performance
    § 11:60. Action for Declaratory Judgment

---

## A. RIGHT TO RENEWAL ABSENT COVENANT

### § 11:1. Generally

p. 471, n. 1—I. S. J. Management Corp. v Delancy Clothing, Inc. (1990) 152 Misc 2d 13, 574 NYS2d 612-Month-to-month commercial tenants do not have a constitutionally protected property interest that entitles them to continue as tenants except for good cause.

*Add text after fourth full paragraph on p. 471:*

East Four-Forty Associates v Ewell, cited on p. 471 of the text, is reported in 138 Misc 2d 235, 527 NYS2d 204. The Appellate Division, First Department, disagreed with the East Four-Forty Associates case and held that Rent Stabilization Code § 2523(b)(2) is valid and that a brother of the named tenant who maintained the apartment as his primary residence from the incep-

§ 11:1

tion of the tenancy is entitled to the protection of this section of the Code.[3.1]

3.1. Festa v Leshen (1989, 1st Dept) 145 AD2d 49, 537 NYS2d 147.

p. 471, n. 4—"Primary residence," for purposes of entitlement to renewal of a lease to a stabilized apartment, means an ongoing, substantial, physical nexus with the premises for actual living purposes which can be demonstrated by objective empirical evidence; it is not equivalent to domicile, although it is a factor to be considered. Sommer v Ann Turkel, Inc. (AT1, 1987) 137 Misc 2d 7, 522 NYS2d 765, later proceeding 139 Misc 2d 892, 530 NYS2d 946.

Epsom Downs, Inc. v Allen (App Term, 1st Dept) NYLJ 4-16-93. The Appellate Term affirmed the trial court decision that respondent primarily resides in California and therefore does not maintain an "ongoing substantial, physical nexus" in the subject premises. In reaching its decision the court relied on the facts that respondent is employed as an actor in California, resides with his four-year old son in California, and listed various California addresses on several important documents, including bank accounts, mortgage applications for joint-owned California properties and certain income tax returns.

Law Center Foundation v DeWitt (App Term, 1st Dept) NYLJ 4-16-93. This court reversed the trial court and found that respondent did not maintain an "ongoing, substantial, physical nexus" with the stabilized premises. Here the court emphasized that respondent listed a Florida address on various key documents, including her driver license, motor vehicle registration, a 1987 federal income tax return, certain utility bills and credit card statements during the relevant time period. In addition, tenant filed a 1988 New York City non-resident income tax return and successfully applied for a Florida homestead exemption in January 1988.

In Crossland Federal Savings Bank

LANDLORD AND TENANT

v Wasserman (Dist Ct Nassau County) NYLJ 12-16-92, p. 25, col. 3. The court found that respondent-tenants were entitled to a renewal of their lease and were not primary residents in the State of Florida. In this case the court found that the tenants had filed a New York State resident tax return with their Florida address on the mailing label; had listed their New York home as their permanent home address; never filed a Florida tax return; had no Florida bank account but used a New York cash management account at Merrill Lynch for checking purposes (for which statements were mailed to Florida after July 1991); had New York licenses (the husband had a Florida driver's license that was issued to part-time residents); their car was registered and insured in Florida; tenants' Social Security check was deposited in New York; they maintained credit cards with both New York and Florida addresses; and had filed an application for a homestead exemption on property in Florida.

The court found "that the filing for the Homestead Exemption is not sufficient to overcome the many other factors which link the respondents to New York and is insufficient to prove the respondents' intent to give up the old (New York) domicile and adopt a new one (Florida). The Court is fully aware that a person requesting the Homestead Exemption is declaring Florida his/her permanent place of abode. However, it is insufficient to overcome the other factors in this case."

p. 472, n. 5—Tenant vacated a rent controlled apartment to reside in a nursing home. The appellate court refused to overturn a decision by the Division of Housing and Community Renewal that a daughter was protected by rent control laws because she was in continuous occupancy since her birth. Tener v New York State Div. of Housing & Community Renewal (1990, 1st Dept) 159 App Div 2d 270, 552 NYS2d 271.

p. 472, n. 7—Where tenant of a rent-stabilized apartment uses it for Com-

## RENEWAL OF LEASES § 11:8

mercial purposes, and the landlord seeks to evict him on the ground that the apartment is not the tenant's primary residence, the tenant must be given the 120-150-day notice before the expiration of the lease, or, if landlord seeks to evict the tenant on the ground that the commercial use is a violation of a residential tenancy, the tenant must be served with a 7-day notice to cure (see § 30:64, text). 30 Pilot Street Corp. v Williams (NYC Civ Ct Bx Co 1988) 140 Misc 2d 688, 531 NYS2d 848 (observing that Tuba Corp. v Laurence S. Freundlich, Inc. (1985) 120 Misc 2d 337, 489 NYS2d 834, and Coronet Properties Co. v Jennie & Co. Film Productions, Inc. (1983) 121 Misc 2d 873, 469 NYS2d 325, holding that a 30-day notice is all that is required in this situation, are no longer valid precedents, since they have been superseded by Golub v Frank (1985) 65 NY2d 900, 493 NYS2d 451, 483 NE2d 126, and Rent Stabilization Code § 2524 (see § 30:64, text).

*Add text at end of section on p. 472:*

The courts are divided as to the validity and enforceability of the provisions of the Rent Stabilization Code.[7.1] which afford qualified members of a named tenant of a rent stabilized apartment, who have lived with the named tenant during a period of the term, succession rights to the apartment, that is, the right to a renewal lease after the named tenant dies or moves out of the apartment.[7.2]

On the other hand, the courts have consistently recognized the existence of succession rights to apartments regulated by the New York City Rent Control Law.[7.3]

7.1. Rent Stabilization Codes §§ 2523.5(b)(1) and (2), 2520.6(d)0.

7.2. *Held invalid and unenforceable:* East Four-Forty Associates v Ewell (1988) 138 Misc 2d 235, 527 NYS2d 204. *Held valid and enforceable:* NCL Realty v Sunga (1988) NYLJ May 31, 1988, p. 21, col. 3; Garry v Blankroth (NYC Civ Ct NY Co 1988) 139 Misc 2d 961, 529 NYS2d 446.

Also, see Lesser v Park 65 Realty Corp. (1988, 1st Dept) 140 AD2d 169, 527 NYS2d 787, app dismd without op 72 NY2d 1042, 534 NYS2d 940, 531 NE2d 660, which held the succession provisions of the Rent Stabilization Code are to be given retroactive effect.

7.3. New York City Rent Control Law (NYC Adm Code § 26-403(m); NY State Rent & Eviction Regs § 2104.6(d).

Sullivan v Brevard Associates (1985) 66 NY2d 489, 498 NYS2d 96, 488 NE2d 1208; North Star Graphics, Inc. v Spitzer (1987, 1st Dept) 135 AD2d 401, 521 NYS2d 699, app dismd without op 72 NY2d 841, 530 NYS2d 556, 526 NE2d 47.

## § 11:8. Mobile Home Park Tenancy

p. 476, n. 4—In People ex rel. Higgins v Peranzo (1992, 3d Dept) 179 App Div 2d 871, 579 NYS2d 453, the court ruled that respondent was not guilty of violating RPL § 233(e), which requires a mobile home park operator to offer every mobile home tenant "prior to occupancy" the opportunity to sign a one-year lease. The court found that because respondent purchased the mobile home park after tenants' occupancy had commenced, respondent could not comply with the literal requirements of RPL § 233(e)

People ex rel. Higgins v Orsland (1992, 3d Dept) 183 App Div 2d 175, 589 NYS2d 640. The Appellate Division held that no statutory ambiguities result from the interpretation of RPL § 233(e), which requires a mobile home park owner to offer in writing a one-year lease to every mobile home tenant prior to occupancy, and RPL

## § 11:8

§ 233(i)(1), which requires an owner to reasonably approve as a mobile home tenant the purchaser of a mobile home already situated in a park for the remainder of a seller's term. The two provisions can be read together to provide a mobile home purchaser with the flexibility to accept a new one year lease or assume the remainder of the seller's term; this in turn provides the selling tenant with protection when selling the mobile home.

People ex rel. Higgins v Bradley (1989) 145 Misc 2d 1071, 549 NYS2d 344. In finding that respondent had failed to offer tenants a one-year written lease prior to their occupancy of the premises, the court awarded plaintiff, inter alia, an allowance of $1,000 for the costs of prosecuting the action and assessed a civil penalty against respondent in the amount of $500.

In Clarkson Mobile Home Park, Inc. v Ecklund (1987) 141 Misc 2d 83, 532 NYS2d 615, the court held that a rental increase on the tenants of a mobile home park was invalid where the landlord failed to offer a written lease to the tenants prior to the occupancy as required by RPL § 233(e).

**p. 476, n. 6**—The statutory reference should be amended to Real Prop L § 233(g)(3).

## B. COVENANT TO RENEW

### § 11:11. Necessity of Certainty

**p. 478, n. 18**—Provision in lease that the rent for the renewal is to be renegotiated between the parties is unenforceable for uncertainty, since it is an agreement to agree. Ping Lum v YWCA (1988, 4th Dept) 143 AD2d 498, 533 NYS2d 163.

## LANDLORD AND TENANT

## E. EXERCISING RIGHT TO RENEW

### § 11:34. Necessity of Strict Performance of Conditions Precedent

**p. 501, n. 17**—Dan's Supreme Supermarkets v Redmont Realty Co. (1995, App Div, 2d Dept) 628 NYS2d 790.

### § 11:35. Necessity of Timely Notice to Renew

**p. 501, n. 19**—Dan's Supreme Supermarkets v Redmont Realty Co. (1995, App Div, 2d Dept) 628 NYS2d 790. The court reversed the lower court decision and denied tenant's request for a preliminary injunction preventing landlord from leasing the premises to another party. Tenants had attempted to exercise the option to renew the lease nine months after the deadline set forth in the lease had passed. Since the execution of a lease by the landlord with another party was imminent the tenant could not establish that the landlord would not suffer any prejudice from the granting of the preliminary injunction precluding the exercise of the option, therefore the court also reversed the lower court on this issue and dismissed tenant's application.

**p. 502, n. 2**—Dan's Supreme Supermarkets v Redmont Realty Co. (1995, App Div, 2d Dept) 628 NYS2d 790.

### § 11:36. When Performance of Other Provisions of Lease Necessary

**p. 504, n. 9**—Tenant's violation of provision of lease that tenant comply with all laws, rules, orders, ordinances and regulations, precluded tenant from validly exercising option to renew, and equity would not relieve tenant from its default where tenant failed to demonstrate valuable im-

## RENEWAL OF LEASES § 11:40

provements to the property which would convert the loss of the option to renew into a forfeiture, and failed to demonstrate that the breach was de minimis, and resulted in no harm to landlord. TSS-Seedman's, Inc. v' Nicholas (1988, 2d Dept) 143 AD2d 223, 531 NYS2d 827.

### § 11:39. Equitable Relief from Failure to Give Timely Notice of Election to Renew

p. 507, n. 16—American Power Industries, Ltd. v Rebel Realty Corp. (1988, 2d Dept) 145 AD2d 454, 535 NYS2d 99 (4 months' notice instead of 6 excused because tenant would suffer a forfeiture, tenant had made substantial repairs and improvements which indicated that tenant had anticipated a 10-year rather than a 5-year occupancy, landlord suffered no prejudice, and evidence showed that landlord knew that tenant intended to renew).

p. 507, n. 17—The test for determining whether or not a tenant should be relieved of a default in exercising an option is threefold: The tenant must show (1) that the default was excusable; (2) that the default will result in a substantial forfeiture by the tenant; and (3) that the landlord will not be prejudiced. Mass Properties Co. v 1820 New York Ave. Corp. (1989, 2d Dept) 152 AD2d 727, 544 NYS2d 180.

Where the notice of renewal was only six (6) days late, that the lessee bank had expended approximately $180,000.00 in construction of a two-story building and remained at the location for over 20 years and had developed a clientele of approximately 1,500 customers, the court determined that a substantial forfeiture would result to plaintiff bank if a renewal was not permitted.

Finding that defendant would not be prejudiced by a renewal the court affirmed a judgment of the lower court declaring that plaintiff bank had effectively exercised its option to renew the lease. Nanuet Nat. Bank v Saramo Holding Co. (1989, 2d Dept) 153 App Div 2d 927, 545 NYS2d 734, app den 75 NY2d 705, 552 NYS2d 927, 552 NE2d 175; Bench 'N' Gavel Restaurant, Ltd. v Time Equities, Inc. (1991, 2nd Dept) 169 App Div 2d 755, 565 NYS2d 121.

Dan's Supreme Supermarkets v Redmont Realty Co. (1995, App Div, 2d Dept) 628 NYS2d 790.

p. 508, n. 1—Waldbaum, Inc. v Fifth Ave. of Long Island Realty Assocs. (1994, 2d Dept) 200 App Div 2d 664, 606 NYS2d 764, app gr 84 NY2d 802, 617 NYS2d 136, 641 NE2d 157. See also § 23:53, infra.

p. 509, n. 2—Although the failure to timely notify a landlord of an intention to exercise an option to renew a lease will forfeit a tenant's right to renew, courts have recognized that principles of equity can intervene to relieve a tenant from such untimely notice if 1) the tenant's failure is the result of inadvertence, 2) the tenant has made valuable and substantial improvements to the property with the intent to renew the lease, 3) the tenant would sustain a substantial loss if the lease is not renewed, and 4) the landlord is not prejudiced by the delay in notice. Duchess Radiology Assocs. P. C. v Narotzky (1993, 3d Dept) 192 App Div 2d 1049, 597 NYS2d 238. Under the circumstances where a new lease was imminent with another tenant the court held that tenant had failed to establish its entitlement to injunctive relief. Dan's Supreme Supermarkets v Redmont Realty Co. (1995, App Div, 2d Dept) 628 NYS2d 790; Souslian Wholesale Beer & Soda, Inc. v 380-4 Union Ave. Realty Corp. (1990, 2d Dept) 166 App Div 2d 435, 560 NYS2d 491, app den 78 NY2d 858, 575 NYS2d 454, 580 NE2d 1057.

### § 11:40. Waiver of Performance of Conditions to Renewal

p. 510, n. 9—Dove Hunters Pub v Posner (1995, 1st Dept) 211 App Div

§ 11:40

2d 494, 621 NYS2d 327. The court granted landlord possession of the premises when tenant failed to cure violations of a substantial obligation of the tenancy before the issuance of the notice of termination, and tenant's claim of waiver was without merit in view of the nonwaiver clause in the lease.

## H. REMEDIES FOR BREACH OF COVENANT TO RENEW

### § 11:59. Specific Performance

p. 530, n. 10—Kumble v Windsor Plaza Co. (1990, 1st Dept) 161 AD2d 259, 555 NYS2d 290, app dismd, motion den 76 NY2d 843, 560 NYS2d 126, 559 NE2d 1285 and app den 76 NY2d 709, 561 NYS2d 913, 563 NE2d 284. In this case the court reviewed the so called "fee on a fee" situation in its relationship to the landlord-tenant context. The court noted that there is nothing in Real Property Law 234 to exclude a "fee on a fee," and that "persuasive if not binding authority strongly suggests that statutes creating a right to attorneys' fees are served by its allowance." The court further stated that a "fee on a fee" would discourage unnecessary litigation in the "hotly contested and emotional field" of landlord-tenant relations.

### § 11:60. Action for Declaratory Judgment

p. 530, n. 11—The Court of Appeals pointed out that it has been the rule in this state that a landlord who is uncertain as to whether a lease must be renewed can ask a court to declare the rights of the parties and resolve the dispute before the time for renewal arrives. 615 Co. v Mikeska (1989, 1st Dept) 146 AD2d 452, 536 NYS2d 690, affd 75 NY2d 987, 557 NYS2d 262, 556 NE2d 1069.

# CHAPTER 12

# RENT

A. IN GENERAL
  § 12:1. Nature and Definition
  § 12:6. Attorney's Fees as Rent
  § 12:7. Attorney's Fees as Rent; Mobile Homes
  § 12:12. Implied Agreement to Pay Rent

B. PAYMENT OF RENT
  § 12:26. Provision for Acceleration

---

## A. IN GENERAL
## § 12:1. Nature and Definition

p. 534, n. 5—Payments made to a landlord by U. S. Dept. of Housing and Urban Development on behalf of a tenant in a federally subsidized housing unit constitutes rent. W. 180th Street Associates v Bryant, NYLJ 8-28-90 at 22, col. 3 (Civ. Ct., NY Co.). See § 30:16, infra.

## § 12:6. Attorney's Fees as Rent

p. 537, n. 6—Barba v Lindissimo Boutique, Inc. (1991) 149 Misc 2d 117, 564 NYS2d 698. A lease between plaintiff and respondent provided the recovery of attorneys' fees incurred by the plaintiff in the case of any default by defendant relating to the use of the premises by the tenant. An action commenced by the City of New York against the plaintiff alleging that the premises were being used illegally was subsequently settled. Plaintiff commenced this action against tenant to recover damages sustained in defending against that action and to recover attorneys' fees incurred in connection with the lawsuit. The court granted plaintiff's motion for summary judgment finding defendant liable to the plaintiff for an improper use of the premises by a subtenant.

p. 537, n. 7—Clemons Management Corp. v Quick Quality Copies (1995, Civ Ct) 164 Misc 2d 144, 623 NYS2d 498. A demand for legal fees as additional rent in a nonpayment summary proceeding against a commercial tenant does not render the petition defective.

Where there is a provision in a lease for attorney's fees the landlord may recover legal fees in the unsuccessful defense of an RPAPL article 7-A proceeding brought by the tenants. Thenebe v Ansonia Assocs. (1996, App Div, 1st Dept) 640 NYS2d 552, app dismd 89 NY2d 858.

p. 537, n. 8—In an action by the tenant for summary judgment and injunction relief the Landlord's request for attorneys fees was denied since attorneys' fees and litigation costs are not ordinarily recoverable as an element of damages absent some contractual or statutory right. Camatron Sewing Machine, Inc. v F.M. Ring Assoc.,

§ 12:6    LANDLORD AND TENANT

Inc. (1992, 1st Dept) 179 App Div 2d 165, 582 NYS2d 396.

Paroff v Muss (1991, 2d Dept) 171 App Div 2d 782, 567 NYS2d 502. In an action for a judgment declaring the rights and duties of the parties with respect to a clause contained in a commercial lease granting an option to certain parking places, the court denied plaintiff's application for attorneys fees since the action was instituted by the tenants for alleged default by the landlord under the lease, stating that a "party must pay its own attorneys' fees and disbursements unless an award is authorized by agreement between the parties or by statute or by court rule. . . ."

Nester v McDowell (1993) 81 NY2D 410, 599 NYS2d 507. Plaintiff owner commenced an ejectment action and since RPL § 234 is not implicated in this case the plaintiff is not entitled to attorney's fees.

p. 537, n. 9—Provision restricting attorney's fees to breaches of lease does not entitle either landlord or tenant to attorney's fees where tenant refuses or fails to renew his lease. 5700-5800-5900 Arlington Ave. Associates v Medina (NYC Civ Ct Bx Co, 1987) 136 Misc 2d 943, 519 NYS2d 521.

Tenant of rent stabilized apartment who prevailed in holdover proceeding on the basis of the invalidity of a proposed cooperative conversion eviction plan was entitled to recover reasonable attorney's fees, since the holdover proceeding concerned an obligation of the lease, to wit, to surrender possession at the expiration of the lease; and the lease contained a provision for attorney's fees in favor of the landlord. Troy v Oberlander (1989, 1st Dept) 146 AD2d 460, 536 NYS2d 73.

p. 538, n. 10—313 West 100th Street Tenants Assn. v Kepasi Realty Corp. (1989) 143 Misc 2d 566, 545 NYS2d 54. An award for time spent in seeking attorney's fees is not authorized.

p. 538, n. 12—Landlord who was successful in a summary holdover proceeding is entitled to attorney's fees incurred in defending subsequent multiple applications, motions, proceedings and actions initiated by the tenant. Simithis v 4 Keys Leasing & Maintenance Co. (1989, 1st Dept) 151 App Div 2d 339, 542 NYS2d 595; Chatanow Assoc., Inc. v 527 MDI Property, Inc. (1990, 1st Dept) 161 AD2d 258, 55 NYS2d 50.

p. 539, n. 13—Duell v Condon (1994, 1st Dept) 200 App Div 2d 549, 606 NYS2d 690, app gr (1st Dept) 202 App Div 2d 1075, 610 NYS2d 775. Where the lease contained a standard attorneys' fees clause, it became reciprocally binding upon the landlord by operation of law (RPL § 234) and tenant-respondent was entitled to the award of legal fees.

p. 539, n. 14—If a lease does not contain a provision entitling landlord to attorney's fees, tenant may not recover any. Eleven Waverly Associates v Waering (1987) 134 Misc 2d 1093, 515 NYS2d 381.

Respondent's application for legal fees in a non-payment summary proceeding which was settled by stipulation that provided, inter alia, for a 25% abatement in rent was denied. The court determined that where each side prevails in part each side must bear the responsibility for its own legal fees, Concourse Village, Inc. v Heard, NYLJ 9-21-89 at 24, col. 4 (Civ Ct., Bx. Co.).

Add text after carryover paragraph on p. 539:

Two cases by the Appellate Division, First Department, set forth the basis whereby a tenant may recover legal fees from a landlord in a summary proceeding. In Lynch v Leibman,[14.1] a jury found that petitioner had breached his implied warranty of habitability and held in favor of the tenant and granted respondent's motion for attorney's fees. The court held that there is no legal authority for the proposition that a partial recovery by the landlord precludes an award of counsel fees to the tenant.

In Bunny Realty v Miller,[14.2] the landlord initiated a non-payment proceeding after respondent began withholding rent in an attempt to force landlord into supplying respondent with mandated services. After trial the Civil Court held in favor of the tenants and awarded abatements of rent in their favor. The tenants thereafter moved pursuant to RPL § 234 for an award of attorney's fees. The lease permits the landlord to recover legal fees for obtaining possession of the premises and the Appellate Term interpreted that section to mean that because it does not specifically contain the words "due to the tenant's default"' it somehow limits the tenant's reciprocal rights in the lease. In reversing this decision, the Appellate Division held that acceptance of the Appellate Term's argument would enable landlords to entirely undermine the effectiveness of RPL § 234 "through artful draftmanship."

The rule now is that a partial recovery by a landlord of back rent does not preclude an award of counsel fees to the tenant in non-payment cases. Ginsberk v Canders (App Term, 1st Dept) NYLJ, 4-20-93.

14.1. Lynch v Leibman (1991, 1st Dept) 177 AD2d 453, 576 NYS2d 550.

Excelsior 57th Corporation v Winters (App Term, 1st Dept) NYLJ 5-25-94, p. 25, col 1. The Appellate Term affirmed the trial court decision but modified landlord's recovery for rent to the sum of $109,524.32 from $119,924.32; vacated the award of attorney's fees to landlord; and granted attorney's fees to the tenant. The award of a rent abatement in the sum of $10,400.00 was based upon the tenants' apartment having been completely uninhabitable due to a flood. In granting attorney's fees, relying on Bunny Realty v Miller and Lynch v Leibman, the court held that "the complete abatement awarded to tenant for four months, during which they were required to relocate so that renovations could proceed, supports an award of attorney's fees in tenants favor."

In Park Towers Tenants Corp. v Gashi (App Term, 1st Dept) NYLJ 9-21-94, p. 21, col. 1. the court held that since the landlord had not prevailed on the issue of late charges it was not the "prevailing party" and was therefore not entitled to the recovery of attorneys' fees. In addition the tenant was not the successful party since he withheld payment of the "agreed upon base maintenance without justification" and was also not entitled to attorneys' fees. The court held that "[t]his is a case where each side should bear the expense of its own legal fees, and not look to the other for reimbursement."

14.2. Bunny Realty v Miller (1992, 1st Dept) 180 AD2d 460, 579 NYS2d 952.

p. 540, n. 16—The Maplewood Management Inc. case cited in the note to the text was reversed in (1988, 2d Dept) 143 AD2d 978, 533 NYS2d 612, which held that an award of attorney's fees may be made under the statute to a tenant who did not become legally obligated to pay the fee either because he represented himself or because he obtained free legal assistance; the legislature's primary intent in enacting the statute was to deter landlords from engaging in what was perceived to be the undesirable practice of bringing meritless eviction proceedings against indigent tenants in the expectation that these tenants would be unable to obtain the legal assistance necessary to defend themselves in such proceedings; and to hold that it requires an award of a fee only when a tenant can afford to pay an attorney would negate the deterrent effect of the statute.

Although the successful attorney for respondent billed her client at the rate of $100.00 per hour the court awarded her $125.00 per hour based upon the reasonable value of her services. Milman v Cataldi (1988) 139 Misc 2d 1067, 529 NYS2d 449.

p. 540, n. 17—But, in Cier Industries Co. v Hessen (1988, 1st Dept) 136 AD2d 145, 526 NYS2d 77, it was held that a landlord was entitled to attorneys' fees, pursuant to the standard fee clause, upon being awarded final judgment in a holdover proceeding based on the ground that tenant did not occupy the premises as his primary residence. Although failure to occupy the premises as his primary residence was not a breach of a covenant of the lease, this act deprived the tenant of a right to a renewal; and, therefore, his continued occupancy of the premises after the expiration of his term constituted a breach of the lease; Chatanow Assoc., Inc. v 527 MDN Property, Inc. (1990, 1st Dept) 161 AD2d 258, 555 NYS2d 50.

After the court granted defendant's motion to dismiss plaintiff's action for rent on the ground that the lease was invalid, defendant moved to recover attorneys' fees pursuant to RPL 234.

The court determined that there is no merit to the defendant's contention that the lease was declared invalid for the purpose of the plaintiff's claim, but still remains valid for the purpose of his counterclaims. Rivertower Assoc. v Chalfen (1990, 1st Dept) 167 App Div 2d 309, 562 NYS2d 54.

Duell v Condon (1995) 84 NY2d 773, 622 NYS2d 891, 647 NE2d 96. Although tenant was not a signatory to the original lease between the landlord and respondent's deceased parents, the court held that the tenant was entitled to attorney's fees as the successful tenant in a holdover proceeding commenced by the landlord. RPL 234 may be applied in a proceeding involving a statutory tenant who was not a signatory to the original lease.

Since attorney's fees are only available to a tenant under RPL § 234 pursuant to a valid clause in a valid lease this defendant was not entitled to attorney's fees since in a prior proceeding between the parties the court had determined there had been no valid lease agreement between the parties. Rivertower Assoc. v Chalfen (1990, 1st Dept) 167 App Div 2d 309, 562 NYS2d 54.

p. 541, n. 1—11 Park Place Assocs. v Barnes (1995, App Div, 1st Dept) 633 NYS2d 19. In this nonpayment proceeding the court awarded attorney's fees of $100,000 in legal fees and $7,066 in disbursements to the landlord on the grounds that plaintiff's attorney provided exhaustive "computer documentation" in support of this case.

## § 12:7. Attorney's Fees as Rent; Mobile Homes

p. 541, n. 3—Frontier Management Corp. v Holmgren (1992, Sup App T) 154 Misc 2d 526, 595 NYS2d 652. RPL § 233(o) permits a mobile home park owner to recover legal fees in a summary proceeding whenever the lease so provides. In this case, the original rules and regulations of the mobile home park in effect, at the time respondent entered into possession did not provide for legal fees to the landlord in the event of tenant's breach. In this nonpayment proceeding respondent is not obligated to pay counsel fees, since the original rules and regulations signed by the tenant made no mention of counsel fees as additional rent.

§ 12:12. Implied Agreement to Pay Rent

p. 559, n. 11—Respondent remained in possession beyond the expiration of the term of the lease. Two weeks later the roof as well as other supporting structures caved in causing the building to collapse. The New York City Building Department ordered that the building remain vacant. Petitioner commenced a holdover summary proceeding and also requested use and occupation. The court held that it is the landlord's burden to prove the reasonable value of the use and occupation and if the premises have no reasonable value because of their condition or if the tenant has been unable to use the premises, there cannot be an award as it would thwart the rationale and purpose of Real Prop Law § 220. 438 W. 19th St. Operating Corp. v Metropolitan Oldsmobile, Inc. (1989) 142 Misc 2d 170, 536 NYS2d 669.

B. PAYMENT OF RENT

§ 12:26. Provision for Acceleration

*Add text at end of section on p. 576:*

Where a tenant is locked out of the leased premises, and the lease is terminated, the landlord may not recover, as rents, subsequent installments of rent due under the lease (see § 23:71), and therefore may not recover accelerated rents under a clause providing therefor upon default in making payments of common area charges, since the provision for accelerated rents is a provision for liquidated damages and is unenforceable where it would provide, as in this situation, landlord with damages greatly disproportionate to the probable loss.[17.1]

17.1. Benderson v Poss (1988, 4th Dept) 142 AD2d 937, 530 NYS2d 362.

# CHAPTER 13
# DEPOSIT TO SECURE PERFORMANCE OF LEASE

## A. IN GENERAL
§ 13:2. Importance of Determining Nature of Deposit
§ 13:5. Immateriality of Names Used, in Determining Nature of Deposit
§ 13:6. Criteria for Determining Nature of Deposit

## C. DUTY WITH RESPECT TO DEPOSIT ON CONVEYANCE OF LEASED PROPERTY
§ 13:22. Liability of Grantee or Assignee for Deposits Made by Tenant on Conveyance of Rent Stabilized Dwelling Units

## D. CONVERSION OF DEPOSIT
§ 13:27. Deposit as Trust Fund

---

## A. IN GENERAL

### § 13:2. Importance of Determining Nature of Deposit

*Add text at end of section on p. 585:*

A liquidated damage clause does not bar the equitable relief of specific performance unless there is explicit language in the lease that it is to be the sole remedy for a breach. Thus, where a lease provides that landlord shall not rent to a business in competition with tenants, and that if he does, the tenant's rent shall be computed under a different formula, tenant, in event of landlord's breach of that provision, could obtain specific performance, since there was no language that a different computation of rent was to be tenant's sole remedy.[5.1]

[5.1] Papa Gino's of America, Inc. v Plaza at Latham Associates (1988, 3d Dept) 135 AD2d 74, 524 NYS2d 536, later app (3d Dept) 144 AD2d 172, 535 NYS2d 116.

## § 13:5. Immateriality of Names Used in Determining Nature of Deposit

p. 587, n. 16—See § 13:6, infra.

## § 13:6. Criteria for Determining Nature of Deposit

p. 588, n. 18—LeRoy v Sayers (1995, 1st Dept) 217 App Div 2d 63, 635 NYS2d 217. In an action involving a breach of a lease the court held that the amount stipulated as liquidated damages in the lease did not bear a reasonable relation to the actual amount of the probable damages that would occur in the event of lessee's default and that the amount therefore constituted a penalty. The court stated that the "rule has evolved that a liquidated damages clause will be enforced if the sum stated is reasonably proportionate to the loss anticipated and the amount of actual loss would be difficult if not impossible to calculate. . . Whether a contractual provision is enforceable presents a question of law for the court."

## C. DUTY WITH RESPECT TO DEPOSIT

## ON CONVEYANCE OF LEASED PROPERTY

## § 13:22. Liability of Grantee or Assignee for Deposits Made by Tenant on Conveyance of Rent Stabilized Dwelling Units

*The phrase "any grantee of assignee" in the fifth line of the section should read: "any grantee or assignee."*

## D. CONVERSION OF DEPOSIT

## § 13:27. Deposit as Trust Fund

p. 608, n. 10—LeRoy v Sayers (1995, 1st Dept) 217 App Div 2d 63, 635 NYS2d 217. A landlord has a duty not to commingle the contract deposit with his own funds and upon a breach of that duty forfeits the right to avail himself of the deposit for any purpose. If there is a commingling a tenant has an immediate right to the funds.

## CHAPTER 14

## TENANT'S OBLIGATION TO PAY TAXES AND WATER CHARGES

B. COVENANT TO PAY TAXES
§ 14:9. Special Assessments
§ 14:13. Covenant to Pay Increase in Taxes
§ 14:23. Covenant to Pay Taxes "Levied or Imposed During Term"

---

### B. COVENANT TO PAY TAXES

### § 14:9. Special Assessments

p. 628, n. 1—Covenant to pay any increase in real estate tax assessment does not include an assessment for a sewer extension project. Allstate Management Corp. v Grand Union Co. (1988, 3d Dept) 142 AD2d 344, 535 NYS2d 779.

### § 14:13. Covenant to Pay Increase in Taxes

p. 636, n. 5—S.B.S. Assocs. v Weissman-Heller, Inc. (1993, 1st Dept) 190 AD2d 529, 593 NYS2d 28. A tax escalator clause in a lease, the court held, is designed to afford relief to a landlord where an increase assessment required actual payment by the landlord.

### § 14:23. Covenant to Pay Taxes "Levied or Imposed During Term"

p. 646, n. 11—8-14 West 38th Street Corp. v W. & J. Sloane, Inc. (1992, 1st Dept) 181 AD2d 545, 582 NYS2d 2. In interpreting a lease clause the court held that the "parties to a lease may mutually agree to have some installments of rent payable after the expiration date of the lease."

# CHAPTER 15

# TENANT'S RIGHTS IN THE USE OF THE LEASED PREMISES

A. IN GENERAL
  § 15:4. Sharing of Apartment

B. WASTE
  § 15:7. Structural Alterations as Waste

C. WHEN TENANT MAY MAKE ALTERATIONS
  § 15:11. Generally
  § 15:13. Consent Granted by Lease "To Make Inside Alterations Provided Premises Not Injured"
  § 15:20. Right of Tenants in Multiple Dwellings to Install Locks

F. MISCELLANEOUS
  § 15:33. Protection from Harassment of Landlord

G. EXPRESS RESTRICTIONS ON USE OF PREMISES BY TENANT
  § 15:39. Specification of Purpose as Description or Limitation of Use of Premises; Forms
  § 15:44. Restriction by Rules and Regulations of Landlord
  § 15:47. Mobile Home Parks

H. WAIVER OF EXPRESS RESTRICTION
  § 15:55. Waiver Binding on Grantee

J. RESTRICTION ON LESSOR'S USE OF OTHER PREMISES
  § 15:59. Generally
  § 15:62. Remedies at Law Against Lessor for Breach
  § 15:64. Measure of Damages for Breach
  § 15:67. Equitable Relief Against Competing Tenant

§ 15:4                  LANDLORD AND TENANT

## A. IN GENERAL
### § 15:4. Sharing of Apartment

p. 672, n. 15—Real Prop L § 235-f applies to proprietary leases or occupancy agreements entered into by shareholders of a cooperative corporation for residential premises. Southridge Cooperative Section No. 3, Inc. v Menendez (NYC Civ Ct Queens Co 1988) 141 Misc 2d 823, 535 NYS2d 299 (no impediment exists to the application of RPL § 235-f to a federally insured cooperative).

p. 673, n. 18—Vidod Realty Co. v Calvin (1989) 147 Misc 2d 488, 557 NYS2d 825. In this case the court held that a roommate and her children are permitted without the consent of the landlord pursuant to RPL 235-f(3).

The Appellate Term reversed the lower court in declining to enforce the strict language of Section 235-f and stated that the language of the statute is plain and unambiguous and must be enforced as written. 425 Realty Co. v Herrera (1990) 146 Misc 2d 790, 559 NYS2d 442.

p. 674, n. 20—Landlord commenced a holdover summary proceeding on the grounds that occupancy by one tenant's girl friend violated Real Prop Law § 235-f(4). The lower court dismissed the petition declining to enforce the strict language of the statute. In reversing the decision Appellate term held that the plain language of Real Property Law § 235-f must be enforced as written. 425 Realty Co. v Herrera (1990) 146 Misc 2d 790, 559 NYS2d 442.

## B. WASTE
### § 15:7. Structural Alterations as Waste

p. 678, n. 19—Haberman v Hawkins (1991, 1st Dept) 170 App Div 2d 377, 566 NYS2d 279. Petitioner-landlord's application to recover possession of a rent controlled unit alleging that respondent-tenant made unauthorized alterations at the premises was denied. The court found that the tenant presented at trial, sufficient evidence to support the affirmative defense of estoppel and waiver. In supporting defendant's position the court found it was evident that the tenant replaced the windows after a discussion with the landlord and that the landlord waited four years before alleging that the tenant was in substantial violation of the lease.

In Sussman v Plainview-Old Bethpage Sch. Dist. (1994, 2d Dept) 209 App Div 2d 609, 619 NYS2d 120, the court granted defendant-landlord's motion to dismiss a personal injury action against it since it had no duty to maintain the interior portion of the leased premises where the injured plaintiff allegedly fell on a slippery floor.

## C. WHEN TENANT MAY MAKE ALTERATIONS
### § 15:11. Generally

p. 680, n. 7—Haberman v Hawkins (1991, 1st Dept) 170 App Div 2d 377, 566 NYS2d 279.

### § 15:13. Consent Granted by Lease "To Make Inside Alterations Provided Premises Not Injured"

Add footnote 10.1 at end of second line on p. 681:

10.1. Where alterations are expressly permitted in a lease they cannot be considered waste. Med Mac Realty Co. v Lerner (1989, 2d Dept) 154 App Div 2d 656, 547 NYS2d 65, app dismd without op 75 NY2d 1004, 557 NYS2d 311, 556 NE2d 1118.

### § 15:20. Right of Tenants in Multiple Dwellings to Install Locks

p. 687, n. 8—111 Tenants Corp. v

# TENANT'S RIGHTS § 15:47

Stromberg (1996, Civ Ct) 168 Misc 2d 1014, 640 NYS2d 1018 A tenant's failure to unconditionally surrender a duplicate key as required by the clear terms of the proprietary lease constitutes a breach of a substantial obligation of her tenancy.

## F. MISCELLANEOUS RIGHTS

### § 15:33. Protection from Harassment of Landlord

p. 698, n. 17—Hartman v New York State Div. of Housing & Community Renewal (1990, 1st Dept) 158 AD2d 330, 551 NYS2d 18, app den 76 NY2d 705, 560 NYS2d 128, 559 NE2d 1287; Malik v Higgins (1991, 2d Dept) 173 App Div 2d 791, 570 NYS2d 652. Plaintiff commenced an action to enjoin defendant from holding hearings by DHCR to determine whether plaintiff had harassed tenants in an apartment which he owned. The court upheld the decision denying the motion for a preliminary injunction finding that plaintiff had "clearly failed to establish his likelihood of success on the merits, irreparable injury absent the granting of the preliminary injunction, and that the equities are balanced in his favor" and that he has an adequate remedy at law to review the determination of DHCR.

Crowell v Le Sannom Bldg. Corp. (1991, 1st Dept) 177 App Div 2d 372, 576 NYS2d 125. The issue before this court is the applicability of RPL 235-b to a residential loft apartment. The court held that, since the building was never used for manufacturing or warehouse purposes, but used for commercial purposes, RPL 235-b does not apply. "If the reach of the statute is to be expanded, it should be accomplished by legislative amendment, not judicial construction."

## G. EXPRESS RESTRICTIONS ON USE OF PREMISES BY TENANT

### § 15:39. Specification of Purpose as Description or Limitation of Use of Premises; Forms

p. 707, n. 9—The minimal sale of video tapes and cassettes does not, but the rental of video tapes and cassettes and the sale and repair of video equipment does, violate a lease provision restricting the use of the leased premises as a drug store. Anzalone v Normant Drugs, Inc. (S Ct Queens Co 1987) 136 Misc 2d 995, 519 NYS2d 601.

### § 15:44. Restriction by Rules and Regulations of Landlord

p. 712, n. 9—Ludwig v 25 Plaza Tenants Corp. (1992, 2d Dept) 184 App Div 2d 623, 584 NYS2d 907. In this case the court held that a clause in the lease, providing that no waiver of any of its terms shall be deemed to have been made unless in a writing expressly approved by the Directors, was fully enforceable.

### § 15:47. Mobile Home Parks

The title of § 233 of the Real Property Law has been amended to read: Manufactured home parks; duties, responsibilities

Real Property Law § 233(f) has been amended and reads as follows:

1. A manufactured home park owner or operator may promulgate rules and regulations governing the rental or occupancy of a manufactured home lot provided such rules and regulations

89

shall not be unreasonable, arbitrary or capricious. The copy of all rules and regulations shall be delivered by the manufactured home park owner or operator to all manufactured home tenants at the commencement of occupancy. The copy of the rules and regulations shall be posted in a conspicuous place upon the manufactured home park grounds.

2. If a rule or regulation is not applied uniformly to all manufactured home tenants of the manufactured home park there shall be rebuttable presumption that such rule or regulation is unreasonable, arbitrary and capricious, provided, however, that an inconsistency between a rule or regulation and a lease term contained in a lease signed before the date the rule or regulation is effective shall not raise a rebuttable presumption that such rule is unreasonable, arbitrary or capricious.

3. Any rule or regulation which does not conform to the requirements of this section or which has not been supplied or posted as required by paragraph one of this subdivision shall be unenforceable and may be raised by the manufactured home tenant as an affirmative defense in any action to evict on the basis of a violation of such rule or regulation.

4. No rules or regulations may be changed by the manufactured home park owner or operator without specifying the date of implementation of said changed rules and regulations, which date shall be no fewer than 30 days after written notice to all tenants.

5. A mobile home park owner or operator may not prohibit the placement of a for sale sign on any mobile home. The rule or regulation may be promulgated limiting the maximum size of such sign; provided, that it does not prohibit signs the size of which do not exceed the smaller of three feet by two feet or the maximum size allowed by law or governmental regulation or ordinance, if any.

Real Property Law § 233(g) has been amended and reads as follows:

1. No tenant shall be charged a fee for other than rent, utilities and charges for facilities and services available to the tenant. All fees, charges or assessments must be reasonably related to services actually rendered.

2. A manufactured home

park owner or operator shall be required to fully disclose in writing all fees, charges, assessments, including rental fees, rules and regulations prior to a manufactured home tenant assuming occupancy in the manufactured home park.

3. No fees, charges, assessments or rental fees may be increased by manufactured home park owner or operator without specifying the date of implementation of said fees, charges, assessments or rental fees which date shall be no less than 90 days after written notice to all manufactured home tenants. Failure on the part of the manufactured home park owner or operator to fully disclose all fees, charges or assessments shall prevent the manufactured home park owner or operator from collecting said fees, charges or assessments, and refusal by the manufactured home tenant to pay any undisclosed charges shall not be used by the manufactured home park owner or operator as a cause for eviction in any court of law.

4. (a) Whenever money shall be deposited or advanced on a contract or license agreement for the use or rental of premises and the manufactured home, if rented, in a manufactured home park as security for performance of the contract or agreement or to be applied to payments upon such contract or agreement when due, such money with interest accruing thereon, if any, until repaid or so applied, shall continue to be the money of the person making such deposit or advance and shall be a trust fund in the possession of the person with whom such deposit or advance shall be made and shall not be mingled with other funds or become an asset of the park owner, operator or his agent.

(b) Whenever the person receiving money so deposited or advanced shall deposit such money in a banking organization, such person shall thereupon notify in writing each of the persons making such security deposit or advance, giving the name and address of the banking organization in which the deposit of security money is made, and the amount of such deposit. Deposits in a banking organization pursuant to the provisions of this subdivision shall be made in a banking organization having a place of business within the state. If the person depositing such security money in a banking organization shall deposit same in an interest bearing account, he shall be entitled to receive, as administration expenses, a sum equivalent to one percent per annum upon the security money so deposited, which shall be in lieu of all other administrative and custodial expenses. The balances of the interest paid by the banking organization shall be the money of the person making the deposit or advance and shall either be held in trust by the person with whom such deposit or advance shall be made, until repaid or applied for the use or rental of the leased premises, or annually paid to the person making the deposit of security money.

(c) Whenever the money so deposited or advanced is for the rental of a manufactured home park lot on property on which are located six or more manufactured home park lots, the person receiving such money shall, subject to the provisions of this section, deposit it in an interest bearing account in a banking organization within the state which account shall earn interest at a rate which shall be the prevailing rate earned by other such deposits made with the banking organizations in such area.

(d) In the event that a lease terminates other than at the time that a banking organization in such area regularly pays interest, the person depositing such security money shall pay over to his manufactured home tenant such interest as he is able to collect at the date of such lease termination.

(e) Any provision of such a contract or agreement whereby a person who so deposits or advances money waives any provision of this subdivision is void.

Real Property Law § 233(h) has been amended and reads as follows:

No manufactured home park owner shall:

1. Require a manufactured home tenant therein to purchase from said manufactured home park owner or operator skirting or equipment for tying down manufactured homes, or any other equipment. However, the manufactured home park owner or operator may determine by rule or regulation the style or quality of such equipment to be purchased by the manufactured home tenant from the vendor of the manufactured home tenant's choosing, providing

such equipment is readily available.

2. Charge any manufactured home tenant who chooses to install an electric or gas appliance in his manufactured home an additional fee solely on the basis of such installation unless such installation is performed by the manufactured home park owner or operator at the request of the manufactured home tenant, nor shall the manufactured home park owner or operator restrict the installation, service or maintenance of any such appliance, restrict the ingress or egress of repairers to enter the manufactured home park for the purpose of installation, service or maintenance of any such appliance, or restrict the making of any interior improvement in such manufactured home, so long as such an installation or improvement is in compliance with applicable building codes and other provisions of law and further provided that adequate utilities are available for such installation or improvement.

3. Require, by contract, rule, regulation or otherwise, a manufactured home dweller to purchase from the manufactured home park owner or any person acting directly or indirectly on behalf of the park owner, commodities or services incidental to placement or rental within such park; nor shall the park owner restrict access to the manufactured home park to any person employed, retained or requested by the manufactured home dweller to provide such commodity or service, unless the manufactured home park owner establishes that such requirement or restriction is necessary to protect the property of such park owner from substantial harm or impairment.

4. Require a manufactured home owner or a prospective manufactured home owner to purchase his or her manufactured home from the manufactured home park owner or operator, or from any person or persons designated by the manufactured home park owner or operator. Nothing herein shall be construed to prevent a manufactured home park owner or operator from requiring that any new manufactured home to be installed in his or her manufactured home park comply with the rules and regulations of said manufactured home park or conform to the physical facilities

§ 15:47

then existing for installation of a manufactured home in said manufactured home park.

Real Property Law § 233(i) has been amended and reads as follows:

1. No manufactured home park owner or operator shall deny any manufactured home tenant the right to sell his manufactured home within the manufactured home park provided the manufactured home tenant shall give to the manufactured home park owner or operator 20 days' written notice of his intention to sell, provided that if the manufactured home owner is deceased no such notice shall be required from the administrator or executor of the home owner's estate, and provided further that no manufactured home park owner or operator shall restrict access to the manufactured home park to any potential purchaser or representatives of any seller unless the manufactured home park owner establishes that such restriction is necessary to protect the property of such park owner or operator from substantial harm or impairment. No manufactured home park owner or operator shall require the manufactured home owner or subsequent purchaser to remove the manufactured home from the manufactured home park solely on the basis of the sale thereof. The manufactured home park owner or operator may reserve the right to approve the purchaser of said manufactured home as a manufactured home tenant for the remainder of the seller's or deceased tenant's term but such permission may not be unreasonably withheld. If the manufactured home park owner or operator unreasonably withholds his permission or unreasonably restricts access to the manufactured home park, the manufactured home tenant or the executor or administrator of a deceased tenant's estate may recover the costs of the proceedings and attorneys' fees if it is found that the manufactured home park owner or operator acted in bad faith by withholding permission or restricting access.

2. The manufactured home park owner or operator shall not exact a commission or fee with respect to the price realized by the seller unless the manufactured home park owner or operator has acted as agent for the manufactured home owner in the sale pursuant to a written contract.

# TENANT'S RIGHTS § 15:47

3. If the ownership or management rejects a purchaser as a prospective tenant, the selling tenant must be informed in writing of the reasons therefor.

**19.1.** In Ba Mar, Inc. v County of Rockland (1991, 2d Dept) 164 AD2d 605, 566 NYS2d 298, app dismd, app den 78 NY2d 877, 573 NYS2d 67, 577 NE2d 58, later proceeding 78 NY2d 982, 574 NYS2d 935, 580 NE2d 407, the Appellate Division set forth a detailed analysis of the present law involving Mobile Home Parks in relationship to RPL 233. See also, People Ex rel. Higgins v Leier, (1990, 3rd Dept) 164 AD2d 492, 564 NYS2d 539. In this case the Appellate Division stated that the Legislature has manifested its "intent to authorize municipalities to impose real property taxation upon the owners of mobile home parks and to permit the value of mobile homes situated on lots within a park to be included in the assessments. . . . It is the owner, not the mobile home owner, who is responsible for payment of the real property tax."

Halpern v Sullivan County (1991, 3d Dept) 171 App Div 2d 157, 574 NYS2d 837. In reviewing a local law providing mobile home owners additional protection not afforded under RPL § 233, the court held that the state statute established a detailed and comprehensive statutory scheme for the regulation of the rights and obligations of park owners and tenants, thereby evidencing its intent to preempt the field of mobile home legislation. A local law providing mobile home owners within the locality additional protection not afforded under RPL § 233, which governs the legal relationship between mobile home park owners/operators and mobile home owners or tenants in New York, is invalid.

People ex rel. Higgins v Leier (1990, 3d Dept) 164 App Div 2d 492, 564 NYS2d 539. The court determined that a mobile home park owner is precluded from imposing a lump-sum charge on tenants as their pro-rata share of real property taxes in addition to the monthly rent. (RPL § 233 (g)). A park owner may charge only rent, utilities and charges for facilities and services available to the tenant. It is the landlord and not the tenant who is responsible for the payment of the real property taxes (New York Mobile Homes Asso. v Steckel (1961) 9 NY2d 533, 215 NYS2d 487, 175 NE2d 151, 86 ALR2d 270, remittitur amd 10 NY2d 814, 221 NYS2d 517, 178 NE2d 231, app dismd 369 US 150, 7 L Ed 2d 782, 82 S Ct 685) and the statute prevents lot owners from "bilking tenants through unnecessary and excessive fees" (Miller v Valley Forge Village (1978) 43 NY2d 626, 403 NYS2d 207, 374 NE2d 118).

**p. 718, n. 20**—Where respondents admitted in their answer that they gave tenants less than 90 days' notice, the court rejected landowners' contention that the lower court erred in finding respondent guilty of violating RPL § 233(g)(3) without an evidentiary hearing. People ex rel. Higgins v Peranzo (1992, 3d Dept) 179 App Div 2d 871, 579 NYS2d 453.

Finding the respondent in violation of RPL § 233(g)(3) in that it had raised tenants' rent without affording them 90 days' written notice of the rent increase, the court awarded plaintiff an allowance of $1,000 for the costs of prosecuting the action and assessed a civil penalty against respondent in the amount of $500. People ex rel. Higgins v Bradley (1989) 145 Misc 2d 1071, 549 NYS2d 344.

*Add text at end of section on p. 720:*

A "mobile home park" is defined in Real Prop Law § 233(a)(3) as "a contiguous parcel of privately owned land which is used for accommodation of *three or more mobile homes* occupied for year round living." (em-

§ 15:47  LANDLORD AND TENANT

phasis added.) The fact that the owner of the park occupies one of the three units does not remove the parcel from the requirements of Real Prop Law § 233.[20.1]

20.1. People ex rel. Higgins v Bradley (1989) 145 Misc 2d 1071, 549 NYS2d 344.

## H. WAIVER OF EXPRESS RESTRICTION

### § 15:55. Waiver Binding on Grantee

p. 727, n. 13—Sharp v Melendez (1988, 1st Dept) 139 AD2d 262, 531 NYS2d 554, app den 73 NY2d 707, 539 NYS2d 300, 536 NE2d 629.

## J. RESTRICTION ON LESSOR'S USE OF OTHER PREMISES

### § 15:59. Generally

p. 729, n. 5—In Key Drug Co. v Luna Park Realty Assocs. (1995, App Div, 2d Dept) 634 NYS2d 502, the court denied plaintiff's motion for a preliminary injunction stating that the restrictive covenant in the lease did not apply since a similar business had already existed in the shopping center before plaintiff taking possession of its leased premises.

### § 15:62. Remedies at Law Against Lessor for Breach

p. 738, n. 6—See § 15:59, supra.

### § 15:64. Measure of Damages for Breach

p. 739, n. 10—Won's Cards v Samsondale/Haverstraw Equities (1994, 2d Dept) 203 App Div 2d 277, 609 NYS2d 667. In this case the court stated that there are only two proper measures in an action to recover damages for a landlord's breach of a restrictive covenant in a lease: (1) the reduction in the rental value of the property with the covenant against competition broken and with the covenant unbroken; and (2) the loss of business profits of the wronged tenant.

### § 15:67. Equitable Relief Against Competing Tenant

p. 742, n. 5—Won's Cards, Inc. v Samsondale/Haverstraw Equities, Ltd. (1991, 3d Dept) 165 AD2d 157, 566 NYS2d 412.

See § 15:59, supra.

# CHAPTER 16

# FIXTURES

A. IN GENERAL
   § 16:1. Fixture Defined
   § 16:2. Trade and Domestic Fixtures Defined

## A. IN GENERAL

### § 16:1. Fixture Defined

p. 746, n. 4—Chittenden Falls Realty Corp. v Cray Valley Prods. (1994, 3d Dept) 208 AD2d 1114, 618 NYS2d 118; 230 Park Ave. Assoc. v Penn Cent. Corp. (1991, 1st Dept) 178 AD2d 185, 577 NYS2d 46

p. 747, n. 6—In re New York (G & C Amusements, Inc.) (1982) 55 NY2d 353, 449 NYS2d 671, 434 NE2d 1038, reh den 56 NY2d 805; Whitehall Corners v State (1994, 2d Dept) 210 AD2d 398, 620 NYS2d 126.

### § 16:2. Trade and Domestic Fixtures Defined

p. 747, n. 10—Chittenden Falls Realty Corp. v Cray Valley Prods. (1994, 3d Dept) 208 AD2d 1114, 618 NYS2d 118. "It is the general rule that as between a landlord and tenant, machinery and equipment affixed to the leased premises by the tenant for the purpose of trade or manufacture carried on by the tenant remain personalty to the extent that the tenant retains the right to remove such trade fixtures, subject to the limitation that the removal must be accomplished without substantial or material injury to the freehold."